UNIVERSITY CASEBOOK SERIES®

CONTRACTS

CASES AND MATERIALS

NINTH EDITION

E. ALLAN FARNSWORTH
Late Alfred McCormack Professor of Law
Columbia University

CAROL SANGER
Barbara Aronstein Black Professor of Law
Columbia University

NEIL B. COHEN
Jeffrey D. Forchelli Professor of Law
Brooklyn Law School

RICHARD R.W. BROOKS
Emilie M. Bullowa Professor of Law
New York University

LARRY T. GARVIN
Lawrence D. Stanley Professor of Law
Ohio State University

FOUNDATION
PRESS

University Casebook Series is a trademark registered in the U.S. Patent and Trademark Office.

© 1965, 1972, 1980, 1988, 1995, 2001 FOUNDATION PRESS
© 2008 By THOMSON REUTERS/FOUNDATION PRESS
© 2013 by LEG, Inc. d/b/a West Academic Publishing
© 2019 LEG, Inc. d/b/a West Academic
      444 Cedar Street, Suite 700
      St. Paul, MN 55101
      1-877-888-1330

Printed in the United States of America

ISBN: 978-1-63460-653-0

CS: *To Artemio, Ines and Little Ziggy*

NBC: *To Amy, Emily, Liz and Claudia*

RRWB: *To Heidi, Travers and Tilly*

LTG: *To Robin, Hannah, Philip and Samuel*

PREFACE

Welcome to the first-year study of Contracts. In this preface we provide a brief introduction to the course and its foundational role in the law school curriculum, and to this casebook and our aspirations for its use. We admit from the start that we are contracts enthusiasts: we think that the public principles that govern private ordering are both fascinating and distinctively important. Our aim here is to provide you with a set materials that demonstrates the doctrinal, intellectual, and policy dimensions of this rich subject with the hope that you too will become intrigued.

As editors, our primary role has been to select, organize, and edit the cases that make up the bulk of the next thousand or so pages, as well as to direct your attention to statutes, particularly Article 2 of the Uniform Commercial Code, that govern many contracts. We have also provided textual passages to introduce cases and concepts and to summarize areas of law that cannot be treated at length in the introductory course. Many contractual issues that arise in this casebook await further study in upper-level courses such as commercial law, real estate transactions, employment and labor law, securities regulation, remedies and international business transactions, each of which has essential contractual underpinnings. The bargaining process is also key to aspects of other, less commercial, areas such as family law (*e.g.*, surrogacy agreements), criminal law (*e.g.*, plea bargaining), and public international law (*e.g.*, treaties and conventions). As you see, this basic course in Contracts provides the conceptual elements necessary for many of the subjects you will study over the next few years.

The casebook's organization is not strictly chronological; we do not begin with the process of contract formation. Instead, we start with a general introduction to the twin topics of enforceable promises and the consequences of their breach. An initial question here is how the legal system determines which promises are to be enforced by the state and which are left to non-governmental forces, such as morality or market behavior. You may find it helpful during the course to return regularly to the Table of Contents to see the relations among the topics. The Table of Contents may be especially useful when you begin outlining a particular area.

Casebooks sometimes have distinctive tones. Ours is intended as a guided discussion with its readers. Thus you are often asked to watch for and consider a particular issue before reading a series of cases or statutes. We note as well that this casebook is largely ecumenical in its outlook. The materials are situated within a variety of disciplines— history, economics, philosophy, socio-legal studies, and ethics. Similarly, the cases presented here arose from a wide range of settings in which a promise has been broken and a remedy sought. Many of the cases are commercial, but especially in the 19th century, as the concept of bargained-for exchange was developing, cases not infrequently arose from promises made but not kept in the family context. We have generally integrated discussions of the law governing contracts for the sale of goods, governed mainly by the Uniform Commercial Code, with discussions of the common law, rather than treating the sale of goods material separately.

Finally, as part of the discursive aspirations of this book, we hope you will not hesitate to write to us with questions, comments, or suggestions. Our exchanges with our students and with other readers have helped us immeasurably in developing this material.

Best wishes in your studies.

CAROL SANGER
NEIL B. COHEN
RICHARD R. W. BROOKS
LARRY T. GARVIN

April 2019

NOTES ON EDITING

In presenting the materials in this book the editors have used the following conventions.

Cases. Descriptions and restatements of the facts of a case, and any insertion within an opinion, if prepared by the editors, are enclosed in brackets. Some opinions are abridged and presented with adjustments in format and style. Statutory references in an opinion are as stated by the court.

Citations. Here are the conventions for four sources that are regularly cited throughout the casebook.

The Restatement, Second, of Contracts (1980) is referred to simply as "Restatement," except when it is compared with the initial Restatement of Contracts (1932) or compared with another Restatement. References to the initial Restatement of Contracts carry a designation such as "original" or "first."

Article 2 of the Uniform Commercial Code is sometimes referred to as "UCC," or "the Code." All references to the UCC are to the current Official Text.

The United Nations Convention on Contracts for the International Sale of Goods, sometimes referred to as the Vienna Convention, is cited as "CISG." The Restatement, Articles 1 and 2 of the UCC, the CISG, and other useful sources are found in *Selections for Contracts* (*Selections*), which accompanies this text.

Finally, the Farnsworth treatise, formally cited, for example, as "2 E. Allan Farnsworth, Farnsworth on Contracts § 6.2, at 110 (4th ed., Zachary Wolfe, ed. 2018)" is cited here as "Farnsworth on Contracts § 6.2."

Parallel citations to cases in materials reproduced, including opinions, have in general been deleted unless they carry information (*e.g.,* a page reference). A citation to a decision does not normally include an indication of subsequent case history having no effect on the merit or authority of the decision cited, or of an opinion associated with it (*e.g.,* "certiorari denied").

Notes and Problems. When a question or problem is accompanied by a reference to a case, the reference is intended only to support a line of thought, or suggest an analogy, and not to supply "the answer."

Footnotes. A lettered footnote within an opinion or other quoted text indicates that the note was inserted by the editors; a numbered footnote indicates a footnote in the original text. When a footnote in an opinion or other reproduced text has been omitted, the footnotes retained have been renumbered in sequence.

Pronouns and Gender. To avoid occasional awkwardness or confusion in distinguishing one party from another, we have, when useful, characterized promisors as women and promisees as men, and used pronouns accordingly.

ACKNOWLEDGMENTS

The 9th Edition of this casebook extends our indebtedness to scores of distinguished scholars in Contracts from whom we have benefitted over the years. We specially want to acknowledge the contributions of two earlier editors: E. Allan Farnsworth, whose influence remains powerful not only in this casebook but in the larger world of contracts scholarship and practice, and William F. Young, a generous and insightful editor of this casebook for some forty years. Colleagues past and present have also played their part and we are grateful for generous discussions with Barbara Aronstein Black, the late Marvin Chirelstein, Ian Ayres, Kevin Davis, Victor Goldberg, Liam Murphy and Seana Shiffrin. Our students Alexander Adler, Karen Brill, Tilden Brooks, Elisabeth Campbell, Michael Demeroukas-Fetterman, Benjamin Hartman, Jaden Powell, Swara Saraiya and Hana Yamahiro, provided invaluable research help on the 9th Edition, and Ghislaine Pagès was a superb administrative and editorial assistant.

Lastly, we acknowledge the permission granted by the Virginia Law Review Association to reprint an excerpt from Robert S. Summers, *Good Faith" in General Contract Law and the Sales Provisions of the Uniform Commercial Code,* 54 Va. L. Rev. 195 (1968); by the Harvard Law Review Association to reprint an excerpt from Steven J. Burton, *Breach of Contract and the Common Law Duty to Perform in Good Faith,* 94 Harv. L. Rev. 369 (1980); and by the College of Law, State University of Iowa, to reprint an excerpt from Steven J. Burton, *Good Faith Performance of a Contract within Article 2 of the Uniform Commercial Code,* 67 Iowa L. Rev. 1 (1981). Permission of the copyright holders was conveyed through Copyright Clearance Center, Inc.

The 9th Edition locates the study of contracts in the developing doctrinal dynamics of the 21st century. We therefore thank our users and their students whose insights into these cases and materials continue to make this casebook sharper and more interesting. Keep those cards and emails coming!

SUMMARY OF CONTENTS

TABLE OF CONTENTS

TABLE OF CASES

The principal cases are in bold type.

UNIVERSITY CASEBOOK SERIES®

CONTRACTS

CASES AND MATERIALS

NINTH EDITION

CHAPTER 1

LEGAL BASES FOR RECOGNIZING AND ENFORCING PROMISES

SECTION 1. PROMISSORY LIABILITY: AN INTRODUCTION

Most people have an informal sense of contracts. Almost everyone of consenting age has entered into a contract, often with little hesitation or ceremony. Consider, for example, the arrangement you have with your cell phone company or the agreement established when you accepted the offer of admission from your law school. You are no doubt already familiar with such common-sense notions of contracts. The aim of this book is to provide more formal content to those general understandings. We are interested in what "contract" means as a matter of law.

The Restatement of Contracts, Second, defines contract as "a promise or set of promises for the breach of which the law gives a remedy, or the performance of which the law in some way recognizes as a duty." Restatement § 1. As the language indicates, not all promises are legally binding; the law does not provide a remedy for every broken promise. There may, of course, be moral or social sanctions for breaking a promise, but our primary inquiry here concerns the distinctive contributions of *law*. How does the law determine which promises to enforce?

We take up that question with two cases that focus on the promise itself. The first considers whether a binding (or enforceable) promise was created by a doctor's assertion that he would make a young man's injured hand "a hundred percent perfect." The second case addresses whether an enforceable promise should be found in the printed materials of a boat manufacturer stating that its boats could attain a "maximum speed of 30 miles per hour." These cases begin our consideration of why some promises are found to be legally enforceable and others not. The section concludes with a brief introduction to theories of why some promises *should* be legally enforceable. In Section 2, we turn to the issue of how the law enforces promises, by taking an initial look at remedies for breach.

Beyond the "why" and "how" of promissory enforcement, these opening materials also serve as an introduction to the question of "where" the law of promissory obligation is to be found: the basic sources and authorities that govern most contractual relationships. We have already mentioned the influential Restatement of Contracts, a comprehensive statement of general common law contract principles first promulgated by the American Law Institute (ALI) in 1932. The Restatement, Second, appeared in 1981. In this book, unless otherwise indicated, a reference to the "Restatement" refers to the Restatement, Second. While not enacted law itself, the Restatement has been aptly described by a former ALI director as "common law 'persuasive authority' with a high degree of persuasion." Herbert Goodrich, *Restatement and Codification*, *in* David Dudley Field: Centenary Essays 241, 244–45 (Alison Reppy ed., 1949). For more on the history of the Restatements, see the *Selections for Contracts*.

Statutes, on the other hand, are a direct and binding source of authority. Of particular relevance to contract law is Article 2 of the Uniform Commercial Code, which, as we shall see in our second case, applies in cases involving the sale of goods. We will highlight various other sources of contract law as we encounter them in the materials that follow. Of course, the primary sources relied on in most casebooks, including this one, are cases—the judicial opinions that constitute the common law. We begin our study of promises with an old chestnut from the American common law of contracts, Hawkins v. McGee.

Hawkins v. McGee

New Hampshire Supreme Court, 1929.
84 N.H. 114, 146 A. 641.

■ BRANCH, JUSTICE. The operation in question consisted in the removal of a considerable quantity of scar tissue from the palm of the plaintiff's right hand and the grafting of skin taken from the plaintiff's chest in place thereof. The scar tissue was the result of a severe burn caused by contact with an electric wire, which the plaintiff received about nine years before the time of the transactions here involved. There was evidence to the effect that before the operation was performed the plaintiff and his father went to the defendant's office, and that the defendant, in answer to the question, "How long will the boy be in the hospital?" replied, "Three or four days, not over four; then the boy can go home and it will be just a few days when he will go back to work with a good hand." Clearly this and other testimony to the same effect would not justify a finding that the doctor contracted to complete the hospital treatment in three or four days or that the plaintiff would be able to go back to work within a few days thereafter. The above statements could only be construed as expressions of opinion or predictions as to the probable duration of the treatment and plaintiff's resulting disability, and the fact that these estimates were exceeded would impose no contractual liability upon the defendant. The only substantial basis for the plaintiff's claim is the testimony that the defendant also said before the operation was decided upon, "I will guarantee to make the hand a hundred per cent perfect hand or a hundred per cent good hand." The plaintiff was present when these words were alleged to have been spoken, and, if they are to be taken at their face value, it seems obvious that proof of their utterance would establish the giving of a warranty in accordance with his contention.

The defendant argues, however, that, even if these words were uttered by him, no reasonable man would understand that they were used with the intention of entering "into any contractual relation whatever," and that they could reasonably be understood only "as his expression in strong language that he believed and expected that as a result of the operation he would give the plaintiff a very good hand." It may be conceded, as the defendant contends, that, before the question of the making of a contract should be submitted to a jury, there is a preliminary question of law for the trial court to pass upon, i.e. "whether the words could possibly have the meaning imputed to them by the party who founds his case upon a certain interpretation," but it cannot be held that the trial court decided this question erroneously in the present case. It is unnecessary to determine at this time whether the argument of the defendant, based upon "common knowledge of the uncertainty which attends all surgical operations," and the improbability that a surgeon would ever contract to make a damaged part of the human body "one hundred per cent perfect," would, in the absence of countervailing considerations, be regarded as conclusive, for there were other factors in the present case which tended to support the contention of the plaintiff. There was evidence that the defendant repeatedly solicited from the plaintiff's father the opportunity to perform this operation, and the theory was advanced by plaintiff's counsel in cross-examination of defendant that he sought an opportunity to "experiment on skin grafting," in which he had had little previous experience. If the jury accepted this part of plaintiff's contention, there would be a reasonable basis for the further conclusion that, if defendant spoke the words attributed to him, he did so with the intention that they should be accepted at their face value, as an inducement for the granting of consent to the operation by the plaintiff and his father, and there was ample evidence that they were so accepted by them. The question of the making of the alleged contract was properly submitted to the jury.

[The Court then discussed the proper measure of compensation for Hawkins, a subject to which we return in Section 2 when we take up the issue of damages as part of the larger question of what it means for the law to give a remedy.]

NOTES

(1) *One Hundred Percent.* Although Dr. McGee made a number of statements to the boy's father regarding the outcome of treatment, he does not appear to have used the word "promise" in any of them. What, then, makes any of the statements a promise? Consider the role of language, its context, and the nature of the transaction in *Hawkins.* See Restatement §§ 2 and 4. Would you find a promise if, before performing reconstructive knee surgery, a surgeon tells the patient that "the operation could give you a knee

that was stronger than before" and that the patient would, "if committed, play basketball again"? See Anglin v. Kleeman, 665 A.2d 747 (N.H. 1995).

(2) *Statutory Override.* Common-law rulings by courts sometimes give way to contrary judgments by legislatures. Consider the following example. In 1971, the Michigan Supreme Court affirmed a judgment for damages for breach of contract against a surgeon who, according to his patient's testimony, had said before a stomach operation, "After this operation, you can throw your pillbox away" and "Once you have an operation it takes care of all your troubles." Guilmet v. Campbell, 188 N.W.2d 601 (Mich. 1971). Three years later, the Michigan legislature enacted a statute providing that an "agreement, promise, contract, or warranty of cure relating to medical care or treatment" is void unless evidenced by a signed writing. Mich.Comp.L.Ann. 566.132(1)(g). Why might the legislature have enacted such a statute?

We note the interplay between courts, legislatures, and other law-making bodies such as regulatory agencies at various points throughout this book. As you read, think about the strengths and advantages of each with regard to making or reforming contract law. Keep in mind such factors as institutional competence, legitimacy, and the practical necessities of law-making.

(3) *The One-L Seamless Web.* Before moving on, a word about one structural limitation of the traditional law school curriculum. First-year courses are sometimes taught—somewhat misleadingly—as though they had little substantive relation to one another. But contracts for the sale of property, say, require an underlying understanding of what counts as property and can therefore be subject to transfer. Land obviously qualifies, but what about leaseholds, or ideas, or embryos? These questions are sometimes resolved in the context of a contract action, as we will see in connection with commercial surrogacy at p. 744 below. More often, however, contract law proceeds against the background of existing rules of property, civil procedure, torts, and so on. We will from time to time point out the significance of these other foundational areas for the contract issue at hand, and throughout this course urge you to keep an eye on the connections between contract law and your other subjects.

Bayliner Marine Corp. v. Crow

Supreme Court of Virginia, 1999.
257 Va. 121, 509 S.E.2d 499.

■ KEENAN, JUSTICE. In this appeal, the dispositive issue is whether there was sufficient evidence to support the trial court's ruling that the manufacturer of a sport fishing boat breached an express warranty and implied warranties of merchantability and fitness for a particular purpose.

In the summer of 1989, John R. Crow was invited by John Atherton, then a sales representative for Tidewater Yacht Agency, Inc. (Tidewater), to ride on a new model sport fishing boat known as a 3486 Trophy

Convertible, manufactured by Bayliner Marine Corporation (Bayliner). During an excursion lasting about 20 minutes, Crow piloted the boat for a short period of time but was not able to determine its speed because there was no equipment on board for such testing.

When Crow asked Atherton about the maximum speed of the boat, Atherton explained that he had no personal experience with the boat or information from other customers concerning the boat's performance. Therefore, Atherton consulted two documents described as "prop matrixes," which were included by Bayliner in its dealer's manual.

Atherton gave Crow copies of the "prop matrixes," which listed the boat models offered by Bayliner and stated the recommended propeller sizes, gear ratios, and engine sizes for each model. The "prop matrixes" also listed the maximum speed for each model. The 3486 Trophy Convertible was listed as having a maximum speed of 30 miles per hour when equipped with a size "20×20" or "20×19" propeller. The boat Crow purchased did not have either size propeller but, instead, had a size "20×17" propeller.

At the bottom of one of the "prop matrixes" was the following disclaimer: "This data is intended for comparative purposes only, and is available without reference to weather conditions or other variables. All testing was done at or near sea level, with full fuel and water tanks, and approximately 600 lb. passenger and gear weight."

Atherton also showed Crow a Bayliner brochure describing the 1989 boat models, including the 3486 Trophy Convertible. The brochure included a picture of that model fully rigged for offshore fishing accompanied by the statement that this model "delivers the kind of performance you need to get to the prime offshore fishing grounds."

In August 1989, Crow entered into a written contract for the purchase of the 3486 Trophy Convertible in which he had ridden. The purchase price was $120,000, exclusive of taxes. The purchase price included various equipment to be installed by Tidewater, including a generator, a cockpit cover, a "Bimini top," a winch, a spotlight, radar, a navigation system, an icemaker, fishing outriggers, an automatic pilot system, extra fuel gauges, a second radio, and air-conditioning and heating units. The total weight of the added equipment was about 2,000 pounds. Crow did not test drive the boat after the additional equipment was installed or at any other time prior to taking delivery.

When Crow took delivery of the boat in September 1989, he piloted it onto the Elizabeth River. He noticed that the boat's speed measuring equipment, which was installed in accordance with the contract terms, indicated that the boat's maximum speed was 13 miles per hour. Crow immediately returned to Tidewater and reported the problem.

During the next 12 to 14 months, while Crow retained ownership and possession of the boat, Tidewater made numerous repairs and adjustments to the boat in an attempt to increase its speed capability.

Despite these efforts, the boat consistently achieved a maximum speed of only 17 miles per hour, except for one period following an engine modification when it temporarily reached a speed of about 24 miles per hour. In July 1990, a representative from Bayliner wrote Crow a letter stating that the performance representations made at the time of purchase were incorrect, and that 23 to 25 miles per hour was the maximum speed the boat could achieve.

In 1992, Crow filed a motion for judgment against Tidewater, Bayliner, and Brunswick Corporation, the manufacturer of the boat's diesel engines. Crow alleged, among other things, that Bayliner breached express warranties, and implied warranties of merchantability and fitness for a particular purpose.

At a bench trial in 1994, Crow, Atherton, and Gordon W. Shelton, III, Tidewater's owner, testified that speed is a critical quality in boats used for offshore sport fishing in the Tidewater area of Virginia because of the distance between the coast and the offshore fishing grounds. According to these witnesses, a typical offshore fishing site in that area is 90 miles from the coast. Therefore, the speed at which the boat can travel to and from fishing sites has a major impact on the amount of time left in a day for fishing.

Crow testified that because of the boat's slow speed, he could not use the boat for offshore fishing, that he had no other use for it, and that he would not have purchased the boat if he had known that its maximum speed was 23 to 25 miles per hour.

The trial court entered judgment in favor of Crow against Bayliner on the counts of breach of express warranty and breach of implied warranties of merchantability and fitness for a particular purpose. . . . On appeal, we review the evidence in the light most favorable to Crow, the prevailing party at trial.

Crow argues that the "prop matrixes" he received created an express warranty by Bayliner that the boat he purchased was capable of a maximum speed of 30 miles per hour. We disagree.

[UCC § 2–313] provides, in relevant part:

Express warranties by the seller are created as follows:

(a) Any affirmation of fact or promise made by the seller to the buyer which relates to the goods and becomes part of the basis of the bargain creates an express warranty that the goods shall conform to the affirmation or promise.

(b) Any description of the goods which is made a part of the basis of the bargain creates an express warranty that the goods shall conform to the description.

The issue whether a particular affirmation of fact made by the seller constitutes an express warranty is generally a question of fact. See id., Official Comment 3; Daughtrey v. Ashe, 243 Va. 73, 78 (1992). In

Daughtrey, we examined whether a jeweler's statement on an appraisal form constituted an express warranty. We held that the jeweler's description of the particular diamonds being purchased as "v.v.s. quality" constituted an express warranty that the diamonds were, in fact, of that grade. Id. at 77, 413 S.E.2d at 338.

Unlike the representation in Daughtrey, however, the statements in the "prop matrixes" provided by Bayliner did not relate to the particular boat purchased by Crow, or to one having substantially similar characteristics. By their plain terms, the figures stated in the "prop matrixes" referred to a boat with different sized propellers that carried equipment weighing substantially less than the equipment on Crow's boat. Therefore, we conclude that the statements contained in the "prop matrixes" did not constitute an express warranty by Bayliner about the performance capabilities of the particular boat purchased by Crow.

Crow also contends that Bayliner made an express warranty regarding the boat's maximum speed in the statement in Bayliner's sales brochure that this model boat "delivers the kind of performance you need to get to the prime offshore fishing grounds." While the general rule is that a description of the goods that forms a basis of the bargain constitutes an express warranty, [UCC § 2–313(2)] directs that "a statement purporting to be merely the seller's opinion or commendation of the goods does not create a warranty."

The statement made by Bayliner in its sales brochure is merely a commendation of the boat's performance and does not describe a specific characteristic or feature of the boat. The statement simply expressed the manufacturer's opinion concerning the quality of the boat's performance and did not create an express warranty that the boat was capable of attaining a speed of 30 miles per hour. Therefore, we conclude that the evidence does not support the trial court's finding that Bayliner breached an express warranty made to Crow.

[The Court also found that Bayliner had not violated the "implied warranty of merchantability" provided in UCC § 2–314. Discussion of implied warranties is left to Chapter 5.]

Reversed and final judgment.

NOTES

(1)   *UCC Primer.* Article 2 of the Uniform Commercial Code ("the UCC" or "the Code") is the primary source of law for transactions involving the sale of goods in the United States. The Code itself is the product of the American Law Institute and the National Conference of Commissioners on Uniform State Laws, now known as the Uniform Law Commission (ULC). Article 2 has been enacted in substantially identical form in all the states except Louisiana. It is fundamental to the study of contract law, and cases exploring its structure and how it differs from the common law appear throughout this book. For a discussion of what constitutes "goods" and which law governs contracts involving both goods and non-goods, see Note 1 on page 574.

(2) *Express Warranties.* UCC § 2–313 provides that sellers may create express warranties through a number of mechanisms without resort to specific terms like "warrant" or "guarantee." These mechanisms include affirmations of facts or promises, descriptions, and physical samples or models which are part of the basis of the bargain between the parties: UCC § 2–313(1).

According to Crow, what promise or express warranty had Atherton broken? By what mechanism had the supposed warranty been made? Why should an express warranty result even if the seller did not intend to make one? What if Atherton had told Crow during their negotiations that "in my opinion this boat will go 30 miles per hour no trouble"? See UCC § 2–313(2).

(3) *Implied Warranties.* Suppose that another purchaser contracted with a boat manufacturer for the sale of a speed boat and that, as in the principal case, the contract was silent with regard to the boat's speed. Assuming that there had been no brochure or any discussion of speed between the parties prior to the sale, would any promise have been broken if, when the purchaser revved the engine of his new boat, it was able to achieve a maximum speed of only 2 miles per hour? See UCC § 2–314 (2). Which of the provisions of that subsection might apply? How do implied warranties alter the force or applicability of the familiar saying *caveat emptor*?

Theories of Promissory Liability

According to Restatement § 1, the law of contract is the law of enforceable promises.[a] But why should law enforce promises at all? In a well-known article from the last century, legal philosopher Morris Cohen suggested that "[t]he simplest answer is that of the intuitionists, namely, that promises are sacred per se, that there is something inherently despicable about not keeping a promise, and that a properly organized society should not tolerate this." At the same time, Cohen thought it doubtful that:

> "many of us would want to live in an entirely rigid world in which one would be obliged to keep all one's promises instead of the present more viable system, in which a vaguely fair proportion is sufficient. Many of us indeed would shudder at the idea of being bound by every promise, no matter how foolish, without any chance of letting increased wisdom undo past foolishness. Certainly, some freedom to change one's mind is necessary for free intercourse between those who lack

---

[a] Not all sources of contract law speak in terms of promises. Article 2 of the UCC characterizes contracts as resulting from agreements, as does the Convention on the International Sale of Goods (CISG), codifying the law of international sale of goods. The French Civil Code also defines a contract as an agreement by which one or more persons legally obligate themselves to transfer, to do, or not to do something.

omniscience." Morris Cohen, The Basis of Contract, 46 Harv. L.
Rev. 553, 571–74, 580–583 (1932).

Few would argue with the notion that promises carry moral force. Yet,
when the force of law is brought to bear on promises, commonsense
notions become more complicated and more contested. "Nowhere,"
declared Oliver Wendell Holmes,[b] "is the confusion between legal and
moral ideas more manifest than in the law of contract." The Path of the
Law, 10 Harv. L. Rev. 457 (1897).

Conceding that law is justified in enforcing some, but not all,
promises, the pertinent question then becomes, what distinguishes the
promises that law will enforce from those it will not? To address this
question, a number of theoretical arguments have been proposed, some
more compelling than others. Pursuing these lines of argument in any
detail would take us well outside the doctrinal focus of this casebook.
However, as we shall see, theoretical perspectives can usefully inform the
application of doctrine. For example, as the court observed in Mills v.
Wyman, p. 73 below, "[g]eneral rules of law established for the protection
and security of honest and fair-minded men, who may inconsiderately
make promises without any equivalent, will sometimes screen men of a
different character from engagements which they are bound *in foro
conscientiae* to perform."

Every theoretical argument justifying promissory liability
emphasizes certain underlying values served by contract doctrine. Take,
for instance, two competing theories that ground legal enforcement in the
promisor's autonomy or will. The "contract as promise" thesis holds that
law is justified in enforcing a promise when an individual "intentionally
invoke[s] a convention whose function is to give grounds—moral
grounds—for another to expect the promised performance." See, Charles
Fried, *Contract as Promise*, at p. 16 (1981). Morality alone, however,
won't tell us which promises are or ought to be legally enforceable,
because all promises carry some moral force. The competing "consent
theory" grounds enforcement less in a general moral duty to keep
promises than in consensual undertakings that reveal an "intention to
create a legally enforceable obligation." See Randy E. Barnett, *A Consent
Theory of Contract*, 86 Colum. L. Rev. 269, 300 (1986).

Both "contract as promise" and the "consent theory" look to the
promisor's will—in making a promise or voluntarily taking on a legal
duty—in locating the basis for judicial enforcement. A third theoretical
basis of promissory obligation flips the focus from the promisor's will to
the promisee's reliance. When a promisee reasonably relies on a promise
to his detriment, law may, and in many cases does, enforce the promise,

---

[b]　Oliver Wendell Holmes, Jr. (1841–1935) fought in the Civil War, practiced law in
Boston, served briefly as professor of law at Harvard, and then for 20 years was justice and later
chief justice of the Supreme Judicial Court of Massachusetts. In 1902, President Theodore
Roosevelt appointed him to the Supreme Court of the United States, where the quality of his
dissenting opinions won him the title of the "Great Dissenter." He resigned because of his great
age in 1932. His most famous work is *The Common Law* (1881), based on a series of lectures.

even against the promisor's will, in order to protect the promisee. Reliance theories are most clearly implicated in the various estoppel doctrines that enforce promises where the promise has triggered reasonable, foreseeable, and justifiable detrimental action by the promisee.

Still other rival theoretical arguments for promissory liability focus less on the interests of the parties, whether promisors or promisees, and more on broader criteria such as economic efficiency, predictability, fairness, social justice, and distribution. For example, as Morris Cohen observed, "[t]here can be no doubt that from an empirical or historical point of view, the ability to rely on the promises of others adds to the confidence necessary to social intercourse and enterprise." Whether or not these broader criteria undergird the whole of contract law, aspects of each are reflected in the various doctrines we will study. As you read the cases going forward, be alert to the competing normative values articulated in the doctrines and opinions recognizing or denying liability for promises. Predictability, for instance, is a central motivating feature of the consideration doctrine, the topic of Section 3, and fairness, social justice and distribution run through the doctrine of unconscionability, discussed in Chapter 6. Theories of economic efficiency have been most effective, and perhaps also most controversial, in the doctrines involving contract remedies, the topic to which we now turn.

SECTION 2.   REMEDYING BREACH

We all know what it means to keep a promise. Simply put, it means doing what was promised. But what does it mean to *enforce* a promise that has not been kept? Restatement § 1 defines a contract in terms of both a legal duty to perform a promise and the provision of a remedy if performance does not occur. How does the law determine the appropriate remedy? Although the answer is taken up in detail in Chapter 8, some consideration of remedies is useful at the outset to get a sense of what is at stake practically and conceptually when a promise is broken.

The cases that follow introduce two fundamental assumptions made by courts in the development of remedies. The first is that the law is primarily concerned with relief of aggrieved promisees and not with punishment of promisors. The second assumption is that the primary purpose of the remedy is to give promisees "the benefit of the bargain" by protecting expectation interests. As expressed in Restatement § 344(a), the objective of protecting a promisee's expectation interest is to put the promisee "in as good a position as he would have been in had the contract been performed." While easily stated, the complexities of figuring out just how to measure that interest are tested by the jury instructions at issue in the next two cases, Hawkins v. McGee and Sullivan v. O'Connor.

Hawkins v. McGee

New Hampshire Supreme Court, 1929.
84 N.H. 114, 146 A. 641.

[The background facts of this case regarding Dr. McGee's legal obligation for his promise to Hawkins "to make the hand a hundred per cent perfect" are found at p. 2. We now turn to the court's discussion of the remedy for the breach of Dr. McGee's promise.]

The substance of the charge to the jury on the question of damages appears in the following quotation: "If you find the plaintiff entitled to anything, he is entitled to recover for what pain and suffering he has been made to endure and for what injury he has sustained over and above what injury he had before." To this instruction the defendant seasonably excepted. By it, the jury was permitted to consider two elements of damage: (1) pain and suffering due to the operation; and (2) positive ill effects of the operation upon the plaintiff's hand. Authority for any specific rule of damages in cases of this kind seems to be lacking, but, when tested by general principle and by analogy, it appears that the foregoing instruction was erroneous.

"By 'damages,' as that term is used in the law of contracts, is intended compensation for a breach, measured in the terms of the contract." Davis v. New England Cotton Yarn Co., 77 N. H. 403, 404, 92 A. 732, 733. The purpose of the law is "to put the plaintiff in as good a position as he would have been in had the defendant kept his contract." 3 Williston Cont. § 1338. The measure of recovery "is based upon what the defendant should have given the plaintiff, not what the plaintiff has given the defendant or otherwise expended." 3 Williston Cont. § 1341. "The only losses that can be said fairly to come within the terms of a contract are such as the parties must have had in mind when the contract was made, or such as they either knew or ought to have known would probably result from a failure to comply with its terms." Davis v. New England Cotton Yarn Co., 77 N. H. 403, 404, 92 A. 732, 733. The present case is closely analogous to one in which a machine is built for a certain purpose and warranted to do certain work. In such cases, the usual rule of damages for breach of warranty in the sale of chattels is applied, and it is held that the measure of damages is the difference between the value of the machine, if it had corresponded with the warranty and its actual value, together with such incidental losses as the parties knew, or ought to have known, would probably result from a failure to comply with its terms. Hooper v. Story, 155 N. Y. 171, 175, 49 N. E. 773 [additional citations omitted].

The rule thus applied is well settled in this state. "As a general rule, the measure of the vendee's damages is the difference between the value of the goods as they would have been if the warranty as to quality had been true, and the actual value at the time of the sale, including gains prevented and losses sustained, and such other damages as could be reasonably anticipated by the parties as likely to be caused by the vendor's failure to keep his agreement, and could not by reasonable care on the part of the vendee have been avoided." Union Bank v. Blanchard, 65 N. H. 21, 23, 18 A. 90, 91. We therefore conclude that the true measure of the plaintiff's damage in the present case is the difference between the value to him of a perfect hand or a good hand, such as the jury found the defendant promised him, and the value of his hand in its present condition, including any incidental consequences fairly within the contemplation of the parties when they made their contract. Damages not thus limited, although naturally resulting, are not to be given.

The extent of the plaintiff's suffering does not measure this difference in value. The pain necessarily incident to a serious surgical operation was a part of the contribution which the plaintiff was willing to make to his joint undertaking with the defendant to produce a good hand. It was a legal detriment suffered by him which constituted a part of the consideration given by him for the contract. It represented a part of the price which he was willing to pay for a good hand, but it furnished no test of the value of a good hand or the difference between the value of the hand which the defendant promised and the one which resulted from the operation.

It was also erroneous and misleading to submit to the jury as a separate element of damage any change for the worse in the condition of the plaintiff's hand resulting from the operation, although this error was probably more prejudicial to the plaintiff than to the defendant. Any such ill effect of the operation would be included under the true rule of damages set forth above, but damages might properly be assessed for the defendant's failure to improve the condition of the hand, even if there were no evidence that its condition was made worse as a result of the operation.

Defendant's request No. 7 was as follows: "If you should get so far as to find that there was a special contract guaranteeing a perfect result, you would still have to find for the defendant unless you also found that a further operation would not correct the disability claimed by the plaintiff." In view of the testimony that the defendant had refused to perform a further operation, it would clearly have been erroneous to give this instruction. The evidence would have justified a verdict for an amount sufficient to cover the cost of such an operation, even if the theory underlying this request were correct.

NOTES

(1) *Jury Instructions*. In civil trials in the United States, the judge and jury have different roles, with the judge not only generally supervising the trial but also determining the rules of law that govern the matter at dispute. The jury in turn finds facts and renders a verdict based on the rules of law applied to those facts. The link between the judicial function and the jury function is typically provided by instructions given by the judge to the jury at the end of the trial and before the jury begins to deliberate. "[Jury]

instructions explain the law applicable to the case and direct the jurors to reach a verdict in accordance with certain legal definitions and instructions. The effect of jury instructions on juror deliberation and decision-making is an essential part of the jury's fulfillment of its duties." Elizabeth G. Thornburg, The Power and the Process: Instructions and the Civil Jury, 66 Fordham L. Rev. 1837, 1840 (1998). In *Hawkins*, the New Hampshire Supreme Court ordered a new trial in part because the judge had erroneously instructed the jury about the substance of the law the jury was to apply in calculating Hawkins's damages.

(2) *Money Damages*. The legal system cannot, by fiat, make young Mr. Hawkins's hand "a hundred percent perfect," and ordering Dr. McGee to keep operating until he achieved the desired result would certainly be an unappealing prospect. This case introduces a more typical reaction of the law to a party's breach of its promise—awarding the promisee money damages. But how much money should be awarded? Instructions about that issue were the subject of this portion of the *Hawkins* opinion. According to the court, damages, "as that term is used in the law of contracts, is intended compensation for a breach, measured in the terms of the contract. . . The purpose of the law is 'to put the plaintiff in as good a position as he would have been in had the defendant kept his contract.' " How to put the promisee in that position, however, can be the subject of difficult analysis and differing views, and will draw much attention throughout a course in contract law. In addition, there are competing theories about the purpose of monetary remedies in contract law, as introduced in the next case.

In the following case, the Supreme Judicial Court of Massachusetts considered how three interests—expectation, reliance, and restitution—play out in the context of an action brought against a plastic surgeon for his failure to improve the plaintiff's appearance as he had promised to do. Our focus in *Sullivan* is not on the promise, but as in the excerpt from *Hawkins* just above, on the nature of the remedy.

Sullivan v. O'Connor

Supreme Judicial Court of Massachusetts, 1973.
363 Mass. 579, 296 N.E.2d 183.

[Alice Sullivan alleged she had entered into a contract with Dr. James O'Connor for plastic surgery "to enhance her beauty and improve her nose," but that as a result of the surgery, her appearance had been worsened. She charged O'Connor with negligence and with breach of contract. A jury awarded her $13,500 on the latter count, rejecting her charge of negligence. The evidence provided support for findings as follow. O'Connor had promised Sullivan that, in two operations, he would make her nose shorter and more pleasing in relation to her other features. Having failed in that, he performed a third operation. Sullivan remained disfigured; and her appearance could not be improved by further surgery. Sullivan had paid a fee to O'Connor, and hospital expenses, for a total of $622.65. She was a professional entertainer, as

O'Connor had known. She failed to demonstrate, however, that she had lost employment by reason of her change of appearance.

O'Connor appealed, contending that the trial judge had erred in instructing the jury about the issue of damages. Sullivan had also objected to those instructions, on the ground that the judge had not instructed the jury that she was entitled to the difference between the value of her nose as promised and the diminished value of her nose after the operations. However, Sullivan indicated on appeal that she was willing to waive that objection if the appellate court denied O'Connor's appeal.

The opinion describes the instructions about damages given to the jury, and O'Connor's objections to them.]

■ KAPLAN, JUSTICE. The judge instructed the jury, first, that the plaintiff was entitled to recover her out-of-pocket expenses incident to the operations. Second, she could recover the damages flowing directly, naturally, proximately, and foreseeably from the defendant's breach of promise. These would comprehend damages for any disfigurement of the plaintiff's nose—that is, any change of appearance for the worse—including the effects of the consciousness of such disfigurement on the plaintiff's mind, and in this connection the jury should consider the nature of the plaintiff's profession. Also consequent upon the defendant's breach, and compensable, were the pain and suffering involved in the third operation, but not in the first two. As there was no proof that any loss of earnings by the plaintiff resulted from the breach, that element should not enter into the calculation of damages.

By his exceptions the defendant contends that the judge erred in allowing the jury to take into account anything but the plaintiff's out-of-pocket expenses (presumably at the stipulated amount). The defendant excepted to the judge's refusal of his request for a general charge to that effect, and, more specifically, to the judge's refusal of a charge that the plaintiff could not recover for pain and suffering connected with the third operation or for impairment of the plaintiff's appearance and associated mental distress.

The plaintiff on her part excepted to the judge's refusal of a request to charge that the plaintiff could recover the difference in value between the nose as promised and the nose as it appeared after the operations. However, the plaintiff in her brief expressly waives this exception and others made by her in case this court overrules the defendant's exceptions; thus she would be content to hold the jury's verdict in her favor.

We conclude that the defendant's exceptions should be overruled.

[In an omitted part of the decision, the Court discussed whether a doctor's promise should be unenforceable on policy grounds, concluding that the law allows "actions based on alleged contract, but insist[s] on clear proof . . . that a given result was promised." The Court then turned to the question of damages.]

If an action on the basis of contract is allowed, we have next the question of the measure of damages to be applied where liability is found. Some cases have taken the simple view that the promise by the physician is to be treated like an ordinary commercial promise, and accordingly that the successful plaintiff is entitled to a standard measure of recovery for breach of contract—"compensatory" ("expectancy") damages, an amount intended to put the plaintiff in the position he would be in if the contract had been performed, or, presumably, at the plaintiff's election, "restitution" damages, an amount corresponding to any benefit conferred by the plaintiff upon the defendant in the performance of the contract disrupted by the defendant's breach. See Restatement: Contracts § 329 and comment a, §§ 347, 384(1). Thus in Hawkins v. McGee, 84 N.H. 114, 146 A. 641, the defendant doctor was taken to have promised the plaintiff to convert his damaged hand by means of an operation into a good or perfect hand, but the doctor so operated as to damage the hand still further. The court, following the usual expectancy formula, would have asked the jury to estimate and award to the plaintiff the difference between the value of a good or perfect hand, as promised, and the value of the hand after the operation. (The same formula would apply, although the dollar result would be less, if the operation had neither worsened nor improved the condition of the hand.) If the plaintiff had not yet paid the doctor his fee, that amount would be deducted from the recovery. There could be no recovery for the pain and suffering of the operation, since that detriment would have been incurred even if the operation had been successful; one can say that this detriment was not "caused" by the breach. But where the plaintiff by reason of the operation was put to more pain than he would have had to endure, had the doctor performed as promised, he should be compensated for that difference as a proper part of his expectancy recovery. It may be noted that on an alternative count for malpractice the plaintiff in the *Hawkins* case had been nonsuited; but on ordinary principles this could not affect the contract claim, for it is hardly a defense to a breach of contract that the promisor acted innocently and without negligence. The New Hampshire court further refined the *Hawkins* analysis in McQuaid v. Michou, 85 N.H. 299, all in the direction of treating the patient-physician cases on the ordinary footing of expectancy.

Other cases, including a number in New York, without distinctly repudiating the *Hawkins* type of analysis, have indicated that a different and generally more lenient measure of damages is to be applied in patient-physician actions based on breach of alleged special agreements to effect a cure, attain a stated result, or employ a given medical method. This measure is expressed in somewhat variant ways, but the substance is that the plaintiff is to recover any expenditures made by him and for other detriment (usually not specifically described in the opinions) following proximately and foreseeably upon the defendant's failure to carry out his promise. Robins v. Finestone, 308 N.Y. 543, 546. This, be it noted, is not a "restitution" measure, for it is not limited to restoration of the benefit conferred on the defendant (the fee paid) but includes other expenditures, for example, amounts paid for medicine and nurses; so also it would seem according to its logic to take in damages for any worsening of the plaintiff's condition due to the breach. Nor is it an "expectancy" measure, for it does not appear to contemplate recovery of the whole difference in value between the condition as promised and the condition actually resulting from the treatment. Rather the tendency of the formulation is to put the plaintiff back in the position he occupied just before the parties entered upon the agreement, to compensate him for the detriments he suffered in reliance upon the agreement. This kind of intermediate pattern of recovery for breach of contract is discussed in the suggestive article by Fuller and Perdue, *The Reliance Interest in Contract Damages*, 46 Yale L.J. 52, 373, where the authors show that, although not attaining the currency of the standard measures, a "reliance" measure has for special reasons been applied by the courts in a variety of settings, including noncommercial settings. See 46 Yale L.J. at 396–401.[1]

For breach of the patient-physician agreements under consideration, a recovery limited to restitution seems plainly too meager, if the agreements are to be enforced at all. On the other hand, an expectancy recovery may well be excessive. The factors, already mentioned, which have made the cause of action somewhat suspect, also suggest moderation as to the breadth of the recovery that should be permitted. Where, as in the case at bar and in a number of the reported cases, the doctor has been absolved of negligence by the trier, an expectancy measure may be thought harsh. We should recall here that the fee paid by the patient to the doctor for the alleged promise would usually be quite disproportionate to the putative expectancy recovery. To attempt, moreover, to put a value on the condition that would or might have resulted, had the treatment succeeded as promised, may sometimes put an exceptional strain on the imagination of the fact finder. As a general consideration, Fuller and Perdue argue that the reasons for granting damages for broken promises to the extent of the expectancy are at their strongest when the promises are made in a business context, when they have to do with the production or distribution of goods or the allocation of functions in the market place; they become weaker as the context shifts from a commercial to a noncommercial field. 46 Yale L.J. at 60–63.

There is much to be said, then, for applying a reliance measure to the present facts, and we have only to add that our cases are not

---

[1] Some of the exceptional situations mentioned where reliance may be preferred to expectancy are those in which the latter measure would be hard to apply or would impose too great a burden; performance was interfered with by external circumstances; the contract was indefinite. See 46 Yale L.J. at 373–386; 394–396.

unreceptive to the use of that formula in special situations. We have, however, had no previous occasion to apply it to patient-physician cases.[2]

The question of recovery on a reliance basis for pain and suffering or mental distress requires further attention. We find expressions in the decisions that pain and suffering (or the like) are simply not compensable in actions for breach of contract. The defendant seemingly espouses this proposition in the present case. True, if the buyer under a contract for the purchase of a lot of merchandise, in suing for the seller's breach, should claim damages for mental anguish caused by his disappointment in the transaction, he would not succeed; he would be told, perhaps, that the asserted psychological injury was not fairly foreseeable by the defendant as a probable consequence of the breach of such a business contract. See Restatement of Contracts, § 341, and comment *a*. But there is no general rule barring such items of damage in actions for breach of contract. It is all a question of the subject matter and background of the contract, and when the contract calls for an operation on the person of the plaintiff, psychological as well as physical injury may be expected to figure somewhere in the recovery, depending on the particular circumstances. The point is explained in Stewart v. Rudner, 349 Mich. 459, 469. Cf. Frewen v. Page, 238 Mass. 499; McClean v. University Club, 327 Mass. 68. Again, it is said in a few of the New York cases, concerned with the classification of actions for statute of limitations purposes, that the absence of allegations demanding recovery for pain and suffering is characteristic of a contract claim by a patient against a physician, that such allegations rather belong in a claim for malpractice. See Robins v. Finestone, 308 N.Y. 543, 547; Budoff v. Kessler, 153 N.Y.S.2d 654. These remarks seem unduly sweeping. Suffering or distress resulting from the breach going beyond that which was envisaged by the treatment as agreed, should be compensable on the same ground as the worsening of the patient's condition because of the breach. Indeed it can be argued that the very suffering or distress "contracted for"—that which would have

---

[2]   In Mt. Pleasant Stable Co. v. Steinberg, 238 Mass. 567, the plaintiff company agreed to supply teams of horses at agreed rates as required from day to day by the defendant for his business. To prepare itself to fulfill the contract and in reliance on it, the plaintiff bought two "Cliest" horses at a certain price. When the defendant repudiated the contract, the plaintiff sold the horses at a loss and in its action for breach claimed the loss as an element of damages. The court properly held that the plaintiff was not entitled to this item as it was also claiming (and recovering) its lost profits (expectancy) on the contract as a whole. Cf. Noble v. Ames Mfg. Co., 112 Mass. 492. (The loss on sale of the horses is analogous to the pain and suffering for which the patient would be disallowed a recovery in Hawkins v. McGee, 84 N.H. 114, 146 A. 641, because he was claiming and recovering expectancy damages.) The court in the *Mt. Pleasant* case referred, however, to Pond v. Harris, 113 Mass. 114, as a contrasting situation where the expectancy could not be fairly determined. There the defendant had wrongfully revoked an agreement to arbitrate a dispute with the plaintiff (this was before such agreements were made specifically enforceable). In an action for the breach, the plaintiff was held entitled to recover for his preparations for the arbitration which had been rendered useless and a waste, including the plaintiff's time and trouble and his expenditures for counsel and witnesses. The context apparently was commercial but reliance elements were held compensable when there was no fair way of estimating an expectancy. See, generally, annotation, 17 A.L.R.2d 1300. A noncommercial example is Smith v. Sherman, 4 Cush. 408, 413–414, suggesting that a conventional recovery for breach of promise of marriage included a recompense for various efforts and expenditures by the plaintiff preparatory to the promised wedding.

Mobil Oil Exploration & Producing Southeast v. United States, 530 U.S. 604, 624 (2000) (Breyer, J.).

———

Remedies Based on Compensatory Measures

When the law seeks to remedy breach by compensating the promisee, what amount of money should the promisor pay? We have already encountered one answer: whatever it takes to protect the promisee's expectation interest. In that case, the award should be just enough money to make the promisee as well off as actual performance would have made her. On this account, the promisee's injury consists of being worse off than if the promise had been performed, and expectation damages "undo" the effect of breach on the promisee. Expectation damages are widely acknowledged as the customary measure of relief for breach of contract. However, concerns of expediency, judicial economy, or other policy considerations, such as those discussed in Sullivan v. O'Connor, will often promote other measures of compensation for breach of contract. After *expectation*, the three most commonly recognized damage measures are *reliance*, *restitution*, and *disgorgement*.

Reliance damages are based on a promisee's reliance interests, which are subverted when he has changed his position to his detriment by relying on the promise. The promisee may, for example, have incurred expenses in preparing to perform his part of the deal. Reliance damages would reimburse those expenses among other losses "caused by reliance." Restatement § 344(b). Here the promisee's injury consists of being worse off than if the promise had not been made in the first place. Hence, reliance damages are often said to "undo" the effect of promise on the promisee. As explained in Restatement § 344(b), reliance damages put the promisee "in as good a position as he would have been in had the contract not been made."

Restitution *damages* must be distinguished from *liability* based on actions arising from claims of "restitution and unjust enrichment." A vast body of law and doctrine on these subjects will significantly inform our discussion of contractual and quasi-contractual obligation throughout the book. At this point, however, we are focused on the more limited notion of restitution damages, which may be adequately characterized in terms of the promisee's "interest in having restored to him any benefit that he has conferred on the other party." Restatement § 344(c). The promisee may, for example, have given the promisor a down payment or performed some work that benefited the promisor before being paid anything. Although a promisee may rely extensively on a promise, such as making up-front payments to the promisor and incurring other expenditures with respect to third parties, restitution damages concern only that aspect of reliance which confers a benefit to the promisor. As such, restitution damages may be said to put the *promisor* in the position in which she would have been had the contract not been made.

Damages based on disgorgement arise from situations wherein a promisor has realized some gain from breaching. Plainly operative in the disgorgement damage measure is the ancient principle of law that one ought not profit from one's own wrongdoing. See Restatement (Third) of Restitution and Unjust Enrichment § 39. The disgorgement measure theoretically aims to put the *promisor* in the position she would have been in had the wrong—which is to say, the breach of contract—not occurred. Achieving this result in practice, however, is often challenging. Complicating matters further is the fact that disgorgement is often advanced to serve an interest other than sanctioning the promisor, such as approximating the promisee's expectation interest. In the next case, Naval Institute, this complication arises as the court seeks to compensate Naval by calculating the extent of profits it lost on account of Berkley's breach.

United States Naval Institute v. Charter Communications, Inc.

United States Court of Appeals, Second Circuit, 1991.
936 F.2d 692.

■ KEARSE, CIRCUIT JUDGE. This case returns to us following our remand in United States Naval Institute v. Charter Communications, Inc., 875 F.2d 1044 (2d Cir.1989) ("Naval I") for the fashioning of relief in favor of plaintiff United States Naval Institute ("Naval") against defendant Charter Communications, Inc., and Berkley Publishing Group (collectively "Berkley"), for breach of an agreement with respect to the publication of the paperback edition of The Hunt For Red October ("Red October" or the "Book"). On remand, the district court awarded Naval $35,380.50 in damages [and] $7,760.12 as profits wrongfully received by Berkley. Naval appeals from so much of the judgment as failed to award a greater amount as profits. Berkley cross-appeals from the judgment as a whole and from such parts of it as awarded moneys to Naval. For the reasons below, we reverse the award of profits; we affirm the award of damages.

I.   Background

Naval, as the assignee of the author's copyright in Red October, entered into a licensing agreement with Berkley in September 1984 (the "Agreement"), granting Berkley the exclusive license to publish a paperback edition of the Book "not sooner than October 1985." Berkley shipped its paperback edition to retail outlets early, placing those outlets in position to sell the paperback prior to October 1985. As a result, retail sales of the paperback began on September 15, 1985, and early sales were sufficiently substantial that the Book was near the top of paperback bestseller lists before the end of September 1985.

Naval commenced the present action when it learned of Berkley's plans for early shipment, and it unsuccessfully sought a preliminary injunction. After trial, the district judge dismissed the complaint. He ruled that Berkley had not breached the Agreement because it was entitled, in accordance with industry custom, to ship prior to the agreed publication date. On appeal, we reversed. Though we upheld the district court's finding that the Agreement did not prohibit the early shipments themselves, we concluded that if the "not sooner than October 1985" term of the Agreement had any meaning whatever, it meant at least that Berkley was not allowed to cause such voluminous paperback retail sales prior to that date, and that Berkley had therefore breached the Agreement. Naval I, 875 F.2d at 1049–51. Accordingly, we remanded for entry of a judgment awarding Naval appropriate relief.

On the remand, Naval asserted that it was entitled to recovery for copyright infringement, and it sought judgment awarding it all of Berkley's profits from pre-October 1985 sales of the Book; it estimated those profits at $724,300. Berkley, on the other hand, [contended] that Berkley could not be held liable for copyright infringement; it argued that Naval therefore had at most a claim for breach-of-contract [and] argued that the profits attributed to it by Naval were inflated. [On remand, the district judge] concluded that Naval was entitled to recover damages for copyright infringement, comprising actual damages suffered by Naval plus Berkley's profits "attributable to the infringement," 17 U.S.C. § 504(b).

The court calculated Naval's "actual damages from Berkley's wrongful pre-October 'publication'" as the profits Naval would have earned from hardcover sales in September 1985 if the competing paperback edition had not then been offered for sale. July 17 Order at 8. Noting the downward trend of hardcover sales of the Book from March through August 1985, the court found that there was no reason to infer that Naval's September 1985 sales would have exceeded its August 1985 sales. The court calculated Naval's lost sales as the difference between the actual hardcover sales for those two months, and awarded Naval $35,380.50 as actual damages.

The district judge held that Berkley's profits "attributable to the infringement" were only those profits that resulted from "sales to customers who would not have bought the paperback but for the fact it became available in September." July 17 Order at 10. He found that most of the September paperback sales were made to buyers who would not have bought a hardcover edition in September, and therefore only those September sales that displaced hardcover sales were attributable to the infringement. Berkley's profit on the displacing copies totaled $7,760.12, and the court awarded that amount to Naval.

II. Discussion

A. Naval's Claim of Copyright Infringement. [The court rejected this claim because an exclusive licensee cannot be liable for infringing the copyright conveyed to it, even though it is liable for breach of contract.]

B. Contract Damages. Since the purpose of damages for breach of contract is to compensate the injured party for the loss caused by the breach, 5 Corbin On Contracts § 1002, at 31 (1964), those damages are generally measured by the plaintiff's actual loss, see, e.g., Restatement (Second) of Contracts § 347 (1981). While on occasion the defendant's profits are used as the measure of damages, see, e.g., Cincinnati Siemens-Lungren Gas Illuminating Co. v. Western Siemens-Lungren Co., 152 U.S. 200, 204–07 (1894), this generally occurs when those profits tend to define the plaintiff's loss, for an award of the defendant's profits where they greatly exceed the plaintiff's loss and there has been no tortious conduct on the part of the defendant would tend to be punitive, and punitive awards are not part of the law of contract damages. See generally Restatement (Second) of Contracts § 356 comment a ("The central objective behind the system of contract remedies is compensatory, not punitive."); id. comment b (agreement attempting to fix damages in amount vastly greater than what approximates actual loss would be unenforceable as imposing a penalty); id. § 355 (punitive damages not recoverable for breach of contract unless conduct constituting the breach is also a tort for which such damages are recoverable). § 355 (punitive damages not recoverable for breach of contract unless conduct constituting the breach is also a tort for which such damages are recoverable).

Here, the district court found that Berkley's alleged $724,300 profits did not define Naval's loss because many persons who bought the paperback in September 1985 would not have bought the book in hardcover but would merely have waited until the paperback edition became available. This finding is not clearly erroneous, and we turn to the question of whether the district court's finding that Naval suffered $35,380.50 in actual damages was proper.

In reaching the $35,380.50 figure, the court operated on the premise that, but for the breach by Berkley, Naval would have sold in September the same number of hardcover copies it sold in August. Berkley challenges that premise as speculative and argues that since Naval presented no evidence as to what its September 1985 sales would have been, Naval is entitled to recover no damages. It argues alternatively that the court should have computed damages on the premise that sales in the second half of September, in the absence of Berkley's premature release of the paperback edition, would have been made at the same rate as in the first half of September. Evaluating the district court's calculation of damages under the clearly erroneous standard of review, we reject Berkley's contentions.

The record showed that, though there was a declining trend of hardcover sales of the Book from March through August 1985, Naval continued to sell its hardcover copies through the end of 1985, averaging some 3,000 copies a month in the latter period.[c] It plainly was not error for the district court to find that the preponderance of the evidence indicated that Berkley's early shipment of 1,400,000 copies of its paperback edition, some 40% of which went to retail outlets and led to the Book's rising close to the top of the paperback bestseller lists before the end of September 1985, caused Naval the loss of some hardcover sales prior to October 1985.

As to the quantification of that loss, we think it was within the prerogative of the court as finder of fact to look to Naval's August 1985 sales. Though there was no proof as to precisely what the unimpeded volume of hardcover sales would have been for the entire month of September, any such evidence would necessarily have been hypothetical. But it is not error to lay the normal uncertainty in such hypotheses at the door of the wrongdoer who altered the proper course of events, instead of at the door of the injured party. See, e.g., Lamborn v. Dittmer, 873 F.2d 522, 532–33 (2d Cir. 1989); Lee v. Joseph E. Seagram & Sons, Inc., 552 F.2d 447, 455–56 (2d Cir. 1977). See generally. Restatement (Second) of Contracts § 352 comment *a* ("Doubts are generally resolved against the party in breach."). The court was not required to use as the starting point for its calculations Naval's actual sales in the first half of September, *i.e.,* those made prior to the first retail sale of the paperback edition. Berkley has not called to our attention any evidence in the record to indicate that the sales in a given month are normally spread evenly through that month. Indeed, it concedes that "[t]o a large degree, book sales depend on public whim and are notoriously unpredictable. " (Berkley brief on appeal at 31 n. 15.) Thus, nothing in the record foreclosed the possibility that, absent Berkley's breach, sales of hardcover copies in the latter part of September would have outpaced sales of those copies in the early part of the month. Though the court accurately described its selection of August 1985 sales as its benchmark as "generous[ ]," it was not improper, given the inherent uncertainty, to exercise generosity in favor of the injured party rather than in favor of the breaching party." (Berkley brief on appeal at 31 n. 15.) Thus, nothing in the record foreclosed the possibility that, absent Berkley's breach, sales of hardcover copies in the latter part of September would have outpaced sales of those copies in the early part of the month. Though the court accurately described its selection of August 1985 sales as its benchmark as "generous[ ]," it was not improper, given the inherent uncertainty, to exercise generosity in favor of the injured party rather than in favor of the breaching party.

---

[c]   It is unclear where Judge Kearse got the figure of only "some 3,000 copies a month" used in the paragraph after the next, but it might be a misprint for 30,000, an approximation of the August figure.

In all the circumstances, we cannot say that the district court's calculation of Naval's damages was clearly erroneous.

Conclusion

For the foregoing reasons, we reverse so much of the judgment as granted Naval $7,760.12 as an award of Berkley's profits. In all other respects, the judgment is affirmed.

NOTES

(1) *Measuring Promisee's Loss.* How did the district court go wrong in awarding Berkley's profits on pre-October paperback sales to Naval Institute? How does that award square with protecting Naval's expectation interest? How does it square with the assumption that the law's concern is with relief of promisees and not punishment of promisors?

(2) *Conceptualizing Disgorgement.* Are there any cases where "the defendant's profits tend to define the plaintiff's loss," as Judge Kearse put it? Professor E. Allan Farnsworth[d] described such cases, like *Cincinnati Siemens-Lungren* cited in *Naval Institute*, as follows:

"Suppose that a seller of a business makes a valid contract not to compete with the buyer and then breaks the covenant by operating a competing business. If the buyer claims damages, the court will often receive evidence of the profits that the seller made from the competing business as evidence of the profit that the buyer lost as a result of the breach. But a court will not assume that the buyer could have made the same sales that the seller did." *Your Loss or My Gain? The Dilemma of the Disgorgement Principle in Breach of Contract Cases*, 94 Yale L.J. 1339, 1366 (1985).

In other words, where the breaching promisor's profits match the amount the promisee would have gained had the promise been performed, disgorgement and expectation produce the same figure, and disgorgement may be ordered. Nonetheless, the purposes of the two measures of recovery are distinct. Protecting the promisee's expectation interest "undoes" the breach with regard to the promisee; the effect of disgorgement is to "undo" the breach with regard to the promisor, who must forego the gains of the breach.

(3) *Reconsidering Disgorgement.* The disgorgement of profits is not uncommon in non-contract cases; as the district judge concluded in *Naval Institute*, "Naval was entitled to recover damages for copyright infringement, comprising actual damages suffered by Naval *plus Berkley's profits* 'attributable to the infringement.' 17 U.S.C. § 504(b)." This provision of the

---

[d] E. Allan Farnsworth (1928–2005) was an eminent contract law scholar, and from 1965 until his death, an editor of this casebook. He taught for 50 years at the Columbia Law School, from which he graduated in 1952. He represented the United States in matters of international trade law at the United Nations and at UNIDROIT. In 1971, following Professor Robert Braucher, Farnsworth became the Reporter for the Restatement, Second, of Contracts. His treatise *Farnsworth on Contracts* is a standard text. In 1998, Prof. Farnsworth published *Changing Your Mind: The Law of Regretted Decisions*, and in 2004, *Alleviating Mistakes: Reversal and Forgiveness for Flawed Perceptions.*

Copyright Act requires the infringer to disgorge profits to prevent the infringer from unfairly benefiting from a wrongful act.

If the measure of disgorgement damages is conceptualized not from the perspective of the *promisee* but from the perspective of the breaching promisor, then disgorgement even in contract cases may not be quite so uncommon. From this perspective, the consequence of disgorgement is to put breaching promisors (rather than injured promisees) in the position they would have been in had the contract been performed. See Steven Thel and Peter Siegelman, You *Do* Have to Keep Your Promises: A Disgorgement Theory of Contract Remedies, 52 Wm. & Mary L. Rev. 1181 (2011). Examples include specific performance (where disgorgement and expectation clearly merge) and the UCC remedy of cover, discussed in Chapter 8. We take up the topic of disgorgement again on p. 39 when considering the efficient allocation of resources and damages.

(4)   *Fault.* As we saw in *Naval Institute*, to succeed in a contract action, the plaintiff must prove the actual amount of damages it has suffered, which Naval had some trouble doing: the amount of profits it would have earned was uncertain. In finding that Naval had come close enough, Judge Kearse stated that "it is not error to lay the normal uncertainty at the door of the wrongdoer who altered the proper course of events, instead of at the door of the injured party." Should the reason a party fails to perform matter in the assessment of damages? Should the law care if the breach is willful or innocent, deliberate or unavoidable? Look for instances where the court appears to take fault into account when deciding a case, despite the fundamental assumption, discussed below at pp. 30–34, that the law does not generally seek to punish promisors.

(5)   *Puzzler.* Why was the transaction in *Naval Institute* not governed by Article 2 of the Code?

———

Remedies Based on Specific Relief

When determining a remedy for a breach of contract, courts typically seek to put the promisee in the position it would have been in had the promise been kept. The most direct way to accomplish this aim is for courts to compel performance of exactly what was promised, using the remedy known as specific performance. Specific performance, however, is often unavailable (promised goods may be no longer available) or undesired (would young Hawkins have wanted Dr. McGee to give it another try?). In addition, ordering a party to do what was promised might require continuing judicial supervision, a task courts are reluctant and perhaps ill-equipped to take on, especially when the performance involves a service or extends over time. These considerations lead to a common assumption animating contract remedies in the United States: the appropriate form of relief is compensation for the breach, rather than requiring the promisor to perform. Courts order specific performance only sparingly, and in cases where monetary compensation is "inadequate." See Restatement § 359. The classic case for specific performance concerns the sale of land, because courts have traditionally regarded each tract of land as unique and therefore not susceptible to substitution. Land sales and other transactions in realty, however, are not the only contractual agreements with unique values recognized by courts as subject to orders of specific performance, as illustrated in the following case.

Morris v. Sparrow
Supreme Court of Arkansas, 1956.
225 Ark. 1019, 287 S.W.2d 583.

■ ROBINSON, JUSTICE. Appellee Archie Sparrow filed this suit for specific performance, seeking to compel appellant Morris to deliver possession of a certain horse, which Sparrow claims Morris agreed to give him as part consideration for work done by Sparrow. The appeal is from a decree requiring the delivery of the horse.

Morris owns a cattle ranch near Mountain View, Arkansas, and he also participates in rodeos. Sparrow is a cowboy, and is experienced in training horses; occasionally he takes part in rodeos. He lives in Florida; while at a rodeo in that state, he and Morris made an agreement that they would go to Morris' ranch in Arkansas and, later, the two would go to Canada. After arriving at the Morris ranch, they changed their plans and decided that, while Morris went to Canada, Sparrow would stay at the ranch and do the necessary work. The parties are in accord that Sparrow was to work 16 weeks for a money consideration of $400. But, Sparrow says that as an additional consideration he was to receive a brown horse called Keno, owned by Morris. However, Morris states that Sparrow was to get the horse only on condition that his work at the ranch was satisfactory, and that Sparrow failed to do a good job. Morris paid Sparrow the amount of money they agreed was due, but did not deliver the horse.

At the time Sparrow went to Morris' ranch, the horse in question was practically unbroken; but during his spare time, Sparrow trained the horse and, with a little additional training, he will be a first class roping horse.

First there is the issue of whether Sparrow can maintain, in equity, a suit to enforce, by specific performance, a contract for the delivery of personal property. Although it has been held that equity will not ordinarily enforce, by specific performance, a contract for the sale of chattels, it will do so where special and peculiar reasons exist which render it impossible for the injured party to obtain relief by way of damages in an action at law. Certainly when one has made a roping horse out of a green, unbroken pony, such a horse would have a peculiar and unique value; if Sparrow is entitled to prevail, he has a right to the horse instead of its market value in dollars and cents.

Morris claims that the part of the agreement whereby Sparrow was to receive the horse was conditional, depending on Sparrow doing a good job, and that he did not do such a job. Both parties were in Chancery Court and the Chancellor had a better opportunity than this court to evaluate the testimony of the witnesses; we cannot say the Chancellor's finding in favor of Sparrow is against the preponderance of the evidence.

Affirmed.

NOTES

(1) *A Priceless Roping Horse?* Why was a money damage award an inadequate remedy for Sparrow? The court describes Keno, the horse, as having "a peculiar and unique value." There is, and has long been, a robust market for the sale and breeding of thoroughbred horses, notwithstanding the unique value of these horses that feature in competitive racing. Is there something so unique about a roping horse, *per se*, that would render money damages too uncertain, too speculative, or otherwise inadequate?

(2) *Value, but Not "in Dollars and Cents."* Might there be something revealing in the court's observation that "if Sparrow is entitled to prevail, he has a right to the horse instead of its market value in dollars and cents"? Why a right to the horse, as opposed to its money value, assuming it can be determined? Perhaps the court gave weight to the value of affection between Sparrow and Keno. See e.g., Houseman v. Dare, 966 A.2d 24 (N.J. Super. App. Div. 2009), wherein Doreen Houseman filed suit against her ex-boyfriend, seeking specific performance of an oral agreement to have possession of "a dog she and defendant Eric Dare jointly owned when they separated and ended their engagement to be married." The Superior Court awarded her $1,500 in damages. Houseman appealed. The appellate court granted equitable relief for breach of the oral agreement to transfer possession of a pet dog, where the dog has "special subjective value based on one party's sincere affection for and attachment to it," as opposed to "a sentiment assumed for the purpose of litigation out of greed, ill-will or other sentiment or motive similarly unworthy of protection in a court of equity." Id. at 28.

(3) *Bargaining Around Court Orders.* An order of specific performance does not necessarily imply that parties will actually perform. Parties may always engage in private bargaining or settlement discussions, even after a final court order. See discussion of Coase Theorem, p. 39. When mutually advantageous to litigants, a new agreement contrary to the court's order may be reached. Over the course of litigating their dispute to a final order, however, parties tend to dig into their positions and animosity tends to increase. How likely, do you imagine, parties are willing to meet each other to negotiate a new agreement at the end of a contentious dispute? See Ward Farnsworth, *Do Parties to Nuisance Cases Bargain After Judgment? A Glimpse Inside the Cathedral*, 66 U. Chi. L. Rev. 373 (1999).

(4) *Canned Tomatoes.* The Curtice Brothers Company, operator of a tomato canning business, sued James Catts and others for breach of contract and sought specific performance of Catts's promise to deliver "the entire

product of certain land planted with tomatoes." In granting specific performance, the court emphasized the importance of Curtice Brothers' planning and investment.

"Complainants' factory has a capacity of about one million cans of tomatoes. The season for packing lasts about six weeks. The preparations made for this six weeks of active work must be carried out in all features to enable the business to succeed. These preparations are primarily based upon the capacity of the plant. Cans and other necessary equipments, including labor, must be provided and secured in advance with reference to the capacity of the plant during the packing period. The condition which arises from the breach of the contracts is not merely a question of the factory being compelled to pay a higher price for the product. Losses sustained in that manner could, with some degree of accuracy, be estimated. The condition which occasions the irreparable injury by reason of the breaches of the contracts is the inability to procure at any price at the time needed and of the quality needed the necessary tomatoes to insure the successful operation of the plant. The business and its needs are extraordinary in that the maintenance of all of the conditions prearranged to secure the pack are a necessity to insure the successful operation of the plant." Curtice Bros. Co. v. Catts, 66 A. 935, 936 (N.J. Ch. 1907)

What relationship might there be, if any, between the short packing season of only six weeks and protecting the investments of the business? We will encounter this question again in Alaska Packers' Ass'n v. Domenico at p. 438, where the court similarly made reference to the shortness of the packing season and the firm's planning and investment activities.

(5) *Personal Service Contracts and Moral Hazard.* A court will not order specific performance of a contract to provide a service that is personal in nature. One concern is the difficulty of passing judgment on the quality of performance. A second concern is the undesirability of compelling the continuance of personal relations after disputes have arisen and confidence and loyalty have been shaken (and, in some instances, of imposing what might seem like involuntary servitude).

Catts, in the case above, sought to avoid specific performance by claiming that specific performance would amount to compelling personal services. The court held that Catts "may be restrained from selling the crop to others, and, if necessary, a receiver can be appointed to harvest the crop." The difficulties courts face in monitoring performance, along with the concern that a party compelled to perform by a judicial order may not have the best incentives to perform well, create the risk that individuals will take less than ideal actions knowing that they will not be made fully accountable for their actions, so-called "moral hazard." Appointing a receiver to perform the task may help but is not a complete solution to the moral hazard problem. Can you see why?

(6) *Negative Injunctions.* Though courts are reluctant to compel performance of contracts to provide services that are personal in nature, they are quite willing to enjoin parties from other performances in appropriate circumstances. The classic case is Lumley v. Wagner, (1852) 42 Eng. Rep.

687, 693, which arose out of a contract in which Johanna Wagner, an opera singer from the court of Prussia, agreed to sing exclusively for Benjamin Lumley, proprietor of Her Majesty's Theatre in London, for a period of three months. When Frederick Gye, proprietor of the Royal Italian Opera in London, persuaded Wagner to break her contract and sing at his theater, Lumley obtained an injunction restraining her from doing so. On appeal, the Lord Chancellor upheld the injunction. "It is true that I have not the means of compelling her to sing, but she has no cause of complaint if I compel her to abstain from the commission of an act which she has bound herself not to do, and thus possibly cause her to fulfil her engagement."

As indicated above, a court will not grant an injunction unless the remedy in damages would be inadequate. This requirement is met if the employee's services are unique or extraordinary, either because of special skill that the employee possesses, as in Wagner's case, or because of special knowledge that the employee has acquired of the employer's business.

Injunctions are especially common in the world of sports, where the availability of such relief is enhanced by the belief that the requirement "that the player be an athlete of exceptional talent is met prima facie in cases involving professional athletes." Nassau Sports v. Peters, 352 F.Supp. 870, 876 (E.D.N.Y. 1972).

Stipulated Remedies and Punitive Damages

In *Hawkins* and *Bayliner*, the question of liability turned on whether there was an agreed standard of performance ("a hundred percent perfect hand" or "maximum speed of 30 miles per hour") that was satisfied. Can parties also agree to standards for remedies? The answer is yes, with some important limitations. For example, in a contract for the sale of goods, parties can agree to modify or limit statutory remedies (by, for example, limiting a seller's obligation in the case of defective goods to repair or replacement of those goods), in which case the limitation on remedies will be given effect unless the limit is so severe that the remedies will fail of their "essential purpose." In addition, parties can, by agreement, "liquidate" damages (by agreeing to an amount of damages for a party's breach or a formula to determine the amount, so long as the amount is reasonable in light of a number of factors stated in UCC § 2–718(1); if the amount is unreasonably large, it will be held void as a penalty). The common law takes a similar approach.

What explains the willingness of courts to enforce contractual provisions that limit standard remedies, often significantly, while being unwilling to enforce liquidated damages that rise substantially above standard remedies? A number of answers may be plausibly offered to address this question, yet the most conventional account is grounded in the deep and longstanding reluctance to award punitive damages for breach of contract in the common law. When a stipulated remedy appears too generous to one side or too punitive to the other, judges are required to negotiate a "fuzzy line between penalty clauses and liquidated-damages clauses." See Lake River Corp. v. Carborundum Co. on p. 997. Liquidated-damages clauses are enforceable; penalty clauses are not. That much is clear. Difficulties lie in determining on which side of the line to place an apparently punitive award. On this account, the challenge is not due to the fact that the remedy is liquidated, but rather because it is, or appears to be, punitive; and as a general matter, as illustrated in the next case, punitive damages are not typically awarded for breach of contract.

White v. Benkowski

Supreme Court of Wisconsin, 1967.
37 Wis.2d 285, 155 N.W.2d 74.

[In 1962, Virgil and Gwynneth White bought a house that lacked its own water supply but was connected by pipes to a well on the adjacent property of Paul and Ruth Benkowski. The Whites entered into a written contract with the Benkowskis under which the Benkowskis promised to supply water to the Whites' home for ten years unless the municipality supplied it, the well became inadequate, or the Whites drilled their own well. In exchange, the Whites agreed to pay the Benkowskis $3 a month and half the cost of any future repairs or maintenance. Although the relationship between the neighbors began as a friendly one, by 1964 it had deteriorated and become hostile. During March and June, the Benkowskis shut off the water supply on nine occasions for periods in the late afternoon and early evening that were, according to Mrs. White's records, well under an hour. Mr. Benkowski claimed this was done either to allow accumulated sand in the pipes to settle or to remind the Whites that their water use was excessive. The Whites sued the Benkowskis for breach of contract, seeking compensatory and punitive damages. The jury found the Benkowskis had shut off the water maliciously in order to harass the Whites. It awarded the Whites compensatory damages of $10 and punitive damages of $2,000. On motions after the verdict, the award was reduced to $1 in compensatory damages and no punitive damages. The Whites appealed.]

■ WILKIE, JUSTICE. Two issues are raised on this appeal.

1. Was the trial court correct in reducing the award of compensatory damages from $10 to $1?

2. Are punitive damages available in actions for breach of contract?

Reduction of Jury Award

The evidence of damage adduced during the trial here was that the water supply had been shut off during several short periods. Three incidents of inconvenience resulting from these shut-offs were detailed by the plaintiffs. Mrs. White testified that the lack of water in the bathroom on one occasion caused an odor and that on two other occasions she was forced to take her children to a neighbor's home to bathe them. Based on this evidence, the court instructed the jury that:

"in an action for a breach of contract the plaintiff is entitled to such damages as shall have been sustained by him which resulted naturally and directly from the breach if you find that the defendants did in fact breach the contract. Such damages include pecuniary loss and inconvenience suffered as a natural result of the breach and are called compensatory damages. In this case the plaintiffs have proved no pecuniary damages which you or the Court could compute. In a situation where there has been a breach of contract which you find to have damaged the plaintiff but for which the plaintiffs have proven no actual damages, the plaintiffs may recover nominal damages.

"By nominal damages is meant trivial-a trivial sum of money."

Plaintiffs did not object to this instruction. In the trial court's decision on motions after verdict it states that the court so instructed the jury because, based on the fact that the plaintiffs paid for services they did not receive, their loss in proportion to the contract rate was approximately 25 cents. This rationale indicates that the court disregarded or overlooked Mrs. White's testimony of inconvenience. In viewing the evidence most favorable to the plaintiffs, there was some injury. The plaintiffs are not required to ascertain their damages with mathematical precision, but rather the trier of fact must set damages at a reasonable amount. Notwithstanding this instruction, the jury set the plaintiffs' damages at $10. The court was in error in reducing that amount to $1.

The jury finding of $10 in actual damages, though small, takes it out of the mere nominal status. The award is predicated on an actual injury. This was not the situation present in Sunderman v. Warnken.[1] Here there was credible evidence which showed inconvenience and thus actual injury, and the jury's finding as to compensatory damages should be reinstated.

Punitive Damages

"If a man shall steal an ox, or a sheep, and kill it, or sell it; he shall restore five oxen for an ox, and four sheep for a sheep."[2]

Over one hundred years ago this court held that, under proper circumstances, a plaintiff was entitled to recover exemplary or punitive damages.[3] In Wisconsin compensatory damages are given to make whole the damage or injury suffered by the injured party. On the other hand, punitive damages are given "on the basis of punishment to the injured party not because he has been injured, which injury has been

---

[1]   (1947), 251 Wis. 471, 29 N.W.2d 496.

[2]   Exodus 22:1.

[3]   McWilliams v. Bragg (1854), 3 Wis. 377 (*424).

compensated with compensatory damages, but to punish the wrongdoer for his malice and to deter others from like conduct."[4]

Simpson states: "Although damages in excess of compensation for loss are in some instances permitted in tort actions by way of punishment in contract actions the damages recoverable are limited to compensation for pecuniary loss sustained by the breach."[5] Corbin states that as a general rule punitive damages are not recoverable for breach of contract.[6]

In Wisconsin, the early case of Gordon v. Brewster[7] involved the breach of an employment contract. The trial court instructed the jury that if the nonperformance of the contract was attributable to the defendant's wrongful act of discharging the plaintiff, then that would go to increase the damages sustained. On appeal, this court said that the instruction was unfortunate and might have led the jurors to suppose that they could give something more than actual compensation in a breach of contract case. We find no Wisconsin case in which breach of contract (other than breach of promise to marry) has led to the award of punitive damages.

Persuasive authority from other jurisdictions supports the proposition (without exception) that punitive damages are not available in breach of contract actions. This is true even if the breach, as in the instant case, is willful. Although it is well recognized that breach of a contractual duty may be a tort, in such situations the contract creates the relation out of which grows the duty to use care in the performance of a responsibility prescribed by the contract. Not so here. No tort was pleaded or proved.

Reversed in part by reinstating the jury verdict relating to compensatory damages and otherwise affirmed. Costs to appellant.

NOTES

(1) *Questions.* Why was only $10 awarded to the Whites as compensatory damages? What did that amount represent? How was it calculated? How did the jury come up with the $2,000 punitive damage award?

Why shouldn't punitive damages be awarded in such a case? What effect would the availability of punitive damages have on parties tempted to breach their contracts? Would it make sense to award punitive damages in cases where the breach was malicious, as in *White*, or should the law be indifferent as to why a party fails to perform? Might the possibility of a punitive damage award affect a party's decision not only whether to breach a contract, but also whether to enter into it in the first place?

---

[4]   Malco, Inc. v. Midwest Aluminum Sales (1961), 14 Wis.2d 57, 66, 109 N.W.2d 516, 521.

[5]   Simpson, Contracts, (2d ed. hornbook series), p. 394, sec. 195.

[6]   5 Corbin, Contracts, p. 438, sec. 1077.

[7]   (1858), 7 Wis. 309 (*355).

(2) *Nominal Damages.* A plaintiff who, like the Whites in the case above, proves a breach of contract but fails to prove damages is traditionally awarded nominal damages (six cents or one dollar); Judge Posner has observed that "for reasons we do not understand every victim of a breach of contract, unlike a tort victim, is [so] entitled." Chronister Oil Co. v. Unocal Ref. & Mktg., 34 F.3d 462, 466 (7th Cir. 1994). Yet such an award serves as a declaration of the plaintiff's rights and may also carry with it an award of court costs.

(3) *Flirting with Punitive Damages.* Although not traditionally granted for breach of contract, punitive or exemplary damages may be granted for tortious conduct that is sufficiently "outrageous." See Restatement, Second, of Torts § 908 (1979). Many courts have departed from the strict rule that denies punitive damages for breach of contract when the breach is accompanied by "fraudulent" conduct or by an "independent" tort sufficiently outrageous to justify such damages. See generally Restatement § 355; Farnsworth on Contracts § 12.8. The use of punitive damages has been noticeable, for example, in connection with claims against insurers for their regular refusal to provide coverage to or settle claims with their insured. See Comunale v. Traders & Gen. Ins. Co., 328 P.2d 198 (Cal. 1958); Vernon Fire & Cas. Ins. Co. v. Sharp, 349 N.E.2d 173 (Ind. 1976).

In 1984, the Supreme Court of California suggested that a new tort of "bad faith breach" might extend beyond insurance cases to other contractual breaches. Seaman's Direct Buying Service v. Standard Oil Company of California, 686 P.2d 1158 (Cal. 1984). While the suggestion triggered much litigation and academic discussion, four years later a differently composed state Supreme Court refused to apply *Seaman's* to an employer's discharge of an at-will employee, and denounced the "uncritical acceptance . . . of the insurance model into the employment context, without careful consideration of the fundamental policies underlying the development of tort and contract law in general or of significant differences between the insurer/insured and employer/employee relationships." Foley v. Interactive Data Corp., 765 P.2d 373 (Cal. 1988). The following year, the Ninth Circuit stated that *Foley* "solidly reaffirms the notion that the bad faith denial of the existence of a contract is a cause of action wholly distinct from the breach of the covenant of good faith and fair dealing." Air-Sea Forwarders, Inc. v. Air Asia Co., 880 F.2d 176, 187 (9th Cir. 1989).

Nonetheless, there are other distinct circumstances where a promisor's breach of promise may result in punitive damages. For example, when a promisor, at the time a promise is made, has no intention of performing, the promisee may bring an action for promissory fraud. This cause of action is discussed more fully in Chapter 4 in the section on misrepresentation.

The Economics of Remedies: An Introductory Note

As noted on p. 9, Justice Holmes expressed his concern about the confusion of law and morality in no uncertain terms. Holmes advocated an approach to the study of contracts informed more by external legal sanctions than by moral intuitions. "When I emphasize the difference between law and morals I do so with reference to a single end, that of learning and understanding the law." Oliver Wendell Holmes, Jr., The Path of the Law, 10 Harv. L. Rev. 457, 459 (1897). As a pedagogic device, Holmes introduced a character, the so-called "bad man," lacking all virtue and morals and who behaved only in response to his own selfish interests and the sanctions imposed by law and society. From the view of the bad man, Holmes argued, the *legal* obligation to honor contractual promises is unclouded by vague notions of morality: "The duty to keep a contract at common law means a prediction that you must pay damages if you do not keep it, and nothing else." Oliver Wendell Holmes, Jr., The Path of the Law, 10 Harv. L. Rev. 457, 462 (1897). The promisor's obligation under this approach is reduced to a choice between performing a specified act and paying for its non-performance.

Though often characterized as immoral, Holmes's "perform-or-pay" approach might be better understood as an *amoral* system, where "[p]rices do the work of morals" in guiding behavior.[e] Holmes joins a long line of political theorists—including Hobbes, Bentham, and Adam Smith—all of whom understood sanctions as useful means of enlisting self-interested individual behavior to promote social welfare. Consider in this regard this excerpt from Adam Smith in *The Wealth of Nations*:

> [M]an has almost constant occasion for the help of his brethren, and it is vain for him to expect it from their benevolence only. He will be more likely to prevail if he can interest their self love in his favour, and shew them that it is for their own advantage to do for him what he requires of them. Whoever offers to another a bargain of any kind, proposes to do this: Give me that which I want, and you shall have this which you want, is the meaning of every such offer; and it is in this manner that we obtain from one another the far greater part of those good offices which we stand in need of. We address ourselves, not to their humanity but to their self love, and never talk to them of our own necessities but of their advantages. Nobody but a beggar chooses to depend chiefly upon the benevolence of his fellow citizens.

Adam Smith, An Inquiry into the Nature and Causes of the Wealth of Nations 11 (1811 ed., bk. 1, ch. II).

Efficient Performance and Breach

Building on Smith's claim to mutual gain through self-interested motivations and Holmes's perform-or-pay vision of contracts, scholars from a school of thought known as *law and economics* have developed a distinctive approach to contract remedies. This school of thought, which has achieved considerable influence over the past several decades,

---

[e]   Samuel Bowles, *Policies Designed for Self-interested Citizens May Undermine "The Moral Sentiments": Evidence from Economic Experiments*, 320 Science 1605 (2008).

emphasizes the incentive effects of legal remedies. Most notably, law and economics scholars observe that a promisor will exercise an "option" to breach and pay expectation damages instead of performing only when it is economically efficient to do so. That is, she will breach when her gain from breaching exceeds the amount of damages she will have to pay to leave the promisee just as well off as he would have been had the promisor performed. In principle, then, breaches of this sort make promisors better off without making promisees worse off.

This observation, known as the "efficient breach hypothesis," may be illustrated with a simple example. Say a promisor has promised to sell a piece of machinery to a promisee. The machinery will cost the promisor $300 to produce and is worth $1,000 to the promisee (the maximum amount the promisee is willing to pay for it). Exchange will produce $700 of surplus, because the promisee's value of the machinery ($1,000) is greater than the promisor's costs to produce it ($300). Say they agreed on a price of $600. This means the promisor gets $300 of the surplus (the $600 price minus her costs of $300) and the promisee gets $400 (the $1,000 value to him of the machinery minus the $600 price). At the time they enter into the contract, the performance is expected to be mutually advantageous.

Now the twist. Assume that at some date before performance, a second buyer approaches the promisor and offers $1,200 for the machinery. The promisor has only one unit and cannot procure another. Suppose further that the promisee and the second buyer are unable to transact with each other, perhaps because neither knows of the other's existence and it would be too costly for them to identify each other. The question then becomes, should the promisor sell the machinery to the first buyer (the promisee) as agreed, or should he sell the machinery to the second buyer at the higher price? The efficient breach hypothesis says the latter course is the better economic option for all parties involved. Why? The promisee will be fully compensated for his expectation by the payment of $400 in damages (because that is the amount that the promisee would have gained from the promisor's full performance). The second buyer gets the machinery that she values at least as much as $1,200. Finally, if the promisor had performed the original contract, she would have gained $300 (recall $600 sale price minus $300 cost to produce), but by breaching the contract and selling to the second buyer, the promisor is left with a gain of $500 after paying expectation damages to the promisee ($1,200 sale price minus $300 cost to produce minus $400 damages paid to the promisee). This suggests that, under the assumptions of this example, the promisor can break her promise and enjoy a gain, without leaving the promisee any worse off.

Transactions that make no one worse off, while making someone else better off, are called Pareto-improving transactions, so named after the 19th-century Italian economist Vilfredo Pareto. Pareto improvement is an important measure of what economists identify as efficiency, but it is not the only measure. Suppose that, in the example above, the promisor breaks her promise to the promisee and sells the machinery for $1,200. At this point an efficient outcome is realized, even *without* compensating the promisee, because the goods were allocated to a higher-value user. That is, the machinery then ends up in the hands of the second buyer, who values it more than the promisee. This measure of efficiency is known as Kaldor-Hicks efficiency. Note, however, that unless the promisee receives at least his expectation damages, this outcome would not be Pareto improving. Without this compensation, the promisee is worse off on account of the breach. Compensating the promisee for the breach is irrelevant under the Kaldor-Hicks approach, so long as the promisor's gains from the breach exceed the promisee's loss. Yet we should not lose sight of distinctions between economic theories and rules of law. The irrelevance of compensating the promisee may be a plausible feature of economic efficiency, but it is certainly not irrelevant to the promisee; nor is it to the law.

Efficient Investment and Planning

Our discussion of efficiency thus far has focused only on the moment when a party decides whether to perform or breach. Economics, however, is the study of incentives broadly conceived, and the question of whether parties have incentive to act efficiently will arise at every point where contracting parties make choices. These include searching for contractual partners, entering into a contract, relying on a contract, modifying or enforcing a contract, and so forth. Economic analyses suggest no single remedy, whether based on money damages or specific relief, satisfies the demands of efficiency at all points concerning the transaction. This does not deprive the economic approach of value, however; it merely highlights the inevitable trade-offs that occur even within the singular perspective of efficiency.

Consider, for instance, the question of whether to rely on or plan around a given contract. Surely law and policy-makers want to encourage parties to rely or plan on contractual performance. These activities tend to make exchange more valuable. Yet economic analyses have demonstrated that standard remedies may encourage an inefficient degree of reliance. To illustrate, recall Archie Sparrow, the cowboy who spent so much of his spare time training Keno to make it a first-class roping horse. No doubt he invested his time and effort in this way based on his expectation of receiving the horse at the end of the 16-week contract period. Would he have invested as much of his time and effort if he knew that instead of getting Keno he would only get money damages in the event that Chip Morris should break the contract? The answer depends on the *measure* of money damages. However, if he was assured of getting Keno through an award of specific performance, he would have every reason to invest his energies as he did.

How does the availability of various remedies for breach affect the willingness of parties to plan and invest resources in reliance on contracts? This question has been the central focus of an extensive literature over the past 40 years.[f] The standard conclusion is that parties will not invest sufficiently unless they expect to receive the full marginal return of those investments. For example, if Morris can breach his contract with Sparrow and pay only a pittance, then Sparrow will have greatly reduced incentives to invest his time in training that horse. But if Morris is required specifically to perform (or pay money damages that take into account the value of Sparrow's investments), then Sparrow's incentive to underinvest goes away.

But can remedies encourage too much investment? When Sparrow relies by investing as though he will get performance with certainty, he takes no account of the possibility that performance may not be forthcoming or perhaps *should not* be forthcoming. This issue returns us to the concept of efficient breach. When a breaching promisor can fully compensate the promisee, breach may be Pareto efficient: the promisee can be left no worse off and the promisor better off by the breach. Failure to account for the likelihood of efficient breach when making investment decisions can lead parties to invest too much. After all, they may not get the goods, or other performances, on which they had counted. In such cases, the investments tailored to and useful only in conjunction with expected but unrealized performances would be wasted. Specific performance can encourage exactly this kind of excessive or wasteful investment by leading parties to disregard the possibility of breach and encouraging them to invest as though they are certain to receive performance: either the promisor will perform or the court will order specific performance. The same is true for money damages that compensate promisees fully for their investments.

We are left with indeterminacy. Without meaningful remedies, parties will not invest adequately in contractual exchanges. With very strong remedies, like specific performance and damages that fully account for investment expenditures, parties invest too much. Underinvestment and overinvestment resulting from weak and strong contract enforcement are viewed among many economists as the central problems of economic organization and exchange, while others see them as a second-order efficiency concern at best. How might other institutions and practices, legal and otherwise, interact with contract remedies to abate these problems? For example, might overinvestment worries be curbed if remedies tend to fall short of full expectancy due to uncompensated legal fees and limits on recovery like foreseeability (discussed at pp. 964–979), certainty (see pp. 981–988), and so on? These are empirical questions of great practical importance that may not have been asked but for the theoretical economic analyses of remedies.

---

[f]   *See* Oliver Williamson, Markets and Hierarchies (1975); Benjamin Klein, Robert G. Crawford and Armen A. Alchian, *Vertical Integration, Appropriable Rents, and the Competitive Contracting Process*, 21 J.L. & Econ. 297 (1978); Oliver Hart and John Moore, *Foundations of Incomplete Contracts*, 66 Rev. Econ. Stud. 115 (1999).

The economics of remedies is an essential aspect of the study of contracts. Contract remedies provide incentives that guide behavior. At the same time, of course, other principles, including morality and fairness, also guide contractual behavior. For example, the promisor who has been offered $1,200 by the second buyer might decide that breaking her promise to sell the machinery to the promisee would cause harm to her reputation and self-esteem that is worth more to her than the $200 gain. On some accounts, this may be factored into her economic calculation of the cost to her of the breach. On other accounts, her decision is guided by independent moral considerations not reducible to an economic calculus. Cf. Lon L. Fuller, The Law in Quest of Itself 93 (1940), on the Holmesian "bad man": "[I]t will be noted that it is a peculiar sort of bad man who is worried about judicial decrees and is indifferent to extra-legal penalties, who is concerned about a fine of two dollars but apparently not about the possible loss of friends and customers." We do not have to choose one approach over another in our study of contracts; behavior is guided by many considerations. Whether economic efficiency is compatible with other normative objectives, like fairness, is an interesting question, but one we needn't answer here. See Richard R.W. Brooks, *The Efficient Performance Hypothesis*, 116 Yale L.J. 568 (2006), Daniel Friedmann, *The Efficient Breach Fallacy*, 18 J. Legal Stud. 1, 13–14 (1989).

Remedies and Coasean Bargaining

Remedies for breach of contract are not self-enforcing. Parties often settle their disputes without going to court. Even after a court has issued an award or order, they may bargain to reach a settlement, which suggests that no particular remedy is fully determinative of economic outcomes. This suggestion underlies a foundational claim in the law and economics literature known as the Coase Theorem. An initial grasp of the Coase Theorem may be reached by contrasting it with the efficient breach hypothesis discussed above. Whereas that hypothesis relies on a specific remedy, i.e., expectation damages, to produce an efficient allocation of resources, the Coase Theorem more profoundly asserts any remedy under the right conditions will lead to efficiency. It therefore shifts the normative impulse away from promoting any single remedy to a focus on the conditions that encourage efficient bargaining—so-called Coasean bargaining—in the shadow of legal remedies. To appreciate the claim and its implications consider the following controversy.

In 1942, Kansas, Nebraska, and Colorado entered negotiations, concluding with an enforceable agreement allocating water rights to the Republican River, which runs through the three States. Disputes are ripe in situations such as these, where an upriver party can draw excessively from a water source to the significant detriment of those downriver. The compact aimed to curtail disputes by clarifying the parties' respective claims to draw water from the Republican River Basin, a watershed encompassing parts of all three States. Disputes among the states persisted, nonetheless, increasing through the 1980s and 1990s, and culminating with a claim before the U.S. Supreme Court that Nebraska, which sits upriver to Kansas, breached the Compact in 2005 and 2006 by taking too much water from the river basin. In Kansas v. Nebraska, 135 S.Ct. 1042 (2015), the Court agreed that Nebraska had breached the agreement.

Turning to damages, Justice Kagan[g] looked to the report of the Special Master appointed to the case:

> After determining that Kansas lost $3.7 million from Nebraska's breach, the Special Master considered the case for an additional monetary award. Based on detailed evidence, not contested here, he concluded that an acre-foot of water is substantially more valuable on farmland in Nebraska than in Kansas. Kansas v. Nebraska, 135 S. Ct. 1042, 1056 (2015).

In other words, as Justice Kagan observed, Nebraska's gain from breach "was 'much larger than Kansas' loss, likely by more than several multiples'," which is to say, this was an "efficient breach." Yet, in addition to compensation for the loss of $3.7 million, "[g]iven the circumstances, the Master thought that Nebraska should have to disgorge part of that additional gain, to the tune of $1.8 million. Id., at 1056. In a dissenting opinion by Justice Thomas,[h] he limited his agreement with the majority opinion to only the following:

> I agree with the Court's conclusion that Nebraska knowingly, but not deliberately, breached the Republican River Compact, and I agree that there is no need to enter an injunction ordering Nebraska to comply with the Compact. But that is where my agreement ends.

Though differing on so much else, the Justices agreed to deny injunctive relief. What might account for this consensus to not enter an injunction "to prevent future violations"? United States v. W.T. Grant Co., 345 U.S. 629, 633 (1953). When someone breaks an enforceable promise, particularly one concerning an interest in land, isn't it reasonable for the Court to enjoin the breaking of the promise going forward? Perhaps, but from an economic perspective, it may be said that enjoining Nebraska from pursing its more valuable uses of water would lead to an inefficient outcome.

---

[g] Elena Kagan (1960–), an Associate Justice of the Supreme Court of the United States, attended Princeton University, University of Oxford and then Harvard Law School. She taught at the University of Chicago and Harvard, where she was dean of the law school before becoming Solicitor General of the United States. Kagan, who was nominated by President Barack Obama, has served on the Supreme Court since 2010.

[h] Clarence Thomas (1948–), an Associate Justice of the Supreme Court of the United States, attended the College of the Holy Cross and Yale Law School. In 1981, he was appointed by President Ronald Reagan to the Chairmanship of the Equal Employment Opportunity Commission (EEOC). Thomas, who was a Judge on the United States Court of Appeals for the District of Columbia Circuit until nominated by President George H. W. Bush, has been on the court since 1991.

Given the Special Master's conclusion that an acre-foot of water can be put to uses multiple times more valuable to Nebraska than Kansas, an injunction order would indeed appear to lead to an inefficient allocation of water resources. What if, however, we assume that notwithstanding the prior disagreements, Kansas and Nebraska are able to bargain with each other at relatively low costs, particularly now that their respective rights and obligations have been clarified by the Court? Wouldn't it be in their interest to strike a new agreement—one might say "bargain around the court order"—whereby Nebraska gets the water it values more and Kansas is compensated, or even more than compensated, for its loss?

Suppose, for instance, that Nebraska values the water at $18.5 million over the same period during which the loss of water would cost Kansas $3.7 million, and then there is a significant surplus of almost $15 million to be had if the two states can agree to "contract around" the Court order. Hence, so long as their costs of bargaining are sufficiently low—i.e., lower than $15 million—the water will be put to its more efficient uses on Nebraska farmland. The example illustrates a more general conclusion of the Coase Theorem. Named after Ronald Coase,[i] the Coase Theorem states that when transaction costs of bargaining are zero (or sufficiently small) and legal entitlements are well-defined, parties will bargain to reach an allocatively efficient outcome under any remedial award or order. That is, bargaining will result in resources going to those who value them the most, irrespective of the remedy provided by the court, whether the remedy is a specific order such as an injunction or *any* money damage award.

The Coase Theorem is often misread as suggesting that the remedies themselves have no efficiency implications. Nothing could be further from the truth. Coase did not believe that transaction costs are typically absent. He argued just the opposite: because transaction costs are always present, the remedy may indeed affect the allocation of goods. With regard to efficiency, then, much turns on the transaction costs associated with various remedial regimes. This insight has sparked a large literature attempting to characterize the circumstances wherein a transaction costs analysis would favor one type of remedy over another. These analyses focus on the costs of bargaining, search costs, the legal costs of determining damages, the monitoring costs of specific performance, etc., as well as the psychological costs and biases associated with certain remedies. No general efficiency argument has been put forth in favor of a singly preferred remedy. Nor is one likely to appear. Perhaps this is as it should be. The value of Coase's insight is that it focuses our

---

[i]   Ronald H. Coase, (1910–2013), was a British-born economist who made a number of foundational insights in economics and law. Coase attended the London School of Economics. In the 1950s, he relocated to the United States, teaching first at University at Buffalo, followed by a move in 1958 to University of Virginia and then, in 1964, to the University of Chicago Law School, where he remained for the rest of his long professional career. He was awarded the Nobel Memorial Prize in Economic Sciences in 1991.

attention on the transaction costs of contracting and asks us to think about the desirability of particular remedies given these constraints.

NOTES

(1) *Framing the Compact.* Is contract law an appropriate conceptualization of compacts among states? Justice Thomas in his Kansas v. Nebraska dissenting opinion pointed to "principles of contract law that we have traditionally applied to compact disputes between sovereign States." Invoking other principles at his first Inaugural Address, on the eve of the American Civil War, President Abraham Lincoln described what he took to be the compact among the United States and his commitment to "the maintenance inviolate of the rights of the States," cautioning against a contractual framing and unilateral and potentially "efficient" breach:

> Again: If the United States be not a government proper, but an association of States in the nature of contract merely, can it, as a contract, be peaceably unmade by less than all the parties who made it? One party to a contract may violate it—break it, so to speak—but does it not require all to lawfully rescind it?

The Avalon Project, http://avalon.law.yale.edu/19th_century/lincoln1.asp.

(2) *Efficient Breach and the Costs of Enforcement.* While the Coase Theorem takes all prospective costs associated with bargaining around a remedy as a central presupposition to its claim, most statements of the efficient breach hypothesis ignore the cost to the parties of enforcing rights. But what if it is very costly for the promisee to hire an attorney in order to prove the promisor's performance was defective, or to prove the amount of its own damages? How might taking those costs into account change the analysis?

(3) *Knowing, Deliberate, Willful and Opportunistic Breach.* How does, or should, the mental calculation or state of mind of the breacher influence the remedy? American contract law typically treats breach in terms of strict liability, without looking to fault or accessing supra-compensatory awards for breach. See Richard A. Posner, *Let Us Never Blame a Contract Breaker*, 107 Mich. L. Rev. 1349 (2009). Note that the Special Master in Kansas v. Nebraska concluded that Nebraska breached knowingly, but not deliberately. Still, he recommended an award of partial disgorgement damages on top of compensation damages for Kansas. What "circumstances" do you imagine influenced the Special Master's thoughts leading to supra-compensatory damages? Writing for the Majority, Justice Kagan observed, "we agree with the Master's judgment that a relatively small disgorgement award suffices here." Why not disgorge the entire gain from Nebraska's breach? Would that be unfair to Nebraska? Would it be inefficient in this case or for future disputes? See Caprice Roberts, *Supreme Disgorgement*, 68 Fla. L. Rev. 1413 (2016).

(4) *Penalties and Reliance Investments.* Sometimes a promisee can encourage the promisor's timely performance by stipulating liquidated damages. Of course, the promisor must agree to the stipulated damages and will likely demand compensation for being accountable for an award greater

than the legal default. If the promisor agrees to the stipulated award, the promisee may feel more confident when relying on the contract because the promisor's commitments are more credible, given the heightened remedy. Consider the effect of such confidence on the incentives of parties to invest. If two sophisticated parties contract to provide efficient incentives to invest using a liquidated damages clause, should the court refuse to enforce the clause even if it appears punitive?

(5) *Limits to the Coasean Conceptualization.* The Coase Theorem offers a powerful conceptual apparatus that law students often encounter across first-year as well as upper-level courses. That is because the "theorem" applies abstractly to any right or remedy, public or private. It is for this reason that it is important to appreciate its limitations and to see what it is meant to address. Of course, the Coase Theorem makes no claims on non-consequential values such as, for instance, dignity. States regulate conditions of labor, sale of human organs, *inter alia,* for many such reasons. Take, for example, the Thirteenth Amendment of the U.S. Constitution, which enjoins slavery. Even if two individuals, for whatever reasons, found it in their interest to contract around that prohibition, the Coase Theorem would offer few insights beyond telling us that a couple of stooges found it mutually advantageous to strike such a bargain. Problems of broader application arise here not merely because the Coase Theorem assumes away or ignores consequential impacts outside of the parties' agreement (including effects on third parties)—these are so-called "externalities"—but more pointedly because it doesn't address such other values. Moreover, even with regard to purely consequential considerations, the Coase Theorem makes no claims about distributive fairness, investment efficiency, or wealth effects that result from distinct assignments of legal entitlements.

(6) *What About Colorado?* In Kansas v. Nebraska there were actually two defendants, Nebraska and Colorado, so there would be three parties to any Coasean bargain. When three or more parties are bargaining, however, it may be impossible to reach an efficient outcome, despite legal entitlements being well-defined and zero transactions costs of bargaining being assumed. This is yet another indication of the importance and distinctiveness concerning the assignment of legal entitlements, even when the unattainable Coasean assumptions are posited. See Lloyd S. Shapley, *A Value for n-person Games*, 28 Ann. Math. Stud. 307 (1953) and Varouj A. Aivazian and Jeffrey L. Callen. *The Coase Theorem and the Empty Core*, 24 J. L. & Econ. 175 (1981).

———

Remedies in Action

Ordinary contracts are not self-executing. Parties must often act to secure their contracts rights. In our discussion of remedies for breach, we have thus far largely ignored the costs of this activity—the costs of obtaining relief—or subsumed it under the encompassing but not quite revealing label "transaction costs." Of course, to some extent the cost of obtaining relief in court is subsidized by the availability of the public machinery of justice. Litigants are not charged, except as taxpayers, for the services of judges or juries in resolving their disputes. In addition, the successful claimant may ordinarily recover its court costs, such as filing fees, court reporter fees, and charges for the serving of process or subpoenas. Such costs are typically set by statute and are often modest in scope. See, for example, Colo. Rev. Stat. Ann. § 13–17–202. But in contrast to the situation in many countries, the successful claimant in the United States is not generally allowed to recover its attorney's fees from the losing party. Unless specifically provided for by the contract itself, even winning parties are left to pay their own, often substantial, lawyers' fees, as well as other costs of litigation, such as the cost of *enforcing* a judgment against an obdurate defendant. If litigation costs are not part of the typical damage recovery, expectation damages will not put the plaintiff in the same position as if the contract had been performed. See Restatement § 344(a). The inability to recover litigation costs helps explain why many contractual disputes are either settled out of court or not brought in the first place.

The reluctance to enlist law to settle disputes also introduces us to the concept of the "law in action," a phrase associated with the law and society approach to the study of contracts. A central premise of this more sociological approach is that doctrine and theory only get us so far in understanding how contract law actually works: "law in action" is contrasted with "law on the books." As Stewart Macaulay discovered in his important 1963 study of practices among disputing businesses, much of what occurs following a breach of contract is "non-contractual":

> Disputes are frequently settled without reference to the contract or potential or actual legal sanctions. There is a hesitancy to speak of legal rights or to threaten to sue in these negotiations. Even where the parties have a detailed and carefully planned agreement which indicates what is to happen if, say, the seller fails to deliver on time, often they will never refer to the agreement but will negotiate a solution when the problem arises apparently as if there had never been any original contract.

Stewart Macaulay, *Non-Contractual Relations in Business: A Preliminary Study*, 28 Am. Soc. Rev. 55, 61 (1963).

Of course, non-contractual practices such as negotiation and modification tell only part of the story. In each of the cases in this book, the parties, or at least one of them, has chosen to litigate. Where the transaction is a substantial one between business firms, litigation is often justified because its costs are small in relation to the amount in dispute or because of the precedential value of a judicial decision. But what of the typical consumer transaction in which the stakes are often smaller, whether the aggrieved party is the merchant (often trying to collect) or the consumer (perhaps refusing to pay)?

Between the two, the merchant is typically in the better position. The merchant is more likely to engage professionals such as lawyers or trade associations to draft its contract, which may provide for liquidated damages and attorneys' fees. The merchant may also be able to provide for security, such as by taking a deposit where goods have not been delivered or by preserving the right to repossess goods that have been delivered. In contrast, the ordinary consumer is less likely to know or be able to afford a lawyer, and less likely to have specifically bargained for favorable contract terms or even to know what terms are favorable. For the argument that the more sophisticated "repeat players" in the legal system tend to acquire and maintain structural advantages over one-shot players, who infrequently participate in litigation and legal strategy. See Marc Galanter, *Why the "Haves" Come Out Ahead: Speculations on the Limits of Legal Change*, 9 L. & Soc. Rev. 95 (1974). Of course it is important to recognize that the big-guy/little-guy story of merchant versus consumer is not always an accurate dividing line for determining party sophistication and advantage. Small businesses, for example, typically behave like consumers (little guys) but are treated at law like large businesses. See Larry T. Garvin, *Small Business and the False Dichotomies of Contract Law*, 40 Wake Forest L. Rev. 295 (2005).

A variety of solutions, many procedural in nature, have been put forth to even out disparities in at least a consumer's ability to bring or defend claims. One solution is to "sweeten the pot" by increasing the successful consumer's recovery through statutes that allow civil penalties, multiple (e.g., treble) damages, or attorney's fees. Other solutions include allowing consumers to join as claimants in class actions, providing free or inexpensive legal services, or authorizing public agencies, such as the Federal Trade Commission (FTC), to bundle claims for investigation and to distribute any recovery to the aggrieved consumers; see discussion of Administrative Measures on p. 627. In 2012, as part of the Dodd-Frank Wall Street Reform and Consumer Protection Act, the Consumer Financial Protection Bureau was created within the FTC. Its stated aim is to "enhance consumer confidence by enforcing existing federal consumer protection laws" and to "empower consumers" by providing information about their statutory rights. See Bureau of Consumer Protection, http://www.consumer.ftc.gov.

Still other mechanisms for reducing the costs and complexities of litigation focus on the forum. Take, for instance, the provision of small claims courts, such as the New York Civil Court, which has jurisdiction over civil matters not exceeding $25,000. As stated on the Court's website:

> Our court is where everyday people come to resolve their everyday legal problems. Whether you are a local merchant, a consumer, a debtor, or a creditor, the Civil Court is dedicated to providing access to fair and efficient justice. http://www.courts. state.ny.us/courts/nyc/smallclaims/index.shtml.

Parties who seek redress in such courts typically represent themselves, appearing *pro se* (without the formal assistance of counsel). Another procedural mechanism, as suggested above, is the class action suit, in which multiple claimants come together to sue a common defendant. While the details of class litigation are left mainly for procedure courses, we consider some aspects of them in Chapter 6 in connection with mandatory arbitration clauses that *prohibit* their use.

Firms too have sought to simplify dispute resolution. One approach is the turn away from courts to methods of alternative dispute resolution (ADR). The most important of these is arbitration. According to Soia Mentschikoff,[j] an early scholar of commercial arbitration in the United States, the four essential aspects of arbitration are that "(1) it is resorted to only by agreement of the parties; (2) it is a method not of compromising disputes but of deciding them; (3) the person making the decision has no formal connection with our system of courts; but (4) before the award is known it is agreed to be 'final and binding.'" Soia Mentschikoff, *The Significance of Arbitration—A Preliminary Inquiry*, 17 L. & Contemp. Probs. 698, 699 (1952). Arbitration is therefore a "creature of contract": parties choose their own scheme of dispute resolution. Proponents of arbitration claim speed, flexibility, increased confidentiality, decreased costs, and decision-maker expertise among its advantages. While these claims are sometimes contested, arbitration undeniably is becoming more important in dispute resolution. For example, international commercial arbitration has become the main way to resolve transnational commercial disputes.

Beyond its use in transnational and domestic commercial disputes, arbitration has grown in importance as arbitration clauses are increasingly incorporated by companies and employers into ordinary consumer and employment contracts. A series of recent U.S. Supreme Court cases interpreting these *mandatory* arbitration clauses has caused some commentators to fear that, whatever the benefits of arbitration in general, mandatory arbitration may now be less an alternative mode of dispute resolution than the dominant mode, and that this in turn may endanger access to courts by would-be litigants. See Jean R. Sternlight, *Tsunami: AT & T Mobility LLC v. Concepcion Impedes Access to Justice*, 90 Or. L. Rev. 703 (2012). We will come back to the questions raised by mandatory arbitration in Chapter 6, when we discuss standard form contracts and unconscionability.

Finally, in addition to varying the forum in which disputes are resolved, certain industries have created private, trade-specific codes to govern their disputes. Professor Lisa Bernstein has explained that in the cotton industry, for example, disputes are subject to arbitration in merchant tribunals that are not only sensitive to the particularities of

---

[j]   Soia Mentschikoff, (1915–1984) born in Moscow to American parents, earned her A. B. from Hunter College and her LL.B. from Columbia Law School. She taught at Harvard Law School, where she was the first woman to be offered a permanent position on its faculty. Leaving an extraordinary imprint on U.S. commercial law, Mentschikoff was Associate Chief Reporter to the Uniform Commercial Code and Dean of the University of Miami Law School, a position she took after many years of teaching at the University of Chicago Law School.

the cotton industry but also quick and inexpensive. The cotton industry "has succeeded in creating and maintaining a private legal system in which transaction costs . . . and collection costs are low." Lisa Bernstein, *Private Commercial Law in the Cotton Industry: Creating Cooperation through Rules, Norms, and Institutions*, 99 Mich. L. Rev. 1724 (2001).

NOTES

(1) *Efficient Breach and the Bench.* How has the concept of efficient breach been received in practice by judges? Since the early 1980s, there have been a hundred or so cases that expressly employ the term. For example, Judge Richard Posner,[k] discussing efficient breach in relation to an award of punitive damages, observed that "if the promisor has discovered that his performance is worth more to someone else," then "efficiency is promoted by allowing him to break his promise, provided he makes good on the promisee's actual losses. If he is forced to pay more than that, an efficient breach may be deterred, and the law doesn't want to bring about that result." Patton v. Mid-Continent Systems, Inc., 841 F.2d 742, 750 (7th Cir. 1988).

Other courts have also taken account of the concept. In refusing to enforce a contract upon a finding that one company had struck too hard a bargain with another, a California court stated: "Hard bargaining, 'efficient' breaches and reasonable settlements of good faith disputes are all acceptable, even desirable, in our economic system. That system can be viewed as a game in which everybody wins, to one degree or another, so long as everyone plays by the common rules. Those rules are not limited to precepts of rationality and self-interest. They include equitable notions of fairness and propriety which preclude the wrongful exploitation of business exigencies to obtain disproportionate exchanges of values. Such exchanges make a mockery of freedom of contract and undermine the proper functioning of our economic system." Rich and Whillock, Inc. v. Ashton Development, Inc., 157 Cal.App.3d 1154, 1159 (Ct. App. 1984).

How should "notions of fairness and propriety" guide the law of remedies? Have you seen examples of this in the cases so far?

(2) *The Social Value of Contract Law.* Professor Karl Llewellyn[l] concluded "that the real major effect of law will be found not so much in the cases in which law officials actually intervene, nor yet in those in which such intervention is consciously contemplated as a possibility, but rather in contributing to, strengthening, stiffening attitudes toward performance as

---

[k]   Richard Allen Posner (1939–), after clerking for Justice William Brennan and occupying several legal positions in the federal government, taught briefly at Stanford University Law School and then for more than a decade at the University of Chicago Law School. In 1981 he was appointed to the United States Court of Appeals for the Seventh Circuit, where from 1993 to 2000 he served as Chief Judge. His many books include the influential Economic Analysis of Law.

[l]   Karl Nickerson Llewellyn (1893–1962) practiced law in New York for two years and taught law at Yale, Columbia, and Chicago law schools. One of the school of "legal realists," Llewellyn was well known for his contributions to the field of jurisprudence, and also to the fields of commercial law and contracts. He was Chief Reporter of the Uniform Commercial Code, and the author of many books, including The Bramble Bush: On Our Law and Its Study, which was written especially for first-year law students.

what is to be expected and what 'is done'. This work of the law machine at the margin, in helping keep the level of social practice and expectation up to where it is, as against slow canker, is probably the most vital single aspect of contract law. For in this aspect each hospital case is a case with significance for the hundreds of thousands of normal cases." Llewellyn, *What Price Contract?—An Essay in Perspective*, 40 Yale L.J. 704, 725 n. 47 (1931). For a discussion of the nonlegal sanctions that may encourage promisors to keep their promises, see David Charny, *Nonlegal Sanctions in Commercial Relationships*, 104 Harv. L. Rev. 373 (1990).

(3)   *Bargaining in the Shadow of Law*. In considering "the work of law," Llewellyn referred to cases in which legal intervention is "not consciously contemplated as a possibility." But what is the work of law when legal action is contemplated or has already been commenced by one of the parties? Does law matter when parties decide to settle a dispute outside the courtroom? In an important 1979 article, Professors Robert Mnookin and Lewis Kornhauser suggested that disputing parties often bargain with one another against the knowledge, or "in the shadow," of what the law is likely to do if they do not agree. See Mnookin and Kornhauser, *Bargaining in the Shadow of the Law: The Case of Divorce*, 88 Yale L.J. 950 (1979). In this way, the background legal rules—say, that fault will not be penalized—provide parties with certain bargaining chips, or "endowments," and that these endowments, among other factors, enhance a party's negotiating power. The concept of bargaining in the shadow of law provides another example of a behavioral or socio-legal approach, as law hovers over the process of dispute settlement.

SECTION 3.   CONSIDERATION AS A BASIS FOR ENFORCEMENT

(A) FUNDAMENTALS OF CONSIDERATION

Starting from the premise that not all promises are legally enforceable, we quickly arrive at the basic question of how to determine which ones are. To address this question, we must begin with an historical perspective. Enforceability under early English law was closely tied to the common law actions of covenant, debt, and assumpsit, and, even today, no adequate answer to our basic question can ignore this aspect of legal history.

The first of these actions, *covenant*, was used to enforce contracts made under seal. Once a written promise was sealed and delivered, the action of covenant was available to enforce it, and it made no difference whether the promisor had bargained for or received anything in exchange for the promise, or whether the promisee had in any way changed position in reliance on it. In medieval England, the seal was a piece of wax affixed to the document and bearing an impression identifying the person who had executed it. At first its use was confined to the nobility, but later it spread to commoners. With the growth of literacy and the use of the personal signature as a means of authentication, the requirement of formality was so eroded that a seal could consist of any written or printed symbol intended to serve as a seal. The word "Seal" and the letters "L.S." (*locus sigilli*) were commonly used for this purpose.

Three functions performed by such legal formalities as the seal have been described by Professor Lon Fuller.[m] The first is "evidentiary"—that is, providing trustworthy evidence of the existence and terms of the contract in the event of controversy. The second function is "cautionary"—that is, bringing home to the parties the significance of their acts, inducing "the circumspective frame of mind appropriate in one pledging his future." The third function of the seal, or of any other form, is "channeling," or marking the promise as one intended to be legal and therefore to be resolved within the system of laws. Using the seal as the example, Fuller explained: "The seal not only insures a satisfactory memorial of the promise and induces deliberations in the making of it. It serves also to mark or signalize the enforceable promise; it furnishes a simple and external test of enforceability." See Lon L. Fuller, *Consideration and Form*, 41 Colum. L. Rev. 799, 800–801 (1941); Lon L. Fuller, Anatomy of the Law 36–37 (1968). Of course, the ability of the seal to perform these functions and its distinctive effect on the enforceability of promises have declined as its legal status has changed. The seal has been abolished in roughly half of the states and seriously curtailed in the rest. The enactment of the Uniform Commercial Code dealt another significant blow to the seal with its announcement that "every effect of the seal which relates to 'sealed instruments' as such is wiped out insofar as contracts for sale are concerned." Comment 1 to UCC § 2–203. Where the seal still retains some effect, it is generally limited to raising a rebuttable presumption of consideration or making applicable a longer period of limitations.

What supplanted the seal as the primary criterion of the enforceability of a promise was the circumstance that the promise was, or was not, given in exchange for something. This development is reflected in the second of the three common law actions, *debt*, which was used to enforce some types of unsealed promises to pay a definite sum of money. These included a promise to repay money that had been loaned and a promise to pay for goods that had been delivered or for work that had been done. Because these were situations in which the contemplated exchange was completed on one side, they appealed to the primitive notion that the promisor (or debtor) had something belonging to the promisee (or creditor) that the former ought to surrender. The proprietary element present in this notion is reflected in the popular

---

[m] Lon L. Fuller (1902–1978) had a long teaching career at Oregon, Illinois, Duke, Columbia, and, for the last three decades of his life, Harvard, where he taught contracts and jurisprudence. In philosophical works he presented alternatives to positivist attitudes toward law, sometimes using partly fanciful cases in imaginary and contrasting opinions. See, e.g., Fuller, *The Case of the Speluncean Explorers*, 62 Harv. 616 (1949). His article, with one of his students, William Perdue, on the reliance interest in contracts prompted an extensive reexamination of the subject. It is cited in Note 2, p. 19 above, and throughout this chapter.

expression that a depositor who is owed money by a bank "*has* money in the bank." What the promisee had given the promisor was sometimes called the "*quid pro quo*" and, as the underlying principles of contract law developed, the promisor's obligation in debt was considered to rest upon receipt of a *benefit* from the promisee.

The third and ultimately the most important common law action, *assumpsit*, grew out of cases in which the promisee sought to recover damages for physical injury to person or property on the basis of a consensual undertaking. In one such case, a ferryman who undertook to carry the plaintiff's horse across a river was held liable when he overloaded the boat and the horse drowned. In another, a carpenter who undertook to build a house for the plaintiff was held liable when he did so unskillfully. The underlying theme of these decisions was that of misfeasance—the promisor, having undertaken (*assumpsit*) to do something, had done it in a manner inconsistent with that undertaking to the detriment of the promisee. The decisions did not go so far as to impose liability for nonfeasance—where the promisor had done *nothing* in pursuance of the undertaking—for example, if the carpenter in the earlier example had failed to build the house at all. It was not until the latter half of the 15th century that the common law courts began to make this extension. When they did, they imposed a requirement, analogous to that in the misfeasance cases, that the promisee must have incurred a *detriment* in reliance on the promise—as where the owner had changed position by selling an old house in reliance on the carpenter's promise to build a new one.

Finally, by the end of the 16th century, the courts made a second major extension of the action of assumpsit and held that a party that had given only a promise in exchange for the other's promise had incurred a detriment by having its freedom of action fettered, because it was bound in turn by its own promise. By this circular argument, the common law courts began to enforce exchanges of promises. Here is the opinion in what is said to be the earliest case recognizing that a promise, not even partly performed, could be consideration for a return promise:

> Note, that a promise against a promise will maintain an action upon the case, as in consideration that you do give me £10 on such a day, I promise to give you £10 such a day after.

Strangborough v. Warner, 74 Eng. Rep. 686 (Q.B. 1588). See Holdsworth, *Debt, Assumpsit and Consideration*, 11 Mich. L. Rev. 347, 351 (1913).

Eventually the action of assumpsit was allowed to supplant that of debt for the enforcement of promises. By the beginning of the 17th century, the common law courts had succeeded in developing the action of assumpsit as a general basis for the enforcement of promises. By that time, the term "consideration" had come to be used as a word of art to express the sum of the conditions necessary for such an action to lie. It was therefore a tautology that a promise, if not under seal, was enforceable only where there was "consideration," for this was to say no more than that it was enforceable only where the action of assumpsit would lie. Bound up in the concept of consideration were several elements. Most important, from the *quid pro quo* of debt came the idea that there must have been an exchange arrived at by way of bargain. To the extent that debt inspired the concept of consideration, there was the notion that there must be a *benefit* to the promisor. To the extent that assumpsit inspired it, there was the notion that there must be a *detriment* to the promisee.

The cases that follow refine our understanding of the doctrine of consideration and its development into this century. Consideration is now a fundamental feature of a contractual relationship, "the glue that binds the parties to a contract together." In re Owen, 303 S.E.2d 351 (N.C.App. 1983). The concept of benefit and detriment have receded, but the centrality of a bargained-for exchange between the parties remains, lending at least some support to the claim of the English legal historian, F.W. Maitland, that "[t]he forms of action we have buried, but they still rule us from their graves." Frederic W. Maitland, The Forms of Action at Common Law 2 (1936 ed.). For a thorough treatment of this historical background, see A.W. Brian Simpson, A History of the Common Law of Contract (1975). See also Patrick S. Atiyah, The Rise and Fall of Freedom of Contract (1979) and E. Allan Farnsworth, *The Past of Promise: An Historical Introduction to Contract*, 69 Colum. L. Rev. 576 (1969). To be sure, the criterion of consideration as the *sine qua non* for promissory enforcement has, like the seal, been partially supplanted in its turn by other criteria of enforceability, such as reliance. These too are developed in the following sections in this chapter. For now, however, our focus is on consideration: its logic, its vocabulary, and its development. Before doing so, a brief word on a few broad categories of cases you will encounter as you proceed through this casebook.

———

Typical Categories of Agreements

Throughout the 19th century, text writers on contract law devoted considerable attention to specific types of agreements, such as contracts with common carriers and innkeepers, and for pawns and pledges, that were on the periphery of general contract law. When, in 1920, Samuel Williston[n] launched the first edition of his magisterial contracts treatise, he announced that he sought to "treat the subject of contracts as a whole, and to show the wide range of application of its principles." This conception of a body of contract law generally applicable to agreements

---

[n] Samuel Williston (1861–1963) joined the faculty of the Harvard Law School in 1890, after practicing law for a short period in Boston, and taught there until his retirement in 1938. His principal fields were contracts and sales. His multi-volume work, *A Treatise on the Law of Contracts*, was first published in 1920 and became one of the most widely used legal treatises in the United States. He was the Reporter for the Restatement of Contracts and the draftsman of several uniform laws, including the Uniform Sales Act.

of all sorts was confirmed in 1932, when the ALI promulgated its original Restatement of Contracts, for which Williston served as Reporter. Half a century later, a federal court of appeals affirmed this view: In response to a party's plea to limit an earlier holding involving the sale of software in the case of ProCD v. Zeidenberg, p. 288 below, the judge responded, "Where's the sense in that? *ProCD* is about the law of contracts, not the law of software." Hill v. Gateway 2000, Inc., 105 F.3d 1147 (7th Cir.1997). Consistent with this conception, this book seeks to show how contract principles apply to a wide variety of transactions.

At the same time, many transactions fall into recognizable categories with distinctive rules and practices. Some of these distinctive features derive from historical practice or common business sense; others reflect larger policy concerns. We note six such categories here: contracts for sales of goods, real estate transactions, construction contracts, employment agreements, consumer contracts, and family contracts. When a case involving one of these categories appears, it is preceded by a description of some of the common features of the category. As other types of agreements appear throughout the book—franchise and distributorship contracts, publishing contracts, government contracts, consumer contracts, and so on—you may discern and organize distinctive features of those categories as well.

And now to the first of the six typical categories that we'll cover: family contracts.

———

Family Contracts

The agreement in the following venerable case—an uncle's promise to a nephew made during a family celebration—is typical of agreements between relatives and others in close personal relationships. Unlike most commercial agreements, family agreements are frequently informal and oral, lacking in detail, and may not be preceded by significant bargaining. The parties may or may not be sophisticated transactors, but they are likely to be in a confidential relationship with one another and therefore are less likely to bargain "at arm's length." Whatever their importance within a particular family, family agreements are rarely of great moment to the economy, although in certain historical periods the accumulation and protection of family capital was often secured by keeping it "in the family" through elaborate contractual formalities.

Because family agreements may involve matters long understood to be outside the proper scope of judicial intervention, an initial question is therefore whether a promise made between family members is enforceable at all. (That question explains the presence of a number of such cases in this chapter.)

The traditional answer has been: No. Goods or services given or pledged by one family member to another were assumed to be motivated by altruism or by domestic obligation (not always the same thing), and were decidedly *not* bargains motivated by gain. Policy concerns, such as family privacy and domestic harmony, further explained judicial reluctance to find a bargain between intimates. As an English court explained in denying a wife recovery on her husband's promise of a stated monthly allowance, "it would be the worst possible example to hold that agreements such as this resulted in legal obligations which could be enforced in the Courts," for "each house is a domain into which the King's writ does not run and to which his officers do not seek to be admitted." Balfour v. Balfour, [1919] 2 K.B. 571, 579 (C.A.). An American court justified a similar decision by declaring that to enforce such a promise would "open an endless field for controversy and bickering." Graham v. Graham, 33 F.Supp. 936 (E.D.Mich.1940).

In recent years, the differences between family agreements and commercial ones have narrowed as contractual relationships among relatives and other intimates have found greater legal acceptance. Sophisticated contracts, now often drafted by lawyers, are used to order matters once considered wholly unsuited for private agreement or public enforcement. Parties, married and unmarried, arrange aspects of their relationships from start to finish through pre-nuptial agreements, cohabitation contracts, mid-marriage agreements and divorce and property settlements. People increasingly contract with one another for the purpose of creating and ordering vertical relationships—that is, between parents and children. For example, contract has come to play a role in parental acquisition of children, whether through surrogacy contracts, open adoption agreements, or the sale of genetic material. We explore such agreements in later chapters but begin here with a relatively straightforward promise from uncle to nephew.

Hamer v. Sidway

Court of Appeals of New York, 1891.
124 N.Y. 538, 27 N.E. 256.

Appeal from an order of the general term of the supreme court in the fourth judicial department, reversing a judgment entered on the decision of the court at special term. The plaintiff presented a claim to the executor of William E. Story, Sr., for $5,000 and interest from the 6th day of February, 1875. She acquired it through several mesne assignments from William E. Story, 2d. The claim being rejected by the executor, this action was brought.

It appears that William E. Story, Sr., was the uncle of William E. Story, 2d; that at the celebration of the golden wedding of Samuel Story and wife, father and mother of William E. Story, Sr., on the 20th day of March, 1869, in the presence of the family and invited guests, he promised his nephew that if he would refrain from drinking, using tobacco, swearing, and playing cards or billiards for money until he became 21 years of age, he would pay him the sum of $5,000. The nephew assented thereto, and fully performed the conditions inducing the promise. When the nephew arrived at the age of 21 years, and on the 31st day of January, 1875, he wrote to his uncle, informing him that he had performed his part of the agreement, and had thereby become entitled to the sum of $5,000. The uncle received the letter, and a few days later, and on the 6th day of February, he wrote and mailed to his nephew the following letter:

BUFFALO, FEB. 6, 1875.

"W.E. STORY, JR.:

"DEAR NEPHEW—Your letter of the 31st ult. came to hand all right, saying that you had lived up to the promise made to me several years ago. I have no doubt but you have, for which you shall have five thousand dollars as I promised you. I had the money in the bank the day you was 21 years old that I intend for you, and you shall have the money certain. Now, Willie, I do not intend to interfere with this money in any way till I think you are capable of taking care of it and the sooner that time comes the better it will please me. I would hate very much to have you start out in some adventure that you thought all right and lose this money in one year. The first five thousand dollars that I got together cost me a heap of hard work. . . . It did not come to me in any mysterious way, and the reason I speak of this is that money got in this way stops longer with a fellow that gets it with hard knocks than it does when he finds it. Willie, you are 21 and you have many a thing to learn yet. This money you have earned much easier than I did besides acquiring good habits at the same time and you are quite welcome to the money; hope you will make good use of it. I was ten long years getting this together after I was your age. Now, hoping this will be satisfactory, I stop. . . .

TRULY YOURS,
"W.E. STORY.

"P.S.—You can consider this money on interest."

The nephew received the letter and thereafter consented that the money should remain with his uncle in accordance with the terms and conditions of the letters. The uncle died on the 29th day of January, 1887, without having paid over to his nephew any portion of the said $5,000 and interest.

■ PARKER, JUDGE. The question which provoked the most discussion by counsel on this appeal°, and which lies at the foundation of plaintiff's

---

° The opinion of the intermediate court, from which this appeal was taken, recites further interesting facts: the uncle had long planned to make a gift of $5,000 to young William; the uncle later loaned $2,500 to William, who went into bankruptcy along with his father and listed no claim against his uncle among his assets; the uncle subsequently gave $11,000 worth of goods to William and his father, taking promissory notes and a general release from both that was broad enough to cover this claim; but it was claimed by the plaintiff on trial that, prior to William's bankruptcy, he had already assigned the $5,000 claim to his wife, so that it was no longer one of his assets and was not later affected by the release. See Hamer v. Sidway, 64 N.Y.Sup.Ct. 229 (1890).

asserted right of recovery, is whether by virtue of a contract defendant's testator William S. Story became indebted to his nephew William E. Story, 2d, on his twenty-first birthday in the sum of five thousand dollars. The trial court found as a fact that "on the 20th day of March, 1869, William E. Story agreed to and with William E. Story, 2d, that if he would refrain from drinking liquor, using tobacco, swearing, and playing cards or billiards for money until he should become 21 years of age, then he, the said William E. Story, would at that time pay him, the said William E. Story, 2d, the sum of $5000 for such refraining, to which the said William E. Story, 2d, agreed," and that he "in all things fully performed his part of said agreement."

The defendant contends that the contract was without consideration to support it, and, therefore, invalid. He asserts that the promisee by refraining from the use of liquor and tobacco was not harmed but benefited; that that which he did was best for him to do independently of his uncle's promise, and insists that it follows that unless the promisor was benefited, the contract was without consideration, a contention which, if well founded, would seem to leave open for controversy in many cases whether that which the promisee did or omitted to do was, in fact, of such benefit to him as to leave no consideration to support the enforcement of the promisor's agreement. Such a rule could not be tolerated, and is without foundation in the law. The Exchequer Chamber, in 1875, defined consideration as follows: "A valuable consideration in the sense of the law may consist either in some right, interest, profit, or benefit accruing to the one party, or some forbearance, detriment, loss, or responsibility given, suffered, or undertaken by the other." Courts "will not ask whether the thing which forms the consideration does in fact benefit the promisee or a third party, or is of any substantial value to any one. It is enough that something is promised, done, forborne, or suffered by the party to whom the promise is made as consideration for the promise made to him." Anson's Prin. of Con. 63.

"In general, a waiver of any legal right at the request of another party is a sufficient consideration for a promise." Parsons on Contracts, 444.

"Any damage, or suspension or forbearance of a right, will be sufficient to sustain a promise." Kent, Vol. 2, 465, 12th Ed.[p]

---

[p]　James Kent (1763–1847) began practice after three years as an apprentice and was active in Federalist politics. Hamilton introduced him to the writings of European authors on the civil law, which were to influence his later work. In 1793, largely through his Federalist connections, he was made Professor of Law at Columbia College. He attracted few students, and soon resigned to become a judge on the New York Supreme Court, then the highest court in the state. In 1814 he became Chancellor. Upon his retirement in 1823, he lectured again at Columbia for three years. Out of these lectures grew the "Commentaries on American Law," in four volumes, which became one of the most important American law books of the century. (It is the source of the quotation above.) Kent lived to prepare six editions; subsequent ones were revised by others. For his work on the Court of Chancery, he has been called the creator of equity in the United States.

Pollock, in his work on contracts, page 166, after citing the definition given by the Exchequer Chamber already quoted, says: "The second branch of this judicial description is really the most important one. Consideration means not so much that one party is profiting as that the other abandons some legal right in the present or limits his legal freedom of action in the future as an inducement for the promise of the first."

Now, applying this rule to the facts before us, the promisee used tobacco, occasionally drank liquor, and he had a legal right to do so. That right he abandoned for a period of years upon the strength of the promise of the testator that for such forbearance he would give him $5000. We need not speculate on the effort which may have been required to give up the use of those stimulants. It is sufficient that he restricted his lawful freedom of action within certain prescribed limits upon the faith of his uncle's agreement, and now having fully performed the conditions imposed, it is of no moment whether such performance actually proved a benefit to the promisor, and the court will not inquire into it, but were it a proper subject of inquiry, we see nothing in this record that would permit a determination that the uncle was not benefited in a legal sense. Few cases have been found which may be said to be precisely in point, but such as have been support the position we have taken.

In Shadwell v. Shadwell, 9 C.B.N.S. 159, an uncle wrote to his nephew as follows:

"MY DEAR LANCEY—I am so glad to hear of your intended marriage with Ellen Nicholl, and as I promised to assist you at starting, I am happy to tell you that I will pay you 150 pounds yearly during my life and until your annual income derived from your profession of a chancery barrister shall amount to 600 guineas, of which your own admission will be the only evidence that I shall require.

"YOUR AFFECTIONATE UNCLE,
"CHARLES SHADWELL."

It was held that the promise was binding and made upon good consideration.

In Lakota v. Newton, an unreported case in the Superior Court of Worcester, Mass., the complaint averred defendant's promise that "if you (meaning plaintiff) will leave off drinking for a year I will give you $100," plaintiff's assent thereto, performance of the condition by him, and demanded judgment therefor. Defendant demurred on the ground, among others, that the plaintiff's declaration did not allege a valid and sufficient consideration for the agreement of the defendant. The demurrer was overruled.

In Talbott v. Stemmons, 89 Ky. 222, the step-grandmother of the plaintiff made with him the following agreement: "I do promise and bind myself to give my grandson, Albert R. Talbott, $500 at my death, if he will never take another chew of tobacco or smoke another cigar during my life from this date up to my death, and if he breaks this pledge he is to refund double the amount to his mother." The executor of Mrs. Stemmons demurred to the complaint on the ground that the agreement was not based on a sufficient consideration. The demurrer was sustained and an appeal taken therefrom to the Court of Appeals, where the decision of the court below was reversed. In the opinion of the court it is said that "the right to use and enjoy the use of tobacco was a right that belonged to the plaintiff and not forbidden by law. The abandonment of its use may have saved him money or contributed to his health; nevertheless, the surrender of that right caused the promise, and having the right to contract with reference to the subject-matter, the abandonment of the use was a sufficient consideration to uphold the promise." Abstinence from the use of intoxicating liquors was held to furnish a good consideration for a promissory note in Lindell v. Rokes, 60 Mo. 249. The cases cited by the defendant on this question are not in point.

[In an omitted part of the opinion the court held that the action was not barred by the statute of limitations because under the uncle's letter he held the money in trust and not merely as a debtor.] Order reversed and judgment of special term affirmed.

NOTES

(1) *Benefit, Detriment, and Bargain.* What was the consideration for the uncle's promise to pay $5,000? How did the court's definition of detriment differ from that urged by the defendant? What role do benefit and detriment play under Restatement §§ 71 and 79? Was there consideration for the uncle's promise under those sections? What if the uncle had promised his nephew $5,000 in exchange for the young man's promise to foreswear illegal substances?

How clear is it that there was consideration for promise of the affectionate uncle in Shadwell v. Shadwell ("My dear Lancey . . ."), cited by the court as being "precisely on point"?

(2) *Holmes and the "Bargain Theory" of Consideration.* Oliver Wendell Holmes, Jr., an early advocate of the "bargain theory" of consideration later espoused in the Restatement, spoke of "reciprocal conventional inducement": "It is said that consideration must not be confounded with motive. It is true that it must not be confounded with what may be the prevailing or chief motive in actual fact. A man may promise to paint a picture for five hundred dollars, while his chief motive may be a desire for fame. A consideration may be given and accepted, in fact, solely for the purpose of making a promise binding. But, nevertheless, it is the essence of a consideration, that, by the terms of the agreement, it is given and accepted as the motive or inducement of the promise. Conversely, the promise must be made and accepted as the conventional motive or inducement for furnishing the consideration. The root of the whole matter is the relation of reciprocal conventional inducement, each for the other, between consideration and promise." Holmes, The Common Law 293–94 (1881).

Holmes reaffirmed this when he went on the bench: "[T]he promise and the consideration must purport to be the motive each for the other, in whole or at least in part. It is not enough that the promise induces the detriment or that the detriment induces the promise if the other half is wanting." Holmes, J., in Wisconsin & Michigan Railway Co. v. Powers, 191 U.S. 379 (1903). Compare Restatement § 71(2) with § 81(1).

(3) *"Sufficiency" of Consideration.* The term "sufficient consideration" appears at several points in Restatement ("the Restatement"), embodied a concept of the "sufficiency" of consideration. Although consideration did not have to be "adequate," it had to be "sufficient." See the Restatement, §§ 76–81. The Restatement Second abandoned this concept. Under its terminology the question is simply whether there is "consideration," with no qualifying adjective. See Restatement § 79. In declining to assess whether a particular lease provision was inadequate, one court relied on the "time-honored principle" that an informed decision by a party is "that what it is receiving is worth what it is giving may not later be second-guessed by that party, nor may the party ask a court to engage in such post-hoc revisionism." GLS Development v. Wal-Mart Stores, 944 F.Supp. 1384 (N.D.Ill. 1996). Whether or not consideration can ever be so paltry as to suggest impermissible overreaching by one of the parties is taken up in Chapter 4.

(4) *The Peppercorn.* Under the bargain theory of consideration, can a gratuitous promise be made enforceable by a mere token payment, arranged by the parties for the sole purpose of satisfying the requirement of consideration? Holmes concluded that because courts would not in general "inquire into the amount of such consideration . . ., consideration is as much a form as a seal." Krell v. Codman, 28 N.E. 578 (Mass. 1891). The term "peppercorn" is often used to describe consideration that is of trifling value.

Will such a device be given effect? There is some authority, most of it old, that it will be—e.g., Thomas v. Thomas, 2 Q.B. 851, 114 Eng.Rep. 330 (1842). Illustration 1 to the Restatement § 84 states:

> A wishes to make a binding promise to his son B to convey to B Blackacre, which is worth $5,000. Being advised that a gratuitous promise is not binding, A writes to B an offer to sell Blackacre for $1. B accepts. B's promise to pay $1 is sufficient consideration.

In contrast, the Restatement Second, takes the opposite view. Illustration 5 to § 71 states:

> A desires to make a binding promise to give $1,000 to his son B. Being advised that a gratuitous promise is not binding, A offers to buy from B for $1,000 a book worth less than $1. B accepts the offer knowing that the purchase of the book is a mere pretense. There is no consideration for A's promise to pay $1,000.

Why should promisors not be able to bind themselves through the pro forma use of consideration? Why might parties want to bind themselves legally in the absence of a bargain? Ought the law differentiate between a peppercorn inserted for the purpose of tying the promisor to the mast and cases in which the consideration is intended as a sham from a promissory point of view? See Meyer v. South Dakota Dept. of Social Services, 581

N.W.2d 151 (S.D. 1998), in which the owner of a ranch sought to reduce his estate for purposes of Medicaid eligibility through a series of "gift/lendback" transactions with his adult children. The owner wrote checks to his children who endorsed the checks and gave them back to the owner, who deposited them into his account uncashed. The owner then gave the children a mortgage on the ranch to secure the "loans" they had made him. The court quoted Williston: "nothing can be treated as consideration that is not intended as such by the parties." 3 Williston on Contracts § 7.2 (4th ed., Richard A. Lord, ed., 1992).

(5) *Promise for Performance or Promise for Promise?* In the principal case, the uncle promised to pay his nephew in exchange for his nephew's *refraining* from various vices, and not for his nephew's *promise* to refrain. See Restatement § 71(1). Why might the uncle have sought actual performance rather than his nephew's promise? Distinctions between contracts in which the promise is exchanged for performance and those in which two promises are exchanged are discussed at p. 94 below and again in Chapter 2 in connection with contract formation. Agreements in which only one party makes a promise are often called *unilateral* contracts; agreements in which each party makes a promise to the other are often called *bilateral*. Bilateral contracts are much more common and economically significant than unilateral contracts. Why might this be?

(6) Hamer *Lives.* In Dahl v. HEM Pharmaceuticals, 7 F.3d 1399 (9th Cir. 1993), a drug company promised a year's free supply of an experimental drug to subjects who participated in a one-year clinical trial to test the drug's efficacy. Dahl participated for the full year, at which time HEM refused to supply the drug any further, claiming its promise to do so was unsupported by consideration. On appeal, the court said: "Somehow the category of unilateral contracts appears to have escaped HEM's notice. The deal was, 'if you submit to our experiment, we will give you a year's supply of Ampligen at no charge.' This form of agreement resembles that in the case taught in the first year of law school, Hamer v. Sidway." Id. at 1404.

PROBLEM

Discounting Retirement. Thomas Hurley has worked as general superintendent for Marine Contractors for eight years, during which Marine has made annual payments into an Employee Retirement Plan and Trust Fund, a legally separate entity whose sole trustee is also the president of Marine. Hurley now plans to leave Marine, and is entitled under the terms of the trust to payment of his vested share after a five-year waiting period. Marine wants Hurley to make a binding promise to Marine not to compete with it after he leaves its employ. In return, Marine's president, as trustee, is willing to have the trust pay Hurley his vested share immediately. Will payment by the trust to Hurley be consideration for Hurley's promise to Marine? Does the answer depend on whether you are looking for a benefit, a detriment, or a bargain? See Marine Contractors Co., Inc. v. Hurley, 310 N.E.2d 915 (Mass. 1974).

Gratuitous Promises

Suppose that the uncle in *Hamer* had given his nephew $5,000 in cash at the golden wedding anniversary and had told him that it was a gift that he could keep on condition that he refrain from drinking, smoking, swearing, and gambling until he was 21. Surely the nephew, having met the condition, could have kept the money if the uncle's executor had attempted to get it back.

If the law recognizes gratuitous *transfers*, with or without strings attached, why should it not recognize gratuitous *promises*? Why did the court have to find that there was consideration? What explains the reluctance to create a regime of enforceable gift promises? We have already seen the suggestion that social cooperation might best be achieved by a system of "free enterprise." Is it the fact that gratuitous promises serve no useful economic function? Do gift promises raise dangers as to proof? See Richard A. Posner, *Gratuitous Promises in Economics and Law*, 6 J. Legal Stud. 411 (1977).

What sorts of rules or legal mechanisms would you suggest if it were thought desirable to enable promisors to make enforceable gratuitous promises? To what extent should those rules take account of such factors as the promisor's motives, the social utility of the promise, the formality with which it was made and the availability of alternate means of making gifts?

NOTES

(1) *Sweetheart Stadium?* In the 1990s, a group of taxpayers in Washington State sought to enjoin a bond ordinance enacted to raise money for a new stadium for the Seattle Mariners, a baseball team. The taxpayers argued that the consideration received by the city under the terms of the stadium lease between the city and the team was so "grossly inadequate" as to make the lease a gift, one prohibited under the state constitution, which forbids gifts of public monies to private organizations. The taxpayers pointed to the lease's profit-sharing requirement (with little expectation of profit), nominal rent, and easy-out terms for the team.

Noting that "courts do not inquire into the adequacy of consideration," the Washington Supreme Court found consideration in the Mariners' obligations to play home games, maintain the stadium, and share profits. It affirmed the trial court's declaratory order validating the bonds. King County v. Taxpayers of King County, 949 P.2d 1260 (Wash.1997).

Is the traditional rule regarding consideration appropriate in the context of a constitutional challenge? A dissent in the stadium case argued that it is not:

> If a public official may transfer $100 of the taxpayer property for a $5 return to the taxpayer, they are $95 poorer. The return is inadequate regardless of the legal sufficiency of the consideration. The purpose of the [constitutional] provision is to avoid

transactions which plunder the public purse to the benefit of private corporate wealth.

Id. at 1278. The dissenting justices would have required a trial on the question of the adequacy of the return. The Arizona Supreme Court agreed. In 2010, the Court held that although "courts do not ordinarily examine the proportionality of consideration between parties contracting at arm's length, leaving such issues to the marketplace," a different test applies when the adequacy of consideration is challenged under the Gift Clause of the state constitution. Turken v. Gordon, 224 P.3d 158 (Ariz. 2010). In that case, the City of Phoenix had agreed to pay a private developer an extraordinary price of over $97,000,000 for the use of parking spaces over a specified period of time. Applying the new test prospectively, the Court held that the Gift Clause "prohibits subsidies to private entities, and paying far more than the fair market value . . . would plainly be a subsidy." Id. at 166. Applying the new test prospectively, the Court held that the Gift Clause "prohibits subsidies to private entities, and paying far more than the fair market value would plainly be a subsidy." Id. at 166.

(2) *Comparative Approaches.* One argument against enforcing gratuitous promises is that enforcement leaves no room for a promisor's regret or for changed circumstances. But might not some reasons for changing one's mind be anticipated and accommodated? French and German laws, for example, permit the revocation of *gifts* by means of implied conditions in cases where the donor is subsequently impoverished (German law), or cases of "donee ingratitude" (French law). See John P. Dawson, Gifts and Promises (1980) at 53, 140–141; see also Richard Hyland, Gifts: A Study in Comparative Law (2009). Louisiana, a civil law jurisdiction, provides for revocation of an inter vivos gift where the donee "has attempted to take the life of the donor" or "has been guilty. . . of cruel treatment, crimes, or grievous injury." Farnsworth on Contracts § 2.18a, n.21.

Consider also an Israeli rule that permits revocation of a gift *promise,* even after reliance by the promisee, "if the retraction is warranted by disgraceful conduct towards the [promisor or the promisor's family]," 22 Laws of State of Israel 113. Is it significant in these latter cases that the promisee appears to have had some responsibility for the promisor's regret? For a thorough investigation of the subject, see E. Allan Farnsworth, Changing One's Mind: The Law of Regretted Decisions (2000).

Settlement Agreements

Despite the well-known, perhaps well-deserved, reputation for litigiousness in the U.S., only a tiny percentage of civil cases actually go to trial. See John H. Langbein, *The Disappearance of Civil Trial in the United States,* 122 Yale L.J. 522 (2012). Most parties settle their cases, and for a number of reasons: risk aversion, trial costs, concerns about privacy. When a plaintiff gives up a valid claim in exchange for something, consideration is no obstacle to the settlement. But what if the plaintiff's claim turns out to be invalid? Has the defendant in such a case given up something for nothing?

Dyer v. National By-Products, Inc.

Supreme Court of Iowa, 1986.
380 N.W.2d 732.

■ SCHULTZ, JUSTICE. The determinative issue in this appeal is whether good faith forbearance to litigate a claim, which proves to be invalid and unfounded, is sufficient consideration to uphold a contract of settlement. The district court determined, as a matter of law, that consideration for the alleged settlement was lacking because the forborne claim was not a viable cause of action. We reverse and remand.

On October 29, 1981, Dale Dyer, an employee of National By-Products, lost his right foot in a job-related accident. Thereafter, the employer placed Dyer on a leave of absence at full pay from the date of his injury until August 16, 1982. At that time he returned to work as a foreman, the job he held prior to his injury. On March 11, 1983, the employer indefinitely laid off Dyer.

Dyer then filed the present lawsuit against his employer claiming that his discharge was a breach of an oral contract. He alleged that he in good faith believed that he had a valid claim against his employer for his personal injury. Further, Dyer claimed that his forbearance from litigating his claim was made in exchange for a promise from his employer that he would have lifetime employment. The employer specifically denied that it had offered a lifetime job to Dyer after his injury.

Dyer then filed the present lawsuit against his employer claiming that his discharge was a breach of an oral contract. He alleged that he in good faith believed that he had a valid claim against his employer for his personal injury. Further, Dyer claimed that his forbearance from litigating his claim was made in exchange for a promise from his employer that he would have lifetime employment.

The district court sustained the employer's motion on the basis that: (1) no reciprocal promise to work for the employer for life was present, and (2) there was no forbearance of any viable cause of action, apparently on the ground that workers' compensation provided Dyer's sole remedy. On appeal, Dyer claims that consideration for the alleged contract of lifetime employment was his forbearance from pursuing an action against his employer.

The employer, on the other hand, maintains that workers' compensation benefits are Dyer's sole remedy for his injury and that his claim for damages is unfounded. It then urges that forbearance from asserting an unfounded claim cannot serve as consideration for a contract. For the purpose of this discussion, we shall assume that Dyer's tort action is clearly invalid and he had no basis for a tort suit against either his employer or his fellow employees. We recognize that the fact issue, as to whether Dyer in good faith believed that he had a cause of action based in tort against the employer, remains unresolved. The determinative issue before the district court and now on appeal is whether the lack of consideration for the alleged promise of lifetime employment has been established as a matter of law.

Preliminarily, we observe that the law favors the adjustment and settlement of controversies without resorting to court action. Olson v. Wilson & Co., 244 Iowa 895, 899, 58 N.W.2d 381, 384 (1953). Compromise is favored by law. White v. Flood, 258 Iowa 402, 409, 138 N.W.2d 863, 867 (1965). Compromise of a doubtful right asserted in good faith is sufficient consideration for a promise. Id.

The more difficult problem is whether the settlement of an unfounded claim asserted in good faith is consideration for a contract of settlement. Professor Corbin presents a view favorable to Dyer's argument when he states:

> [F]orbearance to press a claim, or a promise of such forbearance, may be a sufficient consideration even though the claim is wholly ill-founded. It may be ill-founded because the facts are not what he supposes them to be, or because the existing facts do not have the legal operation that he supposes them to have. In either case, his forbearance may be a sufficient consideration, although under certain circumstances it is not. The fact that the claim is ill-founded is not in itself enough to prevent forbearance from being a sufficient consideration for a promise. Corbin on Contracts § 140, at 595 (1963).

Further, in the same section, it is noted that:

> The most generally prevailing, and probably the most satisfactory view is that forbearance is sufficient if there is any reasonable ground for the claimant's belief that it is just to try to enforce his claim. He must be asserting his claim "in good faith"; but this does not mean he must believe that his suit can be won. It means that he must not be making his claim or threatening suit for purposes of vexation, or in order to realize on its "nuisance value."

Id. § 140, at 602.

Indeed, we find support for the Corbin view in language contained in our cases. See White v. Flood, 258 Iowa at 409, 138 N.W.2d at 867 ("[C]ompromise of a doubtful right asserted in good faith is sufficient consideration for a promise."); . . . Messer v. Washington National Insurance Co., 233 Iowa 1372, 1380, 11 N.W.2d 727, 731 (1943) ("[I]f the parties act in good faith, even when they know all the facts and there is promise without legal liability on which to base it, the courts hesitate to disturb the agreements of the parties. . . . ") [additional citations omitted].

The Restatement (Second) of Contracts section 74 (1979), supports the Corbin view and states:

Settlement of Claims

(1)   Forbearance to assert or the surrender of a claim or defense which proves to be invalid is not consideration unless

(a)   the claim or defense is in fact doubtful because of uncertainty as to the facts or the law, or

(b)   the forbearing or surrendering party believes that the claim or defense may be fairly determined to be valid.

The Comment states:

b.   Requirement of good faith. The policy favoring compromise of disputed claims is clearest, perhaps, where a claim is surrendered at a time when it is uncertain whether it is valid or not. Even though the invalidity later becomes clear, the bargain is to be judged as it appeared to the parties at the time; if the claim was then doubtful, no inquiry is necessary as to their good faith. Even though the invalidity should have been clear at the time, the settlement of an honest dispute is upheld. But a mere assertion or denial of liability does not make a claim doubtful, and the fact that invalidity is obvious may indicate that it was known. In such cases Subsection (1)(b) requires a showing of good faith.

However, not all jurisdictions adhere to this view. Some courts require that the claim forborne must have some merit in fact or at law before it can provide consideration and these jurisdictions reject those claims that are obviously invalid. See Bullard v. Curry-Cloonan, 367 A.2d 127, 131 (D.C.App.1976) ("[A]s a general principle, the forbearance of a cause of action advanced in good faith, which is neither absurd in fact nor obviously unfounded in law, constitutes good and valuable consideration."); Frasier v. Carter, 92 Idaho 79, 437 P.2d 32, 34 (1968) (The forbearance of a claim which is not utterly groundless is sufficient consideration to support a contract.); Charles v. Hill, 260 N.W.2d 571, 575 (Minn.1977) ("[A] wholly baseless or utterly unfounded claim is not consideration for a contract."); Agristor Credit Corporation v. Unruh, 571 P.2d 1220, 1224 (Okla.1977) (In order to constitute consideration for a contract, "claim forborne must be reasonably doubtful in law or fact.").

In fact, we find language in our own case law that supports the view which is favorable to the employer in this case. See Vande Stouwe v. Bankers' Life Co., 218 Iowa 1182, 1190, 254 N.W. 790, 794 (1934) ("A claim that is entirely baseless and without foundation in law or equity will not support a compromise."); Peterson v. Breitag, 88 Iowa 418, 422–23, 55 N.W. 86, 88 (1893) ("It is well settled that there must at least be some appearance of a valid claim to support a settlement to avoid litigation."); ... Sullivan v. Collins, 18 Iowa 228, 229 (1865) (A compromise of a claim is not a sufficient consideration to sustain a note, when such claim is not sustainable in law or in equity, or, at least doubtful in some respect.). Additionally, Professor Williston notes that:

> While there is a great divergence of opinion respecting the kind of forbearance which will constitute consideration, the weight of authority holds that although forbearance from suit on a clearly invalid claim is insufficient consideration for a promise, forbearance from suit on a claim of doubtful validity is sufficient consideration for a promise if there is a sincere belief in the validity of the claim. 1 Williston on Contracts § 135, at 581 (3rd ed. 1957).

We believe, however, that the better reasoned approach is that expressed in the Restatement (Second) of Contracts section 74. Even the above statement from Williston, although it may have been the state of the law in 1957, is a questionable assessment of the current law. In fact, most of the cases cited in the cumulative supplement to Williston follow the "good faith and reasonable" language. 1 Williston on Contracts § 135B (3rd ed. 1957 & Supp.1985). Additionally, Restatement (Second) of Contracts section 74 is cited in that supplement. Id. As noted before, as a matter of policy the law favors compromise and such policy would be defeated if a party could second guess his settlement and litigate the validity of the compromise. The requirement that the forbearing party assert the claim in good faith sufficiently protects the policy of law that favors the settlement of controversies. Our holdings which are to the contrary to this view are overruled.

In the present case, the invalidity of Dyer's claim against the employer does not foreclose him, as a matter of law, from asserting that his forbearance was consideration for the alleged contract of settlement. However, the issue of Dyer's good faith must still be examined. In so doing, the issue of the validity of Dyer's claim should not be entirely overlooked: Although the courts will not inquire into the validity of a claim which was compromised in good faith, there must generally be reasonable grounds for a belief in order for the court to be convinced that the belief was honestly entertained by the person who asserted it. Sufficient consideration requires more than the bald assertion by a claimant who has a claim, and to the extent that the validity or invalidity of a claim has a bearing upon whether there were reasonable grounds for believing in its possible validity, evidence of the validity or invalidity of a claim may be relevant to the issue of good faith. 15A Am.Jur.2d Compromise and Settlement § 17, at 790. We conclude that the evidence of the invalidity of the claim is relevant to show a lack of honest belief in the validity of the claim asserted or forborne.

Under the present state of the record, there remains a material fact as to whether Dyer's forbearance to assert his claim was in good faith. Summary judgment should not have been rendered against him. Accordingly, the case is reversed and remanded for further proceedings consistent with this opinion.

REVERSED AND REMANDED.

NOTES

(1) *Questions.* What was the problem with the claim Dyer agreed not to pursue? Was any aspect of it doubtful as a matter of fact or law? How can forbearing on a legally non-existent claim satisfy the requirement of bargained-for exchange? Does the impossibility of Dyer's tort suit bear at all on the question of whether his forbearance complied with the factors set out in Restatement § 74?

Why might parties in general prefer to settle valid claims rather than litigate them? What broader policies are promoted by settlement? Private ordering? Efficiency? Fairness? See Michael Moffitt, *Three Things to be Against ("Settlement" Not Included)*, 78 Fordham L. Rev. 1203 (2009).

(2) *The Claimant's Belief.* In *Dyer*, what factual issue was the trial court to determine on remand? How does a claimant prove a good faith belief? Is the good faith belief in the validity of the claim measured by an objective or subjective standard?

Consider the following case. In 1951, Hilda Boehm, an unmarried woman, gave birth to a baby girl. After informing Louis Fiege that he was the father, the parties entered into an agreement: Boehm promised not to file a paternity action against Fiege in exchange for Fiege's promise to pay child support during the child's minority. In 1953, Fiege learned from Boehm's physician that blood tests indicated he could not have been the father. Fiege stopped paying support, and Boehm sued for breach of their settlement agreement. A jury found for Boehm, and Fiege appealed on the ground that the contract lacked consideration because Boehm's forbearance was based on an invalid claim. Fiege v. Boehm, 123 A.2d 316 (Ct. App. Md. 1951). Held: For Boehm.

The appellate court found that Boehm's promise to forbear was good consideration. Not only did Boehm honestly believe her claim to be well founded (subjective), but the claim also had a reasonable basis of support (objective). What facts might warrant Boehm's good faith belief in the validity of her claim? Could she have enforced promises for child support against two promisors?

How does Boehm's claim against Fiege differ from that of Dyer in the principal case?

(3) *Settlement Agreements and Legal Ethics.* While *Dyer* concerned forbearance in the context of a personal injury claim, the settlement of doubtful claims also arises in connection with nuisance litigation or "strike suits." These are lawsuits with a sufficiently low chance of prevailing at trial that they would not have been brought but for the prospect of settlement. Why are frivolous suits not always met with blanket refusals to negotiate? A legal economist has observed that "since refusing to take a valid claim seriously can be quite costly, a frivolous plaintiff may be able to take advantage of the defendant's uncertainty regarding the claim's validity to

extract a substantial settlement." Avery Katz, *The Effect of Frivolous Lawsuits on the Settlement of Claims*, 10 Intl. Rev. L. & Econ. 3, 4 (1990).

What is a lawyer's responsibility with regard to filing dubious pleadings? Rule 11(b) of the Federal Rules of Civil Procedure provides that by presenting a pleading to a court an attorney certifies that to the best of his or her knowledge, after a reasonable inquiry, the pleading "is not being presented for any improper purpose, such as to harass or to cause unnecessary delay or needless increase in the cost of litigation." An attorney further certifies, by virtue of signing a pleading, that there is evidentiary support for any fact it asserts. Courts may order sanctions against attorneys who violate Rule 11(b). Comparable rules govern state court pleadings; see, for example, the Signing of Pleadings in Texas Code Annotated § 9.01.

(4) *Plea Bargains.* Settlement agreements are not only a common aspect of civil litigation; they also play a significant role in the criminal justice system. Consider that only five percent of federal and state felony prosecutions are resolved by trial; the remainder are settled through plea bargains entered into between criminal defendants and prosecutors. See Padilla v. Kentucky, 130 S. Ct. 1473, 1485 (2010). Typically, the defendant agrees to plead guilty in exchange for some concession by the prosecutor, such as a sentencing recommendation or a dismissal of other charges. Who is giving up what in this arrangement? What are the advantages for prosecutors, for defendants, and for the administration of justice? Ought the law have particular concerns when a party's forbearance has a constitutional dimension? If the government fails to make the promised sentencing recommendation, what remedy might the defendant seek? See United States v. Ramsey, 503 F.Supp.2d 554 (N.D.N.Y. 2007).

(5) *Forbearing Political Participation.* Community benefits agreements (CBAs) are contracts negotiated and executed between real estate developers and community groups. Typically these agreements require the developer to provide benefits to the community, such as local hiring, living wages and affordable housing, in exchange for the community groups' promise to not oppose the project. Is a promise to refrain from political participation valid consideration? What if the community group or a renegade member of the community group had a change of heart and sought to organize protests after the agreement was formed? Would the developer have a remedy, and how might it be enforced? Citizens cannot offer their votes as consideration. How are CBAs distinguishable from vote-selling? See Vicki Been, *Community Benefits Agreements: New Local Government Tool or Another Variation on the Exactions Theme?*, 77 U. Chi. L. Rev. 5, 5–6 (2010); Naved Sheikh, *Community Benefits Agreements: Can Private Contracts Replace Public Responsibility?*, 18 Cornell J. L. & Pub. Pol'y 223, 233–40 (2009).

(B) THE REQUIREMENT OF EXCHANGE: ACTION IN THE PAST

Feinberg v. Pfeiffer Co.

Saint Louis Court of Appeals, Missouri, 1959.
322 S.W.2d 163.

Action on alleged contract by defendant to pay plaintiff a specified monthly amount upon her retirement from defendant's employ. The Circuit Court, City of St. Louis, rendered judgment for plaintiff, and defendant appealed.

■ DOERNER, COMMISSIONER. This is a suit brought in the Circuit Court of the City of St. Louis by plaintiff, a former employee of the defendant corporation, on an alleged contract whereby defendant agreed to pay plaintiff the sum of $200 per month for life upon her retirement. A jury being waived, the case was tried by the court alone. Judgment below was for plaintiff for $5,100, the amount of the pension claimed to be due as of the date of the trial together with interest thereon, and defendant duly appealed.

The parties are in substantial agreement on the essential facts. Plaintiff began working for the defendant, a manufacturer of pharmaceuticals, in 1910, when she was but 17 years of age. By 1947 she had attained the position of bookkeeper, office manager, and assistant treasurer of the defendant, and owned 70 shares of its stock out of a total of 6,503 shares issued and outstanding. Twenty shares had been given to her by the defendant or its then president, she had purchased 20, and the remaining 30 she had acquired by a stock split or stock dividend. Over the years she received substantial dividends on the stock she owned, as did all of the other stockholders. Also, in addition to her salary, plaintiff from 1937 to 1949, inclusive, received each year a bonus varying in amount from $300 in the beginning to $2,000 in the later years.

On December 27, 1947, the annual meeting of the defendant's Board of Directors was held at the Company's offices in St. Louis, presided over by Max Lippman, its then president and largest individual stockholder. The other directors present were George L. Marcus, Sidney Harris, Sol Flammer, and Walter Weinstock, who, with Max Lippman, owned 5,007 of the 6,503 shares then issued and outstanding. At that meeting the Board of Directors adopted the following resolution, which, because it is the crux of the case, we quote in full:

"The Chairman thereupon pointed out that the Assistant Treasurer, Mrs. Anna Sacks Feinberg, has given the corporation many years of long and faithful service. Not only has she served the corporation devotedly, but with exceptional ability and skill. The President pointed out that although all of the officers and directors sincerely hoped and desired that Mrs. Feinberg would continue in her present position for as long as she felt able, nevertheless, in view of the length of service which she has contributed provision should be made to afford her retirement privileges and benefits which should become a firm obligation of the corporation to be available to her whenever she should see fit to retire from active duty, however many years in the future such retirement may become effective. It was, accordingly, proposed that Mrs. Feinberg's salary which is presently $350.00 per month, be increased to $400.00 per month, and that Mrs. Feinberg would be given the privilege of retiring from active duty at any time she may elect to see fit so to do upon a retirement pay of $200.00 per month for life, with the distinct understanding that the retirement plan is merely being adopted at the present time in order to afford Mrs. Feinberg security for the future and in the hope that her active services will continue with the corporation for many years to come. After due discussion and consideration, and upon motion duly made and seconded, it was—

"Resolved, that the salary of Anna Sacks Feinberg be increased from $350.00 to $400.00 per month and that she be afforded the privilege of retiring from active duty in the corporation at any time she may elect to see fit so to do upon retirement pay of $200.00 per month, for the remainder of her life."

At the request of Mr. Lippman his sons-in-law, Messrs. Harris and Flammer, called upon the plaintiff at her apartment on the same day to advise her of the passage of the resolution. Plaintiff testified on cross-examination that she had no prior information that such a pension plan was contemplated, that it came as a surprise to her, and that she would have continued in her employment whether or not such a resolution had been adopted. It is clear from the evidence that there was no contract, oral or written, as to plaintiff's length of employment, and that she was free to quit, and the defendant to discharge her, at any time.

Plaintiff did continue to work for the defendant through June 30, 1949, on which date she retired. In accordance with the foregoing resolution, the defendant began paying her the sum of $200 on the first of each month. Mr. Lippman died on November 18, 1949, and was succeeded as president of the company by his widow. Because of an illness, she retired from that office and was succeeded in October, 1953, by her son-in-law, Sidney M. Harris. Mr. Harris testified that while Mrs. Lippman had been president she signed the monthly pension check paid plaintiff, but fussed about doing so, and considered the payments as gifts. After his election, he stated, a new accounting firm employed by the defendant questioned the validity of the payments to plaintiff on several occasions, and in the Spring of 1956, upon its recommendation, he consulted the Company's then attorney, Mr. Ralph Kalish. Harris testified that both Ernst and Ernst, the accounting firm, and Kalish told him there was no need of giving plaintiff the money. He also stated that he had concurred in the view that the payments to plaintiff were mere gratuities rather than amounts due under a contractual obligation, and that following his discussion with the Company's attorney plaintiff was sent a check for $100 on April 1, 1956. Plaintiff declined to accept the reduced amount, and this action followed. Additional facts will be referred to later in this opinion.

Appellant's next complaint is that there was insufficient evidence to support the court's findings that plaintiff would not have quit defendant's employ had she not known and relied upon the promise of defendant to pay her $200 a month for life, and the finding that, from her voluntary retirement until April 1, 1956, plaintiff relied upon the continued receipt of the pension installments. The trial court so found, and, in our opinion, justifiably so. Plaintiff testified, and was corroborated by Harris, defendant's witness, that knowledge of the passage of the resolution was communicated to her on December 27, 1947, the very day it was adopted. She was told at that time by Harris and Flammer, she stated, that she could take the pension as of that day, if she wished. She testified further that she continued to work for another year and a half, through June 30, 1949; that at that time her health was good and she could have continued to work, but that after working for almost forty years she thought she would take a rest. Her testimony continued:

"Q. Now, what was the reason—I'm sorry. Did you then quit the employment of the company after you—after this year and a half? A. Yes.

"Q. What was the reason that you left? A. Well, I thought almost forty years, it was a long time and I thought I would take a little rest.

"Q. Yes. A. And with the pension and what earnings my husband had, we figured we could get along.

"Q. Did you rely upon this pension? A. We certainly did.

"Q. Being paid? A. Very much so. We relied upon it because I was positive that I was going to get it as long as I lived.

"Q. Would you have left the employment of the company at that time had it not been for this pension? A. No.

"Mr. Allen: Just a minute, I object to that as calling for a conclusion and conjecture on the part of this witness.

"The Court: It will be overruled.

"Q. (Mr. Agatstein continuing): Go ahead, now. The question is whether you would have quit the employment of the company at that time had you not relied upon this pension plan? A. No, I wouldn't.

"Q. You would not have. Did you ever seek employment while this pension was being paid to you—A. (interrupting): No.

"Q. Wait a minute, at any time prior—at any other place? A. No, sir.

"Q. Were you able to hold any other employment during that time? A. Yes, I think so.

"Q. Was your health good? A. My health was good."

It is obvious from the foregoing that there was ample evidence to support the findings of fact made by the court below.

We come, then, to the basic issue in the case. While otherwise defined in defendant's third and fourth assignments of error, it is thus succinctly stated in the argument in its brief: "whether plaintiff has proved that she has a right to recover from defendant based upon a legally binding contractual obligation to pay her $200 per month for life."

It is defendant's contention, in essence, that the resolution adopted by its Board of Directors was a mere promise to make a gift, and that no contract resulted either thereby, or when plaintiff retired, because there was no consideration given or paid by the plaintiff. It urges that a promise to make a gift is not binding unless supported by a legal consideration; that the only apparent consideration for the adoption of the foregoing resolution was the "many years of long and faithful service" expressed therein; and that past services are not a valid consideration for a promise. Defendant argues further that there is nothing in the resolution which made its effectiveness conditional upon plaintiff's continued employment, that she was not under contract to work for any length of time but was free to quit whenever she wished, and that she had no contractual right to her position and could have been discharged at any time.

Plaintiff concedes that a promise based upon past services would be without consideration, but contends that there were two other elements which supplied the required element: First, the continuation by plaintiff in the employ of the defendant for the period from December 27, 1947, the date when the resolution was adopted, until the date of her retirement on June 30, 1949. And, second, her change of position, i.e., her retirement, and the abandonment by her of her opportunity to continue in gainful employment, made in reliance on defendant's promise to pay her $200 per month for life.

We must agree with the defendant that the evidence does not support the first of these contentions. There is no language in the resolution predicating plaintiff's right to a pension upon her continued employment. She was not required to work for the defendant for any period of time as a condition to gaining such retirement benefits. She was told that she could quit the day upon which the resolution was adopted, as she herself testified, and it is clear from her own testimony that she made no promise or agreement to continue in the employ of the defendant in return for its promise to pay her a pension. Hence there was lacking that mutuality of obligation which is essential to the validity of a contract.

Consideration for a promise has been defined in the Restatement of the Law of Contracts, Section 75, as:

"(1) Consideration for a promise is

(a) an act other than a promise, or

(b) a forbearance, or

(c) the creation, modification or destruction of a legal relation, or

(d) a return promise,

bargained for and given in exchange for the promise."

As the parties agree, the consideration sufficient to support a contract may be either a benefit to the promisor or a loss or detriment to the promisee.

[The rest of the opinion is set out at p. 125, below. There Feinberg prevails on her contention that the defendant's promise resulted in a "change of position" on her part.]

NOTES

(1) *The Missing Ingredient.* Feinberg conceded "that a promise based on past services would be without consideration." Why was it so clear to everyone that her 37 years of service, prior to the resolution of December 27, 1947, could not be consideration for Pfeiffer's promise?

(2) *Drafting.* Suppose that Max Lippman had called in his lawyer in December 1947, and said, "I want you to draw up a resolution that will make sure that Mrs. Feinberg will get a pension of $200 a month as long as she lives." How might the lawyer have drafted such a document? Would it have helped to include the words, *"in consideration of* her many years of long and faithful service"?

PROBLEM

In 1985, the Prentis family entered into an endowment contract, or gift agreement, with Wayne State University ("WSU") under which the Prentis's family foundation would give $1,500,000 to WSU and WSU would name its cancer center the Meyer L. Prentis Comprehensive Cancer Center. The payments were completed in 1990. In 1995, the Karmanos family offered WSU a significant gift on the condition that the center be renamed the Barbara Ann Karmanos Cancer Institute. The center accepted. The Prentis family sued for breach of contract. Should they prevail?

In answering, consider the following language. In paragraph 1 of the agreement, the foundation agreed to contribute the money. In paragraph 2, WSU stated as follows:

> In recognition of the significant and long-standing commitment of and leadership and support by the Prentis Foundation in the fields of cancer education, detection and research and the generous financial contributions made over many years by the Prentis Foundation in furtherance thereof; and in further recognition of and appreciation to the Prentis Foundation for the fund it is hereby creating, [WSU and the other parties] do hereby agree that Center shall be renamed and henceforth be known as the Meyer L. Prentis Comprehensive Cancer Center of Metropolitan Detroit.

See Prentis Family Found. v. Barbara Ann Karmanos Cancer Inst., 698 N.W.2d 900 (Mich. Ct. App. 2005).

————

Moral Obligation

Mills v. Wyman

Supreme Judicial Court of Massachusetts, 1825.
3 Pick. 207, 20 Mass. 207.

[Levi Wyman, age 25, fell ill on his return from a sea voyage and, being poor and in distress, was cared for by Daniel Mills for about two weeks. A few days later, after all Mills's expenses had been incurred, Seth Wyman, Levi's father, wrote Mills promising to pay those expenses. When Seth Wyman decided not to pay, Mills sued him. From a direction of nonsuit, Mills appealed.]

■ PARKER, CHIEF JUSTICE. General rules of law established for the protection and security of honest and fair-minded men, who may inconsiderately make promises without any equivalent, will sometimes screen men of a different character from engagements which they are bound in *foro conscientiae* to perform. This is a defect inherent in all human systems of legislation. The rule that a mere verbal promise, without any consideration, cannot be enforced by action, is universal in its application, and cannot be departed from to suit particular cases in which a refusal to perform such a promise may be disgraceful.

The promise declared on in this case appears to have been made without any legal consideration. The kindness and services towards the sick son of the defendant were not bestowed at his request. The son was in no respect under the care of the defendant. He was twenty-five years old, and had long left his father's family. On his return from a foreign country, he fell sick among strangers, and the plaintiff acted the part of the good Samaritan, giving him shelter and comfort until he died. The defendant, his father, on being informed of this event, influenced by a transient feeling of gratitude, promises in writing to pay the plaintiff for the expenses he had incurred. But he has determined to break this promise, and is willing to have his case appear on record as a strong example of particular injustice sometimes necessarily resulting from the operation of general rules.

It is said a moral obligation is a sufficient consideration to support an express promise; and some authorities lay down the rule thus broadly; but upon examination of the cases we are satisfied that the universality of the rule cannot be supported.

A deliberate promise, in writing, made freely and without any mistake, one which may lead the party to whom it is made into contracts and expenses, cannot be broken without a violation of moral duty. But if there was nothing paid or promised for it, the law, perhaps wisely, leaves the execution of it to the conscience of him who makes it. It is only when the party making the promise gains something, or he to whom it is made loses something, that the law gives the promise validity.

[T]here seems to be no case in which it was nakedly decided, that a promise to pay the debt of a son of full age, not living with his father, though the debt were incurred by sickness which ended in the death of the son, without a previous request by the father proved or presumed, could be enforced by action.

For the foregoing reasons we are all of opinion that the nonsuit directed by the Court of Common Pleas was right, and that judgment be entered thereon for costs for the defendant.

NOTES

(1) *The Case Against "Moral Obligation."* Mills v. Wyman accurately reflects the traditional common law view that a promise made in recognition of a "moral obligation" arising out of a benefit previously received is not enforceable. A benefit conferred before a promise is made can hardly be said to have been given in "exchange" for the promise. Williston noted further that "it is essential that the classes of promises which are [enforceable by law] shall be clearly defined. The test of moral consideration must vary with the opinion of every individual. Indeed, as has been said, since there is a moral obligation to perform every promise, it would seem that if morality was to be the guide, every promise would be enforced and if the existence of a past moral obligation is to be the test, every promise which repeats or restates a prior gratuitous promise would be binding." 1 Williston, Treatise on the Law of Contracts § 148 (1st ed. 1920).

(2) *Immoral Without Obligation?* Suppose the letter from Seth Wyman to Daniel Mills had read as follows:

> I received a line from you relating to my Son Levi's sickness and requesting me to come up and see him, but as the going is very bad I cannot come up at the present, but I wish you to take all possible care of him and if you cannot have him at your house I wish you to remove him to some convenient place and if he cannot satisfy you for it I will.

What, if anything, would Wyman have promised by such a letter? Would this language change your views of the elder Wyman? What if, in contradiction of the court's statement, Levi Wyman had in fact not died? For more on the *Mills* case, see Geoffrey R. Watson, *In the Tribunal of Conscience: Mills v. Wyman Reconsidered*, 71 Tul. L. Rev. 1749 (1997).

(3) *Recognized Exceptions.* As the court acknowledged in *Mills*, in certain exceptional situations the common law does enforce certain promises made in recognition of what could be viewed as a "moral obligation." These include a promise to pay a debt no longer legally enforceable because the statutory period of limitations has run, and a promise by an adult reaffirming a promise made when the promisor was a minor and that could

have been avoided on that ground. A promise to pay a debt that has been discharged in bankruptcy constitutes a third exception. See Restatement §§ 82 and 83. What appears to explain these exceptions? (The enforceability of a promise to pay a debt unenforceable because of the promisor's discharge in bankruptcy is now subject to additional requirements under the Bankruptcy Code. 11 U.S.C. § 524(c)–(d).)

Webb v. McGowin

Court of Appeals of Alabama, 1935.
27 Ala.App. 82, 168 So. 196.

Action by Joe Webb against N. Floyd McGowin and Joseph F. McGowin, as executors of the estate of J. Greeley McGowin, deceased. From a judgment of nonsuit, plaintiff appeals.

■ BRICKEN, PRESIDING JUDGE. This action is in assumpsit. The complaint as originally filed was amended. The demurrers to the complaint as amended were sustained, and because of this adverse ruling by the court the plaintiff took a nonsuit, and the assignment of errors on this appeal are predicated upon said action or ruling of the court.

A fair statement of the case presenting the questions for decision is set out in appellant's brief, which we adopt.

"On the 3d day of August, 1925, appellant while in the employ of the W.T. Smith Lumber Company, a corporation, and acting within the scope of his employment, was engaged in clearing the upper floor of Mill No. 2 of the company. While so engaged he was in the act of dropping a pine block from the upper floor of the mill to the ground below; this being the usual and ordinary way of clearing the floor, and it being the duty of the plaintiff in the course of his employment to so drop it. The block weighed about 75 pounds.

"As appellant was in the act of dropping the block to the ground below, he was on the edge of the upper floor of the mill. As he started to turn the block loose so that it would drop to the ground, he saw J. Greeley McGowin, testator of the defendants, on the ground below and directly under where the block would have fallen had appellant turned it loose. Had he turned it loose it would have struck McGowin with such force as to have caused him serious bodily harm or death. Appellant could have remained safely on the upper floor of the mill by turning the block loose and allowing it to drop, but had he done this the block would have fallen on McGowin and caused him serious injuries or death. The only safe and reasonable way to prevent this was for appellant to hold to the block and divert its direction in falling from the place where McGowin was standing and the only safe way to divert it so as to prevent its coming into contact with McGowin was for appellant to fall with it to the ground below. Appellant did this, and by holding to the block and falling with it to the ground below, he diverted the course of its fall in such way that McGowin was not injured. In thus preventing the injuries to McGowin appellant himself received serious bodily injuries, resulting in his right leg being broken, the heel of his right foot torn off and his right arm broken. He was badly crippled for life and rendered unable to do physical or mental labor.

"On September 1, 1925, in consideration of appellant having prevented him from sustaining death or serious bodily harm and in consideration of the injuries appellant had received, McGowin agreed with him to care for and maintain him for the remainder of appellant's life at the rate of $15 every two weeks from the time he sustained his injuries to and during the remainder of appellant's life; it being agreed that McGowin would pay this sum to appellant for his maintenance. Under the agreement McGowin paid or caused to be paid to appellant the sum so agreed on up until McGowin's death on January 1, 1934. After his death the payments were continued to and including January 27, 1934, at which time they were discontinued. Thereupon plaintiff brought suit to recover the unpaid installments accruing up to the time of the bringing of the suit.

"The material averments of the different counts of the original complaint and the amended complaint are predicated upon the foregoing statement of facts."

The action was for the unpaid installments accruing after January 27, 1934, to the time of the suit.

1. The averments of the complaint show that appellant saved McGowin from death or grievous bodily harm. This was a material benefit to him of infinitely more value than any financial aid he could have received. Receiving this benefit, McGowin became morally bound to compensate appellant for the services rendered. Recognizing his moral obligation, he expressly agreed to pay appellant as alleged in the complaint and complied with this agreement up to the time of his death; a period of more than 8 years.

Had McGowin been accidentally poisoned and a physician, without his knowledge or request, had administered an antidote, thus saving his life, a subsequent promise by McGowin to pay the physician would have been valid. Likewise, McGowin's agreement as disclosed by the complaint to compensate appellant for saving him from death or grievous bodily injury is valid and enforceable.

Where the promisee cares for, improves, and preserves the property of the promisor, though done without his request, it is sufficient consideration for the promisor's subsequent agreement to pay for the service, because of the material benefit received.

In Boothe v. Fitzpatrick, 36 Vt. 681, the court held that a promise by defendant to pay for the past keeping of a bull which had escaped from defendant's premises and been cared for by plaintiff was valid, although there was no previous request, because the subsequent promise obviated that objection; it being equivalent to a previous request. On the same principle, had the promisee saved the promisor's life or his body from grievous harm, his subsequent promise to pay for the services rendered would have been valid. Such service would have been far more material than caring for his bull. Any holding that saving a man from death or grievous bodily harm is not a material benefit sufficient to uphold a subsequent promise to pay for the service, necessarily rests on the assumption that saving life and preservation of the body from harm have only a sentimental value. The converse of this is true. Life and preservation of the body have material, pecuniary values, measurable in dollars and cents. Because of this, physicians practice their profession charging for services rendered in saving life and curing the body of its ills, and surgeons perform operations. The same is true as to the law of negligence, authorizing the assessment of damages in personal injury cases based upon the extent of the injuries, earnings, and life expectancies of those injured.

In the business of life insurance, the value of a man's life is measured in dollars and cents according to his expectancy, the soundness of his body, and his ability to pay premiums. The same is true as to health and accident insurance.

It follows that if, as alleged in the complaint, appellant saved J. Greeley McGowin from death or grievous bodily harm, and McGowin subsequently agreed to pay him for the service rendered, it became a valid and enforceable contract.

2.   It is well settled that a moral obligation is a sufficient consideration to support a subsequent promise to pay where the promisor has received a material benefit, although there was no original duty or liability resting on the promisor. [Cases cited.]

The case at bar is clearly distinguishable from that class of cases where the consideration is a mere moral obligation or conscientious duty unconnected with receipt by promisor of benefits of a material or pecuniary nature. Here the promisor received a material benefit constituting a valid consideration for his promise.

3.   Some authorities hold that, for a moral obligation to support a subsequent promise to pay, there must have existed a prior legal or equitable obligation, which for some reason had become unenforceable, but for which the promisor was still morally bound. This rule, however, is subject to qualification in those cases where the promisor having received a material benefit from the promisee, is morally bound to compensate him for the services rendered and in consideration of this obligation promises to pay. In such cases the subsequent promise to pay is an affirmance or ratification of the services rendered carrying with it the presumption that a previous request for the service was made.

4.   The averments of the complaint show that in saving McGowin from death or grievous bodily harm, appellant was crippled for life. This was part of the consideration of the contract declared on. McGowin was

benefited. Appellant was injured. Benefit to the promisor or injury to the promisee is a sufficient legal consideration for the promissor's agreement to pay.

5. Under the averments of the complaint the services rendered by appellant were not gratuitous. The agreement of McGowin to pay and the acceptance of payment by appellant conclusively shows the contrary.

From what has been said, we are of the opinion that the court below erred in the ruling complained of; that is to say in sustaining the demurrer, and for this error the case is reversed and remanded.

Reversed and remanded.

■ SAMFORD, JUDGE (concurring). The questions involved in this case are not free from doubt, and perhaps the strict letter of the rule, as stated by judges, though not always in accord, would bar a recovery by plaintiff, but following the principle announced by Chief Justice Marshall in Hoffman v. Porter, Fed.Cas. No. 6,577, 2 Brock. 156, 159, where he says, "I do not think that law ought to be separated from justice, where it is at most doubtful," I concur in the conclusions reached by the court.

[Part of the short opinion of the Supreme Court of Alabama, denying certiorari, is set out next.]

■ FOSTER, JUSTICE. The opinion of the Court of Appeals here under consideration recognizes and applies the distinction between a supposed moral obligation of the promisor, based upon some refined sense of ethical duty, without material benefit to him, and one in which such a benefit did in fact occur. We agree with that court that if the benefit be material and substantial, and was to the person of the promisor rather than to his estate, it is within the class of material benefits which he has the privilege of recognizing and compensating either by an executed payment or an executory promise to pay. The cases are cited in that opinion. The reason is emphasized when the compensation is not only for the benefits which the promisor received, but also for the injuries either to the property or person of the promisee by reason of the service rendered.

Writ denied.

Harrington v. Taylor

Supreme Court of North Carolina, 1945.
225 N.C. 690, 36 S.E.2d 227.

■ PER CURIAM. The plaintiff in this case sought to recover of the defendant upon a promise made by him under the following peculiar circumstances:

The defendant had assaulted his wife, who took refuge in plaintiff's house. The next day the defendant gained access to the house and began another assault upon his wife. The defendant's wife knocked him down with an axe, and was on the point of cutting his head open or decapitating him while he was laying on the floor, and the plaintiff intervened, caught the axe as it was descending, and the blow intended for defendant fell upon her hand, mutilating it badly, but saving defendant's life.

Subsequently, defendant orally promised to pay the plaintiff her damages; but, after paying a small sum, failed to pay anything more. So, substantially, states the complaint.

The defendant demurred to the complaint as not stating a cause of action, and the demurrer was sustained. Plaintiff appealed.

The question presented is whether there was a consideration recognized by our law as sufficient to support the promise. The Court is of the opinion that, however much the defendant should be impelled by common gratitude to alleviate the plaintiff's misfortune, a humanitarian act of this kind, voluntarily performed, is not such consideration as would entitle her to recover at law.

The judgment sustaining the demurrer is

Affirmed.

NOTES

(1) *The Case for "Moral Obligation."* "Courts have frequently enforced promises on the simple ground that the promisor was only promising to do what he ought to have done anyway. These cases have either been condemned as wanton departures from legal principle, or reluctantly accepted as involving the kind of compromise logic must inevitably make at times with sentiment. I believe that these decisions are capable of rational defense. When we say the defendant was morally obligated to do the thing he promised, we in effect assert the existence of a substantive ground for enforcing the promise. The court's conviction that the promisor ought to do the thing, plus the promisor's own admission of his obligation, may tilt the scales in favor of enforcement where neither standing alone would be sufficient. If it be argued that moral consideration threatens certainty, the solution would seem to lie, not in rejecting the doctrine, but in taming it by continuing the process of judicial exclusion and inclusion already begun in the cases involving infants' contracts, barred debts, and discharged bankrupts." Fuller, *Consideration and Form*, 41 Colum. L. Rev. 799, 821–822 (1941).

(2) *Reconciling* Webb *and* Harrington. These two cases are less than 10 years apart. What factors might explain the difference in outcome?

(3) *Reform by Statute.* New York law does not recognize "moral obligation" as an equivalent of consideration, but a New York statute enacted in 1941 and now found in General Obligations Law § 5–1105 provides: "A promise in writing and signed by the promisor or by his agent shall not be denied effect as a valid contractual obligation on the ground that consideration for the promise is past or executed, if the consideration is expressed in the writing and is proved to have been given or performed and would be a valid consideration but for the time when it was given or performed."

How would the New York statute have affected the preceding cases? Would the common recital "for value received" satisfy the New York statute? Would you favor the adoption of that statute by other states? What about the adoption of a statute enacting Restatement § 86?

(C) THE REQUIREMENT OF BARGAIN

Kirksey v. Kirksey

Supreme Court of Alabama, 1845.
8 Ala. 131.

The plaintiff was the wife of defendant's brother, but had for some time been a widow, and had several children. In 1840, the plaintiff resided on public land, under a contract of lease, she had held over, and was comfortably settled, and would have attempted to secure the land she lived on. The defendant resided in Talladega County, some 60 or 70 miles off. On the 10th October, 1840, he wrote to her the following letter:

"Dear Sister Antillico,—Much to my mortification, I heard that brother Henry was dead, and one of his children. I know that your situation is one of grief and difficulty. You had a bad chance before, but a great deal worse now. I should like to come and see you, but cannot with convenience at present. . . . I do not know whether you have a preference on the place you live on or not. If you had, I would advise you to obtain your preference, and sell the land and quit the country, as I understand it is very unhealthy, and I know society is very bad. If you will come down and see me, I will let you have a place to raise your family, and I have more open land than I can tend; and on account of your situation, and that of your family, I feel like I want you and the children to do well."

Within a month or two after the receipt of this letter, the plaintiff abandoned her possession, without disposing of it, and removed with her family, to the residence of the defendant, who put her in comfortable houses, and gave her land to cultivate for two years, at the end of which time he notified her to remove, and put her in a house, not comfortable, in the woods, which he afterwards required her to leave.

A verdict being found for the plaintiff, for $200, the above facts were agreed, and if they will sustain the action, the judgment is to be affirmed, otherwise it is to be reversed.

■ ORMOND, JUSTICE. The inclination of my mind is that the loss and inconvenience which the plaintiff sustained in breaking up and moving to the defendant's, a distance of sixty miles, is a sufficient consideration to support the promise to furnish her with a house, and land to cultivate, until she could raise her family. My brothers, however, think that the promise on the part of the defendant was a mere gratuity, and that an action will not lie for its breach. The judgment of the court below must therefore be reversed, pursuant to the agreement of the parties.

NOTES

(1) *Conditional Gift or Bargained-for Exchange?* How did the court read the words, "If you will come down and see me, I will let you have a place to raise your family"? As words of bargain for an exchange or as a condition to a gratuitous promise? What factors (language, circumstances, indications of intent) make the sentence appear more like the promise of a gift? More like a proposal of a bargain?

(2) *Lunchtime at Tiffany's.* A father and his daughter became estranged after her mother divorced the father, and the daughter refused to see her father. The father then wrote to his daughter: "If you will meet me at Tiffany's next Monday at noon, I will buy you the emerald ring advertised in this week's *New Yorker*." The daughter met her father at Tiffany's, but he did not buy her the promised ring. Bargained-for exchange or conditional gratuitous promise?

Williston gave this hypothetical: "If a benevolent man says to a tramp, 'If you go around the corner to the clothing shop there, you may purchase an overcoat on my credit,' no reasonable person would understand that the short walk was requested as the consideration for the promise; rather, the understanding would be that in the event of the tramp going to the shop the promisor would make him a gift." This first appeared in 1 Williston, *A Treatise on the Law of Contracts* § 112 (1st ed. 1920). Is the situation of the daughter distinguishable from that of the tramp?

(3) *The Million-Dollar Swipe.* While vacationing in Atlantic City, New Jersey, Rena Gottlieb went to a promotional booth at the Tropicana Casino and joined the Tropicana's Diamond Club by filling out a simple application. She received a card that club members swipe before playing any machine. The swipe provides information about members' gambling habits, which is then used by the casino's marketing department to tailor its promotions. Diamond Club members are entitled to one free spin daily of the Fun House Million Dollar Wheel. After swiping in, Gottlieb spun the wheel, which landed on the million dollar mark. Tropicana refused to pay on the ground that there was no consideration for her participation in the Diamond Club promotion. She sued the Tropicana Casino and Resort for $1,000,000. Bargained-for exchange, conditional gift, or gratuitous promise? *Held*: For plaintiff. Gottlieb v. Tropicana Hotel and Casino, 109 F.Supp.2d 324 (E.D. Pa. 2000):

> Ms. Gottlieb had to go to the casino to participate in the promotion. She had to wait in line to spin the wheel. By . . . allowing her [Diamond Club card] to be swiped into the casino's machine, she was permitting the casino to gather information about her gambling habits. Additionally, by participating in the game, she was a part of the entertainment that casinos, by their very nature, are designed to offer to all of those present. All of these detriments were 'the requested detriment[s] to the promisee induced by the promise' of Tropicana to offer her a chance to win $1 million. Tropicana's motives in offering the promotion were 'in nowise altruistic.' Tropicana offered the promotion in order to generate

patronage of and excitement within the casino. In short, Ms. Gottlieb provided adequate consideration to form a contract with Tropicana.

Id. at 329–30. The case was remanded to determine the factual question of whether the marker firmly landed on the million-dollar mark, or immediately fell off, as the Casino claimed.

PROBLEMS

(1) *Jailhouse Rock.* Steve Jennings, a prisoner in Texas, was a faithful listener to radio station KSCS, which regularly broadcast that it played "at least three-in-a-row, or we pay you $25,000. No bull, more music on KSCS." Jennings sued KSCS, alleging that each time it played "five-in-a-row" it played only three songs, followed by a brief commercial, and then only *two* songs, but that when he notified KSCS on specific occasions of this they refused to pay him $25,000. He also alleged that he then stopped listening to KSCS. KSCS has moved to dismiss on the ground that there was no consideration for its promise. What decision? See Jennings v. Radio Station KSCS, 96.3 FM, Inc., 708 S.W.2d 60 (Tex.App.1986).

(2) *Open and Shut.* Joshua Gnaizda, the 3-year-old son of a prominent public-interest attorney in San Francisco, received what he (or his mother) thought was a tantalizing offer from Time, Inc. The front of the envelope contained two see-through windows. One window showed Joshua's name and address. The other revealed the following statement: "JOSHUA A. GNAIZDA, I'LL GIVE YOU THIS VERSATILE NEW CALCULATOR WATCH FREE just for opening this envelope before Feb. 15, 1985." Beneath the offer was a picture of the watch itself. Joshua's mother opened the envelope and realized she had been deceived by a ploy to get her to open a piece of junk mail. The see-through window had not revealed the full text of Time's offer. Printed below the picture of the watch, and not visible through the see-through window, were the following additional words: "AND MAILING THIS CERTIFICATE TODAY!" The certificate itself clearly required that Joshua purchase a subscription to Fortune magazine in order to receive the watch. Joshua's father sued Time on behalf of Joshua and two others who had been similarly bamboozled. Time moved to dismiss for want of consideration. What result? See Harris v. Time, Inc., 237 Cal. Rptr. 584 (Ct. App. 1987).

(3) *One Person's Trash.* Pennsy Supply, a paving subcontractor, was hired to pave the parking lot of a new high school. The project specifications stated that the paving contractor could use AggRite, a treated ash by-product, as part of the base. AggRite was available from American Ash. American Ash made AggRite available for free so that it could save the cost of disposal. Pennsy picked up and used 11,000 tons of AggRite. The work had to be redone, however, partly because the AggRite was not suited for use as a base for paving. Pennsy thus had to dig up the AggRite. Pennsy asked American Ash to arrange for its removal and disposal (AggRite is considered a hazardous waste material). American Ash declined. Pennsy paid for the disposal itself and then sued American Ash for breach of contract, requesting

damages that included its disposal costs. American Ash has asserted a good many defenses, including that Pennsy received the AggRite as a conditional gift, not as part of a contract supported by consideration. What result? See Pennsy Supply v. Am. Ash Recycling Corp., 895 A.2d 595 (Pa. Super. 2006).

————

Employment Agreements

The next case introduces the category of personal service or employment agreements. For more than six centuries, important aspects of the employment relationship were governed by statute. For example, the Statute of Laborers, 23 Edw. 3 (1349), imposed a duty to work on most able-bodied adults, and later Elizabethan enactments established a minimum one-year duration for all employment contracts. Agreements between master and servant, as the parties were then called, shifted to a contractual model as industrialization and the philosophy of *laissez faire* took hold. A detailed account of the rise of bargaining, including collective bargaining, and of current statutory regimes such as minimum-wage, safety, and anti-discrimination law, is left to courses on labor and employment law. As you read the employment cases that follow, consider how background policies regarding the right to work or the prevention of idleness have influenced the development of common law contract doctrine.

Our interest here is how basic contract principles play out in the circumstances of employment, including decisions about hiring and firing. We focus particularly on "at-will" employment, which is a category of employment that is terminable by either party at any time. We begin with the problem of bargained-for exchange between employers and employees when, as is often the case, the terms of the agreement are not entirely settled at a single moment. Determining these terms is crucial to deciding whether an employee has been wrongfully fired. In our first case, however, it is the *employer* who seeks to enforce the promise of an at-will employee. The term at issue concerns post-employment conduct, specifically the employee's promise not to compete with his former employer.

Lake Land Employment Group of Akron, LLC v. Columber.

Supreme Court of Ohio, 2004.
101 Ohio St.3d 242, 804 N.E.2d 27.

■ MOYER, CHIEF JUSTICE. Lake Land Employment Group of Akron, LLC ("Lake Land"), appellant, initiated this action by filing a complaint asserting that its ex-employee, appellee Lee Columber, had breached a noncompetition agreement the parties had executed. The agreement provided that for a period of three years after his termination of employment Columber would not engage in any business within a 50-

mile radius of Akron, Ohio, that competed with the business of Lake Land. Lake Land further claimed that Columber's employment with Lake Land terminated in 2001 and that he thereafter violated the terms of the noncompetition agreement. Lake Land sought money damages and an order prohibiting Columber from engaging in any activities that violated the noncompetition agreement.

Columber answered and admitted that he had been employed by Lake Land from 1988 until 2001. He further admitted that he had signed the noncompetition agreement and that following his discharge from Lake Land he had formed a corporation that is engaged in a business similar to that of Lake Land. Columber pled lack of consideration in his answer. Columber moved for summary judgment, claiming that the noncompetition agreement was unenforceable and that the restrictions in the agreement were overly restrictive and imposed an undue hardship on him.

Columber could remember very little about the presentation or execution of the noncompetition agreement. He could not remember whether he had been told that his continued employment was dependent upon execution of the agreement or whether he had posed questions about the restrictions it contained. He testified that he vaguely remembered signing the agreement after his employer presented it to him and told him to read and sign it. He acknowledged that he had read the agreement, but had not talked to an attorney or anybody else about it. The at-will relationship of the parties continued for ten years thereafter.

The trial court granted summary judgment in Columber's favor. It found no dispute that Columber had been employed by Lake Land beginning in 1988 and that Columber signed the agreement in September 1991. It further found no dispute that there "was no increase of salary, benefits, or other remunerations given as consideration for Columber signing the non-competition agreement" and "no change in his employment status in connection with the signing of the noncompetition agreement." The trial court concluded that the noncompetition agreement lacked consideration, and was unenforceable. The trial court therefore found it unnecessary to determine the reasonableness of the temporal and geographical restrictions in the noncompetition agreement.

The court of appeals affirmed. It certified a conflict, however, between its decision and [those of other Ohio district courts of appeals]. The certified issue is "Is subsequent employment alone sufficient consideration to support a covenant-not-to-compete agreement with an at-will employee entered into after employment has already begun?"

I.   Legal Background

Generally, courts look upon noncompetition agreements with some skepticism and have cautiously considered and carefully scrutinized them. Ingram, *Covenants Not to Compete* (2002), 36 Akron L. Rev. 49, 50.

Under English common law, agreements in restraint of trade, including noncompetition agreements, were disfavored as being against public policy, although partial restraints supported by fair consideration were upheld. In a society in which working men entered skilled trades only by serving apprenticeships, and mobility was minimal, restrictive covenants precluding an ex-employee from competing with his ex-employer "either destroyed a man's means of livelihood, or bound him to his master for life." Raimonde v. Van Vlerah (1975), 325 N.E.2d 544.

Modern economic realities, however, do not justify a strict prohibition of noncompetition agreements between employer and employee in an at-will relationship. "The law upholds these agreements because they allow the parties to work together to expand output and competition. If one party can trust the other with confidential information and secrets, then both parties are better positioned to compete with the rest of the world. By protecting ancillary covenants not to compete, even after an employee has launched his own firm, the law 'makes it easier for people to cooperate productively in the first place.'" KW Plastics v. United States Can Co (Feb. 2, 2001), M.D. Ala. Nos. Civ. A. 99-D-286-N and 99-D-878-N, 2001 WL 135722, quoting Polk Bros., Inc. v. Forest City Ent., Inc. (C.A.7, 1985), 776 F.2d 185, 189.

Jurisdictions throughout the country are split on the issue presented by the certified question. See, generally, Annotation, Sufficiency of Consideration for Employee's Covenant Not to Compete, Entered into after Inception of Employment (1973), 51 A.L.R.3d 825. As summarized by the Supreme Court of Minnesota, "cases which have held that continued employment is not a sufficient consideration stress the fact that an employee frequently has no bargaining power once he is employed and can easily be coerced. By signing a noncompetition agreement, the employee gets no more from his employer than he already has,[1] and in such cases there is a danger that an employer does not need protection for his investment in the employee but instead seeks to impose barriers to prevent an employee from securing a better job elsewhere. Decisions in which continued employment has been deemed a sufficient consideration for a noncompetition agreement have focused on a variety of factors, including the possibility that the employee would otherwise have been discharged, the employee was actually employed for a substantial time after executing the contract, or the employee received additional compensation or training or was given confidential information after he signed the agreement." (Citations omitted.) Davies & Davies Agency, Inc. v. Davies (Minn. 1980) 298 N.W.2d 127, 130.

More recently, some courts have found sufficient consideration in an at-will employment situation where a *substantial* period of employment ensues after a noncompetition covenant is executed, especially when the

---

[1]   Note, however, that an at-will employee does not already have a right to come to work in the future at all, let alone under past terms of employment. Although both parties may very well contemplate continuation of the relationship, either may terminate it at any time.

continued employment is accompanied by raises, promotion, or similar tangible benefits. 6 Lord, Williston on Contracts (4th Ed.1995), Section 13:13. These courts thereby implicitly find that the execution of a noncompetition agreement changes the prior employment relationship from one purely at will. Id. at 577–584. In effect, these courts infer a promise on the part of the employer to continue the employment of his previously at-will employee for an indefinite yet substantial term. Under this approach, however, neither party knows whether the agreement is enforceable until events occur after its execution.

This diversity of approach to the issue is reflected in opinions of the courts of appeals of this state.

II.   Formation of Binding Contract

[In a passage omitted here the court reviewed some elementary characteristics of contract law, and of at-will employment agreements.]

[E]ither an employer or an employee in a pure at-will employment relationship may legally terminate the employment relationship at any time and for any reason. Mers v. Dispatch Printing Co. (1985), 19 Ohio St.3d 100, 103. In the event that an at-will employee quits or is fired, he or she provides no further services for the employer and is generally entitled only to wages and benefits already earned.

It follows that either an employer or an employee in an at-will relationship may propose to change the terms of their employment relationship at any time. If, for instance, an employer notifies an employee that the employee's compensation will be reduced, the employee's remedy, if dissatisfied, is to quit. Similarly, if the employee proposes to the employer that he deserves a raise and will no longer work at his current rate, the employer may either negotiate an increase or accept the loss of his employee. In either event the employee is entitled to be paid only for services already rendered pursuant to terms to which they both have agreed. Thus, mutual promises to employ and to be employed on an ongoing at-will basis, according to agreed terms, are supported by consideration: the promise of one serves as consideration for the promise of the other.

The presentation of a noncompetition agreement by an employer to an at-will employee is, in effect, a proposal to renegotiate the terms of the parties' at-will employment. Where an employer makes such a proposal by presenting his employee with a noncompetition agreement and the employee assents to it, thereby accepting continued employment on new terms, consideration supporting the noncompetition agreement exists. The employee's assent to the agreement is given in exchange for forbearance on the part of the employer from terminating the employee.

We therefore hold that consideration exists to support a noncompetition agreement when, in exchange for the assent of an at-will employee to a proffered noncompetition agreement, the employer continues an at-will employment relationship that could legally be terminated without cause.

III. Caveat

We concur in the view that in cases involving noncompetition agreements, "as in other cases, it is still believed to be good policy to let people make their own bargains and their own valuations." 15 Corbin on Contracts (Interim Ed.2002) 96–97, Section 1395. Professor Corbin suggests that courts should inquire into the sufficiency of consideration in cases involving noncompetition agreements by examining the extent and character of the consideration received by the promisor-employee, "even though we do not do so in ordinary contract cases." Id. at 94–95.

Our decision today does no more than recognize that consideration exists where an at-will employer and an at-will employee continue their employment relationship, rather than terminate it, after the employer imposes a new requirement for employment, i.e., execution of a noncompetition agreement by the employee. While we are not prepared to abandon our long-established precedent that courts may not inquire into the adequacy of consideration, we do not disagree with Corbin's conclusion that the validity of a restraining contract such as a noncompetition agreement should be "determined by weighing as best we can the sum-total of all factors standing together." Id. at 97. We simply recognize that weighing of these factors should not be performed in the context of an inquiry concerning the sufficiency of consideration. That balancing instead should occur in the context of our established precedent recognizing that only reasonable noncompetition agreements are enforceable.

Our refusal to sanction judicial inquiry into the adequacy of consideration in cases similar to the one at bar does not exclude consideration of other requisites of a contract. It remains the law that noncompetition agreements, like other purported contractual arrangements, may be voidable or unenforceable for reasons other than lack of consideration.

IV. Disposition

Both Columber and his employer had a legal right to terminate their at-will employment relationship when Columber was presented with the noncompetition agreement in 1991. Neither party exercised that legal right to terminate the employment relationship, and, in fact, Columber continued working for the appellant for an additional ten years. Accordingly, the noncompetition agreement is not void for lack of consideration, and summary judgment in Columber's favor should not have been entered on that basis.

Although the trial court erred in entering summary judgment based on its determination that the noncompetition agreement lacked consideration, it must yet determine whether the noncompetition agreement is reasonable pursuant to controlling precedent. We therefore reverse the judgment of the court of appeals and remand the cause for further proceedings.

Judgment reversed and cause remanded.

■ RESNICK, JUSTICE, dissenting. Courts everywhere are sharply divided on the present certified issue. However, I adhere to the principle that continued employment in an at-will situation does not by itself constitute consideration. I respectfully dissent.

As the majority confirms, "a contract is not binding unless supported by consideration," which is generally defined as "a detriment to the promisee or a benefit to the promisor." Thus, in order for the September 1991 noncompetition agreement executed between appellant, Lake Land Employment Group of Akron, LLC, and appellee, Lee Columber, to be binding, either Lake Land must have given something for it or Columber must have received something in return. Yet, when all is said and done, the only difference in the parties' employment relationship before and after September 1991 is the noncompetition agreement.

The majority's holding that "[c]onsideration exists to support a noncompetition agreement when . . . the employer continues an at-will employment relationship . . ." belies itself. If the same at-will employment relationship continues, where is the consideration? The employer has relinquished nothing, since it retains exactly the same preexisting right it always had to discharge the employee at any time, for any reason, for no reason, with or without cause. The employee has gained nothing, for he has not been given or promised anything other than that which he already had, which is "employment which need not last longer than the ink is dry upon [his] signature." Kadis v. Britt (1944), 224 N.C. 154, 163, 29 S.E.2d 543. It is precisely because the same at-will employment relationship continues that there is no consideration.

In fact, the majority endeavors to transform this mutual exchange of nothing into consideration by formulating such artful euphemisms as "forbearance on the part of an at-will employer from discharging an at-will employee," "mutual promises to employ and to be employed on an ongoing at-will basis," and "a proposal to renegotiate the terms of the parties' at-will employment." But in the end, the employer simply winds up with both the noncompetition agreement and the continued right to discharge the employee at will, while the employee is left with the same preexisting "nonright" to be employed for so long as the employer decides not to fire him. The only actual "forbearance," "proposal," or "promise" made by the employer in this situation is declining to fire the employee until he executes the noncompetition agreement.

Moreover, the majority's holding and supporting rationale would allow the enforcement of a noncompetition agreement that was exacted from an employee who, at the time of execution, had already acquired all the knowledge his or her position affords and who was fired the day after affixing his or her signature to the document. In cryptic fashion, the majority is essentially holding that a restrictive covenant may henceforth be exacted from an at-will employee without any supporting consideration . . .

Since the noncompetition agreement in this case lacked consideration and therefore was unenforceable, I would affirm the judgment of the court of appeals.

■ PFEIFER, JUSTICE, dissenting. I concur with Justice Resnick's dissent— an employer's agreement not to terminate an employee if the employee signs a noncompetition agreement does not constitute consideration. It constitutes coercion.

But the majority has found otherwise. In doing so, the majority must acknowledge that the execution of a noncompetition agreement for which forbearance from discharge is the consideration alters the at-will nature of the employment relationship. Any promise of continued employment removes the employment from the realm of an at-will relationship. For some undefined time, the employer must continue to employ the signer of the agreement. How long a period is enough? The absence of a specified term for the forbearance from discharge will leave courts to determine what period is reasonable.

Employers could prevent noncompetition agreements from intruding into the at-will relationship by not tying consideration to continued employment. A separate, monetary consideration could ensure that the noncompetition agreement stays a separate arrangement.

NOTES

(1) *Questions.* What is the significance of Columber's status as an at-will employee in the court's determination that his promise not to compete was supported by consideration? Do you agree with Chief Justice Moyer or with Justice Resnick (a "mutual exchange of nothing")? Does the majority opinion rest on policy considerations, the straightforward application of doctrine, or both? What policy considerations weigh in favor of Columber? In favor of Lake Land Employment?

(2) *Dueling Dissents.* Although Justice Pfeifer professed to agree with Justice Resnick, the two dissents appear to disagree with regard to the effect of the court's ruling. Justice Resnick concludes that "in the end, the employer simply winds up with both the noncompetition agreement and the continued right to discharge the employee at will." Contrast this with Justice Pfeifer's understanding that "the execution of the noncompetition agreement alters the at-will nature of the employment relationship." How does it do so? If Justice Pfeifer is right, how would a court go about deciding what period of time is reasonable? If these are opposing views, which is the more favorable to employees?

(3) *Jurisdictional Differences.* The Supreme Court of Minnesota has held that "where no raises or promotions resulted, where other employees with similar access were not asked to sign, the mere continuation of employment . . . is not enough." Jostens, Inc. v. National Computer Systems,

Inc., 318 N.W.2d 691, 703–04 (Minn.1982). The decision typifies judicial hostility in a number of states to promises not to compete. For additional helpful analyses, see Cynthia Estlund, *Between Rights and Contract: Arbitration Agreements and Non-Compete Covenants as a Hybrid Form of Employment Law*, 155 U. Pa. L. Rev. 379 (2006), and Katherine Stone, *Revisiting the At-Will Employment Doctrine: Imposed Terms, Implied Terms, and the Normative World of the Workplace* 36 Indus. L.J. 84 (2007).

Only a few months after *Jostens*, the same court said: "We look upon restrictive covenants with disfavor, carefully scrutinizing them because they are agreements in partial restraint of trade." National Recruiters, Inc. v. Cashman, 323 N.W.2d 736, 740 (Minn.1982). Judicially imposed constraints on such agreements are discussed further in the materials on public policy in Chapter 4.

PROBLEM

A Revolting Development. In 1997, American Energy Services (AES) was in financial trouble. The AES employees, all of them at-will, knew of the situation and informed officers of AES that they doubted whether the company would survive. In order to keep the employees from resigning, an AES vice-president promised the employees that, "in the event of sale or merger of AES, the original [eight] employees remaining with AES at that time would get 5% of the value of any sale or merger of AES." Seven of the eight were still with AES in 2001 when another company bought it. The seven demanded their proceeds; when they did not get them, they sued. AES defended in part on the grounds that the promise was illusory, because the employees were not bound to do anything under the alleged contract. What result? Would it matter if the employees were not at will, but rather were hired under long-term employment agreements in force both when AES made the promise and when AES was bought? What if the eight original employees had each signed a document stating that anyone who leaves AES before a sale or merger would not share in the proceeds of that transaction? See Vanegas v. American Energy Servs., 302 S.W.3d 299 (Tex. 2009).

————

Employee Handbooks

In *Lake Land Employment*, the question was whether or not the *employee's* promise not to compete was supported by consideration. Questions about the term of employment also arise with regard to the enforceability of *employers'* promises, often in the context of employee handbooks. Typically, and often some time after they have been hired, employees receive handbooks setting out company policies on matters ranging from vacation schedules to job security. Is the employer bound by these policies? Most employees do not bargain for the policies, and many may not have read or in some cases have even received a handbook. The following case is illustrative.

Mettille, a loan officer and at-will employee at the Pine River State Bank, was fired by the bank president, Griffith, for serious deficiencies in processing over $600,000 worth of loans. Griffith had earlier prepared and distributed a printed Employee Handbook with information on various bank policies including "job security" and "disciplinary policy." In firing Mettille, Griffith failed to follow Handbook rules relating to "disciplinary policy." Mettille argued that Griffith was bound by those policies. Griffith countered that the handbook was intended only as a source of information for employees on bank procedures and that, in any case, it could not be part of an employee's employment contract because it was unsupported by consideration. In an action by Mettille against the bank, he won a money judgment. The Supreme Court of Minnesota affirmed the judgment, stating:

> An employer's offer of a unilateral contract may very well appear in a personnel handbook as the employer's response to the practical problem of transactional costs. Given these costs, an employer, such as the bank here, may prefer not to write a separate contract with each individual employee. Mettille's continued performance of his duties despite his freedom to quit constitutes an acceptance of the bank's offer and affords the necessary consideration for that offer, with the bank gaining the advantages of a more stable and, presumably, more productive work force.

Pine River State Bank v. Mettille, 333 N.W.2d 622, 627–30 (Minn.1983).

The Court compared this approach with its cases holding that employee noncompete covenants signed after the initial employment contract "are not enforceable absent a showing of independent consideration involving something more than just continued services." Id. at 630 n.5. The Court noted that, with regard to the covenants not to compete, "a different public policy is at play, namely, the law's disfavor with restraints on trade, so that noncompete covenants are treated as a special circumstance and, therefore, these cases are not decided strictly according to the principles of contract formation." Id.

NOTES

(1) *Promise or Policy?* Not all representations in a handbook become terms of an at-will employee's contract. The court found that Pine River State Bank's statements about job security, as distinguished from its disciplinary policy, were "no more than a general statement of policy" in contrast to the "definite language" used to set out the disciplinary policy. Id. at 630. Consider the following paragraph from another Employee Handbook:

> ACKNOWLEDGMENT: This employee handbook describes important information about the Company and I understand that I should consult the Business Manager regarding any questions not answered in the handbook. The provisions contained in this handbook are presented as a matter of information only and do not

constitute an employment contract. I have entered into my employment relationship with the Company voluntarily and acknowledge that there is no specified length of employment. At any time, either I or the Company can terminate the relationship at-will, with or without cause or notice, as long as there is no violation of applicable federal or state law. I also understand that because business judgments and needs may change from time to time, the guidelines described herein are not conditions of employment. The Company has the right to change this handbook at any time and without advance notice. I have received a copy of Pflueger Group's Employee Handbook and I have read and understand the information outlined in the handbook. I have asked any questions I may have concerning its contents and will comply with all policies and procedures to the best of my ability.

What purposes is it intended to serve? (The paragraph is taken from Douglass v. Pflueger, found at p. 418 below.)

(2) *Modifications of Employee Handbooks.* To the extent that the terms of an employee handbook become part of an employment contract, can an employer unilaterally change or modify its terms so as to reduce the employee's rights? Several courts have answered: No. "If the disclaimer modifies an existing employment contract requiring termination for cause, the employer must provide consideration to make the disclaimer effective." Worley v. Wyoming Bottling Company, Inc., 1 P.3d 615, 621 (Wyo.2000); see also Doyle v. Holy Cross Hospital, 708 N.E.2d 1140 (Ill.1999). Would a clause in a handbook addressing "the Company's right to change this handbook," as in the form provided in Note 1 above, change the employer's right to modify? The modification of contract terms is examined more generally in Chapter 4.

(3) *An Administrative Law Model?* In In re Certified Question (Bankey v. Storer Broadcasting), 443 N.W.2d 112 (Mich.1989), the court held that an employer *may* alter the terms of employment for existing employees by unilaterally changing its written policy statements even without prior notification to the employees that it has reserved the right to do so. In that case, the employer had replaced an existing "discharge for cause" provision with a term providing for employment "at the will of the company." The court held that as long as the new policy was applied consistently, the employees were bound. Explaining that the purpose of the change was "to promote an environment conducive to collective productivity," the court stated that it is "[t]he benefit to the employer of promoting such an environment, rather than the traditional contract-forming mechanisms of mutual assent or individual detrimental reliance, [that] gives rise to a situation 'instinct with obligation.' " 443 N.W.2d at 118.

In answer to a similar certified question from the Ninth Circuit, the Arizona Supreme Court held that an employer *cannot* unilaterally change a handbook provision. The Arizona court rejected *Bankey* as using an "administrative law model." The court stated: "We do not agree that a party to a contract containing a term that proves to be inconvenient, uneconomic, or unpleasant should have the right, like an administrative agency, 'to change the rules prospectively through proper procedures.' " Demasse v. ITT Corp., 984 P.2d 1138, 1149 (Ariz.1999).

––––––––

Rewards

The sheriff of Dallas County, A.H. Ledbetter, offered a reward of $500 for the capture and return of Holly Vann, an escaped convict. A bounty hunter, S.H. Broadnax, captured Vann, brought him in, and sued for the reward. The trial court dismissed the petition, believing that it omitted a fact essential to the claim. On appeal, this question was certified to the Texas Supreme Court: "Was notice or knowledge to plaintiff of existence of the reward when the recapture was made essential to his right to recover?" The answer given was "Yes": A reward offer "may be accepted by anyone who performs the service called for when the acceptor knows that it has been made and acts in performance of it, but not otherwise." Broadnax v. Ledbetter, 99 S.W. 1111 (Tex.1907). Put in terms of Restatement § 71(2), the service that Broadnax rendered was not given by him in exchange for Ledbetter's promise. Although the details of offer and acceptance are not taken up until the next chapter, it may useful to think now about the relationship between consideration and offer and acceptance. Offer and acceptance can be understood as the mechanism by which the parties exchange consideration. In *Broadnax*, for example, the issue might have been framed in terms of offer and acceptance. Contract formation requires a manifestation of mutual assent. Restatement § 2(1). Broadnax could in principle have manifested his assent by bringing in Vann, but when he actually brought Vann in he was not assenting to anything. Restatement § 23. More on this in Chapter 2.

Could Broadnax have recovered if he had captured Vann while ignorant of the reward but had learned of it before returning Vann to jail? Is his solution to release Vann and recapture him? See Restatement § 51. Could Broadnax have recovered if he had known of the reward but had captured Vann and turned him in because he was a close friend and wished to save him from mob violence? See Restatement § 81(2). For a case where three sets of claimants—including the attorney with whom the outlaw had conferred—sought unsuccessfully to recover the same reward, see Taft v. Hyatt, 180 P. 213 (Kan.1919).

NOTES

(1) *Comparative Perspective.* Under the law of some countries, such as Germany, a promise of reward is treated "not as an offer which would require acceptance in order to ripen into a contract, but as a unilateral jural act which as such is effective and binding without acceptance." 1 Rudolf B. Schlesinger (ed.), Formation of Contracts: A Study of the Common Core of Legal Systems 101–02 (1968). Would such a concept be a desirable one in the

of payment. Had Sheriff Ledbetter promised the reward in exchange for Broadnax's *promise* to capture and return Vann, when would the reward be due? Chapter 7 addresses the issue of conditions in more detail.

(2) *Rights and Duties.* The relationships between the parties in unilateral and bilateral contracts can be analyzed in terms of *right* and *duty.* A is said to have a *right* that B shall do an act when, if B does not do the act, A can initiate legal proceedings against B, and B in such a situation is said to have a *duty* to do the act. *Right* and *duty* are correlatives. In this strict sense there can never be a *right* without a *duty,* nor a *duty* without a *right.* The *right-duty* relationship is one between two parties. The *right* describes the relationship from one end and the *duty* from the other. Since, in a "unilateral" contract, there is a promise on one side only, there is a *duty* on one side only, and a *right* on the other side; and since in a "bilateral" contract there is a promise on each side, there is a *right* and a *duty* on each side.

For the precise use of terms such as *right* and *duty,* the legal profession is indebted to the work of Professor Wesley Newcomb Hohfeld,[a] whose system of "Hohfeldian terminology" is set forth in Fundamental Legal Conceptions (1919). Review the language of Restatement § 1. How does it incorporate the language of right and duty?

———

What Constitutes a Promise?

It has long been clear that the consideration for a promise can be found in a return promise. The Restatement informs us that, with some exceptions, "a promise that is bargained for is consideration if the promised performance would be consideration." Restatement § 75. But what exactly counts as a promise? The following cases explore how courts determine from language and context whether a performance has in fact been promised, or whether only the *illusion* of performance has been held out.

Strong v. Sheffield

Court of Appeals of New York, 1895.
144 N.Y. 392, 39 N.E. 330.

[Action on a promissory note. A judgment for plaintiff, Benjamin B. Strong, against defendant, Louisa A. Sheffield, was reversed by the General Term of the Supreme Court.

---

[a] Wesley Newcomb Hohfeld (1879–1918) practiced law briefly in San Francisco before joining the Stanford law faculty in 1905. In 1914 he left Stanford to teach at Yale until his death at the age of 39. He made a lasting contribution to legal literature through his development of the eight terms of "Hohfeldian terminology" in his book Fundamental Legal Conceptions. Corbin wrote, "He was a severe taskmaster, requiring his students to master his classification of 'fundamental conceptions' and to use accurately the set of terms by which they were expressed. They found this, in the light of the usage of the other professors [at Yale], almost impossible." Their resistance resulted in a petition to the president of Yale that Hohfeld's appointment not be extended. The petition was ignored and generations of law students have continued to master Hohfeld's terms.

Benjamin Strong brought this action against Louisa Sheffield, his niece. Strong had sold a business to her husband, Gerardus ("Rard"), on credit. Later, the buyer's debt was embodied in a promissory note, payable on demand. Mrs. Sheffield endorsed the note, an act which the law treats as a promise to pay if her husband, the "maker" of the note, did not. What, if anything, she got in exchange for that was a matter in issue.

The trial court gave judgment for Strong. That was reversed on a first appeal. Then Strong appealed.]

■ ANDREWS, CHIEF JUSTICE. The contract between a maker or endorser of a promissory note and the payee forms no exception to the general rule that a promise, not supported by a consideration, is nudum pactum. The law governing commercial paper which precludes an inquiry into the consideration as against bona fide holders for value before maturity, has no application where the suit is between the original parties to the instrument. It is undisputed that the demand note upon which the action was brought was made by the husband of the defendant and endorsed by her at his request and delivered to the plaintiff, the payee, as security for an antecedent debt owing by the husband to the plaintiff. The debt of the husband was past due at the time, and the only consideration for the wife's endorsement, which is or can be claimed, is that as part of the transaction there was an agreement by the plaintiff when the note was given to forbear the collection of the debt, or a request for forbearance, which was followed by forbearance for a period of about two years subsequent to the giving of the note.

[According to the record in the case, Mrs. Sheffield was reluctant to endorse the note.q Strong testified that he had said: "Rard, I will give you my word as a man that if you will give me a note, with your wife's endorsement . . . I will not pay that note away; I will not put it in any bank for collection, but I will hold it until such time as I want my money" Strong testified also that Gerardus had said, on delivering the note, "You won't pay this note away?", and that Strong answered, "No, I will keep it until such time as I want it." An example of "paying the note away" would have been for Strong to sell the note, giving the buyer the right to collect it on demand.]

There is no doubt that an agreement by the creditor to forbear the collection of a debt presently due is a good consideration for an absolute or conditional promise of a third person to pay the debt or for any obligation he may assume in respect thereto. Nor is it essential that the creditor should bind himself at the time to forbear collection or to give time. If he is requested by his debtor to extend the time, and a third

---

q   The record on appeal indicates that Benjamin Strong was Louisa Sheffield's uncle. He had sold his business on credit to Louisa's husband, Gerardus, and then sought Gerardus's note with Louisa's endorsement as security for the debt. Louisa was reluctant to endorse her husband's note because she had her own successful business and did not want to hurt her credit by having it known that she had undertaken a debt of her husband.

person undertakes in consideration of forbearance being given to become liable as surety or otherwise, and the creditor does in fact forbear in reliance upon the undertaking, although he enters into no enforceable agreement to do so, his acquiescence in the request, and an actual forbearance in consequence thereof for a reasonable time, furnishes a good consideration for the collateral undertaking. In other words, a request followed by performance is sufficient, and mutual promises at the time are not essential unless it was the understanding that the promisor was not to be bound, except on condition that the other party entered into an immediate and reciprocal obligation to do the thing requested. . . . The note in question did not in law extend the payment of the debt. It was payable on demand, and although being payable with interest it was in form consistent with an intention that payment should not be immediately demanded, yet there was nothing on its face to prevent an immediate suit on the note against the maker or to recover the original debt.

In the present case the agreement made is not left to inference, nor was it a case of request to forbear, followed by forbearance, in pursuance of the request, without any promise on the part of the creditor at the time. The plaintiff testified that there was an express agreement on his part to the effect that he would not pay the note away, nor put it in any bank for collection. [The court then quoted Strong's testimony as recited above.] Upon this alleged agreement the defendant endorsed the note. It would have been no violation of the plaintiff's promise if, immediately on receiving the note, he had commenced suit upon it. Such a suit would have been an assertion that he wanted the money and would have fulfilled the condition of forbearance. The debtor and the defendant, when they became parties to the note, may have had the hope or expectation that forbearance would follow, and there was forbearance in fact. But there was no agreement to forbear for a fixed time or for a reasonable time, but an agreement to forbear for such time as the plaintiff should elect. The consideration is to be tested by the agreement, and not by what was done under it. It was a case of mutual promises, and so intended. We think the evidence failed to disclose any consideration for the defendant's endorsement, and that the trial court erred in refusing so to rule.

The order of the General Term reversing the judgment should be affirmed, and judgment absolute directed for the defendant on the stipulation with costs in all courts.

Ordered accordingly.

NOTES

(1)   *Questions.* Restatement § 77 mentions the "illusory" or "apparent" promise as a type that is not consideration. Did Strong make any promise of substance? Could he have been held liable for breach of contract in any circumstances? If there is no consideration when Strong refrains from calling

the note, why is there consideration when Lake Land refrains from firing Columber?

(2) *Drafting.* Suppose that Louisa Sheffield had written to Strong: "I will be responsible for my husband's debt if you will not bother him about it for two years." Would she have been liable to Strong if he had done nothing about the note for that period? What difference is there between this situation and the case as it stands? The precise rule of this case is reversed by UCC § 3–303(a)(3).

(3) *Sexually Transmitted Debt.* Why might Louisa have agreed to endorse Gerardus's note in the first place? Empirical studies suggest that spouses, and perhaps particularly wives, commonly co-sign or otherwise act as sureties for the debts of the other spouse, and many of them may be less experienced in financial matters than was Louisa Sheffield. For a study of surety spouses in England, see Belinda Fehlberg, Sexually Transmitted Debt (1997), suggesting that spousal promises to act as sureties should be subject to special scrutiny. Do you agree? See also Barclay's Bank v. O'Brien, [1993] 4 All E.R. 417 (H.L.). We return to the question of pressuring in bargaining in Chapter 4.

PROBLEM

The Case of the Unexpected Heir. Under the terms of their divorce settlement agreement, Gerald kept the family farm and Nancy took mortgages on the farm to secure periodic payments that Gerald was to make to her. Gerald later had financial difficulties and sought to refinance previous bank loans, but he found that he could not do so because of Nancy's mortgages. Nancy agreed to give up her right to any additional payments and to satisfy the mortgages in return for Gerald's promise to make a will leaving the farm to their son Ronn, reserving the right to sell a portion of the land in order to continue farming if "future economic exigencies require." Although Gerald made a will and obtained refinancing as promised, Nancy began foreclosure proceedings. She argued that Gerald's promise was illusory because he had reserved a right to convey the farm. Should Nancy prevail? See Harrington v. Harrington, 365 N.W.2d 552 (N.D.1985).

Contracts for the Sale of Real Estate

Sales of land and other real estate transactions, including leases, are often quite complex. The following case, in which a developer sought to buy land in order to construct a shopping center, is an example. A commercial transaction of this kind typically involves not only the buyer (often called "purchaser") and at least one seller (often called "vendor") and their agents but also third parties such as lenders, title companies, and potential lessees of the completed development. Each contributes to the intricacy of the transaction. This structural complexity explains in part why contracts for the sale of real estate have been characterized by more formality than, say, contracts for the sale of goods. Even in residential sales, the parties are frequently represented by lawyers and the required documents are lengthy and detailed.

In both residential and commercial real estate transactions, a number of intervening activities commonly take place between the contract signing and the formal "closing," at which a deed is exchanged for the payment of the price. These typically include the buyer verifying the seller's title to the property, obtaining financing, and—as in the case that follows—lining up enough satisfactory tenants to make the prospective shopping center viable. It is not uncommon for a deal to fall apart during this period (formally called the executory interval).

Real property is a uniquely valuable form of wealth, and real estate transactions are of great salience to the economy in general as well as individual homeowners, current and prospective. For many, the most financially significant transaction of a lifetime is the purchase or sale of a home. In recent years, individual interests in home ownership and its broader economic implications have become deeply entwined. Shoddy lending practices associated with the most basic home loans contributed greatly to the world-wide financial crisis in the fall of 2008 and the ensuing economic recession, the worst since the Great Depression of the 1930s. The financial crisis put new demands on contract doctrine as homeowners have turned to courts for redress and as legislatures attempt to police transactional aspects of the problem. We will look more closely at these issues when we take up the case of Dixon v. Wells Fargo in Chapter 2. We turn now, however, to a more ordinary category of dispute, one between a real estate developer and a recalcitrant seller.

Mattei v. Hopper

Supreme Court of California, 1958.
51 Cal.2d 119, 330 P.2d 625.

■ SPENCE, JUSTICE. Plaintiff [Mattei] brought this action for damages after defendant [Hopper] allegedly breached a contract by failing to convey her real property in accordance with the terms of a deposit receipt which the parties had executed. After a trial without a jury, the court concluded that the agreement was "illusory" and lacking in "mutuality." From the judgment accordingly entered in favor of defendant, plaintiff appeals.

Plaintiff was a real estate developer. He was planning to construct a shopping center on a tract adjacent to defendant's land. For several months, a real estate agent attempted to negotiate a sale of defendant's property under terms agreeable to both parties. After several of plaintiff's proposals had been rejected by defendant because of the inadequacy of the price offered, defendant submitted an offer. Plaintiff accepted on the same day.

The parties' written agreement was evidenced on a form supplied by the real estate agent, commonly known as a deposit receipt. Under its terms, plaintiff was required to deposit $1,000 of the total purchase price of $57,500 with the real estate agent, and was given 120 days to "examine the title and consummate the purchase." At the expiration of that period, the balance of the price was "due and payable upon tender of a good and sufficient deed of the property sold." The concluding paragraph of the deposit receipt provided: "Subject to Coldwell Banker & Company obtaining leases satisfactory to the purchaser." This clause and the 120-day period were desired by plaintiff as a means for arranging satisfactory leases of the shopping center buildings prior to the time he was finally committed to pay the balance of the purchase price and to take title to defendant's property.

Plaintiff took the first step in complying with the agreement by turning over the $1,000 deposit to the real estate agent. While he was in the process of securing the leases and before the 120 days had elapsed, defendant's attorney notified plaintiff that defendant would not sell her land under the terms contained in the deposit receipt. Thereafter, defendant was informed that satisfactory leases had been obtained and that plaintiff had offered to pay the balance of the purchase price. Defendant failed to tender the deed as provided in the deposit receipt.

Initially, defendant's thesis that the deposit receipt constituted no more than an offer by her, which could only be accepted by plaintiff notifying her that all of the desired leases had been obtained and were satisfactory to him, must be rejected. Nowhere does the agreement mention the necessity of any such notice. Nor does the provision making the agreement "subject to" plaintiff's securing "satisfactory" leases necessarily constitute a condition to the existence of a contract. Rather, the whole purchase receipt and this particular clause must be read as merely making plaintiff's performance dependent on the obtaining of "satisfactory" leases. Thus a contract arose, and plaintiff was given the power and privilege to terminate it in the event he did not obtain such leases. (See 3 Corbin, Contracts (1951), § 647, pp. 581–585.) This accords with the general view that deposit receipts are binding and enforceable contracts. (Cal.Practice Hand Book, Legal Aspects of Real Estate Transactions (1956), p. 63.)

However, the inclusion of this clause, specifying that leases "satisfactory" to plaintiff must be secured before he would be bound to perform, raises the basic question whether the consideration supporting the contract was thereby vitiated. When the parties attempt, as here, to make a contract where promises are exchanged as the consideration, the promises must be mutual in obligation. In other words, for the contract to bind either party, both must have assumed some legal obligations. Without this mutuality of obligation, the agreement lacks consideration and no enforceable contract has been created. . . . Or, if one of the promises leaves a party free to perform or to withdraw from the agreement at his own unrestricted pleasure, the promise is deemed illusory and it provides no consideration. . . . Whether these problems are couched in terms of mutuality of obligation or the illusory nature of a promise, the underlying issue is the same—consideration.

While contracts making the duty of performance of one of the parties conditional upon his satisfaction would seem to give him wide latitude in avoiding any obligation and thus present serious consideration problems, such "satisfaction" clauses have been given effect. They have been divided into two primary categories and have been accorded different treatment on that basis. First, in those contracts where the condition calls for satisfaction as to commercial value or quality, operative fitness, or mechanical utility, dissatisfaction cannot be claimed arbitrarily, unreasonably, or capriciously, and the standard of a reasonable person is used in determining whether satisfaction has been received. However, it would seem that the factors involved in determining whether a lease is satisfactory to the lessor are too numerous and varied to permit the application of a reasonable man standard as envisioned by this line of cases. Illustrative of some of the factors which would have to be considered in this case are the duration of the leases, their provisions for renewal options, if any, their covenants and restrictions, the amounts of the rentals, the financial responsibility of the lessees, and the character of the lessees' businesses.

This multiplicity of factors which must be considered in evaluating a lease shows that this case more appropriately falls within the second line of authorities dealing with "satisfaction" clauses, being those involving fancy, taste, or judgment. Where the question is one of judgment, the promisor's determination that he is not satisfied, when made in good faith, has been held to be a defense to an action on the contract. Although these decisions do not expressly discuss the issues of mutuality of obligation or illusory promises, they necessarily imply that the promisor's duty to exercise his judgment in good faith is an adequate consideration to support the contract. None of these cases voided the contracts on the ground that they were illusory or lacking in mutuality of obligation. Defendant's attempts to distinguish these cases are unavailing, since they are predicated upon the assumption that the deposit receipt was not a contract making plaintiff's performance conditional on his satisfaction. As seen above, this was the precise nature of the agreement. Even though the "satisfaction" clauses discussed in the above-cited cases dealt with performances to be received as parts of the agreed exchanges, the fact that the leases here which determined plaintiff's satisfaction were not part of the performance to be rendered is not material. The standard of evaluating plaintiff's satisfaction—good faith—applies with equal vigor to this type of condition and prevents it from nullifying the consideration otherwise present in the promises exchanged.

Moreover, the secondary authorities are in accord with the California cases on the general principles governing "satisfaction" contracts. "A promise conditional upon the promisor's satisfaction is not illusory since it means more than that validity of the performance is to depend on the arbitrary choice of the promisor. His expression of dissatisfaction is not conclusive. That may show only that he has become dissatisfied with the contract; he must be dissatisfied with the performance, as a performance of the contract, and his dissatisfaction must be genuine." (Restatement, Contracts (1932), § 265, comment *a*.)

If the foregoing cases and other authorities were the only ones relevant, there would be little doubt that the deposit receipt here should not be deemed illusory or lacking in mutuality of obligation because it contained the "satisfaction" clause. However, language in two recent cases led the trial court to the contrary conclusion. The first case, Lawrence Block Co. v. Palston, 123 Cal.App.2d 300, 266 P.2d 856, 858, stated that the following two conditions placed in an offer to buy an apartment building would have made the resulting contract illusory: "O.P.A. Rent statements to be approved by Buyer" and "Subject to buyer's inspection and approval of all apartments." These provisions were said to give the purchaser "unrestricted discretion" in deciding whether he would be bound to the contract and to provide no "standard" which could be used in compelling him to perform. 123 Cal.App.2d at pages 308–309, 266 P.2d at pages 861–862. However, this language was not necessary to the decision.

The other case, Pruitt v. Fontana, 143 Cal.App.2d 675, 300 P.2d 371, 377, presented a similar situation. The court concluded that the written instrument with a provision making the sale of land subject to the covenants and easements being "approved by the buyers" was illusory. It employed both the reasoning and language of *Lawrence Block Co.* in deciding that this clause provided no "objective criterion" preventing the buyers from exercising an "unrestricted subjective discretion" in deciding whether they would be bound. 143 Cal.App.2d at pages 684–685, 300 P.2d at page 377. But again, this language was not necessary to the result reached. The buyers in *Pruitt* refused to approve all of the easements of record, and the parties entered into a new and different oral agreement. The defendant seller was held to be estopped to assert the statute of frauds against this subsequent contract, and the judgment of dismissal entered after the sustaining of demurrers was reversed.

While the language in these two cases might be dismissed as mere dicta, the fact that the trial court relied thereon requires us to examine the reasoning employed. Both courts were concerned with finding an objective standard by which they could compel performance. This view apparently stems from the statement in *Lawrence Block Co.* that "The standard 'as to the satisfaction of a reasonable person' does not apply where the performance involves a matter dependent on judgment." 123 Cal.App.2d at page 309, 266 P.2d at page 862. By making this assertion without any qualification, the court necessarily implied that there is no other standard available. Of course, this entirely disregards those cases which have upheld "satisfaction" clauses dependent on the exercise of judgment. In such cases, the criterion becomes one of good faith. Insofar as the language in *Lawrence Block Co.* and *Pruitt* represented a departure from the established rules governing "satisfaction" clauses, they are hereby disapproved.

We conclude that the contract here was neither illusory nor lacking in mutuality of obligation because the parties inserted a provision in their contract making plaintiff's performance dependent on his satisfaction with the leases to be obtained by him.

The judgment is reversed.

NOTES

(1) *Satisfied?* If, after signing the deposit receipt, Mattei had changed his mind about the purchase, could he have avoided liability simply by saying that he was "dissatisfied" with the deal? Would Hopper have been bound if Mattei had inserted a clause permitting him to do this? The meaning of "good faith" is explored further in later chapters.

After negotiations, parties often leave some matters for their lawyers. Do you see a difference in legal effect between a provision that says "subject to my lawyer's approval of our agreement" and one that says "subject to my lawyer's approval of documents tendered when the deal is closed"?

(2) *Holdouts.* Why might Hopper have refused to sell? Perhaps she came to regret the price she had agreed to and was seeking a way out of the contract? Why might this be?

One possibility is that Hopper was a "holdout," or at least a would-be holdout. Holdouts are parties who seek to extract gains by delaying or otherwise raising the costs of contractual formation. The paradigmatic context of holdouts occurs when a real estate developer attempts to assemble adjacent parcels of land for the site of a new project. See Andrew Alpern & Seymour B. Durst, Holdouts! (1984). From an economic perspective, the developer should be able to buy the desired parcels at their current value and still find it worthwhile to proceed with the project. When, however, the parcels are held by multiple separate owners, efficient trade becomes significantly less likely due to the "holdout problem." The last landowner to sell (or perhaps in Hopper's case, the last one to find out about the project) may be able to demand a higher price knowing that the developer is, to some extent, locked in by virtue of the earlier purchases.

When developers encounter a holdout, they have several options: they can go elsewhere (preferably to a site that has a single owner); they can pay the price demanded; they can discretely purchase the land through false fronts and straw buyers; or they can fix a total price that they will pay for the land and let the landowners deal with splitting the pie themselves. They might also, under certain circumstances, appeal to a state or municipal government to exercise its power of eminent domain on their behalf; see Kelo v. City of New London, 545 U.S. 469 (2005).

(3) *Property and Contract.* We noted earlier that the substantive connections among first-year courses are many. Consider for a moment

connections between contract formation and the doctrine of eminent domain mentioned at the end of Note 2 above. Assume that in the principal case, the county (rather than a private developer) had sought Hopper's land to use for a new highway but that Hopper refused to sell because she thought the price offered was too low. Might the availability of eminent domain, as provided for by the Fifth Amendment, influence negotiations over price between Hopper and the private developer? Do property owners in such circumstances bargain under the shadow of constitutional law? For one study about how prices are set generally in takings cases, see Curtis Berger, *The Nassau County Study: An Empirical Look into the Practices of Condemnation*, 67 Colum. L. Rev. 430 (1967).

Contracts for the Sale of Goods

You have already been introduced to this category of contracts in the *Bayliner* case on p. 4 above. Contracts for the sale of goods have long been regarded as distinctive, as evidenced by the reduction of much of the common law of sales to statutory form in England in 1893 by the Sale of Goods Act and in the United States in 1906 by the Uniform Sales Act, later replaced by Article 2 of the Uniform Commercial Code (UCC). The law of international sales of goods is now codified in the United Nations Convention on Contracts for the International Sale of Goods (CISG) (found in Selections for Contracts). In addition, the International Institute for the Unification of Private Law (UNIDROIT) has promulgated the UNIDROIT Principles for International Commercial Contracts (also found in Selections for Contracts).

UCC Article 2 reflects the characteristics of sale of goods transactions in a number of ways. Because agreements to buy and sell goods are often made quickly and informally, the requirements for contract formation tend to be less demanding than in contracts for the sale of real property. The parties to sales contracts are often "repeat players" who have dealt with similar goods and often with each other over time, so that their particular understandings as well as customs and practices within the trade may give added content to their agreements. Terms and entire forms are often standardized.

The nature of goods as the subject of a contract is also significant with regard to remedies. Unlike land, where every parcel is regarded as unique, most goods are considered *fungible*: one item of a particular sort is typically understood to be as good as any other. ("Widgets" have been the inevitable law school example.) Because it is generally assumed that goods of all sorts are available on the market, market price plays an important role in the calculation of damages under Article 2.

Structural Polymer Group, Ltd. v. Zoltek Corp.

United States Court of Appeals for the Eighth Circuit, 2008.
543 F.3d 987.

■ COLLOTON, CIRCUIT JUDGE. A jury awarded Structural Polymer Group and Structural Polymer Systems (together SP) $36,044,895 in lost profits from Zoltek Corporation for breach of a requirements contract for the sale of carbon fiber. The district court reduced the award to $21,138,518, finding the remainder of the award duplicative. Zoltek appeals the district court's denial of its motion for a new trial and motion for judgment as a matter of law. Structural Polymer cross-appeals the district court's modification of the jury's damages award. We affirm.

I.

Zoltek is a Missouri corporation that manufactures and sells carbon fiber. SP are British corporations that manufacture a strong, light-weight building material produced using carbon fiber called "prepreg." Prepreg is made by weaving carbon fiber into textile-like sheets and then impregnating the sheets with liquid resin. The prepreg sheets are then sold to builders who can mold them into different shapes for a variety of applications. Used in this way, prepreg is a common substitute for fiberglass. One common application for prepreg is the manufacture of wind energy turbine blades.

The parties entered into a Supply Agreement in November 2000. Under the disputed agreement, Zoltek promised to manufacture and sell to SP all of SP's requirements between November 6, 2000, and December 31, 2010, for "Large Filament Count Carbon Fibers (Carbon Fibers) as defined by PANEX 33 specifications," at "then-current market price." SP, in turn, promised to "obtain their total requirements for suitable quality, in the reasonable opinion of [SP], Carbon Fibers from [Zoltek]," the volume not to exceed "the amount actually purchased by [SP] in the preceding Contract Year plus one million (1,000,000) pounds." "Large Filament Count," or large-tow carbon fiber, contains 48,000 or more filaments per bundle. "Small-tow" carbon fiber, by contrast, contains fewer than 48,000 filaments per bundle, commonly 24,000 or fewer filaments per bundle. Small-tow is more expensive to produce, but superior in quality.

When the Supply Agreement was formed, most manufacturers used small-tow carbon fiber. The purpose of the agreement was to develop a new market for large-tow fiber as a less expensive alternative to small-tow fiber in the wind-energy industry.

Before April 2002, Zoltek produced a large-tow carbon fiber product called Panex 33. SP purchased 28,219.17 and 20,943.91 pounds of Panex 33 from Zoltek under the Supply Agreement in 2000 and 2001, respectively. SP placed an order for 1,763.70 pounds of Panex 33 in 2002, but returned it due to alleged quality defects. In April 2002, Zoltek stopped manufacturing Panex 33, and started making a large-tow carbon fiber product called Panex 35. SP ordered no Panex 33 or 35 in 2003. SP ordered and received 548,935 pounds of Panex 35 in 2004.

The dispute in this case centers on two orders that SP placed with Zoltek in 2005 and 2006 that were never filled. SP ordered 1,480,138 pounds of Panex 35 in 2005, and claims that it was entitled to 2,480,138 pounds of Panex 35 in 2006.

On February 22, 2005, SP sued Zoltek for breach of contract alleging lost profits through December 31, 2006, and future lost profits through December 31, 2010. Because the parties disputed whether the Supply Agreement entitled SP to both Panex 33 and Panex 35, SP's damages expert made alternative lost profit calculations: $21,138,518 in then-current lost profits under Count I corresponding to 3,960,276 pounds of Panex 35, and $14,906,377 in then-current lost profits under Count II corresponding to 3,000,000 pounds of Panex 33.

On November 29, 2006, a jury awarded SP lost profits under both counts through December 31, 2006, but declined to award SP future lost profits. The district court vacated the award under Count II as duplicative, giving SP a final sum of $21,138,518. Zoltek filed motions under Federal Rule of Civil Procedure 59(a) for a new trial, and under Rule 50(b) for judgment as a matter of law, in connection with both the liability and damages phases of the proceedings, and the district court denied both motions. Zoltek appeals the district court's denial of those motions. SP cross-appeals the district court's vacation of the jury's award under Count II of the complaint.

II.

Zoltek argues that the district court erred in four ways. First, Zoltek argues that the district court erred by refusing to allow it to raise two arguments to the jury. Zoltek sought to urge that the Supply Agreement was void for lack of mutuality of obligation. The district court concluded that Zoltek's argument was an affirmative defense, which Zoltek waived by failing to plead it, and the district court then denied as untimely Zoltek's motion to amend its complaint to add a mutuality defense. Second, the district court ruled that Zoltek failed to make a submissible case that SP had abandoned the Supply Agreement. Third, Zoltek argues that the district court failed to remedy unfairly-prejudicial testimony at trial. Fourth, Zoltek argues that the jury's damages award to SP was not based on adequate evidence, that the district court erred by allowing SP to amend its damages calculations twenty-two days before trial, that SP's revised damages calculations were inadequate as a matter of law, and that the district court instructed the jury incorrectly in connection with the damages phase of the proceedings.

A.

We first consider Zoltek's objection to the district court's resolution of arguments concerning mutuality of obligation. Zoltek urged that the Supply Agreement was "unenforceable as a requirements contract due to a lack of mutuality," which is in essence an argument that SP failed to show that the Supply Agreement was supported by valid consideration. See Restatement (Second) of Contracts § 79 (1981) ("If the requirement of consideration is met, there is no additional requirement of . . . 'mutuality of obligation.' "); USA Chem, Inc. v. Lewis, 557 S.W.2d 15, 24 (Mo.Ct.App.1977); Famous Brands, Inc. v. David Sherman Corp., 814 F.2d 517, 521 (8th Cir.1987). . . .

[W]e agree with the district court that the Supply Agreement was supported by adequate consideration as a matter of law. Under Missouri law, "whether consideration is sufficient to establish a contract is normally a question of law for the court and not a question of fact for the jury." Allison v. Agribank, FCB, 949 S.W.2d 182, 188 (Mo.Ct.App.1997). Missouri law long has followed a rule that "[w]hen a party relies upon a writing or a number of writings to establish a contract, it is unquestionably the province of the court to determine from the writing or writings whether or not a contract was entered into." Nelson v. Cal Hirsch & Sons' Iron & Rail Co., 102 Mo.App. 498, 77 S.W. 590, 594 (1903).

Zoltek advances three reasons why the contract lacked mutuality of obligation. All three are based on an allegation that SP's requirements under the agreement are "hopelessly manipulable" and determined by SP's subjective preferences, rather than by objective criteria outside of SP's control. Specifically, Zoltek argues that "SP could at all times order or not order Zoltek fiber as it wanted" because (1) SP had zero requirements for large-tow fiber when the contract was formed, (2) the price protection clause gave SP the option "to purchase carbon fibers from other producers" whenever SP wanted to, and (3) SP was free to buy small-tow fiber, which Zoltek alleges is "interchangeable" with large-tow fiber, in place of large-tow whenever it pleased.

First, we disagree with Zoltek that the Supply Agreement lacks mutuality if SP had zero requirements for large-tow fiber when the contract was formed. A duty of good faith is implied in requirements contracts under Missouri law, see Mo.Rev.Stat. § 400.2–306(1) (1994); Home Shopping Club, Inc. v. Roberts Broad. Co., 989 S.W.2d 174, 179 (Mo.Ct.App.1998), and this "implied obligation of good faith is enough to avoid finding a contract null and void due to an illusory promise." Magruder Quarry & Co. v. Briscoe, 83 S.W.3d 647, 650–51 (Mo.Ct.App.2002); see also National Refining Co. v. Cox, 227 Mo.App. 778, 57 S.W.2d 778, 781 (1933). The Supply Agreement bound SP to order product from Zoltek in good faith, and if SP failed to purchase anything from Zoltek during the term of the agreement, then the contract allowed Zoltek to allege that SP acted in bad faith by failing to make purchases. An assertion of bad faith, however, is an argument that SP breached the agreement, not that the agreement lacked mutuality or consideration in the first place. The district court's ruling on Zoltek's proposed defense did not foreclose it from arguing to the jury that SP breached the agreement.

Second, we disagree with Zoltek that the price protection clause in the contract made SP's obligation illusory. The price protection clause gave Zoltek a right of first refusal to sell large-tow carbon fiber to SP for the same price as offered by a third party seller. If Zoltek offered to match the price offered by another supplier, then SP was obligated to purchase from Zoltek. We think the Missouri courts are likely to agree with the observation in a leading treatise that this mechanism does not render the contract illusory:

The seller may not promise to meet such prices, but the seller may be given the option of doing so. If the seller meets such prices, the buyer must buy of the seller or not at all. If the seller does not meet such prices, the buyer has the privilege of buying elsewhere. Such promises are not illusory and the contract is valid. Arthur Linton Corbin, et al., 2–6 Corbin on Contracts § 6.8.

Zoltek's authorities do not persuade us to the contrary. They demonstrate only that if SP had an unfettered option to purchase from another supplier during the term of the contract, then this option would destroy the exclusivity of the arrangement, and demonstrate lack of consideration. E.g., In re Modern Dairy of Champaign, Inc., 171 F.3d 1106, 1108 (7th Cir.1999); Harvey v. Fearless Farris Wholesale, Inc., 589 F.2d 451, 459 (9th Cir.1978); Loizeaux Builders Supply Co. v. Donald B. Ludwig Co., 144 N.J.Super. 556, 366 A.2d 721, 724 (1976); Propane Indus., Inc. v. General Motors Corp., 429 F.Supp. 214, 221 (W.D.Mo.1977). The inclusion in the Supply Agreement of a right of first refusal for Zoltek to retain its exclusive right to supply SP, so long as it matched a market price offered by another supplier, is sufficient to create mutuality of obligation and consideration.

Third, we do not agree with Zoltek that if small-tow and large-tow fiber are "interchangeable," then the Supply Agreement lacked mutuality. There was a good deal of evidence at trial that small-tow and large-tow fiber are distinct products, with different qualities and applications. But assuming for the sake of argument that a jury could find that small-tow and large-tow fibers are in fact "interchangeable," as Zoltek contends, the authorities cited by Zoltek do not establish that the Supply Agreement is void for lack of mutuality. These cases illustrate, rather, that when a buyer contracts to purchase its requirements for a product from a particular seller, but then—without a "good faith" basis to do so-purchases an interchangeable product from a third party instead, the buyer may have breached the requirements contract. E.g., Fike Corp. v. Great Lakes Chemical Corp., 332 F.3d 520, 524 (8th Cir.2003); Empire Gas Corp. v. American Bakeries Co., 840 F.2d 1333, 1339–41 (7th Cir.1988); Loudenback Fertilizer Co. v. Tenn. Phosphate Co., 121 F. 298, 303 (6th Cir.1903). Zoltek was free to argue on this basis that SP's purchase of small-tow fiber from parties other than Zoltek was a breach of the agreement to purchase large-tow fiber exclusively from Zoltek, but the jury found that SP performed its obligations under the contract. SP's obligation to purchase in good faith all of its requirements for large-tow fiber exclusively from Zoltek was sufficient consideration to make the contract valid.

For these reasons, we agree with the district court's alternative holding that "on the face of the agreement, there is mutuality of obligation and, therefore, consideration."

III.

In its cross-appeal, SP argues that the district court erred by granting Zoltek's motion to alter or amend judgment pursuant to Federal Rule of Civil Procedure 59(e). The verdict form submitted to the jury included alternative damages calculations corresponding to 3,000,000 pounds of Panex 33 and 3,960,276 pounds of Panex 35. The jury awarded SP damages under both calculations. The district court concluded that SP had argued throughout the case that the Supply Agreement entitled them to "either Panex 33 or Panex 35," but not to both, and therefore vacated the lesser of the two awards as duplicative.

We conclude that the district court did not abuse its discretion. SP's complaint pleaded Counts I and II in the alternative, demanding that Zoltek "supply the unfulfilled quantities of PANEX 35 or, in the alternative, PANEX 33," and alleging that the contract was modified to "substitute" Panex 35 for Panex 33. SP's damages expert presented "alternative" damages calculations—one that assumed the Supply Agreement encompassed both Panex 33 and Panex 35, and a second that assumed that only Panex 33 was covered. The Supply Agreement referred to Panex 33 only, and established a maximum quantity that SP was entitled to order. The jury evidently accepted SP's contention that it also was entitled to order Panex 35 under the agreement, because it was an improved version of Panex 33, but the agreement did not provide that SP could order the maximum quantity of both Panex 33 and Panex 35.

Under the Supply Agreement, SP was entitled to order the quantity of carbon fiber ordered in the immediately preceding year, plus one million pounds. Thus, between 2004 and 2005, SP was entitled either to 3,960,276 pounds of Panex 35, or 3,000,000 pounds of Panex 33, but not both. The jury's award under both Count I and Count II gave SP profit corresponding to 6,960,276 pounds of large-tow carbon fiber when at most SP was entitled to 3,960,276 pounds. Therefore, the district court acted within its discretion when it determined that the jury's award under both counts was duplicative and altered the judgment accordingly.

For these reasons, the judgment of the district court is affirmed.

NOTE

Output Contracts. In contrast to a "requirements" contract, an "output" contract is one that calls on the seller to deliver and the buyer to take all of the goods, or all of a certain sort, that may be produced by the seller. Note the common characteristic of exclusivity in both requirement and output contracts. What protections does the Code provide for buyers and for sellers under these circumstances?

If a buyer announces it will not make any purchases at all, prior to the seller having commenced or completed its manufacture of the goods, how should the court measure the quantity for the purposes of assessing damages?

PROBLEM

This Contract Is Toast. Suppose the Staehl Bread Company and Walker Cattle Farms had a ten-year contract for the sale of all the toasted bread crumbs Staehl made (Walker used the bread crumbs to feed its prize cows). After a year or two, Staehl Bread gave notice to Walker that making the bread crumbs had become unprofitable, so it would cease their manufacture four weeks hence. Walker sued for breach of contract. Has Staehl Bread breached the contract? Isn't losing money a good reason not to continue in a line of business? Or must Staehl Bread continue making bread crumbs for Walker, even as Staehl Bread's losses become ruinous? See UCC § 2–306 cmt. 2. And if the seller is in breach, how would we measure the damages for breach, given the need to predict what the seller's output will be eight or so years after the trial? How might the parties draft their agreement to protect the buyer against the seller's decision to stop making the product? Cf. Feld v. Henry S. Levy & Sons, Inc., 335 N.E.2d 320 (N.Y. 1975).

Introduction to Wood v. Lucy, Lady Duff-Gordon

The cases so far have focused on statements that at least one of the parties regarded as an express promise. The following case concerns a promise that the court agrees was not "expressed in so many words" but instead, was "fairly to be implied." What was it implied from? In Note 1 following Hawkins v. McGee, p. 2 above, you were asked to consider the language, context, and nature of the transaction in determining whether Dr. McGee's statement was a promise. As you read Judge Cardozo's famous opinion below, consider how those factors contribute to the court's conclusion that, despite the absence of an explicit statement or promise, the writing is nonetheless "instinct with obligation."

Wood v. Lucy, Lady Duff-Gordon

Court of Appeals of New York, 1917.
222 N.Y. 88, 118 N.E. 214.

Appeal from Supreme Court, Appellate Division, First Department.

■ CARDOZO, JUDGE.[r] The defendant styles herself "a creator of fashions." Her favor helps a sale. Manufacturers of dresses, millinery, and like

---

[r]   Benjamin Nathan Cardozo (1870–1938) practiced in New York City after law school. He served as judge and later chief judge of the New York Court of Appeals, for which most of his significant opinions were written. President Hoover appointed him to the Supreme Court of the United States in 1932, upon Holmes's retirement. Cardozo's best-known jurisprudential work is a series of lectures entitled *The Nature of the Judicial Process* (1921).

articles are glad to pay for a certificate of her approval. The things which she designs, fabrics, parasols, and what not, have a new value in the public mind when issued in her name. She employed the plaintiff to help her, to turn this vogue into money. He was to have the exclusive right, subject always to her approval, to place her indorsements on the designs of others. He was also to have the exclusive right to place her own designs on sale, or to license others to market them. In return she was to have one-half of "all profits and revenues" derived from any contracts he might make. The exclusive right was to last at least one year from April 1, 1915, and thereafter from year to year unless terminated by notice of 90 days. The plaintiff says that he kept the contract on his part, and that the defendant broke it. She placed her indorsement on fabrics, dresses, and millinery without his knowledge, and withheld the profits. He sues her for the damages, and the case comes here on demurrer.[s]

The agreement of employment is signed by both parties. It has a wealth of recitals. The defendant insists, however, that it lacks the elements of a contract. She says that the plaintiff does not bind himself to anything. It is true that he does not promise in so many words that he will use reasonable efforts to place the defendant's indorsements and market her designs. We think, however, that such a promise is fairly to be implied. The law has outgrown its primitive stage of formalism when the precise word was the sovereign talisman, and every slip was fatal. It takes a broader view today. A promise may be lacking, and yet the whole writing may be "instinct with an obligation," imperfectly expressed (Scott, J., in McCall Co. v. Wright, 133 App.Div. 62, 117 N.Y.S. 775; Moran v. Standard Oil Co., 211 N.Y. 187, 198, 105 N.E. 217). If that is so, there is a contract.

The implication of a promise here finds support in many circumstances. The defendant gave an exclusive privilege. She was to have no right for at least a year to place her own indorsements or market her own designs except through the agency of the plaintiff. The acceptance of the exclusive agency was an assumption of its duties. Phoenix Hermetic Co. v. Filtrine Mfg. Co., 150 N.Y.S. 193; W.G. Taylor Co. v. Bannerman, 120 Wis. 189; Mueller v. Mineral Spring Co., 88 Mich. 390. We are not to suppose that one party was to be placed at the mercy of the other. Hearn v. Stevens & Bro., 97 N.Y.S. 566; Russell v. Allerton,

---

[s]   In dismissing the complaint, the Appellate Division explained that "the plaintiff by this contract promises to collect the revenues derived from the indorsements, sales and licenses and to pay the cost of collecting them out of his half thereof, and to account to the defendant each month. But this promise on his part is not binding on him unless he places indorsements, makes sales or grants licenses, and nowhere in the contract has he bound himself to get these indorsements, or make the sales or grant the licenses. . . . It is quite apparent that in this respect the defendant gives everything and the plaintiff nothing and there is a lack of mutuality in the contract. . . . In fact the plaintiff in the nature of the case could not perform any of his various dependent agreements unless he placed indorsements, made sales or granted licenses to manufacture. And as the contract did not bind him to do any of these things, there is no provision of the contract which the defendant could enforce against him." 164 N.Y.S. at 577.

108 N.Y. 288. Many other terms of the agreement point the same way. We are told at the outset by way of recital that:

"The said Otis F. Wood possesses a business organization adapted to the placing of such indorsements as the said Lucy, Lady Duff-Gordon, has approved."

The implication is that the plaintiff's business organization will be used for the purpose for which it is adapted. But the terms of the defendant's compensation are even more significant. Her sole compensation for the grant of an exclusive agency is to be one-half of all the profits resulting from the plaintiff's efforts. Unless he gave his efforts, she could never get anything. Without an implied promise, the transaction cannot have such business "efficacy, as both parties must have intended that at all events it should have." Bowen, L.J., in The Moorcock, 14 P.D. 64, 68. But the contract does not stop there. The plaintiff goes on to promise that he will account monthly for all moneys received by him, and that he will take out all such patents and copyrights and trademarks as may in his judgment be necessary to protect the rights and articles affected by the agreement. It is true, of course, as the Appellate Division has said, that if he was under no duty to try to market designs or to place certificates of indorsement, his promise to account for profits or take out copyrights would be valueless. But in determining the intention of the parties the promise has a value. It helps to enforce the conclusion that the plaintiff had some duties. His promise to pay the defendant one-half of the profits and revenues resulting from the exclusive agency and to render accounts monthly was a promise to use reasonable efforts to bring profits and revenues into existence. For this conclusion the authorities are ample.

The judgment of the Appellate Division should be reversed, and the order of the Special Term affirmed, with costs in the Appellate Division and in this court.

[Three judges dissented.]

NOTES

(1) *Questions.* What is the rationale for the implication of a promise? To what extent does it turn on the fact that Lady Duff-Gordon gave Wood "an exclusive privilege"? Or on other of the "many circumstances" referred to by Cardozo? What were these circumstances? For a detailed comparison of the contract between Wood and Lucy with an explicit exclusive dealings contract between Wood and another entrepreneur, see Victor P. Goldberg, *Desperately Seeking Consideration: The Unfortunate Impact of U.C.C. Section 2–306 on Contract Interpretation*, 68 Ohio St. L.J. 103 (2007).

How does the statement of the rule in UCC § 2–306(2) guide your analysis of the case? (Would the UCC, if enacted at the time, have applied?)

(2) *What if Wood Wouldn't?* Might there be consideration even without the duty of reasonable efforts implied by Cardozo? Certainly the usual

answer is: No. But suppose Wood was the top agent in New York, one who could make the fortune of anyone he chose to take on as a client. Indeed, he would not even consider adding a client unless the potential client agreed in advance that, if he did, Wood would have the exclusive right to market the client's name and image, and that he would pay the client whatever portion of the revenue he thought appropriate. Illusory? Or, if this is the only way to become one of Wood's clients, isn't the potential client bargaining for the chance to be represented by Wood? Is it sufficient to rely on the contractual duty of good faith and fair dealing?

(3)   *Corbin and Llewellyn on Cardozo.* Professor Arthur Linton Corbin[t] wrote this of Cardozo:

> It cannot be said that he made any extensive changes in the existing law of contract. To state the facts of the cases, the decision, and the reasoning of the opinion will not show the overthrow of old doctrine or the establishment of new. Instead, it will show the application of existing doctrines with wisdom and discretion; an application that does not leave those doctrines wholly unaffected, but one that carries on their evolution as is reasonably required by the new facts before the court. When Cardozo is through, the law is not exactly as it was before, but there has been no sudden shift or revolutionary change.

Arthur L. Corbin, *Mr. Justice Cardozo and the Law of Contracts*, 39 Colum. L. Rev. 56, 56–57, 52 Harv. L. Rev. 408, 408–09, 48 Yale L.J. 426, 426–27 (1939).

Professor Karl Llewellyn used Lady Duff-Gordon to illustrate Cardozo's mastery in presenting the facts of a case.

> You must remember that Cardozo was a truly great advocate, and the fact that he became a great judge didn't at all change the fact that he was a great advocate. And if you will watch, in the very process of your listening to the facts, you will find two things happening. The one is that . . . you arrive at the conclusion that the case has to come out one way. And the other is, that it fits into a legal frame that says, 'How comfortable it will be, to bring it out that way. No trouble at all. No trouble at all.'

Karl Llewellyn, *A Lecture on Appellate Advocacy*, 29 U. Chi. L. Rev. 627, 637–38 (1962). Llewellyn quoted the first five sentences of the opinion, noting how the defendant "is subtly made into a nasty person," and then continued:

> Does this sound . . . like a business deal? Does a business deal sound like a legally enforceable view? Nothing is being said about that. But watch it grow on you. And if I hadn't stopped to tell you about it, it would have grown until you just took it, without a word.

---

[t]   Arthur Linton Corbin (1874–1967) practiced law in Colorado for four years after his graduation from law school in 1899. He taught at the Yale Law School from 1903 until his retirement in 1943 and became a leading authority on the law of contracts. His eight-volume treatise, *Corbin on Contracts*, which began to appear in 1950, ranks as one of the great legal treatises. He also served as Special Advisor, and as Reporter for the Chapter on Remedies, for the First Restatement of Contracts.

Id. Can you give a similar reading to other parts of the opinion?

Might Cardozo have drawn his characterization of the defendant from the contract drafted by Lady Duff-Gordon's lawyer?

(4) *Termination Clauses*. Parties often use termination clauses to reduce the risks that they assume by contracting. The contract in Lady Duff-Gordon was, for example, terminable by either party without liability after one year. (As Judge Richard Posner has noted, "a year can be a long time in the fashion business." Richard A. Posner, Cardozo: A Study in Reputation 96 (1990).)

If a termination clause is read as giving a party the power to terminate at any time at will, without more, that party's promise will be held to be illusory. For example, a license agreement for the manufacture of Orange Crush gave the licensee the exclusive right and the duty to manufacture the soft drink in a specified territory, but provided that the licensee could terminate the contract at any time. In a suit by the licensee against the licensor, the court held that the licensee's promise was not consideration for the licensor's because the licensee "did not promise to do anything and could at any time cancel the contract." Miami Coca-Cola Bottling Co. v. Orange Crush Co., 296 F. 693 (5th Cir.1924).

If, however, a termination clause is read as restricting the right of termination in some way—for example, by requiring that notice be given some period of time before the termination becomes effective or be given in writing—the promise will not be considered illusory.

(5) *Termination Under the Code*. UCC § 2–309(3) requires "reasonable notification" for termination, except on the happening of an agreed event. Suppose a termination clause explicitly negates any duty of notification. Does that leave the agreement without consideration? Comment 8 to the section says: "An agreement dispensing with notification or limiting the time for the seeking of a substitute arrangement is, of course, valid under this subsection unless the results of putting it into operation would be the creation of an unconscionable state of affairs."

————

Substitutes for Consideration

The doctrine of consideration has been subjected to attacks for more than two centuries. Why, critics ask, should a promisor not be able to make a binding promise without receiving something in return from, and without reliance by, the promisee? Attempts at reform have focused on this problem, particularly with regard to gratuitous promises, and various substitutes have been suggested.

As long ago as 1765, in a case involving past consideration, Lord Mansfield[u] declared that a writing might substitute for consideration:

---

[u] William Murray, first Earl of Mansfield (1705–1793), was a rival of William Pitt the Elder in school, in Parliament and in politics. He favored strict measures with the American rebels. His friend Alexander Pope helped him practice advocacy and later praised his eloquence in verse. Dr. Johnson said of him, "much can be made of a Scot if caught young." Mansfield

"The ancient notion about the want of consideration was for the sake of evidence only: for when it is reduced into writing there was no objection to the want of consideration. In commercial cases amongst merchants, the want of consideration is not an objection." Pillans and Rose v. Van Mierop and Hopkins, [1765] 97 Eng. Rep. 1035 (K.B.). His rule was short-lived, for 13 years later it was rejected by the House of Lords, which concluded that, "All contracts are, by the laws of England, distinguished into agreements by specialty [i.e., agreements under seal], and agreements by parol; nor is there any such third class as some of the counsel have endeavored to maintain, as contracts in writing. If they be merely written and not specialties, they are parol, and a consideration must be proved." Rann v. Hughes, [1788] 101 Eng. Rep. 1014 (H.L.). Nonetheless, the view that the formality of putting a promise in writing should operate as an alternative to consideration continued to have some appeal among commentators, especially when the abolition of the seal raised the doctrine of consideration to even greater prominence.

This appeal has not yielded much general legislation. In the 1920's, the National Conference of Commissioners on Uniform State Laws prepared the Uniform Written Obligations Act. Drafted by Samuel Williston, it provided that a promise is not "unenforceable for lack of consideration, if the writing also contains an additional express statement, in any form of language, that the signer intends to be legally bound." This was enacted only in Pennsylvania and Utah, and was repealed by Utah not long after. A couple of states enacted statutes that gave signed writings the legal effect of a seal. Otherwise statutory reform of consideration in the United States has been limited to specific types of contracts, most commonly modifications. These statutes will be discussed in Chapter 4.

A few states have general statutes that facilitate the making of binding gratuitous promises by recognizing some form of writing as a substitute for consideration. California, for example, makes a writing presumptive evidence of consideration. Cal.Civ.Code § 1614 (West 2001). In addition, Article 2 of the Uniform Commercial Code dispenses with the requirement of consideration in certain limited circumstances, as indicated on p. 237 and Note 2, p. 441 below.

Civil law countries commonly have procedures by which a promisor may appear before a notary, a lawyer who holds an appointment from the state and who has no counterpart in common law countries, and make an irrevocable gratuitous promise. See Arthur T. von Mehren, *Civil Law Analogues to Consideration: An Exercise in Comparative Analysis*, 72 Harv. L. Rev. 1009, 1057–62 (1959). One explanation offered for the refusal by the American legal system to provide a similar mechanism is

achieved greatness as a judge, being Lord Chief Justice from 1756 to 1788. One of his chief services was in rationalizing mercantile law. In commercial cases he made effective use of special "juries" of merchants, whose advice about their practices was sometimes instrumental in transforming custom into law. See generally Norman S. Poser, Lord Mansfield: Justice in the Age of Reason (2013).

paternalism, the view that a promisor's preferences regarding the enforceability of the promise should be disregarded for the promisor's own good.[v] See E. Allan Farnsworth, *Promises and Paternalism*, 41 Wm. & Mary L. Rev. 385 (2000). We consider the general question of whether legal constraints on a party's ability to contract are better understood as paternalism or protection in Chapters 4 and 6.

In a provocative article, Professors Daniel Farber and John Matheson proposed a rule that would enforce any promise "made in furtherance of an economic activity." See Daniel A. Farber and John H. Matheson, *Beyond Promissory Estoppel: Contract Law and the Invisible Handshake*, 52 U. Chi. L. Rev. 903, 929 (1985); see also Edward Yorio and Steve Thel, *The Promissory Basis of Section 90*, 101 Yale L.J. 111 (1991). Farber and Matheson argued that because firms commonly make promises for which they expect economic benefits—the promise to keep a plant open, for example—without receiving any specific bargained-for exchange but with the expectation of eventual economic benefit, such promises should be enforced. They concluded that a "rule that enforces promises designed 'to induce the creation of economic activity' simply 'reinforces the traditional free-will basis of promissory liability, albeit in an expanded context of relational and institutional interdependence.'" Farber and Matheson suggest that courts are already implementing the proposed rule using reliance to enforce commercial promises in cases where the plaintiff has shown little or no reliance at all; see Vastoler v. American Can Co., cited in Note 2, p. 132 below. For criticism of the empirical basis of their argument, see Robert Hillman, *Questioning the New Consensus on Promissory Estoppel: An Empirical and Theoretical Study*, 98 Colum. L. Rev. 580 (1998).

In their proposal Farber and Matheson drew a clear line between gratuitous promises that further economic activity and those that don't. "Unlike promises made in an economic setting, [non-commercial gratuitous promises] are not generally made to coordinate activities or generate reliance beneficial to the promisor. The presumption of utility that underlies our proposed enforcement of promises in furtherance of economic activity thus does not apply." Why is it that non-commercial gift promises find no haven, even among proposals that would abandon consideration in commercial dealings?

Consider also Judge Posner's view regarding the economic value of gratuitous promises. See Richard A. Posner, *Gratuitous Promises in Economics and Law*, 6 J. Legal Stud. 411 (1977). On this account, a promise's value depends in part on how likely it is that the promise will be kept. A rational promisee therefore discounts the promise to take the possibility of breach into account. This can work to the disadvantage of

---

[v]   Civil law countries have found it necessary to devise escape hatches for promisors whose finances deteriorate to the point of insolvency or whose promisees, having received the duly notarized gratuitous promises, become ungrateful. See Melvin Eisenberg, *Donative Promises*, 47 U. Chi. L. Rev. 1 (1979).

both the promisor and the promisee. If the promisor is reliable, she would like the prospective promisee to know that; the more valuable the promise, the greater the effect the promise will have on the promisee's actions.

One way to make a gratuitous promise worth more is to provide a means of enforcing it that the promisor may elect or not as she pleases. A low-risk promisor would commit herself readily; a high-risk promisor might want to keep her options open. It thus makes sense for courts to enforce gratuitous promises, because doing so makes the promises more valuable.

PROBLEM

Reviewing the Situation. Grateful for various forms of personal assistance (driving, shopping, companionship) received from a close friend over the years, Jack Tallas, a retired businessman, wrote out a memorandum stating his intention to change his will to make the friend "an heir for the sum of $50,000." Tallas had the memorandum notarized and gave a notarized copy of the memo to his friend to keep. When Tallas died, never having changed his will, the friend sued his estate for $50,000. Assuming, as the court did, that there was no fraud, duress, or misrepresentation, is there any legal basis to support the friend's claim? Consideration? Moral obligation? The writing? The notarization? If your answer is "None of the above," why should the promise not be enforced? Is the concern that the cautionary or evidentiary functions performed by consideration, p. 48 above, have not been met? Is there more Tallas could have done? See DeMentas v. Tallas, 764 P.2d 628 (Utah 1988).

SECTION 4.   RELIANCE AS A BASIS OF ENFORCEMENT

We have already considered reliance as one interest a court might protect when providing a remedy to an aggrieved promisee. The focus in this section, however, is not on reliance as an interest to be remedied, but rather as a theory for enforcing promises in the first place. Here we examine the role of reliance—a change of position by the promisee—as a basis for enforcement of the promise separate and distinct from consideration. As we shall see, recognizing this function of reliance serves to ameliorate injustices that sometimes result from a want of consideration. Consider Mrs. Feinberg, or Sister Antillico, on pp. 68 and 80, respectively. At the same time, by abandoning the requirement of consideration, the doctrine of reliance may risk unfair or unsatisfactory outcomes. In reading the following cases, compare the advantages and limitations offered by reliance as a ground for enforcing promises with those offered by consideration.

Ricketts v. Scothorn

Supreme Court of Nebraska, 1898.
57 Neb. 51, 77 N.W. 365.

■ SULLIVAN, JUSTICE. In the District Court of Lancaster county, the plaintiff, Katie Scothorn, recovered judgment against the defendant, Andrew D. Ricketts, as executor, of the last will and testament of John C. Ricketts, deceased. The action was based upon a promissory note, of which the following is a copy: "May the first, 1891. I promise to pay to Katie Scothorn on demand, $2,000 to be at 6 per cent. per annum. J.C. Ricketts." In the petition the plaintiff alleges that the consideration for the execution of the note was that she should surrender her employment as bookkeeper for Mayer Bros., and cease to work for a living. She also alleges that the note was given to induce her to abandon her occupation, and that, relying on it, and on the annual interest, as a means of support, she gave up the employment in which she was then engaged. These allegations of the petition are denied by the administrator.

The material facts are undisputed. They are as follows: John C. Ricketts, the maker of the note, was the grandfather of the plaintiff. Early in May—presumably on the day the note bears date—he called on her at the store where she was working. What transpired between them is thus described by Mr. Flodene, one of the plaintiff's witnesses: "A. Well, the old gentleman came in there one morning about nine o'clock, probably a little before or a little after, but early in the morning, and he unbuttoned his vest, and took out a piece of paper in the shape of a note; that is the way it looked to me; and he says to Miss Scothorn, 'I have fixed out something that you have not got to work any more.' He says, 'none of my grandchildren work, and you don't have to.' Q. Where was she? A. She took the piece of paper and kissed him, and kissed the old gentleman, and commenced to cry." It seems Miss Scothorn immediately notified her employer of her intention to quit work, and that she did soon after abandon her occupation. The mother of the plaintiff was a witness, and testified that she had a conversation with her father, Mr. Ricketts, shortly after the note was executed, in which he informed her that he had given the note to the plaintiff to enable her to quit work; that none of his grandchildren worked, and he did not think she ought to. For something more than a year the plaintiff was without an occupation, but in September, 1892, with the consent of her grandfather, and by his assistance, she secured a position as bookkeeper with Messrs. Funke & Ogden. On June 8, 1894, Mr. Ricketts died. He had paid one year's interest on the note, and a short time before his death expressed regret that he had not been able to pay the balance. In the summer or fall of 1892 he stated to his daughter, Mrs. Scothorn, that if he could sell his farm in Ohio he would pay the note out of the proceeds. He at no time repudiated the obligation.

We quite agree with counsel for the defendant that upon this evidence there was nothing to submit to the jury, and that a verdict should have been directed peremptorily for one of the parties. The testimony of Flodene and Mrs. Scothorn, taken together, conclusively establishes the fact that the note was not given in consideration of the plaintiff pursuing, or agreeing to pursue, any particular line of conduct. There was no promise on the part of the plaintiff to do, or refrain from doing, anything. Her right to the money promised in the note was not made to depend upon an abandonment of her employment with Mayer Bros., and future abstention from like service. Mr. Ricketts made no condition, requirement, or request. He exacted no quid pro quo. He gave the note as a gratuity, and looked for nothing in return. So far as the evidence discloses, it was his purpose to place the plaintiff in a position of independence, where she could work or remain idle, as she might choose. The abandonment by Miss Scothorn of her position as bookkeeper was altogether voluntary. It was not an act done in fulfillment of any contract obligation assumed when she accepted the note.

The instrument in suit, being given without any valuable consideration, was nothing more than a promise to make a gift in the future of the sum of money therein named. Ordinarily, such promises are not enforceable, even when put in the form of a promissory note. But it has often been held that an action on a note given to a church, college, or other like institution, upon the faith of which money has been expended or obligations incurred, could not be successfully defended on the ground of a want of consideration. In this class of cases the note in suit is nearly always spoken of as a gift or donation, but the decision is generally put on the ground that the expenditure of money or assumption of liability by the donee on the faith of the promise constitutes a valuable and sufficient consideration. It seems to us that the true reason is the preclusion of the defendant, under the doctrine of estoppel, to deny the consideration.

Under the circumstances of this case, is there an equitable estoppel which ought to preclude the defendant from alleging that the note in controversy is lacking in one of the essential elements of a valid contract? We think there is. An estoppel in pais is defined to be "a right arising from acts, admissions, or conduct which have induced a change of position in accordance with the real or apparent intention of the party against whom they are alleged." Mr. Pomeroy has formulated the following definition: "Equitable estoppel is the effect of the voluntary conduct of a party whereby he is absolutely precluded, both at law and in equity, from asserting rights which might, perhaps, have otherwise existed, either of property, of contract, or of remedy, as against another person who in good faith relied upon such conduct, and has been led thereby to change his position for the worse, and who on his part acquires some corresponding right, either of property, of contract, or of remedy." 2 Pom. Eq. Jur. 804. According to the undisputed proof, as shown by the record before us, the plaintiff was a working girl, holding a position in which she earned a salary of $10 per week. Her grandfather, desiring to put her in a position of independence, gave her the note, accompanying it with the remark that his other grandchildren did not work, and that she would not be obliged to work any longer. In effect, he suggested that she might abandon her employment, and rely in the future upon the bounty which he promised. He doubtless desired that she should give up her occupation, but, whether he did or not, it is entirely certain that he contemplated such action on her part as a reasonable and probable consequence of his gift. Having intentionally influenced the plaintiff to alter her position for the worse on the faith of the note being paid when due, it would be grossly inequitable to permit the maker, or his executor, to resist payment on the ground that the promise was given without consideration. The petition charges the elements of an equitable estoppel, and the evidence conclusively establishes them. If errors intervened at the trial, they could not have been prejudicial. A verdict for the defendant would be unwarranted. The judgment is right, and is

Affirmed.

NOTE

(1) *Questions.* What was the promise on which Scothorn relied? What form did her reliance take? What if, during the brief exchange between Ricketts and Scothorn, Ricketts had not mentioned work at all, but had simply handed his granddaughter the promissory note? What result if the conversation took place as it did, and Scothorn decided to keep on working but relied on the promise by buying a horse so that she could get to work more conveniently? Might another court have found a bargained-for exchange and so have enforced Ricketts's note as a promise supported by consideration? Compare, particularly, Hamer v. Sidway, p. 53 above. How might Ricketts have structured his promise so as to ensure its enforcement?

(2) *Equitable Versus Promissory Estoppel.* In the last paragraph of the *Ricketts* decision, the court states that the evidence "conclusively establishes" the elements of an equitable estoppel claim; the court quotes a passage from the Pomeroy treatise ("Mr. Pomeroy") stating that a crucial element of equitable estoppel is that the plaintiff has relied on "an act, admission, or conduct" by the defendant—that is to say, a representation of *fact* that causes the plaintiff to change her position. But in *Ricketts*, Katie relied not on a representation of fact but on her grandfather's *promise:* hence the term promissory estoppel. For a good discussion of the difference between equitable estoppel and promissory estoppel, see Youngblood v. Auto-Owners Ins. Co., 158 P.3d 1088 (Utah 2007).

Why is the court in *Ricketts* not more explicit about what it is doing: that is, expanding the nature of conduct on which another may rely at law from statements of fact to mere promises? The next section on the development of promissory estoppel suggests some answers. Consider why the four categories of promises discussed below might have been particularly agreeable or sympathetic to courts as they honed this new category of enforceable promises.

From Equitable Estoppel to Promissory Estoppel

Holmes said, "It would cut up the doctrine of consideration by the roots, if a promisee could make a gratuitous promise binding by subsequently acting in reliance on it." Commonwealth v. Scituate Savings Bank, 137 Mass. 301, 302 (1884). Nevertheless, a number of 19th and early 20th-century cases, including *Ricketts,* recognized reliance as a basis for the enforcing of promises. For the most part, these cases fall into the following four categories.

Family Promises. As in *Ricketts,* a promise is made by one family member to another, on which the other relies. In earlier centuries, many such cases involved a parent's promise to leave the family farm to the son if the son stays and works the property, or to the daughter if she doesn't marry but cares for her aging parents instead. For a catalogue of such cases and an analysis of why such promises traditionally failed as enforceable contracts, see Hendrik Hartog, *Someday This Will All Be Yours: Inheritance, Adoption, and Obligation in Capitalist America,* 79 Ind. L.J. 345 (2004).

Promises to Convey Land. The recipient of a promise to convey land relied on it by moving onto the land and making improvements. An early example is Freeman v. Freeman, 43 N.Y. 34 (1870). Would the facts in *Kirksey,* above, have brought that case within this category?

Promises Coupled with Gratuitous Bailments. A person entrusted temporarily with another's property makes a promise to the owner respecting the property, on which the owner relies. The leading case is Siegel v. Spear & Co., 138 N.E. 414 (N.Y.1923). Siegel bought furniture on credit from Spear, giving Spear a mortgage on it and agreeing not to remove it from his apartment without Spear's consent until it was paid for. When he decided to leave the city for the summer, Siegel saw Spear's credit man, McGrath, who agreed to store the furniture free of charge. When Siegel stated that he would first have to get some property insurance, McGrath responded that it wouldn't be necessary: "I will do it for you; it will be a good deal cheaper; . . . when you get the next bill— you can send a check for that with the next installment." Siegel then sent the furniture to Spear's storehouse, where a month later it was destroyed by fire. It had not been insured. Siegel sued Spear and won, and Spear appealed. The Court of Appeals affirmed. Although the gratuitous bailment itself imposed no duty on Spear to insure the furniture, such a duty arose from McGrath's promise followed by the delivery of the furniture by Siegel.

Charitable Subscriptions. A person promises to contribute to a not-for-profit organization. Enforcement of such promises may be desirable for policy reasons. As one court put it,

> This promise was made to a charitable corporation, and for that reason we are not confined to the same orthodox concepts which once were applicable to every situation arising within a common law jurisdiction. There can be no denying that the strong desire on the part of the American courts to favor charitable institutions has established a doctrine which once would have been looked upon as legal heresy.

Danby v. Osteopathic Hosp. Ass'n of Delaware, 104 A.2d 903, 904 (Del.Ch.1954). Courts have sometimes enforced promises to charities by finding an exchange among subscribers of promises for the benefit of (and enforceable by) the charitable organization, especially when one subscriber appears as the "bellwether" of the flock and has promised a large sum on the condition that other subscribers raise a specified amount. See Congregation B'Nai Sholom v. Martin, 173 N.W.2d 504 (Mich.1969). (How could you draft a pledge form to help your favorite charity take advantage of this possibility?) Charitable subscriptions have also been enforced by finding that the charity has done or has promised to do something in exchange for the subscriber's promise.

The most widely-known and influential decision on charitable subscriptions rests on this last ground and contains only dictum concerning the effect of reliance. The case is Allegheny College v. National Chautauqua County Bank of Jamestown, 159 N.E. 173 (N.Y.1927). Mary Yates Johnston promised to pay $5,000 to Allegheny College by a writing denoted an "Estate Pledge" that stipulated that "this gift shall be known as the Mary Yates Johnston memorial fund, the proceeds from which shall be used to educate students preparing for the ministry." The sum was not payable until 30 days after her death, but $1,000 was paid while she was alive and set aside by the college for the specified purpose. She later repudiated her promise, and after her death, the college brought an action against her executor for the unpaid balance.

Writing for the New York Court of Appeals, Cardozo found consideration for her promise in the return promise of the college to set up the memorial fund which arose "by implication" from its acceptance of the $1,000. "The college could not accept the money and hold itself free thereafter from personal responsibility to give effect to the condition." Id. at 175. In the course of his opinion, Cardozo went out of his way to speak to the effect of reliance.

> [T]here has grown up of recent days a doctrine that a substitute for consideration or an exception to its ordinary requirements can be found in what is styled 'a promissory estoppel'. . . . Whether the exception has made its way in this state to such an extent as to permit us to say that the general law of consideration has been modified accordingly, we do not now attempt to say. Cases such as Siegel v. Spear & Co. [the bailment case discussed above] may be signposts on the road. Certain, at least, it is that we have adopted the doctrine of

promissory estoppel as the equivalent of consideration in connection with our law of charitable subscriptions.

Id. For a detailed account of the case, see Alfred S. Konefsky, *How to Read, or at Least Not Misread, Cardozo in the* Allegheny College *Case*, 36 Buffalo L. Rev. 645 (1987); see also Leon Lipson, *The* Allegheny College *Case*, 23 Yale L. Rep. No. 3, 11 (1977).

————

Restatement, First, § 90

Cardozo's dictum in *Allegheny College* was surely influenced by what was to become Restatement, First, § 90, whose text had been considered at the annual meeting of the American Law Institute in 1926—in a session presided over by Cardozo, Vice-President of the ALI. The section reads:

§ 90.   Promise Reasonably Inducing Definite and Substantial Action

> A promise which the promisor should reasonably expect to induce action or forbearance of a definite and substantial character on the part of the promisee and which does induce such action or forbearance is binding if injustice can be avoided only by enforcement of the promise.

Although the section avoids the use of the term "promissory estoppel," it states in general terms the principle that had been applied in the four categories of cases just described. During the discussion of Restatement, First, § 90 on the floor of the American Law Institute, Samuel Williston, as Reporter, stated:

> Either the promise is binding or it is not. If the promise is binding it has to be enforced as it is made. As I said to Mr. Coudert, I could leave this whole thing to the subject of quasi contracts so that the promisee under those circumstances shall never recover on the promise but he shall recover such an amount as will fairly compensate him for any injury incurred; but it seems to me you have to take one leg or the other. You have either to say the promise is binding or you have to go on the theory of restoring the status quo.

4 American Law Institute Proceedings, Appendix, 103–04 (1926).

What do you make of Williston's comment above? Although often characterized as a champion of the consideration doctrine, Williston believed the historical basis of contract enforcement rested more in justifiable reliance rather than consideration. That "the historically authentic basis of common contract, for him, was not bargain but reliance[,] had, naturally, an effect upon his attitude toward promissory estoppel, quintessentially the doctrine that protects reliance." Barbara A. Black, *Samuel Williston at the ALI: Promissory Estoppel*, Colum. L. School Working Paper Series (2019).

Feinberg v. Pfeiffer Co.

Saint Louis Court of Appeals, Missouri, 1959.
322 S.W.2d 163.

[The facts and the first part of the opinion in this case are at p. 68 above. The court there rejected Mrs. Feinberg's contention that her continuation in the employ of Pfeiffer Co. from December 27, 1947, the date of the resolution, until her retirement on June 30, 1949, was consideration for Pfeiffer's promise to pay her $200 per month for life upon her retirement. In this portion of the opinion, the court considered Mrs. Feinberg's second contention that the company's promise was enforceable because of her reliance on it, "*i.e.,* her retirement, and the abandonment by her of her opportunity to continue in gainful employment."]

■ DOERNER, COMMISSIONER. But as to the second of these contentions we must agree with plaintiff. By the terms of the resolution defendant promised to pay plaintiff the sum of $200 a month upon her retirement.

[The court quoted Restatement, First, § 90.] Was there such an act on the part of plaintiff, in reliance upon the promise contained in the resolution, as will estop the defendant, and therefore create an enforceable contract under the doctrine of promissory estoppel? We think there was. One of the illustrations cited under Section 90 of the Restatement is: "2. A promises B to pay him an annuity during B's life. B thereupon resigns a profitable employment, as A expected that he might. B receives the annuity for some years, in the meantime becoming disqualified from again obtaining good employment. A's promise is binding." This illustration is objected to by defendant as not being applicable to the case at hand. The reason advanced by it is that in the illustration B became "disqualified" from obtaining other employment *before* A discontinued the payments, whereas in this case the plaintiff did not discover that she had cancer and thereby became unemployable until *after* the defendant had discontinued the payments of $200 per month. We think the distinction is immaterial. The only reason for the reference in the illustration to the disqualification of A is in connection with that part of Section 90 regarding the prevention of injustice. The injustice would occur regardless of when the disability occurred. Would defendant contend that the contract would be enforceable if the plaintiff's illness had been discovered on March 31, 1956, the day before it discontinued the payment of the $200 a month, but not if it occurred on April 2nd, the day after? Furthermore, there are more ways to become disqualified for work, or unemployable, than as the result of illness. At the time she retired plaintiff was 57 years of age. At the time the payments were discontinued she was over 63 years of age. It is a matter of common knowledge that it is virtually impossible for a woman of that age to find satisfactory employment, much less a position comparable to that which plaintiff enjoyed at the time of her retirement.

The fact of the matter is that plaintiff's subsequent illness was not the "action or forbearance" which was induced by the promise contained in the resolution. As the trial court correctly decided, such action on plaintiff's part was her retirement from a lucrative position in reliance upon defendant's promise to pay her an annuity or pension. [The court quoted from *Ricketts v. Scothorn*, p. 119 above.]

The Commissioner therefore recommends, for the reasons stated, that the judgment be affirmed.

■ PER CURIAM. The foregoing opinion is adopted as the opinion of the court. The judgment is, accordingly, affirmed.

PROBLEM

Parallel Pension Promise? In January 1972, Edward J. Hayes announced his intention to retire from Plantations Steel the following July after 25 years of continuous service. About a week before his retirement, he had a conversation with a Plantations Steel officer who said that though Hayes was not eligible for a pension, the company "would take care" of him. Hayes retired and sought no other employment, and the company paid him $5,000 a year through 1976. When payments were discontinued on the ground that the promise was unsupported by consideration, Hayes sued, relying on *Feinberg*. What result? Do the facts in Hayes's case differ significantly from those in Feinberg's? Hayes v. Plantations Steel Co., 438 A.2d 1091 (R.I.1982).

————

Restatement, Second, § 90

In view of the great influence § 90 of the Restatement, First, has had on the enforcement of promises, § 90 of the Restatement, Second, (otherwise simply referred to as the Restatement herein) set out below, merits particularly careful reading. What has happened to the requirement in the Restatement, First, that the reliance be of "a definite and substantial character"? Is there a relation between this deletion and the addition of the second sentence in (1)? Note also the liberalization in Subsection (2) of the rule as to charitable subscriptions.

§ 90. Promise Reasonably Inducing Action or Forbearance

(1) A promise which the promisor should reasonably expect to induce action or forbearance on the part of the promisee or a third person and which does induce such action or forbearance is binding if injustice can be avoided only by enforcement of the promise. The remedy granted for breach may be limited as justice requires.

(2) A charitable subscription or a marriage settlement is binding under Subsection (1) without proof that the promise induced action or forbearance.

NOTES

(1) *Remedies and the Requirements of Justice.* Fuller and Perdue posed the following case:

> An uncle promises his nephew $1,000 as a gift. The nephew decides to go into business, and, reserving the promised sum for use in paying his rent, spends a large sum of money laying in a stock of goods. The uncle declines to perform his promise; the nephew is forced to abandon his plans, and sells his stock of goods at a sacrifice of $2,000.

See Lon L. Fuller & William R. Perdue, Jr., *The Reliance Interest in Contract Damages*, 46 Yale L.J. 52, 80 (1936).

How much should the nephew recover in the preceding hypothetical?

(2) *Charitable Subscriptions Revisited.* Reread paragraph (2) of Restatement, Second, § 90 above. How does paragraph (2) differ from Cardozo's dictum in *Allegheny College*, at p. 123 above? Does it suggest that all promises made to charities are now enforceable? In fact, the state of the law on charitable subscriptions remains unsettled; most jurisdictions have not even addressed the matter above. Does it suggest that all promises made to charities are now enforceable? In fact, the state of the law on charitable subscriptions remains unsettled; most jurisdictions have not even addressed the matter.

For an example of a court that continues to require reliance, see King v. Trustees of Boston Univ., 647 N.E.2d 1196 (Mass.1995), involving the ownership of the papers of Dr. Martin Luther King, Jr. In a 1964 letter, Dr. King named the Boston University Library as the repository of his papers and authorized their removal to Boston University. His letter stated further that "[i]n the event of my death, all such materials deposited with the University shall become from that date the absolute property of Boston University." Id. at 1999. Coretta Scott King, Dr. King's widow, later sought to recover his papers on the ground that his statement was at best a gratuitous promise. A Massachusetts jury found for the University and King appealed. *Held*: Affirmed.

The court held that either consideration or reliance was required and that the jury could have concluded that the University's efforts in caring for the papers constituted consideration or reliance on Dr. King's promise to transfer ownership of the papers at the time of his death. King v. Trustees of Boston University, 647 N.E.2d 1196 (Mass.1995). Might the University have shown other forms of reliance on their possession of the papers? For a case in which the same court found no injustice in declining to enforce an oral promise to give $25,000 to a synagogue, see Congregation Kadimah Toras-Moshe v. DeLeo, 540 N.E.2d 691 (Mass.1989)

(3) *Decline and Fall.* In the provocatively titled *The Death of Contract*, Professor Grant Gilmore[w] described the "decline and fall" of "the general

---

[w] Grant Gilmore (1910–1982), first a scholar of Romance languages, practiced law in New York for two years before teaching law at Yale and for some years at Chicago. He was a principal architect of Article 9 of the Uniform Commercial Code, which deals with secured transactions,

theory of contract," as espoused by Langdell, Holmes, and Williston. He referred to "the Restatement's schizophrenia" and quoted from the Restatement, First, § 75 (found in Feinberg v. Pfeiffer Co. at p. 125 above), and Restatement, First, § 90 (p. 126 above).

> Perhaps what we have here is Restatement and anti-Restatement or Contract and anti-Contract. . . . The one thing that is clear is that these two contradictory propositions cannot live comfortably together: in the end one must swallow the other up. . . . Clearly enough the unresolved ambiguity in the relationship between [the two sections] has now been resolved in favor of the promissory estoppel principle of § 90 which has, in effect, swallowed up the bargain principle of § 75. The wholly executory exchange where neither party has yet taken any action would seem to be the only situation in which it would be necessary to look to § 75—and even there, as the Comment somewhat mysteriously suggests, the 'probability of reliance' may be a sufficient reason for enforcement without inquiring into whether or not there was any 'consideration.' . . . Speaking descriptively, we might say that what is happening is that 'contract' is being reabsorbed into the mainstream of 'tort.'

Grant Gilmore, The Death of Contract 61–65, 72, 87 (1974).

Gilmore's remark about the "wholly executory exchange where neither party has yet taken any action" has not gone unnoticed. An English contracts scholar, Professor Patrick Atiyah, has argued that the case for enforcing such exchanges is not compelling and that "there are signs of an increasing reluctance to impose liability in wholly executory contracts, that is, on promises which have neither been paid for, nor relied upon." Patrick S. Atiyah, Promises, Morals and Law 5–6 (1981). Can you find any of those signs? See Melvin Eisenberg, *The Bargain Principle and Its Limits*, 95 Harv. L. Rev. 741 (1982).

PROBLEM

Applied Measures of Recovery. Assuming that each of the following plaintiffs were allowed to recover under the rule stated in Restatement § 90, which of them might appropriately be limited to recovery based on the reliance interest? Katie Scothorn? Anna Feinberg? Antillico Kirksey?

Wright v. Newman

Supreme Court of Georgia, 1996.
266 Ga. 519, 467 S.E. 533.

■ CARLEY, JUSTICE. Seeking to recover child support for her daughter and her son, Kim Newman filed suit against Bruce Wright. Wright's answer admitted his paternity only as to Newman's daughter and DNA testing subsequently showed that he is not the father of her son. The trial court

and wrote a two-volume work on that subject as well as shorter works on admiralty, contracts, and legal history.

nevertheless ordered Wright to pay child support for both children. As to Newman's son, the trial court based its order upon Wright's "actions in having himself listed on the child's birth certificate, giving the child his surname and establishing a parent-child relationship. . . . " According to the trial court, Wright had thereby allow[ed] the child to consider him his father and in so doing deterr[ed Newman] from seeking to establish the paternity of the child's natural father [,] thus denying the child an opportunity to establish a parent-child relationship with the natural father.

We granted Wright's application for a discretionary appeal so as to review the trial court's order requiring that he pay child support for Newman's son. Wright does not contest the trial court's factual findings. He asserts only that the trial court erred in its legal conclusion that the facts authorized the imposition of an obligation to provide support for Newman's son. If Wright were the natural father of Newman's son, he would be legally obligated to provide support. OCGA § 19–7–2. Likewise, if Wright had formally adopted Newman's son, he would be legally obligated to provide support. OCGA § 19–8–19(a)(2). However, Wright is neither the natural nor the formally adoptive father of the child and "the theory of 'virtual adoption' is not applicable to a dispute as to who is legally responsible for the support of minor children." Ellison v. Thompson, 240 Ga. 594, 596 (1978).

Although Wright is neither the natural nor the formally adoptive father of Newman's son . . ., it does not necessarily follow that, as a matter of law, he has no legal obligation for child support. A number of jurisdictions have recognized that a legally enforceable obligation to provide child support can be "based upon parentage or contract. . . ." Albert v. Albert, 415 So.2d 818, 819 (Fla.App.1982). Georgia is included among those jurisdictions. Foltz v. Foltz, 238 Ga. 193, 194, 232 S.E.2d 66 (1977). Accordingly, the issue for resolution is whether Wright can be held liable for child support for Newman's son under this state's contract law.

There was no formal written contract whereby Wright agreed to support Newman's son. Nevertheless, under this state's contract law, [a] promise which the promisor should reasonably expect to induce action or forbearance on the part of the promisee or a third person and which does induce such action or forbearance is binding if injustice can be avoided only by enforcement of the promise. The remedy granted for breach may be limited as justice requires. OCGA § 13–3–44(a). This statute codifies the principle of promissory estoppel. Insilco Corp. v. First Nat. Bank of Dalton, 248 Ga. 322(1) (1981). In accordance with that principle, "[a] party may enter into a contract invalid and unenforceable, and by reason of the covenants therein contained and promises made in connection with the same, wrongfully cause the opposite party to forego a valuable legal right to his detriment, and in this manner by his conduct waive the right to repudiate the contract and become estopped to deny the opposite party any benefits that may accrue to him under the terms of the agreement." Pepsi Cola Bottling Co. of Dothan, Ala., Inc. v. First Nat. Bank of Columbus, 248 Ga. 114, 116–117(2) (1981).

The evidence authorizes the finding that Wright promised both Newman and her son that he would assume all of the obligations and responsibilities of fatherhood, including that of providing support. As the trial court found, this promise was evidenced by Wright's listing of himself as the father on the child's birth certificate and giving the child his last name. Wright is presumed to know "the legal consequences of his actions. Since parents are legally obligated to support their minor children, [he] accepted this support obligation by acknowledging paternity." Marshall v. Marshall, 386 So.2d 11, 12 (Fla.App.1980). There is no dispute that, at the time he made his commitment, Wright knew that he was not the natural father of the child. Compare NPA v. WBA, 8 Va.App. 246, 380 S.E.2d 178 (1989). Thus, he undertook his commitment knowingly and voluntarily. Moreover, he continued to do so for some 10 years, holding himself out to others as the father of the child and allowing the child to consider him to be the natural father.

The evidence further authorizes the finding that Newman and her son relied upon Wright's promise to their detriment. As the trial court found, Newman refrained from identifying and seeking support from the child's natural father. Had Newman not refrained from doing so, she might now have a source of financial support for the child and the child might now have a natural father who provided emotional, as well as financial, support. If, after 10 years of honoring his voluntary commitment, Wright were now allowed to evade the consequences of his promise, an injustice to Newman and her son would result. Under the evidence, the duty to support which Wright voluntarily assumed 10 years ago remains enforceable under the contractual doctrine of promissory estoppel and the trial court's order which compels Wright to discharge that obligation must be affirmed.

Judgment affirmed.

■ SEARS, JUSTICE, concurring. I write separately only to address the dissenting opinion's misperception that Newman has not relied upon Wright's promise to her detriment. It is an established principle in Georgia that a promise which the promisor should reasonably expect to induce action or forbearance on the part of the promisee or a third person and which does induce such action or forbearance is binding if injustice can be avoided only by enforcement of the promise.

Bearing these principles in mind, and as explained very well in the majority opinion, it is clear that Wright's commitment to Newman to assume the obligations of fatherhood as regards her son are enforceable. Specifically, it is abundantly clear that Wright should have known that Newman would rely upon his promise, especially after he undertook for ten years to fulfill the obligations of fatherhood. In this regard, it could hardly have escaped Wright's notice that Newman refrained from seeking to identify and obtain support from the child's biological father while Wright was fulfilling his commitment to her.

Promissory estoppel requires only that the reliance by the injured party be reasonable. Moreover, contrary to the dissent's implicit assertion, promissory estoppel does not require that the injured party exhaust all other possible means of obtaining the benefit of the promise from any and all sources before being able to enforce the promise against the promisor. In this regard, it is illogical to argue that Newman, after reasonably relying upon Wright's promise for ten years, can now simply seek to determine the identity of the biological father and collect support from him. . . . This requirement would be an imposing, if not an impossible, burden, and would require Newman not only to identify the father (if possible), but also to locate him, bring a costly legal action against him, and to succeed in that action.

Finally, there can be no doubt that, unless Wright's promise to Newman is enforced, injustice will result. Given the approximately ten years that have passed since the child's birth, during which time Wright, for all purposes, was the child's father, it likely will be impossible for Newman to establish the identity of the child's biological father, bring a successful paternity action, and obtain support from that individual. Consequently, if Wright is allowed to renege on his obligation, Newman likely will not receive any support to assist in the cost of raising her son, despite having been promised the receipt of such by Wright. Furthermore, an even greater injustice will be inflicted upon the boy himself. A child who has been told by any adult, regardless of the existence of a biological relationship, that he will always be able to depend upon the adult for parenting and sustenance, will suffer a great deal when that commitment is broken. And when a child suffers under those circumstances, society-at-large suffers as well.

Because Wright's promise is capable of being enforced under the law, and because I believe that Wright's promise must be enforced in order to prevent a grave miscarriage of justice, I concur fully in the majority opinion.

■ BENHAM, CHIEF JUSTICE, dissenting. I respectfully dissent. While I agree with the majority opinion's statement that liability for child support may be based on promissory estoppel in a case where there is no statutory obligation or express contract, there is a critical element that must be shown for promissory estoppel to apply. In addition to making a showing of expectation and reasonable reliance, a person asserting liability on the theory of promissory estoppel must show that she relied on the promise to her detriment.

The majority states that Newman and her son incurred detriment by refraining from identifying and seeking support from the child's natural father. However, Newman has not alleged, nor does the record reveal, that she does not know the identity of the natural father, nor does she show that the natural father is dead or unable to be found.

Consequently, Newman has not shown that she is now unable to do what she would have had to do ten years ago—seek support from the natural father.

In fact, Wright contends, and Newman does not refute, that Newman severed the relationship and all ties with Wright when the child was approximately three years old. For approximately the next five years, until the child was eight, Newman and Wright did not communicate. Only for the past two years has Wright visited with the child. Importantly, Wright contends that during the past seven years he did not support the child. Thus, taking Wright's undisputed contentions as true, any prejudice incurred by Newman because of the passage of ten years in time is not due to Wright's actions, since, at least for the past seven years, Newman has been in the same situation-receiving no support payments from Wright. Thus, although Wright may be morally obligated to support the ten-year-old child, he is not legally obligated to do so because Newman has failed to show that she or the child incurred any detriment by Wright's failure to fulfill his promise made ten years ago.

For the foregoing reasons, I dissent.

NOTES

(1) *Questions*. What was the promise on which Newman was found to rely? Was Wright's payment of child support to Newman a case of promissory or equitable estoppel? What was the factual basis of the majority's decision to enforce Wright's promise in its entirety? What was the legal basis? What factual and doctrinal concerns trouble the dissenting judge? What is the position of the concurring judge? Is it possible to apply the last sentence of Section 90 without finding reliance first? Is there a hint of that in the concurrence?

(2) *Detriment*. In discussing Section 90, courts often speak of detriment, as in the case above, as if the promisee's reliance were not sufficient. Does Section 90 mention "detriment"?

In Vastoler v. American Can Co., 700 F.2d 916 (3d Cir.1983), Vastoler sued his employer for breach of a promise for greater pension benefits. Vastoler claimed he had relied on the promise when he accepted a promotion from working as an hourly lithographer to become a salaried supervisor. The trial court granted summary judgment for the employer on the ground that, because the promotion had been to Vastoler's financial *advantage*, there was a "complete absence of any detriment, let alone a substantial one." The Court of Appeals reversed, concluding that there was "a genuine issue of material fact concerning Vastoler's detrimental reliance upon the Company's promise." The court noted that Vastoler "asserted that he remained with [the] Company because of his pension benefits." It also found "that the trial judge erred in failing to recognize that absorption of the stress and anxiety inherent in supervisory positions could be one of the factors that constitutes detrimental reliance." This explains, the court said, "why some qualified people do not want to be President of Fortune 500 corporations, nominee for the Presidency of the United States, or foreman of their plants."

Was the court, in effect, applying a rule similar to that of Restatement § 90(2)? The court in *Vastoler* used reliance to enforce a promise where the plaintiff seemed to show little or no reliance. Does the case suggest that courts may in fact be implementing the Farber and Matheson proposal discussed at p. 117.

Cohen v. Cowles Media Company

Minnesota Supreme Court, 1992.
479 N.W.2d 387.

[Dan Cohen, an associate of a gubernatorial candidate, informed reporters for the *Minneapolis Star* and the *Pioneer Press Dispatch* of the arrest for unlawful assembly and the conviction for shoplifting of the opposing candidate for lieutenant governor. Although the reporters promised to keep Cohen's identity confidential, the newspapers' editors overruled those promises. When the stories were published, Cohen was fired by his advertising firm, and he sued the publishers of the papers for breach of contract.

The jury awarded Cohen $200,000 in compensatory damages, but the Minnesota Supreme Court held that, though the papers may have had a moral and ethical commitment to keep their source anonymous, the parties were not thinking in terms of a legally binding contract. It also held that to allow Cohen to recover under the doctrine of promissory estoppel would violate the papers' First Amendment rights. The Supreme Court of the United States granted certiorari and held that the First Amendment was not offended by use of the doctrine to enforce confidentiality agreements because it had only "incidental effects" on news gathering and reporting. It remanded the case.]

■ SIMONETT, JUSTICE. This case comes to us on remand from the United States Supreme Court. We previously held that plaintiff's verdict of $200,000 could not be sustained on a theory of breach of contract. On remand, we now conclude the verdict is sustainable on the theory of promissory estoppel and affirm the jury's award of damages.

Under promissory estoppel, a promise which is expected to induce definite action by the promisee, and does induce the action, is binding if injustice can be avoided only by enforcing the promise. First of all, the promise must be clear and definite. As a matter of law, such a promise was given here. Secondly, the promisor must have intended to induce reliance on the part of the promisee, and such reliance must have occurred to the promisee's detriment. Here again, these facts appear as a matter of law.

This leads to the third step in a promissory estoppel analysis: Must the promise be enforced to prevent an injustice? [T]his is a legal question for the court, as it involves a policy decision.

It is perhaps worth noting that the test is not whether the promise should be enforced to do justice, but whether enforcement is required to prevent an injustice. As has been observed elsewhere, it is easier to recognize an unjust result than a just one, particularly in a morally ambiguous situation. Cf. Edmond Cahn, The Sense of Injustice (1964). The newspapers argue it is unjust to be penalized for publishing the whole truth, but it is not clear this would result in an injustice in this case. For example, it would seem veiling Cohen's identity by publishing the source as someone close to the opposing gubernatorial ticket would have sufficed as a sufficient reporting of the "whole truth."

Cohen, on the other hand, argues that it would be unjust for the law to countenance, at least in this instance, the breaking of a promise. We agree that denying Cohen any recourse would be unjust. What is significant in this case is that the record shows the defendant newspapers themselves believed that they generally must keep promises of confidentiality given a news source. The reporters who actually gave the promises adamantly testified that their promises should have been honored. The editors who countermanded the promises conceded that never before or since have they reneged on a promise of confidentiality. A former Minneapolis Star managing editor testified that the newspapers had "hung Mr. Cohen out to dry because they didn't regard him very highly as a source." The Pioneer Press Dispatch editor stated nothing like this had happened in her 27 years in journalism. The Star Tribune's editor testified that protection of sources was "extremely important." Other experts, too, stressed the ethical importance, except on rare occasions, of keeping promises of confidentiality. It was this long-standing journalistic tradition that Cohen, who has worked in journalism, relied upon in asking for and receiving a promise of anonymity.

Neither side in this case clearly holds the higher moral ground, but in view of the defendants' concurrence in the importance of honoring promises of confidentiality, and absent the showing of any compelling need in this case to break that promise, we conclude that the resultant harm to Cohen requires a remedy here to avoid an injustice. In short, defendants are liable in damages to plaintiff for their broken promise.

NOTE

Questions. The case above was the second time the Supreme Court decided the matter. In its initial decision (*Cohen I*), the Court concluded that although "the newspapers may have had a moral and ethical commitment to keep their sources anonymous, this was not a situation where the parties were thinking in terms of a legally binding commitment." Do you agree? A dissenting judge in *Cohen I* argued that "the news media should be compelled to keep their promises like anyone else" and should therefore be liable "on either a contract or promissory estoppel theory." If, as the majority suggested in *Cohen I,* the newspapers' commitment was only "moral and ethical," was Cohen justified in relying on it?

A context of bargaining for terms gives some assurance that the promisors made them with serious intent. Reliance on a promise may well give some assurance that the recipient took it seriously but does not demonstrate that the promisor *meant* it so. Is there anything in Section 90 that warrants a court taking account of the degree of circumspection that accompanied the making of a promise? As to the principal case, can it be doubted that both Cohen and the reporters took seriously their promise of confidentiality? Might not their understanding be characterized as a bargain?

PROBLEM

The Ear of the Beholder. In 1977, the Township of Ypsilanti, Michigan created an industrial development district for General Motors' Willow Run plant and subsequently gave it a series of property tax abatements. Prior to the 1988 abatements, Harvey Williams, the plant manager, made the following statement as part of General Motors' presentation.

> Good evening, my name is Harvey Williams and I am the plant manager of the Buick Oldsmobile Cadillac group's Willow Run plant. We are pleased to have this opportunity to appear before the Ypsilanti Township Board of Trustees. This application for an industrial facilities exemption certificate is for an investment totalling $75,000,000.00 for machinery and equipment. This will enable our plant to assemble a new full size car in the 1991 model year. This new rear wheel drive car is substantially larger than our current model. And specifically it will generate major booth, oven and conveyor changes in the paint shop and assembly line process, changes in the body, trim and chassis department. This change will also provide additional flexibility at our assembly plant. Essentially we would now have the capability to produce either front or rear wheel drive cars with minimum modifications to our facility. Upon completion of this project and favorable market demand, it will allow Willow Run to continue production and maintain continuous employment for our employees. I would like to introduce Russell Hughes, our controller, who will review pertinent charts pertaining to our request.

In 1991, General Motors announced that, because of record losses, it had decided to consolidate the work done at Willow Run with that done at Arlington, Texas, and to close the Willow Run plant. The Township sought and obtained an injunction barring General Motors from transferring production from the Willow Run plant, and General Motors appealed.

How would you argue the case for the Township? For General Motors? Where in Williams's speech do you find a promise? See Charter Township of Ypsilanti v. General Motors Corp., 506 N.W.2d 556 (Mich.App.1993). See also Local 1330, United Steel Workers v. United States Steel Corp., 631 F.2d 1264 (6th Cir.1980).

D & G Stout, Inc. v. Bacardi Imports, Inc.

United States Court of Appeals, Seventh Circuit, 1991.
923 F.2d 566.

■ CUDAHY, CIRCUIT JUDGE. D & G Stout, Inc., operating at all relevant times under the name General Liquors, Inc. (General), was distributing liquor in the turbulent Indiana liquor market in 1987. When two of its major suppliers jumped ship in early 1987, General faced a critical dilemma: sell out at the best possible price or continue operating on a smaller scale. It began negotiating with another Indiana distributor on the terms of a possible sale. Bacardi Imports, Inc. (Bacardi), was still one of General's remaining major suppliers. Knowing that negotiations were ongoing for General's sale, Bacardi promised that General would continue to act as Bacardi's distributor for Northern Indiana. Based on this representation, General turned down the negotiated selling price it was offered. One week later, Bacardi withdrew its account. Realizing it could no longer continue to operate, General went back to the negotiating table, this time settling for an amount $550,000 below the first offer. The question is whether General can recover the price differential from Bacardi on a theory of promissory estoppel. The district court believed that as a matter of law it could not, and entered summary judgment for defendant Bacardi. We disagree, and so we remand for trial.

I.

General was (and D & G Stout, Inc., is) an Indiana corporation with its main place of business in South Bend. Bacardi is a corporation organized in New York and doing business primarily in Miami, Florida. General served at Bacardi's will as its wholesale distributor in Northern Indiana for over 35 years. During the 1980s, liquor suppliers in Indiana undertook an extensive effort to consolidate their distribution, the effect of which was to reduce the number of distributors in the state from approximately twenty in 1980 to only two in 1990.

General weathered the storm until April 1987, when two of its major suppliers withdrew their lines, taking with them the basis of more than fifty percent of General's gross sales. By June, General recognized that it must choose between selling out and scaling back operations in order to stay in business. Despite the recent setbacks, General calculated that remaining operational was possible as long as it held on to its continuing two major suppliers, Bacardi and Hiram Walker.

About this time (and probably in connection with the same forces concentrating distribution) Bacardi lost its distributor in Indianapolis and southern Indiana. Bacardi decided to convene a meeting on July 9, 1987, of applicants for the open distributorship. General's president, David Stout, attended the meetings as an observer, with no designs on the new opening. Stout did intend to seek assurances from Bacardi about its commitment to General in Northern Indiana. While in Indianapolis, Stout was approached by National Wine & Spirits Company (National), which expressed an interest in buying General. Stout agreed to begin negotiations the following weekend. Stout also received the assurances from Bacardi he sought: after listening to Stout's concerns and hearing about his contemplated sale of General, Bacardi emphatically avowed that it had no intention of taking its line to another distributor in Northern Indiana. This promise was open-ended—no one discussed how long the continuing relationship might last.

During the ensuing two weeks, General carried on negotiations with National to reach a price for the purchase of General's assets. Bacardi kept in close contact with General to find out whether it would indeed sell. The negotiations yielded a final figure for Stout to consider. On July 22 and again on July 23—with negotiations concluded and only the final decision remaining—Stout again sought assurances from Bacardi. The supplier unequivocally reconfirmed its commitment to stay with General, and Stout replied that, as a result, he was going to turn down National's offer and would continue operating. Later on the 23rd, Stout rejected National's offer. That same afternoon, Bacardi decided to withdraw its line from General.

General learned of Bacardi's decision on July 30. The news spread quickly through the industry, and by August 3, Hiram Walker had also pulled its line, expressing a belief that General could not continue without Bacardi on board. By this time, sales personnel were abandoning General for jobs with the two surviving distributors in Indiana (one of which was National). General quickly sought out National to sell its assets, but National's offer was now substantially reduced. The ensuing agreement, executed on August 14 and closed on August 28, included a purchase price $550,000 lower than the one National offered in mid-July. Stout's successor company brought suit under the diversity jurisdiction against Bacardi, claiming that the supplier was liable by reason of promissory estoppel for this decline in the purchase price. Judge Miller entered summary judgment for Bacardi, holding that the promises plaintiff alleged were not the type upon which one may rely under Indiana law. Plaintiff appeals.

II.

We have generally stated General's version of the facts, many of which are undisputed. On appeal, Bacardi does not argue the facts and is apparently willing to rest on Judge Miller's legal analysis. Both parties also agree with Judge Miller that Indiana law governs this case and we do not question this conclusion. Before us then is the legal question whether the plaintiff has alleged any injury which Indiana's law of promissory estoppel redresses.

Indiana has adopted the Restatement's theory of promissory estoppel:

A promise which the promisor should reasonably expect to induce action or forbearance on the part of the promisee and a third person and which does induce such action or forbearance is binding if injustice can be avoided only by the enforcement of the promise. The remedy for breach may be limited as justice requires.

Restatement (Second) of Contracts § 90(1) (1981); Eby v. York-Division, Borg-Warner, 455 N.E.2d 623, 627 (Ind.App.1983); Pepsi-Cola General Bottlers, Inc. v. Woods, 440 N.E.2d 696, 698 (Ind.App.1982). The district judge dismissed the complaint on the ground that Bacardi's alleged promise was not one on which it should reasonably have expected General to rely.

The district court first noted that the relationship between General and Bacardi had always been terminable at will. Because Bacardi's promises that it would continue to use General as its distributor contained no language indicating that they would be good for any specific period,[1] the court reasoned that the relationship remained terminable at will. It then concluded that the promise was not legally enforceable, and thus was not one on which General reasonably might rely. We agree with each of these conclusions but the last. Notwithstanding the continuation of an at-will relationship between Bacardi and General, the promises given between July 9 and July 23 were not without legal effect.

In Indiana, as in many states, an aspiring employee cannot sue for lost wages on an unfulfilled promise of at-will employment. Pepsi-Cola, 440 N.E.2d 696; accord Ewing v. Board of Trustees of Pulaski Memorial Hosp., 486 N.E.2d 1094, 1098 (Ind.App.1985) (employment contract for indefinite tenure is unenforceable for future employment). Because the employer could have terminated the employee without cause at any time after the employment began, the promise of a job brings no expectation of any determinable period of employment or corresponding amount of wages. The promise is therefore unenforceable under either a contract or a promissory estoppel theory in an action for lost wages. Nevertheless, lost wages are not the only source of damages flowing from a broken promise of employment, enforceable or not. Indiana courts acknowledge certain damages as recoverable when the employer breaks a promise of employment, even if the employment is to be terminable at will. For example, in Eby v. York-Division, Borg-Warner, 455 N.E.2d at 627, a plaintiff who gave up a job and moved from Indiana to Florida on a promise of employment sued for recovery of preparation and moving expenses incurred on the basis of the promise. The court found that the defendant could have expected the plaintiff and his wife to move in reliance on the promise of employment and therefore might be liable for reneging. See also Pepsi-Cola, 440 N.E.2d 696).

---

[1]   Given the context of the promise, we see a plausible argument that the promise was one for a term, namely that Bacardi would stay on at least until the rush toward consolidation passed. But the district judge found differently, and we need not question his factual conclusion in light of our legal analysis.

Our review of Indiana law thus leaves us a simple if somewhat crude question: are the damages plaintiff seeks here more like lost future wages or like moving expenses? We can better answer the question if we determine why Indiana draws this distinction. Unlike lost wages, moving expenses represent out-of-pocket losses; they involve a loss of something already possessed. It would be plausible, although not very sophisticated, to distinguish between the loss of something yet to be received and the loss of something already in hand. But this is not precisely where Indiana draws the distinction, nor where we would draw it if it were our choice to make. *Eby* itself involved not only moving expenses, but wages lost at plaintiff's old job during the few days plaintiff was preparing to move. 455 N.E.2d at 625. Those wages were not out-of-pocket losses: plaintiff had no more received those wages than he had received wages from his promised employment.

In fact, the line Indiana draws is between expectation damages and reliance damages. In future wages, the employee has only an expectation of income, the recovery of which promissory estoppel will not support in an at-will employment setting. In wages forgone in order to prepare to move, as in moving expenses themselves, the employee gave up a presently determinate sum for the purpose of relocating. Both moving expenses and forgone wages were the hopeful employee's costs of positioning himself for his new job; moving expenses happen to be out-of-pocket losses, while forgone wages are opportunity costs. Both are reliance costs, not expectancy damages.

Thus, the question has become whether the loss incurred from the price drop was attributable to lost expectations of future profit or resulted from an opportunity forgone in reliance on the promise. At first blush, the injury might seem more like the loss of future wages. Bacardi was a major supplier whose business was extremely valuable to General. While the loss of this "asset" might cause a decline in General's market value as measured by the loss of future income from the sale of Bacardi's products, this loss is not actionable on a promissory estoppel theory. Those damages would presumably be measured by the present value of General's anticipated profit from the sale of Bacardi's products, and Indiana will not grant relief based on promissory estoppel to compensate an aggrieved party for such expectancy damages.

But the fact is that recovery of lost profits is not a question before us. Bacardi's account was never an "asset" that National could acquire by purchasing General. As counsel for the defendant candidly but carefully explained, National never assumed that it would retain the Bacardi account by buying General; in fact, National assumed the opposite. Bacardi's major competitor in the rum distilling business distributed through National, and the two top distillers in a given category of liquor would not choose the same distributor. Both before and after Bacardi decided to withdraw its products, all National wanted from General were its assets other than the Bacardi account. But Bacardi's repudiation of its promise ostensibly affected the price of General's business so drastically because, as everyone in the industry understood, General's option to stay in business independently was destroyed by Bacardi's withdrawal of its account. Thus, through its repudiation, Bacardi destroyed General's negotiating leverage since General no longer had the alternative of continuing as an independent concern. Thus, Bacardi's repudiation turned General's discussions with National from negotiations to buy a going concern into a liquidation sale. Instead of bargaining from strength, knowing it could reject a junk-value offer and carry on its business, General was left with one choice: sell at any price.

Under these facts, General had a reliance interest in Bacardi's promise. General was in lively negotiations with National and it repeatedly informed Bacardi of this fact. General had a business opportunity that all parties knew would be devalued once Bacardi announced its intention to go elsewhere. The extent of that devaluation represents a reliance injury, rather than an injury to General's expectation of future profit. The injury is analogous to the cost of moving expenses incurred as a result of promised employment in *Eby* and *Pepsi-Cola*.

Nor were these promises merely meaningless restatements of an understood at-will relationship. With its current business opportunity, General stood at a crossroads. Circumstances foreshadowed a costly demise for the company, but it was able to negotiate an alternative. Far from confirming the obvious, Bacardi wrote its assurances on a clean slate with full knowledge that General was just as likely to reject the offered relationship as embrace it. That this was the situation is indicated most clearly by Bacardi's repeated calls to check on Stout's impending decision. Bacardi reassured Stout of its commitment in full knowledge that he planned to reject National's offer and with the reasonable expectation that an immediate pull out would severely undermine General's asking price. Like the plaintiffs in *Eby* who moved based on the promise of a job, General incurred a cost in rejecting the deal that was non-recoverable once Bacardi's later decision became known.

There may always exist the potential for a quandary in a promissory estoppel action based on a promise of at-will employment. When could Bacardi terminate the relationship with General without fear of liability for reliance costs, once it made the assurances in question? Obviously we do not hold that General and Bacardi had formed a new, permanent employment relationship. How long an employee can rely on the employer's promise is not a matter we can decide here. The issue is one of reasonable reliance, and to the extent that there might be questions, they should be for trial.

III.

We have, of course, reviewed this case in the posture of summary judgment. General's allegations still must be proven at trial. However, under Indiana law, we think that Bacardi's promise was of a sort on which General might rely, with the possibility of damages for breach. For that reason the judgment of the district court is

Reversed and remanded.

NOTES

(1) *Questions.* What exactly was the promise on which General relied? What was the nature of General's reliance? Was Bacardi's statement that "it had no intention of taking its line to another distributor" a promise? Why did the at-will doctrine not make any reliance by General unreasonable from the start?

(2) *Outcome on Remand.* Judge Cudahy recited General's claim that "Bacardi emphatically avowed that it had no intention of taking its line to another distributor in Northern Indiana." On remand, however, the district court found as a fact that Bacardi's promise had been "contingent on future events" since it was "subject to the conditions that General would continue to meet Bacardi's expectation in sales and no market changes would occur." Nevertheless, the district court held that "the conditional nature of Bacardi's commitment does not make General's reliance unreasonable." The court awarded General "damages incurred in reliance on Bacardi's promise" equal to "the difference between National's initial offer and the final sale price"— a total of $394,050. The damages awarded look suspiciously like the "lost opportunities" denied to the plaintiff in Note 2, p. 19 above. Can you distinguish the two cases with regard to the availability of lost opportunities in one, but not the other?

(3) *At-Will Relationships.* We have already seen some of the difficulties in conceptualizing interests in at-will relationships in Lake Land Employment Group of Akron, LLC v. Columber, p. 83 above. How do you think that the Ohio Supreme Court would have addressed the remedies issue in this case?

PROBLEM

Promising to Undo Harm. As the materials above have suggested, promissory estoppel is commonly invoked to enforce a promise unsupported by consideration: there has been no breach of contract, and yet justice requires a remedy by virtue of the promisee's justified reliance on the promise. Might promissory estoppel function in the context of a failed tort? Consider the reasoning in Barnes v. Yahoo, 570 F.3d 1096 (9th Cir. 2009), described by the court as stemming from "a dangerous, cruel, and highly indecent use of the internet for the apparent purpose of revenge." Id. at 1098. After the plaintiff, Celia Barnes, broke off a lengthy relationship with her boyfriend, he began posting nude picture of Barnes (taken without her knowledge) on a Yahoo website. Posing as Barnes, the boyfriend also directed male correspondents to fraudulent profiles of Barnes suggesting that she was looking for sex. In consequence, Barnes received email and telephonic solicitations from strangers.

In accordance with Yahoo policies, Barnes mailed Yahoo a copy of her photo ID and a signed statement denying her involvement with the profiles and requesting their immediate removal. Yahoo made no response and the undesired advances continued. Barnes sent Yahoo several more written requests over a period of time but received no reply from Yahoo. A day before a local news program was to run a report on the matter, Yahoo's Director of Communications, Ms. Osako, called Barnes and asked her to fax directly the previous statements she had mailed. Osako told Barnes that she would "personally walk the statements over to the division responsible for stopping unauthorized profiles and they would take care of it." The profiles were not taken down, until two months later when Barnes filed a lawsuit against Yahoo.

Barnes sued on two grounds: the tort of "negligent undertaking" and her reliance on Osako's promise to remove the false profiles. Yahoo argued that under the Communications Decency Act of 1996, 47 U.S.C. § 230(c)(1), it was immune from liability for the negligent provision of services that Yahoo undertook to provide. The trial court agreed and dismissed Barnes's tort claim; the Ninth Circuit affirmed because Yahoo came within a statutorily protected role as a publisher.

However, with regard to Yahoo's *promise* to Barnes, the court saw things differently:

> To undertake a thing, within the meaning of the tort, is to do it. Promising is different because it is not synonymous with the performance of the action promised. That is, whereas one cannot undertake to do something without simultaneously doing it, one can, and often does, promise to do something without actually doing it at the same time. Contract liability here would come not from Yahoo's publishing conduct, but from Yahoo's manifest intention to be legally obligated to do something, which happens to be removal of material from publication. Contract law treats the outwardly manifested intention to create an expectation on the part of another as a legally significant event. That event generates a legal duty distinct from the conduct at hand, be it the conduct of a publisher, of a doctor, or of an overzealous uncle.

570 F.3d at 1107. The court then held that insofar as Barnes alleged a breach of contract claim under the theory of promissory estoppel, subsection 230(c)(1) of the Act did not preclude her cause of action. Putting aside the complexities of the Communications Indecency Act, how would you analyze Barnes's claim against Yahoo, applying each of the elements of Section 90?

SECTION 5.   RESTITUTION AS AN ALTERNATIVE BASIS FOR RECOVERY

So far we have been concerned with recovery based on the enforcement of promises. We turn now to an entirely different basis of recovery: restitution. The term is not entirely new; we encountered the concept of restitution in our introductory exploration of damages at p. 13. There we saw that a promisee may be entitled to the return of benefits bestowed upon the promisor, as when the promisee has given the promisor a down payment on a purchase but the promisor subsequently refuses to sell. See Restatement § 344(c).

In this section, we examine restitution not simply as a measure of damage but as a theory of recovery. As stated in the Comment to Section 1 of the Restatement, Third, of Restitution and Unjust Enrichment, "liability in restitution derives from the receipt of a benefit whose retention without payment would result in the unjust enrichment of the defendant at the expense of the claimant." And unjust enrichment may occur even when there has been no promise. The underlying principle is that "gains produced through another's loss are unjust and should be restored." John P. Dawson, *The Self-Serving Intermeddler*, 87 Harv. L. Rev. 1409 (1974).

Benefits whose retention by the recipient would be unjust arise in a number of circumstances. Sometimes benefits have been bestowed in error, as when a person overpays a bill by mistake. The recipient owes restitution in the amount of the excess payment. Mistakes also arise in the employment context, as when Worker A misunderstands the scope of his duties and performs services for which Worker B is being paid. Worker A will have a claim in restitution to recover the money paid to Worker B for the services actually performed by Worker A. See Restatement (Third) of Restitution and Unjust Enrichment § 9 ill. 9. A number of cases deal with the problem of improvements to land mistakenly made on the wrong property; see generally Restatement (Third) of Restitution and Unjust Enrichment § 10 ill. 3 ("Mistaking the location of his own land, A builds a house on property belonging to B. A has a claim in restitution against B.").

A limiting principle, however, is that one who acts *officiously* in conferring a benefit (as opposed to acting erroneously) cannot get restitution from the recipient. One so acting is often called a volunteer or, using a term of legal snark, an *officious intermeddler*. The Restatement (Third) states the applicable rule: absent circumstances that justify a claimant's intervention—and we will look at the possibility of such circumstances in the cases that follow—there is no liability in restitution "for an unrequested benefit voluntarily conferred." § 2(3). Judge Posner approaches the matter from an economic perspective:

> If while you are sitting on your porch drinking Margaritas a trio of itinerant musicians serenades you with mandolin, lute, and hautboy, you have no obligation, in the absence of a contract, to pay them for their performance, no matter how much you enjoyed it. . . . When voluntary transactions are feasible (in economic parlance, when the transactions costs are low), it is better and cheaper to require the parties to make their own terms than for a court to try to fix them—better and cheaper that the musicians should negotiate a price with you in advance

than for them to go running to a court for a judicial determination of the just price of their performance.

Indiana Lumbermens Mut. Ins. Co. v. Reinsurance Results, Inc., 513 F.3d 652, 656–57 (7th Cir.2008).

Yet there may be circumstances that justify compensating a person for benefits received that were not negotiated beforehand. The following case, involving medical services provided to an unconscious accident victim, begins to sort out differences between deserving claimants and officious intermeddlers and highlights the difficulties of determining a just price in cases of unjust enrichment.

A final word regarding the vocabulary of restitution. Sometimes the term *quasi-contract* is used to describe a ground for recovering money in an action at common law, when the claim is not based on a true contract but instead seeks redress for unjust enrichment. *Quantum meruit* ("as much as is deserved") describes a type of action used for centuries in enforcing duties of payment for services. A related action for the worth of goods was *quantum valebant* ("as much as they were worth"). The term quantum meruit is often used interchangeably (if inexactly) with quasi-contract. *Restitution* is a broader term used to embrace all of the grounds for recovery based on unjust enrichment.

Cotnam v. Wisdom

Supreme Court of Arkansas, 1907.
83 Ark. 601, 104 S.W. 164.

Action by F.L. Wisdom and another against T.T. Cotnam, administrator of A.M. Harrison, deceased, for services rendered by plaintiffs as surgeons to defendant's intestate. Judgment for plaintiffs. Defendant appeals. Reversed and remanded.

Instructions 1 and 2, given at the instance of plaintiffs, are as follows: "(1) If you find from the evidence that plaintiffs rendered professional services as physicians and surgeons to the deceased, A.M. Harrison, in a sudden emergency following the deceased's injury in a street car wreck, in an endeavor to save his life, then you are instructed that plaintiffs are entitled to recover from the estate of the said A.M. Harrison such sum as you may find from the evidence is a reasonable compensation for the services rendered. (2) The character and importance of the operation, the responsibility resting upon the surgeon performing the operation, his experience and professional training, and the ability to pay of the person operated upon, are elements to be considered by you in determining what is a reasonable charge for the services performed by plaintiffs in the particular case."

■ HILL, CHIEF JUSTICE. The first question is as to the correctness of [the first] instruction. [T]he facts are that Mr. Harrison was thrown from a street car, receiving serious injuries which rendered him unconscious, and while in that condition the appellees were notified of the accident and summoned to his assistance by some spectator, and performed a difficult operation in an effort to save his life, but they were unsuccessful, and he died without regaining consciousness. The appellant says: "Harrison was never conscious after his head struck the pavement. He did not and could not, expressly or impliedly, assent to the action of the appellees. He was without knowledge or will power. However merciful or benevolent may have been the intention of the appellees, a new rule of law, of contract by implication of law, will have to be established by this court in order to sustain the recovery." Appellant is right in saying that the recovery must be sustained by a contract by implication of law, but is not right in saying that it is a new rule of law, for such contracts are almost as old as the English system of jurisprudence. They are usually called "implied contracts." More properly they should be called "quasi contracts" or "constructive contracts." See 1 Page on Contracts, sec. 14; also 2 Page on Contracts, sec. 771.

The following excerpts from Sceva v. True, 53 N.H. 627, are peculiarly applicable here: "We regard it as well settled by the cases referred to in the briefs of counsel, many of which have been commented on at length by Mr. Shirley for the defendant, that an insane person, an idiot, or a person utterly bereft of all sense and reason by the sudden stroke of an accident or disease may be held liable, in assumpsit, for necessaries furnished to him in good faith while in that unfortunate and helpless condition. And the reasons upon which this rests are too broad, as well as too sensible and humane, to be overborne by any deductions which a refined logic may make from the circumstances that in such cases there can be no contract or promise, in fact, no meeting of the minds of the parties. The cases put it on the ground of an implied contract; and by this is not meant, as the defendant's counsel seems to suppose, an actual contract—that is, an actual meeting of the minds of the parties, an actual, mutual understanding, to be inferred from language, acts, and circumstances by the jury—but a contract and promise, said to be implied by the law, where, in point of fact, there was no contract, no mutual understanding, and so no promise. The defendant's counsel says it is usurpation for the court to hold, as a matter of law, that there is a contract and a promise, when all the evidence in the case shows that there was not a contract, nor the semblance of one. It is doubtless a legal fiction, invented and used for the sake of the remedy. If it was originally usurpation, certainly it has now become very inveterate, and firmly fixed in the body of the law. Illustrations might be multiplied, but enough has been said to show that when a contract or promise implied by law is spoken of, a very different thing is meant from a contract in fact, whether express or tacit. The evidence of an actual contract is generally to be found either in some writing made by the parties, or in verbal communications which passed between them, or in their acts and conduct considered in the light of the circumstances of each particular case. A contract implied by law, on the contrary, rests upon no evidence. It has no actual existence. It is simply a mythical creation of the law. The law says it shall be taken that there was a promise, when in point of fact, there was none. Of course this is not good logic, for the obvious and sufficient reason that it is not true. It is a legal fiction, resting wholly for its support on a plain legal obligation, and a plain legal right. If it were true, it would not be a fiction. There is a class of legal rights, with their correlative legal duties, analogous to the obligations quasi ex contractu of the civil law which seem to lie in the region between contracts on the one hand, and torts on the other, and to call for the application of a remedy not strictly furnished either by actions ex contractu or actions ex delicto. . . . "

In its practical application it sustains recovery for physicians and nurses who render services for infants, insane persons, and drunkards. And services rendered by physicians to persons unconscious or helpless by reason of injury or sickness are in the same situation as those rendered to persons incapable of contracting, such as the classes above described. The court was therefore right in giving the instruction in question.

There was evidence in this case proving that it was customary for physicians to graduate their charges by the ability of the patient to pay, and hence, in regard to that element, this case differs from the Alabama case [Morrisette v. Wood, 123 Ala. 384, 26 So. 307]. This could not apply to a physician called in an emergency by some bystander to attend a stricken man whom he never saw or heard of before; and certainly the unconscious patient could not, in fact or in law, be held to have contemplated what charges the physician might properly bring against him. In order to admit such testimony, it must be assumed that the surgeon and patient each had in contemplation that the means of the patient would be one factor in determining the amount of the charge for the services rendered. While the law may admit such evidence as throwing light upon the contract and indicating what was really in contemplation when it was made, yet a different question is presented when there is no contract to be ascertained or construed, but a mere fiction of law creating a contract where none existed in order that there might be a remedy for a right. This fiction merely requires a reasonable compensation for the services rendered. The services are the same be the patient prince or pauper, and for them the surgeon is entitled to fair compensation for his time, service, and skill. It was therefore error to admit this evidence, and to instruct the jury in the second instruction that in determining what was a reasonable charge they could consider the "ability to pay of the person operated upon."

It was improper to let it go to the jury that Mr. Harrison was a bachelor and that his estate was left to nieces and nephews. This was relevant to no issue in the case, and its effect might well have been prejudicial. While this verdict is no higher than some of the evidence would justify, yet it is much higher than some of the other evidence would justify, and hence it is impossible to say that this was a harmless error.

Judgment is reversed, and cause remanded.

■ BATTLE and WOOD, JJ., concur in sustaining the recovery, and in holding that it was error to permit the jury to consider the fact that his estate would go to collateral heirs; but they do not concur in holding that it was error to admit evidence of the value of the estate, and instructing that it might be considered in fixing the charge.

NOTES

(1) *Questions.* Would the result have been different if Dr. Wisdom had treated Harrison in response to a call from Harrison's daughter, who had said, "Give him the best care you can and I will pay you for it"? What fee would Dr. Wisdom have been entitled to from the daughter under those circumstances? For a case rejecting Cotnam v. Wisdom on the issue of the admissibility of the patient's ability to pay, see In re Agnew's Estate, 231 N.Y.S. 4 (Surrogate's Ct.1928). Are there grounds, policy or otherwise, for admitting such evidence? The Restatement (Third) of Restitution and Unjust Enrichment agrees with the rule in the principal case that "[u]njust enrichment [in such circumstances] is measured by a reasonable charge." § 20.

Would the result have been different if *you* had seen Harrison lying injured in the street, stopped to treat him, and had done so successfully? Recovery? What underlies Comment b of the Restatement (Third) of Restitution and Unjust Enrichment § 20 cmt. *b* (Protection Of Another's Life Or Health), which observes that even though a rescue by a bystander "may confer a benefit of inestimable value," the heroic bystander receives nothing? Is the problem one of calculating the services provided by an amateur? A dissatisfaction with uncompensated labor? Or, as suggested by Comment b to § 20, is there something morally troubling about paying for all services? Comment b specifically notes:

> The imposition of restitutionary liability in such circumstances... transforms an act of self-sacrifice into a contentious exchange of values. The law avoids these unedifying consequences by presuming that an emergency rescue is a gratuitous act. The heroic bystander receives nothing; the heroic professional receives a "reasonable and customary charge" for professional services, but nothing extra for heroism.

Restatement (Third) of Restitution and Unjust Enrichment § 20 cmt. b (2001). Recall the court's argument in *Webb* that saving life has "material, pecuniary" value, supported by the fact that "physicians practice their profession charging for services rendered in saving life." Would Webb have had a claim against McGowin in restitution?

(2) *The Protection of Property.* The *Webb* court relied upon Boothe v. Fitzpatrick, the case of the promise "to pay for the past keeping of a bull which had escaped and been cared for." See p. 76. Aside from the promise by the owner of the bull, would the keeper of the bull have had a claim against its owner? Should emergency interventions by bystanders to protect property be treated differently than interventions to protect a person's life or health?

Might the answer depend on the nature of the property—livestock, chattels, or real property? What is the appropriate measure of recovery in such a case? See Restatement (Third) of Restitution and Unjust Restitution § 21 (Protection Of Another's Property). Note under the Restatement (Third), restitution for services provided to protect health *or* property is available only when "circumstances justify the decision to intervene without request." § 21(1). Why the limiting proviso?

(3) *Comparative Recompense.* Consider the doctrine known to civil law systems (those derived from Roman law) as *negotiorum gestio* ("management of the affairs [of another]"). It provides that a person who, without invitation but in compelling circumstances, takes charge of the affairs of another is entitled to compensation for services rendered in the other's interest. How does this doctrine differ from that in Cotnam v. Wisdom? What problems do you see in the application of such a doctrine? See Samuel J. Stoljar, *Restitution—Unjust Enrichment and Negotiorum Gestio*, in International Encyclopedia of Comparative Law (1984).

PROBLEM

The Suggestion Box. Schott, an employee of Westinghouse, twice submitted an idea concerning the construction of circuit breaker panels pursuant to a Westinghouse program inviting its employees to submit suggestions for cash awards. On the suggestion form, above the line for the employee's signature, appeared the stipulation, "I agree that the decision of the local Suggestion Committee on all matters pertaining to this suggestion will be final." The Committee twice rejected Schott's suggestion, stating that it would require heavy preliminary expenditures but would be reconsidered if circuit breaker redesign was undertaken for other reasons. Within a year, however, Westinghouse had made the suggested change but refused to pay Schott, explaining that it had been made as "the result of independent action taken without knowledge of your suggestion." What factors weigh in Schott's favor in an action against Westinghouse for unjust enrichment? What facts favor Westinghouse? Might Schott have a claim for breach of contract? In Schott v. Westinghouse Electric Corp., 259 A.2d 443 (Pa.1969), two judges answered the last question with a "Yes."

Callano v. Oakwood Park Homes Corp.

Superior Court of New Jersey, 1966.
91 N.J.Super. 105, 219 A.2d 332.

■ COLLESTER, JUDGE A.D. Defendant Oakwood Park Homes Corp., (Oakwood) appeals from a judgment of $475 entered in favor of plaintiffs Julia Callano and Frank Callano in the Monmouth County District Court.

The case was tried below on an agreed stipulation of facts. Oakwood, engaged in the construction of a housing development, in December 1961 contracted to sell a lot with a house to be erected thereon to Bruce Pendergast, who resided in Waltham, Massachusetts. In May 1962, prior to completion of the house, the Callanos, who operated a plant nursery, delivered and planted shrubbery pursuant to a contract with Pendergast. A representative of Oakwood had knowledge of the planting.

Pendergast never paid the Callanos the invoice price of $497.95. A short time after the shrubbery was planted Pendergast died. Thereafter, on July 10, 1962 Oakwood and Pendergast's estate cancelled the contract of sale. Oakwood had no knowledge of Pendergast's failure to pay the Callanos. On July 16, 1962 Oakwood sold the Pendergast property, including the shrubbery located thereon, to Richard and Joan Grantges for an undisclosed amount.

The single issue is whether Oakwood is obligated to pay plaintiffs for the reasonable value of the shrubbery on the theory of *quasi*-contractual liability. Plaintiffs contend that defendant was unjustly enriched when the Pendergast contract to purchase the property was cancelled and that an agreement to pay for the shrubbery is implied in law. Defendant argues that the facts of the case do not support a recovery by plaintiffs on the theory of *quasi*-contract.

Contracts implied by law, more properly described as *quasi* or constructive contracts, are a class of obligations which are imposed or created by law without regard to the assent of the party bound, on the ground that they are dictated by reason and justice. They rest solely on a legal fiction and are not contract obligations at all in the true sense, for there is no agreement; but they are clothed with the semblance of contract for the purpose of the remedy, and the obligation arises not from consent, as in the case of true contracts, but from the law or natural equity. Courts employ the fiction of *quasi* or constructive contract with caution. 17 C.J.S. Contracts § 6, pp. 566–570 (1963).

In cases based on *quasi*-contract liability, the intention of the parties is entirely disregarded, while in cases of express contracts and contracts implied in fact the intention is of the essence of the transaction. In the case of actual contracts the agreement defines the duty, while in the case of *quasi*-contracts the duty defines the contract. Where a case shows that it is the duty of the defendant to pay, the law imparts to him a promise to fulfill that obligation. The duty which thus forms the foundation of a *quasi*-contractual obligation is frequently based on the doctrine of unjust enrichment. It rests on the equitable principle that a person shall not be allowed to enrich himself unjustly at the expense of another, and on the principle of whatsoever it is certain a man ought to do, that the law supposes him to have promised to do. St. Paul Fire, etc., Co. v. Indemnity Ins. Co. of No. America, 32 N.J. 17, 22, 158 A.2d 825 (1960).

The key words are *enrich* and *unjustly*. To recover on the theory of *quasi*-contract the plaintiffs must prove that defendant was enriched, *viz.*, received a benefit, and that retention of the benefit without payment therefor would be unjust.

It is conceded by the parties that the value of the property, following the termination of the Pendergast contract, was enhanced by the reasonable value of the shrubbery at the stipulated sum of $475. However, we are not persuaded that the retention of such benefit by defendant before it sold the property to the Grantges was inequitable or unjust.

Quasi-contractual liability has found application in a myriad of situations. See Woodruff, Cases on Quasi-Contracts (3d ed. 1933). However, a common thread runs throughout its application where liability has been successfully asserted, namely, that the plaintiff expected remuneration from the defendant, or if the true facts were known to plaintiff, he would have expected remuneration from defendant, at the time the benefit was conferred. See Rabinowitz v. Mass. Bonding & Insurance Co., 119 N.J.L. 552, 197 A. 44 (E. & A. 1937); Power-Matics, Inc. v. Ligotti, 79 N.J.Super. 294, 191 A.2d 483 (App.Div.1963); Shapiro v. Solomon, 42 N.J.Super. 377, 126 A.2d 654 (App.Div.1956). It is further noted that *quasi*-contract cases involve either some direct relationship between the parties or a mistake on the part of the person conferring the benefit.

In the instant case the plaintiffs entered into an express contract with Pendergast and looked to him for payment. They had no dealings with defendant, and did not expect remuneration from it when they provided the shrubbery. No issue of mistake on the part of plaintiffs is involved. Under the existing circumstances we believe it would be inequitable to hold defendant liable. Plaintiffs' remedy is against Pendergast's estate, since they contracted with and expected payment to be made by Pendergast when the benefit was conferred. A plaintiff is not entitled to employ the legal fiction of *quasi*-contract to "substitute one promisor or debtor for another." Cascaden v. Magryta, 247 Mich. 267, 225 N.W. 511, 512 (Sup.Ct.1929).

Plaintiffs place reliance on De Gasperi v. Valicenti, 198 Pa.Super. 455, 181 A.2d 862 (Super.Ct.1962), where recovery was allowed on the theory of unjust enrichment. We find the case inapposite. It is clear that recovery on *quasi*-contract was permitted there because of a fraud perpetrated by defendants. There is no contention of fraud on the part of Oakwood in the instant case.

Recovery on the theory of *quasi*-contract was developed under the law to provide a remedy where none existed. Here, a remedy exists. Plaintiffs may bring their action against Pendergast's estate. We hold that under the facts of this case defendant was not unjustly enriched and is not liable for the value of the shrubbery.

Reversed.

NOTES

(1) *Questions.* Which, if any, of the players in the case—Oakwood, the Grantges, the Pendergast estate—were enriched by the transaction? Why did the Callanos not sue Pendergast's estate? Why not the Grantges? How might the Callanos have better protected themselves in this transaction? You may find it useful to know that ordinarily contractual obligations survive the death of a party to that contract and become obligations of the estate (but no further; if the estate's assets are inadequate to meet an obligation, the heirs and executors will not as such become liable).

(2) *The Case of the Contractor's Claim.* In Johnson v. Larson, 779 N.W.2d 412 (S.D. 2010), Larson arranged that Johnson would remove rock from his land in exchange for the value of the rock, with a later agreement that Johnson could store the rock on Larson's land in exchange for installing drain tile. Some time later, Penny asked whether he could have the rock; believing that Johnson had abandoned the rock, Larson said yes, and Penny removed the rock gratis. Naturally, Johnson then showed up, demanding the rock. Left rockless, Johnson then sued Larson and Penny. Were Penny and Larson unjustly enriched?

The court held that Johnson had no cause of action in unjust enrichment against Larson; "there was no room for a court to imply a promise by Larson to pay Johnson, as the parties expressly fixed their rights and obligations: Johnson's remedy lay in a claim for breach of contract." 779 N.W.2d at 416. In contrast, the court held that there was no contract between Johnson and Penny, so an unjust enrichment action was available—indeed, "[t]he transfer between Johnson and Penny is the very type of event contemplated by the doctrine of unjust enrichment." 779 N.W.2d at 417.

Can this case be distinguished from *Callano*? One writer suggests:

> Where benefit is conferred on a stranger through performance of one's own contract various intermediate solutions could be thought of. The most plausible would be to permit restitution of the benefit to the stranger when the remedy of the gain-producer against his own obligor had failed or was certain to fail. Restitution would then serve as a surrogate, being held in reserve to insure the gain-producer against deficits in the return promised him.

John P. Dawson, *The Self-Serving Intermeddler*, 87 Harv. L. Rev. 1409, 1457–58 (1974). Are *Callano* and *Johnson* consistent with this suggestion? For an analysis in economic terms, see Anthony T. Kronman and Richard A. Posner, The Economics of Contract Law 59–64 (1979).

(3) *Measure of Recovery.* If recovery is allowed in cases like *Callano*, how should it be measured? The Restatement offers two alternatives: "the reasonable value to the [defendant] of what he received in terms of what it would have cost him to obtain it from a person in the claimant's position" and "the extent to which the [defendant's] property has increased in value or his other interests advanced." See Restatement § 371. Which measure would be more generous? Do we know that on selling the lot to the Grantges, Oakwood got a price enhanced by the value of the shrubbery? Should it matter?

(4) *Mechanics' Liens. Callano* introduces a problem of great practical importance: the rights of subcontractors on construction jobs. Commonly in such cases, two contracts are involved, one between an owner and a general contractor, and another between the general contractor and a subcontractor. It is clear that if, after the subcontractor has performed, it is not paid by the general contractor, it has no contractual right to payment from the owner. It is also clear, under reasoning like that in *Callano*, that it has no right to restitution from the owner, even though its work has conferred a benefit on the owner.

Every state legislature has addressed the situation in statutes commonly called "mechanics' lien" laws. They protect laborers, suppliers, contractors and others who make improvements on real property, by giving them a lien on that property to secure payment for those improvements.

Why did the Callanos and Johnson not have mechanics' liens on the properties concerned? Although a New Jersey statute provides for a lien on property for improvements, including "planting thereon any shrubs," it applies only to "debts contracted by the owner." N.J. Stat. Ann. § 2A:44A–4. Oakwood, not Pendergast, was the "owner" of the property. Similarly, a Tennessee statute provides for a lien where improvements have been made on a house, but only by "contract with the owner or the owner's agent." Tenn.Code Ann. § 66–11–102(a).

(5) *Wrestling with Unjust Enrichment.* The court in *Callano* observed that Oakwood might have been accountable if it had perpetrated a fraud. Compare Ventura v. Titan Sports, Inc., 65 F.3d 725 (8th Cir.1995). Jesse Ventura, in 1987 a wrestler and "heel commentator," hired Barry Bloom to negotiate his contract with Titan Sports, owners of the World Wrestling Federation. (According to the court, "[a] heel commentator is a color commentator who plays the role of 'the bad guy.' ") Bloom asked for royalties for any videotape sales in which Ventura appeared but was told that only "feature" performers got royalties. Wanting to secure the job with Titan, Ventura agreed to waive any claim to royalties. When Ventura found out that other non-feature performers were getting royalties, he brought an action for fraud, misappropriation of publicity rights, and unjust enrichment. The jury awarded Ventura $800,000 on the latter claim. On appeal, Titan argued that the express contractual provision waiving royalties barred Ventura's claim for unjust enrichment. *Held*: Affirmed. The court said: "Had Ventura known that Titan did not abide by its stated policy, he would not have accepted a deal which did not compensate him for [the sale of his likeness]. . . . The fraud rescinded or set aside the contract, opening the door to his quantum meruit claim."

Pyeatte v. Pyeatte

Court of Appeals of Arizona, 1982.
661 P.2d 196.

■ CORCORAN, JUDGE. This is an appeal by the husband from an award of $23,000 in favor of the wife as ordered in a decree of dissolution. Two issues are before us: (1) The validity of an oral agreement entered into by the husband and wife during the marriage, whereby each spouse agreed to provide in turn the sole support for the marriage while the other spouse was obtaining further education; and, (2) whether the wife is entitled to restitution for benefits she provided for her husband's educational support in a dissolution action which follows closely upon the husband's graduation and admission to the Bar. The word "agreement" is used as a term of reference for the stated understanding between the husband and wife and not as a legal conclusion that the agreement is enforceable at law as a contract.

The husband, H. Charles Pyeatte (appellant), and the wife, Margrethe May Pyeatte (appellee), were married in Tucson on December 27, 1972. At the time of the marriage both had received bachelor's degrees. Appellee was coordinator of the surgical technical program at Pima College. Appellant was one of her students. In early 1974, the parties had discussions and reached an agreement concerning postgraduate education for both of them.

Appellee testified that they agreed she "would put him through three years of law school without his having to work, and when he finished, he would put [her] through for [her] masters degree without [her] having to work."

Appellant concedes the existence of an agreement. Although there was a claim by appellant that his agreement with appellee was qualified by certain contingencies, there is substantial evidence in the record to support the findings made by the trial court after the trial:

The Court is of the opinion that there was a definite agreement that the respondent [appellant] would pay for the support of petitioner [appellee] while the petitioner [appellee] obtained her master's degree without her having to work. The Court is further of the opinion that there was no contingency expressed or implied that this would not be carried out or enforced in the event of a divorce. Petitioner [appellee] carried out her part of the agreement in supporting the respondent [appellant] while he obtained his law degree.

Appellant attended law school in Tucson, Arizona, from 1974 until his graduation. He was admitted to the State Bar shortly thereafter.

After appellant's admission to the Bar, the couple moved to Prescott, Arizona, where appellant was employed by a law firm. Both parties realized that appellant's salary would not be sufficient to support the marriage and pay for appellee's education for a master's degree simultaneously. Appellee then agreed to defer her plans for a year or two until her husband got started in his legal career. In the meantime, she obtained part-time employment as a teacher.

In April 1978, appellant told appellee that he no longer wanted to be married to her, and in June of 1978, she filed a petition for dissolution. Trial was had in March of 1979, and a decree of dissolution was granted.

At the time of the trial, there was little community property and no dispute as to division of any community or separate property. Spousal maintenance was neither sought by nor granted to appellee.

The trial court determined that there was an agreement between the parties, that appellee fully performed her part of that agreement, that appellant had not performed his part of the agreement, and that appellee had been damaged thereby.

Based on appellee's expert testimony on the cost of furthering her education, in accordance with the agreement, the trial court awarded judgment of $23,000 against appellant as damages for breach of contract, with additional directions that the judgment be payable through the court clerk on a quarterly basis in a sum of not less than ten percent of appellant's net quarterly income.

The trial court directed appellant to use his best efforts to produce income and to keep accurate records of his income-producing activities, which records would be available to appellee upon request but not more frequently than on a quarterly basis. The court also retained jurisdiction of the case for the purpose of supervising the administration of the payment of the judgment and the keeping of records by the appellant. Appellant filed a timely notice of appeal from the judgment.

On appeal, appellant argues that the agreement did not rise to the level of a binding contract because, among other things, the terms thereof were not definite and could not be legally enforced.

Appellee advances three theories as grounds upon which the trial court's award should be upheld:

1.   The agreement between the parties was a binding contract. Appellant's failure to perform after appellee had fully performed her obligations renders appellant liable in damages.

2.   Appellant's education was obtained through the exhaustion of the community resources. Appellee argues that her financing of appellant's education was an extraordinary expenditure and that the trial court's award should be sustained as a lien upon appellant's separate estate to the extent of those expenditures pursuant to A.R.S. § 25–318.

3.   If the agreement is not enforceable as a binding contract, appellee is nevertheless entitled to restitution in quantum meruit to prevent appellant's unjust enrichment because he received his education at appellee's expense.

We will address each argument in turn.

The Contract Claim

Although the terms and requirements of an enforceable contract need not be stated in minute detail, it is fundamental that, in order to be binding, an agreement must be definite and certain so that the liability of the parties may be exactly fixed. Terms necessary for the required definiteness frequently include time of performance, place of performance, price or compensation, penalty provisions, and other material requirements of the agreement.

Upon examining the parties' agreement in this instance, it is readily apparent that a sufficient mutual understanding regarding critical provisions of their agreement did not exist. For example, no agreement was made regarding the time when appellee would attend graduate school and appellant would be required to assume their full support.

The agreement lacks a number of other essential terms which prevent it from becoming binding. Appellee's place of education is not mentioned at all, yet there are masters programs available throughout the country. Whether or not they would be required to relocate in another state should she choose an out-of-state program was not agreed upon. Appellant testified at trial that "that particular problem was really never resolved." Nor was there any agreement concerning the cost of the program to which appellee would be entitled under this agreement. There can be several thousand dollars' difference in tuition, fees, and other expenses between any two masters programs depending upon resident status, public versus private institutions, and other factors. Appellant testified that at the time of the "contract," neither he nor his wife had any idea as to the specific dollar amounts that would be involved.

Appellee urges us to enforce this agreement because contracts should be interpreted, whenever reasonable, in such a way as to uphold the contract, and that this is particularly true where there has been performance by one party. We are aware of these general legal concepts, and also note that reasonableness can be implied by the courts when interpreting agreements.

The court's function, however, cannot be that of contract maker. Nor can the court create a contract simply to accomplish a purportedly good purpose. [citations omitted] Our review of the record persuades us that the essential terms and requirements of this agreement were not sufficiently definite so that the obligations of the parties to the agreement could be determined:

> A party will not be subjected to a contractual obligation where the character of that obligation is so indefinite and uncertain as to its terms and requirements that it is impossible to state with certainty the obligations involved.

Aztec Film Productions v. Tucson Gas and Electric Co., 11 Ariz. App. 241, 243, 463 P.2d 547, 549 (1969).

Based on its ruling that the agreement was enforceable, the trial court awarded appellee $23,000, the amount established by expert testimony as necessary to further her education in accordance with the agreement. On the basis of our determination that the agreement in this case is unenforceable, there can be no recovery for amounts necessary to further appellee's education.

Having decided that the agreement was not enforceable for the reasons stated above, we need not consider appellant's other arguments regarding that issue.

Statutory Reimbursement under A.R.S. § 25–318

Appellee advances that she is entitled to reimbursement of her expenditures for appellant's legal education under A.R.S. § 25–318. This section provides in part that the court, in disposing of property in a dissolution, may consider "excessive or abnormal expenditures of community, joint tenancy and other property held in common."

She contends that appellant left the marriage with an asset—his legal education—which was obtained by the exhaustion of the community. Appellee argues that her husband's education was an extraordinary expenditure which inured to his benefit and for which she paid and that she is entitled to equitable reimbursement in the form of a lien upon appellant's separate estate under A.R.S. § 25–318. We do not agree. A.R.S. § 25–318 concerns disposition of property, and we have already decided that one spouse's education cannot be characterized as property to be divided between the parties. Wisner v. Wisner, 129 Ariz. 333, 631 P.2d 115 (App. 1981).

The question of characterizing education and professional degrees or licenses as marital property is one which has been addressed in the context of dissolution in this and a number of other jurisdictions. This 352 court in Wisner adopted the view of the majority of those jurisdictions which have considered the issue and rejected the argument that an educational degree, professional license or the increased earning potential each represents is community property subject to valuation and division upon dissolution.

The Restitution Claim

Appellee's last contention is that the trial court's award should be affirmed as an equitable award of restitution on the basis of unjust enrichment. She argues that appellant's education, which she subsidized and which he obtained through the exhaustion of community assets constitutes a benefit for which he must, in equity, make restitution.

Contracts implied-in-law or quasi-contracts, also called constructive contracts, are inferred by the law as a matter of reason and justice from the acts and conduct of the parties and circumstances surrounding the transactions . . . and are imposed for the purpose of bringing about justice without reference to the intentions of the parties.

The mere fact that one party confers a benefit on another, however, is not of itself sufficient to require the other to make restitution. Retention of the benefit must be unjust.

Historically, restitution for the value of services rendered has been available upon either an "implied-in-fact" contract or upon quasi-contractual grounds. D. Dobbs, Remedies § 4.2 at 237 (1973); 1 Williston,

Contracts § 3 and 3A at 10–15 (3d ed. 1957). An implied-in-fact contract is a true contract, differing from an express contract only insofar as it is proved by circumstantial evidence rather than by express written or oral terms. In contrast, a quasi-contract is not a contract at all, but a duty imposed in equity upon a party to repay another to prevent his own unjust enrichment. . . . To support her claim for restitution on the basis of an implied-in-fact contract, appellee must demonstrate the elements of a binding contract. For the reasons we have previously discussed, we cannot find the necessary mutual assent or certainty as to the critical terms of the agreement sufficient to establish such a contract.

While a quasi-contractual obligation may be imposed without regard to the intent of the parties, such an obligation will be imposed only if the circumstances are such that it would be unjust to allow retention of the benefit without compensating the one who conferred it. See Williston, supra. One circumstance under which a duty to compensate will be imposed is when there was an expectation of payment or compensation for services at the time they were rendered.

[A]n obligation to pay, ordinarily, will not be implied in fact or by law if it is clear that there was indeed no expectation of payment, that a gratuity was intended to be conferred, that the benefit was conferred officiously, or that the question of payment was left to the unfettered discretion of the recipient. Osborn v. Boeing Airplane Co., 309 F.2d at 102.

Although we found that the spousal agreement failed to meet the requirements of an enforceable contract, the agreement still has importance in considering appellee's claim for unjust enrichment because it both evidences appellee's expectation of compensation and the circumstances which make it unjust to allow appellant to retain the benefits of her extraordinary efforts.

[The court next addresses whether restitution or quasi-contract based on unjust enrichment is appropriately applied in marital context.]

The Measure of Recovery

A variety of methods of computing the unjust enrichment may be employed in ascertaining the working spouse's compensable interest in the attainment of the student spouse's education, degree or license.

The award to appellee should be limited to the financial contribution by appellee for appellant's living expenses and direct educational expenses.

The portion of the judgment in the amount of $23,000 is reversed and remanded for proceedings in accordance with this opinion.

NOTES

(1) *Three Claims.* What was the fatal infirmity in Margrethe's breach of contract claim against Charles? In response to Margrethe's urging the

court to fix the problem through interpretation, the court observed that its function "cannot be that of a contract maker." Can you explain the doctrinal logic of the court's response?

Would a claim by Margrethe based on promissory estoppel have been a more successful approach? If the judge was sympathetic to Margrethe's situation, why didn't he simply divide the couple's property to reflect an off-set for her contributions to Charles's degree?

Why does the court find unjust enrichment is the appropriate basis for Margrethe's claim? How was Charles's enrichment *unjust*? What did the lower court's award of $23,000 represent? How should the lower court calculate Margrethe's recovery for unjust enrichment? Suppose that the Pyeattes had not divorced until ten years after Charles' graduation from law school, during which time Margrethe had lived the life of a successful law firm partner's spouse. How might such facts affect her restitutionary claim? See Cal. Fam. Code § 2641 (Community Contributions to Education or Training).

Margrethe's third (and losing) claim drew from an Arizona statute permitting a court, when disposing of a divorcing couple's property, to reimburse one spouse for "excessive or abnormal expenditure of [the couple's] community property" by the other. A more complete study of community property awaits you in your Property course; for our purposes now, the term refers to a special category of property (money or assets) that is under the legal control of *both* spouses (the community) during the marriage. What is the nature of the statutory claim offered by A.R.S. § 25–318?

Despite the court's endorsement of restitution on the *Pyeatte* facts, it held that the reimbursement statute was inapplicable in this case. In Arizona, a community property state, a degree earned by one spouse during a marriage is not considered property subject to division upon divorce. While this is the rule in almost every state, note that it is *not* the rule in New York, where a law (or other) degree, or even a career, earned during the marriage by one spouse, with contributions made by the other, may be considered "marital property" subject to monetary evaluation and division upon divorce. See O'Brien v. O'Brien, 66 N.Y.2d 576 (1985).

(2) *Restitution Between Spouses.* Restitutionary claims between spouses have traditionally failed because the services of each are presumed to be gratuitous. As the Supreme Court of North Carolina explained, the rule denying restitution "is particularly applicable where a husband makes improvements to his wife's land because of the presumption that the improvements constitute a gift." Wright v. Wright, 289 S.E.2d 347 (N.C.1982). Historically, the presumption of a gift extended to other family relationships as well. The Pennsylvania Supreme Court refused to grant restitution to an adult son despite evidence of his father's promise to pay for the son's labor, observing that "we do not infer a contract of hiring, because the principle of family affection is sufficient to account for the family association. . . ." Hertzog v. Hertzog, 29 Pa. 465, 468 (Pa.1857). See generally, Hendrik Hartog, Someday All of This Will Be Yours: A History of Inheritance and Old Age (2012).

(3) *Restitution Between Cohabitants.* When a sexual relationship between unmarried cohabitants was included among the benefits bestowed, courts traditionally refused to grant restitution on public policy grounds. See Hewitt v. Hewitt, 394 N.E.2d 1204 (Ill.1979). Restitution has been permitted when sexual services were found to be severable from other forms of enrichment, such as improvements to property. In Watts v. Watts, 405 N.W.2d 303 (Wis.1987), the Supreme Court of Wisconsin held that "unmarried cohabitants may raise claims based upon unjust enrichment following the termination of their relationship where one of the parties attempts to retain an unreasonable amount of the property acquired through the efforts of both."

In 2011, section 28(1) of the Restatement (Third) of Restitution and Unjust Enrichment recognized that "substantial, uncompensated contributions in the form of property or services" made by one person "living together in a relationship resembling marriage" to the asset of the other person "has a claim in restitution against the owner as necessary to prevent unjust enrichment upon the dissolution of the relationship."

CHAPTER 2

CREATING CONTRACTUAL OBLIGATIONS

SECTION 1.   THE NATURE OF ASSENT

It is said that "a contract may be made in any manner sufficient to show agreement," (UCC § 2–204(1)), but how agreement can be demonstrated is not always obvious. Typically, we conclude that agreement to a transaction is present when both parties have manifested assent to it. See Restatement § 17(1). What kind of assent to a bargain is necessary to bind a party? Different answers are given by two contrasting theories of contract, commonly described as "objective" and "subjective." They are illustrated by the following excerpts taken from opinions by two distinguished jurists, Judge Learned Hand[a] and his colleague on the bench Judge Jerome Frank,[b] concurring in a case in which Hand wrote the opinion of the court.

According to Hand:

> A contract has, strictly speaking, nothing to do with the personal, or individual, intent of the parties. A contract is an obligation attached by the mere force of law to certain acts of the parties, usually words, which ordinarily accompany and represent a known intent. If, however, it were proved by twenty bishops that either party when he used the words intended something else than the usual meaning which the law imposes upon them, he would still be held, unless there were some mutual mistake or something else of the sort.

Hotchkiss v. National City Bank of New York, 200 F. 287, 293 (S.D.N.Y.1911).

According to Frank:

> In the early days of this century a struggle went on between the respective proponents of two theories of

---

[a]   Learned Hand (1872–1961) was admitted to the practice of law in New York in 1897, appointed to the United States District Court for the Southern District of New York in 1909 and to the United States Court of Appeals for the Second Circuit in 1924. He retired in 1961, after 52 years of service as a federal judge. Justice Cardozo called him "the greatest living American jurist," and he was so regarded by many of his contemporaries. His extrajudicial utterances may be sampled in The Spirit of Liberty (1952) and The Bill of Rights (1958).

[b]   Jerome New Frank (1889–1957) practiced in Chicago and New York for more than twenty years before going to Washington in 1933, where he served first as a government lawyer and then as a member and later chairman of the Securities and Exchange Commission. In 1941 he was appointed to the United States Court of Appeals for the Second Circuit. He also lectured at the Yale Law School and was associated with the philosophy of law known as "legal realism." One of his best known books is Law and the Modern Mind (1930).

contracts, (a) the 'actual intent' theory—or 'meeting of the minds' or 'will' theory—and (b) the so-called 'objective' theory.[1] Without doubt, the first theory had been carried too far: Once a contract has been validly made, the courts attach legal consequences to the relation created by the contract, consequences of which the parties usually never dreamed—as, for instance, where situations arise which the parties had not contemplated. As to such matters, the 'actual intent' theory induced much fictional discourse which imputed to the parties intentions they plainly did not have.

But the objectivists also went too far. They tried (1) to treat virtually all the varieties of contractual arrangements in the same way, and (2), as to all contracts in all their phases, to exclude, as legally irrelevant, consideration of the actual intention of the parties or either of them, as distinguished from the outward manifestation of that intention. The objectivists transferred from the field of torts that stubborn anti-subjectivist, the 'reasonable man'; so that, in part at least, advocacy of the 'objective' standard in contracts appears to have represented a desire for legal symmetry, legal uniformity, a desire seemingly prompted by aesthetic impulses. Whether (thanks to the 'subjectivity' of the jurymen's reactions and other factors) the objectivists' formula, in its practical workings, could yield much actual objectivity, certainty, and uniformity may well be doubted. At any rate, the sponsors of complete 'objectivity' in contracts largely won out in the wider generalizations of the Restatement of Contracts and in some judicial pronouncements.

Ricketts v. Pennsylvania R. Co., 153 F.2d 757, 761 (2d Cir.1946).

Bear these theories in mind as you read the next three cases concerning assent. Lucy v. Zehmer, directly below, involves a transaction for the sale of a farm after some back and forth over drinks and a promise written out on the back of a restaurant receipt. Specht v. Netscape, on p. 168, moves us from what the court called "the world of paper" to online transactions. The third case, Lamps Plus, Inc. v. Varela, considers assent in the context of an employment relationship. When reading these cases,

---

[1]   "The 'actual intent' theory, said the objectivists, being 'subjective' and putting too much stress on unique individual motivations, would destroy that legal certainty and stability which a modern commercial society demands. They depicted the 'objective' standard as a necessary adjunct of a 'free enterprise' economic system. In passing, it should be noted that they arrived at a sort of paradox. For a 'free enterprise' system is, theoretically, founded on 'individualism'; but, in the name of economic individualism, the objectivists refused to consider those reactions of actual specific individuals which sponsors of the 'meeting-of-the-minds' test purported to cherish. 'Economic individualism' thus shows up as hostile to real individualism. This is nothing new: The 'economic man' is of course an abstraction, a 'fiction.' "

question whether the court has gone too far or not far enough in excluding the parties' actual intent.

Lucy v. Zehmer

Supreme Court of Appeals of Virginia, 1954.
196 Va. 493, 84 S.E.2d 516.

■ BUCHANAN, JUSTICE. This suit was instituted by W.O. Lucy and J.C. Lucy, complainants, against A.H. Zehmer and Ida S. Zehmer, his wife, defendants, to have specific performance of a contract by which it was alleged the Zehmers had sold to W.O. Lucy a tract of land owned by A.H. Zehmer in Dinwiddie county containing 471.6 acres, more or less, known as the Ferguson farm, for $50,000. J.C. Lucy, the other complainant, is a brother of W.O. Lucy, to whom W.O. Lucy transferred a half interest in his alleged purchase.

The instrument sought to be enforced was written by A.H. Zehmer on [Saturday,] December 20, 1952, in these words: "We hereby agree to sell to W.O. Lucy the Ferguson Farm complete for $50,000.00, title satisfactory to buyer," and signed by the defendants, A.H. Zehmer and Ida S. Zehmer.[c]

The answer of A.H. Zehmer admitted that at the time mentioned W.O. Lucy offered him $50,000 cash for the farm, but that he, Zehmer,

---

[c]   Here is a photocopy from the record:

[Front]

[Back]

considered that the offer was made in jest; that so thinking, and both he and Lucy having had several drinks, he wrote out "the memorandum" quoted above and induced his wife to sign it; that he did not deliver the memorandum to Lucy, but that Lucy picked it up, read it, put it in his pocket, attempted to offer Zehmer $5 to bind the bargain, which Zehmer refused to accept, and realizing for the first time that Lucy was serious, Zehmer assured him that he had no intention of selling the farm and that the whole matter was a joke. Lucy left the premises insisting that he had purchased the farm.

Depositions were taken and the decree appealed from was entered holding that the complainants had failed to establish their right to specific performance, and dismissing their bill. The assignment of error is to this action of the court.

The defendants insist that the evidence was ample to support their contention that the writing sought to be enforced was prepared as a bluff or dare to force Lucy to admit that he did not have $50,000; that the whole matter was a joke; that the writing was not delivered to Lucy and no binding contract was ever made between the parties.

It is an unusual, if not bizarre, defense. When made to the writing admittedly prepared by one of the defendants and signed by both, clear evidence is required to sustain it.

In his testimony Zehmer claimed that he "was high as a Georgia pine," and that the transaction "was just a bunch of two doggoned drunks bluffing to see who could talk the biggest and say the most." That claim is inconsistent with his attempt to testify in great detail as to what was said and what was done. It is contradicted by other evidence as to the condition of both parties, and rendered of no weight by the testimony of his wife that when Lucy left the restaurant she suggested that Zehmer drive him home. The record is convincing that Zehmer was not intoxicated to the extent of being unable to comprehend the nature and consequences of the instrument he executed, and hence that instrument is not to be invalidated on that ground. C.J.S. Contracts, § 133, b., p. 483; Taliaferro v. Emery, 124 Va. 674, 98 S.E. 627. It was in fact conceded by defendants' counsel in oral argument that under the evidence Zehmer was not too drunk to make a valid contract.

The evidence is convincing also that Zehmer wrote two agreements, the first one beginning "I hereby agree to sell." Zehmer first said he could not remember about that, then that "I don't think I wrote but one out." Mrs. Zehmer said that what he wrote was "I hereby agree," but that the "I" was changed to "We" after that night. The agreement that was written and signed is in the record and indicates no such change. Neither are the mistakes in spelling that Zehmer sought to point out readily apparent.

The appearance of the contract, the fact that it was under discussion for forty minutes or more before it was signed; Lucy's objection to the first draft because it was written in the singular, and he wanted Mrs. Zehmer to sign it also; the rewriting to meet that objection and the signing by Mrs. Zehmer; the discussion of what was to be included in the sale, the provision for the examination of the title, the completeness of the instrument that was executed, the taking possession of it by Lucy with no request or suggestion by either of the defendants that he give it back, are facts which furnish persuasive evidence that the execution of the contract was a serious business transaction rather than a casual, jesting matter as defendants now contend.

If it be assumed, contrary to what we think the evidence shows, that Zehmer was jesting about selling his farm to Lucy and that the transaction was intended by him to be a joke, nevertheless the evidence shows that Lucy did not so understand it but considered it to be a serious business transaction and the contract to be binding on the Zehmers as well as on himself. The very next day he arranged with his brother to put up half the money and take a half interest in the land. The day after that he employed an attorney to examine the title. The next night, Tuesday, he was back at Zehmer's place and there Zehmer told him for the first time, Lucy said, that he wasn't going to sell and he told Zehmer, "You know you sold that place fair and square." After receiving the report from his attorney that the title was good he wrote to Zehmer that he was ready to close the deal.

Not only did Lucy actually believe, but the evidence shows he was warranted in believing, that the contract represented a serious business transaction and a good faith sale and purchase of the farm.

In the field of contracts, as generally elsewhere, "We must look to the outward expression of a person as manifesting his intention rather than to his secret and unexpressed intention. The law imputes to a person an intention corresponding to the reasonable meaning of his words and acts.'" First Nat. Exchange Bank of Roanoke v. Roanoke Oil Co., 169 Va. 99, 114.

At no time prior to the execution of the contract had Zehmer indicated to Lucy by word or act that he was not in earnest about selling the farm. They had argued about it and discussed its terms, as Zehmer admitted, for a long time. Lucy testified that if there was any jesting it was about paying $50,000 that night. The contract and the evidence show that he was not expected to pay the money that night. Zehmer said that after the writing was signed he laid it down on the counter in front of Lucy. Lucy said Zehmer handed it to him. In any event there had been what appeared to be a good faith offer and a good faith acceptance, followed by the execution and apparent delivery of a written contract. Both said that Lucy put the writing in his pocket and then offered Zehmer $5 to seal the bargain. Not until then, even under the defendants' evidence, was anything said or done to indicate that the matter was a joke. Both of the Zehmers testified that when Zehmer asked his wife to sign he whispered that it was a joke so Lucy wouldn't hear and that it was not intended that he should hear.

The mental assent of the parties is not requisite for the formation of a contract. If the words or other acts of one of the parties have but one reasonable meaning, his undisclosed intention is immaterial except when an unreasonable meaning which he attaches to his manifestations is known to the other party. Restatement of the Law of Contracts, Vol. I, § 71, p. 74.

An agreement or mutual assent is of course essential to a valid contract but the law imputes to a person an intention corresponding to the reasonable meaning of his words and acts. If his words and acts, judged by a reasonable standard, manifest an intention to agree, it is immaterial what may be the real but unexpressed state of his mind. C.J.S. Contracts, § 32, p. 361; 12 Am.Jur., Contracts, § 19, p. 515.

So a person cannot set up that he was merely jesting when his conduct and words would warrant a reasonable person in believing that he intended a real agreement.

Whether the writing signed by the defendants and now sought to be enforced by the complainants was the result of a serious offer by Lucy and a serious acceptance by the defendants, or was a serious offer by Lucy and an acceptance in secret jest by the defendants, in either event it constituted a binding contract of sale between the parties.

The complainants are entitled to have specific performance of the contract sued on. The decree appealed from is therefore reversed and the cause is remanded for the entry of a proper decree requiring the defendants to perform the contract in accordance with the prayer of the bill.

Reversed and remanded.

NOTES

(1) *Questions.* Does either the objective or subjective theory alone adequately explain the decision in this case? Did Zehmer believe that Lucy intended to sell the Ferguson Farm? What facts suggest an affirmative answer? Why is Zehmer's honest belief alone not sufficient to bind Lucy? What more does the court require?

The United States Court of Appeals for the Tenth Circuit has stated that "contracts are not formed by comparing mental states; they are formed by what the parties *communicate*." Navair, Inc. v. IFR Americas, 519 F.3d 1131 (10th Cir. 2008). Are there risks in this position? What are its benefits? Recall Jerome Frank's questioning of whether such an approach could actually yield the hoped-for certainty and uniformity claimed by the objectivist formula. Can you develop any practical alternatives?

(2) *Jesting and Bluffing.* What result if the price offered for the Zehmer farm had been $50 rather than $50,000? In Keller v. Holderman, 11 Mich. 248 (1863), Holderman, as a "frolic and banter," gave Keller a $300 check for a watch worth about $15. Holderman had no money in the bank and intended to insert a condition in the check rendering him not liable. This he neglected

to do. Keller sued Holderman on the check and had judgment. Holderman appealed. *Held:* Reversed.

"When the Court below found as a fact that 'the whole transaction between the parties was a frolic and a banter, the plaintiff not expecting to sell, nor the defendant intending to buy the watch at the sum for which the check was drawn,' the conclusion should have been that no contract was ever made by the parties. " How does this use of the price differ from that of a peppercorn discussed above at Note 4, p. 58?

In addition to contending that "the whole matter was a joke," the Zehmers, in the case above, further contended that the writing "was prepared as a bluff or dare to force Lucy to admit that he did not have $50,000." What result if Lucy, knowing this, had "called their bluff" by raising the money from his brother? Should a distinction be made between jesting on the one hand, and bluffing or daring on the other? Are both "jokes"?

(3) *The Right Stuff.* John Leonard watched a television commercial touting a range of items ("Pepsi Stuff") that consumers could acquire by redeeming "Pepsi Points" obtained by buying specially marked packages of Pepsi products. The commercial showed a suburban high school student using various items from the Pepsi collection, with legends identifying each item and the number of Pepsi Points for which it could be obtained ("SHADES 175 PEPSI POINTS"; "LEATHER JACKET 1450 PEPSI POINTS"), and arriving at school in a fighter jet. On the same screen as the fighter jet, a similar legend appeared on the screen, stating "HARRIER JET 7,000,000 PEPSI POINTS." Using an official order form, Leonard ordered one Harrier Jet, enclosing 15 Pepsi Points and a check for $700,000. (Pepsi permitted consumers to buy additional points for 10 cents a point.) Pepsi did not send Leonard the Harrier Jet. Instead, it returned Leonard's check, explaining that the "Harrier jet in the Pepsi commercial is fanciful and simply intended to create a humorous and entertaining ad." Leonard then sued Pepsico, arguing that it was bound to sell him the Harrier Jet in exchange for the Pepsi Points and $700,000. Held: For Pepsico.

Noting "the obvious absurdity of the commercial," the court held that "no objective person could reasonably have concluded that the commercial actually offered consumers a Harrier Jet. The commercial is the embodiment of what defendant [Pepsi] appropriately characterizes as 'zany humor.' " "In light of the Harrier Jet's well documented function in attacking and destroying surface and air targets, depiction of such a jet as a way to get to school in the morning is clearly not serious. " Leonard v. Pepsico, 88 F.Supp.2d 116, 129 (S.D.N.Y.1999), aff'd, 210 F.3d 88 (2d Cir. 2000).

Do you agree? What result in the *Pepsico* case under *Lucy*? The court in *Leonard*, noting that the price of a Harrier Jet is roughly $23 million, stated that "[e]ven if an objective, reasonable person were not aware of this fact, he would conclude that purchasing a fighter plane for $700,000 is a deal too good to be true." *Id.* Is a price too good to be true always an indication that no offer has been made? Compare Restatement § 19(3).

(4) *Proving Subjective Intent.* If a party's subjective intent is to play any role in contract law, how is that intent to be proved? As Grant Gilmore

explained, "If the actual state of the parties' minds is relevant, then each litigated case must become an extended factual inquiry into what was 'intended,' 'meant,' 'believed,' and so on. If, however, we can restrict ourselves to the 'externals' (what the parties 'said' or 'did'), then the factual inquiry will be much simplified." Grant Gilmore, The Death of Contract 42 (1974).

Contract law's preference for the objective has not, however, completely solved the problem of proof. Suppose, for example, that Lucy had actually known that the Zehmers were joking even though this was not objectively apparent. Does this mean that a witness's testimony as to intent simply goes unchallenged? A number of safeguards suggest that the answer is No. These include: the availability of pretrial discovery to reveal prior inconsistent statements or other such evidence; confidence in a jury's ability to discern when a witness is untruthful; and the fact that the person whose intent is at issue may well be a corporation or other organization leading to the possibility of conflicting sources of information regarding intent, such as testimony from disaffected former employees or email trails.

For the argument that the application of subjective intent "brings the formation of contracts into harmony with the rules governing contract interpretation, consideration, and gap-filling," see Lawrence Solan, *Contract as Agreement*, 83 Notre Dame L. Rev. 353 (2007).

Specht v. Netscape Communications Corp.

United States Court of Appeals, Second Circuit, 2002.
306 F.3d 17.

■ SOTOMAYOR, CIRCUIT JUDGE.[d] This is an appeal from a judgment of the Southern District of New York denying a motion by defendants-appellants Netscape Communications Corporation and its corporate parent, America Online, Inc. (collectively, "defendants" or "Netscape"), to compel arbitration and to stay court proceedings. In order to resolve the central question of arbitrability presented here, we must address issues of contract formation in cyberspace. Principally, we are asked to determine whether plaintiffs-appellees ("plaintiffs"), by acting upon defendants' invitation to download free software made available on defendants' webpage, agreed to be bound by the software's license terms (which included the arbitration clause at issue), even though plaintiffs could not have learned of the existence of those terms unless, prior to executing the download, they had scrolled down the webpage to a screen located below the download button. We agree with the district court that a reasonably prudent Internet user in circumstances such as these would not have known or learned of the existence of the license terms before

---

[d]   Sonia Sotomayor (1954–____) became an Associate Justice of the Supreme Court in 2009, having been appointed by President Barack Obama. Sotomayor began her career as an Assistant District Attorney in the New York County District Attorney's Office (1979–1984). After several years in private practice in New York City, she served on the United States Court of Appeals for the Second Circuit (1998–2009) and on the United States District Court for the Southern District of New York (1991–1998). Sotomayor received her B.A. from Princeton University in 1976 and her J.D. from Yale Law School in 1979.

responding to defendants' invitation to download the free software, and that defendants therefore did not provide reasonable notice of the license terms. In consequence, plaintiffs' bare act of downloading the software did not unambiguously manifest assent to the arbitration provision contained in the license terms.

BACKGROUND

I. Facts

In three related putative class actions, plaintiffs alleged that, unknown to them, their use of SmartDownload transmitted to defendants private information about plaintiffs' downloading of files from the Internet, thereby effecting an electronic surveillance of their online activities in violation of two federal statutes, the Electronic Communications Privacy Act, 18 U.S.C. §§ 2510 et seq., and the Computer Fraud and Abuse Act, 18 U.S.C. § 1030.

In the time period relevant to this litigation, Netscape offered on its website various software programs, including Communicator and SmartDownload, which visitors to the site were invited to obtain free of charge. It is undisputed that five of the six named plaintiffs—Michael Fagan, John Gibson, Mark Gruber, Sean Kelly, and Sherry Weindorf—downloaded Communicator from the Netscape website. These plaintiffs acknowledge that when they proceeded to initiate installation of Communicator, they were automatically shown a scrollable text of that program's license agreement and were not permitted to complete the installation until they had clicked on a "Yes" button to indicate that they accepted all the license terms.[1] If a user attempted to install Communicator without clicking "Yes," the installation would be aborted. All five named user plaintiffs expressly agreed to Communicator's license terms by clicking "Yes." The Communicator license agreement that these plaintiffs saw made no mention of SmartDownload or other plug-in programs, and stated that "[t]hese terms apply to Netscape Communicator and Netscape Navigator" and that "all disputes relating to this Agreement (excepting any dispute relating to intellectual property rights)" are subject to "binding arbitration in Santa Clara County, California."

Although Communicator could be obtained independently of SmartDownload, all the named user plaintiffs, except Fagan, downloaded and installed Communicator in connection with downloading SmartDownload. Each of these plaintiffs allegedly arrived at a Netscape webpage captioned "SmartDownload Communicator" that urged them to "Download With Confidence Using SmartDownload!" At or near the bottom of the screen facing plaintiffs was the prompt "Start

---

[1] This kind of online software license agreement has come to be known as "clickwrap" because it "presents the user with a message on his or her computer screen, requiring that the user manifest his or her assent to the terms of the license agreement by clicking on an icon. The product cannot be obtained or used unless and until the icon is clicked." Specht, 150 F.Supp.2d at 593–94 (footnote omitted).

Download" and a tinted button labeled "Download." By clicking on the button, plaintiffs initiated the download of SmartDownload. Once that process was complete, SmartDownload, as its first plug-in task, permitted plaintiffs to proceed with downloading and installing Communicator, an operation that was accompanied by the clickwrap display of Communicator's license terms described above.

The signal difference between downloading Communicator and downloading SmartDownload was that no clickwrap presentation accompanied the latter operation. Instead, once plaintiffs Gibson, Gruber, Kelly, and Weindorf had clicked on the "Download" button located at or near the bottom of their screen, and the downloading of SmartDownload was complete, these plaintiffs encountered no further information about the plug-in program or the existence of license terms governing its use. The sole reference to SmartDownload's license terms on the "SmartDownload Communicator" webpage was located in text that would have become visible to plaintiffs only if they had scrolled down to the next screen.

Had plaintiffs scrolled down instead of acting on defendants' invitation to click on the "Download" button, they would have encountered the following invitation: "Please review and agree to the terms of the Netscape SmartDownload software license agreement before downloading and using the software."

Even for a user who, unlike plaintiffs, did happen to scroll down past the download button, SmartDownload's license terms would not have been immediately displayed in the manner of Communicator's clickwrapped terms. Instead, if such a user had seen the notice of SmartDownload's terms and then clicked on the underlined invitation to review and agree to the terms, a hypertext link would have taken the user to a separate webpage entitled "License & Support Agreements." The first paragraph on this page read, in pertinent part:

The use of each Netscape software product is governed by a license agreement. You must read and agree to the license agreement terms BEFORE acquiring a product. Please click on the appropriate link below to review the current license agreement for the product of interest to you before acquisition. For products available for download, you must read and agree to the license agreement terms BEFORE you install the software. If you do not agree to the license terms, do not download, install or use the software.

Below this paragraph appeared a list of license agreements, the first of which was "License Agreement for Netscape Navigator and Netscape Communicator Product Family (Netscape Navigator, Netscape Communicator and Netscape SmartDownload)." If the user clicked on that link, he or she would be taken to yet another webpage that contained the full text of a license agreement that was identical in every respect to the Communicator license agreement except that it stated that its "terms apply to Netscape Communicator, Netscape Navigator, and Netscape

SmartDownload." The license agreement granted the user a nonexclusive license to use and reproduce the software, subject to certain terms. Among the license terms was a provision requiring virtually all disputes relating to the agreement to be submitted to arbitration.

DISCUSSION

I. Standard of Review and Applicable Law

A district court's denial of a motion to compel arbitration is reviewed de novo. The determination of whether parties have contractually bound themselves to arbitrate a dispute—a determination involving interpretation of state law—is a legal conclusion also subject to de novo review. The findings upon which that conclusion is based, however, are factual and thus may not be over-turned unless clearly erroneous. The district court properly concluded that in deciding whether parties agreed to arbitrate a certain matter, a court should generally apply state-law principles to the issue of contract formation. The district court further held that California law governs the question of contract formation here; the parties do not appeal that determination. [citations omitted]

III. Whether the User Plaintiffs Had Reasonable Notice of and Manifested Assent to the SmartDownload License Agreement

Whether governed by the common law or by Article 2 of the Uniform Commercial Code ("UCC"), a transaction, in order to be a contract, requires a manifestation of agreement between the parties. California's common law is clear that "an offeree, regardless of apparent manifestation of his consent, is not bound by inconspicuous contractual provisions of which he is unaware, contained in a document whose contractual nature is not obvious."

Arbitration agreements are no exception to the requirement of manifestation of assent. "This principle of knowing consent applies with particular force to provisions for arbitration." Windsor Mills, 101 Cal.Rptr. at 351. Clarity and conspicuousness of arbitration terms are important in securing informed assent. "If a party wishes to bind in writing another to an agreement to arbitrate future disputes, such purpose should be accomplished in a way that each party to the arrangement will fully and clearly comprehend that the agreement to arbitrate exists and binds the parties thereto." Commercial Factors Corp. v. Kurtzman Bros., 131 Cal.App.2d 133, 134–35, 280 P.2d 146, 147–48 (1955). Thus, California contract law measures assent by an objective standard that takes into account both what the offeree said, wrote, or did and the transactional context in which the offeree verbalized or acted.

A. The Reasonably Prudent Offeree of Downloadable Software

Defendants argue that plaintiffs must be held to a standard of reasonable prudence and that, because notice of the existence of SmartDownload license terms was on the next scrollable screen, plaintiffs were on "inquiry notice" of those terms. We disagree[.] It is true that "[a] party cannot avoid the terms of a contract on the ground that he or she failed to read it before signing." Marin Storage & Trucking, 89 Cal.App.4th at 1049, 107 Cal.Rptr.2d at 651. But courts are quick to add: "An exception to this general rule exists when the writing does not appear to be a contract and the terms are not called to the attention of the recipient. In such a case, no contract is formed with respect to the undisclosed term." Id.

Most of the cases cited by defendants in support of their inquiry-notice argument are drawn from the world of paper contracting. See, e.g., Taussig v. Bode & Haslett, 134 Cal. 260, 66 P. 259 (1901) (where party had opportunity to read leakage disclaimer printed on warehouse receipt, he had duty to do so); In re First Capital Life Ins. Co., 34 Cal.App.4th 1283, 1288, 40 Cal.Rptr.2d 816, 820 (1995) (purchase of insurance policy after opportunity to read and understand policy terms creates binding agreement); King v. Larsen Realty, Inc., 121 Cal.App.3d 349, 356, 175 Cal.Rptr. 226, 231 (1981) (where realtors' board manual specifying that party was required to arbitrate was "readily available," party was "on notice" that he was agreeing to mandatory arbitration); Cal. State Auto. Ass'n Inter-Ins. Bureau v. Barrett Garages, Inc., 257 Cal.App.2d 71, 76, 64 Cal.Rptr. 699, 703 (1967) (recipient of airport parking claim check was bound by terms printed on claim check, because a "ordinarily prudent" person would have been alerted to the terms).

As the foregoing cases suggest, receipt of a physical document containing contract terms or notice thereof is frequently deemed, in the world of paper transactions, a sufficient circumstance to place the offeree on inquiry notice of those terms. "Every person who has actual notice of circumstances sufficient to put a prudent man upon inquiry as to a particular fact, has constructive notice of the fact itself in all cases in which, by prosecuting such inquiry, he might have learned such fact." Cal.Civ.Code § 19. These principles apply equally to the emergent world of online product delivery, pop-up screens, hyperlinked pages, clickwrap licensing, scrollable documents, and urgent admonitions to "Download Now!". What plaintiffs saw when they were being invited by defendants to download this fast, free plug-in called SmartDownload was a screen containing praise for the product and, at the very bottom of the screen, a "Download" button. Defendants argue that under the principles set forth in the cases cited above, a "fair and prudent person using ordinary care" would have been on inquiry notice of SmartDownload's license terms. Shacket, 651 F.Supp. at 690.

We are not persuaded that a reasonably prudent offeree in these circumstances would have known of the existence of license terms. Plaintiffs were responding to an offer that did not carry an immediately visible notice of the existence of license terms or require unambiguous manifestation of assent to those terms. Moreover, the fact that, given the position of the scroll bar on their computer screens, plaintiffs may have been aware that an unexplored portion of the Netscape webpage remained below the download button does not mean that they reasonably should have concluded that this portion contained a notice of license terms. Plaintiffs testified, and defendants did not refute, that plaintiffs were in fact unaware that defendants intended to attach license terms to the use of SmartDownload.

We conclude that in circumstances such as these, where consumers are urged to download free software at the immediate click of a button, a reference to the existence of license terms on a submerged screen is not sufficient to place consumers on inquiry or constructive notice of those terms.

C. Online Transactions

After reviewing the California common law and other relevant legal authority, we conclude that under the circumstances here, plaintiffs' downloading of SmartDownload did not constitute acceptance of defendants' license terms. Reasonably conspicuous notice of the existence of contract terms and unambiguous manifestation of assent to those terms by consumers are essential if electronic bargaining is to have integrity and credibility. We hold that a reasonably prudent offeree in plaintiffs' position would not have known or learned, prior to acting on the invitation to download, of the reference to SmartDownload's license terms hidden below the "Download" button on the next screen. We affirm the district court's conclusion that the user plaintiffs, including Fagan, are not bound by the arbitration clause contained in those terms.

CONCLUSION

For the foregoing reasons, we affirm the district court's denial of defendants' motion to compel arbitration and to stay court proceedings.

NOTES

(1) *Questions.* What action was argued by Netscape to constitute assent in *Specht*? Can a keystroke ever constitute a party's intent to be bound? How does the plaintiffs' challenge to its assent in Specht differ with the seller's challenge to assent in *Lucy v. Zehmer*? Does it matter that the party disputing their assent is the offeror in one case, and the offeree in the other?

Recall that in *Lucy,* the question was whether there was a contract at all. In this case, there was apparently no doubt that there was a contract for the deal as a whole; the question, instead, was whether Specht agreed to a particular term. What is the significance of the difference?

(2) *Inquiry Notice.* Must an "offeree of downloadable software," as the court describes the plaintiffs, have actually read the terms of the deal before clicking can constitute assent? According to *Specht,* what does it take to bind a person who clicks on "I agree"? Compare Netscape's presentation of terms in *Specht* from a procedure where the seller's technician showed the buyer the terms on the technician's laptop, and the buyer was unable to complete the transaction without clicking on one of three boxes ("Exit Registration," "I Accept," or "I Reject") located under the Terms of Service, see Hancock v. AT

& T (10th Cir. 2012). Would you find intent by an offeree who clicks on "I Accept" in the latter case?

Lamps Plus, Inc. v. Varela

United States Supreme Court, 2019.
587 U.S. ___, 139 S. Ct. 1407.

■ CHIEF JUSTICE ROBERTS.[e] Petitioner Lamps Plus is a company that sells light fixtures and related products. In 2016, a hacker impersonating a company official tricked a Lamps Plus employee into disclosing the tax information of approximately 1,300 other employees. Soon after, a fraudulent federal income tax return was filed in the name of Frank Varela, a Lamps Plus employee and respondent here.

Like most Lamps Plus employees, Varela had signed an arbitration agreement when he started work at the company. But after the data breach, he sued Lamps Plus in Federal District Court in California, bringing state and federal claims on behalf of a putative class of employees whose tax information had been compromised. Lamps Plus moved to compel arbitration on an individual rather than classwide basis, and to dismiss the lawsuit. In a single order, the District Court granted the motion to compel arbitration and dismissed Varela's claims without prejudice. But the court rejected Lamps Plus's request for individual arbitration, instead authorizing arbitration on a classwide basis. Lamps Plus appealed the order, arguing that the court erred by compelling class arbitration.

The Ninth Circuit affirmed. The court acknowledged that *Stolt-Nielsen* [Stolt-Nielsen S. A. v. AnimalFeeds Int'l Corp., 559 U.S. 662 (2010)] prohibits forcing a party "to submit to class arbitration unless there is a contractual basis for concluding that the party *agreed* to do so" and that Varela's agreement "include[d] no express mention of class proceedings." But that did not end the inquiry, the court reasoned, because the fact that the agreement "does not expressly refer to class arbitration is not the 'silence' contemplated in *Stolt-Nielsen*." In *Stolt-Nielsen*, the parties had *stipulated* that their agreement was silent about class arbitration. Because there was no such stipulation here, the court concluded that *Stolt-Nielsen* was not controlling.

The Ninth Circuit then determined that the agreement was ambiguous on the issue of class arbitration . . . [and] followed California law to construe the ambiguity against the drafter, a rule that "applies

---

    e   John G. Roberts, Jr. (1955–____) became the Chief Justice of the United States in 2005, following his nomination by President George W. Bush. Roberts received an A.B. (1976) and a J.D. (1979) from Harvard University, after which he clerked for Judge Henry J. Friendly on the United States Court of Appeals for the Second Circuit and for then-Associate Justice William H. Rehnquist on the Supreme Court during the 1980 Term. During the 1980s, he served as Special Assistant to the Attorney General, as Associate Counsel to President Ronald Reagan in the White House Counsel's Office, and as Principal Deputy Solicitor General from 1989–1993. From 1986–1989 and 1993–2003, he practiced law in Washington, D.C., and was appointed to the United States Court of Appeals for the District of Columbia Circuit in 2003.

with peculiar force in the case of a contract of adhesion" such as this. Because Lamps Plus had drafted the agreement, the court adopted Varela's interpretation authorizing class arbitration.

III

The Ninth Circuit applied California contract law to conclude that the parties' agreement was ambiguous on the availability of class arbitration. In California, an agreement is ambiguous "when it is capable of two or more constructions, both of which are reasonable." Following our normal practice, we defer to the Ninth Circuit's interpretation and application of state law and thus accept that the agreement should be regarded as ambiguous.

We therefore face the question whether, consistent with the FAA, an ambiguous agreement can provide the necessary "contractual basis" for compelling class arbitration. We hold that it cannot—a conclusion that follows directly from our decision in *Stolt-Nielsen*. Class arbitration is not only markedly different from the "traditional individualized arbitration" contemplated by the FAA, it also undermines the most important benefits of that familiar form of arbitration. Epic Systems Corp. v. Lewis, 584 U.S. ___, ___ (2018) (slip op., at 8). The statute therefore requires more than ambiguity to ensure that the parties actually agreed to arbitrate on a classwide basis.

A

The FAA requires courts to "enforce arbitration agreements according to their terms." *Epic Systems*, 584 U.S., at ___ (slip op., at 5) (quoting American Express Co. v. Italian Colors Restaurant, 570 U.S. 228, 233 (2013)). Although courts may ordinarily accomplish that end by relying on state contract principles, state law is preempted to the extent it "stands as an obstacle to the accomplishment and execution of the full purposes and objectives" of the FAA, AT&T Mobility LLC v. Concepcion, 563 U.S. 333, 352 (2011). At issue in this case is the interaction between a state contract principle for addressing ambiguity and a "rule[ ] of fundamental importance" under the FAA, namely, that arbitration "is a matter of consent, not coercion." *Stolt-Nielsen*, 559 U.S., at 681 (internal quotation marks omitted).

"[T]he first principle that underscores all of our arbitration decisions" is that "[a]rbitration is strictly a matter of consent." Granite Rock Co. v. Teamsters, 561 U.S. 287, 299 (2010).

Consent is essential under the FAA because arbitrators wield only the authority they are given. That is, they derive their "powers from the parties' agreement to forgo the legal process and submit their disputes to private dispute resolution." *Stolt-Nielsen*, 559 U.S., at 682. Parties may generally shape such agreements to their liking by specifying with whom they will arbitrate, the issues subject to arbitration, the rules by which they will arbitrate, and the arbitrators who will resolve their disputes. *Id.*, at 683–684. Whatever they settle on, the task for courts and arbitrators at bottom remains the same: "to give effect to the intent of the parties." *Id.*, at 684.

In carrying out that responsibility, it is important to recognize the "fundamental" difference between class arbitration and the individualized form of arbitration envisioned by the FAA. In individual arbitration, "parties forgo the procedural rigor and appellate review of the courts in order to realize the benefits of private dispute resolution: lower costs, greater efficiency and speed, and the ability to choose expert adjudicators to resolve specialized disputes." *Id.*, at 685. Class arbitration lacks those benefits. It "sacrifices the principal advantage of arbitration—its informality—and makes the process slower, more costly, and more likely to generate procedural morass than final judgment." *Concepcion*, 563 U.S., at 348.

Because of these "crucial differences" between individual and class arbitration, *Stolt-Nielsen* explained that there is "reason to doubt the parties' mutual consent to resolve disputes through classwide arbitration." 559 U.S., at 687, 685–686. And for that reason, we held that courts may not infer consent to participate in class arbitration absent an affirmative "contractual basis for concluding that the party *agreed* to do so." *Id.*, at 684. Silence is not enough; the "FAA requires more." *Id.*, at 687.

Our reasoning in *Stolt-Nielsen* controls the question we face today. Like silence, ambiguity does not provide a sufficient basis to conclude that parties to an arbitration agreement agreed to "sacrifice[ ] the principal advantage of arbitration." *Concepcion*, 563 U.S., at 348.

This conclusion aligns with our refusal to infer consent when it comes to other fundamental arbitration questions. . . . Neither silence nor ambiguity provides a sufficient basis for concluding that parties to an arbitration agreement agreed to undermine the central benefits of arbitration itself.

* * *

Courts may not infer from an ambiguous agreement that parties have consented to arbitrate on a classwide basis. The doctrine of *contra proferentem* cannot substitute for the requisite affirmative "contractual basis for concluding that the part[ies] *agreed* to [class arbitration]." *Stolt-Nielsen*, 559 U.S., at 684.

We reverse the judgment of the Court of Appeals for the Ninth Circuit and remand the case for further proceedings consistent with this opinion.

It is so ordered.

■ JUSTICE GINSBURG,[f] dissenting[g].

Joining Justice Kagan's dissenting opinion in full, I write separately to emphasize once again how treacherously the Court has strayed from the principle that "arbitration is a matter of consent, not coercion." *Stolt-Nielsen*, 681.

Congress enacted the Federal Arbitration Act (FAA) in 1925 "to enable merchants of roughly equal bargaining power to enter into binding agreements to arbitrate *commercial* disputes." *Epic Systems* (Ginsburg, J., dissenting) (slip op., at 19) (emphasis in original). The Act was not designed to govern contracts "in which one of the parties characteristically has little bargaining power." Prima Paint Corp. v. Flood & Conklin Mfg. Co., 388 U.S. 395, 403, n. 9 (1967); see Gilmer v. Interstate/Johnson Lane Corp., 500 U.S. 20, 42 (1991) (Stevens, J., dissenting) ("I doubt that any legislator who voted for [the FAA] expected it to apply . . . to form contracts between parties of unequal bargaining power, or to the arbitration of disputes arising out of the employment relationship."); Miller, Simplified Pleading, Meaningful Days in Court, and Trials on the Merits: Reflections on the Deformation of Federal Procedure, 88 N.Y. U. L. Rev. 286, 323 (2013) (The FAA was "enacted in 1925 with the seemingly limited purpose of overcoming the then-existing 'judicial hostility' to the arbitration of contract disputes between businesses.").

The Court has relied on the FAA, not simply to overcome once-prevalent judicial resistance to enforcement of arbitration disputes between businesses. In relatively recent years, it has routinely deployed the law to deny to employees and consumers "effective relief against powerful economic entities." DIRECTV, Inc. v. Imburgia, 577 U.S. ___, ___ (2015) (Ginsburg, J., dissenting) (slip op., at 9). Arbitration clauses, the Court has decreed, may preclude judicial remedies even when submission to arbitration is made a take-it-or-leave-it condition of employment or is imposed on a consumer given no genuine choice in the matter.

Piling Pelion on Ossa, the Court has hobbled the capacity of employees and consumers to band together in a judicial or arbitral forum. The Court has pursued this course even though "neither the history nor present practice suggests that class arbitration is fundamentally

---

[f]   Ruth Bader Ginsburg (1933–____) graduated from Cornell University in 1954 and Columbia Law School in 1959. After clerking for Judge Edmund Palmieri on the United States District Court for the Southern District of New York, she joined the legal academy, teaching at Rutgers Law School from 1963 to 1972 and Columbia Law School from 1972–1980. In the 1970s she became the director of the Women's Rights Project of the ACLU. There she developed a litigation strategy aimed at achieving gender equality and argued a series of landmark gender discrimination cases before the Supreme Court, starting with *Frontiero v. Richardson* in 1973. Justice Ginsburg was appointed to the Supreme Court in 1993 by President Bill Clinton, having served on the United States Court of Appeals for the District of Columbia from 1980 to 1993.

[g]   There were dissenting opinions in this case by Justices Breyer, Ginsburg, Kagan, and Sotomayor.

incompatible with arbitration itself." AT&T Mobility LLC v. Concepcion, 563 U.S. 333, 362 (2011) (Breyer, J., dissenting).

Employees and consumers forced to arbitrate solo face severe impediments to the "vindication of their rights." *Stolt-Nielsen*, 559 U.S., at 699 (Ginsburg, J., dissenting). "Expenses entailed in mounting individual claims will often far outweigh potential recoveries." *Epic*, 584 U.S., at ___ (Ginsburg, J., dissenting) (slip op., at 27); see American Express Co. v. Italian Colors Restaurant, 570 U.S. 228, 246 (2013) (Kagan, J., dissenting) ("[The defendant] has put [the plaintiff] to this choice: Spend way, way, way more money than your claim is worth, or relinquish your . . . rights."); *Concepcion*, 563 U.S., at 365 (Breyer, J., dissenting) ("What rational lawyer would have signed on to represent the [plaintiffs] for the possibility of fees stemming from a $30.22 [individual] claim?").

Today's decision underscores the irony of invoking "the first principle" that "arbitration is strictly a matter of consent," to justify imposing individual arbitration on employees who surely would not choose to proceed solo. Respondent Frank Varela sought redress for negligence by his employer leading to a data breach affecting 1,300 employees. The widely experienced neglect he identified cries out for collective treatment. Blocking Varela's path to concerted action, the Court aims to ensure the authenticity of consent to class procedures in arbitration. Shut from the Court's sight is the "Hobson's choice" employees face: "accept arbitration on their employer's terms or give up their jobs." *Epic*, 584 U.S., at ___, n. 2 (Ginsburg, J., dissenting) (slip op., at 7, n. 2).

Recent developments outside the judicial arena ameliorate some of the harm this Court's decisions have occasioned. Some companies have ceased requiring employees to arbitrate sexual harassment claims or have extended their no-forced-arbitration policy to a broader range of claims. And some States have endeavored to safeguard employees' opportunities to bring sexual harassment suits in court. These developments are sanguine, for "[p]lainly, it would not comport with the congressional objectives behind a statute seeking to enforce civil rights . . . to allow the very forces that had practiced discrimination to contract away the right to enforce civil rights in the courts." Barrentine v. Arkansas-Best Freight System, Inc., 450 U.S. 728, 750 (1981) (Burger, C. J., dissenting).

Notwithstanding recent steps to counter the Court's current jurisprudence, mandatory individual arbitration continues to thwart "effective access to justice" for those encountering diverse violations of their legal rights. The Court, paradoxically reciting the mantra that "[c]onsent is essential," *ante*, at 7, has facilitated companies' efforts to deny employees and consumers the "important right" to sue in court, and to do so collectively, by inserting solo-arbitration-only clauses that parties lacking bargaining clout cannot remove. CompuCredit Corp. v.

Greenwood, 565 U.S. 95, 115 (2012) (Ginsburg, J., dissenting). When companies can "muffl[e] grievance[s] in the cloakroom of arbitration," the result is inevitable: curtailed enforcement of laws "designed to advance the well-being of [the] vulnerable." *Epic*, 584 U.S., at ___ (Ginsburg, J., dissenting) (slip op., at 26). "Congressional correction of the Court's elevation of the FAA over" the rights of employees and consumers "to act in concert" remains "urgently in order." *Id.*, at ___ (slip op., at 2).

NOTES

(1) *Finding Ambiguity.* On what basis did the Ninth Circuit find that the parties' agreement on class arbitration was ambiguous? How do Chief Justice Roberts and Justice Ginsburg differ regarding the consequences of that ambiguity with respect to judicial recognition of class arbitration in this case?

(2) *Forms of Consent.* Both the plaintiffs in *Specht* and in *Lamps Plus* were found not to have consented to a contested arbitration term. How did their "non-consent" manifest itself in the two cases?

———

Intent to Be Bound

Certain cases in the last chapter were presented as if parties made deals without much fuss: Hawkins agreed to the hand surgery; Story 2d forebore from vice. Yet some negotiation is a common precursor to most agreements, even seemingly straightforward ones. (Recall that Dr. McGee really wanted to practice the surgery on Hawkins, and so sweetened the deal to secure his consent.) For more complex deals—the acquisition of companies, real estate developments, divorce settlements—negotiations are usually more protracted and may take shape over an extended period of time. Negotiating parties in these transactions may want to record, or perhaps lock in, terms that have been agreed upon, yet not be contractually bound to that term until a final agreement is reached, and often not until that agreement takes formal written form. During this process, it is therefore important to ask: even when parties have assented, just what have they have agreed to?

"Mutual assent has many implications for contract law theory and doctrine. Importantly, it sets the boundary between the precontractual and the contractual stages. Prior to attaining a consensus, while an agreement is still being negotiated, no liability arises between the parties. At some point in time, the positions of the parties (or, more correctly, their outward manifestations) meet, and full expectation liability emerges." Omri Ben-Shahar, *Contracts without Consent: Exploring a New Basis for Contractual Liability*, 152 U. Penn. L. Rev. 1829 (2004). Assent is a necessary condition for contractual liability, but it is not sufficient. For example, let's say that two parties agree on what they consider to be the essential terms of a contract, leaving the details to be worked out by their lawyers in a final, formal document that the parties expect to sign. If one of the parties then refuses to sign the formal document, can the other enforce their agreement?

The answer depends on whether the parties *intended* to conclude their agreement at the earlier point in time. In that regard, courts have developed two widely-accepted common law principles:

> (a) that absent an expressed intent that no contract shall exist, mutual assent between the parties, even though oral or informal, to exchange acts or promises is sufficient to create a binding contract; and (b) that to avoid the obligation of a binding contract, at least one of the parties must express an intention not to be bound until a writing is executed.

Consarc Corp. v. Marine Midland Bank, N.A., 996 F.2d 568, 570 (2d Cir.1993).

But how does a court determine whether or not a party has sufficiently expressed an intention not to be bound in the absence of a formal document? In Winston v. Mediafare Entertainment Corp., 777 F.2d 78 (2d Cir.1985), the court listed "several factors that help." These factors are:

> (1) whether there has been an express reservation of the right not to be bound in the absence of a writing; (2) whether there has been partial performance of the contract; (3) whether all of the terms of the alleged contract have been agreed upon; and (4) whether the agreement at issue is the type of contract that is usually committed to writing.

Id. at 80. Despite such guidance, cases involving this question are frequently before the courts. For two classic discussions, see Charles Knapp, *Enforcing the Contract to Bargain*, 44 N.Y. U. L. Rev. 673 (1969) and E. Allan Farnsworth, *Precontractual Liability and Preliminary Agreements: Fair Dealing and Failed Negotiations*, 87 Colum. L. Rev. 217 (1987).

Other forms of precontractual commitment include "gentlemen's agreements" and letters of intent.[h] We will engage with letters of intent more fully on p. 316 in connection with precontractual liability; for now it is enough to consider them along the lines of "agreements in principle" in which negotiating parties keep a record of, or memorialize, matters on which accord has been reached. At the same time, letters of intent typically include language that seeks to prevent the letter from signaling an intent to be bound, such as "This letter is not intended to create nor should it be construed as creating any legal obligation." White

---

[h] "A gentlemen's agreement is . . . an agreement which is not an agreement, made between two persons neither of whom is a gentleman, whereby each expects the other to be strictly bound without himself being bound at all." Wilma Fall, Letters of Comfort, 1990 J. S. Afr. L. 73 (1990) (quoting Chemo Leasing v. Rediffusion, 1 FTLR 201 CA, (1987)).

Construction Co. v. Martin Marietta Materials, 633 F.Supp.2d 1302 (M.D.Fla.2009).

Let us consider one further form of preliminary agreement, an agreement to negotiate. May parties bind themselves not to a particular term, but to the process of achieving the terms? The answer is Yes. As one court stated, in a contract to negotiate,

> the parties exchange promises to conform to a specific course of conduct during negotiations, such as negotiating in good faith, exclusively with each other, or for a specific period of time. Under a contract to negotiate, the parties do not intend to be bound if negotiations fail to reach ultimate agreement on the substantive deal. [N]o breach occurs if the parties fail to reach agreement on the substantive deal. The contract to negotiate is breached only when one party fails to conform to the specific course of conduct agreed upon.

Keystone Land & Development Co. v. Xerox Corp., 94 P.3d 945 (Wash. 2004). How does a contract to negotiate differ from an "agreement to agree," defined by the court in Keystone Land as "an agreement to do something which requires a further meeting of the minds of the parties and without which it would not be complete"?

NOTES

(1) *Preliminary   Binding   Agreements/Preliminary   Binding Commitments.* In Teachers Insurance & Annuity Association v. Tribune Co., 670 F.Supp. 491 (S.D.N.Y.1987), Judge Pierre Leval distinguished between two types of binding preliminary agreements, often designated "Tribune I" and "Tribune II." The decision has had wide influence and has been described as follows by the Second Circuit in Adjustrite Systems v. GAB Business Services, 145 F.3d 543, 548 (2d Cir.1998).

A *Tribune* Type I contract "is a fully binding preliminary agreement, which is created when the parties agree on all the points that require negotiation (including whether to be bound) but agree to memorialize their agreement in a more formal document. Such an agreement is fully binding; it is 'preliminary in form—only in the sense that the parties desire a more elaborate formalization of the agreement. [I]t binds both sides to their ultimate contractual objective in recognition that, 'despite the anticipation of further formalities,' a contract has been reached."

A *Tribune* Type II contract, "dubbed a 'binding preliminary commitment' by Judge Leval, is created when the parties agree on certain major terms, but leave other terms open for further negotiation. The parties 'accept a mutual commitment to negotiate together in good faith in an effort to reach final agreement.'" In contrast to a Type I agreement, a Type II agreement "'does not commit the parties to their ultimate contractual objective but rather to the obligation to negotiate the open issues in good faith in an attempt to reach the objective within the agreed framework.' Indeed if a final contract is not agreed upon, the parties may abandon the transaction as long as they have made a good faith effort to close the deal and have not insisted on conditions that do not conform to the preliminary writing."

Some courts have sought to distinguish between open terms that are "deal breakers" and those that are not. See A/S Apothekernes Laboratorium v. I.M.C. Chemical, 873 F.2d 155 (7th Cir.1989). How might a party make certain, throughout negotiations, that every open term is a deal breaker? See Budget Marketing, Inc. v. Centronics Corp., 927 F.2d 421 (8th Cir.1991).

(2) *Of Oil and Honor.* One celebrated case involving "formal contract contemplated" was a so-called "handshake deal" between the Pennzoil Company and the Getty Oil Company. Getty, having negotiated a sale of stock to Pennzoil, refused to perform and sold the stock to Texaco, Inc. Pennzoil's first legal sally was an attempt to charge Getty with breach of contract in Delaware. When that failed, Pennzoil shifted its ground to Texas and sued Texaco there for interfering with the alleged Getty contract. This action produced a verdict against Texaco for $10.53 billion and (after much maneuvering, including a reduction of $2 billion in the jury's punitive-damage award and a visit to the Supreme Court of the United States) led to Texaco's bankruptcy. Its bankruptcy petition was designed to effectuate a $3 billion settlement agreement between the parties. For a description of the Pennzoil-Getty dealings see Texaco, Inc. v. Pennzoil Co., 729 S.W.2d 768 (Tex.App.1987). See also T. Petzinger, Oil and Honor: The Texaco-Pennzoil Wars (1987).

————

Intent in Context

Lucy v. Zehmer, above, suggests that a promisor may not be bound if the promise, whether from its content or from the circumstances of its making, is insufficiently sincere to indicate the promisor's intent to be bound. In addition to disregarding jests, courts and sometimes legislatures are also reluctant to enforce a statement on the ground that no binding promise was intended. One area where this reluctance is observed, touched upon in Chapter 1, concerns optimistic statements made by doctors to patients. See Note 2, p. 4 above. In an omitted passage from Sullivan v. O'Connor, p. 13, the court observed that "patients may transform such statements into firm promises in their own minds. " Statements made for social purposes or among family members provide a second category in which the promisor may not have intended to make a legally enforceable promise.

In thinking further about the nature or quality of assent necessary to make a promise binding, consider Professor Edwin Patterson's[i] suggestion that:

---

[i] Edwin W. Patterson (1889–1965) practiced for four years in Kansas City and then taught at the Universities of Texas, Colorado, and Iowa and at Columbia. He was one of the Advisers for the Restatement of Restitution. Among his writings are books on contracts, insurance and jurisprudence, including four editions of the predecessor of this casebook.

A good legal rule as to the enforceability of promises should make contracting available to non-lawyers who will take the pains to clarify their ideas as to what they want to contract about; yet it should not make contracting so easy that it hooks the unwary signer or the casual promisor. The first may be called freedom *to* contract, the second, freedom *from* contract. These are, of course, counsels of perfection.

NOTES

(1) *Dining Together.* Should a court enforce a promise made for a social purpose, such as a promise to be a guest at a dinner party? Would it make a difference if the host had gone to considerable expense to make elaborate preparations in honor of the guest? What if the broken promise was one to marry and the plaintiff's expenses had included a wedding dress and the rental of a hall for the reception? See Ferraro v. Singh, 495 A.2d 946 (Pa.Super.1985).

(2) *Hunting Together.* Two friends, Mitzel and Hauck, went duck hunting in a car driven by Hauck. While taking a curve on a country road at 74 miles per hour, Hauck lost control and crashed the car, injuring Mitzel, who then sued Hauck. South Dakota law provides that "no person transported as a guest" has a cause of action against the driver for negligence. Mitzel testified that he was not a guest: "I told him I would accompany him on this trip to look for ducks. I would take my time and go along on this trip and look for ducks on the agreement he would take the car." From a judgment for Hauck, plaintiff appealed. *Held*: For Hauck.

"It is not every agreement that results in a binding, legally enforceable contract. Neither party may intend the writing to be a contract; it must contemplate the assumption of legal rights and duties. This is not to say that contracts may not be implied in fact or in law. [Yet to] spell out a contract from this hunting trip of these young men would 'transcend reality,' and transform this sport and similar social affairs to a new legal field. It was not a commercial arrangement or one that removed [plaintiff] from his status as a guest." Mitzel v. Hauck, 105 N.W.2d 378, 380 (S.D.1960).

(3) *Living Together.* What effect should be given promises made between spouses or cohabitants? In Balfour v. Balfour, p. 53 above, the court denied the wife recovery on her husband's promise to pay her an allowance on the ground that such promises "are not contracts because the parties did not intend that they should be attended by legal consequences." Although this strict traditional view persists in judicial reluctance to enforce agreements between husband and wife, it has been relaxed considerably. As for unmarried couples, one court has said that "[o]rdinary contract principles are not suspended for unmarried persons living together, whether or not they engage in sexual activity." Boland v. Catalano, 521 A.2d 142 (Conn.1987).

(4) *Ethics in Educating a Client.* When a party's intent is key to a determination regarding formation, how is a lawyer to ascertain a client's state of mind at the earlier time? It is popular wisdom that a client's report regarding intent may be influenced by what the client knows of the law.

Hence there are situations in which it is at least questionable for a lawyer to give legal advice "to assist his client in developing evidence relevant to the [client's] state of mind." See Code of Professional Responsibility (Ethical Consideration 7–6). Precepts issued by the American Bar Association emphasize, however, that a lawyer *may* properly assist a client in that way, and "may discuss the legal consequences of any proposed course of conduct with a client." Rule 1.2(d) of the Model Rules of Professional Conduct.

For a colloquy on the question "whether it is proper to give your client legal advice when you have reason to believe that the knowledge you give him will tempt him to commit perjury," see Monroe Freedman, *Professional Responsibility of the Criminal Defense Lawyer: The Three Hardest Questions*, 64 Mich. L. Rev. 1469, 1478–82 (1966), and John Noonan, *The Purposes of Advocacy and the Limits of Confidentiality*, 64 Mich. L. Rev. 1485, 1488 (1966). In a later book, Professor Freedman conceded that there comes a point where "nothing less than 'brute rationalization' can purport to justify a conclusion that the lawyer is seeking in good faith to elicit truth rather than actively participating in the creation of perjury." Monroe Freedman, Lawyers' Ethics in an Adversary System 73, 75 (1975).

Although the problem has drawn attention chiefly in connection with defense preparations in criminal matters, in which intent is often a critical fact, counsel's explanation of the law might also bear on a client's recollection regarding a contractual transaction. Recall Mitzel, Note 2, above, who testified that he went duck hunting "on the agreement" that his friend would drive.

Whether or not a contract has been formed often depends on choosing between conflicting accounts of a conversation. Recall the conflicting testimony in Lucy v. Zehmer. Does the decision in that case ease or intensify qualms that lawyers may have about educating their clients about contract law?

Section 2.   The Offer

The process by which parties arrive at a bargain varies widely according to the circumstances. It is common to treat the process as involving two distinct steps: first, an offer by one party and, second, an acceptance by the other. In practice, however, the process of contract formation is often more complicated and muddled.

[H]owever suited [the rules of offer and acceptance] may have been to the measured cadence of contracting in the nineteenth century, they have little to say about the complex processes that lead to major deals today. During the negotiation of such deals there is often no offer or counter-offer for either party to accept, but rather a gradual process in which agreements are reached piecemeal in several 'rounds' with a succession of drafts. When the ultimate agreement is reached, it is often expected that it will be embodied in a document or documents that will be exchanged by the parties at a closing.

E. Allan Farnsworth, *Precontractual Liability and Preliminary Agreements: Fair Dealing and Failed Negotiations*, 87 Colum. L. Rev. 217, 219 (1987). Article 2 of the UCC addresses this aspect of formation explicitly in section 2–204: "An agreement sufficient to make a contract for sale may be found even though the moment of its making is undetermined."

Nonetheless, it is useful in developing the basics of contract formation to begin with the assumption of a clear offer followed by a clear acceptance.

What then is an offer? The Restatement defines an offer as "the manifestation of willingness to enter into a bargain, so made as to justify another person in understanding that his assent to that bargain is invited and will conclude it." Restatement § 24. In comparison, Corbin defines an offer as

> an act whereby one person confers upon another the power to create contractual relations between them. It must be an act that leads the offeree reasonably to believe that a power to create a contract is conferred upon him. It is on this ground that we must exclude invitations to deal or acts of mere preliminary negotiation, and acts *evidently* done in jest or without intent to create legal relations. All these are acts that do not lead others reasonably to believe that they are empowered 'to close the contract.'

Arthur Corbin, *Offer and Acceptance, and Some of The Resulting Legal Relations*, 26 Yale L.J. 169, 181–82 (1917). Consider whether Corbin's more expansive definition comes closer to describing the legal effect of an offer than to defining the term.

Keep these two different definitions in mind as you read the next case, Why might the court proceed so carefully, even reluctantly, to find a contract? What lessons does the case below and in Note 2 on p. 187 suggest with regard to drafting offers?

Note that in these cases, the means of communication are somewhat old-fashioned: letters, telegraphs, and telegrams. Today phones, email, messaging and other forms of electronic media serve as the means by which offers are typically made; see, for example, International Casings Group, Inc. v. Premium Standard Farms, Inc., 358 F.Supp.2d 863 (W.D.Mo.2005), in which the court examines a lengthy email correspondence between the parties. Yet the importance for purposes of contract formation is less the medium than the intent revealed by the communication; see Brighton Investment, Ltd. v. Har-ZVI, 88 A.D.3d 1220, 932 N.Y.S.2d 214 (2011) ("an exchange of emails may constitute an enforceable contract, even if a party subsequently fails to sign implementing documents, when the communications are "sufficiently clear and concrete" to establish such an intent").

Owen v. Tunison

Supreme Judicial Court of Maine, 1932.
131 Me. 42, 158 A. 926.

Action by W.H. Owen against R.G. Tunison for breach of contract.

■ BARNES, JUSTICE. This case is reported to the law court, and such judgment is to be rendered as the law and the admissible evidence require.

Plaintiff charges that defendant agreed in writing to sell him the Bradley block and lot, situated in Bucksport, for a stated price in cash, that he later refused to perfect the sale, and that plaintiff, always willing and ready to pay the price, has suffered loss on account of defendant's unjust refusal to sell, and claims damages.

From the record it appears that defendant, a resident of Newark N.J., was, in the fall of 1929, the owner of the Bradley block and lot.

With the purpose of purchasing, on October 23, 1929, plaintiff wrote the following letter:

"Dear Mr. Tunison:

"Will you sell me your store property which is located on Main St. in Bucksport, Me. running from Montgomery's Drug Store on one corner to a Grocery Store on the other, for the sum of $6,000.00?"

Nothing more of this letter need be quoted.

On December 5, following, plaintiff received defendant's reply apparently written in Cannes, France, on November 12, and it reads:

"In reply to your letter of Oct. 23rd which has been forwarded to me in which you inquire about the Bradley Block, Bucksport, Me.

"Because of improvements which have been added and an expenditure of several thousand dollars it would not be possible for me to sell it unless I was to receive $16,000.00 cash.

"The upper floors have been converted into apartments with baths and the b'l'dg put into first class condition.

> "VERY TRULY YOURS,
> "[SIGNED] R.G. TUNISON."

Whereupon, and at once, plaintiff sent to defendant, and the latter received, in France, the following message:

"Accept your offer for Bradley block Bucksport Terms sixteen thousand cash send deed to Eastern Trust and Banking Co Bangor Maine Please acknowledge."

Four days later he was notified that defendant did not wish to sell the property, and on the 14th day of January following brought suit for his damages.

Granted that damages may be due a willing buyer if the owner refuses to tender a deed of real estate, after the latter has made an offer in writing to sell to the former, and such offer has been so accepted, it remains for us to point out that defendant here is not shown to have written to plaintiff an offer to sell.

There can have been no contract for the sale of the property desired, no meeting of the minds of the owner and prospective purchaser, unless there was an offer or proposal of sale. It cannot be successfully argued that defendant made any offer or proposal of sale.

In a recent case the words, "Would not consider less than half" is held "not to be taken as an outright offer to sell for one-half." Sellers v. Warren, 116 Me. 350, 102 A. 40, 41.

Where an owner of millet seed wrote, "I want $2.25 per cwt. for this seed f.o.b. Lowell," in an action for damages for alleged breach of contract to sell at the figure quoted above, the court held: "He [defendant] does not say, 'I offer to sell to you.' The language used is general, and such as may be used in an advertisement, or circular addressed generally to those engaged in the seed business, and is not an offer by which he may be bound, if accepted, by any or all of the persons addressed." Nebraska Seed Co. v. Harsh, 98 Neb. 89, 152 N.W. 310, 311, and cases cited in note L.R.A. 1915F, 824.

Defendant's letter of December 5 in response to an offer of $6,000 for his property may have been written with the intent to open negotiations that might lead to a sale. It was not a proposal to sell.

Judgment for defendant.

NOTES

(1) *Offer Versus Non-Offer.* In his letter of November 12, did Tunison indicate an intention to empower Owen "to close the contract"? Consider the language "it would not be possible for me to sell it unless I were to receive $16,000 cash." Was the problem in the statement a matter of the price or of Tunison's intent to sell or both? What result if Tunison had said, "I will sell for $16,000"? What if he had said, "I will not entertain an offer for less than $16,000"? Could Tunison have expected Owen to respond with an offer of more than $16,000? If your answer is No, was it not reasonable for Owen to infer that he could close the deal by acceding to that price?

(2) *Buying Bumper Hall Pen.* In a case from 1893, a would-be buyer, Harvey, was interested in purchasing a piece of property known as Bumper Hall Pen. Facey, the BHP owner, had been negotiating for its sale to local municipality for £900. Harvey telegraphed Facey, "Will you sell us Bumper Hall Pen? Telegraph lowest cash price—answer paid." Facey replied by telegram, "Lowest price for Bumper Hall Pen £900." Harvey then telegraphed back, "We agree to buy Bumper Hall Pen for the sum of nine hundred pounds asked by you." When Facey refused to sell, Harvey sued for specific performance. The Privy Council held for Facey on the ground that no

contract had been concluded. Harvey v. Facey, [1893] A.C. 552 (Privy Council) (Jamaica). Do you find an offer in any of the three telegrams? Applying Restatement § 24, identify the infirmities in each.

Is it significant that Harvey presumably knew that he was not the only potential buyer for Bumper Hall Pen? What result if Harvey's first telegram had read, "What is the lowest price at which you will sell me Bumper Hall Pen?" Redraft Facey's telegram so that it clearly would have been an offer.

(3) *Addressee of Offer*. Generally, an offer can be accepted only by the person the offeror has invited to furnish the consideration. Although one might expect this principle to have frequent application, as when an offer is addressed to an enterprise that may have changed its corporate identity, in fact, there are few cases exemplifying the principle. Why might that be so?

In another 19th-century case, Boulton, the manager of a leather "pipe hose" business, bought out the owner, Brocklehurst. Later the same day a regular customer named Jones, who had a running account with Brocklehurst, sent him an order for merchandise. Boulton received the order and supplied the goods without notifying Jones of the change of ownership. When Jones refused to pay, Boulton sued for the price. *Held:* for Jones. "When a contract is made, in which the personality of the contracting party is or may be of importance, as a contract with a man to write a book, or the like, or where there might be a setoff, no other person can interpose and adopt the contract." Boulton v. Jones, 157 Eng.Rep. 232 (1857) (Exchequer Chamber) (Bramwell, B.).

Was the personality of Brocklehurst likely to be of importance in this transaction? In sales transactions generally?

PROBLEM

Neighborly Buy-Out. In May, Joseph Oliver spoke individually to several neighbors about his plans to dispose of his ranch. On June 13, one of them, J.W. Southworth who Oliver knew had long wanted to buy the property, asked Oliver if his plans for selling "continued to be in force." Oliver responded that he expected soon to be able to put a price on the property. Southworth then said that he had the money available, that Oliver "didn't have to worry," and that "everything was ready to go." Four days later, Oliver sent a letter to four neighbors, including Southworth, enclosing "the information that I had discussed with you," as follows:

> Selling [ranch as described] at the assessed market value of $324,419. Terms available—29% down—balance over 5 years at 8% interest. Negotiate sale date for December 1, 1976 or January 1, 1977.

Has Oliver made an offer to sell his ranch? See Southworth v. Oliver, 587 P.2d 994 (Or.1978). Assume that his letter began: "I am sending this letter to you and three other neighbors." Develop reasoning that is based on that sentence and that leads to this conclusion: None of the recipients could have understood, reasonably, that the letter was an offer.

Fairmount Glass Works v. Crunden-Martin Woodenware Co.

Court of Appeals of Kentucky, 1899.
106 Ky. 659, 51 S.W. 196.

Action by the Crunden-Martin Woodenware Company against the Fairmount Glass Works to recover damages for breach of contract. Judgment for plaintiff, and defendant appeals. Affirmed.

■ HOBSON, JUDGE. On April 20, 1895, appellee wrote appellant the following letter:

"St. Louis, Mo., April 20, 1895. Gentlemen: Please advise us the lowest price you can make us on our order for ten car loads of Mason green jars, complete, with caps, packed one dozen in a case, either delivered here, or f.o.b. cars your place, as you prefer. State terms and cash discount. Very truly, Crunden-Martin W.W. Co."

To this letter appellant answered as follows:

"Fairmount, Ind. April 23, 1895. Crunden-Martin Wooden Ware Co., St. Louis, Mo.—Gentlemen: Replying to your favor of April 20, we quote you Mason fruit jars, complete, in one-dozen boxes, delivered in East St. Louis, Ill.: Pints, $4.50, quarts, $5.00, half gallons, $6.50 per gross, for immediate acceptance, and shipment not later than May 15, 1895; sixty days' acceptance,[j] or 2 off, cash in ten days. Yours truly, Fairmount Glass Works.

"Please note that we make all quotations and contracts subject to the contingencies of agencies or transportation delays or accidents beyond our control."

For reply thereto, appellee sent the following telegram on April 24, 1895:

"Fairmount Glass Works, Fairmount, Ind.: Your letter twenty-third received. Enter order ten car loads as per your quotation. Specifications mailed. Crunden-Martin W.W. Co."

In response to this telegram, appellant sent the following:

"Fairmount, Ind., April 24, 1895. Crunden-Martin W.W. Co., St. Louis, Mo.: Impossible to book your order. Output all sold. See letter. Fairmount Glass Works."

Appellee insists that, by its telegram sent in answer to the letter of April 23d, the contract was closed for the purchase of 10 car loads of Mason fruit jars. Appellant insists that the contract was not closed by this telegram, and that it had the right to decline to fill the order at the time it sent its telegram of April 24. This is the chief question in the case. The court below gave judgment in favor of appellee, and appellant has appealed, earnestly insisting that the judgment is erroneous.

---

[j]   In this context the word "acceptance" is not used to denote a response to an offer. Rather, here it refers to a form of commitment used to assure payment in 60 days.

We are referred to a number of authorities holding that a quotation of prices is not an offer to sell, in the sense that a completed contract will arise out of the giving of an order for merchandise in accordance with the proposed terms. There are a number of cases holding that the transaction is not completed until the order so made is accepted. 7 Am. & Eng.Enc.Law (2d Ed.) p. 138; Smith v. Gowdy, 8 Allen, Mass., 566; Beaupre v. Telegraph Co., 21 Minn. 155. But each case must turn largely upon the language there used. In this case we think there was more than a quotation of prices, although appellant's letter uses the word "quote" in stating the prices given. The true meaning of the correspondence must be determined by reading it as a whole. Appellee's letter of April 20th, which began the transaction, did not ask for a quotation of prices. It reads: "Please advise us the lowest price you can make us on our order for ten carloads of Mason green jars. State terms and cash discount." From this appellant could not fail to understand that appellee wanted to know at what price it would sell ten car loads of these jars; so when, in answer, it wrote: "We quote you Mason fruit jars pints $4.50, quarts $5.00, half gallons $6.50, per gross, for immediate acceptance; 2 off, cash in ten days,"—it must be deemed as intending to give appellee the information it asked for. We can hardly understand what is meant by the words "for immediate acceptance," unless the latter was intended as a proposition to sell at these prices if accepted immediately. In construing every contract, the aim of the court is to arrive at the intention of the parties. In none of the cases to which we have been referred on behalf of appellant was there on the face of the correspondence any such expression of intention to make an offer to sell on the terms indicated. The expression in appellant's letter, "for immediate acceptance," taken in connection with appellee's letter, in effect, at what price it would sell it the goods, is, it seems to us, much stronger evidence of a present offer, which, when accepted immediately, closed the contract. Appellee's letter was plainly an inquiry for the price and terms on which appellant would sell it the goods, and appellant's answer to it was not a quotation of prices, but a definite offer to sell on the terms indicated, and could not be withdrawn after the terms had been accepted.

[The court quoted further from Crunden-Martin's telegram of April 24 and a letter in which it gave "specifications": shipment not later than May 15; first carload to contain 55 gross quart jars and other specified quantities of pint and half-gallon jars; and "The jars and caps to be strictly first-quality goods." Referring to the latter expression, Fairmount observed that it was not in its offer of April 23, and contended that, because the offer had not been "accepted as made", Fairmount was not bound. The court observed that this objection came late in the day. The court further stated: "Crunden-Martin offers proof tending to show that these words, in the trade in which parties were engaged, conveyed the same meaning as the words used in Fairmount's letter and were only a different form of expressing the same idea. Fairmount's conduct would seem to confirm this evidence." (In this quotation the parties' names have been substituted for "appellant" and "appellee.")]

Appellant also insists that the contract was indefinite, because the quantity of each size of the jars was not fixed, that ten car loads is too indefinite a specification of the quantity sold, and that appellee had no right to accept the goods to be delivered on different days. The proof shows that "ten car loads" is an expression used in the trade as equivalent to 1,000 gross, 100 gross being regarded as a car load. The offer to sell the different sizes at different prices gave the purchaser the right to name the quantity of each size, and, the offer being to ship not later than May 15th, the buyer had the right to fix the time of delivery at any time before that. The petition, if defective, was cured by the judgment, which is fully sustained by the evidence.

Judgment affirmed.

NOTES

(1) *The Fairmount Letter.* Suppose that Fairmount's letter of April 23 had not been in response to a preliminary letter from Crunden-Martin. Would the result have been the same? What significance should be attached to the use of the expression "we quote you" in the Fairmount letter? What facts make "quote" mean "offer"?

(2) *The Salt-Trade Case.* Consider the foregoing questions in relation to the decision in Moulton v. Kershaw, 18 N.W. 172 (Wis.1884). Kershaw wrote to Moulton:

> In consequence of a rupture in the salt trade we are authorized to offer Michigan fine salt in full car load lots of 80 to 95 barrels, delivered at your city at 85 cents per barrel to be shipped per C. & N.W.R.R. Co. only. At this price it is a bargain as the price in general remains unchanged. Shall be pleased to receive your order.

Moulton immediately wired Kershaw, "Your letter of yesterday received and noted. You may ship me two thousand barrels Michigan fine salt as offered in your letter." Kershaw failed to ship the salt, and Moulton sued for breach of contract. The trial court overruled Kershaw's demurrer and Kershaw appealed. *Held:* Reversed. "The language is not such as a business man would use in making an offer to sell a definite amount of property."

Suppose Kershaw's communication to Moulton had read, "we are authorized to offer one to 25 carloads Michigan fine salt," etc. Would the result have been different? What would be the objection to construing Kershaw's communication as an offer to sell any reasonable quantity of salt—say one to twenty-five car load lots—leaving it to the offeree to name the precise quantity? Has not Kershaw committed himself in advance to supply any reasonable quantity? What result if Kershaw's communication had read, "we are authorized to offer you all the Michigan fine salt you will order," etc.?

Advertisements as Offers

Proposals to engage in a transaction are sometimes addressed to a very wide audience. Advertisements by sellers to the general public provide a familiar example. Are such proposals offers? The general rule is that an advertisement is not an offer, but rather an invitation by the seller to the buyer to make an offer to purchase.

What about reward notices, which are also typically made to a general audience? Do they empower the offeree to "close the contract," in Corbin's phrase? What does Broadnax v. Ledbetter, discussed on p. 93 above, suggest?

If advertisements were held to be offers, what would be a store's position if the demand for its advertised wares exceeded its supply? Might the problem of unexpected demand be solved if sellers were required to have on hand a reasonable supply of advertised merchandise? Another solution might require "first come, first served" to be read into every advertisement. This appears to be the approach of French law, under which "the great majority of authorities consider such a proposal to be an offer, even if it can be accepted only by one of those to whom it is addressed. But such an offer is subject to the condition, as to each offeree, that it has not already been accepted by a quicker-acting offeree." 1 Rudolf B. Schlesinger (ed.), Formation of Contracts: A Study of the Common Core of Legal Systems 359 (1968). Which approach do you prefer? Which better protects the parties' expectations?

What about reward notices, which are also typically made to a general audience? Do they empower the offeree to "close the contract," in Corbin's phrase? What does Broadnax v. Ledbetter, discussed on p. 93 above, suggest?

Whether an advertisement can *ever* be an offer is considered in Lefkowitz v. Great Minneapolis Surplus Store, p. 194 below.

————

Consumer Contracts

One important class of contracts—familiar to all readers of this book—consists of contracts between businesses and consumers. Businesses typically have superior bargaining power and, as repeat players, greater expertise and experience with respect to the matters addressed in the contract. This understandably leads to concerns that the standard doctrines of contract law, which tend to assume that the parties are of roughly equal sophistication and bargaining power, may not provide sufficient protection for consumers. As the Reporters for the American Law Institute's draft Restatement of Consumer Contracts put it:

> Consumer contracts present a fundamental challenge to the law
> of contracts, arising from the asymmetry in information,

sophistication, and stakes between the parties to these contracts—the business and the consumers. On one side stands a well-informed and counseled business party, entering numerous identical transactions, with the tools and sophistication to understand and draft detailed legal terms and design practices that serve its commercial goals. On the other side stand consumers who are informed only about some aspects of the transaction, but rarely about the list of standard terms. These consumers enter the transaction solely for personal or household purposes, without any professional understanding of its legal contours. It is both irrational and infeasible for most consumers to keep up with the increasingly complex terms provided by businesses in the multitude of transactions, large and small, entered into daily.[k]

The responses of the legal system to these concerns have taken many forms. At both the state and federal level, legislation has been enacted and regulations promulgated to protect consumers. Some of that legislation and regulation focuses primarily on disclosure—attempting to assure that consumers have sufficient information to make up for existing asymmetries and make an informed choice as to whether to enter into a particular contract. Other approaches focus on substantive limits on the terms of contracts to which a consumer is a party. These laws and rules are considered in depth in courses on consumer law.

Even in the absence of relevant legislation or regulation, though, issues arise that force the common law of contracts to come to grips with the consumer context in applying general doctrines of contract law in the consumer context. Sometimes this involves application of a standard rule with sensitivity to its context; other times, it involves application of rules that are facially neutral but, by their nature, apply most often in the consumer context. Occasionally, judges develop new rules that recognize the imbalance between businesses and consumers. Of course, a great many disputes about consumer contracts are resolved by application of existing contract doctrines with no adjustment for the consumer context. As might be expected, the entire area is the subject of continuing controversy, both as to the need for protection for consumers and the nature of that protection (including disputes as to whether particular measures are protective or paternalistic).

As you read cases involving contracts between businesses and consumers, consider the extent to which courts have, or have not, taken that context into account. Consider further whether it is the role of courts, as opposed to legislators and regulators, to do so.

---

[k]   Restatement of the Law, Consumer Contracts (May 2017 Discussion Draft), Reporters' Introduction.

Lefkowitz v. Great Minneapolis Surplus Store

Supreme Court of Minnesota, 1957.
86 N.W.2d 689.

■ MURPHY, JUSTICE. This is an appeal from an order of the Municipal Court of Minneapolis denying the motion of the defendant for amended findings of fact, or, in the alternative, for a new trial. The order for judgment awarded the plaintiff the sum of $138.50 as damages for breach of contract.

This case grows out of the alleged refusal of the defendant to sell to the plaintiff a certain fur piece which it had offered for sale in a newspaper advertisement. It appears from the record that on April 6, 1956, the defendant published the following advertisement in a Minneapolis newspaper:

Saturday 9 A.M. Sharp 3 Brand New Fur Coats Worth to $100.00

First Come First Served $1 Each

On April 13, the defendant again published an advertisement in the same newspaper as follows:

SATURDAY 9 A.M.

2 BRAND NEW PASTEL

MINK 3-SKIN SCARFS

Selling for $89.50

Out they go

Saturday. Each $1.00

1 BLACK LAPIN STOLE BEAUTIFUL,

worth $139.50 . . . . $1.00

FIRST COME FIRST SERVED[1]

The record supports the findings of the court that on each of the Saturdays following the publication of the above-described ads the plaintiff was the first to present himself at the appropriate counter in the defendant's store and on each occasion demanded the coat and the stole so advertised and indicated his readiness to pay the sale price of $1. On both occasions, the defendant refused to sell the merchandise to the plaintiff, stating on the first occasion that by a 'house rule' the offer was intended for women only and sales would not be made to men, and on the second visit that plaintiff knew defendant's house rules.

The trial court properly disallowed plaintiff's claim for the value of the fur coats since the value of these articles was speculative and uncertain. The only evidence of value was the advertisement itself to the effect that the coats were 'Worth to $100.00,' how much less being

---

[1] The text of the ad for the furs appeared in a small bubble along with scores of other items in bubbles on a crowded full page.

speculative especially in view of the price for which they were offered for sale. With reference to the offer of the defendant on April 13, 1956, to sell the '1 Black Lapin Stole * * * worth $139.50 * * *' the trial court held that the value of this article was established and granted judgment in favor of the plaintiff for that amount less the $1 quoted purchase price.'

1.   The defendant contends that a newspaper advertisement offering items of merchandise for sale at a named price is a 'unilateral offer' which may be withdrawn without notice. He relies upon authorities which hold that, where an advertiser publishes in a newspaper that he has a certain quantity or quality of goods which he wants to dispose of at certain prices and on certain terms, such advertisements are not offers which become contracts as soon as any person to whose notice they may come signifies his acceptance by notifying the other that he will take a certain quantity of them. Such advertisements have been construed as an invitation for an offer of sale on the terms stated, which offer, when received, may be accepted or rejected and which therefore does not become a contract of sale until accepted by the seller; and until a contract has been so made, the seller 1 may modify or revoke such prices or terms. Montgomery Ward & Co. v. Johnson, 209 Mass. 89, 95 N.E. 290; Nickel v. Theresa Farmers Co-op. Ass'n, 247 Wis. 412, 20 N.W.2d 117; Craft v. Elder & Johnson Co., 38 N.E.2d 416, 34 Ohio L.A. 603; Annotation, 157 A.L.R. 746.

The defendant relies principally on Craft v. Elder & Johnston Co. supra. In that case, the court discussed the legal effect of an advertisement offering for sale, as a one-day special, an electric sewing machine at a named price. The view was expressed that the advertisement 'was not an offer made to any specific person but was made to the public generally. Thereby it would be properly designated as a unilateral offer and not being supported by any consideration could be withdrawn at will and without notice.' It is true that such an offer may be withdrawn before acceptance. Since all offers are by their nature unilateral because they are necessarily made by one party or on one side in the negotiation of a contract, the distinction made in that decision between a unilateral offer and a unilateral contract is not clear. On the facts before us we are concerned with whether the advertisement constituted an offer, and, if so, whether the plaintiff's conduct constituted an acceptance.

There are numerous authorities which hold that a particular advertisement in a newspaper or circular letter relating to a sale of articles may be construed by the court as constituting an offer, acceptance of which would complete a contract. The test of whether a binding obligation may originate in advertisements addressed to the general public is 'whether the facts show that some performance was promised in positive terms in return for something requested.' 1 Williston, Contracts (Rev. ed.) s 27.

The authorities above cited emphasize that, where the offer is clear, definite, and explicit, and leaves nothing open for negotiation, it constitutes an offer, acceptance of which will complete the contract.

Whether in any individual instance a newspaper advertisement is an offer rather than an invitation to make an offer depends on the legal intention of the parties and the surrounding circumstances. Annotation, 157 A.L.R. 744, 751; 77 C.J.S., Sales, s 25b; 17 C.J.S., Contracts, s 389. We are of the view on the facts before us that the offer by the defendant of the sale of the Lapin fur was clear, definite, and explicit, and left nothing open for negotiation. The plaintiff having successful managed to be the first one to appear at the seller's place of business to be served, as requested by the advertisement, and having offered the stated purchase price of the article, he was entitled to performance on the part of the defendant. We think the trial court was correct in holding that there was in the conduct of the parties a sufficient mutuality of obligation to constitute a contract of sale.

2.   The defendant contends that the offer was modified by a 'house rule' to the effect that only women were qualified to receive the bargains advertised. The advertisement contained no such restriction. This objection may be disposed of briefly by stating that, while an advertiser has the right at any time before acceptance to modify his offer, he does not have the right, after acceptance, to impose new or arbitrary conditions not contained in the published offer.

[AFFIRMED.]

NOTES

(1)   Lefkowitz had also shown up in response to the first ad run by the store but was denied recovery then as well. Why? What aspect of advertisement as offer was missing from the store's first ad? That ruling is criticized in Ian Ayres and Robert Gertner, *Filling Gaps in Incomplete Contracts: An Economic Theory of Default Rules*, 99 Yale L.J. 87, 105–106 (1989).

On the first occasion the store had also refused to sell to Lefkowitz, saying that by a "house rule" the offer was intended for women only; sales would not be made to men. Considering this additional fact (and putting aside questions of discrimination), do you agree with the court's decision that Lefkowitz could recover under the second advertisement?

(2)   *Case Comparison.* In Leonard v. Pepsico, described at Note 3, p. 167, the would-be purchaser of the Harrier Jet, relying on *Lefkowitz*, argued that the Pepsi Stuff television commercial was an offer. The court held it was not: "First, the commercial cannot be regarded in itself as sufficiently definite, because it specifically reserved the details of the offer to a separate writing, the Catalog.[m] The commercial itself made no mention of the steps a

---

[m]   It also communicated additional words of reservation: "Offer not available in all areas. See details on specially marked packages."

potential offeree would be required to take to accept the alleged offer of a Harrier Jet. The advertisement in *Lefkowitz*, in contrast, 'identified the person who could accept.' Second, even if the Catalog had included a Harrier Jet among the items that could be obtained by redemption of Pepsi Points, the absence of any words of limitation such as 'first come, first served,' renders the alleged offer sufficiently indefinite that no contract could be formed." 88 F.Supp.2d at 124.

(3) *Consumer Protection.* In Geismar v. Abraham & Strauss, 439 N.Y.S.2d 1005 (Dist.Ct.1981), a disappointed shopper sued a department store that had advertised a set of china dishes regularly priced at $280 for only $39.95, but had refused to sell them at that price. The court held that since the advertisement was not an offer, there was no breach of contract. But it went on to hold that she could recover $50 under a New York statute providing that any person "injured" by advertising "which is misleading in a material respect" is entitled to recover actual damages or $50, whichever is greater. Many other states have enacted laws dealing with false advertising, such as the Uniform Deceptive Trade Practices Act. In addition, Section 5 of the Federal Trade Commission Act (15 U.S.C. § 45) declares "unfair or deceptive acts or practices" to be unlawful as a matter of federal law.

Consumers may also be protected by bait-and-switch legislation that makes unlawful "the disparagement by acts or words of the advertised product" and "the failure to have available a sufficient quantity of the advertised product to meet reasonably anticipated demands, unless the advertisement clearly and adequately discloses that supply is limited." 16 C.F.R. § 238.3 (2016).

(4) *Competitive Bidding.* Contracting parties may fix the contract price, leave it to negotiation, or determine it by competitive bidding. A party who chooses to determine it by competitive bidding may invite open bids at an auction, as is often done in the sale of goods or land, or may invite sealed bids, as is common in the letting of building contracts.

If a party invites competitive bids, is this an offer to be accepted by the highest bidder when the bid is made? Or is it merely an invitation for offers by bids that can then be accepted or rejected by the one who has invited them? The law has taken the latter view, that it is the bidder who makes the offer. Can you see why? This is the general rule stated in UCC § 2–328 with respect to the sale of goods by auction. Under that section the auctioneer may, however, make an offer by advertising the sale to be "without reserve." Note that if the sale is "without reserve," the auctioneer is bound not to withdraw after a bid is made. The bidder is not similarly bound.

The rather elaborate provisions of UCC § 2–328 (sale by auction) are, of course, expressly applicable only to the sale of goods. UCC § 2–102. Might they be extended by analogy to the sale of land? Comment 1 to UCC § 1–103 considers that possibility:

> The courts have often recognized that the policies embodied in an act are applicable in reason to subject-matter that was not expressly included in the language of the act and did the same where reason and policy so required, even where the subject-matter

had been intentionally excluded from the act in general. Nothing in the Uniform Commercial Code stands in the way of the continuance of such action by the courts.

See Chevalier v. Town of Sanford, 475 A.2d 1148 (Me.1984), (a land auction case in which the court reasoned by analogy to UCC § 2–328).

Although UCC § 2–328 describes a sale by auction as "complete when the auctioneer so announces by the fall of the hammer or in other customary manner," thousands of auctions daily are now concluded with a click rather than a hammer, as buyers bid on on-line auction websites such as eBay. Millions of auctions can be found at any time on that and other sites, governed by rules that bidders and sellers agree to as a condition of using the site. An on-line seller may also condition the offer to sell by setting a "reserve price" that must be met in order for the seller to be bound; see Note 4, p. 197–198 above.

PROBLEM

The Midas Touch. In 1985, as part of the Liberty-Ellis Island Commemorative Coin Act, the United States Mint produced a limited run of 500,000 gold five dollar coins. Announcements were sent to lists of coin collectors, who were informed that "[i]f the Mint receives your reservation by December 31, 1985, you will enjoy a favorable Pre-Issue Discount saving you up to 16% on your coins." The Mint received over 756,000 orders, and a number of buyers were sorely disappointed when their order forms were returned. (The court noted that many buyers "developed a more serious case of disappointment when it became apparent that the gold coins had increased in value by approximately 200% with the first months of 1986.") Two such buyers, Mary and Anthony Mesaros, sued for breach of contract, arguing that their order forms ("YES, please accept my order for the U.S. Liberty Coins I have indicated. I understand that all sales are final. Verification of my order will be made by the Department of Treasury, US Mint") were acceptances of the Mint's advertised offer. Did the Mesaros have a contract with the United States? See Mesaros v. United States, 845 F.2d 1576, 1578 (Fed.Cir.1988).

Construction Contracts

Construction contracts are the last of the "typical categories" of cases we highlight here. Given the construction industry's significant role in the economy, such agreements are of great importance. In consequence, disputes arising from construction contracts often result in litigation. The complexity of the typical transaction, with a general contractor perched between an owner and a subcontractor, invites sophisticated analysis that is often useful by analogy in other transactions involving intermediaries, also called brokers or middlemen. See Note 2, p. 604.

Some of the most intractable disputes in construction contracts involve claims of improper performance. This is not surprising given the length of time required to build a particular project and the difficulty of complying with the details of plans and specifications; such claims are dealt with in later chapters. We begin, however, with the problem of mistake in the formation stage. For major construction projects, the process of offer and acceptance typically involves a complicated bidding process in which general contractors compete with each other by submitting bids that are in turn based on bids received from subcontractors, who also compete with each other. Bidding is particularly common, and often highly regulated, when the construction is for a branch of government rather than a private landowner. Why might that be?

Mistakes in Offers

Mistakes occur, or are at least noticed, at various points throughout the contracting process. They may be made by one party (unilateral mistake) or by both parties (bilateral mistake). In this section, we are concerned with unilateral mistakes in offers that are computational in nature or that result from an error in the transmission of the offer, the sort of mistake that Professor Melvin Eisenberg calls "intellectual blunders." Melvin Eisenberg, *Mistake in Contract Law*, 91 Calif. L. Rev. 1573, 1577 (2003). In Chapter 9, we consider *mutual* mistakes that are sometimes in the nature of a misunderstanding between the parties about the terms of their agreement than the more flatfooted errors at issue at here.

Mistakes in offers tend to occur in situations where the contracting process is complex, is subject to deadlines, and involves input from multiple parties. This explains why mistakes commonly arise in bids (offers) submitted by contractors for work on construction projects. Not only must the contractor solicit, select, and coordinate bids from multiple subcontractors across the building trades in exact compliance with the owner's specifications, but the entire process occurs within a short and frequently pressured time frame:

> Subcontractor and supplier bidders may fear that their bids will be undercut by their competition, so they often wait to submit their bids until the last hour or two before the general contractor's bid is due. Frequently, a subcontractor or materialman will discover after submitting his bid that he has made a mistake, perhaps because one of the general contractors informs him that he is either substantially higher or substantially lower than other bidders. He must then frantically review the plans (if he still has access to them), correct his mistake, and telephone his corrected price to all concerned. While this last-minute subcontractor bidding is being received, the general contractor is collating and comparing the prices and

the qualifying restrictions that he has received, adding in factors for his own workforce and supervision, and adjusting the total as later prices are received by phone.

Comment, *The Subcontractor's Bid: An Option Contract Arising Through Promissory Estoppel*, 34 Emory L.J. 421, 425–28 (1985).

In Elsinore Union Elementary School District v. Kastorff, for example, the contractor made what the court identified as "an honest clerical error" in his bid on a building contract after he failed to include anything for plumbing in his bid. When the bids were opened, Kastorff's was the lowest by some $11,000. Noticing this, the school superintendent asked Kastorff if his numbers were correct. After checking with his assistant, Kastorff replied that they were, and was awarded the contract. After realizing his mistake the next day, Kastorff informed the school district he could not do the job for the amount bid. The school district refused to release him from the contract. When Kastorff refused to perform, the school district hired the second lowest bidder, and sued Kastorff for the difference between the two bids. Judgment was given for the school district, and Kastorff appealed. Held: Reversed.

The Supreme Court of California agreed with the trial court that "the bid had been submitted as the result of an excusable and honest mistake of a material and fundamental character, that [Kastorff] had not been negligent in preparing the proposal, that it had acted promptly to notify the board of the mistake and to rescind the bid, and that the board had accepted the bid with knowledge of the error. Under the circumstances, the "bargain" for which the board presses appears too sharp for law and equity to sustain." 353 P.2d 713 (Cal.1960). What factors appear to have made Kastorff's mistake excusable?

A second area in which mistakes occur with some regularity is in settlement agreements. As you read the next case, consider if there are similarities in the circumstances of formation between construction contracts and settlements agreements.

NOTES

(1) *Knowledge of Mistake.* If an offeree knows or has reason to know, of the offeror's material mistake at the time of acceptance, the offeror is not bound. "One cannot snap up an offer or bid knowing that it was made in mistake." Tyra v. Cheney, 152 N.W. 835 (Minn.1915).

Professor Eisenberg argues that granting relief for a bidder, in a case like *Kastorff*, is the morally correct thing to do. Melvin Eisenberg, *Mistake in Contract Law*, 91 Calif. L. Rev. 1573, 1586 (2003). On that view, should the size of the party's computational error matter? Is it any more immoral to take advantage of a known thousand-dollar mistake than of a ten-dollar mistake? In Kastorff's case, the court took note of the magnitude of his mistake.

(2) *Mistakes in Bidding*. As noted in the excerpt on subcontractors' bids, p. 199 above, "Mistakes come in a variety of flavors. There may be mistakes in construing the language of the plans and specification, in estimating quantities required, in unit pricing, in multiplying quantities by unit prices, in transferring data from one work-sheet to another, in typing the bid form, and many others." Id. Courts considering bidders' claims for relief for mistake have often distinguished between mistakes that are "clerical" or "computational" from those of "judgment." Consider a dealer in lumber, invited to bid on a sale of shingles required to roof a building. What mistakes might the dealer make that would be certainly ones of judgment? Is it apparent why the courts disfavor giving relief for mistakes of that kind? See M.A. Mortenson v. Timberline Software Corp., 998 P.2d 305 (Wash.2000), where the mistake was attributable to faulty computer software.

Does the provision of relief to a contractor like Kastorff tempt low bidders to manufacture evidence of mistakes in computation when the mistake was really one of misjudgment? Professor Melvin A. Eisenberg has discounted that threat on the ground that typically, when a computational error has been made, "the work papers, surrounding circumstances, or both, clearly demonstrate" the error. See Melvin Eisenberg, cited in Note 1 above, at 1587.

(3) *Statutory Sequel*. More than a decade after the decision in *Kastorff*, mentioned in the text above, the California legislature enacted the following statute:

> A bidder [on a public contract] shall not be relieved of the bid unless by consent of the awarding authority nor shall any change be made in the bid because of mistake, but the bidder may bring an action against the public entity in a court of competent jurisdiction in the county in which the bids were opened for the recovery of the amount forfeited, without interest or costs.

> The bidder shall establish to the satisfaction of the court that:

> (a) A mistake was made.

> (b) He or she gave the public entity written notice within five days after the opening of the bids of the mistake, specifying in the notice in detail how the mistake occurred.

> (c) The mistake made the bid materially different than he or she intended it to be.

> (d) The mistake was made in filling out the bid and not due to error in judgment or to carelessness in inspecting the site of the work, or in reading the plans or specifications.

Cal. Pub. Cont. Code §§ 5101 & 5103. Why might the legislature have enacted this statute? What result in *Kastorff* under this statute?

(4) *Knowledge Versus Reason to Know*. An offeror who has submitted a mistaken bid may claim that the magnitude of the mistake was such that it should have been apparent from the face of the offer. What sorts of circumstances might warrant suspicion on the part of the offeree? See

Sumerel v. Goodyear Tire & Rubber Co., 232 P.3d 128 (Colo. Ct. App. 2009), presented in full in Chapter 9, involving the settlement agreement of a lawsuit, in which the plaintiffs' counsel argued that a $500,000 misstatement of the amount of a settlement in an email was binding. (Plaintiffs' counsel attributed the overstatement "to a possible desire on [defendant's] part to 'sweeten the pot.'") As the court admonished: "In our view, the present case is a prototype for a purported offer that was "on its face manifestly too good to be true." The jury had already spoken, and the parties had agreed on the relevant accrual dates. All that should have been left was a simple mathematical calculation. [T]he proper course [of conduct] was obvious to us: plaintiffs' counsel should have called [defendant's counsel], identified the discrepancy, and concluded the matter without further delay. [T]he law will not countenance the patently inequitable result that plaintiffs seek."

Heifetz Metal Crafts, Inc. v. Peter Kiewit Sons' Co., 264 F.2d 435 (8th Cir.1959), provides another good example. There Kiewit was preparing a bid for the construction of a hospital and Heifetz offered to do the kitchen work for $99,500, $52,000 less than Kiewit's next lowest quotation. Kiewit lowered its bid by $52,000, which made it $17,942,200, the lowest by $9,000. After Kiewit was awarded the contract and had accepted the Heifetz offer, Heifetz discovered that in preparing its quotation it had overlooked some subsidiary kitchen installations required by the plans. It sought rescission and argued that since its quotation was one-third less than the next lowest, Kiewit should have realized that there had been a mistake. The court rejected this contention and held that the contract was enforceable. It relied upon testimony by Kiewit's employees that they were ignorant of the mistake, upon Kiewit's lack of familiarity with the kitchen equipment field, and upon "testimony indicating that at times some contractor would have a special reason for desiring to obtain a particular job and would submit a figure controlled by that consideration." It noted that "the figures submitted by subcontractors on the electrical work for the project has varied from $1,400,000 to $1,850,000 and on the lathing and plastering work from $672,000 to $1,028,000; and the 'mechanical spread' had been between $3,647,000 and $6,000,000."

Is it of any significance that a general contractor will sometimes pass over a low bid to accept one from a subcontractor with which the general contractor has a personal or business connection, and that subcontractors sometimes deliberately make losing bids to break up such combinations? Is it of any significance that subcontractors sometimes bid low in the expectation that changes will later be made to provide for profitable extra work?

(5) *Errors in Advertising*. What should a merchant to do when it finds that it has misstated the price for advertised goods? One solution is to withdraw the ad, before opportunistic shoppers have proceeded to checkout. Another, given a serious understatement of price, is simply to dishonor orders from shoppers, on the ground that shoppers should have known the price was "too good to be true." Is there protective language a merchant might include in every ad, such as "One to a customer"? See Mark Budnitz,

Consumers Surfing for Sales in Cyberspace: What Constitutes Acceptance and What Legal Terms and Conditions Bind the Consumer?, 16 Ga. St. U. L. Rev. 741 (2000).

PROBLEMS

(1) *Transmission Problems.* In the market for a car, Donovan read an advertisement placed by Lexus of Westminster in his local newspaper, the Daily Pilot. The advertisement presented a number of used cars for sale, including a sapphire blue 1995 Jaguar XJ6, VIN 720603, listed for $25,995. Donovan went down to the dealership, took the advertised car for a test drive, and told the sales representative that he would buy it. The sales representative immediately informed Donovan that the advertised price was a mistake. Although Donovan began to write a check for the advertised price, he was informed that the car could only be sold for $37,016. Donovan refused to pay the higher price and sued the dealership for breach of contract. Donovan v. RRL Corp., 88 Cal. Rptr.2d 143 (Ct.App. 1999).

> In that case, the appellate court made the following observation:

> A first year law student would not be surprised to be called upon to answer the questions we address here. Does an advertisement for a specific used car at a designated price constitute an offer that may be accepted by tendering the purchase price? Does a statute prohibiting an automobile dealer from refusing to sell a vehicle at the advertised price affect the answer? Finally, does the answer change if the erroneous price inserted in the advertisement was the result of an error? We believe the answers are respectively 'possibly,' 'yes,' and 'no.' However, since such cryptic answers would not entitle our hypothetical law student to a passing grade, we must explain these answers below.

Id. at 144. Do you agree with the court's answers? As a *real* first year law student, what are your explanations? A few additional facts may help: the newspaper had made a typographical error which caused the 1995 Jaguar to be advertised at the price of a 1994 Jaguar; the dealership failed to proofread the advertising copy received from the Daily Pilot; a California statute makes it unlawful for an automobile dealer to "[f]ail to sell a vehicle to any person at the advertised total price, exclusive of taxes and [certain other specified fees]"; and Donovan did not know the market price of a 1995 Jaguar.

In 2001, the California Supreme Court reversed the appellate court decision. Donovan v. RRL Corp., 27 P.3d 702 (Cal.2001). On what grounds might the lower court have failed to get a passing grade?

(2) *Errors on Line?* Foley, in the market for a boat, examined a 55′ Hatteras Convertible ("Material Girls") owned by Yale and Donna Turner, but decided not to make an offer. Five months later, the Turners informed Foley that the boat was listed on eBay as a "reserve auction" (reserving the sellers' right not to sell unless an undisclosed minimum reserve price was met). Although Foley was the highest bidder, he had not met the reserve price, so no sale was concluded. A week later, the boat was listed again on eBay as a reserve auction; again the reserve price was not met. The boat was

then listed again, but this time as a "No Reserve" auction with an opening bid of $100,000. Foley was the highest bidder (at $135,000) and received an eBay generated email informing him that he had "won." The Turners refused to sell him the boat on the grounds that their agent had mistakenly listed the auction as "No Reserve."

Assuming that the Turners' agent was authorized to act for them (and leaving further questions about agency for course on torts), are the Turners obligated to sell the boat to Foley? How would you describe the nature of an offer created by a reserve auction? See Foley v. Yacht Management Group, Inc., 2009 WL 2020776 (N.D. Ill. 2009).

SECTION 3.   THE ACCEPTANCE

What is an acceptance? Restatement § 50 defines it as "a manifestation of assent to the terms thereof made by the offeree in a manner invited or required by the offer." Corbin, in turn, defines an acceptance as "a voluntary act of the offeree whereby he exercises the power conferred upon him by the offer, and thereby creates the set of legal relations called a contract. What acts are sufficient to serve this purpose? We must look first to the terms in which the offer was expressed, either by words or by other conduct. The offeror has, in the beginning, full power to determine the acts that are to constitute acceptance." Arthur L. Corbin, *Offer and Acceptance, and Some of the Resulting Legal Relations*, 26 Yale L.J. 169, 199 (1917).

Assuming that there has been an offer, the offeree by exercising the power of acceptance "thereby creates," in Corbin's words, "the set of legal relations called a contract." One of the most important consequences of this "set of legal relations" is that the offeror is no longer free to change its mind and withdraw from the relationship without incurring liability. (In Hohfeldian terminology, see Note 2, p. 96, "the offeree has, before the contract is made, a power to create a contract by means of acceptance. A power is the capacity to change a legal relationship.") By what means, then, may the offeree exercise this power of acceptance? If, as Corbin says, the offeror has "full power to determine the acts that are to constitute acceptance," the first step in answering this question is to look at the offer to see what sort of acceptance it invited.

We already know from Chapter 1 that an offeror may bargain either for a performance or for a promise. As suggested at Note 5, p. 59, the more economically significant transactions usually involve the latter sort of bargain, in which the offeror seeks the assurance of another promise in return for its own. When a promise is sought, can it be inferred from conduct of the offeree? Can mere silence ever count? Must the offeree notify the offeror of the acceptance? This section considers these and related questions concerning the components of an acceptance.

Wucherpfennig v. Dooley

Supreme Court of North Dakota, 1984.
351 N.W.2d 443.

■ SAND, JUSTICE. Donald Wucherpfennig appealed from a district court judgment dismissing his claim for specific performance of an alleged contract for the sale of land. We affirm.

Donald Wucherpfennig, Elizabeth Dooley, and Louise Grettum are the children of Fred and Harriet Wucherpfennig. Fred died in 1964 and Harriet died in 1977. The family farm, consisting of four quarters of land, passed to Donald, Elizabeth, and Louise by their parents' wills. The quarter which includes the farmstead, known as the "home quarter," was devised as follows: two-thirds undivided interest to Donald, one-sixth undivided interest each to Elizabeth and Louise. Each of the three children received a one-third undivided interest in the remaining three quarters.

During the probate of Harriet's estate, Elizabeth expressed an interest in selling her share of the property to Donald. On 4 January 1979, Elizabeth sent to Robert Case, the attorney handling the probate of the estate, a letter which stated:

"Now if Don wants to buy my share of the real estate, I will sell it to him for $200 an acre, provided it is a cash deal & handled promptly."

Case responded by letter dated 13 January 1979, stating that Donald was "interested" in purchasing Elizabeth's interest in the property. Case subsequently followed up with another letter, dated 17 February 1979, the entire text of which states:

"Donald has made arrangements with the Federal Land Bank to secure funds to purchase your interest in the estate farmland and we are therefore ready to proceed with this transaction. Please let me know the exact dollar amount that you expect to receive for your interest in the land. I must know also if you are willing to sign the agreement relating to Special Use Valuation. Please let me hear from you regarding these matters."

Elizabeth did not respond to this letter, but revoked her offer to sell the land to Donald for $200 per acre by a letter dated 9 March 1979.

Donald brought an action seeking to enforce the contract which he alleges was formed by Elizabeth's offer of 4 January and his acceptance as communicated in Case's letter of 17 February. Donald also sought, in the alternative, partition of the property. By consent of the parties the specific performance action was tried first.

The district court found that there was no acceptance of Elizabeth's offer, and that even if there had been an acceptance the resulting contract could not have been specifically enforced. Judgment dismissing Donald's claim for specific performance was entered, and Donald appealed.

The court listed four separate bases for dismissal of the action, and any one of these, standing alone, would be sufficient to support a denial of specific performance. Therefore, in order to warrant reversal on appeal the appellant must establish that all four of these conclusions are erroneous. Because we agree with the district court that there was no acceptance, it is unnecessary for us to reach the remaining issues.

The acceptance of an offer must be absolute, unequivocal, and unconditional, and it may not introduce additional terms or conditions. Section 9–03–21, N.D. C.C.; Cooke v. Blood Systems, Inc., 320 N.W.2d 124, 128 (N.D.1982); Grossman v. McLeish Ranch, 291 N.W.2d 427, 430 (N.D.1980); Greenberg v. Stewart, 236 N.W.2d 862, 868 (N.D.1975). In order to form a contract, the offer and acceptance must express assent to the same thing. Grossman, supra, 291 N.W.2d at 430; Greenberg, supra, 236 N.W.2d at 868. A valid acceptance must be unequivocally expressive of an intent to create thereby, without more, a contract. Markmann v. H.A. Bruntjen Co., 249 Minn. 281, 286, 81 N.W.2d 858, 862 (1957); Minar v. Skoog, 235 Minn. 262, 266, 50 N.W.2d 300, 302 (1951).

There is no dispute that Elizabeth offered to sell the property for $200 per acre. Donald claims that Case's letter of 17 February unequivocally accepted that offer. However, Case's letter merely states that Donald "has made arrangements . . . to secure funds" and that they were "ready to proceed with this transaction." In the next sentence of the letter, Case asks Elizabeth to let him know the exact dollar amount that she expected to receive for the land.

The language of the 17 February letter does not embody an absolute, unequivocal, and unconditional acceptance of Elizabeth's offer, and is not expressive of an intent to create, without more, a contract. The terms of the letter appear to be more in the nature of negotiations with a view toward reaching an agreement in the future. Case states that Donald is "ready to proceed" and asks what amount Elizabeth expects to receive for her interest in the property. These are hardly the words of an unequivocal, unconditional acceptance of Elizabeth's offer.

In addition, the testimony of Donald at trial lends further support to the conclusion that the parties never assented to the same terms. In response to a question by Elizabeth's counsel asking why an exact dollar amount was not included in the 17 February letter, Donald stated:

"A. The exact dollar amount would have been $37,200.00. And that would have been somewhat less than she would have thought she was entitled to. And had we sent a contract at that time with the $37,200.00 in it, I'm sure she wouldn't have signed it."

The parties can hardly be said to have mutually assented to the terms of a contract when Donald admits that he believed Elizabeth was expecting more than $37,200, the amount he intended to pay, and that she would not have agreed to that amount.

We conclude that Donald did not accept Elizabeth's offer prior to her revocation of the offer on 9 March 1979, and thus there is no contract between the parties. The judgment of the district court dismissing Donald's claim for specific performance is affirmed.

NOTE

Expression of Acceptance. On May 16, a Seattle retailer ordered men's fall suits on a printed form supplied by the manufacturer's salesman that provided that the manufacturer was not bound until acceptance by one of its officers in New Jersey. On May 23, the manufacturer, by form letter, advised the retailer that, "You may be assured of our very best attention to this order." On July 18, the manufacturer wrote to "cancel" the order. The retailer sued the manufacturer for damages for breach of contract; the defendant responded that there was no contract. Based on the decision in *Wucherpfennig*, had the manufacturer accepted the retailer's offer? Hill's, Inc. v. William B. Kessler, Inc., 246 P.2d 1099 (Wash 1952).

International Filter Co. v. Conroe Gin, Ice & Light Co.

Commission of Appeals of Texas, 1925.
277 S.W. 631.

Action by the International Filter Company against the Conroe Gin, Ice & Light Company. Judgment for defendant was affirmed in 269 S.W. 210, and plaintiff brings error. Reversed and remanded.

■ NICKELS, JUDGE. Plaintiff in error, an Illinois corporation, is a manufacturer of machinery, apparatus, etc., for the purification of water in connection with the manufacture of ice, etc., having its principal office in the city of Chicago. Defendant in error is a Texas corporation engaged in the manufacture of ice, etc., having its plant, office, etc., at Conroe, Montgomery County, Tex. [Hereafter plaintiff in error is referred to as International Filter, and defendant in error as Conroe Gin.]

On February 10, 1920, through its traveling solicitor, Waterman, International Filter, submitted to Conroe Gin, acting through Henry Thompson, its manager, a written instrument, addressed to Conroe Gin, which (with immaterial portions omitted) reads as follows:

"Gentlemen: We propose to furnish, f.o.b. Chicago, one No. two Junior (steel tank) International water softener and filter to purify water of the character shown by sample to be submitted. Price: Twelve hundred thirty ($1,230.00) dollars. This proposal is made in duplicate and becomes a contract when accepted by the purchaser and approved by an executive officer of the International Filter Company, at its office in Chicago. Any modification can only be made by duly approved supplementary agreement signed by both parties.

"This proposal is submitted for prompt acceptance, and unless so accepted is subject to change without notice.

"RESPECTFULLY SUBMITTED,
"INTERNATIONAL FILTER CO.
"W.W. WATERMAN."

On the same day the "proposal" was accepted by Conroe Gin through notation made on the paper by Thompson reading as follows:

"ACCEPTED FEB. 10, 1920.
"CONROE GIN, ICE & LIGHT CO.,
"BY HENRY THOMPSON, MGR."

The paper as thus submitted and "accepted" contained the notation, "Make shipment by Mar. 10." The paper, in that form, reached the Chicago office of International Filter, and on February 13, 1920, P.N. Engel, its president and vice president, indorsed thereon: "O.K. Feb. 13, 1920, P.N. Engel." February 14, 1920, International Filter wrote and mailed, and in due course Conroe Gin received, the following letter:

"FEB. 14, 1920.

"Attention of Mr. Henry Thompson, Manager.

"Conroe Gin, Ice & Light Co., Conroe, Texas-Gentlemen: This will acknowledge and thank you for your order given Mr. Waterman for a No. 2 Jr. steel tank International softener and filter, for 110 volt, 60 cycle, single phase current—for shipment March 10th.

"Please make shipment of the sample of water promptly so that we may make the analysis and know the character of the water before shipment of the apparatus. Shipping tag is inclosed, and please note, the instructions to pack to guard against freezing.

"YOURS VERY TRULY,
"INTERNATIONAL FILTER CO.
"M.B. JOHNSON."

By letter of February 28, 1920, Conroe Gin undertook to countermand the "order," which countermand was repeated and emphasized by letter of March 4, 1920. By letter of March 2, 1920 (replying to the letter of February 28th), International Filter denied the right of countermand, etc., and insisted upon performance of the "contract." The parties adhered to the respective positions thus indicated, and this suit resulted.

International Filter sued for breach of the contract alleged to have been made in the manner stated above. The defense is that no contract was made because: (1) Neither Engel's indorsement of "O.K.," nor the letter of February 14, 1920, amounted to approval "by an executive officer of the International Filter Company, at its office in Chicago." (2) Notification of such approval, or acceptance, by International Filter was required to be communicated to Conroe Gin; it being insisted that this requirement inhered in the terms of the proposal and in the nature of the transaction and, also, that Thompson, when he indorsed "acceptance" on the paper stated to Waterman, as agent of International Filter, that such notification must be promptly given; it being insisted further that the letter of February 14, 1920, did not constitute such acceptance or notification of approval, and therefore Conroe Gin, on February 28, 1920, etc., had the right to withdraw or countermand, the unaccepted offer. Thompson testified in a manner to support the allegation of his statement to Waterman. There are other matters involved in the suit which must be ultimately determined, but the foregoing presents the issues now here for consideration.

The case was tried without a jury, and the judge found the facts in favor of Conroe Gin on all the issues indicated above, and upon other material issues. The judgment was affirmed by the Court of Civil Appeals, 269 S.W. 210.

We agree with the honorable Court of Civil Appeals upon the proposition that Mr. Engel's indorsement of "O.K." amounted to an approval "by an executive officer of the International Filter Company, at its office in Chicago," within the meaning of the so-called "proposal" of February 10th. The paper then became a "contract," according to its definitely expressed terms, and it became then, and thereafter it remained, an enforceable contract, in legal contemplation, unless the fact of approval by the filter company was required to be communicated to the other party and unless, in that event, the communication was not made.

We are not prepared to assent to the ruling that such communication was essential. There is no disposition to question the justice of the general rules stated in support of that holding, yet the existence of contractual capacity imports the right of the offerer to dispense with notification; and he does dispense with it "if the form of the offer," etc., "shows that this was not to be required." 9 Cyc. 270, 271; Carlill v. Carbolic Smoke Ball Co., 1 Q.B. 256 (and other references in note 6, 9 Cyc. 271).

The Conroe Gin, Ice & Light Company executed the paper for the purpose of having it transmitted, as its offer, to the filter company at Chicago. It was so transmitted and acted upon. Its terms embrace the offer, and nothing else, and by its terms the question of notification must be judged, since those terms are not ambiguous.

The paper contains two provisions which relate to acceptance by the filter company. One is the declaration that the offer shall "become a contract when approved by an executive officer of the International Filter Company, at its Chicago office." The other is thus stated: "This proposal is submitted for prompt acceptance, and unless so accepted is subject to change without notice." The first provision states "a particular mode of acceptance as sufficient to make the bargain binding," and the filter company (as stated above) followed "the indicated method of acceptance." When this was done, so the paper declares, the proposal "became a contract." The other provision does not in any way relate to a different method of acceptance by the filter company. Its sole reference is to the time within which the act of approval must be done; that is to say, there was to be a "prompt acceptance," else the offer might be changed "without notice." The second declaration merely required the approval therein before stipulated for to be done promptly; if the act was so done, there is nothing in the second provision to militate against, or to conflict with, the prior declaration that, thereupon, the paper should become "a contract."

A holding that notification of that approval is to be deduced from the terms of the last-quoted clause is not essential in order to give it meaning or to dissolve ambiguity. On the contrary, such a construction of the two provisions would introduce a conflict, or ambiguity, where none exists in the language itself, and defeat the plainly expressed term wherein it is said that the proposal "becomes a contract . . . when approved by an executive officer." There is not anything in the language used to justify a ruling that this declaration must be wrenched from its obvious meaning and given one which would change both the locus and time prescribed for the meeting of the minds. The offerer said that the contract should be complete if approval be promptly given by the executive officer at Chicago; the court cannot properly restate the offer so as to make the offerer declare that a contract shall be made only when the approval shall have been promptly given at Chicago and that fact shall have been communicated to the offerer at Conroe. In our opinion, therefore, notice of the approval was not required.

The letter of February 14th, however, sufficiently communicated notice, if it was required. Here the fact of acceptance in the particular method prescribed by the offerer is established aliunde the letter—Engel's "O.K." indorsed on the paper at Chicago did that. The form of notice, where notice is required, may be quite a different thing from the acceptance itself; the latter constitutes the meeting of the minds, the former merely relates to that pre-existent fact. The rules requiring such notice, it will be marked, do not make necessary any particular form or manner, unless the parties themselves have so prescribed. Whatever would convey by word or fair implication, notice of the fact would be sufficient. And this letter, we think, would clearly indicate to a reasonably prudent person, situated as was the defendant in error, the fact of previous approval by the filter company. If the Gin, Ice & Light Company had acted to change its position upon it as a notification of that fact, it must be plain that the filter company would have been estopped to deny its sufficiency.

We recommend that the judgment of the Court of Civil Appeals be reversed, and that the cause be remanded to that court for its disposition of all questions not passed upon it by it heretofore and properly before it for determination.

■ CURETON, CHIEF JUDGE. Judgment of the Court of Civil Appeals reversed, and cause remanded to the Court of Civil Appeals for further consideration by that court, as recommended by the Commission of Appeals.

NOTES

(1) *Questions.* Which party was the offeror in this case? Who prepared the offer? Which of the following constituted the acceptance: The buyer's notation "Accepted Feb. 10, 1920"? The seller's indorsement "O.K. Feb. 13, 1920"? The seller's Feb. 14, 1920 letter? What function does each of these perform in the formation process?

(2) *Expressions of Acceptance.* The Court of Civil Appeals reasoned that International Filter's letter of February 14 "did not constitute an acceptance of appellee's proposal." International Filter Co. v. Conroe Gin, Ice & Light Co., 269 S.W. 210, 215 (Ky. App. 1925). It relied on Courtney Shoe Co. v. E.W. Curd & Son, 134 S.W. 146 (Ky.1911). In that case a manufacturer wrote, "Your order . . . is at hand and will receive our prompt and careful attention," but sent a second letter eight days later rejecting the order on the ground that the salesman had made the sale without authority. It was held that the first letter was not an acceptance. Assume, for the moment, that the February 14 letter was the only response to the proposal signed by Conroe Gin. Do you agree with the Court of Civil Appeals?

(3) *Control of Representatives.* When a seller is a large organization with salespersons ("traveling solicitors" in the opinion above) who are expected to use a carefully prepared standard form for all contracts, there is still a risk that the salespersons will make written changes on the form during their negotiations with customers. What does this fact suggest about the purpose behind home-office approval clauses? See Restatement, Second, of Agency § 167 as to the effect of such language as: "No agent of seller has authority to change the terms hereof." What additional benefits or risks might such a clause provide the seller? The buyer? A home-office approval clause enables parties to limit the authority of certain employees to enter into certain contracts.

(4) *Notice in Bilateral Contracts.* Can you distinguish the position of International Filter from that of the offeree who merely thinks or mutters "I accept"? See Restatement §§ 54 and 56. For a case holding that the mere signing of the contract by the offeree was not acceptance even though the contract said that it would be binding "when . . . signed by both parties," see Kendel v. Pontious, 261 So.2d 167 (Fla.1972). If notice of acceptance is necessary for an offer that seeks a promise, on what basis did the court find that no notice was required in International Filter? Whether notice is required in unilateral contracts is discussed, on p. 218. Do you have an intuition about whether it should be?

PROBLEM

"Awesome" Acceptance? Through its website, Smoking Everywhere, Inc. sold an alternative to regular cigarettes called "electronic cigarettes," or "E-Cigs." To generate web traffic to its site, Smoking Everywhere entered into a contract with CX Digital Media, Inc., ("CX Digital"), a specialist in on-line advertising. Smoking Everywhere agreed to pay CX Digital a commission of $45 for every customer referral or "lead" that resulted from an ad placed by CX Digital or its affiliates, subject to a limit of 200 per day. A dispute arose when Smoking Everywhere refused to pay a CX Digital invoice for more than 200 referrals a day. CX Digital argued that the parties' original agreement had been modified to provide for compensation for an unlimited number of leads. At trial, the CX Digital produced the following transcript, part of a day-long instant-message conversation, between Nick Touris, a Smoking Everywhere vice-president, and Pedram Soltani, an account manager at CX Digital:

> pedramcx (2:49:45 PM): A few of our big guys are really excited about the new page and they're ready to run it
>
> pedramcx (2:50:08 PM): We can do 2000 orders/day by Friday if I have your blessing
>
> pedramcx (2:52:13 PM): those 2000 leads are going to be generated by our best affiliate and he's legit
>
> nicktouris (4:43:09 PM): NO LIMIT
>
> pedramcx (4:43:21 PM): awesome!

In determining whether a contract had been formed, how would you analyze this sequence of exchanges? What claim must CX Digital make for the meaning of the message "awesome!"? Do you agree? What if, instead of "awesome!", pedramcx had sent an upbeat emoji (☺)? See CX Digital Media, Inc. v. Smoking Everywhere, Inc., 09-62020-CIV, 2011 WL 1102782 (S.D. Fla. Mar. 23, 2011).

White v. Corlies & Tift
Court of Appeals of New York, 1871.
46 N.Y. 467.

Appeal from judgment of the General Term of the first judicial district, affirming a judgment entered upon a verdict for plaintiff.

The action was for an alleged breach of contract.

The plaintiff was a builder, with his place of business in Fortieth Street, New York City.

The defendants were merchants at 32 Day Street.

In September, 1865, the defendants furnished the plaintiff with specifications for fitting up a suite of offices at 57 Broadway, and requested him to make an estimate of the cost of doing the work.

On September 28th, the plaintiff left his estimate with the defendants, and they were to consider upon it, and inform the plaintiff of their conclusions.

On the same day the defendants made a change in their specifications, and sent a copy of the same, so changed, to the plaintiff for his assent under his estimate, which he assented to by signing the same and returning it to the defendants.

On the day following the defendants' bookkeeper wrote the plaintiff the following note:

"NEW YORK, SEPTEMBER 29.

"Upon an agreement to finish the fitting up of offices 57 Broadway in two weeks from date, you can begin at once.

"The writer will call again, probably between 5 and 6 this p.m.

"W H R.
FOR J.W. CORLIES & CO.,
32 DEY ST."

No reply to this note was ever made by the plaintiff; and on the next day the same was countermanded by a second note from the defendants.

Immediately on receipt of the note of September 29th, and before the countermand was forwarded, the plaintiff commenced a performance by the purchase of lumber and beginning work thereon.

And after receiving the countermand, the plaintiff brought this action for damages for a breach of contract.[n]

The court charged the jury as follows: "From the contents of this note which the plaintiff received, was it his duty to go down to Dey Street (meaning to give notice of assent), before commencing the work?

In my opinion it was not. He had a right to act upon this note and commence the job, and that was a binding contract between the parties."

To this defendants excepted.

■ FOLGER, JUDGE. We do not think that the jury found, or that the testimony shows, that there was any agreement between the parties, before the written communication of the defendants of September 30th[o] was received by the plaintiff. This note did not make an agreement. It was a proposition, and must have been accepted by the plaintiff before either party was bound, in contract, to the other. The only overt action

---

[n] Some additional facts, taken from the record on appeal of White's testimony may be helpful. Corlies' initial request was to have the office done in black walnut, a hard wood, within 21 days. White replied that he could not do the job in a hard wood in that time. Corlies then requested an estimate for white pine, a soft wood. White left the estimate on September 28, but did not indicate the time within which he would finish. Corlies made a change in the specifications to which White assented. There followed the letter of September 29 from Corlies. The countermand from Corlies said that it had decided to do the office in black walnut and requested an estimate for that in place of pine. Record, pp. 7–12.

[o] It appears the court meant September 29.

which is claimed by the plaintiff as indicating on his part an acceptance of the offer, was the purchase of the stuff necessary for the work, and commencing work, as we understand the testimony, upon that stuff.

We understand the rule to be, that where an offer is made by one party to another when they are not together, the acceptance of it by that other must be manifested by some appropriate act. It does not need that the acceptance shall come to the knowledge of the one making the offer before he shall be bound. But though the manifestation need not be brought to his knowledge before he becomes bound, he is not bound, if that manifestation is not put in a proper way to be in the usual course of events, in some reasonable time communicated to him. Thus a letter received by mail containing a proposal may be answered by letter by mail, containing the acceptance. And in general, as soon as the answering letter is mailed, the contract is concluded. Though one party does not know of the acceptance, the manifestation thereof is put in the proper way of reaching him.

In the case in hand, the plaintiff determined to accept. But a mental determination not indicated by speech, or put in course of indication by act to the other party, is not an acceptance which will bind the other. Nor does an act, which in itself, is no indication of an acceptance, become such, because accompanied by an unevinced mental determination. Where the act uninterpreted by concurrent evidence of the mental purpose accompanying it, is as well referable to one state of facts as another, it is no indication to the other party of an acceptance, and does not operate to hold him to his offer.

Conceding that the testimony shows that the plaintiff did resolve to accept this offer, he did no act which indicated an acceptance of it to the defendants. He, a carpenter and builder, purchased stuff for the work. But it was stuff as fit for any other like work. He began work upon the stuff, but as he would have done for any other like work. There was nothing in his thought, formed but not uttered, or in his acts that indicated or set in motion an indication to the defendants of his acceptance of their offer, or which could necessarily result therein.

But the charge of the learned judge was fairly to be understood by the jury as laying down the rule to them, that the plaintiff need not indicate to the defendants his acceptance of their offer; and that the purchase of stuff and working on it after receiving the note, made a binding contract between the parties. In this we think the learned judge fell into error.

Judgment reversed, and new trial ordered.

NOTES

(1) *An Ambiguity.* According to Judge Folger's first paragraph, the bookkeeper's note of September 29 was a proposal, and not an acceptance of an offer made by White in the estimate he left with Corlies & Tift. That might

be explained in two ways. One is that the estimate was not an offer. Were there any facts that suggest that White's estimate may have constituted an offer? Might "I estimate . . . " constitute an offer just as well as "we quote you Mason fruit jars"?

The other explanation is that the opening phrase of the September 29 note—*"Upon an agreement"*—was understood to mean "When we have agreed about finishing the fitting up the offices (and not before). . . . " The brief on appeal for Corlies & Tift characterized the phrase this way, as one "demanding an agreement." Consider an alternate reading: "With reference to the work of fitting up. . . . " That reading may comport better with 19th-century diction, and with the opinion as a whole.

(2) *Problems of Manifestation.* Assuming that the bookkeeper's note constituted an offer, does the court's opinion imply that White might have accepted it by some kind of activity? If so, what kind of activity might count? Activity at a lumberyard? At his shop? If not, what sense can be made of ". . . you can begin at once"?

The court stated a familiar rule about contracts created by correspondence: posting a letter sometimes constitutes the acceptance of an offer. (The "mailbox rule" is further considered at p. 249 below.) In such instances, however, the offeror is at risk, for no more than a few days, of having made a commitment that it is unaware of. Corlies & Tift would have borne that risk if White could have bound it to a contract simply by busying himself with "stuff" suited only for offices at 57 Broadway. On the other hand, Corlies & Tift gave some indication of willingness to bear that risk: "you can begin at once."

Ever-Tite Roofing Corporation v. Green

Court of Appeal of Louisiana, Second Circuit, 1955.
83 So.2d 449.

■ AYRES, JUDGE. This is an action for damages allegedly sustained by plaintiff as the result of the breach by the defendants of a written contract for the re-roofing of defendants' residence. Defendants denied that their written proposal or offer was ever accepted by plaintiff in the manner stipulated therein for its acceptance, and hence contended no contract was ever entered into. The trial court sustained defendants' defense and rejected plaintiff's demands and dismissed its suit at its costs. From the judgment thus rendered and signed, plaintiff appealed.

Defendants executed and signed an instrument June 10, 1953, for the purpose of obtaining the services of plaintiff in re-roofing their residence situated in Webster Parish, Louisiana. The document set out in detail the work to be done and the price therefore to be paid in monthly installments. This instrument was likewise signed by plaintiff's sale representative, who, however, was without authority to accept the contract for and on behalf of the plaintiff. This alleged contract contained these provisions:

"This agreement shall become binding only upon written acceptance hereof, by the principal or authorized officer of the Contractor, or upon commencing performance of the work. This contract is Not Subject to Cancellation. This written agreement is the only and entire contract covering the subject matter hereof and no other representations have been made unto Owner except these herein contained. No guarantee on repair work, partial roof jobs, or paint jobs."

Inasmuch as this work was to be performed entirely on credit, it was necessary for plaintiff to obtain credit reports and approval from the lending institution which was to finance said contract. With this procedure defendants were more or less familiar and knew their credit rating would have to be checked and a report made. On receipt of the proposed contract, plaintiff requested a credit report, which was made and submitted by plaintiff to the lending agency. Additional information was requested by this institution, which then gave its approval.

The day immediately following this approval, which was either June 18 or 19, 1953, plaintiff engaged its workmen and two trucks, loaded the trucks with the necessary roofing materials and proceeded from Shreveport to defendants' residence for the purpose of doing the work and performing the services allegedly contracted for the defendants. Upon their arrival at defendants' residence, the workmen found others in the performance of the work which plaintiff had contracted to do. Defendants notified plaintiff's workmen that the work had been contracted to other parties two days before and forbade them to do the work.

The basis of the judgment appealed was that defendants had timely notified plaintiff before "commencing performance of work" notice to plaintiff's workmen upon their arrival with the materials that defendants did not desire them to commence the actual work was sufficient and timely to signify their intention to withdraw from the contract. With this conclusion we find ourselves unable to agree.

Defendants evidently knew this work was to be processed through plaintiff's Shreveport office. The record discloses no unreasonable delay on plaintiff's part in receiving, processing or accepting the contract or in commencing the work contracted to be done. No time limit was specified in the contract within which it was to be accepted or within which the work was to be begun. It was nevertheless understood between the parties that some delay would ensue before the acceptance of the contract and the commencement of the work, due to the necessity of compliance with the requirements relative to financing the job through a lending agency. The evidence as referred to hereinabove shows that plaintiff proceeded with due diligence.

The general rule of law is that an offer proposed may be withdrawn before its acceptance and that no obligation is incurred thereby. This is, however, not without exceptions. For instance, Restatement of the Law of Contracts stated:

"(1) The power to create a contract by acceptance of an offer terminates at the time specified in the offer, or, if no time is specified, at the end of a reasonable time.

"What is a reasonable time is a question of fact depending on the nature of the contract proposed, the usages of business and other circumstances of the case which the offeree at the time of his acceptance either knows or has reason to know."

These principles are recognized in the Civil Code. LSA-C.C. Art. 1800 provides that an offer is incomplete as a contract until its acceptance and that before its acceptance the offer may be withdrawn. However, this general rule is modified by the provisions of LSA-C.C. Arts. 1801, 1802, 1804 and 1809, which read as follows:

"Art. 1809. The obligation of a contract not being complete, until the acceptance, or in cases where it is implied by law, until the circumstances, which raise such implication, are known to the party proposing; he may therefore revoke his offer or proposition before such acceptance, but not without allowing such reasonable time as from the terms of his offer he has given, or from the circumstances of the case he may be supposed to have intended to give to the party, to communicate his determination."

[S]ince the contract did not specify the time within which it was to be accepted or within which the work was to have been commenced, a reasonable time must be allowed therefor in accordance with the facts and circumstances and the evident intention of the parties. A reasonable time is contemplated where no time is expressed. What is a reasonable time depends more or less upon the circumstances surrounding each particular case. The delays to process defendants' application were not unusual. The contract was accepted by plaintiff by the commencement of the performance of the work contracted to be done. This commencement began with the loading of the trucks with the necessary materials in Shreveport and transporting such materials and the workmen to defendants' residence. Actual commencement or performance of the work therefore began before any notice of dissent by defendants was given plaintiff. The proposition and its acceptance thus became a completed contract.

By their aforesaid acts defendants breached the contract. They employed others to do the work contracted to be done by plaintiff and forbade plaintiff's workmen to engage upon that undertaking. By this breach defendants are legally bound to respond to plaintiff in damages.

[Reversed.]

NOTES

(1) *Means of Acceptance.* What means of acceptance were authorized by the Greens' offer to Ever-Tite? What was the purpose of the words 'or upon commencing performance of the work?' Could the court have read this

language more favorably to the Greens? Was the contract between the Greens and Ever-Tite bilateral or unilateral? What is the difference an offer such as the one made by the Greens above, and an offer seeking performance?

(2) *Case Comparison.* Can the Ever-Tite case be distinguished from White v. Corlies & Tift? What is the critical language of the offer in each case?

————

Notification of Acceptance in Unilateral Contracts

As White v. Corlies & Tift suggests, if an offeror proposes a "bilateral" contract and invites acceptance by means of a promise, it is ordinarily understood that the offeree must at least take steps to see that the promise is, in the words of the opinion in that case, "in some reasonable time communicated" to the offeror. The court stressed the fact that White had neither indicated his determination to accept by *speech* nor "put in course of indication" to Corlies & Tift of anything he had *done.* See Restatement § 56. (Can the *International Filter* and *Ever-Tite* cases be reconciled with this rule?)

The necessity of giving notice is less obvious if the offer proposes a "unilateral" contract, inviting acceptance by means of performance and not a promise. A celebrated case is Carlill v. Carbolic Smoke Ball Co., [1893] 1 Q.B. 256 (C.A.). It arose out of the following advertisement:

> £100 reward will be paid by the Carbolic Smoke Ball Company to any person who contracts the increasing epidemic influenza, colds or any disease caused by taking cold, after having used the ball three times daily for two weeks according to the printed directions supplied with each ball.[p] £1000 is deposited with the Alliance Bank, Regent Street shewing our sincerity in the matter.

After buying and using a smokeball as directed, Carlill contracted influenza. When the Company refused to pay, she sued and was awarded £100 in damages. The Company argued that Carlill had failed to notify it of her acceptance, but its appeal was dismissed.

As Lindley, L.J., explained, the advertisement was not "a mere puff" but an offer under which "the reward is offered to any person who contracts the epidemic or other disease within a reasonable time after having used the smoke ball." The fact that Carlill had not notified the Company of her acceptance was not fatal to her claim. According to

———

[p]   The smoke ball was a small compressible hollow ball filled with carbolic acid in powder form, worn around the neck on a cord. When the ball was squeezed, the powder was forced through a small opening in the ball and created a small cloud of smoke. For more on the case, including pictures of the advertisement, facts on the smokeball, and the lethality of carbolic acid in more than small amounts, see Simpson, *Quackery and Contract Law: The Case of the Carbolic Smoke Ball,* 14 J. Legal Stud. 345 (1985), reprinted in A.W.B. Simpson, Leading Cases in the Common Law 259, 262–64 (1995).

Bowen, L.J., "One cannot doubt that, as an ordinary rule of law, an acceptance of an offer made ought to be notified to the person who makes the offer, in order that the two minds may come together. But there is this clear gloss to be made upon that doctrine, that as notification of acceptance is required for the benefit of the person who makes the offer, the person who makes the offer may dispense with notice to himself, if he thinks it desirable to do so . [I]f the person making the offer, expressly or impliedly intimates in his offer that it will be sufficient to act on the proposal without communicating acceptance of it to himself, performance of the condition is a sufficient acceptance without notification."

How can one tell if the offer has dispensed with notice? Bowen explained: "In many cases you look to the offer itself. In many cases you extract from the character of the transaction and in the advertisement cases it seems to me to follow as an inference to be drawn from the transaction itself that a person is not to notify his acceptance of the offer before he performs the condition, but that if he performs the condition notification is dispensed with. It seems to me that from the point of view of common sense no other idea could be entertained."

NOTES

(1) *Questions.* Was the acceptance of the Carbolic Smoke Ball Company's offer: (a) the purchase of the smoke ball; (b) its use in accordance with directions; (c) the plaintiff's contracting influenza; or (d) all of the above? Which of these acts was bargained for? Recall that a promise may be conditional, so that its performance becomes due only if a specified event occurs. See Note 1, p. 95 above. Was the promise conditional in the Carbolic Smoke Ball case?

(2) *Notice from Afar.* A leading American case on the necessity of notice of acceptance of a unilateral offer is Bishop v. Eaton, 37 N.E. 665, 667 (Mass.1894). In that case Frank Eaton, in Nova Scotia, had written to Bishop, in Illinois, that if Bishop would help Eaton's brother, Harry, to get money, "I will see that it is paid." Bishop did help Harry get money by signing his note as surety when Harry got a loan. When Harry did not repay the loan, Bishop did, and sued Frank on his promise. The court thought that this was a case in which notice of acceptance should have been given, since the loan was made in Illinois and Frank was in Nova Scotia. "Ordinarily there is no occasion to notify the offeror of the acceptance of such an offer, for the doing of the act is a sufficient acceptance, and the promisor knows that he is bound when he sees that action has been taken on the faith of his offer. But if the act is of such a kind that knowledge of it will not quickly come to the promisor, the promisee is bound to give him notice of his acceptance within a reasonable time after doing that which constitutes the acceptance." The court concluded, however, that notice had been given.

PROBLEM

Acceptance and Rejection. The Chicago Medical School distributed a bulletin for prospective students stating that it selected applicants "on the basis of scholarship, character, and motivation," in addition to "academic achievement." Robert Steinberg received a bulletin, applied for admission, and paid the School the required $15 fee. Following his rejection, Steinberg learned that candidates were also evaluated on nonacademic criteria, such as their family's ability to make large donations. He argues that by failing to evaluate his application according to the stated criteria, the School is in breach of its contract with him. Can you state a theory of contract liability? Who made the offer? See Steinberg v. Chicago Medical School, 371 N.E.2d 634 (Ill.1977).

Shipment of Goods as Acceptance

Is a seller's shipment of goods, in response to a buyer's order, an acceptance? The question usually arises when the buyer attempts to revoke an order after the seller has shipped the goods in response to the buyer's order. UCC § 2–206(1)(b) provides that an order "for prompt or current shipment shall be construed as inviting acceptance either by a prompt promise to ship or by the prompt or current shipment of conforming or non-conforming goods."

Why does UCC § 2–206(1)(b) state that shipment of *non-conforming* goods will constitute acceptance? That situation is taken up in the opinion that follows.

Corinthian Pharmaceutical Systems, Inc. v. Lederle Laboratories

United States District Court, S.D. Indiana, Indianapolis Division, 1989.
724 F.Supp. 605.

■ MCKINNEY, DISTRICT JUDGE. Defendant Lederle Laboratories is a pharmaceutical manufacturer and distributor that makes a number of drugs, including the DTP vaccine. Plaintiff Corinthian Pharmaceutical is a distributor of drugs that purchases supplies from manufacturers such as Lederle Labs and then resells the product to physicians and other providers. One of the products that Corinthian buys and distributes with some regularity is the DTP vaccine.

Lederle periodically issued a price list to its customers for all of its products. Each price list stated that all orders were subject to acceptance by Lederle at its home office, and indicated that the prices shown "were in effect at the time of publication but are submitted without offer and are subject to change without notice." The price list further stated that changes in price "take immediate effect and unfilled current orders and back orders will be invoiced at the price in effect at the time shipment is made."

From 1985 through early 1986, Corinthian made a number of purchases of the vaccine from Lederle Labs. During this period of time, the largest single order ever placed by Corinthian with Lederle was for 100 vials. When Lederle Labs filled an order it sent an invoice to Corinthian.

During this period of time, product liability lawsuits concerning DTP increased, and insurance became more difficult to procure. As a result, Lederle decided in early 1986 to self-insure against such risks. In order to cover the costs of self-insurance, Lederle concluded that a substantial increase in the price of the vaccine would be necessary.

In order to communicate the price change to its own sales people, Lederle's Price Manager prepared "PRICE LETTER NO. E-48." This document was dated May 19, 1986, and indicated that effective May 20, 1986, the price of the DTP vaccine would be raised from $51.00 to $171.00 per vial. Price letters such as these were routinely sent to Lederle's sales force, but did not go to customers. Corinthian Pharmaceutical did not know of the existence of this internal price letter until a Lederle representative presented it to Corinthian several weeks after May 20, 1986.

Additionally, Lederle Labs also wrote a letter dated May 20, 1986, to its customers announcing the price increase and explaining the liability and insurance problems that brought about the change. Corinthian somehow gained knowledge of this letter on May 19, 1986, the date before the price increase was to take effect. In response to the knowledge of the impending price increase, Corinthian immediately ordered 1000 vials of DTP vaccine from Lederle. Corinthian placed its order on May 19, 1986, by calling Lederle's "Telgo" system. The Telgo system is a telephone computer ordering system that allows customers to place orders over the phone by communicating with a computer. After Corinthian placed its order with the Telgo system, the computer gave Corinthian a tracking number for its order. On the same date, Corinthian sent Lederle two written confirmations of its order. On each form Corinthian stated that this "order is to receive the $64.32 per vial price."

On June 3, 1986, Lederle sent invoice 1771 to Corinthian for 50 vials of DTP vaccine priced at $64.32 per vial. The invoice contained the standard Lederle conditions noted above. The 50 vials were sent to Corinthian and were accepted. At the same time, Lederle sent its customers, including Corinthian, a letter regarding DTP vaccine pricing and orders. This letter stated that the "enclosed represents a partial shipment of the order for DTP vaccine, which you placed with Lederle on May 19, 1986." The letter stated that under Lederle's standard terms and conditions of sale the normal policy would be to invoice the order at the price when shipment was made. However, in light of the magnitude of the price increase, Lederle had decided to make an exception to its terms and conditions and ship a portion of the order at the lower price. The letter further stated that the balance would be priced at $171.00, and that shipment would be made during the week of June 16. The letter closed, "If for any reason you wish to cancel the balance of your order, please contact [us] . . . on or before June 13."

Based on these facts, plaintiff Corinthian Pharmaceutical brings this action seeking specific performance for the 950 vials of DTP vaccine that Lederle Labs chose not to deliver. [Lederle moved for summary judgment urging] a number of alternative grounds for disposing of this claim, including that no contract for the sale of 1000 vials was formed, that if one was formed, it was governed by Lederle's terms and conditions, and that the 50 vials sent to Corinthian were merely an accommodation.

Discussion

Despite the lengthy recitation of facts and summary judgment standards, this is a straightforward sale of goods problem resembling those found in a contracts or sales casebook. The fundamental question is whether Lederle Labs agreed to sell Corinthian Pharmaceuticals 1,000 vials of DTP vaccine at $64.32 per vial. As shown below, the undisputed material facts mandate the conclusion as a matter of law that no such agreement was ever formed.

Initially, it should be noted that this is a sale of goods covered by the Uniform Commercial Code, and that both parties are merchants under the Code. The parties do not discuss which state's laws are to apply to action, but because the Code is substantially the same in all states having any connection to this dispute, the Court will, for ease of reference, refer in general to the UCC with relevant interpretations from Indiana and other states.

The starting point in this analysis is where did the first offer originate. An offer is "the manifestation of willingness to enter into a bargain, so made as to justify another person in understanding that his assent to that bargain is invited and will conclude it." H. Greenberg, Rights and Remedies Under U.C.C. Article 2 § 5.2 at 50 (1987) [hereinafter "Greenberg, U.C.C. Article 2"], (quoting 1 Restatement (Second), Contracts § 4 (1981)). The only possible conclusion in this case is that Corinthian's "order" of May 19, 1986, for 1,000 vials at $64.32 was the first offer. Nothing that the seller had done prior to this point can be interpreted as an offer.

First, the price lists distributed by Lederle to its customers did not constitute offers. It is well settled that quotations are mere invitations to make an offer, particularly where, as here, the price lists specifically stated that prices were subject to change without notice and that all orders were subject to acceptance by Lederle.

Second, neither Lederle's internal price memorandum nor its letter to customers dated May 20, 1986, can be construed as an offer to sell 1,000 vials at the lower price. There is no evidence that Lederle intended

Corinthian to receive the internal price memorandum, nor is there anything in the record to support the conclusion that the May 20, 1986, letter was an offer to sell 1,000 vials to Corinthian at the lower price. If anything, the evidence shows that Corinthian was not supposed to receive this letter until after the price increase had taken place. Moreover, the letter, just like the price lists, was a mere quotation (i.e., an invitation to submit an offer) sent to all customers. As such, it did not bestow on Corinthian nor other customers the power to form a binding contract for the sale of one thousand, or, for that matter, one million vials of vaccine.

Thus, as a matter of law, the first offer was made by Corinthian when it phoned in and subsequently confirmed its order for 1,000 vials at the lower price. The next question, then, is whether Lederle ever accepted that offer.

Under the Code, an acceptance need not be the mirror-image of the offer. UCC § 2–207. However, the offeree must still do some act that manifests the intention to accept the offer and make a contract. Under § 2–206, an offer to make a contract shall be construed as inviting acceptance in any manner and by any medium reasonable in the circumstances. The first question regarding acceptance, therefore, is whether Lederle accepted the offer prior to sending the 50 vials of vaccine.

The record is clear that Lederle did not communicate or do any act prior to shipping the 50 vials that could support the finding of an acceptance. When Corinthian placed its order, it merely received a tracking number from the Telgo computer. Such an automated, ministerial act cannot constitute an acceptance. See, e.g., Foremost Pro Color, Inc. v. Eastman Kodak Co., 703 F.2d 534, 539 (9th Cir.1983) (logging purchase orders as received did not manifest acceptance); Southern Spindle & Flyer Co. v. Milliken & Co., 53 N.C.App. 785, 281 S.E.2d 734, 736 (1981) (seller's acknowledgement of receipt of purchase order did not constitute assent to its terms). Thus, there was no acceptance of Corinthian's offer prior to the delivery of 50 vials.

The next question, then, is what is to be made of the shipment of 50 vials and the accompanying letter. Section 2–206(1)(b) of the Code speaks to this issue:

> [A]n order or other offer to buy goods for prompt or current shipment shall be construed as inviting acceptance either by a prompt promise to ship or by the prompt or current shipment of conforming or non-conforming goods, *but such a shipment of non-conforming goods does not constitute an acceptance if the seller seasonably notifies the buyer that the shipment is offered only as an accommodation to the buyer.*

§ 2–206 (emphasis added). Thus, under the Code a seller accepts the offer by shipping goods, whether they are conforming or not, but if the seller ships non-conforming goods and seasonably notifies the buyer that the shipment is a mere accommodation, then the seller has not, in fact, accepted the buyer's offer. See Greenberg, U.C.C. Article 2 § 5.5 at 53.

In this case, the offer made by Corinthian was for 1,000 vials at $64.32. In response, Lederle Labs shipped only 50 vials at $64.32 per vial, and wrote Corinthian indicating that the balance of the order would be priced at $171.00 per vial and would be shipped during the week of June 16. The letter further indicated that the buyer could cancel its order by calling Lederle Labs. Clearly, Lederle's shipment was non-conforming, for it was for only 1/20th of the quantity desired by the buyer. See § 2–106(2) (goods or conduct are conforming when they are in accordance with the obligations under the contract); Michiana Mack, Inc. v. Allendale Rural Fire Protection, 428 N.E.2d 1367, 1370 (Ind.App.1981) (non-conformity describes goods and conduct). The narrow issue, then, is whether Lederle's response to the offer was a shipment of non-conforming goods not constituting an acceptance because it was offered only as an accommodation under § 2–206.

An accommodation is an arrangement or engagement made as a favor to another. Black's Law Dictionary (5th ed. 1979). The term implies no consideration. Id. In this case, then, even taking all inferences favorably for the buyer, the only possible conclusion is that Lederle Labs' shipment of 50 vials was offered merely as an accommodation; that is to say, Lederle had no obligation to make the partial shipment, and did so only as a favor to the buyer. The accommodation letter, which Corinthian is sure it received, clearly stated that the 50 vials were being sent at the lower price as an exception to Lederle's general policy, and that the balance of the offer would be invoiced at the higher price. The letter further indicated that Lederle's proposal to ship the balance of the order at the higher price could be rejected by the buyer. Moreover, the standard terms of Lederle's invoice stated that acceptance of the order was expressly conditioned upon buyer's assent to the seller's terms.

Under these undisputed facts, § 2–206(1)(b) was satisfied. Where, as here, the notification is properly made, the shipment of nonconforming goods is treated as a counteroffer just as at common law, and the buyer may accept or reject the counteroffer under normal contract rules. 2 W. Hawkland, Uniform Commercial Code Series § 2–206:04 (1987).

Thus, the end result of this analysis is that Lederle Lab's price quotations were mere invitations to make an offer, that by placing its order Corinthian made an offer to buy 1,000 vials at the low price, that by shipping 50 vials at the low price Lederle's response was non-conforming, but the non-conforming response was a mere accommodation and thus constituted a counteroffer. Accordingly, there being no genuine issues of material fact on these issues and the law being in favor of the seller, summary judgment must be granted for Lederle Labs.

For all these reasons, the defendant's motion for summary judgment is granted.

NOTES

(1) *Questions.* What functions does each of the following events play in the process of contract formation: Lederle's letter to customers? Corinthian's telephone order? Telgo's assignment of a tracking number? Lederle's shipment to Corinthian and accompanying letter?

If the seller's shipment is not an acceptance of the buyer's offer but is a counter-offer, what means of acceptance does that counter-offer invite? See UCC § 2–206(1). (For cases not within the scope of UCC Article 2, compare Restatement §§ 32 and 62.)

The court quickly disposed of the argument that the tracking number was an acceptance by Lederle: "Such an automated, ministerial act cannot constitute an acceptance." Why should that be so? Was the fact of automation or the ministerial purpose that made the computer-generated response legally insignificant in this case?

(2) *Non-Conforming.* According to Comment 4 to UCC § 2–206, subsection (1)(b) "deals with the situation where a shipment made following an order is shown by a notification of shipment to be referable to that order but has a defect." If that refers to defective *goods,* the situation in the main case was different. Perhaps, although the statute speaks of non-conforming *goods,* the Comment refers to defective *shipment.* In either case the court's application of the subsection may make good sense. What of an order calling for goods to be "shipped within ten days"? Is a shipment after that a non-conforming one? Observe that the statute speaks of promptness by offerees.

Observe also that, by shipping non-conforming goods, an offeree—one who does not say they are sent as an accommodation—commits itself to supply goods that conform to the order. For example, by shipping wormy apples, a grower might bind itself to ship apples without worms.

To what other situations might the subsection apply? To one in which apples are ordered, and oranges are shipped? Are oranges defective apples?

(3) *Preparation for Shipment of Goods as Acceptance?* What if a buyer attempts to revoke an order after the seller has incurred expense in preparing to ship the goods but has not actually shipped them? In Doll & Smith v. A. & S. Sanitary Dairy Co., 211 N.W. 230 (Iowa 1926), the Dairy Company ordered advertising materials from Doll & Smith ("Doll"), through an agent. Two days after Doll received the order in New York, the Dairy Company wired a cancellation of the order. In an action by Doll it contended that he had incurred expenses in response to the order, having referred it to a factory and paid a commission to the agent. A judgment in favor of the Dairy Company was affirmed on appeal: "No case for damages is made." Id. Can this decision be reconciled with the *Ever-Tite* case, above?

Silence Not Ordinarily Acceptance

The general rule is that silence alone is not acceptance. "So fundamental is the tenet that, even as the master of the offer, the offeror is powerless to alter the rule." Farnsworth on Contracts § 3.15. The offeror who appends to an offer, "Unless I hear from you within 48 hours, you will be deemed to have accepted my offer," cannot hold the offeree who fails to reject. The rule, along with some real or apparent exceptions to it, is stated in Restatement § 69.

In a Massachusetts case from 1893, however, the court concluded that a silent retention amounted to an acceptance. A seller sued for $108.50, the price of 2,350 eelskins that he had sent to the buyer. Holmes wrote:

> The plaintiff was not a stranger to the defendant, even if there was no contract between them. He had sent eelskins in the same way four or five times before, and they had been accepted and paid for. . . . [S]ending them [imposed] on the defendant a duty to act about them; and silence on its part, coupled with a retention of the skins for an unreasonable time, might be found by the jury to warrant the plaintiff in assuming that they were accepted, and thus to amount to an acceptance.

Hobbs v. Massasoit Whip Co., 33 N.E. 495. What, beyond mere silence, was there in this case?

What if the parties are reversed and it is the *buyer* who asserts that the seller has accepted by silent retention of the buyer's order? American Bronze Corp. v. Streamway Products, 456 N.E.2d 1295, 1300 (Ohio App.1982), is such a case. For over 20 years, Streamway had called in orders to American by telephone and followed them up with written purchase orders, at which time American would begin production. When American refused to fill three orders, Streamway claimed damages and, from a denial of its claim, appealed. The Ohio Court of Appeals reversed and remanded, citing UCC § 2–204(1). "The filling of these orders in this manner as a regular practice constituted a valid acceptance and thus created a binding contract. Absent a notice of rejection Streamway would be justified in believing that American had indeed begun production." Id. What, beyond mere silence, was there in *this* case?

NOTE

Unsolicited Merchandise. A persistent consumer complaint concerns the practice of sending unsolicited merchandise, often coupled with the suggestion that the recipient will be liable for the price if it is not returned. As you might suppose, this suggestion is not the law: the recipient who lays the merchandise on a shelf and does not use it incurs no liability. Nonetheless, the practice is at best irritating and at worst deceptive. A number of states have enacted statutes dealing with it. See, *e.g.,* N.Y.Gen.Bus.L. § 396–2a. Federal laws regulating the mails also restrict such practices. See, e.g., 39 U.S.C. § 3009.

Marketing programs for book or CD clubs depend on a subscriber's agreement that merchandise not specifically ordered will be paid for in the absence of an instruction to the contrary. Is it significant that these arrangements "typically provide some up-front benefits to the offeree," such as an introductory bonus, and place mailing costs on the offeror? See Avery Katz, *The Strategic Structure of Offer and Acceptance: Game Theory and the Law of Contract Formation*, 89 Mich. L. Rev. 215, 264–65, 271–72 (1990). Professor Katz suggests an efficiency argument for the offeree's "right to be let alone." More simply, it might be thought that freedom *from* contract is a more important ideal than is freedom *to* contract. See Edwin Patterson, *An Apology for Consideration*, 58 Colum. L. Rev. 929, 948 (1958).

The Significance of Contract Formation for Anti-Discrimination Law

Beyond the basic obligation of performance, concluding whether and when a contract exists has important consequences for such other areas of law as civil rights law. Congress enacted the Civil Rights Act of 1866 in response to "Black Codes" (passed throughout the South in the wake of the American Civil War) limiting the contractual capacity, *inter alia*, of the recently freed slaves. The Act, codified as 42 U.S.C. § 1981(a), states, "All persons within the jurisdiction of the United States shall have the same right in every State and Territory to *make and enforce contracts* . . . as is enjoyed by white citizens[.]" (emphasis added). Against that background, consider these facts.

> On the morning of October 12, 1987, plaintiff's husband telephoned to the hair salon Command Performance in the King of Prussia Mall, to set up an appointment for his wife, Edith Perry. . . . On the date in question, Helene Kugler was scheduled to wash and set Ms. Perry's hair, as she had done previously. Not long after Ms. Perry arrived at the salon, Ms. Kugler explained to her that she had a bad cold and was not feeling well. She asked Ms. Perry if she would mind if another hairdresser were to do her hair. Ms. Perry consented. However, according to plaintiff's complaint and her deposition testimony, when Ms. Kugler asked Beth Abbott, another operator, to do plaintiff's hair, Ms. Abbott responded loudly, "No, no, no, no! I don't do black hair. No, no, no, no! Not today!" Ms. Abbott went on to exclaim, "I just don't do black people's hair! Oh, no, I'm not going to do your hair, I'm from New Hampshire and I don't deal with blacks!"
>
> Throughout Ms. Abbott's protest, Ms. Perry grew increasingly distraught and started to cry. She called the security police. Her husband was located within the mall to escort her from the salon. Plaintiff claims that she was traumatized by this incident and that as a result she suffered from hives and insomnia. In addition, she has pursued

treatment with a psychiatrist. Perry v. Command Performance, 913 F.2d 99, 100 (3d Cir. 1990).

Perry brought a § 1981 action against the beauty salon as well as a claim of intentional infliction of emotional distress under Pennsylvania law. Vacating a district court dismissal on summary judgment, the appellate court remanded the case to determine whether Perry was in the process of making a contract at the time of the incident or if "contract was made at the time of the scheduling of the appointment." Id., at 102. Do you find an offer and an acceptance in the transaction described? If so, when and by what actions?

At the time of *Perry*, § 1981 was viewed as applying to intentional discrimination in the *making* of a contract, such as a refusal on the basis of race to enter into a contract or offering "terms different than those afforded white patrons," but not applicable to discrimination *after* formation or under a contract." Id., at 101. A year after *Perry,* Congress amended § 1981, as part of the Civil Rights Act of 1991, adding, "For purposes of this section, the term 'make and enforce contracts' includes the making, performance, modification, and termination of contracts, and the enjoyment of all benefits, privileges, terms, and conditions of the contractual relationship." 42 U.S.C. § 1981(b).

Consider also Barfield v. Commerce Bank, 484 F.3d 1276 (10th Cir. 2007), in which Chris Barfield, an African-American man, entered a Commerce Bank branch in Wichita, Kansas, and requested change for a $50 bill. He was refused change on the ground that he was not an account-holder. The next day, a white friend of Barfield's father made the same request of the bank, and was given change without being asked whether he was an account-holder. When Barfield's father came in a few minutes later and asked for change, he was told he would not be given change unless he was an account-holder. The Barfields filed suit under 42 U.S.C. § 1981, alleging racial discrimination in the impairment of the ability to contract. The bank defended in part on the grounds that there was no consideration. Was there consideration on these facts? We return to § 1981 when considering the uncommon context of courts awarding punitive damages for breach of contract in Chapter 8, p. 885.

SECTION 4.   TERMINATION OF THE POWER OF ACCEPTANCE

After a party has made an offer, conferring on another the power of acceptance, that power can be terminated (1) by lapse of the offer, (2) by its revocation by the offeror, (3) by the offeror's death or incapacity, or (4) by the offeree's rejection.

This section begins with lapse—the expiration of the period within which an offer can be accepted. How long does an offer remain "open" when an offeror neglects to state a period for acceptance: When does it become too late for the offeree to accept?

Revocation is considered next. The basic rule in common-law countries is that an offeror can terminate an ordinary offer, at any time before it has been accepted, by revoking it. An exception to this rule occurs when the offeror has made a "firm offer" or otherwise created an option contract. In contrast to ordinary offers, option contracts are offers that are—for a time—not subject to revocation. Irrevocability is the defining characteristic of an option contract.

Attention then briefly turns to a third terminating event: the death or the incapacity of the offeror. While posing interesting conceptual problems (the rule holds whether or not the offeree learns of the death), the practical import of the rule has been greatly reduced since the typical offeror is now often a deathless corporate entity.

The fourth terminating event is rejection, an act by the offeree which puts an end to an ordinary offer. Here we examine what counts as a rejection under the common law "mirror image" rule. The materials also consider the effect of rejecting a firm offer.

One final topic rounds out this Section. When the offeree has sent an acceptance to the offeror, or the offeror has sent a revocation of the offer to the offeree, when does the acceptance or revocation become effective: when it is sent, or when it is received? The traditional answers are found in the "mailbox rule," discussed below.

(A) LAPSE OF AN OFFER

After some period of time, an offer lapses. If no period is specified in the offer, it lapses after a reasonable time. What is a reasonable time depends, of course, on the circumstances. Take an offer to buy or sell. If the subject matter undergoes rapid fluctuation in price, as is often the case for goods, this will typically shorten the amount of time that is considered reasonable. The following cases illustrate some other factors used in determining what is a reasonable time for this purpose.

In Akers v. J.B. Sedberry, Inc., 286 S.W.2d 617 (Tenn.App.1955), Akers, while in a conference with the president of his employer, offered orally to resign. The president ignored the offer and the conference continued. A few days later the president advised Akers by wire that his offer was accepted, and that Akers was to discontinue his association with the Sedberry firm. Akers sued for breach of contract and a decree in his favor was affirmed. "Ordinarily, an offer made by one to another in a face to face conversation is deemed to continue only to the close of their conversation, and cannot be accepted thereafter." Caldwell v. E.F. Spears & Sons, 216 S.W. 83 (Ky.1919).

In Loring v. City of Boston, 48 Mass. 409 (1844), the City of Boston had run in the daily papers an advertisement offering a $1,000 reward for the apprehension and conviction of any person setting fire to any building within the city limits. The advertisements continued for about a week in May, 1837, and did not appear again. In January, 1841, there was a fire in Boston, and Loring, with the reward in mind, pursued the arsonist to New York, arrested him, returned him to Boston, had him indicted and prosecuted, produced evidence that convicted him, and then sued the city for the reward. There was evidence that fire alarms had been frequent before the advertisements but much less so from that time until the end of 1841.

The Supreme Judicial Court of Massachusetts denied recovery. Since the purposes of such an offer are to excite the vigilance of the public and, perhaps, to alarm offenders, the offer of the reward must be notorious in order to be effective. Three years and eight months was not a reasonable time under the circumstances. "In that length of time, the exigency under which it was made having passed, it must be presumed to have been forgotten by most of the officers and citizens of the community, and cannot be presumed to have been before the public as an actuating motive to vigilance and exertion on this subject; nor could it justly and reasonably have been so understood by the plaintiffs." But cf. Carr v. Mahaska County Bankers Ass'n, 269 N.W. 494 (Iowa 1936).

NOTES

(1) *Tardy Acceptances.* What is the effect of an expression of acceptance that arrives too late to operate as an acceptance? Can the offeror choose simply to disregard the delay and treat the message as an acceptance? Or is it a counter-offer, so that no contract results unless the original offeror, in turn, expresses acceptance?

(2) *Counting the Offers.* In Newman v. Schiff, 778 F.2d 460, 462 (8th Cir.1985), the plaintiff was a tax lawyer who claimed $100,000 for supplying citations to the Internal Revenue Code in response to a challenge made on a television call-in show: "If anybody calls this show—I have the Code—and cites any section of this Code that says an individual is required to file a tax return, I will pay them $100,000." The challenge had been made in the evening, on the program Nightwatch; the plaintiff had learned of it from watching a brief segment that was rebroadcast on CBS Morning News. (He called a number at CBS different from the one announced on Nightwatch for call-ins.) Was the plaintiff right in thinking two offers had been made? Under an objective approach, was the plaintiff justified in thinking an offer had been made on the morning program?

PROBLEM

Courtroom Countdown. After falling at a university's ice rink, a claimant sued the university for negligence. A jury trial was held. During a 10-minute recess prior to the closing arguments, the university's counsel, Orlando, offered the claimant, through her counsel Haaz, $750,000 to settle the case. At the end of the conversation, Orlando told Haaz, "You've got to get back to me." While making the statement, Orlando looked at the clock and "placed his palms sideward." When the trial resumed, Haaz was granted two minutes to talk to his client. There was no further communication between counsel. During Orlando's closing argument, the claimant authorized Haaz to accept the settlement offer. Haaz then gave his closing argument. At a sidebar conference following the closings, Haaz stated that his client had accepted the offer, to which Orlando replied, "I don't know if it's still there, judge." Prior to jury deliberations, the claimant moved to enforce the settlement agreement. Had it lapsed? The period between the offer and the statement of acceptance was seventy minutes. What is a reasonable time in such a case? See Yaros v. Trustees of University of Pennsylvania, 742 A.2d 1118 (Pa. 1999). The jury later returned a verdict for the university; does this fact help in deciding the question of lapse? In understanding the timing of the purported acceptance?

(B) REVOCATION OF OFFERS

Grotius, the great 17th-century Dutch jurist, favored the rule that prevails at the common law: an offer is freely revocable. But the opposing rule has its adherents. In Germany and some other civil-law countries an offer is irrevocable for a reasonable time unless the offeror expresses a different intention. See 1 *Formation of Contracts: A Study of the Common Core of Legal Systems* 780–83 (Rudolf B. Schlesinger and Pierre G. Bonassies eds., 1968).

Which rule is preferable? One disadvantage of the German rule is that during the period of irrevocability, the offeree can take advantage of changing economic conditions to speculate at the expense of the offeror. Although Germany and the other countries that have this rule have historically experienced much greater economic upheavals than has the United States, they have been able to live with the rule, at least in part, because it can easily be avoided by expressly reserving the power to revoke or providing that the communication is not an offer at all. The extent to which the offeror in the United States can avoid the common law rule by expressly relinquishing the power to revoke is discussed in connection with "firm offers" under Article 2, p. 237 below.

When is a communication a revocation? In Hoover Motor Express Co. v. Clements Paper Co., 241 S.W.2d 851 (Tenn.1951), Hoover had made an offer to Clements to buy real estate. Although the offer had been made on November 19, and Williams, Clements' vice-president, had been authorized in December to accept it, he had not done so by January 13. On that day Williams telephoned Hoover and "told him that we were ready to go through with it and I would like to discuss it with him." Hoover replied, "Well, I don't know if we are ready. We have not decided, we might not want to go through with it." Clements later sent an acceptance, but the court held that it was too late. Hoover's remark on the telephone "brought home to Williams that Hoover no longer consented to the transaction." Compare the court's treatment of the claimed revocation in this case with the courts' treatment of the claimed offers in Owen v. Tunison and in Harvey v. Facey, above. Are they consistent?

In the case of offers addressed to the general public, such as rewards and most advertisements, it is ordinarily impossible for the offeror actually to communicate a revocation to all of the persons who are aware of the offer. Consider the offers in the *Broadnax* case, p. 93 above, and the *Lefkowitz* case, p. 194 above. The offeror can, of course, be required to give a notice of revocation publicity equal (and usually similar) to that given the offer. But if this has been done, is the offeror nevertheless bound by the acceptance of an offeree who was aware of the offer but missed the notice of revocation? The answer is that the offeror is not bound, in spite of the requirement that a revocation be actually communicated to the offeree. See Restatement § 46.

How would one revoke an offer of a reward posted on a bulletin board? Would taking it down be sufficient? When would the revocation take effect? See Carr v. Mahaska County Bankers Ass'n, 269 N.W. 494 (Iowa 1936). In that case, the bank's reward notice has been posted in 1930, taken down in 1931 or 1932, and the reward claimed for the capture of a robber in 1935. Affirming judgment for the claimant who sought the reward, the Supreme Court of Iowa distinguished between the rewards for the discovery of perpetrators of crimes already committed, and those that were "contemplative" and "had to do with the robbing of some bank in Mahaska County, should it happen some day." From the nature of the rewards, the court stated "the public could reasonably assume that the offer once made was intended to continue into the future to accomplish [its] evident purpose."

For an interesting historical example of revocation by publication involving a reward issued by Secretary of War Stanton for Suratt, one of Booth's accomplices in the assassination of President Lincoln, see Shuey v. United States, 92 U.S. 73 (1875).

Limiting the Power of Revocation: Option Contracts

A promise made by an offeror that effectively limits the offeror's power to revoke the offer is often called an option or, in the language of the Restatement § 25, an option contract. Usually an option expresses, directly or indirectly, a fixed period during which the offer stays open, usually phrased as the time by which the offeree must exercise, or "pick up," the option. The following material explores four ways that an option may be created: (i) a promise to hold the offer open which is supported by consideration, (ii) a "firm offer" under Article 2 of the UCC, (iii) an offer seeking performance rather than a return promise (an offer to enter into a unilateral contract) which generates the beginning of the sought performance by the offeree, and (iv) reliance by the offeree.

We begin with a well-known case from the 19th century which addresses the first way to create an option contract.

Dickinson v. Dodds

In the Court of Appeal, Chancery Division, 1876.
LR 2 Ch.D. 463.

On Wednesday, the 10th of June, 1874, the defendant John Dodds signed and delivered to the plaintiff, George Dickinson, a memorandum, of which the material part was as follows:

"I hereby agree to sell to Mr. George Dickinson the whole of the dwelling-houses, garden ground, stabling, and outbuildings thereto belonging, situate at Croft, belonging to me, for the sum of £800. As witness my hand this tenth day of June, 1874.

£800 [Signed] John Dodds."

"P.S.—This offer to be left over until Friday, 9' o'clock a.m. J.D. (The twelfth), 12th June, 1874. [Signed] J. Dodds."

The bill alleged that Dodds understood and intended that the plaintiff should have until Friday, 9 a.m., within which to determine whether he would or would not purchase, and that he should absolutely have until that time the refusal of the property at the price of £800, and that the plaintiff in fact determined to accept the offer on the morning of Thursday, the 11th of June, but did not at once signify his acceptance to Dodds, believing that he had the power to accept it until 9 a.m. on Friday.

In the afternoon of the Thursday the plaintiff was informed by a Mr. Berry that Dodds had been offering or agreeing to sell the property to Thomas Allan, the other defendant. Thereupon the plaintiff, at about half past seven in the evening, went to the house of Mrs. Burgess, the mother-in-law of Dodds, where he was then staying, and left with her formal acceptance in writing of the offer to sell the property. According to the evidence of Mrs. Burgess this document never in fact reached Dodds, she having forgotten to give it to him.

On the following (Friday) morning, at about seven o'clock, Berry, who was acting as agent for Dickinson, found Dodds at Darlington Railway station, and handed to him a duplicate of the acceptance by Dickinson, and explained to Dodds its purport. He replied that it was too late, as he had already sold the property. A few minutes later Dickinson himself found Dodds entering a railway carriage, and handed him another duplicate of the notice of acceptance, but Dodds declined to receive it, saying: "You are too late. I have sold the property."

It appeared that on the day before, Thursday, the 11th of June, Dodds had signed a formal contract for the sale of the property to the defendant Allan for £800, and received from him a deposit of £40.

The bill in this suit prayed that the defendant Dodds might be decreed specifically to perform the contract of the 10th of June, 1874; that he might be restrained from conveying the property to Allan; that Allan might be restrained from taking any such conveyance; that, if any such conveyance had been or should be made, Allan might be declared a trustee of the property for, and might be directed to convey the property to, the plaintiff; and for damages.

Dickinson won a decree of specific performance. Dodds and Allan appealed.

■ JAMES, LORD JUDGE, after referring to the document of the 10th of June, 1874, continued:

The document, though beginning "I hereby agree to sell," was nothing but an offer, and was only intended to be an offer, for the plaintiff himself tells us that he required time to consider whether he would enter into an agreement or not. Unless both parties had then agreed, there was no concluded agreement then made; it was in effect and substance only an offer to sell. The plaintiff, being minded not to complete the bargain at that time, added this memorandum: "This offer to be left over until Friday, 9 o'clock a.m. 12th June, 1874." That shows it was only an offer. There was no consideration given for the undertaking or promise, to whatever extent it may be considered binding, to keep the property unsold until 9 o'clock on Friday morning; but apparently Dickinson was of opinion, [and probably Dodds was of the same opinion] that he (Dodds) was bound by that promise, and could not in any way withdraw from it, or retract it, until 9 o'clock on Friday morning, and this probably explains a good deal of what afterwards took place. But it is clear settled law, on one of the clearest principles of law, that this promise, being a mere (nudum pactum) was not binding, and that at any moment before a complete acceptance by Dickinson of the offer, Dodds was as free as Dickinson himself.

The plaintiff says in effect that, having heard and knowing that Dodds was no longer minded to sell to him, and that he was selling or sold to some one else, thinking that he could not in point of law withdraw his offer, meaning to fix him to it, and endeavoring to bind him: "I went to the house where he was lodging, and saw his mother-in-law, and left with her an acceptance of the offer, knowing all the while that he had entirely changed his mind. I got an agent to watch for him at 7 o'clock the next morning, and I went to the train just before 9 o'clock, in order that I might catch him and give him my notice of acceptance just before 9 o'clock, and when that occurred he told my agent, and he told me, 'You are too late,' and he then threw back the paper." It is to my mind quite clear that before there was any attempt at acceptance by the plaintiff, he was perfectly well aware that Dodds had changed his mind, and that he had in fact agreed to sell the property to Allan. It is impossible, therefore to say there was ever that existence of the same mind between the two parties which is essential in point of law to the making of an agreement. I am of opinion, therefore, that the plaintiff has failed to prove that there was any binding contract between Dodds and himself.

■ MELLISH, LORD JUDGE. I am of the same opinion. Well, then, this being only an offer, and the law says—and it is clearly rule of law—that, although it is said that the offer is to be left open until Friday morning at 9 o'clock, that did not bind Dodds. Assuming Allan to have known (there is some dispute about it, and Allan does not admit that he knew of it, but I will assume that he did) that Dodds had made the offer to Dickinson, and had given him until Friday morning at 9 o'clock to accept it, still in point of law that could not prevent Alan from making a more favorable offer than Dickinson, and entering at once into a binding agreement with Dodds.

Then Dickinson is informed by Berry that the property has been sold by Dodds to Allan. Berry does not tell us from whom it heard it, but he says that he did hear it, that he knew it, and that he informed Dickinson of it. Now, stopping there, the question which arises is this: If an offer has been made for the sale of the property, and before that offer is accepted the person who has made the offer enters into a binding agreement to sell the property to somebody else, and the person to whom the offer was first made receives notice in some way that the property has been sold to another person, can he after that make a binding contract by the acceptance of the offer? I am of opinion that he cannot. The law may be right or wrong in saying that a person who has given to another a certain time within which to accept an offer is not bound by his promise to give that time; but, if he is not bound by that promise, and may still sell the property to some one else, and if it be the law that, on order to make a contract, the two minds must be in agreement at some one time, that is, at the time of the acceptance, how is it possible that when the person to whom the offer has been made the offer has sold the property to someone else, and that, in fact, he has not remained in the same mind to sell it to him, he can be at liberty to accept the offer and thereby make a binding contract? It seems to me that would be simply absurd. If a man makes an offer to sell a particular horse in his stable, and says, "I will give you until the day after to-morrow to accept the offer," and the next day goes and sells the horse to somebody else, and receives the purchase money from him, can the person to whom the offer was originally made then come and say, "I accept," so as to make a binding contract, and so as to be entitled to recover damages for the non-delivery of the horse? If the rule of law is that a mere offer to sell property, which can be withdrawn at any time, and which is made dependent on the acceptance of the person to whom it is made, is a mere nudum pactum, how is it possible that the person to whom the offer has been made can by acceptance make a binding contract after he knows that the person who has made the offer has sold the property to some one else? . . . I am clearly of opinion that there was no binding contract for the sale of this property by Dodds to Dickinson; and, even if there had been, it seems to me that the sale of the property to Allan was first in point to time. However, it is not necessary to consider, if there had been two binding contracts, which of them would be entitled to priority in equity, because there is no binding contract between Dodds and Dickinson.

NOTES

(1) *Indirect Communication of Revocation.* The opinion gives several versions of what Dickinson knew about what Dodds was doing. What exactly did Berry tell Dickinson? That Dodds had made an *offer* to sell the property or that he had made a *contract* to sell the property? Does it make a difference what Dickinson was told, or by whom? See Restatement § 43.

(2) *All in the Timing.* What can be said in support of a system in which the existence of a contract depends on the exact sequence of "acceptance" and "revocation"? When offeror and offeree meet at a railway station, is it not absurd that their legal relations can depend on who speaks first? See E. Allan Farnsworth, *Mutuality of Obligation in Contract Law*, 3 Dayton L. Rev. 271 (1978).

(3) *Asymmetrical Advantages?* Are there asymmetrical advantages to an option contract? In a rapidly fluctuating market, may the offeree not have the opportunity to speculate during the period when the offeror is bound but the offeree is not? Given this risk, why would an informed offeror enter into an option contract? The traditional answer is that the offeror is compensated for the risk through a higher contract price. We might say that the offeree has paid for the chance to speculate during the time when the offeror is bound. Is it unfair then, if during that period the offeree then decides to take advantage of the fluctuating market? What are the assumptions that underlie the traditional answer? Under what circumstances might those assumptions fail?

(4) *Lapse or Revocation?* Consider the following case. In 1911, private land owners dedicated a property to a township for public use. State law required that any such dedication, or offer of public use, be accepted by a formal governmental resolution. (Why might that be?) Raymond and Jean Marx bought the property in the 1970s, and in 1993, they brought a quiet title action seeking to have the land declared theirs and not the township's. The township argued that in 1979 it had passed a resolution accepting all dedicated lands not yet accepted. Had the offer lapsed by 1979? It helps to know that an offer to dedicate land is generally understood as an on-going offer. Nonetheless, in Marx v. Department of Commerce, 558 N.W.2d 460 (Mich.App.1996), the court found that the 68-year delay was too long. But see Ackerman v. Spring Lake Twp., 163 N.W.2d 230 (Mich.App.1968), holding that a 28 year delay in accepting dedication was timely. The court in *Marx* also found that the offer had been withdrawn, noting that withdrawal, or revocation, of an offer, differs from lapse in that the "former requires an affirmative act, while the latter stems from inaction." What action constituted the revocation in *Marx*?

PROBLEM

Hedging One's Bets. A offered in writing to sell B Greenacre for $1,000, offer to remain open five days. On the fourth day, B received a report from the county recorder of deeds that the recorder had received for recording a deed of Greenacre from A to C executed that day. Thinking there might be some chance that the recorder was wrong, B notified A of acceptance on the fifth day. The information given by the recorder proved to be erroneous. A denied having a contract with B. Was A right about that? See Restatement § 43, indicating that A is right if the report was "reliable." Might the report have been reliable, although erroneous?

"Firm Offers" Under Article 2

In the early common law an irrevocable offer or option could be created by making the promise under seal. Upon the abolition of the seal, however, the doctrine of consideration became the exclusive means to this end. Decisions such as in Dickinson v. Dodds and its progeny have been subject to some criticism. "Until the nineteenth century was well advanced there seems to have been no serious concern over means for making offers 'firm.' [Then in 1876 in Dickinson v. Dodds] an English court concluded with great confidence that a time limit fixed by the offeror could not prevent revocation before the time limit had expired, for in the absence of consideration any restriction on the power to revoke was simply *nudum pactum*. American decisions have dutifully followed this line ever since and thereby made the consideration test a still more prominent target of public ridicule. The difficulties were all manufactured by treating offers as a subordinate form of promise." John P. Dawson, Gifts and Promises 211–13 (1980).

The technique of giving a nominal sum in exchange for a promise of irrevocability may make sense for offers involving real property, where the parties might be more likely to anticipate the possibility of revocation and so account for it more formally. It is less satisfactory for more informal transactions, such as those for the sale of goods, where the offeror is less likely to clothe a promise in the trappings of consideration. (Compare the circumstances surrounding the typical sale of goods with a sale of real property.)

Section 2–205 of the UCC ("Firm Offers") is an important provision that, in certain cases, enables an offeree to enforce an offer which, by its terms, states that it will be held open, even though the promise to hold it open was not supported by consideration. What conditions must be satisfied in order for the rule to apply? Under the Article 2 rule, how long can a firm offer unsupported by consideration be held open?

NOTES

(1) *Merchants Under Article 2.* Compare the definition of merchant in UCC § 2–104 with language of UCC § 2–205. Can one who does not deal in goods of the kind be bound to a firm offer under UCC § 2–205? Consider, for example, a manufacturer seeking to buy a new piece of factory equipment or to sell a used piece of factory equipment. Would such a manufacturer hold "himself out as having knowledge or skill peculiar to the practices involved in the transaction"? What practices? (According to Comment 2, professional

status "may be based upon specialized knowledge as to the goods, specialized knowledge as to business practices, or specialized knowledge as to both and which kind of specialized knowledge may be sufficient is indicated by the nature of the provisions.")

(2)   *New York Statute.* In addition to UCC § 2–205, New York has the following statute of broader applicability, first enacted in 1941 (along with its statute on "moral obligation" in Note 3, p. 79 above), and subsequently amended to take account of the later-enacted Uniform Commercial Code:

> Except as otherwise provided in section 2–205 of the uniform commercial code with respect to an offer by a merchant to buy or sell goods, when an offer to enter into a contract is made in a writing signed by the offeror, or by his agent, which states that the offer is irrevocable during a period set forth or until a time fixed, the offer shall not be revocable during such period or until such time because of the absence of consideration for the assurance of irrevocability. When such a writing states that the offer is irrevocable but does not state any period of time of irrevocability, it shall be construed to state that the offer is irrevocable for a reasonable time. (New York General Obligations Law § 5–1109.)

(3)   *Recitals.* If a sum of money is paid as consideration for an option, this fact is usually recited. What is the effect of such a recital if no payment is made? Some courts have held it to be of no effect. Others have held that it makes the offer irrevocable, either as a binding acknowledgment of payment or as a promise to pay. Restatement § 87 favors the latter view, with the qualifications that the recital be in a signed writing and that the proposed exchange be fair. Comment *b* to that section explains, "The signed writing has vital significance as a formality, while the ceremonial manual delivery of a dollar or a peppercorn is an inconsequential formality."

Promises Seeking Performance and Restatement § 45

Consider a notorious hypothetical put by Professor Maurice Wormser nearly a 100 years ago:

> Suppose A says to B, 'I will give you $100 if you walk across the Brooklyn Bridge'. B starts to walk across the Brooklyn Bridge and has gone about one-half of the way across. At that moment A overtakes B and says to him, 'I withdraw my offer.' Has B then any rights against A? Let us now suppose that after A has said, 'I withdraw my offer,' B continues to walk across the Brooklyn Bridge and completes the act of crossing. Under these circumstances, has B any rights against A?" Wormser concluded that he had none. "What A wanted from B, what A asked for, was the act of walking across the bridge. Until that was done, B had not given to A what A had requested. The acceptance by B

of A's offer could be nothing but the act on B's part of crossing the bridge. It is elementary that an offeror may withdraw his offer until it has been accepted. It follows logically that A is perfectly within his rights in withdrawing his offer before B has accepted it by walking across the bridge—the act contemplated by the offeror and the offeree as the acceptance of the offer.

I. Maurice Wormser, *The True Conception of Unilateral Contracts*, 26 Yale L.J. 136–37 (1916).

Restatement § 45 states a rule, based on the former Restatement § 45 and couched in language of "option contract," that supports a different result. It states that if "an offer invites an offeree to accept by rendering a performance and does not invite a promissory acceptance, an option contract is created when the offeree tenders or *begins* the invited performance" (emphasis supplied). In reading this section in its entirety it helps to understand that one cannot "tender" a performance that is to extend over a period of time, such as crossing a bridge.

Indeed, long after Wormser first wrote of the Brooklyn Bridge hypothetical, he admitted: "Since that time I have repented, so that now, clad in sackcloth, I state frankly, that my point of view has changed. I agree, at this time, with the rule set forth in the Restatement." Book Review, 3 J. Legal Ed. 145 (1950).

Note that the problem posed by the hypothetical and addressed in Restatement § 45 can be avoided if the offer seeks a promise as acceptance and either a promise is given in so many words or one can be inferred from the offeree's conduct. The Restatement allows an offeree to choose the means of acceptance—"either by promising to perform what the offer requests or by rendering the performance"—when the offer itself was unclear about the type of response invited. See Restatement § 32.

NOTE

Would it be preferable to limit recovery by B in the Brooklyn Bridge hypothetical to damages based on B's reliance rather than B's expectation interest? See Fuller and Perdue, *The Reliance Interest in Contract Damages: 2*, 46 Yale L.J. 373, 410–17 (1937).

PROBLEM

The Move to Maine. Sarah Hodgkin, a widow who lived alone on her farm in Maine, wrote to her daughter and son-in-law, the Brackenburys, in Missouri, offering them the use and income of her farm if they would move to Maine and take care of Mrs. Hodgkin during her life. The letter closed, "you to have the place when I have passed away." The Brackenburys moved to Maine and began performance, but after a few weeks, relations between the parties soured. When Mrs. Hodgkin sought to evict the Brackenburys, they sued to enforce her promise. What result? Brackenbury v. Hodgkin, 102 A. 106 (Me.1917). Would it make a difference if Hodgkin's letter had read: "If

you will agree to move to Lewiston and care for me on the home place. . . . ”
See Davis v. Jacoby, 34 P.2d 1026 (Cal.1934).

What if Hodgkin had died after the Brackenburys had sold their home
and business in Missouri and begun the journey to Maine? See the discussion
of Death of an Offeror at p. 246 below.

Revocability and Reliance

Can a promisee's reliance on an offer, in contrast to reliance on a
promise, make the offer irrevocable? The orthodox response is found in
Judge Learned Hand's opinion in James Baird Co. v. Gimbel Bros., Inc.,
64 F.2d 344 (2d Cir.1933). In that case, a general contractor received a
bid from a subcontractor that the general contractor then used in making
up his own bid. When the subcontractor realized that he had made a
clerical error in his bid, he sought to revoke the bid, which the general
contractor had not yet accepted. The general contractor argued that his
use of subcontractor's bid was a form of reliance that made the
subcontractor's bid irrevocable at least until the general's own bid was
accepted or not.

Judge Hand held that promissory estoppel is inapplicable to a
bargain promise seeking a promise in return, even if the promise
occasioned reliance by the promisee. The subcontractor could withdraw
its bid because “an offer for an exchange is not meant to become a promise
until a consideration has been received, either a counter-promise or
whatever is stipulated. To extend it would be to hold the offeror
regardless of the stipulated condition of his offer.” The subcontractor's
offer could impose a duty to render a performance only when the general
contractor “promised to take and pay for it. There is no room in such a
situation for the doctrine of ‘promissory estoppel.’ ”

This afforded protection along traditional lines to the offeror, who
asks for something (acceptance by the offeree), and is not to be bound
until he gets it; the offer is conditional on acceptance. Hand's theory is
that section 90 of the Restatement was originally intended to cover only
the non-bargain situation—the transaction in which no exchange is
asked or contemplated—and the drafting history of the section supports
this position. “The element of exchange which marks off the bargain
promise also” limits promissory estoppel. Hand also noted that in the
context of construction bidding, contractors have “a ready escape from
their difficulty by insisting upon a contract before they used the figures;
and in commercial transactions it does not in the end promote justice to
seek strained interpretations in aid of those who do not protect
themselves.”

As you study the following case, keep in mind that Justice Traynor
had to confront Hand's position that in the world of exchange
transactions there is no place for section 90, which was intended only to

cover the relied-upon gift promise. How does Traynor counter Hand on this?

Drennan v. Star Paving Co.
Supreme Court of California, In Bank, 1958.
51 Cal.2d 409, 333 P.2d 757.

General contractor brought action against paving subcontractor to recover damages because of refusal of subcontractor to perform paving according to bid which subcontractor submitted to general contractor. The Superior Court, Kern County, William L. Bradshaw, J., entered judgment adverse to the subcontractor, and the subcontractor appealed.

■ TRAYNOR, JUSTICE.[q] Defendant appeals from a judgment for plaintiff in an action to recover damages caused by defendant's refusal to perform certain paving work according to a bid it submitted to plaintiff.

On July 28, 1955, plaintiff, a licensed general contractor, was preparing a bid on the "Monte Vista School Job" in the Lancaster school district. Bids had to be submitted before 8:00 p.m. Plaintiff testified that it was customary in that area for general contractors to receive the bids of subcontractors by telephone on the day set for bidding and to rely on them in computing their own bids. Thus on that day plaintiff's secretary, Mrs. Johnson, received by telephone between fifty and seventy-five subcontractors' bids for various parts of the school job. As each bid came in, she wrote it on a special form, which she brought into plaintiff's office. He then posted it on a master cost sheet setting forth the names and bids of all subcontractors. His own bid had to include the names of subcontractors who were to perform one-half of one per cent or more of the construction work, and he had also to provide a bidder's bond of ten per cent of his total bid of $317,385 as a guarantee that he would enter the contract if awarded the work.

Late in the afternoon, Mrs. Johnson had a telephone conversation with Kenneth R. Hoon, an estimator for defendant. He gave his name and telephone number and stated that he was bidding for defendant for the paving work at the Monte Vista School according to plans and specifications and that his bid was $7,131.60. At Mrs. Johnson's request he repeated his bid. Plaintiff listened to the bid over an extension telephone in his office and posted it on the master sheet after receiving the bid form from Mrs. Johnson. Defendant's was the lowest bid for the paving. Plaintiff computed his own bid accordingly and submitted it with the name of defendant as the subcontractor for the paving. When the bids

q   Roger Traynor (1900–1983) was a member of the law faculty of the University of California at Berkeley from 1930 to 1940 and specialized in tax law. He served from 1940 to 1964 as associate justice of the Supreme Court of California and from 1964 to 1970 as its chief justice. Some of his opinions on contract law are discussed in Stewart Macaulay, *Mr. Justice Traynor and the Law of Contracts*, 13 Stan. L. Rev. 812 (1961).

were opened on July 28th, plaintiff's proved to be the lowest, and he was awarded the contract.

On his way to Los Angeles the next morning plaintiff stopped at defendant's office. The first person he met was defendant's construction engineer, Mr. Oppenheimer. Plaintiff testified: "I introduced myself and he immediately told me that they had made a mistake in their bid to me the night before, they couldn't do it for the price they had bid, and I told him I would expect him to carry through with their original bid because I had used it in compiling my bid and the job was being awarded them. And I would have to go and do the job according to my bid and I would expect them to do the same."

Defendant refused to do the paving work for less than $15,000. Plaintiff testified that he "got figures from other people" and after trying for several months to get as low a bid as possible engaged L & H Paving Company, a firm in Lancaster, to do the work for $10,948.60.

The trial court found on substantial evidence that defendant made a definite offer to do the paving on the Monte Vista job according to the plans and specifications for $7,131.60, and that plaintiff relied on defendant's bid in computing his own bid for the school job and naming defendant therein as the subcontractor for the paving work. Accordingly, it entered judgment for plaintiff in the amount of $3,817.00 (the difference between defendant's bid and the cost of the paving to plaintiff) plus costs.

Defendant contends that there was no enforceable contract between the parties on the ground that it made a revocable offer and revoked it before plaintiff communicated his acceptance to defendant.

There is no evidence that defendant offered to make its bid irrevocable in exchange for plaintiff's use of its figures in computing his bid. Nor is there evidence that would warrant interpreting plaintiff's use of defendant's bid as the acceptance thereof, binding plaintiff, on condition he received the main contract, to award the subcontract to defendant. In sum, there was neither an option supported by consideration nor a bilateral contract binding on both parties.

Plaintiff contends, however, that he relied to his detriment on defendant's offer and that defendant must therefore answer in damages for its refusal to perform. Thus the question is squarely presented: Did plaintiff's reliance make defendant's offer irrevocable?

Section 90 of the Restatement of Contracts states: "A promise which the promisor should reasonably expect to induce action or forbearance of a definite and substantial character on the part of the promisee and which does induce such action or forbearance is binding if injustice can be avoided only by enforcement of the promise." This rule applies in this state.

Defendant's offer constituted a promise to perform on such conditions as were stated expressly or by implication therein or annexed thereto by operation of law. (See 1 Williston, Contracts [3rd ed.], § 24A, p. 56, § 61, p. 196.) Defendant had reason to expect that if its bid proved the lowest it would be used by plaintiff. It induced "action of a definite and substantial character on the part of the promisee."

Had defendant's bid expressly stated or clearly implied that it was revocable at any time before acceptance we would treat it accordingly. It was silent on revocation, however, and we must therefore determine whether there are conditions to the right of revocation imposed by law or reasonably inferable in fact. In the analogous problem of an offer for a unilateral contract, the theory is now obsolete that the offer is revocable at any time before complete performance. Thus section 45 of the Restatement of Contracts provides: "If an offer for a unilateral contract is made, and part of the consideration requested in the offer is given or tendered by the offeree in response thereto, the offeror is bound by a contract, the duty of immediate performance of which is conditional on the full consideration being given or tendered within the time stated in the offer, or, if no time is stated therein, within a reasonable time." In explanation, comment *b* states that the "main offer includes as a subsidiary promise, necessarily implied, that if part of the requested performance is given, the offeror will not revoke his offer, and that if tender is made it will be accepted. Part performance or tender may thus furnish consideration for the subsidiary promise. Moreover, merely acting in justifiable reliance on an offer may in some cases serve as sufficient reason for making a promise binding (see § 90)."

Whether implied in fact or law, the subsidiary promise serves to preclude the injustice that would result if the offer could be revoked after the offeree had acted in detrimental reliance thereon. Reasonable reliance resulting in a foreseeable prejudicial change in position affords a compelling basis also for implying a subsidiary promise not to revoke an offer for a bilateral contract.

The absence of consideration is not fatal to the enforcement of such a promise. It is true that in the case of unilateral contracts the Restatement finds consideration for the implied subsidiary promise in the part performance of the bargained—for exchange, but its reference to section 90 makes clear that consideration for such a promise is not always necessary. The very purpose of section 90 is to make a promise binding even though there was no consideration "in the sense of something that is bargained for and given in exchange." (See 1 Corbin, Contracts 634 et seq.) Reasonable reliance serves to hold the offeror in lieu of the consideration ordinarily required to make the offer binding. In a case involving similar facts the Supreme Court of South Dakota stated that "we believe that reason and justice demand that the doctrine [of section 90] be applied to the present facts. We cannot believe that by accepting this doctrine as controlling in the state of facts before us we will abolish the requirement of a consideration in contract cases, in any different sense than an ordinary estoppel abolishes some legal requirement in its application. We are of the opinion, therefore, that the defendants in executing the agreement [which was not supported by consideration] made a promise which they should have reasonably expected would induce the plaintiff to submit a bid based thereon to the Government, that such promise did induce this action, and that injustice can be avoided only by enforcement of the promise." Northwestern Engineering Co. v. Ellerman, 10 N.W.2d 879, 884; see also, Robert Gordon, Inc. v. Ingersoll-Rand Co., 7 Cir.; cf. James Baird Co. v. Gimbel Bros., 2 Cir., 64 F.2d 344.

When plaintiff used defendant's offer in computing his own bid, he bound himself to perform in reliance on defendant's terms. Though defendant did not bargain for this use of its bid neither did defendant make it idly, indifferent to whether it would be used or not. On the contrary it is reasonable to suppose that defendant submitted its bid to obtain the subcontract. It was bound to realize the substantial possibility that its bid would be the lowest, and that it would be included by plaintiff in his bid. It was to its own interest that the contractor be awarded the general contract; the lower the subcontract bid, the lower the general contractor's bid was likely to be and the greater its chance of acceptance and hence the greater defendant's chance of getting the paving subcontract. Defendant had reason not only to expect plaintiff to rely on its bid but to want him to. Clearly defendant had a stake in plaintiff's reliance on its bid. Given this interest and the fact that plaintiff is bound by his own bid, it is only fair that plaintiff should have at least an opportunity to accept defendant's bid after the general contract has been awarded to him.

It bears noting that a general contractor is not free to delay acceptance after he has been awarded the general contract in the hope of getting a better price. Nor can he reopen bargaining with the subcontractor and at the same time claim a continuing right to accept the original offer. See, R.J. Daum Const. Co. v. Child, Utah, 247 P.2d 817, 823. In the present case plaintiff promptly informed defendant that plaintiff was being awarded the job and that the subcontract was being awarded to defendant.

Defendant contends, however, that its bid was the result of mistake and that it was therefore entitled to revoke it. It relies on the rescission cases of M.F. Kemper Const. Co. v. City of Los Angeles, 37 Cal.2d 696, 235 P.2d 7, and Brunzell Const. Co. v. G.J. Weisbrod, Inc., 134 Cal.App.2d 278, 285 P.2d 989. See also, Lemoge Electric v. San Mateo County, 46 Cal.2d 659, 662, 297 P.2d 638. In those cases, however, the bidder's mistake was known or should have been known to the offeree, and the offeree could be placed in status quo. Of course, if plaintiff had reason to believe that defendant's bid was in error, he could not justifiably rely on it, and section 90 would afford no basis for enforcing it. Robert Gordon, Inc. v. Ingersoll-Rand, Co., 7 Cir. Plaintiff, however, had no reason to know that defendant had made a mistake in submitting its bid, since there was usually a variance of 160 per cent between the highest and lowest bids for paving in the desert around Lancaster. He committed himself to performing the main contract in reliance on defendant's figures. Under these circumstances defendant's mistake, far from relieving it of its obligation, constitutes an additional reason for enforcing it, for it misled plaintiff as to the cost of doing the paving. Even had it been clearly understood that defendant's offer was revocable until accepted, it would not necessarily follow that defendant had no duty to exercise reasonable care in preparing its bid. It presented its bid with knowledge of the substantial possibility that it would be used by plaintiff; it could foresee the harm that would ensue from an erroneous underestimate of the cost. Moreover, it was motivated by its own business interest. Whether or not these considerations alone would justify recovery for negligence had the case been tried on that theory (see Biakanja v. Irving, 49 Cal.2d 647, 650, 320 P.2d 16), they are persuasive that defendant's mistake should not defeat recovery under the rule of section 90 of the Restatement of Contracts. As between the subcontractor who made the bid and the general contractor who reasonably relied on it, the loss resulting from the mistake should fall on the party who caused it.

Leo F. Piazza Paving Co. v. Bebek & Brkich, 141 Cal.App.2d 226, 296 P.2d 368, 371, and Bard v. Kent, 19 Cal.2d 449, 122 P.2d 8, 139 A.L.R. 1032, are not to the contrary. In the *Piazza* case the court sustained a finding that defendants intended, not to make a firm bid, but only to give the plaintiff "some kind of an idea to use" in making its bid; there was evidence that the defendants had told plaintiff they were unsure of the significance of the specifications. There was thus no offer, promise, or representation on which the defendants should reasonably have expected the plaintiff to rely. The *Bard* case held that an option not supported by consideration was revoked by the death of the optionor. The issue of recovery under the rule of section 90 was not pleaded at the trial, and it does not appear that the offeree's reliance was "of a definite and substantial character" so that injustice could be avoided "only by the enforcement of the promise."

The judgment is affirmed.

NOTES

(1) *Questions.* Justice Traynor found in Star Paving's offer a promise to hold it open for a time, although he said that the offer was "silent on revocation." He did not find that promise in § 45 of the First Restatement. Why not? If, as seems evident, the form of acceptance invited by Star Paving's offer was a promise by Drennan, when did Star Paving expect to receive that promise? Only after Drennan should be awarded the school job? So it seems from the opinion. Does the opinion suggest how soon?

Would the decision have been simpler if Drennan had said "I accept" before introducing himself? See Note 2, p. 236 above.

(2) *Preparing to Cross the Brooklyn Bridge.* The rationale of the *Drennan* case is reflected in Restatement § 87(2). Would this rule protect B in the Brooklyn Bridge hypothetical if B had spent time and money in preparing to cross the bridge, but had not begun to cross it when A revoked?

(3) *Subcontractor Reliance?* Is a general contractor who uses a subcontractor's bid in its own bid obliged to accept the subcontractor's bid, once the general contractor is awarded the contract? If under *Drennan*, a subcontractor is obliged to hold its bid open because of reliance on it by the general contractor, should not the same be true in reverse? The Supreme Court of Minnesota has answered No, dismissing what it called "a superficial equity notion." In bidding on a municipal project, a general contractor named Madsen had used a bid by the Holman Erection Company to do steel erection. That fact was disclosed in a public record, as was required. The municipality selected Madsen, who engaged another firm to do the steel erection work.

In an action against Madsen, Holman contended that Madsen had accepted Holman's bid by using it and winning the general contract. The court ruled otherwise, affirming a summary judgment in favor of Madsen. Holman Erection Co. v. Orville E. Madsen & Sons, Inc., 330 N.W.2d 693 (Minn. 1983).

The court explained that subcontractors do not rely on a general contractor's use of their bids. A subcontractor is likely to have submitted its bid to a number of general contractors, and the cost of that is "part of the overhead of doing business." (Holman had submitted like bids to six other general contractors bidding against Madsen.) The court said also that the low bidder among competing subcontractors "is not always the one chosen to do the work or the one listed as the potential subcontractor. Reliability, quality of work, and capability to handle the job are all considerations weighted by the general in choosing the subcontractors." Another consideration, apparently operative in *Holman Erection*, is the requirement that a contractor attempt to engage the services of minority-owned firms in certain enterprises.

(C) DEATH OF AN OFFEROR

Restatement § 48 sets out the generally accepted rule that an offeree's power of acceptance is terminated by the offeror's death or supervening incapacity. Corbin said of this rule that there is not "any compelling necessity for its existence," pointing out that if a man contracts to pay debts and then dies, "the law has no difficulty in creating legal relations with the dead man's personal representative, and there would be no greater difficulty in declaring the power of acceptance to survive as against the offeror's representative." Arthur L. Corbin, *Offer and Acceptance, and Some of the Resulting Legal Relations*, 26 Yale L.J. 169, 198 (1917).

Under the original draft of the first Restatement, as written by Professor Williston and his advisers, the unknown death of the offeror did not revoke the offer, but the Council of the American Law Institute changed the rule. Professor Williston concluded that "though the amount of actual authority is not impressive, there is a very general opinion among lawyers that death, even though unknown, does revoke an offer and does revoke an agency," and it was vital that the Restatement rule for contracts coincide with that for agency. 3 Proceedings of the American Law Institute 198 (1925). The Restatement preserves this rule, admitting that it "seems to be a relic of the obsolete view that a contract requires a 'meeting of the minds,' and it is out of harmony with the modern doctrine that a manifestation of assent is effective without regard to actual mental assent." Comment *a* to § 48 of the First Restatement. Should the rule be limited to situations in which the offeree has not relied on the assumed contract in ignorance of the fact of the offeror's death?

Death or incapacity of the offeree has the same effect as that of the offeror under § 48. The death or incapacity of the offeror does not terminate the offeree's power of acceptance under an option contract. The death of a party *after* a contract has been formed may, depending on how pivotal the person's role in the enterprise, affect obligations under the contract and is taken up on pp. 157 and 1054.

PROBLEM

In Memoriam. A client, Benjamin Earle, comes to see you with the following story. "About four years ago I had a conversation with my aunt, Mary Dewitt, who lived in Massachusetts, and she said to me something like this, as best I can remember: 'Ben there are few left to come to my funeral. I have thought a great deal of you for coming to your uncle's funeral and bringing that large box of flowers in the terrible snowstorm we had, when our friends could not reach here from Boston, and you coming from Philadelphia. I want you to attend my funeral, Ben, if you outlive me, and I think you will, and I will pay all expenses and I will give you five thousand dollars. I want you to come.' I replied that I would come if I was living and if they informed me in time to get there and if I was able. We talked about it a little more on the occasion of my mother's funeral two years later. Aunt Mary died a few months ago and I went to Massachusetts for her funeral. Soon after the funeral, I received in the mail this paper, bearing the date of our conversation and signed by Aunt Mary." The paper reads, "If Benjamin A. Earle should come to my funeral, I order my executor to pay him the sum of five thousand dollars. Mary Dewitt." The executor has refused to pay and Mr. Earle wants to know whether he has a claim against the estate for $5,000 and his expenses. Advise him. These facts are drawn from Earle v. Angell, 32 N.E. 164 (Mass.1892). See Hamer v. Sidway, p. 53 above.

You may need more facts. What recollections by Earle of events in years past would help to support his claim? In Note 4, p. 183 above, you have been cautioned about prefacing your questions to Earle with an exposition of contract law; according to the Model Rules, a lawyer "shall not . . . counsel or assist a witness to testify falsely." Rule 3.4(b). Compare this, from the Freedman book cited in that note.

> It is not the lawyer's function to prejudice his client as a perjurer. He cannot presume that the client will make unlawful use of his advice. . . . Before [a client] begins to remember essential facts, the client is entitled to know what his own interests are . . . To decide otherwise would . . . penalize the less well-educated defendant.

Does this mean that in advising Earle you should take account of his level of education?

(D) THE CONSEQUENCES OF REJECTION

Does rejection bar an offeree from subsequently accepting the offer? In *Minneapolis & St. Louis Railway Co. v. Columbus Rolling-Mill Co.,* below on p. 248, the court answered Yes. Affirming a judgment for the rolling-mill company in an action for breach by the railway, the court held as follows:

> A proposal to accept, or an acceptance, upon terms varying from those offered, is a rejection of the offer, and puts an end to the negotiation, unless the party who made the original offer renews it, or assents to the modification suggested.[r] The other party having once rejected the offer, cannot afterwards revive it by tendering an acceptance of it.

Minneapolis & St. Louis Railway Co. v. Columbus Rolling-Mill Co., 119 U.S. 149 (1886).

Why is this? One argument is that it would be unjust to allow an offeree who has rejected an offer to reconsider and accept if the offeror has already substantially relied on the rejection. What if the offer was irrevocable? Does the holder of a power to accept under an option contract put an end to the power by rejecting the "offer?" Probably not, though the authorities are sparse. In one of them, Humble Oil held an option contract to acquire some subdivision lots, fixed to expire on June 4. Early in May it wrote to the owner: "Humble . . . hereby exercises its option. . . . The contract of sale is hereby amended to provide that Seller shall extend all utility lines to the property before the date of closing." Twelve days later it wrote again: "The exercise of said option is not qualified and you may disregard the proposed amendment. . . . " Later, Humble sued on a supposed contract of sale. What decision? How different would the case be if Humble had first written: "We have decided not to purchase your property"? *Humble Oil & Refining Co. v. Westside Investment Corp.,* 428 S.W.2d 92 (Tex.1968). See Restatement § 37.

It would be possible to distinguish between the *Humble Oil* case, in which the grantor of the option had received consideration for it, and one in which an offer is irrevocable as a "firm offer" under UCC § 2–205. (Imagine that the Columbus Rolling-Mill had added to its December 8

---

[r]   For contracts for the sale of goods, this rule is changed by UCC § 2–207.

letter: "Offer firm until then—Dec. 20th.") Is there any reason to make the distinction?

To vary the facts of the rolling-mill case, suppose that the railway, holding a firm offer from the rolling-mill company to sell 2,000 tons of rails for March delivery, rejected the offer on December 16, but purported to accept it on December 18. On December 17, however, the company committed all its March output to another customer. How would you explain whether the company is under an obligation to the railway?

(E) THE "MAILBOX RULE": CONTRACTS BY CORRESPONDENCE

How do the rules for the bargaining process apply when the parties are at a distance and bargain by correspondence? Suppose, for example, that one party has sent the other an offer and that the offeree has dispatched an acceptance which has not yet been received by the offeror. Is it too late for the offeror to change its mind and revoke the offer? Is it too late for the offeree to change its mind and reject the offer? And is there a contract if the acceptance is somehow lost and is never received by the offeror?

The tendency of the common law has been to answer these questions on the assumption that dispatch of the acceptance, not its receipt, is the moment of acceptance and, therefore, the moment at which the contract is made—after which the offeror's power to revoke is terminated, the offeree's power to reject is ended, and the risks of transmission are on the offeror. Because the early cases involved acceptance by post, this came to be known as the "mailbox rule." A question to be answered in the 21st century, when even parties who bargain at a distance frequently do so by near-instantaneous means of communication, is the extent to which the "mailbox rule" will retain significance in contract formation.

The origin of the rule is found in the celebrated case of Adams v. Lindsell, [1818] 106 Eng. Rep. 250 (K.B.), where the Court of King's Bench held that a firm of wool dealers that had made an offer by post to sell "eight hundred tons of wether fleeces" could not revoke the offer after the offeree, a firm of woolen manufacturers, had put a letter of acceptance in the post. The overwhelming weight of authority in the United States supports the "mailbox rule" of Adams v. Lindsell. See Restatement § 63 and Comment *a*, which gives this explanation:

> It is often said that an offeror who makes an offer by mail makes the post office his agent to receive the acceptance, or that the mailing of a letter of acceptance puts it irrevocably out of the offeree's control. Under United States postal regulations, however, the sender of a letter has long had the power to stop delivery and reclaim the letter. A better explanation of the rule that the acceptance takes effect on dispatch is that the offeree needs a dependable basis for his decision whether to accept. In

many legal systems such a basis is provided by a general rule that an offer is irrevocable unless it provides otherwise. The common law provides such a basis through the rule that a revocation of an offer is ineffective if received after an acceptance has been properly dispatched.

The implications for the mailbox rule in an era of email and other electronic means of communication are the subject of the next case.

Restatement § 63 makes the mailbox rule applicable only if the acceptance is "made in a manner and by a medium invited by [the] offer." It would not, therefore, ordinarily apply to acceptance by mail of an offer made by telegram, and such an acceptance would be effective only on receipt. A revocation, however, is generally held to be effective only on receipt, not on dispatch. See Restatement § 42.

It has generally been assumed that the "mailbox rule," laid down in connection with the termination of the offeror's power to *revoke*, applies as well in connection with the termination of the offeree's power to *reject*. In other words, once the offeree has dispatched an acceptance, it is too late for the offeree to change its mind and reject the offer. See Restatement § 63. This is, of course, not a necessary result since it would be possible to frame a rule that would deprive the offeror of its power to revoke the offer upon dispatch of the acceptance by the offeree, but leave the offeree free to reject the offer, at least as long as the offeror receives the rejection before receiving the acceptance. The two rules can best be contrasted by considering the case of the overtaking rejection.

Suppose that on Monday, Buyer receives by mail an offer from Seller of goods. On Tuesday, Buyer mails Seller a letter of acceptance which arrives on Friday. On Wednesday, however, Buyer calls Seller to explain that, although Buyer has mailed a letter of acceptance which has not yet reached Seller, Buyer wants to reject the offer and Seller should ignore the letter of acceptance when it arrives. If the "mailbox rule" is applied, it is too late for Buyer to reconsider and Seller can hold Buyer to the contract formed when the acceptance was mailed. If, on the other hand, acceptance becomes effective on receipt, Buyer remains free to change its mind while the letter is in transit, and Seller cannot hold Buyer to a contract. This rule would benefit Buyer who, while the letter is in transit, would be free to watch the market and speculate, having in effect an "option contract" for that period, while Seller would be unable to revoke its offer.

Of course, the "mailbox rule" similarly disadvantages one of the parties. Suppose that the rejection does not mention the letter of acceptance, as where Buyer on Wednesday sends an overtaking telegram which is received on Thursday and says simply, "Reject your offer." Under these facts, Seller is prejudiced if it relies on the telegram of rejection, sells the goods to another buyer before receiving the letter of acceptance on Friday, and is then held to a contract with Buyer under the "mailbox rule." Might Buyer be estopped to enforce the contract in such a case? See Comment *c* and Illustration 7 to Restatement § 63.

United States Life Insurance Company v. Wilson

Court of Special Appeals of Maryland, 2011.
198 Md.App. 452, 18 A.3d 110.

[The holder of a life insurance policy, Dr. John Griffith, had failed to keep up with his premium payments, and his policy expired. The insurer sent Dr. Griffith an "Application For Reinstatement Of Coverage" which provided that "within 31 days after the end of the Grace Period," the Policy could be reinstated simply by paying the overdue premium, without the need to submit evidence of insurability and obtain the approval of U.S. Life. The Grace Period ended on July 14, 2007; the last day Griffith could reinstate the policy merely by paying the overdue premium was August 14, 2007. The Application further stated that the payment should be "mail[ed]" to the insurer's program administrator. On July 23, 2007, Dr. Griffith accessed his on-line bank account with Bank of America and electronically directed that payment be made to the program administrator in the amount of $369.46, the full amount required for reinstatement. The electronic check was delivered to the program administrator on July 30. However, on July 28, Dr. Griffith was killed in a bicycle accident while on vacation.]

■ EYLER, JUSTICE. The principal issue in this case is whether a policy of insurance on the life of John G. Griffith, M.D., was in force the day he died. We hold that it was.

In the Circuit Court for Baltimore City, Elizabeth Wilson, Dr. Griffith's widow and the appellee, filed a breach of contract action against the United States Life Insurance Company in the City of New York ("US Life") and AMA Insurance Agency, Inc. ("AMAIA"), the appellants, claiming they had failed to pay the death benefit and accidental death benefit on a policy insuring Dr. Griffith's life ("the Policy"). The appellants maintained that the Policy no longer was in force when Dr. Griffith died. Ms. Wilson acknowledged that the Policy had lapsed but maintained that it had been reinstated before Dr. Griffith died. The court agreed with Ms. Wilson and granted summary judgment in her favor.

In this appeal, the appellants present two questions for review, which we have rephrased:

    I.   Did the circuit court err in ruling on the summary judgment record that the Policy was in force when Dr. Griffith died?

    II.   Did the circuit court err in ruling on the summary judgment record that AMAIA was jointly and severally liable with U.S. Life for payment under the Policy? [Discussion on this issue is omitted.]

Insurance contracts initially are formed when an insurer unconditionally accepts an insured's application, which constitutes an offer, for coverage. Martin v. Government Employees Ins. Co., 206 Ill.App.3d 1031, 1039–40 (Ill.App.Ct.1990). Accord, Mitchell v. AARP Life Ins. Program, 140 Md.App. 102, 117–18 (2001). From then on, the life insurance policy operates as a unilateral contract, 29 APPLEMAN ON INSURANCE 2d ("APPLEMAN") § 179.03, at 230 (2006), i.e., one that is formed by performance. See 1 WILLISTON ON CONTRACTS § 4:8, at 462 (4th ed., Richard A. Lord, 2007) (observing that a unilateral contract is one in which one party makes a promise and the other party renders an act or forbearance). "The periodic payment of premiums is the mechanism by which the insured opts to keep the insurance policy in force." APPLEMAN § 179.0–3, at 230. Failure to pay the premiums will result in coverage lapsing.

Life insurance policies have standard non-forfeiture clauses that allow for reinstatement after a lapse in coverage. See APPLEMAN § 179.03, at 273. The "REINSTATEMENT" clause in the Policy in this case is such a standard non-forfeiture clause.[2] According to APPLEMAN, courts in a majority of American jurisdictions are of the view that "reinstatement [of a life insurance policy] does not involve the creation of a new contract but, instead, reinstates the original contract, under which the insured has the right to reinstatement on compliance with its requirements." APPLEMAN § 179.03, at 275. Thus, under the majority rule, reinstatement does not involve the formation of a new life insurance policy. Rather, once the requirements for reinstatement are fulfilled, the original life insurance contract is "revived." In that circumstance, there is no need for acceptance by the insurer. . . . A minority of jurisdictions take the contrary position that a reinstatement request by the insured is no different than an original insurance application: that is, it is an offer by the insured to enter into a new life insurance contract, which does not become effective until accepted by the insurer. See Johnson v. Prudential Ins. Co., 589 F.Supp. 30 (D.D.C.1983), aff'd, 744 F.2d 878 (1984) (applying District of Columbia law).

The Illinois appellate courts have not addressed this issue. We conclude that, if presented with the issue in this case, the Illinois courts would follow the majority rule. Aside from its being a rule followed by most of the jurisdictions considering the issue, here the circumstances under which Dr. Griffith was acting to reinstate the Policy militate strongly in favor of application of the majority rule.

Under the policy, when the relevant time frame for reinstatement is "within 31 days after the end of the Grace Period" (as it is here), the "REINSTATEMENT" clause is a promise by the insurer to reinstate coverage upon performance by the insured of a single act payment of the overdue premium. In that situation, the insurer is not being asked to consider and either accept or reject an offer by the insured to enter into a life insurance contract. Thus, the plain language of the "REINSTATEMENT" clause of the Policy establishes that, upon payment by the insured of the overdue premium within 31 days after the end of the grace period, the Policy is revived. In other words, in that situation, the "REINSTATEMENT" clause is an offer of a unilateral contract to revive the Policy, with the insurer promising that revival will take place upon the insured's performing by paying the overdue premium.

It is within the context of Dr. Griffith's acceptance by performance (that is, by payment of the overdue premium) of U.S. Life's offer to revive the Policy that we must determine when payment took place. At common law, what is often called the "mailbox rule," the "dispatch rule," or sometimes the "postal acceptance rule" is the widely-adopted convention for pinpointing the time that an offer is accepted and a contract is formed. Illinois, like Maryland, recognizes the rule, by which "the mailed acceptance of an offer is effective when mailed, not when received or acknowledged." Martin, 206 Ill.App.3d at 1042. See also Hinc v. Lime-O-Sol Co., 382 F.3d 716, 719 (7th Cir.2004) (discussing Illinois law and citing RESTATEMENT (SECOND) OF CONTRACTS § 63 (1979), and stating, "The common law mailbox rule provides that once an offer is made, acceptance is effective when the offeree puts the signed contract in the mail"). Accord, Cochran v. Norkunas, 398 Md. 1 (2007) ("The well established rule is that in the absence of any limitation or provision to the contrary in the offer, the acceptance of the offer is complete and the contract becomes binding on both parties when the offeree deposits the acceptance in the post box."); Reserve Insurance Co., 249 Md. at 117, 238 A.2d 536 (explaining that the "postal acceptance rule" first was adopted in Adams v. Lindsell, 1 Barn & Ald. 681, 106 Eng. Rep. 250 (1818, King's Bench)).

Section 63(a) of the RESTATEMENT (SECOND) OF CONTRACTS (1979), while not using any of the familiar mailbox rule nomenclature, recognizes with respect to the time that acceptance of an offer takes effect that, unless an offer states otherwise, "an acceptance made in a manner and by a medium invited by the offer is operative and completes the manifestation of mutual assent as soon as put out of the offeree's possession, without regard to whether it ever reaches the offeror." The rationale for the rule, as explained in comment (a) to that subsection, is, essentially, certainty and predictability. The comment observes that, even though it may be possible under United States postal regulations for a sender to stop delivery and reclaim a letter, it remains the case that one to whom an offer has been made "needs a dependable basis for his decision whether to accept," and has such a basis when he knows that, once properly dispatched, his acceptance is binding and the offer cannot be revoked. Id.

In 2 WILLISTON ON CONTRACTS § 6:32 (4th ed. Richard A. Lord, 2007) ("WILLISTON"), the author explains that the "dispatch rule" applies equally to bilateral and unilateral contracts. If an offer for a unilateral contract calls for the performance of an act by the offeree that can be accomplished by sending money through the mail, including in the form of a check, "as soon as the money is sent it would become the property of the offeror, and the offeror would become bound to perform its promise for which the money was the consideration." Id. at 441–42 (footnote omitted). The offeror must have authorized the use of the particular medium (in the cases above, the mail) as a means of acceptance, and the acceptance must have been properly dispatched. See WILLISTON §§ 6:35 and 6:36, respectively.

In addressing with particularity when acceptance is dispatched, WILLISTON states: "An acceptance is dispatched within the meaning of the rule under consideration when it is put out of the possession of the offeree and within the control of the postal authorities, telegraph operator, or other third party authorized to receive it." § 6:37, at 484. However, "mere delivery of an acceptance to a messenger with directions to mail it amounts to no acceptance until the messenger actually deposits it in the mail." Id. The treatise continues:

> The private delivery service, under the modern view, would have to be independent of the offeree, reliable both in terms of its delivery obligations and record keeping, and of a type that would customarily be used to communicate messages of this sort. Such agencies as the United Parcel Service, Federal Express, or even private messenger services in urban areas would qualify, and as soon as the communication leaves the offeree's possession and is placed with an authorized recipient of the instrumentality, an effective dispatch will be deemed to have occurred.

WILLISTON § 6:37, at 486–87. See also CORBIN ON CONTRACTS § 3.24, at 440 (Revised ed. Joseph M. Perillo) (1993) (stating that the dispatch rule establishes when the contract is formed so as to uniformly and definitely designate which of the parties is to carry the risk of "loss and inconvenience").

We conclude that the long-recognized mailbox rule governing the time of formation of a contract by written acceptance applies in the case at bar to control the time the Policy was reinstated, that is, when coverage under the Policy was revived. The transaction at issue here is not wholly traditional, that is, one in which a paper document, whether a check or otherwise, is mailed by the offeree to the offeror, in that it began electronically, as an on-line banking directive by Dr. Griffith on July 23, 2007. The Bank of America documents in the summary judgment record show, however, that the directive was acted upon by preparation of a paper check drawn on a JP Morgan Chase Bank, N.A. account under Dr. Griffith's name, and bearing his "Authorized Signature"; and that the paper check then was "sent" to AMAIA on July 25, 2007, coming into AMAIA's physical possession on July 30, 2007.

The transaction thus resembles a traditional acceptance by writing mailed to the offeror, in that a writing (the check) was "sent" to AMAIA, even though its creation was directed electronically and it was created not by the offeree but by his bank. A writing thus was generated by actions taken by Dr. Griffith; the writing complied with that which was necessary to accept the reinstatement offer; and the writing was "sent," which was a permissible mode of acceptance, and subsequently was delivered to AMAIA, the proper recipient. The nature of the transaction, involving the sending of a written acceptance, is such that, just like a transaction in which a written acceptance is prepared in writing and mailed, or a written acceptance is prepared by telegram and sent, the mailbox rule is a necessary tool to establish the time that the new agreement—here, one to revive a prior contract—was formed. See WILLISTON § 6:33, at 448 (explaining that the dispatch rule for acceptance by mail generally has been applied by analogy to acceptance by telegraph). The nature of the transaction is not akin to those that have been determined to be outside the sphere of the dispatch rule. See WILLISTON § 6:34, at 450 (explaining that the dispatch rule has not been applied to "'substantially instantaneous two-way communication devices,'" such as telephones or teletypes, as they do not resemble communication by mail (quoting RESTATEMENT (SECOND) OF CONTRACTS (1979) § 64)).

Application of the mailbox rule to the undisputed material facts in this case produces the legal conclusion that the date of payment of the overdue premium was July 25, 2007. On July 23, 2007, Dr. Griffith electronically instructed Bank of America, as his agent, to make payment to AMAIA. The evidence viewed most favorably to the appellants supports a reasonable inference that Dr. Griffith could have reinstructed Bank of America not to make the payment; therefore, as of July 23, 2007, he had set in motion the means to accept the offer of reinstatement but still had the power to reverse course. On July 25, 2007, however, Bank of America remitted payment to AMAIA by sending it a check, drawn on the J.P. Morgan Chase Bank, N.A. account, for $369.46. At that point, the permissible means for acceptance was in motion and, so far as is established by the common law mailbox rule, was beyond Dr. Griffith's power to stop. This would be true whether Bank of America sent the check through the United States Postal Service, a courier service, or otherwise.

For all these reasons, we hold that the Policy was reinstated effective July 25, 2007, three days before Dr. Griffith died, and therefore was in force when he died.

NOTES

(1) *Question.* What key fact in the case made the application of the common law mailbox rule straightforward, despite the modern means of communication?

(2) *Option Contracts.* The Pennsylvania Academy of Fine Arts (PAFA) held a lease on a parking lot that was to expire on July 31, 1989. The lease contained an option to purchase, and this provision: "All notices hereunder shall be in writing and shall be delivered or mailed by certified mail or

registered mail." The option was, according to the lease, to be exercised at least six months before the expiration of the lease. On July 30, PAFA prepared a letter to the lessor giving notice of its intent to purchase, and a check for a deposit. The letter, with check enclosed, was sent on July 31 by certified mail, return receipt requested. The lessor returned the check, saying that because she did not receive the letter until August 3, she considered the notice invalid. In an action by PAFA to enforce the lease, it was granted summary judgment; the lessor appealed. *Held:* Affirmed. Pennsylvania Academy of Fine Arts v. Grant, 590 A.2d 9 (Pa.Super.1991).

Is this decision consistent with Restatement § 63(b)?

(3) *International Approaches.* In contrast to the common law, the CISG provides that an acceptance is effective "at the moment the indication of assent reaches the offeror." CISG art. 18(2), 23. Revocations, however, follow the "mailbox rule" and are effective only if received before an acceptance has been dispatched. CISG 16(1). The UNIDROIT Principles are in agreement. See Articles 2.4(2) and 2.6(2).

PROBLEM

As a result of a dispute regarding the distribution of profits, Ellefson, a member of the metal band Megadeth, sued the band for fraud. Negotiations ensued in an effort to settle the case. The parties, through their respective counsel, drafted a "Settlement and General Release," which was amended several times over a period of weeks. On May 13, 2004, the defendants informed Ellefson by email that they were going to "terminate this deal as of 5PM PST on Friday 5/14/04, if we do not have a signed agreement in hand." The agreement itself was then finalized and sent to the defendants at 4:45 p.m. on May 14. However, Ellefson's signature page was not faxed to the defendants until 5:16 p.m. On May 20, the defendants' lawyer sent all parties, by regular mail, fully-executed copies of the agreement. On May 24, Ellefson's lawyer informed the defendants that his client was "withdrawing from these negotiations." The defendants' lawyer responded that "we don't know what you are talking about there is a signed agreement in place." On June 2, Ellefson received the finalized agreement that had been mailed on May 20.

The defendants filed a motion to enforce the settlement agreement. Should the court grant the motion? See Ellefson v. Megadeth, Inc., 2005 WL 82022 (S.D.N.Y. 2005). In deciding the case, the court noted that "the issue presented by this motion is reminiscent of a first year law school contracts exam." In answering the question, it may help to review Note 1 on Tardy Acceptances, p. 230 above.

SECTION 5. ACCEPTANCE VARYING OFFER: CONTRACT FORMATION AND CONTRACT TERMS

(A) THE COMMON LAW APPROACH AND THE MIRROR IMAGE RULE

In Section 4 Part D, we saw that the rejection of an offer by the offeree terminates the power of acceptance: the offeree cannot thereafter accept. We start this Section with a closer examination of what counts as a rejection.

Certainly an unequivocal statement such as "I hereby reject your offer" constitutes a rejection, but what other communications have the same effect? For example, what if the offeree's response expresses interest in the transaction proposed by the offeror but on terms that are not identical to those in the offer?

The traditional common law answer is that an acceptance must be on the *exact* terms proposed by the offer. "In order that an offer and acceptance may result in a binding contract the acceptance must be absolute, unconditional, and identical with the terms of the offer. It must in every respect meet and correspond with the offer; any qualification of or departure from those terms invalidates the offer." St. Louis Smelting & Refining Co. v. Nix, 101 Okla. 197, 224 P. 982 (1924). This is usually called "the mirror image rule." If there is any variation, the purported acceptance operates as a rejection, and at the same time constitutes a counter-offer to the original offeror.

An example of the mirror image rule is provided by Ardente v. Horan, 366 A.2d 162 (R.I.1976). In Ardente, a prospective buyer who had received an offer of residential property signed an agreement, which his lawyer returned with a check and a letter that said:

> My clients are concerned that the following items remain with the real estate: a) dining room set and tapestry wall covering in dining room; b) fireplace fixtures throughout; c) the sun parlor furniture. I would appreciate your confirming that these items are a part of the transaction, as they would be difficult to replace." When the offerors/sellers refused to convey the property, the offeree/buyer sought specific performance. He lost on the ground that an acceptance "must be definite and unequivocal. An acceptance which is equivocal or upon condition or with a limitation is a counteroffer and requires acceptance by the original offeror before a contractual relationship can exist.

Id. at 163, 165. The rigors of the rule that an acceptance must be the mirror image of the offer may be mitigated in practice. First, a court may decide that what seemed to be an additional or different term in the acceptance was really an "implied term" in the offer, so that language at first appearing to vary the terms of the offer did not really do so. An example is the court's treatment of the buyer's addition, "the jars and caps to be strictly first-quality goods," near the end of the opinion in *Fairmount Glass*, p. 189 above. Second, a court may conclude that the language of the acceptance relating to an additional or different term is only suggestive, or precatory. Might the court have read the language in *Ardente v. Horan*, described just above, in this manner? This would have resulted in a contract on the terms of the offeror, who could then have decided whether or not to modify that contract by accepting the offeree's additional proposal.

To take an example from the area of plea bargaining, in *State v. Rios*, 974 A.2d 366 (Md. App. 2009), the prosecutor had offered criminal defendant Jeffrey Rios a deal under which Rios would plead guilty to certain charges in exchange for a specialized type of guilty plea known as an "Alford plea." Before accepting the offer, Rios's lawyer asked the prosecutor, "Would you consider a nolo plea to reckless endangerment?" (Unlike an Alford plea, a nolo plea does not result in a conviction.). The motions court had held that this question constituted a counter-offer, thereby rejecting the original offer, which the prosecutor sought to withdraw. Rios appealed. Held: Reversed. The appellate court stated:

> A common type of counter-offer is the qualified or conditional acceptance, which purports to accept the original offer but makes acceptance expressly conditional on assent to additional or different terms [citation omitted]. Such a counter-offer must be distinguished from an unqualified acceptance which is accompanied by a proposal for modification of the agreement or for a separate agreement. *A mere inquiry regarding the possibility of different terms, a request for a better offer, or a comment upon the terms of the offer, is ordinarily not a counter-offer.* Such responses to an offer may be too tentative or indefinite to be offers of any kind; or they may deal with new matters rather than a substitution for the original offer; or their language may manifest an intention to keep the original offer under consideration.

Id. at 369 (emphasis added). In the same comment to § 39, Illustration 2 provides the following example which is analogous to the facts of this case:

> A makes the same offer to B as that stated in Illustration 1 [an offer to sell land for $5000, offer to remain open for 30 days], and B replies, "Won't you take less?" A answers "No." An acceptance thereafter by B within the thirty-day period is effective. B's inquiry was not a counter-offer, and A's original offer stands.

The appellate court in *Rios* concluded that "[b]ecause [defense counsel's] question about the possibility of a better offer was not a counter offer, he did not reject the prosecutor's offer. Therefore, [defense counsel's] subsequent communication of his client's acceptance, prior to the time the prosecutor attempted to withdraw the offer, was effective, and the parties formed a plea agreement that was binding upon the State (subject to court approval)." State v. Rios, 974 A.2d 366, 371 (Md. App. 2009).

Disputes tend to arise in two kinds of cases. In the first, one party claims that a contract was made while the other maintains the contrary. This was the case in Ardente, where the sellers seized on the variation to justify their refusal to convey. When the market rises, sellers are tempted to find pretexts for getting out of their bargains; when the market falls, buyers are so tempted. The more rigorous the application of the mirror image rule, the more attractive recourse to such pretexts becomes.

In the second kind of case, some performance has taken place, following an exchange of messages showing that the parties believed they had reached a contract. But the terms proposed by the parties were never an exact match. When a dispute arises with respect to that performance, the parties typically differ about whose terms control, and each insists on its own. Under the mirror-image rule, the party that sent the last message before performance began usually prevails. This is because each message operated as a rejection of the other's prior message, and as a counter-offer. Performance, or the beginning of performance, by the recipient constituted acceptance of the terms of the final offer in the series. Accordingly, under the mirror image rule, it is advantageous to have fired the "last shot" before that.

NOTE

Back and Forth Firing. Under the common-law rule described above that provides an advantage to the party who fired the "last shot," (the so-called last-shot rule), a question sometimes arises as to which of the parties was the last to fire before performance. Consider the following long-standing disagreement. MPS, an employment agency, sent the Dresser-Rand company a quotation for labor on a form that included a non-solicitation clause barring Dresser-Rand from hiring MPS employees. Dresser-Rand returned a purchase order, taking specific exception to the non-solicitation clause. Although the parties remained at loggerheads over the clause; over the next five years MPS regularly supplied Dresser-Rand with employees, each time sending a contract with a non-solicitation clause. Dresser-Rand regularly refused to sign, although it always paid MPS for its services. When Dresser-Rand hired MPS employees in violation of the non-solicitation clause, MPS sued for breach of contract. Each party argued that its terms have been accepted by the other. Following summary judgment for Dresser-Rand, MPS appealed. *Held*: Affirmed.

"MPS signified through its course of conduct that it was willing to supply labor to Dresser-Rand despite Dresser-Rand's consistent rejection of any non-solicitation agreement. In effect, MPS accepted Dresser-Rand's counter-offer, which plainly eliminated the non-solicitation clause." In reaching its conclusion, the majority was influenced by "North Carolina's suspicion of direct contractual restraints on employee mobility." Mechanical Plant Services, Inc. v. Dresser Rand Company, 116 F.3d 1474 (4th Cir.1997).

Might one argue on the same facts that Dresser-Rand accepted *MPS's* offer? One judge dissented on the ground that "Our job here is not to pick between these equally plausible conclusions. Put another way, it is not up to us to determine which party actually 'fired the last shot' and consequently, which party 'accepted' the other party's offer. That is why we have juries, and the question of mutual assent on these facts should not be resolved on summary judgment." Id.

(B) THE "BATTLE OF THE FORMS"

As we saw in Fairmount Glass Works, p. 189 above, a contract for a sale of goods is often the result of an exchange of several messages, rather than a single document signed by both parties. In routine transactions these messages typically consist of standardized printed forms containing several paragraphs of standard terms, with blanks filled in by the parties to fit the particular transaction. A characteristic sequence includes a "request for quotation," answered by a "quotation" form. (Compare the letters exchanged in Fairmount.) The ensuing steps are likely to be a "purchase order" followed by a "sales acknowledgment." Note that, typically, it was the buyer that, by its purchase order, made the initial offer and the seller that, by its varying acknowledgment, fired the "last shot," declining to enter into a contract on the buyer's terms (thereby rejecting the buyer's offer) and indicating willingness to enter into a contract on its terms (thereby making a counter-offer). When the buyer accepted the goods, it was taken to have accepted the seller's counter-offer and was bound by the seller's terms.

Because each party's form typically contains terms tailored to the benefit of that party, a mismatch of terms is likely. Yet neither the buyer nor the seller may have focused or even noticed the mismatched standard terms. The parties are likely to assume that they have a "deal" in light of their agreement regarding the transaction-specific, or "dickered," terms inserted in the blanks on the forms.

Transactions of this sort are referred to as involving a "battle of the forms," and—not surprisingly—arise most often when parties use standardized forms to express offers and acceptances. These transactions raise an interesting series of questions. Does the exchange of forms create a contract, despite their failure to "mirror" one another? (This question is of particular importance if, before performance, one of the parties abandons the transaction.) If a contract is formed, what are its terms? And what happens if the exchange of forms does not create a contract but the parties nonetheless perform, only to engage in a subsequent dispute about that performance?

We are about to investigate how the Uniform Commercial Code abandoned (we suggest "transcended") the mirror image rule (and the "last shot" rule that followed from it) in favor of a more fine-tuned approach to acceptances that vary offers. But to understand why such reform was undertaken, it is useful to have a more detailed picture of how standard forms are created and exchanged, and why the exchange of such ordinary documents so regularly evolved into a "battle." Professor Stewart Macaulay provides this more extensive description, which is based on his study of Wisconsin businesses:

A firm will have a set of terms and conditions for purchases, sales, or both printed on the business documents used in these exchanges. Thus the things to be sold and the price may be planned particularly for each transaction, but standard provisions will further elaborate the performances and cover the other subjects of planning. Typically, these terms and conditions are lengthy and printed in small type on the back of the forms. For example, 24 paragraphs in eight point type are printed on the back of the purchase order form used by the Allis Chalmers Manufacturing Company.

In larger firms such "boiler plate" provisions are drafted by the house counsel or the firm's outside lawyer. In smaller firms such provisions may be drafted by the industry trade association, may be copied from a competitor, or may be found on forms purchased from a printer. In any event, salesmen and purchasing agents, the operating personnel, typically are unaware of what is said in the fine print on the back of the forms they use. Yet often the normal business patterns will give effect to this standardized planning. For example, purchasing agents may have to use a purchase order form so that all transactions receive a number under the firm's accounting system. Thus, the required accounting record will carry the necessary planning of the exchange relationship printed on its reverse side. If the seller does not object to this planning and accepts the order, the buyer's "fine print" will control. If the seller does object, differences can be settled by negotiation.

This type of standardized planning is very common. [However], standardized planning can break down. [T]he seller may fail to read the buyer's 24 paragraphs of fine print and may accept the buyer's order on the seller's own acknowledgment-of-order form. Typically this form will have ten to 50 paragraphs favoring the seller, and these provisions are likely to be different from or inconsistent with the buyer's provisions. The seller's acknowledgment form may be received by the buyer and checked by a clerk. She will read the *face* of the acknowledgment but not the fine print on the back of it because she has neither the time nor ability to analyze the small print on the 100 to 500 forms she must review each day. The face of the acknowledgment—where the goods and the price are specified—is likely to correspond with the face of the purchase order. If it does, the two forms are filed away. At this point, both buyer and seller are likely to assume they have planned an exchange and made a contract. Yet they have done neither, as they are in disagreement about all that appears on the back of their forms. This practice is common enough to have a name. Law teachers call it "the battle of the forms." Stewart Macaulay, *Non-Contractual Relations in Business: A Preliminary Study*, 28 Am. Soc. Rev. 55, 57–59 (1963).

NOTE

Boilerplate. The term "boilerplate" refers to the standard clauses lifted from formbooks and inserted repeatedly into standard form contracts, so it is said, like metal plate is riveted to a boiler. See Sharon Steel Corp. v. Manhattan Bank, 691 F.2d 1039 (2d Cir.1982). As the court stated in that case, boilerplate provisions "do not depend upon particularized intentions of the parties." See Stephen J. Choi and G. Mitu Gulati, *Contract as Statute*, 104 Mich. L. Rev. 1129 (2006). See generally, Omri Ben-Shahar, *Boilerplate: Foundations of Market Contracts Symposium*, 104 Mich. L. Rev. 821 *et seq.* (2006). Boilerplate is further discussed in Chapter 6 at p. 618.

(C) UCC § 2–207: TRANSCENDING THE MIRROR IMAGE RULE

In UCC § 2–207 ("Additional Terms in Acceptance or Confirmation"), Article 2 made a marked shift from the common law rules applied to transactions involving a "battle of the forms." Each of the provision's three subsections contains an aspect of this dramatic change, as indicated in the following overview.

To begin, Article 2 abandoned the "mirror image" rule of contract formation in favor of an analysis more attentive to the kinds of commercial practices described above by Professor Macaulay: inconsistent boilerplate passing unheeded between parties that intend to enter into a contractual relationship. This abandonment is accomplished first through UCC § 2–207(1), which provides that an "expression of acceptance" may indeed "operate as an acceptance even though it states terms additional to or different from those offered and agreed upon." This is not the case, however, if "acceptance is expressly made conditional on assent to the additional or different terms."

Accordingly, we can see that UCC § 2–207(1) provides for two methods of contract formation. If the expression of acceptance that contains additional or different terms is expressly conditional on the offeror's assent to those terms, and the offeror does assent to those terms, we have a traditional agreement. If, however, the expression of acceptance is *not* expressly conditional on the offeror's assent, then UCC § 2–207(1) provides that a contract is formed ("the expression of acceptance operates as an acceptance") even though the communications of the offeror and offeree are not identical and the offeror does not express assent to the offeree's terms.

What if the communications of the parties do not form a contract (because, say, the expression of acceptance contains additional or different terms and is expressly made conditional on the offeror's assent to those terms) and the offeror never assents, but the parties (perhaps unaware of the inconsistencies in their communications) proceed to perform the transaction? In that case, UCC § 2–207(3) provides a third method of contract formation: "Conduct by both parties which recognizes the existence of a contract is sufficient to establish a contract for sale although the writings of the parties do not otherwise establish a contract."

When the operation of UCC § 2–207(1) or UCC § 2–207(3) results in a contract being formed, what are its terms? After all, the communications of the parties are not identical; there is no "mirror image." As a result, the law must decide whose terms will prevail, or whether the contract will be governed by rules suggested by neither party.

For contracts formed by UCC § 2–207(1), the issue is addressed in UCC § 2–207(2). That section provides an elaborate scheme, explored in the cases below, that determines whether the "additional" terms found in the expression of acceptance are part of the contract. (The materials that follow also explore the interesting question of the fate of terms that are "different," rather than "additional.")

What are the terms of contracts formed under UCC § 2–207(3)? That arnsworth

Note that, in separating the determination of formation of the contract in subsection (1) from the determination of the content of the contract in subsection (2), UCC § 2–207 contemplates that the terms of the contract may be determined at a different time than the time at which the contract is formed. There is, for example, the possibility that an "additional term" will become part of the contract later when, after receiving notice of it, the offeror lets a reasonable time elapse without giving "notification of objection" to the additional term. UCC § 2–207(2).

As many courts and commentators have observed, UCC § 2–207 is a challenging exercise in statutory analysis. Almost every phrase of the provision has been the subject of intense debate and substantial litigation. As the court in the next principal case noted, in an omitted part of the opinion, UCC § 2–207 "has been described as a 'murky bit of prose.'" More colorfully, another court observed that "§ 2–207 is a defiant, lurking demon patiently waiting to condemn its interpreters to the depths of despair." *Reaction Molding Technologies, Inc. v. General Electric Co.,* 585 F.Supp. 1097, 1104 (E.D. Pa. 1984). UCC § 2–207 therefore provides the opportunity for a close reading of a complicated statute. Moreover, as the court in the *Reaction Molding* case indicated, "§ 2–207 must and can be conquered."

NOTE

Expressions of Acceptance. Under UCC § 2–207(1), not all responses to an offer operate as acceptances. Not only must the expression of acceptance be definite, seasonable, and sent within a reasonable time, it must also be "an expression of acceptance"—*i.e.,* sufficiently responsive to the offer to indicate the intent to enter into a contract. A response that differs radically from the offer, particularly with regard to dickered terms, such as price or

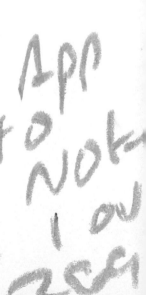

quantity, may fail as an acceptance and end the inquiry into contract formation then and there. See Koehring Co. v. Glowacki, 253 N.W.2d 64 (Wis.1977).

Under UCC § 2–207(1), the acceptance may, by its own terms, prevent its operation as an acceptance if it is "expressly made conditional on assent to the additional or different terms." This phrase has prompted two much litigated questions, taken up in the cases that follow: (1) Exactly what language or conduct by the offeree makes the acceptance "expressly conditional," and (2) what constitutes "assent" by the offeror?

(D) CONTRACT FORMATION UNDER ARTICLE 2

1.   CONTRACT FORMATION THROUGH THE EXCHANGE OF FORMS

Dorton v. Collins & Aikman Corp.

United States Court of Appeals, Sixth Circuit, 1972.
453 F.2d 1161.

■ CELEBREZZE, CIRCUIT JUDGE. [Dorton and his partners did business in Tennessee as "The Carpet Mart." Collins & Aikman was a Delaware corporation having its principal place of business in New York. Over a three-year period, in 55 transactions, The Carpet Mart bought carpets from Collins & Aikman. Ultimately, however, The Carpet Mart brought an action against Collins and Aikman in a Tennessee court, claiming damages for fraud and misrepresentation about the quality of the carpets.] The Carpet Mart maintains that in May, 1970, in response to a customer complaint, it learned that not all of the carpets were manufactured from 100% Kodel polyester fiber but rather some were composed of a cheaper and inferior carpet fiber. After the cause was removed to the District Court on the basis of diversity of citizenship, Collins & Aikman moved for a stay pending arbitration, asserting that The Carpet Mart was bound to an arbitration agreement which appeared on the reverse side of Collins & Aikman's printed sales acknowledgment forms. Holding that there existed no binding arbitration agreement between the parties, the District Court denied the stay. For the reasons set out below, we remand the case to the District Court for further findings.

[The court described the dealings between the parties. Upon receiving an order telephoned to the Collins & Aikman order department in Dalton, Georgia, and after a report from its credit department, Collins & Aikman typed the information concerning the particular order on one of its printed acknowledgment forms. One legend or another on the face specified when the order "shall become a contract," *e.g.*,

(a) when signed and delivered by Buyer to Seller and accepted in writing by Seller or (b) when Buyer has received and retained this order for ten days without objection, or (c) when Buyer has accepted delivery of any part of the merchandise, or when Buyer has otherwise indicated acceptance of the terms hereof.

Also:

acceptance (or "order") subject to all of the terms and conditions on the face and reverse side hereof.]

The small print on the reverse side of the forms provided, among other things, that all claims arising out of the contract would be submitted to arbitration in New York City. Absent a delay in the mails. The Carpet Mart always received the acknowledgment forms prior to receiving the carpets. In all cases The Carpet Mart took delivery of and paid for the carpets without objecting to any terms contained in the acknowledgment form.

In holding that no binding arbitration agreement was created between the parties through the transactions above, the District Court relied on T.C.A. § 47–2–207 [UCC § 2–207]. [The court] found that Subsection 2–207(3) controlled the instant case [and it] concluded that the arbitration clause on the back of Collins & Aikman's sales acknowledgment had not become a binding term in the 50-odd transactions with The Carpet Mart.

In reviewing this determination by the District Court, we are aware of the problems which courts have had in interpreting Section 2–207. Yet despite the lack of clarity in its language, Section 2–207 manifests definite objectives which are significant in the present case.

[S]pecifically Subsection 2–207(1) was intended to alter the "ribbon matching" or "mirror" rule of common law, under which the terms of an acceptance or confirmation were required to be identical to the terms of the offer or oral agreement, respectively. 1 W. Hawkland, supra, at 16; R. Nordstrom, Handbook of the Law of Sales, Sec. 37, at 99–100 (1970). Under the common law, an acceptance or a confirmation which contained terms additional to or different from those of the offer or oral agreement constituted a rejection of the offer or agreement and thus became a counter-offer. The terms of the counter-offer were said to have been accepted by the original offeror when he proceeded to perform under the contract without objecting to the counter-offer. Thus, a buyer was deemed to have accepted the seller's counter-offer if he took receipt of the goods and paid for them without objection.

Under Section 2–207 the result is different. This section of the Code recognizes that in current commercial transactions, the terms of the offer and those of the acceptance will seldom be identical. Rather, under the current "battle of the forms," each party typically has a printed form drafted by his attorney and containing as many terms as could be envisioned to favor that party in his sales transactions. Whereas under common law the disparity between the fineprint terms in the parties' forms would have prevented the consummation of a contract when these forms are exchanged, Section 2–207 recognizes that in many, but not all, cases the parties do not impart such significance to the terms on the printed forms. Thus, under Subsection (1), a contract is recognized notwithstanding the fact that an acceptance or confirmation contains terms additional to or different from those of the offer or prior agreement, provided that the offeree's intent to accept the offer is definitely expressed, see Sections 2–204 and 2–206, and provided that the offeree's acceptance is not expressly conditioned on the offeror's assent to the additional or different terms. When a contract is recognized under Subsection (1), the additional terms are treated as "proposals for addition to the contract" under Subsection (2), which contains special provisions under which such additional terms are deemed to have been accepted when the transaction is between merchants. Conversely, when no contract is recognized under Subsection 2–207(1)—either because no definite expression of acceptance exists or, more specifically, because the offeree's acceptance is expressly conditioned on the offeror's assent to the additional or different terms—the entire transaction aborts at this point. If, however, the subsequent conduct of the parties—particularly, performance by both parties under what they apparently believe to be a contract—recognizes the existence of a contract, under Subsection 2–207(3) such conduct by both parties is sufficient to establish a contract, notwithstanding the fact that no contract would have been recognized on the basis of their writings alone. Subsection 2–207(3) further provides how the terms of contracts recognized thereunder shall be determined.

With the above analysis and purposes of Section 2–207 in mind, we turn to their application in the present case.

[The court considered two possibilities: the defendant's forms were either "acceptances" or they were "confirmations." For resolving this, the court directed the trial court to determine "whether oral agreements were reached between the parties prior to the sending of Collins & Aikman's acknowledgment forms." In an affidavit by a partner in The Carpet Mart there was testimony indicating that they were.

In either event, the court suggested, the plaintiff's oral orders may have embodied an arbitration provision, such that in this respect the defendant's forms were not "additional to or different from" the orders: "we believe that a specific finding on this point will be required on remand."[1]]

[The court next addressed the question whether or not if "additional or different," the defendant's forms were within the proviso of UCC § 2–207(1): "acceptance expressly made conditional on assent to the additional or different terms."] Although Collins & Aikman's use of the words "subject to" suggests that the acceptances were conditional to some extent we believe that [the proviso] was intended to apply only to an

---

[1]   It is not inconceivable that a buyer might request that all claims be submitted to arbitration, see Universal Oil Products v. S.C.M. Corp., 313 F.Supp. 905 (D.Conn.1970), or that a buyer might orally submit to the seller's known policy of arbitration in order to facilitate acceptance of the offer.

acceptance which clearly reveals that the offeree is unwilling to proceed with the transaction unless he is assured of the offeror's assent to the additional or different terms therein. See 1 Hawkland, [A Transactional Guide to the Uniform Commercial Code (1964)] § 1.090303, at 21. That the acceptance is predicated on the offeror's assent must be "directly and distinctly stated or expressed rather than implied or left to inference." Webster's Third International Dictionary (defining "express").

Although the UCC does not provide a definition of "assent," it is significant that Collins & Aikman's printed acknowledgment forms specified at least seven types of action or inaction on the part of the buyer which—sometimes at Collins & Aikman's option—would be deemed to bind the buyer to the terms therein. These ranged from the buyer's signing and delivering the acknowledgment to the seller—which indeed could have been recognized as the buyer's assent to Collins & Aikman's terms—to the buyer's retention of the acknowledgment for ten days without objection—which could never have been recognized as the buyer's assent to the additional or different terms where acceptance is expressly conditional on that assent.[2]

To recognize Collins & Aikman's acceptances as "expressly conditional on [the buyer's] assent to the additional . . . terms" therein, within the proviso of Subsection 2–207(1), would thus require us to ignore the specific language of that provision.[3] Such an interpretation is not justified in view of the fact that Subsection 2–207(1) is clearly designed to give legal recognition to many contracts where the variance between the offer and acceptance would have precluded such recognition at common law.

Because Collins & Aikman's acceptances were not expressly conditional on the buyer's assent to the additional terms within the proviso of Subsection 2–207(1), a contract is recognized under Subsection (1), and the additional terms are treated as "proposals" for addition to the contract under Subsection 2–207(2).[4] Since both Collins & Aikman and

---

[2] The common law has never recognized silence or inaction as a mode of acceptance. See 1 W. Hawkland, supra, § 1.090301, at 17. Under the counter-offer approach which Section 2–207 was designed to modify, the offeror had to take receipt of and pay for the goods without objection before he was deemed to have accepted the terms of the counter-offer. And although Subsection 2–207(2)(c) provides that certain additional terms can be accepted by the offeror's failure to object, nothing in the Code suggests that silence or inaction can be recognized as an offeror's assent in the present context.

[3] We are aware that at least two Courts of Appeals have not chosen to read the Subsection 2–207(1) proviso as strictly as we do here. See Roto-Lith, Ltd. v. F.P. Bartlett & Co., 297 F.2d 497, 499–500 (1st Cir.1962); Construction Aggregates Corp. v. Hewitt-Robins, Inc., 404 F.2d 505, 509 (5th Cir.1968) (dictum). But see Matter of Doughboy Industries, Inc., and Pantasote Co., 17 A.D.2d 216, 233 N.Y.S.2d 488 (1962). We believe, however, that the approach adopted here is dictated by both the language of the proviso and the purpose of Subsection 2–207(1). [The decision in *Roto-Lith* was "almost uniformly criticized by the courts and commentators as an aberration in Article 2 jurisprudence," Gardner Zemke Co. v. Dunham Bush, Inc., 850 P.2d 319, 323 (N.M.1993), and was finally overturned in Ionics v. Elmwood Sensors, Inc. 110 F.3d 184 (1st Cir.1997). For a thorough discussion, see JOM, Inc. v. Adell Plastics, Inc., 193 F.3d 47 (1st Cir.1999).]

[4] Apparently believing that Collins & Aikman's acknowledgments were acceptances "expressly . . . conditional on assent to the additional or different terms" under the Subsection

The Carpet Mart are clearly "merchants" as that term is defined in Subsection 2–104(1), the arbitration provision will be deemed to have been accepted by The Carpet Mart under Subsection 2–207(2) unless it materially altered the terms of The Carpet Mart's oral offers. T.C.A. § 47–2–207(2)(b) [UCC § 2–207(2)(b)].[5] We believe that the question of whether the arbitration provision materially altered the oral offer under Subsection 2–207(2)(b) is one which can be resolved only by the District Court on further findings of fact in the present case.[6] If the arbitration provision did in fact materially alter The Carpet Mart's offer, it could not become a part of the contract "unless expressly agreed to" by The Carpet Mart. T.C.A. § 47–2–207 [UCC § 2–207], Comment No. 3.

We therefore conclude that if on remand the District Court finds that Collins & Aikman's acknowledgments were in fact acceptances and that the arbitration provision was additional to the terms of The Carpet Mart's oral orders, contracts will be recognized under Subsection 2–207(1). The arbitration clause will then be viewed as a "proposal" under Subsection 2–207(2) which will be deemed to have been accepted by The Carpet Mart unless it materially altered the oral offers.

[Next the court considered the possibility that the acknowledgment forms were not acceptances but, rather, were confirmations of prior oral agreements between the parties. It said that "an application of Section 2–207 similar to that above will be required."]

Assuming that the District Court finds that the arbitration provision was not a term of the oral agreements between the parties, the arbitration clause will be treated as a "proposal" for addition to the

---

2–207(1) proviso, the District Court recognized contracts between the parties under Subsection 2–207(3) since the subsequent performance by both parties clearly recognized the existence of a contract. Absent our conclusion that Collins & Aikman's acknowledgments do not fall within the Subsection 2–207(1) proviso, we believe that the District Court correctly applied Subsection 2–207(3) to Collins & Aikman's "acceptances" notwithstanding the fact that some of the language of that Subsection appears to refer to the typical situation under Section 2–207 where there exist both a written offer and a written acceptance. Although we recognize the value that writings by both parties serve in sales transactions, where Subsection 2–207(3) is otherwise applicable we do not believe the purposes of that Subsection should be abandoned simply because the offeror chose to rely on his oral offer. In such a case, we believe that the District Court's comparison of the terms of the oral offer and the written acceptance under Subsection (3) would have been correct.

[5]   The parties do not dispute the fact that The Carpet Mart made no objections to the terms embodied in Collins & Aikman's acknowledgments. Therefore, Subsection 2–207(2)(c) is not relevant in the present case. And although it is not inconceivable that an oral offer could "expressly [limit] acceptance to the terms of the offer" under Subsection 2–207(2)(a), The Carpet Mart has never asserted that this was the nature of its offers to Collins & Aikman. We are therefore concerned with only Subsection 2–207(2)(b).

[6]   While T.C.A. § 47–2–207 [UCC § 2–207], Official Comment Nos. 4 and 5 provide examples of terms which would and would not materially alter a contract, an arbitration clause is listed under neither. Although we recognize the rule "that the agreement to arbitrate must be direct and the intention made clear, without implication, inveiglement or subtlety," Matter of Doughboy Industries, Inc., and Pantasote Co., 17 A.D.2d 216, 218, 233 N.Y.S.2d 488, 492 (1962) (indicating in dictum that an arbitration clause would materially alter a contract under 2–207(2)(b)), we believe the question of material alteration necessarily rests on the facts of each case. See American Parts Co. v. American Arbitration Ass'n, 8 Mich.App. 156, 171, 154 N.W.2d 5, 14 (1967).

contract under Section 2–207(2). Regardless of whether the District Court finds Collins & Aikman's acknowledgment forms to have been acceptances or confirmations, if the arbitration provision was additional to, and a material alteration of, the offers or prior oral agreements, The Carpet Mart will not be bound to that provision absent a finding that it expressly agreed to be bound thereby.

For the reasons set forth above, the case is remanded to the District Court for further findings consistent with this opinion.

NOTES

(1) *Questions.* What is the difference between "an expression of acceptance" and a "written confirmation"? Is there a functional difference between the two under UCC § 2–207(1)? How did the trial court get from subsection (1) to subsection (3)?

(2) *Non-Merchants Under Subsection (2).* What result in *Dorton* had the buyer not been Carpet Mart but an individual consumer? What if the buyer had been a business buying carpets not for resale but for use on its own premises? These questions are considered in greater depth at page 271.

2. CONTRACT FORMATION BY CONDUCT

C. Itoh & Co. (America) Inc. v. Jordan Int'l Co.

United States Court of Appeals, Seventh Circuit, 1977.
552 F.2d 1228.

[Itoh sent Jordan a purchase order for steel coils. Jordan sent back its acknowledgment form, which contained the following provision:

> Seller's acceptance is, however, expressly conditional on Buyer's assent to the additional or different terms and conditions set forth below and printed on the reverse side. If these terms are not acceptable, Buyer should notify Seller at once.

One of the provisions on the reverse side of Jordan's form was an arbitration clause that had no counterpart in Itoh's purchase order. After the steel had been delivered and paid for, Itoh sued Jordan claiming that the steel was defective and had been delivered late. Jordan moved to stay the proceedings pending arbitration. From a denial of its motion, Jordan appealed.]

■ SPRECHER, CIRCUIT JUDGE. The instant case involves the classic "battle of the forms". [Since] it is clear that the statement contained in Jordan's acknowledgment form comes within the Section 2–207(1) proviso, the exchange of forms between Jordan and Itoh did not result in the formation of a contract under Section 2–207(1), and Jordan's form became a counteroffer. Thus, "[s]ince [Itoh's] purchase order and [Jordan's] counter-offer did not in themselves create a contract, Section 2–207(3) would operate to create one because the subsequent performance by both parties constituted 'conduct by both parties which recognizes the existence of a contract.' " Construction Aggregates [Corp. v. Hewitt-Robins, 404 F.2d 505 (7th Cir.1968), cert. denied, 395 U.S. 921 (1969)], at 509.

What are the terms of a contract created by conduct under Section 2–207(3) rather than an exchange of forms under Section 2–207(1)? The second sentence of Section 2–207(3) provides that where, as here, a contract has been consummated by the conduct of the parties, "the terms of the particular contract consist of those terms on which the writings of the parties agree, together with any supplementary terms incorporated under any other provisions of this Act." Since it is clear that the Jordan and Itoh forms do not "agree" on arbitration, the only question which remains *under the Code* is whether arbitration may be considered a supplementary term incorporated under some other provision of the Code.

We have been unable to find any case authority shedding light on the question of what constitutes "supplementary terms" within the meaning of Section 2–207(3) and the Official Comments to Section 2–207 provide no guidance in this regard. We are persuaded, however, that the disputed additional terms (i.e., those terms on which the writings of the parties do not agree) which are necessarily excluded from a Subsection (3) contract by the language, "terms on which the writings of the parties agree," cannot be brought back into the contract under the guise of "supplementary terms." Accordingly, we find that the "supplementary terms" contemplated by Section 2–207(3) are limited to those supplied by the standardized "gap-filler" provisions of Article Two. Since provision for arbitration is not a necessary or missing term which would be supplied by one of the Code's "gap-filler" provisions unless agreed upon by the contracting parties, there is no arbitration term in the Section 2–207(3) contract which was created by the conduct of Jordan and Itoh in proceeding to perform even though no contract had been established by their exchange of writings.

We are convinced that this conclusion does not result in any unfair prejudice to a seller who elects to insert in his standard sales acknowledgment form the statement that acceptance is expressly conditional on buyer's assent to additional terms contained therein. Such a seller obtains a substantial benefit under Section 2–207(1) through the inclusion of an "expressly conditional" clause. If he decides after the exchange of forms that the particular transaction is not in his best interest, Subsection (1) permits him to walk away from the transaction without incurring any liability so long as the buyer has not in the interim expressly assented to the additional terms. Moreover, whether or not a seller will be disadvantaged under Subsection (3) as a consequence of inserting an "expressly conditional" clause in his standard form is within his control. If the seller in fact does not intend to close a particular deal unless the additional terms are assented to, he can protect himself by not delivering the goods until such assent is forthcoming. If the seller does intend to close a deal irrespective of whether or not the buyer assents to the additional terms, he can hardly complain when the contract formed under Subsection (3) as a result of the parties' conduct is held not to include those terms. Although a seller who employs such an "expressly conditional" clause in his acknowledgment form would undoubtedly appreciate the dual advantage of not being bound to a contract under Subsection (1) if he elects not to perform and of having his additional terms imposed on the buyer under Subsection (3) in the event that performance is in his best interest, we do not believe such a result is contemplated by Section 2–207. Rather, while a seller may take advantage of an "expressly conditional" clause under Subsection (1) when he elects not to perform, he must accept the potential risk under Subsection (3) of not getting his additional terms when he elects to proceed with performance without first obtaining buyer's assent to those terms. Since the seller injected ambiguity into the transaction by inserting the "expressly conditional" clause in his form, he, and not the buyer, should bear the consequence of that ambiguity under Subsection (3).

Affirmed.

NOTES

(1) *Conduct as Assent to Conditional Acceptance.* Why did Itoh's acceptance of and payment for the steel not constitute assent to Jordan's "additional or different terms"? (Recall that in Dorton v. Collins & Aikman, above, the court observed that "the UCC does not provide a definition of 'assent.'")

(2) *Case Comparison.* The transaction in *Itoh* fell into subsection (3) by operation of the "assent made expressly conditional" language in subsection (1). Compare the trial court's decision in *Dorton*, p. 264 above, in which the trial court was reversed for making the same move. What explains the difference in the two decisions?

(E) DETERMINING CONTRACT TERMS UNDER ARTICLE 2

When a contract is formed by UCC § 2–207(1), we are faced with a problem that did not exist under the mirror image rule—determining the terms of that contract. After all, the offeror communicated one set of terms and the offeree communicated a set of terms that was not identical. Once it is determined that these non-identical communications create a contract under UCC § 2–207(1), whose terms should govern? The common law did not need to face this question because the exchange of non-identical terms did not create a contract (unless one party accepted the other's "last shot" verbally or by performance, in which case the terms of the last shot governed).

1.   ADDITIONAL TERMS

When the acceptance contains terms that are *additional* to those in the offer, the answer is found in UCC § 2–207(2). Note that the second sentence of that subsection applies only in transactions "between merchants." We have already encountered the concept of a "merchant" at Note 3, p. 8; and, perhaps in an excess of particularity, the Code drafters have also defined the phrase "between merchants." See UCC § 2–104(3).

The first sentence of UCC § 2–207(2) (the only sentence that is applicable if either of the parties to the contract is not a merchant) provides that the additional terms are "proposals for addition to the contract." What does this mean? How would such a proposal be accepted?

Between merchants (the most common battle-of-the-forms scenario), the second sentence of UCC § 2–207(2) is also applicable. That sentence provides that the additional terms automatically become part of the contract unless one of three situations described in the subsection is present. The situations described in UCC §§ 2–207(2)(a) and 2–207(2)(c) are self-evident. (See if you can construct examples in which additional terms do not become part of the contract because of those provisions.)

Application of UCC § 2–207(2)(b)—requiring determination of whether the additional terms "materially alter" the contract—has proven to be much more challenging. Some courts have held that certain sorts of additional terms are always material. See, *e.g.*, Air Products and Chemicals, Inc. v. Fairbanks Morse, Inc., 58 Wis.2d 193, 206 N.W.2d 414 (1973), holding that a disclaimer of an implied warranty of merchantability is always material. Other courts, however, have applied a more nuanced approach.

Bayway Refining Co. v. Oxygenated Marketing & Trading A.G.

United States Court of Appeals, Second Circuit, 2000.
215 F.3d 219.

■ JACOBS, CIRCUIT JUDGE. [OMT, the buyer, faxed an offer to buy 60,000 barrels of MTBE from Bayway, the seller. Bayway's response, which operated as an acceptance, contained an additional term referred to as the "Tax Clause." The Tax Clause provided that "Buyer shall pay seller the amount of any federal, state and local excise, gross receipts, import, motor fuel, superfund and spill taxes and all other federal, state and local taxes however designated, other than taxes on income, paid or incurred by seller directly or indirectly with respect to the oil or product sold hereunder and/or on the value thereof." OMT did not object to Bayway's acceptance or to the incorporation of the Tax Clause, and accepted delivery of the MTBE barrels. The transaction created a tax liability of $464,035.12, which Bayway paid. Invoking the Tax Clause, Bayway demanded payment of the $464,035.12 in taxes in addition to the purchase price of the MTBE. OMT denied that it had agreed to assume the tax liability and refused to pay that invoice item. The district court held that the Tax Clause was properly incorporated into the contract, and OMT appealed.]

We affirm for substantially the reasons stated by the district court. We hold—on an issue of first impression in this Court—that in a "battle of the forms" case governed by UCC § 2–207(2)(b), the party opposing the inclusion of an additional term bears the burden of proving that the term works a material alteration. Viewing the evidence in the light most favorable to OMT, we conclude that OMT failed to shoulder that burden. Finally, we hold that the district court properly admitted the evidence concerning industry custom and practice.

A.   Battle of the Forms.

It was undisputed in the district court that Bayway's [response] is effective to form a contract as an acceptance—even though it stated or referenced additional terms (including the Tax Clause)—because it was not made expressly conditional on OMT's assent to the additional terms. *See* UCC § 2–207(1). Therefore, under UCC § 2–207(2), the Tax Clause is a proposal for an addition to the contract. The parties are both merchants within the meaning of the UCC *See* UCC § 2–104(1), (3). The Tax Clause therefore is presumed to become part of the contract unless one of the three enumerated exceptions applies. *See* UCC § 2 207(2). In its defense, OMT invokes the "material alteration" exception of UCC § 2–207(2)(b).

1.   *Burden of Proof.*

UCC § 2–207(2)(b) is an exception to the general rule of § 2–207(2) that additional terms become part of a contract between merchants. That general rule is in the nature of a presumption concerning the intent of the contracting parties. Thus if neither party introduced any evidence, the Tax Clause would, by the plain language of UCC § 2–207(2), become part of the contract. To implement that presumption, the burden of proving the materiality of the alteration must fall on the party that opposes inclusion. Accordingly, we hold that under UCC § 2–207(2)(b) the party opposing the inclusion of additional terms shoulders the burden of proof. In so doing, we join almost every court to have considered this issue.

2.   *Materiality and* Per Se *Materiality.*

A material alteration is one that would "result in *surprise* or *hardship* if incorporated without express awareness by the other party." UCC § 2–207, cmt. 4 (emphasis added).

Certain additional terms are deemed material as a matter of law. For example, an arbitration clause is *per se* a material alteration in New York because New York law requires an express agreement to commit disputes to arbitration. *See* Marlene Indus. v. Carnac Textiles, Inc., 45 N.Y.2d 327, 408 N.Y.S.2d 410, 413, 380 N.E.2d 239 (1978); *see also* UCC § 2–207 cmt. 4 (listing as examples of *per se* material alterations, *inter alia,* waivers of warranties of merchantability or fitness for a particular purpose and clauses granting the seller the power to cancel upon the buyer's failure to meet any invoice). OMT characterizes the Tax Clause as a broad-ranging indemnity clause, and analogizes it to these *per se* material alterations. We reject the analogy. The Tax Clause allocates responsibility for the tax payable on a specific sale of goods. *See* Union Carbide Corp. v. Oscar Mayer Foods Corp., 947 F.2d 1333, 1335, 1337 (7th Cir.1991) (distinguishing between "open-ended" tax liability, which is a material alteration, from "responsibility for taxes shown on an individual invoice," which is not). And unlike an arbitration clause, which waives a range of rights that are solicitously protected, the Tax Clause is limited, discrete and the subject of no special protection. Unable to show that the Tax Clause is a material alteration *per se,* OMT must prove that in this case the Tax Clause resulted in surprise or hardship.

3.   *Surprise.*

Surprise, within the meaning of the material alteration exception of UCC § 2–207(2)(b), has both the subjective element of what a party actually knew and the objective element of what a party should have known. *See* American Ins. Co. v. El Paso Pipe & Supply Co., 978 F.2d 1185, 1191 (10th Cir.1992); *In re Chateaugay,* 162 B.R. at 956–57. A profession of surprise and raised eyebrows are not enough: "[C]onclusory statements, conjecture, or speculation by the party resisting the motion will not defeat summary judgment." Kulak v. City of New York, 88 F.3d 63, 71 (2d Cir.1996). To carry the burden of showing surprise, a party must establish that, under the circumstances, it cannot be presumed that a reasonable merchant would have consented to the additional term. *See Union Carbide,* 947 F.2d at 1336.

OMT has adduced evidence that the Tax Clause came as an amazement to OMT's executives, who described the term's incorporation as "contract by ambush" and a "sl[e]ight-of-hand proposal." Thus OMT has sufficiently exhibited its subjective surprise. As to objective surprise, however, OMT has alleged no facts and introduced no evidence to show that a reasonable petroleum merchant would be surprised by the Tax Clause. *See In re Chateaugay,* 162 B.R. at 957 (including as types of evidence proving objective surprise "the parties' prior course of dealing and the number of written confirmations that they exchanged, industry custom and the conspicuousness of the term"). OMT had no prior contrary course of dealing with Bayway, and offered nothing concerning trade custom or practice.

Ordinarily, our inquiry into surprise would end here. However, in response to OMT's claim of surprise, Bayway introduced evidence that the Tax Clause reflects custom and practice in the petroleum industry, and on appeal OMT argues that Bayway's own evidence raises a genuine issue of material fact as to whether such a trade practice exists. Although the evidence was introduced by Bayway, we are "obligated to search the record and independently determine whether or not a genuine issue of fact exists." Jiminez v. Dreis & Krump Mfg. Co., 736 F.2d 51, 53 (2d

Cir.1984) (quoting Higgins v. Baker, 309 F.Supp. 635, 639 (S.D.N.Y.1970)) (internal quotation marks omitted).

Upon our review of the evidence, we conclude that Bayway has adduced compelling proof that shifting tax liability to a buyer is the custom and practice in the petroleum industry. Two industry experts offered unchallenged testimony that it is customary for the buyer to pay all the taxes resulting from a petroleum transaction. One expert stated that "[t]his practice is so universally understood among traders in the industry, that I cannot recall an instance, in all my years of trading and overseeing trades, when the buyer refused to pay the seller for excise or sales taxes."

OMT cites the standard contracts of five major petroleum companies that Bayway introduced to illustrate contract terms similar to the Tax Clause. OMT argues that only three of the five place the tax liability on the buyer, and that there is therefore an issue of fact as to whether the Tax Clause would objectively surprise a merchant in this industry.

OMT misconstrues the evidence. Three of the contracts—those of CITGO Petroleum, Conoco, and Enron—mirror the Tax Clause. A fourth, Chevron's, differs from the others only in that the cost of the taxes is added into the contract price rather than separately itemized. Thus Chevron's standard contract affords OMT no support.

The fifth example, the Texaco contract, is silent as to the tax allocation issue in this case. But on this unrebutted record of universal trade custom and practice, silence supports no contrary inference.

Moreover, common sense supports Bayway's evidence of custom and practice. The federal excise tax is imposed when taxable fuels are sold "to any person who is not registered under [26 U.S.C. § 4101]." 26 U.S.C. § 4081(a)(1)(A)(iv). The buyer thereby controls whether any tax liability is incurred in a transaction. A trade practice that reflects a rational allocation of incentives (as trade practices usually do) would place the burden of the tax on the party that is in the position to obviate it—here, on OMT as the buyer.

Viewing Bayway's evidence in the light most favorable to OMT, we conclude that allocating the tax liability to the buyer is the custom and practice in the petroleum industry. OMT could not be objectively surprised by the incorporation of an additional term in the contract that reflects such a practice.

4. *Hardship.*

To recapitulate: A material alteration is one that would "result in surprise *or hardship* if incorporated without express awareness by the other party." UCC § 2–207 cmt. 4 (emphasis added). Although this Official Comment to the UCC seemingly treats hardship as an independent ground for finding that an alteration is material, courts have expressed doubt: "You cannot walk away from a contract that you can fairly be deemed to have agreed to, merely because performance turns out to be a hardship for you, unless you can squeeze yourself into the impossibility defense or some related doctrine of excuse." *Union Carbide,* 947 F.2d at 1336 ("Hardship is a consequence [of material alteration], not a criterion. (Surprise can be either.)"); *see also, e.g.,* Suzy Phillips Originals, Inc. v. Coville, Inc., 939 F.Supp. 1012, 1017–18 (E.D.N.Y.1996) (citing *Union Carbide* with approval and limiting the test for material alteration to surprise); *In re Chateaugay,* 162 B.R. at 957 (same).

We need not decide whether hardship is an independent ground of material alteration, because even if it were, OMT failed to raise a genuine issue of material fact as to hardship. OMT's only evidence of hardship is (generally) that it is a small business dependent on precarious profit margins, and it would suffer a loss it cannot afford. That does not amount to hardship in the present circumstances.

Typically, courts that have relied on hardship to find that an additional term materially alters a contract have done so when the term is one that creates or allocates an open-ended and prolonged liability. *See, e.g.,* St. Charles Cable TV, Inc. v. Eagle Comtronics, Inc., 687 F.Supp. 820, 827 (S.D.N.Y.1988) (finding a hardship in "shift[ing] all risks for any dispute to the buyers"), *aff'd,* 895 F.2d 1410 (2d Cir.1989) (unpublished table disposition); Charles J. King, Inc. v. Barge LM-10, 518 F.Supp. 1117, 1120 (S.D.N.Y.1981).

The Tax Clause places on a buyer a contractual responsibility that bears on a specific sale of goods, that is (at least) not uncommon in the industry, and that the buyer could avoid by registration. The cry of hardship rings hollow, because any loss that the Tax Clause imposed on OMT is limited, routine and self-inflicted.

OMT failed to raise a factual issue as to hardship or surprise. Summary judgment was therefore appropriately granted in favor of Bayway.

NOTES

(1) *Surprise or Hardship?* In an effort to lower its prices by avoiding a local Chicago sales tax, Union Carbide, a supplier of sausage casings, instructed its customers to send their purchase orders to a Union Carbide address outside Chicago. Oscar Mayer Foods entered into several contracts for casings with Union Carbide in this manner. Several years later the relevant tax authorities decided this arrangement was improper and assessed Union Carbide $88,000 in back taxes. Union Carbide paid the sum and then sought to recover it from Oscar Mayer under the terms of an indemnity provision printed on the back of Union Carbide's invoices.[s] Among the issues to be decided by the trial court was whether the indemnity provision materially altered the offer under UCC § 2–207(2). From a

---

[s]   "Buyer shall pay Seller the amount of all governmental taxes . . . that Seller may be required to pay with respect to the production, sale, or transportation of any materials delivered hereunder." 947 F.2d at 1334.

summary judgment for the defendants that the alteration was material, Union Carbide appealed. *Held*: Affirmed.

> An alteration is material if consent to it cannot be presumed. That is our gloss; the cases more commonly speak of 'unreasonable surprise'. But it comes to the same thing. What is expectable, hence unsurprising, is okay. What is unexpected, hence surprising, is not. Not infrequently the test is said to be 'surprise or hardship,' but this is a misreading of Official Comment 4 to UCC § 2–207. Hardship is a consequence, not a criterion. You cannot walk away from a contract that you can be fairly deemed to have agreed to, merely because your performance turns out to be a hardship for you.

Union Carbide Corp. v. Oscar Mayer Foods Corp., 947 F.2d 1333, 1335 (7th Cir.1991) (Posner, J.).

The court used the facts of the case for a useful review of the applicability of UCC § 2–207: "Every actual purchase of sausage casings involved an exchange of four documents: the standing order, the price book, the release order, the invoice. Such a pattern of sequential exchange of documents governing a single sale is a prototypical situation for the application of UCC § 2–207." 947 F.2d at 1336.

(2) *Battlegrounds of Materiality*. Provisions requiring arbitration and limiting warranties are commonplace occasions for considering whether an additional term would materially alter a contract under Article 2. The issue has also arisen in connection with terms about choice of forum, M.K.C. Equipment Company v. M.A.I.L. Code, Inc., 843 F.Supp. 679 (D.Kan.1994), and time for payment (St. Paul Structural Steel Co. v. ABI Contracting, Inc., 364 N.W.2d 83 (N.D.1985)).

2. DIFFERENT TERMS

So far the materials in this section have focused on contracts formed under UCC § 2–207(1) in which the "expression of acceptance" contained terms that were "in addition to" those in the offer. But how does UCC § 2–207 work when the terms in the expression of acceptance *differ* from, rather than add to, the terms in the offer? What has been called the "notorious distinction between 'different' and 'additional' terms" appears upon comparing subsections (1) and (2) of UCC § 2–207. Pace Communs., Inc. v. Moonlight Design, Inc., 31 F.3d 587, 592 (7th Cir.1994). The following case reviews the textual conundrum and competing judicial approaches to a solution. As the trial court in that case observed, "Mischief lurks in the words 'additional to or different from.' " *Id.* at 1174.

Northrop Corp. v. Litronic Industries

United States Court of Appeals, Seventh Circuit, 1994.
29 F.3d 1173.

[Litronic offered to sell the Northrop, a giant defense firm, printed wire boards. The offer contained a 90-day warranty stated to be in lieu of any other warranties. Northrop's return invoice contained a warranty period unlimited in duration. After 90 days had passed, Northrop attempted to return some of the wire boards as defective. Litronic refused to accept them, arguing that the 90-day warranty period had lapsed. A preliminary question before the court was how to treat terms that were "different" but not "additional" to those of the offer under subsection (2). From a judgment for Northrup, Litronic appealed.]

■ POSNER, CHIEF JUDGE: [The Code does not explain] what happens if the offeree's response contains different terms (rather than additional ones) within the meaning of section 2–207(1). There is no consensus on that question. See James J. White & Robert S. Summers, Uniform Commercial Code 33–36 (3d ed. 1988); John E. Murray, Jr., *The Chaos of the 'Battle of the Forms': Solutions*, 39 Vand. L. Rev. 1307, 1354–65 (1986). We know there is a contract because an acceptance is effective even though it contains different terms; but what are the terms of the contract that is brought into being by the offer and acceptance? One view is that the discrepant terms in both the nonidentical offer and the acceptance drop out, and default terms found elsewhere in the Code fill the resulting gap. Another view is that the offeree's discrepant terms drop out and the offeror's become part of the contract. A third view, possibly the most sensible, equates "different" with "additional" and makes the outcome turn on whether the new terms in the acceptance are materially different from the terms in the offer—in which event they operate as proposals, so that the offeror's terms prevail unless he agrees to the variant terms in the acceptance—or not materially different from the terms in the offer, in which event they become part of the contract. John L. Utz, *More on the Battle of the Forms: The Treatment of 'Different' Terms Under the Uniform Commercial Code*, 16 U.C.C. L.J. 103 (1983). This interpretation equating "different" to "additional," bolstered by drafting history which shows that the omission of "or different" from section 2–207(2) was a drafting error, substitutes a manageable inquiry into materiality for a hair-splitting inquiry into the difference between "different" and "additional." It is hair-splitting ("metaphysical," "casuistic," "semantic," in the pejorative senses of these words) because all different terms are additional and all additional terms are different.

The majority view is that the discrepant terms fall out and are replaced by a suitable UCC gap-filler. E.g., Daitom, Inc. v. Pennwalt Corp., supra, 741 F.2d at 1578–80; The magistrate judge followed this approach and proceeded to section 2–309, which provides that nonconforming goods may be rejected within a "reasonable" time (see also § 2–601(1)), and she held that the six months that Northrop took to reject Litronic's boards was a reasonable time because of the complexity of the required testing. The leading minority view is that the discrepant terms in the acceptance are to be ignored, Valtrol, Inc. v. General Connectors Corp., 884 F.2d 149, 155 (4th Cir.1989); Reaction Molding Technologies,

Inc. v. General Electric Co., 588 F.Supp. 1280, 1289 (E.D.Pa.1984), and that would give the palm to Litronic. Our own preferred view—the view that assimilates "different" to "additional," so that the terms in the offer prevail over the different terms in the acceptance only if the latter are materially different, has as yet been adopted by only one state, California. Steiner v. Mobil Oil Corp., 20 Cal.3d 90, 141 Cal.Rptr. 157, 569 P.2d 751, 759 n. 5 (1977). Under that view, as under what we are calling the "leading" minority view, the warranty in Litronic's offer, the 90-day warranty, was the contractual warranty, because the unlimited warranty contained in Northrop's acceptance was materially different.

Because Illinois in other UCC cases has tended to adopt majority rules, e.g., Rebaque v. Forsythe Racing, Inc., 134 Ill.App.3d 778, 89 Ill.Dec. 595, 598, 480 N.E.2d 1338, 1341 (1985), and because the interest in the uniform nationwide application of the Code—an interest asserted in the Code itself (see § 1–102)—argues for nudging majority views, even if imperfect (but not downright bad), toward unanimity, we start with a presumption that Illinois, whose position we are trying to predict, would adopt the majority view. We do not find the presumption rebutted. The idea behind the majority view is that the presence of different terms in the acceptance suggests that the offeree didn't really accede to the offeror's terms, yet both parties wanted to contract, so why not find a neutral term to govern the dispute that has arisen between them? Of course the offeree may not have had any serious objection to the terms in the offer at the time of contracting; he may have mailed a boilerplated form without giving any thought to its contents or to its suitability for the particular contract in question. But it is just as likely that the discrepant terms in the offer itself were the product of a thoughtless use of a boilerplate form rather than a considered condition of contracting. And if the offeror doesn't want to do business other than on the terms in the offer, he can protect himself by specifying that the offeree must accept all those terms for the parties to have a contract. UCC § 2–207(2)(a).

What we are calling the leading minority view may tempt the offeror to spring a surprise on the offeree, hoping the latter won't read the fine print. Under the majority view, if the offeree tries to spring a surprise (the offeror can't, since his terms won't prevail if the acceptance contains different terms), the parties move to neutral ground; and the offeror can, we have suggested, more easily protect himself against being surprised than the offeree can protect himself against being surprised. The California rule dissolves all these problems, but has too little support to make it a plausible candidate for Illinois, or at least a plausible candidate for our guess as to Illinois's position.

Affirmed.

NOTES

(1) *The Knockout Rule.* The decision in *Northrop* was based on what is commonly called the "knockout rule." Under this approach, when the

difference between the seller's terms and the buyer's are material, the two terms cancel each other out, and the contested term is to be supplied by a Code gap-filler. Why did the court in *Northrop* decide to apply to knockout rule despite its preference for a different ("possibly the most sensible") rule? What result with regard to warranties under the view preferred by the court?

A recent empirical study of how firms conduct the battle suggests that "it is difficult for either side to win the battle of the forms with clever drafting, at least if we define 'winning' as making the other side be held to your non-dickered terms. By the same token, it is easy with good drafting never to lose the battle of the forms, at least if 'losing' equals letting your side get stuck with the other party's boilerplate terms." Daniel Keating, Exploring the Battle of the Forms in Action, 98 Mich.L.Rev. 2678, 2682 (2000).

(2) *Fairness and the Knockout Doctrine.* According to one court, the overriding goal of Article 2 is "to discern the bargain struck by the contracting parties. However, there are times where the conduct of the parties makes realizing that goal impossible. In such cases, we find guidance in the Code's commitment to fairness, good faith, and conscionable conduct." Gardner Zemke Co. v. Dunham Bush, Inc., n. 3, p. 267 above. Does the knockout doctrine, by substituting Code gap-fillers for the discordant terms of the parties further the Code's "commitment to fairness"?

Some would argue that it does, in part by enhancing the importance of Code gap-fillers, notably the warranty sections which in most cases work to the general advantage of *buyers*. "Sellers should not be permitted, by surreptitious manipulation of section 2–207, to obtain contract terms that cannot be obtained either through statutory amendment of the UCC gap-filler provisions or by negotiation with the buyer. If warranty, remedy, and arbitration terms are so important to sellers, then those terms are and must be negotiated. [I]f the seller 'is not willing to sacrifice the time and effort that this requires, then he should be willing to abide by the rules of Article 2.' " Roszkowski and Wladis, *Revised UCC Section 2–207: Analysis and Recommendations*, 49 Bus. Law. 1065, 1070 (1994). Others contend that sellers are driven to the strategic use of forms exactly to avoid the imposition of gap-fillers such as the warranty of merchantability provided in UCC § 2–314 that, in their view, unreasonably favor buyers.

(3) *Drafting § 2–207.* Professor James J. White includes the example of different versus additional among the textual "troubles" of UCC § 2–207; see James J. White, *Contracting Under Amended 2–207*, 2004 Wis. L. Rev. 723 (2004). White's critique includes a "delightful" 1980 letter from Professor Grant Gilmore to UCC drafter Robert Summers discussing the impossibility of discerning what the drafters intended in § 2–207 in light of the hodge-podge method of drafting. Id. at 724–25.

(4) *Strategies in the "Battle"?* To "win" the battle of the forms, what clauses might a seller insert in its "quotation" or "sales acknowledgment" forms? What clauses might a buyer insert in its "purchase order" forms? Do those clauses present risks as well as rewards?

When parties have an on-going relationship, one method for avoiding the battle altogether is to negotiate an overriding master agreement to govern all their dealings. Still another is for a trade association to work out standard terms to which its members agree. See, for example, Professor Lisa Bernstein's studies of private codes in the grain and diamond industries, *Merchant Law in a Merchant Court*, 144 U. Pa. L. Rev. 1765 (1996), and *Opting Out of the Legal System: Extra Contractual Relations in the Diamond Industry*, 21 J. Legal Stud. 115 (1992).

Electronic data interchange is another means of reducing sales terms to an agreed "transaction set" to be used between trading partners in all future sales. Professor Keating suggests that these practices may mean the battle of the forms has not been as ferocious as may have been supposed. See Keating, Note 1 above, at 279.

PROBLEM

Misplaced Strategies. Buyer sent Seller a purchase order containing an arbitration clause. Seller returned an invoice silent on arbitration, but stating that "This document is not an Expression of Acceptance or Confirmation document as contemplated in Section 2–207. The acceptance of any order entered by Buyer is expressly conditional on [Buyer's] assent to any additional or conflicting terms herein." After Seller shipped and Buyer received the goods (bulk nylon fiber or nylon tow), the goods spontaneously combusted, destroying several of Buyer's buildings. (Buyer alleged that a static electric charge in the nylon ignited, causing the fire.) Seller resisted Buyer's lawsuit on the ground that the Buyer was bound to the arbitration clause in its purchase order. What result? See Commerce & Industry Insurance Co. v. Bayer Corp., 742 N.E.2d 567 (Mass.2001).

(F) CONTRACT FIRST, TERMS LATER: UCC § 2–207 OR A NEW METHOD OF CONTRACT FORMATION?

An increasingly common transactional scenario is presented when the parties have seemingly entered into a basic contract, but subsequently one party communicates additional terms, sometimes accompanied by language conditioning the contract on acquiescence to those terms. Consider, for example, a disclaimer of warranty included in a package insert, seen only after the product has been purchased and brought home. Does UCC § 2–207 apply to such a transaction? If so, what is the status of the parties' contract and of the additional terms in the package?

The cases that follow investigate the problem of post-agreement terms in three common settings: terms found on box tops, terms found encoded on disks, and terms enclosed in the box containing purchased goods. In reading these cases consider the following question: Are there reasons to distinguish between consumer transactions and commercial transactions?

Step-Saver Data Systems, Inc. v. Wyse Technology

United States Court of Appeals, Third Circuit, 1991.
939 F.2d 91.

■ WISDOM, CIRCUIT JUDGE: The "Limited Use License Agreement" printed on a package containing a copy of a computer program raises the central issue in this appeal. The trial judge held that the terms of the Limited Use License Agreement governed the purchase of the package, and, therefore, granted the software producer, The Software Link, Inc. ("TSL"), a directed verdict on claims of breach of warranty brought by a disgruntled purchaser, Step-Saver Data Systems, Inc. We disagree with the district court's determination of the legal effect of the license, and reverse and remand the warranty claims for further consideration.

[In the spring of 1986 Step-Saver obtained several copies of Wyse Technology's program "Advanced Multilink," which it tested with a view to incorporating it into a multi-user electronic system ("the system"). It decided to do so.] From August of 1986 through March of 1987, Step-Saver purchased and resold 142 copies of the Multilink Advanced program. Step-Saver would typically purchase copies of the program in the following manner. First, Step-Saver would telephone TSL and place an order. (Step-Saver would typically order twenty copies of the program at a time.) TSL would accept the order and promise, while on the telephone, to ship the goods promptly. After the telephone order, Step-Saver would send a purchase order, detailing the items to be purchased, their price, and shipping and payment terms. TSL would ship the order promptly, along with an invoice. The invoice would contain terms essentially identical with those on Step-Saver's purchase order: price, quantity, and shipping and payment terms. No reference was made during the telephone calls, or on either the purchase orders or the invoices with regard to a disclaimer of any warranties.

Printed on the package of each copy of the program, however, would be [form language purporting to express the complete agreement between the parties (the "box-top license"), including] five terms relevant to this action:

(1) The box-top license provides that the customer has not purchased the software itself, but has merely obtained a personal, non-transferable license to use the program.

(2) The box-top license, in detail and at some length, disclaims all express and implied warranties except for a warranty that the disks contained in the box are free from defects.

. . .

(5) The box-top license states: "Opening this package indicates your acceptance of these terms and conditions. If you do not agree with them, you should promptly return the package unopened to the person from whom you purchased it within

fifteen days from date of purchase and your money will be refunded to you by that person."

Step-Saver began marketing the system in November of 1986, and sold one hundred forty-two systems mostly to law and medical offices before terminating sales of the system in March of 1987. Almost immediately upon installation of the system, Step-Saver began to receive complaints from some of its customers.[1] At least twelve of Step-Saver's customers filed suit against Step-Saver because of the problems with the multi-user system.

[Efforts by the parties having failed to resolve the problems, Step-Saver brought an action against TSL, charging it with breaches of warranties and seeking indemnity for costs in resolving the customers' suits. Wyse Technology, a manufacturer of terminals, also a defendant, was exonerated in the trial court and on appeal.]

The district court, without much discussion, held, as a matter of law, that the box-top license was the final and complete expression of the terms of the parties' agreement. Because the district court decided the questions of contract formation and interpretation as issues of law, we review the district court's resolution of these questions *de novo*.

Step-Saver contends that the contract for each copy of the program was formed when TSL agreed, on the telephone, to ship the copy at the agreed price.[2] The box-top license, argues Step-Saver, was a material alteration to the parties' contract which did not become a part of the contract under UCC § 2–207.

A.   *Does UCC § 2–207 Govern the Analysis?*

As a basic principle, we agree with Step-Saver that UCC § 2–207 governs our analysis. We see no need to parse the parties' various actions to decide exactly when the parties formed a contract. TSL has shipped the product, and Step-Saver has accepted and paid for each copy of the program. The parties' performance demonstrates the existence of a contract. The dispute is, therefore, not over the existence of a contract, but the nature of its terms. When the parties' conduct establishes a contract, but the parties have failed to adopt expressly a particular writing as the terms of their agreement, and the writings exchanged by the parties do not agree, UCC § 2–207 determines the terms of the contract.

---

[1]   According to the testimony of Jeffrey Worthington, an employee of Step-Saver, 20 to 25 of the purchasers of the multi-user system had serious problems with the system that were never resolved.

[2]   See UCC § 2–206(1)(b) and comment 2. Note that under UCC § 2–201, the oral contract would not be enforceable in the absence of a writing or part performance because each order typically involved more than $500 in goods. However, courts have typically treated the questions of formation and interpretation as separate from the question of when the contract becomes enforceable. See, e.g., C. Itoh & Co. v. Jordan Int'l Co., 552 F.2d 1228, 1232–33 (7th Cir.1977); Southeastern Adhesives Co. v. Funder America, 89 N.C.App. 438, 366 S.E.2d 505, 507–08 (N.C.App.1988). . . .

Under the common law of sales, and to some extent still for contracts outside the UCC, an acceptance that varied any term of the offer operated as a rejection of the offer, and simultaneously made a counteroffer. [T]he terms of the party who sent the last form, typically the seller, would become the terms of the parties' contract. This result was known as the "last shot rule".

The UCC, in § 2–207, rejected this approach. Instead, it recognized that, while a party may desire the terms detailed in its form if a dispute, in fact, arises, most parties do not expect a dispute to arise when they first enter into a contract. As a result, most parties will proceed with the transaction even if they know that the terms of their form would not be enforced.[3] The insight behind the rejection of the last shot rule is that it would be unfair to bind the buyer of goods to the standard terms of the seller, when neither party cared sufficiently to establish expressly the terms of their agreement, simply because the seller sent the last form. In the absence of a party's express assent to the additional or different terms of the writing, section 2–207 provides a default rule that the parties intended, as the terms of their agreement, those terms to which both parties have agreed,[4] along with any terms implied by the provisions of the UCC.

The reasons that led to the rejection of the last shot rule, and the adoption of section 2–207, apply fully in this case.

B.   Application of § 2–207

TSL advances two reasons why its box-top license should be considered a conditional acceptance under UCC § 2–207(1). First, TSL argues that the express language of the box-top license, including the phrase "opening this product indicates your acceptance of these terms", made TSL's acceptance "expressly conditional on assent to the additional or different terms". Second, TSL argues that the box-top license, by permitting return of the product within fifteen days if the purchaser[5] does not agree to the terms stated in the license (the "refund offer"), establishes that TSL's acceptance was conditioned on Step-Saver's assent to the terms of the box-top license, citing Monsanto Agricultural Products Co. v. Edenfield.[6] While we are not certain that a conditional acceptance

---

[3]   As Judge Engel has written: "Usually, these standard terms mean little, for a contract looks to its fulfillment and rarely anticipates its breach. Hope springs eternal in the commercial world and expectations are usually, but not always, realized." McJunkin Corp. v. Mechanicals, Inc., 888 F.2d at 481 (6th Cir. 1989).

[4]   The parties may demonstrate their acceptance of a particular term either "orally or by informal correspondence", UCC 2–207, comment 1, or by placing the term in their respective form.

[5]   In the remainder of the opinion, we will refer to the transaction as a sale for the sake of simplicity, but, by doing so, do not mean to resolve the sale-license question.

[6]   426 So.2d 574 (Fla.Dist.Ct.App.1982).

analysis applies when a contract is established by performance,[7] we assume that it does and consider TSL's arguments.

To determine whether a writing constitutes a conditional acceptance, courts have established three tests. [The court described various applications that courts have given to the concluding phrase in subsection (1) of UCC § 2–207, and then recited some further facts about the dealings between the parties.]

Based on these facts, we conclude that TSL did not clearly express its unwillingness to proceed with the transactions unless its additional terms were incorporated into the parties' agreement. The box-top license did not, therefore, constitute a conditional acceptance under UCC § 2–207(1).

> 3. Did the parties's course of dealing establish that the parties had excluded any express or implied warranties associated with the software program?

TSL argues that because Step-Saver placed its orders for copies of the Multilink Advanced program with notice of the terms of the box-top license, Step-Saver is bound by the terms of the box-top license. Essentially, TSL is arguing that, even if the terms of the box-top license would not become part of the contract if the case involved only a single transaction, the repeated expression of those terms by TSL eventually incorporates them within the contract.

While one court has concluded that terms repeated in a number of written confirmations eventually become part of the contract even though neither party ever takes any action with respect to the issue addressed by those terms, most courts have rejected such reasoning.

[W]e are not convinced that TSL's unilateral act of repeatedly sending copies of the box-top license with its product can establish a course of dealing between TSL and Step-Saver that resulted in the adoption of the terms of the box-top license.

With regard to more specific evidence as to the parties' course of dealing or performance, it appears that the parties have not incorporated the warranty disclaimer into their agreement. First, there is the evidence that TSL tried to obtain Step-Saver's express consent to the disclaimer and limitation of damages provision of the box-top license. Step-Saver refused to sign the proposed agreements. Second, when first notified of the problems with the program, TSL spent considerable time and energy attempting to solve the problems identified by Step-Saver.

---

[7] Even though a writing is sent after performance establishes the existence of a contract, courts have analyzed the effect of such a writing under UCC § 2–207. See Herzog Oil Field Serv. v. Otto Torpedo Co., 391 Pa.Super. 133, 570 A.2d 549, 550 (Pa.Super.Ct.1990); McJunkin Corp. v. Mechanicals, Inc., 888 F.2d at 487. The official comment to UCC 2–207 suggests that, even though a proposed deal has been closed, the conditional acceptance analysis still applies in determining which writing's terms will define the contract.

Course of conduct is ordinarily a factual issue. But we hold that the actions of TSL in repeatedly sending a writing, whose terms would otherwise be excluded under UCC § 2–207, cannot establish a course of conduct between TSL and Step-Saver that adopted the terms of the writing.

[The court rejected arguments of public policy advanced by TSL.]

C.   The Terms of the Contract

Under section 2–207, an additional term detailed in the box-top license will not be incorporated into the parties' contract if the term's addition to the contract would materially alter the parties' agreement.[8] Step-Saver alleges that several representations made by TSL constitute express warranties, and that valid implied warranties were also a part of the parties' agreement. Because the district court considered the box-top license to exclude all of these warranties, the district court did not consider whether other factors may act to exclude these warranties. The existence and nature of the warranties is primarily a factual question that we leave for the district court,[9] but assuming that these warranties were included within the parties' original agreement, we must conclude that adding the disclaimer of warranty and limitation of remedies provisions from the box-top license would, as a matter of law, substantially alter the distribution of risk between Step-Saver and TSL. Therefore, under UCC § 2–207(2)(b), the disclaimer of warranty and limitation of remedies terms of the box-top license did not become a part of the parties' agreement.

[T]he box-top license should have been treated as a written confirmation containing additional terms. Because the warranty disclaimer and limitation of remedies terms would materially alter the parties' agreement, these terms did not become a part of the parties' agreement. We remand for further consideration the express and implied warranty claims against TSL.

NOTES

(1)   *Questions.* How many "expressions of acceptance" might one find in *Step-Saver*? Why does the court reject TSL's argument that the box-top was a conditional acceptance under subsection (1)? How does the court finally characterize the box-top? On what basis did the court decide that the warranty disclaimer and limitation of remedies provisions were material alterations under subsection (2)?

---

[8]   UCC § 2–207(2)(b).

[9]   For example, questions exist as to: (1) whether the statements by TSL were representations of fact, or mere statements of opinion; (2) whether the custom in the trade is to exclude warranties and limit remedies in contracts between a software producer and its dealer; (3) whether Step-Saver relied on TSL's alleged representations, or whether these warranties became a basis of the parties' bargain; and (4) whether Step-Saver's testing excluded some or all of these warranties. From the record, it appears that most of these issues are factual determinations that will require a trial, as did the warranty claims against Wyse. But we leave these issues open to the district court on remand.

(2) *Assenting to Material Terms*. In Union Carbide Corp. v. Oscar Mayer Foods, discussed at Note 1, p. 276 above, the court stated that "Even if the alteration is material, the other party can, of course, decide to accept it." In that case, involving the materiality of an indemnity clause for taxes, the court thought it important to separate the issues of materiality from that of consent, noting that "[t]hey are close but distinct." The court observed:

> If the new term does not effect a material alteration, silence is consent, period. If it does effect a material alteration, the party who proposed it must present additional evidence, beyond the term itself, to show that he was reasonable to infer consent to the new term from the other party's failure to object (silence); ordinarily this will be evidence of prior dealings.

947 F.2d at 1336.

The case provides a good workout of this close but distinctive relationship. Union Carbide argued that Oscar Mayer had agreed to the indemnity clause by paying all the sales taxes that appeared on the Union Carbide invoices without complaint:

> What difference does it make, asks Union Carbide, if the [tax] increase took the form of an assessment of back taxes? It makes a big difference, amounting to a material alteration to which Oscar Mayer did not consent either explicitly or implicitly. . . . To assume responsibility for taxes shown on an individual invoice is quite different from assuming an open-ended, indeed, incalculable, liability for back taxes. . . . [T]his is not a case where consent can be realistically inferred from Oscar Mayer's silence in the face of a succession of acceptances (Union Carbide's invoices) containing the new term.

947 F.2d at 1337.

(3) *Assent and Arbitration*. The fact that arbitration terms are in widespread use sometimes contributes to the conclusion that a particular term was assented to. In Pervel Industries, Inc. v. TM Wallcovering, Inc., 871 F.2d 7 (2d Cir.1989), the court said:

> Where, as here, a manufacturer has a well established custom of sending purchase order confirmations containing an arbitration clause, a buyer who has made numerous purchases over a period of time, receiving in each instance a standard confirmation form which it either signed and returned or retained without objection, is bound by the arbitration provision. This is particularly true in industries such as fabrics and textiles where the specialized nature of the product has led to the widespread use of arbitration clauses and knowledgeable arbitrators.

Conversely, the fact that a term diverges from trade usage and the like may be a reason to doubt that it was assented to. Business persons, it is said, "do not consider the boilerplate printed on the reverse side of their forms to be part of the deal unless it coincidentally reflects some aspect of custom, usage, course of dealing, or practice that they understand as implicit in the resulting transactional relationship." Thomas J. McCarthy, *An Introduction:*

The Commercial Irrelevancy of the "Battle of the Forms," 49 Bus. Law. 1019, 1026 (1994). If this is correct, how far should the courts consult such practices for indications that a given term was or was not assented to?

The New York Court of Appeals has said that an arbitration term "is a material addition which can become part of a contract only if it is expressly assented to by both parties." Marlene Industries Corp. v. Carnac Textiles, Inc., 380 N.E.2d 239, 242 (N.Y.1978). Can that statement be reconciled with the excerpt quoted from *Pervel Industries* above? See Diskin v. J.P. Stevens & Co., Inc., 836 F.2d 47 (1st Cir.1987). The problem of mandatory arbitration clauses is discussed in Chapter 6.

(4) *International Approaches.* A provision comparable to UCC § 2–207 appears as Article 19 of the Convention on Contracts for the International Sale of Goods. (Provisions of the Convention, together with an introduction, can be found in Selections for Contracts.) Among the many additional terms considered to alter "materially" the terms of an offer, under that provision are those relating to "the extent of one party's liability to the other or the settlement of disputes." Does this expression embrace all terms that "substantially alter the distribution of risk" between the parties? If so, and if the *Step-Saver* case had been governed by the Convention, would the result have been the same?

In contrast to the approach in the CISG, the UNIDROIT Principles leave the determination of materiality to the "circumstances of each case" and, like the UCC, provides that "surprise to the offerer" is important to that assessment; see *UNIDROIT Principles* art. 2.11, cmt. 2.

ProCD, Inc. v. Zeidenberg

United States Court of Appeals, Seventh Circuit, 1996.
86 F.3d 1447.

[Every box containing ProCD's software declared that it came with restrictions stated in an enclosed license. This license, encoded on the CD-ROM disks as well as printed in the manual, and which appeared on a user's screen every time the software ran, limited use of the application program and listings to non-commercial purposes. Matthew Zeidenberg bought a consumer package of ProCD's software from a retail outlet but decided to ignore the license. He formed a company to resell the information in ProCD's database at a price less than ProCD charges its commercial customers. ProCD filed suit seeking an injunction against further dissemination that exceeds the rights specified in the licenses.]

■ EASTERBROOK, CIRCUIT JUDGE.[t] The district court held the licenses ineffectual because their terms do not appear on the outside of the packages. The court added that a purchaser does not agree to—and

---

[t]   Frank Easterbrook (1948–___) served for several years in the Department of Justice and then joined the University of Chicago law faculty, where he made important scholarly contributions in the fields of corporate and anti-trust law and has been an influential proponent of economic analysis to law. In 1985 he was appointed to the United States Court of Appeals, Seventh Circuit.

cannot be bound by terms that were secret at the time of purchase. 908 F.Supp. at 654.

Following the district court, we treat the licenses as ordinary contracts accompanying the sale of products, and therefore as governed by the common law of contracts and the Uniform Commercial Code. Whether there are legal differences between "contracts" and "licenses" (which may matter under the copyright doctrine of first sale) is a subject for another day. Zeidenberg [argues], and the district court held, that placing the package of software on the shelf is an "offer," which the customer "accepts" by paying the asking price and leaving the store with the goods. Peeters v. State, 142 N.W. 181 (1913). In Wisconsin, as elsewhere, a contract includes only the terms on which the parties have agreed. One cannot agree to hidden terms, the judge concluded. So far, so good—but one of the terms to which Zeidenberg agreed by purchasing the software is that the transaction was subject to a license. Zeidenberg's position therefore must be that the printed terms on the outside of a box are the parties' contract—except for printed terms that refer to or incorporate other terms. But why would Wisconsin fetter the parties' choice in this way? Vendors can put the entire terms of a contract on the outside of a box only by using microscopic type, removing other information that buyers might find more useful (such as what the software does, and on which computers it works), or both. The "Read Me" file included with most software, describing system requirements and potential incompatibilities, may be equivalent to ten pages of type; warranties and license restrictions take still more space. Notice on the outside, terms on the inside, and a right to return the software for a refund if the terms are unacceptable (a right that the license expressly extends), may be a means of doing business valuable to buyers and sellers alike. See Farnsworth on Contracts § 4.26 (1990); Restatement (2d) of Contracts § 211 comment *a* (1981) ("Standardization of agreements serves many of the same functions as standardization of goods and services; both are essential to a system of mass production and distribution. Scarce and costly time and skill can be devoted to a class of transactions rather than the details of individual transactions."). Doubtless a state could forbid the use of standard contracts in the software business, but we do not think that Wisconsin has done so.

Transactions in which the exchange of money precedes the communication of detailed terms are common. Consider the purchase of insurance. The buyer goes to an agent, who explains the essentials (amount of coverage, number of years) and remits the premium to the home office, which sends back a policy. On the district judge's understanding, the terms of the policy are irrelevant because the insured paid before receiving them. Yet the device of payment, often with a "binder" (so that the insurance takes effect immediately even though the home office reserves the right to withdraw coverage later), in advance of the policy, serves buyers' interests by accelerating effectiveness and reducing transactions costs. Or consider the purchase of an airline ticket. The traveler calls the carrier or an agent, is quoted a price, reserves a seat, pays, and gets a ticket, in that order. The ticket elaborates terms, which the traveler can reject by canceling the reservation. To use the ticket is to accept the terms, even terms that in retrospect are disadvantageous. See Carnival Cruise Lines, Inc. v. Shute, 499 U.S. 585 (1991). Just so with a ticket to a concert. The back of the ticket states that the patron promises not to record the concert; to attend is to agree. A theater that detects a violation will confiscate the tape and escort the violator to the exit. One could arrange things so that every concertgoer signs this promise before forking over the money, but that cumbersome way of doing things not only would lengthen queues and raise prices but also would scotch the sale of tickets by phone or electronic data service.

Consumer goods work the same way. Someone who wants to buy a radio set visits a store, pays, and walks out with a box. Inside the box is a leaflet containing some terms, the most important of which usually is the warranty, read for the first time in the comfort of home. By Zeidenberg's lights, the warranty in the box is irrelevant; every consumer gets the standard warranty implied by the UCC in the event the contract is silent; yet so far as we are aware no state disregards warranties furnished with consumer products. Drugs come with a list of ingredients on the outside and an elaborate package insert on the inside. The package insert describes drug interactions, contraindications, and other vital information—but, if Zeidenberg is right, the purchaser need not read the package insert, because it is not part of the contract.

Next consider the software industry itself. Only a minority of sales take place over the counter, where there are boxes to peruse. A customer may place an order by phone in response to a line item in a catalog or a review in a magazine. Much software is ordered over the Internet by purchasers who have never seen a box. Increasingly software arrives by wire. There is no box; there is only a stream of electrons, a collection of information that includes data, an application program, instructions, many limitations ("MegaPixel 3.14159 cannot be used with BytePusher 2.718"), and the terms of sale. The user purchases a serial number, which activates the software's features. On Zeidenberg's arguments, these unboxed sales are unfettered by terms—so the seller has made a broad warranty and must pay consequential damages for any shortfalls in performance, two "promises" that if taken seriously would drive prices through the ceiling or return transactions to the horse-and-buggy age.

According to the district court, the UCC does not countenance the sequence of money now, terms later. [Yet] only three cases (other than ours) touch on the subject, and none directly addresses it. See Step-Saver Data Systems, Inc. v. Wyse Technology, 939 F.2d 91 (3d Cir.1991); Vault Corp. v. Quaid Software Ltd., 847 F.2d 255, 268–70 (5th Cir.1988); Arizona Retail Systems, Inc. v. Software Link, Inc., 831 F.Supp. 759 (D.Ariz.1993). As their titles suggest, these are not consumer transactions. Step-Saver is a battle-of-the-forms case, in which the parties exchange incompatible forms and a court must decide which prevails. See Northrop Corp. v. Litronic Industries, 29 F.3d 1173 (7th Cir.1994) (Illinois law); Douglas G. Baird & Robert Weisberg, *Rules, Standards, and the Battle of the Forms: A Reassessment of § 2–207*, 68 Va. L. Rev. 1217, 1227–31 (1982). Our case has only one form; UCC § 2–207 is irrelevant. Vault holds that Louisiana's special shrinkwrap-license statute is preempted by federal law, a question to which we return. And Arizona Retail Systems did not reach the question, because the court found that the buyer knew the terms of the license before purchasing the software.

What then does the current version of the UCC have to say? We think that the place to start is § 2–204(1): "A contract for sale of goods may be made in any manner sufficient to show agreement, including conduct by both parties which recognizes the existence of such a contract." A vendor, as master of the offer, may invite acceptance by conduct, and may propose limitations on the kind of conduct that constitutes acceptance. A buyer may accept by performing the acts the vendor proposes to treat as acceptance. And that is what happened. ProCD proposed a contract that a buyer would accept by using the software after having an opportunity to read the license at leisure. This Zeidenberg did. He had no choice, because the software splashed the license on the screen and would not let him proceed without indicating acceptance. So although the district judge was right to say that a contract can be, and often is, formed simply by paying the price and walking out of the store, the UCC permits contracts to be formed in other ways. ProCD proposed such a different way, and without protest Zeidenberg agreed. Ours is not a case in which a consumer opens a package to find an insert saying "you owe us an extra $10,000" and the seller files suit to collect. Any buyer finding such a demand can prevent formation of the contract by returning the package, as can any consumer who concludes that the terms of the license make the software worth less than the purchase price. Nothing in the UCC requires a seller to maximize the buyer's net gains.

Section 2–606, which defines "acceptance of goods", reinforces this understanding. A buyer accepts goods under § 2–606(1)(b) when, after an opportunity to inspect, he fails to make an effective rejection under § 2–602(1). ProCD extended an opportunity to reject if a buyer should find the license terms unsatisfactory; Zeidenberg inspected the package, tried out the software, learned of the license, and did not reject the goods. We refer to § 2–606 only to show that the opportunity to return goods can be important; acceptance of an offer differs from acceptance of goods after delivery, see Gillen v. Atalanta Systems, Inc., 997 F.2d 280, 284 n. 1 (7th Cir.1993); but the UCC consistently permits the parties to structure their relations so that the buyer has a chance to make a final decision after a detailed review.

Reversed and Remanded.

NOTES

(1) *Case Comparisons.* The court's decision in *ProCD* distinguishes *Step-Saver*, noting that the transaction in that case involved *two* forms, thereby properly triggering a "battle of the forms" analysis. *Does* UCC § 2–207 require two forms? (Review the court's analysis of a possible reading of the facts in *Dorton*, p. 264.) In what ways, if any, is a box-top license different from shrinkwrap terms?

The *ProCD* opinion also noted that unlike *ProCD*, *Step-Saver* was not a consumer transaction. Should the rules of contract formation differ depending on whether the transaction is commercial or consumer in nature? How does UCC § 2–207(2) account for this difference? Assuming that buyer Zeidenberg was not a merchant, what result in *ProCD* if the court had applied UCC § 2–207(2)?

(2) *Case Archeology.* Zeidenberg, a graduate student in computer science at the University of Wisconsin at the time he bought the Select Phone program, consulted with law professor John Kidwell about his proposed use of the program in light of existing copyright law. Professor Kidwell told Zeidenberg that "You're probably legally in the clear, but you'll definitely be sued." For an interview with Zeidenberg, see William Whitford, *Freedom from Contract Symposium: Appendix*, 2004 Wis. L. Rev. 821.

Hill v. Gateway 2000, Inc.

United States Court of Appeals, Seventh Circuit, 1997.
105 F.3d 1147.

■ EASTERBROOK, CIRCUIT JUDGE. A customer picks up the phone, orders a computer, and gives a credit card number. Presently a box arrives, containing the computer and a list of terms, said to govern unless the customer returns the computer within 30 days. Are these terms effective as the parties' contract, or is the contract term-free because the order-taker did not read any terms over the phone and elicit the customer's assent?

One of the terms in the box containing a Gateway 2000 system was an arbitration clause. Rich and Enza Hill, the customers, kept the computer more than 30 days before complaining about its components and performance. They filed suit in federal court arguing, among other things, that the product's shortcomings make Gateway a racketeer (mail and wire fraud are said to be the predicate offenses), leading to treble damages under RICO for the Hills and a class of all other purchasers. Gateway asked the district court to enforce the arbitration clause; the judge refused, writing that "[t]he present record is insufficient to support a finding of a valid arbitration agreement between the parties or that the plaintiffs were given adequate notice of the arbitration clause." Gateway took an immediate appeal, as is its right. 9 U.S.C. § 16(a)(1)(A).

ProCD, Inc. v. Zeidenberg, 86 F.3d 1447 (7th Cir.1996), holds that terms inside a box of software bind consumers who use the software after an opportunity to read the terms and to reject them by returning the product. Likewise, Carnival Cruise Lines, Inc. v. Shute, 499 U.S. 585, enforces a forum-selection clause that was included among three pages of terms attached to a cruise ship ticket. *ProCD* and *Carnival Cruise Lines* exemplify the many commercial transactions in which people pay for products with terms to follow; *ProCD* discusses others. 86 F.3d at 1451–52. The district court concluded in *ProCD* that the contract is formed when the consumer pays for the software; as a result, the court held, only terms known to the consumer at that moment are part of the contract, and provisos inside the box do not count. Although this is one way a contract could be formed, it is not the only way: "A vendor, as master of the offer, may invite acceptance by conduct, and may propose limitations on the kind of conduct that constitutes acceptance. A buyer may accept by performing the acts the vendor proposes to treat as acceptance." *Id.* at 1452. Gateway shipped computers with the same sort of accept-or-return offer *ProCD* made to users of its software. *ProCD* relied on the Uniform Commercial Code rather than any peculiarities of Wisconsin law; both Illinois and South Dakota, the two states whose law might govern relations between Gateway and the Hills, have adopted the UCC; neither side has pointed us to any atypical doctrines in those states that might be pertinent; *ProCD* therefore applies to this dispute.

Plaintiffs ask us to limit *ProCD* to software, but where's the sense in that? *ProCD* is about the law of contract, not the law of software. Payment preceding the revelation of full terms is common for air transportation, insurance, and many other endeavors. Practical considerations support allowing vendors to enclose the full legal terms with their products. Cashiers cannot be expected to read legal documents to customers before ringing up sales. If the staff at the other end of the phone for direct-sales operations such as Gateway's had to read the four-page statement of terms before taking the buyer's credit card number, the droning voice would anesthetize rather than enlighten many potential buyers. Others would hang up in a rage over the waste of their time. And oral recitation would not avoid customers' assertions (whether true or feigned) that the clerk did not read term X to them, or that they did not remember or understand it. Writing provides benefits for both sides of commercial transactions. Customers as a group are better off when vendors skip costly and ineffectual steps such as telephonic recitation, and use instead a simple approve-or-return device. Competent adults are bound by such documents, read or unread. For what little it is worth, we add that the box from Gateway was crammed with software. The computer came with an operating system, without which it was useful only as a boat anchor. See Digital Equipment Corp. v. Uniq Digital Technologies, Inc., 73 F.3d 756, 761 (7th Cir.1996). Gateway also included many application programs. So the Hills' effort to limit *ProCD* to software would not avail them factually, even if it were sound legally—which it is not.

For their second sally, the Hills contend that ProCD should be limited to executory contracts (to licenses in particular), and therefore does not apply because both parties' performance of this contract was complete when the box arrived at their home. This is legally and factually wrong: legally because the question at hand concerns the *formation* of the contract rather than its *performance*, and factually because both contracts were incompletely performed. *ProCD* did not depend on the fact that the seller characterized the transaction as a license rather than as a contract; we treated it as a contract for the sale of goods and reserved the question whether for other purposes a "license" characterization might be preferable. 86 F.3d at 1450. All debates about characterization to one side, the transaction in *ProCD* was no more executory than the one here: Zeidenberg paid for the software and walked out of the store with a box under his arm, so if arrival of the box with the product ends the time for revelation of contractual terms, then the time ended in *ProCD* before Zeidenberg opened the box. But of course ProCD had not completed performance with delivery of the box, and neither had Gateway. One element of the transaction was the warranty, which obliges sellers to fix defects in their products. The Hills have invoked Gateway's warranty and are not satisfied with its response, so they are not well positioned to say that Gateway's obligations were fulfilled when the motor carrier unloaded the box. What is more, both ProCD and Gateway promised to help customers to use their products. Long-term service and information obligations are common in the computer business, on both hardware and software sides. Gateway offers "lifetime service" and has a round-the-clock telephone hotline to fulfill this promise. Some vendors spend more money helping customers use their products than on developing and manufacturing them. The document in Gateway's box includes promises of future performance that some consumers value highly; these promises bind Gateway just as the arbitration clause binds the Hills.

Next the Hills insist that *ProCD* is irrelevant because Zeidenberg was a "merchant" and they are not. Section 2–207(2) of the UCC, the infamous battle-of-the-forms section, states that "additional terms [following acceptance of an offer] are to be construed as proposals for addition to a contract. Between merchants such terms become part of the contract unless . . . ". Plaintiffs tell us that *ProCD* came out as it did only because Zeidenberg was a "merchant" and the terms inside ProCD's box were not excluded by the "unless" clause. This argument pays scant attention to the opinion in *ProCD,* which concluded that, when there is only one form, "sec. 2–207 is irrelevant." 86 F.3d at 1452. The question in *ProCD* was not whether terms were added to a contract after its formation, but how and when the contract was formed-in particular, whether a vendor may propose that a contract of sale be formed, not in the store (or over the phone) with the payment of money or a general "send me the product," but after the customer has had a chance to inspect both the item and the terms. *ProCD* answers "yes," for merchants and consumers alike. Yet again, for what little it is worth we observe that the Hills misunderstand the setting of *ProCD*. A "merchant" under the UCC "means a person who deals in goods of the kind or otherwise by his occupation holds himself out as having knowledge or skill peculiar to the practices or goods involved in the transaction", § 2–104(1), Zeidenberg bought the product at a retail store, an uncommon place for merchants to acquire inventory. His corporation put ProCD's database on the Internet for anyone to browse, which led to the litigation but did not make Zeidenberg a software merchant.

At oral argument the Hills propounded still another distinction: the box containing ProCD's software displayed a notice that additional terms were within, while the box containing Gateway's computer did not. The difference is functional, not legal. Consumers browsing the aisles of a store can look at the box, and if they are unwilling to deal with the prospect of additional terms can leave the box alone, avoiding the transactions costs of returning the package after reviewing its contents. Gateway's box, by contrast, is just a shipping carton; it is not on display anywhere. Its function is to protect the product during transit, and the information on its sides is for the use of handlers rather than would-be purchasers.

"Fragile!" "This Side Up!" ✳ ⏽↑↑

Perhaps the Hills would have had a better argument if they were first alerted to the bundling of hardware and legal-ware after opening the box and wanted to return the computer in order to avoid disagreeable terms, but were dissuaded by the expense of shipping. What the remedy would be in such a case—could it exceed the shipping charges?—is an interesting question, but one that need not detain us because the Hills knew before they ordered the computer that the carton would include *some* important terms, and they did not seek to discover these in advance. Gateway's ads state that their products come with limited warranties and lifetime support. How limited was the warranty—30 days, with service contingent on shipping the computer back, or five years, with free onsite service? What sort of support was offered? Shoppers have three principal ways to discover these things. First, they can ask the vendor to send a copy before deciding whether to buy. The Magnuson-Moss Warranty Act requires firms to distribute their warranty terms on request, 15 U.S.C. § 2302(b)(1)(A); the Hills do not contend that Gateway would have refused to enclose the remaining terms too. Concealment would be bad for business, scaring some customers away and leading to excess returns from others. Second, shoppers can consult public sources (computer magazines, the Web sites of vendors) that may contain this information. Third, they may inspect the documents after the product's delivery. Like Zeidenberg, the Hills took the third option. By keeping the computer beyond 30 days, the Hills accepted Gateway's offer, including the arbitration clause.

NOTES

(1) *Rolling Contract Formation.* The analysis in *Hill* is sometimes described as recognizing a doctrine of "rolling contract formation." This approach was followed in Brower v. Gateway 2000, 676 N.Y.S.2d 569, 572 (App.Div.1998). "There is no agreement or contract upon the placement of the order or even upon the receipt of the goods. . . . It is only after the consumer has affirmatively retained the merchandise for more than 30 days—within which the consumer has presumably examined and even used the product(s) and read the agreement—that the contract has been effectuated." Id. at 572. In *Brower*, because thirty days had passed, the court found that a contract had been formed on the terms inside the box; however, it declined to enforce the terms on the grounds of unconscionability. The case is discussed further on p. 671 below.

(2) *Rolling Too Far?* In *Hill,* Judge Easterbrook concluded that the contract was created only when the Hills accepted Gateway's offer by keeping the computer beyond 30 days. Suppose that after the Hills had agreed to buy the computer at a particular price and Gateway had charged their credit card, but before delivery of the computer, Gateway refused to sell the computer except at a price higher than that agreed upon. Does Judge Easterbrook mean to say that such refusal would not constitute a breach of contract by Gateway? If so, does that result square with the policy of UCC § 2–207 favoring contract formation?

Revising Article Two

In ProCD on p. 288 above, Judge Easterbrook asked what "the current version" of the UCC had to say about the facts of the case. The phrase anticipated a revision of Article 2 which had been undertaken by the ALI and ULC in the 1990s. Drafters sought to clean up problems and restore uniformity to a code which, over 40 years of use and interpretation, had developed its own body of case law. Yet while a revised text was promulgated in 2003, there was substantial opposition to some of its provisions and no state enacted it. The ALI and ULC withdrew the new text from consideration in 2011. For accounts of the controversies surrounding the revision, see generally, Symposium, *Perspectives on the Uniform Laws Revision Process*, 52 Hastings L.J. 603 (2001).

As for whether a revision of the UCC that is meritorious but seems unlikely to achieve uniform enactment throughout the United States should be promulgated, see Neil B. Cohen, *Taking Democracy Seriously*, 52 Hastings L.J. 667 (2001).

SECTION 6.   PRECONTRACTUAL LIABILITY

Up to this point we have been concerned with situations in which an offer has been made. Although the law governing contract formation is usually analyzed in terms of the classic rules of offer and acceptance, most major contractual commitments are the product of lengthy negotiations in which it is often difficult later to identify particular messages of offer and acceptance. If the negotiations succeed, a contract will result. But what if the negotiations fail? May a disappointed party have a claim against the other? If so, on what theory of recovery? And what measure of recovery is appropriate under circumstances? And what measure of recovery is appropriate under such circumstances? If no contract has been entered into, does it make sense to talk in terms of expectation damages?

One possibility is a claim in restitution. If during the course of negotiations one party has conferred a benefit on the other, the recipient may be required to restore the benefit, or its value. To take a clear case, a prospective buyer of land who had made a down payment during negotiations that fail to result in a contract is entitled to repayment.

Claimants seeking recovery for services performed during negotiations have rarely succeeded, however. Songbird Jet Ltd. v. Amax, Inc., 581 F.Supp. 912, 926–27 (S.D.N.Y.1984), illustrates the obstacles faced by such claimants. Amax, the owner of a corporate jet then under construction by Falcon Jet, negotiated with Songbird which sought to purchase the jet as a broker for resale to a third party. When the negotiations fell through, Songbird claimed compensation from Amax for its services. The court denied recovery for Songbird's locating and contracting with French, a Texas oil man, as ultimate buyer: if there was any enrichment of Amax at all, it was not "unjust" because such activities "are regularly engaged in by parties endeavoring to reach a mutual accommodation" and are "the common grist of negotiations." Id. at 926. The court also denied recovery for Songbird's suggestion of the idea of an advantageous "tax benefits transaction": this "idea was neither novel nor original" but was instead "a publicized tax saving device known not only to Amax but to the jet industry at large." Id. The court conceded that Songbird's claim for monitoring services to expedite Falcon Jet's delivery so that the "tax benefit transaction" would not be lost "stands on a somewhat different footing." Id. at 927. Nevertheless, in view of Songbird's contract for resale to French, these "services were entirely voluntary and were designed to and had the effect of protecting [its] own interests, . . . even if they incidentally benefited Amax." Id.

The claimant managed to overcome such obstacles in Precision Testing Laboratories, Ltd. v. Kenyon Corp., 644 F.Supp. 1327, 1350–51 (S.D.N.Y.1986). While Ellis and Kenyon were negotiating a contract to develop emission systems for imported automobiles, Ellis provided substantial labor and technical work in bringing Kenyon's test car to certification level. When the negotiations fell through, Ellis sued Kenyon claiming unjust enrichment. The court held for Ellis, distinguishing *Songbird* on the ground that there Songbird's "services were designed to promote [its] own interests," whereas here "Ellis' services were designed to benefit" Kenyon, and the issuance of a certificate of conformity by the Environmental Protection Administration was clearly such a benefit. The fact that Ellis himself gained knowledge from the experience "does not detract from the lengthy period of time he and his technicians spent working toward bringing Kenyon's car to certification level."

Even when successful, a restitution claim leaves the claimant uncompensated for reliance costs that produced no benefit to the other party. On what ground might a negotiating party recover reliance losses? Misrepresentation is a possibility: a negotiating party may not with impunity misrepresent its intention to come to terms, and liability for misrepresentation includes reliance losses. But rare are the situations in which a party has had a motive for making such a misrepresentation.

Markov v. ABC Transfer & Storage Co., 457 P.2d 535, 537–38, 539 (Wash.1969), involved such a rare situation. The lessor of a warehouse misrepresented to the lessee that it intended to renew the lease for three years, while "it was at the same time quietly negotiating for the sale of its premises." Id. at 537–38. The lessor's motive was to have the premises occupied while negotiating for their sale and to be assured that, should those negotiations fail, the lease could be renewed. When, only a few weeks before the lease expired, the purchaser of the warehouse gave the startled lessee notice to vacate the premises, the lessee claimed damages from the lessor for fraud. The Supreme Court of Washington concluded that the lessor had fraudulently promised "to renew the lease . . . and to negotiate the amount of rentals in good faith," Id. at 539, and upheld an award of damages based on the lessee's reliance losses, including not only the extra expense incurred as a result of the precipitous move to another warehouse but also profits lost when the lessee's principal customers left because no preparations had been made for that move.

The next four cases suggest more fruitful bases of recovery for pre-contractual loss than restitution or misrepresentation. The first two are what we might think of as "little guy" transactions, involving negotiations between individuals and large companies: the first an attempt to buy a franchise; the second an attempt to modify a home loan during the mortgage crisis of the late 2000s. The second two cases involve dealings between entities of relatively equal status and sophistication. In none of the cases did the parties ever agree to the terms of a contract or conclude a deal.

This raises a question that is common to each case: can there be liability when the parties have failed to reach a bargain? As you read the following cases, consider not only the different doctrinal basis of the holdings (there appear to be two) but the facts and factors in each that contribute to the decisions.

Hoffman v. Red Owl Stores

Supreme Court of Wisconsin, 1965.
26 Wis.2d 683, 133 N.W.2d 267.

[Joseph Hoffman and his wife owned and operated a bakery in Wautoma, Wisconsin. In November, 1959, he contacted Red Owl, which operated a supermarket chain, seeking to obtain a franchise for a Red Owl store in Wautoma. He mentioned that he had only $18,000 to invest and was assured that this would be sufficient. In February, 1961, on the advice of Red Owl's representative, Lukowitz, he acquired a small grocery store as a means of gaining experience. After three months, the store was operating at a profit, and Lukowitz advised him to sell it, assuring him that Red Owl would find him a larger store elsewhere. Hoffman did so in June, 1961, although he was reluctant to lose the summer tourist business. He was again assured that $18,000 would suffice to obtain a franchise. In September, on Lukowitz's advice, Hoffman put $1,000 down on a lot in Chilton selected by Red Owl. Later in September, after meeting with Hoffman to prepare a financial statement, Lukowitz told him, "[E]verything is ready to go. Get your money together and we are set." Lukowitz then told Hoffman to sell his bakery. Hoffman did that in November for $10,000, suffering a loss of $2,000. He then paid $125 a month's rent on a house in Chilton, and then spent $140 in moving his family to Neenah, at Red Owl's suggestion that he get experience by working at a Red Owl store there. When that job did not materialize, Hoffman went to work on the night shift at an Appleton bakery.

By this time, Lukowitz and Hoffman had considered a variety of arrangements under which Red Owl would get some third party to acquire the Chilton lot, build the building, and lease it to Hoffman. They had also agreed on some of the terms of a 10-year lease, with an option for Hoffman to renew the lease or purchase the property. Late in November they met with Red Owl's credit manager and drew up a proposed financing statement showing Hoffman contributing $24,100. $4,600 was an actual cash contribution, and another $7,500 was to be borrowed from his father-in-law. A week or two later, Lukowitz said that according to the home office, if Hoffman could get another $2,000 for promotion, the deal could go through for $26,000. Hoffman got his father-in-law to agree to put up $13,000 if he could come in as a partner. The home office, however, insisted that the father-in-law sign an agreement that the $13,000 was either a gift or a loan subordinate to all general creditors. Early in February, 1962, the negotiations collapsed when Hoffman refused to accede to a proposed financial statement that showed his contribution as $34,000, including $13,000 from his father-in-law as an outright gift. The Hoffmans sued Red Owl and the jury gave a special verdict, assessing damages as $16,735 for the sale of the Wautoma store, $2,000 for the sale of the bakery, $1,000 for taking up the option on the Chilton lot, $140 for moving expenses to Neenah, and $125 for house rental in Chilton. The trial court confirmed the verdict, except for the figure of $16,735 for the sale of the Wautoma store, as to which it ordered a new trial. Red Owl appealed. The Hoffmans also appealed from the order of a new trial.]

■ CURRIE, CHIEF JUSTICE. The record here discloses a number of promises and assurances given to Hoffman by Lukowitz in behalf of Red Owl upon which plaintiffs relied and acted upon to their detriment. There remains for consideration the question of law raised by defendants that agreement was never reached on essential factors necessary to establish a contract between Hoffman and Red Owl. Among these were the size, cost, design, and layout of the store building; and the terms of the lease with respect to rent, maintenance, renewal, and purchase options. This poses the question of whether the promise necessary to sustain a cause of action for promissory estoppel must embrace all essential details of a proposed transaction between promisor and promisee so as to be the equivalent of an offer that would result in a binding contract between the parties if the promisee were to accept the same.

Originally the doctrine of promissory estoppel was invoked as a substitute for consideration rendering a gratuitous promise enforceable as a contract. See Williston, Contracts (1st ed.), p. 307, sec. 139. In other words, the acts of reliance by the promisee to his detriment provided a substitute for consideration. If promissory estoppel were to be limited to only those situations where the promise giving rise to the cause of action must be so definite with respect to all details that a contract would result were the promise supported by consideration, then the defendants' instant promises to Hoffman would not meet this test. However, sec. 90 of Restatement, 1 Contracts, does not impose the requirement that the promise giving rise to the cause of action must be so comprehensive in scope as to meet the requirements of an offer that would ripen into a contract if accepted by the promisee. Rather the conditions imposed are:

(1) Was the promise one which the promisor should reasonably expect to induce action or forbearance of a definite and substantial character on the part of the promisee?

(2) Did the promise induce such action or forbearance?

(3) Can injustice be avoided only by enforcement of the promise?[1]

We deem it would be a mistake to regard an action grounded on promissory estoppel as the equivalent of a breach of contract action. As Dean Boyer points out, it is desirable that fluidity in the application of the concept be maintained. 98 University of Pennsylvania Law Review (1950), 459, at page 497. While the first two of the above listed three requirements of promissory estoppel present issues of fact which ordinarily will be resolved by a jury, the third requirement, that the

---

[1] See Boyer, 98 University of Pennsylvania Law Review (1950), 459, 460. "Enforcement" of the promise embraces an award of damages for breach as well as decreeing specific performance.

remedy can only be invoked where necessary to avoid injustice, is one that involves a policy decision by the court. Such a policy decision necessarily embraces an element of discretion.

We conclude that injustice would result here if plaintiffs were not granted some relief because of the failure of defendants to keep their promises which induced plaintiffs to act to their detriment.

[With regard to damages, the court concluded that all those awarded to Hoffman by the trial court had been properly awarded. As noted above, that court had not awarded him the $16,735 claimed for the sale of the Wautoma store.]

We turn now to the damage item with respect to which the trial court granted a new trial, *i.e.*, that arising from the sale of the Wautoma grocery-store fixtures and inventory. The trial court ruled that [recovery on that account] would be limited to the difference between the sales price received and the fair market value of the assets sold, giving consideration to any goodwill attaching thereto by reason of the transfer of a going business. There was no direct evidence presented as to what this fair market value was on June 6, 1961. The evidence did disclose that Hoffman paid $9,000 for the inventory, added $1,500 to it and sold it for $10,000 or a loss of $500. His 1961 federal income tax return showed that the grocery equipment had been purchased for $7,000 and sold for $7,955.96. Plaintiffs introduced evidence of the buyer that during the first eleven weeks of operation of the grocery store his gross sales were $44,000 and his profit was $6,000 or roughly 15 percent. On cross-examination he admitted that this was gross and not net profit. Plaintiffs contend that in a breach of contract action damages may include loss of profits. However, this is not a breach of contract action.

The only relevancy of evidence relating to profits would be with respect to proving the element of goodwill in establishing the fair market value of the grocery inventory and fixtures sold. Therefore, evidence of profits would be admissible to afford a foundation for expert opinion as to fair market value.

Where damages are awarded in promissory estoppel instead of specifically enforcing the promisor's promise, they should be only such as in the opinion of the court are necessary to prevent injustice. Mechanical or rule of thumb approaches to the damage problem should be avoided.

At the time Hoffman bought the equipment and inventory of the small grocery store at Wautoma he did so in order to gain experience in the grocery store business. At that time discussion had already been had with Red Owl representatives that Wautoma might be too small for a Red Owl operation and that a larger city might be more desirable. Thus Hoffman made this purchase more or less as a temporary experiment. Justice does not require that the damages awarded him, because of selling these assets at the behest of defendants, should exceed any actual loss sustained measured by the difference between the sales price and the fair market value.

Since the evidence does not sustain the large award of damages arising from the sale of the Wautoma grocery business, the trial court properly ordered a new trial on this issue.

Order affirmed.

NOTES

(1) *Questions*. What does the court award Hoffman in damages and on what basis? Do you agree with the outcome, and on what grounds? Was Lukowitz just running Hoffman around? But for what purpose? Should Hoffman have shown more backbone? See William Whitford and Stewart Macaulay, Hoffman v. Red Owl: *The Rest of the Story*, 61 Hastings L.J. 801 (2009–2010).

Although Red Owl has been of great interest to legal scholars, the holding is not uniformly followed. In Green Industries, Inc. v. Biller, 608 F.2d 274, 280–81 (7th Cir.1979), Green and a subsidiary sought to recover their expenses in reliance on a promise to sell them stock. The expenses were, predominately, substantial attorneys' fees incurred for drafting the sales transaction. In upholding summary judgment for the sellers, the court distinguished *Red Owl*. The alleged stock-sale agreement was "not a reasonable basis for reliance" because it "was subject to numerous conditions, some of which were under the control of third parties." Id. Even if the sellers had kept the alleged promises "the sale may very well have failed on the basis of the many contingencies." Id. at 281. See Robert Scott, Hoffman v. Red Owl Stores *and the Myth of Precontractual Reliance*, 68 Ohio St. L.J. 71 (2007).

(2) *Franchise Agreements*. Starting perhaps with fast food, most of us are familiar with franchises from a consumer's point of view. But consider the following, more structural description of a franchise agreement:

> The franchise system is a method of selling products and services identified by a particular trade name which may be associated with a patent, a trade secret, a particular product design or management expertise. The franchisee usually purchases some products from the franchisor and makes royalty payments on the basis of units sold, in exchange for the right to offer products for sale under the trademark. The franchise agreement establishes the relationship between the parties and usually regulates the quality of the product, sales territory, the advertising and other details; and it usually requires that certain supplies be purchased from the franchisor.

Kosters v. Seven-Up Co., 595 F.2d 347 (6th Cir.1979). The nature of franchise agreement prompts consideration of the relative status and sophistication of two parties; this is discussed further in Chapter 6 in connection with termination clauses.

(3) *At-Will Employment.* John Grouse, a pharmacist in Minneapolis, applied for and was offered a position with Group Health Plan in the same city. Grouse then told Cyrus Elliott, Group Health's chief pharmacist, that he had to give his current employer two weeks' notice, which he did. The same day, Grouse received an offer from a Veterans' Administration hospital in Virginia, but rejected it because of Group Health's offer. Sometime in the next few days, Elliott was told by Donald Shoberg, Group Health's general manager, that the company required a favorable written reference, a background check, and Shoberg's approval before hiring Grouse. When references were not forthcoming, Shoberg then hired someone else. Grouse had difficulty regaining full time employment and sued for damages. The trial judge dismissed his complaint, and Grouse appealed. *Held:* Reversed and remanded for a trial on the issue of damages.

> The parties focus their arguments on whether an employment contract which is terminable at will can give rise to an action for damages if anticipatorily repudiated. Group Health contends that recognition of a cause of action on these facts would result in the anomalous rule that an employee who is told not to report to work the day before he is scheduled to begin has a remedy while an employee who is discharged after the first day does not. We cannot agree since under appropriate circumstances we believe section 90 would apply even after employment has begun. Relief may be limited to damages measured by the promisee's reliance. [T]he appellant had a right to assume he would be given a good faith opportunity to perform his duties to the satisfaction of respondent once he was on the job. He was not only denied that opportunity but resigned the position he already held in reliance on the firm offer which respondent tendered him.

Grouse v. Group Health Plan, Inc., 306 N.W.2d 114, 116 (Minn.1981). The court's reference to a "firm offer" should be understood to mean "definite offer," and not a "firm offer" under UCC § 2–205. Why is this? How should Grouse's damages be calculated on a new trial?

(4) *Rough Justice and Public Policy.* Kajima, a general contractor, submitted a bid of some $69 million to the Los Angeles Metropolitan Transportation Authority (MTA) for the construction of a station and tunnel. Despite a California statute requiring the contracts be awarded to the "lowest responsible bidder," the MTA accepted a bid of nearly $1 million more from another firm, under a misapplication of a California statute requiring the use of Disadvantaged Business Enterprises. Kajima itself could have qualified as a Disadvantaged Business Enterprise. Kajima sued the MTA for bid preparation costs of some $45,000 and lost profits on the MTA contract. From a decision for the MTA, Kajima appealed. *Held:* Reversed as to bid preparation costs. Wilson v. Los Angeles County Metropolitan Transportation Authority, 1 P.3d 63, 69 (Cal.2000). The court said:

> [W]hen a public entity solicits bids, it represents, consistent with the statutory mandate, that if the contract is awarded, it well be awarded to the lowest responsible bidder. [If] the contract is awarded to a higher bidder, the elements of a promissory estoppel

cause of action appear to be established. It is important to note, however, that [promissory estoppel] fits these circumstances imperfectly. Promissory estoppel was developed to do rough justice when a party lacking contractual protection relied on another's promise to its detriment. Here, we use promissory estoppel primarily to further certain public policies by creating a damages remedy for a public entity's statutory violation.

Id. at 68–69. The court added however, that the remedy should be limited to what "justice requires." "Allowing recovery of lost profits 'could drain the public fisc in response to mere carelessness on the part of low level government officials.'" Id. at 70. Why is the fit with reliance imperfect? On what basis did the court grant relief?

Dixon v. Wells Fargo, N.A.

United States District Court, D. Massachusetts, 2011.
798 F.Supp.2d 336.

■ YOUNG, DISTRICT JUDGE.

I.   INTRODUCTION

Frank and Deana Dixon (collectively "the Dixons") bring this cause of action against Wells Fargo Bank, N.A. ("Wells Fargo"), seeking (1) an injunction prohibiting Wells Fargo from foreclosing on their home; (2) specific performance of an oral agreement to enter into a loan modification; and (3) damages.

B.   Facts Alleged

The Dixons reside at their home in Scituate, Plymouth County, Massachusetts. Wells Fargo is a corporation doing business in the Commonwealth of Massachusetts. Wells Fargo alleges that it is the holder of a mortgage on the Dixons' home.

On or about June 8, 2009, the Dixons orally agreed with Wells Fargo to take the steps necessary to enter into a mortgage loan modification. As part of this agreement, Wells Fargo instructed the Dixons to stop making payments on their loan. It was contemplated that the unpaid payments would be added to the note as modified. In addition, Wells Fargo requested certain financial information, which the Dixons promptly supplied.

Notwithstanding the Dixons' diligent efforts and reliance on Wells Fargo's promise, Wells Fargo has failed, and effectively refused, to abide by the oral agreement to modify the existing mortgage loan.

On or about December 8, 2010, the Dixons received notice from the Massachusetts Land Court that Wells Fargo was proceeding with a foreclosure on their home. The return date on the order of notice in the Land Court was January 10, 2011, and so the Dixons sought a temporary restraining order in the Superior Court to prevent the loss of their home.

The Dixons state that, on information and belief, the fair market value of their home is in excess of the mortgage loan balance and any arrearage.

II. ANALYSIS

B.   Promissory Estoppel

The gravamen of the Dixons' complaint is that Wells Fargo promised to engage in negotiations to modify their loan, provided that they took certain "steps necessary to enter into a mortgage modification." On the basis of Wells Fargo's representation, the Dixons stopped making payments on their loan and submitted the requested financial information—only to learn subsequently that the bank had initiated foreclosure proceedings against them. They contend that Wells Fargo ought to have anticipated their compliance with the terms of its promise to consider them for a loan modification. Not only was it reasonable that they would rely on the promise, but also their reliance left them considerably worse off, for by entering into default they became vulnerable to foreclosure.

The question whether these allegations are sufficient to state a claim for promissory estoppel requires a close look at the doctrine's evolution in the law of Massachusetts. In Loranger Const. Corp. v. E.F. Hauserman Co., 376 Mass. 757 (1978), the Supreme Judicial Court recognized the enforceability of a promise on the basis of detrimental reliance, but declined to "use the expression 'promissory estoppel,' since it tends to confusion rather than clarity." Id. at 760–61, 384 N.E.2d 176. The court reasoned that "[w]hen a promise is enforceable in whole or in part by virtue of reliance, it is a 'contract,' and it is enforceable pursuant to a 'traditional contract theory' antedating the modern doctrine of consideration." Id. at 761, 384 N.E.2d 176. Since Loranger, the court has adhered to its view that "an action based on reliance is equivalent to a contract action, and the party bringing such an action must prove all the necessary elements of a contract other than consideration." Rhode Island Hosp. Trust Nat'l Bank v. Varadian, 419 Mass. 841, 850 (1995).

"An essential element in the pleading and proof of a contract claim is, of course, the 'promise' sought to be enforced." Kiely v. Raytheon Co., 914 F.Supp. 708, 712 (D.Mass.1996) (O'Toole, J.). Thus, even where detrimental reliance acts as a substitute for consideration, the promise on which a claim for promissory estoppel is based must be interchangeable with an offer "in the sense of 'commitment.'" The promise must demonstrate "an intention to act or refrain from acting in a specified way, so as to justify a promisee in understanding that a commitment has been made." Varadian, 419 Mass. at 849–50, 647 N.E.2d 1174 (quoting Restatement (Second) of Contracts § 2 (1981)).

In addition to demonstrating a firm commitment, the putative promise, like any offer, must be sufficiently "definite and certain in its terms" to be enforceable. "[I]f an essential element is reserved for the future agreement of both parties, as a general rule, the promise can give rise to no legal obligation until such future agreement." 1 Richard A. Lord, Williston on Contracts § 4:29 (4th ed. 1990); see Lucey v. Hero Int'l Corp., 361 Mass. 569, 574–75, 281 N.E.2d 266 (1972).

The longstanding reluctance of courts to enforce open-ended "agreements to agree" reflects a belief that, unless a "fall-back standard" exists to supply the missing terms, there is no way to know what ultimate agreement, if any, would have resulted.

Moreover, parties ought to be allowed to step away unscathed if they are unable to reach a deal. Cf. R.W. Int'l Corp. v. Welch Food, Inc., 13 F.3d 478, 484–85 (1st Cir.1994). To impose rights and duties at "the stage of 'imperfect negotiation,' " Lafayette Place Assocs., 427 Mass. at 517, 694 N.E.2d 820, would be to interfere with the liberty to contract—or not to contract.

Wells Fargo would have this Court end its inquiry here. The complaint plainly alleges that the parties had an "agreement to enter into a loan modification agreement," but as matter of law "[a]n agreement to reach an agreement is a contradiction in terms and imposes no obligations on the parties thereto." Rosenfield, 290 Mass. at 217, 195 N.E. 323. As such, the complaint would appear to fail to state a claim.

During the course of opposing Wells Fargo's motion to dismiss, however, the Dixons have made clear that they do not seek specific performance of a promised loan modification. They admit that there was no guarantee of a modification by Wells Fargo, only a verbal commitment to determine their eligibility for a modification if they followed the bank's prescribed steps. Thus, the Dixons' request that Wells Fargo be held to its promise to consider them for a loan modification is not a covert attempt to bind the bank to a final agreement it had not contemplated. There is no risk that this Court, were it to uphold the promissory estoppel claim, would be "trapping" Wells Fargo into a vague, indefinite, and unintended loan modification masquerading as an agreement to agree.

Furthermore, because the parties had not yet begun to negotiate the terms of a modification, the Court questions whether Wells Fargo's promise ought to even be characterized as a preliminary agreement to agree. Instead, it more closely resembles an "agreement to negotiate." See Farnsworth, supra at 263–69;

To be sure, Massachusetts courts have tended to treat agreements to negotiate as variants of open-ended agreements to agree. The view that "[a]n agreement to negotiate does not create a binding contract," Sax, 639 F.Supp.2d at 171, again reflects a concern that a promise of further negotiations is too indefinite, too undefined in scope, to be enforceable. This is particularly true where the parties have not specified the terms on which they will continue negotiating. See Farnsworth, supra at 264. Conventional wisdom holds that courts ought not "strain[ ] to find an agreement to negotiate in the absence of a clear indication of assent" by the parties to a governing standard of conduct, e.g., "good faith" or "best efforts." Id. at 266–67, because "there is no meaningful content in a general duty to negotiate, standing alone," Steven J. Burton & Eric G. Anderson, Contractual Good Faith § 8.4.2, at 361 (1995) As with open-ended agreements to agree, judicial enforcement of vague agreements to negotiate would risk imposing on parties contractual obligations they had not taken on themselves.

In this case, Wells Fargo and the Dixons had not yet contemplated the terms of a loan modification, but they had contemplated negotiations. Their failure to elaborate on the boundaries of that duty to negotiate, however, would seem to militate against enforcement of it. Yet, Wells Fargo made a specific promise to consider the Dixons' eligibility for a loan modification if they defaulted on their payments and submitted certain financial information. See Burton & Anderson, supra § 8.2.2, at 332–33 (recognizing that, while there is no general duty to negotiate in good faith, public policy favors imposing noncontractual liability "when one person wrongfully harms another" by making a promise intended to induce reliance). . . . Importantly, it was not a promise made in exchange for a bargained—for legal detriment, as there was no bargain between the parties; rather, the legal detriment that the Dixons claim to have suffered was a direct consequence of their reliance on Wells Fargo's promise.

Admittedly, the courts of Massachusetts have yet to formally embrace promissory estoppel as more than a consideration substitute. Nonetheless, without equivocation, they have adopted section 90 of the Restatement (Second) of Contracts, which reads, "A promise which the promisor should reasonably expect to induce action or forbearance on the part of the promisee or a third person and which does induce such action or forbearance is binding if injustice can be avoided only by enforcement of the promise." Nowhere in the comments to section 90 nor in section 2 of the Restatement, which defines the word "promise," is there an explicit "requirement that the promise giving rise to the cause of action must be so comprehensive in scope as to meet the requirements of an offer that would ripen into a contract if accepted by the promisee." Hoffman v. Red Owl Stores, Inc., 26 Wis.2d 683 (1965). In fact, the Restatement "has expressly approved" promissory estoppel's use to protect reliance on indefinite promises.

Massachusetts's continued insistence that a promise be definite—at least to a degree likely not met in the present case—is arguably in tension with its adoption of the Restatement's more relaxed standard. This tension is not irreconcilable, however. Tracing the development of promissory estoppel through the case law reveals a willingness on courts' part to enforce even an indefinite promise made during preliminary negotiations where the facts suggest that the promisor's words or conduct were designed to take advantage of the promisee. The promisor need not have acted fraudulently, deceitfully, or in bad faith. McLearn v. Hill, 276 Mass. 519, 524–25 (1931). Rather, "[f]acts falling short of these elements may constitute conduct contrary to general principles of fair dealing and to the good conscience which ought to actuate individuals and which it is the design of courts to enforce." Id. at 524.

Typically, where the Massachusetts courts have applied the doctrine of promissory estoppel to enforce an otherwise unenforceable promise, "there has been a pattern of conduct by one side which has dangled the other side on a string." Pappas Indus. Parks, Inc. v. Psarros, 24 Mass.App.Ct. 596, 598, 511 N.E.2d 621 (1987) (citing Greenstein v. Flatley, 19 Mass.App.Ct. 351, 352–54, 474 N.E.2d 1130 (1985). In Greenstein, where a landlord submitted a lease to a prospective tenant and then strung him along for more than four months before repudiating the lease he had submitted, the Massachusetts Appeals Court concluded that the conduct of the landlord "was calculated to misrepresent the true situation to the [tenant], keep him on a string, and make the [tenant] conclude—reasonably—that the deal had been made and that only a bureaucratic formality remained." 19 Mass.App.Ct. at 356, 474 N.E.2d 1130. Because this conduct "was misleading, it fit[ ] comfortably 'within at least the penumbra of some common-law, statutory, or other established concept of unfairness.'" Id.; Avery Katz, *When Should an Offer Stick? The Economics of Promissory Estoppel in Preliminary Negotiations*, 105 Yale L.J. 1249, 1254 (1996) ("The doctrine of promissory estoppel is commonly explained as promoting the same purposes as the tort of misrepresentation: punishing or deterring those who mislead others to their detriment and compensating those who are misled.")

In Cohoon v. Citizens Bank, No. 002774, 2000 WL 33170737 (Mass.Super. Nov. 11, 2000) (Agnes, J.), the parties orally agreed to a discounted payoff in full satisfaction of the plaintiff's original mortgage obligation. The defendant encouraged the plaintiff to default on a mortgage payment to ensure approval of the discounted payoff. Until that time, the plaintiff had made timely payments. Once in default, however, the defendant sold the note to a buyer who promptly commenced foreclosure. The court upheld the plaintiff's claim for promissory estoppel because, "[t]aking the facts in the light most favorable to the plaintiff, it could be found that [the defendant] encouraged [the plaintiff] to delay mortgage payment and, as a result of that reliance, the eventual buyer took advantage of [the plaintiff's] vulnerable state by initiating foreclosure on [the plaintiff's] property interest." While the court indicated that, to prevail at trial, the plaintiff would need to establish that he "was misled or induced to believe that by defaulting he would achieve the discounted purchase of the note that he was seeking," he was at least entitled to "th[is] opportunity to prove facts in support of his claim of detrimental reliance."

In the present case, Wells Fargo convinced the Dixons that to be eligible for a loan modification they had to default on their payments, and it was only because they relied on this representation and stopped making their payments that Wells Fargo was able to initiate foreclosure proceedings. While there is no allegation that its promise was dishonest, Wells Fargo distinctly gained the upper hand by inducing the Dixons to open themselves up to a foreclosure action. In specifically telling the Dixons that stopping their payments and submitting financial information were the "steps necessary to enter into a mortgage modification," Wells Fargo not only should have known that the Dixons would take these steps believing their fulfillment would lead to a loan modification, but also must have intended that the Dixons do so. The bank's promise to consider them for a loan modification if they took those steps necessarily "involved as matter of fair dealing an undertaking on [its] part not to [foreclose] based upon facts coming into existence solely from" the making of its promise. Wells Fargo's decision to foreclose without warning was unseemly conduct at best. In the opinion of this Court, such conduct presents "an identifiable occasion for applying the principle of promissory estoppel." Greenstein, 19 Mass.App.Ct. at 356–57.

As the cases reveal, where, like here, the promisor opportunistically has strung along the promisee, the imposition of liability despite the preliminary stage of the negotiations produces the most equitable result. In cases of opportunism, "[the] willingness to impose a liability rule can be justified as efficient since such intervention may be the most cost-effective means of controlling opportunistic behavior, which both parties would seek to control ex ante as a means of maximizing joint gains. Because private control arrangements may be costly, the law-supplied rule may be the most effective means of controlling opportunism and maximizing joint gain." Juliet P. Kostritsky, *The Rise and Fall of Promissory Estoppel or Is Promissory Estoppel Really as Unsuccessful as Scholars Say It Is: A New Look at the Data*, 37 Wake Forest L. Rev. 531, 574 (2002); see Katz, supra at 1309 (contending that promissory estoppel can help "regulat[e] the opportunistic exercise of bargaining power" during preliminary negotiations); Schwartz & Scott, supra at 667 (remarking that protecting the party who has relied "will deter some strategic behavior").

There remains the concern that, by imposing precontractual liability for specific promises made to induce reliance during preliminary negotiations, courts will restrict parties' freedom to negotiate by reading in a duty to bargain in good faith not recognized at common law. While this concern does not fall on deaf ears, it can be effectively minimized by limiting the promisee's recovery to his or her reliance expenditures.

The Dixons have not alleged that a duty of good faith governed their negotiations with Wells Fargo over a loan modification, and thus this Court need not address the issue. The fact that the parties already were bound to the special contractual relationship of mortgagor-mortgagee, however, lends support to today's conclusion that Wells Fargo's conduct, at a minimum, was "shabby and doubtless would not be followed by conscientious mortgagees." Williams, 417 Mass. at 385.

This Court, therefore, holds that the complaint states a claim for promissory estoppel: Wells Fargo promised to engage in negotiating a loan modification if the Dixons defaulted on their payments and provided certain financial information, and they did so in reasonable reliance on that promise, only to learn that the bank had taken advantage of their default status by initiating foreclosure proceedings. Assuming they can prove these allegations by a preponderance of the evidence, their damages appropriately will be confined to the value of their expenditures in reliance on Wells Fargo's promise.

SO ORDERED.

NOTES

(1) *Reliance in the Mortgage Context.* In a footnote that extends for over a page, the court in *Dixon* cites 24 cases from 2011 in which other federal district courts nationwide *rejected* claims by defaulting homeowners that a lender's conduct before or during foreclosure satisfied the elements of promissory estoppel. Why might this be? Which (if any) of Restatement § 90 requirements do you find do you find lacking in the facts of *Dixon*?

(2) *Measure of Recovery.* If the Dixons prevail at trial, what measure of damages might they receive and in what amount? Expectation? Reliance? The court in *Dixon* observed that, assuming liability, "[a] balancing of the equities would seem to weigh in favor of limiting recovery to the detriment sustained. Returning their loan to non-default status would put them back in their previous position. By the same reasoning, they would be required to resume their mortgage payments in their original amount, with the missed payments being added into the loan balance amortized over the life of the loan. If the Dixons were unable to resume their payments, Wells Fargo could then proceed in foreclosure."

(3) *Truth and Consequences.* In 2016, Wells Fargo's long-time CEO John Stumpf retired, a month after appearing before the U.S. Senate Banking Committee and after the Company admitted to firing over several years approximately 5,300 workers, who had engaged in a series of rampant fraudulent and deceptive banking practices. Two years later, the Company apologized for foreclosing on hundreds of "homeowners after improperly denying them loan modifications that could have allowed them to stay in their homes." James R. Koren, Wells Fargo Foreclosed on 400 People Who May Have Had a Chance to Keep Their Homes, Los Angeles Times, Aug. 3, 2018.

(4) *"Some Ruminations."* In an omitted conclusion from *Dixon*, the court attempted to contextualize its holding, which it acknowledged was an anomaly, in the context of a particular economic crisis:

> Current estimates have twenty-five percent of houses 'underwater,' and some analysts predict as much as forty-eight percent of all residential properties nationwide will have a negative equity

between their mortgage balances and their property values before the housing market recovers. Robin S. Golden, *Building Policy Through Collaborative Deliberation: A Reflection on Using Lessons from Practice to Inform Responses to the Mortgage Foreclosure Crisis*, 38 Fordham Urb. L.J. 733, 734 (2011) (footnotes omitted).

This case is but a microcosm of much larger economic issues; to a significant extent, our national economy may depend upon promptly sorting out the issues raised here. Clogging the operation of the mortgage foreclosure system with court delay simply will not work. Either individual rights will be submerged, and people will lose their homes unlawfully, or home mortgage liquidity will atrophy, the larger economy will suffer, and potential home buyers will be denied homeownership, although financially able to support mortgage payments.

What do you make of the court's self-described "ruminations"?

Cyberchron Corp. v. Calldata Systems Development, Inc.

United States Court of Appeals, Second Circuit, 1995.
47 F.3d 39.

[Both parties appeal from a judgment on a claim of promissory estoppel awarding Cyberchron Corporation ("Cyberchron") $162,824.19 for direct labor and materials costs incurred in reliance upon statements and conduct of Calldata Systems Development ("Calldata"). Judge Spatt, the district court judge, denied recovery on Cyberchron's contract and quantum meruit claims.]

■ MAHONEY, CIRCUIT JUDGE:

BACKGROUND

A. The Events at Issue.

Cyberchron is engaged in the business of providing customized computer hardware for military and civilian use. Calldata is a subsidiary of Grumman Data Systems Corp. ("Grumman"). Grumman had a contract with the United States Marine Corps to provide a combat command control system for a Marine Corps defense program known as the Advanced Tactical Air Command Central ("ATACC"). The equipment at issue in this case is a "rugged computer work station," consisting of a video processor, a work station, and a color monitor (the "Equipment") that was to be provided for the ATACC program.

During the years 1989 and 1990, the parties were involved in extended negotiations as a result of which Cyberchron attempted to produce the Equipment. Although Cyberchron ultimately produced some Equipment, none was ever delivered to Calldata or Grumman, and no payment for it was ever made to Cyberchron, resulting in this lawsuit. The key problem precluding contractual agreement was the inability of the parties to agree upon the weight of the Equipment, and the penalties to be assessed against Cyberchron for the delivery of Equipment that exceeded the contractually agreed weight.

After protracted preliminary negotiations, Grumman delivered a purchase order dated May 15, 1990 to Cyberchron (including subsequent amendments, the "Purchase Order") that set forth a total weight per unit of Equipment (consisting of the three components, video processor, work station, and color monitor) of 145 pounds and specified severe penalties for exceeding that weight.

Cyberchron never agreed to the terms of the Purchase Order, but had previously commenced production of the Equipment despite the absence of any agreement regarding the matter. Grumman and Calldata encouraged Cyberchron in that course. Indeed, in a letter to Cyberchron dated June 26, 1990, Grumman "insisted" that Cyberchron continue to perform its "contractually binding obligations" under the Purchase Order.

The district court made a factual determination, in which we perceive no clear error, that in mid-July 1990 a Grumman representative directed Cyberchron to proceed with production of the Equipment as if there had been agreement on the weight issue, asserting that the terms of the purchase order would be resolved later. In addition, on or about July 30, 1990, Cyberchron submitted a progress payment request in the amount of $495,207.58, representing eighty percent of claimed costs, including overhead charges, incurred by Cyberchron through July 20, 1990. Grumman's business manager, Gerald Glinka, testified that although the purchase order was undefinitized, Grumman would have paid the full amount of this progress payment but for a court order, issued in a suit brought by Digital Equipment Corporation against Grumman and Cyberchron which was eventually dismissed, that barred any payments to Cyberchron by Grumman. The order was subsequently vacated.

Ultimately, agreement between the parties was never achieved. By letter dated September 6, 1990, Calldata directed Cyberchron to show cause within ten days why the Purchase Order should not be terminated. Cyberchron's detailed response dated September 13, 1990 was rejected by Calldata in a letter dated September 25, 1990, in which Calldata "terminated the [Purchase Order] for default effective immediately."

The district court determined, in findings that are not clearly erroneous, that Grumman had commenced negotiations with alternate suppliers of the Equipment in August 1990, and entered into a contract with Codar Technology, Inc. dated September 26, 1990 for equipment "which Grumman conceded was inferior to the Cyberchron equipment and weighed more, according to [a Grumman witness]".

B.   *The Ruling of the District Court.*

The district court found that no enforceable agreement ever existed because there was no agreement on "two of the most essential, material and substantial terms of the proposed contract, namely, the weights of the three components [of the Equipment] and the weight penalties." As a result, Cyberchron's contract claim and Calldata's contractually based counterclaim were dismissed. Cyberchron's claim of quantum meruit was also dismissed "in view of the lack of any benefit to the defendant, the failure by the plaintiff to fully perform, and the absence of any unjust enrichment by the defendant." Neither party appeals any of these dismissals.

However, the District Court found that because of the mid-July 1990 representations and promises that had been made to Cyberchron, Cyberchron was entitled to reliance damages of $162,824.10 for out-of-pocket labor and materials costs incurred after July 15, 1990 and before the termination of negotiations on September 25, 1990, under a theory of promissory estoppel.

The court denied any recovery for lost profits, or for administrative and general overhead, but allowed prejudgment interest from December 18, 1990, the date of the commencement of this litigation. The court did not address the issue of "shutdown" expenses occurring after September 25, 1990.

DISCUSSION

A. *Recovery on the TLP.*

[The court held that the termination liability provision (TLP) of the Purchase Order did not provide a ground for recovery by Cyberchron.]

B. *Promissory Estoppel.*

"In New York, promissory estoppel has three elements: 'a clear and unambiguous promise; a reasonable and foreseeable reliance by the party to whom the promise is made, and an injury sustained by the party asserting the estoppel by reason of the reliance.'" Arcadian Phosphates, Inc. v. Arcadian Corp., 884 F.2d 69, 73 (2d Cir. 1989) (quoting Esquire Radio & Elecs., Inc. v. Montgomery Ward & Co., 804 F.2d 787, 793 (2d Cir. 1986)).

As noted by Judge Spatt, an unconscionable injury is sometimes required to fulfill the third requirement. In addition, some courts will apply the doctrine only when enforcement is necessary to avoid injustice. See Werner v. Xerox Corp., 732 F.2d 580, 582–83 (7th Cir. 1984) (citing Hoffman v. Red Owl Stores, Inc., 133 N.W.2d 267 (1965)); see also Restatement (Second) of Contracts § 90 (1981). In any event, as will appear, we regard the injury inflicted upon Cyberchron as unconscionable, and believe that injustice can be avoided in this case only by invoking the doctrine of promissory estoppel on Cyberchron's behalf.

Judge Spatt expressly found that Calldata pressured Cyberchron to produce the Equipment, and "assured Cyberchron [in August 1990] that if it did the work, the negotiation problem could be resolved." 831 F.Supp. at 103. The district court also found that in mid-July 1990, Grumman's [manager of procurement, Calvin] Wilhelm directed Cyberchron's Paul "to proceed 'as if the new set of weights was approved and we would work out the definitization of the purchase order later.'" Id. at 102. Later, when Paul asked Wilhelm to put this reassurance in writing, Wilhelm refused. Id. at 114. Paul then stated that: "'If I have your assurance that we will resolve the issues in the very near future—we will proceed.'" Wilhelm responded: "'You should proceed.'" Id.

After an August 8, 1990 meeting, Robert C. Drost, Grumman's director of material, took over the Cyberchron negotiations. Id. at 103. Drost assured Paul that "'everything would be fine'" but insisted that Cyberchron had to "'keep pushing, keep performing. to maintain the schedule.'" Id. at 105. Drost testified that Cyberchron "'had the responsibility and obligation'" to "'continue performing,'" and that "'one can assume'" that Cyberchron would be paid for that continued performance. Id. The district court found that between August 8 and August 28, 1990, Paul was in constant conversation with Grumman personnel, all of whom demanded that Cyberchron continue to manufacture and deliver the Equipment "'as if the weights were approved.'" Id. at 114. We have no basis to conclude that the trial judge's evaluation of this developing scenario was clearly erroneous.

We accordingly accept the district court's determination that starting in mid-July, there was (1) a clear and unambiguous promise, (2) reasonable and foreseeable reliance thereon, and (3) an unconscionable injury, resulting in injustice that could be remedied only by invoking the doctrine of promissory estoppel. In sum, we agree with Judge Spatt's assessment that:

> Grumman's conduct exerting pressure on Cyberchron to produce the units at great expense, and then abruptly terminating the transaction to purchase heavier, inferior equipment at a later date from another company, was unconscionable. At the same time that Grumman was pressuring Cyberchron to produce, with the promise of payment, it was already negotiating with another company to do the work. 831 F. Supp. at 116.

We reject, however, Cyberchron's argument that promissory estoppel recovery should be extended to the periods prior to mid-July 1990. We are unprepared to conclude that the commitments made at that juncture should be interpreted to validate recovery of the expenses incurred by Cyberchron prior to any promise sufficient to undergird Cyberchron's claim of promissory estoppel.

C. Damages.

Based upon documentary evidence, the district court awarded Cyberchron "reliance damages" for materials purchased in the amount of $53,588.40 and labor costs incurred in the amount of $109,235.79 between July 15 and September 25, 1990, totalling $162,824.19. 831 F.

Supp. at 118. The court specifically declined to provide any award for administrative or engineering overhead on the bases that: (1) these expenses were not proved to have been specifically incurred for the Grumman/Calldata transaction; (2) Cyberchron offered proof of overhead expenses for the six months ended June 30, 1990 rather than the period July 15–September 25, 1990; and (3) the overhead expenses were not proper "reliance damages" but rather were speculative and conjectural. 831 F. Supp. at 117–18. In addition, no award was provided for "shutdown" expenses occurring after September 25, 1990.

Cyberchron does not contend for benefit-of-the-bargain damages on this appeal, but argues that it should have been awarded overhead and "shutdown" expenses. Neither party points to any controlling New York law regarding when overhead costs are recoverable. We believe that a workable rule would be to allow recovery of reasonable overhead costs when it is shown that there is a demonstrable past history of ongoing business operations, without requiring proof that a specific alternative project would have absorbed the overhead costs at issue. If such a showing can be made in this case, we see no reason for a blanket bar against the recovery of reasonable overhead expenses as long as they are normally allocated to specific projects in accordance with Cyberchron's standard cost accounting practices.

[The court also held that Cyberchron was entitled to recovery of its shutdown costs, even though they were incurred after termination of negotiations and therefore outside the July 15–September 25 time frame, to the extent that these costs were incurred due to reliance upon the Calldata promises.]

CONCLUSION

We affirm the judgment of the district court insofar as it allowed recovery to Cyberchron on a theory of promissory estoppel, but vacate the judgment and remand for a redetermination of damages in accordance with this opinion.

NOTES

(1) *Questions.* What was the scope of the promise that *was* enforceable on the ground of promissory estoppel? In order to show a breach of that promise did Cyberchron have to prove that Grumman/Calldata negotiated in bad faith?

(2) *UNIDROIT Principles.* Might an obligation to negotiate in good faith arise from the mere fact of prolonged negotiations, without such explicit language as that in *Cyberchron*? See UNIDROIT Principles art. 2.15(2), under which "a party who negotiates or breaks off negotiations in bad faith is liable for the losses caused to the other party."

An obligation to negotiate in good faith has found favor in some civil law systems, but American courts have been firm in according parties the freedom to negotiate without risk of precontractual liability imposed by law.

This "freedom from contract" is enhanced by the judicial reluctance to read a proposal as an offer in the first place. The assumption is that a party entering negotiations in the hope of the gain that will result from agreement bears the risk of whatever loss results if the other party breaks off the negotiations. See E. Allan Farnsworth, *Precontractual Liability and Preliminary Agreements: Fair Dealing and Failed Negotiations*, 87 Colum. L. Rev. 217, 239–43 (1987).

————

Express Agreements and Precontractual Liability

Up to now, we have been looking at theories of reliance and restitution, advanced when negotiations have failed. This is not to say, however, that parties willing to undertake the obligation of negotiating in good faith may not do so by express agreement. This is the subject of the following case.

Channel Home Centers, Division of Grace Retail Corp. v. Grossman

United States Court of Appeals, Third Circuit, 1986.
795 F.2d 291.

■ BECKER, CIRCUIT JUDGE. This diversity case presents the question whether, under Pennsylvania law, a property owner's promise to a prospective tenant, pursuant to a detailed letter of intent, to negotiate in good faith with the prospective tenant and to withdraw the lease premises from the marketplace during the negotiation, can bind the owner for a reasonable period of time where the prospective tenant has expended significant sums of money in connection with the lease negotiations and preparation and where there was evidence that the letter of intent was of significant value to the property owner. We hold that it may. We therefore vacate and reverse the district court's determination that there was no enforceable agreement, and remand the case for trial. [The district court had made that determination on the view that there was insufficient documentation for enforcement of the owner's letter of intent, a view that was erroneous according to the appellate court.]

Appellant Channel Home Centers ("Channel"), a division of Grace Retail Corporation, operates retail home improvement stores throughout the Northeastern United States, including Philadelphia and its suburbs. Appellee Frank Grossman, a real estate broker and developer, with his sons Bruce and Jeffrey Grossman, either owns or has a controlling interest in appellees Tri-Star Associates ("Tri-Star"), Baker Investment Corporation ("Baker"), and Cedarbrook Associates, a Pennsylvania Limited Partnership ("Cedarbrook").

Between November, 1984 and February, 1985, the Grossmans, through Baker, were in the process of acquiring ownership of Cedarbrook Mall ("the mall") located in Cheltenham Township, Pennsylvania, a northern suburb of Philadelphia. During these months, Baker was the equitable owner of the mall, Tri-Star was acting as the mall's leasing agent, and legal title was in Equitable Life Assurance Society. It was anticipated that, upon closing in February, 1985, Baker would become both legal and equitable owner of the mall. The Grossmans intended to revitalize the mall, which had fallen on hard times prior to their acquisition, through an aggressive rehabilitation and leasing program.

In the third week of November, 1984, Tri-Star wrote to Richard Perkowski, Director of Real Estate for Channel, informing him of the availability of a store location in Cedarbrook Mall which Tri-Star believed Channel would be interested in leasing. Perkowski expressed some interest, and met the Grossmans on November 28, 1984. After Perkowski was given a tour of the premises, the terms of a lease were discussed. Frank Grossman testified that "we discussed various terms, and these terms were, some were loose, some were more or less terms." App. at 364a, 496a–497a.

In a memorandum dated December 7, 1984, to S. Charles Tabak, Channel's senior vice-president for general administration, Perkowski outlined the salient lease terms that he had negotiated with the Grossmans. On or about the same date, Tabak and Leon Burger, President of Channel, visited the mall site with the Grossmans. They indicated that Channel desired to lease the site. Frank Grossman then requested that Channel execute a letter of intent that, as Grossman put it, could be shown to "other people, banks or whatever." Tabak testified that the Grossmans wanted to get Channel into the site because it would give the mall four "anchor" stores. Apparently, Frank Grossman was anxious to get Channel's signature on a letter of intent so that it could be used to help Grossman secure financing for his purchase of the mall.

On December 11, 1984, in response to Grossman's request, Channel prepared, executed, and submitted a detailed letter of intent setting forth a plethora of lease terms which provided, *inter alia,* that

> [t]o induce the Tenant [Channel] to proceed with the leasing of the Store, you [Grossman] will withdraw the Store from the rental market, and only negotiate the above described leasing transaction to completion.
>
> Please acknowledge your intent to proceed with the leasing of the store under the above terms, conditions and understanding by signing the enclosed copy of the letter and returning it to the undersigned within ten (10) days from the date hereof.

App. at 31a.

Frank Grossman promptly signed the letter of intent and returned it to Channel. Grossman contends that Perkowski and Tabak also agreed orally that a draft lease be submitted within thirty (30) days. Perkowski and Tabak denied telling Grossman that a lease would be forthcoming within 30 days or any finite period of time.

Thereafter, both parties initiated procedures directed toward satisfaction of lease contingencies. The letter of intent specified that execution of the lease was expressly subject to each of the following: (1) approval by Channel's parent corporation, W.R. Grace & Company ("Grace"), of the essential business terms of the lease; (2) approval by Channel of the status of title for the site; and (3) Channel's obtaining, with Frank Grossman's cooperation, all necessary permits and zoning variances for the erection of Channel's identification signs.

On December 14, 1984, Channel directed the Grace legal department to prepare a lease for the premises. Channel's real estate committee approved the lease site on December 20, 1984. Channel planning representatives visited the premises on December 21, 1984, to obtain measurements for architectural alterations, renovations and related construction. Detailed marketing plans were developed, building plans drafted, delivery schedules were prepared and materials and equipment deemed necessary for the store were purchased. The Grossmans applied to the Cheltenham Township building and zoning committee for permission to erect commercial signs for Channel and other tenants of the mall.

On January 11, 1985, Frank Shea, Esquire, of the Grace legal department sent to Frank Grossman two copies of a forty-one (41) page draft lease and, in a cover letter, requested copies of several documents to be used as exhibits to the lease. On January 16, 1985, Frank Shea received the following letter from Bruce Grossman:

Dear Mr. Shea:

As you requested, enclosed please find the following documents:

1)   A copy of a recent title report for the Cedarbrook Mall (the "Mall"),

2)   A legal description of the Mall,

3)   A site plan of the Mall, and

4)   A description of the Landlord's construction.

As we discussed, we have commenced work on the Channel location at the Mall and would, therefore, appreciate your assistance in expediting the execution of the Channel lease.

I look forward to hearing from you soon.

Very truly yours,

BAKER INVESTMENT CORPORATION

/s/ Bruce S. Grossman,

Executive Vice President

On January 21, 1985, Frank Shea received a copy of a letter from Frank Grossman to Richard Perkowski dated January 17, 1985. It provided:

> At Frank Shea's request, enclosed is a site plan for the Cedarbrook Mall and also a copy of the proposed pylon sign design.

> We look forward to executing the lease agreement in the very near future. If you have any questions, please feel free to call me.

Bruce Grossman called Shea on January 23, 1985 to discuss the lease. The only item Grossman could recall discussing pertained to the "use" clause in the lease, specifically whether Channel could use the site for warehouse facilities at some future point. Apparently, Grossman then related other areas of concern and Shea suggested that a telephone conference be arranged with all parties the following week. Grossman agreed. According to Grossman, Shea was supposed to initiate the conference call; however, when the call was not forthcoming, Grossman did not attempt to reach Shea or anyone else at Channel. Shea understood that the Grossmans were going to discuss the lease among themselves and get back to him.

On or about January 22, 1985, Stephen Erlbaum, Chairman of the Board of Mr. Good Buys of Pennsylvania, Inc. ("Mr. Good Buys"), contacted Frank Grossman. Like Channel, Mr. Good Buys is a corporation engaged in the business of operating retail home improvement centers; it is a major competitor of Channel in the Philadelphia area. Erlbaum advised Grossman that Mr. Good Buys would be interested in leasing space at Cedarbrook Mall, and sent Grossman printed information about Mr. Good Buys.

On January 24, 1985, construction representatives from Channel met at the mall site to go over building alterations and designs. The next day, January 25, 1985, Erlbaum and other representatives from Mr. Good Buys met with the Grossmans and toured Channel's proposed lease location. When Erlbaum expressed an interest in leasing this site, lease terms were discussed.

On February 6, 1985, Frank Grossman notified Channel that "negotiations terminated as of this date" due to Channel's failure to submit a signed and mutually acceptable lease for the mall site within thirty days of the December 11, 1984 letter of intent. (This was the first and only written evidence of the purported thirty-day time limit. The letter of intent contained no such term.) On February 7, 1985, Mr. Good Buys and Frank Grossman executed a lease for the Cedarbrook Mall. Mr. Good Buys agreed to make base-level annual rental payments which were substantially greater than those agreed to by Channel in the December 11, 1984 letter of intent. Channel's corporate parent, Grace, approved the terms of Channel's proposed lease on February 13, 1985.

Channel argues that the letter, coupled with the surrounding circumstances, constitutes a binding agreement to negotiate in good faith. Appellees rejoin that a promise to negotiate in good faith or to use best efforts to reduce to formal writing an agreement between the parties is enforceable only if the parties have in fact reached agreement on the underlying transaction. Appellees further argue that even if the agreement were an otherwise enforceable contract, the letter of intent and any promises contained therein are unenforceable by virtue of Channel's lack of consideration.[1] The parties agree that Pennsylvania law applies to the case.

Channel does not contend that the letter of intent is binding as a lease or an agreement to enter into a lease. Rather it is Channel's position that this document is enforceable as a mutually binding obligation *to negotiate in good faith.* By unilaterally terminating negotiations with Channel and precipitously entering into a lease agreement with Mr. Good Buys, Channel argues, Grossman acted in bad faith and breached his promise to "withdraw the Store from the rental market and only negotiate the above-described leasing transaction to completion."

Although no Pennsylvania court has considered whether an agreement to negotiate in good faith may meet [the conditions of enforceability], the jurisdictions that have considered the issue have held that such an agreement, if otherwise meeting the requisites of a contract, is an enforceable contract.[2] We are satisfied that Pennsylvania would follow this rule. Applying Pennsylvania law, then, we must ask (1) whether both parties manifested an intention to be bound by the agreement; (2) whether the terms of the agreement are sufficiently definite to be enforced; and (3) whether there was consideration.

In determining the parties' intentions concerning the letter of intent, we must examine the entire document and the relevant circumstances surrounding its adoption. The letter of intent, signed by both parties, provides that "[t]o induce the Tenant [Channel] to proceed with the leasing of the Store, you [Grossman] will withdraw the Store from the rental market, and only negotiate the above described leasing transaction to completion." The agreement thus contains an unequivocal promise by Grossman to withdraw the store from the rental market and to negotiate the proposed leasing transaction with Channel to completion.

---

[1]   The district court also rejected Channel's additional contention that the letter of intent should be enforced under the doctrine of promissory estoppel. In light of our disposition on appeal, we need not reach the propriety of the district court's determinations that neither a unilateral contract analysis nor the doctrine of promissory estoppel is applicable to the instant case. [Footnote transposed.]

[2]   Good faith in the bargaining or formation stages of the contracting process is distinguishable from the common law duty to perform in good faith. See Restatement of Contracts (Second) § 205 (1979) ("Every contract imposes upon each party a duty of good faith and fair dealing in its performance and its enforcement.")

Evidence of record supports the proposition that the parties intended this promise to be binding. After the letter of intent was executed, both Channel and the Grossmans initiated procedures directed toward satisfaction of lease contingencies. Channel directed its parent corporation to prepare a draft lease; Channel planning representatives visited the lease premises to obtain measurements for architectural alterations, renovations, and related construction. Channel developed extensive marketing plans; delivery schedules were prepared and material and equipment deemed necessary for the store were purchased. The Grossmans applied to the township zoning committee for permission to erect Channel signs at various locations on the mall property. Channel submitted a draft lease on January 11, 1985, and the parties, through correspondence and telephone conversations and on-site visits, exhibited an intent to move toward a lease as late as January 23, 1985. Accordingly, the letter of intent and the circumstances surrounding its adoption both support a finding that the parties intended to be bound by an agreement to negotiate in good faith.

We also believe that Grossman's promise to "withdraw the Store from the rental market and only negotiate the above described leasing transaction to completion," viewed in the context of the detailed letter of intent (which covers most significant lease terms), is sufficiently definite to be specifically enforced, provided that Channel submitted sufficient legal consideration in return.

Appellees argue that "[n]o money or thing of value was paid, either at the time of the letter or at any other time that would convert an agreement to negotiate into some enforceable type of contract." Brief of Appellees at 16. We disagree. It seems clear that the execution and tender of the letter of intent by Channel was of substantial value to Frank Grossman. At the time the letter of intent was executed, Grossman was in the process of obtaining financing for his purchase of the mall. When it became apparent to Grossman that Channel—a major corporate tenant—was seriously interested in leasing the mall site, he requested that Channel sign a letter of intent which, as Grossman put it, could be shown to "other people, banks or whatever with a view to getting permanent financing." App. at 366a–367a. Fully aware of Grossman's desire to obtain financing, Channel sought to solidify its bargaining position by requesting that Grossman also sign the letter of intent and promise to "withdraw the store from the rental market and only negotiate the above-described leasing transaction to completion." There being evidence that value passed from each party to the other, we conclude that the record would support a finding that Channel's execution and tender of the letter of intent conferred a bargained for benefit on Grossman which was valid consideration for Grossman's return promise to negotiate in good faith.

In sum, we agree with Channel that the record contains evidence that supports a finding that the parties intended to enter into a binding agreement to negotiate in good faith. We further hold that the agreement had sufficient specificity to make it an enforceable contract if the parties so intended, and that consideration passed between the parties. We will therefore remand this case to the district court for trial.

At least two significant issues must be resolved at trial. First, although our review of the record reveals that there is sufficient evidence to support a finding that the parties intended to be bound by the letter of intent, we do not hold that the evidence requires this conclusion. At trial, evidence will decide this issue.

As noted above, there is also some dispute over whether there was a time limit on the negotiations that was not specified in the letter of intent. Because the district court erroneously concluded that the letter of intent was unenforceable as a matter of law, it made no factual findings with regard to this critical term. If, as appellees suggest, Channel orally agreed to forward a draft lease within 30 days of the date on which the letter of intent was executed, Channel's failure to do so could have terminated the agreement. Alternatively, if, as Channel argues, the parties did not fix a definite time for the duration of negotiations, then a reasonable time would be applicable, and a determination must be made as to what constitutes a reasonable time under all the circumstances.

The judgment of the district court will therefore be reversed, and the case remanded for further proceedings consistent with this opinion.

NOTES

(1) *Measure of Damages.* If the Grossmans were held liable on remand, how would Channel's damages be measured? In terms of its expectation? In terms of its reliance? If Channel could show that it had passed up other opportunities to lease premises in reliance on Grossman's promise to negotiate, would damages based on those lost opportunities be recoverable? Is this one of the relatively rare instances referred to in Note 2, p. 19 above, where courts take account of lost opportunities? Are there reasons why this might be so?

A conventional objection to the recovery of expectation damages when negotiations fail is that a court cannot know what agreement would have been reached and therefore has no way to measure lost expectation. Goodstein Construction Corp. v. City of New York, 604 N.E.2d 1356, 1361 (N.Y.1992). But in Venture Associates Corp. v. Zenith Data Systems Corp., 96 F.3d 275 (7th Cir.1996), Judge Posner said that

> if the plaintiff can prove that had it not been for the defendant's bad faith the parties would have made a final contract, then the loss of the benefit of the contract is a consequence of the defendant's bad faith, and, provided that it is a foreseeable consequence, the defendant is liable for that loss—liable, that is, for the plaintiff's consequential damages. The difficulty, which may well be insuperable, is that since by hypothesis the parties had not agreed on *any* of the terms of their contract, it may be impossible to

determine what those terms would have been and hence what profit the victim of bad faith would have had. But this goes to the practicality of the remedy, not the principle of it.

96 F.3d 275 at 278–79. See Farnsworth on Contracts § 3.26b. As we will see in *Oglebay Norton*, p. 332 below, a court might even grant specific performance for breach of a promise to negotiate.

(2) *The Meaning of Bad Faith.* What would amount to bad faith in negotiation? In PSI Energy v. Exxon Coal USA, 17 F.3d 969 (7th Cir.1994), Judge Easterbrook said:

> An obligation to negotiate 'in good faith' nixes trickery and certain forms of obduracy, but it does not require one side in negotiations to reveal its bargaining strategy or its reservation price, to disclose every tidbit that would be of use to the other side, or to refrain from taking advantage of its opportunities.

Id. at 972. Would it be bad faith to renege on an agreed term? Recall that a *Tribune* Type II contract requires agreement "on certain major terms." To engage in negotiations with another party (as Grumman did with Codar in *Cyberchron*)? To terminate negotiations without warning in order to make a contract with another party (as Grumman presumably did to make a contract with Codar in *Cyberchron*)? See Farnsworth on Contracts § 3.26b.

SECTION 7. THE REQUIREMENT OF DEFINITENESS

In *Channel Home Centers*, p. 316 above, the court asked first "whether both parties manifested an intention to be bound by the agreement" and second "whether the terms of the agreement are sufficiently definite to be enforced." The preceding sections of this chapter explored the first question: Did both parties assent to be bound? This section explores the second: Is an agreement definite enough to be enforced? Both questions must be answered in the affirmative for there to be a contract.

The requirement of definiteness serves two basic functions. In order for a court to determine whether or not a contract has been broken, it must first know with some certainty what the terms of the contract are. The concept of definiteness is also implicit in the principle that the promisee's expectation interest is to be protected. In calculating the damages that will put a promisee in the position it would have been in had the promise been performed, a court must be able to determine with some precision what the promise was. For requirement of definiteness in Article 2, see UCC § 2–204(3); in the Restatement, see § 33.

The effect of indefiniteness can be seen from Varney v. Ditmars, 111 N.E. 822 (N.Y.1916). Varney, an architectural draftsman, sued Ditmar, his employer, on Ditmar's promise to pay Varney "a fair share of my profits," in addition to a stated salary. The court denied recovery of profits on the ground that the amount was a matter of "pure conjecture" and might be "any amount from a nominal sum to a material part according to the particular views of the person whose guess is considered."

In deciding whether or not an agreement is sufficiently definite, a court may piece together terms from such sources as preliminary negotiations, prior communications, external sources such as governmental regulations and applicable trade usages. A course of dealing between the parties prior to the transaction, or a course of performance between them after their agreement may also provide terms. See UCC § 1–303. Indefiniteness may also be cured, sometimes, by resort to a term implied by law, in the way that the duty to use reasonable efforts was supplied in Wood v. Lucy, Lady Duff-Gordon, p. 111 above.

Terms such as good faith and reasonable efforts are regarded as sufficiently definite if their content can be determined by reference to some external standard. Probably that would have been done in Wood v. Lucy, Lady Duff-Gordon, had it been necessary to determine what efforts were required of Wood in the circumstances. The processes by which language is interpreted, and terms such as "reasonable efforts" and "good faith" are supplied and construed, are explored in Chapter 5. Consider now a case illustrating certain consequences of indefiniteness.

Toys, Inc. v. F.M. Burlington Company

Supreme Court of Vermont, 1990.
582 A.2d 123.

[F.M. Burlington Company, a mall owner, entered into a five year lease with Toys, Inc., a retailer. The lease gave Toys an option to renew for an additional five years, requiring Toys to notify Burlington in writing of its intention to exercise the option one year before the lease expired. The lease further provided that "the fixed minimum rental [for the renewal period] shall be renegotiated to the then prevailing rate within the mall." In February, Toys gave timely written notice to Burlington of its intent to renew. Burlington confirmed Toy's exercise of the option and stated the then prevailing rate per square foot in the mall. A week later Toys replied that its renewal had been premised on a "substantially different understanding of the prevailing rate."

For the next ten months, the parties engaged in what the court called "paper jousting" as they attempted to negotiate a rent structure for the renewal period, creating and extending various deadlines for doing so along the way. By November, no agreement had been reached, and Burlington advised Toys that it was listing the location for rent. Toys then left the mall, found alternative space, and sued for breach of contract. Burlington argued, that owing to Toys's failure to accept the prevailing rate stated in February and a second rent proposal made by Burlington in July, the renewal option had lapsed. The trial court granted summary judgment, holding that the lease had created a binding option. Burlington appealed on the ground that the option was too indefinite.]

■ DOOLEY, JUSTICE. We agree with the trial court that summary judgment for plaintiff was appropriate. The lease provision created a valid option for plaintiff to renew for an additional five years. Defendant characterizes the lease renewal provision as merely an agreement to agree and therefore not enforceable. If defendant's construction were correct, the lease provision would not create an enforceable option. See Reynolds v. Sullivan, 136 Vt. 1, 3, 383 A.2d 609, 611 (1978). In Reynolds we held that a preliminary option agreement that was vague and uncertain in its terms "would be an impossibility to enforce." Id. The test is whether the option agreement contains "all material and essential terms to be incorporated in the subsequent document." Id. The agreement in Reynolds was labeled as preliminary and specifically provided that the parties "agree to enter an agreement for an option" and that "more specific terms will be stated in the option to purchase." Id. at 2, 383 A.2d at 610.

It is not necessary under Reynolds that the option agreement contains all the terms of the contract as long as it contains a practicable, objective method of determining the essential terms. See Krupinsky v. Birsky, 278 A.2d 757, 760 (Vt.1971) (option contract valid even though it "did not fix a price certain" where "it did appoint a mode of determining the price"); Restatement (Second) of Contracts § 33 comment a, § 34(1) (1981) ("The terms of a contract may be reasonably certain even though it empowers one or both parties to make a selection of terms in the course of performance."). We must construe the option agreement in a way to give it binding effect if possible. See Agway, Inc. v. Marotti, 540 A.2d 1044, 1046 (Vt.1988) (before voiding a contract for vagueness, indefiniteness or uncertainty of expression, Court must attempt to construe the contract to avoid the defect). We are also mindful that defendant drafted the language of the option clause and that a doubtful provision in a written instrument is construed against the party responsible for drafting it. See Trustees of Net Realty v. AVCO Financial Services, 520 A.2d 981, 983 (Vt.1986).

The option agreement states that "the fixed minimum rental shall be renegotiated to the then prevailing rate within the mall." We believe that this language sets forth a definite, ascertainable method of determining the price term for the lease extension. Within days after plaintiff stated its original intent to exercise its option, defendant replied by quoting the "prevailing rate within the mall" at that time. Neither defendant nor plaintiff have disputed the accuracy of this calculation.

Defendant puts much emphasis on the use of the term "renegotiate" in the renewal clause, as showing an intent to reach a future agreement. While the choice of wording could have been more precise, we agree with the plaintiff that the term means that the then-existing "prevailing rate" would be determined by agreement, and does not mean that the parties would start from a clean slate in renegotiating a rent term. Even if we give defendant the benefit of all inferences and reasonable doubt, we find no genuine issue of fact bearing on whether there was an enforceable option to renew and hold as a matter of law that a valid option existed.

NOTES

(1) *Questions*. What consideration supported the option? What did the exercise of the option require? Could the parties have drafted the rent term more clearly?

(2) *Open Price Terms*. Would you expect a similar result if the option provision in *Toys* had been: "Tenant shall be provided one option to extend the lease for five years at annual rentals to be agreed upon"? See Joseph Martin, Jr., Delicatessen, Inc. v. Schumacher, 417 N.E.2d 541 (N.Y.1981). Consider a contract for the sale of goods, which "if [the parties] so intend," can be concluded even though they leave the price term "open." UCC § 2–305. Why might the law be more indulgent of indefiniteness with regard to price in agreements for the sale of goods than in landlord-tenant agreements? We return to this question later in the chapter.

(3) *The Case of the Business Opportunity*. In Lee v. Joseph E. Seagram & Sons, Inc., 552 F.2d 447 (2d Cir.1977), a jury found that when Seagram contracted in writing to buy a wholesale liquor distributorship (Capitol City), it had orally agreed with some of its owners to provide them, within a reasonable time, with a Seagram distributorship in another city, in a location acceptable to them, "whose price would require roughly an amount equal to the capital obtained by [those owners] for the sale of their interest in Capitol City." Id. at 450. In an action by the promisees, a judgment was entered against Seagram and it appealed. It contended in part that the oral agreement was so vague and indefinite as to be unenforceable. Held: Affirmed. The plaintiffs had testified about the financial record of Capitol City and produced expert testimony about the industry standard for valuing a liquor distributorship.

Why do you suppose the parties were not more precise in defining their obligations with respect to the new distributorship? What answer can be given to Seagram's further point that the oral agreement was illusory, owing to the promisees' "unbridled discretion" to accept or to reject any new situation that Seagram might proffer? Suppose that the promisee had been an investor negotiating to buy Capitol City, and that Seagram had persuaded the investor to break off negotiations by making a comparable promise. Same result?

(4) *Offers of Job Security*. In Sayres v. Bauman, 425 S.E.2d 226 (W.Va.1992), the claimants were employees of a firm whose ownership changed hands. There was evidence that before the buy-out, they were told that "you won't lose your job because a new company is buying us out." Id. at 231. The plaintiffs continued in their jobs for more than a year under the new ownership but were then discharged. Might the statement attributed to the former owners be construed as an offer to the employees of job security— one that the employees accepted by continuing on their jobs? In an action by

the employees for wrongful discharge, the court reversed a judgment for the plaintiffs, saying: "an oral promise which has as its effect the alteration of an 'at will' employment relationship must contain terms that are both ascertainable and definitive in nature to be enforceable." Id. at 227.

Recall that statements of company policy, announced in handbooks or manuals for employees, have often been found to be incorporated in the terms of employment for personnel already in place, as well as for new recruits. The "handbook" cases frequently permit employees to escape the rigors of the doctrine of at-will employment. See the discussion of Employee Handbooks, p. 90 above. In Berube v. Fashion Centre, Ltd., 771 P.2d 1033 (Utah 1989), according to the lead opinion, the defendant employer had "created and distributed a disciplinary action policy which was read and understood by the plaintiff," thereby limiting the grounds on which it could discharge her. The court reversed a judgment for the employer and ordered a retrial on the theory of an implied-in-fact contract. On these facts, was an offer any more evident than in *Sayres*?

(5) *Restitution*. A party who has, in the course of performing an agreement that is unenforceable for indefiniteness, conferred a benefit upon the other party, is entitled to restitution. For example, in Varney v. Ditmars, above, the court suggested that if the architectural draftsman's work was worth more than his salary, he would have had a right to restitution measured by the difference. Similarly, in Pyeatte v. Pyeatte, p. 152 above, the court refused to enforce the husband's promise to put his wife through a master's degree program, finding the agreement too indefinite as to timing, place, duration, and costs: "Such a loosely worded agreement can hardly be said to have fixed [his] liability with certainty." But although the agreement "failed to meet the requirements of an enforceable contract, [it] still has importance in considering [her] claim for unjust enrichment because it both evidences [her] expectation of compensation and the circumstances which make it unjust to allow [him] to retain the benefits of her extraordinary efforts." The court then awarded the former wife restitution. Why were the Pyeattes not more precise? Which recovery—restitution or expectation—would have been greater?

PROBLEM

Forbearing on a Claim. Review Note 1, p. 98 above. Suppose that Louisa Sheffield had written to Strong: "I will be responsible for my husband's debt if you will not bother him about it for a reasonable time." Would she have been accountable to Strong if he had done nothing about the note for two years? See Baker v. Citizens State Bank of St. Louis Park, 349 N.W.2d 552 (Minn.1984). Farmers Union Oil Co. of New England v. Maixner, 376 N.W.2d 43 (N.D.1985).

Indefiniteness and Contractual Incompleteness

Contracts need not specify all their essential terms at formation in order to be enforceable. It is enough for agreements to provide means for making those terms sufficiently definite by the time performance is due. Take, for example, output and requirements contracts, which usually have undetermined delivery quantities at the time of formation; see discussion in *Structural Polymer Group, Ltd.*, p. 106. Consider also *Fairmount Glass*, p. 189, where the seller complained "that the contract was indefinite, because the quantity of each size of the jars was not fixed", but the court held that the agreement was not unenforceable because the buyer had "the right to name the quantity of each size" before shipment. The same is true when other particulars of performance are to be specified by one of the parties. See UCC § 2–311.

A degree of indefiniteness is common to all contracts. Yet agreements may be indefinite in several ways. In addition to vague terms, an agreement may be indefinite because of contractual incompleteness. Contracts are "incomplete" in two distinct senses. First, relevant terms may simply be absent, leaving gaps in the contract. Courts are quite familiar with this type of incompleteness and, in many circumstances, will fill in what is missing, either through conventional gap-filling rules, or, where appropriate, by implying a term; recall the duty of reasonable efforts supplied by Cardozo in Wood v. Lucy, Lady Duff-Gordon, p. 111 above. (UCC gap-fillers rules are explored more thoroughly in section 6 of Chapter 5.)

"The second form of contractual incompleteness is more subtle. A contract may also be incomplete in that it is insensitive to relevant future contingencies[:] specified duties are not tailored to economically relevant future events." Ian Ayres and Robert Gartner, *Filling Gaps in Incomplete Contracts: An Economic Theory of Default Rules*, 99 Yale L.J. (1990) 87 at 92 n.29. Imagine, for example, a simple contract where a seller agrees to ship to buyer a fixed quality and quantity of rice by December 31. The agreement is "complete" in the sense that the specified shipment is required by the end of the calendar year in all eventualities. What if war or weather, however, disrupts shipping routes for an extended period of time? A contract that is more meaningfully complete would specify what should occur should such contingencies arise. While the simple contract is literally complete, a more thoroughgoing notion of contractual completeness would require the parties to specify exact actions and obligations for important contingencies that arise in such states of the world. "Courts seldom recognize the second form of contractual incompleteness. That is, they are generally unwilling to alter (they strictly enforce) the terms of a contract that is insufficiently state-contingent." Id.

Why do contract parties leave their agreements incomplete? Consider the following possibilities:

(a) They do not want to take the time or pay attorneys for their time to work through every eventuality, or they are willing to rely on the terms that a court will supply in the event of dispute arises.

(b) They are reluctant to raise difficult issues for fear that the deal may fall through.

(c) They do not, due to bounded rationality or bias, foresee problems that might arise.

(d) They cannot adequately describe certain features of their agreement at formation.

(e) They choose to withhold business information in order to retain an advantage.

Do other reasons come to mind? Might the reason in a particular case affect the court's willingness to overlook some indefiniteness?

Indefiniteness and Relational Contracting

A completely contingent contract, surely hypothetical, provides a specific course of action for every possible eventuality or contingency that might occur under the agreement. For the reasons stated above—the costs of writing fully contingent agreements, limited foreseeability, bounded rationality, indescribability and so on—all contracts are incomplete in the strong sense of the term. But some contractual exchanges are subject to more incompleteness than others. Contractual incompleteness tends to be more pronounced in agreements between parties who deal with one another on a regular basis ("repeat players") or who interact over an extended period, giving rise to what are often called "relational contracts." The expression derives from an influential article by Stewart Macaulay, *Non-Contractual Relations in Business: A Preliminary Study*, 28 Am. Soc. Rev. 55 (1963).

The study of relational contracts was advanced significantly by Ian Macneil, *Contracts: Adjustment of Long-Term Economic Relations Under Classical, Neoclassical, and Relational Contract Law*, 72 Nw. U. L. Rev. 854 (1978); see also Macneil, *Relational Contract Theory: Challenges and Queries*, 94 Nw. U. L. Rev. 877 (2000). Macneil proposed a spectrum of contractual exchanges. At one end sits the "transactional" ideal type, characterized by discrete, simple, immediate, one-shot, impersonal exchanges, like one-off sales transactions made at a bazaar or in the spot market. The deal is as complete as it needs to be for its discrete purpose. At the other end of the spectrum, the "relational" ideal exhibits exchange characteristics that are complex, extended, repeated and often quite personal. Transactions in family businesses, franchise arrangements, as well as those among partners, joint-venturers and between principals and their agents are common examples of more relational exchanges.

While various bodies of law have specifically adapted to the contours of these transactions—including agency, employment, family and partnership law among others—the material covered in this casebook, so-called "neoclassical contract law", is also pertinent to relational exchanges. Charles Goetz and Robert Scott, for example, long ago described how "best efforts" and "termination" clauses (discussed in Chapters 6 and 1, respectively) respond to the unique challenges in long-term relational contracts:

> These rules serve the important purpose of saving most bargainers the cost of negotiating a tailor-made arrangement. All relevant risks thus can be assigned optimally either by legal rule or through individualized agreement because future contingencies are not only known and understood at the time the bargain is struck, but can also be addressed by efficacious contractual responses.

Charles Goetz and Robert Scott, *Principles of Relational Contracts*, 67 Va. L. Rev. 1089, 1091 (1981). For parties in relational exchanges, Goetz and Scott point out, "a complete contingent contract may not be a feasible contracting mechanism. Where the future contingencies are peculiarly intricate or uncertain, practical difficulties arise that impede the contracting parties' efforts to allocate optimally all risks at the time of contracting." Id., at 1090. On the other hand, the very fact that their exchanges are relational will often render the objective of contractual completeness less consequential. Why might parties in relational exchanges be less concerned with addressing every contingency, such as the effect of defective performance, than parties to other sorts of parties? Authority, status, trust, social role, familial ties and habits inter alia can all influence behavior in relational contexts, making strict contractual enforcement of ex ante specified terms less essential. Also of central importance is the role of reputation in relational exchanges. See David Charny, *Nonlegal Sanctions in Commercial Relationships*, 104 Harv. L. Rev. 373 (1990). In recent years economists have developed a rich literature based on repeated games to advance reputation as an alternative to formal contractual enforcement. See, e.g., George Baker, Robert Gibbons and Kevin J. Murphy, *Relational Contracts and the Theory of the Firm*, 117 Q. J. Econ. 39 (2002); Avinash Dixit, Lawlessness and Economics: Alternative Modes of Governance (2004).

Indefiniteness and Contract Price

Parties sometimes intentionally leave aspects of their agreements unspecified at formation and subsequently fill-in the blanks at a later date when more information is available. For example, a buyer of goods to be shipped may specify a dock or warehouse delivery location just prior to delivery. Deferred decisions of this sort are common and to be expected.

But what about leaving indefinite something as basic as the contract price? This too is not uncommon.

Suppose that over a long term a seller wants to be assured of an outlet for a fixed quantity of a product and that a buyer wants to be assured of a source of supply for the same quantity. Neither party, however, wants to take the risk of a shift in the market: the seller does not want to risk a rise in prices before delivery, and the buyer does not want to risk a fall. How can they make an agreement that will be legally enforceable and yet will allow the price of the goods to fluctuate?

One possibility is to leave the price term open; the price will then be "a reasonable price at the time for delivery." See UCC § 2–305. Of course this leaves open opportunities for dispute over what is "reasonable." If the parties anticipated too much dispute over determining the "reasonable price," they might stipulate a schedule of prices, which would set the contact price based on observed contingencies. Professors Benjamin Hermalin and Michael Katz suggest exactly this approach in their 'fill-in-the-price' mechanism, where "[t]he initial contract is incomplete in the sense that the price is initially 'left blank' and is only later 'filled in.' But in a more important sense, it is complete: All contingencies (including the process by which the blanks are to be filled in) are covered." Benjamin E. Hermalin and Michael L. Katz, *Judicial Modification of Contracts Between Sophisticated Parties: A More Complete View of Incomplete Contracts and Their Breach*, 9 J. Law, Econ. & Org. 230, 232 (1993). As the title of their article indicates, parties must be very sophisticated if they are to devise a fully contingent price schedule. As much as Hermalin and Katz supposed extremely rational actors, they were perhaps even more motivated by a skepticism concerning the capacity of courts to determine prices ex post. In their framework, "the courts' role is simply to make sure that the various monetary transfers (payments and 'liquidated damages') called for by the contract are made." Id. Courts, however, are often reluctant to enforce liquidated damages without inquiry into their content and compensatory purpose (as elaborated in the remedies material in Chapter 8) and for this reason courts may not play as deferential a role to the parties' contract as Professors Hermalin and Katz would demand.

Parties skeptical of judicial capacity to determine and fill-in an appropriate price may use an alternative mechanism, such as designating a third party (perhaps one with some transaction-specific expertise) to fix the price if the parties should disagree. Again, see UCC § 2–305. Arbitrators are a prominent example of such third-parties, toward whom courts are required to show great deference under Federal Arbitration Act. After the arbitrator renders a ruling on the price term, the parties may then enforce that award in court. In this two-step approach, might a liquidated price term that would not survive the scrutiny of judges be nonetheless enforceable in their courts?

Another possibility is to use an "escalator clause" under which the price will be fixed according to a formula tied in some way to the market; see the Eastern Airlines case, p. 1076 below. Would it be easier to draft such an agreement if there were an ascertainable market price for the raw materials required by the seller to produce his product? An ascertainable market price for the product itself? (On ascertainable market price, see UCC §§ 2–723 and 2–724.) Would prices charged by competing sellers or to competing buyers be useful?

Helpful analogies can be found in common commercial lease clauses, wherein rent is tied to gross profits, and in collective bargaining agreements clauses, in which wages are tied to the cost of living, and in the clauses of construction contracts that tie the price to costs ("cost-plus" contracts). An interesting variant is patterned after the "most favored nation" clause found in treaties. See, for example, Reynolds Metals Co. v. United States, 438 F.2d 983 (Ct.Cl.1971), in which the United States promised Reynolds to amend their contract "if later agreements with the Aluminum Company of America and/or the Kaiser Aluminum and Chemical Company are, in your opinion, more favorable than the agreement which has been executed with you." What standard might a court apply to the term "in your opinion"? An objective one, subjective one, or both? 'Most favored counterparty' clauses are now quite common in contracts between buyers and sellers as well as in settlement agreements. See Thomas P. Lyon, *Most Favored Customer Clauses*, *in The New Palgrave Dictionary of Economics and the Law* (Peter Newman ed., 1998); Kathryn E. Spier, *The Use of "Most-Favored-Nation" Clauses in Settlement of Litigation*, 34 RAND J. of Econ. 78 (2003).

Although there are a number of ways to specify a flexible, if somewhat indefinite, pricing mechanism at contract formation, such specification does not, however, assure that an unanticipated contingency will not develop and unravel the mechanism. What then? The final case of this chapter raises this challenge and returns us to the question of assent. As we shall see, the parties have been in a long-term, cooperative relational contract whose terms became indefinite over the course of the contract's performance. The case raises questions about the vitality of assent when a flexible price mechanism appears to fail. In reading the case, keep the following questions in mind: What evidence does the court assemble to assess whether or not the parties intended to remain bound over time? Could these sophisticated actors have avoided the problem through better contractual specification?

Oglebay Norton Co. v. Armco, Inc.

Supreme Court of Ohio, 1990.
52 Ohio St.3d 232, 556 N.E.2d 515.

[In 1957, Armco made a long-term contract with Oglebay requiring Oglebay to have adequate shipping capacity available and requiring Armco to use that capacity for the transportation of iron ore on the Great

Lakes. The contract provided for a primary and a secondary price mechanism:

> *Armco agrees to pay* for all iron ore transported hereunder the *regular net contract rates for the season* in which the ore is transported, *as recognized by the leading iron ore shippers* in such season for the transportation of iron ore. *If*, in any season of navigation hereunder, *there is no regular net contract rate recognized by the leading iron ore shippers for such transportation, the parties shall mutually agree upon a rate* for such transportation, *taking into consideration the contract rate being charged for similar transportation* by the leading independent vessel operators engaged in transportation of iron ore from The Lake Superior District. (Emphasis supplied by the court.)]

During the next 23 years the parties modified the contract four times, each time extending the time and entailing substantial capital investment by Oglebay to meet Armco's requirements. After the fourth modification, which extended the contract to the year 2010, Oglebay began a $95 million capital improvement program.

From 1957 through 1983 the parties established the contract shipping rate by reference to a rate published in Skillings Mining Review, in accord with the contract's primary price mechanism. After a serious downturn in the iron ore industry in 1983, Armco challenged the rate quoted by Oglebay and the parties negotiated a mutually satisfactory rate for the 1984 season. After that, however, the parties were unable to agree on a rate and, in April of 1986, Oglebay sought a declaratory judgment, asking the court to declare the contract rate to be the correct rate or, in the absence of such a rate, to declare a reasonable rate. Armco denied that the rate sought by Oglebay was the "contract rate" and denied that the court had jurisdiction to declare a rate of its own accord. The parties continued to perform pending resolution of the dispute. In August of 1987, Armco filed a supplementary counterclaim seeking a declaration that the contract was no longer enforceable.

In November of 1987, the trial court issued its declaratory judgment, fixing $6.25 as the rate for the 1986 season and holding that, if the parties were unable to agree on a rate for the upcoming seasons, they must notify the court, which would appoint a mediator and require the parties' chief executive officers to meet and "mutually agree upon a rate." The court of appeals affirmed and a motion was made to certify the record.]

■ PER CURIAM. This case presents three mixed questions of fact and law. First, did the parties intend to be bound by the terms of this contract despite the failure of its primary and secondary pricing mechanisms? Second, if the parties did intend to be bound, may the trial court establish $6.25 per gross ton as a reasonable rate for Armco to pay Oglebay for shipping Armco ore during the 1986 shipping season? Third, may the trial court continue to exercise its equitable jurisdiction over the parties, and may it order the parties to utilize a mediator if they are unable to mutually agree on a shipping rate for each annual shipping season? We answer each of these questions in the affirmative and for the reasons set forth below affirm the decision of the court of appeals.

I

Appellant Armco argues that the complete breakdown of the primary and secondary contract pricing mechanisms renders the 1957 contract unenforceable, because the parties never manifested an intent to be bound in the event of the breakdown of the primary and secondary pricing mechanisms. Armco asserts that it became impossible after 1985 to utilize the first pricing mechanism in the 1957 contract, i.e., examining the published rate for a leading shipper in the "Skillings Mining Review," because after 1985 a new rate was no longer published. Armco asserts as well that it also became impossible to obtain the information necessary to determine and take into consideration the rates charged by leading independent vessel operators in accordance with the secondary pricing mechanism. This is because that information was no longer publicly available after 1985 and because the trial court granted the motions to quash of non-parties, who were subpoenaed to obtain this specific information. Armco argues that since the parties never consented to be bound by a contract whose specific pricing mechanisms had failed, the trial court should have declared the contract to be void and unenforceable.

The trial court recognized the failure of the 1957 contract pricing mechanisms. Yet the trial court had competent, credible evidence before it to conclude that the parties intended to be bound despite the failure of the pricing mechanisms. The evidence demonstrated the long-standing and close business relationship of the parties, including joint ventures, interlocking directorates and Armco's ownership of Oglebay stock. As the trial court pointed out, the parties themselves contractually recognized Armco's vital and unique interest in the combined dedication of Oglebay's bulk vessel fleet, and the parties recognized that Oglebay could be required to ship up to 7.1 million gross tons of Armco iron ore per year.

Whether the parties intended to be bound, even upon the failure of the pricing mechanisms, is a question of fact properly resolved by the trier of fact. . . . Since the trial court had ample evidence before it to conclude that the parties did so intend, the court of appeals correctly affirmed the trial court regarding the parties' intent. We thus affirm the court of appeals on this question.

II

Armco also argues that the trial court lacked jurisdiction to impose a shipping rate of $6.25 per gross ton when that rate did not conform to the 1957 contract pricing mechanisms. The trial court held that it had the authority to determine a reasonable rate for Oglebay's services, even though the price mechanism of the contract had failed, since the parties intended to be bound by the contract. The court cited 1 Restatement of the Law 2d, Contracts (1981) 92, Section 33, and its relevant comments to support this proposition. Comment e to Section 33 explains in part:

"[Where the parties] intend to conclude a contract for the sale of goods and the price is not settled, the price is a reasonable price at the time of delivery if (c) the price is to be fixed in terms of some agreed market or other standard as set or recorded by a third person or agency and it is not so set or recorded. Uniform Commercial Code § 2–305(1)." Id. at 94–95.

The court therefore determined that a reasonable rate for Armco to pay to Oglebay for transporting Armco's iron ore during the 1986 shipping season was $6.00 per gross ton with an additional rate of twenty-five cents per gross ton when self-unloading vessels were used. The court based this determination upon the parties' extensive course of dealing, "the detriment to the parties respectively, and valid comparisons of market price which reflect [the] economic reality of current depressed conditions in the American steel industry."

The court of appeals concluded that the trial court was justified in setting $6.25 per gross ton as a "reasonable rate" for Armco to pay Oglebay for the 1986 season, given the evidence presented to the trial court concerning various rates charged in the industry and given the intent of the parties to be bound by the agreement.

III

Armco also argues that the trial court lacks equitable jurisdiction to order the parties to negotiate or in the failure of negotiations, to mediate, during each annual shipping season through the year 2010. The court of appeals ruled that the trial court did not exceed its jurisdiction in issuing such an order.

3 Restatement of the Law 2d, Contracts (1981) 179, Section 362, entitled "Effect of Uncertainty of Terms," is similar in effect to Section 33 and states:

"Specific performance or an injunction will not be granted unless the terms of the contract are sufficiently certain to provide a basis for an appropriate order."

Comment b to Section 362 explains:

"Before concluding that the required certainty is lacking, however, a court will avail itself of all of the usual aids in determining the scope of the agreement. Expressions that at first appear incomplete may not appear so after resort to usage or the addition of a term supplied by law." Id. at 179.

Ordering specific performance of this contract was necessary, since, as the court of appeals pointed out, "the undisputed dramatic changes in the market prices of great lakes shipping rates and the length of the contract would make it impossible for a court to award Oglebay accurate damages due to Armco's breach of the contract." We agree with the court of appeals that the appointment of a mediator upon the breakdown of court-ordered contract negotiations neither added to nor detracted from the parties' significant obligations under the contract.

It is well-settled that a trial court may exercise its equitable jurisdiction and order specific performance if the parties intend to be bound by a contract, where determination of long-term damages would be too speculative. See 3 Restatement of the Law 2d, Contracts, supra, at 171–172, Section 360(a), Comment b; Columbus Packing Co. v. State, ex rel. Schlesinger (1919), 126 N.E. 291, 293–294. Indeed, the court of appeals pointed out that under the 1962 amendment, Armco itself had the contractual right to seek a court order compelling Oglebay to specifically perform its contractual duties.

The court of appeals was correct in concluding that ordering the parties to negotiate and mediate during each shipping season for the duration of the contract was proper, given the unique and long-lasting business relationship between the parties, and given their intent to be bound and the difficulty of properly ascertaining damages in this case. The court of appeals was also correct in concluding that ordering the parties to negotiate and mediate with each shipping season would neither add to nor detract from the parties' significant contractual obligations. This is because the order would merely facilitate in the most practical manner the parties' own ability to interact under the contract. Thus we affirm the court of appeals on this question.

Judgment affirmed.

NOTES

(1) *Relationship-Specific Investments and Holdups.* What is the significance, if any, of Oglebay's capital improvement plan? See the discussion of holdups on p. 780. The threat of holdups is commonplace in long-term relational exchanges where one party makes an investment that is to some extent sunk, which is to say an investment that has a lower return outside of the relationship or transaction. The economic consequences of holdups following relationship-specific investments has received considerable academic attention. For a summary, see Richard R.W. Brooks, *The Holdup Game*, in The Elgar Companion to Ronald H. Coase (Claude Ménard and Elodie Bertrand, eds., 2016).

(2) *Inferring Intent.* What, if anything, should be made of the four contract modifications? Would the court's assessment of the parties' intent to be bound differ if their inability to agree on a price had occurred at the formation stage? Did Oglebay's investment in capital improvement imply an intent to be bound?

(3) *Express Default Pricing Mechanisms.* Parties who anticipate the inability to agree on renegotiating a price term in a long-term contract may provide their own default formula, should agreement prove impossible.

Consider the following clause from a contract between a coal supplier and a utility company for the renegotiated price of coal:

If the parties are unable to reach agreement, BUYER will accept SELLER's last offer or present SELLER with a firm, written offer which it has received from another supplier, which it is willing to accept, for the supply of coal called for under the remaining term of this Agreement (herein referred to as a "competitive offer"). It shall also provide SELLER with documentary proof of such offer, and permit SELLER to examine all supporting data and information submitted with the offer. SELLER shall have the right to meet such competitive offer.

Why did the contract require the competing offer be a firm offer?

The clause is taken from PSI Energy, Inc. v. Exxon Coal USA, Inc., 17 F.3d 969 (7th Cir.1994), mentioned at Note 2, p. 323 above. In that litigation, the seller (Exxon Coal) argued that the firm offer received by the buyer (PSI) from another coal supplier was not competitive because delivery and other terms were different from and incommensurate with those in the Exxon-PSI contract. According to Exxon, it was therefore not required to meet the offer, and its last offer (of $30 per ton) would be the price. From a trial court ruling for PSI, Exxon appealed. Held: Reversed. The court observed:

Under the contract, when the parties do not agree and there is no valid competitive offer, the seller's last offer prevails. Not 'the market price' in the abstract, but the seller's last offer. Persons negotiating such a contract would understand that this default rule gives the seller the whip hand; it is simultaneously an element of compensation for taking the risk of developing a new mine (which cost Exxon several hundred million dollars,) and a goad to accommodation. Knowing that it is apt to pay more than the market price if it fails to come up with a competitive offer, PSI had every incentive to be scrupulous in finding a proper bid. We concluded on the prior appeal that it had failed. Now we quantify the price of that failure: $30 per ton.

Id. at 969 (Easterbrook, J.).

(4) *Remedies.* Generally in those cases where the court orders specific performance or enjoins a threatened breach, it must know the scope of the party's promise with greater precision than when it awards monetary damages, because failure to obey the court's order may subject the promisor to the court's contempt power. Why then in Oglebay did the Supreme Court of Ohio approve specific performance with so little apparent hesitation? What exactly did the trial court order the parties to do? Is the remedy not so extraordinary under the terms of the particular contract at issue in the case?

CHAPTER 3

STATUTES OF FRAUDS

SECTION 1. INTRODUCTION

When we use the word *contract*, we commonly have two different things in mind. One is the somewhat abstract idea of an enforceable promise, to paraphrase Restatement § 1. The other is a document that embodies that promise. (Note that the UCC definition of "contract" in UCC § 1–201(b)(12) covers only the former.) As we have seen, however, a promise generally need not be in writing to be enforced; consider Hawkins v. McGee and Sullivan v. O'Connor, for example.

Just because oral promises may be enforceable does not mean that it is a good idea to make one's promises orally. True, even huge contracts are sealed with a handshake. But oral promises are subject to the memories of those who made them, memories that may fade or transmute with time—and which have been known to change in the face of a dispute. Over time, the terms of oral contracts may resemble the game of "Telephone," with a word whispered at the start of a chain coming out very differently at the end.

The law therefore treats oral contracts and written contracts somewhat differently. One of the ways in which it does so concerns how the law determines what the terms of a written contract are and what they mean. This topic is discussed in Chapter 5. The other is more fundamental: whether the contract is enforceable at all. That is this chapter's subject.

Whether oral contracts are enforceable is almost entirely governed by statutes, generically called "statutes of frauds" after the first of its kind, An Act for Prevention of Fraud and Perjuries, 29 Car. 2, c. 3 (1677).[a] The original Statute of Frauds listed six categories of contracts that would be enforceable only if in a signed writing: (1) a contract by an executor or administrator of an estate to answer for a duty of the decedent (the *executor-administrator* provision); (2) a contract to answer for the debt of another (the *suretyship* provision); (3) a contract made upon consideration of marriage (the *marriage* provision); (4) a contract for the sale of an interest in land (the *land contract* provision); (5) a contract that is not to be performed within one year of its making (the *one-year* provision); and (6) a contract for the sale of goods (the *sale of goods* provision). Nor are these the only writing requirements in the statute books. In Professor Farnsworth's words, "legislators have an abiding faith in formality." Farnsworth on Contracts § 6.2, at 110.

---

[a] In this chapter, the "Statute of Frauds" is the 1677 act and its U.S. descendants. Lower-case denotes the more general term for any statute that requires a writing for a contract to be enforceable.

Contracts to arbitrate, to cohabitate, to take a security interest in property one doesn't possess, to borrow, to lease, to guarantee a medical result, to waive a statute of limitations, to ratify a contract made by an infant, to provide for property distributions upon divorce, to modify franchise agreements, to pay brokers for arranging the sale of real estate—all have writing requirements in at least a handful of states, and in some cases all or nearly all. And this is merely a sampling.

It would be difficult to come up with a single explanation of why *these* contracts, of all the types of contracts in the world, have merited legislative attention. It might also be a challenge to explain why the United States, almost alone in the world, finds writing requirements so alluring. Certainly other nations lack our abiding faith. England has repealed almost all of its Statute of Frauds. Most nations had nothing to repeal; statutes of frauds abroad are vestigial compared with ours. Reflecting this, the international sales convention (CISG) has no statute of frauds. CISG Art. 11. Neither does the UNIDROIT Principles of International Commercial Contracts. Whichever national law may be right or wrong for any particular writing requirement, this rampant and vigorous disagreement about the need for a writing suggests that the Statute of Frauds sits on a fault line of contract law and theory.

Our discussion begins with a look at the functions that a statute of frauds may serve. Then this chapter looks at the scope of the most common statutes of frauds, such as contracts requiring more than a year for full performance, contracts requiring the transfer of an interest in real property, and contracts to be potentially liable for the debt of another. The next section deals with what needs to be in the record or records that satisfy a statute of frauds. We will then compare the requirements of the general Statute of Frauds with those governing the sale of goods in UCC § 2–201, which is based on rather a different set of assumptions than was the 1677 statute. Finally, we will look at the exceptions to statutes of frauds, concluding with a discussion of the ethical issues surrounding the use of the Statute of Frauds and with another look at the rationales for writing requirements.

(A) WHAT A STATUTE OF FRAUDS DOES AND DOES NOT DO

Before we can start thinking about the scope and uses of a statute of frauds, we need to look briefly at how a statute of frauds operates and what the consequences are if a contract does not comply with the statute. The starting point for any statute of frauds analysis is whether there is a contract at all. The statute of frauds requires that a contract be in writing to be *enforceable,* not to exist in the first place. An oral contract, even one that falls under a statute of frauds, is still a contract.

The next step is to decide whether the contract falls under any statute of frauds and, if so, which and how many. The term of art used here is whether a contract is *within* a statute of frauds. The problems of scope—whether a contract is within a statute of frauds—will occupy us for much of this chapter.

Once we know whether there is a contract and whether that contract falls within one or more statutes of frauds, we then ask whether the contract is set forth in a writing or writings that meet the statutory requirements of form and content. These include such matters as who must have signed the writing, whether the contract may be set forth in more than one writing, which contract terms must be in the writing, and so on. The legal shorthand for this is whether the writings *satisfy* the statute of frauds.

As with most legal rules, there are exceptions, and the Statute of Frauds has its share. For example, reliance upon a contract may take it outside the Statute of Frauds. So may part performance. So may admitting that the contract exists. Some of these exceptions are within the Statute itself. Others—most—have been added to the various statutes of frauds by the courts.

The many judicially-created exceptions to the Statute of Frauds show two important things about this area of law. First, although in almost every state the principal Statute of Frauds is, as the name says, a statute, the courts usually treat it as though it is part of the common law. More than in most statutory areas, the case law has produced not just interpretations, but also requirements and exceptions not found in the Statute itself. As we will soon see, statutes of frauds themselves normally say something about scope, but very little about content, and even less about exceptions. Judicial exceptions to the Statute of Frauds are almost as old as the Statute of Frauds itself. The original statute took effect in 1677; the first published decision invoking a exception to the statute came in 1686, and there is evidence that courts started carving out exceptions as early as 1681. Butcher v. Stapely, 1 Vernon 364, 22 Eng. Rep. 524 (Ch. 1686) (part-performance exception for land contracts). The courts have remained active ever since.

Second, the presence of so many exceptions to the Statute of Frauds properly suggests that the courts are reluctant to read the statute very broadly. In part this results from some centuries-old discontent with the statute itself. England, the home of the Statute of Frauds, repealed most of it in 1954. Law Reform (Enforcement of Contracts) Act, 2 & 3 Eliz. 2, c. 34 (1954). This discontent results in part from the draconian nature of a statute of frauds. If a contract falls within a statute of frauds and is not set forth in a sufficient writing, then the contract is unenforceable. This is so even if all the evidence set forth makes sense only if there is an enforceable contract. The main purpose of the 1677 Statute of Frauds was, logically enough, to prevent the fraud potentially resulting from perjury. To accomplish this goal, is it necessary to make oral contracts unenforceable, even where there is no dispute whether such a contract exists? This question has troubled courts, which frequently have responded by reading the scope provisions narrowly and by creating and expanding the range of exceptions to the statute.

A point from the first paragraph of this subsection needs to be discussed further. What is the difference between saying that a contract is unenforceable and saying that the contract does not exist? In either case, the promisor has no contractual obligations that a court will recognize, so the promisee will lose if it sues for breach of contract. Indeed, some legislatures have blurred the line with statutes providing that a non-complying contract is "invalid" or "void." Cal. Civ. Code § 1624(a) ("invalid"); N.Y. Gen. Oblig. Law § 5–701(a) ("void").[b]

In many cases there is no real difference between void and unenforceable. But in many others the distinction makes a huge difference. Most fundamentally, a statute of frauds is a defense that must usually be pleaded specially. Fed. R. Civ. P. 8(c). If it is not raised by the defendant, the defense is lost. Furthermore, a contract may initially be unenforceable because of the statute, but may become enforceable later, something that can be true only if there is already a contract. Another common difference arises when a writing satisfies a statute of frauds as to one party but not another—for example, when one party has signed a writing and the other has not. If the contract is void, there is nothing to enforce against either party, but the courts have uniformly concluded that the contract is enforceable against the party that has satisfied the statute.

In addition, because the Statute of Frauds is only a defense to enforcement, the sole result of not complying with the Statute of Frauds is losing a cause of action for breach of contract. So, for example, the Statute of Frauds does not invalidate defenses raised outside actions for breach of contract, such as responding to an action for conversion by proving one's contractual entitlement to the goods. Even within an action for breach, the Statute of Frauds does not affect whether a defendant may raise a defense, even if the contract is unenforceable against the plaintiff. Restatement §§ 140 & 143. The contract may also be admissible in court for any purpose other than to enforce the contract, such as in a cause of action for restitution or as a defense to a charge of trespass. It may be the basis of a claim for tortious misrepresentation. And it may be effective against a third person who is neither a transferee nor a successor to a party to it, as in a cause of action for wrongful inducement to breach. Restatement § 144.

One must also bear in mind that the Statute of Frauds is a statute. In all but two states, the writing requirements of the 1677 Statute of Frauds are found in the statute books. Some of these state Statutes of Frauds are modelled closely on their English predecessor. Others carry

---

[b]   Even in those states, though, the courts have read the statute to make non-complying contracts unenforceable, rather than void from the start. Bed, Bath & Beyond of La Jolla v. La Jolla Village Square Venture Ptnrs., 60 Cal. Rptr. 2d 830 (Ct. App. 1997); McCooey v. Forstmann Leff Assocs., 594 N.Y.S.2d 13 (App. Div. 1993).

out much the same function with substantially different wording. The Selections book contains a number of representative general Statutes of Frauds. Even a casual look shows that they differ in both wording and scope. The latter is more a matter of happenstance than anything else. Writing requirements are strewn throughout every state's code; although the most general or time-honored among them are collected as *the* Statute of Frauds, whether other writing requirements are included depends mainly on the whims of the state's codifier.

The only other point to raise now is a matter of interpretation. By now, using the Restatement as a guide to the common law of contract should be second nature. If, however, a contract falls within the scope of Article 2 of the UCC, then the language of that Article comes to the fore and the Restatement is useful mainly on those issues that Article 2 does not address. It may thus be a little surprising to see in the Restatement a substantial treatment of the Statute of Frauds. Restatement Sections 110–150. Why? The Statute of Frauds is a statute and thus would be expected to displace the common law. What is gained by restating the common law in a statutory area?

The Restatement itself makes little mention of this apparent anomaly, but there are some reasons to treat the Restatement much the same for the Statute of Frauds as for the common law. First, the Statute of Frauds has developed a huge body of case law explicating its every section. That case law has at times splintered, and even when it has not, it has sometimes veered in directions not easily anticipated by resort to the text of the statute. The traditional role of a Restatement—to clarify the common law, meaning principally the case authority—is thus relevant here. In addition, as the text following will show, the courts have engrafted many exceptions or limits on the Statute of Frauds. These seldom have been codified. The consequence is the growth of a sort of common law of the Statute of Frauds, which again is within the expected scope of a Restatement.

PROBLEMS

1. Look at Ohio Rev. Code § 1335.05 (second paragraph) and Tex. Bus. & Com. Code § 26.01(b)(8), both of which may be found in *Selections*. In light of *Hawkins v. McGee* and *Sullivan v. O'Connor,* what policies do these provisions further? Are these policies important enough or broad enough to warrant inclusion in the state's general Statute of Frauds?

2. Compare Cal. Civil Code § 1624(a)(3), N.Y. Gen. Oblig. L. § 5–703(1), and Ohio Rev. Code § 1335.04, all of which are in the Selections book. Based on these provisions, in each of these states must a one-year lease of real property be in a sufficient writing in order to be enforceable? See Ohio Rev. Code § 5301.08.

(B) BACKGROUND[c]

The Statute of Frauds of 1677 came about because of the collision of two early causes of action, the writ of assumpsit and the writ of debt. We normally think of assumpsit as the predecessor of the modern action for breach of contract; indeed, some jurisdictions still refer to actions for breach of contract as sounding in assumpsit. See, e.g., Hall v. Laroya, 238 P.3d 714 (Haw. App. 2010) (suit to collect attorney's fees is "in the nature of assumpsit"). But, as discussed in chapter 1, pp. 48–51, there were two other common-law writs. One, the action of covenant, dealt only with contracts under seal. The action of covenant bears a clear relation to the Statute of Frauds, but it had little effect on the development of contract precisely because it required strict attention to formality. The other, the action of debt, required less formality. Perhaps as a result it affected the growth of contract more than did covenant. Debt had its own limits, though, because the action in debt required an actual exchange. Executory contracts fell outside its scope.

Assumpsit filled the gap. At first it was more or less a cause of action for breach of implied warranty, or rather for negligent performance of contractual obligations. The logical next step was to go from misfeasance to nonfeasance—from faulty performance to the lack of performance. By the start of the seventeenth century, the common-law courts had extended assumpsit to cover bilateral executory contracts. Assumpsit by then had also triumphed over the action in debt. Until the middle of the sixteenth century, actions that could fall under either assumpsit or debt had to be brought under debt. Over time, assumpsit gradually supplanted debt, first by covering promises to pay debts, then debts alone, and then bargains without debts.

By the early 1600s, then, assumpsit had largely taken over the field of contract. This had two huge problems, though, stemming from the rules of procedure. First, the rules of evidence did not permit either party to give testimony, nor did they in civil matters until 1851. This meant that a liar could suborn perjury, perhaps through the testimony of friends or servants, without violating an oath sworn in court. In contrast, in a cause of action for debt the debtor could defend by denying the debt while under oath, if a certain number of oath-helpers swore that the defendant was telling the truth. This lack of testimony from the contracting parties was not much of a problem when an action in assumpsit was based wholly on the contents of documents. But proof of an oral contract was complicated greatly by the absence of the testimony of the parties to the contract. As John Langbein observed, "in a transactional setting the knowledge that the parties would not be allowed to testify about the transaction if it fell into contention must have encouraged prudent transaction planners to attempt to channel significant matters in

---

[c]   The account that follows is drawn largely from 2 Arthur L. Corbin, Corbin on Contracts § 275 (1950), 6 William Holdsworth, A History of English Law 379–97 (1924), and A.W.B. Simpson, A History of the Common Law of Contract 599–620 (1975).

writing." John H. Langbein, *Historical Foundations of the Law of Evidence: A View from the Ryder Sources*, 96 Colum. L. Rev. 1168, 1185 (1996). In addition, there was no right to a jury trial in debt, but there was in assumpsit. The juries of that time were supposed to decide cases based mainly on their own familiarity with the people and events before the court, not on the testimony that the trial brought forth. By the middle of the seventeenth century, evidence introduced in court had become an important basis for a jury's verdict, but only one basis. Consider, for example, an important decision from 1670 on the right of a jury to rule contrary to the views of the judge without incurring penalties. The court based its decision for the jury in part on the proposition that the evidence seen by the judge was not the same as the evidence known to the jury, so a judge could not declare with certainty that the jury had erred. Bushell's Case, 124 Eng. Rep. 1006 (C.P. 1670).

The combination meant that it was all too easy for someone to bring an action in assumpsit, and all too easy for a jury to rule based on its predilections or prejudices rather than on the facts of the case. When the only types of action for breach of contract were covenant and debt, this wasn't a problem. The sealed contract required in covenant cut off both perjurers and rogue juries. There was no such requirement in debt, but there was a requirement that there have been an actual payment by the promisee; it thus was insufficient merely to invent an exchange of oral promises. But the action in assumpsit did cover exchanges of promises, and the problem grew ever more severe. One way out would have been to allow sworn testimony and place some restraints upon juries. As we know, this eventually happened, though not for another two centuries or so. Another was to put a bit of covenant into assumpsit by requiring some sort of writing for a contract to be enforceable. That solution gave us the Statute of Frauds. Even then, however, lawmakers recognized that not every contract should be included. Some were simply too minor to warrant the time and cost of preparing a writing. On the other hand, some promises were particularly prone to false claims, and many of those caused tremendous problems if the false claims were upheld—for example, contracts to wed and contracts to pay the debt of another. Parliament thus drew up a list of contracts that could be enforced only if they were in a sufficiently detailed document, and the Statute of Frauds emerged.

(C) WHY A STATUTE OF FRAUDS?

Interpreting a statute is much easier when you know what it was intended to do. For the Statute of Frauds, this would seem an easy task; it was intended to cut down on fraud. But that is only the first level of analysis. Is that all the Statute of Frauds does? Are there other functions it serves?

In chapter 1, p. 49, we saw the three functions of form set out by Lon Fuller in "Consideration and Form"—the evidentiary, cautionary, and channeling functions. Any analysis of form must start there, but it cannot end there. Fuller's three functions may be the three most important, but they do not cover the field. In a classic article, Professor Perillo discussed nine functions in some detail and mentioned two others in passing. Joseph M. Perillo, *The Statute of Frauds in the Light of the Functions and Dysfunctions of Form,* 43 Fordham L. Rev. 39, 43–69 (1974). We will concentrate on Fuller's analysis, but we will take a look at some of the rationales delineated by Perillo.

Starting, then, with Fuller: The evidentiary function is the most obvious and the most referred-to of the three. Certainly a writing that describes the parties and the transaction is evidence that the parties in fact made a contract. This can be useful, not just in judicial proceedings, but for the contracting parties themselves; by setting down the contract's main terms in a document, they do not have to rely upon the fading memories of the original negotiators when they seek to perform or to evaluate the performance of others. Conversely, a prospective perjurer is less likely to lie if doing so requires not just a flexible interpretation of the oath but also some skills at forgery, and an associated willingness to face criminal sanctions if the forgery is detected.

The cautionary function furthers a few distinct goals. Writings take more time to prepare than oral promises, and the extra time allows the parties to an agreement to think further about their transaction and possibly change or abandon it. They also avoid the mistakes that may result from faulty memories or sloppy phrasing. Finally, whether a party is willing to put an agreement in writing, and what the party is willing to put into that writing, provides information about the party's seriousness and reliability.

Last, the channeling function lets the parties to a contract tell the court that they really do want their promises to be enforced. This helps a court decide whether the parties intended to be bound, and thus makes the court's deliberations less costly and more accurate. Additionally, it is useful for the parties to a contract to have some simple and unambiguous way to make their contracts enforceable—a so-called "safe harbor." They can use the safe harbor, or they can take their chances on some other method that may be more costly, less reliable, or both. (In practice, many, if not most, attempts to enforce contracts made without a sufficient writing come from informal dealings, typically by non-lawyers. It seems likely that the parties to these contracts did not take the possibility of breach or disagreement adequately into account. This should surprise no one. Those who form contracts think more about performance than about breach, both because the overwhelming majority of contracts are performed in full and because parties entering into a relationship, financial or otherwise, tend to be overly optimistic about its chances for success.)

Of the functions Professor Perillo identified, the most important for our purposes are the *clarifying function* and the *managerial function.*

The clarifying function is the working-out of disagreements, ambiguities, and omissions as a result of having to put a contract into writing. The managerial function is the use of standard writings to control subordinate employees and make it possible for everyone in an organization to have one reliable source for the terms of each agreement. These overlap somewhat with Fuller's three functions, but they do tease out specific advantages to written agreements that are imperfectly captured by Fuller's categories.

Each of these functions furthers some aspect of contracting behavior, but none of them does so without a cost. Critics of the Statute of Frauds argue that these costs far exceed any benefits the Statute yields. The most obvious cost is the cost of preparing and executing the writing, a cost incurred whether a contract really needed to be in writing or not. Another cost arises if a contract actually was formed but is rendered unenforceable by the Statute of Frauds, thus defeating the expectations of at least one party to the contract. Indeed, the Statute of Frauds may even be used to produce fraud. If one party to a contract knows that the contract falls within the Statute of Frauds and the other doesn't, the more knowledgeable party may prefer to keep the contract oral. If the contract is profitable, then that party will perform; if it is less profitable than some alternative, that party may choose not to perform and will then assert the Statute of Frauds as a defense. (Ethical issues may arise from using this "technical" defense, especially if the defendant's lawyer knows that the parties really did make a contract but that the Statute of Frauds would bar its enforcement. These are discussed in Section Six below.)

As we go through the most important provisions of the Statute of Frauds and its successors, it may be helpful to keep these functions in mind. To what extent are they served by a particular writing requirement? Would these functions be served if there were no writing requirement, leaving the parties to a contract to decide for themselves whether to put that contract in writing? Do the costs of a statute of frauds exceed whatever benefits it may produce? Are there other ways to produce these benefits while minimizing the associated costs?

NOTE

Questions. As mentioned earlier, Article 11 of CISG expressly rejects a writing requirement: "A contract of sale need not be concluded in or evidenced by writing and is not subject to any other requirement as to form." (Recall that CISG applies to international contracts for the sale of goods, excluding consumer transactions.) In light of the functions served by a statute of frauds, does Article 11 go too far? Or is a statute of frauds unnecessary for contracts of the sort governed by CISG?

SECTION 2.   CONTRACTS WITHIN THE STATUTE OF FRAUDS

Here we study the boundaries of the most important provisions of the Statute of Frauds—the one-year provision, the land contract provision, and the suretyship provision. (We will discuss the UCC Article 2 statute of frauds separately.)

(A) DURATION OF PERFORMANCE: THE ONE-YEAR AND LIFETIME CLAUSES

An agreement that cannot be performed within the year following its making is unenforceable unless circumstances persuade a court otherwise. This provision has brought about more controversy than any other part of the modern Statute of Frauds. Along with the controversy has been a large and unsettled body of case law. In the words of one scholar, "Creative decisions, attempting to minimize the effect of a statutory provision with no clear-cut policy basis, have led to a quibbler's paradise in which arid distinctions devoid of functional content reign supreme." Joseph M. Perillo, *The Statute of Frauds in the Light of the Functions and Dysfunctions of Form,* 43 Fordham L. Rev. 39, 78 (1974).

The controversy and uncertainty are caused in large part by the weak link between the one-year provision and the main reasons advanced for statutes of frauds. Fuller's analysis is a good place to start. For example, it often is said that a statute of frauds ensures that the parties to a contract know exactly what they agreed upon. This avoids disputes due to faulty or convenient memories, departed employees, imperfectly communicated terms, and so forth. But form isn't free; putting a contract into written form and executing it properly takes time and money. The law should therefore separate contracts that are as a class worth putting into writing from those that are not. How well does the one-year provision manage this? Bear in mind two things about the one-year provision. (1) The year runs from the time of contracting to the time for completed performance, not from the time of contracting to the time of a dispute as to the terms of the contract. (2) The performance need not take more than one solid year to complete.

A related justification for the one-year provision is proof in court, which falls under both the evidentiary and channeling functions described by Fuller. Certainly figuring out the terms of a contract is easier when those terms are in a signed document instead of just the skulls of the negotiators. (As we shall see in Chapter 5, however, even a signed writing may not keep the parties from bringing in wagonloads of extra material to supplement or interpret it.) But remember that the one year does not run from the time of contracting to the time for proof of the contract's terms, but rather from the time of contracting to the time set for completed performance. The statute of limitations for breaches of contract in most jurisdictions is six years, and depositions may not take place until a year or more after the promisee files a complaint. From the evidentiary vantage, whether a contract cannot or may not be completed within one year makes little difference against the six or seven years that may elapse between making the contract and taking depositions or answering requests for production in a resulting lawsuit.

Another rationale is that the time and bother required to put a contract into writing can operate as a sort of "cooling-off period." A contracting party, upon reflection, may think better of his agreement and want to get out. If the other party refuses to permit this, the party seeking escape can simply not sign the writing, so the writing would not be enforceable on him. This is related to the cautionary function, but it is not quite the same. The cautionary function is supposed to affect whether a contract is formed in the first place, not whether it is formed but is not enforceable. If the parties did not objectively intend to make an oral contract, then a writing requirement serves the cautionary function directly. If they have already made a contract, however, it is too late to give caution. Does the one-year provision adequately separate those contracts that require the caution of an executed writing from those that do not? Does the one-year provision guide contracting parties to put important contracts into signed writings? Does it help clarify the terms of a contract or promote efficient management? Answering these questions may not make one fonder of the one-year provision.

PROBLEM

In or Out? Which of the following promises fall within the one-year provision of the Statute of Frauds? Are your conclusions consistent with the stated purposes of the one-year provision? With the functions of form?

   a.   You promise to take care of my pet yak for one afternoon thirteen months from now.

   b.   You promise to take care of my pet yak for the next eleven months.

————

Judges frequently note their distaste for the one-year provision, as the next case shows. It also shows a common method of limiting the scope of the one-year provision.

C. R. Klewin, Inc. v. Flagship Properties, Inc.

Supreme Court of Connecticut, 1991.
220 Conn. 569, 600 A.2d 772.

■ PETERS, CHIEF JUSTICE. The sole question before us in this certified appeal is whether the provision of the statute of frauds, General Statutes § 52–550(a)(5)[1] requiring a writing for an Agreement that is not to be

---

[1]   General Statutes § 52–550 provides in pertinent part: "(a) No civil action may be maintained in the following cases unless the agreement, or a memorandum of the agreement, is made in writing and signed by the party, or the agent of the party, to be charged (5) upon any agreement that is not to be performed within one year from the making thereof."

performed within one year from the making thereof, renders unenforceable an oral contract that fails to specify explicitly the time for performance when performance of that contract within one year of its making is exceedingly unlikely. This case comes to this court upon our grant of an application for certification from the United States Court of Appeals for the Second Circuit.

[Flagship was the developer of a project, called ConnTech, near the main campus of the University of Connecticut. The master plan called for the construction of housing for hundreds of students and teachers, a hotel and convention center, and twenty industrial buildings. At a meeting in March of 1986 between Flagship representatives and representatives of G. R. Klewin, the latter named a percentage fee for acting as construction manager for the project. The meeting ended with a handshake and the statement, "We've got a deal."

Construction began on the first phase of the project—"Celeron Square"—in May of 1987. For that phase the parties entered into a written agreement. By the time it was completed, in mid-October, Flagship had become dissatisfied with Klewin's work. In March of 1988 it engaged another firm to do the sitework for Celeron Square II, the next phase. Having been replaced as construction manager, Klewin brought an action against Flagship, charging it with, among other things, breach of a contract for work on the entire project.]

Flagship moved for summary judgment, claiming, *inter alia*, that enforcement of the alleged oral contract was barred by the statute of frauds. The district court granted summary judgment, reasoning that (1) "the contract was not of an indefinite duration or openended" because full performance would take place when all phases of the ConnTech Project were completed, and (2) the contract "as a matter of law" could not possibly have been performed within one year. In drawing this second conclusion, the court focused on the sheer scope of the project and Klewin's own admission that the entire project was intended to be constructed in three to ten years.

Klewin appealed. [In the absence of controlling precedent about Connecticut law, the federal appellate court] certified to this court the following questions:

A.   Whether under the Connecticut Statute of Frauds, Conn. Gen. Stat. § 52–550(a)(5), an oral contract that fails to specify explicitly the time for performance is a contract of "indefinite duration," as that term has been used in the applicable Connecticut precedent, and therefore outside of the Statute's proscriptions?

B.   Whether an oral contract is unenforceable when the method of performance called for by the contract contemplates performance to be completed over a period of time that exceeds one year, yet the contract itself does not explicitly negate the possibility of performance within one year? We answer "yes" to the first question, and "no" to the second.

Modern scholarly commentary has found much to criticize about the continued viability of the statute of frauds. The statute has been found wanting because it serves none of its purported functions very well; see J. Perillo, [*The Statute of Frauds in the Light of the Functions and Dysfunctions of Form*, 43 Fordham L. Rev. 39 (1974)]; and because it permits or compels economically wasteful behavior; see M. Braunstein, *"Remedy, Reason, and the Statute of Frauds: A Critical Economic Analysis,"* 1989 Utah L. Rev. 383. It is, however, the one-year provision that is at issue in this case that has caused the greatest puzzlement among commentators. As Professor Farnsworth observes, "of all the provisions of the statute, it is the most difficult to rationalize." [At this point the court quoted at some length from the Farnsworth treatise on Contracts. The court followed with "see also" citations as follows.] Goldstick v. ICM Realty, 788 F.2d 456, 464 (7th Cir. 1986); D & N Boening, Inc. v. Kirsch Beverages, Inc., 63 N.Y.2d 449, 454, 472 N.E.2d 992 (1984); 1 Restatement (Second), Contracts (1979) § 130, *comment a*; J. Calamari & J. Perillo, Contracts (3d Ed. 1987) §§ 19–18, p. 807.[2]

Historians have had difficulty accounting for the original inclusion of the one-year provision.[3] Some years after the statute's enactment, one English judge stated that "the design of the statute was, not to trust to the memory of witnesses for a longer time than one year." Smith v. Westall, 1 Ld.Raym. 316, 317, 91 Eng.Rep. 1106, 1107 (1697). That explanation is, however, unpersuasive, since, as Farnsworth notes, the language of the statute is ill suited to this purpose. One eminent historian suggested that because such contracts are continuing contracts, it might be very difficult to give evidence of their formation, inasmuch as the rules of evidence of that time prohibited testimony by the parties to an action or any person who had an interest in the litigation. 6 W. Holdsworth, *supra*, p. 392. That argument, however, proves too much, since it would apply equally to all oral contracts regardless of the duration of their performance. The most extensive recent study of the history of English contract law offers plausible explanations for all of the other provisions, but acknowledges that this one is "curious." A. Simpson, A History of the Common Law of Contract (1975) p. 612. More recently, it has been suggested that the provision "may have been intended to prevent oral perjury in actions of assumpsit against customers who had forgotten the details of their purchases." P. Hamburger, *"The Conveyancing Purposes of the Statute of Frauds,"* 27 Am. J. Leg. Hist. 354, 376 n.85 (1983).

---

[2] Even the statute's most notable defender chose not to mention the one-year provision when he contended that the statute is "in essence better adapted to our needs than when it was first passed." K. Llewellyn, *"What Price Contract? An Essay in Perspective,"* 40 Yale L.J. 704, 747 (1931).

[3] The language of the original English statute was nearly identical to that of the provision we are now considering, including "any agreement that is not to be performed within the space of one year from the making thereof."

In any case, the one-year provision no longer seems to serve any purpose very well, and today its only remaining effect is arbitrarily to forestall the adjudication of possibly meritorious claims. For this reason, the courts have for many years looked on the provision with disfavor, and have sought constructions that limited its application. See, *e.g.*, Landes Construction Co. v. Royal Bank of Canada, 833 F.2d 1365, 1370 (9th Cir. 1987) (noting policy of California courts "of restricting the application of the statute to those situations precisely covered by its language"); Cunningham v. Healthco, Inc., 824 F.2d 1448, 1455 (5th Cir.1987) (one-year provision does not apply if the contract "conceivably" can be performed within one year); Hodge v. Evans Financial Corporation, 823 F.2d 559, 561 (D.C.Cir.1987) (statute of frauds "has long been construed narrowly and literally"); Goldstick v. ICM Realty, *supra*, 464 ("Courts tend to take the concept of 'capable of full performance' quite literally because they find the one-year limitation irksome.").

II

Our case law in Connecticut, like that in other jurisdictions, has taken a narrow view of the one-year provision of the statute of frauds now codified as § 52–550(a)(5). In Russell v. Slade, 12 Conn. 455, 460 (1838), this court held that "it has been repeatedly adjudged, that unless it appear *from the agreement itself*, that it is *not* to be performed within a year, the statute does not apply. The statute of frauds plainly means an agreement *not* to be performed within the space of a year, and *expressly* and *specifically* so agreed. A *contingency* is not within it; nor any case that *depends upon contingency*. It does *not* extend to cases where the thing only *may* be performed within the year." (Emphases in original; citation and internal quotation marks omitted.)

A few years later, in Clark v. Pendleton, 20 Conn. 495, 508 (1850), the statute was held not to apply to a contract that was to be performed following a voyage that both parties expected to take one and one-half years. . . . In this century, in Appleby v. Noble, 101 Conn. 54, 57, 124 A. 717 (1924), this court held that "[a] contract is not within this clause of the statute unless *its terms are so drawn* that it cannot by any possibility be performed fully within one year." (Emphasis added.) In Burkle v. Superflow Mfg. Co., 137 Conn. 488, 492–93, 78 A.2d 698 (1951), we delineated the line that separates contracts that are within the one-year provision from those that are excluded from it. "Where *the time for performance is definitely fixed at more than one year*, the contract is, of course, within the statute. . . . If no time is *definitely fixed* but full performance may occur within one year through the happening of a contingency upon which the contract depends, it is not within the statute." (Emphases added; citations omitted.)

More recently, in Finley v. Aetna Life & Casualty Co., 202 Conn. 190, 197, 520 A.2d 208 (1987), we stated that " '[u]nder the prevailing interpretation, the enforceability of a contract under the one-year provision does not turn on the actual course of subsequent events, nor on the expectations of the parties as to the probabilities. Contracts of uncertain duration are simply excluded; the provision covers *only* those contracts whose performance *cannot possibly* be completed within a year.' (Emphasis added.) 1 Restatement (Second), Contracts, [§ 130, comment a]."

In light of this unbroken line of authority, the legislature's decision repeatedly to reenact the provision in language virtually identical to that of the 1677 statute suggests legislative approval of the restrictive interpretation that this court has given to the one-year provision. "[T]he action of the General Assembly in re-enacting the statute, including the clause in question is presumed to have been done in the light of those decisions." Turner v. Scanlon, 146 Conn. 149, 156, 148 A.2d 334 (1959); see also Ralston Purina Co. v. Board of Tax Review, 203 Conn. 425, 439– 40, 525 A.2d 91 (1987).

III

Bearing this history in mind, we turn to the questions certified to us by the federal court. Our case law makes no distinction, with respect to exclusion from the statute of frauds, between contracts of uncertain or indefinite duration and contracts that contain no express terms defining the time for performance. The two certified questions therefore raise only one substantive issue. That issue can be framed as follows: in the exclusion from the statute of frauds of all contracts except those "whose performance cannot possibly be completed within a year"; (emphasis omitted) Finley v. Aetna Life & Casualty Co., *supra*, 197; what meaning should be attributed to the word "possibly"? One construction of "possibly" would encompass only contracts whose completion within a year would be inconsistent with the express terms of the contract. An alternate construction would include as well contracts such as the one involved in this case, in which, while no time period is expressly specified, it is (as the district court found) realistically impossible for performance to be completed within a year. We now hold that the former and not the latter is the correct interpretation. "The critical test . . . is whether 'by its terms' the agreement is not to be performed within a year," so that the statute will not apply where "the alleged agreement contain[s] [no] provision which directly or indirectly regulated the time for performance." Freedman v. Chemical Construction Corporation, 43 N.Y.2d 260, 265, 372 N.E.2d 12 (1977). "It is the law of this state, as it is elsewhere, that a contract is not within this clause of the statute unless *its terms are so drawn that* it cannot by any possibility be performed fully within one year." (Emphasis added.) Burkle v. Superflow Mfg. Co., *supra*, 492.

Flagship contends, to the contrary, that the possibility to which this court referred in *Burkle* must be a reasonable possibility rather than a theoretical possibility. It is true that in *Burkle* this court rejected the argument that "since all the members of a partnership [that was a party to the contract] may possibly die within a year, the contract is not within the statute." We noted that "[n]o case has come to our attention where the rule that the possibility of death within a year removes a contract from the statute has been extended to apply to the possibility of the death of more than one individual." Id., 494. In *Burkle*, however, we merely refused to extend further yet another of the rules by which the effect of the provision has been limited. *Burkle* did not purport to change the well established rule of narrow construction of the underlying one-year provision.

Most other jurisdictions follow a similar rule requiring an express contractual provision specifying that performance will extend for more than one year. Only "[a] few jurisdictions, contrary to the great weight of authority . . . hold that the intention of the parties may put their oral agreement within the operation of the Statute." 3 S. Williston, Contracts (3d Ed. W. Jaeger 1960) § 495, pp. 584–85. In "the leading case on this section of the Statute"; id., p. 578; the Supreme Court of the United States undertook an extensive survey of the case law up to that time and concluded that "[i]t appears to have been the settled construction of this clause of the statute in England, before the Declaration of Independence, that an oral agreement which, according to the intention of the parties, *as shown by the terms of the contract*, might be fully performed within a year from the time it was made, was not within the statute, although the time of its performance was uncertain, and might probably extend, and be expected by the parties to extend, and did in fact extend, beyond the year. The several States of the Union, in reenacting this provision of the statute of frauds in its original words, must be taken to have adopted the known and settled construction which it had received by judicial decisions in England." (Emphasis added.) Warner v. Texas & Pacific R. Co., 164 U.S. 418, 422–23 (1896). "The parties may well have expected that the contract would continue in force for more than one year; it may have been very improbable that it would not do so; and it did in fact continue in force for a much longer time. But they made no stipulation which in terms, or by reasonable inference, required that result. The question is not what the probable, or expected, or actual performance of the contract was; but whether the contract, according to the reasonable interpretation *of its terms*, required that it should not be performed within the year." (Emphasis added.) Id., 434; see also Walker v. Johnson, 96 U.S. 424, 427 (1877); McPherson v. Cox, 96 U.S. 404, 416–17 (1877).

Because the one-year provision "is an anachronism in modern life . . . we are not disposed to expand its destructive force." Farmer v. Arabian American Oil Co., 277 F.2d 46, 51 (2d Cir.1960).[4] When a contract contains no express terms about the time for performance, no sound reason of policy commends judicial pursuit of a collateral inquiry into whether, at the time of the making of the contract, it was realistically possible that performance of the contract would be completed within a

---

[4]   In this case, one of the issues before the Second Circuit was whether the oral agreement could have been performed within a year.

year. Such a collateral inquiry would not only expand the "destructive force" of the statute by extending it to contracts not plainly within its terms, but would also inevitably waste judicial resources on the resolution of an issue that has nothing to do with the merits of the case or the attainment of a just outcome.[5] See 2 A. Corbin, *supra*, § 275, p. 14 (the statute "has been in part the cause of an immense amount of litigation as to whether a promise is within the statute or can by any remote possibility be taken out of it. This latter fact is fully evidenced by the space necessary to be devoted to the subject in this volume and by the vast number of cases to be cited").

We therefore hold that an oral contract that does not say, in express terms, that performance is to have a specific duration beyond one year is, as a matter of law, the functional equivalent of a contract of indefinite duration for the purposes of the statute of frauds. Like a contract of indefinite duration, such a contract is enforceable because it is outside the proscriptive force of the statute regardless of how long completion of performance will actually take.

The first certified question is answered "yes." The second certified question is answered "no."

NOTES

(1) *Questions.* Would the outcome have been different if the agreement, as alleged, had contained either of the following terms? (a) "Klewin will not be required to do site work for Celeron Square II within twelve months of this agreement." (b) "Klewin's fee is to be, at a minimum, $9 million, payable in full not later than four years from this date."

(2) *Analogs.* In D & N Boening, Inc. v. Kirsch Beverages, Inc., a New York case cited to in *C. R. Klewin*, the court gave the following catalog of earlier New York cases in which oral agreements were upheld as being fully performable within one year:

[W]here either party had the option to terminate the agreement on seven months' notice; where the agreement merely set the terms of

---

[5]   We recognize, as Flagship observed at oral argument, that comment *a* to § 130 of the Restatement (Second) of Contracts (1979) . . . includes an illustration that is inconsistent with the result that we are reaching today. Contrary to illustration 3 (which is drawn from Warner v. Texas & Pacific R. Co., 164 U.S. 418 (1896)), which supports our holding, illustration 4 states: "A orally promises B to sell him five crops of potatoes to be grown on a specified farm in Minnesota, and B promises to pay a stated price on delivery. The contract is within the Statute of Frauds. It is impossible in Minnesota for five crops of potatoes to mature in one year." The illustration is adapted from illustration 11 to § 198 of the Restatement (First) of Contracts (1928), which does not include case citations. The Restatement (Second) supports the illustration by citing Adams v. Big Three Industries, Inc., 549 S.W.2d 411 (Tex.Civ.App.1977). The *Adams* court held that "when no time for performance has been specified, a 'reasonable time' will be implied, and what is a reasonable time must be determined from all the circumstances, the situation of the parties, and the subject matter of the contract. . . . Where an agreement, by its terms or the nature of the performance required, cannot be performed within one year, it necessarily comes within the purview of the statute. . . . If, as here, the contract is not a written one and depends upon disputed facts, the determination of what constitutes a reasonable time is a question of fact." (Citations omitted.) Id., 414–15. In our view, illustration 3 more closely represents the law of this state.

anticipated prospective purchases but did not bind either party to any particular transaction; where defendant had the option to discontinue at any time the activities upon which the agreement was conditioned; where defendant had the option of selling at any time the property on lease to plaintiff for four years; where no provision in the agreement directly or indirectly regulated the time for performance despite the extreme unlikelihood of its completion within one year; where employment was terminable for any just and sufficient cause wherever dismissal was deemed necessary for the welfare of the company.

In *Boening* itself, the alleged agreement was to last as long as the claimant performed satisfactorily, exerted its best efforts, and acted in good faith. (The claimant had been appointed the exclusive distributor, in parts of Long Island, of a chocolate drink called "Yoo-Hoo.") The court said there was no way the performances on either side could be concluded within a year, except by a breach on one side or the other. Compare the paragraph near the end of the foregoing opinion, beginning "We therefore hold. . . . " Is the *Boening* case consistent with that paragraph?

(3)   *Possible, Practicable, or Predicted?* Chief Justice Peters noted in passing that not all courts narrow the scope of the one-year provision to the degree in *Klewin.* Most jurisdictions do follow the approach in *Klewin,* not requiring a writing for promises that could be performed within one year only by efforts that no actual promisor would undertake or by the occurrence of events that almost certainly would not happen within a century, much less a year. See Nasso v. Seagal, 263 F.Supp.2d 596 (E.D.N.Y. 2002) (contract was "susceptible of fulfillment" within one year even though promisor argued that "it would defy common sense to contend that four feature films would be produced and released within one year"). But a significant minority of jurisdictions read the one-year provision more expansively. These readings fall into two categories. In one, the court looks at whether performance within one year is actually possible, rather than possible in theory. See Dean v. Myers, 466 So.2d 952 (Ala. 1985) (joint venture to build condominiums; within statute because there was no "reasonable possibility of performance within a year"). In the other, the court looks at the intent of the parties; even if the promisor could have performed within a year, the contract will fall within the Statute of Frauds if the parties contemplated performance over a longer period. See Sawyer v. Mills, 295 S.W.3d 79 (Ky. 2009) (agreement to pay employee one million dollars at the rate of ten thousand dollars per month is within one-year provision; even though it would have been possible for the employer to make the payments within one year, the employer "clearly balked" at agreeing to a lump-sum payment and thus the parties did not intend performance to take less than one year).

Informal Extensions of Employment

Often a person, having been hired for a term, remains on the job when the term is over. Suppose the original employment agreement was set forth in a writing that satisfied the Statute of Frauds. Once that contract comes to an end, the employer and employee may keep going under either an express contract or a contract implied by conduct. An express agreement was described by witnesses in Rash v. J.V. Intermediate, Ltd. [J.V.], 498 F.3d 1201 (10th Cir.2007). According to them, when Rash's initial employment with J.V. was over the parties "just kept going," and the employer's president said to Rash, "Clayton, as long as you're with J.V., that contract is good 'til the end." Does the agreement to extend employment have to be in a sufficient writing? The courts go in different directions.

One view is that the parties can bind themselves to a term in the written agreement by making an "oral renewal" of the agreement, at least if the renewal is for a period no longer than a year. In re Arbitration (Acadia Company v. Edlitz), 165 N.E.2d 411 (N.Y.1960). At the other extreme is Farone v. Bag'n Baggage, Ltd., 165 S.W.3d 795 (Tex.Civ.App.2005). In that case the parties disagreed about Farone's rights long after the close of a term covered by his only written employment agreement. The court said: "there may have been implied agreements to continue the original contract; but, without a further writing during each period of extension of the original two year agreement, any subsequent agreements are not enforceable." *Id.* at 801.

Farone was distinguished in Rash v. J.V. Intermediate, Ltd. (applying Texas law). What *Farone* means, that court thought, is that the parties to an employment contract cannot extend it orally *for a period more than a year*. In Rash's case the trial court had found that the parties had, by implication, extended his employment month to month. *Farone* was therefore distinguishable. "[N]othing [there] precludes parties from impliedly renewing a contract or extending its time period beyond its express terms *indefinitely or for less than one year.*" *Id.* at 1214.

————

Lifetime Agreements

On the face of it, a lifetime agreement should not fall within the one-year provision of the Statute of Frauds. Even the most robust person may be in the wrong place at the wrong time, as disasters continually remind us. The intuitive answer is generally the correct one; because we may die at any time, a lifetime agreement may be performed in full within a year. See Doherty v. Doherty Ins. Agency, 878 F.2d 546 (1st Cir. 1989) ("contract for lifetime employment is not subject to the statute of frauds, because the contract may be performed within one year if the employee happens to die").

Now consider the following four promises.

1. A promises to work for B for five years.

2. A promises to work for B for the rest of A's life.

3.   A promises to work for B for five years or the rest of A's life, whichever is shorter.

4.   A promises to work for B for five years, but performance is excused upon A's death.

The first promise falls within the one-year provision, because by its terms it cannot be completed until more than one year has passed. The second promise does not fall within the one-year provision, because A may die within one year. The other two have proved vexing.

In practice, promises 3 and 4 are the same. A has promised to work for B for five years. If A dies before the five years have passed, A is no longer obligated to work for B. This is true whether death is described as the end of the contract or as an excuse for non-performance. In theory, however, promises 3 and 4 are very different. In promise 3, A has set up alternative ways to perform. As long as one of these ways is outside the Statute of Frauds, the contract as a whole is outside the Statute of Frauds. In contrast, promise 4 does not say that A has performed in full if she dies before five years have passed. It says that she may perform only by working for five years, but her failure to perform will be excused if she dies during the term of the contract.

The one-year provision of the Statute of Frauds follows theory rather than practice. Promise 3 can be performed within one year, so it is outside the Statute of Frauds. Promise 4 cannot be performed within one year, so it is within the Statute of Frauds. This is perfectly logical, given the Statute of Frauds's requirement that the performance be completed within one year. Non-performance is not the same thing as performance, even though the non-performance may have been excused.

But look at promises 3 and 4 from the perspective of B, a non-lawyer. To someone untrained in the law, the promises are two ways of saying the same thing. A works for B for five years; if she dies first, she doesn't have to perform. B might thus use the two promises interchangeably, seeing no practical difference between them, but with calamitous results if B tries to enforce an oral version of promise 4.

NOTE

In and Out? Promises 3 and 4 raise the related issue of how alternative promises fit within the one-year provision of the Statute of Frauds. For example, what if we combine the yak-sitting problems earlier and ask whether your promise either to take care of my pet yak for the next eleven months or to take care of my pet yak for one afternoon thirteen months from now falls within the one-year provision. A hasty reading of Restatement § 130(1) would suggest yes: this provision applies "[w]here *any* promise in a contract cannot be fully performed within a year." But courts and commentators agree that alternative promises are to be treated as though they are not distinct promises, but different ways of fulfilling the same promise. Accordingly, if *either* alternative can be performed within one year, the one-year Statute of Frauds does not apply. See Professional Bull Riders, Inc. v. AutoZone, Inc., 113 P.3d 757 (Colo. 2005).

Termination Clauses

Termination clauses pose the same problems as death. "A promises to work for B for five years, but B may fire A at any time upon giving one month's notice" in practice means that A's employment may well be for less than one year. Her *employment*, but not her *performance*. A still can perform in full only by working for five years. B may well fire her within the first year, but that doesn't mean that A has performed in full—only that her performance was curtailed. Here, however, the case law looks better for the party wanting to keep an agreement outside the Statute of Frauds. Insofar as there is a trend, it is toward holding that a contract with a termination clause is not within the Statute of Frauds if one of the parties can terminate the contract within one year of its making. See Bennett v. Atomic Prods. Corp., 903 N.Y.S.2d 154 (App. Div. 2010) (contract to develop and market medical equipment not within Statute of Frauds, because the defendant had the right to terminate it at will by ending its sale of the products).

NOTES

(1)   Would the contract above be enforceable if the termination clause permitted termination only for cause? Compare Collins v. Allied Pharmacy Mgt., 871 S.W.2d 929 (Tex. Civ. App. 1994) ("the possibility of termination for cause does not take a [contract for more than one year] outside the statute of frauds") with Foley v. Interactive Data Corp., 765 P.2d 373 (Cal. 1988) (clause permitting termination for cause "does not render an employment agreement unenforceable under the statute of frauds").

(2)   What if a contract of employment was to be in effect "for six months, with an option on the part of the employee to extend it for four years"? Is this within the one-year provision of the Statute of Frauds? Does it matter whether the employee is the plaintiff or the defendant? Would your answer change if the contract provided for employment for four years and six months, with the option to terminate it after six months?

(B) INTERESTS IN REAL PROPERTY

The land contract provision encompasses contracts "to transfer to any person any interest in land," in the words of Restatement § 125(1). Legislatures, courts, and commentators have generally left it alone, apart from an early need to rephrase the original and ambiguous language. Indeed, when Great Britain repealed most of the Statute of Frauds, it left behind the land contract provision. But why?

The explanation for this clause has shifted somewhat over time. One early justification was the importance of real property as a source and

Leases of real property also are within the land-contract Statute of Frauds. A lease transfers some of the rights of ownership; during the term of the lease, the landlord's right to enter and occupy the property is greatly curtailed. What is true for leases is true for subleases. Berdick v. Costilla, 97 So. 3d 316 (Fla. Dist. Ct. App. 2012). Most legislatures have carved out one important exception to this rule: short-term leases of real property, sometimes but not usually limited to leases for residential purposes. Cal. Civ. Code § 1624(a)(3); N.Y. Gen. Oblig. Law § 5–703. What policies might this carve-out serve?

PROBLEM

The Law of the Land. Which, if any, of the following contracts would fall within the land contract provision of the statute of frauds, and why?

a. An owner's contract with a real estate broker to sell the owner's land for a commission.

b. An option to purchase a piece of real property.

c. An agreement revoking a contract for the sale of real property.

d. An agreement resolving a disputed boundary between two pieces of real property.

(C) THE SURETYSHIP CLAUSE

Suretyship Agreements

Before we can discuss the suretyship provision of the Statute of Frauds, we should discuss what a suretyship contract is. This type of contract makes one person liable for the obligations of another. Co-signers on loans are generally sureties. So are bail bondsmen. We traditionally refer to the person liable for the obligations of another person as the *surety* and to the person whose obligations the surety shares as the *principal*. There are actually two common terms for this relation: *suretyship* and *guaranty*. A surety normally is jointly and severally liable with the principal, whereas a guarantor normally agrees to fulfill the principal's obligations only after the principal has failed to do so. Drawing lines between these is not necessary for our purposes. For the sake of simplicity, we will refer collectively to these contracts as suretyship contracts. Both the surety and the principal are liable to the *obligee* (sometimes called a creditor) for the same performance, though the obligee can get no more than one performance from the two obligors.[d]

---

[d] The Restatement (Third) of Suretyship and Guaranty avoids this messy terminology by using its own terms. The person to whom the obligation is owed is still called the obligee, but the principal is called the *principal obligor* and the surety or guarantor is called the *secondary obligor*. Restatement § 1. The obligation owed by the principal obligor to the obligee is called the *underlying obligation* and the contractual obligation owed by the secondary obligor to the obligee is called the *secondary obligation*. Id.

An example may help. Suppose Paige wanted to borrow money from Olivia. Olivia, aware that Paige has been financially imprudent, told Paige that she would lend Paige the money only if someone with good credit would agree to guarantee that the loan would be repaid. Paige's sister, Sarah, had excellent credit, and agreed to make that promise. In this scenario, Paige is the principal, Sarah is the surety, and Olivia is the obligee (or creditor). The same terms would apply if Paige had already borrowed money from Olivia, but breached their loan agreement, and Olivia demanded that Paige get a co-signer or else she would sue to collect the debt. If Sarah promised to repay Olivia, then once again Sarah would be a surety, Paige the principal, and Olivia the obligee.

In this example there are two distinct duties owed to the obligee. One is the duty the principal (or principal obligor) owes to the obligee—here, Paige's obligation to repay Olivia. The other is the duty the surety (or secondary obligor) owes to the obligee—here, Sarah's promise to pay Olivia. The second duty is the one relevant to this provision of the Statute of Frauds.

Like the land-contract provision of the Statute of Frauds, the suretyship provision has not been particularly controversial. No state has repealed it, and Great Britain spared this provision when it demolished most of its Statute of Frauds. Unlike some other provisions of the Statute of Frauds, the suretyship provision is generally thought to serve the same useful purposes it did in 1677. First among these is its evidentiary function. Even a scrupulous obligee faced with a defaulting principal might misremember or exaggerate casual comments by a third party to the extent that they would amount to a promise. And not all obligees are scrupulous. A writing requirement should prevent the errors of the scrupulous obligee and deter the lies of the unscrupulous obligee. Moreover, suretyship contracts pose problems that most other contracts do not. For instance, the surety is not paid by the obligee, so there is less evidence of a suretyship agreement. See Restatement (Third) of Suretyship and Guaranty § 11 cmt. *b*.

The suretyship provision also serves the cautionary function. Writing requirements slow down those subject to them. It is easy to make an offhand promise to guarantee a loan without appreciating how serious the consequences may be. Having to put that promise into a signed writing may allow the promisor to reconsider her well-meaning but reckless promise. This is especially important because many sureties, like Sarah above, are not paid for their promises. If these promises do not feel particularly businesslike, then it is less likely that those who make them will do so with businesslike caution.

1. SCOPE

Not every promisor who agrees to take on the debt of another is a surety. The law draws a distinction between a promise that guarantees the principal's duty to the obligee and one that does not. Only the former falls within the Statute of Frauds. The original Statute referred to performing the duty "of another," not of one's own. There are two major situations in which that distinction is important. One is if the surety is taking the place of the principal rather than merely guaranteeing that the principal will perform. If that occurs, then the newcomer is a principal, not a surety. If Sarah told Olivia, not that she would guarantee Paige's debt, but that she would take on Paige's obligations, and if Olivia agreed, then Sarah is not a surety. By accepting Sarah's offer, Olivia discharged Paige from any further liability under the contract. Sarah is not answering for the debt of another; she is answering for her own debt. This is called a *novation*.

The other situation arises when the third party directly enters into a contract with the obligee to pay for a benefit that the obligee will give to the recipient. Then the third party is not agreeing to pay the debt of another; she is the only party who ever had an obligation, and so is not guaranteeing the debt of anyone other than herself. Under our hypothetical, this would happen if Sarah entered into a contract with Olivia for a loan whose proceeds were to go to Paige. In the terms of art, the promisor's liability is *original* rather than *collateral*. This distinction is explored in the case below.

Langman v. Alumni Association of the University of Virginia

Virginia Supreme Court, 1994.
442 S.E.2d 669.

[The Alumni Association accepted a "gift" that later proved to be a burden. The gift was a deed to a commercial property called "Ferdinand's Arcade." One of the donors was Dr. M.W. Langman. The Association acknowledged the gift and had the deed recorded. When the donors had bought the property, they incurred a debt and granted a lien (mortgage) on the property to secure the debt. Their deed to the Association referred to the debt, and continued:

> The Grantee [Association] does hereby assume payment of such obligation and agrees to hold the Grantors harmless from further liability on such obligation.

Dr. Langman brought this action against the Association a few years later. The loan charges and expenses of operating the Arcade had outrun the income it produced. Langman had had to pay part of the debt that came due following the gift, and she sought reimbursement under the debt-assumption clause quoted above.[e]

---

[e]   The other donor, Caleb Stowe, had borne some of the post-transfer charges, writing that off as a gift. Following a business failure, however, he had discontinued payments on the debt.

The trial court ruled for the Association, finding that it had "no clear understanding of the deed's contents" and that there had been no meeting of the minds with respect to the debt.[f] Langman appealed].

■ BARBARA MILANO KEENAN, JUSTICE. [First, the court rejected some findings by the trial court, saying that the evidence supporting them had been erroneously admitted.]

A grantee who accepts a deed becomes contractually bound by its provisions, and becomes liable to perform any promise or undertaking imposed by the deed on the grantee, including a promise to assume an existing mortgage.

[Next, the court described an argument made by the Association, based on the suretyship clause of the Virginia Statute of Frauds, as quoted in the footnote.[g] From this provision, the Association argued that it was not liable because it had not signed a written agreement to assume the mortgage.] The Alumni Association asserts that, because Langman would remain secondarily liable on the mortgage debt even after an effective assumption of the debt, the Alumni Association's agreement to assume the mortgage was a "collateral" promise falling within the scope of Code § 11–2(4). We disagree.

A grantee who assumes an existing mortgage is not a surety. The grantee makes no promise to the mortgagee to pay the debt of another, but promises the grantor to pay to the mortgagee the debt the grantee owes to the grantor. This is an original undertaking. Blanton v. Keneipp, 155 Va. 668, 678 (1931).

A collateral undertaking to which Code § 11–2(4) applies is one in which the promisor is merely a surety or guarantor, receives no direct benefit, and is liable only if the debtor defaults. Colonial Ford Truck Sales, Inc. v. Schneider, 325 S.E.2d 91, 93–94 (Va.1985). Here, the Alumni Association received a direct benefit and did not merely act as surety for the grantors. Therefore, we conclude that the trial court did not err in ruling that the statute of frauds does not bar enforcement of the mortgage assumption clause.

PROBLEM

The Very Thrifty Caterpillar. Caterpillar, Inc. made a promise to see that a provider of skilled nursing, Rosewood Care Center, would be paid for giving care to Betty Jo Cook. Cook, an employee of Caterpillar, had suffered a workplace injury, had been hospitalized for some months, and had made a

---

f   Further findings: The debt-assumption clause was mistakenly placed in the deed by an unknown draftsman; the Association "did not knowingly accept the gift with contractual conditions"; the deed contained provisions contrary to the parties' intentions; and, by disavowing its obligation, the Association had "sufficiently rejected the gift to require a finding . . . that the conveyance is ineffective."

g   Unless a promise, contract, agreement, representation, assurance, or ratification, or some memorandum or note thereof, is in writing and signed by the party to be charged or his agent, no action shall be brought in any of the following cases.

workers' compensation claim against Caterpillar. Rosewood admitted Cook as a patient at the request of Dr. Norma Just, employed by Caterpillar to arrange for medical care in this and like cases. Dr. Just told Rosewood that Cook's care would be "100% covered," and she asked that the bills be sent to Caterpillar's workers' compensation division. Caterpillar did not pay all of the bills. Rosewood sued for breach. Caterpillar asserted the suretyship provision of the Statute of Frauds. And Rosewood argued that Caterpillar's promise was original, not collateral.

Which is it? What kinds of evidence might be helpful in this connection? What of testimony by Dr. Just that she meant, on behalf of Caterpillar, to assure Rosewood that it would not suffer from Cook's failure to pay? Or testimony on behalf of Rosewood that it understood Dr. Just to mean "Don't bother Cook; we'll just pay for her care"? See Rosewood Care Center v. Caterpillar, Inc., 877 N.E.2d 1091 (Ill. 2007).

A court might prefer evidence less subjective than testimony about someone's state of mind. What more objective evidence might be introduced?

2.   THE MAIN PURPOSE RULE

So far we have looked at exceptions that apply because the promisor is not a surety at all. Now we will consider an important exception that applies even though the promisor *is* a surety. Suppose the surety acted, not to benefit the principal, but to benefit itself. Then most of the reasons for protecting the surety fall away. In the words of the Restatement (Third) of Suretyship and Guaranty, if the surety's

> main purpose is its own pecuniary or business advantage, the gratuitous or sentimental element often present in suretyship is eliminated, the likelihood of disproportion in the values exchanged between [surety] and obligee is reduced, and the commercial context commonly provides evidentiary safeguards [; consequently,] there is less need for cautionary or evidentiary formality.

§ 11 cmt. k. The *main purpose* or *leading object* rule is much litigated. A representative case follows.

Central Ceilings, Inc. v. National Amusements, Inc.

Appeals Court of Massachusetts, 2007.
70 Mass.App.Ct. 172, 873 N.E.2d 754.

[Central Ceilings (Central) was engaged in March of 2000 to do carpentry and other work on a projected theater complex, the owner of which was National Amusements. Central was a subcontractor; the prime contractor was the Old Colony Construction Corporation (Old Colony). By mid-summer all three firms were under some stress. The date for which completion of the complex had been first scheduled had just passed. Completion had been rescheduled for September 3. A delay beyond that seemed likely. The owner cared about delay, partly because it hoped to outstrip competitors. Old Colony had its own problems—unpaid bills and a cash shortage. That led Central to worry about getting payments from Old Colony. Agents of the three firms conferred about their concerns on or about July 1. At the conference, Central's agent, McPherson, said to National's agent, Brady, "you've got to guarantee me the payment. You've got to guarantee me that I will get funded for this project." Brady said that he would guarantee McPherson.

Central continued work, having been promised that National would pay, in time, what Old Colony owed it on the project. Months later, when National learned that it owed nothing more to Old Colony, it resisted paying Central. Central sued National for breach of contract, and won a verdict and judgment for some $600,000. National appealed, invoking, among other defenses, the suretyship provision of the Statute of Frauds.

The court said: "The principal issue before us ... is whether enforcement of the oral agreement is barred by the Statute of Frauds." The relevant part of the applicable statute (Massachusetts General Laws chapter 259) is as follows:

§ 1. Certain Contracts Actionable Only if in Writing.

No action shall be brought:

Second, To charge a person upon a special promise to answer for the debt, default or misdoings of another;

Unless the promise, contract or agreement upon which such action is brought, or some memorandum or note thereof, is in writing and signed by the party to be charged therewith or by some person thereunto by him lawfully authorized.]

■ PERETTA, JUDGE. National argues on appeal that Brady's alleged oral promise to McPherson at the meeting prior to July 4, 2000, was, at best, a promise "to answer for the debt . . . of another," G. L. c. 259, § 1, Second, and was unenforceable as it was not in writing.

In ruling on National's posttrial motions, the judge [below] applied the long-recognized exception to the Statute, the so-called "leading object" or "main purpose" exception. In Ames v. Foster, 106 Mass. 400, 403 (1871), the court stated:

[A] case is not within the statute, where, upon the whole transaction, the fair inference is, that the leading object or purpose and the effect of the transaction was the purchase or acquisition by the promisor from the promisee of some property, lien or benefit which he did not before possess, but which enured to him by reason of his promise, so that the debt for which he is liable may fairly be deemed to be a debt of his own, contracted in such purchase or acquisition.

See Nelson v. Boynton, 44 Mass. 396, 400 (1841) (cited in *Ames, supra*, and in which "original" and "collateral" promises are distinguished for purposes of Statute); Hayes v. Guy, 348 Mass. 754, 756, 205 N.E.2d 699

(1965) (discussing "main purpose" exception to Statute and citing Williston, Contracts [3rd ed.] § 472); Barboza v. Liberty Contractors Co., 18 Mass.App.Ct. 971, 972, 469 N.E.2d 1303 (1984) (same, citing Restatement [Second] of Contracts § 116 [1979]).

[National contended that the alleged agreement was outside the Statute only if it constituted a "novation"—if, that is, it substituted one party for another. The agreement would have been a novation if it had released Old Colony from its obligation to Central, putting National in place as the obligor instead.]

Novation, however, is but one ground on which a promise is removed from the operation of the Statute. The "leading object" exception to the Statute addresses a separate and distinct set of circumstances. They are that (1) a third party is indebted; (2) there is no novation; and (3) the third party's duty to the creditor will be terminated by the performance promised by the defendant. See 4 Corbin, Contracts, *supra* § 16.12 at 362. Under the "leading object" exception to the Statute, an oral agreement that does not effect a novation may nonetheless be enforceable if the facts and circumstances of the transaction show that the promise was given primarily or solely to serve the promisor's own interests.

In another line of decisions, it is recognized that a property owner's promise to pay subcontractors or suppliers may, in appropriate circumstances, come within the "leading object" exception to the Statute. See Hayes v. Guy, 348 Mass. at 756–757; Barboza v. Liberty Contractors Co., 18 Mass.App.Ct. at 971. See also Gegan, *Some Exceptions to the Suretyship Statute of Frauds: A Tale of Two Courts*, 79 St. John's L. Rev. 319, 353 (2005). Based upon these authorities the question now before us is whether the circumstances presented in the instant case are such as to bring it within the "leading object" exception to the Statute.

There was evidence here to show that (1) National wanted to open the theater at the Project by the end of August so as to capture large audiences over the Labor Day weekend and thereby tap the revenue and business opportunities associated with a movie premier and the Labor Day weekend; (2) as of the beginning of July, the work to be completed for the anticipated opening would have to be completed in a "tight time frame"; (3) Central was one of the "core" subcontractors on the Project and was responsible for significant portions of the work to be completed; (4) Central had completed its preliminary work and was poised to start building; and (5) given the circumstances, Central was one of the few subcontractors in Massachusetts, if not the only one, capable of delivering the necessary work in the time frame desired by National.

Under these circumstances, we conclude that the evidence was sufficient to warrant a finding that National's promise—made through Brady, who was found by the jury to have the apparent authority to make such a promise—was given to secure Central's continued and expedited performance at the Project and that the satisfaction of any obligation on the part of Old Colony was merely incidental to that promise. See *Hayes* at 757; *Barboza* at 971–72.

PROBLEM

The School of Self-Interest. The holder of a mortgage on "Isabella's Arcade" objected to a transfer of the property by the owner (mortgagor) to her college, with the owner continuing to pay the mortgage from other assets. In order to meet the mortgagee's objection, the college gave the mortgagee an oral undertaking that it would satisfy the donor's debt if she failed to do so. The mortgagee withdrew its objection and the gift was made. The donor defaulted on the mortgage. Does the suretyship clause bar enforcement of the college's promise? Or does the main-purpose doctrine apply?

Of Nursing Care and Caterpillar's Main Purpose

Refer again to the facts of Rosewood Care Center v. Caterpillar, as stated at p. 365 above. Rosewood contended that Caterpillar's alleged oral promise to pay for Cook's care was enforceable because of the main-purpose exception to the statute. Caterpillar denied that the main purpose of any promise it might have made was to promote its own interest. Indeed, Caterpillar denied that it had received any benefit from the agreement. Citing authorities, the Illinois court said that most jurisdictions had adopted the exception, and that it had long been a part of Illinois law. The court disposed of the issue in the two following paragraphs:

"Whether the 'main purpose' or 'leading object' of the promisor is to promote a pecuniary or business advantage to it is generally a question for the trier of fact. 9 R. Lord, Williston on Contracts § 22:20, at 308 (4th ed.1999). In making this determination, the following factors may be considered: 'prior default, inability or repudiation of the principal obligor; forbearance of the creditor to enforce a lien on property in which the promisor has an interest or which he intends to use; equivalence between the value of the benefit and the amount promised; lack of participation by the principal obligor in the making of the surety's promise; a larger transaction to which the suretyship is incidental.' Restatement (Second) of Contracts § 116, Comment *b*, at 300 (1981). See also Restatement (Third) of Suretyship & Guaranty § 11, Comment to Subsection (3)(c) (1996); P. Alces, Law of Suretyship & Guaranty, § 4:20 (1996). The crux of this inquiry is the reason the promisor made the promise, *i.e.*, the impetus for the promise. See [Davis v. Patrick], 141 U.S. at 488 ('there is a marked difference between a promise which, without any interest in the subject-matter of the promise in the promisor . . . and that which, though operating upon the debt of a third party, is also and mainly for the benefit of the promisor').

"Here, a decision on what was Caterpillar's 'main purpose' or 'leading object' in making the promise cannot be made based on the allegations in the complaint. What is required is evidence from which one can ascertain whether the reason for Caterpillar's promise was in fact or apparently desired by Caterpillar mainly for its own advantage. The determination must be made by the trier of fact based on evidence to be presented by the parties. [T]his cause must be remanded for further proceedings to determine the 'leading object' or 'main purpose' of Caterpillar's promise."

NOTE

Question. Apart from its satisfaction in aiding an injured person, what advantage could Caterpillar have expected from inducing Rosewood to care for Cook?

SECTION 3.   SATISFYING THE STATUTE OF FRAUDS

If a contract falls within a statute of frauds, then it must be set forth in a signed writing in order to be enforceable—as it is usually put, in order to *satisfy* that statute of frauds. In this section, we will consider what must be in a writing, and what form that writing must take, if it is to satisfy the parts of the Statute of Frauds we have covered thus far. We will also see what constitutes a signature for these purposes. These questions take on special significance in our increasingly digital age. How can a 1677 statute deal adequately with electronic communications? (Indeed, how did it deal with earlier waves of technology, such as the telegram, the typewriter, the audio recording, and the talking motion picture?) To that end we will look at fairly recent state and federal legislation that attempts to resolve the special problems of the digital world.

As we go through these formal requirements, we should look back at the functions of form as laid out by Professor Fuller and Professor Perillo. How well are they served by the requirements actually adopted by legislatures or implied by courts? In particular, do modern applications of these writing requirements strike the appropriate balance between certainty and flexibility?

Finally, consider how Statute of Frauds cases arise. There have been no studies of who drafted the writings offered to satisfy the main Statutes of Frauds. One gets the impression that most of the reported opinions in the area are not based upon contracts drafted by counsel. What might that tell us about how effective statutes of frauds have been in channeling contracting parties toward desirable methods of recording their contracts? How do formal requirements mesh with a contracting world consisting mainly of non-lawyers? And keep in mind that lawyers deal with statutes of frauds in very different capacities. Litigators do what they can with the writings that the parties set down. Transactional lawyers seek to avoid statute of frauds disputes rather than to figure out what to do if a client brings a dispute to the office. How might a lawyer's different roles affect how lawyers view the Statute of Frauds and how they would prefer it to be stated and interpreted?

(A) THE CONTENT OF A WRITING

To satisfy a statute of frauds, a writing must have some content beyond the signature of the party to be bound. But how much content? That depends on which functions the writing is supposed to serve. One of the arguments made in support of a statute of frauds is that a writing will contain the terms of the contract—not merely as evidence that there is a contract, but as evidence of the rights and duties that the contract creates. The parties thus would not be subject to the risks of faulty or convenient memories, which should remove some grounds for later disputes. If this argument is to have any weight, a writing that satisfies the statute of frauds must contain the main terms of the contract. If, on the other hand, the writing serves only to provide evidence that a contract exists, then it need not be particularly complete. Similarly, one might expect greater detail in a writing that serves more functions than in one serving just the evidentiary function. To take one example, the land contract provision serves the channeling function, by providing a clear path to enforcement, and perhaps the clarifying function as well.

1. IDENTIFYING WHO, WHAT, AND WHETHER

What any particular statute of frauds requires thus depends greatly on what the writing is supposed to do. There are, however, some basic requirements shared by most statutes of frauds, varied as necessary for different types of contracts. (The Article 2 Statute of Frauds, UCC § 2–201, departs significantly from this model. We will discuss it in the next section of this chapter.) For a writing to satisfy the general Statute of Frauds, it must do four things with reasonable certainty. First, it must identify the parties to the contract. Second, it must show that those parties made a contract. Third, it must set forth the nature of the contract, including some indication of what the parties contracted about. Fourth, it must state the essential terms of the contract.

With one exception, the first three of these requirements have yielded little litigation. It is easy for the contracting parties to write down who has made a contract with whom for what. Even if one of the parties goes unnamed, the courts usually have been forgiving when it is clear from context who that party was. Nor is it necessary that an agent disclose a principal; if the agent purchases the property, the agent need provide only its own name. Nor does the subject-matter of the contract prove much of a hurdle, because parties who have gone to the trouble of writing down their contracts find it easy to state generally what the contracting parties are supposed to do.

The exception comes with contracts for the sale or transfer of land. The courts normally require that the contract describe the land clearly enough that the seller knows what she is conveying and the buyer knows what he is buying. Just what this means varies from state to state. At one extreme, a few jurisdictions require that real property be described as specifically as it would in a deed. See Martin v. Seigel, 212 P.2d 107 (Wash. 1950). In those jurisdictions, it is not sufficient to use a street address in a writing that was to satisfy the Statute of Frauds. Only the full legal description of the property will suffice. At the other extreme, many courts have stated that the writing need not itself identify the property sold. As one court put it, "while a perfect description is not required, the contract must furnish the key to identifying the land intended to be conveyed." Park Regency Partners v. Gruber, 608 S.E.2d 667 (Ga. App. 2004). With the key in hand, the parties may use evidence outside the contract itself to complete the description. In other words, "[t]he purpose of a description in a written conveyance is not to identify the land, but to afford a means of identification." Ardmore, Inc. v. Rex Group, Inc., 377 S.W.3d 45 (Tex. Civ. App. 2012).

PROBLEM

Where Am I? Suppose your state has adopted the approach laid out in *Park Regency Partners* for describing real property. You have been asked to review a batch of contracts to sell farms in order to determine whether they adequately describe the land. For each, determine (a) whether the description is sufficiently specific on its own, (b) whether it is sufficiently specific only when supported by oral and other outside evidence, or (c) whether the description is too vague to serve as a key, whatever the state of the outside evidence might be. If the description falls under (b), suggest types of outside evidence that would make the definition clear enough to satisfy the Statute of Frauds.

1. 187.5 acres in Land Lot 170. See O'Dell v. Pine Ridge Invs., 667 S.E.2d 912 (Ga. App. 2008).

2. My property at Miller and Concord. See Butler v. Lovoll, 620 P.2d 1251 (Nev. 1980).

3. Thirty acres from my eighty-four and one-eighth acre parcel. See Zuk v. Zuk, 55 A.3d 102 (Pa. Super. 2012).

4. Whatever areas you want from the south end of my property at 1313 Mockingbird Lane. See Jacobson v. Gulbransen, 623 N.W.2d 84 (S.D. 2001).

2. STATING THE ESSENTIAL TERMS

Whether a writing is sufficient commonly turns on whether it states the "essential terms" of the contract. This requirement is not found within either the original Statute of Frauds or most state Statutes of Frauds, but it has become the most common way to determine whether a particular memorandum contains the agreement at issue. Restatement

§ 131 cmt. *g.* There is no one test for distinguishing essential terms from inessential; what is essential depends on the circumstances of the dispute and of the underlying contract. Thus, for example, the date by which an option to purchase real estate must be exercised has usually been found essential. If, however, the context makes clear that the exact timing is not critical, it is not necessary that the writing contain the date. See Shellabarger v. Shellabarger, 317 S.W.3d 77 (Mo. App. 2010).

Why this uncertainty? It stems in part from the varied functions the Statute of Frauds serves and from the varied purposes served by each of these functions. For example, the evidentiary function should be met adequately by a bare-bones memorandum if the purpose is merely to provide evidence that a contract was made. But if the evidentiary purpose is to state the terms of a contract so that the parties or a judge may be certain in the future just what those terms are, then the memorandum would have to be far more detailed. The "essential terms" might then be enough, but even peripheral terms can be the sources of dispute and litigation. The channeling function also leads to different requirements. If by channeling we mean only that we want to provide a clear way for parties to make their contracts enforceable, then pretty much any writing that identifies the parties and the subject-matter of the contract and states that the parties did in fact make a contract will be good enough. Sometimes, however, the channeling function is described in the same terms as Professor Perillo's managerial function— a way for the parties to a contract to control employees who will actually perform and to ensure that there is one reliable source containing the terms of the agreement. Only a very complete writing would further this interest significantly. And the cautionary function may encompass just the slowing down that occurs when the parties must prepare a writing, or it may also encompass the sort of warning that may come when a contracting party sees exactly what she is getting herself into if she signs. Once again, whether a writing serves this function adequately depends on what aspect of the function is most important.

The most important point here is not exactly which terms are or are not essential, but how one goes about determining which terms are or are not essential. Here the courts largely agree that one may go outside the four corners of the memorandum to provide the necessary context. So, for example, the parties to a contract need not state a specific price, quantity, or the like, so long as the writing contains a method for determining what that term will be. See Wakelam v. Hagood, 263 P.3d 742 (Idaho 2011). Nor is it necessary to provide a formula, if there is some other way to fill the gap. The parties may have established a course of dealing that is implicitly part of the contract. They may be part of a trade that has its own customs and usages that commonly go unexpressed in memoranda. For that matter, the law may imply a term. For example, a memorandum of an employment agreement needs to state only the fact and nature of employment and the names of the employer and employee. If the salary is missing, the law will imply reasonable compensation. Trueforge Global Mach. Corp. v. Viraj Group, 923 N.Y.S.2d 146 (App. Div. 2011).

Even courts that normally are strict about letting in evidence outside of a final writing are generally willing to be more lenient regarding the Statute of Frauds. For example, Missouri strictly limits whether this sort of evidence may supplement a written agreement. See Kenney v. Vansittert, 277 S.W.3d 713 (Mo. Ct. App. 2008) ("In Missouri, to determine if a writing is [complete], we look to the face of the document itself—without looking to the surrounding facts and circumstances.").[h] Nevertheless, its courts routinely look outside the writing to determine whether the writing plus the outside material will collectively satisfy the Statute of Frauds. See In re Estate of Looney, 975 S.W.2d 508 (Mo. Ct. App. 1998) (contract to sell land: memorandum did not contain adequate description of real property, but the court found a sufficiently detailed description in tax receipts).

(B) ISSUES OF FORM

There is more to assessing a writing than determining whether it clearly states the necessary terms, with or without the aid of outside evidence. Two questions about form have provoked much litigation. First, what form must the writing take? Second, is the Statute of Frauds satisfied if no one writing contains everything needed, but a group of writings does?

The courts have allowed many different types of writings to satisfy the Statute of Frauds, including writings that neither party intended to provide evidence of the contract. This is consistent with the evidentiary function of the Statute of Frauds. If the proffered evidence shows that the parties made a contract and provides sufficient detail, it does not matter who made the writing or why it was made. Certainly it is not necessary that the writing be devoted to stating the contract, or that it be in the usual form of a contract. The courts have found the Statute of Frauds satisfied by, among other things, a letter, a receipt, a check, a price list, the minutes of a meeting, and a will. See Farnsworth on Contracts § 6.7.

PROBLEM

The Write Stuff. In light of the purposes of the Statute of Frauds, consider whether each of the following would satisfy the formal requirements of the Statute of Frauds. If you do not have the facts needed to reach a conclusion, determine what facts might be relevant.

1. A signed letter from an employer to an employee stating that "This is to confirm the following changes in the commissions payable to you under your employment contract with us,"

---

[h] Whether evidence outside a final writing may be admitted to supplement it is governed by the *parol evidence rule,* which is discussed in Chapter 5.

going on to list several reductions inconsistent with the terms of their five-year oral contract. See SAR Group Ltd. v. E.A. Dion, Inc., 2011 WL 2201063 (Mass. App. Ct. June 8, 2011).

2. A memorandum summing up the terms of an oral contract to sell land that was made by the seller purely for the seller's reference and was not delivered to the buyer. Compare Rulon-Miller v. Carhart, 544 A.2d 340 (Me. 1988) with Schwinn v. Griffith, 303 N.W.2d 258 (Minn. 1981).

3. A video of two people in a bar making a contract for the sale of real property. Compare Londono v. City of Gainesville, 768 F.2d 1223 (11th Cir. 1985) with Sonders v. Roosevelt, 476 N.E.2d 996 (N.Y. 1985).

4. A guarantee recorded in a properly signed and executed writing that has been lost. See Brooks v. Toperzer, 441 A.2d 1177 (N.H. 1982). (If the writing were lost, how would one prove that it existed?)

5. A written and signed offer that was accepted orally. Restatement § 131 cmt. *f*.

———————

The final issue to consider is whether the signed memorandum required by the Statute of Frauds can consist of two or more documents, not all of which are signed and no one of which contains all the terms of the agreement. Here we see some tension between principle and practice. In principle, this should pose no problems. If the function of the Statute of Frauds is to provide tangible evidence that those involved actually made a contract, that function could be served regardless of how many documents made up the writing. "All that is required is that these writings shall so clearly evidence the fact that a contract was made, and what are its terms, that there is no serious possibility that the assertion of the contract is false." 2 Arthur L. Corbin, Corbin on Contracts § 512, at 744–45 (1950).

In practice, however, this is not so easy. The main problem is how the various writings are to be linked together. Certainly this is not a problem when each expressly refers to the others. Nor is it generally a problem if the writings were stored together—kept in the same envelope, for example. The hardest cases arise when the writings do not have express internal cross-references. One classic example follows.

Crabtree v. Elizabeth Arden Sales Corp.

New York Court of Appeals, 1953.
110 N.E.2d 551.

■ FULD, JUDGE. In September of 1947, Nate Crabtree entered into preliminary negotiations with Elizabeth Arden Sales Corporation, manufacturers and sellers of cosmetics, looking toward his employment as sales manager. Interviewed on September 26th, by Robert P. Johns, executive vice-president and general manager of the corporation, who had apprised him of the possible opening, Crabtree requested a three-year contract at $25,000 a year. Explaining that he would be giving up a secure well-paying job to take a position in an entirely new field of endeavor which he believed would take him some years to master he insisted upon an agreement for a definite term. And he repeated his desire for a contract for three years to Miss Elizabeth Arden, the corporation's president. When Miss Arden finally indicated that she was prepared to offer a two-year contract, based on an annual salary of $20,000 for the first six months, $25,000 for the second six months and $30,000 for the second year, plus expenses of $5,000 a year for each of those years, Crabtree replied that that offer was "interesting." Miss Arden thereupon had her personal secretary make this memorandum on a telephone order blank that happened to be at hand:

"EMPLOYMENT AGREEMENT WITH NATE CRABTREE

Date Sept. 26–1947 6: PM

At 681–5th Ave * * *

Begin 20000.

6 months 25000.

6 months 30000.

5000. per year

Expense money

(2 years to make good)

Arrangement with

Mr Crabtree

By Miss Arden

Present Miss Arden

Mr John

Mr Crabtree

Miss OLeary"

A few days later, Crabtree phoned Mr. Johns and telegraphed Miss Arden; he accepted the "invitation to join the Arden organization," and Miss Arden wired back her "welcome." When he reported for work, a "payroll change" card was made up and initialed by Mr. Johns, and then forwarded to the payroll department. Reciting that it was prepared on September 30, 1947, and was to be effective as of October 22d, it specified the names of the parties, Crabtree's "Job Classification" and, in addition, contained the notation that "This employee is to be paid as follows:

"First six months $20,000. per annum
of employment

Next six months of   25,000. per annum
employment

After one year of   30,000. per annum
employment

> Approved by RPJ (initialed)"

After six months of employment, Crabtree received the scheduled increase from $20,000 to $25,000, but the further specified increase at the end of the year was not paid. Both Mr. Johns and the comptroller of the corporation, Mr. Carstens, told Crabtree that they would attempt to straighten out the matter with Miss Arden, and, with that in mind, the comptroller prepared another "pay-roll change" card, to which his signature is appended, noting that there was to be a "Salary increase" from $25,000 to $30,000 a year, "per contractual arrangements with Miss Arden." The latter, however, refused to approve the increase and, after further fruitless discussion, plaintiff left defendant's employ and commenced this action for breach of contract.

At the ensuing trial, defendant denied the existence of any agreement to employ plaintiff for two years, and further contended that, even if one had been made, the statute of frauds barred its enforcement. The trial court found against defendant on both issues and awarded plaintiff damages of about $14,000, and the Appellate Division, two justices dissenting, affirmed. Since the contract relied upon was not to be performed within a year, the primary question for decision is whether there was a memorandum of its terms, subscribed by defendant, to satisfy the statute of frauds, Personal Property Law, § 31.

Each of the two payroll cards—the one initialed by defendant's general manager, the other signed by its comptroller—unquestionably constitutes a memorandum under the statute. That they were not prepared or signed with the intention of evidencing the contract, or that they came into existence subsequent to its execution, is of no consequence; it is enough, to meet the statute's demands, that they were signed with intent to authenticate the information contained therein and that such information does evidence the terms of the contract. Those two writings contain all of the essential terms of the contract the parties to it, the position that plaintiff was to assume, the salary that he was to receive except that relating to the duration of plaintiff's employment. Accordingly, we must consider whether that item, the length of the contract, may be supplied by reference to the earlier unsigned office memorandum, and, if so, whether its notation, "2 years to make good," sufficiently designates a period of employment.

The statute of frauds does not require the "memorandum * * * to be in one document. It may be pieced together out of separate writings, connected with one another either expressly or by the internal evidence of subject-matter and occasion." Marks v. Cowdin, supra, 226 N.Y. 138, 145, 123 N.E. 139, 141 [Cardozo, J.—eds.], see, also, 2 Williston, op cit., p. 1671; Restatement, Contracts, § 208, subd. (a). Where each of the separate writings has been subscribed by the party to be charged, little if any difficulty is encountered. See, e. g., Marks v. Cowdin, supra, 226 N.Y. 138, 144–145. Where, however, some writings have been signed, and others have not as in the case before us there is basic disagreement as to what constitutes a sufficient connection permitting the unsigned papers to be considered as part of the statutory memorandum. The courts of some jurisdictions insist that there be a reference, of varying degrees of specificity, in the signed writing to that unsigned, and, if there is no such reference, they refuse to permit consideration of the latter in determining whether the memorandum satisfies the statute. That conclusion is based upon a construction of the statute which requires that the connection between the writings and defendant's acknowledgment of the one not subscribed, appear from examination of the papers alone, without the aid of parol evidence. The other position which has gained increasing support over the years is that a sufficient connection between the papers is established simply by a reference in them to the same subject matter or transaction. The statute is not pressed "to the extreme of a literal and rigid logic," Marks v. Cowdin, supra, 226 N.Y. 138, 144, 123 N.E. 139, 141, and oral testimony is admitted to show the connection between the documents and to establish the acquiescence, of the party to be charged, to the contents of the one unsigned.

The view last expressed impresses us as the more sound, and, indeed although several of our cases appear to have gone the other way, this court has on a number of occasions approved the rule, and we now definitively adopt it, permitting the signed and unsigned writings to be read together, provided that they clearly refer to the same subject matter or transaction.

The language of the statute "Every agreement * * * is void, unless * * * some note or memorandum thereof be in writing, and subscribed by the party to be charged," Personal Property Law, § 31—does not impose the requirement that the signed acknowledgment of the contract must appear from the writings alone, unaided by oral testimony. The danger of fraud and perjury, generally attendant upon the admission of parol evidence, is at a minimum in a case such as this. None of the terms of the contract are supplied by parol. All of them must be set out in the various writings presented to the court, and at least one writing, the one establishing a contractual relationship between the parties, must bear the signature of the party to be charged, while the unsigned document must on its face refer to the same transaction as that set forth in the one that was signed. Parol evidence to portray the circumstances surrounding the making of the memorandum serves only to connect the separate documents and to show that there was assent, by the party to be charged, to the contents of the one unsigned. If that testimony does not convincingly connect the papers, or does not show assent to the unsigned paper, it is within the province of the judge to conclude, as a matter of law, that the statute has not been satisfied. True, the possibility still remains that, by fraud or perjury, an agreement never in fact made may occasionally be enforced under the subject matter or transaction test. It is better to run that risk, though, than to deny enforcement to all agreements, merely because the signed document made no specific mention of the unsigned writing. As the United States Supreme Court declared, in sanctioning the admission of parol evidence to establish the connection between the signed and unsigned writings. "There may be cases in which it would be a violation of reason and common sense to ignore a reference which derives its significance from such (parol) proof. If there is ground for any doubt in the matter, the general rule should be enforced. But where there is no ground for doubt, its enforcement would aid, instead of discouraging, fraud." Beckwith v. Talbot, supra, 95 U.S. 289, 292, 24 L.Ed. 496.

Turning to the writings in the case before us the unsigned office memo, the payroll change form initialed by the general manager Johns, and the paper signed by the comptroller Carstens it is apparent, and most patently, that all three refer on their face to the same transaction. The parties, the position to be filled by plaintiff, the salary to be paid him, are all identically set forth; it is hardly possible that such detailed information could refer to another or a different agreement. Even more, the card signed by Carstens notes that it was prepared for the purpose of a "Salary increase per contractual arrangements with Miss Arden." That certainly constitutes a reference of sorts to a more comprehensive "arrangement," and parol is permissible to furnish the explanation.

The corroborative evidence of defendant's assent to the contents of the unsigned office memorandum is also convincing. Prepared by defendant's agent, Miss Arden's personal secretary, there is little likelihood that that paper was fraudulently manufactured or that defendant had not assented to its contents. Furthermore, the evidence as to the conduct of the parties at the time it was prepared persuasively demonstrates defendant's assent to its terms. Under such circumstances, the courts below were fully justified in finding that the three papers constituted the "memorandum" of their agreement within the meaning of the statute.

Nor can there be any doubt that the memorandum contains all of the essential terms of the contract. Only one term, the length of the employment, is in dispute. The September 26th office memorandum contains the notation, "2 years to make good." What purpose, other than to denote the length of the contract term, such a notation could have, is hard to imagine. Without it, the employment would be at will, and its inclusion may not be treated as meaningless or purposeless. Quite obviously, as the courts below decided, the phrase signifies that the parties agreed to a term, a certain and definite term, of two years, after which, if plaintiff did not "make good," he would be subject to discharge. And examination of other parts of the memorandum supports that construction. Throughout the writings, a scale of wages, increasing plaintiff's salary periodically, is set out; that type of arrangement is hardly consistent with the hypothesis that the employment was meant to be at will. The most that may be argued from defendant's standpoint is that "2 years to make good" is a cryptic and ambiguous statement. But, in such a case, parol evidence is admissible to explain its meaning. Having in mind the relations of the parties, the course of the negotiations and plaintiff's insistence upon security of employment, the purpose of the phrase or so the trier of the facts was warranted in finding was to grant plaintiff the tenure he desired.

The judgment should be affirmed, with costs.

NOTES

(1) *Questions.* How can the use of parol evidence to link the documents be consistent with a writing requirement? Wouldn't requiring that the documents be linked internally, without reference to outside materials, be more faithful to the Statute of Frauds?

(2) *Problem: Snatching Defeat from the Jaws of Victory?* Hannah sought to buy Fair Castle from Sam. After many meetings and telephone conversations, Sam agreed. Hannah drafted a contract consistent with their agreement, signed it, and sent it to Sam. Sam received the contract but did not sign it. Not long after, Sam was offered considerably more by Jillian and decided to sell to her instead. Sam told Hannah about this in a telephone conversation. Hannah sued for breach of contract; Sam asserted a Statute of Frauds defense. Sam's attorney asked him for any documents potentially relevant to the case. In response, Sam sent his attorney his copy of the contract, along with a signed cover letter saying "Here is my copy of the contract Hannah and I agreed to." Does Sam's response satisfy the Statute of Frauds? How would Hannah ever learn about it, given the attorney-client privilege? See Fesmire v. Digh, 683 S.E.2d 803 (S.C. App. 2009). See also the discussion below of ethical aspects of the Statute of Frauds.

Signing

Crabtree shows us how a court deals with a collection of documents that together provide all the essential terms of a contract but separately do not. It also shows how a signature on one document may be attributed to the others, which allows the parties to meet the requirement that a writing be signed in order to satisfy a statute of frauds.

The rationale for a signature requirement has been repeated for centuries: If a writing must bear a signature in order to make the contract enforceable, then fewer would-be fraudsters will commit fraud, whether because they cannot forge a signature well enough or because they are afraid that they will be thrown in jail if they are caught. A signed document thus provides substantial assurance that the document in fact contains the terms of an actual contract. In Fuller's terms, a signature meets the evidentiary requirement. The need for this sort of requirement was greater before parties could give sworn testimony, but this requirement remains at least a mild deterrent to fraud. Moreover, this rule serves not just the evidentiary function, but the other functions as well. Channeling works best when it involves an act not routinely performed in other settings. The seal is a good example of that principle; very few people would go to the bother of dripping melted wax on a document if there were nothing to be gained, so we can be reasonably sure that a party who seals a document really means for it to be enforced. A signature has much the same effect—not to the same degree, but we do not ordinarily sign documents unless we think doing so will have some consequences. Similarly, signing a document is somewhat cautionary, in that it requires one step beyond merely preparing a writing. If a party to a potential contract learns that the contract must be put in writing and signed before it becomes effective, that party gets notice that there may be more terms on the way, and may think twice about committing to the contract until he sees the final terms.

Putting these together, we get something like the UCC definition of "signed." Under the Code, " 'Signed' includes using any symbol executed or adopted with present intention to adopt or execute a writing." UCC § 1 201(b)(37). The UCC emphasizes the intent of the signer and de-emphasizes the manner of expressing intent, as does the case law that has grown around the Statute of Frauds. Thus, for example, a printed or scanned signature will usually suffice. So will a printed letterhead. The question is whether any particular symbol shows the requisite intent.

PROBLEMS

(1) *Sign Right . . . Where?* Diane wanted to buy a three-year extended warranty for her car. The best deal she found was at Tropical Chevrolet, and she agreed to buy a warranty shortly after she visited the dealership. Tropical's sales manager gave Diane a contract to sign, showing her the signature line on the bottom of the third page. He then left the office for a few minutes. When he returned, Diane had gone. The contract he had given her was signed, but on the top of the first page, not on the signature line on the third page. Diane refused to make the payments due on the contract. Tropical sued. Diane asserted a Statute of Frauds defense, arguing that the contract fell within the one-year provision and that she hadn't signed it. Tropical pointed to the signature on the first page of the written contract. Does this written contract satisfy the signature requirement of the Statute of Frauds? Does Diane have any plausible replies to Tropical's argument?

(2) *Manual Labor.* Robin was a teacher at the Computer Training Academy (CTA). She was hired on a three-year oral contract. Shortly after Robin arrived, she was given a copy of the CTA employees' manual, which contained, among other things, a set of policies governing what rights a teacher would have if discharged. After one year, Larry, a new headmaster, was hired, and immediately fired Robin without giving her any of the procedural rights laid out in the manual. Robin has sued CTA for breach of contract, in part because CTA failed to deliver on its procedural promises.

CTA has asserted a Statute of Frauds defense, arguing that even if the employees' manual was a contract, it was never signed and therefore was not enforceable. Robin pointed to the manual itself, which bore the CTA logo in large print on the cover and at many spots inside. Was the manual signed for the purposes of the Statute of Frauds? Is there anything you might look for inside the manual that might guide your answer? If you represent CTA, how would you suggest it forestall future litigation of this sort without making any changes in the policies?

(C) THE STATUTE OF FRAUDS IN THE DIGITAL AGE

Some years before the end of the 20th century it became apparent that the words "writing," "signed," and "subscribed" in statutes of frauds were threats to electronic commerce. Two statutory responses have emerged in the United States—one state and one federal. Because the federal statute has a "reverse-preemption" provision, we will start with the state statute.

The state statute governing electronic transactions is the Uniform Electronic Transactions Act ("UETA"), drafted by the Uniform Law Commissioners and enacted in all but three states. It is the major United States source of validation for electronic agreements not represented in signed writings. UETA applies to contracts for the sale of goods that are governed by Article 2 and to most contracts governed by the common law. UETA § 3. It provides that "if a law requires a record to be in writing, an *electronic record* satisfies the law," and that "if a law requires a signature, an *electronic signature* satisfies the law." UETA §§ 7(c) & (d). The terms italicized here are defined in UETA § 2. These provisions, taken together, allow the electronic equivalents of signed writings to satisfy a statute of frauds that has not been amended to accommodate electronic commerce.

UETA is relevant only when the parties to a transaction agree to conduct that transaction electronically, as "determined from the context and surrounding circumstances, including the parties' conduct." UETA § 5(b). UETA also is mainly a default rule, so contracting parties may choose to validate electronic transactions but regulate them outside of UETA. UETA § 5(d). In addition, UETA excludes certain transactions from its scope. These transactions include any governed by the state's law of wills and trusts or by the UCC, apart from Articles 2 and 2A. UETA § 3(b). UETA also includes a placeholder subsection for those states that want to exclude other transactions or statutes. UETA § 3(b)(4). The Legislative Note following § 3 mentions several possibilities for inclusion, such as the laws governing non-testamentary trusts, powers of attorney, real estate transactions, and consumer transactions. The states differ greatly in their inclination to extend § 3's exclusions. For example, California has excluded dozens of statutory provisions from UETA, such as those requiring notice before foreclosure, repossession, eviction, insurance cancellation, and utility cut-off. Cal. Civ. Code. §§ 1633.3(b)(4) & (c). In contrast, Ohio excluded no additional transactions whatever from its version of UETA. Ohio Rev. Code § 1306.02(B).

The federal statute is the Electronic Signatures in Global and National Commerce Act, 15 U.S.C. § 7001 *et seq.*, otherwise known as "E-SIGN." It covers much the same ground as UETA, and in the main reaches the same results. One important exception is that it contains express consumer protections, which were left wide open in UETA. E-SIGN § 101(c), 15 U.S.C. § 7001(c). Which is preferable seems largely academic, though, because E-SIGN provides that its § 101 is superseded if a state enacts UETA "as approved and recommended for enactment in all the States by the National Conference of Commissioners on Uniform State Laws in 1999," leaving aside the different state exclusions in UETA § 3(b)(4). E-SIGN § 102(a)(1), 15 U.S.C. § 7002(a)(1). Because every state except Illinois, New York, and Washington has adopted UETA—three large exceptions, but still only three—E-SIGN has a fairly modest reach.

Comparable action on the global front is illustrated by the Convention on the Use of Electronic Communications in International Contracts, recently adopted by the United Nations. This was based largely on UETA and almost always yields the same result.

SECTION 4.   THE STATUTE OF FRAUDS AND THE SALE OF GOODS

Before we can turn to the exceptions to statutes of frauds, we must look at the statute of frauds in Article 2 of the Uniform Commercial Code—UCC § 2–201. In this section we will look at its scope and its formal requirements; we will deal with its exceptions when we go through exceptions in general.

The Article 2 Statute of Frauds merits its own section for a few reasons, but one above all: It rests on different assumptions than did its 1677 predecessor, and thus contains very different requirements. The original Statute of Frauds did contain a section on contracts for the sale of goods for a price of £10 or more (roughly $2,000 today). The rationales were the same here as for the rest of the 1677 Statute, and it provoked much the same degree of obloquy. Consider, for example, the comments of Sir James Fitzjames Stephen, Judge of the High Court from 1879 to 1891 and Professor of Common Law at the Inns of Court:

> [I]t is in the nature of things impossible that [the Statute of Frauds provision on sales of goods] ever should have any operations, except that of enabling a man to escape from the discussion of the question whether he has or has not been guilty of a deliberate fraud by breaking his word.... [I]n the vast majority of cases its operation is simply to enable a man to break a promise with impunity, because he did not write it down with sufficient formality. The cases in which a man of honour would

condescend to avail himself of it must, I should think, be very rare indeed.

Stephen, *Section Seventeen of the Statute of Frauds,* 1 L. Q. Rev. 1, 4–5 (1885).

We have already seen how Karl Llewellyn, the Chief Reporter for the UCC and the Reporter for Article 2, tried to adapt the law to standard commercial behavior. When the Code was being drafted, businesses engaged in the same sort of informal contracting that they do today. Logically, then, Llewellyn would have rejected putting a Statute of Frauds into Article 2, in order to avoid having perfectly good and readily acknowledged contracts held unenforceable because of the operation of a purely formal rule. Far from rejecting a sales Statute of Frauds, however, Llewellyn wrote and spoke vigorously in its favor, calling it "an amazing product" and "in essence better adapted to our needs than when it was first passed." Karl N. Llewellyn, *What Price Contract?—An Essay in Perspective,* 40 Yale L.J. 704, 747 (1930).

Llewellyn's defense of the Statute of Frauds rests little on its anti-fraud rationale. He focused instead on its effect "both in encouraging permanent trustworthy record of agreements, and in inducing care in the making of that record." *Id.* at 748. The potential harms of a Statute of Frauds he thought diminished by the practices and demands of modern business. Sound commercial practice virtually dictated that contracts be put in writing. Consequently, a Statute of Frauds would have little effect on the costs of doing business and create few opportunities for the unwary to be taken advantage of. (But what about its effects on non-merchants?)

This did not mean that Llewellyn entirely approved of the Statute of Frauds as it then existed. Llewellyn found two circumstances especially deplorable. One was its use to get out of performing inconvenient contracts. An unscrupulous party could argue that the contract omitted an essential term; if the finder of fact held for that party, then the contract would become unenforceable because it was fatally incomplete. See New York Law Revision Commission, Record of Hearings on the Uniform Commercial Code 99–100 (1954) (testimony of Karl Llewellyn). The other was the ability of a defendant to invoke the Statute of Frauds even though she admitted that she had made a contract with the plaintiff; in the absence of the required writing, the contract would be unenforceable.

With those in mind, we can now review the Article 2 Statute of Frauds and see how it responds to Llewellyn's concerns.

UCC § 2–201(1) contains the core of the Statute of Frauds. It provides:

(1)   Except as otherwise provided in this section a contract for the sale of goods for the price of $500[i] or more is not enforceable by way of action or defense unless there is some writing sufficient to indicate that a contract for sale has been made between the parties and signed by the party against whom enforcement is sought or by his authorized agent or broker. A writing is not insufficient because it omits or incorrectly states a term agreed upon but the contract is not enforceable under this paragraph beyond the quantity of goods shown in such writing.

The critical part of this section is what the signed writing must contain in order to be sufficient against the signer. The general Statute of Frauds required that all essential terms be included, though there was a good deal of uncertainty at the margins about what terms were essential and whether it was actually necessary that they be stated expressly in the writing. Here the requirements are straightforward and modest. Just how modest they are may be shown by applying them to a range of fact patterns.

NOTES

(1)   *Problem: A Good(s) Writing.* Determine whether each of the following writings would satisfy UCC § 2–201(1) and the definition of "signed" in § 1–201(b)(37). Are there any additional facts that you need to make any or all of these determinations? Would they also satisfy the general Statute of Frauds?

a.   A letter from a buyer cancelling its previous purchase order for ordinary equipment valued at $10,000. The cancellation letter was received before the seller shipped the goods.

b.   A letter from a buyer repudiating a previously negotiated oral contract.

c.   A letter evidencing a contract for the sale of goods at a price of $25,000 which the buyer never sent but which remains in the buyer's files.

d.   A seller's invoice showing the terms of a contract, but misstating the terms for payment.

e.   A writing that shows a contract was made for the sale of a certain quantity of goods, identifies the parties, and is initialed by both parties, but which does not indicate which party is buyer or seller and which contains no information on price or time and place of delivery.

---

[i]   This figure has not changed since the Code was first proposed for enactment in 1951. In fact, the UCC took this figure from the Uniform Sales Act of 1906. If adjusted for inflation, the 1951 figure would now be around $4,800 and the 1906 figure would now be around $14,000. What types of transactions would no longer be within UCC § 2–201(1) were these higher figures in the statute? How might this affect our analysis of the merits of § 2–201(1)?

f.   An oral contract for the sale of $10 of fruit every month for three years (for a total price of $360).

(2)   *Question.* To what extent does UCC § 2–201(1) fit with Llewellyn's assessment of the sales Statute of Frauds?

———

As the comments above suggest, the only specific term a writing needs to state is the quantity. Otherwise the Code provides gap-fillers to use if a term cannot be given meaning by any other means. A quantity gap-filler would be more than a little problematic. The memorandum need not state the quantity accurately or completely, but the contract would then be enforceable only to the extent that it states the quantity.

SECTION 5.   EXCEPTIONS TO THE STATUTE OF FRAUDS

We have already seen that the courts have limited the effects of statutes of frauds in two ways. Sometimes they have narrowed the scope of a statute, most notably the scope of the one-year provision. Sometimes they have broadened the range of writings and signatures that will satisfy a statute of frauds, whether by holding even modest evidence sufficient or by using evidence outside the writings to fill in missing terms or to link together incomplete records. We will now look at a third way of limiting their effects—by creating exceptions.

Most exceptions to the Statute of Frauds are rooted in reliance. There are two basic types of reliance, each of which has given rise to a category of exceptions. One type of reliance is performing the contract in full or in part on the belief that it was enforceable. Another type arises as an offshoot of estoppel; the breaching party is estopped to deny that it has made a contract if the other party has in some manner relied on the statements of the breaching party. Each serves the evidentiary function of the statute of frauds, because the party seeking to enforce the contract would not have acted as it did had there not been a contract in place. Indeed, there often is some sort of writing in these cases, so the performance or preparation becomes more a means of verifying that the writing is genuine than the sole means of establishing that there is a contract.

The first of these types of reliance also involves restitution. If the breached-against party has performed, then the other party has presumably derived some benefit from that performance. The law deals with this possibility by allowing the breached-against party to recover in restitution, even though the underlying contract is not itself enforceable. Restatement (Third) of Restitution and Unjust Enrichment § 31(1)(b) & cmt. *f.* As we saw in Chapter 1, restitution is not always a satisfactory cause of action. In particular, it usually does not take into account either the breached-against party's potential gains from performance or that party's out-of-pocket costs that did not enrich the breaching party. *Cf.* Restatement (Third) of Restitution and Unjust Enrichment § 31 cmt. *c.* But restitution ordinarily is not available when the breached-against party has the option of suing for breach of contract. Whether restitution is available thus has a part in setting the bounds of the reliance-based exceptions to the Statute of Frauds.

The two important exceptions that do not involve reliance are both found in UCC § 2–201, though to some degree the courts have used them outside sales of goods. They reflect Karl Llewellyn's emphasis on giving effect to sound commercial practice. One, found in UCC § 2–201(2), is based on the unremarkable idea that those who deal with merchants may expect them to read their mail. The other, found in UCC § 2–201(3)(b), is based on the equally unremarkable idea that anyone who admits entering into a contract should be bound by that contract. We will discuss those after we go through the reliance-based exceptions.

(A) RELIANCE-BASED EXCEPTIONS

These exceptions have in common that the breached-against party has in some way relied upon a contract unenforceable because it is not set forth in a signed writing that satisfies the Statute of Frauds. Their exact contours vary greatly, however, because reliance may clash with other parts of the law—restitution and equitable remedies most importantly. We will therefore go through each   part or full performance and preparation to perform—in order to determine how these legal doctrines have shaped each exception.

1.   THE PART-PERFORMANCE EXCEPTION

The exceptions based on performance vary tremendously based on the particular provision of the Statute of Frauds that is relevant. For example, these exceptions do not exist for contracts within the suretyship provision. Partial performance may satisfy the evidentiary aspect of the suretyship provision, but it does not satisfy the cautionary aspect nearly as well as does a writing requirement. Moreover, a party does not ordinarily seek to enforce a surety contract until that party's performance is complete, so allowing this exception would gut the suretyship provision. On the other hand, there is a *full*-performance exception to the one-year provision. Restatement § 130. Partial performance does not suffice, because the one-year provision generally becomes relevant only after performance has begun. Why full performance is an exception to the one-year provision is difficult to explain, except perhaps as a way to avoid the messy valuation problems that would arise in restitution.

The two provisions most affected by the part-performance exception are the sale-of-goods provision and the real-property provision. The sale-of-goods exceptions are codified as UCC §§ 2–201(3)(a) & (3)(c). The first of these creates an exception if (1) the goods are to be specially manufactured for the buyer, (2) the goods cannot be sold to others in the ordinary course of the seller's business, and (3) the seller has substantially begun making the goods or making commitments to get the goods. Reliance is not an express element of this defense, but it might as well be; the seller would not have started making these otherwise unsalable goods were there no contract. This exception goes beyond partial performance, in that the substantial beginning of manufacture need not benefit the buyer. The second applies "with respect to goods for which payment has been made and accepted or which have been received and accepted." UCC § 2–201(3)(c). Note that *both* parties must act in order for this exception to apply. Otherwise it would be possible for a fraudster simply to ship goods to an unsuspecting recipient in the hopes that the recipient would either accept the goods expressly or do so by the passage of time. (For more on acceptance under Article 2 of the UCC, see Chapters 2 and 7.) But when both parties act in a way consistent with the existence of a contract, then the Code makes their contract enforceable, writing or no writing. This serves both the evidentiary function of the Statute of Frauds and Llewellyn's desire to give effect to sound commercial behavior. If a buyer and a seller act as though they have a binding contract, then they should have one in fact. (In practice, § 2–201(3)(c) applies mainly to partial performance of a contract within Article 2. If the court can apportion price and performance according to the terms of the contract, then the court has a basis for awarding damages.)

The most important use of the part-performance doctrine comes in contracts for the sale of interests in real property. Often a seller lets a buyer start improving the property under contract even before title has passed, which can create a problem if the seller thinks better of the deal. On the other side, a buyer who has started paying for the property presumably does not do so out of the desire to make the owner a handsome gift.

Part performance as an exception to the land-contract Statute of Frauds differs materially from its Article 2 counterpart. For largely historical reasons, this exception applies only when the breached-against party seeks specific performance of the contract. It also requires reliance expressly, not just as the basis for other elements of the test. The courts often use a heightened evidentiary standard—"clear and convincing evidence" is common. See Restatement § 129 cmt. *b*. Finally, specific performance is a drastic remedy, so it is available only when there are no reasonable alternatives. If the contract itself is not enforceable, the main alternative is restitution; even though restitution may not be entirely compensatory, it nevertheless is usually considered adequate.

There are two key issues in part-performance litigation under the land-contract provision of the Statute of Frauds. First, is the putative performance actually performance of the contract at issue, or is it consistent with another type of contract? For example, merely making monthly payments on property one occupies is consistent with both a purchase and a lease, and consequently is not "unequivocally referable" to the contract. Burns v. McCormick, 135 N.E. 273 (N.Y. 1922) (Cardozo, J.); see also 151 Mulberry St. Corp. v. Italian American Museum, 957

N.Y.S.2d 698 (App. Div. 2013) (improvements made consistent with both oral option to purchase property and with oral lease). Second, if there has been partial performance, is it both possible and necessary to give an equitable remedy, or should the breached-against party instead be relegated to restitution? Both issues are addressed in the following decision.

Beaver v. Brumlow

New Mexico Court of Appeals, 2010.
231 P.3d 628.

■ VIGIL, JUDGE. This case is about a verbal agreement made by Warren and Betty Beaver (Sellers) to sell land for a home site to Michael and Karen Brumlow (Buyers). Sellers reneged on the agreement after Mr. Brumlow left Sellers' employment and started working for a competitor. The trial court ordered specific performance of the oral agreement, and Sellers appeal. Sellers acknowledge that the evidence was sufficient for the trial court to find that they made the agreement with Buyers. Nevertheless, Sellers contend that specific enforcement of the verbal agreement is barred pursuant to the statute of frauds. We disagree and affirm.

BACKGROUND

Buyer Michael Brumlow worked for Sellers in their race horse transportation business for approximately ten years, beginning in 1994, and ending in 2004. In October 2000, Sellers purchased twenty-four acres of property in the Village of Ruidoso Downs, and in approximately June or July of 2001, Mr. Brumlow asked Seller Warren Beaver if he would sell some of the land to put a home on. Mr. Beaver agreed, and the parties walked the specific boundaries of the property that Sellers would sell to Buyers.

Sellers allowed Buyers to rely on their representations to Buyers that Sellers would sell Buyers the subject property. Buyers went into possession of the land with Sellers' consent. In reliance on Sellers' agreement to sell, Buyer Karen Brumlow cashed in her IRA and 401-K retirement plans, at a substantial penalty, to pay for the home and improvements. Buyers purchased a double-wide home and moved it onto the property. Mr. Beaver signed an application with the Village of Ruidoso Downs for placement of the home on the property he agreed to sell to Buyers. In reliance on the agreement, Buyers also skirted the mobile home, poured concrete footers and a concrete foundation for the home, built a deck and two sets of stairs to access the home, had electricity and a water supply run to the property, had a septic system installed, had a propane system installed, brought a Tuff Shed for storage onto the property, and landscaped the property. Mr. Beaver signed the application/approval required by the Village of Ruidoso Downs for the construction of the septic system. In reliance on the agreement, Buyers spent approximately $85,000.

Sellers sought legal advice as to the manner in which to sell the property to Buyers, and the parties discussed with Sellers' attorney the requirement of a survey, and either a real estate contract or a note and mortgage. A fair inference from the record is that formal documents were not prepared and executed because Sellers discovered that their property was encumbered with a mortgage containing a due on sale clause. Throughout their time on the land, Buyers repeatedly requested that their contract be formalized, and Sellers responded, "We will work it out."

A date certain was never determined for the sale of the property or transfer of title to the property, nor was a price actually determined. However, Mr. Brumlow assumed he would pay whatever the market would bear in that particular neighborhood. He testified he thought the price would be "whatever it was worth."

Sellers drove by Buyers' home location daily during the time Buyers were making improvements to the land and setting up the home without ever expressing an intent not to sell the subject property to Buyers. Sellers never attempted to interrupt Buyers' quiet possession of the property during the years of possession. Sellers allowed Buyers to rely on their representations to Buyers that Sellers would sell Buyers the subject property for years without notifying Buyers they intended to renege on their promise.

In March 2004, Mr. Brumlow gave Mr. Beaver a two-week notice of termination of his employment with Sellers, intending to go to work for a competitor of Sellers in the race horse transportation business. The relationship between the parties rapidly deteriorated, and Sellers changed their mind and decided not to sell the agreed upon tract of land to Buyers because of hurt or anger. Sellers then attempted to restructure the agreement as a "lease" as opposed to a sale, and then attempted to terminate the "lease" and evict Buyers. Sellers prepared and required Buyers to sign an "Agreement." The "Agreement" required Buyers to pay Sellers $400 per month, and Buyers complied, believing it was payment for the land. When Buyers began writing "Land Payment" on the checks, Sellers stopped cashing the checks and alleged that the "Agreement" was for rental, although the "Agreement" did not contain the words "Rent," "Rental," "Lease," or "Leasehold." Buyers attempted to amicably resolve the dispute by offering to pay cash in the amount of the fair market value for the property and to have the property surveyed at their expense. Sellers refused.

Sellers then filed a suit for ejectment against Buyers, seeking to remove them from the property by alleging that Buyers were in violation of a rental agreement. Buyers denied the existence of a rental agreement and affirmatively alleged that their occupancy was pursuant to an agreement to purchase the property. Buyers also filed counterclaims which included claims for breach of contract, fraud, and prima facie tort. Sellers pleaded the statute of frauds as a defense.

The trial court concluded that Sellers entered into a contract with Buyers to sell them a specific portion of their land and that Sellers reneged on their agreement to sell the property to Buyers. The trial court further determined that Sellers changed their mind three years after making the contract, chose not to honor it, and attempted to unilaterally restructure the contract into a lease, which was never intended. In committing these acts, the trial court concluded, Sellers committed a prima facie tort, which they knew would harm Buyers. Addressing the statute of frauds defense, the trial court concluded that while the parties had no written agreement, the verbal agreement was proven by clear, cogent, and convincing evidence and that part performance of the contract by both Buyers and Sellers was sufficient to remove the contract from the statute of frauds. Furthermore, the trial court concluded, requiring a cash payment of the fair market value, as determined by a professional appraiser, was a proper equitable remedy.

The trial court allowed Buyers a choice of remedy: money damages for the prima facie tort or specific performance of the contract. Buyers chose specific performance. The property was appraised at a value of $10,000 by a professional appraiser, and a survey of the property to be sold was prepared. The final judgment directs that Buyers tender to Sellers the amount of $10,000 by depositing that amount into the trust account of Buyers' attorney within thirty days from the entry of the judgment, and that Sellers prepare and execute a good and sufficient warranty deed to Buyers for the property as described in the testimony of Mr. Brumlow and as depicted on the survey of the property. Upon receipt of the warranty deed executed by Sellers, payment of the $10,000 is to be made to Sellers. All other claims and counterclaims were dismissed with prejudice. Sellers appeal.

Sellers contend that specific enforcement of the oral contract is barred pursuant to the statute of frauds because: (1) Buyers' part performance was not "unequivocally referable" to the verbal agreement; and (2) the verbal agreement was not certain as to the purchase price and time of performance. Sellers also argue that specific performance was improper because Buyers had an adequate remedy at law in damages. For the following reasons, we disagree and affirm.

* * *

THE STATUTE OF FRAUDS

While the underlying reasons justifying adoption of the statute of frauds no longer exist, retention of the statute has been justified for three primary reasons: the statute still serves an evidentiary function, and thereby lessens the danger of perjured testimony (the original reason for the statute); the requirement of a writing causes the parties to reflect on the importance of the agreement; and the writing requirement makes it easier to distinguish agreements which are enforceable from those which are not.

PART PERFORMANCE

Notwithstanding its language, judicial construction of the statute of frauds has resulted in limiting its application in order to overcome the harshness and injustice of a literal and mechanical application of its terms. . . . One well settled exception, recognized in New Mexico, is the doctrine of part performance. Alvarez v. Alvarez, 72 N.M. 336, 341, 383 P.2d 581, 584 (1963).

"Where an oral contract not enforceable under the statute of frauds has been performed to such extent as to make it inequitable to deny effect thereto, equity may consider the contract as removed from operation of the statute of frauds and decree specific performance." Id. In this case, the trial court concluded:

> [T]he evidence is clear, cogent and convincing so as to remove the case from the application of the [s]tatute of [f]rauds and that there is significant partial performance by both parties, [Buyers] in expending so much time, energy and money developing the parcel of property and [Sellers] in applying for permission to have the personal property placed on the land, seeking advice of counsel as to the manner in which to sell the property and allowing [Buyers] to rely on their representations and to reside on the property for years. The [c]ourt finds that applying the [s]tatute of [f]rauds would be unfair and inequitable.

Sellers do not contend that proof of the oral contract is lacking; in fact, they concede that the evidence is sufficient. Moreover, Sellers do not argue that the partial performance of Buyers was insufficient to overcome the statute of frauds or that their own partial performance was insufficient. Sellers' sole argument is that the character of Buyers' performance was not sufficiently indicative of an oral agreement to sell land to qualify as partial performance. See Burns v. McCormick, 135 N.E. 273, 273 (N.Y. 1922) ("Not every act of part performance will move a court of equity, though legal remedies are inadequate, to enforce an oral agreement affecting rights in land. There must be performance 'unequivocally referable' to the agreement, performance which alone and without the aid of words of promise is unintelligible or at least extraordinary unless as an incident of ownership, assured, if not existing."); Woolley v. Stewart, 118 N.E. 847, 848 (N.Y. 1918) ("An act which admits of explanation without reference to the alleged oral contract or a contract of the same general nature and purpose is not, in general, admitted to constitute a part performance."), quoted with approval in Alvarez, 72 N.M. at 342, 383 P.2d at 585.

> A court of equity [therefore] requires that a part performance relied on to take the case out of the statute [of frauds] should be

> of a character, not only consistent with the reasonable presumption that what was done was done on the faith of such a contract, but also that it would be unreasonable to presume that it was done on any other theory.

Alvarez, 72 N.M. at 342, 383 P.2d at 585 (internal quotation marks and citation omitted).

Sellers argue that Buyers' acts are not "unequivocally referable" to their agreement because Buyers' actions could also be consistent with those taken by a person who needs a place to live and who is given an opportunity to reside on another person's property. Sellers argue that if there is an alternative explanation for the actions taken in reliance of the oral contract, those actions are not "unequivocally referable" to the contract, and application of the part performance doctrine is improper. We disagree.

In Nashan v. Nashan, 119 N.M. 625, 630–31, 894 P.2d 402, 407–08 (Ct. App. 1995), we discussed the interrelationship of the factors that may be considered in determining whether a contract to convey land has been proven and whether it would be inequitable to enforce the contract. We said:

> Whatever the purpose of each test, however, the main questions are the same for a court faced with a case such as this one: was there actually an oral agreement such as that alleged by the plaintiff, and if so would it be inequitable to deny enforcement to the agreement? The factors should not be applied mechanically to determine whether the plaintiff's performance has met a particular test. Instead, the case must be viewed as a whole to determine whether specific performance of the agreement is required.

Id. at 631, 894 P.2d at 408. Thus, we reject the suggestion that the "unequivocally referable" concept means that outside of the contract, there can be no other plausible explanation for the part performance. We did not say that the performance must relate exclusively to the oral contract; rather, the performance must lead an outsider to "naturally and reasonably" conclude that the contract alleged actually exists. Two key specific factors, approved by this Court and many other courts, in coming to such a conclusion, are taking possession of the property, and making valuable, permanent, and substantial improvements to the property. Id. at 630–31, 894 P.2d at 407–08. Where these two factors coincide, specific performance usually results. Id.

In this case, Buyers went into possession of the specific land Sellers agreed to convey with Sellers' consent. In reliance on the agreement, Buyers cashed IRA and 401-K retirement plans at a substantial penalty, purchased a double-wide mobile home, and with Sellers' consent, moved it onto the property. Buyers also erected valuable temporary and permanent improvements on the land, and landscaped the property with

Sellers' consent. In reliance on the agreement, Buyers spent approximately $85,000 in purchasing the home and making improvements. We hold Buyers' actions were sufficient part performance in reliance on the oral agreement to take the agreement outside of the statute of frauds.

SUFFICIENCY OF THE VERBAL AGREEMENT

The trial court concluded:

> [T]he terms of the contract were that [Sellers] would sell to [Buyers] the piece of property included in the demarcation of the landmarks as testified to by [Mr. Brumlow]. While the purchase price was never agreed upon, the [c]ourt finds that [Buyers] should pay to [Sellers] the fair market value of the property as determined by an objective appraiser, in one lump sum, within sixty days of the [c]ourt's decision. Imposing fair market value and requiring a cash payment is the equitable remedy.

Sellers assert that by ruling that the purchase price would be established by an appraisal and that the terms of the payment would be in cash payable within thirty days, the trial court "formulated an agreement between the parties that never existed" and it "enforced terms and conditions on the parties that they had not had a meeting of the minds upon."

This case is analogous to Colcott v. Sutherland, 36 N.M. 370, 16 P.2d 399 (1932), in which our Supreme Court suggested that a claim for specific performance of a contract involving land will not fail for failure to specify a price where the contract is otherwise complete, and there has been part performance of the contract by a transfer of possession. Id. at 374–75, 16 P.2d at 401–02. In Colcott, the buyer alleged that the owner agreed to sell the buyer two acres from a parcel he owned for the sum of $150 per acre, provided that the buyer gave the seller an option to buy the land back if the buyer decided to move a gin he was planning on constructing on the land in the future. Id. at 371–72, 16 P.2d at 400. In reliance on the agreement, the buyer alleged he went into possession of the land and constructed the gin at a cost of $25,000. Id. at 372, 16 P.2d at 400. However, the parties never agreed on a price at which the seller could repurchase the property, nor did they agree on a means for determining the repurchase price. Id. at 374, 16 P.2d at 401. On this basis, the seller asserted that the allegations failed to state a claim for specific performance because there was no contract. Id. at 373–74, 16 P.2d at 400–01. Our Supreme Court said:

> The parties having thus agreed, what is the effect of the omission to stipulate the price for a repurchase? [The seller] contends that it results in incompleteness and uncertainty fatal to the remedy of specific performance. [The buyer] says there is no incompleteness or uncertainty, since the law's implication

binds the parties to a reasonable price, and equity has means to determine it. *This may be entirely sound.*

Id. at 374–75, 16 P.2d at 401 (emphasis added) (citing John Norton Pomeroy & John C. Mann, Specific Performance of Contracts § 148, at 380–82 (3d ed. 1926)). However, the suit was not for specific performance of the seller's option to repurchase; it was to enforce the contract to sell to the buyer. Accordingly, the Court did not decide whether an action would lie for specific performance of the option itself.

Buyers proved to the satisfaction of the trial court by clear, cogent, and convincing evidence that Sellers entered into a contract to sell specific land to Buyers, as reflected in its conclusions of law quoted above. In addition, there was significant specific part performance by both Buyers and Sellers in reliance on the contract they made. In particular, Buyers cashed their retirement plans, went into possession of the property, moved their home onto the property, and made significant improvements to the land at a total cost of approximately $85,000, all with the knowledge and consent of Sellers for several years. Buyers assumed they would have to pay whatever the property was worth, and Sellers consulted an attorney to draft the sale documents. When Buyers repeatedly asked that the contract be formalized, Sellers' response was, "We will work it out." Thus, it is through no fault of Buyers that formal contract documents were not written with a set price and terms. Under these circumstances, it was within the equitable jurisdiction of the trial court to set the price at the fair market value as determined by an objective appraiser. We take particular note that Sellers do not dispute on appeal the fairness of the price established by the trial court.

Sellers would have us invalidate what was unquestionably a valid contract based on a mechanical application of contract law. We decline to do so. See Herrera v. Herrera, 1999-NMCA-034, ¶ 13, 126 N.M. 705, 974 P.2d 675 (noting that the purpose of the statute of frauds is to prevent fraud and perjury, not to prevent the performance or enforcement of oral contracts that have been made or to create a loophole of escape for a person who seeks to repudiate a contract he admits was made). Sellers do not seem to acknowledge that this is a case under the equitable jurisdiction of the trial court. "In the general juristic sense, equity means the power to meet the moral standards of justice in a particular case by a tribunal having discretion to mitigate the rigidity of the application of strict rules of law so as to adapt the relief to the circumstances of the particular case." Henry L. McClintock, Principles of Equity § 1, at 1 (2d ed. 1948). We hold that there was no error committed by the trial court by decreeing specific performance of the contract for Sellers to sell, and Buyers to buy, the subject property for its fair market value.

* * *

ADEQUACY OF REMEDY AT LAW

[The court held that damages would not be adequate to compensate the buyers. Land is unique, so there was no way to assess damages accurately. Although it would be possible to calculate the value of the buyers' work, that wasn't what the buyers sought in either their contract or their suit.]

CONCLUSION

The judgment of the trial court is affirmed.

NOTES

(1) *Many Eggs, But How Many Baskets?* Was it prudent for the Beavers to rest their whole case on the Statute of Frauds? Were there any other arguments apparent from the facts? If the Statute of Frauds was their best hope to prevail, how might they have framed their argument to make it more appealing?

(2) *The Laugh's on You.* Is this an instance of the "laughing defendant" problem attacked by Llewellyn in UCC § 2–201(3)(b), discussed *infra*? Does the court's discussion suggest any distaste for this sort of argument? See Section 6, "Ethical Practices and the Statute of Frauds."

(3) *Unequivocal?* Consider the court's discussion of whether the buyers' performance was unequivocally referable to the contract at issue. How broadly or narrowly does the court interpret what is an unequivocal reference? Is this consistent with the bases for the land-contract provision of the Statute of Frauds? And why have the test at all, instead of letting the finder of fact determine whether the buyers relied on the contract as they would determine any other question of fact?

(4) *The Restatement Approach.* The part-performance exception for land contracts may be found in Restatement § 129. It contains the basic elements mentioned earlier: reasonable reliance on the contract, continuing assent by the other party to the first party's reliance, and the avoidance of injustice only by enforcement of the contract.

PROBLEM

Managing to Rely. Philip lived in a rented house that was part of a large development. He was interested in buying that house, and asked the development's owner whether he could do so. The owner said that she would sell the house to him, but that she needed someone to manage the development. If Philip would manage the development for three years, she would convey the land to him at the end for no additional consideration. In the meantime, Philip could continue living in the house, and she would pay Philip a modest but adequate salary for his work. Philip agreed. Over the next three years, he managed the properties for the promised wage and lived in his old house, paying rent as before (though on his checks he wrote "partial payment for house"). As the three years came toward their end, Philip remodeled the kitchen and bathrooms in the house and finished the basement. When the three years were up, Philip requested the deed. The owner refused. Philip sued for breach. The owner invoked the Statute of Frauds. Do any of the provisions of the Statute of Frauds apply to this transaction? Do any exceptions to those provisions apply here? Would it matter whether the owner knew of the remodeling? Would Philip's case be helped or hurt if he had moved into the house as part of his contract, rather than some years before? See Kazlauskas v. Emmert, 275 P.3d 171 (Or. Ct. App. 2012); Richard v. Richard, 900 A.2d 1170 (R.I. 2006).

2. ESTOPPEL

The estoppel exception to the Statute of Frauds closely resembles the promissory estoppel exception to consideration doctrine. Indeed, the Restatement uses almost identical language for each. Compare Restatement § 90(1) with Restatement § 139(1). These exceptions have somewhat different purposes, however, which have led to different approaches to analysis.

The original use of estoppel to assert the Statute of Frauds fit within the established doctrine of equitable estoppel, discussed in Chapter 1 at p. 121. The breached-against party could invoke estoppel only if it had relied on a misrepresentation by the breaching party. If, for example, the breaching party had falsely stated that it would execute a writing (as in Beaver v. Brumlow?), then it could be estopped from asserting the Statute of Frauds as a defense to enforcement. See Seymour v. Oelrichs, 106 P. 88 (Cal. 1909). The same would apply if one party falsely assured the other that no writing was necessary, at least if the assurance came in a context that would justify the recipient in relying upon it. See Loeb v. Gendel, 179 N.E.2d 7 (Ill. 1961) (husband, a lawyer, told wife that an agreement was enforceable). In these cases, equitable estoppel would prevent the use of the Statute of Frauds as a means of committing fraud. But there is no fraud in ordinary promissory estoppel cases; the promisee relies upon the promise that falls within the Statute of Frauds, not upon some misrepresentation surrounding the writing requirement.

This remained the situation until Justice Traynor's classic opinion in *Monarco v. LoGreco,* which is the next case in this Chapter. It was the main source for Restatement § 139, as well as the bulk of the case law since. As you read *Monarco,* keep in mind how Justice Traynor limits the scope of the court's holding.

Monarco v. Lo Greco

Supreme Court of California, 1950.
35 Cal.2d 621, 220 P.2d 737.

■ TRAYNOR, JUSTICE. Natale and Carmela Castiglia were married in 1919 in Colorado. Carmela had three children, John, Rosie and Christie [Lo Greco], by a previous marriage. Rosie was married to Nick Norcia. Natale had one grandchild, plaintiff Carmen Monarco, the son of a deceased daughter by a previous marriage. Natale and Carmela moved to California where they invested their assets, amounting to approximately $4,000, in a half interest in agricultural property. Rosie and Nick Norcia acquired the other half interest. Christie, then in his early teens, moved with the family to California. Plaintiff remained in Colorado. In 1926, Christie, then 18 years old, decided to leave the home of his mother and step-father and seek an independent living. Natale and Carmela, however, wanted him to stay with them and participate in the family venture. They made an oral proposal to Christie that if he stayed home and worked they would keep their property in joint tenancy so that it would pass to the survivor who would leave it to Christie by will except for small devises to John and Rosie. In performance of this agreement Christie remained home and worked diligently in the family venture. He gave up any opportunity for further education or any chance to accumulate property of his own. He received only his room and board and spending money. When he married and suggested the possibility of securing some present interest to support his wife, Natale told him that his wife should move in with the family and that Christie need not worry, for he would receive all the property when Natale and Carmela died. Natale and Carmela placed all of their property in joint tenancy and in 1941 both executed wills leaving all their property to Christie with the exception of small devises to Rosie and John and $500 to plaintiff. Although these wills did not refer to the agreement, their terms were agreed upon by Christie, Natale and Carmela. The venture was successful, so that at the time of Natale's death his and Carmela's interest was worth approximately $100,000. Shortly before his death Natale became dissatisfied with the agreement and determined to leave his half of the joint property to his grandson, the plaintiff. Without informing Christie or Carmela he arranged the necessary conveyances to terminate the joint tenancies and executed a will leaving all of his property to plaintiff. This will was probated and the court entered its decree distributing the property to plaintiff. After the decree of distribution became final, plaintiff brought these actions for partition of the properties and an accounting. By cross-complaint Carmela asked that plaintiff be declared a constructive trustee of the property he received as a result of Natale's breach of his agreement to keep the property in joint tenancy. On the basis of the foregoing facts the trial court gave judgment for defendants and cross-complainant, and plaintiff has appealed.

The controlling question is whether plaintiff is estopped from relying upon the statute of frauds (Civil Code § 1624; Code Civ.Proc. § 1973) to defeat the enforcement of the oral contract. [The provision referred to put contracts to make a will within the Statute of Frauds. It has since been repealed, and its successor, Cal. Prob. Code § 21700(a), allows oral proof of a contract to make a will if the claimant can present clear and convincing evidence of a promise enforceable in equity. Cal. Prob. Code § 21700(a)(4).] The doctrine of estoppel to assert the statute of frauds has been consistently applied by the courts of this state to prevent fraud that would result from refusal to enforce oral contracts in certain circumstances. Such fraud may inhere in the unconscionable injury that would result from denying enforcement of the contract after one party has been induced by the other seriously to change his position in reliance on the contract, or in the unjust enrichment that would result if a party who has received the benefits of the other's performance were allowed to rely upon the statute. In many cases both elements are present. Thus, not only may one party have so seriously changed his position in reliance upon, or in performance of, the contract that he would suffer an unconscionable injury if it were not enforced, but the other may have reaped the benefits of the contract so that he would be unjustly enriched if he could escape its obligations.

In this case both elements are present. In reliance on Natale's repeated assurances that he would receive the property when Natale and Carmela died, Christie gave up any opportunity to accumulate property of his own and devoted his life to making the family venture a success. That he would be seriously prejudiced by a refusal to enforce the contract is made clear by a comparison of his position with that of Rosie and Nick Norcia. Because the Norcias were able to make a small investment when the family venture was started, their interest, now worth approximately $100,000, has been protected. Christie, on the other hand, forbore from demanding any present interest in the venture in exchange for his labors on the assurance that Natale's and Carmela's interest would pass to him on their death. Had he invested money instead of labor in the venture on the same oral understanding, a resulting trust would have arisen in his favor. Byers v. Doheny, 105 Cal.App. 484, 493–495, 287 P. 988; see, Restatement, Trusts, § 454, comment *j*. illus. 12. His twenty years of labor should have equal effect. On the other hand, Natale reaped the benefits of the contract. He and his devisees would be unjustly enriched if the statute of frauds could be invoked to relieve him from performance of his own obligations thereunder.

It is contended, however, that an estoppel to plead the statute of frauds can only arise when there have been representations with respect to the requirements of the statute indicating that a writing is not necessary or will be executed or that the statute will not be relied upon as a defense. This element was present in the leading case of Seymour v. Oelrichs, 156 Cal. 782, 106 P. 88, 134 Am.St.Rep. 154, and it is not surprising therefore that it has been listed as a requirement of an estoppel in later cases that have held on their facts that there was or was not an estoppel. Those cases, however, that have refused to find an estoppel have been cases where the court found either that no unconscionable injury would result from refusing to enforce the oral contract, or that the remedy of quantum meruit for services rendered was adequate. In those cases, however, where either an unconscionable injury or unjust enrichment would result from refusal to enforce the contract, the doctrine of estoppel has been applied whether or not plaintiff relied upon representations going to the requirements of the statute itself. Likewise in the case of partly performed oral contracts for the sale of land specific enforcement will be decreed whether or not there have been representations going to the requirements of the statute, because its denial would result in a fraud on the plaintiff who has gone into possession or made improvements in reliance on the contract. In reality it is not the representation that the contract will be put in writing or that the statute will not be invoked, but the promise that the contract will be performed that a party relies upon when he changes his position because of it. Moreover, a party who has accepted the benefits of an oral contract will be unjustly enriched if the contract is not enforced whether his representations related to the requirements of the statute or were limited to affirmations that the contract would be performed.

It is settled that neither the remedy of an action at law for damages for breach of contract nor the quasi-contractual remedy for the value of services rendered is adequate for the breach of a contract to leave property by will in exchange for services of a peculiar nature involving the assumption or continuation of a close family relationship. The facts of this case clearly bring it within the foregoing rule.

The judgments are affirmed.

NOTES

(1) *Flexibility*. Comment *b* to Restatement § 139 states: "Like § 90 this Section states a flexible principle, but the requirement of consideration is more easily displaced than the requirement of a writing. The reliance must be foreseeable by the promisor, and enforcement must be necessary to avoid injustice. Subsection (2) lists some of the relevant factors in applying the latter requirement."

One entry in the list of relevant factors is "the extent to which the action or forbearance [on the part of the promisee or a third party] corroborates evidence of the making and terms of the promise." On the facts of *Monarco*, do you see strong corroboration in the conduct of Christie Lo Greco?

(2) *The Case of the Ungrateful Grandfather*. In Estate of Horrigan, 757 So.2d 165 (Miss.1999), Horrigan orally promised his grandchildren, Ted and Christy, that he would leave them the main interest in his home. Relying on this promise, Ted and Christy invested most of their savings, roughly $22,000, in renovating the home. On Horrigan's death, it was found that his will left the property to his widow. The court of probate awarded the property to Horrigan's widow, as the will provided, but charged the property with a lien in favor of Ted and Christy for the amount of their investment, with interest. On review, this disposition was affirmed. Specific performance was not an available remedy, according to the appellate court.

Both in *Horrigan* and in *Monarco*, the courts characterized the relief as a constructive trust. But in *Monarco* the relief granted to Christie Lo Greco amounted to specific performance. According to § 139 of the Restatement, the remedy granted for breach, by reason of reliance, "is to be limited as justice requires." Does this limitation explain the difference between the forms of relief granted in *Monarco* and in *Horrigan*? Is it apparent that justice to the Horrigan grandchildren did not require specific performance?

(3) *Part Performance: Reprise.* Consider *Horrigan* (foregoing Note) as an instance of a contract for a transfer of real property. Is it apparent why part performance by Ted and Christy did not make their contract enforceable? The opinion in the case recites this further fact: Ted and Christy had taken up residence in the house in question. On that account the court directed that they be charged rent for their use of the property. Note, however, that they did not invest in the property as a purchaser usually does, expecting near-term use of the improvements.

(4) *Roger Traynor, Traditionalist?* Compare the court's holding in *Monarco* with Restatement § 139. Does Justice Traynor's opinion contain any limits not found within the Restatement? If so, which makes more sense given the purposes of the Statute of Frauds and the facts that would allow a court in equity to disregard those purposes?

(5) *Estoppel Marches on.* The version of estoppel laid out in *Monarco* and Restatement § 139 has generally been adopted by courts dealing with the original Statute of Frauds or its progeny. How widely accepted estoppel is depends on which provision of the Statute of Frauds the breaching party seeks to invoke and the breached-against party seeks to estop the other from invoking. For example, courts seem fairly willing to recognize estoppel to assert the one-year provision, which is consistent with their hostility to that provision elsewhere. See McIntosh v. Murphy, 469 P.2d 177 (Haw. 1970). They are considerably less enthusiastic when the suretyship provision has been invoked, perhaps because reliance speaks more to the evidentiary aspect of the Statute of Frauds than to the cautionary aspect so important for guarantees. Land contracts fall somewhere near the middle. Compare Kiernan v. Creech, 268 P.3d 312 (Alaska 2012) (recognizing promissory estoppel; collecting cases) with Bradley v. Sanchez, 943 So.2d 218 (Fla. Dist. Ct. App. 2006) (rejecting promissory estoppel). One does still see decisions rejecting promissory estoppel altogether, though this is very much a minority position. But see Olympic Holding Co. v. Ace Ltd., 909 N.E.2d 93 (Ohio 2009) (completely rejecting promissory estoppel; but see dissent by O'Donnell, J., collecting cases that show 26 states that recognize a reliance exception and only eight that do not).

PROBLEM

Home on the Range. Ross and Wesley were grandsons of Albert, a ranch owner. Albert orally promised Ross and Wesley that he would convey the ranch to them if they worked for him until his death and if, once Albert died, they would take care of Albert's son, their uncle, until his death. Over the next decade they managed the ranch's operations without compensation. Ross and Wesley also invested money, resources, and labor, for, among other things, an irrigation system. Ross was eligible to receive a certain amount of federal funding to install irrigation systems, which he used to benefit this ranch and another owned by Albert. Then Albert sold the ranch to Clyde.

Ross and Wesley sued Albert for breach of contract and unjust enrichment. Albert raised a Statute of Frauds defense; Ross and Wesley countered with the part-performance exception and with estoppel. Should Albert be able to assert the Statute of Frauds successfully? Suppose Albert had worked on property owned by Ross and Wesley both before and after the oral promise. How, if at all, might this affect your analysis? If their breach of contract action is blocked, could they still succeed using unjust enrichment? If so, for what types of enrichment? See Wilberg v. Hyatt, 285 P.3d 1249 (Utah App. 2012).

Estoppel and UCC § 2–201

Whether estoppel to raise the Statute of Frauds as a defense applies to actions to enforce contracts for the sale of goods within Article 2 of the UCC has proved surprisingly controversial. The debate concerns the interaction between two Code provisions, UCC §§ 1–103(b) and 2–201(1).

UCC § 1–103(b) provides (with emphasis added) that

> *Unless displaced by the particular provisions of [the Uniform Commercial Code]*, the principles of law and equity, including . . . the law relating to . . . estoppel . . . shall supplement its provisions.

This provision suggests that, as is the case outside the UCC, estoppel may be used to enforce some contracts whose enforcement would otherwise be barred by a statute of frauds.

But UCC § 1–103(b) may be limited by the opening seven words of UCC § 2–201(1): "Except as otherwise provided *in this section. . . .*" The italicized passage suggests that the only exceptions to the Article 2 statute of frauds must be found in that section, which contains no reference to estoppel.

A representative opinion favoring estoppel is B & W Glass, Inc. v. Weather Shield Mfg., 829 P.2d 809 (Wyo. 1992). The court said that the "Except" phrase in subsection (1) does not displace general principles of law, such as estoppel:

> The effect [of the opening phrase of § 2–201(1)] is to alert the reader that the remaining subsections are disjunctive, and it serves to advise the reader of the proposition that the statutory exceptions to the statute of frauds are contained in subsections [(1) and (2) of § 2–201].

The Wyoming court found support in Comment 1 to UCC § 1–103 (as that Comment appeared before the 2001 revision to Article 1), indicating that displacement of general principles is to be found only where another Code provision is explicit on the point. "Neither the text of § 2–201 nor the comments following it specifically refer to estoppel," the court said.

For the minority view that UCC § 2–201 displaces estoppel, see Lige Dickson Co. v. Union Oil Co., 635 P.2d 103 (Wash. 1981). There the court pointed to the exceptions listed under UCC § 2–201(3) and concluded that they were exclusive. When the Code was proposed to the states, "[i]t was hoped that commercial transactions could take place across state boundaries without the stultifying effect caused by differences in states' laws." Adopting an estoppel exception "would allow parties to circumvent the UCC [and] we cannot help but foresee increased litigation and confusion as being the necessary result of the eroding of the UCC if [estoppel] is adopted in this case."

NOTES

(1) *Clarity Rejected.* A revised version of Article Two that was proposed in 2003 but never enacted (see p. 296) would have resolved this issue in favor of estoppel by deleting the first seven words of § 2–201(1): "Except as otherwise provided in this section." In the words of comment 2 to the amended § 2–201, "This change was made to provide that the statement of the three statutory exceptions in subsection (3) should not be read as limiting under subsection (1) the possibility that a promisor will be estopped to raise the statute-of-frauds defense in appropriate cases." When discussing this section, members of the drafting committee treated the amendment as a clarification rather than as a change. These amendments have been withdrawn, but they may have some persuasive value.

(2) *Restitution and Reliance.* Restitution is, like estoppel, a "principle of law," although not one mentioned by name in UCC § 1–103(b). On examining UCC § 2–201, does it appear that this liability is displaced with respect to unenforceable agreements for sales of goods? See Allied Grape Growers v. Bronco Wine Co., 249 Cal. Rptr. 872 (Ct. App. 1988) (connecting estoppel exception with unjust enrichment); Miss. Livestock Producers Ass'n v. Hood, 758 So.2d 447 (Miss. Ct. App. 2000) (restitution available).

(B) UCC § 2–201(2): THE SOUNDS OF SILENCE

It has long been common for those who make oral contracts to make a memorandum of the agreement they reached, whether the transaction is within the Statute of Frauds or not. These memoranda do not satisfy the Statute of Frauds, though, unless they are signed—and even then, they satisfy the Statute of Frauds only if the signer is the party against whom enforcement is sought. The drafter presumably would like to know whether her memorandum is accurate and would like the memorandum to satisfy the Statute of Frauds against the other party. The alternative would be to prepare a contract for the other party to sign, which adds to the time and cost of contracting.

The Code deals with this problem in § 2–201(2), sometimes called the "read your mail" exception or the "merchant" exception. It provides:

(2)   Between merchants if within a reasonable time a writing in confirmation of the contract and sufficient against the sender is

received and the party receiving it has reason to know its contents, it satisfies the requirements of subsection (1) against such party unless written notice of objection to its contents is given within ten days after it is received.

Although this subsection consists of only a single sentence, it contains six distinct elements before this exception takes effect. These are:

— The recipient of a message has let ten days go by without having responded to it, or if any response was made within that time it was not a "written notice of objection to [the] contents" of the message.

— The recipient had "reason to know" the contents of the message.

— The message was "a writing in confirmation of the contract."

— The message was "sufficient against the sender."

— The message was sent "within a reasonable time"; and

— Both the sender and the recipient were "merchants."

The effect of § 2–201(2) is for a writing to satisfy the Statute of Frauds against its recipient, even though the recipient did not sign the writing. Sending a writing of this sort thus has a salutary effect, no matter what the response. If there is no response, then the writing satisfies the Statute of Frauds. If the recipient responds, then the parties can resolve any points of disagreement and end up with a contract that more accurately represents the bargain-in-fact. Either way, sending the writing will move the contracting process along.

PROBLEMS

(1) *The Farmer in the Deal.* Cargill Incorporated, a major dealer in agricultural products, brought an action against Jorgenson Farms ("Farms"), alleging breach of a contract to supply it with 80,000 bushels of corn. Part of its evidence was a document titled "Contract #27985." James Jorgenson, a co-owner of Farms, acknowledged he had received that document in October 2003, in a packet of information. But Jorgenson said that he had not noticed the packet until later because October was "harvest time for us and I was busy in the fields." When Jorgenson did notice the document, he protested that there had been no agreement. In the previous July, however, Cargill had mailed to Farms what it called a "confirmation" of an oral sale agreement. This "confirmation" stated that it was to be signed and returned to Cargill. It also said: "Please sign and date the original copy of this contract. The original must be returned to Buyer. . . . " Cargill contended that Farms had acquiesced in the supposed contract because it had failed to respond.

Did either of the papers that Cargill sent Farms amount to what UCC § 2–201(2) calls a *confirmation*? And was either of them "sufficient against the sender [Cargill]"? See Cargill Inc. v. Jorgenson Farms, 719 N.W.2d 226 (Minn. App. 2006).

(2) *The Case of the Officious Spam Filter.* Ponzi, the owner of an office supply store, concocted a way to earn a huge amount of money. He sent emails that superficially looked like spam to a great many businesses, whose spam filters flagged the emails accordingly. In the email was a memorandum, signed by Ponzi, purporting to confirm an oral contract with the recipient for the sale of a large quantity of grossly overpriced office supplies. He reasoned that if the recipient read the email and objected, he would apologize, but nothing more should happen. If the recipient ignored or simply didn't see the mail, however, then Ponzi would wait ten days, send the truck filled with office supplies to the recipient, and demand payment under the terms of their contract.

Ponzi's plan didn't work. Why not?

(3) *Try, Try Again.* After he was released from prison for his first office-supply idea, Ponzi decided to take a more subtle approach. He approached local merchants, offering to sell them cleaning supplies at a very low price. If they agreed, then he offered to write up the deal and send the write-up to them as a confirmation of their conversation. The buyers invariably agreed. Ponzi then went back to his computer and sent an emailed invoice containing both the purchase actually contracted for and a large quantity of grossly overpriced office supplies. As before, he waited ten days and then sent the truck. Ponzi figured that this plan was destined to succeed, because the confirmation would bind the recipient under § 2–201(2) if the recipient didn't make a timely objection, and a confirmation under § 2–207 would establish the terms of the oral contract.

Ponzi's new plan didn't work. Why not? See § 2–201 cmt. 3.

St. Ansgar Mills, Inc. v. Streit
Supreme Court of Iowa, 2000.
613 N.W.2d 289.

■ CADY, JUSTICE. A grain dealer appeals from an order by the district court granting summary judgment in an action to enforce an oral contract for the sale of corn based on a written confirmation. The district court held the oral contract was unenforceable because the written confirmation was not delivered within a reasonable time after the oral contract as a matter of law. We reverse the decision of the district court and remand for further proceedings.

I.   Background Facts and Proceedings.

St. Ansgar Mills, Inc. is a family-owned agricultural business located in Mitchell County. As a part of its business, St. Ansgar Mills buys corn from local grain farmers and sells corn to livestock farmers for feed. The price of the corn sold to farmers is established by trades made on the Chicago Board of Trade for delivery with reference to five contract months. The sale of corn for future delivery is hedged by St. Ansgar Mills through an offsetting futures position on the Chicago Board of Trade.

A sale is typically made when a farmer calls St. Ansgar Mills and requests a quote for a cash price of grain for future delivery based on the Chicago Board of Trade price for the delivery.[1] The farmer then accepts or rejects the price. If the price is accepted, St. Ansgar Mills protects the price through a licensed brokerage house by acquiring a hedge position on the Chicago Board of Trade. This hedge position, however, obligates St. Ansgar Mills to purchase the corn at the stated price at the time of delivery. Thus, St. Ansgar Mills relies on the farmer who purchased the grain to accept delivery at the agreed price.

[Duane Streit, the defendant, raised hogs and, assisted by his father, John Streit, operated a "hog finishing operation" which he had acquired from John in 1993.]

Duane and his father have been long-time customers of St. Ansgar Mills. Since 1989, Duane entered into numerous contracts with St. Ansgar Mills for the purchase of large quantities of corn and other grain products. Duane would generally initiate the purchase agreement by calling St. Ansgar Mills on the telephone to obtain a price quote. If an oral contract was made, an employee of St. Ansgar Mills would prepare a written confirmation of the sale and either mail it to Duane to sign and return, or wait for Duane or John to sign the confirmation when they would stop into the business.

John would regularly stop by St. Ansgar Mills sometime during the first ten days of each month and pay the amount of the open account Duane maintained at St. Ansgar Mills for the purchase of supplies and other materials. On those occasions when St. Ansgar Mills sent the written confirmation to Duane, it was not unusual for Duane to fail to sign the confirmation for a long period of time. He also failed to return contracts sent to him. Nevertheless, Duane had never refused delivery of grain he purchased by telephone prior to the incident which gave rise to this case.

On July 1, 1996, John telephoned St. Ansgar Mills to place two orders for the purchase of 60,000 bushels of corn for delivery in December 1996 and May 1997. This order followed an earlier conversation between Duane and St. Ansgar Mills. After the order was placed, St. Ansgar Mills completed the written confirmation but set it aside for John to sign when he was expected to stop by the business to pay the open account. The agreed price of the December corn was $3.53 per bushel. The price of the May corn was $3.73 per bushel.

John failed to follow his monthly routine of stopping by the business during the month of July. St. Ansgar Mills then asked a local banker who was expected to see John to have John stop into the business.

---

[1]   This is not the exclusive method of sale. Another type of sale is based on an order contingent upon the cash price of the corn reaching a specific level. This type of sale, however, was not involved in this case.

John did not stop by St. Ansgar Mills until August 10, 1996. On that date, St. Ansgar Mills delivered the written confirmation to him.

Duane later refused delivery of the corn orally purchased on July 1, 1996. The price of corn had started to decline shortly after July 1, and eventually plummeted well below the quoted price on July 1. After Duane refused delivery of the corn, he purchased corn for his hog operations on the open market at prices well below the contract prices of July 1. St. Ansgar Mills later told Duane it should have followed up earlier with the written confirmation and had no excuse for not doing so.

St. Ansgar Mills then brought this action for breach of contract. It sought damages of $152,100, which was the difference between the contract price of the corn and the market price at the time Duane refused delivery.

Duane filed a motion for summary judgment. He claimed the oral contract alleged by St. Ansgar Mills was governed by the provisions of the Uniform Commercial Code, and was unenforceable as a matter of law under the statute of frauds. He claimed the written confirmation delivered to John on August 10, 1996 did not satisfy the statute of frauds for two reasons. First, he was not a merchant. Second, the confirmation was not received within a reasonable time after the alleged oral agreement.

The district court determined a jury question was presented on whether Duane was a merchant under the Uniform Commercial Code. However, the district court found the written confirmation did not satisfy the writing requirements of the statute of frauds because the delivery of the confirmation to John, as Duane's agent, did not occur within a reasonable time after the oral contract as a matter of law. The district court found the size of the order, the volatility of the grain market, and the lack of an explanation by St. Ansgar Mills for failing to send the confirmation to Duane after John failed to stop by the business as expected made the delay between July 1 and August 10 unreasonable as a matter of law.

St. Ansgar Mills appeals. It claims a jury question was presented on the issue of whether a written confirmation was received within a reasonable time.

III. Statute of Frauds.

Although the statute of frauds has been deeply engrained into our law, many of the forces which originally gave rise to the rule are no longer prevalent. J. White & R. Summers, [Uniform Commercial Code § 2–1, at 51 (2d ed. 1980)—hereinafter "White & Summers"]. This, in turn, has caused some of the rigid requirements of the rule to be modified.

One statutory exception or modification to the statute of frauds which has surfaced applies to merchants. UCC § 2–201(2). Under [that provision], the writing requirements of UCC § 2–201(1) are considered to be satisfied if, within a reasonable time, a writing in confirmation of the contract which is sufficient against the sender is received and the merchant receiving it has reason to know of its contents, unless written notice of objection of its contents is given within ten days after receipt. Id. Thus, a writing is still required, but it does not need to be signed by the party against whom the contract is sought to be enforced. The purpose of this exception was to put professional buyers and sellers on equal footing by changing the former law under which a party who received a written confirmation of an oral agreement of sale, but who had not signed anything, could hold the other party to a contract without being bound. See White & Summers § 2–3, at 55; Kimball County Grain Coop. v. Yung, 263 N.W.2d 818, 820 (Neb.1978). It also encourages the common, prudent business practice of sending memoranda to confirm oral agreements. White & Summers § 2–3, at 55.

While the written confirmation exception imposes a specific ten-day requirement for a merchant to object to a written confirmation, it employs a flexible standard of reasonableness to establish the time in which the confirmation must be received. The Uniform Commercial Code specifically defines a reasonable time for taking action in relationship to "the nature, purpose and circumstances" of the action. UCC § 2–201(2). Additionally, the declared purpose of the Uniform Commercial Code is to permit the expansion of commercial practices through the custom and practice of the parties. See UCC § 1–102 cmt. 2 (course of dealings, usage of trade or course of performance are material in determining a reasonable time). Furthermore, the Uniform Commercial Code relies upon course of dealings between the parties to help interpret their conduct. UCC § 1–205(1). Thus, all relevant circumstances, including custom and practice of the parties, must be considered in determining what constitutes a reasonable time under UCC § 2–201(2).

There are a host of cases from other jurisdictions which have considered the question of what constitutes a reasonable time under the written confirmation exception of the Uniform Commercial Code. See Gestetner Corp. v. Case Equip. Co., 815 F.2d 806, 810 (1st Cir.1987) (roughly five month delay reasonable in light of merchants' relationship and parties' immediate action under contract following oral agreement); Serna, Inc. v. Harman, 742 F.2d 186, 189 (5th Cir.1984) (three and one-half month delay reasonable in light of the parties' interaction in the interim, and non-fluctuating prices, thus no prejudice); Cargill, Inc. v. Stafford, 553 F.2d 1222, 1224 (10th Cir.1977) (less than one month delay unreasonable despite misdirection of confirmation due to mistaken addressing); Starry Constr. Co. v. Murphy Oil USA, Inc., 785 F.Supp. 1356, 1362–63 (D. Minn.1992) (six month delay for confirmation of modification order for additional oil unreasonable as a matter of law in light of Persian Gulf War, thus increased prices and demand); Rockland Indus., Inc. v. Frank Kasmir Assoc., 470 F.Supp. 1176, 1179 (N.D.Tex.1979) (letter sent eight months after alleged oral agreement for two-year continuity agreement unreasonable in light of lack of evidence supporting reasonableness of delay); *Yung*, 263 N.W.2d at 820 (six month delay in confirming oral agreement delivered one day prior to last possible day of delivery unreasonable); *Azevedo*, 471 P.2d at 666 (ten week delay reasonable in light of immediate performance by both parties following oral agreement); Lish v. Compton, 547 P.2d 223, 226–27 (Utah 1976) (twelve day delay "outside the ambit which fair-minded persons could conclude to be reasonable" in light of volatile price market and lack of excuse for delay other than casual delay). Most of these cases, however, were decided after a trial on the merits and cannot be used to establish a standard or time period as a matter of law. Only a few courts have decided the question as a matter of law under the facts of the case. Compare *Starry*, 785 F.Supp. at 1362–63 (granting summary judgment), and *Lish*, 547 P.2d at 226–27 (removing claim from jury's consideration), with Barron v. Edwards, 206 N.W.2d 508, 511 (Mich.Ct.App.1973) (remanding for further development of facts, summary judgment improper). However, these cases do not establish a strict principle to apply in this case. The resolution of each case depends upon the particular facts and circumstances.

In this case, the district court relied upon the large amount of the sale, volatile market conditions, and lack of an explanation by St. Ansgar Mills for failing to send the written confirmation to Duane in determining St. Ansgar Mills acted unreasonably as a matter of law in delaying delivery of the written confirmation until August 10, 1996. Volatile market conditions, combined with a large sale price, would normally narrow the window of reasonable time under UCC § 2–201(2). However, they are not the only factors to consider. Other relevant factors which must also be considered in this case reveal the parties had developed a custom or practice to delay delivery of the confirmation. The parties also maintained a long-time amicable business relationship and had engaged in many other similar business transactions without incident. There is also evidence to infer St. Ansgar Mills did not suspect John's failure to follow his customary practice in July of stopping by the business was a concern at the time. These factors reveal a genuine dispute over the reasonableness of the delay in delivering the written confirmation, and make the resolution of the issue appropriate for the jury. Moreover, conduct is not rendered unreasonable solely because the acting party had no particular explanation for not pursuing different conduct, or regretted not pursuing different conduct in retrospect. The reasonableness of conduct is determined by the facts and circumstances existing at the time.

Considering our principles governing summary adjudication and the need to resolve the legal issue by considering the particular facts and circumstances of each case, we conclude the trial court erred by granting summary judgment. We reverse and remand the case for further proceedings.

Reversed and remanded.

NOTE

On remand, what would you want to prove if you represented the plaintiff? The defendant? What testimony would help you make your case?

(C) UCC § 2–201(3)(b): THE JUDICIAL ADMISSIONS EXCEPTION

As noted above, Karl Llewellyn was greatly irritated by the possibility that a breaching party could both agree that he made a contract and successfully assert the Statute of Frauds because that contract was not in writing. The "laughing defendant," as this sort of person became known, was a prime example of someone using the Statute of Frauds as a means of committing fraud.

Llewellyn looked for a way to prevent a defendant from both admitting that a contract existed and successfully asserting the Statute of Frauds. He came up with one in UCC § 2–201(3)(b). Under this subsection, the laughing defendant would be able to laugh no more. If the party against whom enforcement was sought "admits in his pleading, testimony or otherwise in court that a contract for sale was made," then it is enforceable up to the quantity of goods admitted.

Just how far this subsection extends has been litigated sporadically. The general approach is to extend it to cover depositions, most notably, but also interrogatories and requests for admissions. A more difficult question is what exactly qualifies as an admission that a contract was made. If a party to a contract testifies that she in fact made a contract with the other party, that testimony should fall safely within the judicial admissions exception. How to procure this testimony can be tricky.

A corollary to the judicial admissions section is the need to give the party seeking these admissions a reasonable time in which to conduct discovery. That does not make this exception into a license for a fishing expedition in the other party's waters. It is always possible that a defendant will break down under the plaintiff's withering cross-examination, but it is far from probable; on the other hand, the plaintiff does have to have some time in which to secure the desired admissions. Exactly where to draw this line has been a matter of considerable dispute. In a very influential opinion by Judge Posner, the court held that the defendant could cut off the plaintiff's investigations by submitting a sworn affidavit. DF Activities Corp. v. Brown, 851 F.2d 920 (7th Cir. 1988). In Judge Posner's words, if "defendant swears in an affidavit that there was no contract, we see no point in keeping the lawsuit alive," for though "defendant *may* blurt out an admission in a deposition, this is hardly likely." This rather restrictive rule has been adopted outside the Seventh Circuit, but the courts generally head in other directions. The center of gravity for the judicial admissions exception is probably the proposal that the plaintiffs get one round of discovery as a matter of course, with more only after establishing a real likelihood of success. The single round may yield documents that collectively satisfy the Statute of Frauds. Moreover, additional information from discovery may make depositions more productive. Finally, just because a CEO is not aware that some of her workers have breached contracts, committed torts, and so forth does not mean that these torts or contract breaches didn't happen. The CEO cannot be expected to know everything. A sworn affidavit reflects only the finite knowledge and authority of its author. See Dennco, Inc. v. MacNeill Eng'g Co., 2005 WL 3578132 (D.N.H. 2005).

The judicial admissions exception has been adopted outside Article 2 by a substantial minority of courts. See Gibson v. Arnold, 288 F.3d 1242 (10th Cir. 2002). Almost all of the others simply haven't yet reached the issue.

PROBLEM

The Whole *Truth?* You represent the plaintiff in an action for breach of an oral contract. You are all but certain that the defendant actually did make a contract with the plaintiff, but thought better of it a little later and sought to get out by any means possible. It has come time to depose the defendant. What questions would you ask the defendant in order to get the defendant to make the requisite admissions? If you represented the defendant, how might you prepare your client in order to avoid making damaging admissions?

SECTION 6.   ETHICAL PRACTICE AND STATUTES OF FRAUDS

The Statute of Frauds is as much a part of the law as anything else in the statute books. But like statutes of limitations, its use may be both unimpeachable and disquieting. In each case, somebody seems to be getting away with something. Leaving aside the Holmesian bad man and his modern kin, most people find getting away with something morally dubious, not to say dishonest or sleazy. It is as though the defendant is thumbing his nose at the frustrated plaintiff. We thus see many of these defenses stigmatized as merely "technical," which implies that they are in some way inferior to grander principles of law and ethics. Consider, for example, the opinion in *Beaver v. Brumlow, supra* at p. 389. At the end, the court had this to say:

> Sellers would have us invalidate what was unquestionably a valid contract based on a mechanical application of contract law. We decline to do so. See Herrera v. Herrera, 1999-NMCA-034, ¶ 13, 126 N.M. 705, 974 P.2d 675 (noting that the purpose of the statute of frauds is to prevent fraud and perjury, not to prevent the performance or enforcement of oral contracts that have been made or to create a loophole of escape for a person who seeks to repudiate a contract he admits was made). Sellers do not seem to acknowledge that this is a case under the equitable

jurisdiction of the trial court. "In the general juristic sense, equity means the power to meet the moral standards of justice in a particular case by a tribunal having discretion to mitigate the rigidity of the application of strict rules of law so as to adapt the relief to the circumstances of the particular case." Henry L. McClintock, Principles of Equity § 1, at 1 (2d ed. 1948). We hold that there was no error committed by the trial court by decreeing specific performance of the contract for Sellers to sell, and Buyers to buy, the subject property for its fair market value.

A lawyer's perspective is different when she is asked to oppose a claim on a "technical" ground. Consider one who is asked to defend a client against the enforcement of an agreement that the client acknowledges having made. If the lawyer believes that a statute of frauds stands in the way of enforcement, she may have some compunction about invoking it. On the other hand, lawyers are expected to be zealous in representing clients.

Is it unethical of the lawyer to invoke the statute? Unethical *not* to invoke it? The U.S. authorities generally favor the statute's use. The Restatement (Third) of the Law Governing Lawyers speaks of "the general rule that a lawyer may act guided only by the objective of furthering the interests of the lawyer's client." Comment *b* to Section 94. Invoking a defense on behalf of one's client, however technical that defense might be, furthers the client's interests. Dean Robert Stevens thought it a prevailing practice among lawyers "automatically to plead the Statute of Limitations to a stale claim and the Statute of Frauds when there is known to be no writing signed by the defendant, or his agent, evidencing the contract sued upon." The statutes are there and supply the defenses, he said, "and the attorney would not be giving full and competent service to his client if he did not advise him of them and advance them for him." Stevens, *Ethics and the Statute of Frauds,* 37 Cornell L. Q. 355 (1952).

But Stevens saw a dilemma for a lawyer asked by a client to defend against a claim based on an oral agreement that the client privately concedes having made. Courts almost unanimously approve that practice, but the lawyer's conscience may not. "[W]hat is the lawyer to do? Conscience tells him that the practice is wrong, but the literature from insurance companies reminds him of liability for malpractice." *Id.* at 356. The lawyer might both tell her client about the defense and recommend that it not be pursued, but what if the client wishes to press on?

Whether to invoke technical defenses like a statute of frauds or a statute of limitations has troubled lawyers at least as far back as the first American writings on legal ethics. In 1836, David Hoffman put at the end of his *Course of Legal Study* a list of resolutions for a well-conducted lawyer. Among them Hoffman put:

My client's conscience, and my own, are distinct entities: and though my vocation may sometimes justify my maintaining as facts, or principles, in doubtful cases, what may be neither one nor the other, I shall ever claim the privilege of solely judging to what extent to go. In *civil* cases, if I am satisfied from the evidence that the *fact* is against my client, he must excuse me if I do not see as he does, and do not press it: and should the *principle* also be wholly at variance with sound law, it would be dishonourable folly in me to endeavor to incorporate it into the jurisprudence of this country . . . [vol. 2, p. 755]

According to the American Bar Association, "a lawyer can be a zealous advocate on behalf of a client and at the same time assume that justice is being done." But this precept is qualified by this introductory phrase: "When an opposing party is well represented. . . ." Preamble to Model Rules of Professional Conduct (2002). One scholar has said that the answer depends on whether or not the lawyer holds "a good faith belief that the assertion of the doctrine or rule in the particular case will further a policy behind the doctrine or rule." Kenney Hegland, *Quibbles,* 67 Tex. L. Rev. 1491, 1494 (1989). That did not suit Professor John Sutton, who answered that Professor Hegland would leave it to each lawyer on his own "to make the decision concerning fairness and justice." *Outlawing Unjust Rules of Law: A Response to* Quibbles, 67 Tex. L. Rev. 1517, 1522 (1989).

Leaving aside the rules of ethics for the moment, what should a lawyer do when a client admits to making and breaching a contract that the lawyer knows is unenforceable because of a statute of frauds? More particularly, what if the lawyer finds this statute of frauds odious and thinks its use reprehensible? And should the lawyer's freedom of action be affected by when this defense appears—before the lawyer accepts the client, or very early in the representation, or not long before trial? Turning back to the rules of ethics, how does the lawyer's duty to represent her client zealously mesh with the attorney's right not to accept a client, or, though limited, to withdraw from the representation?

And consider actual statutes of frauds, both the original and the later versions we have studied. Are there any limits or exceptions to these statutes that make it less likely that the so-called "laughing defendant" will succeed? If we take Professor Hegland's suggestion, what *are* the policies behind a statute of frauds? Are there cases in which invoking the statute would not further these policies? And what if the statute does indeed further those policies, but the attorney finds the policies odious and reprehensible?

NOTE

Technicalities. Lack of consideration sometimes looks like a technical defense. In Mills v. Wyman, p. 73 above, Seth Wyman broke a promise to pay for emergency care given by Mills to his son, and found not liable because

Mills gave no consideration for the promise. The court heaped scorn upon Wyman and his defense, calling the outcome a "strong example of particular injustice." Many attorneys would have qualms about advancing the defense. When a statute of frauds is an effective defense for a self-confessed promise-breaker, is it any more "technical" than the defense that worked for Seth Wyman? Any less so?

CHAPTER 4

POLICING THE BARGAINING PROCESS

Although a contract may meet the general requirements for enforceability, such as agreement, consideration and, when relevant, compliance with the statute of frauds, there are circumstances where the law may refuse nonetheless to enforce the bargain. For example, when a promise is extracted through lawless threat ("Your money or your life!") or through outright fraud, one would not expect the courts to enforce the deal. Of course, bargaining abuses in a commercial society are usually more subtle and often less egregious than these. Sometimes the difficulty lies in the particular characteristics of a party to the bargain. Should bargains be enforced where one party is underage, "under the influence," or unsophisticated relative to the other party? Other times the problem concerns not the bargaining *process* but rather the bargaining *result*: When the old homestead is sold for a song, but there is no proof of anything approaching force or fraud, should law stand content and enforce the sale?

A variety of mechanisms have been adopted for policing what our society views as bargaining abuses. In this endeavor, there are three basic types of policing concerns: the *status* of the party seeking relief from a promise, the *behavior* of parties during the bargaining process, and the *substance* of the resulting bargain. While this chapter focuses primarily on the first two, a brief discussion of all three is in order, in part to indicate at the outset the often tangled relation among them.

The first concern attends chiefly to the *status* of the parties. In their strongest form, status-based policing measures disqualify certain classes of persons from committing themselves by contract. Minors, married women, and the mentally infirm have been among the historic classes, and are treated in Section 1. It is useful in considering status-based policing to pay attention to the underlying characteristics and presumptions on which the disqualification, or some lesser form of regulation, is based. Are they innate, as in the case of minors, who are understood to be immature and inexperienced or in any event are deemed to be? Are they circumstantial, as perhaps in the case of protections placed around consumers? And should contractual incapacities be determined by using bright line *rules*—the age of majority, for example—or are *standards*—like maturity or soundness of mind—more appropriate and perhaps fine-tuned?

The second policing concern focuses on the *behavior* of the parties during the bargaining process. The treatment of duress illustrates the difficult problem of how the law should deal with disparities in bargaining power between parties. What sorts of pressure or duress ought the law take into account in refusing to enforce a promise? How do courts distinguish among degrees of persuasion, pressure, and duress? What sorts of inequalities between the parties should the law take into account in policing a bargain? Informational asymmetries? Emotional and economic dependencies? Wealth disparities? In short, what limits or requirements should the law place on how the parties treat one another in the process of striking a deal?

The third concern looks to the *substance* of the bargain. Recall from your study of consideration in Chapter 1 that exchanges of unequal value are commonly enforced: Courts will not inquire into the adequacy of the consideration. Yet the law has introduced a variety of judicial and legislative policing measures that treat particularly lopsided bargains with disfavor. Limits on the substance of a bargain are the principal subject of Chapter 6.

What motivates courts in their policing efforts? To some extent, the answer combines moral conviction with a sense of institutional integrity. In the dramatic phrasing of an older case concerning an agreement to pay a bribe, "no court should be required to serve as paymaster of the wages of crime, or referee between thieves." Stone v. Freeman, 298 N.Y. 268, 271 (1948). Put another way, although we accept that contracts are a matter of private ordering—we say that parties can make whatever deal they want and rely on the state for its enforcement—still, contract law must take its place alongside other bodies of law such as criminal law, torts, corporate law, and family law from which public policies may be drawn. Policing the process or the substance of private bargains is a way of coordinating the social and moral values of the broader legal system.

We might also look to an account given by law and economics scholars: Courts are reluctant to enforce agreements involving bargaining failures, such as fraud, for reasons of efficiency. A bargain based on fraud or mistake, when unraveled, might reveal that the parties would not otherwise have entered into the agreement and that their joint welfare would be *reduced* by enforcement.

Whatever the origins of judicial action for policing the bargaining process, other important governmental actors have now entered the arena. The powers of legislatures and administrative agencies are regularly deployed to police both the bargaining process and bargains themselves. As we shall see, many, though not all, legislative and regulatory attempts to set proper conditions for fair and effective bargaining are directed at consumer protection.

This chapter focuses primarily on concerns regarding status and behavior, recognizing that the substance of a deal is sometimes an indication that something has gone awry in the bargaining process. Section 1 begins with the question of capacity. What limits does the law place on who can bind themselves contractually? Section 2 turns to the question of pressure and other irregularities in the conduct of the parties leading up the contract. How does the law define and attempt to address the problem of duress? How do courts determine whether a decision to enter or to modify a contract reflects the promisor's will or results instead from excessive pressure? Finally, Section 3 considers other forms of overreaching, including undue influence, non-disclosure and misrepresentation.

SECTION 1. CAPACITY

What classes of persons are considered by the law to have less than full power to contract? We focus on two important categories of incapacity: minority and mental infirmity.

In thinking about contractual incapacity, it is important to consider both the underlying bases and the broader consequences of such a determination. To take an historical example, the incapacities of married women under the common law were based not on impaired mental faculties but on the doctrine of coverture, brought about as a legal consequence of marriage. "By marriage, the husband and wife are one person in law; that is, the very being of the woman is suspended during the marriage, or at least is incorporated and consolidated into that of the husband: under whose wing, protection, and *cover*, she performs everything . . . [T]herefore all deeds executed, and all acts done, by her during her coverture, are void." 1 *Blackstone, Commentaries on the Law of England*, 442–443 (1765). The inability to enter to binding contracts ("all acts by her are void") justified the disqualification of married women from various forms of employment, including the practice of law, for as lawyers they would be unable to contract even with clients. See Bradwell v. Illinois, 83 U.S. 130 (1873). These incapacities were largely removed by Married Women's Property Acts enacted during the middle and late nineteenth century. See Richard Chused, *Married Women's Property Law: 1800–1850*, 71 Geo. L.J. 1359 (1983).

As you read, keep an eye on the bases for and consequences of other incapacities. We begin our study with minors, or "infants," as those not yet 21 were traditionally called. In 1971, the scope of minority shrank with the passage of the 26th Amendment, which lowered the age of majority to 18 for purposes of voting in federal elections. Enacted against the background of the Vietnam War, the slogan that helped win the day was "Old Enough to Die, Old Enough to Vote." Within a few years, the states too had established 18 as the age not only for voting but for contractual capacity.

Yet there are exceptions. Consider the federal "Credit CARD Act of 2009" which established 21 as the age required to contract for a credit card without a cosigner. Pub. L. No. 111–24, § 1, 123 Stat. The legislation has been criticized by Professor Andrew Schwartz on the grounds that it "rolls back the clock to medieval times," undermines the dignity of eighteen-year-olds, and hampers entrepreneurship to the detriment of enterprising youth and society in general. Andrew A. Schwartz, *Old Enough to Fight, Old Enough to Swipe: A Critique of the Infancy Rule in the Federal Credit Card Act,* 2011 Utah L. Rev. 407. Prof. Schwartz notes that Bill Gates founded Microsoft and Mark Zuckerberg started Facebook when each was 19; neither would have been able to obtain credit independently under the 2009 Act.

Why might Congress have restricted credit card contracts to those 21 and over? (What does "CARD" stand for?) Certainly minors now constitute a significant share of the consumer market. Are minors today significantly different from those of your parents' or grandparents' generations in other respects? If so, how? In thinking about limits on the contractual capacity, keep in mind that under the common law, most of those whose capacity was limited were regarded as "favorites" of the law. On the other hand, as the Restatement, Third, of Restitution and Unjust Enrichment reminds us, "[l]egal incapacity is legal disability, and a person who lacks the capacity to undertake a legally binding obligation is foreclosed from participating in transactions that may be advantageous or even vitally necessary;" § 33 cmt. c. As you read the following materials, consider whether contractual incapacity constitutes a benefit or a burden to those so favored.

Douglass v. Pflueger Hawaii, Inc.

Supreme Court of Hawai'i, 2006.
110 Hawai'i 520, 135 P.3d 129.

■ MOON, CHIEF JUSTICE. This appeal concerns the sole question whether plaintiff-appellant Adrian D. Douglass, a minor at the time he was hired by defendant-appellee Pflueger Hawaii, Inc. dba Pflueger Acura (Pflueger), is contractually bound by an arbitration provision set forth in Pflueger's Employee Handbook. Douglass appeals the December 30, 2003 order of the Circuit Court of the First Circuit, the Honorable Victoria S. Marks presiding, granting Pflueger's motion to stay action and to compel arbitration of the claims asserted by Douglass in his complaint. Douglass' claims stem from his allegations of sexual harassment and assault committed by his supervisor, an employee of Pflueger.

On appeal, Douglass contends that the circuit court erred in compelling arbitration because: (1) Douglass was a minor child who did not have the legal capacity to bind himself as a party to "an enforceable, valid, and irrevocable" arbitration agreement; (2) the arbitration provision contained in the Employee Handbook is not a valid and enforceable contract; and (3) Douglass produced sufficient evidence in opposition to Pflueger's motion to compel for the court to have sustained the motion and allow the case to proceed to trial. Douglass further contends that Pflueger waived its right to compel arbitration because it knowingly and voluntarily accepted the benefits of the judicial process.

For the reasons discussed infra, we vacate the December 30, 2003 order staying the instant action and compelling arbitration and remand this case for further proceedings consistent with this opinion.

I. BACKGROUND

On or about August 31, 2001, Pflueger hired Douglass as a lot technician at the Pflueger Acura car lot in Honolulu, Hawai'i. At that time, Douglass was seventeen years old (less than four months shy of the age of majority, i.e., eighteen years), having graduated from high school in the spring of 2001. On September 13, 2001, Douglass attended an employee orientation, where he received Pflueger's Employee Handbook [hereinafter, the Employee Handbook or the Handbook]. The Employee Handbook contained, inter alia, policies and procedures regarding Pflueger's anti-harassment/discrimination policies and an arbitration provision. The provision located on page 20 of the Handbook provides:

> Arbitration Agreement
>
> Any and all claims arising out of the employee's employment with the Company and his/her termination shall be settled by final binding arbitration in Honolulu, Hawaii, in accordance with the arbitration provisions of the Federal Arbitration Act and the rules and protocol prevailing with the American Arbitration Association. The parties agree not to institute any action in any court located in the State of Hawaii or elsewhere against the other arising out of the claims covered by this paragraph.

At the September 13, 2001 meeting, Douglass signed an acknowledgment form, located at page 60 in the Employee Handbook.

On or about November 29, 2001, Douglass was injured on the job when a coworker sprayed him on the buttocks area with an air hose. Subsequently, on May 2, 2002, Douglass filed a complaint with the Hawai'i Civil Rights Commission (HCRC). In response to his request to withdraw his HCRC complaint and pursue the matter in court, the HCRC, on September 25, 2002, issued a right-to-sue letter to Douglass, pursuant to HRS § 368–12 (1993).[1] Thereafter, on December 17, 2002, Douglass filed an action against Pflueger in the circuit court. In his complaint, Douglass alleged five employment law claims: (1) Hostile, Intimidating and/or Offensive Working Environment; (2) Unsafe Working Environment; (3) Sexual Assault and Sexual Discrimination; (4) Negligent Training (of its Supervisor); and (5) Negligent Supervision.

Thereafter, on December 1, 2003, Pflueger filed its motion to "stay this action and to compel arbitration in this dispute in accordance with

---

[1] HRS § 368–12 provides: Notice of right to sue. The commission [(HCRC)] may issue a notice of right to sue upon written request of the complainant. Within ninety days after receipt of a notice of right to sue, the complainant may bring a civil action under this chapter. The commission may intervene in a civil action brought pursuant to this chapter if the case is of general importance.

the [a]rbitration [a]greement set forth in [the] Employee [H]andbook." The circuit court heard Pflueger's motion on December 29, 2003. At the conclusion of the parties' oral argument, the circuit court granted the motion, stating:

> Well, I'm going to grant the motion. I think you have a situation where, as Ms. Petrus [Pflueger's counsel] says, you have a person who accepts the benefits of some of the contractual provisions and then tries to disavow one other contractual provision, and I don't think that's appropriate. And your argument is that if it wasn't specifically discussed or if they don't have a specific memory about it, that somehow would allow anybody to disavow any contract that they sign. I don't find that particularly persuasive.

On December 30, 2003, the circuit court issued its written order granting Pflueger's motion to compel arbitration. On January 27, 2004, Douglass timely filed his appeal.

III. DISCUSSION

As previously stated, the parties have raised issues regarding the validity and enforceability of the alleged arbitration agreement and possible waiver of such an agreement. The threshold question, however, is whether Douglass, as a minor, has an absolute right to disaffirm his employment contract with Pflueger, including the condition that "[a]ny and all claims arising out of the employee's employment with the Company and his/her termination shall be settled by final binding arbitration[.]"

A. The Infancy Doctrine

Hawai'i has long recognized the common law rule—referred to as "the infancy doctrine" or "the infancy law doctrine"—that contracts entered into by minors are voidable. See, e.g., Jellings v. Pioneer Mill Co., 30 Haw. 184 (1927); Zen v. Koon Chan, 27 Haw. 369 (1923); McCandless v. Lansing, 19 Haw. 474 (1909). Under this doctrine, a minor may, upon reaching the age of majority, choose either to ratify or avoid contractual obligations entered into during his or her minority. See 4 Richard A. Lord, Williston on Contracts § 8:14 (4th ed. 1992); see also Restatement (Second) of Contracts, §§ 7, 12, and 14 (1979); 7 Joseph M. Perillo, Corbin on Contracts § 27.4 (2002 ed.). Traditionally, the reasoning behind the infancy doctrine was based on the well-established common law principles that the law should protect children from the detrimental consequences of their youthful and improvident acts. As the California Court of Appeals explained in Michaelis v. Schori, 24 Cal. Rptr. 2d 380 (Cal. Ct. App. 1993):

> The rule has traditionally been that the law shields minors from their lack of judgment and experience and under certain conditions vests in them the right to disaffirm their contracts. Although in many instances such disaffirmance may be a

hardship upon those who deal with an infant, the right to avoid his contracts is conferred by law upon a minor for his protection against his own improvidence and the designs of others. It is the policy of the law to protect a minor against himself and his indiscretions and immaturity as well as against the machinations of other people and to discourage adults from contracting with an infant. Any loss occasioned by the disaffirmance of a minor's contract might have been avoided by declining to enter into the contract.

Id. at 381; see also Dodson v. Shrader, 824 S.W.2d 545, 547 (Tenn. 1992) ("[T]he underlying purpose of the infancy doctrine . . . is to protect minors from their lack of judgment and from squandering their wealth through improvident contracts with crafty adults who would take advantage of them in the marketplace.")

The rule that a minor's contracts are voidable, however, is not absolute. An exception to the rule is that a minor may not avoid a contract for goods or services necessary for his health and sustenance. See 5 Richard A. Lord, Williston on Contracts § 9:18 (4th ed. 1993). As the Maryland Court of Appeals summarized in Schmidt v. Prince George's Hospital, 784 A.2d 1112 (Md. Ct. App. 2001):

By the common law, persons, under the age of twenty-one years,[2] are not bound by their contracts, except for necessaries. They are allowed to contract for their benefit with power in most cases, to recede from their contract when it may prove prejudicial to them, but in their contract for necessaries, such as board, apparel, medical aid, teaching and instruction, and other necessaries, they are absolutely bound, and may be sued and charged in execution; but it must appear that the things were absolutely necessary, and suitable to their circumstances, and whoever trusts them does so at his peril, or as it is said, deals with them at arms' length. Their power, thus[,] to contract for necessaries, is for their benefit, because the procurement of these things is essential to their existence, and if they were not permitted so to bind themselves they might suffer. Id. at 1116.

It is apparent that the Hawai'i Legislature has, through the enactment of several statutory provisions codified the principle that contracts relating to medical care, hospital care, and drug or alcohol abuse treatment are contracts for "necessaries" (i.e., medical aid). These statutes explicitly provide that minors who enter into contracts for the medical services described therein cannot later disaffirm them by reason of their minority status.

---

[2]   In Hawai'i, the age of majority was reduced from twenty to eighteen years of age, effective March 28, 1972. 1972 Haw. Sess. L. Act 2, § 1 at 2, 28; see also Sen. Stand. Comm. Rep. No. 74–72, in 1972 Senate Journal, at 777.

Inasmuch as none of the parties to this appeal contend that Douglass' employment was "a necessary," it would appear that under the well-recognized infancy doctrine, Douglass would be entitled to disaffirm his employment contract, including the purported arbitration agreement. However, a review of Hawaii's child labor law—specifically HRS § 390–2 (1993 & Supp. 2005)—evinces the legislature's intent to incorporate the rationale underlying the common law infancy doctrine—that is, to protect children from the detrimental consequences of their youthful and improvident acts—into the statutory scheme and impose upon the Department of Labor and Industrial Relations (DLIR) the responsibility of promulgating rules and regulations to effectuate such intent. Under Hawaii's child labor law, "[n]o minor under eighteen years of age shall be employed or permitted to work in, about, or in connection with any gainful occupation at any time except as otherwise provided in this section." HRS § 390–2(a). To avoid violating child labor laws, employers and minors must meet certain requirements set forth in the statute as follows (emphasis added):

> (b)   A minor who has attained the age of *sixteen years but not eighteen years* may be employed during periods when the minor is not legally required to attend school or when the minor is excused by school authorities from attending school; provided that the employer of the minor records and keeps on file the number of *a valid certificate of age issued to the minor* by the department [of labor and industrial relations (DLIR)].

With respect to contracts of employment, it is apparent that, by relaxing the requirements for sixteen-and seventeen-year-olds to obtain employment, the legislature clearly viewed minors in this particular age group—being only one to two years from adulthood—as capable and competent to contract for gainful employment and, therefore, should be bound by the terms of such contracts. Similarly, inasmuch as the parent or guardian of a minor under sixteen is required to sign the application for a certificate of employment, which contains specific information regarding the nature and conditions of that employment, before entering into an employment contract, any such contract is equally binding on said minor. However, consistent with the policy of protecting minors until they attain the age of majority, the legislature provided an additional safeguard by authorizing the DLIR to "suspend, revoke or invalidate" any certificate of employment or age previously issued if the minor's employment is later found to be detrimental to the minor. See HRS § 390–4, quoted supra note 7. Thus, based on the foregoing reasoning, we conclude that, inasmuch as the protections of the infancy doctrine have been incorporated into the statutory scheme of Hawaii's child labor law, the general rule that contracts entered into by minors are voidable is not applicable in the employment context.

In applying the foregoing discussion to the circumstances of the instant case, we recognize that the record does not indicate whether

Douglass had, in fact, obtained an age certificate prior to his employment with Pflueger. However, even if he did not, Douglass should, nevertheless, be bound by the terms of his employment contract with Pflueger. First, there is nothing in the statutory scheme of the child labor law that renders Douglass' employment invalid or illegal based on his failure to obtain an age certificate. Second, it is undisputed that Douglass was, at the time he was hired, a seventeen-year-old high school graduate, who was only four months away from majority. And, third, there is nothing in the record to suggest that "the nature or condition of [Douglass'] employment [as a lot technician was] such as to injuriously affect [his] health, safety or well-being or contribute towards [his] delinquency" so as to trigger the suspension, revocation, or invalidation authority bestowed upon the DLIR director pursuant to HRS § 390–4. In other words, whether Douglass did or did not obtain an age certificate is irrelevant; it does not change the fact that Hawaii's child labor law provides for the protections of the infancy doctrine and renders inapplicable the general rule that contracts entered into by minors are voidable in the employment context. To conclude otherwise would be inconsistent with the clear legislative policy that sixteen-and seventeen-year-old minors do not, in accordance with the common law infancy doctrine, have an absolute right to disaffirm their employment contracts.

Accordingly, we hold that the circuit court properly rejected Douglass' argument that he is entitled to disaffirm his employment contract, including the arbitration provision, by reason of his minority status. Mossman v. Hawaiian Trust Co., Ltd., 45 Haw. 1, 15–16 (1961) (agreeing with determination of the trial court, but for different reason); see also Koolau Agric. Co., Ltd. v. Comm'n on Water Res. Mgmt., 83 Hawai'i 484, 493 (1996) (same).

[In an omitted section, the court held that although Douglass was not entitled to disaffirm the employment agreement in its entirety, the arbitration provision was not enforceable because its location in the Handbook failed to alert Douglass to its presence or scope, and therefore had not been assented to.]

Accordingly, we hold that, under the circumstances of this case, Douglass cannot be compelled to arbitrate his claims against Pflueger.

NOTES

(1) *Ages of Majority?* What bothered the circuit court judge in the hearing below? Should it matter in applying the infancy doctrine rule that Douglass was "only four months away from majority"? On what basis did the Supreme Court of Hawai'i decide to modify the common-law infancy doctrine?

If a seller reasonably believes a minor has lied about his age, why should the minor be allowed to rely upon his infancy? Does this not clash with the objective standard advanced in *Lucy v. Zehmer*, p. 163 above? Or is misrepresenting one's age exactly the kind of folly the infancy doctrine is intended to protect against?

(2)   *Necessaries*. What makes a good or service a necessary? What is the doctrine's purpose? The court in *Douglass* above noted in an omitted footnote that "[s]ome courts have narrowed the definition of 'necessaries' to exclude products or services that another person, such as a parent or guardian, is obligated to provide for the minor." But are all minors equal with regard to what counts as necessaries? A New York court observed that except when applied to such things as are obviously requisite for the maintenance of existence," the term "is a relative term and depends on the social position and situation in life of the infant as well as upon his own fortune and that of his parents. What would be necessary in a legal sense for an infant with ample means of his own might not be so for one with no means at all." Int'l Text-Book Co. v. Connelly, 99 N.E. 722, 725 (N.Y. 1912).

Viewed in that light, might employment ever be considered a necessary? A car? Housing? In Rivera v. Reading Housing Authority, 819 F.Supp. 1323, 1332–34 (E.D. Pa. 1993), a teenage mother's application for public housing was rejected:"[I]f a minor is living with a parent or guardian who is able and willing to furnish the minor with housing, housing is not a necessary. [For the Housing Authority] to assume the risks of entering into unenforceable contracts would be to jeopardize sound fiscal policy as well as a fair allocation of scarce housing resources."

What about a contract for lawyer's fees? In Zelnick v. Adams, 561 S.E.2d 711 (Va. 2002), the Supreme Court of Virginia held that a contract for legal services entered into on a minor's behalf to secure a portion of his grandfather's estate is "within the 'general class of necessaries' that may defeat a plea of infancy." Remanding the case for further fact-finding, the Supreme Court noted that "if minors are not required to pay for legal services, they will not be able to protect their various interests." Are legal services "absolutely necessary" as described on page 418 in *Pflueger*? If a suit could be brought *after* a minor turned 18, should the services be considered necessaries?

(3)   *Disaffirmance*. A contract entered into by a minor is voidable (not void, as with married women at common law). It may be disaffirmed in its entirety by the minor during minority or within a reasonable time thereafter. In Milicic v. Basketball Marketing Co., Inc. 857 A.2d 689 (Pa. 2004), a 16-year-old Serbian basketball player, relatively unknown in the United States, signed an exclusive endorsement agreement with a sports management company. By his 18th birthday, the player, then a top NBA draft pick, offered to buy out the contract. When the company refused, the player, Darko Milicic, disaffirmed. Describing him as "a child, living in a foreign country" at the time he signed the agreement, the court upheld the disaffirmance and, quoting from an earlier case reviewed one policy consideration underlying disaffirmance: "minors should not be bound by mistakes resulting from . . . the overbearance of unscrupulous adults."

The power to disaffirm may be limited by statute, see Okla. Stat. Tit. 15 § 19 (one-year limit), or lost if the contract received judicial approval at the time of its making; see Cal. Fam. Code § 6750–51, governing contracts of minors who contract for "artistic or creative services" or for athletic performances. It may also be lost through parental consent. In 1983, Brooke Shields, an "infant model," sought to disaffirm a contract entered into by her mother, selling the rights to nude photos of Shields taken when she was ten. The court held that a New York statute authorizing parental consent abrogated Shields' common-law right to disaffirm. Shields v. Gross, 58 N.Y.2d 338, 350 (1983).

The right to disaffirm may also be lost through *ratification*, when, having reached the age of majority, the former minor "does any distinct and decisive act clearly showing an intention to affirm" the contract. For example, in Fletcher v. Marshall, 632 N.E.2d 1105 (Ill. App. Ct. 1994), Fletcher, at age 17, co-signed a lease. After he turned 18, he continued to pay the rent. Note that in this case, the ratification consisted not of words ("I'm in!") but of part performance.

(4) *Restitution for Minors: The Traditional Rule.* Upon disaffirming a contract, a minor can get restitution of all payments already made to a seller, but the goods must be returned. Thus, in *Milicic*, Note 2 above, immediately upon disaffirming, and apparently by then well-advised, the player "began returning all monies and products (or their equivalent value)" received under the agreement. The requirement of restoration serves to prevent unjust enrichment of the buyer, but does not necessarily prevent loss to the seller; goods purchased by minors—cars, electronics—may well be the worse for wear. Yet policy concerns often prevail: "he who deals with a minor does so at his own peril." See Keser v. Chagnon, 410 P.2d 637 (Colo. 1966).

What if the minor contracted not for goods which could be restored but for services which could not? In Mitchell v. Mizerski, 1995 WL 118429 (Neb. App. 1995), a Nebraska court stated that "[d]ue to the nature of the consideration furnished by Mizerski, *i.e.*, paint and body work on the [minor's vehicle], there was nothing that could be returned by Travis. Although this result appears unjust to Mizerski, Nebraska law imposes such consequence upon adults who enter into contracts with minors, as a means to discourage such contracts."

Does the infancy doctrine produce perverse incentives? In Dodson v. Shrader, 824 S.W.2d 545 (Tenn. 1992), a 16-year-old bought a used pick-up truck for $4900, and despite knowing the truck had developed a mechanical problem, drove it for ten months until it "blew up." Upon the minor's disaffirmance, the trial court ordered the seller to reimburse the entire purchase price. On appeal, held: Reversed.

Noting the "glory of the common law" to adapt to "changes produced by time and circumstance," the Tennessee Supreme Court held that the seller should receive "reasonable compensation for the use of, depreciation, and willful or negligent damage to the article purchased, while in the minor's hands:"

The rule is best adapted to modern conditions under which minors are permitted to, and do in fact, transact a great deal of business, long before they have reached the age of legal majority. It seems intolerably burdensome for everyone concerned if merchants and business people cannot deal with them safely, in a fair and reasonable way. Such a doctrine can only lead to the corruption of principles and encourage young people in the habits of trickery and dishonesty.

Might the requirement of restitution protect minors as well? See Scott Eden Management v. Kavovit, 563 N.Y.S.2d 1001, 1004 (Sup. Ct. 1990). There the court noted that if minors can rescind contracts with talent agents immediately signing a lucrative contract, while still retaining all the benefits of the contract, "no reputable manager will expend any efforts on behalf of an infant." See also Statler v. Dodson, 466 S.E.2d 497 (W. Va. 1995).

(5) *Restitution for Persons: The New Rule.* Section 33 of the Restatement (Third) of Restitution and Unjust Enrichment provides that "[a] person who renders performance under an agreement that is unenforceable by reason of the other party's legal incapacity has a claim in restitution against the recipient as necessary to prevent unjust enrichment." How does this provision change the traditional rule? Is there an exception for necessaries?

Section 33 has met with criticism on several fronts. Professor Perillo observes that "[t]here is very little authority outside of New Hampshire for this view of the law;" see Joseph M. Perillo, *Restitution in a Contractual Context and the Restatement (Third) of Restitution & Unjust Enrichment*, 68 Wash. & Lee L. Rev. 1007, 1017 (2011). Professors Preston and Crowther argue that Section 33 "has gutted the infancy doctrine through the back door of a remedies restatement, without confronting it head on in a contracts restatement, and, more importantly, without the input of the state legislatures, which have enacted the infancy doctrine in every state." Cheryl B. Preston & Brandon T. Crowther, *Minor Restrictions: Adolescence Across Legal Disciplines, the Infancy Doctrine, and the Restatement (Third) of Restitution and Unjust Enrichment*, 61 U. Kan. L. Rev. 343, 349 (2012).

What age would you set for the contractual incapacity of minors? Might individualized judicial hearings on the maturity of a particular minor in a particular transaction be preferred to a bright line rule? Should status changes in other areas of life—teenage marriage, for example—create a presumption of contractual maturity?

Ortelere v. Teachers' Retirement Bd.

New York Court of Appeals, 1969.
25 N.Y.2d 196, 250 N.E.2d 460.

[Grace Ortelere was a 60-year-old New York City schoolteacher who had suffered a nervous breakdown diagnosed as involving "involutional psychosis, melancholia type," and was on leave for mental illness. Her psychiatrist suspected that she also suffered from cerebral arteriosclerosis. Her husband had quit his job as an electrician to stay home and care for her. She had an account of $70,925 in the public retirement system in which she had participated for over 40 years. In

1965, without telling her husband, she obtained a loan from the system in the largest amount possible, $8,760, and made an irrevocable election to take the maximum retirement benefits of $450 a month during her lifetime. This revoked an earlier election under which she would have received only $375 a month but her husband would have taken the unexhausted reserve on her death. The new election left him with no benefits in the event of her death. Two months later she died of cerebral arteriosclerosis. Her husband sued to set aside her election on the ground of mental incompetence. Her psychiatrist testified that she was incapable of making a decision of any kind and that victims of involutional melancholia "can't think rationally. They will even tell you 'I don't know whether I should get up or whether I should stay in bed.' Everything is impossible to decide." From a judgment for Mr. Ortelere, the Board appealed to the Appellate Division, which reversed and dismissed the complaint. The plaintiff appealed.]

■ BREITEL, JUDGE.[a] The particular issue arises on the evidently unwise and foolhardy selection of benefits by a 60-year-old teacher, on leave for mental illness and suffering from cerebral arteriosclerosis. The teacher died a little less than two months after making her election of maximum benefits, payable to her during her life, thus causing the entire reserve to fall in. She left her surviving husband of 38 years and two grown children.

Traditionally, in this State and elsewhere, contractual mental capacity has been measured by what is largely a cognitive test. Under this standard the "inquiry" is whether the mind was "so affected as to render him wholly and absolutely incompetent to comprehend and understand the nature of the transaction". A requirement that the party also be able to make a rational judgment concerning the particular transaction qualified the cognitive test. Conversely, it is also well recognized that contractual ability would be affected by insane delusions intimately related to the particular transaction.

These traditional standards governing competency to contract were formulated when psychiatric knowledge was quite primitive. They fail to account for one who by reason of mental illness is unable to control his conduct even though his cognitive ability seems unimpaired. When these standards were evolving it was thought that all the mental faculties were simultaneously affected by mental illness. This is no longer the prevailing view.

Of course the greatest movement in revamping legal notions of mental responsibility has occurred in the criminal law. The nineteenth century cognitive test embraced in the *M'Naghten* rules has long been

---

[a]   Charles D. Breitel (1908–1991) was appointed to the New York Supreme Court in 1950 after law practice in New York City and service with Thomas E. Dewey, first on his staff when Dewey was district attorney and later as his counsel when Dewey was governor. He was elevated to the Appellate Division in 1952 and to the Court of Appeals in 1967, serving as Chief Judge from 1974 to 1978.

out [all] the checks, yes." See Richard Danzig and Geoffrey Watson, 272 (2004). What do you make of Mr. Ortelere's testimony?

Under the Employee Retirement Income Security Act (ERISA), 29 U.S.C. §§ 1001 *et seq.*, a person in Mrs. Ortelere's position could not now, except in some cases of exigency, elect a lifetime annuity depriving his or her spouse of a survivor's annuity, without the spouse's written, witnessed consent.

(3)   *Capacities Compared.* Farnum v. Silvano, 540 N.E.2d 202 (Mass. App. 1989), was an action by the seller of a home to rescind the sale. The seller was a 90-year-old woman who sometimes exhibited distressing delusions (*e.g.*, that her one story house had a second story). The purchaser was a young man who had kept up her lawn and who had her confidence. He had paid about 56% of the fair market value of the home, while obtaining a mortgage loan on the property for much more than the fair market value. The trial court concluded that the seller had conveyed her home during a lucid interval and ruled for the defendant. She appealed. *Held:* Reversed, and rescission ordered. The court cited *Ortelere,* and said: "Acting during a lucid interval can be the basis for executing a will. Competence to enter into a contract presupposes something more than a transient surge of lucidity." What explains the differing measures for capacity with regard to wills and contracts?

Cundick v. Broadbent

United States Court of Appeals, Tenth Circuit, 1967.
383 F.2d 157.

[Darwin Cundick was a 59-year-old sheep rancher who had on occasion sold his lamb crop to J.R. Broadbent. At a meeting between the two men in September, 1963, they signed a one-page contract in longhand by which Cundick agreed to sell all of his ranching properties to Broadbent. Mr. and Mrs. Cundick then took the contract to their lawyer, who refined and amplified it into an eleven-page document, which the parties signed in his office. In October, 1963, the agreement was amended, again with a lawyer's aid, so as to increase the price to Cundick and in another respect favorable to him. Under the amended agreement, more than 2,000 acres of range land went for about $40,000. (An expert later valued it at $89,000.) Also included was Cundick's interest in a development company of which Broadbent was a director, at a price of $46,750. (A witness for Cundick later valued this at $184,000, and one for Broadbent at $73,743.) As late as February, 1964, Cundick was executing documents to carry out the sale. In March, when the price had been paid and the sale was almost completed, Cundick sought to rescind. His wife, who had been appointed his guardian *ad litem* ("for the purpose of suing"), brought an action against Broadbent to set aside the agreement. She asserted that her husband had been mentally incompetent to contract, and that in any event he was mentally infirm and Broadbent had knowingly overreached him. The evidence showed that Cundick had

had psychiatric treatment in 1961. Thereafter his family doctor saw him many times about various ailments, but nothing was said or done about a mental condition before the suit was commenced. The court ordered examinations in 1964; they disclosed premature arteriosclerosis. Two neurosurgeons and a psychologist testified that Cundick had been incapable, the previous September, of transacting important business affairs, and that he was a "confused and befuddled man with very poor judgment." There was no medical evidence to the contrary. The trial court nevertheless found: "The acts and conduct of Cundick between September 2, 1963, and the middle of February, 1964, were the acts, conduct and behavior of a person competent to manage his affairs and cognizant of the effect of his actions." It also found that the contract was not unconscionable, unfair or inequitable. From a dismissal of the action, Mrs. Cundick appealed.]

■ MURRAH, CHIEF JUDGE. At one time, in this country and in England, it was the law that since a lunatic or non compos mentis had no mind with which to make an agreement, his contract was wholly void and incapable of ratification. But, if his mind was merely confused or weak so that he knew what he was doing yet was incapable of fully understanding the terms and effect of his agreement, he could indeed contract, but such contract would be voidable at his option. But in recent times courts have tended away from the concept of absolutely void contracts toward the notion that even though a contract be said to be void for lack of capacity to make it, it is nevertheless ratifiable at the instance of the incompetent party. The modern rule, and the weight of authority, seems to be [that] ". . . the contractual act by one claiming to be mentally deficient, but not under guardianship, absent fraud, or knowledge of such asserted incapacity by the other contracting party, is not a void act but at most only voidable at the instance of the deficient party; and then only in accordance with certain equitable principles." Rubenstein v. Dr. Pepper Co., 8 Cir., 228 F.2d 528 [(1955)].

In recognition of different degrees of mental competency the weight of authority seems to hold that mental capacity to contract depends upon whether the allegedly disabled person possessed sufficient reason to enable him to understand the nature and effect of the act in issue. Even average intelligence is not essential to a valid bargain. "Mere weakness of body or mind, or of both, do not constitute what the law regards as mental incompetency sufficient to render a contract voidable. A condition which may be described by a physician as senile dementia may not be insanity in a legal sense." Kaleb v. Modern Woodmen of America, 51 Wyo. 116 (1937). Weak-mindedness is, however, highly relevant in determining whether the deficient party was overreached and defrauded. . . .

There was, to be sure, evidence of a change in [Cundick's] personality and attitude toward his business affairs during [the period between his mental examinations in 1961 and 1964]. But the record is conspicuously silent concerning any discussion of his mental condition among his family and friends in the community where he lived and operated his ranch. Certainly, the record is barren of any discussion or comment in Broadbent's presence. It seems incredible that Cundick could have been utterly incapable of transacting his business affairs, yet such condition be unknown on this record to his family and friends, especially his wife who lived and worked with him and participated in the months-long transaction which she now contends was fraudulently conceived and perpetrated.

The narrated facts of this case amply support the trial court's finding to the effect that Broadbent did not deceive or overreach Cundick. [Although] there is positive evidence that the property was worth very much more than what Broadbent paid for it, . . . there was evidence to the effect that after the original contract was signed and some complaint made about the purchase price, the parties agreed to raise the price and the contract was so modified.

[Affirmed.]

■ HILL, CIRCUIT JUDGE (dissenting). . . . The evidence relied upon by the majority is actually trivial and inconsequential as compared with the undisputed medical testimony . . . It is inconceivable to me that any mentally competent person, with a lifetime of experience as a successful rancher and stockman, would dispose of his ranch interests at a price equal to less than one-half of the actual value.

NOTES

(1) *Case Comparison.* Are the *Ortelere* and *Cundick* cases distinguishable? To what extent do the differences among the opinions in those cases reflect the different orientations regarding status, behavior, and substance introduced at p. 417 above?

(2) *Appearances.* Claims of incapacity raise several issues of proof. In Hakimoglu v. Trump Taj Mahal Assocs., 876 F.Supp. 625 (D.N.J. 1994), intoxication was raised as a defense to an action by a casino to recover $700,000 in gambling debts. The gambler argued that he had been plied with martinis by the casino; the casino argued that Hakimoglu was not "visibly and obviously drunk." The court said that as the party asserting intoxication, Hakimoglu had "the burden of coming forward with evidence from which a reasonable fact-finder [could] conclude that he was intoxicated." It remanded the case for a jury determination of Hakimoglu's apparent state at the time the credits were extended, as recorded by surveillance cameras and other observers.

(3) *Particularized Incapacities.* Are there other conditions that so impair a person's ability to comprehend a particular transaction as to make a transaction of that kind reversible by that person? What about grief, in connection with buying a coffin for a loved one? Or are emotional states different in kind from the disabling condition in *Ortelere*?

What about elderly persons, who may be particularly vulnerable to certain kinds of blandishments (or threats) from unscrupulous vendors and service providers? Should the elderly be treated in the same way as minors, with a presumption of incapacity and the right to disaffirm? There may, of course, be difficulties in drawing a bright-line rule at this end of the age spectrum, but are they different in kind from those arising from treating all minors alike?

One statutory mechanism used to police transactions involving the elderly is a "penalty enhancement," a civil fine of $10,000 or so, that is added to a criminal sentence in cases of fraud where the "defendant knew or should have known that the victim of the offense was unusually vulnerable due to age. . . . " See United States v. Williams, 1997 WL 573379 (N.D. Ill. 1997), affirming a conviction for aggravated home repair. Another is the appointment of a guardian or conservator. California, for example, provides for the judicial appointment of conservators for any person who, for specified reasons, is "likely to be deceived or imposed upon by artful or designing persons." See Bd. of Regents of State Univ., State of Wisconsin v. Davis, 533 P.2d 1047 (Cal. 1975). What virtues and hazards do you see in these approaches?

Kenai Chrysler Center, Inc. v. Denison

Supreme Court of Alaska, 2007.
167 P.3d 1240.

[Kenai Chrysler Center, Inc., sold a car to David Denison, a developmentally disabled young adult, who was subject to the legal guardianship of his parents. David, who lived independently, had used his debit card to buy the car. When David's parents found out about the purchase, his mother immediately informed Kenai Chrysler that David had no legal authority to enter into a contract and the contract was void. When she tried to return the car, the manager of Kenai Chrysler informed her that "the company sold cars to 'a lot of people who aren't very smart,'" and refused to take it back. The Denisons then sued Kenai Chrysler, seeking both a declaration that the contract was void by virtue of the guardianship and an injunction to prevent Kenai Chrysler from receiving further payments as required under the contract. At the close of discovery, the Denisons moved for summary judgment on this issue. From a judgment for the plaintiffs, the defendant appealed.]

■ BRYNER, CHIEF JUSTICE. Kenai Chrysler points out that Alaska has not expressly held that a valid guardianship order automatically voids an attempt by the ward to create a binding contract. In Kenai Chrysler's view, the party contracting with the ward should at least be entitled to restitution.

[The argument] lacks merit. Under the Restatement (Second) of Contracts, the existence of a valid legal guardianship precludes the formation of a valid contract with the guardianship's ward.[1] In keeping with the Restatement's view, we ruled in Pappert v. Sargent that a party who attempted to enter into a contract with a ward would be entitled to restitution only in the absence of actual or constructive knowledge of the ward's incompetence.[2] Kenai Chrysler nevertheless cites *Pappert* as a case supporting its position that a genuine issue of material fact existed as to whether the dealership had notice of David's guardianship. But Kenai Chrysler misreads *Pappert.* The incompetent party in Pappert was not under a legal guardianship, and the circumstances of the disputed transaction in that case failed to create any reason to suspect incompetence. By contrast, in the present case, David Denison was a ward under a formal guardianship order that declared him incompetent to enter into a contract. And under the Restatement (Second) of Contracts, the guardianship order gave notice to the public of David's incapacity:

> The guardianship proceedings are treated as giving public notice of the ward's incapacity and establish his status with respect to transactions during guardianship even though the other party to a particular transaction may have no knowledge or reason to know of the guardianship: the guardian is not required to give personal notice to all persons who may deal with the ward.[3]

Since Kenai Chrysler had constructive notice of David's incapacity, it was not entitled to restitution under Pappert v. Sargent. Kenai Chrysler's position also ignores Alaska's territorial case law. In The Emporium v. Boyle, the Alaska territorial court followed opinions from several states recognizing that "an adjudication of insanity is notice to all the world of the fact that from that time on neither the lunatic nor his estate can be held upon any contract except those completed before that time."[4] Applying this principle, the court in *The Emporium* held that a letter of credit authorizing another person to purchase goods on account was automatically revoked when the person who wrote the letter was declared incompetent. This conclusion was justified, the court explained, "because the world was charged with notice of the adjudication."[5]

Based on these authorities, we conclude that the superior court correctly interpreted and applied the law. We also reject Kenai Chrysler's suggestions that factual issues concerning David's state of mind at the time of the sale precluded summary judgment on the Denisons' claim for declaratory relief.

---

[1]   See Restatement (Second) of Contracts § 13 (1981).

[2]   Pappert v. Sargent, 847 P.2d 66, 69 (Alaska 1993).

[3]   Restatement (Second) of Contracts § 13, cmt. a (1981).

[4]   The Emporium v. Boyle, 7 Alaska 80, 82 (1923).

[5]   Id.; accord Huntington Nat'l Bank v. Toland, 71 Ohio App.3d 576 (1991) ("[T]he probate record of judgment is deemed to provide constructive notice to the world of the ward's legal disability.").

NOTE

Questions. What is "constructive notice"? How does the legal position of David Denison differ from that of Adrian Douglass, the plaintiff in the *Pflueger* case above, with regard to contracting for a non-necessary good or service? What protections can a seller take to protect itself from a person of legal age who is nonetheless under a legal guardianship?

SECTION 2.   OVERREACHING

Under the leadership of equity, courts have traditionally been insistent that no advantage should be gained through gross unfairness in the process of bargaining. The three forms of overreaching condemned in classical equity are duress, fraud, and mistake. When a contract is found to result from one of these infirmities, the ordinary remedy is to allow the victim to rescind or avoid it. As with minors, the contract is said to be "avoidable." As equity merged with law, all courts in which contract actions are brought are now competent to avoid a contract without requiring an independent proceeding for rescission.

In Section (A) we begin our study of the common law defenses with duress. The term refers to impermissible pressure exerted by one party over another either during pre-contractual bargaining, or, as is often the case, during the attempted renegotiation of an existing deal. Here the doctrine of consideration, studied in Chapter 1, makes a comeback as courts assess whether a particular term was bargained for or was instead accepted under duress or undue influence.

Section (B) then moves to the issues of misrepresentation and fraud. Here we consider one party's obligation (and the limits on such obligation) to make accurate representations to the other party during the process of bargaining. As we shall see, not only fraud, in the sense of deliberate trickery or deceit, but even an innocent misrepresentation may be a ground for avoiding a contract. Indeed, the law sometimes requires that a party possessing information material to the exchange must either disclose it or refrain from exploiting the ignorance of the other. (The third concern of equity, mistake, is taken up in Chapter 9.)

(A) PRESSURE IN BARGAINING

When a person has used compulsion to obtain a benefit, the victim can sometimes compel restoration: money paid and property transferred under duress may be recovered. Similarly, a promise obtained by duress may not be enforced against the victim. Moses v. Macferlan, [1760] 97 Eng. Rep. 676 (K.B.). In that case Lord Mansfield said that an action for money had and received lies "for money got through imposition (express or implied); or extortion; or oppression; or an undue advantage taken of the plaintiff's situation, contrary to laws made for the protection of persons under those circumstances." In early English cases from which the current doctrine stems, such relief was confined to situations in which coercion took the form of imprisonment or threats of confinement or bodily harm. Later, threats of purely economic injury became a ground for relief when "duress of goods" (a threat to a person's property) was recognized. Economic coercion has now generally become a potential source of duress.

A number of policy considerations, as well as some surviving technical obstacles, limit the use of duress as a commonplace defense in contract actions. One important limitation is the insistence that the victim had no reasonable alternative but to assent to the contract. Restatement § 175(1).

A second limitation concerns the substance of the threat. As indicated above, threats to business interests, as well as to life or limb, may now constitute duress. Making someone an offer "they cannot refuse" is not a permissible business practice. Yet not all threats constitute duress. Certainly one who yields to a threat of criminal or tortious injury may be given relief. In contrast, it has also been held that a threat of *lawful* action cannot be wrongful: "It is not duress to threaten to do what there is a legal right to do." Chouinard v. Chouinard, 568 F.2d 430 (5th Cir. 1978).

This qualification has particular application to cases in which a dispute is settled under the threat of a lawsuit. As it is not unlawful to institute legal proceedings, a party threatened with suit may not buy its way out and thereafter complain of the bargain. Yet there are limitations even on the threat of suit. As we saw in Fiege v. Boehm, Note 2, p. 66 above, and Note 3, p. 66 above, on strike suits, one does not have the right to bring a suit without some basis for the underlying claim other than party's "belie[f] that the claim or defense may be fairly determined to be valid." Thus it is not *quite* the rule that one may rightfully threaten any kind of rightful act. "An unjust and inequitable threat is wrongful, although the threatened act would not be a violation of duty in the sense of an independent actionable wrong in the law of crimes, torts, or contracts." McCubbin v. Buss, 144 N.W.2d 175 (Neb. 1966). As you read the cases in this section consider Lake Land Employment v. Columber, p. 83 above, and whether Lake Land's request that Columber sign a covenant not to compete rose to the level of duress.

NOTES

(1) *Duress by Threat of Suit.* When a party seeks relief from a contract on the ground of coercion, it is not uncommon to find that the complaining party is itself adept at coercive practices. An example is Undersea Eng. & Const. Co. v. Int'l Tel. & Tel. Corp., 429 F.2d 543, 549 (9th Cir. 1970). In that case the plaintiff, Undersea, had been a subcontractor on a job for which the defendant, ITT, was the general contractor. Disputes between them led to extended negotiations, and to a settlement which Undersea later sought to void. ITT was depicted as a billion-dollar corporation having elephantine power over Undersea. The court observed, however, that before the

settlement "Undersea was using every threat of economic and moral pressure to coerce and force ITT to settle rather than face a law suit with threatened world-wide publicity."

(2) *Duress in Context.* Should the law be concerned with *why* a threat of lawful action was effective against the party complaining of it? Put another way, should the law take account of the social or emotional origins of particular threats, such as the consequences to a young man of being threatened with a paternity suit? Or the humiliation of canceling a wedding the day before unless the bride signs a prenuptial agreement?

What about a wife who is threatened with a divorce by her husband unless she signs a mid-marriage or "post-nuptial" property agreement? In Pacelli v. Pacelli, 725 A.2d 56, 58, 61 (N.J. Sup. 1999), a wife agreed to a property settlement in the case of an eventual divorce in exchange for her husband's promise not to file for divorce immediately. The court compared the wife's circumstances with that of a fiancé: "[Mrs. Pacelli] faced a more difficult choice than the bride who is presented with a demand for a pre-nuptial agreement. The cost to her would have been the destruction of a family and the stigma of a failed marriage. She testified on several occasions that she signed the agreement to preserve the family and to make sure that her sons were raised in an intact family. Our point is that the context in which [Mr. Pacelli] made his demand was inherently coercive. [Mrs. Pacelli's] access to eminent counsel is of little relevance because her decision was dictated not by a consideration of her legal rights, but by her desire to preserve the family."

The court held that, while it need not decide if "such agreements are so inherently and unduly coercive that they should not be enforced, . . . at the very least, [their content] must be closely scrutinized and carefully evaluated." It concluded that the terms of the Pacelli agreement were "not fair and just."

PROBLEM

Parental Concern. A farm couple mortgaged their property to a bank for the purpose (they said) of preventing their son Glen from going to prison. Glen had been found to have defrauded creditors of his business, a farm-implement dealership. The president of the bank, to which the parents gave both a guaranty of Glen's debt and the mortgage, testified that no threats were made to induce the execution of these papers. But a trial court found otherwise and rescinded the agreement. On the bank's appeal, the court found it incredible that the parents would hazard the fruits of fifty years of toil to try to bail out a business "which was in debt to the extent of $628,000 plus, absent the threat and concern that the son might go to prison."

Before the guaranty was given, Glen's father had consulted a lawyer (whose advice he disregarded) and Glen's mother had berated the bank president for lending him so much money. Should the trial court's decree be reversed? Would it matter that Glen implored his parents to sign? What if the bank had relied on the guaranty by purchasing the claims of other creditors of Glen's business? See Haumont v. Security State Bank, 374 N.W.2d 2 (Neb. 1985).

The Pre-Existing Duty Rule: Promises to Fulfill Contractual Obligations That Already Exist

"Performance of a legal duty owed to a promisor which is neither doubtful nor the subject of honest dispute is not consideration." Restatement § 73. This is a recent version of an old rule that has given rise to some dissatisfaction. Professor Edwin Patterson observed that it is "on the whole, that adjunct of the doctrine of consideration which has done most to give it a bad name." Patterson, *An Apology for Consideration*, 58 Colum. L. Rev. 929, 936–38 (1958). On the other hand, as illustrated in the following well-known case, some decisions upholding the rule have long been followed, though not without criticism in recent years. The case raises a question often played out on more subtle facts: When is the modification of a contract properly seen as resulting from the genuine assent of the party to whom performance is owed, and when is a renegotiated deal more likely the result of coercion?

Alaska Packers' Ass'n v. Domenico

United States Court of Appeals, Ninth Circuit, 1902.
117 F. 99.

[A group of workmen had individually signed contracts with Alaska Packers to sail from San Francisco to Pyramid Harbor, Alaska, "as sailors and fishermen, agreeing to do 'regular ship's duty, both up and down, discharging and loading; and to do any other work whatsoever when requested to do so by the captain or agent of the Alaska Packers' Association." Under the agreement, Alaska Packers was to pay each of the workmen "$50 for the season, and two cents for each red salmon in the catching of which he took part."

Upon arrival at Pyramid Harbor, where Alaska Packers "had about $150,000 invested in a salmon cannery," the workmen "stopped work in a body" and demanded $100 for their services, stating that "unless they were paid this additional wage they would stop work entirely, and return to San Francisco." Since it was impossible to get substitute workers, the superintendent signed an agreement to pay the larger amount. Upon the return of the men to San Francisco at the end of the season, Alaska Packers paid them in accordance with the first agreement, and the employees sued in admiralty to recover the additional compensation. From judgment for the workmen (the "libelants") [the term used in admiralty proceedings for plaintiffs], Alaska Packers appealed.]

■ ROSS, CIRCUIT JUDGE. On the trial in the court below, the libelants undertook to show that the fishing nets provided by the respondent were defective, and that it was on that account that they demanded increased wages. On that point, the evidence was substantially conflicting, and the finding of the court was against the libelants the court saying:

> 'The contention of libelants that the nets provided them were rotten and unserviceable is not sustained by the evidence. The defendants' interest required that libelants should be provided with every facility necessary to their success as fishermen, for on such success depended the profits defendant would be able to realize that season from its packing plant, and the large capital invested therein. In view of this self-evident fact, it is highly improbable that the defendant gave libelants rotten and unserviceable nets with which to fish. It follows from this finding that libelants were not justified in refusing performance of their original contract.' 112 Fed. 554.

The evidence being sharply conflicting in respect to these facts, the conclusions of the court, who heard and saw the witnesses, will not be disturbed.

The real questions in the case as brought here are questions of law, and, in the view that we take of the case, it will be necessary to consider but one of those. Assuming that the appellant's superintendent at Pyramid Harbor was authorized to make the alleged contract of May 22d, and that he executed it on behalf of the appellant, was it supported by a sufficient consideration? From the foregoing statement of the case, it will have been seen that the libelants agreed in writing, for certain stated compensation, to render their services to the appellant in remote waters where the season for conducting fishing operations is extremely short, and in which enterprise the appellant had a large amount of money invested; and, after having entered upon the discharge of their contract, and at a time when it was impossible for the appellant to secure other men in their places, the libelants, without any valid cause, absolutely refused to continue the services they were under contract to perform unless the appellant would consent to pay them more money. Consent to such a demand, under such circumstances, if given, was, in our opinion, without consideration, for the reason that it was based solely upon the libelants' agreement to render the exact services, and none other, that they were already under contract to render. The case shows that they willfully and arbitrarily broke that obligation.

Certainly, it cannot be justly held, upon the record in this case, that there was any voluntary waiver on the part of the appellant of the breach of the original contract. The company itself knew nothing of such breach until the expedition returned to San Francisco, and the testimony is uncontradicted that its superintendent at Pyramid Harbor, who, it is claimed, made on its behalf the contract sued on, distinctly informed the libelants that he had no power to alter the original or to make a new contract, and it would, of course, follow that, if he had no power to change the original, he would have no authority to waive any rights thereunder.

The circumstances of the present case bring it, we think, directly within the sound and just observations of the Supreme Court of Minnesota in the case of King v. Railway Co., 61 Minn. 482:

> No astute reasoning can change the plain fact that the party who refuses to perform, and thereby coerces a promise from the other party to the contract to pay him an increased compensation for doing that which he is legally bound to do, takes an unjustifiable advantage of the necessities of the other party. Surely it would be a travesty on justice to hold that the party so making the promise for extra pay was estopped from asserting that the promise was without consideration. A party cannot lay the foundation of an estoppel by his own wrong, where the promise is simply a repetition of a subsisting legal promise. There can be no consideration for the promise of the other party, and there is no warrant for inferring that the parties have voluntarily rescinded or modified their contract. The promise cannot be legally enforced, although the other party has completed his contract in reliance upon it.

In Lingenfelder v. Brewing Co., 103 Mo. 578, the court, in holding void a contract by which the owner of a building agreed to pay its architect an additional sum because of his refusal to otherwise proceed with the contract, said:

> It is urged upon us by respondents that this was a new contract. New in what? Jungenfeld was bound by his contract to design and supervise this building. Under the new promise, he was not to do anything more or anything different. What benefit was to accrue to Wainwright? He was to receive the same service from Jungenfeld under the new, that Jungenfeld was bound to tender under the original, contract. What loss, trouble, or inconvenience could result to Jungenfeld that he had not already assumed? No amount of metaphysical reasoning can change the plain fact that Jungenfeld took advantage of Wainwright's necessities, and extorted the promise of five per cent. on the refrigerator plant as the condition of his complying with his contract already entered into.

> To permit plaintiff to recover under such circumstances would be to offer a premium upon bad faith, and invite men to violate their most sacred contracts that they may profit by their own wrong. That a promise to pay a man for doing that which he is already under contract to do is without consideration is conceded by respondents. The rule has been so long imbedded in the common law and decisions of the highest courts of the various states that nothing but the most cogent reasons ought to shake it. (Citing a long list of authorities.) But it is 'carrying coals to Newcastle' to add authorities on a proposition so universally accepted, and so inherently just and right in itself.

[W]hen a party merely does what he has already obligated himself to do, he cannot demand an additional compensation therefor; and although, by taking advantage of the necessities of his adversary, he obtains a promise for more, the law will regard it as nudum pactum, and will not lend its process to aid in the wrong.

It results from the views above expressed that the judgment must be reversed.

NOTES

(1) *Questions.* What factors support the court's conclusion? Discussing *Alaska Packers*, Judge Posner concluded that due to the circumstances, the fishermen had a temporary monopoly on labor and that "[t]he exploitation of temporary monopolies is the functional meaning of the legal concept of economic duress." Trompler v. NLRB, 338 F.3d 747, 751–52 (7th Cir. 2003). Is there anything to be said on the fishermen's side? For background on the case and on the Alaskan salmon canning fishing industry at the turn of the century, see Deborah Threedy, *A Fish Story: Alaska Packers' Association v. Domenico*, 2000 Utah L. Rev. 185.

(2) *Rejection and Reformation of the Rule.* In some states the pre-existing duty rule has been largely rejected by judicial decision. In Alabama, for example, the rule is that "an executory contract may be modified by the parties without any new consideration other than mutual consent." Winegardner v. Burns, 361 So.2d 1054 (Ala. 1978).

Other states have suspended the rule legislatively in certain circumstances. For example, a New York statute provides:

> *Written agreement for modification or discharge.* An agreement, promise or undertaking to change or modify, or to discharge in whole or in part, any contract, obligation, or lease, or any mortgage or other security interest in personal or real property, shall not be invalid because of the absence of consideration, provided that the agreement, promise or undertaking changing, modifying, or discharging such contract, obligation, lease, mortgage or security interest, shall be in writing and signed by the party against whom it is sought to enforce the change, modification or discharge, or by his agent.

N.Y. Gen. Oblig. L. § 5–1103.

How would the Alaska Packers case have been decided under the New York statute?

Article 2 of the UCC permits the modification of a contract without consideration. See UCC § 2–209(1). How does the Article 2 approach differ from that of the New York statute quoted above? The CISG and the UNIDROIT Principles are in general accord with Article 2. See CISG art. 29 and UNIDROIT Principles art. 3.2.

(3) *Duress Nonetheless?* Might a modifying agreement that is within UCC § 2–209(1), or the New York statute quoted above, be voidable for

duress if it was induced by one party's threat to break the contract? Comment 2 to UCC § 2–209 states, in part, that "modifications made thereunder must meet the test of good faith imposed by this Act and the extortion of a 'modification' without legitimate commercial reason is ineffective as a violation of the duty of good faith." See E. Allan Farnsworth, *Good Faith Purchase and Commercial Reasonableness Under the Uniform Commercial Code*, 30 U. Chi. L. Rev. 666, 675–76 (1963). Which part of the UCC definition of good faith might be violated by an extorted modification?

A thoughtful review of the pre-existing duty rule by Professor Robert Hillman concluded that it has been dismissed too summarily in UCC § 2–209. He recommended that a person relying on a concession under certain modifying agreements be put to proof that the concession was not unfairly coerced. See Robert Hillman, *Policing Contract Modifications under the UCC: Good Faith and the Doctrine of Economic Duress*, 64 Iowa L. Rev. 849 (1979).

(4)   *Pre-Existing Statutory Duty*? Michael Borelli and Hilda Borelli were married in 1980. In 1988, Michael suffered a stroke and thereafter required round-the-clock nursing care. Unhappy at being cared for in a rehabilitation center, Michael agreed to transfer certain real property to Hilda upon his death in exchange for her promise to care for him at home for the duration of his illness. Hilda agreed, and took care of Michael until his death, in 1989. Under the terms of Michael's will, Hilda received $100,000; the remainder of his estate, including the promised properties, were left to Michael's daughter by his first marriage. In an action by Hilda for specific performance, the trial court dismissed the complaint on the ground that the agreement was without consideration. Hilda appealed. *Held*: Affirmed. Borelli v. Brusseau, 16 Cal. Rptr. 2d 16 (Ct. App. 1993).

The court considered two provisions of the California Civil Code: Section 5100 ("Husband and wife contract toward each other obligations of mutual respect, fidelity, and support"), and Section 5132 ("[A] married person shall support the person's spouse while they are living together"); and concluded that "[p]ersonal performance of a personal duty created by the contract of marriage does not constitute a new consideration supporting the indebtedness alleged in this case." The court also found on policy grounds that "deathbed negotiating" was "antithetical to the institution of marriage as the Legislature has defined it." *Id.* at 20.

The dissent noted that "[h]ad there been no marriage and had they been total strangers, there is no doubt Mr. Borelli could have validly contracted to receive [the claimant's] services in exchange for certain of his property. The mere existence of a marriage certificate should not deprive otherwise competent adults of the 'utmost freedom of contract' they would otherwise possess. In this context, public policy should not be equated with coerced altruism." *Id.* at 23, 25.

(5)   *Reliance Redux*. If a promisor is relieved of her promise by virtue of the pre-existing duty rule, might the promisee enforce the promise on a reliance theory?

PROBLEM

Work Reduction. Refer again to Ever-Tite Roofing Corp. v. Green, p. 215 above. Suppose these changes in the facts: Ever-Tite's workmen arrived at the Greens' residence, found no other roofer engaged, and advised the Greens that although new gutters were called for in the signed agreement, Ever-Tite had discontinued gutter work. They persuaded the Greens to initial an amendment to the agreement stating "gutter installation eliminated." Would the Greens be bound by the amendment? See Engle v. Shapert Constr. Co., 443 F.Supp. 1383 (M.D. Pa. 1978). Would it matter whether or not Article 2 of the Code applies to a sale and installation of roofing materials?

Avoiding the Pre-Existing Duty Rule: Rescission and Modification

Are parties to a contract ever free to disavow their agreements and bargain with one another anew? Are they always free to do so? In Schwartzreich v. Bauman-Basch, Inc., 131 N.E. 887, 888 (N.Y. 1921), Schwartzreich had contracted in writing to work as a clothing designer for Bauman-Basch for one year, beginning several weeks later, at a salary of $90 a week. During the period before this employment was to begin, Schwartzreich received an offer of $115 a week to do similar work elsewhere. When he informed Mr. Bauman of this development, Bauman promised to pay him at the weekly rate of $100 if Schwartzreich would reject the other offer. Bauman's testimony about the conversation was as follows:

> "I called him in the office, and I asked him, 'Is that true that you want to leave us?' and he said 'Yes,' and I said, 'Mr. Schwartzreich, how can you do that; you are under contract with us?' He said, 'Somebody offered me more money.' . . . I said, 'How much do they offer you?' He said, 'They offered him $115 a week.' . . . I said, 'I cannot get a designer now, and, in view of the fact that I have to send my sample line out on the road, I will give you a hundred dollars a week rather than to let you go.' He said, 'If you will give me $100, I will stay.' "

The parties then prepared and signed a new contract just like the earlier one except for the pay rate. At the same time they tore their signatures off the earlier contract. Schwartzreich began work in November, as scheduled, but was discharged soon after. He sued for his wages, which the jury awarded him based on the $100 rate. The trial court set aside the verdict, but it was reinstated on appeal.

According to the appellate court, the situation was one in which "an existing contract is terminated by consent of both parties and a new one executed in its place and stead." (This is commonly called a substituted agreement.) The court quoted from Williston:

A rescission followed shortly afterwards by a new agreement in regard to the same subject-matter would create the legal obligations provided in the subsequent agreement.

"Very little difference may appear," the court said, "in a mere change of compensation in an existing and continuing contract and a termination of one contract and the making of a new one for the same time and work, but at an increased compensation. There is, however, a marked difference in principle." Do you see the difference?

NOTES

(1) *Questions.* In *Schwartzreich,* how many contracts did the parties enter into? What was the significance, if any, of the ceremony in which the signatures were torn off the original contract? Would the decision have been different if they had not been torn off until after the parties had signed the new one? If so, is this any way to do business?

The decision in *Schwartzreich* was cited as a source of commercial uncertainty in a study by the New York Law Revision Commission, leading to the enactment of the New York statute on written modifications, set out in Note 3, p. 79 above. There was concern that jury determinations would be unpredictable about whether one contract has been rescinded and replaced by another, or whether the original remained in force with a modification of its terms. N.Y. Law Rev. Comm., *Second Annual Report* 255 (Leg. Doc. No. 65, 1936).

(2) *Lawyers' Roles.* The owners of a farm became dissatisfied with the price they had agreed to accept for it. The buyers agreed to an increase when the sellers' attorney told them that his clients were willing to go to court to get out of the initial agreement, and that they would find litigation expensive. See Recker v. Gustafson, 279 N.W.2d 744 (Iowa 1979).

Are there circumstances in which you, as the lawyer for the sellers, would have declined to negotiate for them in the manner stated? If so, would your decision turn on whether or not the buyers also were advised by counsel? Would it matter that the initial agreement was afflicted (as it was in the case cited) with problems such as definiteness and the statute of frauds?

If an attorney *for the buyers* had advised them to agree to the price increase, would that attorney be at liberty, later, to question the consideration for it? See Rickett v. Doze, 603 P.2d 679 (Mont. 1979).

(3) *Restatement.* The two-step process of rescission and modification avoids the pre-existing duty rule as long as the contract is executory, that is, not fully performed on either side. Restatement § 89 provides more directly for the modification of promises "not fully performed on either side." Why is the rule limited to executory contracts?

Restatement § 89 provides three circumstances in which a promise modifying a contractual duty is binding. The Restatement uses the facts of *Schwartzreich* as an illustration to the section but does not indicate which clause it illustrates. Should the job offer at $115 a week be regarded as a circumstance not anticipated when the contract was made, so that a $10 raise was "fair and equitable" under Restatement § 89(a)? Might subsection (b) or (c) apply?

(4) *The Sheep and the Goats.* It has been urged that the courts should endeavor "to separate the sheep from the goats" by enforcing the new promise in favor of the honest contractor and refusing to enforce it in favor of the dishonest or extortionate contractor. Arthur Corbin, *Does a Preexisting Duty Defeat Consideration?*, 27 Yale L.J. 362, 373 (1918). What facts, provable in court, might provide the basis for separating "the sheep from the goats"?

The traditional rationale employed in support of the pre-existing duty doctrine is that it prevents overreaching and blackmail. See Samuel Williston, *Successive Promises of the Same Performance*, 8 Harv. L. Rev. 27 (1894). As Professor Charles Fried notes, however, the modern trend is toward recognition of promises whose legitimacy the strict consideration doctrine placed in doubt, so long as the sincerity of the obligation is clear and the commitment freely made. Charles Fried, Contract as Promise 39 (2nd ed. 2015).

Watkins & Son v. Carrig
Supreme Court of New Hampshire, 1941.
91 N.H. 459, 21 A.2d 591.

Assumpsit for work done. By a written contract between the parties the plaintiff agreed to excavate a cellar for the defendant for a stated price. Soon after the work was commenced solid rock was encountered. The plaintiff's manager notified the defendant, a meeting between them was held, and it was orally agreed that the plaintiff should remove the rock at a stipulated unit price about nine times greater than the unit price for excavating upon which the gross amount to be paid according to the written contract was calculated. The rock proved to constitute about two-thirds of the space to be excavated.

A referee found that the oral agreement "superseded" the written contract, and reported a verdict for the plaintiff based on the finding. To the acceptance of the report and an order of judgment thereon the defendant excepted. Further facts appear in the opinion. Transferred by Burque, C.J.

■ ALLEN, CHIEF JUSTICE. When the written contract was entered into, no understanding existed between the parties that no rock would be found in the excavating. The plaintiff's manager made no inquiry or investigation to find out the character of the ground below the surface, no claim is made that the defendant misled him, and the contract contains no reservations for unexpected conditions. It provides that "all material" shall be removed from the site, and its term that the plaintiff is "to excavate" is unqualified. In this situation a defence of mutual mistake is not available. A space of ground to be excavated, whatever its character, was the subject matter of the contract, and the offer of price on that basis was accepted. Leavitt v. Dover, 67 N.H. 94. If the plaintiff was unwise in taking chances, it is not relieved, on the ground of mistake, from the burden incurred in being faced with them. The case differs from that of King Co. v. Aldrich, 81 N.H. 42, in which the parties did not contract for the property delivered in purported performance of the contract actually made.

The referee's finding that the written contract was "superseded" by an oral contract when the rock was discovered is construed to mean that the parties agreed to rescind the written contract as though it had not been made and entered into an oral one as though it were the sole and original one. The defendant either thought that the contract did not require the excavation of rock on the basis of the contract price or was willing to forego his rights under the contract in respect to rock. It was important to him that the work should not be delayed, and other reasons may have contributed to induce him to the concession he made. In any event, he consented to a special price for excavating rock, whatever his rights under the contract. The plaintiff on the strength of the promise proceeded with the work.

But the defendant contends that the facts do not support a claim of two independent and separate transactions, one in rescission of the written contract as though it were nugatory, and one in full substitution of it. All that is shown, as he urges, is one transaction by which he was to pay more for the excavating than the written contract provided, with that contract otherwise to remain in force. And upon the basis of this position he relies upon the principle of contract law that his promise to pay more was without consideration, as being a promise to pay the plaintiff for performance of its obligation already in force and outstanding. Whether the contract was rescinded with a new one to take its place or whether it remained in force with a modification of its terms, is not important. In the view of a modification, the claim of a promise unsupported by consideration is as tenable as under the view of a rescission. A modification involves a partial rescission.

In the situation presented the plaintiff entered into a contractual obligation. Facts subsequently learned showed the obligation to be burdensome and the contract improvident. On insistent request by the plaintiff, the defendant granted relief from the burden by a promise to pay a special price which overcame the burden. The promise was not an assumption of the burden; the special price was fair and the defendant received reasonable value for it.

The issue whether the grant of relief constituted a valid contract is one of difficulty. The basic rule that a promise without consideration for it is invalid leads to its logical application that a promise to pay for what the promisor already has a right to receive from the promise is invalid. The promisee's performance of an existing duty is no detriment to him, and hence nothing is given by him beyond what is already due the promisor. But the claim is here made that the original contract was rescinded, either in full or in respect to some of its terms, by mutual consent, and since any rescission mutually agreed upon is in itself a contract, the claim of a promise to pay for performance of a subsisting duty is unfounded. The terms of the contract of rescission are of course valid if the rescission is valid. The defendant's answer to this claim is well stated in this quotation from Williston, Contr., 2d Ed., § 130a: "But calling an agreement an agreement for rescission does not do away with the necessity of consideration, and when the agreement for rescission is coupled with a further agreement that the work provided for in the earlier agreement shall be completed and that the other party shall give more than he originally promised, the total effect of the second agreement is that one party promises to do exactly what he had previously bound himself to do, and the other party promises to give an additional compensation therefor."

With due respect for this eminent authority, the argument appears to clothe consideration with insistence of control beyond its proper demands. With full recognition of the legal worthlessness of a bare promise and of performance of a subsisting duty as a void consideration, a result accomplished by proper means is not necessarily bad because it would be bad if the means were improper or were not employed.

In common understanding there is, importantly, a wide divergence between a bare promise and a promise in adjustment of a contractual promise already outstanding. A promise with no supporting consideration would upset well and long-established human interrelations if the law did not treat it as a vain thing. But parties to a valid contract generally understand that it is subject to any mutual action they may take in its performance. Changes to meet changes in circumstances and conditions should be valid if the law is to carry out its function and service by rules conformable with reasonable practices and understandings in matters of business and commerce. Merger of the rescission and promise into one transaction does not destroy them as elements composing the transaction.

The case is one of a simple relinquishment of a right pertaining to intangible personalty. The defendant intentionally and voluntarily yielded to a demand for a special price for excavating rock. In doing this he yielded his contract right to the price it provided. Whether or not he thought he had the right, he intended, and executed his intent, to make no claim of the right. The promise of a special price for excavating rock necessarily imported a release or waiver of any right by the contract to hold the plaintiff to the lower price the contract stipulated. In mutual understanding the parties agreed that the contract price was not to control. The contract right being freely surrendered, the issue of contract law whether the new promise is valid is not doubtful. If the totality of the transaction was a promise to pay more for less, there was in its inherent makeup a valid discharge of an obligation. Although the transaction was single, the element of discharge was distinct in precedence of the new promise.

The foregoing views are considered to meet the reasonable needs of standard and ethical practices of men in their business dealings with each other. Conceding that the plaintiff threatened to break its contract because it found the contract to be improvident, yet the defendant yielded to the threat without protest, excusing the plaintiff, and making a new arrangement. Not insisting on his rights but relinquishing them, fairly he should be held to the new arrangement. The law is a means to the end. It is not the law because it is the law, but because it is adapted and adaptable to establish and maintain reasonable order. If the phrase justice according to law were transposed into law according to justice, it would perhaps be more accurately expressive. In a case like this, of conflicting rules and authority, a result which is considered better to establish "fundamental justice and reasonableness" (Cavanaugh v. Boston & M. Railroad, 76 N.H. 68, 72, 79 A. 694, 696), should be attained. It is not practical that the law should adopt all precepts of moral conduct, but it is desirable that its rules and principles should not run counter to them in the important conduct and transactions of life.

Exceptions overruled.

NOTES

(1) *Questions*. Why was the "insistent request" of the excavator not found to be as coercive as the demands of the fishermen in *Alaska Packers*, p. 438 above? How did the court overcome the rule regarding rescission set out in *Schwartzreich*, p. 443 above? The opinion discusses the importance of "changes [in agreements] to meet changes in circumstances." How good is the argument that circumstances changed in this case? In reflecting about that, consider that the official nickname of New Hampshire is "the Granite State." Is there an argument that Watkins & Son assumed the risk that performance might be burdensome?

(2) *Transactional Constraints*? What prevents purely opportunistic attempts to renegotiate terms? Economists suggest a number of constraints. "The party demanding modification on threat of breach will need to take account of: the impact of this on future dealings with the other party if repeat transactions are envisaged; the reputation effects on other potential trading partners in the market; ease of substitution by the party from whom the modification is demanded; initial contract terms that may make the latter party unreceptive to a modification (for example, liquidated damage or penalty clauses . . .); the possibility of the latter party obtaining specific relief in the form of an injunction or specific performance; exposure to a damages claim in the event that modification is refused and breach occurs." Varouj Aivazian, Michael Trebilcock, & Michael Penny, *The Law of Contract Modification: The Uncertain Quest for a Bench Mark of Enforceability*, 22 Osgoode Hall L.J. 173, 174 (1984). Which of these constraints, if any, might have operated in *Watkins & Son*? In *Alaska Packers*?

Yielding to Threat

How resistant must the pressured party be? And in the face of what degree of impermissible behavior? Is threatening extended civil litigation insufficiently severe? In Denbow v. Tesch, 278 N.W. 16 (S.D. 1938), a brother threatened his sister that unless she signed an agreement dividing their parents' estate, he would "law and law it" in court and she would get nothing. The sister signed and later sought to have the agreement cancelled. In upholding the agreement, the court stated: "Suffice it to say that if it be assumed that this feeble threat was effective in coercing the signature of the plaintiff, it is not such a threat as will support a conclusion that the consent of the plaintiff was procured through duress and menace." Do you agree?

And what degree of fortitude is required if the threat or pressure is more substantial? The homeowner in *Watkins & Son* seemed to cave quickly. Did he meet the standard of duress and resistance suggested by one court of "restraint or danger, either actually inflicted or impending, which is sufficient in severity or apprehension to overcome the mind of a person of ordinary firmness"? Carrier v. William Penn Broadcasting Co., 233 A.2d 519 (Pa. 1967). Other courts imply even stricter tests: duress, as they describe it, must deprive a person of free exercise of will, see Raymundo v. Hammond Clinic Ass'n, 449 N.E.2d 276 (Ind. 1983), or destroy a person's volition, see Konsuvo v. Netzke, 220 A.2d 424 (N.J. 1966). Such expressions, often somewhat metaphorical, appear largely in cases where relief was *granted,* and often in cases where no such total mastery over the innocent party existed.

A classical passage rejecting the "no will" conception of duress is from Holmes: "It always is for the interest of a party under duress to choose the lesser of two evils. But the fact that a choice was made according to interest does not exclude duress. It is the characteristic of duress properly so called." Union Pacific R. Co. v. Public Service Comm., 248 U.S. 67 (1918) (duress by a state agency). On the other hand, it is regularly acknowledged that a perfectly honorable agreement may be made with a person who must either accede to it or face some repugnant alternative. Tidwell v. Critz, 282 S.E.2d 104 (Ga. 1981). "The question is one of degree." Hellenic Lines, Ltd. v. Louis Dreyfus Corp., 372 F.2d 753 (2d Cir. 1967).

NOTES

(1) *Objective or Subjective?* By what standard is the loss of "free will" measured? As one court has stated, "It was said in the early books that there could not be duress by threats unless the threats were such as 'to put a brave man in fear'; then came the qualified standard of something sufficient to overcome the will of a person of 'ordinary firmness'; but the tendency of more

recent cases, and the rules comporting with reason and principle, is that any 'unlawful threats' which do in fact 'overcome the will of the person threatened, and induce him to do an act which he would not otherwise have done constitutes duress. The age, sex, capacity, relation of parties and all attendant circumstances must be considered.'" Rubenstein v. Rubenstein, 120 A.2d 11, 14 (N.J. 1956). (In that case the threats to a husband from his wife included gang violence and arsenic poisoning.)

How is evidence that a party's will has been overcome to be adduced? In *Rubenstein*, the court said that it may be proved by the party's own testimony.

(2) *Hard Choices.* In considering whether assent has been coerced or whether it simply results from a universe of bleak choices, consider the following case. Nicole, a 17-year-old unmarried high-school student, executed consent forms surrendering her two day old baby for adoption. Ten days later, and after the statutory period for rescission had passed, she sought to revoke her consent on the ground of duress. She argued that her mother had told her she could not continue to reside in her parents' home if she elected to keep the baby. From a Family Court order vacating Nicole's consent, the adoptive parents appealed. *Held*: Reversed. In re Baby Boy L., 534 N.Y.S.2d 706, 708 (App. Div. 1988).

"[S]uggestions, persuasion, arguments or entreaties in favor of adoption do not constitute the 'kind of force' which would sustain a finding of duress.... [M]aternal pressure ... did not necessarily render the circumstances ... coercive nor did the entreaties of her mother impair Nicole's ability to exercise her free will. Instead it appears that Nicole was confronted by an emotionally difficult choice and that she elected to defer to the judgment of her mother." *Id.* at 108.

What if the pressure to relinquish parental rights comes not from a parent, but from the state department of social services that is otherwise threatening to remove the child involuntarily? Assume further that only if a birth mother agrees to surrender her child voluntarily can she negotiate with the adopting parents for postadoption visitation. For the complexities of this problem in the context of open adoption, see Carol Sanger, *Bargaining for Motherhood: Postadoption Visitation Agreements*, 41 Hofstra L. Rev. 309 (2012).

(3) *Promoting Trust in Contracts.* In Selmer Co. v. Blakeslee-Midwest Co., 704 F.2d 924 (7th Cir. 1983) (Posner, J.), the court upheld a settlement agreement between a contractor and a subcontractor, explaining that the financial difficulties of the subcontractor did not present a factual issue of duress. "The fundamental issue in a duress case is whether the statement that induced the promise is the kind of offer to deal that we want to discourage, and hence that we call a 'threat.' If contractual protections are illusory, people will be reluctant to make contracts. Allowing contract modifications to be avoided in circumstances such as those in *Alaska Packers* assures prospective contract parties that signing a contract is not stepping into a trap, and by thus encouraging people to make contracts promotes the efficient allocation of resources."

If Alaska Packers had been held chargeable with the higher wage it promised, what measures might it have taken to avoid stepping into the same trap in later fishing seasons? See the excerpt quoted in Note 2, p. 448 above, on transactional constraints. Would anything suggested there have served Alaska Packers' purpose?

PROBLEM

Hawaiian Housing. Richards contracted to build housing in Hawaii for the Marine Air Corps, using a subcontractor's bid of $49,000 for the metal work. By error, the subcontractor, Air Conditioning Company (AC), had calculated its bid on the assumption that galvanized sheet metal would be used rather than zinc alloy. When AC informed Richards that it would not do the work for the bid price, Richards "blew up." Over the next two months, hard bargaining ensued, during which Richards insisted that AC was bound by its bid price. At length, Richards and AC executed a contract for the metal work at $62,000. After paying some $50,000 as the work progressed, Richards refused to pay more. In fact, he never intended to pay the higher price. When sued for the remainder, Richards relied on the pre-existing duty rule, and cited the Alaska Packers case. Some additional facts may be useful. AC did not inform Richards of its error for about a month after it had discovered its error and learned of the award of the main contract. The second lowest bid was $83,000. Richards's architect had estimated the cost of the metal work at $16,000. One of the bids it received was for more than $173,000.

What result? Is *Alaska Packers* easily distinguishable? Was Richards in a good position to assert the rule, having retreated from the position that AC was bound by its bid?

Avoiding the Pre-Existing Duty Rule: New Consideration

Two problematic aspects of the pre-existing duty rule are presented in two well-known cases: *Foakes v. Beer* and *De Cicco v. Schweitzer*. Each involved the court's use of the doctrine of consideration in determining if the rule applied.

Although the doctrine of consideration underlies the rule, it also offers an escape route. As one court has explained, "any consideration for the new undertaking, however insignificant, satisfies this rule. For instance, an undertaking to pay part of the debt before maturity, or at a place other than that where the obligor was legally bound to pay, or to pay in property, regardless of its value, or to effect a composition with creditors by the payment of less than the sum due, has been held to constitute a consideration sufficient in law." Levine v. Blumenthal, 186 A. 457 (N.J. 1936), aff'd on opinion of Supreme Court, 189 A. 54 (N.J. Err. App. 1937). The same thought was expressed much earlier by Lord Coke in Pinnel's Case, decided in 1602, cited as 5 Coke's Rep. 117a (in Vol. 3,

Part V), 77 Eng. Rep. 237 (Common Pleas): "by no possibility, a lesser sum can be satisfaction to the plaintiff for a greater sum: but the gift of a horse, hawk or robe, etc. in satisfaction is good." But on the utter irrelevance of Pinnel's Case, see Larry T. Garvin, *Scapegoats and the Common Law: Pinnel's Case,* Cumber v. Wane, *and the Legal Duty Rule,* in The Best and Worst of Contracts Decisions: An Anthology, 45 Fla. St. U. L. Rev. 887, 974 (2018).

What modern equivalent of a "horse, hawk or robe" might suitably be used to make a creditor's concession to a debtor binding? Restatement § 73 states that a performance "similar" to that owing "is consideration if it differs from what was required . . . in a way which reflects more than a pretense of a bargain." Does the concluding phrase encourage lawyers to concoct trivial new objects of bargaining? Or does this use of consideration enable parties to modify their arrangements in accordance with business practices?

Partial Payment

A controversial application of the pre-existing duty rule arises in cases in which *part* of a debt has been paid as part of the creditor's agreement for forgiving the rest. Recall that consideration is only a test of the enforceability of an *executory* promise, one that has not been fully performed. See Note 2, p. 441 above. Does the pre-existing rule prevent enforcement by the debtor of the creditor's forgiveness agreement?

The leading case is Foakes v. Beer, [1884] 9 App. Cas. 605 (H.L.). In that case Mrs. Beer, the creditor, had obtained a judgment against Dr. Foakes, her debtor. She then agreed to forgo interest on her judgment and Dr. Foakes paid the principal amount in installments. Still later, she sued to recover the unpaid interest and prevailed. The law lords found a controlling precedent in Pinnel's Case, above. There it was said that "payment of a lesser sum on the day [*i.e.,* on or after the due date of a money debt] cannot be any satisfaction of the whole." In agreeing to pay the judgment, Dr. Foakes did no more than he was obliged to do in any event.

The rule of Foakes v. Beer has often been doubted or denounced. One eminent judge called it a relic of antique law, and "evidence of the former capacity of lawyers and judges to make the requirement of consideration an overworked shibboleth rather than a logical and just standard of accountability." Rye v. Phillips, 282 N.W. 459 (Minn. 1938). Even Lord Blackburn, a concurring judge in Foakes v. Beer, had reservations at the time of the decision. As he explained, "all men of business, whether merchants or tradesmen, do every day recognize and act on the ground that prompt payment of a part of their demand may be more beneficial to them than it would be to insist on their rights and enforce payment of the whole." L.R. 9 A.C. at 617, 622.

Some scholars have gone further and challenged the general rule about pre-existing duty, as it affects the modification of contracts. One thoughtful appraisal is that of Professor Patterson, who observed: "The nineteenth century, striving to bring unity out of diversity, included too many different ideas under the general heading of consideration." An Apology for Consideration, p. 182 above.

————

Pre-Existing Duty to a Third Party

A second, less common problem concerning the scope of the pre-existing duty rule is whether the rule applies in cases where a contractual duty "pre-exists," but is owed not to the promisor but to a third party. This was the issue presented in De Cicco v. Schweizer, 117 N.E. 807 (N.Y. 1917), and decided by Justice Cardozo. Four days before the wedding of Blanche Schweizer, the groom and the bride's parents entered into an agreement conferring on Blanche an annual payment for as long as she and her fiancée should live. Her father expressed his promise of the annuity in a sentence beginning:

> Whereas, Miss Blanche Josephine Schweizer . . . is now affianced to and is to be married to the above said Count Oberto Giacomo Giovanni Francesco Maria Gulinelli: Now in consideration of all that is herein set forth the said Mr. Joseph Schweizer promises.

The first payment ($2,500) was made on the wedding day. After the tenth payment, no more was paid. The couple assigned their rights in the contract to Attilio De Cicco, and he sued the father-in-law, Schweizer. (The court assumed, properly, that De Cicco's right to enforce the contract was as good as that of either Blanche or the Count. Assignment is taken up in Chapter 10 below.)

When the case reached the New York Court of Appeals, Judge Cardozo first stated the defendant's contention "that Count Gulinelli was already affianced to Miss Schweizer, and that the marriage was merely the fulfillment of an existing legal duty." (It is helpful to keep in mind that at this time, a breach of a promise to marry was a viable cause of action; one could not break off an engagement with impunity.) Turning to the law, he accepted the premise of the defendant's argument that "a promise by A. to B. to induce him not to break his contract with C. is void." He then developed a distinction, showing that Schweizer's promise was not of that character. Instead, he reasoned, it was a promise to induce the Count ("B.") not to join with Blanche ("C.") in a voluntary rescission of their engagement. Although neither could rightfully withdraw without the other's consent, *together* they were free to terminate the engagement or postpone the marriage. The consideration, then, for Schweizer's promise was that they did not do so.

The opinion then seeks to make this reading plausible: "It does not seem a far-fetched assumption [in relation to contracts to marry] that one will release where the other has repented . . . one does not commonly apply pressure to coerce the will and action of those who are anxious to proceed. The attempt to sway their conduct by new inducements is an implied admission that both may waver. . . . " And in a final paragraph, Cardozo took higher ground, appealing to "those considerations of public policy which cluster about contracts that touch the marriage relation." Do you find the reasoning in the case plausible, or far-fetched? What was Cardozo trying to accomplish?

In a later opinion, Cardozo cited *De Cicco v. Schweizer* as a "signpost on the road" toward general acceptance of the doctrine of promissory estoppel. See Allegheny College v. National Chautauqua County Bank, referred to at p. 123 above. Do you see a connection between the case and that doctrine? See also Restatement § 90, Illustration 8.

In *Central Ceilings, Inc. v. National Amusements, Inc.*, p. 366 above, National Amusements made an argument that its promise to Central Ceilings was supported by no consideration other than the latter's performance of its contract with a third party ("Old Colony"). The argument failed. The court rejected, in effect, the rule of New York law stated this way in *De Cicco v. Schweitzer*: "a promise by A. to B. to induce him not to break his contract with C. is void."

NOTES

(1)   *The Jockey's Case.* Mike McDevitt was a jockey who had accepted employment from Shaw to drive a mare named Grace in the Kentucky Futurity. Stokes owned "relatives" of the mare, and stood to gain if she should win. Stokes promised McDevitt a bonus of $1,000 for winning the race. McDevitt won, but Stokes refused to pay, and McDevitt sued him. From judgment for the defendant on a demurrer to the plaintiff's complaint, the plaintiff appealed. *Held:* Affirmed. "To hold that [McDevitt] would not have won the race . . . but for the agreement of [Stokes] to pay him the $1,000 . . . would be to say that he would have been recreant to the obligation arising out of his employment by Shaw . . ." McDevitt v. Stokes, 192 S.W. 681 (Ky. 1917). Does this case illustrate (to use Cardozo's words just above) "a promise by A. to B. to induce him not to break his contract with C."?

(2)   *Prisoner's Dilemma.* Can one bargain around a pre-existing duty owed not to a specific third party but to the state at large? Consider the following case. Prosecuted for organized fraud under Florida law, defendant Brian Schneir entered into a cooperation agreement with the prosecutor. Schneir agreed to testify truthfully against his co-defendants in return for a guilty plea to one felony charge and a two-year sentence. The agreement further provided that if Schneir violated the agreement, the deal was off and he could be sentenced up to the maximum of thirty years. In his pre-trial deposition, Schneir repeatedly lied under oath and upon his conviction, the court sentenced him to twelve years in prison. Schneir appealed on the grounds that he was nonetheless entitled to receive the two-year sentence

because the cooperation agreement had been modified to provide that if after the deposition, Schneir truthfully testified at trial, he would receive the two-year sentence. He had so testified. Held: Affirmed. Schneir v. State, 43 So.3d 135 (Fla. App. 2010). Do you see any pre-existing duty problems with Schneir's argument?

The court held as follows: "[E]ven if an understanding that the State would, in essence, forgive the breach had been established, any such promise would have been unenforceable. This is because, like an initial contract, a modification . . . requires lawful consideration for its validity. See Newkirk Construction Corp. v. Gulf County, 366 So.2d 813 (Fla. 1979). The only performance, however, even allegedly required of him by the "modification" was that Schneir testify truthfully at the trial. But he was obligated to do just that by the express terms of the original contract he had already broken, as well as by the obligation imposed on any citizen. It is well settled that a promise to perform what one is already required to do by an existing contract or otherwise is not valid consideration." Can you think of other examples that might constitute "otherwise"? See Note 4, p. 442.

─────────

Duress in Business Transactions

While coercive behavior may be easier to detect or to condemn when the pressured party is an individual, duress also occurs in commercial dealings between businesses. This form of economic duress is often referred to as "business compulsion." How should courts assess pressure in such cases? What are the requirements of resistance for a business? Do commercial enterprises so regularly anticipate modifications of their arrangements that the pre-existing duty rule might be said to operate anachronistically? Consider these questions in connection with the following case, which, like *Alaska Packers'* and others described above, is about duress.

Austin Instrument, Inc. v. Loral Corporation

Court of Appeals of New York, 1971.
29 N.Y.2d 124, 324 N.Y.S.2d 22, 272 N.E.2d 533.

■ FULD, CHIEF JUDGE.[b] The defendant, Loral Corporation, seeks to recover payment for goods delivered under a contract which it had with the plaintiff Austin Instrument, Inc., on the ground that the evidence establishes, as a matter of law, that it was forced to agree to an increase in price on the items in question under circumstances amounting to economic duress.

In July of 1965, Loral was awarded a $6,000,000 contract by the Navy for the production of radar sets. The contract contained a schedule

─────────

[b]   Stanley H. Fuld (1903–2003) practiced law in New York City from 1926 to 1935, when he became assistant district attorney. In 1946 he was appointed to the New York Court of Appeals. He became chief judge in 1967 and served until 1974.

of deliveries, a liquidated damages clause applying to late deliveries and a cancellation clause in case of default by Loral. The latter thereupon solicited bids for some 40 precision gear components needed to produce the radar sets, and awarded Austin a subcontract to supply 23 such parts. That party commenced delivery in early 1966.

In May, 1966, Loral was awarded a second Navy contract for the production of more radar sets and again went about soliciting bids. Austin bid on all 40 gear components but, on July 15, a representative from Loral informed Austin's president, Mr. Krauss, that his company would be awarded the subcontract only for those items on which it was low bidder. The Austin officer refused to accept an order for less than all 40 of the gear parts and on the next day he told Loral that Austin would cease deliveries of the parts due under the existing subcontract unless Loral consented to substantial increases in the prices provided for by that agreement—both retroactively for parts already delivered and prospectively on those not yet shipped—and placed with Austin the order for all 40 parts needed under Loral's second Navy contract. Shortly thereafter, Austin did, indeed, stop delivery. After contacting 10 manufacturers of precision gears and finding none who could produce the parts in time to meet its commitments to the Navy,[1] Loral acceded to Austin's demands; in a letter dated July 22, Loral wrote to Austin that "We have feverishly surveyed other sources of supply and find that because of the prevailing military exigencies, were they to start from scratch as would have to be the case, they could not even remotely begin to deliver on time to meet the delivery requirements established by the Government. . . . Accordingly, we are left with no choice or alternative but to meet your conditions."

Loral thereupon consented to the price increases insisted upon by Austin under the first subcontract and the latter was awarded a second subcontract making it the supplier of all 40 gear parts for Loral's second contract with the Navy.[2] Although Austin was granted until September to resume deliveries, Loral did, in fact, receive parts in August and was able to produce the radar sets in time to meet its commitments to the Navy on both contracts. After Austin's last delivery under the second subcontract in July, 1967, Loral notified it of its intention to seek recovery of the price increases.

On September 15, 1967, Austin instituted this action against Loral to recover an amount in excess of $17,750 which was still due on the second subcontract. On the same day, Loral commenced an action against Austin claiming damages of some $22,250—the aggregate of the price increases under the first subcontract—on the ground of economic duress. The two actions were consolidated and, following a trial, Austin was awarded the sum it requested and Loral's complaint against Austin was

---

[1] The best reply Loral received was from a vendor who stated he could commence deliveries sometime in October.

[2] Loral makes no claim in this action on the second subcontract.

dismissed on the ground that it was not shown that "it could not have obtained the items in question from other sources in time to meet its commitment to the Navy under the first contract." A closely divided Appellate Division affirmed (316 N.Y.S.2d 528, 532). There was no material disagreement concerning the facts; as Justice Steuer stated in the course of his dissent below, "[t]he facts are virtually undisputed, nor is there any serious question of law. The difficulty lies in the application of the law to these facts." (316 N.Y.S.2d 534.)

The applicable law is clear and, indeed, is not disputed by the parties. A contract is voidable on the ground of duress when it is established that the party making the claim was forced to agree to it by means of a wrongful threat precluding the exercise of his free will. The existence of economic duress or business compulsion is demonstrated by proof that "immediate possession of needful goods is threatened" or, more particularly, in cases such as the one before us, by proof that one party to a contract has threatened to breach the agreement by withholding goods unless the other party agrees to some further demand. However, a mere threat by one party to breach the contract by not delivering the required items, though wrongful, does not in itself constitute economic duress. It must also appear that the threatened party could not obtain the goods from another source of supply and that the ordinary remedy of an action for breach of contract would not be adequate.

We find without any support in the record the conclusion reached by the courts below that Loral failed to establish that it was the victim of economic duress. On the contrary, the evidence makes out a classic case, as a matter of law, of such duress.[3]

It is manifest that Austin's threat—to stop deliveries unless the prices were increased—deprived Loral of its free will. As bearing on this, Loral's relationship with the Government is most significant. As mentioned above, its contract called for staggered monthly deliveries of the radar sets, with clauses calling for liquidated damages and possible cancellation on default. Because of its production schedule, Loral was, in July, 1966, concerned with meeting its delivery requirements in September, October and November, and it was for the sets to be delivered in those months that the withheld gears were needed. Loral had to plan ahead and the substantial liquidated damages for which it would be liable, plus the threat of default, were genuine possibilities. Moreover, Loral did a substantial portion of its business with the Government, and it feared that a failure to deliver as agreed upon would jeopardize its chances for future contracts. These genuine concerns do not merit the label " 'self-imposed, undisclosed and subjective' " which the Appellate Division majority placed upon them. It was perfectly reasonable for

---

[3] The suggestion advanced that we are precluded from reaching this determination because the trial court's findings of fact have been affirmed by the Appellate Division ignores the question to be decided. That question, undoubtedly one of law (see Cohen and Karger, Powers of the New York Court of Appeals [1952], § 115, p. 492), is, accepting the facts found, did the courts below properly apply the law to them.

Loral, or any other party similarly placed, to consider itself in an emergency, duress situation.

[T]he parts needed for the October schedule were delivered in late August and early September. Even so, Loral had to "work . . . around the clock" to meet its commitments. Considering that the best offer Loral received from the other vendors it contacted was commencement of delivery sometime in October, which, as the record shows, would have made it late in its deliveries to the navy in both September and October, Loral's claim that it had no choice but to accede to Austin's demands is conclusively demonstrated.

We find unconvincing Austin's contention that Loral, in order to meet its burden, should have contacted the Government and asked for an extension of its delivery dates so as to enable it to purchase the parts from another vendor. Aside from the consideration that Loral was anxious to perform well in the Government's eyes, it could not be sure when it would obtain enough parts from a substitute vendor to meet its commitments. The only promise which it received from the companies it contacted was for *commencement* of deliveries, not full supply, and, with vendor delay common in this field, it would have been nearly impossible to know the length of the extension it should request. It must be remembered that Loral was producing a needed item of military hardware. Moreover, there is authority for Loral's position that nonperformance by a subcontractor is not an excuse for default in the main contract. (See, e.g., McBride & Wachtel, Government Contracts, § 35.10, [11].) In light of all this, Loral's claim should not be held insufficiently supported because it did not request an extension from the Government.

Loral, as indicated above, also had the burden of demonstrating that it could not obtain the parts elsewhere within a reasonable time, and there can be no doubt that it met this burden. The 10 manufacturers whom Loral contacted comprised its entire list of "approved vendors" for precision gears and none was able to commence delivery soon enough.[4] As Loral was producing a highly sophisticated item of military machinery requiring parts made to the strictest engineering standards, it would be unreasonable to hold that Loral should have gone to other vendors, with whom it was either unfamiliar or dissatisfied, to procure the needed parts. As Justice Steuer noted in his dissent, Loral "contacted all the manufacturers whom it believed capable of making these parts" (316 N.Y.S.2d at p. 534), and this was all the law requires.

It is hardly necessary to add that Loral's normal legal remedy of accepting Austin's breach of the contract and then suing for damages would have been inadequate under the circumstances, as Loral would still have had to obtain the gears elsewhere with all the concomitant

---

[4] Loral, as do many manufacturers, maintains a list of "approved vendors," that is, vendors whose products, facilities, techniques and performance have been inspected and found satisfactory.

consequences mentioned above. In other words, Loral actually had no choice, when the prices were raised by Austin, except to take the gears at the "coerced" prices and then sue to get the excess back.

Austin's final argument is that Loral, even if it did enter into the contract under duress, lost any rights it had to a refund of money by waiting, until July, 1967, long after the termination date of the contract, to disaffirm it. It is true that one who would recover moneys allegedly paid under duress must act promptly to make his claim known. . . . In this case, Loral delayed making its demand for a refund until three days after Austin's last delivery on the second subcontract. Loral's reason— for waiting until that time—is that it feared another stoppage of deliveries which would again put it in an untenable situation. Considering Austin's conduct in the past, this was perfectly reasonable, as the possibility of an application by Austin of further business compulsion still existed until all of the parts were delivered.

In sum, the record before us demonstrates that Loral agreed to the price increases in consequence of the economic duress employed by Austin. Accordingly, the matter should be remanded to the trial court for a computation of its damages.

The order appealed from should be modified, with costs, by reversing so much thereof as affirms the dismissal of defendant Loral Corporation's claim and, except as so modified, affirmed.

■ BERGAN, JUDGE (dissenting). Whether acts charged as constituting economic duress produce or do not produce the damaging effect attributed to them is normally a routine type of factual issue.

Here the fact question was resolved against Loral both by the Special Term and by the affirmance at the Appellate Division. It should not be open for different resolution here.

When the testimony of the witnesses who actually took part in the negotiations for the two disputing parties is examined, sharp conflicts of fact emerge. Under Austin's version the request for a renegotiation of the existing contract was based on Austin's contention that Loral had failed to carry out an understanding as to the items to be furnished under that contract and this was the source of dissatisfaction which led both to a revision of the existing agreement and to entering into a new one.

This is not necessarily and as a matter of law to be held economic duress. On this appeal it is needful to look at the facts resolved in favor of Austin most favorably to that party. Austin's version of events was that a threat was not made but rather a request to accommodate the closing of its plant for a customary vacation period in accordance with the general understanding of the parties.

Moreover, critical to the issue of economic duress was the availability of alternative suppliers to the purchaser Loral.

Austin asserted and Loral admitted on cross-examination that there were many suppliers listed in a trade registry but that Loral chose to rely only on those who had in the past come to them for orders and with whom they were familiar. It was, therefore, at least a fair issue of fact whether under the circumstances such conduct was reasonable and made what might otherwise have been a commercially understandable renegotiation an exercise of duress.

The order should be affirmed.

■ BURKE, SCILEPPI and GIBSON, JUDGES, concur with FULD, CHIEF JUDGE.

■ BERGAN, JUDGE., dissents and votes to affirm in a separate opinion in which BREITEL and JASEN, JUDGES, concur.

NOTES

(1) *Questions.* Suppose that Loral had renounced its agreement with Austin a year before it did, shortly after acceding to Austin's demands. Laying aside the problem of duress, would Loral have been justified in renouncing the price increases? Would it have been justified in renouncing the purchase order under the second Navy contract? What is the answer to these questions under UCC § 2–209(1)? If Loral had consented to Austin's demand for price increases without protesting as it did in the letter of July 22, but had not meant to pay as agreed, would that have been an instance of bad faith on Loral's part? See United States for Use and Benefit of Crane Co. v. Progressive Enterprises, Inc., 418 F.Supp. 662 (E.D. Va. 1976).

Loral concerned the sale of goods and was therefore governed by Article 2, which contains no rules with respect to duress. How therefore could Loral raise the issue of duress? See UCC § 1–103(b). For contextualized consideration of these questions, see Meredith R. Miller, *Revisiting* Austin v. Loral*: A Study in Economic Duress, Contract Modification and Framing*, 2 Hastings Bus. L.J. 357 (2006).

(2) *Objective Standard?* Did the court apply the test for duress that the danger must have been sufficient to "overcome the mind of a person of ordinary firmness?" See discussion at p. 449 above. Holmes once remarked that to apply a requirement of ordinary courage in duress cases is "an attempt to apply an external standard of conduct in the wrong place." Silsbee v. Webber, 50 N.E. 555 (Mass. 1898). And Holmes was usually insistent on objective criteria in the law.

(3) *Yielding to Threat of Suit Revisited.* If the threat is one to sue for a money judgment, one obvious mode of resistance is to defend the suit. Some legal proceedings, however, such as mortgage foreclosure, commonly put the debtor in a situation of some urgency. Even so, the debtor may have recourse to injunctive relief, or to damages for abuse of legal process. To forego such a remedy, in favor of a settlement, is naturally prejudicial to the debtor in making a subsequent complaint of duress. Should the law insist on its preference that wrongful threats be met by resort to the courts? Professor John Dawson observes that if the "freedom to litigate" is prized, to control

abuses of it by injunction or tort recoveries impairs that freedom more directly than to do so through relief for duress. "The most that is sought," in the latter form, "is judicial review of a settlement, after surrender to the pressure. The object is neither to transfer nor to prevent losses but to cancel out the gain." John Dawson, *Duress Through Civil Litigation: I*, 45 Mich. L. Rev. 571, 577 (1947).

PROBLEM

Financial Stress. Alyeska Pipeline contracted with Totem Marine, a newly formed corporation, to transport pipe from Houston to Alaska. Impediments were met in loading and sailing, which caused long delays and substantial wrangling between the parties. The goods were finally offloaded in Long Beach, California, and the contract was terminated. Totem then presented Alyeska with a $300,000 bill for its services and requested prompt payment as it is likely to go into bankruptcy unless its own creditors are paid. Officials of Alyeska have negotiated with Totem's attorney, and are prepared to offer it $100,000 in full settlement. As counsel to Alyeska, are you confident in advising your client that the settlement with Totem, if accepted, will be upheld? What distinctions are there between this case and Austin Instrument v. Loral Corp.? See Totem Marine Tug & Barge v. Alyeska Pipeline Serv. Co., 584 P.2d 15 (Alaska 1978).

Undue Influence

Although this chapter emphasizes the bargaining *process*, the two other policing concerns, substance and status, are often intertwined with judicial determinations about unfairness in bargaining: A bad bargain sometimes indicates that something untoward has happened in the bargaining process, and pressure in bargaining may implicate issues of status. The following materials focus on the relation between bargaining and the relative status of the parties. What degree of disparity is necessary before the parties are unable to bargain with one another "at arm's length"? As we shall see, the disparities that seem to matter are not always monetary, but instead may derive from the degree of influence one party has—and uses—over the other.

Howe v. Palmer

Appeals Court of Massachusetts, 2011.
956 N.E.2d 249.

■ TRAINOR, JUDGE. The defendants, Ronald F. Palmer and Jeanette M. Palmer (collectively, Palmers), appeal from a jury verdict finding that a 2000 deed from the plaintiff, Virgil D. Howe, to the Palmers was the product of undue influence and that the Palmers had intentionally inflicted emotional distress on Howe. In answer to special questions, the jury found that Howe did not know nor should he reasonably have known prior to March 1, 2003, that he had been harmed (for purposes of applying the discovery rule and the statute of limitations) and that he did not unreasonably delay bringing suit so as to prejudice the Palmers. Judgment entered rescinding the deed and awarding damages for emotional distress in the amount of $60,000 plus interest and costs. The Palmers appeal the judgment, arguing that the trial judge should have allowed their motions for a directed verdict as to the two claims, as well as their motion for judgment notwithstanding the verdict. We affirm.

Background. We recite the facts the jury could have found. Howe owned a farm in Deerfield, an inheritance from his mother. His wife, Esther, was not on the deed. By all accounts, Howe is a simple man with severe dyslexia and slow mental processing. These issues contributed to a difficult childhood where he was treated harshly and subjected to severe discipline by school administrators, as well as being teased and bullied by his peers and classmates. As an adult, he was easily intimidated; in fact, Ronald Palmer (Palmer) testified that because Howe is "who he is," "he could be made to go along with things he may not really want to go along with." The Palmers befriended the Howes in the mid-1990s and Palmer became Howe's only friend. Howe confided in Palmer concerning his (Howe's) weak financial position and his fear that he would lose his farm, "his inheritance." Palmer offered to help and advised Howe to pray on it. In the fall of 1998, the Palmers spent one week on the farm with the Howes. The Palmers asked a lot of questions about expenses and about Esther's children from her two previous marriages. After the Palmers spent their "trial" week with the Howes, Palmer told a friend, "[G]ive me a year and I'll have my retirement." Ultimately, by agreement, the Palmers moved into the Howes' home in January or February of 1999 to share expenses for a period of six months to one year. The inside of the house was cluttered and dirty, and the outside was littered with abandoned and rusting vehicles and other machine parts. Apparently the house was uninsurable.

In the spring of 1999, the parties started cleaning up the property, but Howe was a somewhat reluctant participant. During "house meetings," Palmer intimidated Howe about the cleaning, forced him to part with items he desired to keep, and yelled at him to keep his word and to speed up his work. Howe became uncomfortable living with Palmer and found it difficult to face him when he came home from his job working on the adjacent farm. Although Palmer professed that he never expected to be paid for the work he did cleaning up the Howe home and property, he decided unilaterally to take a "commission" on the profits of a tag sale the parties held in the summer of 1999. Jeanette Palmer kept the balance of the proceeds for household expenses. In addition to the tag sale, more than fifteen tons of "junk" was removed by a junk hauler. Howe never was informed how much, if any, money was realized from that transaction. Howe, fearful of Palmer, did not protest.

Despite the fact that there was no such agreement before moving on to the farm, after six months, Palmer convinced Howe that he owed him $20,000 to $25,000 for his (Palmer's) assistance in cleaning up the property, and that the only way Howe could settle his debt was to sell the farm or convey a fifty percent interest in it to the Palmers. Howe agreed to do so because he "felt like there was no other option." Jeanette Palmer contacted a lawyer, and on March 7, 2000, Howe signed a deed giving the Palmers a fifty percent interest in the property as his joint tenants by the entirety, subject to a life estate for Esther Howe. Although the lawyer inquired as to separate representation for Howe, Howe did not have the money for such representation. Howe had ongoing feelings of "fear and intimidation" at the time the deed was executed.

It is unclear exactly when, but at some point in 2000, the parties and Esther Howe decided to create a Christian ministry on the farm, and called it "Shepherds Haven." Through a correspondence course, the Palmers became ministers of Full Gospel International of Pennsylvania. They had a "spiritual board" of four to five people at the farm. On November 9, 2000, Howe signed a document agreeing to be counseled by Reverend Carol Pomeroy. He also agreed that if he could not "change" himself by March 31, the ministry would be disbanded. Those who wished to continue the ministry to God would leave the farm, and Howe would reimburse them financially for all the time, effort, and work they put into the farm.

Howe's stepdaughter, who was concerned when she learned about the deed to the Palmers, had a discussion with Howe around the time the deed was signed. During the discussion, he told her that he "had been having a bad attitude about everything that was going on at the farm" and asked her to "pray that his attitude would change." He also told her he was "in counseling" with Pomeroy, a friend of the Palmers, and "that he now felt that what was happening out there was okay." The Palmers told Howe that his prior pastor was not "Holy Spirit filled" and, therefore, would not be an appropriate counselor. In addition, they forbade Howe to tell anyone outside of the ministry what went on at Shepherds Haven. Palmer yelled at Howe if Howe did not support him without question, and the jury could have found that the counseling was designed to change Howe's behavior and his resistance to cooperating with, and being "loyal" to, Palmer. Esther testified that she and Howe were "learning to submit," to be "loyal," and to "[go] along with [Palmer's] leadership." Pomeroy reported to Palmer upon completing each session with Howe.

Some months later, Howe and his wife reconciled despite the Palmers' efforts to keep them apart by telling Esther that Howe had abandoned her. Esther eventually left the property as well, and this action was commenced on March 1, 2006, less than one year after Howe left the property.

Discussion. Undue influence. It is well established that the obligations of documents such as deeds, wills, and contracts can be avoided by showing that they were procured by means of fraud or undue influence. See, e.g., Brodie v. Evirs, 313 Mass. 741, 744–745 (1943); Henchey v. Cox, 348 Mass. 742, 746–747 (1965); Bruno v. Bruno, 384 Mass. 31, 33–34 (1981); Tetrault v. Mahoney, Hawkes & Goldings, 425 Mass. 456, 464 (1997). Fraud and undue influence are separate and distinct grounds for invalidating such documents, and their proof proceeds from different theories. See generally Wellman v. Carter, 286 Mass. 237, 253 (1934). In the case of fraud, the victim proceeds of his own free will but is affected by a false representation of a fact that induced the execution of the document. Ibid. Undue influence, however, creates a situation where the victim's own free will is destroyed or overcome such that what he does, his action, is contrary to his true desire and free will. Neill v. Brackett, 234 Mass. 367, 369–370 (1920). Wellman, supra. Rood v. Newberg, 48 Mass.App.Ct. 185, 191–192. We are dealing here with a claim of undue influence. The party challenging the validity of the document, on the ground that it was procured and executed as a result of undue influence, bears the burden of proving the allegation by a preponderance of the evidence. See, e.g., Cleary v. Cleary, 427 Mass. 286, 290 (1998). Undue influence has been defined to mean "whatever destroys free agency and constrains the person whose act is under review to do that which is contrary to his own untrammelled desire." Neill, 234 Mass. at 369. There are numerous means by which undue influence may be exerted upon an individual. The means may be overt or subtle, and one method is no more determinative of the outcome than another. Undue influence "may be caused by physical force, by duress, by threats, or by importunity. It may arise from persistent and unrelaxing efforts in the establishment or maintenance of conditions intolerable to the particular individual. It may result from more subtle conduct designed to create an irresistible ascendancy by imperceptible means. It may be exerted either by deceptive devices, or by material compulsion without actual fraud. Any species of coercion, whether physical, mental or moral, which subverts the sound judgment and genuine desire of the individual, is enough to constitute undue influence." Ibid. Our analysis is made easier when dramatic or overt means are employed, but ultimately the nature, extent, or degree of the means employed "is inconsequential so long as it is sufficient to substitute the dominating purpose of another for the free expression of the wishes of the person signing the instrument. Any influence to be unlawful must overcome the free will and eliminate unconstrained action. The nature of fraud and undue influence is such that they often work in veiled and secret ways. The power of a strong will over an irresolute character or one weakened by disease, overindulgence or age may be manifest although not shown by gross or palpable instrumentalities." Ibid.

"Four [factors] are usually present in a case of undue influence: 'an (1) unnatural disposition [is] made (2) by a person susceptible to undue influence to the advantage of someone (3) with an opportunity to exercise undue influence and (4) who in fact has used that opportunity to procure the contested disposition through improper means.'" Rostanzo v. Rostanzo, 73 Mass.App.Ct. 588, 604–605 (2009), quoting from O'Rourke v. Hunter, 446 Mass. 814 (2006). A claim of undue influence therefore can be made out upon a showing that a third party, here Palmer, "by means of coercion, overpowered the mind of the [victim, here Howe] and caused him to [sign a document] that embodied [Palmer's] 'dominating purpose' rather than the 'wishes of the person signing the instrument,' i.e., [Howe]." Id. at 604, quoting from Neill, supra. This burden shifts when a person in a fiduciary relationship with the grantor or principal benefits from the transaction. Cleary v. Cleary, 427 Mass. 286, 290 (1998).

The Palmers do not now contend, nor did they at trial, that there was insufficient evidence to support a finding that the deed was procured by undue influence. Rather, the Palmers argue that even if one of them unduly influenced Howe, the deed should be enforceable by the other because they each have separate enforceable legal rights in the deed. It is well settled, however, that an instrument procured by undue influence is voidable by the person who was unduly influenced. Willett v. Herrick, 258 Mass. 585, 603 (1927). Howe has not ratified the deed, so neither of the Palmers would have any right to its enforcement if the statute of limitations is determined not to prevent the claim of undue influence.

Amended final judgment affirmed.

NOTES

(1) *Confidential Relations.* A finding of a confidential relationship is often central to avoiding a contract on the basis of overreaching. In general, when the party asserting rights under the contract is the one in whom confidence was reposed, the claimant must show that the bargain was "fair, conscientious, and beyond the reach of suspicion." Young v. Kaye, 279 A.2d 759 (Pa. 1971). In that case, an elderly man was imposed upon by an ex-convict who provided him with services and won his confidence as a "tax consultant." As examples of confidential relations, the court mentioned guardian and ward, principal and agent, attorney and client. Beyond such standard examples, however, the list is not pre-determined. The key is not the type of relationship, but its nature; a confidential relation "is not restricted to any specific association. . . but is deemed to exist whenever the relative position of the parties is such that one has power and means to take advantage of or exert undue influence over the other." Id. at 763. Thus an automobile dealer and a customer were found be in a confidential relation; see Browder v. Hanley Dawson Cadillac, 379 N.E.2d 1206 (Ill. App. 1978) For a celebrated case in which an heiress argued that through the abuse of a confidential relation, she had been induced to support a religious organization over a period of years, see In re The Bible Speaks, 869 F.2d 628 (1st Cir. 1989), *cert. denied*, 493 U.S. 816 (1989).

(2) *Time Pressures.* In Howe v. Palmer, the Palmers' influence over Howe developed over time as Howe was, in a sense, groomed for servility. In other cases, the undue influence (or overreaching) occurs in a short period of

vulnerability brought on by special circumstances such as the period surrounding a funeral, see Moore v. Moore 22 P. 589; a deathbed decision, see Rothberg v. Walt Disney Co., 168 F.3d 501 (1999); or a deadline for action set by the dominant party in which the servient party is told he must make a decision, see Odorizzi v. Bloomfield School District, 246 Cal.App.2d 123 (1966).

(3) *Patterns of Behavior.* In a 1966 California case, an elementary school teacher was "arrested on criminal charges of homosexual activity." Odorizzi v. Bloomfield School District, 246 Cal.App.2d 123 (1966). Shortly thereafter, the superintendent of the school district and the school principal visited Odorizzi at his apartment, telling him that if he resigned his position immediately, the school district would not publicized the incident. Odorizzi thereupon formally resigned. When the criminal charges were subsequently dropped, Odorizzi sought to rescind his resignation on the grounds that he had lost his free will to decide due to the circumstances of the transaction. The court agreed. In its decision, it listed factors which commonly appear in cases of overreaching:

> [Overpersuasion is generally accompanied by certain characteristics which tend to create a pattern. The pattern usually involves several of the following elements: (1) discussion of the transaction at an unusual or inappropriate time, (2) consummation of the transaction in an unusual place, (3) insistent demand that the business be finished at once, (4) extreme emphasis on untoward consequences of delay, (5) the use of multiple persuaders by the dominant side against a single servient party, (6) absence of third-party advisers to the servient party, (7) statements that there is no time to consult financial advisers or attorneys. If a number of these elements are simultaneously present, the persuasion may be characterized as excessive.]

Which of these factors were present in Howe v. Palmer?

(4) *Background Law.* Recall the concept of "bargaining in the shadow of law" introduced in Note 3, p. 48 above. What law cast a shadow on the bargaining between Odorizzi in the preceding note and the school superintendent? As different activities fall in and out of a state's criminal code—forms of sexual behavior, marijuana use—might the opportunity for overreaching another change accordingly? Should the legal nature of the threat influence a finding of overreaching? What if the grounds for overreaching (the threat to expose legal drug use, for example) are unobjectionable but a social stigma still attaches to the behavior?

Note how the court in Howe distinguishes among fraud, undue influence, duress, and capacity. While there are defining characteristics of each, the line between them often appears less bright than fuzzy.

(5) *Statutory Solutions.* Is a court less likely to find undue influence in a consumer transaction where the buyer can simply walk away? For a statutory response to situations where the buyer is not able to walk away, states often provide for "cooling off periods;" see, for example, Ky. Rev. St. Ann. § 367.420 (Buyer's Right to Cancel Home Solicitation Sale). Do home

telephone solicitations present a similar problem? What about contracts with residents of nursing homes?

(6) *Undue Influence at Home.* Are agreements between spouses particularly susceptible to "overpersuasion"? Consider one spouse's promise to guarantee the debt of the other, either personally, as did Louisa Sheffield, p. 96 above, or by pledging the family home as security for a loan to the other, as in Barclay's Bank v. O'Brien, Note 3, p. 99 above. In the latter case, the British Law Lords noted that "a high proportion of privately owned wealth is invested in the matrimonial home" and that such wealth would become "economically sterile" if suretyship agreements were too easily set aside on the grounds of spousal pressure. But they observed that "[i]n a substantial proportion of marriages it is still the husband who has the business experience and the wife is willing to follow his advice without bringing a truly independent mind and will to bear on financial decisions." 4 All E.R. at 422. In view of these two propositions, the court held that a creditor is "put on inquiry" when a wife offers to stand as surety for her husband in cases when the transaction is on its face not to the financial advantage of the wife *and* there is a substantial risk that "in procuring the wife to act as surety, the husband has committed a legal or equitable wrong that entitles the wife to set aside the transaction." 4 All E.R. at 429. The court further stated that "the underlying risk of one cohabitee exploiting the emotional involvement and trust of the other" is not limited to married couples, and extended the rule announced to any case where "the surety is cohabitating with the principal debtor."

If a creditor is "put on inquiry," what steps might it take to make sure the wife's consent is obtained properly? Should the requirement apply to spouses generally?

PROBLEM

Andrew Gengaro, a member of Local 3144, AFSCME, worked for the city of New Haven. In February, 2004, Gengaro was suspended indefinitely from his employment pending an investigation into allegations of sexual harassment. Following a hearing, representatives of the city and Local 3144, on Gengaro's behalf, negotiated a confidential settlement agreement. Under the settlement, Gengaro agreed to resign in exchange for $7500, payment of accrued vacation and sick leave, and the city's promise not to oppose a claim by Gengaro for unemployment compensation. Both parties agreed not to disparage the other publicly regarding the circumstances of Gengaro's resignation. In signing the agreement, Gengaro acknowledged that he was advised to consult with an attorney, that he had at least twenty-one days to decide whether to execute the agreement, and that he could revoke the agreement within a seven day period after signing.

Ten months later, Gengaro filed a complaint against both the city and Local 3144, seeking to rescind the agreement on grounds of undue influence, claiming the following: that the city told him that if he did not sign the agreement, his employment would be terminated; that the union told him that if he did not sign the agreement, the union would not continue to represent his interests; and that at the time he signed the agreement, he had " serious financial difficulties . . .; was a care provider to an elderly family member. . .; and would have seen embarrassing allegations made public." Thus, Gengaro argued, "he had no reasonable alternative but to acquiesce to the [city's] ultimatum and accept the settlement agreement."

From an order for summary judgment to city and union, Gengaro appealed. Gengaro v. City of New Haven, 984 A.2d 1133 (Conn. App. 2009).

What verdict on appeal? And on what grounds? Was Gengaro overpersuaded? Does it matter on these facts?

In answering, consider the court's summary of the law of undue influence in Connecticut: "(1) a person who is subject to influence; (2) an opportunity to exert undue influence; (3) a disposition to exert undue influence; and (4) a result indicating undue influence. . . . Relevant factors include age and physical and mental condition of the one alleged to have been influenced, whether he had independent or disinterested advice in the transaction . . . consideration or lack or inadequacy thereof for any contract made, necessities and distress of the person alleged to have been influenced, his predisposition to make the transfer in question, the extent of the transfer in relation to his whole worth . . . active solicitations and persuasions by the other party, and the relationship of the parties." Consider also that prior to filing the complaint, Gengaro had received the major part of the benefits due him under the settlement agreement.

———

(B) CONCEALMENT AND MISREPRESENTATION

According to Chancellor Kent, "*Cicero de Officiis*, lib. 3. sec. 50–57, states the case of a corn merchant of Alexandria arriving at Rhodes in a time of great scarcity, with a cargo of grain, and with knowledge that a number of other vessels, with similar cargoes, had already sailed from Alexandria for Rhodes, and whom he had passed on the voyage. He then puts the question, whether the Alexandrine merchant was bound in conscience to inform the buyers of that fact, or to keep silence, and sell his wheat for an extravagant price; and he answers it by saying, that, in his opinion, good faith would require of a just and candid man, a frank disclosure of the fact." 2 Kent's Commentaries 491* n. c. (3d ed. 1836).

What is the requirement that the law, as opposed to the demand of conscience, makes for disclosing facts in a bargaining context? Many courts have said that they will not insist on the degree of disclosure that a person of exceptional scruple might make. On the other hand, in allowing bargaining advantages to be secured by persons of little scruple, the law may attach a competitive disadvantage to conscientious conduct. See Laidlaw v. Organ, 15 U.S. 178, 195 (1817), in which a buyer, having learned hours before the general population that the British blockade of New Orleans was to be lifted by virtue of the signing of the Treaty of Ghent, bought a huge quantity of tobacco at a most advantageous price from a seller without this information. The seller later sought to have the transaction rescinded for fraud. In dictum, Chief Justice John Marshall stated that the buyer was not bound to communicate the information to the seller because "it would be difficult to circumscribe the contrary doctrine within proper limits." Is there any benefit in the law making an effort to do so?

NOTES

(1) *Investment in Knowledge.* Should there be special rules about information derived from research, training, and experience? It is generally understood that dealers in certain types of merchandise, such as antiques and rare coins, for example, trade on their expertise and experience and are not expected to disclose to their customers all the elements that enter into their evaluations. The expense of acquiring such expertise would not be justified if it did not yield bargaining advantages. To some extent the same consideration affects the degree of disclosure required in most commercial exchanges. Compare the market expertise of middlemen, mentioned in Note 2, p. 604 below.

A justification for enforcing the option is given in Anthony Kronman, *Mistake, Disclosure, Information, and the Law of Contracts*, 7 J. Leg. Studies 1, 33 (1978). Certain information, Professor Kronman has argued, is "in essence a property right," at least when produced by a "deliberate search for socially useful information." The law tends (he said) to recognize such a right, and "not to recognize it where the information has been casually acquired"—so enhancing efficiency in resource allocation. Beyond deliberately and casually acquired information, what other distinctions might support "a property right" in knowledge? Economist Jack Hirshleifer argued that "discovery" of information that might otherwise not come to surface should be privileged above information that is simply learned early ("foreknowledge") but would likely become common knowledge in time. Jack Hirshleifer, *The Private and Social Value of Information and the Reward to Inventive Activity*, 61 Am. Econ. Rev. 561 (1971). Robert Cooter & Thomas Ulen, *Law and Economics* 357–9 (6th ed. 2012), would give greater protection to "productive information"—that is, information that increase wealth in society—than merely "redistributive information," which only leads to shifts in wealth. See generally Melvin A. Eisenberg, *Disclosure in Contract Law*, 91 Cal. L. Rev. 1645 (2003).

(2) *The Kidd Creek Strike.* The discovery of an extremely valuable ore deposit near Timmins, Ontario, touched off an immense number of trades. The finder, Texas Gulf Sulphur Company, detected the deposit through aerial searches for electromagnetic "anomalies." Having found one, it purchased mineral rights and options from landowners in the vicinity. When the deposit was verified, but not publicly announced, officers of the firm made purchases of its stock. Some of the officers were successfully charged with violations of the securities laws, for wrongful use of "inside" information. See S.E.C. v. Texas Gulf Sulphur Co., 446 F.2d 1301 (2d Cir. 1971). One of the landowners sued the firm for wrongful use of its information in dealing with him: it had failed to disclose "an unusually promising indication of economic mineralization on [his] property."

Swinton v. Whitinsville Sav. Bank

Supreme Judicial Court of Massachusetts, 1942.
311 Mass. 677, 42 N.E.2d 808.

■ QUA, JUSTICE. The declaration alleges that on or about September 12, 1938, the defendant sold the plaintiff a house in Newton to be occupied by the plaintiff and his family as a dwelling; that at the time of the sale the house "was infested with termites, an insect that is most dangerous and destructive to buildings"; that the defendant knew the house was so infested; that the plaintiff could not readily observe this condition upon inspection; that "knowing the internal destruction that these insects were creating in said house," the defendant falsely and fraudulently concealed from the plaintiff its true condition; that the plaintiff at the time of his purchase had no knowledge of the termites, exercised due care thereafter, and learned of them about August 30, 1940; and that, because of the destruction that was being done and the dangerous condition that was being created by the termites the plaintiff was put to great expense for repairs and for the installation of termite control in order to prevent the loss and destruction of said house.

There is no allegation of any false statement or representation, or of the uttering of a half truth which may be tantamount to a falsehood. There is no intimation that the defendant by any means prevented the plaintiff from acquiring information as to the condition of the house. There is nothing to show any fiduciary relation between the parties, or that the plaintiff stood in a position of confidence toward or dependence upon the defendant. So far as appears the parties made a business deal at arm's length. The charge is concealment and nothing more; and it is concealment in the simple sense of mere failure to reveal, with nothing to show any peculiar duty to speak. The characterization of the concealment as false and fraudulent of course adds nothing in the absence of further allegations of fact. Province Securities Corp. v. Maryland Casualty Co., 269 Mass. 75, 92, 168 S.E. 252.

If this defendant is liable on this declaration every seller is liable who fails to disclose any nonapparent defect known to him in the subject of the sale which materially reduces its value and which the buyer fails to discover. Similarly it would seem that every buyer would be liable who fails to disclose any nonapparent virtue known to him in the subject of the purchase which materially enhances its value and of which the seller is ignorant. See Goodwin v. Agassiz, 283 Mass. 358, 186 N.E. 659. The law has not yet, we believe, reached the point of imposing upon the frailties of human nature a standard so idealistic as this. That the particular case here stated by the plaintiff possesses a certain appeal to the moral sense is scarcely to be denied. Probably the reason is to be found in the facts that the infestation of buildings by termites has not been common in Massachusetts and constitutes a concealed risk against which buyers are off their guard. But the law cannot provide special rules for termites and can hardly attempt to determine liability according to the varying probabilities of the existence and discovery of different possible defects in the subjects of trade. The rule of nonliability for bare nondisclosure has been stated and followed by this court in [seven cases cited]. It is adopted in the American Law Institute's Restatement of Torts, § 551. See Williston on Contracts, Rev.Ed., §§ 1497, 1498, 1499.

The order sustaining the demurrer is affirmed, and judgment is to be entered for the defendant. Keljikian v. Star Brewing Co., 303 Mass. 53, 55–63, 20 N.E.2d 465.

So ordered.

NOTES

(1) *Questions.* Does it follow from this holding that the plaintiff could not have *rescinded* the sale on establishing the facts he alleged? If the decision had been to the contrary, overruling the defendant's demurrer, would it follow that the plaintiff could have rescinded the sale? (An answer to this question is suggested by the next main case.) If the sale had not been executed, and the seller had brought an action against the buyer for specific performance, would it have succeeded?

(2) *Latent Defects: Caveat Emptor?* For a statute requiring that sellers of homes disclose defects known to them unless the property is sold "as is," see Va. Code §§ 55–517 *et seq.* (2018). In addition to statutory protection, some courts require that dangerous conditions be disclosed. Some impose a warranty, in cases of sales by builders, that a home is fit for habitation.

In a case like *Swinton,* some courts start with the proposition that a seller of a home should disclose to the buyer a so-called latent defect—a deleterious condition, known to the seller, that is not readily observable. "[W]e are certain," a New Jersey court has said, that *Swinton* "does not represent our sense of justice or fair dealing." Weintraub v. Krobatsch, 317 A.2d 68 (N.J. 1974). Another court contrasted the sale of a simple farm home with the sale of a modern residence of complex construction. While the ancient rule of *caveat emptor* "may have had some merit in the agrarian society in which it was applied," the court thought, it is "no longer an expression of American mores." Holcomb v. Zinke, 365 N.W.2d 507 (N.D. 1985). But see Johnson v. Davis, 480 So.2d 625 (Fla. 1985) (Boyd, C.J., dissenting): although it "sounds progressive, high-minded, and idealistic," a decision to blur the distinction between misrepresentation and nondisclosure can be expected to distort the real-estate market. *Id.* at 629, 631.

What justification might be given for imposing a broad disclosure requirement in connection with the sale of a new home by the builder, but otherwise adhering to the *Swinton* rule? Is the general availability of termite insurance relevant? Compare Compass Point Condominium Owners Ass'n v. First Fed. Sav. & Loan Ass'n, 641 So.2d 253 (Ala.1994) (the court held that the seller has no duty to disclose existence of water damage; that there was no fraudulent concealment; and distinguished its abrogation of caveat emptor for sales of new homes), with Hill v. Jones, 725 P.2d 1115 (Ariz. App. 1986) (holding that seller has duty to disclose the existence of termite damage which materially affects the value of the property). In the case of a builder-vendor, is an implied warranty more suitable, as protection for the buyer, than a disclosure requirement?

(3) *Remedies.* The authorities cited in the foregoing note suggest an array of remedies for concealment. In *Weintraub*, the buyers were sued initially for specific performance and countered with a rescission claim. In *Johnson*, the sellers were required to repay the amounts they had received from the buyers, with interest. In *Holcomb* (as in *Weintraub*), the court ordered rescission of the contract. It charged the sellers for the buyers' expenses in curing defects, but charged the buyers with the reasonable rental value of the home. In *Compass Point*, the buyers claimed punitive damages. In the Virginia statute, one of the remedies provided for a buyer is recovery of the "actual damages suffered" as a result of an undisclosed defect.

What might a buyer hope to recover in a breach-of-warranty action against the seller? If that action is available to a buyer, should the buyer be permitted to choose rescission instead?

(4) *Career Changes.* A congregation employed a rabbi to provide spiritual leadership on the strength of two services he conducted, a few conversations, and a sparse resume ("references on request"). Thereafter it emerged that he had been convicted for defrauding an insurance company and had been disbarred as an attorney for bribing a police officer. In an action by the employer for rescission of the contract, summary judgment was granted for the plaintiff. See Jewish Ctr. of Sussex County v. Whale, 397 A.2d 712 (N.J. 1978) (concealment), *aff'd*, 432 A.2d 521 (N.J. 1981) (misrepresentation).

In another case, an applicant for a teaching position failed to disclose to his Catholic employer at the time he was hired that, years earlier, under a different first name, had been an ordained priest who had left the church and married. When the university learned these facts, it discharged him and he sued for breach of contract. What result under *Swinton*? See Fuller v. De Paul Univ., 12 N.E.2d 213 (Ill. 1938).

PROBLEM

Disclosure and DNA. What is the status of an agreement to pay child support entered into as part of a divorce settlement on the assumption that paying father is the biological father of the children, when DNA testing later shows that he is not? For one such case, see Paternity of Cheryl, 746 N.E.2d 488 (Mass. 2001). Does it matter, for purposes of a disclosure analysis, whether the parents are married or not? Should such a contract be set aside on grounds of mistake? Should the father be able to obtain restitution from the mother for monies already paid?

Kannavos v. Annino

Supreme Judicial Court of Massachusetts, 1969.
356 Mass. 42, 247 N.E.2d 708.

[In 1961 or 1962, Mrs. Carrie Annino bought a one-family dwelling in Springfield: No. 11, Ingersoll Grove. She converted it into a multi-family building with eight apartments, without obtaining a building permit, and in knowing violation of the city zoning ordinance. The house was in a "Residence A" district, where multi-family uses were prohibited. In 1965 a real-estate broker was employed to try to sell the property. He placed newspaper ads, of which the following is an example: "Income gross $9,600 yr. in lg. single house, converted to 8 lovely, completely furn. (includ. TV and china) apts. 8 baths, ideal for couple to live free with excellent income. By apt. only. Foote Realty."

Apostolos Kannavos read one of the ads, and got in touch with the broker, Foote. Foote showed him the house, and gave him income and expense figures supplied by Mrs. Annino. Without the aid of a lawyer, Kannavos contracted to buy the property, and did so, borrowing money from a bank for the purpose, and giving it a mortgage. At the closing, attorneys for the seller and for the mortgagee were present, and the latter prepared the papers. Mrs. Annino and Foote knew that Kannavos's reason for buying was to rent the apartments. He was unaware of any zoning or building permit violation, and would not have purchased the property if he had known of any such violation. It was worth substantially less if operated only as a single-family dwelling than it was as an apartment building.

Soon after the sale, the city started legal proceedings to abate the non-conforming use of the building.[c] Kannavos brought a bill in equity against Mrs. Annino to rescind the purchase. The trial court overruled a demurrer, and granted rescission on the basis of findings by a master. Mrs. Annino appealed.

It appeared that Kannavos had immigrated from Greece in 1957, when he was about thirty years old. In this country he had learned English, and become a self-employed hairdresser. It was found that he made no inquiry of anyone about zoning or building permits before or during the closing, and that no statements were made to him on these subjects. Everything that was said to him by or on behalf of the seller was substantially true.]

■ CUTTER, JUSTICE. We assume that, if the vendors had been wholly silent and had made no references whatsoever to the use of the Ingersoll Grove houses, they could not have been found to have made any misrepresentation. See Swinton v. Whitinsville Sav. Bank, 311 Mass.

---

[c] As to other, similar properties that Kannavos (and an associate) also bought from Mrs. Annino, the city also asserted violations of the building code, but the opinion does not make it clear whether or not No. 11 was in question on this score.

677, 678–679, 42 N.E.2d 808, 141 A.L.R. 965,[1] where this court affirmed an order sustaining a demurrer to a declaration in an action of tort brought by a purchaser of a house. The court (p. 679) indicated that it was applying a long standing "rule of nonliability for *bare nondisclosure*" (emphasis supplied).

As in the *Swinton* case, the parties here were dealing at arm's length, the vendees were in no way prevented from acquiring information, and the vendors stood in no fiduciary relationship to the vendees. In two aspects, however, the present cases differ from the *Swinton* case: viz. (a) The vendees themselves could have found out about the zoning violations by inquiry through public records, whereas in the *Swinton* case the purchaser would have probably discovered the presence of termites only by retaining expert investigators; and (b) there was something more here than the "bare nondisclosure" of the seller in the *Swinton* case.

(a)   We deal first with the affirmative actions by the vendors, their conduct, advertising, and statements. Was enough said and done by the vendors so that they were bound to disclose more to avoid deception of the vendees and reliance by them upon a half truth? In other words, did the statements made by the vendors in their advertising and otherwise take the cases out of the "rule of nonliability for bare nondisclosure" applied in the *Swinton* case?

Although there may be "no duty imposed upon one party to a transaction to speak for the information of the other if he does speak with reference to a given point of information, voluntarily or at the other's request, he is bound to speak honestly and to divulge all the material facts bearing upon the point that lie within his knowledge. Fragmentary information may be as misleading as active misrepresentation, and half-truths may be as actionable as whole lies. . . . " See Harper & James, Torts, § 7.14. See also Restatement: Torts, § 529; Williston, Contracts (2d ed.) §§ 1497–1499. The existence of substantially this principle was assumed in the *Swinton* case, 311 Mass. 677, 678, 42 N.E.2d 808, 141 A.L.R. 965, in the first sentence of the passage from that case quoted above. Massachusetts decisions have applied this principle. See Kidney v. Stoddard, 7 Metc. 252, 254–255 (a father represented that his son was entitled to credit but failed to disclose that the son was a minor; statement treated as a fraudulent representation); Burns v. Dockray, 156 Mass. 135, 137, 30 N.E. 551 (assertion that title was good [see Lyman v. Romboli, 293 Mass. 373, 374, 199 N.E. 916] but omitting to refer to the possible insanity of one whose incompetence might cloud title); Van

---

[1]   The *Swinton* case may not represent the law elsewhere. See Restatement 2d: Torts, § 551 (Tent. Draft No. 11, April 15, 1965), p. 43; Prosser, Torts (3d ed.), § 101, p. 711. Cf. discussions of situations in landlord and tenant cases like Cutter v. Hamlen, 147 Mass. 471, 474, 18 N.E. 397, 1 L.R.A. 429; Stumpf v. Leland, 242 Mass. 168, 172–174, 136 N.E. 399; Cooper v. Boston Housing Authority, 342 Mass. 38, 40, 172 N.E.2d 117. For general consideration of silence as misrepresentation, see Restatement: Restitution, § 8; Williston, Contracts (2d ed.) § 1497.

Houten v Morse, 162 Mass. 414, 417–419, 38 N.E. 705, 26 L.R.A. 430 (partial disclosure by a woman to her fiancé about a prior divorce). See also . . . Boston Five Cents Sav. Bank v. Brooks, 309 Mass. 52, 55–56, 34 N.E.2d 435, 437 ("Deception need not be direct. . . . Declarations and conduct calculated to mislead . . . which . . . do mislead one . . . acting reasonably are enough to constitute fraud"). Cf. Wade v. Ford Motor Co., 341 Mass. 596, 597–598, 171 N.E.2d 282.

The master's report provides ample basis for treating the present cases as within the decisions just cited. The original advertisements in effect offered the houses as investment properties and referred to them as single houses converted to apartments. The investment aspect of the houses was emphasized by Foote's action in furnishing income and expense figures. There was an express assertion that 11 Ingersoll Grove was "being rented to the public for multi-family purposes" and that Kannavos and Bellas "could continue to operate . . . [the other properties] as multi-dwelling property." The master's conclusions indicate that this statement applied to all the properties.[2] The buildings were divided into apartments. The sales included refrigerators, stoves, and other furnishings appropriate for apartment use as well as real estate. The vendors knew that the vendees were planning to continue to use the buildings for apartments, and yet the vendors still failed to disclose the zoning and building violations. We conclude that enough was done affirmatively to make the disclosure inadequate and partial, and, in the circumstances, intentionally deceptive and fraudulent.

(b) The second difference between these cases and the *Swinton* case is the character of the defect not disclosed.

In the *Swinton* case, the presence of predatory insects threatened the structure sold. In the absence of any seller's representations whatsoever, there was no duty to disclose this circumstance, even though doubtless it would have been difficult to discover. In the present cases, the defect in the premises related to a matter of public regulation, the zoning and building ordinances. Its applicability to these premises could have been discovered by these vendees or by the vendees' counsel if, acting with prudence, they had retained counsel, which they did not. The bank mortgagee's counsel presumably was looking only to the protection of the bank's security position. Nevertheless, where there is reliance on fraudulent representations or upon statements and action treated as fraudulent, our cases have not barred plaintiffs from recovery merely because they "did not use due diligence . . . [when they] could readily have ascertained from . . . records" what the true facts were. See Yorke v. Taylor, 332 Mass. 368, 373, 124 N.E.2d 912. There this court allowed rescission because of the negligent misrepresentation, innocent but false, of the current assessed value of the property being sold. Here the

---

[2] In any event some discussions with respect to all these properties in the same neighborhood were going on about the same time and the later transaction appears to have been commenced either before or about the time the earlier one was completed.

representations made by the advertising and the vendors' conduct and statements in effect were that the property was multi-family housing suitable for investment and that the housing could continue to be used for that purpose. Because the vendors did as much as they did do, they were bound to do more. Failing to do so, they were responsible for misrepresentation. We think the situation is comparable to that in Yorke v. Taylor, 332 Mass. 368, 374, 124 N.E.2d 912, even though there the misrepresentation was "not consciously false" and here it was by half truth.

We hold that the vendors' conduct entitled the vendees to rescind. See Yorke v. Taylor, 332 Mass. 368, 371–372, 374, 124 N.E.2d 912; Restatement: Contracts, §§ 472, 489; Restatement: Restitution, § 28; Williston, Contracts (2d ed.) §§ 1497–1500. There was, in our opinion, much more than "bare nondisclosure" as in the *Swinton* case. Cf. Spencer v. Gabriel, 328 Mass. 1, 2, 101 N.E.2d 369; Donahue v. Stephens, 342 Mass. 89, 92, 172 N.E.2d 101.

[The court affirmed the decree below overruling the demurrer. However, it reversed the final decree so that there might be further consideration of the relief, in view of a fire that had occurred at No. 11 after that decree.]

NOTES

(1) *Questions.* Does it follow from the decision above that Kannavos could have maintained an action in deceit against Annino? The requisites of that action, and the remedy it affords, are dealt with in detail in courses on torts. Thus contract remedies are not the only guarantees of minimum decencies in the bargaining process.

(2) *Fraud in Release.* John Hand sued his former employer, Dayton-Hudson (D-H), for breach of contract and age discrimination after his job as an attorney was eliminated. D-H moved for summary judgment on the ground that Hand had released it from these claims. Upon firing Hand, D-H had offered him $38,000 for a general release of any claim he might have against it. The release form was given to Hand for study. He conceived a "clever scheme" for turning the tables (as he put it) on D-H. He retyped the document so as to mimic the original, but inserted the term, "except as to claims of age discrimination and breach of contract." Not suspecting the change, D-H executed the copy and paid Hand $38,000. Assuming that Hand's conduct was fraudulent, and that D-H's failure to read the copy was excusable, should Hand be permitted to return the amount paid him and maintain his claims? Or should he be bound by the release as D-H understood it? For opinions on reformation to conform a writing to an agreement to which one of the parties did not assent, see Hand v. Dayton-Hudson, 775 F.2d 757 (6th Cir. 1985).

(3) *No-Reliance Clauses.* A party may try to protect itself from an allegation of fraud by including a "no-reliance clause" in the contract. The clause is an attempt to remove one of the necessary elements of a subsequent

claim for fraud by virtue of the party's declaration that it has not relied on anything but its own judgment. For example, in Extra Equipamentos E Exportação Ltda v. Case Corp., 541 F.3d 719 (7th Cir. 2011) (Posner, J.), the no-reliance clause in a settlement agreement between the parties (the "Release") stated: "Both parties represent and warrant that in making this Release they are relying on their own judgment, belief and knowledge and the counsel of their attorneys of choice. The parties are not relying on representations or statements made by the other party or any person representing them except for the representations and warranties expressed in this Release." Judge Posner informs us, "In the trade, no-reliance clauses are called 'big boy' clauses (as in: 'we're big boys and can look after ourselves')."

Sometime later, Extra Equipamentos ("Extra") brought an action in fraud and promissory fraud against Case alleging that during the negotiation of the release, Case's representative had stated it would retain Extra as a distributor if Extra signed the release, but that Case had no intention of fulfilling that promise at the time it was made. Should Extra be permitted to introduce evidence of Case's promise regarding the distributorship? Might any of the following matter in your answer: whether the terms were boilerplate or negotiated? Whether the complaining party had counsel? Whether the parties were knowledgeable in business, that is, were indeed "big boys"? See Forest Oil Corp. v. McAllen, 268 S. W.3d 51 (Tex. 2008) for these and other factors.

How does a no-reliance clause differ in application and in kind from the parol evidence rule, discussed in Chapter 5, at p. 489 below?

PROBLEM

Consider the following two cases, briefly sketched. How would the Massachusetts court in *Kannavos* have decided them?

a. In response to a dealer's advertisement, a shopper bought a used car after a test drive. The salesman had told the shopper it was air-conditioned (repeating a statement in the advertisement), "and that Chrysler was a nice car and all that jazz." The shopper bought the car, and now knows—as the salesman knew earlier—that the knobs marked "air" were for ventilation only. Is the agreement voidable? See Williams v. Rank & Son Buick, Inc., 170 N.W.2d 807 (Wis. 1969) (fraud action; 4–3 decision).

b. A cattleman and a potential buyer discussed with one another sales that had occurred earlier in the day at a local sales barn. (The buyer had attended the earlier sales.) The cattleman contracted to sell 360 head at $60 a hundredweight to that same buyer. Now he knows—as the buyer knew earlier—that some cattle had been sold at the barn for as much as $62 a hundredweight. Is the contract voidable? See Kanzmeier v. McCoppin, 398 N.W.2d 826 (Iowa 1987).

Fraud and Misrepresentation

Concealment and nondisclosure are varieties of misrepresentation, which is both a ground for rescinding a contract and the predicate for a tort action. With regard to the latter, the plaintiff must establish that the defendant made the misrepresentation knowing it to be false, or at least with reckless disregard for its truth. This element, known as *scienter,* was insisted on in 19th-century English cases, and remains influential in many courts today. In contract law it generally has not had the same force, owing partly to the equitable character of rescission. See Halpert v. Rosenthal, 267 A.2d 730 (R.I. 1970), a "termite case" making the distinction. As a rule, a party to a contract may avoid the contract even if the other party obtained its assent by an innocent misrepresentation, *i.e.,* one that the party making it believed to be true. What difference between the functions of tort and contract law might explain this difference in sensitivity to the nature of a falsehood?

In both tort and contract law relief for misrepresentation is restricted in ways that merit at least a mention. (To the extent that they are distinctive, the principles of tort law will not be pursued here.) It has sometimes been held that a misrepresentation of *law* is innocuous. Yet because the author of a misrepresentation of law is frequently better placed to know the law than the victim of it—a lawyer speaking to a client, an insurance agent to a customer—the inequality of competence succeeds as a ground for giving relief. See *Kannavos*, p. 473 above.

The misrepresentation must be a material one. This requirement is prominent in insurance litigation, where a misrepresentation by a policy buyer relating to health is a commonplace ground for rejecting a claim. Various standards of materiality have been expressed, and while none is applied uniformly, they serve the common function of justifying a certain control by judges over the more volatile behavior of juries.

Some degree of diligence is required of a party who relies on another's statement, though whether a party has been negligent in relying depends partly on the victim's capacities, partly on the nature of the transaction, and partly on the plausibility of the representation. The question of diligence should be distinguished from the question whether any credence was placed in the representation at all. There can be no complaint about a statement by one who heard it and proceeded to investigate its accuracy: "reliance and verification are incompatible." Hayat Carpet Cleaning Co., Inc. v. Northern Assur. Co., 69 F.2d 805 (2d Cir. 1934) (L. Hand, J.). In the currently preferred formulation, the complainant must show not mere reliance, but *justifiable* reliance.

Finally, the traditional rule is that the misrepresentation must be one of fact, and not of opinion. That tradition is rattled by the next principal case, which describes a suspicious representation embedded in an array of other questionable bargaining techniques.

NOTE

What the Document Means. "A representation as to the legal effect of a document is regarded as a statement of opinion rather than of fact and will not ordinarily support an action for fraud." Fina Supply, Inc. v. Abilene Nat'l Bank, 726 S.W.2d 537 (Tex. 1987).

In that case a bank (defendant) had given a formal assurance to a customer (plaintiff) that the customer could require the bank to pay certain obligations of a third party. The customer, Fina, dealt in large quantities of oil. The document expressing the bank's assurance had been amended from time to time. In litigation between Fina and the bank about the scope of the bank's assurance, Fina charged that a bank employee had misled it about the effect of the amendments. Fina charged the bank with fraud and sought reformation of the document (letter of credit) expressing the bank's undertaking. From a judgment for Fina, the bank appealed. *Held:* Reversed.

The court stated that "where the parties are in an equal bargaining position with equal access to legal advice, there is no room for application of the doctrine that misrepresentations of points of law will be considered misrepresentations of fact if they were so intended and understood."

Promissory Fraud

The law distinguishes between a promise that has not been performed and a promise that at the time of its making the promisor never intended to perform. The first is a simple breach for which the promisee is entitled to expectation damages. The second gives rise to an action at the intersection of tort and contract called promissory fraud, and for which the promisee may recover punitive as well as compensatory damages. The key feature of promissory fraud is that " 'the promisor, at the time of making certain representations, lacked any intention to perform them.' " Junk v. Aon Corp., 2007 WL 4292034 (S.D.N.Y. 2007) (citations omitted).

But why, in such a case should the promisee receive punitive damages? If the promise has not been kept, do not traditional expectation damages make him whole? One possibility is that the law regards lying about one's intent to perform more egregious than simply not performing. The law does, however, tolerate, if not encourage, efficient breach where we rely on expectation damages—but no more than that—to prevent the plaintiff from being any worse off than he would have been had the promise been kept. Is intending not to perform—dissembling about perspective performance—worse than deliberately not performing?

Is there perhaps a moral dimension to misrepresenting one's intent in these circumstances? Consider the comment to UCC § 2–609 (right to adequate assurance of performance), which we deal with more fully in Chapter 7. The Comment reminds us that "the essential purpose of a contract between commercial men is actual performance and [that] they do not bargain merely for a promise, or for a promise plus the right to win a law suit and that a continuing sense of reliance and security that the promised performance will be forthcoming when due, is an important feature of the bargain." Section 2–609 supplies a mechanism for promisees who have reasonable grounds for anxiety about whether performance will be forthcoming or not. Promissory fraud similarly recognizes that promisees bargained for a sense of security and reliance when entering a contract, and that their security is fundamentally undermined if the promisor has never intended to perform.

Professors Ian Ayres and Gregory Klass suggest that the nature of the undermining caused by what they call "insincere promises" is economic. They explain that a promisee must have credible information about the promisor's intent in order to "determine how much to invest in precautions against the possibility of nonperformance and to spend in ways that will increase his profits if the promisor does perform. . . . Promissory fraud is not a doctrine where tort principles just happen to overlap with contractual behavior. Rather, legal liability for insincere promising has a well-defined function within the apparatus of the law of contracts. It promotes the credible transfer of information about the promisor's intent, information that can tell a promise whether it is in his interest to enter into the contract, with whom he should contract, and how much he should invest in reliance." See generally Ian Ayres and Gregory Klass, Insincere Promises: The Law of Misrepresented Intent 8 (2005). On this account, punitive damages create the right disincentive for promisors "intentionally or recklessly misrepresenting the probability of performance." Id. at 81.

NOTES

(1) *Promissory Fraud in Employment.* In Junk v. Aon Corporation, mentioned above, Aon had recruited Junk to join its offices in New York. According to Junk, an Aon vice-president had promised that if Junk accepted Aon's offer, he would work exclusively on a revolutionary new software program that Aon was about to "roll out." When Junk expressed concern regarding the delay in development of the product, the vice-president said, "No. no. no. I have guys working on it as we speak and it will be done in three months." Junk then accepted the job and moved to New York, but when he got there, there was no new software to work on. Junk sued for promissory fraud, showing, among other things, that Aon had not started development of the product at the time the vice-president spoke to Junk, nor had it allocated any funds for the research and development for the project. Aon moved to dismiss the complaint for Junk's failure to state a claim for promissory fraud, among other things. Aon introduced undisputed evidence that Junk's contract contained the following provision: "Employment with Aon Consulting is for no specified period and constitutes at-will employment." The motion was denied, and Aon appealed. How would you analyze these facts? What other facts might be helpful? See Junk v. Aon Corp., 2007 WL 4292034 (S.D.N.Y. 2007).

(2) *Hoffman, Redux.* In Hoffman v. Red Owl, p. 299 above, would Joseph Hoffman have an action for promissory fraud against Red Owl's representative Lukowitz? Is there a difference between "negligent promising" and promissory fraud?

(3) *Promissory Fraud in the Academy.* Claims for promissory fraud have also arisen in the educational context. Consider the following: A student brought an action against the administrators of his university, claiming that when the student transferred to the university, the dean had promised him that music courses listed in the school's catalogue would be offered. The student provided proof that at the time of the dean's promise, the dean knew that the school had neither qualified instructors nor the necessary equipment for the courses. What result? Held: For the student; see Byrd v. Lamar, 846 So.2d 334 (Ala. 2002).

For an example closer to home, see Rodi v. S. New Eng. Sch. of Law, 532 F.3d 11 (1st Cir. 2008), in which a student attending an unaccredited law school relied upon the dean's statement in 1997 that the school was likely to receive American Bar Association accreditation before the student was graduated, in deciding whether to transfer. (Because the school failed to achieve ABA accreditation, the student upon graduation was unable to sit for the New Jersey bar examination.) At the time the dean made the statements expressing optimism about accreditation, he was aware of serious criticisms of the school by the ABA committee. What result? Held: For the school.

How might the following facts have fit into the court's analysis? A) the law school catalogue contained a disclaimer providing: "The Law School makes no representation to any applicant or student that it will be approved by the American Bar Association prior to the graduation of any matriculating student;" b) decisions about accreditation are solely in the hands of the ABA; c) the statement upon which the student relied was that "There should be no cause for pessimism about the school's ultimate achievement of ABA approval;" and d) "prior to his statement in September of 1997 Larkin had been exposed as a flawed prognosticator." Id. at 18.

Speakers of Sport v. ProServ

United States Court of Appeals, Seventh Circuit, 1999.
178 F.3d 862.

■ POSNER, CHIEF JUDGE. [In 1991, Ivan Rodriguez, a highly successful catcher with the Texas Rangers baseball team, signed the first of several one-year, terminable-at-will contracts with Speakers of Sports, an agency representing professional athletes. Hoping to lure Rodriguez away from Speakers, in 1995, ProServ, another sports agency, invited Rodriguez to its offices and promised to get him between $2 and $4 million in endorsements if he signed with them. Rodriguez signed, although ProServ failed to get him any significant endorsements and one year later he switched to still another agent who landed him a five-year, $42 million contract with the Rangers. Speakers then brought suit against ProServ, charging that their promise of endorsements to Rodriguez was fraudulent and had induced him to terminate his contract with Speakers. The trial court granted ProServ's motion for summary judgment, and Speakers appealed. One question before the appellate court concerned the legal characterization of ProServ's promises to Rodriguez.]

There is in general nothing wrong with one sports agent trying to take a client from another if this can be done without precipitating a breach of contract. That is the process known as competition, which though painful, fierce, frequently ruthless, sometimes Darwinian in its pitilessness, is the cornerstone of our highly successful economic system. Competition is not a tort, Keeble v. Hickeringill, 11 East. 574, 103 Eng. Rep. 1127 (K.B. 1706 or 1707) [citations omitted], but on the contrary provides a defense (the "competitor's privilege") to the tort of improper interference.

There would be few more effective inhibitors of the competitive process than making it a tort for an agent to promise the client of another agent to do better by him, Triangle Film Corp. v. Artcraft Pictures Corp., 250 F. 981 (2d Cir. 1918) (L. Hand, J.)—which is pretty much what this case comes down to. It is true that Speakers argues only that the competitor may not make a promise that he knows he cannot fulfill, may not, that is, compete by fraud. Because the competitor's privilege does not include a right to get business from a competitor by means of fraud, it is hard to quarrel with this position in the abstract, but the practicalities are different. If the argument were accepted and the new agent made a promise that was not fulfilled, the old agent would have a shot at convincing a jury that the new agent had known from the start that he couldn't deliver on the promise. Once a case gets to the jury, all bets are off. The practical consequence of Speakers' approach, therefore, would be that a sports agent who lured away the client of another agent with a promise to do better by him would be running a grave legal risk.

The promise of endorsements was puffing not in the most common sense of a cascade of extravagant adjectives but in the equally valid sense of a sales pitch that is intended, and that a reasonable person in the position of the "promisee" would understand, to be aspirational rather than enforceable—an expression of hope rather than a commitment. It is not as if ProServ proposed to employ Rodriguez and pay him $2 million a year. That would be the kind of promise that could found an enforceable obligation. ProServ proposed merely to get him endorsements of at least that amount. They would of course be paid by the companies whose products Rodriguez endorsed, rather than by ProServ. ProServ could not force them to pay Rodriguez, and it is not contended that he understood ProServ to be warranting a minimum level of endorsements in the sense that if they were not forthcoming ProServ would be legally obligated to make up the difference to him.

It is possible to make a binding promise of something over which one has no control; such a promise is called a warranty. All-Tech Telecom, Inc. v. Amway Corp., supra, 174 F.3d at 868–69; L.S. Heath & Son, Inc.

v. AT & T Information Systems, Inc., 9 F.3d 561, 570 (7th Cir. 1993); Metropolitan Coal Co. v. Howard, 155 F.2d 780, 784 (2d Cir. 1946) (L. Hand, J.); Restatement (Second) of Contracts § 2 and comment d (1981); Oliver Wendell Holmes, Jr., The Common Law 298–301 (1881). But it is not plausible that this is what ProServ was doing—that it was guaranteeing Rodriguez a minimum of $2 million a year in outside earnings if he signed with it. The only reasonable meaning to attach to ProServ's so-called promise is that ProServ would try to get as many endorsements as possible for Rodriguez and that it was optimistic that it could get him at least $2 million worth of them. So understood, the "promise" was not a promise at all. But even if it was a promise (or a warranty), it cannot be the basis for a finding of fraud because it was not part of a scheme to defraud evidenced by more than the allegedly fraudulent promise itself.

Affirmed.

NOTE

The court distinguished between puffing, fraud, promissory fraud, and misrepresentation. What are these distinctions? Why didn't Speakers sue Rodriguez for breach of contract? What might Speakers have been seeking in damages? For all there is to say about puffing, see David A. Hoffman, *The Best Puffery Article Ever*, 91 Iowa L. Rev. 1395 (2006).

Vokes v. Arthur Murray, Inc.

District Court of Appeal of Florida, Second District, 1968.
212 So.2d 906.

■ PIERCE, JUDGE. Plaintiff Mrs. Audrey E. Vokes, a widow of 51 years and without family, had a yen to be "an accomplished dancer" with the hopes of finding "new interest in life." So, on February 10, 1961, a dubious fate, with the assist of a motivated acquaintance, procured her to attend a "dance party" at Davenport's "School of Dancing" where she whiled away the pleasant hours, sometimes in a private room, absorbing the accomplished sales technique [of J.P. Davenport, the owner of the Arthur Murray franchise], during which her grace and poise were elaborated upon and her rosy future as "an excellent dancer" was painted for her in vivid and glowing colors. As an incident to this interlude, he sold her eight ½-hour dance lessons to be utilized within one calendar month therefrom, for the sum of $14.50 cash in hand paid, obviously a baited "come-on."

Thus she embarked upon an almost endless pursuit of the terpsichorean art during which, over a period of less than sixteen months, she was sold fourteen "dance courses" totaling in the aggregate 2302 hours of dancing lessons for a total cash outlay of $31,090.45, all at Davenport's dance emporium.

These dance lesson contracts and the monetary consideration therefor of over $31,000 were procured from her by means and methods of Davenport and his associates which went beyond the unsavory, yet legally permissible, perimeter of "sales puffing" and intruded well into the forbidden area of undue influence, the suggestion of falsehood, the suppression of truth, and the free exercise of rational judgment, if what plaintiff alleged in her complaint was true. From the time of her first contact with the dancing school in February, 1961, she was influenced unwittingly by a constant and continuous barrage of flattery, false praise, excessive compliments, and panegyric encomiums, to such extent that it would be not only inequitable, but unconscionable, for a Court exercising inherent chancery power to allow such contracts to stand.

She was incessantly subjected to overreaching blandishment and cajolery. She was assured she had "grace and poise"; that she was "rapidly improving and developing in her dancing skill"; that the additional lessons would "make her a beautiful dancer, capable of dancing with the most accomplished dancers"; that she was "rapidly progressing in the development of her dancing skill and gracefulness," etc., etc. She was given "dance aptitude tests" for the ostensible purpose of "determining" the number of remaining hours instructions needed by her from time to time.

[The court described a succession of contracts Vokes signed for more and more lessons to be added onto the hundred of unused lessons she had already purchased, each contract induced by the promise of eligibility for such awards as a "Gold Medal" for achievement.]

All the foregoing sales promotions, illustrative of the entire fourteen separate contracts, were procured by defendant Davenport and Arthur Murray, Inc., by false representations to her that she was improving in her dancing ability, that she had excellent potential, that she was responding to instructions in dancing grace, and that they were developing her into a beautiful dancer, whereas in truth and in fact she did not develop in her dancing ability, she had no "dance aptitude," and in fact had difficulty in "hearing that musical beat." The complaint alleged that such representations to her "were in fact false and known by the defendant to be false and contrary to the plaintiff's true ability, the truth of plaintiff's ability being fully known to the defendants, but withheld from the plaintiff for the sole and specific intent to deceive and defraud the plaintiff and to induce her in the purchasing of additional hours of dance lessons."

[The trial court held that the complaint failed to state a cause of action and dismissed it with prejudice.]

The material allegations of the complaint must, of course, be accepted as true for the purpose of testing its legal sufficiency. Defendants contend that contracts can only be rescinded for fraud or misrepresentation when the alleged misrepresentation is as to a material fact, rather than an opinion, prediction or expectation, and that the statements and representations set forth at length in the complaint were in the category of "trade puffing," within its legal orbit.

It is true that "generally a misrepresentation, to be actionable, must be one of fact rather than of opinion." Tonkovich v. South Florida Citrus Industries, Inc., Fla.App.1966, 185 So.2d 710; Kutner v. Kalish, Fla.App.1965, 173 So.2d 763. But this rule has significant qualifications, applicable here. It does not apply where there is a fiduciary relationship between the parties, or where there has been some artifice or trick employed by the representor, or where the parties do not in general deal at "arm's length" as we understand the phrase, or where the representee does not have equal opportunity to become apprised of the truth or falsity of the fact represented. As stated by Judge Allen of this Court in Ramel v. Chasebrook Construction Company, Fla.App.1961, 135 So.2d 876:

> "... A statement of a party having ... superior knowledge may be regarded as a statement of fact although it would be considered as opinion if the parties were dealing on equal terms."

It could be reasonably supposed here that defendants had "superior knowledge" as to whether plaintiff had "dance potential" and as to whether she was noticeably improving in the art of terpsichore. ...

Even in contractual situations where a party to a transaction owes no duty to disclose facts within his knowledge or to answer inquiries respecting such facts, the law is if he undertakes to do so he must disclose the whole truth. Ramel v. Chasebrook Construction Company, supra; Beagle v. Bagwell, Fla.App.1964, 169 So.2d 43. From the face of the complaint, it should have been reasonably apparent to defendants that her vast outlay of cash for the many hundreds of additional hours of instruction was not justified by her slow and awkward progress, which she would have been made well aware of if they had spoken the "whole truth."

We repeat that where parties are dealing on a contractual basis at arm's length with no inequities or inherently unfair practices employed, the Courts will in general "leave the parties where they find themselves." But in the case sub judice, from the allegations of the unanswered complaint, we cannot say that enough of the accompanying ingredients, as mentioned in the foregoing authorities, were not present which otherwise would have barred the equitable arm of the Court to her. In our view, from the showing made in her complaint, plaintiff is entitled to her day in Court.

It accordingly follows that the order dismissing plaintiff's last amended complaint with prejudice should be and is reversed.

NOTES

(1) *Questions.* How do the representations made to Vokes differ from those made to Kannavos (p. 473)? How did the court overcome the traditional rule limiting misrepresentations to statement of facts?

(2) *Mrs. Vokes's Pursuits.* What exactly about the transaction between Mrs. Vokes and Arthur Murray is objectionable? That Vokes paid to be flattered? That she paid too much to be flattered? That she bought worthless services? What factors (and language) did the court array to entitle Vokes to the court's "equitable arm"? Is anything about the decision itself objectionable? Does Judge Pierce's description of the facts contain a hint of "insinuendo"? In what sense was Vokes's initial presence "procured"? If Vokes had been employed at the time she signed up for the dancing lessons, and had at that time elected an irrevocable pension option, would grounds exist to set aside her election, should it later prove improvident? See *Ortelere*, p. 426, above.

What mechanisms are appropriate for policing what one scholar has called the "grotesque" bargain in *Vokes*? See Robert Gordon, *Unfreezing Legal Realities: Critical Approaches to Law*, 15 Fla. St. U. L. Rev. 195 (1987). California, among other states, has enacted a Dance Studio Act providing that any contract for dancing lessons entered into "in reliance upon any willful and false . . . or misleading information . . . shall be void and unenforceable." Cal. Civ. Code § 1812.60 (West 1969). It also requires that "[e]very contract for dance studio lessons . . . shall provide that performance of the agreed-upon lessons will begin within six months from the date the contract is entered into." Cal.Civ. Code § 1812.54. In People v. Arthur Murray, Inc., 47 Cal. Rptr. 700 (Ct. App. 1965), the court upheld the Act against a constitutional challenge, stating that special regulation was appropriate in a "class of business so habitually fraught with fraud and sharp practices."

CHAPTER 5

DETERMINING THE PARTIES' OBLIGATIONS UNDER THE CONTRACT

To this point, this book has primarily examined the law governing the creation of enforceable contracts: Has there been assent? Are the parties' promises supported by consideration? Is the agreement evidenced by a writing or other record if required by the Statute of Frauds? Has the bargaining process been unobjectionable? Little attention has been paid, however, to the legal system's determination of what obligations the parties have incurred by virtue of their agreement. That subject—determining the obligations of the parties under their contract—is the focus of this chapter.

Not surprisingly, the starting point for determining the obligations of the parties to a contract is their language. One might expect that the words of the parties would also be the ending point, that the obligations of the parties are ascertained by a court simply applying their words. But this puts too much faith in the parties' ability (or desire) to "put it all in writing" or "get it all down." Even when parties reduce their agreement to writing, they may omit some terms or express others unclearly. How does such omission or imperfection in expressing the deal come about?

Part of the answer concerns the contracting process itself. Transactions come in all shapes and sizes. Some transactions are extensively negotiated and reduced to writing by attorneys who produce draft documents that have been extensively vetted by both sides before being finalized. Considerable time and effort are expended on these transactions to assure that all matters agreed to during negotiations are detailed in the documents. Notwithstanding the time and effort, these documents are (for the reasons considered at p. 328–329, above) imperfect or "incomplete" representations of the parties' agreement.

Even if more time and effort could perfect the document, many transactions are simply not worth the expense of intensive attorney involvement. Moreover, there is often insufficient time for such efforts to take place. Less formally negotiated transactions, where the parties themselves create a writing or use a previously prepared form document, do not avoid the basic problem. In any case, when the parties reduce their agreement to writing (for certainty and evidentiary reasons as well as, perhaps, satisfying the Statute of Frauds), it is almost certain that some relevant matters discussed or negotiated will either not appear in the writing or be recorded imperfectly therein.

Omissions and imperfections in written agreements often go unnoticed, especially if the transaction is fully performed by both parties. But what happens when a dispute arises regarding an allegation that a term was agreed upon but not included in the writing? At that point, the party who would benefit from the allegedly agreed-upon term not reflected in the writing will seek to enforce it, while the other party (who may have a strategic incentive to fail to remember such an oral—also referred to as "parol"—agreement) may disagree that such an agreement was ever made. How does the law deal with such a dispute about terms allegedly agreed upon but not included in the writing?

Before addressing the question of omissions, consider a related issue of ambiguity. When parties reach a deal, their agreement is expressed in words. But words are only imperfect proxies for the ideas they represent. Sometimes the words used by the parties admit more than one meaning; for example, a word may have one meaning in general discourse and a special meaning in a particular business context. When a transaction has been reduced to writing and a dispute arises as to the meaning of what has been written down, should a court simply do its best to interpret the writing on its own? Or may the parties assist the court by providing extrinsic evidence—something outside the writing—regarding the meaning of the terms of the contract?

Similarly, there may be matters that were never explicitly discussed or negotiated but which were implicit, or so it is claimed, in the express agreement. What happens when a dispute arises and one party claims that, although the matter was not addressed in so many words in the agreement, it was included in the agreement even though it was never written or perhaps even expressed orally? The problem here is not differing assertions of the meaning of words used by the parties but, rather, differing assertions about matters that were implicit in the "deal" but never reduced to words. How does the law deal with such disputes?

These distinct problems—whether a writing fully reflects the parties' agreement and what the written terms mean—have one thing in common. In both cases, one or both of the parties may want to use facts outside the written document in order to determine the nature of the full agreement between them. To address the first problem—that of agreed-upon terms missing from the writing—contract doctrine elaborates a set of directives embodied in the so-called "parol evidence rule," which is the subject of the first section of this chapter. The second problem, concerning ambiguity, is dealt with using various rules of "contract interpretation," which are considered in Sections 2 and 3. Other matters addressed in this chapter include the use of extrinsic evidence to supplement or qualify the parties' agreement (Section 4), the limits of interpretation (Section 5), and supplemental contract terms supplied by law (Section 6).

SECTION 1.   THE PAROL EVIDENCE RULE

What should a court do when one party to a contract seeks to enforce a term allegedly agreed upon prior to or contemporaneously with the formation of the contract, but which does not appear in the writing reflecting the contract? One approach could be to treat the problem in the same way the court treats most other factual disputes: by hearing the evidence and ascertaining the facts. The evidence in such a case might consist of the writing, testimony of the parties, and other forms of evidence such as email or other correspondence between the parties. All of that evidence would go before the fact-finder, and none of it would have a privileged place in the proof process. The fact finder would then decide, based on the entirety of the evidence, whether the assertion that the term was agreed to is true.

For the most part, the law of contract has *not* taken that path. Instead, one of the more challenging rules in contract law, the "parol evidence rule," has evolved to address this issue. The parol evidence rule may preclude a determination that an agreement made prior to or contemporaneously with the writing—but not reflected in it—is part of the contract. The rule is not aptly named. Although called a rule of "parol" evidence, it is not limited to oral agreements, but also operates to exclude writings, such as letters or emails, as well. Nor is it, strictly speaking, a rule of "evidence" (such as the hearsay rule) that bars admissibility of certain types of evidence to prove an ultimate matter of fact. Rather the parol evidence rule is a rule of substantive law that, when it applies, precludes any proof that the terms of the contract are other than as expressed in the writing.

As the cases demonstrate, courts applying the parol evidence rule consider a number of factors including whether the asserted term is within the scope of the writing or, rather, is "collateral" to it, whether the asserted term contradicts the writing, whether the writing appears to be the parties' final expression with respect to the matters it addresses, and whether the parties intended the writing to embody all the terms of their transaction.

The rule is also controversial. In England, the Law Commission called it "a technical rule of uncertain ambit which, at best, adds to the complications of litigation without affecting the outcome and, at worst, prevents the courts from getting at the truth." The Law Commission, *Law of Contract, The Parol Evidence Rule 25*, Working Paper No. 70 (1976). The Commission's provisional recommendation that the rule be abolished was not, however, carried out.

Others have defended the rule. "The parol evidence rule is maligned in some circles as the vestige of an era when judges were hostile to plaintiffs and mistrusted juries, and thus as an arbitrary barrier to getting at the truth. But it has stubbornly refused to die and in fact it serves an important social purpose. Not all parties to contracts want to entrust their fate to the vagaries of juries unversed in the usages of business. . . . " Olympia Hotels Corp. v. Johnson Wax Dev. Corp., 908 F.2d 1363, 1373 (7th Cir. 1990) (Posner, J.).

NOTE

Rule of Substantive Law. Characterizing the parol evidence rule as "substantive" has some important practical consequences. Here are two.

First, in our adversary trial system it is traditionally the responsibility of the party seeking to preclude the admission of evidence to make timely objection to its admission in order to give the trial judge an opportunity to rule before the evidence is admitted. Failure to object is ordinarily a waiver of any ground of complaint against admission, and the evidence becomes part of the proof in the case. By way of contrast, a failure to object to evidence that would establish the existence of an agreement not reflected in the writing does not bar a later assertion of the parol evidence rule. Gajewski v. Bratcher, 221 N.W.2d 614 (N.D. 1974).

Second, in our federal court system, under the *Erie* doctrine, federal courts apply state substantive law "to any issue or claim which has its source in state law." C. Wright, A. Miller and E. Cooper, 19 *Federal Prac. & Proc. Juris.* § 4520 (3d ed. 2010). Thus, a federal court adjudicating a state law claim must apply the parol evidence rule of the appropriate state. Betz Labs., Inc. v. Hines, 647 F.2d 402 (3d Cir. 1981).

Mitchill v. Lath

Court of Appeals of New York, 1928.
247 N.Y. 377, 160 N.E. 646.

■ ANDREWS, JUDGE. In the fall of 1923 the Laths owned a farm. This they wished to sell. Across the road, on land belonging to Lieutenant Governor Lunn, they had an icehouse which they might remove. Mrs. Mitchill looked over the land with a view to its purchase. She found the icehouse objectionable. Thereupon the defendants orally promised and agreed, for and in consideration of the purchase of their farm by the plaintiff, to remove the said icehouse in the spring of 1924. Relying upon this promise, she made a written contract to buy the property for $8,400, for cash and mortgage and containing various provisions usual in such papers. Later receiving a deed, she entered into possession, and has spent considerable sums in improving the property for use as a summer residence. The defendants have not fulfilled their promise as to the icehouse, and do not intend to do so. We are not dealing, however, with their moral delinquencies. The question before us is whether their oral agreement may be enforced in a court of equity.

This requires a discussion of the parol evidence rule—a rule of law which defines the limits of the contract to be construed. It is more than a rule of evidence, and oral testimony, even if admitted, will not control the written contract unless admitted without objection. It applies, however, to attempts to modify such a contract by parol. It does not affect a parol collateral contract distinct from and independent of the written agreement. It is, at times, troublesome to draw the line. Williston, in his work on Contracts (section 637) points out the difficulty. 'Two entirely distinct contracts,' he says, 'each for a separate consideration, may be made at the same time, and will be distinct legally. Where, however, one agreement is entered into wholly or partly in consideration of the simultaneous agreement to enter into another, the transactions are necessarily bound together. * * * Then if one of the agreements is oral and the other in writing, the problem arises whether the bond is sufficiently close to prevent proof of the oral agreement.' That is the situation here. It is claimed that the defendants are called upon to do more than is required by their written contract in connection with the sale as to which it deals.

The principle may be clear, but it can be given effect by no mechanical rule. As so often happens it is a matter of degree, for, as Prof. Williston also says, where a contract contains several promises on each side it is not difficult to put any one of them in the form of a collateral agreement. If this were enough, written contracts might always be modified by parol. Not form, but substance, is the test.

In applying this test, the policy of our courts is to be considered. We have believed that the purpose behind the rule was a wise one, not easily to be abandoned. Notwithstanding injustice here and there, on the whole it works for good. Old precedents and principles are not to be lightly cast aside, unless it is certain that they are an obstruction under present conditions. New York has been less open to arguments that would modify this particular rule, than some jurisdictions elsewhere. Thus in Eighmie v. Taylor, 98 N. Y. 288, it was held that a parol warranty might not be shown, although no warranties were contained in the writing.

Under our decisions, before such an oral agreement as the present is received to vary the written contract, at least three conditions must exist: (1) The agreement must in form be a collateral one; (2) it must not contradict express or implied provisions of the written contract; (3) it must be one that parties would not ordinarily be expected to embody in the writing, or, put in another way, an inspection of the written contract, read in the light of surrounding circumstances, must not indicate that the writing appears 'to contain the engagements of the parties, and to define the object and measure the extent of such engagement.' Or, again, it must not be so clearly connected with the principal transaction as to be part and parcel of it.

The respondent does not satisfy the third of these requirements. It may be, not the second. We have a written contract for the purchase and sale of land. The buyer is to pay $8,400 in the way described. She is also to pay her portion of any rents, interest on mortgages, insurance premiums, and water meter charges. She may have a survey made of the premises. On their part, the sellers are to give a full covenant deed of the premises as described, or as they may be described by the surveyor, if the survey is had, executed, and acknowledged at their own expense; they sell the personal property on the farm and represent they own it; they agree that all amounts paid them on the contract and the expense of examining the title shall be a lien on the property; they assume the risk of loss or damage by fire until the deed is delivered; and they agree to pay the broker his commissions. Are they to do more? Or is such a claim inconsistent with these precise provisions? It could not be shown that the plaintiff was to pay $500 additional. Is it also implied that the defendants are not to do anything unexpressed in the writing?

That we need not decide. At least, however, an inspection of this contract shows a full and complete agreement, setting forth in detail the obligations of each party. On reading it, one would conclude that the reciprocal obligations of the parties were fully detailed. Nor would his opinion alter if he knew the surrounding circumstances. The presence of the icehouse, even the knowledge that Mrs. Mitchill thought it objectionable, would not lead to the belief that a separate agreement existed with regard to it. Were such an agreement made it would seem most natural that the inquirer should find it in the contract. Collateral in form it is found to be, but it is closely related to the subject dealt with in the written agreement—so closely that we hold it may not be proved.

■ LEHMAN, JUDGE. (dissenting). I accept the general rule as formulated by Judge Andrews. I differ with him only as to its application to the facts shown in the record. The plaintiff contracted to purchase land from the defendants for an agreed price. A formal written agreement was made between the sellers and the plaintiff's husband. It is on its face a complete contract for the conveyance of the land. It describes the property to be conveyed. It sets forth the purchase price to be paid. All the conditions and terms of the conveyance to be made are clearly stated. I concede at the outset that parol evidence to show additional conditions and terms of the conveyance would be inadmissible. There is a conclusive presumption that the parties intended to integrate in that written contract every agreement relating to the nature or extent of the property to be conveyed, the contents of the deed to be delivered, the consideration to be paid as a condition precedent to the delivery of the deeds, and indeed all the rights of the parties in connection with the land. The conveyance of that land was the subject-matter of the written contract, and the contract completely covers that subject.

The parol agreement which the court below found the parties had made was collateral to, yet connected with, the agreement of purchase and sale. It has been found that the defendants induced the plaintiff to agree to purchase the land by a promise to remove an icehouse from land not covered by the agreement of purchase and sale. No independent consideration passed to the defendants for the parol promise. To that extent the written contract and the alleged oral contract are bound together. The same bond usually exists wherever attempt is made to prove a parol agreement which is collateral to a written agreement. Hence 'the problem arises whether the bond is sufficiently close to prevent proof of the oral agreement.' See Judge Andrews' citation from Williston on Contracts, § 637.

Judge Andrews has formulated a standard to measure the closeness of the bond. Three conditions, at least, must exist before an oral agreement may be proven to increase the obligation imposed by the written agreement. I think we agree that the first condition that the agreement 'must in form be a collateral one' is met by the evidence. I concede that this condition is met in most cases where the courts have nevertheless excluded evidence of the collateral oral agreement. The difficulty here, as in most cases, arises in connection with the two other conditions.

The second condition is that the 'parol agreement must not contradict express or implied provisions of the written contract.' Judge Andrews voices doubt whether this condition is satisfied. The written contract has been carried out. The purchase price has been paid; conveyance has been made; title has passed in accordance with the terms of the written contract. The mutual obligations expressed in the written contract are left unchanged by the alleged oral contract. When performance was required of the written contract, the obligations of the parties were measured solely by its terms. By the oral agreement the plaintiff seeks to hold the defendants to other obligations to be performed by them thereafter upon land which was not conveyed to the plaintiff. The assertion of such further obligation is not inconsistent with the written contract, unless the written contract contains a provision, express or implied, that the defendants are not to do anything not expressed in the writing. Concededly there is no such express provision in the contract, and such a provision may be implied, if at all, only if the asserted additional obligation is 'so clearly connected with the principal transaction as to be part and parcel of it,' and is not 'one that the parties would not ordinarily be expected to embody in the writing.' The hypothesis so formulated for a conclusion that the asserted additional obligation is inconsistent with an implied term of the contract is that the alleged oral agreement does not comply with the third condition as formulated by Judge Andrews. In this case, therefore, the problem reduces itself to the one question whether or not the oral agreement meets the third condition.

I have conceded that upon inspection the contract is complete. 'It appears to contain the engagements of the parties, and to define the object and measure the extent of such engagement;' it constitutes the contract between them, and is presumed to contain the whole of that contract. That engagement was on the one side to convey land; on the other to pay the price. The plaintiff asserts further agreement based on the same consideration to be performed by the defendants after the conveyance was complete, and directly affecting only other land. It is true, as Judge Andrews points out, that 'the presence of the icehouse, even the knowledge that Mrs. Mitchill thought it objectionable, would not lead to the belief that a separate agreement existed with regard to it'; but the question we must decide is whether or not, *assuming* an agreement was made for the removal of an unsightly icehouse from one parcel of land as an inducement for the purchase of another parcel, the parties would ordinarily or naturally be expected to embody the agreement for the removal of the icehouse from one parcel in the written agreement to convey the other parcel. Exclusion of proof of the oral agreement on the ground that it varies the contract embodied in the writing may be based only upon a finding or presumption that the written contract was intended to cover the oral negotiations for the removal of the icehouse which lead up to the contract of purchase and sale. To determine what the writing was intended to cover, 'the document alone will not suffice. What it was intended to cover cannot be known till we know what there was to cover. The question being whether certain subjects of negotiation were intended to be covered, we must compare the writing and the negotiations before we can determine whether they were in fact covered.' Wigmore on Evidence (2d Ed.) § 2430.

The subject-matter of the written contract was the conveyance of land. The contract was so complete on its face that the conclusion is inevitable that the parties intended to embody in the writing all the negotiations covering at least the conveyance. The promise by the defendants to remove the icehouse from other land was not connected with their obligation to convey except that one agreement would not have been made unless the other was also made. The plaintiff's assertion of a parol agreement by the defendants to remove the icehouse was completely established by the great weight of evidence. It must prevail unless that agreement was part of the agreement to convey and the entire agreement was embodied in the writing.

The fact that in this case the parol agreement is established by the overwhelming weight of evidence is, of course, not a factor which may be considered in determining the competency or legal effect of the evidence. Hardship in the particular case would not justify the court in disregarding or emasculating the general rule. It merely accentuates the outlines of our problem. The assumption that the parol agreement was made is no longer obscured by any doubts. The problem, then, is clearly whether the parties are presumed to have intended to render that parol agreement legally ineffective and nonexistent by failure to embody it in the writing. Though we are driven to say that nothing in the written contract which fixed the terms and conditions of the stipulated conveyance suggests the existence of any further parol agreement, an inspection of the contract, though it is complete on its face in regard to the subject of the conveyance, does not, I think, show that it was intended to embody negotiations or agreements, if any, in regard to a matter so loosely bound to the conveyance as the removal of an icehouse from land not conveyed.

The rule of integration undoubtedly frequently prevents the assertion of fraudulent claims. Parties who take the precaution of embodying their oral agreements in a writing should be protected against the assertion that other terms of the same agreement were not integrated in the writing. The limits of the integration are determined by the writing, read in the light of the surrounding circumstances. A written contract, however complete, yet covers only a limited field. I do not think that in the written contract for the conveyance of land here under consideration we can find an intention to cover a field so broad as to include prior agreements, if any such were made, to do other acts on other property after the stipulated conveyance was made.

In each case where such a problem is presented, varying factors enter into its solution. Citation of authority in this or other jurisdictions is useless, at least without minute analysis of the facts. The analysis I have made of the decisions in this state leads me to the view that the decision of the courts below is in accordance with our own authorities and should be affirmed.

NOTES

(1) *Fact-Finding Versus Preclusion.* One could imagine a fact-finder, after considering all relevant evidence, concluding that Mrs. Mitchill had not proved that the Laths had agreed to remove the icehouse. The opinion of Judge Andrews, though, ends with the statement that the agreement "may not be proved." What is the significance of that difference?

(2) *Rationale.* What are the reasons behind the parol evidence rule? One rationale is that, as Restatement § 213 puts it, the later agreement "discharges prior agreements." Viewed in this way, the rule simply affirms the primacy of a subsequent agreement not only over prior negotiations, which would not be binding in any case, but also over prior agreements, which, though they would be binding, are discharged. See generally Farnsworth on Contracts § 7.2.

Many of the older cases, however, evince a different rationale. As the opinion in the next case explains, Dean Charles McCormick, an expert on the law of evidence, "suggested that the party urging the spoken as against the written word is most often the economic underdog, threatened by severe hardship if the writing is enforced." He argued that the "rule arose to allow the court to control the tendency of the jury to find through sympathy and without a dispassionate assessment of the probability of fraud or faulty memory that the parties made an oral agreement collateral to the written contract, or that the preliminary tentative agreements were not abandoned when omitted from the writing." Does this rationale seem applicable to *Mitchill*? Does it explain why the rule bars prior *writings*? Does it explain why the rule does not bar *subsequent* oral agreements?

(3) *"Integrated" Agreements and the Restatement.* Although Professor James Bradley Thayer said of the parol evidence rule that, "Few things are darker than this, or fuller of subtle difficulties," application of the rule is clarified considerably by the scheme adopted by the Restatement. It involves two steps to be followed by the court. See Restatement §§ 209(2), 210(3).

The first step is to see whether a writing has been adopted by the parties as "a *final* expression of one or more terms of an agreement." If there is no such writing, the rule does not apply. If there is such a writing, the agreement is known as an "integrated agreement," with the consequence that "evidence of prior . . . agreements or negotiations is not admissible in evidence to contradict a term of the writing." Restatement §§ 209, 215.

If there is an integrated agreement, so that the rule applies, the second step is to determine whether the writing has been "adopted by the parties as a *complete* and *exclusive* statement of the terms of the agreement." If this is not the case, the agreement is known as a "partially integrated agreement" and the rule has only the effect described in the previous paragraph. If the writing was adopted as a complete and exclusive statement of the terms of the agreement, however, the agreement is referred to as a "completely integrated agreement," with the additional consequence that evidence even of "a consistent additional term" is not admissible to supplement the written agreement to the extent that the additional term is within the scope of the written agreement. Restatement §§ 210, 216. Such evidence is, however, admissible if the writing is only a "partially integrated agreement."

Masterson v. Sine

Supreme Court of California, 1968.
68 Cal.2d 222, 436 P.2d 561.

■ TRAYNOR, CHIEF JUSTICE. Dallas Masterson and his wife Rebecca owned a ranch as tenants in common. On February 25, 1958, they conveyed it to Medora and Lu Sine by a grant deed. "Reserving unto the Grantors herein an option to purchase the above described property on or before February 25, 1968" for the "same consideration as being paid heretofore plus their depreciation value of any improvements Grantees may add to the property from and after two and a half years from this date." Medora is Dallas' sister and Lu's wife. Since the conveyance Dallas has been adjudged bankrupt. His trustee in bankruptcy and Rebecca brought this declaratory relief action to establish their right to enforce the option.

The case was tried without a jury. Over defendants' objection the trial court admitted extrinsic evidence that by "the same consideration as being paid heretofore" both the grantors and the grantees meant the sum of $50,000 and by "depreciation value of any improvements" they meant the depreciation value of improvements to be computed by deducting from the total amount of any capital expenditures made by defendants['] grantees the amount of depreciation allowable to them under United States income tax regulations as of the time of the exercise of the option.

The court also determined that the parol evidence rule precluded admission of extrinsic evidence offered by defendants to show that the parties wanted the property kept in the Masterson family and that the option was therefore personal to the grantors and could not be exercised by the trustee in bankruptcy.

The court entered judgment for plaintiffs, declaring their right to exercise the option, specifying in some detail how it could be exercised, and reserving jurisdiction to supervise the manner of its exercise and to determine the amount that plaintiffs will be required to pay defendants for their capital expenditures if plaintiffs decide to exercise the option.

Defendants appeal. They contend that the option provision is too uncertain to be enforced and that extrinsic evidence as to its meaning should not have been admitted. The trial court properly refused to frustrate the obviously declared intention of the grantors to reserve an option to repurchase by an overly meticulous insistence on completeness and clarity of written expression. It properly admitted extrinsic evidence to explain the language of the deed to the end that the consideration for the option would appear with sufficient certainty to permit specific enforcement. The trial court erred, however, in excluding the extrinsic evidence that the option was personal to the grantors and therefore nonassignable.

When the parties to a written contract have agreed to it as an "integration"—a complete and final embodiment of the terms of an agreement—parol evidence cannot be used to add to or vary its terms. When only part of the agreement is integrated, the same rule applies to that part, but parol evidence may be used to prove elements of the agreement not reduced to writing.

The crucial issue in determining whether there has been an integration is whether the parties intended their writing to serve as the exclusive embodiment of their agreement. The instrument itself may help to resolve that issue. It may state, for example, that "there are no previous understandings or agreements not contained in the writing," and thus express the parties' "intention to nullify antecedent understandings or agreements." (See 3 Corbin, *Contracts* (1960) § 578, p. 411.) Any such collateral agreement itself must be examined, however, to determine whether the parties intended the subjects of negotiation it deals with to be included in, excluded from, or otherwise affected by the writing. Circumstances at the time of the writing may also aid in the determination of such integration. . . .

California cases have stated that whether there was an integration is to be determined solely from the face of the instrument and that the question for the court is whether it "appears to be a complete . . . agreement." See Ferguson v. Koch, 268 P. 342, 344 (Cal. 1928). Neither of these strict formulations of the rule, however, has been consistently applied. The requirement that the writing must appear incomplete on its face has been repudiated in many cases where parol evidence was admitted "to prove the existence of a separate oral agreement as to any matter on which the document is silent and which is not inconsistent with its terms"—even though the instrument appeared to state a complete agreement. Even under the rule that the writing alone is to be consulted, it was found necessary to examine the alleged collateral agreement before concluding that proof of it was precluded by the writing alone. (See 3 Corbin, Contracts (1960) § 582, pp. 444–446.) It is therefore evident that "The conception of a writing as wholly and intrinsically self-determinative of the parties' intent to make it a sole memorial of one or seven or twenty-seven subjects of negotiation is an impossible one." (9 Wigmore, Evidence (3d ed. 1940) § 2431, p. 103.) For example, a promissory note given by a debtor to his creditor may integrate all their present contractual rights and obligations, or it may be only a minor part of an underlying executory contract that would never be discovered by examining the face of the note.

In formulating the rule governing parol evidence, several policies must be accommodated. One policy is based on the assumption that written evidence is more accurate than human memory. This policy, however, can be adequately served by excluding parol evidence of agreements that directly contradict the writing. Another policy is based on the fear that fraud or unintentional invention by witnesses interested in the outcome of the litigation will mislead the finder of facts. (Mitchill v. Lath, 160 N.E. 646 (N.Y. 1928)). McCormick has suggested that the party urging the spoken as against the written word is most often the economic underdog, threatened by severe hardship if the writing is enforced. In his view the parol evidence rule arose to allow the court to control the tendency of the jury to find through sympathy and without a dispassionate assessment of the probability of fraud or faulty memory that the parties made an oral agreement collateral to the written contract, or that preliminary tentative agreements were not abandoned when omitted from the writing. (See McCormick, Evidence (1954) § 210.) He recognizes, however, that if this theory were adopted in disregard of all other considerations, it would lead to the exclusion of testimony concerning oral agreements whenever there is a writing and thereby often defeat the true intent of the parties. (See McCormick, op. cit. supra, § 216, p. 441.)

Evidence of oral collateral agreements should be excluded only when the fact finder is likely to be misled. The rule must therefore be based on the credibility of the evidence. One such standard, adopted by section 240(1)(b) of the Restatement of Contracts, permits proof of a collateral agreement if it "is such an agreement as might *naturally* be made as a separate agreement by parties situated as were the parties to the written contract." (Italics added; see McCormick, Evidence (1954) § 216, p. 441;

see also 3 Corbin, Contracts (1960) § 583, p. 475, § 594, pp. 568–569; 4 Williston, Contracts (3d ed. 1961) § 638, pp. 1039–1045.) The draftsmen of the Uniform Commercial Code would exclude the evidence in still fewer instances: "If the additional terms are such that, if agreed upon, they would *certainly* have been included in the document in the view of the court, then evidence of their alleged making must be kept from the trier of fact." (Com. 3, § 2–202, italics added.)[1]

The option clause in the deed in the present case does not explicitly provide that it contains the complete agreement, and the deed is silent on the question of assignability. Moreover, the difficulty of accommodating the formalized structure of a deed to the insertion of collateral agreements makes it less likely that all the terms of such an agreement were included. The statement of the reservation of the option might well have been placed in the recorded deed solely to preserve the grantors' rights against any possible future purchasers and this function could well be served without any mention of the parties' agreement that the option was personal. There is nothing in the record to indicate that the parties to this family transaction, through experience in land transactions or otherwise, had any warning of the disadvantages of failing to put the whole agreement in the deed. This case is one, therefore, in which it can be said that a collateral agreement such as that alleged "might naturally be made as a separate agreement." *A fortiori,* the case is not one in which the parties "would certainly" have included the collateral agreement in the deed.

It is contended, however, that an option agreement is ordinarily presumed to be assignable if it contains no provisions forbidding its transfer or indicating that its performance involves elements personal to the parties. The fact that there is a written memorandum, however, does not necessarily preclude parol evidence rebutting a term that the law would otherwise presume.

In the present case defendants offered evidence that the parties agreed that the option was not assignable in order to keep the property in the Masterson family. The trial court erred in excluding that evidence.

The judgment is reversed.

■ PETERS, TOBRINER, MOSK, and SULLIVAN, JUSTICES, concur.

■ BURKE, JUSTICE (dissenting). I dissent. The majority opinion [u]ndermines the parol evidence rule as we have known it in this state since at least 1872 by declaring that parol evidence should have been

---

[1]   Corbin suggests that, even in situations where the court concludes that it would not have been natural for the parties to make the alleged collateral oral agreement, parol evidence of such an agreement should nevertheless be permitted if the court is convinced that the unnatural actually happened in the case being adjudicated. (3 Corbin, Contracts, § 485, pp. 478, 480; cf. Murray, *The Parol Evidence Rule: A Clarification* (1966) 4 Duquesne L.Rev. 337, 341–342.) This suggestion may be based on a belief that judges are not likely to be misled by their sympathies. If the court believes that the parties intended a collateral agreement to be effective, there is no reason to keep the evidence from the jury.

admitted by the trial court to show that a written option, absolute and unrestricted in form, was intended to be limited and nonassignable.

The opinion permits defendants to establish by parol testimony that their grant to their brother (and brother-in-law) of a written option, absolute in terms, was nevertheless agreed to be nonassignable by the grantee (now a bankrupt), and that therefore the right to exercise it did not pass, by operation of the bankruptcy laws, to the trustee for the benefit of the grantee's creditors. And how was this to be shown? By the proffered testimony of the bankrupt optionee himself! Thereby one of his assets (the option to purchase defendants' California ranch) would be withheld from the trustee in bankruptcy and from the bankrupt's creditors.

[T]here was nothing ambiguous about the *granting* language of the option and not the slightest suggestion in the document that the option was to be nonassignable. Thus, to permit such words of limitation to be added by parol is to *contradict* the absolute nature of the grant, and to directly violate the parol evidence rule.

Just as it is unnecessary to state in a deed to "lot X" that the house located thereon goes with the land, it is likewise unnecessary to add to "I grant an option to Jones" the words *"and his assigns"* for the option to be assignable. As hereinafter emphasized in more detail, California statutes expressly declare that it *is* assignable, and only if I add language in writing showing my intent to withhold or restrict the right of assignment may the grant be so limited. Thus, to seek to restrict the grant by parol is to *contradict* the written document in violation of the parol evidence rule.

The right of an optionee to transfer his option to purchase property is one of the basic rights which accompanies the option unless limited under the language of the option itself. To allow an optionor to resort to parol evidence to support his assertion that the written option is not transferable is to authorize him to limit the option by attempting to restrict and reclaim rights with which he has already parted. A clearer violation of two substantive and basic rules of law—the parol evidence rule and the right of free transferability of property—would be difficult to conceive.

In an effort to provide justification for applying the newly pronounced "natural" rule to the circumstances of the present case, the majority opinion next attempts to account for the silence of the writing in this case concerning assignability of the option, by asserting that "the difficulty of accommodating the formalized structure of a deed to the insertion of collateral agreements makes it less likely that all the terms of such an agreement were included." What difficulty would have been involved here, to add the words "this option is nonassignable"? The asserted "formalized structure of a deed" is no formidable barrier.

Comment hardly seems necessary on the convenience to a bankrupt of such a device to defeat his creditors. He need only produce parol testimony that any options (or other property, for that matter) which he holds are subject to an oral "collateral agreement" with family members (or with friends) that the property is nontransferable "in order to keep the property in the family" or in the friendly group. In the present case the value of the ranch which the bankrupt and his wife held an option to purchase has doubtless increased substantially during the years since they acquired the option. The initiation of this litigation by the trustee in bankruptcy to establish his right to enforce the option indicates his belief that there is substantial value to be gained for the creditors from this asset of the bankrupt. Yet the majority opinion permits defeat of the trustee and of the creditors through the device of an asserted collateral oral agreement that the option was "personal" to the bankrupt and nonassignable "in order to keep the property in the family"!

I would hold that the trial court ruled correctly on the proffered parol evidence, and would affirm the judgment.

■ McComb, Justice, concurs.

NOTES

(1) *Questions.* In Restatement terms, how did the agreement in *Masterson* differ from that in *Mitchill*? How did the dissenters in *Mitchill* and *Masterson* differ from the majority? Did Mitchill and the Sines seek to introduce extrinsic evidence to show "consistent additional terms"?

(2) *Test of Complete Integration.* To what may a court look in deciding how to characterize a writing under the parol evidence rule? Chief Justice Traynor referred to the "strict formulations of the rule" under which "whether there was an integration is to be determined solely from the face of the instrument and . . . the question for the court is whether it 'appears to be a complete . . . agreement.'" This view was favored in older cases, of which *Mitchill* appears to be an example. The view of the Restatement is somewhat different. See Comment *b* to Restatement § 210, which states that "a writing cannot of itself prove its own completeness, and wide latitude must be allowed for inquiry into circumstances bearing on the intention of the parties."

(3) *Merger Clauses.* Chief Justice Traynor observed that the "instrument may help to resolve" the issue of whether the agreement is completely integrated. It is a common practice to include in written contracts a clause known as a "merger," "integration," or "entire agreement" clause. Here are two examples:

> There are no promises, verbal understandings, or agreements of any kind, pertaining to this contract other than specified herein.

> This writing constitutes a complete and exclusive statement of all of the terms of our agreement.

Integration is a matter of the parties' intention, such clauses can provide strong evidence of that intention. But are such clauses conclusive? A survey of the cases shows a range of results, some making a merger clause conclusive, others not. Compare Howard v. Perry, 106 P.3d 465 (Idaho 2005) ("the merger clause is not merely a factor to consider in deciding whether the agreement is integrated; it proves the agreement is integrated") and Phelps-Dickson Builders v. Amerimann Partners, 617 S.E.2d 664 (N.C. App. 2005) ("the merger clause bars the parol evidence") with Jenkins v. Eckerd Corp., 913 So.2d 43 (Fla. App. 2005) ("Although the existence of a merger clause does not per se establish that the integration of the agreement is total . . . a merger clause is a highly persuasive statement that the parties intended the agreement to be totally integrated . . ."); Behrens v. S.P. Constr. Co., 904 A.2d 676 (N.H. 2006) ("Though not dispositive, an integration clause is evidence that parties intended a writing to be a total integration."); and Bellman v. Am. Int'l Group, 865 N.E.2d 853 (Ohio 2007) ("Whether a contract is integrated . . . is not dependent upon the existence of an integration clause to that effect, and '[t]he presence of an integration clause makes the final written agreement no more integrated than does the act of embodying the complete terms into the writing.'").

One would expect that the weight given to a merger clause would in any case vary with the circumstances of its use. In a contract between sophisticated parties, hammered out after many revisions by lawyers, a merger clause would logically get great weight. See, e.g., Telecom Int'l Am. v. AT&T Corp., 280 F.3d 175 (2d Cir. 2001) ("presumption of completeness is particularly strong where sophisticated parties have conducted extensive negotiations prior to entering into the agreement"). In the fine print of a form contract handed to an unsophisticated buyer, the clause might not reflect the reasonable expectations of both parties. See, e.g., Seibel v. Layne & Bowler, 641 P.2d 668 (Or. Ct. App. 1982) ("inconspicuous" merger clause "provides little or no evidence of the parties' intentions").

As to merger clauses in international commercial contracts, *see* UNIDROIT Principles art. 2.1.17.

(4) *Unconscionability.* As to whether a merger clause might be held to be unconscionable, see Franklin v. White, 493 N.E.2d 161, 165 (Ind. 1986), in which the court said that "there are rules adequately protecting against the unconscionable use of integration clauses."

(5) *"Collateral Agreements."* The fact that the parties have adopted a writing as an integration of one agreement has, of course, no effect on another, entirely separate agreement. Note that Chief Justice Traynor speaks of a "collateral agreement" in *Masterson*. What was that agreement? What was its consideration? Does the notion of a "collateral agreement," as he uses it, differ from that of "partial integration"?

Bollinger v. Central Pennsylvania Quarry Stripping and Construction Co.

Supreme Court of Pennsylvania, 1967.
425 Pa. 430, 229 A.2d 741

■ MUSMANNO, JUSTICE. Mahlon Bollinger and his wife, Vinetta C. Bollinger, filed an action in equity against the Central Pennsylvania Quarry Stripping Construction Company asking that a contract entered into between them be reformed so as to include therein a paragraph alleged to have been omitted by mutual mistake and that the agreement, as reformed, be enforced.

The agreement, as executed, provided that the defendant was to be permitted to deposit on the property of the plaintiffs, construction waste as it engaged in work on the Pennsylvania Turnpike in the immediate vicinity of the plaintiffs' property. The Bollingers claimed that there had been a mutual understanding between them and the defendant that, prior to depositing such waste on the plaintiffs' property, the defendant would remove the topsoil of the plaintiffs' property, pile on it the waste material and then restore the topsoil in a way to cover the deposited waste. The Bollingers averred that they had signed the written agreement without reading it because they assumed that the condition just stated had been incorporated into the writing.

When the defendant first began working in the vicinity of the plaintiffs' property, it did first remove the topsoil, deposited the waste on the bare land, and then replaced the topsoil. After a certain period of time, the defendant ceased doing this and the plaintiffs remonstrated. The defendant answered there was nothing in the written contract which required it to make a sandwich of its refuse between the bare earth and the topsoil. It was at this point that the plaintiffs discovered that that feature of the oral understanding had been omitted from the written contract. The plaintiff husband renewed his protest and the defendant's superintendent replied he could not remove the topsoil because his equipment for that operation had been taken away. When he was reminded of the original understanding, the superintendent said, in effect, he couldn't help that.

The plaintiffs then filed their action for reformation of the contract, the Court granted the requested relief, and the defendant firm appealed. We said in Bugen v. New York Life Insurance Co., 408 Pa. 472, 184 A.2d 499: "A court of equity has the power to reform the written evidence of a contract and make it correspond to the understanding of the parties. However, the mistake must be mutual to the parties to the contract." The fact, however, that one of the parties denies that a mistake was made does not prevent a finding of mutual mistake. Kutsenkow v. Kutsenkow, 414 Pa. 610, 612, 202 A.2d 68.

Once a person enters into a written agreement he builds around himself a stone wall, from which he cannot escape by merely asserting he had not understood what he was signing. However, equity would completely fail in its objectives if it refused to break a hole through the wall when it finds, after proper evidence, that there was a mistake between the parties, that it was real and not feigned, actual and not hypothetical.

The Chancellor, after taking testimony, properly concluded: "We are satisfied that plaintiffs have sustained the heavy burden placed upon them. Their understanding of the agreement is corroborated by the undisputed evidence. The defendant did remove and set aside the topsoil on part of the area before depositing its waste and did replace the topsoil over such waste after such depositing. It follows it would not have done so had it not so agreed. Further corroboration is found in the testimony that it acted similarly in the case of plaintiffs' neighbor Beltzner."

Decree affirmed, costs on the appellant.

NOTES

(1) *Questions.* How did the situation of the Bollingers differ from that of Mrs. Mitchill? What would Mrs. Mitchill have had to show in order to bring herself within the rule of *Bollinger*?

(2) *Validity of Agreement.* It is generally held that, since the parol evidence rule proceeds on the assumption that there is a written agreement, it does not bar extrinsic evidence to show that the written agreement is not valid. It does not, for example, preclude the use of extrinsic evidence to show that the writing was a sham, not intended to be enforced, or that a recital of a performance as consideration (*e.g.,* "in consideration of the payment of $10, receipt of which is hereby acknowledged") is false. See Restatement § 214(d).

(3) *Fraud.* For the reason suggested in the preceding note, it is also generally held that the parol evidence rule does not preclude the use of extrinsic evidence to show fraud in the inducement of the contract. See, e.g., Riverisland Cold Storage, Inc. v. Fresno-Madera Prod. Credit Ass'n, 291 P.3d 316 (2013). It is important in this respect to distinguish a claim that a party made a fraudulent representation during negotiations, consideration of which is not barred by the rule, from a claim that the party made an express warranty during negotiations, which is barred.

Similarly, the parol evidence rule does not preclude the use of extrinsic evidence to show promissory fraud (where a promisor makes a promise not intending to perform it). Lovejoy Electronics, Inc. v. O'Berto, 873 F.2d 1001 (7th Cir. 1989). *But see* Alling v. Universal Mfg. Corp., 7 Cal.Rptr.2d 718, 734 (Cal.App. 1992) (fraud exception does not apply unless "the false promise is either independent of or consistent with the written instrument").

Would a merger clause preclude the use of extrinsic evidence to show fraud? *See* Restatement § 214. *See also* Keller v. A.O. Smith Harvestore Prods., Inc., 819 P.2d 69, 73 (Colo. 1991) ("general integration clause does not effect a waiver of a claim of negligent misrepresentation not specifically prohibited by the terms of the agreement").

PROBLEM

Reformation of Bids. Ballard was the successful bidder on the Loving High School job. When the parties signed a written contract, they also executed a change order that modified the contract by deducting the cost of paving parking areas. The parties did not realize that this cost of paving had already been deducted from Ballard's total cost of construction in the contract, so that the result was a double deduction. Has Ballard any remedy? Does the answer depend on whether the mistake is discovered before construction has been begun? *See* Ballard v. Chavez, 868 P.2d 646 (N.M. 1994).

Parol Evidence and Contracts for the Sale of Goods

For the treatment of parol evidence issues in Article 2 of the UCC, *see* UCC § 2–202. Note that this section of the UCC addresses issues in addition to those addressed in the common law parol evidence rule. Which parts of UCC § 2–202 address the parol evidence rule? Is UCC § 2–202 consistent, in concept or results, with the Restatement approach? Note also that UCC § 2–202 does not discuss whether parol evidence can be used to show fraud in the inducement of the contract. May common law cases on this point be used in the context of a contract for the sale of goods? See UCC § 1–103(b).

PROBLEM

Contract Integration and Sale of Goods. Amy Miller, a local dentist in the market for a new dental chair, went to the Dentco Supply Company ("Dentco") to look at dental chairs. While she was examining a chair known as the "Super Relaxer," the owner of Dentco came over and said "This is our best selling model. It reclines a full 180 degrees." Dr. Miller responded "That's great. My patients will love it; they're always asking if I can tilt them back further." Dr. Miller and Dentco quickly agreed on a price of $9000 for the chair. They then signed a writing that provided, in its entirety:

> Amy Miller ("Miller") and Dentco Supply Company ("Dentco") hereby agree that Miller will buy, and Dentco will sell, one (1) Super Relaxer dental chair for a price of $9000.00. Dentco will deliver and install said chair no later than December 13. Payment in cash is due upon delivery. This contract represents a complete and exclusive statement of all of the terms of our transaction.

On December 13, Dentco delivered and installed the Super Relaxer. Dr. Miller asked the installer to sit in the chair so that she could see what it would be like to treat a patient sitting in the chair. Dr. Miller tilted the chair as far back as it could go, and immediately noticed that the chair had not inclined even close to 180 degrees. Dr. Miller would like to sue Dentco for breach of contract because the chair did not recline a full 180 degrees, as

Dentco's owner had stated that it would. Does she have a cause of action against Dentco?

————

No-Oral-Modification Clauses

Suppose that a party seeks to prove that the provisions of a carefully drafted written contract were varied by a conversation between the parties *after* the contract was made. The parol evidence rule does not speak to this problem (and thus does not preclude this proof), though it is not dissimilar to the problems to which the rule does speak. If one wants to do business on the basis of the written word (preferably one's own), to the exclusion of oral agreements, one has as much interest in excluding subsequent oral agreements as in excluding prior ones. An owner under a construction contract has a particularly strong interest in preventing claims by a builder for extra work allegedly done under oral modifications by the owner's representative on the site. A typical clause, this one taken from Wagner v. Graziano Constr. Co., 136 A.2d 82 (Pa. 1957), reads:

> No extra work or changes from plans and specifications under this contract will be recognized or paid for, unless agreed to in writing before the extra work is started or the changes made.

Is such a clause effective?

The traditional answer has been that it is not effective. The reasoning is that any prior agreement, including the no-oral-modification clause itself, can be modified by a later agreement. In the colorful prose of Justice Michael Musmanno, "The most ironclad written contract can always be cut into by the acetylene torch of parol modification supported by adequate proof. . . . The hand that pens a writing may not gag the mouths of the assenting parties." *Wagner*, 136 A.2d at 83–84. A century ago, Judge Cardozo wrote: "Those who make a contract may unmake it. The clause which forbids a change may be changed like any other. The prohibition of oral waiver may itself be waived. Every such agreement is ended by the new one which contradicts it. What is excluded by one act is restored by another. You may put it out by the door; it is back through the window." Beatty v. Guggenheim Exploration Co., 225 N.Y. 380, 387–88, 122 N.E. 378, 381 (1919).

In some states, legislatures have responded to this judicial hostility to the enforcement of no-oral-modification clauses. See, e.g., N.Y. General Obligations Law § 15–301(1), which provides that "A written agreement or other written instrument which contains a provision to the effect that it cannot be changed orally, cannot be changed by an executory agreement unless such executory agreement is in writing and signed by the party against whom enforcement of the change is sought or by his agent." Judicial hostility continues, however, in the form of decisions that construe the statute narrowly. See, e.g., Rose v. Spa Realty Assocs., 42 N.Y.2d 338, 366 N.E.2d 1279 (1977).

Moreover, even in those jurisdictions that honor no-oral-modification clauses, a party that seeks to escape the effect of the clause can often do so by showing reliance on the oral modification. As the Supreme Court of Pennsylvania concluded in such a case, "When an owner requests a builder to do extra work, promises to pay for it and watches it performed knowing that it is not authorized in writing, he cannot refuse to pay on the ground that there was no written change order." Universal Builders, Inc. v. Moon Motor Lodge, Inc., 244 A.2d 10, 16 (Pa. 1968).

Article 2 of the Uniform Commercial Code applies a rule that is different than the common law rule. Under UCC § 2–209(2), "A signed agreement which excludes modification or rescission except by a signed writing cannot be otherwise modified or rescinded. . . . " Note, however, that under subsection (4), what may fail to be effective as a modification or rescission may nevertheless be effective as a waiver. And under subsection (5), a material change of position in reliance on the waiver may prevent its retraction. Subsection (5) has been the subject of differing interpretations. *See* the conflicting opinions of Judges Posner and Easterbrook in Wisconsin Knife Works v. Nat'l Metal Crafters, 781 F.2d 1280 (7th Cir. 1986).

On no-oral-modification clauses, see Farnsworth on Contracts § 7.6. See also David Snyder, *The Law of Contract and the Concept of Change: Public and Private Attempts to Regulate Modification, Waiver, and Estoppel*, 1999 Wis. L. Rev. 607.

NOTE

International Approaches. Article 29(2) of the CISG provides that a written contract "which contains a provision requiring any modification or termination by agreement to be in writing may not be otherwise modified or terminated by agreement." Note that this provision, evidently designed to change the rule in common law countries, makes an exception for cases of reliance. UNIDROIT Principles art. 2.18 contains a similar provision.

SECTION 2.   THE USE OF EXTRINSIC EVIDENCE OF THE PARTIES' INTENT

In 1898, in *A Preliminary Treatise on Evidence at Common Law*, Professor James Bradley Thayer stated the prevailing view about the meaning of words: There is no "lawyers' Paradise" where, in Professor Thayer's language, "[A]ll words have a fixed, precisely ascertained meaning and where, if the writer has been careful, a lawyer, having a document referred to him may sit in his chair, inspect the text, and answer all questions without raising his eyes." Twenty years later, Justice Holmes said "A word is not a crystal, transparent and unchanged, it is the skin of a living thought and may vary greatly in color and content according to the circumstances and the time in which it is used." Towne v. Eisner, 245 U.S. 418 (1918).

The admissibility of extrinsic evidence, particularly evidence of the parties' prior negotiations, is one of the most troublesome aspects of contract interpretation. Courts have traditionally employed a two-stage process often referred to as the "plain meaning rule." Because the process is generally used only for completely integrated agreements, it is often regarded as a corollary of the parol evidence rule. In the first stage, the judge determines whether the language in the written agreement, with respect to the dispute in question, admits of only one plausible meaning or, rather, is ambiguous. If the language is *not* ambiguous, extrinsic evidence as to its meaning will be excluded. In the second stage, the court determines the meaning of the contract language. If, in the first stage, the language was found to be "ambiguous," extrinsic evidence as to its meaning will be admitted to inform the court's determination of the meaning of the contract language.

Courts disagree about what evidence may be considered in the first stage to determine whether there is ambiguity. The courts of California and New York are often seen as exemplars of opposite approaches. Consider the following cases from courts of those states.

Pacific Gas & Electric Co. v. G.W. Thomas Drayage & Rigging Co.

Supreme Court of California, 1968.
69 Cal.2d 33, 442 P.2d 641.

■ TRAYNOR, CHIEF JUSTICE. Defendant appeals from a judgment for plaintiff in an action for damages for injury to property under an indemnity clause of a contract.

In 1960 defendant entered into a contract with plaintiff to furnish the labor and equipment necessary to remove and replace the upper metal cover of plaintiff's steam turbine. Defendant agreed to perform the work "at [its] own risk and expense" and to "indemnify" plaintiff "against all loss, damage, expense and liability resulting from . . . injury to property, arising out of or in any way connected with the performance of this contract." Defendant also agreed to procure not less than $50,000 insurance to cover liability for injury to property. Plaintiff was to be an additional named insured, but the policy was to contain a cross-liability clause extending the coverage to plaintiff's property.

During the work the cover fell and injured the exposed rotor of the turbine. Plaintiff brought this action to recover $25,144.51, the amount it subsequently spent on repairs. During the trial it dismissed a count based on negligence and thereafter secured judgment on the theory that the indemnity provision covered injury to all property regardless of ownership.

Defendant offered to prove by admissions of plaintiff's agents, by defendant's conduct under similar contracts entered into with plaintiff, and by other proof that in the indemnity clause the parties meant to cover injury to property of third parties only and not to plaintiff's property. Although the trial court observed that the language used was "the classic language for a third party indemnity provision" and that "one could very easily conclude that its whole intendment is to indemnify third parties," it nevertheless held that the "plain language" of the agreement also required defendant to indemnify plaintiff for injuries to plaintiff's property. Having determined that the contract had a plain meaning, the court refused to admit any extrinsic evidence that would contradict its interpretation.

When a court interprets a contract on this basis, it determines the meaning of the instrument in accordance with the ". . . extrinsic evidence of the judge's own linguistic education and experience." (3 Corbin on Contracts (1960 ed.) [1964 Supp. § 579, p. 225, fn. 56].) The exclusion of testimony that might contradict the linguistic background of the judge reflects a judicial belief in the possibility of perfect verbal expression. (9 Wigmore on Evidence (3d ed. 1940) § 2461, p. 187.) This belief is a remnant of a primitive faith in the inherent potency[1] and inherent meaning of words.[2]

The test of admissibility of extrinsic evidence to explain the meaning of a written instrument is not whether it appears to the court to be plain and unambiguous on its face, but whether the offered evidence is relevant to prove a meaning to which the language of the instrument is reasonably susceptible.

A rule that would limit the determination of the meaning of a written instrument to its four-corners merely because it seems to the court to be clear and unambiguous, would either deny the relevance of the intention of the parties or presuppose a degree of verbal precision and stability our language has not attained.

Some courts have expressed the opinion that contractual obligations are created by the mere use of certain words, whether or not there was any intention to incur such obligations.[3] Under this view, contractual

---

[1] E.g., "The elaborate system of taboo and verbal prohibitions in primitive groups; the ancient Egyptian myth of Khern, the apotheosis of the word, and of Thoth, the Scribe of Truth, the Giver of Words and Script, the Master of Incantations; the avoidance of the name of God in Brahmanism, Judaism and Islam; totemistic and protective names in mediaeval Turkish and Finno-Ugrian languages; the misplaced verbal scruples of the 'Precieuses'; the Swedish peasant custom of curing sick cattle smitten by witchcraft, by making them swallow a page torn out of the psalter and put in dough. . . . " from Ullman, The Principles of Semantics (1963 ed.) 43. (See also Ogden and Richards, The Meaning of Meaning (rev. ed. 1956) pp. 24–47.)

[2] " 'Rerum enim vocabula immutabilia sunt, homines mutabilia,' " (Words are unchangeable, men changeable) from Dig. XXXIII, 10, 7 § 2, de sup. leg. as quoted in 9 Wigmore on Evidence, op. cit. supra, § 2461, p. 187.

[3] "A contract has, strictly speaking, nothing to do with the personal, or individual, intent of the parties. A contract is an obligation attached by the mere force of law to certain acts of the parties, usually words, which ordinarily accompany and represent a known intent." (Hotchkiss v. National City Bank of New York (S.D.N.Y.1911) 200 F. 287, 293)

evidence, that the language of a contract, in the light of all the circumstances, is fairly susceptible of either one of the two interpretations contended for," admission of extrinsic evidence relevant to prove either of such meanings is admissible) from the plain-meaning rule as described at p. 508?

(2) *Ambiguity.* Why do you suppose Justice Traynor included footnote 6, admitting "the existence of an ambiguity" so that the trial court's "exclusion of extrinsic evidence in this case would be an error even under a rule that excluded such evidence when the instrument appeared to the court to be clear and unambiguous on its face"?

(3) *Trend Lines.* Four months after the *Pacific Gas* decision, the California Supreme Court issued its opinion in Delta Dynamics, Inc. v. Arioto, 446 P.2d 785 (Cal. 1968). In that case, Delta Dynamics and Pixey Distributing had entered into an exclusive distributorship contract under which Delta was to supply trigger locks for firearms to Pixey for five years. Pixey agreed to sell a minimum of 50,000 units during the first year and 100,000 units in each of the following four years. If Pixey failed to meet the minimum, the agreement was "subject to termination." In case of breach by either party, "the party prevailing in any action for damages or enforcement of the terms of this Agreement shall be entitled to reasonable attorneys' fees." When Pixey took only 10,000 locks during the first year, Delta terminated and sued Pixey for damages. Pixey contended that Delta's exclusive remedy for Pixey's failure to meet the minimum was to terminate the contract. The trial court excluded extrinsic evidence offered by Pixey to prove this meaning, and Pixey appealed from a judgment for Delta.

Justice Traynor wrote that "the parties may have included the termination clause to spell out with specificity the condition on which Delta would be excused under the contract, or to set forth the exclusive remedy for a failure to meet the quota in any year, or for both such purposes. That clause is therefore reasonably susceptible of the meaning contended for by Pixey. There is nothing in the rest of the contract to preclude that interpretation. It does not render meaningless the provision for the recovery of attorney's fees in the event of an action for damages for breach of the contract, for the attorneys' fees provision would still have full effect with respect to other breaches of the contract. Accordingly, the trial court committed prejudicial error by excluding extrinsic evidence offered to prove the meaning of the termination clause contended for by Pixey.

Masterson, Pacific Gas & Electric, and *Delta Dynamics* were decided within a year of each other. In each case Chief Justice Traynor wrote the majority opinion, but his support on the court declined from case to case. In *Delta Dynamics,* decided by a 4–3 vote, a dissenter, Justice Stanley Mosk, "confessed" to having supported with misgivings the earlier decisions, which, he said, marked "a course leading toward emasculation of the parol evidence rule. Now, however, the trend has become so unmistakably ominous that I must urge a halt." 446 P.2d at 789. Do you agree with Justice Mosk?

Greenfield v. Philles Records, Inc.

Court of Appeals of New York, 2002.
98 N.Y.2d 562, 780 N.E.2d 166, 750 N.Y.S.2d 565.

■ GRAFFEO, JUDGE. In this contract dispute between a singing group and their record producer, we must determine whether the artists' transfer of full ownership rights to the master recordings of musical performances carried with it the unconditional right of the producer to redistribute those performances in any technological format. In the absence of an explicit contractual reservation of rights by the artists, we conclude that it did.

In the early 1960s, Veronica Bennett (now known as Ronnie Greenfield), her sister Estelle Bennett and their cousin Nedra Talley, formed a singing group known as "The Ronettes." They met defendant Phil Spector, a music producer and composer, in 1963 and signed a five-year "personal services" music recording contract (the Ronettes agreement) with Spector's production company, defendant Philles Records, Inc. The plaintiffs agreed to perform exclusively for Philles Records and in exchange, Philles Records acquired an ownership right to the recordings of the Ronettes' musical performances. The agreement also set forth a royalty schedule to compensate plaintiffs for their services. After signing with Philles Records, plaintiffs received a single collective cash advance of approximately $15,000.

The Ronettes recorded several dozen songs for Philles Records, including "Be My Baby," which sold over a million copies and topped the music charts. Despite their popularity, the group disbanded in 1967 and Philles Records eventually went out of business. Other than their initial advance, plaintiffs received no royalty payments from Philles Records.

Beyond their professional relationship, however, was the story of the personal relationship between Spector and plaintiff Ronnie Greenfield. They married in 1968 but separated after a few years. Greenfield initiated a divorce proceeding against Spector in California and a settlement was reached in 1974. As part of that agreement, Spector and Greenfield executed mutual general releases that purported to resolve all past and future claims and obligations that existed between them, as well as between Greenfield and Spector's companies.

Defendants subsequently began to capitalize on a resurgence of public interest in 1960s music by making use of new recording technologies and licensing master recordings of the Ronettes' vocal performances for use in movie and television productions, a process known in entertainment industry parlance as "synchronization." The most notable example was defendants' licensing of "Be My Baby" in 1987 for use in the motion picture "Dirty Dancing." Defendants also licensed master recordings to third parties for production and distribution in the United States (referred to as domestic redistribution), and sold compilation albums containing performances by the Ronettes. While defendants earned considerable compensation from such licensing and sales, no royalties were paid to any of the plaintiffs.

As a result, plaintiffs commenced this breach of contract action in 1987, alleging that the 1963 agreement did not provide Philles Records with the right to license the master recordings for synchronization and domestic redistribution, and demanded royalties from the sales of compilation albums. Although defendants initially denied the existence of a contract, in 1992 they stipulated that an unexecuted copy of the contract would determine the parties' rights. Defendants thereafter argued that the agreement granted them absolute ownership rights to the master recordings and permitted the use of the recordings in any format, subject only to royalty rights. Following extensive pretrial proceedings, Supreme Court ruled in plaintiffs' favor and awarded approximately $3 million in damages and interest.

The Appellate Division affirmed, concluding that defendants' actions were not authorized by the agreement with plaintiffs because the contract did not specifically transfer the right to issue synchronization and third-party domestic distribution licenses. Permitting plaintiffs to assert a claim for unjust enrichment, the Court found that plaintiffs were entitled to the music recording industry's standard 50% royalty rate for income derived from synchronization and third-party licensing. We granted leave to appeal.

We are asked on this appeal to determine whether defendants, as the owners of the master recordings of plaintiffs' vocal performances, acquired the contractual right to issue licenses to third parties to use the recordings in connection with television, movies and domestic audio distribution. The agreement between the parties consists of a two-page document, which apparently was widely used in the 1960s by music producers signing new artists. Plaintiffs executed the contract without the benefit of counsel. The parties' immediate objective was to record and market the Ronettes' vocal performances and "mak[e] therefrom phonograph records and/or tape recordings and other similar devices (excluding transcriptions)." The ownership rights provision of the contract provides:

"All recordings made hereunder and all records and reproductions made therefrom together with the performances embodied therein, shall be entirely [Philles'] property, free of any claims whatsoever by you or any person deriving any rights of interest from you. Without limitation of the foregoing, [Philles] shall have the right to make phonograph records, tape recordings or other reproductions of the performances embodied in such recordings by any method now or hereafter known, and to sell and deal in the same under any trade mark or trade names or labels designated by us, or we may at our election refrain therefrom."

Plaintiffs concede that the contract unambiguously gives defendants unconditional ownership rights to the master recordings, but contend that the agreement does not bestow the right to exploit those recordings in new markets or mediums since the document is silent on those topics. Defendants counter that the absence of specific references to synchronization and domestic licensing is irrelevant. They argue that where a contract grants full ownership rights to a musical performance or composition, the only restrictions upon the owner's right to use that property are those explicitly enumerated by the grantor/artist.

Despite the technological innovations that continue to revolutionize the recording industry, long-settled common-law contract rules still govern the interpretation of agreements between artists and their record producers. The fundamental, neutral precept of contract interpretation is that agreements are construed in accord with the parties' intent. "The best evidence of what parties to a written agreement intend is what they say in their writing"(Slamow v. Del Col, 594 N.E.2d 918 [1992]). Thus, a written agreement that is complete, clear and unambiguous on its face must be enforced according to the plain meaning of its terms (*see e.g.* R/S Assoc. v. New York Job Dev. Auth., 771 N.E.2d 240 [2002]; W.W.W. Assoc. v. Giancontieri, 566 N.E.2d 639 [1990]).

Extrinsic evidence of the parties' intent may be considered only if the agreement is ambiguous, which is an issue of law for the courts to decide (*see W.W.W. Assoc. v. Giancontieri, supra* at 162, 565 N.Y.S.2d 440, 566 N.E.2d 639). A contract is unambiguous if the language it uses has "a definite and precise meaning, unattended by danger of misconception in the purport of the [agreement] itself, and concerning which there is no reasonable basis for a difference of opinion"(Breed v. Insurance Co. of N. Am., 46 385 N.E.2d 1280 [1978]). Thus, if the agreement on its face is reasonably susceptible of only one meaning, a court is not free to alter the contract to reflect its personal notions of fairness and equity (*see e.g.* Teichman v. Community Hosp. of W. Suffolk, 663 N.E.2d 628 [1996]; First Natl. Stores v. Yellowstone Shopping Ctr., 237 N.E.2d 868 [1968]).

The pivotal issue in this case is whether defendants are prohibited from using the master recordings for synchronization, and whatever future formats evolve from new technologies, in the absence of explicit contract language authorizing such uses. Stated another way, does the contract's silence on synchronization and domestic licensing create an ambiguity which opens the door to the admissibility of extrinsic evidence to determine the intent of the parties? We conclude that it does not and, because there is no ambiguity in the terms of the Ronettes agreement, defendants are entitled to exercise complete ownership rights, subject to payment of applicable royalties due plaintiffs. . . .

Defendants further claim that Greenfield is barred from sharing in those royalties because she executed a general release in connection with her divorce from Spector. We look to California law to analyze the scope of Greenfield's release because that is the state where the release was executed and the divorce was finalized. In contrast to the "four corners" rule that New York has long applied, California courts preliminarily consider all credible evidence of the parties' intent in addition to the language of the contract—"[t]he test of admissibility of extrinsic evidence to explain the meaning of a written instrument is not whether it appears to the court to be plain and unambiguous on its face, but whether the offered evidence is relevant to prove a meaning to which the language of the instrument is reasonably susceptible"(Pacific Gas & Elec. Co. v. G.W. Thomas Drayage & Rigging Co., 442 P.2d 641, 644 [1968]).

During proceedings in New York, Supreme Court determined that the extrinsic evidence supported Greenfield's allegation that her right to compensation under the 1963 recording contract was not an intended subject of the release. That finding of fact, affirmed by the Appellate Division, is supported by the record. We find no reason to reverse the Appellate Division's interpretation of California law. Plaintiff Greenfield is therefore entitled to her share of any damages assessed against defendants.

We have reviewed the parties' remaining contentions; they are either academic or meritless.

Accordingly, the order of the Appellate Division should be modified, without costs, and the case remitted to Supreme Court for further proceedings in accordance with this opinion and, as so modified, affirmed.

NOTES

(1) *Only One Interpretation?* Do you agree with the court's conclusion that the recording contract was unambiguous? Would your answer be the same if the phrase "without limitation of the foregoing" had not been included in the sentence granting Philles the right to make phonograph records, tape recordings, or other reproductions of the performances?

(2) *A Split Opinion.* Note that the court's ruling on the second issue in the case was an application of *California* law rather than New York law. Did the court describe California law fairly? How would the first issue in the case have been decided under California law?

———

The court in Greenfield relied on the following case for the proposition that "extrinsic evidence of the parties' intent may be considered only if the agreement is ambiguous, which is an issue of law for the courts to decide." Can the parties use extrinsic evidence, however, to demonstrate ambiguity?

W.W.W. Associates, Inc. v. Giancontieri
Court of Appeals of New York, 1990.
77 N.Y.2d 157, 566 N.E.2d 639.

[The defendants, owners of real property, contracted for its sale to the plaintiff, a real estate investor and developer, with the closing to take place "on or about December 1, 1986." Paragraph 31 of the contract of sale provided that "The parties acknowledge that Sellers have been served with process instituting an action concerned with the real property which is the subject of this agreement. In the event the closing of title is delayed by reason of such litigation it is agreed that closing of title will in a like manner be adjourned until after the conclusion of such litigation provided, *in the event such litigation is not concluded, by or before 6–1–87 either party shall have the right to cancel this contract whereupon the down payment shall be returned and there shall be no further rights hereunder.*" (Emphasis supplied.) The sale did not close on December 1, 1986, as originally contemplated. As June 1, 1987 neared, with the litigation still unresolved, the buyer wrote to the sellers that it was prepared to close and would appear for closing on May 28. On June 2, 1987, the sellers canceled the contract and returned the down payment, which the buyer refused. The buyer brought an action seeking specific performance of the contract to sell the real property. The sellers sought summary judgment dismissing the specific performance action, on the ground that the contract gave them the absolute right to cancel.]

■ KAYE, JUDGE.[a] Plaintiff's claim to specific performance rests upon its recitation of how paragraph 31 originated. Those facts are set forth in the affidavit of plaintiff's vice-president, submitted in opposition to defendants' summary judgment motion.

As plaintiff explains, during contract negotiations it learned that, as a result of unrelated litigation against defendants, a lis pendens had been filed against the property. Although assured by defendants that the suit was meritless, plaintiff anticipated difficulty obtaining a construction loan (including title insurance for the loan) needed to implement its plans to build senior citizen housing units. According to the affidavit, it was therefore agreed that paragraph 31 would be added for plaintiff's sole benefit, as contract vendee. As it developed, plaintiff's fears proved groundless—the lis pendens did not impede its ability to secure construction financing. However, around March 1987, plaintiff claims it learned from the broker on the transaction that one of the defendants had told him they were doing nothing to defend the litigation, awaiting June 2, 1987 to cancel the contract and suggesting the broker might get a higher price.

Defendants made no response to these factual assertions. Rather, its summary judgment motion rested entirely on the language of the Contract of Sale, which it argued was, under the law, determinative of its right to cancel.

---

[a]   Judith S. Kaye (1938–2016). Judith Kaye served as Chief Judge of the New York Court of Appeals from 1993 to 2008 when she reached the mandatory retirement age of 70. A graduate of Barnard College and New York University School of Law, she was the first woman named to the highest court of New York and the first female chief judge. Judge Kaye modernized the New York State judicial system through changes to jury service and through the creation of specialized courts which took a comprehensive approach to such issues as drug addiction and domestic violence, focusing on diversionary programs rather than incarceration. In addition to her decisions against the death penalty and in support of marriage equality, Judge Kaye is also known for her 2003 ruling that New York State was obliged to for provide a "sound basic education" to all public school students.

The trial court granted defendants' motion and dismissed the complaint, holding that the agreement unambiguously conferred the right to cancel on defendants as well as plaintiff. The Appellate Division, however, reversed and, after searching the record and adopting the facts alleged by plaintiff in its affidavit, granted summary judgment to plaintiff directing specific performance of the contract. We now reverse and dismiss the complaint.

Critical to the success of plaintiff's position is consideration of the extrinsic evidence that paragraph 31 was added to the contract solely for its benefit. The Appellate Division made clear that this evidence was at the heart of its decision: "review of the record reveals that under the circumstances of this case the language of clause 31 was intended to protect the plaintiff from having to purchase the property burdened by a notice of pendency filed as a result of the underlying action which could prevent the plaintiff from obtaining clear title and would impair its ability to obtain subsequent construction financing." In that a party for whose sole benefit a condition is included in a contract may waive the condition prior to expiration of the time period set forth in the contract and accept the subject property "as is," plaintiff's undisputed factual assertions—if material—would defeat defendants' summary judgment motion.

We conclude, however, that the extrinsic evidence tendered by plaintiff is not material. In its reliance on extrinsic evidence to bring itself within the "party benefited" cases, plaintiff ignores a vital first step in the analysis: before looking to evidence of what was in the parties' minds, a court must give due weight to what was in their contract.

A familiar and eminently sensible proposition of law is that, when parties set down their agreement in a clear, complete document, their writing should as a rule be enforced according to its terms. Evidence outside the four corners of the document as to what was really intended but unstated or misstated is generally inadmissible to add to or vary the writing. That rule imparts "stability to commercial transactions by safeguarding against fraudulent claims, perjury, death of witnesses . . . infirmity of memory . . . [and] the fear that the jury will improperly evaluate the extrinsic evidence." (Fisch, New York Evidence § 42, at 22 [2d ed].) Such considerations are all the more compelling in the context of real property transactions, where commercial certainty is a paramount concern.

Whether or not a writing is ambiguous is a question of law to be resolved by the courts.

The question next raised is whether extrinsic evidence should be considered in order to create an ambiguity in the agreement. That question must be answered in the negative. It is well settled that "extrinsic and parol evidence is not admissible to create an ambiguity in a written agreement which is complete and clear and unambiguous upon its face." (Intercontinental Planning v. Daystrom, Inc., 24 N.Y.2d 372, 379).

An analysis that begins with consideration of extrinsic evidence of what the parties meant, instead of looking first to what they said and reaching extrinsic evidence only when required to do so because of some identified ambiguity, unnecessarily denigrates the contract and unsettles the law.

NOTES

(1) *Wisdom of the Plain Meaning Rule.* Judge Richard Posner, whose views on the parol evidence rule were quoted earlier at p. 489–490 above, had this to say in defense of the traditional plain meaning rule described on page 508: "The older view . . . which excludes extrinsic evidence if the contract is clear 'on its face,' is not ridiculous. . . . The rule tends to cut down on the amount of litigation, in part by reducing the role of the jury; for it is the jury that interprets contracts when interpretation requires consideration of extrinsic evidence. Parties to contracts may prefer, ex ante (that is, when negotiating the contract, and therefore before an interpretive dispute has arisen), to avoid the expense and uncertainty of having a jury resolve a dispute between them, even at the cost of some inflexibility in interpretation." Fed. Deposit Ins. Corp. v. W.R. Grace & Co., 877 F.2d 614, 621 (7th Cir. 1989).

(2) *International Approaches.* UNIDROIT Principles art. 4.3 states that in interpreting contract language "regard shall be had to all the circumstances, including preliminary negotiations between the parties." Because article 4.3 does not provide for a first stage in which the admissibility of extrinsic evidence is determined, it is not a plain meaning rule. Is it significant in judging the merit of article 4.3 that the principal application of the *Principles* is in international commercial arbitrations where the arbitrators are relatively sophisticated and pre-trial discovery is generally very limited? (Does the matter of pre-trial discovery help to distinguish the plain meaning rule as applied to contracts from the plain meaning rule as applied to legislation?)

(3) *Variation by Contract.* Suppose that parties to a contract governed by California law prefer the rule in *Philles* to that in *Pacific Gas,* as Judge Posner predicted they might. Could they, by a provision in their contract, prevent a court from admitting extrinsic evidence that it would otherwise admit in the first stage? Whether the parties could avoid California law altogether by providing for the application of New York law is a question best left for a course in conflict of laws.

In Garden State Plaza Corp. v. S.S. Kresge Co., 189 A.2d 448 (N.J. Super. Ct. 1963), the court held void as against public policy a clause providing that no "previous negotiations, arrangements, agreements and understandings . . . shall be used to interpret or construe this lease." The clause would, the court said, have it construe the contract "wearing judicial blinders. We are requested to conform to a private agreement mandating our performance of a judicial function in a manner which, under our precedents, is not the path to justice in arriving at the binding meaning of a contract." Do you agree? Would it make a difference if the language in question were "plain"?

————

The United States Court of Appeals for the Ninth Circuit (which includes California) often must apply California law. In the following opinion, this court expressed the view that the approach to contract interpretation exemplified by the *Pacific Gas & Electric Co.* decision "chips away at the foundation of our legal system."

Trident Center v. Connecticut General Life Ins. Co.

United States Court of Appeals for the Ninth Circuit, 1988.
847 F.2d 564.

■ KOZINSKI, CIRCUIT JUDGE. The parties to this transaction are, by any standard, highly sophisticated business people: Plaintiff is a partnership consisting of an insurance company and two of Los Angeles' largest and most prestigious law firms; defendant is another insurance company. Dealing at arm's length and from positions of roughly equal bargaining strength, they negotiated a commercial loan amounting to more than $56 million. The contract documents are lengthy and detailed; they squarely address the precise issue that is the subject of this dispute; to all who read English, they appear to resolve the issue fully and conclusively.

Plaintiff nevertheless argues here, as it did below, that it is entitled to introduce extrinsic evidence that the contract means something other than what it says. This case therefore presents the question whether parties in California can ever draft a contract that is proof to parol evidence. Somewhat surprisingly, the answer is no.

Facts

The facts are rather simple. Sometime in 1983 Security First Life Insurance Company and the law firms of Mitchell, Silberberg & Knupp and Manatt, Phelps, Rothenberg & Tunney formed a limited partnership for the purpose of constructing an office building complex on Olympic Boulevard in West Los Angeles. The partnership, Trident Center, the plaintiff herein, sought and obtained financing for the project from defendant, Connecticut General Life Insurance Company. The loan documents provide for a loan of $56,500,000 at 12 1/4 percent interest for a term of 15 years, secured by a deed of trust on the project. The promissory note provides that "[m]aker shall not have the right to prepay the principal amount hereof in whole or in part" for the first 12 years. [Promissory] Note at 6. In years 13–15, the loan may be prepaid, subject to a sliding prepayment fee. The note also provides that in case of a default during years 1–12, Connecticut General has the option of accelerating the note and adding a 10 percent prepayment fee.

Everything was copacetic for a few years until interest rates began to drop. The 12 1/4 percent rate that had seemed reasonable in 1983 compared unfavorably with 1987 market rates and Trident started looking for ways of refinancing the loan to take advantage of the lower rates. Connecticut General was unwilling to oblige, insisting that the loan could not be prepaid for the first 12 years of its life, that is, until January 1996.

Trident then brought suit in state court seeking a declaration that it was entitled to prepay the loan now, subject only to a 10 percent prepayment fee. Connecticut General promptly removed to federal court and brought a motion to dismiss, claiming that the loan documents clearly and unambiguously precluded prepayment during the first 12 years. The district court agreed and dismissed Trident's complaint. The court also "*sua sponte,* sanction[ed] the plaintiff for the filing of a frivolous lawsuit." Trident appeals both aspects of the district court's ruling.

Discussion

I

Trident makes two arguments as to why the district court's ruling is wrong. First, it contends that the language of the contract is ambiguous and proffers a construction that it believes supports its position. Second, Trident argues that, under California law, even seemingly unambiguous contracts are subject to modification by parol or extrinsic evidence. Trident faults the district court for denying it the opportunity to present evidence that the contract language did not accurately reflect the parties' intentions.

A.   The Contract

As noted earlier, the promissory note provides that Trident "shall not have the right to prepay the principal amount hereof in whole or in part before January 1996." [Promissory] Note at 6. It is difficult to imagine language that more clearly or unambiguously expresses the idea that Trident may not unilaterally prepay the loan during its first 12 years. Trident, however, argues that there is an ambiguity because another clause of the note provides that "[i]n the event of a prepayment resulting from a default hereunder or the Deed of Trust prior to January 10, 1996 the prepayment fee will be ten percent (10%)." [Promissory] Note at 6–7. Trident interprets this clause as giving it the option of prepaying the loan if only it is willing to incur the prepayment fee.

We reject Trident's argument out of hand.

B.   Extrinsic Evidence

Trident argues in the alternative that, even if the language of the contract appears to be unambiguous, the deal the parties actually struck is in fact quite different. It wishes to offer extrinsic evidence that the parties had agreed Trident could prepay at any time within the first 12 years by tendering the full amount plus a 10 percent prepayment fee. As discussed above, this is an interpretation to which the contract, as written, is not reasonably susceptible. Under traditional contract principles, extrinsic evidence is inadmissible to interpret, vary or add to the terms of an unambiguous integrated written instrument. *See* 4 S. Williston, *supra* p. 5, § 631, at 948–49; 2 B. Witkin, California Evidence § 981, at 926 (3d ed. 1986).

Trident points out, however, that California does not follow the traditional rule. Two decades ago the California Supreme Court in Pacific Gas & Electric Co. v. G.W. Thomas Drayage & Rigging Co., 442 P.2d 641 (1968), turned its back on the notion that a contract can ever have a plain meaning discernible by a court without resort to extrinsic evidence. The court reasoned that contractual obligations flow not from the words of the contract, but from the intention of the parties. "Accordingly," the court stated, "the exclusion of relevant, extrinsic, evidence to explain the meaning of a written instrument could be justified only if it were feasible to determine the meaning the parties gave to the words from the instrument alone." 442 P.2d 641. This, the California Supreme Court concluded, is impossible: "If words had absolute and constant referents, it might be possible to discover contractual intention in the words themselves and in the manner in which they were arranged. Words, however, do not have absolute and constant referents." *Id.* In the same vein, the court noted that "[t]he exclusion of testimony that might contradict the linguistic background of the judge reflects a judicial belief in the possibility of perfect verbal expression. This belief is a remnant of a primitive faith in the inherent potency and inherent meaning of words." *Id.* at 37, 442 P.2d 641, 69 Cal. Rptr. 561 (citation and footnotes omitted).[1]

Under *Pacific Gas,* it matters not how clearly a contract is written, nor how completely it is integrated, nor how carefully it is negotiated, nor how squarely it addresses the issue before the court: the contract cannot be rendered impervious to attack by parol evidence. If one side is willing to claim that the parties intended one thing but the agreement provides for another, the court must consider extrinsic evidence of possible ambiguity. If that evidence raises the specter of ambiguity where there was none before, the contract language is displaced and the intention of the parties must be divined from self-serving testimony offered by partisan witnesses whose recollection is hazy from passage of time and colored by their conflicting interests. *See* Delta Dynamics, Inc. v. Arioto, 69 Cal.2d 525, 532, 446 P.2d 785, 72 Cal.Rptr. 785 (1968) (Mosk, J., dissenting). We question whether this approach is more likely to divulge the original intention of the parties than reliance on the seemingly clear

---

[1] In an unusual footnote, the [California Supreme] court compared the belief in the immutable meaning of words with " '[t]he elaborate system of taboo and verbal prohibitions in primitive groups . . . [such as] the Swedish peasant custom of curing sick cattle smitten by witchcraft, by making them swallow a page torn out of the psalter and put in dough. . . .' " *Id.* n. 2 (quoting Ullman, *The Principles of Semantics* 43 (1963)). [Footnote by the court]

words they agreed upon at the time. *See generally* Morta v. Korea Ins. Co., 840 F.2d 1452, 1460 (9th Cir.1988).

Pacific Gas casts a long shadow of uncertainty over all transactions negotiated and executed under the law of California. As this case illustrates, even when the transaction is very sizeable, even if it involves only sophisticated parties, even if it was negotiated with the aid of counsel, even if it results in contract language that is devoid of ambiguity, costly and protracted litigation cannot be avoided if one party has a strong enough motive for challenging the contract. While this rule creates much business for lawyers and an occasional windfall to some clients, it leads only to frustration and delay for most litigants and clogs already overburdened courts.

It also chips away at the foundation of our legal system. By giving credence to the idea that words are inadequate to express concepts, *Pacific Gas* undermines the basic principle that language provides a meaningful constraint on public and private conduct. If we are unwilling to say that parties, dealing face to face, can come up with language that binds them, how can we send anyone to jail for violating statutes consisting of mere words lacking "absolute and constant referents"? How can courts ever enforce decrees, not written in language understandable to all, but encoded in a dialect reflecting only the "linguistic background of the judge"? Can lower courts ever be faulted for failing to carry out the mandate of higher courts when "perfect verbal expression" is impossible? Are all attempts to develop the law in a reasoned and principled fashion doomed to failure as "remnant[s] of a primitive faith in the inherent potency and inherent meaning of words"?

Be that as it may. While we have our doubts about the wisdom of *Pacific Gas,* we have no difficulty understanding its meaning, even without extrinsic evidence to guide us. As we read the rule in California, we must reverse and remand to the district court in order to give plaintiff an opportunity to present extrinsic evidence as to the intention of the parties in drafting the contract. It may not be a wise rule we are applying, but it is a rule that binds us. Erie R.R. Co. v. Tompkins, 304 U.S. 64, 78, 58 S.Ct. 817, 822, 82 L.Ed. 1188 (1938). By holding that language has no objective meaning, and that contracts mean only what courts ultimately say they do, Pacific Gas invites precisely this type of lawsuit. With the benefit of 20 years of hindsight, the California Supreme Court may wish to revisit the issue. If it does so, we commend to it the facts of this case as a paradigmatic example of why the traditional rule, based on centuries of experience, reflects the far wiser approach.

NOTES

(1) *Picking Sides.* This chapter has provided extensive materials about the competing approaches concerning extrinsic evidence and contract interpretation, providing the reader ample opportunity to assess the claimed

advantages and disadvantages of each approach. On balance, which approach do you favor? Why?

(2) *Contracts for the Sale of Goods.* Under Article 2 of the UCC, must a court find that the words of the agreement are ambiguous before extrinsic evidence of their meaning may be considered? Does UCC § 2–202 provide any guidance?

Methods of Interpreting Ambiguous Contracts

In analyzing contract language, it is sometimes useful to distinguish *vagueness* from *ambiguity.* A word is vague when its applicability in marginal situations is uncertain, as is the case for the word "green" to describe a color. For another example, if parties contract for the removal of "all the dirt" on a given tract, may sand from a stratum of subsoil be taken? See Highley v. Phillips, 5 A.2d 824 (Md. 1939) (held: yes). In contrast, a word is ambiguous when it has two entirely different connotations so that it may be at the same time both appropriate and inappropriate, as is the case for "light" when applied to dark feathers. Since "ambiguous" is often used to comprehend the notion of vagueness, as well as the notion of ambiguity in the narrow sense, some writers prefer to use "ambivalent" or "equivocal" instead. For example, if a contract specifies "tons," are they to be long or short tons? Compare Chemung Iron & Steel Co. v. Mersereau Metal Bed Co., 179 N.Y.S. 577 (N.Y. Sup. 1920) (specifying short tons), with Higgins v. California Petroleum & Asphalt Co., 52 P. 1080 (Cal. 1898) (specifying long tons). Drafters sometimes find vague terms useful as a means of delegating decisions to a later adjudicator at such time as a dispute on particular facts arises. Think of "a reasonable time," "good faith and fair dealing," and "best efforts." Use of ambiguous terms is simply bad drafting.

NOTES

(1) *Inconsistent Provisions.* One of the most common results of carelessness in drafting is inconsistency between different parts of a written agreement—a lawyer's version of syntactical ambiguity. *See* Robinhorne Constr. Corp. v. Snyder, 265 N.E.2d 670, 674–75 (Ill. 1970) ("This is the kind of case that has been described as 'one where no principle of law is involved, but only the meaning of careless and slovenly documents'").

(2) *Interpretation in the Agreement Process.* We have already encountered problems of interpretation in the agreement process. *See,* for example, Owen v. Tunison, p. 186 above, and Harvey v. Facey, pp. 187–188 above. The problems of interpretation in those cases are similar, but not identical, to the ones we are about to encounter. In United States v. Braunstein, 75 F.Supp. 137, 139 (S.D.N.Y. 1947), Judge Harold Medina wrote: "It is true that there is much room for interpretation once the parties are inside the framework of a contract, but it seems that there is less in the field of offer and acceptance. Greater precision of expression may be

required, and less help from the court given, when the parties are merely at the threshold of a contract."

(3) *The Role of Punctuation.* Commas are sometimes effective, sometimes not. Consult Overhauser v. United States, 45 F.3d 1085, 1086–87 (7th Cir. 1995), rejecting the assumptions "that there is a clear rule of grammar by which the scope of a qualifying phrase can be determined from the placement of commas" and "that the agreement was drafted by a grammarian or at least by someone knowledgeable about obscure rules of grammar." Judge Posner pointed out that even the Supreme Court of the United States "cannot make up its mind whether to be skeptical or credulous about imputing grammatical expertise to drafters of legal documents and using the imputation to decide interpretive questions."

PROBLEMS

(1) *Drafting Exercises.* Try, in each of the following fact patterns: (1) to state the issue in terms of the contract language; and (2) to redraft the contract language, first for one party and then for the other, making as few changes as possible.

   a. A contract for the sale of a photography studio provides that the seller will not compete with the buyer "for school photography work in any school in Grant County, with the exception of Marion High School and Bennett High School." May the seller compete with the buyer for the photography of Marion College students? *See* Lawrence v. Cain, 245 N.E.2d 663 (Ind. App. 1969).

   b. A lease of premises for a drug store provides for a minimum monthly rental plus a percentage of the "gross sales" of the business. Must the lessee pay a percentage of what it is paid by customers for lottery tickets? Hartig Drug Co. v. Hartig, 602 N.W.2d 794 (Iowa 1999).

   c. A contract between a provider of medical services and a technician employed by it prohibits the technician from competing with the provider for three years "within 50 miles of the Company office." Is the technician prohibited from competing at a location that is a distance of 45 miles, but a 55 mile drive from the Company office? Vantage Technology v. Cross, 17 S.W.3d 637 (Tenn. App. 1999).

   d. A construction contract provides that "All domestic water piping and rainwater piping installed above finished ceilings under this specification shall be insulated." Must the contractor insulate domestic water piping installed below finished ceilings? *See* Paul W. Abbott v. Axel Newman Heating & Plumbing, 166 N.W.2d 323 (Minn. 1969).

(2) *A Matter of Taste.* Tastings, Inc. furnishes cafeteria service to business firms. It is about to employ your client under a two-year contract as manager of its cafeteria operation at a data processing plant. The draft contains the following restrictive covenant:

> For one year after my employment with you ends, I will not
> participate in the management of any cafeteria operated by any
> firm who shall have been your client within the period of one year
> prior to the termination of my employment or with whom you may
> have been negotiating during my employment with you if I have
> participated in such negotiations or had contact with that firm in
> the course of my employment with you.

Do you see any ambiguity in this clause? How can it be corrected? (Suppose
that your client leaves Tastings at the end of two years and takes a job
managing a cafeteria for a firm with which he has had no previous connection
but which had been a client of Tastings three months earlier, before deciding
to operate its own cafeteria?) *See* Servomation Mathias, Inc. v. Englert, 333
F.Supp. 9 (M.D. Pa. 1971).

(3)   *The Ambiguity of "Minerals."* A contract involving the conveyance
of land from a railroad to Colorado landowners reserves to the railroad rights
to "all coal and other minerals." The landowners claim that the term
"minerals" includes oil and gas. Is the term "ambiguous"? If not, who is right?
See McCormick v. Union Pacific R.R. Co., 983 P.2d 84 (Colo. App. 1998).

(4)   *The Ambiguity of "Matriculated."* Raymond Woodcock had student
loans from a bank that came due at "the end of the ninth month following
the month in which I cease to be matriculated." After graduating from law
school and business school, he attended college part-time but not in a degree
program, and then went into bankruptcy. The bank claims that Raymond
was still "matriculated" while he was a part-time student so that the loans
did not become due until a statutory period, prior to bankruptcy, when
student loans coming due are not dischargeable. Raymond claims that he
ceased to be matriculated long before that when he graduated from business
school. Is the term "matriculated" ambiguous? If not, who is right? *See* In re
Woodcock, 45 F.3d 363 (10th Cir. 1995).

(5)   *The Ambiguity of "Exploit."* Emerson granted Orion an exclusive
license to "utilize and exploit" Emerson's trademarks in connection with the
sale of various consumer electronic items. Emerson claimed that the term
"exploit" imposed an express contractual obligation on Orion to use
"reasonable efforts" or "due diligence" in selling and marketing Emerson-
brand products. Orion argued that the term "exploit" "could as easily be
interpreted as granting Orion authority to act in its own self-interest as
imposing a duty to act in Emerson's best interests." Is the term "exploit"
ambiguous? If not, whose meaning prevails? See Emerson Radio Corp. v.
Orion Sales, Inc., 253 F.3d 159 (3rd Cir. 2001).

(6)   *An Offer You Can't Refuse?* The Steuarts gave the McChesneys a
right of first refusal on a farm, under which, if the Steuarts obtained an offer
from a third party, the McChesneys had a right to purchase the farm for a
price "equivalent to the market value of the premises according to the
assessment rolls as maintained by the County of Warren." The agreement
was completely integrated. It is now a decade later, and the assessed value
according to the County's tax rolls is $70,000, having been increased by only
$8,000 when the farm was reassessed a few years ago. The county's practice

is to value real estate for tax purposes at 50% of market value. However, a broker recently appraised the farm at a market value of $500,000 and Lepha Steuart, now a widow, has just received an offer of $350,000 for the farm.

How much must the McChesneys tender in order to exercise their right of first refusal? $500,000? $350,000? $140,000? $70,000? Twice the proper assessed value? Would a court admit evidence concerning the county's established practice in valuing real estate for tax purposes? Would it admit testimony concerning the negotiations from Lepha Steuart and the drafter of the contract? *See* Steuart v. McChesney, 444 A.2d 659 (Pa. 1982).

Canons of Construction

Maxims. Rules of thumb typically referred to as "maxims" of construction are often used in the interpretation of contracts. Examples of such maxims include *ejusdem generis* (of the same kind)[b], *expressio unius est exclusio alterius* (the expression of one thing is the exclusion of another)[c], *noscitur a sociis* (it is known from its associates), and *contra proferentem* (against its author or profferer)[d]. Typically, *contra proferentem* is employed "only as a matter of last resort after all aids to construction have been employed without a satisfactory result." Rottkamp v. Eger, 74 Misc. 2d 858, 864 (Sup. Ct. 1973). See also Lamps Plus, Inc. v. Varela, page 529 below.

Public Interest. In North Gate Corp. v. National Food Stores, Inc., 140 N.W.2d 744 (Wis. 1966), a printed shopping center lease prepared by the lessee for use by its retail food stores throughout the country contained a provision that prohibited the owner of the shopping center from leasing to other retail stores. The court observed that "the intent of the provision" was "to restrict trade and the use of land. Such provisions are to be strictly construed." In Chapter 6, we will see that contracts involving performance that would be in violation of some strongly rooted public interest, often expressed in a statute, may be held to be

---

[b]   Ejusdem generis "provides that when a list of specific words is followed by a broader or more general term, the broader term is interpreted to include only potential members of a class similar to those denoted by the specific words." Peter M. Tiersma, Parchment Paper Pixels: Law and the Technologies of Communication 152 (2010).

To illustrate these, consider a contract dealing with repairing cars. If it says "sedans, SUVs, and minivans," under *expression unius est exclusion alterius* it would not include tractor-trailers, motorcycles, or any other motor vehicle. If the contract read "sedans, SUVs, minivans, and other motor vehicles," *ejusdem generis* would favor reading "motor vehicles" in light of the specified types, so a tractor-trailer, the function of which is transporting cargo, not passengers, would not be included. A motorcycle might be; it does transport passengers, like the three types listed, but it is not a closed vehicle, as they are. Finally, suppose the contract says "vehicles" without providing a definition. If the contract is otherwise about passenger vehicles, then under *noscitur a sociis* the word "vehicles" would be interpreted, in light of its neighbors, to mean "passenger vehicles."

[c]   "For example, the rule that 'each citizen is entitled to vote' implies that noncitizens are not entitled to vote." Black's Law Dictionary (10th ed. 2014).

[d]   "In the interpretation of documents, ambiguities are to be construed unfavorably to the drafter." Id.

unenforceable. As *North Gate* shows, public interest may also affect the interpretation of contracts.

In State ex rel. Youngman v. Calhoun, 231 S.W. 647 (Mo. App. 1921), a physician sold his practice, agreeing not to "establish [himself] as a practicing physician and surgeon within a radius of five miles" of his former office. The court held that he was not precluded from making calls within this area or treating patients from this area who might call at his office outside the area. "The contract in question is clearly one in restraint of trade and personal liberty, and as such should not be construed to extend beyond its fair import." Why? Because of the intention of the parties? See also Sun Oil Co. v. Vickers Refining Co., 414 F.2d 383 (8th Cir.1969) (rejecting Sunray's interpretation under which the contract would have been void because of a violation of the antitrust laws: "Sunray's attorneys, experienced in antitrust work, approved the contract without any question of antitrust consequences").

The Statutory Analogy. There is an obvious similarity between the interpretation of contracts and that of statutes. To what extent is the analogy compelling? For example, are the policies for or against the use of legislative history as an aid to statutory interpretation similar to those for or against the use of negotiations ("transactional history") as an aid to contract interpretation?

Purpose Interpretation. Is there an analogy to what is known as "purpose interpretation" in the field of statutory interpretation? According to the formulation in Heydon's Case, (1584) 76 Eng. Rep. 637; 3 Coke 7a, it involves these steps: (1) examination of the law before enactment of the statute; (2) ascertainment of the "mischief or defect" for which the law did not provide; (3) analysis of the remedy provided by the legislature to "cure the disease"; (4) determination of the "true reason of the remedy"; and then (5) application of the statute so as to "suppress the mischief, and advance the remedy." Can you formulate an analogous technique for contract interpretation?

In the case of a statute, purpose interpretation does not depend on the availability of legislative history, and the court may even find a helpful statement of the purpose of enactment set forth in the preamble or purpose clause of the statute itself. Similarly, it is not uncommon for written contracts to begin with a series of recitals of the surrounding circumstances and of the objectives of the parties. Usually prefixed by the word "whereas," contract recitals are not ordinarily drafted as promises or conditions, and their proper role in the interpretation of the main body of the contract has been a source of bafflement to many a judge and lawyer. Courts in this country have frequently repeated with approval Lord Esher's "three rules": "If the recitals are clear and the operative part is ambiguous, the recitals govern the construction. If the recitals are ambiguous, and the operative part is clear, the operative part must prevail. If both the recitals and the operative part are clear, but they are inconsistent with each other, the operative part is to be preferred." Ex parte Dawes, (1886) 17 Q.B.D. 275, 286 (Eng.). But these, like many rules of interpretation, are easier to state than to apply.

NOTE

"Woe Unto You, Lawyers." Should it make a difference, in interpreting a contract, whether the parties were represented by counsel? In Weiland Tool & Mfg. Co. v. Whitney, 251 N.E.2d 242, 248 (Ill. 1969), the court wrote: "In interpreting the letter . . . we have taken into consideration not only that inferences from ambiguous language must be resolved against its author . . . but also that he is a lawyer with a number of years of trial experience and experience as a legal adviser in commercial transactions. He must have had the ability to express [his intention] in concise and clear English . . . if that were his intention. Since he did not do so, we are further persuaded that this was not his intention." See also Gulf Oil Corp. v. Am. Louisiana Pipe Line Co., 282 F.2d 401 (6th Cir. 1960) (reasoning that the fact that both parties were represented by lawyers suggested that difference in language between two sections of contract was not inadvertent).

PROBLEM

On which maxim of construction would you rely in each of the following situations?

a.   A lease provides that a tenant can keep "sheep, cows, pigs and other animals" on a farm and you want to argue that a tiger is not included.

b.   A lease provides that a tenant can keep "sheep, cows and pigs" on a farm and you want to argue that a wild boar is not included.

c.   A lease provides that a tenant can keep "cats and dogs" in an apartment and you want to argue that a gerbil is not included.

Lamps Plus, Inc. v. Varela

United States Supreme Court, 2019.
587 U.S. ____, 139 S.Ct. 1407.

[The facts of this case were first described in Chapter 2, at p. 174 where the focus was on the requirements for consent to class arbitration. Here we return to the case for its discussion of contract interpretation. Recall that [Lamps Plus fell prey to] a hacker who tricked a Lamps Plus employee into disclosing the tax information of approximately 1,300 of the company's employees, including Frank Varela. Varela sued Lamps Plus in Federal District Court in California, bringing state and federal claims on behalf of a putative class of employees whose tax information had been compromised. Lamps Plus moved to compel arbitration on an individual rather than classwide basis, and to dismiss the lawsuit. The district court rejected Lamps Plus's request for individual arbitration, and instead authorized arbitration on a classwide basis. Lamps Plus appealed the order. The Ninth Circuit affirmed, ruling that the agreement between Varela and Lamps Plus—drafted by Lamps Plus—was ambiguous on the issue of class arbitration, the court would follow California law to construe the ambiguity against the drafter. It therefore adopted Varela's interpretation authorizing class arbitration.]

■ ROBERTS, CHIEF JUSTICE, delivered the opinion of the Court.

Neither silence nor ambiguity provides a sufficient basis for concluding that parties to an arbitration agreement agreed to undermine the central benefits of arbitration itself. The Ninth Circuit reached a contrary conclusion based on California's rule that ambiguity in a contract should be construed against the drafter, a doctrine known as *contra proferentem*. The rule applies "only as a last resort" when the meaning of a provision remains ambiguous after exhausting the ordinary methods of interpretation. 3 A. Corbin, Contracts § 559, pp. 268–270 (1960). At that point, *contra proferentem* resolves the ambiguity against the drafter based on public policy factors, primarily equitable considerations about the parties' relative bargaining strength. See 2 E. Farnsworth, Contracts § 7.11, pp. 300–304 (3d ed. 2004); see also 11 R. Lord, Williston on Contracts § 32:12, pp. 788–792 (4th ed. 2012) (stating that application of the rule may vary based on "the degree of sophistication of the contracting parties or the degree to which the contract was negotiated"); Restatement (Second) of Contracts § 206, pp. 80–81, 105–107 (1979) (classifying *contra proferentem* under "Considerations of Fairness and the Public Interest" rather than with rules for interpreting "The Meaning of Agreements"); 3 Corbin, Contracts § 559, at 270 (noting that *contra proferentem* is "chiefly a rule of public policy"). Although the rule enjoys a place in every hornbook and treatise on contracts, we noted in a recent FAA case that "the reach of the canon construing contract language against the drafter must have limits, no matter who the drafter was." DIRECTV, Inc. v. Imburgia, 577 U.S. ___, ___ (2015) (slip op., at 10). This case brings those limits into focus.

Unlike contract rules that help to interpret the meaning of a term, and thereby uncover the intent of the parties, *contra proferentem* is by definition triggered only after a court determines that it *cannot* discern the intent of the parties. When a contract is ambiguous, *contra proferentem* provides a default rule based on public policy considerations; "it can scarcely be said to be designed to ascertain the meanings attached by the parties." 2 Farnsworth, Contracts § 7.11, at 303. Like the contract rule preferring interpretations that favor the public interest, see *id.*, at 304, *contra proferentem* seeks ends other than the intent of the parties.

■ KAGAN, JUSTICE, dissenting. The Federal Arbitration Act (FAA or Act) requires courts to enforce arbitration agreements according to their terms. But the Act does not federalize basic contract law. Under the FAA, state law governs the interpretation of arbitration agreements, so long as that law treats other types of contracts in the same way. That well-established principle ought to resolve this case against Lamps Plus's request for individual arbitration. In my view, the arbitration agreement Lamps Plus wrote is best understood to authorize arbitration on a classwide basis. But even if the Court is right to view the agreement as ambiguous, a plain-vanilla rule of contract interpretation, applied in California as in every other State, requires reading it against the drafter—and so likewise permits a class proceeding here. Today's opinion is rooted instead in the majority's belief that class arbitration "undermine[s] the central benefits of arbitration itself." But that policy view—of a piece with the majority's ideas about class litigation—cannot justify displacing generally applicable state law about how to interpret ambiguous contracts. I respectfully dissent.

Under the FAA, courts must "enforce arbitration agreements according to their terms." Epic Systems Corp. v. Lewis, 584 U.S. ___, ___ (2018). But the construction of those contractual terms (save for in limited circumstances, addressed below) is "a question of state law, which this Court does not sit to review." The Court has made that crucial point many times. Nothing in the FAA (as contrasted to today's majority opinion) "purports to alter background principles of state contract law regarding" the scope or content of agreements. In short, the FAA does not federalize contract law.

Except when state contract law discriminates against arbitration agreements. As this Court has explained, the FAA came about because courts had shown themselves "unduly hostile to arbitration." Epic Systems, 584 U.S., at ___ (slip op., at 5). To remedy that problem, Congress built an "equal-treatment principle" into the Act, requiring courts to "place arbitration agreements on an equal footing with other contracts." Kindred Nursing Centers L. P. v. Clark, 581 U.S. ___, ___ (2017). So any state rule treating arbitration agreements worse than other contracts "stand[s] as an obstacle" to achieving the Act's purposes—and is preempted. Concepcion, 563 U.S., at 343. That means the FAA displaces any state rule discriminating on its face against arbitration. And the Act likewise preempts any more subtle law "disfavoring contracts that (oh so coincidentally) have the defining features of arbitration Court reiterated last Term, is whether the state law in question "target[s]" arbitration agreements, blatantly or covertly, for substandard treatment. Epic Systems, 584 U.S., at ___ (slip op., at 7). When the law does so, it cannot operate; when, conversely, it treats arbitration agreements the same as all other contracts, the FAA leaves it alone.

Here, California's anti-drafter rule is as even-handed as contract rules come. It does not apply only to arbitration contracts. Nor does it apply (as the rule we rejected in Concepcion did) only a tad more broadly to "dispute-resolution contracts," pertaining to both arbitration and litigation. Instead, the anti-drafter rule, as even the majority admits, applies to every conceivable type of contract—and treats each identically to all others. And contrary to what the majority is left to insist, the rule does not "target arbitration" by "interfer[ing] with [one of its] fundamental attributes"—*i.e.,* its supposed individualized nature. The anti-drafter rule (again, quite unlike *Concepcion*'s ban on class-action waivers) takes no side—favors no outcome—as between class and individualized dispute resolution. All the anti-drafter rule asks about is who wrote the contract. So if, for example, Varela had drafted the agreement here, the rule would have prevented, rather than permitted, class arbitration.

So this case should come out Varela's way even if the agreement is ambiguous. To repeat the simple logic applicable here: Under the FAA, state law controls the interpretation of arbitration agreements unless that law discriminates against arbitration; the anti-drafter default rule is subject to no such objection; the rule therefore compels this Court to hold that the agreement here authorizes class arbitration. That the majority thinks the contract, as so read, seriously disadvantages Lamps Plus, see *ante,* at 7–8, is of no moment (any more than if state law had instead construed the contract to produce adverse consequences for Varela). The FAA was enacted to protect against judicial hostility toward arbitration agreements. But the Act provides no warrant for courts to disregard neutral state law in service of ensuring that those agreements give defendants the best terms possible. The Court has thus (rightly) viewed the use of default rules as a run-of-the-mill aspect of contract interpretation, which (so long as neutrally applied) can support class arbitration.

And nothing particular to the anti-drafter rule justifies a different conclusion, as the majority elsewhere suggests. That rule, proclaims the majority, reflects "public policy considerations," rather than "help[ing] to interpret the meaning of a term" as understood by the parties. *Ante,* at 10. The majority here notes that some commentators have viewed some equitable factors as supporting the rule, see *ante,* at 9–10—which is no doubt right. But see 11 R. Lord, Williston on Contracts § 30:1, p. 11 (4th ed. 2012) (Williston) (stating that the rule is *not* justified by public interest considerations). But if the majority means to claim—as it must to prove its point—that the anti-drafter rule has no concern with what "the part[ies] *agreed* to," *Stolt-Nielsen*, 559 U.S., at 684, then the majority is flat-out wrong. From an *ex ante* perspective, the rule encourages the drafter to set out its intent in clear contractual language, for the other party then to see and agree to. See Ayres & Gertner, 99 Yale L.J., at 91, 105, n. 80 (stating the modern view); 2 W. Blackstone, Commentaries on the Laws of England 380 (1766) (anticipating that view by 200-plus years). And from an *ex post* perspective, the rule enables an interpreter to resolve any remaining uncertainty in line with the parties' likely expectations. Consider this very contract. Lamps Plus, knowing about the anti-drafter rule, still chose *not* to include a term prohibiting class arbitration. And Varela, seeing only the language sending "any and all disputes, claims, or controversies" to arbitration, had no reason to think class disputes barred. The upshot is that the rule (as this Court recognized in another arbitration case) protects against "unintended" consequences.

And even if that were not so evident, the FAA does not empower a court to halt the operation of such a garden-variety principle of state law. Nothing in the Act's text requires the displacement of state contract rules, as the majority implicitly concedes. See *ante*, at 6. Nor do the Act's purposes, so long as the state rule (as is true here) extends to all contracts alike, without disfavoring arbitration. The idea that the FAA blocks a state rule satisfying that standard because (a court finds) the rule has too much "public policy" in it comes only from the majority's collective mind. That approach disrespects the preeminent role of the States in designing and enforcing contract rules. It discards a universally accepted principle of contract interpretation in favor of unsupported assertions about what the parties must have (or could not possibly have) consented to. It subordinates authoritative state law to (at most) the impalpable emanations of federal policy, impossible to see except in just the right light. For that reason, it would never have graced the pages of the U.S. Reports save that this case involves class proceedings.

The heart of the majority's opinion lies in its cataloging of class arbitration's many sins. In that respect, the opinion comes from the same place as (though goes a step beyond) this Court's prior arbitration decisions. See, *e.g., Concepcion*, 563 U.S., at 350 (lamenting that class arbitration "greatly increases risks to defendants" by "aggregat[ing] and decid[ing] at once" the "damages allegedly owed to tens of thousands of potential claimants"). The opinion likewise has more than a little in common with this Court's efforts to pare back class litigation. In this case, the result is to disregard the actual contract the parties signed. And to dismiss the neutral and commonplace default rule that would construe that contract against the drafting party. No matter what either requires, the majority will prohibit class arbitration. Does that approach remind you of anything? It should. Here (again) is *Stolt-Nielsen* as *Concepcion* described it: The panel exceeded its authority by "imposing class procedures based on policy judgments rather than the arbitration agreement itself or some background principle of contract law that would affect its interpretation." 563 U.S., at 347. Substitute "foreclosing" for "imposing" and that is what the Court today has done. It should instead— as the FAA contemplates—have left the parties' agreement, as construed by state law, alone.

NOTES

(1) *Contra Proferentem Reconsidered.* In *Lamps Plus*, Chief Justice Roberts rejects *contra proferentem* as an interpretative aid outright. What is his argument? What is the basis of Justice Kagan's insistence that the maxim *should* be applied to the facts of this case?

(2) *The Federal Arbitration Act Versus State Contract Law.* Justice Kagan writes that the Federal Arbitration Act "does not federalize basic contract law." What is the basis of her claim that the Court's opinion makes exactly that move? How does Chief Justice Roberts overcome the application of state law, including the maxim of *contra proferentem*?

Function of Judge and Jury

A detailed consideration of the respective roles of judge and jury (when trial is by jury) in matters of contract interpretation is best left to a course in evidence or procedure. Nevertheless, a few elementary generalizations may be in order. It is clear that the meaning of language is, strictly speaking, a question of fact. Yet the interpretation of written agreements, as to which there is no dispute over the words used by the parties, has often been withdrawn from the jury by calling it a question of "law" for the judge, rather than a question of "fact" for the jury. One reason for this has been a distrust of unsophisticated, uneducated, and—at least at one time—illiterate jurors. Another reason has been a desire for consistency in interpretation of some kinds of contracts, such as standard insurance policies.

Chief Justice Traynor concluded that it is "solely a judicial function to interpret a written instrument unless the interpretation turns upon the credibility of extrinsic evidence." Parsons v. Bristol Dev. Co., 402 P.2d 839, 842 (Cal. 1965). But Judge Henry Friendly pointed out: "With the courts' growing appreciation of Professor Corbin's lesson that words are seldom so 'plain and clear' as to exclude proof of surrounding circumstances and other extrinsic aids to interpretation the exception bids fair largely to swallow the supposed general rule. Whether determination of meaning be regarded as a question of fact, a question of law, or just itself, reliance on the jury to resolve ambiguities in the light of extrinsic evidence seems quite as it should be, save where the form or subject-matter of a particular contract outruns a jury's competence. . . . " Meyers v. Selznick Co., 373 F.2d 218, 222 (2d Cir. 1966).

NOTE

Scope of Review. If a particular question of interpretation is one for the judge and not for the jury, what is the scope of review of the judge's decision on appeal? In Ram Construction Co., Inc. v. Am. States Ins. Co., 749 F.2d 1049, 1052–53 (3d Cir. 1984), the court reasoned that in matters of interpretation the traditional distribution of functions between judge and jury "rests on outdated common law policy considerations, such as jury illiteracy and lack of respect for writings, as well as such continuing concerns as a judicial desire for uniformity. In instances of contract interpretation, therefore, assignment to judge or jury does not of itself determine the standard of review to be applied on appeal. Interpretation by a trial court of a factual matter is reviewable on a clearly erroneous basis, rather than as a plenary one."[e]

SECTION 3.   THE USE OF EXTRINSIC EVIDENCE FROM COMMERCIAL CONTEXT

Frigaliment Importing Co. v. B.N.S. International Sales Corp.

United States District Court, S.D.N.Y., 1960.
190 F.Supp. 116.

■ FRIENDLY, CIRCUIT JUDGE.[f] The issue is, what is chicken? Plaintiff says "chicken" means a young chicken, suitable for broiling and frying. Defendant says "chicken" means any bird of that genus that meets contract specifications on weight and quality, including what it calls "stewing chicken" and plaintiff pejoratively terms "fowl." Dictionaries give both meanings, as well as some others not relevant here. To support its, plaintiff sends a number of volleys over the net; defendant essays to return them and adds a few serves of its own. Assuming that both parties were acting in good faith, the case nicely illustrates Holmes' remark "that the making of a contract depends not on the agreement of two minds in one intention, but on the agreement of two sets of external signs—not on the parties' having *meant* the same thing but on their having *said* the same thing." The Path of the Law, in Collected Legal Papers, p. 178. I have concluded that plaintiff has not sustained its burden of persuasion that the contract used "chicken" in the narrower sense.

The action is for breach of the warranty that goods sold shall correspond to the description, New York Personal Property Law, McKinney's Consol.Laws, c. 41, § 95. Two contracts are in suit. In the first, dated May 2, 1957, defendant, a New York sales corporation, confirmed the sale to plaintiff, a Swiss corporation, of

"US Fresh Frozen Chicken," Grade A, Government Inspected, Eviscerated

2½–3 lbs. and 1½–2 lbs. each

---

[e]   See also Paragon Resources, Inc. v. National Fuel Gas Distribution Corp., 695 F.2d 991, 995 (5th Cir. 1983) ("[T]he clearly erroneous rule applies when extrinsic evidence is used to interpret an *ambiguous* contract, and ambiguity is a question of law." Therefore the appellate court "must first review the decision that the contract terms are ambiguous." If it agrees with the trial court that they are, it must "accord 'clearly erroneous' deference to its interpretation of that contract in light of extrinsic evidence.").

[f]   Henry J. Friendly (1903–1986) clerked for Justice Brandeis and then practiced law in New York for thirty years before becoming a judge, and later chief judge, on the United States Court of Appeals for the Second Circuit. He was admired for his keen mind and the breadth of his learning, and was renowned for his work on federal common law. His article, *In Praise of Erie—And of the New Federal Common Law*, 39 N.Y. U. L. Rev. 383 (1964), has been described as "one of the classics of American legal scholarship." Seventy-Fifth Anniversary Retrospective: Most Influential Articles, 75 N.Y. U. L. Rev. 1517, 1534–35 (2000).

all chicken individually wrapped in cryovac, packed in secured fiber cartons or wooden boxes, suitable for export

75,000 lbs. 2½–3 lbs. $33.00

25,000 lbs. 1½–2 lbs. $36.50

per 100 lbs. FAS New York[g]

"scheduled May 10, 1957 pursuant to instructions from Penson & Co., New York."

The second contract, also dated May 2, 1957, was identical save that only 50,000 lbs. of the heavier "chicken" were called for, the price of the smaller birds was $37 per 100 lbs., and shipment was scheduled for May 30. The initial shipment under the first contract was short but the balance was shipped on May 17. When the initial shipment arrived in Switzerland, plaintiff found, on May 28, that the 2½–3 lbs. birds were not young chicken suitable for broiling and frying but stewing chicken or "fowl"; indeed, many of the cartons and bags plainly so indicated. Protests ensued. Nevertheless, shipment under the second contract was made on May 29, the 2½–3 lbs. birds again being stewing chicken. Defendant stopped the transportation of these at Rotterdam.

This action followed. Plaintiff says that, notwithstanding that its acceptance was in Switzerland, New York law controls under the principle of Rubin v. Irving Trust Co., 1953, 305 N.Y. 288, 305; defendant does not dispute this, and relies on New York decisions. I shall follow the apparent agreement of the parties as to the applicable law.

Since the word "chicken" standing alone is ambiguous, I turn first to see whether the contract itself offers any aid to its interpretation. Plaintiff says the 1½–2 lbs. birds necessarily had to be young chicken since the older birds do not come in that size, hence the 2½–3 lbs. birds must likewise be young. This is unpersuasive—a contract for "apples" of two different sizes could be filled with different kinds of apples even though only one species came in both sizes. Defendant notes that the contract called not simply for chicken but for "US Fresh Frozen Chicken, Grade A, Government Inspected." It says the contract thereby incorporated by reference the Department of Agriculture's regulations, which favor its interpretation; I shall return to this after reviewing plaintiff's other contentions.

The first hinges on an exchange of cablegrams which preceded execution of the formal contracts. The negotiations leading up to the contracts were conducted in New York between defendant's secretary, Ernest R. Bauer, and a Mr. Stovicek, who was in New York for the Czechoslovak government at the World Trade Fair. A few days after meeting Bauer at the fair, Stovicek telephoned and inquired whether

---

[g]   F.A.S. is a common trade term that means, in this context, that for the stated price the seller will place the chicken "free alongside" a ship at the named port, here New York.

defendant would be interested in exporting poultry to Switzerland. Bauer then met with Stovicek, who showed him a cable from plaintiff dated April 26, 1957, announcing that they "are buyer" of 25,000 lbs. of chicken 2½–3 lbs. weight, Cryovac packed, grade A Government inspected, at a price up to 33 cents per pound, for shipment on May 10, to be confirmed by the following morning, and were interested in further offerings. After testing the market for price, Bauer accepted, and Stovicek sent a confirmation that evening. Plaintiff stresses that, although these and subsequent cables between plaintiff and defendant, which laid the basis for the additional quantities under the first and for all of the second contract, were predominantly in German, they used the English word "chicken"; it claims this was done because it understood "chicken" meant young chicken whereas the German word, "Huhn," included both "Brathuhn" (broilers) and "Suppenhuhn" (stewing chicken), and that defendant, whose officers were thoroughly conversant with German, should have realized this. Whatever force this argument might otherwise have is largely drained away by Bauer's testimony that he asked Stovicek what kind of chickens were wanted, received the answer "any kind of chickens," and then, in German, asked whether the cable meant "Huhn" and received an affirmative response.

Plaintiff's next contention is that there was a definite trade usage that "chicken" meant "young chicken." Defendant showed that it was only beginning in the poultry trade in 1957, thereby bringing itself within the principle that "when one of the parties is not a member of the trade or other circle, his acceptance of the standard must be made to appear" by proving either that he had actual knowledge of the usage or that the usage is "so generally known in the community that his actual individual knowledge of it may be inferred." 9 Wigmore, Evidence (3d ed. 1940) § 2464. Here there was no proof of actual knowledge of the alleged usage; indeed, it is quite plain that defendant's belief was to the contrary. In order to meet the alternative requirement, the law of New York demands a showing that "the usage is of so long continuance, so well established, so notorious, so universal and so reasonable in itself, as that the presumption is violent that the parties contracted with reference to it, and made it a part of their agreement." Walls v. Bailey, 1872, 49 N.Y. 464, 472–473.

Plaintiff endeavored to establish such a usage by the testimony of three witnesses and certain other evidence. Strasser, resident buyer in New York for a large chain of Swiss cooperatives, testified that "on chicken I would definitely understand a broiler." However, the force of this testimony was considerably weakened by the fact that in his own transactions the witness, a careful businessman, protected himself by using "broiler" when that was what he wanted and "fowl" when he wished older birds. Indeed, there are some indications, dating back to a remark of Lord Mansfield, Edie v. East India Co., 2 Burr. 1216, 1222 (1761), that no credit should be given "witnesses to usage, who could not adduce instances in verification." 7 Wigmore, Evidence (3d ed. 1940) § 1954; see McDonald v. Acker, Merrall & Condit Co., 2d Dept.1920, 192 App.Div. 123, 126, 182 N.Y.S. 607. While Wigmore thinks this goes too far, a witness' consistent failure to rely on the alleged usage deprives his opinion testimony of much of its effect. Niesielowski, an officer of one of the companies that had furnished the stewing chicken to defendant, testified that "chicken" meant "the male species of the poultry industry. That could be a broiler, a fryer or a roaster," but not a stewing chicken; however, he also testified that upon receiving defendant's inquiry for "chickens," he asked whether the desire was for "fowl or frying chickens" and, in fact, supplied fowl, although taking the precaution of asking defendant, a day or two after plaintiff's acceptance of the contracts in suit, to change its confirmation of its order from "chickens," as defendant had originally prepared it, to "stewing chickens." Dates, an employee of Urner-Barry Company, which publishes a daily market report on the poultry trade, gave it as his view that the trade meaning of "chicken" was "broilers and fryers." In addition to this opinion testimony, plaintiff relied on the fact that the Urner-Barry service, the Journal of Commerce, and Weinberg Bros. & Co. of Chicago, a large supplier of poultry, published quotations in a manner which, in one way or another, distinguish between "chicken," comprising broilers, fryers and certain other categories, and "fowl," which, Bauer acknowledged, included stewing chickens. This material would be impressive if there were nothing to the contrary. However, there was, as will now be seen.

Defendant's witness Weininger, who operates a chicken eviscerating plant in New Jersey, testified "Chicken is everything except a goose, a duck, and a turkey. Everything is a chicken, but then you have to say, you have to specify which category you want or that you are talking about." Its witness Fox said that in the trade "chicken" would encompass all the various classifications. Sadina, who conducts a food inspection service, testified that he would consider any bird coming within the classes of "chicken" in the Department of Agriculture's regulations to be a chicken. The specifications approved by the General Services Administration include fowl as well as broilers and fryers under the classification "chickens." Statistics of the Institute of American Poultry Industries use the phrases "Young chickens" and "Mature chickens," under the general heading "Total chickens." and the Department of Agriculture's daily and weekly price reports avoid use of the word "chicken" without specification.

Defendant advances several other points which it claims affirmatively support its construction. Primary among these is the regulation of the Department of Agriculture, 7 C.F.R. §§ 70.300–70.370, entitled, "Grading and Inspection of Poultry and Edible Products Thereof." and in particular § 70.301 which recited:

Chickens. The following are the various classes of chickens:

(a)   Broiler or fryer . . .

    (b) Roaster . . .

    (c) Capon . . .

    (d) Stag . . .

    (e) Hen or stewing chicken or fowl . . .

    (f) Cock or old rooster . . .

Defendant argues, as previously noted, that the contract incorporated these regulations by reference. Plaintiff answers that the contract provision related simply to grade and Government inspection and did not incorporate the Government definition of "chicken," and also that the definition in the Regulations is ignored in the trade. However, the latter contention was contradicted by Weininger and Sadina; and there is force in defendant's argument that the contract made the regulations a dictionary, particularly since the reference to Government grading was already in plaintiff's initial cable to Stovicek.

Defendant makes a further argument based on the impossibility of its obtaining broilers and fryers at the 33 cents price offered by plaintiff for the 2½–3 lbs. birds. There is no substantial dispute that, in late April, 1957, the price for 2½–3 lbs. broilers was between 35 and 37 cents per pound, and that when defendant entered into the contracts, it was well aware of this and intended to fill them by supplying fowl in these weights. It claims that plaintiff must likewise have known the market since plaintiff had reserved shipping space on April 23, three days before plaintiff's cable to Stovicek, or, at least, that Stovicek was chargeable with such knowledge. It is scarcely an answer to say, as plaintiff does in its brief, that the 33 cents price offered for the 2½–3 lbs. "chickens" was closer to the prevailing 35 cents price for broilers than to the 30 cents at which defendant procured fowl. Plaintiff must have expected defendant to make some profit—certainly it could not have expected defendant deliberately to incur a loss.

Finally, defendant relies on conduct by the plaintiff after the first shipment had been received. On May 28 plaintiff sent two cables complaining that the larger birds in the first shipment constituted "fowl." Defendant answered with a cable refusing to recognize plaintiff's objection and announcing "We have today ready for shipment 50,000 lbs. chicken 2½–3 lbs. 25,000 lbs. broilers 1½–2 lbs.," these being the goods procured for shipment under the second contract, and asked immediate answer "whether we are to ship this merchandise to you and whether you will accept the merchandise." After several other cable exchanges, plaintiff replied on May 29 "Confirm again that merchandise is to be shipped since resold by us if not enough pursuant to contract chickens are shipped the missing quantity is to be shipped within ten days stop we resold to our customers pursuant to your contract chickens grade A you have to deliver us said merchandise we again state that we shall make you fully responsible for all resulting costs." Defendant argues that if plaintiff was sincere in thinking it was entitled to young chickens, plaintiff would not have allowed the shipment under the second contract to go forward, since the distinction between broilers and chickens drawn in defendant's cablegram must have made it clear that the larger birds would not be broilers. However, plaintiff answers that the cables show plaintiff was insisting on delivery of young chickens and that defendant shipped old ones at its peril. Defendant's point would be highly relevant on another disputed issue—whether if liability were established, the measure of damages should be the difference in market value of broilers and stewing chicken in New York or the larger difference in Europe, but I cannot give it weight on the issue of interpretation. Defendant points out also that plaintiff proceeded to deliver some of the larger birds in Europe, describing them as "poulets"; defendant argues that it was only when plaintiff's customers complained about this that plaintiff developed the idea that "chicken" meant "young chicken." There is little force in this in view of plaintiff's immediate and consistent protests.

When all the evidence is reviewed, it is clear that defendant believed it could comply with the contracts by delivering stewing chicken in the 2½–3 lbs. size. Defendant's subjective intent would not be significant if this did not coincide with an objective meaning of "chicken." Here it did coincide with one of the dictionary meanings, with the definition in the Department of Agriculture Regulations to which the contract made at least oblique reference, with at least some usage in the trade, with the realities of the market, and with what plaintiff's spokesman had said. Plaintiff asserts it to be equally plain that plaintiff's own subjective intent was to obtain broilers and fryers; the only evidence against this is the material as to market prices and this may not have been sufficiently brought home. In any event it is unnecessary to determine that issue. For plaintiff has the burden of showing that "chicken" was used in the narrower rather than in the broader sense, and this it has not sustained.

This opinion constitutes the Court's findings of fact and conclusions of law. Judgment shall be entered dismissing the complaint with costs.

NOTES

(1) *"What Is Chicken"*? Judge Friendly says that "The issue is, what is chicken?" Is this the issue that the court had to decide? He also says that the case "nicely illustrates Holmes' remark 'that the making of a contract depends . . . not on the parties' having *meant* the same thing but on their having *said* the same thing.'" Does it? Would the result have been the same if *both* parties had *meant* broilers although they had *said* "chicken"? Is there any reason to hold the parties to a meaning that *neither* attached to their language? See also Shrum v. Zeltwanger, 559 P.2d 1384 (Wyo. 1977) (asking, what is a cow?); Johnson v. Calvert, 5 Cal. 4th 84 (1993) (asking, what is a mother?).

(2) *Corporate Intent.* Since both parties in *Frigaliment* were corporations, the notion that either "meant" anything or had any "intention" may seem somewhat strained. It would seem even more strained if other

persons, including lawyers, had participated in the negotiations along with Bauer and Stovicek. Courts have not been greatly troubled by the problems of finding a collective "intention" in such cases. (For example, Judge Friendly states that B.N.S. "was only beginning in the poultry trade." Would it have been significant if Bauer had been hired by B.N.S. because of his long experience in that trade?) For a rare instance where such a problem was raised, see Franklin Life Insurance Co. v. Mast, 435 F.2d 1038 (9th Cir. 1970), where the court said, "Whatever may have been the secret intent of Mast, it is clear that the intent of his attorney in fact . . . was to enter into a bona fide agreement."

(3) *Incorporation by Reference.* Are there any special problems that arise in the interpretation of terms, such as the regulations of the Department of Agriculture, that have been incorporated in a contract by reference? Cf. Wilcox v. Wilcox, 406 S.W.2d 152 (Ky. 1966) (involving a divorce settlement in which the husband agreed to make maintenance payments until his daughter reached "the age of majority." The court held that the husband's obligation continued until the child reached 21, the statutory age of majority at the time of the agreement, even though the statutory age had subsequently been lowered to 18.)

If you wanted to incorporate the UNIDROIT Principles, would it suffice to say, "This contract incorporates the UNIDROIT Principles"? See Model Clauses for the Use of the UNIDROIT Principles of International Commercial Contracts, https://unidroit.org/instruments/commercial-contracts/upicc-model-clauses.

(4) *Usage.* Judge Friendly observes that Frigaliment's evidence of trade usage "would be impressive if there were nothing to the contrary"—but "there was." Usage will be taken up later in this chapter. How did the parties attempt to show usage? *See* UCC § 1–303.

PROBLEM

Is Silence Golden? Fredrick Hamann, who taught at the Garden City Community Junior College, wanted a year's leave to take a teacher training course. The college regulations incorporated by reference in his contract of employment provided:

> Professional employees granted leaves will, if possible, be reinstated in positions that are similar to the position held when granted the leave.

When he was offered a leave, he knew that the college interpreted this to mean that it would not be required to re-hire him unless there was a similar position open when he re-applied. However, he consulted a lawyer, who advised that in his judgment the provision should be interpreted to mean that the college was required to re-hire him even though a similar position might not be open. Secure in this knowledge, Hamann said nothing and accepted the leave. When he sought to return, the college told him that he could not do so because there was no similar position available. What do you think of the lawyer's advice? See Hamann v. Crouch, 508 P.2d 968 (Kan. 1973).

Hurst v. W.J. Lake & Co.

Supreme Court of Oregon, 1932.
16 P.2d 627.

[Hurst contracted to sell Lake 350 tons of horse meat scraps at $50 a ton. The specifications stated "minimum 50% protein" and the contract provided that if any of the scraps "analyzes less than 50% of protein" Lake was to have a discount of $5.00 a ton. Lake paid only $45 a ton for 140 tons that contained protein varying from 49.53 to 49.96 per cent. Hurst sued to recover the balance of $5 a ton, alleging that both parties were members of a group of traders in horse meat scraps and that the defendant was aware of a usage, prevalent among that group, under which the terms "minimum 50% protein" and "less than 50% protein" required the buyer to accept all scraps containing 49.5 per cent protein or more and pay for them at the rate provided for scraps containing 50% protein. The trial court entered judgment on the pleadings for the defendant and the plaintiff appealed.]

■ ROSMAN, JUSTICE. [T]he language of the dictionaries is not the only language spoken in America. For instance, the word "thousand" as commonly used has a very specific meaning, but the language of the various trades and localities has assigned to it meanings quite different from that just mentioned. Thus in the bricklaying trade a contract which fixes the bricklayer's compensation at "$5.25 a thousand" does not contemplate that he need lay actually 1,000 bricks in order to earn $5.25, but that he should build a wall of a certain size. Brunold v. Glasser, 25 Misc. 285, 53 N.Y.S. 1021; Walker v. Syms, 118 Mich. 183. In the lumber industry a contract requiring the delivery of 4,000 shingles will be fulfilled by the delivery of only 2,500 when it appears that by trade custom two packs of a certain size are regarded as 1,000 shingles, and that hence the delivery of eight packs fulfills the contract, even though they contain only 2,500 shingles by actual count. Soutier v. Kellerman, 18 Mo. 509. And, where the custom of a locality considers 100 dozen as constituting a thousand, one who has 19,200 rabbits upon a warren under an agreement for their sale at the price of 60 pounds for each thousand rabbits will be paid for only 16,000 rabbits. Smith v. Wilson, 3 Barn. & Adol. 728. Numerous other instances could readily be cited showing the manner in which the meaning of words has been contracted, expanded, or otherwise altered by local usage, trade custom, dialect influence, code agreement, etc.

The defendant cites numerous cases in many of which the courts held that, when a contract is expressed in language which is not ambiguous upon its face the court will receive no evidence of usage, but will place upon the words of the parties their common meaning; in other words, in those decisions the courts ran the words of the parties through a judicial sieve whose meshes were incapable of retaining anything but the common meaning of the words, and which permitted the meaning which the parties had placed upon them to run away as waste material.

Surely those courts did not believe that words are always used in their orthodox sense. The rulings must have been persuaded by other considerations. The rule which rejects evidence of custom has the advantage of simplicity; it protects the writing from attack by some occasional individual who will seek to employ perjured testimony in proof of alleged custom; and, if one can believe that the parol evidence rule is violated when common meaning is rejected in favor of special meaning, then the above rule serves the purpose of the parol evidence rule. Without setting forth the manner in which we came to our conclusion, we state that none of these reasons appeals to us as sufficient to exclude evidence of custom and assign to the words their common meaning only, even though the instrument is nonambiguous upon its face.

[Reversed.]

NOTES

(1) *Trade Usage and the UCC.* State the issue in *Hurst* in terms of the contract language. How will trade usage help to resolve that issue at the trial? Even Holmes endorsed trade usage, as distinguished from private codes or conventions: "when you have the security of a local or class custom or habit of speech, it may be presumed that the writer conforms to the usage of his place or class when that is what a normal person in his situation would do." See Oliver Wendell Holmes, *The Theory of Legal Interpretation*, 12 Harv. L. Rev. 417, 420 (1899). How can Hurst prove usage? Why did the buyer fail in its attempt to prove usage in *Frigaliment*?

(2) *Commercial Context in the UCC.* Note that the UCC has two provisions relating to the use of commercial context: §§ 1–303 and 2–202. Would the buyer in *Frigaliment* have succeeded under the UCC? *See* UCC § 1–303. Under the UCC, what is the difference between a usage of trade and a course of dealing? How would a party like Hurst prove a course of dealing? What impact does UCC § 2–202 have on the admissibility of usage of trade? What impact does UCC § 1–303(e) have? How does the rule in UCC § 1–303(e) differ from a plain meaning rule?

For a critical view of the Code provisions on usage, see Lisa Bernstein, *The Questionable Empirical Basis of Article 2's Incorporation Strategy: A Preliminary Study*, 66 U. Chi. L. Rev. 710 (1999).

(3) *Knowledge of Usage.* Under UCC § 1–303, would a buyer be bound by the usage of trade if the buyer had been unaware of it? Recall that in *Frigaliment* the seller had no knowledge of the usage claimed by the buyer. If the buyer had succeeded in proving that usage, would the seller, who "was only beginning in the poultry trade," have been bound by it? Compare Foxco Industries, Ltd. v. Fabric World, Inc., 595 F.2d 976 (5th Cir. 1979) (reasoning that the buyer is bound by usage of trade association as to meaning of "first quality," though it was not a member and did not know of industry usage), with Flower City Painting Contractors, Inc. v. Gumina Constr. Co., 591 F.2d 162 (2d Cir. 1979) (reasoning that the "neophyte minority painting contractor" with first substantial subcontract did not have reason to know of trade usage).

In Martin Rispens & Son v. Hall Farms, Inc., 621 N.E.2d 1078, 1084 (Ind. 1993), a seller argued that its implied warranty of merchantability under a contract for the sale of seeds from Rispens to Hall Farms had been excluded by a usage of trade under UCC § 2–316(3)(c). The problem, thought the court, is that "Rispens and Hall Farms are not in the same trade; Rispens is in the business of selling seeds while Hall Farms is in the business of planting seeds and producing crops. Thus, Rispens can effectively negate the implied warranty of merchantability only by establishing that Hall Farms was or should have been aware of the asserted usage of trade." But was not Hall Farms in the business of buying seeds? Suppose that in *Frigaliment*, the buyer had been the operator of a large chain of fried chicken restaurants?

PROBLEM

What Is "Slaw"? Williams, a Georgian, contracted to sell "slaw cabbage" to Curtin, a New Yorker, who buys cabbage for processing into cole slaw. Both parties had federal licenses to buy and sell perishable agricultural commodities in interstate commerce. Curtin was to send trucks for the cabbage. Because of the weather, most of the cabbage did not grow to the desired size and the market price for cabbage increased dramatically. Williams, claiming that "slaw cabbage" meant large cabbage according to a usage of trade in Georgia, delivered only the large cabbage to Curtin and sold the rest on the risen market. Curtin, claiming that according to a usage of trade in the interstate cole slaw market, "slaw cabbage" meant all cabbage suitable for making cole slaw, seeks damages for breach of contract. If both usages can be established, which applies? See Williams v. Curtin, 807 F.2d 1046 (D.C. Cir. 1986).

SECTION 4.   THE USE OF EXTRINSIC EVIDENCE TO SUPPLEMENT OR QUALIFY THE AGREEMENT: COURSE OF DEALING, USAGE OF TRADE, AND COURSE OF PERFORMANCE

UCC § 1–303(d) provides that a course of dealing, usage of trade, and course of performance may not only "give particular meaning to . . . terms of an agreement," but may also "supplement or qualify" those terms. In *Frigaliment*, p. 535 above, and *Hurst*, p. 542 above, we saw how usage can give meaning to contract language. The two cases that follow are concerned with how usage and course of dealing may *supplement* or *qualify* contract language.

Nanakuli Paving & Rock Co. v. Shell Oil Co.

United States Court of Appeals, Ninth Circuit, 1981.
664 F.2d 772.

■ HOFFMAN, DISTRICT JUDGE. Nanakuli, the second largest asphaltic paving contractor in Hawaii, had bought all its asphalt requirements from 1963 to 1974 from Shell under two long-term supply contracts; its suit charged Shell with breach of the later 1969 contract. The jury returned a verdict of $220,800 for Nanakuli on its first claim, which is that Shell breached the 1969 contract in January, 1974, by failing to price protect Nanakuli on 7200 tons of asphalt at the time Shell raised the price for asphalt from $44 to $76. Nanakuli's theory is that price-protection, as a usage of the asphaltic paving trade in Hawaii, was incorporated into the 1969 agreement between the parties, as demonstrated by the routine use of price protection by suppliers to that trade, and reinforced by the way in which Shell actually performed the 1969 contract up until 1974. Price protection, appellant claims, required that Shell hold the price on the tonnage Nanakuli had already committed because Nanakuli had incorporated that price into bids put out to or contracts awarded by general contractors and government agencies. The District Judge set aside the verdict and granted Shell's motion for judgment n.o.v., which decision we vacate. We reinstate the jury verdict because we find that, viewing the evidence as a whole, there was substantial evidence to support a finding by reasonable jurors that Shell breached its contract by failing to provide protection for Nanakuli in 1974.

Nanakuli offers two theories for why Shell's failure to offer price protection in 1974 was a breach of the 1969 contract. First, it argues, all material suppliers to the asphaltic paving trade in Hawaii followed the trade usage of price protection and thus it should be assumed, under the UCC, that the parties intended to incorporate price protection into their 1969 agreement. This is so, Nanakuli continues, even though the written contract provided for price to be "Shell's Posted Price at time of delivery," F.O.B. Honolulu. The UCC looks to the actual performance of a contract as the best indication of what the parties intended those terms to mean. Nanakuli points out that Shell had price protected it on the two occasions of price increases under the 1969 contract other than the 1974 increase. In 1970 and 1971 Shell extended the old price for four and three months, respectively, after an announced increase.[1]

Nanakuli's second theory for price protection is that Shell was obliged to price protect Nanakuli, even if price protection was not incorporated into their contract, because price protection was the commercially reasonable standard for fair dealing in the asphaltic paving trade in Hawaii in 1974.

Shell presents three arguments for upholding the judgment n.o.v. or, on cross appeal, urging that the District Judge erred in admitting certain evidence. First, it says, the District Court should not have denied Shell's motion *in limine* to define trade, for purposes of trade usage evidence, as the sale and purchase of asphalt in Hawaii, rather than expanding the

---

[1]   Price protection was practiced in the asphaltic paving trade by either extending the old price for a period of time after a new one went into effect or charging the old price for a specified tonnage, which represented work committed at the old price. In addition, several months' advance notice was given of price increases.

knowledge of those practices or to the degree his ignorance of those practices is not excusable: they were so generally practiced he should have been aware of them.

No UCC cases have been found on this point, but the court's reading of the Code language is similar to that of two of the best-known commentators on the UCC:

> Under pre-Code law, a trade usage was not operative against a party who *was not a member of the trade unless* he actually knew of it or *the other party could reasonably believe he knew of it.*

J. White and R. Summers, Uniform Commercial Code, § 12–6 at 371 (1972) (emphasis supplied). White and Summers add (emphasis supplied):

> This view has been carried forward by 1–205(3). [U]sage of the trade is only binding on *members of the trade* involved *or persons* who know or *should know about it.* Persons who should be aware of the trade usage doubtless *include those who regularly deal with members of the relevant trade,* and also members of a second trade that commonly deals with members of a relevant trade (for example, farmers should know something of seed selling).

White and Summers, supra, § 12–6 at 371. Using that analogy, even if Shell did not "regularly deal" with aggregate supplies, it did deal constantly and almost exclusively on Oahu with one asphalt paver. It therefore should have been aware of the usage of Nanakuli and other asphaltic pavers to bid at fixed prices and therefore receive price protection from their materials suppliers due to the refusal by government agencies to accept escalation clauses.

Shell argued not only that the definition of trade was too broad, but also that the practice itself was not sufficiently regular to reach the level of a usage and that Nanakuli failed to show with enough precision how the usage was carried out in order for a jury to calculate damages. The extent of a usage is ultimately a jury question. The Code provides, "The existence and scope of such a usage are to be proved as facts." Haw.Rev.Stat. § 490:1–205(2). The practice must have "such regularity of observance . . . as to justify an expectation that it will be observed. . . ." Id. The Comment explains:

> The ancient English tests for "custom" are abandoned in this connection. Therefore, it is not required that a usage of trade be "ancient or immemorial," "universal" or the like. [F]ull recognition is thus available for new usages and for usages currently observed by the great majority of decent dealers, even though dissidents ready to cut corners do not agree.

Id., Comment 5. The Comment's demand that "not universality but only the described 'regularity of observance'" is required reinforces the provision only giving "effect to usages of which the parties 'are or should be aware'. . . . " Id., Comment 7. A "regularly observed" practice of protection, of which Shell "should have been aware," was enough to constitute a usage that Nanakuli had reason to believe was incorporated into the agreement.

Waiver Or Course Of Performance

Course of performance under the Code is the action of the parties in carrying out the contract at issue, whereas course of dealing consists of relations between the parties prior to signing that contract. Evidence of the latter was excluded by the District Judge; evidence of the former consisted of Shell's price protection of Nanakuli in 1970 and 1971. Shell protested that the jury could not have found that those two instances of price protection amounted to a course of performance of its 1969 contract, relying on two Code comments. First, one instance does not constitute a course of performance. "A single occasion of conduct does not fall within the language of this section. . . . " Haw.Rev.Stat. § 490:2–208, Comment 4. Although the Comment rules out one instance, it does not further delineate how many acts are needed to form a course of performance. The prior occasions here were only two, but they constituted the only occasions before 1974 that would call for such conduct. In addition, the language used by a top asphalt official of Shell in connection with the first price protection of Nanakuli indicated that Shell felt that Nanakuli was entitled to some form of price protection. On that occasion in 1970 Blee, who had negotiated the contract with Nanakuli and was familiar with exactly what terms Shell was bound to by that agreement, wrote of the need to "bargain" with Nanakuli over the extent of price protection to be given, indicating that some price protection was a legal right of Nanakuli's under the 1969 agreement.

Shell's second defense is that the Comment expresses a preference for an interpretation of waiver.

> 3.   Where it is difficult to determine whether a particular act merely sheds light on the meaning of the agreement or represents a waiver of a term of the agreement, the preference is in favor of "waiver" whenever such construction, plus the application of the provisions on the reinstatement of rights waived, is needed to preserve the flexible character of commercial contracts and to prevent surprise or other hardship.

Id., Comment 3. The preference for waiver only applies, however, where acts are ambiguous. It was within the province of the jury to determine whether those acts were ambiguous, and if not, whether they constituted waivers or a course of performance of the contract. The jury's interpretation of those acts as a course of performance was bolstered by evidence offered by Shell that it again price protected Nanakuli on the only two occasions of post-1974 price increases, in 1977 and 1978.

Express Terms As Reasonably Consistent
With Usage In Course of Performance

Perhaps one of the most fundamental departures of the Code from prior contract law is found in the parol evidence rule and the definition of an agreement between two parties. Under the UCC, an agreement goes beyond the written words on a piece of paper. "'Agreement' means the bargain of the parties in fact as found in their language or by implication from other circumstances including course of dealing or usage of trade or course of performance as provided in this chapter (sections 490:1–205 and 490:2–208)." Id. § 490:1–201(3). Express terms, then, do not constitute the entire agreement, which must be sought also in evidence of usages, dealings, and performance of the contract itself. . . . Course of dealings is more important than usages of the trade, being specific usages between the two parties to the contract. "[C]ourse of dealing controls usage of trade." Id. § 490:1–205(4).

A commercial agreement, then, is broader than the written paper and its meaning is to be determined not just by the language used by them in the written contract but "by their action; read and interpreted in the light of commercial practices and other surrounding circumstances. The measure and background for interpretation are set by the commercial context, which may explain and supplement even the language of a formal or final writing." Id., Comment 1. Performance, usages, and prior dealings are important enough to be admitted always, even for a final and complete agreement; only if they cannot be reasonably reconciled with the express terms of the contract are they not binding on the parties.

Our study of the Code provisions and Comments, then, form the first basis of our holding that a trade usage to price protect pavers at times of price increases for work committed on nonescalating contracts could reasonably be construed as consistent with an express term of seller's posted price at delivery. Since the agreement of the parties is broader than the express terms and includes usages, which may even add terms to the agreement, and since the commercial background provided by those usages is vital to an understanding of the agreement, we follow the Code's mandate to proceed on the assumption that the parties have included those usages unless they cannot reasonably be construed as consistent with the express terms.

Although the Code abandoned the traditional common law test of nonconsensual custom and views usage as a way of determining the parties' probable intent, thus abolishing the requirement that common law custom be universally practiced, trade usages still must be well settled. Here the evidence was overwhelming that all suppliers to the asphaltic paving trade price protected customers under the same types of circumstances.

[In addition, here] the express price term was "Shell's Posted Price at time of delivery." A total negation of that term would be that the buyer was to set the price. It is a less than complete negation of the term that an unstated exception exists at times of price increases, at which times the old price is to be charged, for a certain period or for a specified tonnage, on work already committed at the lower price on nonescalating contracts. Such a usage forms a broad and important exception to the express term, but does not swallow it entirely. Therefore, we hold that, under these particular facts, a reasonable jury could have found that price protection was incorporated into the 1969 agreement between Nanakuli and Shell and that price protection was reasonably consistent with the express term of seller's posted price at delivery.

Good Faith In Setting Price

Nanakuli offers an alternative theory why Shell should have offered price protection at the time of the price increases of 1974. Even if price protection was not a term of the agreement, Shell could not have exercised good faith in carrying out its 1969 contract with Nanakuli when it raised its price by $32 effective January 1 in a letter written December 31st and only received on January 4, given the universal practice of advance notice of such an increase in the asphaltic paving trade. The Code provides, "A price to be fixed by the seller or by the buyer means a price for him to fix in good faith," Haw.Rev.Stat. § 490:2–305(2). For a merchant good faith means "the observance of reasonable commercial standards of fair dealing in the trade." Id. 490:2–103(1)(b). The comment to Section 2–305 explains, "[I]n the normal case a 'posted price' . . . satisfies the good faith requirement." Id., Comment 3. However, the words "in the normal case" mean that, although a posted price will usually be satisfactory, it will not be so under all circumstances. In addition, the dispute here was not over the amount of the increase—that is, the price that the seller fixed—but over the manner in which that increase was put into effect. However, Nanakuli presented evidence that Chevron, in raising its price to $76, gave at least six weeks' advance notice, in accord with the long-time usage of the asphaltic paving trade. Shell, on the other hand, gave absolutely no notice, from which the jury could have concluded that Shell's manner of carrying out the price increase of 1974 did not conform to commercially reasonable standards. In both the timing of the announcement and its refusal to protect work already bid at the old price, Shell could be found to have breached the obligation of good faith imposed by the Code on all merchants.

Because the jury could have found for Nanakuli on its price protection claim under either theory, we reverse the judgment of the District Court and reinstate the jury verdict for Nanakuli in the amount of $220,800, plus interest according to law.

■ KENNEDY, CIRCUIT JUDGE, concurring specially. Our opinion should not be interpreted to permit juries to import price protection or a similarly specific contract term from a concept of good faith that is not based on well-established custom and usage or other objective standards of which the parties had clear notice. Here, evidence of custom and usage regarding price protection in the asphaltic paving trade was not contradicted in major respects, and the jury could find that the parties knew or should have known of the practice at the time of making the contract. In my view, these are necessary predicates for either theory of the case, namely, interpretation of the contract based on the course of its performance or a finding that good faith required the seller to hold the price.

NOTES

(1) *Questions.* Is this a case in which usage was employed, in the words of UCC § 1–303(d), to "give particular meaning to . . . terms of an agreement"? To "supplement" those terms? To "qualify" them? (If the purpose was interpretation, what language was being interpreted?)

Recall that in *Naval Institute*, p. 21 above, the trial court had dismissed Naval Institute's complaint for breach of Berkley's agreement to publish the paperback "not sooner than October" on the ground that Berkley "was entitled, in accordance with industry custom, to ship prior to the agreed publication date." The Second Circuit concluded that if the quoted language "had any meaning whatever, it meant at least that Berkley was not allowed to cause such voluminous paperback retail sales prior to that date." Did Berkley seek to use "industry custom" to interpret the language of the agreement? To supplement it? To qualify it? (If the purpose was interpretation, what language was being interpreted?)

In discussing waiver or course of performance, the court states that there were two prior occasions of price protection before 1974, as well as two after 1974. Would it be useful to know if the increases on those occasions were comparable to the jump from $44 to $76 in 1974?

(2) *At What Time?* Should a court apply a usage of trade as of the time of the making of the contract, or as of the time of its performance? In answer to Shell's objection to the trial court's admission of evidence of usage after 1969, the *Nanakuli* opinion states that the court did "not need to decide whether usage evidence after a contract was signed is admissible to show that a party's reliance on a given usage was justifiable, given its continuation, because part of that evidence dealing with asphalt prices was admissible to show the reasonable commercial standards of fair dealing prevalent in the trade in 1974 and the part dealing with the continuation of price protection by aggregate suppliers, after 1969 was not so extensive as to be prejudicial to Shell." 664 F.2d at 785 n.17.

(3) *Usage and Omitted Cases.* Look back at *Drennan*, p. 241 above. Could a general contractor use usage of trade to show that a subcontractor's bid, which was silent as to revocability, was irrevocable? What facts would be sufficient to establish such a usage? See Albert v. R.P. Farnsworth & Co., 176 F.2d 198 (5th Cir. 1949); *cf.* Industrial Electric-Seattle v. Bosko, 410 P.2d 10 (Wash. 1966).

Figgie International, Inc. v. Destileria Serralles, Inc.

United States Court of Appeals, Fourth Circuit, 1999.
190 F.3d 252.

■ TRAXLER, CIRCUIT JUDGE. This action arises out of a sales agreement between Destileria Serralles, Inc. ("Serralles"), a bottler of rum, and Figgie International, Inc. ("Figgie"), a manufacturer of bottle-labeling equipment. Following Figgie's unsuccessful attempts to provide satisfactory bottle-labeling equipment to Serralles under the agreement, Serralles returned the equipment and received a refund of the purchase price.

When a dispute arose as to whether Serralles was entitled to damages for breach of the agreement, Figgie instituted this declaratory judgment action, seeking a determination that Serralles is limited under the agreement to the exclusive remedy of repair, replacement, or return of the equipment. See S.C.Code Ann. § 36–2–719 (Law.Co-op.1976). Serralles, on the other hand, contends that it is entitled to the full array of remedies provided by the South Carolina Uniform Commercial Code (the "UCC" or "Code"). See S.C.Code Ann. §§ 36–2–712, –714, and –715 (Law.Co-op.1976). The district court granted Figgie's motion for summary judgment and denied Serralles' motion for partial summary judgment. Finding no error in the district court's judgment, we affirm.

I.

Serralles, a distributor of rum and other products, operates a rum bottling plant in Puerto Rico. In June 1993, Serralles and Figgie entered into a written agreement under which Figgie was to provide bottle-labeling equipment capable of placing a clear label on a clear bottle of "Cristal" rum within a raised glass oval. When the bottle-labeling equipment was installed in the Serralles plant in April 1994, however, problems arose immediately. Over the course of the next several months, Figgie attempted to repair the equipment to achieve satisfactory performance. However, by November 1994, the equipment still did not work properly, prompting Figgie to refund the purchase price and Serralles to return the equipment.

Additionally, Serralles requested that Figgie pay for alleged losses caused by the failure of the equipment to perform as expected and by the delay in obtaining alternative equipment. Unable to reach a compromise, Figgie instituted this declaratory judgment action, asserting that it owed no further obligations to Serralles under the agreement because Serralles' remedy for breach was limited to repair, replacement, or refund-both under the written terms and conditions of the sales agreement and pursuant to usage of trade in the bottle-labeling industry.

With regard to the alleged limitation of remedy in the sales agreement, Figgie asserts that standard terms and conditions accompanying the sales agreement contained the following language:

Buyer's exclusive remedies for all claims arising out of this agreement and the transaction to which it pertains shall be the right to return the product at buyer's expense, and, at seller's option, receive repayment of the purchase price plus reasonable depreciation for the repair and/or replacement of the product. Seller shall not be subject to any other obligations or liabilities whatsoever with respect to this transaction, and shall under no circumstances be liable for delays, or for any consequential, contingent or incidental damages.

J.A. 13. Figgie, however, has been unable to produce the original sales agreement, asserting that it was lost during a business reorganization. Hence, Figgie is forced to rely upon standard terms and conditions that purportedly accompanied every sales agreement entered into during the time that the Serralles agreement was executed. Serralles, on the other hand, has produced its copy of the agreement, the last page of which stated that "[t]his quotation is made subject to the additional general terms and conditions of sale printed on the reverse hereof," but the reverse side of the page is blank. Figgie asserts that the absence of the general terms and conditions on Serralles' copy is most certainly a copying mistake, whereas Serralles asserts that they were never part of the agreement.

Although conceding at oral argument that a factual dispute exists as to whether the written standards and conditions accompanied the original sales agreement, Figgie asserts that it is nevertheless entitled to summary judgment because, under the UCC, usage of trade in the bottle-labeling industry would supplement the sales agreement with the identical limited remedy of repair, replacement, or refund. See S.C.Code Ann. § 36–1–205(3) (Law.Co-op.1976). Serralles, of course, disputes that usage of trade imposes this limitation and, alternatively, asserts that because the limited remedy has "fail[ed] of its essential purpose," S.C.Code Ann. § 36–2–719(2), it is entitled to the full array of remedies provided by the UCC. [The section of this opinion addressing the enforceability of the limited remedy may be found in Chapter 8, page 992.]

III.

We first address Serralles' contention that the district court erred in granting Figgie's motion for summary judgment. Specifically, the district court concluded that usage of trade in the bottle-labeling industry supplemented the agreement between Figgie and Serralles with the limited remedy of repair, replacement, or return in the event of a breach. Serralles disputes that usage of trade supplies such a limited remedy and, in any event, contends that the limited remedy failed of its essential purpose.

Because the crux of this appeal centers on whether the agreement between the parties limited Serralles' remedy for breach to repair, replacement, or refund of the purchase price, we begin with the language of S.C.Code Ann. § 36–2–719, which governs modifications or limitations to the remedies otherwise provided by the UCC for the breach of a sales agreement.

Under [Section 36–2–719], parties to a commercial sales agreement may provide for remedies in addition to those provided by the UCC, or limit themselves to specified remedies in lieu of those provided by the UCC. An "[a]greement" for purposes of the UCC is defined as "the bargain of the parties in fact as found in their language or by implication from other circumstances including course of dealing or usage of trade." S.C.Code Ann. § 36–1–201(3) (Law.Co-op.1976) (emphasis added). In turn, the Code provides that "[a] course of dealing between parties and any usage of trade in the vocation or trade in which they are engaged or of which they are or should be aware give particular meaning to and supplement or qualify terms of an agreement." S.C.Code Ann. § 36–1–205(3); see also Weisz Graphics v. Peck Indus. Inc., 304 S.C. 101, 403 S.E.2d 146, 150 (S.C.Ct.App.1991) (holding that industry standard supplemented the express provisions of a written contract).

"Usage of trade" is defined as "any practice or method of dealing having such regularity of observance in a place, vocation or trade as to justify an expectation that it will be observed with respect to the transaction in question." S.C.Code Ann. § 36–1–205(2) (Law.Co-op.1976). Where possible and reasonable, an applicable course of dealing or usage of trade will be construed as consistent with the agreement's express terms. See S.C.Code Ann. § 36–1–205(4) (Law.Co-op.1976).

Serralles contends that the district court erred in concluding that usage of trade in the bottle-labeling industry supplemented the agreement between these parties with the limited remedy of repair, replacement, or refund. We disagree.

In support of its motion for summary judgment, Figgie submitted several affidavits of persons with extensive experience in the bottle-labeling and packaging industry, attesting that sellers in the industry always limit the available remedies in the event of a breach to repair, replacement, or return, and specifically exclude consequential damages. While Serralles asserts that it did not "acquiesce" in this practice, it has offered no evidence to contradict the affidavits submitted by Figgie. Accordingly, the district court correctly concluded that usage of trade would limit Serralles to the exclusive remedy of repair, replacement, or return.

NOTE

Suppose Serralles had found a copy of the original sales agreement, which did not mention limited remedies at all. Same result?

Columbia Nitrogen Corp. v. Royster Co.

United States Court of Appeals, Fourth Circuit, 1971.
451 F.2d 3.

[Royster manufactured and sold mixed fertilizers, the principal components of which are nitrogen, phosphate, and potash. Columbia was primarily a producer of nitrogen, although it also manufactured some mixed fertilizer for several years. Royster had been a major buyer from Columbia, but Columbia had never been a significant buyer from Royster. In the fall of 1966, Royster built a phosphate production facility and, to dispose of what it did not need, negotiated a contract to sell to Columbia a minimum of 31,000 tons of phosphate a year for three years, with an option to extend. The contract stated the price per ton subject to an escalation clause dependent on production costs. It set the quantities under the heading "Products Supplied Under Contract Minimum Tonnage Per Year" and contained a merger clause.

When phosphate prices plunged precipitously, Columbia was unable to resell competitively and ordered less than one tenth of the scheduled tonnage during the first contract year. Royster sold the unaccepted phosphate below the contract price and sued for damages. Columbia sought to show by witnesses with long experience in the trade that because of uncertain crop and weather conditions, farming practices and government agricultural programs, express price and quantity terms in the mixed fertilizer industry are mere projections to be adjusted according to market forces. Columbia also sought to show that in its business dealings with Royster during the previous six years—mainly nitrogen sales to Royster—there was repeated and substantial deviation from stated amount or price. The district court excluded this evidence on the ground that "custom and usage or course of dealing are not admissible to contradict the express, plain, unambiguous language of a valid written contract, which by virtue of its detail negates the proposition that the contract is open to variances in its terms." From a $750,000 judgment for Royster, Columbia appealed on the ground that the proffered evidence was improperly excluded.]

■ BUTZNER, CIRCUIT JUDGE. There can be no doubt that the Uniform Commercial Code restates the well established rule that evidence of usage of trade and course of dealing should be excluded whenever it cannot be reasonably construed as consistent with the terms of the contract. Royster argues that the evidence should be excluded as inconsistent because the contract contains detailed provisions regarding the base price, escalation, minimum tonnage, and delivery schedules. The argument is based on the premise that because a contract appears on its face to be complete, evidence of course of dealing and usage of trade should be excluded. We believe, however, that neither the language nor the policy of the Code supports such a broad exclusionary rule. Section 8.2–202 expressly allows evidence of course of dealing or usage of trade to explain or supplement terms intended by the parties as a final expression of their agreement. When this section is read in light of Va.Code Ann. § 8.1–205(4), it is clear that the test of admissibility is not whether the contract appears on its face to be complete in every detail, but whether the proffered evidence of course of dealing and trade usage reasonably can be construed as consistent with the express terms of the agreement.

For the following reasons it is reasonable to construe this evidence as consistent with the express terms of the contract:

The contract does not expressly state that course of dealing and usage of trade cannot be used to explain or supplement the written contract.

The contract is silent about adjusting prices and quantities to reflect a declining market. It neither permits nor prohibits adjustment, and this neutrality provides a fitting occasion for recourse to usage of trade and prior dealing to supplement the contract and explain its terms.

Minimum tonnages and additional quantities are expressed in terms of "Products Supplied Under Contract." Significantly, they are not expressed as just "Products" or as "Products Purchased Under Contract." The description used by the parties is consistent with the proffered testimony.

Finally, the default clause of the contract refers only to the failure of the buyer to pay for delivered phosphate.[h] During the contract negotiations, Columbia rejected a Royster proposal for liquidated damages of $10 for each ton Columbia declined to accept. On the other hand, Royster rejected a Columbia proposal for a clause that tied the price to the market by obligating Royster to conform its price to offers Columbia received from other phosphate producers. The parties, having rejected both proposals, failed to state any consequences of Columbia's refusal to take delivery—the kind of default Royster alleges in this case. Royster insists that we span this hiatus by applying the general law of contracts permitting recovery of damages upon the buyer's refusal to take delivery according to the written provisions of the contract. This solution is not what the Uniform Commercial Code prescribes. Before allowing damages, a court must first determine whether the buyer has in fact defaulted. It must do this by supplementing and explaining the agreement with evidence of trade usage and course of dealing that is consistent with the contract's express terms. Va.Code Ann. §§ 8.1–205(4), 8.2–202. Faithful adherence to this mandate reflects the reality of the

---

[h]   A footnote in the court's opinion contained excerpts from the contract, including the following default clause: "*Default*—If Buyer fails to pay for any delivery under this contract within 30 days after Seller's invoice to Buyer and then if such invoice is not paid within an additional 30 days after the Seller notifies the Buyer of such default, then after that time the Seller may at his option defer further deliveries hereunder or take such action as in their judgment they may decide including cancellation of this contract. Any balances carried beyond 30 days will carry a service fee of ¾ of 1% per month."

was also called the Peerless, and which sailed from Bombay, to wit, in December.

Demurrer, and joinder therein.

■ MILWARD, LORD JUDGE in support of the demurrer. The contract was for the sale of a number of bales of cotton of a particular description, which the plaintiff was ready to deliver. It is immaterial by what ship the cotton was to arrive, so that it was a ship called the Peerless. The words "to arrive ex Peerless," only mean that if the vessel is lost on the voyage, the contract is to be at an end. [Pollock, C.B. It would be a question for the jury whether both parties meant the same ship called the Peerless.] That would be so if the contract was for the sale of a ship called the Peerless; but it is for the sale of cotton on board a ship of that name. [Pollock, C.B. The defendant only bought that cotton which was to arrive by a particular ship. It may as well be said that if there is a contract for the purchase of certain goods in warehouse A that is satisfied by the delivery of goods of the same description in warehouse B.] In that case there would be goods in both warehouses; here it does not appear that the plaintiff had any goods on board the other Peerless. [Martin, B. It is imposing on the defendant a contract different from that which he entered into. Pollock, C.B. It is like a contract for the purchase of wine coming from a particular estate in France or Spain, where there are two estates of that name.] The defendant has no right to contradict by parol evidence a written contract good upon the face of it. He does not impute misrepresentation or fraud, but only says that he fancied the ship was a different one. Intention is of no avail, unless stated at the time of the contract. [Pollock, C.B. One vessel sailed in October and the other in December.] The time of sailing is no part of the contract.

■ MELLISH, LORD JUDGE, (Cohen with him) in support of the plea. There is nothing on the face of the contract to show that any particular ship called the Peerless was meant; but the moment it appears that two ships called the Peerless were about to sail from Bombay there is a latent ambiguity, and parol evidence may be given for the purpose of showing that the defendant meant one Peerless and the plaintiff another. That being so, there was no consensus ad litem, and therefore no binding contract. He was then stopped by the court.

■ PER CURIAM. There must be judgment for the defendants.

Judgment for the defendants.

NOTES

(1) *Simpson on Raffles.* At least some of the case's fascination is due to the circumstances that "the judges . . . thought the solution to the problem presented to them to be so obvious that they gave judgment for the defendants without troubling to give any reasons for their decision." A.W. Brian Simpson, *Contracts for Cotton to Arrive: The Case of the Two Ships Peerless,* 11 Cardozo L. Rev. 287, 287 (1989)

(2) *Gilmore on Raffles.* Professor Grant Gilmore wrote that "the celebrated case of Raffles v. Wichelhaus . . . is to the ordinary run of case law as the recently popular theater of the absurd is to the ordinary run of theater." He noted that if the ship which sailed first had also arrived first and if the market price had broken between the two arrival dates, the buyer would presumably have pleaded these facts; since he did not, "we may . . . safely assume that there was no such issue to be raised." There was therefore merit to Milward's argument that it was "immaterial by what ship the cotton was to arrive, so [long as] it was a ship called the Peerless." According to Gilmore, this "meant only that 'if the vessel is lost on the voyage, the contract is to be at an end' (that is, the seller would bear the loss but the buyer would have no claim for damages for non delivery)." But "the judges, no doubt mistakenly, believed that the identity of the carrying ship was important." Grant Gilmore, The Death of Contract 35–39 (1974).

(3) *Simpson on Gilmore.* Professor Brian Simpson concluded otherwise in a detailed examination of the background of the contract, which was made in 1862 at the time of the cotton shortage created by the blockade of the southern states during the Civil War. The shortage made cotton prices high and volatile, and caused English spinners to look to India. Speculators were attracted to "arrival" contracts, under which the buyer purchased cotton in transit for forward delivery. Although the time of arrival was of paramount importance to the buyer, it was not common for the contract to specify this time because of the uncertainties involved. One technique that made it possible for the buyer to at least estimate the approximate date of arrival was to name the ship and sometimes the port of departure. The contract in the principal case was such a "ship named" and "port named" contract. Simpson, supra, at 324.

How might the outcome of this debate affect the value of the case as a precedent?

(4) *Holmes on Raffles.* Here is Holmes's analysis of *Raffles*: "[W]hile other words may mean different things, a proper name means one person or thing and no other. . . . In theory of speech your name means you and my name means me, and the two names are different. They are different words. . . . [H]ere the parties have said different things and never have expressed a contract." Oliver Wendell Holmes, *The Theory of Legal Interpretation*, 12 Harv. L. Rev. 417, 418 (1899).

(5) *"What Is Chicken"? (Reprise).* Is the Restatement test too broad? At the end of the *Frigaliment* opinion, Judge Friendly said that "the burden of showing that 'chicken' was used in the narrower rather than in the broader sense" was on the buyer. Its action for breach of warranty therefore failed. *See* UCC § 2–607(4). Recall that in *Frigaliment*, the seller, under the second contract, stopped shipment at Rotterdam as a result of the buyer's protests. Does it follow from the dismissal of the buyer's complaint that the seller would necessarily have prevailed in an action against the buyer for breach of this contract? Would not the seller have had the burden of showing that "chicken" was used in the broader sense? Is it possible that the seller might have failed to sustain this burden?

In a case like *Raffles*, is it possible that the seller might fail to meet the burden of showing that "Peerless" was used in the sense of the ship sailing in December, and that the buyer might also fail to meet the burden of showing that "Peerless" was used in the sense of the ship sailing in October?

Not long after *Frigaliment* was handed down, Judge Friendly had occasion to discuss mutual misunderstanding, and said this: "It may be that Frigaliment Importing Co. v. B.N.S. International Sales Corp. . . . decided by the writer, might better have been placed on that ground, with the loss still left on the plaintiff because of defendant's not unjustifiable change of position." Dadourian Export Corp. v. U.S., 291 F.2d 178, 187 & n.4 (2d Cir. 1961) (Friendly, J., dissenting).

(6)   *Subjective Intent and CISG.* In MCC-Marble Ceramic Center, Inc. v. Ceramica Nuova d'Agostino, *S.P.A.*, 144 F.3d 1384 (11th Cir. 1998), the court stated that, "Contrary to what is familiar practice in United States courts, the CISG appears to permit a substantial inquiry into the parties' subjective intent. . . . " Does the court's statement accord with Restatement § 201, which says that a term to which "the parties have attached the same meaning . . . is interpreted in accordance with that meaning." Is it clear that the parol evidence rule (or the plain meaning rule) applies to testimony of a party, or its representative, with regard to the party's "subjective intent"?

PROBLEM

Wichelhaus v. Raffles. Suppose that Raffles had not shipped cotton on either ship and that Wichelhaus had sued Raffles for breach of contract. What result? Suppose that Wichelhaus, having found no cotton on the October Peerless, had learned for the first time of the December Peerless and decided to wait for it. If the price of cotton had continued to rise, could he have held Raffles to a contract to deliver cotton on the December Peerless?

Colfax Envelope Corp. v. Local No. 458–3M

United States Court of Appeals for the Seventh Circuit, 1994.
20 F.3d 750.

■ POSNER, CHIEF JUDGE. This appeal in a suit over a collective bargaining agreement presents a fundamental issue of contract law, that of drawing the line between an ambiguous contract, requiring interpretation, and a contract that, because it cannot be said to represent the agreement of the parties at all, cannot be interpreted, can only be rescinded and the parties left to go their own ways. Colfax, the plaintiff, is a manufacturer of envelopes. It does some printing of its envelopes, and the seventeen employees who do the printing are represented by the defendant union. Colfax has two printing presses. One prints 78-inch-wide sheets in four colors. The other prints 78-inch-wide sheets in five colors, but most of the time Colfax prints only four-color sheets on it.

Colfax has so few printing employees that it does not bother to participate in the collective bargaining negotiations between the union and the Chicago Lithographers Association, an association for collective bargaining of the other Chicago printing companies whose employees are represented by this union. Instead, whenever the union and the CLA sign a new collective bargaining agreement, the union sends Colfax a summary of the changes that the new agreement has made in the old one. If Colfax is content with the changes, the union sends it a copy of the complete new agreement, which Colfax signs and returns. If Colfax doesn't like the terms negotiated by the CLA, it is free to do its own bargaining with the union.

The collective bargaining agreements specify minimum manning requirements for each type of press used by the printers. The agreement in force between 1987 and 1991 fixed those minima as three men for four-color presses printing sheets 45 to 50 inches wide and four men for four-color presses printing sheets wider than 50 inches. Five-color presses printing sheets more than 55 inches wide required five men unless only four colors were printed, in which event only four men were required. The upshot was that under these agreements, all of which Colfax had signed, Colfax had to man each of its presses (which were 78-inch presses) with four men except on the rare occasions when it printed five-color sheets on its second press, and then it had to add a man.

In 1991 the union negotiated a new agreement with the CLA and sent a summary of the changes to Colfax. The letter enclosing the summary asked Colfax to indicate whether it agreed to the terms in the summary. (This may have been a departure from past practice, in which Colfax signed the complete agreement rather than the summary, but if so neither party makes anything of it.) In a section on manning requirements, the summary lists "4C 60 Press-3 Men" and "5C 78 Press-4 Men." Believing (in part because union members who claimed to be familiar with the new agreement had told Colfax that Colfax would really like the changes in it) that this meant that all presses operated as four-color presses would now require only three men to man them, Colfax's president and majority shareholder, Charles Patten, signed the union's letter, indicating acceptance of the terms in the summary. Later a copy of the actual agreement arrived, but it contained a crucial typo, which supported Patten's understanding of the summary. When a corrected copy of the agreement finally arrived, the manning requirements stated in it were different from what Patten had understood from the summary. Four-color presses between 45 and 60 inches required three men, but all four-color presses over 60 inches required four men. The changes had not benefited Colfax at all, and because it was under competitive pressure, it would have liked to negotiate better terms. Patten refused to sign the agreement but the union took the position that Colfax was bound to it by its acceptance of the summary.

Colfax brought this suit under section 301 of the Taft-Hartley Act, 29 U.S.C. § 185, for a declaration that it has no collective bargaining contract with the union because the parties never agreed on an essential term—the manning requirements for Colfax's printing presses. The union counterclaimed for an order to arbitrate. The union's position was that Colfax had accepted the new agreement, which requires arbitration of all disputes "arising out of the application or interpretation of this contract." The district judge granted summary judgment for the union, concluding that the reference to the new manning requirement for a four-color 60-inch press in the summary of changes that Colfax had accepted referred unambiguously to 60-inch presses and had no application to any other presses, such as Colfax's 78-inch presses. Colfax has appealed.

One way to describe the issue that divides the parties is that they disagree about the meaning of the term "4C 60 Press-3 Men." Colfax believes that it means four-color presses printing sheets 60 inches and over, while the union believes that it means four-color presses 60 inches and under (down to 45 inches). Remember that the previous agreement had allowed the use of three-man crews on four-color presses between 45 and 50 inches. The union interprets the change as extending the upper bound of the three-man range to 60 inches. Ordinarily a dispute over the meaning of a contractual term is, if the contract contains an arbitration clause, for the arbitrator to decide. But sometimes the difference between the parties goes so deep that it is impossible to say that they ever agreed—that they even *have* a contract that a court or arbitrator might interpret. In the famous though enigmatic and possibly misunderstood case of Raffles v. Wichelhaus, 2 H. & C. 906, 159 Eng.Rep. 375 (Ex. 1864), the parties made a contract for the delivery of a shipment of cotton from Bombay to England on the ship *Peerless*. Unbeknownst to either party, there were two ships of that name sailing from Bombay on different dates. One party thought the contract referred to one of the ships, and the other to the other. The court held that there was no contract; there had been no "meeting of the minds." See generally A.W. Brian Simpson, "Contracts for Cotton to Arrive: The Case of the Two Ships *Peerless*," 11 Cardozo L.Rev. 287 (1989).

The premise—that a "meeting of the minds" is required for a binding contract—obviously is strained. 2 E. Allan Farnsworth, *Contracts* § 7.9, at p. 251 (1990). Most contract disputes arise because the parties did not foresee and provide for some contingency that has now materialized—so there was no meeting of minds on the matter at issue—yet such disputes are treated as disputes over contractual meaning, not as grounds for rescinding the contract and thus putting the parties back where they were before they signed it. So a literal meeting of the minds is not required for an enforceable contract, which is fortunate, since courts are not renowned as mind readers. Let us set the concept to one side, therefore, and ask how (else) to explain Raffles v. Wichelhaus and cases like it. It seems to us as it has to other courts that a contract ought to be terminable without liability and the parties thus allowed to go their own ways when there is "no sensible basis for choosing between conflicting understandings" of the contractual language, as the court said in an American *Raffles*-like case, Oswald v. Allen, 417 F.2d 43, 45 (2d

Cir.1969), quoting William F. Young, Jr., "Equivocation in the Making of Agreements," 64 Colum.L.Rev. 619, 647 (1964). In *Oswald* the misunderstanding arose because the parties did not speak the same language (literally). In Balistreri v. Nevada Livestock Production Credit Association, 262 Cal.Rptr. 862 (1989), the parents of an aspiring farmer thought they had pledged property they owned in Sebastopol to secure a loan to their son, and indeed the lender's cover letter described the property as "your Sebastopol residence." But the actual deed of trust listed the parents' home in Petaluma as the collateral. The court held that there had been no meeting of the minds.

Raffles and *Oswald* were cases in which neither party was blameable for the mistake; *Balistreri* was a case in which both were equally blameable, the parents for having failed to read the deed of trust, the lender for having drafted a misleading cover letter. It is all the same. *Restatement (Second) of Contracts* §§ 20(1)(a), (b) (1981). If neither party can be assigned the greater blame for the misunderstanding, there is no nonarbitrary basis for deciding which party's understanding to enforce, so the parties are allowed to abandon the contract without liability. Neel v. Lang, 236 Mass. 61, 127 N.E. 512 (1920); Konic International Corp. v. Spokane Computer Services, Inc., 109 Idaho 527, 529, 708 P.2d 932, 934 (App.1985). These are not cases in which one party's understanding is more reasonable than the other's. Compare *Restatement, supra,* § 20(2)(b). If rescission were permitted in *that* kind of case, the enforcement of every contract would be at the mercy of a jury, which might be persuaded that one of the parties had genuinely held an idiosyncratic idea of its meaning, so that there had been, in fact, no meeting of the minds. Cf. Young, *supra,* at 646. Intersubjectivity is not the test of an enforceable contract.

The clearest cases for rescission on the ground that there was "no meeting of the minds" (or, better, that there was a "latent ambiguity" in the sense that neither party knew that the contract was ambiguous) are ones in which an offer is garbled in transmission. The cases we have cited are all of that character, if "transmission" is broadly construed. Vickery v. Ritchie, 202 Mass. 247, 88 N.E. 835 (1909), provides a further illustration. A landowner and a contractor signed what they believed to be duplicate copies of a contract for the construction of a Turkish bath house. Because of a fraud by the architect for which neither the contractor nor the landowner could be blamed, the copy signed by the landowner stated the price as $23,000 and the copy signed by the contractor stated it as $34,000. Through no fault of their own, the parties had signed different contracts. Or consider Konic International Corp. v. Spokane Computer Services, Inc., *supra.* The seller quoted a price of "fifty-six twenty," which the buyer thought meant $56.20. In fact the seller had meant $5,620. In both cases rescission was permitted, the first being a case in which neither party was at fault, the second one in which both were equally at fault, being careless in their utterance and interpretation, respectively, of an ambiguous oral formula.

Our case is superficially similar. The actual terms of the 1991 agreement were muddied in the summary that the union gave Colfax and that Colfax signed, making it possible that the parties had different understandings. The difference between this case and the others is that Colfax, unlike the hapless promisors in the cases we have cited, should have realized that the contract was unclear. The buyer in *Konic* thought—*really* thought—that he was being quoted a price of $56.20, and no doubt fell off his stool when he discovered that the price was a hundred times greater than he thought. But the expression "4C 60 Press" does not on its face speak to the minimum manning requirement for a 4C 78 Press. The union's interpretation, that the phrase merely extended the upper bound of the old range for three-man four-color presses from 50 to 60 inches, may or may not be correct. The fact that the union restated and clarified the interpretation in the corrected agreement that it sent Colfax is not decisive on the question, because it is the summary rather than the corrected full agreement that is the contract between these parties. But Colfax, if reasonable, could not have doubted from reading the summary that interpretations of the kind that the union and the district judge later placed upon it would be entirely plausible. Colfax had a right to *hope* that its interpretation would prevail but it had no right to accept the offer constituted by the summary on the premise that either its interpretation was correct or it could walk away from the contract. "Heads I win, tails you lose," is not the spirit that animates the principle that latent ambiguity is a ground for rescission of a contract.

It is common for contracting parties to agree—that is, to *signify* agreement—to a term to which each party attaches a different meaning. It is just a gamble on a favorable interpretation by the authorized tribunal should a dispute arise. Parties often prefer to gamble in this way rather than to take the time to try to iron out all their possible disagreements, most of which may never have any consequence. Colfax gambled on persuading an arbitrator that the reference in the summary to the four-color 60-inch press meant what Colfax believes it means. The union gambled on the arbitrator's adopting the meaning that the union later made clear in the full agreement—but, to repeat, if there is a contract it is (the parties agree) the summary, read in light of the collective bargaining agreement that was being modified, that is the contract between these parties.

When parties agree to a patently ambiguous term, they submit to have any dispute over it resolved by interpretation. That is what courts and arbitrators are *for* in contract cases—to resolve interpretive questions founded on ambiguity. It is when parties agree to terms that reasonably appear to each of them to be unequivocal but are not, cases like that of the ship *Peerless* where the ambiguity is buried, that the possibility of rescission on grounds of mutual misunderstanding, or, the term we prefer, latent ambiguity, arises. A reasonable person in Colfax's position would have realized that its interpretation of the term "4C 60 Press-3 Men" might not coincide with that of the other party or of the tribunal to which a dispute over the meaning of the term would be submitted. It threw the dice, and lost, and that is the end of the case. It cannot gamble on a favorable interpretation and, if that fails, repudiate the contract with no liability. *Cf.* Prudential Ins. Co. v. Miller Brewing Co., 789 F.2d 1269, 1278 (7th Cir.1986).

[In the remainder of the opinion, the court held that the arbitrator, rather than a court, should determine whether, "under a proper interpretation of the contract, there really was no meeting of the minds over the manning requirements and therefore that the contract should be rescinded after all."]

NOTES

(1) *A Matter of Terminology?* In *Raffles*, the court concluded that "there was no binding contract." In *Colfax*, the court phrased the issue as one of whether the contract should be rescinded. Is there a difference in meaning between these formulations?

(2) *A Matter of Timing?* Eleven years after the *Colfax* decision, its author qualified his views a bit. Judge Posner wrote, "When neither party is blamable, or both parties are equally blamable, for an incurable uncertainty in their contract, it makes economic sense to allow the contract to be rescinded. For in such a case there is no presumption that one party was trying to repudiate a value-maximizing transaction. But the qualification 'equally blamable' is important, because one function of contract enforcement, as we will see, is to penalize a party who negligently creates interpretive uncertainty." In a footnote, though, he added, "But this is in general rather than in every case. As Scott Hemphill has pointed out to me, rescission should not be ordered if the consequence is a windfall to one of the parties, even if the party was blameless for the mistake giving rise to the claim for rescission. In *Raffles*, the contract was a losing one for the buyers whichever date the cotton was shipped on, so that by rescinding the contract they were able to shift to the seller a loss unrelated to the mutual mistake." Richard A. Posner, *The Law and Economics of Contract Interpretation*, 83 Texas L. Rev. 1581, 1591 n.20 (2005).

SECTION 6.   SUPPLEMENTING THE AGREEMENT WITH TERMS SUPPLIED BY LAW: GAP FILLERS, WARRANTIES, AND MANDATORY TERMS

Until now, this chapter has focused on determining the terms of parties' obligations to each other by ascertaining and interpreting their agreement in fact. As we have seen, though, parties do not write fully specified (or completely contingent) contracts, in which every eventuality is the subject of an explicit (or even implicit) agreement. Rather, the agreement of the parties is, by necessity, incomplete. Although major issues are resolved by bargaining and, in many cases, issues that recur with some frequency are covered by boilerplate terms, other issues that may give rise to dispute may not be the subject of agreement between the parties.

Why is this the case? For one thing, "if all terms were expressly agreed to, even the simplest contracts would become intolerably long." Farnsworth on Contracts § 7.15. Moreover, "businessmen pay more attention to describing the performance in an exchange than to planning for contingencies or defective performance . . . " Stewart Macaulay, Non-Contractual Relations in Business: A Preliminary Study, 28 Am. Soc. Rev. 55, 60 (1963).

(A) FILLING CONTRACTUAL GAPS

What happens when a dispute arises about which there has been no agreement between the parties, either explicit or implicit (*e.g.*, via course of dealing, usage of trade, etc.)? In such a case, the process of ascertaining and interpreting the parties' agreement—the subject of this chapter—will not yield an answer to the dispute. Accordingly, the court may need to supply a contract term to resolve the dispute. This process is usually referred to as "implication."

The process of implication may have one of two bases. The first basis for implication may be the court's findings as to the actual expectations of the parties. (Thus, strictly speaking, this might be more precisely referred to as "inference" rather than "implication," but the latter usage is traditional.) "If the court is persuaded that the parties shared a common expectation with respect to the omitted case, the court will give effect to that expectation, even though the parties did not reduce it to words." Farnsworth on Contracts § 7.16. Because this sort of implication involves the court giving effect to the fact of such a common understanding, the terms incorporated by this process are often referred to as "implied-in-fact" terms.

How is a court to be convinced of the common expectations of the parties in the context of a dispute when the parties may have quite different memories of their expectations? The New York Court of Appeals has stated that "a party who asserts the existence of an implied-in-fact covenant bears a heavy burden, for it is not the function of the courts to remake the contract agreed to by the parties, but rather to enforce it as it exists. Thus, a party making such a claim must prove not merely that it would have been better or more sensible to include such a covenant, but rather that the particular unexpressed promise sought to be enforced is in fact implicit in the agreement viewed as a whole." Rowe v. Great Atl. & Pac. Tea Co., 46 N.Y.2d 62, 385 N.E.2d 566 (1978). Is this the standard applied by Judge Cardozo in Wood v. Lucy, Lady Duff-Gordon, p. 111, above, when he concluded that the agreement in question was "instinct with an obligation?"

In the absence of a common expectation, matters may become more difficult when courts are faced with a number of competing theories. Jeremy Bentham argued that the court should implement the bargain the parties would have made had they considered the matter, thus remedying "the shortsightedness of individuals, by doing for them what they would have done for themselves if their imagination had anticipated the march of nature." *A General View of a Complete Code of Laws, in* 3 *Works of Jeremy Bentham* 191 (J. Bowring ed., 1843). Others have argued against that view, suggesting a different basis for implication. "It might seem that the parties themselves have become so far disembodied spirits that their actual persons should be allowed to rest in peace. In their place there rises the figure of the fair and reasonable man . . . the anthropomorphic conception of justice." Davis Contractors v. Fareham Urban Dist. Council, [1956] A.C. 696, 728 (Eng.). This is the view generally adopted by the Restatement. See Restatement § 204. More recently, the debate has been augmented by a focus on law and economics. *See, e.g.,* Ian Ayres and Robert Gertner, *Filling Gaps in Incomplete Contracts: An Economic Theory of Default Rules,* 99 Yale L.J. 87 (1989). Among the other possibilities noted by Ayres and Gertner is the "penalty default rule . . . designed to give at least one party to the contract an incentive to contract around the default rule and therefore to choose affirmatively the contract provision they prefer." Id. at 91. Since the process just described results in terms supplied pursuant to a legal rule rather than by factual inference, such terms are often referred to as being "implied by law."

(B) FILLING COMMON CONTRACTUAL GAPS BY STATUTE

As discussed above, some issues with respect to which parties tend to omit agreement occur with such frequency that the law has developed "off-the-rack" default terms—terms that courts imply in the absence of agreement between the parties—to address those issues. This practice is extensively developed in Article 2 of the Uniform Commercial Code.

Consider the following example: Brown and Silver, located some distance away from each other, have entered into a contract pursuant to which Brown has agreed to buy 1000 grommets from Silver for $100. All the basic terms of the contract have been specified except for the location at which the grommets will be tendered to Brown. On the date for performance under the agreement, each party awaits performance by the other; Brown assumes that Silver will deliver the grommets to Brown, while Silver assumes that Brown will come to Silver's plant to pick up the grommets. When Silver does not deliver, and Brown does not pick up the grommets at Silver's plant, each believes the other is in breach.

Who is right—Brown or Silver? In the absence of actual agreement as to where tender will take place, and in the absence of any course of dealing or usage of trade relevant to the issue, the process of ascertaining and interpreting the parties' agreement does not yield an answer as to the location of tender. Because issues of this sort arise with some frequency, the drafters of UCC Article 2 provided "gap fillers" to resolve this and several other gaps as a matter of law.

How does UCC Article 2 resolve the gap in the contract between Brown and Silver described above? See UCC § 2–308. When must Brown pay? See UCC § 2–310.

Avoiding the Gaps. Assume that Buyer and Seller are aware of the resolution of the "tender gap" provided in UCC § 2–308, but would prefer to resolve the matter differently. Are they nonetheless constrained by the rule in that section? Would your answer be different if UCC § 2–308 did not contain the phrase "unless otherwise agreed"? See UCC §§ 1–302(a) and 1–302(c).

How Wide the Gaps? As noted above, major issues in a transaction tend to be resolved by negotiation between the parties, which typically leads to an explicit term. Can the law supply a key term when the parties have not bargained with respect to it? For example, assume that Seller and Buyer have agreed to a sale of goods but have failed to reach agreement as to the price of the goods. (Why might they fail to agree with respect to such a key term?) Will the law enforce such an agreement as a contract? If so, what is the contract price? See UCC § 2–305(1).

(C) FILLING GAPS WITH RESPECT TO CHARACTERISTICS OF THE GOODS—IMPLIED WARRANTIES IN ARTICLE 2

In contracts for the sale of goods, it is common for the agreement to be silent about whether the goods must meet any particular standard of quality in order to fulfill the seller's obligation under the contract. One way of dealing with such omissions is through the well-known maxim of *caveat emptor*, or "buyer beware." In other words, if the agreement is silent as to product quality, the contract does not impose any minimum standard; if a buyer wishes to contract only for goods that meet a particular standard, he or she must contract for that result. See, e.g., Seixas v. Woods, 2 Cai. 48, 2 Am. Dec. 215 (N.Y. Sup. Ct. 1804). See generally Walton Hamilton, *The Ancient Maxim Caveat Emptor*, 40 Yale L.J. 1133 (1931).

More recently, the law has taken a different path. In certain circumstances, the law supplies a default term with respect to the standards that a contracting party's performance must fulfill, even when the parties' agreement could easily be interpreted and enforced without such a term. Such implied terms are default terms in the sense that the parties can contract to the contrary. The term "gap fillers" does not adequately describe them, though, since the agreement could be understood and applied even in the absence of the supplied terms.

Such contract terms implied by law usually are referred to as "implied warranties." While the concept of implied warranties is sometimes used in other contexts, their most common use appears to be in sale-of-goods contracts governed by UCC Article 2.

Implied warranties are dealt with extensively in UCC Article 2. The two most important rules are that which provides for an implied warranty of merchantability (UCC § 2–314), and that which establishes an implied warranty of fitness for particular purpose (UCC § 2–315). In addition, there is UCC § 2–312, which provides for a warranty of title and a warranty against infringement. This following material focuses on the implied warranties of merchantability and fitness.

For each of the Article 2 implied warranties, three questions must be addressed. First, in what circumstances does Article 2 make the warranty part of the contract? Second, what is the content of the warranty? Third, may the parties, if they so desire, draft a contract that does not contain the warranty?

The Implied Warranty of Merchantability

When does the implied warranty of merchantability come into existence? According to UCC § 2–314(1), "a warranty that the goods shall be merchantable is implied in a contract for their sale if the seller is a merchant with respect to goods of the kind." This is not the only time that Article 2 applies a special rule for merchants. Indeed, the term appears fourteen times in Article 2. We have already encountered other uses of the term in that Article: Recall that, pursuant to UCC § 2–205, a promise by a merchant to hold an offer open is sometimes irrevocable even when not supported by consideration. Similarly, UCC § 2–207(2), governing the fate of additional terms in an acceptance, contains a rule that applies only "between merchants" And the same is true for the statute of frauds exception in UCC § 2–201(2).

Who qualifies as a merchant? The term "merchant" is defined in UCC § 2–104. Section 2–314 qualifies the term by requiring that the seller be a merchant with respect to goods of the kind that are being sold. Does this mean that a seller of goods can be a merchant without triggering the implied warranty of merchantability?

Consider the definition of "merchant" in deciding whether a contract to sell goods by each of the following sellers would contain an implied warranty of merchantability:

(1) A retired lawyer no longer has use for her late-model automobile. She enters into a contract to sell the automobile to her next-door neighbor.

(2) A used-car dealer enters into a contract to sell a used car from his lot to a buyer.

(3) A used-car dealer has just bought a new desk for his office. He has no use for the old desk, so he enters into a contract

to sell it to a visitor to his showroom who admired it and asked to buy it.

If the seller is a merchant with respect to goods of the kind, the contract for their sale contains a warranty that the goods shall be merchantable. What does it mean for goods to be merchantable? Read UCC § 2–314(2), noting each of the criteria of merchantability. What is the significance of the phrase "at least"?

Most litigation under UCC § 2–314(2) has concerned the second ("fair average quality") and third ("fit for the ordinary purpose for which such goods are used") criteria of merchantability. As courts have frequently noted, "fair average quality" and "fit" set standards that are short of perfect. See, e.g., In re First Hartford Corp., 63 B.R. 479 (Bankr. S.D.N.Y. 1986) ("Satisfaction of this implied warranty entails a finding 'that the article is reasonably fit for the ordinary uses for which it was manufactured and [it] need only be of 'medium quality or goodness' . . . In addition, under a section 2–314 analysis, all we need find is that the [item sold] be reasonably fit for its ordinary uses, not that it be perfect.")

A recurring issue is whether the buyer's use of the goods is "ordinary," as illustrated by the next case.

Koken v. Black & Veatch Construction, Inc.

United States Court of Appeals, First Circuit, 2005.
426 F.3d 39.

■ DYK, CIRCUIT JUDGE. On May 17, 1999, a fire occurred during a torch-cutting operation performed as part of a construction project in Maine. A fire blanket had been used to protect the area beneath the welding. The project was owned by Androscoggin Energy LLC ("Androscoggin") and insured by appellant Reliance Insurance Company ("Reliance"). Appellant Black & Veatch Construction, Inc. ("B & V") was the general contractor. Appellees Redco, Inc. ("Redco") and O'Connor Constructors, Inc. ("O'Connor") were subcontractors.

Although the fire was quickly put out through the use of a fire extinguisher, the chemicals in the fire extinguisher caused damage to the generator. The damage to the generator caused an estimated $9 million in repair and delay costs. This incident led to the claims and cross-claims at issue in this case.

At the heart of the case are allegations that appellee Auburn Manufacturing, Inc. ("Auburn") manufactured the fire blanket and appellee Inpro, Inc. ("Inpro") distributed it and that the blanket was unfit for its ordinary purpose.

The appellants also brought breach of warranty claims against Auburn and Inpro. Presumably, this refers to the implied warranty of merchantability, though in the four lines in its brief addressing the breach of warranty claim, B & V did not bother to say so. This, in itself, would furnish a basis for rejecting B & V's claim. Moreover, even were we inclined to overlook the cursory briefing, we would nonetheless affirm the entry of summary judgment. We explain briefly.

Under the Maine version of the Uniform Commercial Code, "a warranty that the goods shall be merchantable is implied in a contract for their sale if the seller is a merchant with respect to goods of that kind." 11 Me.Rev.Stat. Ann. § 2–314(1) (2004). There is no dispute that both Auburn and Inpro are merchants of fire blankets. To be "merchantable," a good must be "fit for the ordinary purposes for which such goods are used." 11 Me.Rev.Stat. Ann. § 2–314(2)(c) (2004).

The first step of the analysis is whether the good was being used for its ordinary purposes. The plaintiff bears the burden of establishing the ordinary purposes of a good. Binks Mfg. Co. v. Nat'l Presto Indus., 709 F.2d 1109, 1121 (7th Cir.1983). "[T]he ordinary purposes for which goods are used go to uses which are customarily made of the goods in question." UCC § 2–315 cmt. 2 (2004). Examining the record, it is far from clear that Austin was using the fire blanket for its "ordinary purposes." Although there is no evidence that a fire blanket was inappropriate for cutting operations or horizontal capture generally, there also appears to be no evidence that the fire blanket was appropriate for such use. However, Auburn and Inpro appear to have waived this issue below, when they represented that they do "not contend that the wrong blanket was used for the application described by Perry Austin." Therefore, we must address whether the appellants have carried their burden of producing evidence sufficient to support a finding that the blanket was "unfit" for this purpose.

In Lorfano [v. Dura Stone Steps, Inc., 569 A.2d 195 (Me. 1990)], the Supreme Judicial Court held that steps outside a building were fit for their ordinary purpose because they "performed as expected." 569 A.2d at 197. The district court held there was no breach of warranty here because the fire blanket likewise "performed as expected" and was thus fit for its ordinary use. *Recommended Decision* at 25 (citing Lorfano, 569 A.2d at 197). B & V responds that since Austin was surprised that the blanket melted,[1] it obviously did not perform as Austin expected. That is true but not on point. The question is not the subjective expectations of

---

[1]   Austin's testimony may fairly be described as occasionally self-contradictory and lacking in clarity. Viewing the record in the light most favorable to the appellants, the pertinent testimony was as follows:

> Q: So, what you're saying is you were mistaken in your assumption that the blanket would stop a fire?
> A: Yes.
> Q: But you don't think there's anything wrong with the blanket?
> A: Other than the fact that it started melting on me, no.
> . . .
> Q: Did the blanket actually start melting?
> A: It was bubbling up, black.
> . . .
> Q: So, were you pretty surprised to see that?
> A: Oh, yes. Very surprised.

the particular user, but the reasonable expectations of an ordinary user or purchaser. *See* Venezia v. Miller Brewing Co., 626 F.2d 188, 190 (1st Cir.1980) ("Under Massachusetts law the question of fitness for ordinary purposes is largely one centering around reasonable consumer expectations."). For example, in Alevromagiros v. Hechinger Co., 993 F.2d 417 (4th Cir.1993), the Fourth Circuit, applying Virginia law in a product liability and breach of warranty case, held that the standard was objective rather than subjective. An expert witness testified that, "tragically," the industry standards used in the manufacture of the allegedly unfit ladder "did not require triangular braces on the rear portion of a ladder." *Id.* at 420. The court held that this testimony was not sufficient to take the issue of the reasonableness of the standards to the jury, because the expert "testified to no customs of the trade, referred to no literature in the field, and did not identify the reasonable expectations of consumers. His comment that the advisory industry standards "tragically" did not require the use of triangular braces does not constitute proof that industry standards are inadequate. It is merely another example of his own subjective opinion." *Id.* at 421.

As the district court concluded, there is no testimony in the summary judgment record here (for example, by experts in the field) that the ordinary user reasonably expected a fire blanket to prevent the type of melting that Austin observed. Indeed, there is testimony by others, for example, the foreman Paul Gagnon, that while he expected the blanket to contain sparks and small fires, he thought the blanket performed as they expected and that burn-through holes in blankets were not uncommon.

Because B & V failed to produce evidence establishing the expectations of ordinary users beyond the subjective views of a single individual, summary judgment on the breach of warranty claim was properly granted.

NOTES

(1) *Applicability of Article 2 Rules.* Article 2 applies to "transactions in goods." UCC § 2–102. This simple language raises several questions. First, what constitutes "goods" under Article 2? The starting point is UCC § 2–105(1). (What are "things . . . which are movable"? Is land "goods"? Is a 10-ton printing press "goods"?) Second, is an agreement to sell goods that have not yet been manufactured a transaction in goods? See UCC § 2–105(2). Third, what if a transaction involves both goods and non-goods (such as services)? Courts have often answered this question by looking for the "predominant factor" of the contract. In the leading case of Bonebrake v. Cox, 499 F.2d 951, 960 (8th Cir. 1974), the court held that Article 2 applied to a contract for the sale and installation of used bowling equipment for a lump sum, even though the contract involved substantial amounts of labor. The court described the test as whether the "predominant factor . . . is the rendition of service, with goods incidentally involved (e.g., contract with artist for painting) or is a transaction of sale, with labor incidentally involved (e.g., installation of a water heater in a bathroom)."

(2) *You Get What You Pay For.* This case emphasizes that the question of whether goods are merchantable focuses on their "ordinary" use rather than the use to which a buyer has put them. Why should the warranty be limited in this way? What would be the effect on the price of goods if there were an implied warranty that the goods be fit for whatever purpose to which the buyer puts them? Would buyers who use the goods for their ordinary purposes be happy about that result? As you learn, in the pages that follow, about the implied warranty of fitness for particular purpose and about express warranties, consider how those warranties may help a buyer who intends to use the goods atypically.

(3) *Implied Warranty for Services?* Should there be an implied warranty of merchantability for contracts outside the scope of UCC Article 2? For example, what about situations in which a party is in the business of performing services (*e.g.*, house painting, dentistry, or tutoring) rather than selling goods? Article 2 does not govern contracts entered into by those parties, who might be considered "merchants" with respect to the services they offer. In contracts for the provision of services by such a merchant of services, is there an implied warranty analogous to the implied warranty of merchantability, requiring that the services will be provided in such a way that meets minimum standards and that would pass without objection in that business? Surprisingly, this area is not well-developed, and the cases vary from state to state.

The Implied Warranty of Fitness for Particular Purpose

While the implied warranty of merchantability relates to the ordinary use of the goods in question, the law in some circumstances provides protection for a buyer who intends to put goods to non-standard use. This protection, termed the implied warranty of fitness for a particular purpose, is found in UCC § 2–315. That section both describes the situations in which the implied warranty arises and indicates the content of that warranty. With respect to those issues, can you identify the differences between this kind of warranty and the implied warranty of merchantability? Keep those differences in mind as you read the following case.

Lewis v. Mobil Oil Corporation

United States Court of Appeals, Eighth Circuit, 1971.
438 F.2d 500.

■ GIBSON, CIRCUIT JUDGE. In this diversity case the defendant appeals from a judgment entered on a jury verdict in favor of the plaintiff in the amount of $89,250 for damages alleged to be caused by use of defendant's oil.

Plaintiff Lewis has been doing business as a sawmill operator in Cove, Arkansas, since 1956. In 1963, in order to meet competition, Lewis decided to convert his power equipment to hydraulic equipment. He purchased a hydraulic system in May 1963, from a competitor who was installing a new system. The used system was in good operating condition at the time Lewis purchased it. It was stored at his plant until November 1964, while a new mill building was being built, at which time it was installed. Following the installation, Lewis requested from Frank Rowe, a local Mobil oil dealer, the proper hydraulic fluid to operate his machinery. The prior owner of the hydraulic system had used Pacemaker oil supplied by Cities Service, but plaintiff had been a customer of Mobil's for many years and desired to continue with Mobil. Rowe said he didn't know what the proper lubricant for Lewis' machinery was, but would find out. The only information given to Rowe by Lewis was that the machinery was operated by a gear-type pump; Rowe did not request any further information. He apparently contacted a Mobil representative for a recommendation, though this is not entirely clear, and sold plaintiff a product known as Ambrex 810. This is a straight mineral oil with no chemical additives.

Within a few days after operation of the new equipment commenced, plaintiff began experiencing difficulty with its operation. The oil changed color, foamed over, and got hot. The oil was changed a number of times, with no improvement. By late April 1965, approximately six months after operations with the equipment had begun, the system broke down, and a complete new system was installed. The cause of the breakdown was undetermined, but apparently by this time there was some suspicion of the oil being used. Plaintiff Lewis requested Rowe to be sure he was supplying the right kind of oil. Ambrex 810 continued to be supplied.

From April 1965 until April 1967, plaintiff continued to have trouble with the system, principally with the pumps which supplied the pressure. Six new pumps were required during this period, as they continually broke down. During this period, the kind of pump used was a Commercial pump which was specified by the designer of the hydraulic system. The filtration of oil for this pump was by means of a metal strainer, which was cleaned daily by the plaintiff in accordance with the instruction given with the equipment.

In April 1967, the plaintiff changed the brand of pump from a Commercial to a Tyrone pump. The Tyrone pump, instead of using the metal strainer filtration alone, used a disposable filter element in addition. Ambrex 810 oil was also recommended by Mobil and used with this pump, which completely broke down three weeks later. At this point, plaintiff was visited for the first time by a representative of Mobil Oil Corporation, as well as a representative of the Tyrone pump manufacturer.

On the occasion of this visit, May 9, 1967, plaintiff's system was completely flushed and cleaned, a new Tyrone pump installed, and on the pump manufacturer's and Mobil's representative's recommendation, a new oil was used which contained certain chemical additives, principally a "defoamant." Following these changes, plaintiff's system worked satisfactorily up until the time of trial, some two and one-half years later.

Briefly stated, plaintiff's theory of his case is that Mobil supplied him with an oil which was warranted fit for use in his hydraulic system, that the oil was not suitable for such use because it did not contain certain additives, and that it was the improper oil which caused the mechanical breakdowns, with consequent loss to his business. The defendant contends that there was no warranty of fitness, that the breakdowns were caused not by the oil but by improper filtration, and that in any event there can be no recovery of loss of profits in this case.

I.   THE EXISTENCE OF WARRANTIES

Defendant maintains that there was no warranty of fitness in this case, that at most there was only a warranty of merchantability and that there was no proof of breach of this warranty, since there was no proof that Ambrex 810 is unfit for use in hydraulic systems generally. We find it unnecessary to consider whether the warranty of merchantability was breached, although there is some proof in the record to that effect, since we conclude that there was a warranty of fitness.

Plaintiff Lewis testified that he had been a longtime customer of Mobil Oil, and that his only source of contact with the company was through Frank Rowe, Mobil's local dealer, with whom he did almost all his business. It was common knowledge in the community that Lewis was converting his sawmill operation into a hydraulic system, Rowe knew this, and in fact had visited his mill on business matters several times during the course of the changeover. When operations with the new machinery were about to commence, Lewis asked Rowe to get him the proper hydraulic fluid. Rowe asked him what kind of a system he had, and Lewis replied it was a Commercial pump type. This was all the information asked or given. Neither Lewis nor Rowe knew what the oil requirements for the system were, and Rowe knew that Lewis knew nothing more specific about his requirements. Lewis also testified that after he began having trouble with his operations, while there were several possible sources of the difficulty the oil was one suspected source, and he several times asked Rowe to be sure he was furnishing him with the right kind.

Rowe's testimony for the most part confirmed Lewis'. It may be noted here that Mobil does not contest Rowe's authority to represent it in this transaction, and therefore whatever warranties may be implied because of the dealings between Rowe and Lewis are attributable to Mobil. Rowe admitted knowing Lewis was converting to a hydraulic system and that Lewis asked him to supply the fluid. He testified that he did not know what should be used and relayed the request to a superior in the Mobil organization, who recommended Ambrex 810. This is what was supplied.

When the first Tyrone pump was installed in April 1967, Rowe referred the request for a proper oil recommendation to Ted Klock, a

Mobil engineer. Klock recommended Ambrex 810. When this pump failed a few weeks later, Klock visited the Lewis plant to inspect the equipment. The system was flushed out completely and the oil was changed to DTE-23 and Del Vac Special containing several additives. After this, no further trouble was experienced.

This evidence adequately establishes an implied warranty of fitness. Arkansas has adopted the Uniform Commercial Code's provision for an implied warranty of fitness.

Under this provision of the Code, there are two requirements for an implied warranty of fitness: (1) that the seller have "reason to know" of the use for which the goods are purchased, and (2) that the buyer relies on the seller's expertise in supplying the proper product. Both of these requirements are amply met by the proof in this case. Lewis' testimony, as confirmed by that of Rowe and Klock. shows that the oil was purchased specifically for his hydraulic system, not for just a hydraulic system in general, and that Mobil certainly knew of this specific purpose. It is also clear that Lewis was relying on Mobil to supply him with the proper oil for the system, since at the time of his purchases, he made clear that he didn't know what kind was necessary.

Mobil contends that there was no warranty of fitness for use in his particular system because he didn't specify that he needed an oil with additives, and alternatively that he didn't give them enough information for them to determine that an additive oil was required. However, it seems that the circumstances of this case come directly within that situation described in the first comment to this provision of the Uniform Commercial Code:

'§ 1. Whether or not this warranty arises in any individual case is basically a question of fact to be determined by the circumstances of the contracting. Under this section the buyer need not bring home to the seller actual knowledge of the particular purpose for which the goods are intended or of his reliance on the seller's skill and judgment, if the circumstances are such that the seller has reason to realize the purpose intended or that the reliance exists.' [UCC § 2–315], Comment 1 (1961).

Here Lewis made it clear that the oil was purchased for his system, that he didn't know what oil should be used, and that he was relying on Mobil to supply the proper product. If any further information was needed, it was incumbent upon Mobil to get it before making its recommendation. That it could have easily gotten the necessary information is evidenced by the fact that after plaintiff's continuing complaints, Mobil's engineer visited the plant, and, upon inspection, changed the recommendation that had previously been made.

Additionally, Mobil contends that even if there were an implied warranty of fitness, it does not cover the circumstances of this case because of the abnormal features which the plaintiff's system contained, namely an inadequate filtration system and a capacity to entrain excessive air. There are several answers to this contention. First of all, the contention goes essentially to the question of causation—i.e., whether the damage was caused by a breach of warranty or by some other cause—and not to the existence of a warranty of fitness in the first place. Secondly, assuming that certain peculiarities in the plaintiff's system did exist, the whole point of an implied warranty of fitness is that a product be suitable for a specific purpose, and that a seller should not supply a product which is not so suited. Thirdly, there is no evidence in the record that the plaintiff's system was unique or abnormal in these respects. It operated satisfactorily under the prior owner, and the new system has operated satisfactorily after it was adequately cleaned and an additive type oil used.

NOTES

(1) *Non-Merchant Warrantors?* Must a seller of goods be a merchant for the implied warranty of fitness to become part of the contract? Can you imagine a situation in which a non-merchant is the seller and this warranty arises?

(2) *These Shoes Are Made for Walking.* Comment 2 to UCC § 2–315 provides the following guidance for distinguishing the warranty of fitness for *particular* purpose from the warranty of merchantability, which relates to the *ordinary* purposes for which such goods are used: "A 'particular' purpose differs from the ordinary purpose for which the goods are used in that it envisages a specific use by the buyer which is peculiar to the nature of his business whereas the ordinary purposes for which goods are used are those envisaged in the concept of merchantability and go to uses which are customarily made of the goods in question. For example, shoes are generally used for the purpose of walking upon ordinary ground, but a seller may know that a particular pair was selected to be used for climbing mountains."

––––––––

Excluding Implied Warranties from the Contract

While Article 2 contains detailed rules that determine when an implied warranty is part of a contract, those rules do not make implied warranties mandatory. Rather, both UCC § 2–314 and UCC § 2–315 refer to UCC § 2–316 for detailed rules that indicate how a contract for sale of goods can be concluded *without* those warranties. Thus, while implied warranties may be considered to be a type of default rule, UCC § 2–316 provides that it takes more than simple agreement to the contrary to prevent them from becoming part of the contract. It is obvious why a seller would prefer that a contract not contain implied warranties, but why might a buyer agree to a contract without them?

UCC Sections 2–316(2) and 2–316(3) contain several routes by which implied warranties can be kept out of a contract. Focus first on UCC § 2–316(2). For each of the implied warranty of merchantability and the implied warranty of fitness, consider whether particular words must be used to exclude the warranty and whether the words of exclusion may be oral or must be in a writing or other record. If the exclusion is accomplished by a writing, is it effective if the words of exclusion are in the "fine print?"

Note that the opening phrases of both UCC § 2–316(2) and UCC § 2–316(3) subordinate the former subsection to the latter. In what ways does UCC § 2–316(3)(a) qualify or override UCC § 2–316(2)? If the seller states orally that the goods are offered "as is" and the buyer agrees to that, is this sufficient to exclude the implied warranty of fitness? If the "as is" term appears in writing, but is buried in fine print on page 72 of a 96-page agreement, does it suffice to exclude the implied warranty of merchantability?

South Carolina Electric and Gas Co. v. Combustion Engineering, Inc.

Court of Appeals of South Carolina, 1984.
283 S.C. 182, 322 S.E.2d 453.

■ GOOLSBY, JUDGE. The appellant South Carolina Electric and Gas Company (SCE & G) seeks to recover damages in excess of $350,000 that SCE & G alleges it sustained as a result of a fire that occurred when a flexible metal hose ruptured and sprayed heated fuel oil across the surface of a steam generating boiler at the Arthur Williams Station, a power generating plant owned by SCE & G. The circuit court granted summary judgment in favor of the respondent Combustion Engineering, Inc. (Combustion), which manufactured and sold the boiler and its ancillary equipment to SCE & G, and the respondent Daniel International Corporation (Daniel), which constructed the power plant and installed the boiler as well as the pipes and hoses that connected to it.

SCE & G appeals the grant of summary judgment in favor of Combustion on causes of action for (1) breach of an implied warranty that the boiler unit was fit for a particular purpose, (2) breach of an implied warranty that the boiler unit was merchantable, and (3) negligence in the design of the fuel piping.

I.   Case Against Combustion

A.   Implied Warranties

SCE & G entered into the contract with Combustion for the sale of the boiler unit in early 1970. The sales contract contains an item labeled "WARRANTY," that expressly warrants the equipment to be free "from defects in material and workmanship for a period of one year." Because the boiler became operational on March 18, 1973, and the fire that brought on this litigation occurred over two years later on May 19, 1975, the one-year warranty provision had expired at the time of the fire.

The warranty item also contains a disclaimer of warranties provision. It states that "[t]here are no other warranties, whether expressed or implied, other than title."

The circuit court, in granting Combustion summary judgment on each cause of action alleging a breach of an implied warranty, ruled that the disclaimer excludes an implied warranty of merchantability as well as an implied warranty of fitness for a particular purpose.

SCE & G, however, maintains that Combustion was not entitled to summary judgment. It argues that the disclaimer, as a matter of law, does not exclude the implied warranties alleged in its complaint because the disclaimer does not meet the requirements of Subsection (2) of Section 36–2–316 of the South Carolina Code of Laws (1976) and that a question of fact exists as to whether the disclaimer can come within the exceptions to Subsection (2) permitted by Subsection (3) of that statute.

We agree with SCE & G that the disclaimer does not satisfy the requirements of Subsection (2). First of all, the disclaimer nowhere mentions the word "merchantability," as it must do under Subsection (2) to exclude an implied warranty of merchantability.

Further, the written language of disclaimer, as a matter of law, is not "conspicuous," as Subsection (2) requires it to be to exclude an implied warranty of fitness for a particular purpose as well as an implied warranty of merchantability. Indeed, the written agreement is twenty-two typewritten pages in length and is mostly single-spaced. The disclaimer itself appears on page 17 of the agreement in the last sentence of a two-paragraph item. It is indistinctive both as to color and as to type. *See* S.C.Code of Laws § 36–1–210(10) (1976) ("A . . . clause is conspicuous when it is so written that a reasonable person against whom it is to operate ought to have noticed it. . . . Language in the body of a form is 'conspicuous' if it is in larger or other contrasting type or color"); Billings v. Joseph Harris Company, Inc., 220 S.E.2d 361 (1975); Chrysler Corp. v. Wilson Plumbing Company, Inc., 208 S.E.2d 321 (1974).

Moreover, the item containing the disclaimer is misleading in that it is suggestive of "a grant of a warranty rather than a disclaimer" because the heading of the item, printed in underlined capital letters, simply reads "*WARRANTY*." Hartman v. Jensen's Inc., 289 S.E.2d 648 (1982).

But the question remains concerning whether a genuine issue of material fact exists as to whether the disclaimer, as the circuit court found, falls within the exception prescribed by Subsection (3)(a). Subsection (3)(a) permits, as do Subsections (3)(b) and (c), the exclusion of implied warranties when "the circumstances surrounding the transaction are in themselves sufficient to call the buyer's attention to the fact that no implied warranties are made or that a certain implied warranty is excluded." S.C.Code of Laws § 36–2–316 official comment 6 (1976).

In support of its motion for summary judgment, Combustion submitted the affidavit of Kurt W. Johnson that identified several documents exchanged between Combustion and SCE & G relative to the purchase by SCE & G of the boiler from Combustion. The first document, dated August 15, 1968 and entitled "Proposal No. 16268-E," originated with Combustion. It included the disclaimer at issue here. Five months later on January 31, 1969, SCE & G wrote Combustion stating that its August 1968 proposal was unacceptable in certain respects. SCE & G advised Combustion that it required that any purchase order filled by Combustion be subject to certain prescribed conditions. One condition was that Combustion agree "to be bound in relation to [its] equipment by the . . . warranties implied by the laws of the State of South Carolina."

Combustion responded to SCE & G's letter on February 19, 1969, and informed SCE & G that it could not accept the condition relating to implied warranties. Combustion insisted that it "have a limitation on the warranty period and a limitation on the remedy for breach of any warranty, expressed or implied." On February 21, 1969, SCE & G replied to Combustion's letter of two days before and advised Combustion that it agreed that the "warranties implied by [the] laws of the State of South Carolina shall be limited" to the warranty item included in the original proposal.

The parties differ concerning whether the correspondence mentioned above forms part of the contract and whether it constitutes evidence extrinsic to the contract. SCE & G maintains that the correspondence is not part of the contract and that consideration of it by the circuit court to determine whether the disclaimer is effective demonstrates conclusively that the disclaimer is ambiguous. SCE & G relies on the settled rule that the intention of the parties to an ambiguous contract is a question of fact for the jury to determine and is not a question that a court should decide on summary judgment. *See* Wheeler v. Globe & Rutgers Fire Insurance Co., 118 S.E. 609 (1923) ("where a contract is not clear, or is ambiguous and capable of one or more constructions, what the parties really intended, as a matter of fact, should be submitted to a jury").

We need not decide whether the correspondence forms part of the contract because we think that the language of the disclaimer itself is unambiguous. In plain language, the disclaimer excludes all warranties other than the express one-year warranty and the warranty of title.

Although we do not use the correspondence to resolve an ambiguity in the language employed by the disclaimer, we do consider the correspondence to determine whether the language of disclaimer was unbargained for and unexpected by SCE & G, the buyer. If the evidentiary material presented in connection with Combustion's motion for summary judgment shows that no genuine issue of fact exists as to whether the language of disclaimer was unbargained for and unexpected and that, as a matter of fact, the language was bargained for and expected, SCE & G could not rightly claim, irrespective of the requirements of Subsection (2), that the language does not exclude the two implied warranties asserted by Combustion. *See* S.C.Code of Laws § 36–2–316 official comment 1 (1976) (Subsections (2) and (3) designed to protect the buyer from "unexpected and unbargained language of disclaimer"). In such a case, summary judgment for Combustion would be entirely proper.

As we view the record, Combustion was entitled to summary judgment as a matter of law on the causes of action alleging breaches of implied warranties of merchantability and fitness for a particular purpose.

The correspondence exchanged between Combustion and SCE & G relating to the warranty item and submitted in support of Combustion's motion for summary judgment discloses that the language of disclaimer included in the warranty item came as no surprise to SCE & G and that SCE & G in fact bargained with Combustion over a period of seven months concerning it. SCE & G makes no factual showing to the contrary. As the correspondence indicates, the disclaimer, which is written in simple language, was subjected to detailed review by SCE & G and was agreed upon by SCE & G only after Combustion refused to accept SCE & G's condition that Combustion be bound by the "warranties implied by the laws of the State of South Carolina."

In addition, both corporations are commercially sophisticated and possess relatively equal bargaining strength. The sheer size of the transaction itself ($12,139,786.00) and the length of the negotiations (approximately nineteen months) suggest as much. As in *AMF Incorporated v. Computer Automation, Inc.*, 573 F.Supp. 924, 930 (S.D. Ohio 1983), which also involved "commercially sophisticated businesses," it would strain "credulity to hold that a business like [SCE & G] was not, or should not have been, aware of the language disclaiming implied warranties."

We therefore hold that an effective disclaimer of implied warranties under Subsection (3)(a) was shown; thus, the language of the disclaimer at issue here was effective notwithstanding its failure to satisfy the requirements of Subsection (2). *See* Tennessee Carolina Transportation Inc. v. Strick Corp., 196 S.E.2d 711 (1973) (*dictum* that actual awareness by a nonconsumer buyer of a disclaimer prior to entering into a sales contract and possession of substantially equivalent bargaining power satisfies purpose of "conspicuous" requirement); *cf.* Country Clubs, Inc. v. Allis-Chalmers Manufacturing Co., 430 F.2d 1394, 1397 (6th Cir.1970) (exclusion of implied warranty of merchantability upheld under Subsection 3(c) where course of dealing indicated buyer "had acquiesced in the limited warranty provision" and sale involved experienced businessmen dealing at arm's length).

NOTE

Inspection. Note that UCC § 2–316(3)(b) provides an additional circumstance in which implied warranties do not become part of the contract: When a buyer has inspected goods before entering into a contract, there are no implied warranties with respect to defects that ought to have been revealed by inspection. Why do you think that the statute contains this rule?

PROBLEM

Latent Defect. NAK sold Garlock industrial oil seal products that caused significant oil leakage problems in Garlock's equipment. It is uncontested that such oil seal products were not merchantable. Before entering into the contract, NAK sent samples of the oil seal products and Garlock tested them to ensure that they were the proper configuration and dimension, and otherwise met specification requirements. Garlock did the normal tests designated by the American Society for Testing and Materials (ASTM) to check the basic physical properties of the compound of which the seals were made. The seals met specifications and passed the standard ASTM tests. Garlock did not do any functional testing of the samples. If the defect in NAK's products was one that would not be detected by the ASTM tests, is there a warranty of merchantability with respect to that defect? See Garlock Sealing Techs., LLC v. NAK Sealing Techs. Corp., 56 Cal.Rptr.3d 177 (App. 2007).

(D) EXPRESS WARRANTIES

Recall the *Bayliner* case at page 4 above, which introduced the concept of express warranties governed by UCC § 2–313. Conceptually, express warranties differ from implied warranties in that they are the product of bargaining between the parties rather than implication by law. Comment 1 to UCC § 2–313 states that express warranties "rest on 'dickered' aspects of the individual bargain." As such, express warranties may be considered to be merely terms of the agreement between the parties, not worthy of extensive discussion. Nonetheless, UCC § 2–313 contains detailed provisions about how such terms become part of the contract.

Under UCC § 2–313(1), an express warranty may be created in any of three ways. First, an affirmation of fact or promise made by the seller with respect to the goods creates a warranty that they will conform to that affirmation or promise. UCC § 2–313(1)(a). Second, a description of the goods creates a warranty that they will conform to the description. UCC § 2–313(1)(b). Third, a sample or model of the goods creates a warranty that the "whole of the goods" will conform to the sample or model. UCC § 2–313(1)(c).

Three aspects of UCC § 2–313 are noteworthy. First, there is no requirement that the buyer have relied on the affirmation of fact, promise, description, sample, or model in order for it to be part of the contract, but it must have been part of the "basis of the bargain." That phrase has been the subject of extensive litigation. See cases collected at 1 Hawkland UCC Series § 2–313:5 (2019).

Second, "it is not necessary to the creation of an express warranty that the seller use formal words such as 'warrant' or 'guarantee,' or that he have a specific intention to make a warranty . . . ." UCC § 2–313(2). Thus, a seller who has made an affirmation of fact, promise, or the like with respect to the goods cannot escape a finding that there is an express warranty merely by claiming that he did not intend to incur that obligation.

Third, "an affirmation merely of the value of the goods or a statement purporting to be merely the seller's opinion or commendation of the goods does not create a warranty." UCC § 2–313(2). This rule, sometimes known as the "puffing" exception or the "sales talk" exception, is attributed to "common experience [that] discloses that some statements or predictions cannot fairly be viewed as entering into the bargain." We have encountered this rule already in the *Bayliner* case in Chapter 1.

The following case, Keith v. Buchanan, addresses these issues, as well as the connection between express warranty and the implied warranty of fitness—and in the same context as *Bayliner,* the sale of a boat for personal use.

Keith v. Buchanan

California Court of Appeal, 1985.
173 Cal.App.3d 13, 220 Cal.Rptr. 392.

■ OCHOA, ASSOCIATE JUSTICE.

This breach of warranty case is before this court after the trial court granted defendants' motion for judgment at the close of plaintiff's case during the trial proceedings. We hold that an express warranty under section 2313 of the California Uniform Commercial Code was created in this matter, and that actual reliance on the seller's factual representation need not be shown by the buyer. The representation is presumed to be part of the basis of the bargain, and the burden is on the seller to prove that the representation was not a consideration inducing the bargain. We affirm all other aspects of the trial court's judgment but reverse in regard to its finding that no express warranty was created and remand for further proceedings consistent with this opinion.

STATEMENT OF FACTS

Plaintiff, Brian Keith, purchased a sailboat from defendants in November 1978 for a total purchase price of $75,610. Even though plaintiff belonged to the Waikiki Yacht Club, had attended a sailing school, had joined the Coast Guard Auxiliary, and had sailed on many yachts in order to ascertain his preferences, he had not previously owned a yacht. He attended a boat show in Long Beach during October 1978 and looked at a number of boats, speaking to sales representatives and obtaining advertising literature. In the literature, the sailboat which is the subject of this action, called an "Island Trader 41," was described as a seaworthy vessel. In one sales brochure, this vessel is described as "a picture of sure-footed seaworthiness." In another, it is called "a carefully well-equipped, and very seaworthy live-aboard vessel." Plaintiff testified he relied on representations in the sales brochures in regard to the purchase. Plaintiff and a sales representative also discussed plaintiff's desire for a boat which was ocean-going and would cruise long distances.

Plaintiff asked his friend, Buddy Ebsen, who was involved in a boat building enterprise, to inspect the boat. Mr. Ebsen and one of his associates, both of whom had extensive experience with sailboats, observed the boat and advised plaintiff that the vessel would suit his stated needs. A deposit was paid on the boat, a purchase contract was entered into, and optional accessories for the boat were ordered. After delivery of the vessel, a dispute arose in regard to its seaworthiness.

Plaintiff filed the instant lawsuit alleging causes of action in breach of express warranty and breach of implied warranty. The trial court granted defendants' Code of Civil Procedure section 631.8 motion for judgment at the close of plaintiff's case. The court found that no express warranty was established by the evidence because none of the defendants had undertaken in writing to preserve or maintain the utility or performance of the vessel, nor to provide compensation for any failure in utility or performance. It found that the written statements produced at trial were opinions or commendations of the vessel. The court further found that no implied warranty of fitness was created because the plaintiff did not rely on the skill and judgment of defendants to select and furnish a suitable vessel, but had rather relied on his own experts in selecting the vessel.

DISCUSSION

I.   *EXPRESS WARRANTY*

California Uniform Commercial Code section 2313 provides, inter alia, that express warranties are created by (1) any affirmation of fact or promise made by the seller to the buyer which relates to the goods and becomes part of the basis of the bargain, and (2) any description of the goods which is made part of the basis of the bargain. Formal words such as "warranty" or "guarantee" are not required to make a warranty, but the seller's affirmation of the value of the goods or an expression of opinion or commendation of the goods does not create an express warranty. . . .

In deciding whether a statement made by a seller constitutes an express warranty under this provision, the court must deal with three fundamental issues. First, the court must determine whether the seller's statement constitutes an "affirmation of fact or promise" or "description of the goods" under California Uniform Commercial Code section 2313, subdivision (1)(a) or (b) or whether it is rather "merely the seller's opinion or commendation of the goods" under section 2313, subdivision (2). Second, assuming the court finds the language used susceptible to creation of a warranty, it must then be determined whether the statement was "part of the basis of the bargain." Third, the court must determine whether the warranty was breached. (See Sessa v. Riegle (E.D.Pa.1977) 427 F.Supp. 760, 765.)

A warranty relates to the title, character, quality, identity, or condition of the goods. The purpose of the law of warranty is to determine what it is that the seller has in essence agreed to sell. (A.A. Baxter Corp. v. Colt Industries, Inc. (1970) 10 Cal.App.3d 144, 153.) "Express warranties are chisels in the hands of buyers and sellers. With these tools, the parties to a sale sculpt a monument representing the goods. Having selected a stone, the buyer and seller may leave it almost bare, allowing considerable play in the qualities that fit its contours. Or the parties may chisel away inexactitudes until a well-defined shape emerges. The seller is bound to deliver, and the buyer to accept, goods that match the sculpted form. [Fn. omitted.]" (Special Project: Article Two Warranties in Commercial Transactions, Express Warranties— Section 2–313 (1978–79) 64 Cornell L.Rev. 30 (hereafter cited as Warranties in Commercial Transactions) at pp. 43–44.)

A. *Affirmation of fact, promise or description versus statement of opinion, commendation or value.*

"The determination as to whether a particular statement is an expression of opinion or an affirmation of fact is often difficult, and frequently is dependent upon the facts and circumstances existing at the time the statement is made." (Willson v. Municipal Bond Co. (1936) 7 Cal.2d 144, 150, 59 P.2d 974.) Recent decisions have evidenced a trend toward narrowing the scope of representations which are considered opinion, sometimes referred to as "puffing" or "sales talk," resulting in an expansion of the liability that flows from broad statements of manufacturers or retailers as to the quality of their products. Courts have liberally construed affirmations of quality made by sellers in favor of injured consumers. (Hauter v. Zogarts (1975) 14 Cal.3d 104, 112, 120 Cal.Rptr. 681, 534 P.2d 377; see also 55 Cal.Jur.3d, Sales, § 74, p. 580.)

The code comment indicates that the basic question is: "What statements of the seller have in the circumstances and in objective judgment become part of the basis of the bargain?" The commentators indicated that the language of subsection (2) of the code section was included because "common experience discloses that some statements or predictions cannot fairly be viewed as entering into the bargain." [UCC § 2–313 cmt. 8]

Statements made by a seller during the course of negotiation over a contract are presumptively affirmations of fact unless it can be demonstrated that the buyer could only have reasonably considered the statement as a statement of the seller's opinion. Commentators have noted several factors which tend to indicate an opinion statement. These are (1) a lack of specificity in the statement made, (2) a statement that is made in an equivocal manner, or (3) a statement which reveals that the goods are experimental in nature. (See *Warranties in Commercial Transactions, supra,* at pp. 61–65.)

It is clear that statements made by a manufacturer or retailer in an advertising brochure which is disseminated to the consuming public in order to induce sales can create express warranties. In the instant case, the vessel purchased was described in sales brochures as "a picture of sure-footed seaworthiness" and "a carefully well-equipped and very seaworthy vessel." The seller's representative was aware that appellant was looking for a vessel sufficient for long distance ocean-going cruises. The statements in the brochure are specific and unequivocal in asserting that the vessel is seaworthy. Nothing in the negotiation indicates that the vessel is experimental in nature. In fact, one sales brochure assures prospective buyers that production of the vessel was commenced "after years of careful testing." The representations regarding seaworthiness made in sales brochures regarding the Island Trader 41 were affirmations of fact relating to the quality or condition of the vessel.

B.   *"Part of the basis of the bargain" test.*

Under former provisions of law, a purchaser was required to prove that he or she acted in reliance upon representations made by the seller. (Grinnell v. Charles Pfizer & Co. (1969) 274 Cal.App.2d 424, 440, 79 Cal.Rptr. 369.) California Uniform Commercial Code section 2313 indicates only that the seller's statements must become "part of the basis of the bargain." According to official comment 3 to this Uniform Commercial Code provision, "no particular reliance . . . need be shown in order to weave [the seller's affirmations of fact] into the fabric of the agreement. Rather, any fact which is to take such affirmations, once made, out of the agreement requires clear affirmative proof."

The California Supreme Court, in discussing the continued viability of the reliance factor, noted that commentators have disagreed in regard to the impact of this development. Some have indicated that it shifts the burden of proving non-reliance to the seller, and others have indicated that the code eliminates the concept of reliance altogether. (Hauter v. Zogarts, *supra*, 14 Cal.3d at pp. 115–116, 120 Cal.Rptr. 681, 534 P.2d 377.) The court did not resolve this issue, but noted that decisions of other states prior to that time had "ignored the significance of the new standard and have held that consumer reliance still is a vital ingredient for recovery based on express warranty." (*Id.*, at p. 116, fn. 13, 120 Cal.Rptr. 681, 534 P.2d 377; see also Fogo v. Cutter Laboratories, Inc. (1977) 68 Cal.App.3d 744, 760, 137 Cal.Rptr. 417.)

The shift in language clearly changes the degree to which it must be shown that the seller's representation affected the buyer's decision to enter into the agreement. A buyer need not show that he would not have entered into the agreement absent the warranty or even that it was a dominant factor inducing the agreement. A warranty statement is deemed to be part of the basis of the bargain and to have been relied upon as one of the inducements for the purchase of the product. In other words, the buyer's demonstration of reliance on an express warranty is "not a prerequisite for breach of warranty, as long as the express warranty involved became part of the bargain. See White and Summers, Uniform Commercial Code (2d ed. 1980) § 9–4. If, however, the resulting bargain does not rest at all on the representations of the seller, those representations cannot be considered as becoming any part of the 'basis of the bargain.' . . ." (Allied Fidelity Ins. Co. v. Pico (Nev.S.Ct.1983) 656 P.2d 849, 850.)

The official Uniform Commercial Code comment in regard to section 2–313 "indicates that in actual practice affirmations of fact made by the seller about the goods during a bargain are regarded as part of the description of those goods; hence no particular reliance on such statements need be shown in order to weave them into the fabric of the agreement." (Young & Cooper, Inc. v. Vestring (1974) 214 Kan. 311, 521 P.2d 281, 291; Brunner v. Jensen (1974) 215 Kan. 416, 524 P.2d 1175, 1185.) It is clear from the new language of this code section that the concept of reliance has been purposefully abandoned. (Interco Inc. v. Randustrial Corp. (Mo.App.1976) 533 S.W.2d 257, 261; see also Winston Industries, Inc. v. Stuyvesant Insurance Co., Inc. (1975) 55 Ala.App. 525, 317 So.2d 493, 497.)

The change of the language in section 2313 of the California Uniform Commercial Code modifies both the degree of reliance and the burden of proof in express warranties under the code. The representation need only be part of the basis of the bargain, or merely a factor or consideration inducing the buyer to enter into the bargain. A warranty statement made by a seller is presumptively part of the basis of the bargain, and the burden is on the seller to prove that the resulting bargain does not rest at all on the representation.

The buyer's actual knowledge of the true condition of the goods prior to the making of the contract may make it plain that the seller's statement was not relied upon as one of the inducements for the purchase, but the burden is on the seller to demonstrate such knowledge on the part of the buyer. Where the buyer inspects the goods before purchase, he may be deemed to have waived the seller's express warranties. But, an examination or inspection by the buyer of the goods does not necessarily discharge the seller from an express warranty if the defect was not actually discovered and waived. (Doak Gas Engine Co. v. Fraser (1914) 168 Cal. 624, 627, 143 P. 1024 . . .)

Appellant's inspection of the boat by his own experts does not constitute a waiver of the express warranty of seaworthiness. Prior to the making of the contract, appellant had experienced boat builders observe the boat, but there was no testing of the vessel in the water.[i] Such a

---

[i]   Evidence was presented of examination or inspection of the boat after the making of the contract of sale and prior to delivery and acceptance of the vessel. Such an inspection would be

warranty (seaworthiness) necessarily relates to the time when the vessel has been put to sea (Werner v. Montana (1977) 117 N.H. 721, 378 A.2d 1130, 1134–35) and has been shown to be reasonably fit and adequate in materials, construction, and equipment for its intended purposes (Daly v. General Motors Corp. (1978) 20 Cal.3d 725, 739, 144 Cal.Rptr. 380, 575 P.2d 1162; Vittone v. American President Lines (1964) 228 Cal.App.2d 689, 693–694, 39 Cal.Rptr. 758).

In this case, appellant was aware of the representations regarding seaworthiness by the seller prior to contracting. He also had expressed to the seller's representative his desire for a long distance ocean-going vessel. Although he had other experts inspect the vessel, the inspection was limited and would not have indicated whether or not the vessel was seaworthy. It is clear that the seller has not overcome the presumption that the representations regarding seaworthiness were part of the basis of this bargain.

II. *IMPLIED WARRANTY*

Appellant also claimed breach of the implied warranty of fitness for a particular purpose in regard to the sale of the subject vessel.

The reliance elements are important to the consideration of whether an implied warranty of fitness for a particular purpose exists. "If the seller had no reason to know that he was being relied upon, his conduct in providing goods cannot fairly be deemed a tacit representation of their suitability for a particular purpose. And if the buyer did not in fact rely, then the principal justification for imposing a fitness warranty disappears." (See *Warranties in Commercial Transactions, supra,* at p. 89.) The major question in determining the existence of an implied warranty of fitness for a particular purpose is the reliance by the buyer upon the skill and judgment of the seller to select an article suitable for his needs. (Bagley v. International Harvester Co. (1949) 91 Cal.App.2d 922, 925, 206 P.2d 43; Drumar M. Co. v. Morris Ravine M. Co. (1939) 33 Cal.App.2d 492, 495–496, 92 P.2d 424.)

The trial court found that the plaintiff did not rely on the skill and judgment of the defendants to select a suitable vessel, but that he rather relied on his own experts. "Our sole task is to determine 'whether the evidence, viewed in the light most favorable to [respondent], sustains [these] findings.' [Citations.] Moreover, 'in examining the sufficiency of the evidence to support a questioned finding an appellate court must accept as true all evidence tending to establish the correctness of the

---

irrelevant to any issue of express warranty. Although it deals with implied warranties as opposed to express warranties, the Uniform Commercial Code comment 8 to section 2–316 (Cal.U.Com.Code, § 2316) is instructive: "Under paragraph (b) of subdivision (3) warranties may be excluded or modified by the circumstances where the buyer examines the goods or a sample or model of them *before entering into the contract. 'Examination' as used in this paragraph is not synonymous with inspection before acceptance or at any other time after the contract has been made. It goes rather to the nature of the responsibility assumed by the seller at the time of the making of the contract.*" (See U.Com.Code com. 8 to Cal.U.Com.Code, § 2316, West's Ann.Com.Code (1964) p. 308, emphasis added.)

finding as made, taking into account, as well, all inferences which might reasonably have been thought by the trial court to lead to the same conclusion.' [Citations.] If appellate scrutiny reveals that substantial evidence supports the trial court's findings and conclusions, the judgment must be affirmed." (Board of Education v. Jack M. (1977) 19 Cal.3d 691, 697, 139 Cal.Rptr. 700, 566 P.2d 602.)

A review of the record reveals ample evidence to support the trial court's finding. Appellant had extensive experience with sailboats at the time of the subject purchase, even though he had not previously owned such a vessel. He had developed precise specifications in regard to the type of boat he wanted to purchase. He looked at a number of different vessels, reviewed their advertising literature, and focused on the Island Trader 41 as the object of his intended purchase. He also had friends look at the boat before making the final decision to purchase. The trial court's finding that the buyer did not rely on the skill or judgment of the seller in the selection of the vessel in question is supported by substantial evidence.

The trial court's judgment that no express warranty existed in this matter is reversed. The trial court's judgment is affirmed in all other respects. Since considerable contradictory evidence was elicited at trial relating to the asserted breach of warranty of seaworthiness of the subject vessel, and since the trial court made no finding in regard to that issue, the matter is remanded to the trial court for further proceedings consistent with this opinion.

NOTES

(1) *Puffing Versus Fact.* Compare the representations made here with those made in *Bayliner* (p. 4). Why were the statements here warranties but not those in *Bayliner*? What about "a picture of sure-footed seaworthiness" is more than an expression of opinion or puffery?

(2) *The Basis of the Bargain.* How would a seller prove that a particular representation was *not* part of the basis of the bargain? If the representation was made in an advertisement? In a statement from a salesperson?

(3) *An Unfit Warranty.* The court found that, although there was an express warranty, there was no implied warranty of fitness. Consider the elements of each. If, according to the court, Keith was not extended a fitness warranty because of his own knowledge and expertise and those of his friends, why shouldn't that knowledge also bar him from claiming an express warranty?

(4) *The Warranty in the Box.* Many express warranties are transmitted to the buyer in the package containing the product, and are not known to the buyer until she opens the package and the enclosed information packet. How can those warranties become part of the "basis of the bargain," when the buyer didn't see them before making the purchase? See UCC § 2–313 cmt. 7. And if warranties in the box should become part of the basis of the bargain,

what about warranties made in advertising that was not seen by the buyer until after the purchase?

(5) *Disclaiming Express Warranties.* In § 2–316(1), the UCC states that if language creating an express warranty and language disclaiming it cannot reasonably be read as consistent with each other, "negation or limitation is inoperative to the extent that such construction is unreasonable." A seller thus cannot make an express warranty to entice a buyer and then disclaim it at some less obvious time. But § 2–316(1) contains the important proviso, "subject to the provisions of this Article on parol or extrinsic evidence." Although a seller cannot create a warranty with one hand and disclaim it with the other, a seller can effectively disclaim any express warranties it made before the contract was entered into if that contract is completely integrated, or at least integrated with respect to express warranties. See BHC Development, L.C. v. Bally Gaming, Inc., 985 F.Supp.2d 1276 (D.Kan. 2013) (evidence of express warranties of software quality excluded by final signed agreement with merger clause).

(E) SUPPLEMENTING THE CONTRACT WITH MANDATORY TERMS—GOOD FAITH

It is now well-established in the vast majority of states that virtually all contracts contain an obligation of good faith (or "good faith and fair dealing") in their performance and enforcement. For contracts governed by the Uniform Commercial Code, UCC § 1–304 provides that "Every contract or duty within [the Uniform Commercial Code] imposes an obligation of good faith in its performance and enforcement." Similarly, for contracts governed by the common law, Restatement § 205 provides that "Every contract imposes upon each party a duty of good faith and fair dealing in its performance and its enforcement."

The obligation to perform and enforce in good faith is present even if the parties have not bargained for it. Moreover, unlike gap fillers and other default terms, the parties cannot, by agreement, prevent the obligation from becoming part of their contract. See UCC § 1–302(b). Thus, the obligation of good faith is said to be a mandatory term of a contract. In contracts governed by the Uniform Commercial Code, however, there is explicit authorization for the parties to determine by agreement "the standards by which the performance of [the obligation of good faith in the performance and enforcement of the contract] is to be measured if those standards are not manifestly unreasonable." *Id.*

Because the obligation of good faith places limits on a party's actions in performing a contract, consideration of the content of that obligation is deferred until the next chapter, which addresses legal doctrines that police the performance of contracts by the parties.

CHAPTER 6

LIMITS ON THE BARGAIN AND ITS PERFORMANCE

Let us now assume two parties have successfully bargained with one another, a deal has been struck, and that the obligations of each party are clear. Are there circumstances where the law may still refuse to enforce the deal, not out of concern about the bargaining process, the focus of Chapter 4, but out of concern about its content? Are there limits to the now familiar rule that "[p]arties of sufficient mental capacity for the management of their own business have the right to make their own bargains?" Hardesty v. Smith, 3 Ind. 39 (1851). To answer the question, we return to the matter of policing and look at the doctrines and circumstances under which the law has found it appropriate to place limits on the *substance* of a bargain and, through the obligation of "good faith," also on its *performance*.

We start with the treatment of unfair terms under the common law. That there are limiting principles to prevent the routine enforcement of unequal bargains might come as something of a surprise. The core idea of consideration is the *fact* of a bargain, not its content. "If the requirement of consideration is met, there is no additional requirement of . . . equivalence in the values exchanged." Restatement § 79(b). Yet although the law contains an implicit judgment that a promise should be enforced whether or not something of equal value was given for it, courts have developed a variety of common law policing measures, or "conventional controls," as we have called them, to limit certain bargains marked by an inequality of exchange. These are explored in Section 1.

Section 2 introduces two categories of contracts in which unfair or oppressive terms sometimes, though not always, manifest themselves. These are *standard form contracts*, the industry-drafted contracts with which we are all familiar, and *adhesion contracts*, whose terms are not only offered on a take-it-or-leave-it basis but are often oppressively one-sided. How should the law treat terms that have not been "bargained for" in any colloquial sense of the phrase, and that may not have been noticed or read, perhaps by either party, until the dispute arises? Under what circumstances might the contract, or at least those terms, be unenforceable?

The question leads to the second and relatively modern limiting principle. This is the doctrine of unconscionability, which denies enforcement to a contract, or to a particular term within a contract, if it is found to be oppressive. While unconscionability encompasses some of the same procedural concerns about the bargaining process considered in Chapter 4, it also has a substantive dimension directed at the inequality of the exchange. What factors do courts consider in determining whether a contract is procedurally or substantively unconscionable? Does one (or more) unconscionable term taint the entire agreement? The materials in Section 3 explore these questions in the context of commercial, consumer, and employment agreements.

In addition to limits imposed on the content of a bargain, the law also insists on certain decencies in how the parties carry out their contractual obligations. These derive from the obligation developed in the common law that parties must perform in good faith. The Restatement asserts a "duty of good faith and fair dealing" in contract performance and enforcement. Restatement § 205. The Uniform Commercial Code imposes a similar "obligation of good faith." UCC § 1–304. Section 4 takes a closer look at how the concept of good faith has been defined and applied.

The final section of this chapter, Public Policy, deals with bargains challenged not because they threaten the interests of individual parties, as in the case of unfairness or unconscionability, but because they threaten the interests of the public at large. How do courts determine what counts as "public policy"? Some situations are easy, as when contract terms violate the criminal law: a contract to extort money, for example, or a "hit contract." But how do courts discern public policy when the connection between the bargain and a statute is less immediate? What sources do they look to in order to refuse enforcement of a contract on the grounds of public policy, when the parties themselves may be perfectly content with their bargain? As with other policing measures, here too hard questions arise about coordinating judicial and legislative functions in defining and giving effect to public policy.

SECTION 1.   UNFAIRNESS

The function of policing bargains was traditionally a specialty of equity courts, which were empowered to grant specific relief. See the discussion at p. 886 below. Because obtaining a decree of specific performance was not a matter of right in the same sense as was an award of damages, courts of equity often denied specific enforcement in cases when the bargain was procured by sharp practice, or when the exchange appeared highly disproportionate.

By contrast, in cases "at law," courts lacked the inherent discretion to weigh equities, and resorted to more established methods of policing, such as finding that a particularly overbearing provision conflicts with an established public policy. Courts have also manipulated the doctrine of consideration to serve the ideal of fairness, including determinations about whether or not there was any "bargain" at all.

The following three decisions are each concerned with the fairness of the exchange. In each, other values, such as certainty regarding the enforcement of promises or the recognition of individual agency in entering a bargain, compete with the claim of unfairness. How should this trade-off be weighed? Do you agree with the suggestion that: "There does come a point where the additional costs of having personalized transactions may be too great; a little injustice may be a social good"? Arthur Leff, *Injury, Ignorance and Spite—The Dynamics of Coercive Collection*, 80 Yale L.J. 1, 42 (1970). Undoubtedly Leff meant not that injustice is a good in itself, but that in the context of contract law, it might be an acceptable price to pay for such values as certainty. Keep this framework in mind as you proceed through these materials.

McKinnon v. Benedict

Supreme Court of Wisconsin, 1968.
38 Wis.2d 607, 157 N.W.2d 665.

[In 1960 Roderick McKinnon, the owner of a thousand-acre property on Mamie Lake, Wisconsin, assisted Mr. and Mrs. Roy Benedict in buying a resort known as Bent's Camp. The camp consisted of a lodge and some cabins on about 80 acres that were enclosed by the lake and by McKinnon's property. McKinnon promised some help in getting business and in other minor respects, but his principal contribution was in making a loan of $5,000. The Benedicts used the advance as part of a down payment on a land purchase contract with the previous owners of the camp. In exchange, the Benedicts promised McKinnon to cut no trees between their camp and his property, and to make no improvements "closer to [his] property than the present buildings." The term of these restrictions was 25 years. They did not affect all the resort tract, but did affect all the most desirable portion.

Although they repaid the loan to McKinnon in about seven months, the Benedicts' resort business did not prosper. In 1964 they decided to add a trailer park and tent camp, and in the fall and following spring they invested some $9,000 in bulldozing and installing utilities. The summer of 1965 brought with it both McKinnon from Arizona, where he spent the winters, and a suit by McKinnon against the Benedicts seeking to enjoin them from continuing with their projected improvements. The trial court granted the injunction and the Benedicts appealed.]

■ HEFFERNAN, JUSTICE. No action at law has been commenced for damages by virtue of the breach of the restrictions; and, in fact, the plaintiffs in their complaint claim that they have no adequate remedy at law. [The court expounded some "ancient principles of equity," and quoted the Restatement (First) of Contracts § 367.[a]]

---

[a]   Specific enforcement of a contract may be refused if

(a) The consideration for it is grossly inadequate or its terms are otherwise unfair, or

(b) its enforcement will cause unreasonable or disproportionate hardship or loss to the defendant or to third persons, or

(c) it was induced by some sharp practice, misrepresentation, or mistake.

Coupled with the general equitable principle that contracts that are oppressive will not be enforced in equity is the principle of public policy that restrictions on the use of land "are not favored in the law" (Mueller v. Schier (1926), 189 Wis. 70, 82, 205 N.W. 912, 916), and that restrictions and prohibitions as to the use of real estate should be resolved, if a doubt exists, in favor of the free use of the property. Stein v. Endres Home Builders, Inc. (1938) 228 Wis. 620, 629, 280 N.W. 316.[b]

The great hardship sought to be imposed upon the Benedicts is apparent. What was the consideration in exchange for this deprivation of use? The only monetary consideration was the granting of a $5,000 loan, interest free, for a period of seven months. The value of this money for that period of time, if taken at the same interest rate as the 5 percent used on the balance of the land contract, is approximately $145; and it should be noted that this was not an unsecured loan, since McKinnon took a mortgage on the cottage property of the Benedicts in Michigan. In addition, McKinnon stated that he would "help you try" to reach a solution of the problem posed by Mrs. Vair's occupancy of one of the cottages on a fifty-year lease at $5 per year. His one attempt, as stated above, was a failure; and McKinnon's promise to generate business resulted in an occupancy by only one group for less than a week. For this pittance and these feeble attempts to help with the operational problems of the camp, the Benedicts have sacrificed their right to make lawful and reasonable use of their property.

In oral argument it was pointed out that the value of the $5,000 loan could not be measured in terms of the interest value of the money, since, without this advance, Benedict would have been unable to purchase the camp at all. To our mind, this is evidence of the fact that Benedict was not able to deal at arm's length with McKinnon, for his need for these funds was obviously so great that he was willing to enter into a contract that results in gross inequities. Lord Chancellor Northington said "necessitous men are not, truly speaking, free men." Vernon v. Bethell (1762), 2 Eden 110, 113.

We find that the inadequacy of consideration is so gross as to be unconscionable and a bar to the plaintiffs' invocation of the extraordinary equitable powers of the court.

While there is no doubt that there are benefits from this agreement to McKinnon, they are more than outweighed by the oppressive terms that would be imposed upon the Benedicts. McKinnon testified that he and his wife spend only the summer months on their property. Undoubtedly, these are the months when it is most important that there be no disruption of the natural beauty or the quiet and pleasant enjoyment of the property, nevertheless, there was testimony that the

---

[b]   It is actually the dissent in *Stein* that makes the point that "restrictions and prohibitions as to the use of real estate by the grantee should be resolved in favor of the free use of the property." *Id.* at 320 (Rosenberry, C.J., dissenting). The majority comes out the other way and allows a restrictive covenant on the use of the land.

trailer camp could not be seen from the McKinnon home, nor could the campsite be seen during the summer months of the year, when the leaves were on the trees. Thus, the detriment of which the McKinnons complain, that would be cognizable in an equity action, is minimal,[1] while the damage done to the Benedicts is severe.

Considering all the factors—the inadequacy of the consideration, the small benefit that would be accorded the McKinnons, and the oppressive conditions imposed upon the Benedicts—we conclude that this contract failed to meet the test of reasonableness that is the *sine qua non* of the enforcement of rights in an action in equity.

5A Corbin, *Contracts*, sec. 1164, p. 219, points out that, although a contract is harsh, oppressive, and unconscionable, it may nevertheless be enforceable at law; but, in the discretion of the court, equitable remedies will not be enforced against one who suffers from such harshness and oppression.

A fair reading of the transcript indicates no sharp practice, dishonesty, or overreaching on the part of McKinnon. However, there was a wide disparity between the business experience of the parties. McKinnon was a man of stature in the legal field, an investment counsellor, a former officer of a major corporation, and had held posts of responsibility with the United States government, while, insofar as the record shows, Benedict was a retail jeweler and a man of limited financial ability. He no doubt overvalued the promises of McKinnon to assist in getting the operation "well organized" and to solve the lease problem and to "generate business." These factors, in view of Benedict's financial inability to enter into an arms-length transaction, may be explanatory of the reason for the agreement, but the agreement viewed even as of the time of its execution was unfair and based upon inadequate consideration. We, therefore, have no hesitancy in denying the plaintiffs the equitable remedy of injunction.

[Reversed.]

NOTES

(1) *Questions.* If the Benedicts had begun their new business immediately after making the agreement of 1960, would the court have given McKinnon the relief that he sought? May the Benedicts now bulldoze on their property and make improvements wherever they please?

In denying the plaintiffs relief, the court took note of a public policy disfavoring restrictions on the use of land, citing a 1926 case. Are there countervailing public policies that might be invoked today? See, for example,

---

[1] McKinnon testified that the value of his property had depreciated in the amount of $50,000. That testimony was properly admissible, but its probative value was slight, especially since plaintiff's expert real estate witness stated that he was unable to testify to the amount of the depreciated value.

the claim for damages made by homeowners in Oklahoma for a mining company's failure to restore property after strip-mining; Note 1, p. 931.

(2) *Damages at Law.* In denying specific performance to a claimant, the courts sometimes take comfort in the thought that the decision does not deprive the claimant of *all* remedies but only remits it the more perfunctory one of damages. Is that an empty justification in a case like McKinnon v. Benedict? Was there an effective remedy available to McKinnon other than specific performance? Remedies are dealt with in more detail in Chapter 8.

(3) *The Contours of Equitable Discretion.* "Within the ambit of those factors of contract-producing behavior which would result in a denial of specific performance, a bewildering number of permutations work to inform the chancellor's discretion. In these cases one runs continually into the old, the young, the ignorant, the necessitous, the illiterate, the improvident, the drunken, the naïve and the sick, all on one side of the transaction, with the sharp and hard on the other. Language of quasi-fraud and quasi-duress abounds. Certain whole classes of presumptive sillies like sailors and heirs and farmers and women continually wander on and off stage. Those not certifiably crazy, but nonetheless pretty peculiar, are often to be found. And in most of the cases, of course, several of these factors appear in combination. . . . Almost without exception, actions for specific performance were (and are) brought with respect to transactions involving real property." Arthur Leff, *Unconscionability and the Code—the Emperor's New Clause*, 115 U. Pa. L. Rev. 485, 531–34 (1967).

(4) *Class and Contract.* The court in *McKinnon* suggested that "necessitous men are not, truly speaking, free men." The question of comparative wealth arises in cases throughout this chapter. Consider as you proceed how courts and legislatures take account of wealth and other disparities between parties in policing bargains. Is class, like minority, a status to which the law should attend, perhaps creating a presumption of vulnerability?

Tuckwiller v. Tuckwiller

Supreme Court of Missouri, 1967.
413 S.W.2d 274.

[John and Ruby Tuckwiller lived on the family farm in Missouri, which John farmed as a renter. Almost half of the 160 acre farm was owned by Mrs. Metta Hudson Morrison, John's aunt. When she was about 70 years of age, Mrs. Morrison manifested Parkinson's disease. At about the same time she gave up her residence in New York and returned to the Hudson farm, where some rooms were reserved for her use. In April she was hospitalized for about a week, as a result of dizziness and falling. She was thought then to have had a stroke, and showed some mental confusion. But at the first of May her doctor and a friend found her "clear as a bell." She knew, the doctor said, that Parkinsonism is a progressive disease, leaving the victim ultimately dependent entirely on outside care.

Before the April incident, Mrs. Tuckwiller had been urged by Mrs. Morrison to quit a job she held and care for her for the rest of her life, and the subject was discussed again after Mrs. Morrison's release from the hospital. The two were quite congenial. On May 3, Mrs. Morrison signed the following paper, written by Mrs. Tuckwiller:

My offer to Aunt Metta is as follows

I will take care of her for her lifetime; by that I mean provide her 3 meals per day—a good bed—do any possible act of nursing and provide her every pleasure possible.

In exchange she will will me her (Corum) farm at her death keeping all money made from it during her life. She will maintain expense of her medicine.

On May 6, Mrs. Tuckwiller resigned her job, and Mrs. Morrison made an appointment with a lawyer to change her will. Later that day, however, she fainted and fell. She was taken to the hospital, where, except for four days, she remained until her death on June 14. She was 73 at that time. Mrs. Tuckwiller spent much time at the hospital during Mrs. Morrison's final illness, assisting as she could, but Mrs. Morrison was attended by special nurses.

Before leaving for the hospital on May 6, Mrs. Morrison had the date put on the paper set out above, and obtained the signatures of the two ambulance attendants as witnesses. Her will, dated in 1961, was never changed. It provided for the sale of the farm, the proceeds to be used for a student loan fund at Davidson College. The farm had an "inventory value" of $34,400.

Mrs. Tuckwiller brought a bill for specific performance of the contract, which was resisted by the College and Mrs. Morrison's executor, Marion Tuckwiller. The trial court granted the relief, and the defendants appealed.]

■ WELBORN, COMMISSIONER. [I]n determining whether or not a contract is so unfair or inequitable or is unconscionable so as to deny its specific performance, the transaction must be viewed prospectively, not retrospectively. The same rule applies with respect to sufficiency of consideration. Viewed in this light, we find that plaintiff gave up her employment with which she was well satisfied and undertook what was at the time of the contract an obligation of unknown and uncertain duration, involving duties which, in the usual course of the disease from which Mrs. Morrison suffered, would have become increasingly onerous. Viewed from the standpoint of Mrs. Morrison, the contract cannot be considered unfair. She was appreciative of the care and attention which plaintiff had given her prior to the agreement. Although, as defendants suggest, such prior services cannot provide the consideration essential to a binding contract, such prior services and the past relation of the parties may properly be considered in connection with the fairness of the contract and adequacy of the consideration. 5A Corbin on Contracts, § 1165, p.

227. Aware of her future outlook and having no immediate family to care for her, Mrs. Morrison was understandably appreciative of the personal care and attention of plaintiff and concerned with the possibility of routine impersonal care over a long period of time in a nursing home or similar institution. Having no immediate family which might be the object of her bounty, she undoubtedly felt more free to agree to dispose of the farm without insisting upon an exact quid pro quo. Her insistence that the contract be witnessed prior to her hospitalization is clear evidence of her satisfaction with the bargain as was her unsuccessful effort to change her will to carry out her agreement.

Properly viewed from the standpoint of the parties at the time of the agreement, we find that the contract was fair, not unconscionable, and supported by an adequate consideration. Although not conceding that such conclusion is correct, defendants argue, in effect, that in view of the obviously brief duration of plaintiff's services and their value in comparison with the value of the farm, plaintiff should be obliged to accept the offered payment of the reasonable value of her services and denied the relief of specific performance. Defendants point out that the trial court found that valuing the services which plaintiff rendered might be "possible." That conclusion is undoubtedly correct and unquestionably the monetary value of plaintiff's services would have been a quite small proportion (perhaps one percent) of the value of the farm. Once, however, the essential fairness of the contract and the adequacy of the consideration are found, the fact that the subject of the contract is real estate answers any question of adequacy of the legal remedy of monetary damages. "Whenever a contract concerning real property is in its nature and incidents entirely unobjectionable—that is, when it possesses none of those features which . . . appeal to the discretion of the court—it is as much a matter of course for a court of equity to decree a specific performance of it, as it is for a court of law to give damages for the breach of it." Pomeroy's Specific Performance of Contracts (3d ed.), § 10, p. 23.

[Affirmed.]

NOTES

(1) *Questions.* The defendants agreed that Ruby Tuckwiller should get *something.* How would they have calculated her damages? What risks did Ruby assume in this agreement? What risks did each of the parties in McKinnon v. Benedict assume? How is the question of relative risk implicated in the two decisions?

(2) *Professional Services.* In Gladding v. Langrall, Muir & Noppinger, 401 A.2d 662 (Md. 1979), the court rejected a claim of unconscionability in reliance on the principle that a bargain is to be evaluated by reference to the situation existing at the time it was struck. Is this principle of special importance to lawyers who spend many billable hours on claims of questionable value? See Cetenko v. United California Bank, 638 P.2d 1299 (Cal. 1982). Compare Brobeck, Phleger & Harrison v. Telex Corp., 602 F.2d

866 (9th Cir. 1979), in which a law firm recovered a million dollars for filing a petition for certiorari.

What about lawyers who contract for contingent fees? What risk do clients and lawyers take in making such an arrangement? Would you expect the principle to be equally reliable for an attorney as for an accountant, each working for a contingent fee? In *Gladding* the court spoke of "the broader judicial interest in attorney-client contracts, which exist only because of the attorney's status as an officer of the court." The claimant was an accounting firm. It recovered a fee of more than $30,000 (in addition to a retainer of $10,000) for 17 hours of professional services. The fee was a percentage of tax savings effected for the firm's clients through a settlement with the Internal Revenue Service.

Introduction to Black Industries, Inc. v. Bush

The previous two cases concerned the fairness of the terms of the deal and the courts' willingness (in *Tuckwiller*) and refusal (in *McKinnon*) to enforce the bargain struck by the parties on that account. The next case also involves a claim of unfairness, but not between the parties themselves. Instead, the seller has argued that the buyer, a middleman, made excessive profits on his resale of the goods to the government and for that reason, the contract should not be enforced. Note that the case is not a "government contract" as the term is typically used (a contract between a party and the government), but rather one where the government's interests are invoked by a party on policy grounds.

The contract in *Black* arose during the Korean War. You may already have noticed the presence of wars and crises throughout the cases, such as the Vietnam War in Austin v. Loral, and there is more to come, including the 1956 Suez Canal crisis and the OPEC oil crisis of the 1970s. We shall see in Chapter 9 (Impracticability of Performance) that certain calamities—such monumental events as Acts of God, earthquakes, civil commotion—may in some circumstances provide a defense to performance. For now, however, consider more generally whether courts should, or do, take account of background crises in deciding contract disputes between private parties or between private parties and the government.

Black Industries, Inc. v. Bush

United States District Court, D. New Jersey, 1953.
110 F.Supp. 801.

[Black Industries ("Black"), a manufacturer of machine parts, was asked to bid on contracts with The Hoover Company for anvils, holder primers, and plunger supports, and with Standby Products for two of the same items. Black contracted to buy the same items to be included in the Hoover bid from a supplier, George F. Bush, doing business as G.F. Bush Associates ("Bush"). Bush agreed to manufacture anvils at a price of

$4.40 per thousand; holder primers at $11.50 per thousand and plunger supports at a price of $12 per thousand, all in accordance with government specifications provided by Black.

The terms of the contract were set out in a letter from Black to Bush, and signed "as agreed to" by Bush. The letter stated that Black Industries had "spent considerable time, effort and money in developing the contract" to the point where The Hoover Company issued a purchase order. The letter further stated: "The purchase order [from Hoover], when received, will run directly to G. F. Bush and Associates. Your company is to ship the material directly to The Hoover Co. Your company, however, is not to bill The Hoover Co. All shipping invoices, documents of transfer and title are to be forwarded to me, and I shall have the exclusive right to bill, upon [your] billing forms and receive payment therefor in your behalf. It is understood that I shall have the right to receive payment, cash checks made payable to your company under The Hoover Co. contract; and to remit to you [amounts payable under the agreement, while retaining sums] as compensation due me." The letter stated that Black's compensation was to be the difference between Bush's price to Black and Black's price to Hoover. A similar arrangement was in place between Black and Standby products.

The Hoover Company agreed to purchase the parts from Black at a rate of $8.10 per thousand anvils, $16 per thousand holder primers, and $21.20 per thousand plunger supports. After beginning performance of the contract, Bush failed to complete the order, and Black sued for damages of $14,625 for the Hoover contract and $4,460.95 for the Standby contract. Black was to receive a "profit" of 84.09% on anvils, 39.13% on holder primers, and 68.33% on plunger supports under the Hoover contract, and similar percentages under the Standby contract.

In its decision the court noted that the items purchased by Hoover and Standby were to be used to fulfill contracts with United States government in aid of "the defense effort," *i.e.*, the Korean War of 1950–53. Bush moved for summary judgment on the ground that the contract was void against public policy because Black's "profits" were passed on to the government and the public in the form of increased prices. In support of his motion, Bush cited two federal laws intended to prevent excessive profits on war contracts: The Renegotiation Act, 50 U.S.C.A. Appendix, § 1211, and 41 U.S.C.A. § 51.]

■ FORMAN, CHIEF JUDGE. In order to declare a contract, entered by the parties freely and without evidence of fraud, void as against public policy, the contract must be invalid on the basis of recognized legal principles. [In an omitted passage, the court quotes from Muschany v. United States, 324 U.S. 49, 66–67 (1945), as follows: "It is a matter of public importance that good faith contracts of the United States should not be lightly invalidated." Then it discusses three types of illegal contracts, as indicated in the following paragraph.]

The contract in the present case, however, does not fall in any of these categories. It is not a contract by the defendant to pay the plaintiff for inducing a public official to act in a certain manner; it is not a contract to do an illegal act; and it is not a contract which contemplates collusive bidding on a public contract. It should be noted that the first and third categories of cases, upon which the defendant relies most heavily, involve agreements which directly impinge upon government activities. In the case at hand, the contract's only effect on the government was that ultimately the government was to buy the product of which defendant's goods were to be a component. Neither the defendant nor the plaintiff had any dealings with the United States on account of this contract, and therefore the profit accruing to the plaintiff was not to have been earned as a result of either inducing government action or interfering with the system of competitive bidding. This contract cannot, therefore, be declared void as against public policy on the basis of the precedents cited by the defendant.

It is quite possible that the plaintiff was to have received a very high profit on the sale of the parts, either because The Hoover Company agreed to pay too high a price or because the defendant quoted too low a price. Further proof would be required to establish this as a fact. Even if it were proved that the plaintiff was to have received a far greater profit than the defendants for a much smaller contribution, the defendant would nevertheless be bound by his agreement by the familiar rule that relative values of the consideration in a contract between business men dealing at arm's length without fraud will not affect the validity of the contract. The Coast National Bank v. Bloom, 113 N.J.L. 597, 174 A. 576, 95 A.L.R. 528 (E. & A. 1934); Restatement of the Law of Contracts § 81 (1932).

The fact that the government is the ultimate purchaser of the product in which defendant's parts are used is cited by the defendant as a reason to hold that this contract is void as against public policy. To so hold would necessitate either ruling that all contracts are void if they provide for compensation for middlemen, such as Black Industries, between producer and purchaser of goods which ultimately are incorporated in products sold to the government, a result which is not supported by precedent and which would defy the realities of our economic life, or deciding in every case involving such a contract whether the compensation paid a middleman such as the plaintiff here who locates purchasers and assists the producer in other ways, is reasonable. This latter course would, in effect, impose price regulatory functions on the court. There are other and more effective methods of insuring that the government does not pay an unreasonable price for its supplies. The manufacturer selling directly to the United States must conform to procedures such as bidding designed to protect the government, and which should, in conjunction with the ordinary considerations of profits and loss, insure that prime contractors do not pay outlandish prices for the products they buy in order to fulfill a government contract. The contract may be subject to renegotiation. 50 U.S.C.A. Appendix, § 1211 et seq. I do not believe that it is the function of the court to interfere by determining the validity of a contract between ordinary business men on the basis of its beliefs as to the adequacy of the consideration. Consequently, I hold that, assuming the facts to be as stated by the defendant, the contract sued on in this case is not void as against public policy and the defendant's motion for a summary judgment will, therefore, be denied.

Let an order be submitted in accordance with this opinion.

NOTES

(1)   *Price Regulation.* The arguments against courts' inquiring into the "relative value of the consideration in a contract between business men dealing at arm's length without fraud" have been summarized as follows: "(1) The efficient administration of the law of contracts requires that courts shall not be required to prescribe prices. (2) The test of enforceability should be certain and should not be beclouded by such vague terms as 'fair' or 'reasonable' as tests of validity. (3) There is still the somewhat old-fashioned theory that persons of maturity and sound mind should be free to contract imprudently as well as prudently." Edwin Patterson, *An Apology for Consideration*, 58 Colum. L. Rev. 929 (1958).

Does it appear that courts, in specific performance actions, undertake price regulatory functions? Does the equitable power exercised in McKinnon v. Benedict invite litigation in a large proportion of contracts about land? If so, it may tend to impair the value of such contracts as the Tuckwillers made with Mrs. Morrison, in Tuckwiller v. Tuckwiller. Should the courts be cautious, on that account, in attempting supervision over the values exchanged?

(2)   *Intermediaries or "Middlemen."* The court acknowledges that Black might have stood to receive a "far greater profit" than Bush "for a much smaller contribution." What was the nature of Black's contribution in this transaction?

Intermediaries typically perform an "informational" or "search" function by bringing together buyers and sellers who would otherwise be ignorant of one another's needs or existence. They may also perform "risk-shifting" functions, by taking on themselves the risks of market fluctuations that would otherwise be borne by buyers or sellers. Both of these functions are highly developed in well-organized markets. Does it appear that Black's "contribution" involved either an informational or a risk-shifting function? If it involved the former, did Black supply Hoover with enough information about available suppliers to merit the compensation it received? Why did Hoover not contact Bush directly? Why did Bush not contact Hoover directly? Would Bush have been able to charge Black more if he had known how much Hoover was paying Black?

Fairness, Excessive Profits, and Government Contracts

One of Bush's arguments in the case above was that the cost of Black's profits was passed on to the government and to the tax-paying public contrary to "public policy." Referring to existing and "more effective methods," the court suggested that the government is able to take care of itself in this regard, citing the Federal Renegotiation Act of 1942.

Since that time, additional statutory measures have been enacted to protect the government (and taxpayers) from profiteering. The Competition in Contracting Act of 1984 requires that subject to certain exceptions, federal contracts are to be awarded on the basis of "full and open competition." 31 U.S.C. § 3729 *et seq*. Exceptions, which authorize noncompetitive or "no-bid" contracts, include cases in which only one responsible source can provide the goods or services required, and emergency circumstances which require immediate contract awards. For example, a sizable number of contracts awarded in the aftermath of Hurricane Katrina (for roofing, trailers, debris removal) fell under the emergency exception, and were awarded without competitive bidding. See Presidential Council on Integrity and Efficiency, *Oversight of Gulf Coast Hurricane Recovery: A Semiannual Report to Congress* at 9 (Oct. 2006), available at https://www.ignet.gov/sites/default/files/files/hksemi 0406.pdf.

Other mechanisms for avoiding excessive profits are limitations placed on awarding various forms of "cost reimbursement" contracts, rather than fixed price contracts. See Federal Acquisition Regulation (FAR), 48 C.F.R. § 16.301. Might the government ever prefer a cost-plus contract? Under what circumstances? See John Cibinic and Ralph Nash, *Formation of Government Contracts,* 1061 *et seq.* (3d ed. 1998). FAR provides the framework for all government procurement contracts. Such contracts are explored in depth in the Cibinic and Nash treatise.

Excessive profits may also result when a party acts egregiously in the performance of a contract, say, by submitting claims for work not actually done. To protect against such practices Congress enacted the False Claims Act (FCA). Originally enacted in 1863 in response to fraudulent claims submitted to the government during the Civil War, the current version was passed in 1986, see 31 U.S.C. § 3729 *et seq.* It provides that "any person who knowingly presents, or causes to be presented, to an officer or employer of the United States Government a false or fraudulent claim for payment is liable to the United States" for a civil penalty of not more than $10,000 and three times the amount of damages which the government sustains, or treble damages. 31 U.S.C. § 3729(a)(1). Proceedings under the Act may be brought by a private person (called a "relator") acting in the public interest. Actions brought by private persons are called *qui tam* actions, the phrase short for *"qui tam pro domino rege quam pro se ipso in hac parte sequitur"* (who pursues this action on our Lord the King's behalf as well as his own), Rockwell International Corp. v. United States, 549 U.S. 457, 463 n.2 (2007). The United States may choose to intervene in a *qui tam* action, also as a relator. For a *qui tam* action brought in the aftermath of Hurricane Katrina and involving the unethical behavior of counsel, see United States ex rel. Rigsby v. State Farm Insurance Company, 2008 WL 2130314 (S.D. Miss. May 19, 2008).

Claims under the FCA are subject to a number of requirements—the false claim must be presented "knowingly," for example—and are often difficult to prove. In a 2006 case, the United States claimed that a private U.S. contractor had submitted inflated invoices to the Coalition Provisional Authority (CPA) in Iraq for reimbursement of $3,000,000 in costs not actually expended in performing its duties under a $20,000,000 cost-plus contract to provide machinery and security for the Dinar Exchange Contract. (The contract reimbursed the contractor for its actual expenses, plus 25% of actual expenses for replacing Iraqi currency bearing Saddam Hussein's image for dinar without the image.) After a 12-day trial, the jury found for the government on the fraud count, but the district court granted the contractor's motion for summary judgment that it had not presented a false claim to the United States, but to the CPA, which did not qualify as an "instrumentality of the U.S. government." The government appealed. *Held*: Reversed. United States v. Custer Battles LLC, 562 F. 3d 295 (4th Cir. 2009). The Fourth Circuit Court of Appeals found that "ample evidence" had been introduced "to show that the fraudulently inflated invoices were presented to U.S. government employees or officials who were acting in their official capacities," so that the requirements of the False Claims Act had in fact been met.

Overseeing government contracts—their formation, performance completion, billing, and so on—is a vast task, headed in the first instance at the federal level by the Comptroller General of the U.S., and the Government Accountability Office. See, for example, Government Accountability Office, *Rebuilding Iraq: Status of Competition for Iraq Construction Contracts, Report to Congressional Committees* (2006). The Inspector General is also charged with various oversight functions, see 5 U.S.C. App. § 2. See, for example, Special Inspector General for Iraq Reconstruction, *Iraq Reconstruction: Lessons Learned in Contracting and Procurement* (2006), available at https://usiraq.procon.org/sourcefiles/Lessons_Learned_July-06.pdf.

Do government contracts raise policy concerns in addition to those concerning excessive profits? What policies, if any, are supported by the court's observation in Black v. Bush, above, that "good faith contracts of the United States should not be lightly invalidated?"

SECTION 2.　STANDARD FORM AND ADHESION CONTRACTS

The preceding section explored traditional common law principles concerned with the equality of exchange. Just as the policing measures were "conventional," so in a sense were the contracts: *individualized* agreements, tailored to the specifics of the particular deal by the parties themselves. This section focuses on a now ubiquitous type of contract that emerged some two hundred years ago—the *standard form contract*.

Like the mass production of goods, the mass production of contracts may serve the interests of both courts and parties. Among the advantages claimed for their use are the following: they take advantage of the lessons of experience and enable a judicial interpretation of one contract to serve as an interpretation of all contracts; they reduce uncertainty and save time and trouble; they simplify planning and administration and make superior drafting skills more widely available; and they make risks calculable and "[increase] that real security which is the necessary basis of initiative and the assumption of foreseeable risks." Morris Cohen, *The Basis of Contract*, 46 Harv. L. Rev. 553, 558 (1933). From an economic perspective, standard form contracts further "benefit consumers because, in competition, reductions in the cost of doing business show up as lower prices . . . ." Carbajal v. H & R Block Tax Servs, 372 F.3d 903 (7th Cir. 2004) (Easterbrook, J.).

Professor Friedrich Kessler elaborated the matter of risk: "It has been noted that uniformity of terms of contracts typically recurring in a business enterprise is an important factor in the exact calculation of risks. Risks which are difficult to calculate can be excluded altogether. Unforeseeable contingencies affecting performance, such as strikes, fire, and transportation difficulties can be taken care of. The standard clauses in insurance policies are the most striking illustrations of successful attempts on the part of business enterprises to select and control risks assumed under a contract. The insurance business probably deserves credit also for having first realized the full importance of the so-called 'juridical risk', the danger that a court or jury may be swayed by 'irrational factors' to decide against a powerful defendant. . . . Standardized . . . contracts have thus become an important means of excluding or controlling the 'irrational factor' in litigation. In this respect they are a true reflection of the spirit of our time with its hostility to irrational factors in the judicial process, and they belong in the same category as codifications and restatements." Friedrich Kessler, *Contracts of Adhesion—Some Thoughts About Freedom of Contract*, 43 Colum. L. Rev. 629, 631–32 (1943).

On the other hand, standard form contracts, often referred to as "contracts of adhesion," offer the means by which one party may impose its will upon another. How does this come about? There are several means of imposition, which often appear in combination. First, an enterprise may have such disproportionately strong economic power that it can dictate its terms to the weaker party. Second, there may be no opportunity to bargain over terms at all; the standardized contract is often a take-it-or-leave-it proposition. Finally, standardized contracts are often used by a party who has had the advantage of time and expert advice in preparing it while the other party may have no real opportunity to scrutinize, and often no real means to understand, the contract. This difficulty may be compounded by the use of fine print and obfuscating clauses.

The cases in this section present types of standard form contracts probably familiar to readers who have rented an apartment, checked a coat or backpack, bought a car, or purchased travel tickets. In each case, the court is concerned with whether a party to a standardized contract can reasonably be held to have seen, understood, and assented to its unfavorable terms, and accordingly, to be bound by them. The following questions provide a framework for thinking about policing bargains in an impersonal market where the "individuality of the parties which so frequently gave color to the old type of contract has disappeared." Friedrich Kessler, *Contracts of Adhesion—Some Thoughts About Freedom of Contract*, 43 Colum. L. Rev. 629, 631–32 (1943). Should it matter whether a party is a firm in a commercial deal, or an individual in a consumer agreement? How do courts determine public policy, a concept often invoked in deciding whether or not a particular term should be enforced? Finally, how should lawmakers evaluate attempts to ensure fairness in a particular case by means of a rule that may complicate, burden, or increase the expense of contracting, sometimes for those the law seeks to protect?

Before turning to these issues, we take a moment to consider standard form contracts within a larger social framework.

NOTES

(1) *From Status to Contract, and Back.* One of the great generalizations about social history is the thesis of Sir Henry Maine that the history of progressive societies may be described as a movement from status to contract. In *Ancient Law* (1865), Maine stated: "The movement of the progressive societies has been uniform in one respect. Through all its course it has been distinguished by the gradual dissolution of family dependency and the growth of individual obligation in its place. The individual is steadily substituted for the Family, as the unit of which civil laws take account. . . . Nor is it difficult to see what is the tie between man and man which replaces by degrees those forms of reciprocity in rights and duties which have their origin in the Family. It is Contract. . . . All the forms of Status taken notice of in the Law of Persons were derived from, and to some extent are still coloured by, the powers and privileges anciently residing in the Family. If then we employ Status, agreeably with the usage of the best writers, to signify these personal conditions only, and avoid applying the term to such conditions as are the immediate or remote result of agreement, we may say

that the movement of the progressive societies has hitherto been a movement *from Status to Contract.*"

Over a century later, some scholars detected a reverse tendency in the law. They suggested that standard form contracts may be conducive to a regressive regime of status: "With the decline of the free enterprise system due to the innate trend of competitive capitalism towards monopoly, the meaning of contract has changed radically. Society, when granting freedom of contract, does not guarantee that all members of the community will be able to make use of it to the same extent. On the contrary, the law, by protecting the unequal distribution of property, does nothing to prevent freedom of contract from becoming a one-sided privilege. Freedom of contract enables enterprisers to legislate by contract and, what is even more important, to legislate in a substantially authoritarian manner without using the appearance of authoritarian forms. Standard contracts in particular could thus become effective instruments in the hands of powerful industrial and commercial overlords enabling them to impose a new feudal order of their own making upon a vast host of vassals. . . . Thus the return back from contract to status which we experience today was greatly facilitated by the fact that the belief in freedom of contract has remained one of the firmest axioms in the whole fabric of the social philosophy of our culture." Friedrich Kessler, *Contracts of Adhesion—Some Thoughts About Freedom of Contract*, 43 Colum. L. Rev. 629, 640 (1943).

Consider as you read further, whether the law's efforts at policing have thwarted or facilitated the new "feudal order."

(2) *Distinctions Among Standard Form Contracts.* The term "contract of adhesion" was first used in the United States by Professor Patterson, *The Delivery of a Life-Insurance Policy*, 33 Harv. L. Rev. 198, 222 (1919). It was coined by Raymond Saleilles as "contrat d'adhésion" to describe contracts "in which one predominant unilateral will dictates its law to an undetermined multitude rather than to an individual . . . as in all employment contracts of big industry, transportation contracts of big railroad companies and all those contracts which, as the Romans said, resemble a law much more than a meeting of the minds." Raymond Saleilles, *De la Declaration de Volonté* 229 (1901).

Are all standard form contracts contracts of adhesion? In Oblix, Inc. v. Winiecki, 374 F.3d 488 (7th Cir. 2004), the court upheld an employment agreement "offered on a take-it-or-leave-it" basis against the claim that the agreement and an arbitration clause within were "adhesive." Returning to the fundamentals of consideration, Judge Easterbrook stated that the claimant "does not deny the arbitration clause is supported by consideration—her salary. Oblix paid [her] to do a number of things; one of the things it paid her to do was agree to non-judicial dispute resolution."

The mere fact of exchange between the parties may not fully answer the question of whether or not the terms of a contract have been imposed, in contrast to having been meaningfully bargained for. The following case discusses the sorts of factors that help courts make that determination under the common law.

O'Callaghan v. Waller & Beckwith Realty Co.

Supreme Court of Illinois, 1958.
15 Ill.2d 436, 155 N.E.2d 545.

■ SCHAEFER, JUSTICE.[c] This is an action to recover for injuries allegedly caused by the defendant's negligence in maintaining and operating a large apartment building. Mrs. Ella O'Callaghan, a tenant in the building, was injured when she fell while crossing the paved courtyard on her way from the garage to her apartment. She instituted this action to recover for her injuries, alleging that they were caused by defective pavement in the courtyard. Before the case was tried, Mrs. O'Callaghan died and her administrator was substituted as plaintiff. The jury returned a verdict for the plaintiff in the sum of $14,000, and judgment was entered on the verdict. Defendant appealed. The Appellate Court held that the action was barred by an exculpatory clause in the lease that Mrs. O'Callaghan had signed, and that a verdict should have been directed for the defendant. 146 N.E.2d 198. It therefore reversed the judgment and remanded the cause with directions to enter judgment for the defendant. We granted leave to appeal.

In reaching its conclusion the Appellate Court relied upon our recent decision in Jackson v. First National Bank, 114 N.E.2d 721. There we considered the validity of such an exculpatory clause in a lease of property for business purposes. We pointed out that contracts by which one seeks to relieve himself from the consequences of his own negligence are generally enforced "unless (1) it would be against the settled public policy of the State to do so, or (2) there is something in the social relationship of the parties militating against upholding the agreement." 114 N.E.2d at page 725. And we held that there was nothing in the public policy of the State or in the social relationship of the parties to forbid enforcement of the exculpatory clause there involved.

The exculpatory clause in the lease now before us clearly purports to relieve the lessor and its agents from any liability to the lessee for personal injuries or property damage caused by any act or neglect of the lessor or its agents. It does not appear to be amenable to the strict construction to which such clauses are frequently subjected. See 175 A.L.R. 8, 89. The plaintiff does not question its applicability, and she concedes that if it is valid it bars her recovery. She argues vigorously, however, that such a clause is contrary to public policy, and so invalid, in a lease of residential property.

Freedom of contract is basic to our law. But when that freedom expresses itself in a provision designed to absolve one of the parties from the consequences of his own negligence, there is danger that the standards of conduct which the law has developed for the protection of

_____

c   Walter V. Schaefer (1904–1986) practiced law and served in a variety of governmental posts in Chicago between 1928 and 1940, when he became a professor of law at Northwestern University. From 1951 to 1976 he was a member of the Illinois Supreme Court, serving as Chief Judge. He was one of the Advisers for the Restatement Second.

others may be diluted. These competing considerations have produced results that are not completely consistent. This court has refused to enforce contracts exculpating or limiting liability for negligence between common carriers and shippers of freight or paying passengers (Chicago and Northwestern Railway Co. v. Chapman, 24 N.E. 417, 8 L.R.A. 508), between telegraph companies and those sending messages (Tyler, Ullman & Co. v. Western Union Telegraph Co., 60 Ill. 421), and between masters and servants (Campbell v. Chicago, Rock Island and Pacific Railway Co., 90 N.E. 1106). The obvious public interest in these relationships, coupled with the dominant position of those seeking exculpation, were compelling considerations in these decisions, which are in accord with similar results in other jurisdictions. See 175 A.L.R. 8.

On the other hand, as pointed out in the *Jackson* case, the relation of lessor and lessee has been considered a matter of private concern. Clauses that exculpate the landlord from the consequences of his negligence have been sustained in residential as well as commercial leases. . . . There are intimations in other jurisdictions that run counter to the current authority. See Kuzmiak v. Brookchester, Inc., 1955, 111 A.2d 425; Kay v. Cain, 1946, 81 U.S.App.D.C. 24. The New Hampshire court applies to exculpatory clauses in all leases its uniform rule that any attempt to contract against liability for negligence is contrary to public policy. Papakalos v. Shaka, 1941, 18 A.2d 377. But apart from the Papakalos case we know of no court of last resort that has held such clauses invalid in the absence of a statute so requiring.

A contract shifting the risk of liability for negligence may benefit a tenant as well as a landlord. See Cerny-Pickas & Co. v. C.R. Jahn Co., 131 N.E.2d 100. Such an agreement transfers the risk of a possible financial burden and so lessens the impact of the sanctions that induce adherence to the required standard of care. But this consideration is applicable as well to contracts for insurance that indemnify against liability for one's own negligence. Such contracts are accepted, and even encouraged. See Ill.Rev.Stat.1957, chap. 95½, pars. 7–202(1) and 7–315.

The plaintiff contends that due to a shortage of housing there is a disparity of bargaining power between lessors of residential property and their lessees that gives landlords an unconscionable advantage over tenants. And upon this ground it is said that exculpatory clauses in residential leases must be held to be contrary to public policy. No attempt was made upon the trial to show that Mrs. O'Callaghan was at all concerned about the exculpatory clause, that she tried to negotiate with the defendant about its modification or elimination, or that she made any effort to rent an apartment elsewhere. To establish the existence of a widespread housing shortage the plaintiff points to numerous statutes designed to alleviate the shortage (see Ill.Rev.Stat.1957, chap. 67½, *passim*) and to the existence of rent control during the period of the lease. 65 Stat. 145 (1947), 50 U.S.C.A. Appendix, § 1894.

Unquestionably there has been a housing shortage. That shortage has produced an active and varied legislative response. Since legislative attention has been so sharply focused upon housing problems in recent years, it might be assumed that the legislature has taken all of the remedial action that it thought necessary or desirable. One of the major legislative responses was the adoption of rent controls which placed ceilings upon the amount of rent that landlords could charge. But the very existence of that control made it impossible for a lessor to negotiate for an increased rental in exchange for the elimination of an exculpatory clause. We are asked to assume, however, that the legislative response to the housing shortage has been inadequate and incomplete, and to augment it judicially.

The relationship of landlord and tenant does not have the monopolistic characteristics that have characterized some other relations with respect to which exculpatory clauses have been held invalid. There are literally thousands of landlords who are in competition with one another. The rental market affords a variety of competing types of housing accommodations, from simple farm house to luxurious apartment. The use of a form contract does not of itself establish disparity of bargaining power. That there is a shortage of housing at one particular time or place does not indicate that such shortages have always and everywhere existed, or that there will be shortages in the future. Judicial determinations of public policy cannot readily take account of sporadic and transitory circumstances. They should rather, we think, rest upon a durable moral basis. Other jurisdictions have dealt with this problem by legislation. McKinney's Consol.Laws of N.Y.Ann., Real Property Laws, sec. 234, Vol. 49, Part I; Ann.Laws of Mass., Vol. 6, c. 186, sec. 15. In our opinion the subject is one that is appropriate for legislative rather than judicial action.

The judgment of the Appellate Court is affirmed.

■ BRISTOW, JUSTICE, and DAILY, CHIEF JUSTICE (dissenting). We cannot accept the conclusions and analysis of the majority opinion, which in our judgment not only arbitrarily eliminates the concept of negligence in the landlord and tenant relationship, but creates anomalies in the law, and will produce grievous social consequences for hundreds of thousands of persons in this State.

According to the undisputed facts in the instant case, this form lease with its exculpatory clause, was executed in a metropolitan area in 1947, when housing shortages were so acute that "waiting lists" were the order of the day, and gratuities to landlords to procure shelter were common. (U.S.Sen.Rep.1780, Committee on Banking & Currency, vol. II, 81st Cong., 2nd Sess. (1950), p. 2565 et seq.; Cremer v. Peoria Housing Authority, 78 N.E.2d 276.) While plaintiff admittedly did not negotiate about the exculpatory clause, as the majority opinion notes, the record shows unequivocally that the apartment would not have been rented to her if she had quibbled about any clause in the form lease. According to the uncontroverted testimony, "If a person refused to sign a [form] lease in the form it was in, the apartment would not be rented to him."

Apparently, the majority opinion has chosen to ignore those facts and prevailing circumstances, and finds instead that there were thousands of landlords competing with each other with a variety of rental units. Not only was the element of competition purely theoretical—and judges need not be more naive than other men—but there wasn't even theoretical competition, as far as the exculpatory clauses were concerned, since these clauses were included in all form leases used by practically all landlords in urban areas. Simmons v. Columbus Venetian Stevens Building, Inc., Ill.App., 155 N.E.2d 372; 1952 Ill.L.Forum, 321, 328.

Thus, we are *not* construing merely an isolated provision of a contract specifically bargained for by one landlord and one tenant, "a matter of private concern," as the majority opinion myopically views the issue in order to sustain its conclusion. We are construing, instead, a provision affecting thousands of tenants now bound by such provisions, which were foisted upon them at a time when it would be pure fiction to state that they had anything but a Hobson's choice in the matter. Can landlords, by that technique, immunize themselves from liability for negligence, and have the blessings of this court as they destroy the concept of negligence and standards of law painstakingly evolved in the case law? That is the issue in this case, and the majority opinion at no time realistically faces it.

In the instant case we must determine whether the exculpatory clause in the lease offends the public policy of this State. We realize that there is no precise definition of "public policy" or rule to test whether a contract is contrary to public policy, so that each case must be judged according to its own peculiar circumstances. First Trust & Savings Bank of Kankakee v. Powers, 65 N.E.2d 377. None would dispute, however, that there is a recognized policy of discouraging negligence and protecting those in need of goods or services from being overreached by those with power to drive unconscionable bargains.

In determining whether such clauses should be deemed void, the courts have weighed such factors as the importance which the subject has for the physical and economic well-being of the group agreeing to the release; their bargaining power; the amount of free choice actually exercised in agreeing to the exemption; and the existence of competition among the group to be exempted. (Williston, Contracts, vol. 6, p. 4968; *"The Significance of Bargaining Power in the Law of Exculpation,"* 37 Col.L.Rev. 248; 15 Univ.Pitt.L.Rev. 493.) Adjudged by such criteria, it is evident that the subject matter of the exculpatory clause herein— shelter—is indispensable for the physical well being of tenants; that they have nothing even approaching equality of bargaining power with landlords and no free choice whatever in agreeing to the exemption, since they will be confronted with the same clause in other form leases if they seek shelter elsewhere. Although the majority opinion claims that such clauses may also benefit tenants, it is hard for us to envisage a tenant on a waiting list for an apartment, insisting that the lease include a provision relieving him from liability for his negligence in the maintenance of the premises. Consequently, in our judgment, every material ground for voiding the exculpatory clause exists in the lease involved in the instant case.

NOTES

(1) *Questions.* What facts, authorities, and public policies did the majority array to support its conclusion that the liability disclaimer did not violate public policy? The dissent? Which do you find more persuasive?

In denying relief to the tenants, the court in O'Callaghan relied in part on its observation that "the relation of lessor and lessee has been considered a matter of private concern." Yet, in the same era, courts in other states provided relief from contracts of adhesion in areas such as automobile warranties. See, e.g., Henningsen v. Bloomfield Motors, Inc., 161 A.2d 69 (N.J. 1960). Is the relation between an automobile dealer and its customer less a matter of private concern than that between lessor and lessee?

(2) *Current Law.* Most states now provide by statute that provisions in residential leases exculpating the landlord from liability to the tenant for negligence are ineffective. In a few states, variant rules prevail. In Maine, for example, a tenant may accept in writing "specified conditions which may violate the warranty of fitness for human habitation in return for a stated reduction in rent or other specified fair consideration." Me. Rev. Stat. Ann. Tit. 14 §§ 6021(4)(B), (5), and § 6026(5). In Texas, waivers by a tenant of a landlord's responsibilities must be made "knowingly, voluntarily, and for consideration." Tex. Prop. Code § 92.006(e)(4)(D). Under what circumstances might a residential tenant prefer, with full information, to exculpate a landlord from liability for negligence?

In several states, including Illinois, there are statutory limitations on exculpatory provisions in commercial leases as well. 765 ILCS 705/1. What differences between residential and commercial leasing might justify a difference in treatment?

(3) *Strict Construction.* Courts sometimes rely on "rules (or canons) of construction" to bypass claims of contractual unfairness. Consider Galligan v. Arovitch, 219 A.2d 463 (Pa. 1966), in which a tenant in an apartment building suffered injury in a fall on the lawn. She sued the owner for negligence in maintenance. The plaintiff's lease, like Mrs. O'Callaghan's, excluded liability of the owner for injury arising from her use of the hallways and six other common areas, including sidewalks. Judgment was given for the defendant on the pleadings. On appeal, the judgment was reversed. The opinion of the court was based on the location of the injury—the lawn was not mentioned in the lease. "A lawn and a sidewalk are clearly different locations."

Consider the view of Professor Llewellyn: "A court can 'construe' language into patently not meaning what the language is patently trying to say. It can find inconsistencies between clauses and throw out the troublesome one. It can even reject a clause as counter to the whole purpose of the transaction. The difficulty with these techniques of ours is threefold. First, since they all rest on the admission that the clauses in question are permissible in purpose and content, they invite the draftsman to recur to the attack. Give him time, and he will make the grade. Second, since they do not face the issue, they fail to accumulate either experience or authority in the needed direction: that of marking out for any given type of transaction what the *minimum decencies* are which a court will insist upon as essential to an enforceable bargain of a given type, or as being inherent in a bargain of that type. Third, since they purport to construe, although do not really construe nor are intended to, but are instead tools of intentional and creative misconstruction, they seriously embarrass later efforts at true construction, later efforts to get at the true meaning of those wholly legitimate contracts and clauses which call for their meaning to be got at instead of avoided. The net effect is unnecessary confusion and unpredictability, together with inadequate remedy, and evil persisting that calls for remedy. Covert tools are never reliable tools." Karl Llewellyn, *Book Review*, 52 Harv. L. Rev. 700, 702 (1939) (reviewing O. Prausnitz, *The Standardization of Commercial Contracts in English and Continental Law*).

PROBLEM

Abusive Drafting. A landlord, believing that tenants often give credence to lease provisions even if they are unenforceable, asks his attorney to prepare a waiver of tenants' rights that the attorney knows to be unenforceable. How should the attorney respond? See generally Bailey Kuklin, *On the Knowing Inclusion of Unenforceable Contract and Lease Terms*, 6 U. Cin. L. Rev. 845 (1988).

What if the attorney does not know, but only suspects, that the suggested provision is unenforceable? Consider the following Opinion from the Ethics Committee of the Alaska Bar Association: "Disciplinary Rule 7–102(A)(7) states that a lawyer shall not 'counsel or assist his client in conduct that the lawyer knows to be illegal or fraudulent.' Thus, if the lawyer determines that the contract is illegal, then the lawyer must refuse to participate in drafting the contract. . . . The Code of Professional Responsibility does not prohibit an attorney from drafting a contract which might be held voidable or unenforceable, provided that the attorney advises the client of the particular risks involved in the particular contract that is being drafted." AK. Eth. Op. 84–4, 1984 WL 270979 (Alaska Bar. Assn. Eth. Comm. 1984). The New York State Bar is in agreement, see NY Eth. Op. 584, 1987 WL 109300 (N.Y. St. Bar. Assn. Comm. Prof. Eth., 1987). For the problems of leasing apartments in college towns, and a model lease enacted in Davis, California in response to those problems, see Daniel E. Wenner, *Renting in Collegetown*, 84 Cornell L. Rev. 543 (1999).

Graham v. Scissor-Tail, Inc.

Supreme Court of California, En Banc, 1981.
171 Cal.Rptr. 604.

[Bill Graham, "an experienced promoter and producer of musical concerts," entered into a contract with Scissor-Tail, Inc., a corporation representing recording artist Leon Russell. In 1973, Graham and Scissor-Tail agreed to a multi-city concert tour by Russell. Graham signed four contracts, all prepared on an identical form known in the industry as an "American Federation of Musicians (A.F. of M.) Form B Contract." The contract provided that any disputes would be arbitrated by the union's international executive board. Russell's concerts met with mixed success and a dispute arose concerning whether losses from one concert could be off-set against profits from another. The parties were unable to resolve the issue, and Graham filed an action for breach of contract. Scissor-Tail moved to compel arbitration and won. After the international executive board ruled in Scissor-Tail's favor, Graham appealed from a judgment confirming the arbitrator's award on the grounds that the entire contract was unenforceable as a contract of adhesion, and that the arbitration provision was unconscionable.]

■ THE COURT: The term "contract of adhesion," now long a part of our legal vocabulary, has been variously defined in the cases and other legal literature. The serviceable general definition first suggested by Justice Tobriner in 1961, however, has well stood the test of time and will bear little improvement: "The term signifies a standardized contract, which, imposed and drafted by the party of superior bargaining strength, relegates to the subscribing party only the opportunity to adhere to the contract or reject it." (Neal v. State Farm Ins. Cos. (1961) 188 Cal.App.2d 690, 694 [10 Cal.Rptr. 781].)

Such contracts are, of course, a familiar part of the modern legal landscape, in which the classical model of "free" contracting by parties of equal or near-equal bargaining strength is often found to be unresponsive to the realities brought about by increasing concentrations of economic and other power. They are also an inevitable fact of life for all citizens—businessman and consumer alike.

We believe that the contract here in question, in light of all of the circumstances presented, may be fairly described as adhesive. Although defendant and its supporting amicus curiae are strenuous in their insistence that Graham's prominence and success in the promotion of popular music concerts afforded him considerable bargaining strength in the subject negotiations, the record before us fairly establishes that he, for all his asserted stature in the industry, was here reduced to the humble role of "adherent." It appears that all concert artists and groups of any significance or prominence are members of the A.F. of M.; [and] that pursuant to express provision of the A.F. of M.'s constitution and bylaws members are not permitted to sign any form of contract other than that issued by the union. In these circumstances it must be concluded that Graham, whatever his asserted prominence in the industry, was required by the realities of his business as a concert promoter to sign A.F. of M. form contracts with *any* concert artist with whom he wished to do business.

To describe a contract as adhesive in character is not to indicate its legal effect. It is, rather, "the beginning and not the end of the analysis insofar as enforceability of its terms is concerned." (Wheeler v. St. Joseph Hospital, supra, 63 Cal.App.3d 345, 357.) Thus, a contract of adhesion is fully enforceable according to its terms, unless certain other factors are present which, under established legal rules—legislative or judicial—operate to render it otherwise.

Generally speaking, there are two judicially imposed limitations on the enforcement of adhesion contracts or provisions thereof. The first is that such a contract or provision which does not fall within the reasonable expectations of the weaker or "adhering" party will not be enforced against him. (See, e.g., Gray v. Zurich Insurance Co. (1966) 419 P.2d 168; Steven v. Fidelity & Casualty Co. (1962) 377 P.2d 284). The second—a principle of equity applicable to all contracts generally—is that a contract or provision, even if consistent with the reasonable expectations of the parties, will be denied enforcement if, considered in its context, it is unduly oppressive or "unconscionable." We proceed to examine whether the instant contract, and especially that provision thereof requiring the arbitration of disputes before the A.F. of M., should have been denied enforcement under either of these two principles.

We cannot conclude on the record before us that the contractual provision requiring arbitration of disputes before the A.F. of M. was in any way contrary to the reasonable expectations of plaintiff Graham. By his own declarations and testimony, he had been a party to literally thousands of A.F. of M. contracts containing a similar provision; indeed it appears that during the 3 years preceding the instant contracts he had promoted 15 or more concerts with Scissor-Tail, on each occasion signing a contract containing arbitration provisions similar to those here in question. It also appears that he had been involved in prior proceedings before the A.F. of M. regarding disputes with other musical groups arising under prior contracts. Finally, the discussions taking place following the Oakland concert, together with his telegram indicating that he himself would file charges with the A.F. of M. if the matter were not settled to his satisfaction . . . , all strongly suggest an abiding awareness on his part that all disputes arising under the contracts were to be resolved by arbitration before the A.F. of M. For all of these reasons it must be concluded that the provisions requiring such arbitration . . . were wholly consistent with Graham's reasonable expectations upon entering into the contract.

[As to the second judicially imposed limitation on enforcement, the court concluded that "[b]ecause [the A.F.M. arbitration provision] designates an arbitrator who, by reason of its status and identity, is presumptively biased in favor of one party," it was unconscionable.]

NOTES

(1) *Refining Expectations.* What factors made the contract Graham signed one of adhesion? Why, according to the court in this portion of the opinion, was it nonetheless enforceable against Graham?

(2) *Distributive Justice as a Limiting Factor?* Professor Anthony Kronman has argued that "[t]he attack on contracts of adhesion rests upon an unstated conception of distributive fairness; though often overlooked, it is this conception that gives the attack its appeal." Anthony Kronman, *Paternalism and the Law of Contracts*, 92 Yale L.J. 763, 771–72 (1983). Kronman offers the example of a contract for the sale of an oil painting to an eager buyer (Kronman) by the seller, whose "take-it-or-leave-it" terms include the price and a disclaimer regarding authenticity: "Clearly, the fact that I lack bargaining power and must adhere to the terms he proposes does not by itself justify a judicial or legislative effort to tip the balance in my favor. The imbalance in this case, which stems from the fact that he owns the painting and I do not, is unobjectionable because we do not care how control over the painting is distributed.

"We feel differently about the distribution of control over society's available housing stock. The distribution of housing matters more to us than the distribution of paintings: Only the first is likely to seem important from the standpoint of most theories of distributive justice. Those contracts of adhesion that disturb us do so, then, because they reflect an underlying distribution of power or resources that offends our conception of distributive fairness; when distributive concerns are weak or nonexistent, contracts of adhesion are less troubling and the concept of adhesion itself loses meaning."

Do you agree? Can there be a contract of adhesion for, say, the purchase of cruise ship tickets? For two interesting, philosophically-oriented critiques, see Seana Valentine Shiffrin, *Paternalism, Unconscionability Doctrine, and Accommodation*, 29 Phil. & Pub. Aff. 205 (2000), and Rebecca Stone, *Unconscionability, Exploitation, and Hypocrisy*, 22 J. of Pol. Phil. 27 (2014).

Agreeing to Boilerplate

In Graham v. Scissor-Tail, the court found that the presence of a mandatory arbitration clause did not by itself make the contract unenforceable: Whether or not Graham had bargained for or even looked at the clause, he was nonetheless familiar with both the fact of its inclusion or its content: he was, after all, the rock impresario of his day. But is it assumed that *all* parties know or are presumed to know the embedded clauses—the boilerplate,[d] or what used to be called the "fine

---

[d] The term, it is said, likens boilerplate clauses, which are permanently affixed to standard form contracts, to the way metal plate is riveted to boilers.

print"—that have become such a regular feature of modern contracting practices? Should terms inserted into consumer (and other) form contracts by drafters for some perceived or potential advantage be enforceable?

An initial approach is to think about boilerplate within the materials on assent and the bargaining process that you have studied up to now. Consider Professor Llewellyn's influential commentary: "instead of thinking about 'assent' to boiler-plate clauses, we can recognize that so far as concerns the specific, there is no assent at all. What has in fact been assented to, specifically, are the few dickered terms, and the broad type of the transaction, and but one thing more. That one thing more is a blanket assent (not a specific assent) to any not unreasonable or indecent terms the seller may have on his form, which do not alter or eviscerate the reasonable meaning of the dickered terms." Karl Llewellyn, *The Common Law Tradition: Deciding Appeals* 370–71 (1960).

Restatement § 211(3) provides that where a party effectively manifests assent to a standardized expression of agreement, and the other party has reason to believe that he would not have done so if he had known that it contained a particular term, "the term is not part of the agreement." Thus not *all* standardized terms are excluded under the Restatement approach, but rather only those that are "beyond the range of reasonable expectation." Restatement § 211, cmt. f. To be sure, the question of what is reasonably expected becomes more complicated as certain categories of terms—liability disclaimers, mandatory arbitration clauses, and the like—are so often inserted into standard form contracts as to have *become* expected.

What then is the current legal status of, to take one example, the disclaimers that appear as a matter of course on such everyday contracts as tickets and stubs issued to customers by laundries, parking lots, coat checks, and so on? To what extent are exculpatory clauses, printed on unsigned papers incident to everyday transactions, effective? Has the holder assented to the terms of the stub? Consider the following well-known case involving a claim check, reproduced here, by a "parcel room" purporting to limit its liability for checked items that become lost or damaged.

H. & M. PARCEL ROOM, INC.
BROADWAY & 33rd ST., HUDSON TUNNELS
OPEN 7:00 A. M. - CLOSE 1:00 A. M.
(E. S. Time Except When Another Time Is In Effect)

■ **CONTRACT** ■

THIS **CONTRACT** IS MADE ON THE FOLLOWING CONDITIONS AND IN CONSIDERATION OF THE LOW RATE AT WHICH THE SERVICE IS PERFORMED, AND ITS ACCEPTANCE BY THE DEPOSITOR, EXPRESSLY BINDS BOTH PARTIES TO THE **CONTRACT**.
CHARGE—10 CENTS FOR EVERY 24 HOURS OR FRACTION THEREOF, FOR EACH PIECE COVERED BY THIS CONTRACT
LOSS OR DAMAGE—NO CLAIM SHALL BE MADE IN EXCESS OF $25.00 FOR LOSS OR DAMAGE TO ANY PIECE.
UNCLAIMED ARTICLES REMAINING AFTER 90 DAYS MAY BE SOLD AT PUBLIC OR PRIVATE SALE TO SATISFY ACCRUED CHARGES.
PHONE PEnnsylvania 6-2467   H. & M. PARCEL ROOM, INC.

34--971

[C 1224]

A patron left a package at the parcel room and received but did not read the claim check. When another person holding the ticket later returned to reclaim the package, he was told that it had been delivered to someone else by mistake. He sued the parcel room for the alleged value of the contents, $1,000, and the trial court gave judgment for nearly that amount. On successive appeals, the judges were in disagreement, some arguing that recovery should be limited to $25, the maximum provided by the terms of the claim check. In the words of one judge: "The parcel check had conspicuously printed the word 'Contract' on the face thereof near the top in bold face type, clearly legible in red ink. The whole form was exceptionally brief. Plaintiffs had ample opportunity to read the notice on the check stub. The package, alleged to contain valuable furs, was tied up with a piece of cord in a brown paper parcel. The charge for checking was the trivial sum of ten cents."[e]

Nonetheless, the court affirmed the trial court's judgment, holding that "the coupon was presumptively intended as between the parties to serve the special purpose of affording a means of identifying the parcel left by the bailor. In the mind of the bailor the little piece of cardboard . . . did not arise to the dignity of a contract by which he agreed that in the event of the loss of the parcel, even through the negligence of the bailee itself, he would accept therefor a sum which, perhaps, would be but a small fraction of its actual value." Klar v. H. & M. Parcel Room, Inc., 61 N.Y.S.2d 285 (App.Div. 1946), (quoting Healy v. New York Central

---

[e]   An explanation for these facts is suggested by the following report: "Public lockers in Penn Station. Locked trunks in parked cars. This is where the contraband is hidden, deposited there surreptitiously by one party and picked up quietly by another. Is it narcotics, jewels, gold bullion? No, it is furs, or, more accurately, parts of fur garments, awaiting sewing so that the complete garment can be made available for sale. The lined skins are placed in lockers or car-trunks by fur-garment producers willing to use nonunion contractors, usually a one-man sewing shop or a shop with a few workers. After picking up the garments at their convenience, the contractors sew them for 50 per cent less than a unionized shop would. They then return the garments via the same conduits to their unionized clients. Although outlawed in labor-management contracts, the increasing use of such contractors has produced consternation in an already-troubled industry." *The New York Times*, March 26, 1972, Business Section, p. 1.

H.R.R.R. Co. (153 App. Div. 516, 519, 210 N.Y. 646). "While the defendant bailee should be protected in its legal right to limit its responsibility, the public should also be safeguarded against imposition. If the bailee wishes to limit its liability for negligence, it must at least show that it has given adequate notice of the special contract and that it has received the assent thereto of those with whom it transacts business." Klar v. H. & M. Parcel Room, Inc., 61 N.Y.S.2d 285 (App. Div. 1946), aff'd mem., 73 N.E.2d 912 (N.Y. 1947).

NOTES

(1) *Questions.* What competing principles does the court in *Klar* attempt to reconcile? Do you think the solution is a workable one? How would the parcel room case be decided under Restatement § 211(3)? Does that provision take an objective or subjective approach? The court in *Klar* notes that the stub "did not arise to the dignity of a contract" in the bailor's mind. Is this an objective or subjective standard?

In *Klar* and similar cases, it may be said that courts have policed against overreaching by manipulating the principles of contract formation. What are the limits of this method?

(2) *Insurance Contracts.* Although the prevalence of oppressive "take it or leave it" clauses has increased in recent years, insurance contracts have traditionally been a rich source for the regulation of adhesion contracts. In Darner Motor Sales v. Universal Underwriters, 682 P.2d 388, 399 (Ariz. 1984), the court applied the Restatement provision to the terms of an "umbrella" insurance policy favorably to the insured. It characterized the policy as one which, "because of the nature of the enterprise, customers will not be expected to read and over which they have no real power of negotiation." Another technique used to overcome terms that have literally been disclosed, but that would likely come as a surprise to the insured is the "doctrine of reasonable expectations." It holds that when insurance is sold in circumstances that discourage detailed inquiries, the reasonable expectations of the buyer should be honored even though the policy terms do not support them. See Robert Keeton and Alan Widiss, *Insurance Law* § 6.3 (Prac. Ed. 1988). "In general, courts will protect the reasonable expectations of applicants, insureds, and intended beneficiaries regarding the coverage afforded. Even though a careful examination of the policy provisions indicates that such expectations are contrary to the expressed intention of the insurer." For a discussion of *Darner*, see Jean Braucher, *Cowboy Contracts: The Arizona Supreme Court's Grand Tradition of Transactional Fairness*, 50 Ariz. L. Rev. 191, 213–18 (2008).

Should a buyer of automobile insurance get coverage according to an ordinary buyer's reasonable expectations, notwithstanding a policy exclusion? As one court observed: "It is fatuous to suppose the policy owner had any part in the language of the policy besides filling in the blanks. The common wisdom is that very few insurance policy purchasers read all or even substantially all of the purchased contract, and it is not guaranteeable that they would understand it if they did.". Powers v. Detroit Auto. Inter-insurance Exchange, 398 N.W.2d 411 (Mich. 1986), overruled by Wilkie v. Auto-Owners Ins. Co., 664 N.W.2d 776 (Mich. 2003). But see also Sparks v. St. Paul Ins. Co., 495 A.2d 406 (N.J. 1985): ". . . courts have a special responsibility to prevent the marketing of policies that provide unrealistic and inadequate coverage." Why might courts be particularly concerned about hidden or unsuspected limitations in insurance contracts?

(3) *An Economic-Behavioral Approach to Standard Form Contracts.* Why do consumers agree to, accept, or acquiesce to standardized terms? One scholarly line of research emphasizes the fact that consumers tend to overlook some terms and focus on others because of their myopia and other cognitive biases, which more sophisticated sellers are able to exploit in standard form agreements and boilerplate. See Oren Bar-Gill, *Seduction by Contract: Law Economics, and Psychology in Consumer Markets* (2012), which considers how an agreement's so-called "design features"—like small down payments, teaser rates and other salient terms that variously characterize contracts for cell phone services, credit cards, and mortgages— can lead consumers to enter into costly contracts, and how various regulatory responses might address this problem.

While emphasized more in the area of consumer contracts, boilerplate is also a feature of contracts between firms. A recent study by Professors Robert Scott and Mitu Gulati suggests that lawyers in big firms who draft (or re-use) standardized terms do not always remember how a particular term became part of the boilerplate, or even how the term is interpreted and for whose benefit. Robert Scott and Mitu Gulati, *The Three and a Half Minute Transaction: Boilerplate and the Limits of Contract Design* (2012). Do you believe that firms are insulated from the behavioral biases observed in consumer transactions? What arguments might suggest that firms are immune from these biases; what are the arguments to the contrary?

For some of the rich literature on boilerplate, see Omri Ben-Shahar, ed., *Symposium, "Boilerplate" Foundations of Market Contracts*, 104 Mich. L. Rev. 821 (2006).

(4) *Boilerplate and Democratic Law-Making.* Some 40 years ago, in an article called Standard Form Contracts and Democratic Control of Lawmaking Power, Professor David Slawson observed that automobile manufacturers "make more warranty law in a day than most legislatures or courts make in a year." 84 Harv. L. Rev. 529, 530 (1971). What might Slawson mean? Recently Professor Margaret Jane Radin has put the case more provocatively, arguing that "mass-market boilerplate schemes can delete large swaths of legal rights that are granted through democratic processes and instead substitute the system of rights that the firm wishes to impose." Margaret Jane Radin, *Reconsidering Boilerplate: Confronting Normative and Democratic Degradation*, 40 Cap. U. L. Rev. 40, 617 (2012). As an example, Radin asks, why "did the U.S. Congress debate reform of the Copyright Act for years . . . if the resulting legislative regime can be restructured in minutes by a firm promulgating a boilerplate regime?" Id. See also Margaret Jane Radin, *Boilerplate Today: The Rise of Modularity and the Waning of Consent*, 104 Mich. L. Rev. 1223 (2006). Do you agree that

consumer consent is "waning"? That standardized contract terms are overtaking democratic processes?

The "Duty" to Read Contract Terms

The starting point is the common law rule that "in the absence of fraud, one who signs a written agreement is bound by its terms whether he read and understood it or not, or whether he can read or not." Cohen v. Santoianni, 112 N.E.2d 267, 271 (Mass. 1953). In Washington Mutual Finance Group, LLC v. Bailey, 364 F.3d 260, 264–265 (5th Cir. 2004), a group of Mississippi borrowers sought to set aside a loan agreement, arguing, in part, that although the borrowers had signed the agreement, they had not read or understood it because they were illiterate. The trial court found the agreement was unenforceable, and the bank appealed. *Held*: Reversed. "The Mississippi Supreme Court has held that, as a matter of law, an individual's inability to understand a contract is not a sufficient basis for concluding a contract is unenforceable." The court quoted earlier Mississippi cases stating that "the suggestion of illiteracy cannot prevail, for the manifest reason that there cannot be two separate departments in the law of contracts, one for the educated and another for those who are not" and that "a person who cannot read had a duty to find someone to read the contract to him."

What then are the obligations of a party to read and understand the terms of a standardized agreement? What are the obligations, if any, of the imposing party to facilitate such understanding? For while there is a general "duty" to read the contract one signs—or at least there is no relief for those who fail to do so—courts have fashioned various exceptions to relieve a party who has signed a standard form contract that has not fairly disclosed its terms. In one older case, the typography of an insurance policy, long a source of impenetrable documents, was held to present a triable issue of a "fraudulent plot" on the part of the insurer. De Lancey v. Rockingham Farmers' Mut. Fire Insurance Co., 52 N.H. 581 (1873) ("Seldom has the art of typography been so successfully diverted from the diffusion of knowledge to the suppression of it."). Over 100 years later, in McCarthy Well Co. v. St. Peter Creamery, Inc., 410 N.W.2d 312 (Minn. 1987), the court described the contract at issue as "difficult, exceedingly tedious, and even physically painful" to read: "This is not a case of unconscionability as that concept is usually understood. . . . Rather, this is a case where a party is not able to know what the contract terms are because they are unreadable. As a matter of law, the exculpatory clause will not be enforced."

Of course, the duty to read presupposes that the parties are aware there are terms to be read. Legislatures have therefore sought to make parties aware of contract terms. For example, a New York statute regulating retail installment sales requires contracts to include the following admonition to buyers: "Do not sign this agreement before you read it." N.Y. Pers. Prop. L. § 402. To ensure that parties can literally see what they are expected to read, the use of red ink for certain terms is sometimes required, as are suitable font sizes and the placement of captions. Other statutes require only that particular information be "conspicuous." The UCC, for example, requires that certain written limitations on implied warranties be "conspicuous," see UCC § 2–316(2), and defines the term with reference to what "a reasonable person against which it is to operate ought to have noticed." See UCC § 1–201(b)(10).

To ensure that terms are not only visible, but intelligible as well, a number of states have enacted "plain language statutes." The New York version requires that a covered agreement be

> 1.   Written in a clear and coherent manner using words with common and every day meanings;
>
> 2.   Appropriately divided and captioned by its various sections.

The statute covers written residential leases, and written agreements "to which a consumer is a party and the money, property or service which is the subject of the transaction is primarily for personal, family or household purposes." An exception is made for agreements "involving amounts in excess of fifty thousand dollars." Gen. Oblig. L. § 5–702.

Still other statutes require that information particularly relevant to the transaction be included, primarily in industries whose contracts have tended to be obscure and one-sided. Thus the Truth in Lending Act (Title I of the Consumer Credit Protection Act) requires early disclosure by financers of an annual percentage rate (APR), which expresses a ratio between the "finance charge" and the "amount financed"—interest and principal in common parlance.

Does the requirement of disclosure presuppose some level of financial sophistication on the part of those who may borrow money? Are there intrinsic limitations on the utility of disclosure requirements? Are consumers up to the task?

NOTES

(1) *Plain Language in Application.* A characteristic remedy provided for the violation of a plain-language statute is a modest monetary claim, perhaps augmented by an attorney's fee. The New York statute allows recovery of "any actual damages sustained," but it also provides that a violation does not affect the enforceability of an agreement.

Should plain-language requirements also cover situations in which the wording of contractual provisions is clear, but their effect is far from obvious? Should a party's compliance with a plain-language statute insulate it from the legal consequences of oppressive terms that are clearly stated? Consider, as a preview, the terms in the second paragraph of Williams v. Walker-Thomas Furniture Company on p. 637 below.

(2) *Prominent Entities and Average Joes.* In Avenell v. Westinghouse Electric Corp., 324 N.E.2d 583 (Ohio App. 1974), a finding of conspicuousness was made—and approved on appeal—for the reason, among others, that the buyer, the Toledo Edison Company, was a "prominent, sophisticated entity." Is there a difference between this case and one in which the buyer is an "average Joe (or Jane)" but happens to know of the disclaimer? What reason might there be for refusing to recognize a distinction?

A similar issue arose regarding the duty to read. In Fraass Surgical Mfg. Co., Inc. v. United States, 571 F.2d 34 (Ct. Cl. 1978), an Air Force procurement contract assigned a risk to the supplier which, in previous contracts between the same parties, had been assigned to the government. If the government had known that the supplier was unaware of the change, an appropriate remedy would have been to reform the document so as to assign the risks as before. That knowledge was not proved, however. The supplier's president testified that he did not read the contract "because contracts that he had signed in 1963 and 1960 had contained the other clause." The court found this testimony unacceptable: "He is an experienced businessman and should know better."

(3) *On-Line Disclosures.* The Federal Trade Commission (FTC) has published Dot Com (or ".com") Disclosure guidelines which require any disclosure covered by FTC regulations to be "clear and conspicuous." The guidelines advise advertisers with regard to the placement and prominence of disclosures, as well as the physical proximity of the disclaimer to the claim being qualified. For example, advertisers are encouraged to use text or visual cues to encourage consumers to scroll, and to place hyperlinks to disclaimers "as close as possible to the triggering claim." What techniques, if any, might encourage on-line purchasers not to "click through" automatically? See ".com Disclosures: How to Make Effective Disclosures in Digital Advertising," available at http://www.ftc.gov/os/2013/03/130312dotcomdisclosures.pdf.

(4) *Scrolling.* Subscribers to an on-line computer service (MSN) challenged the validity of a forum-selection clause included in the MSN membership agreement. The clause stated: "This agreement is governed by the laws of the State of Washington, USA, and you consent to the exclusive jurisdiction and venue of the courts in King County, Washington in all disputes arising out of or relating to your use of MSN or your MSN membership." The subscribers argued that they had *not* received adequate notice of the clause, and therefore it had not become part of the contract. From a New Jersey trial court judgment dismissing the action on the basis of the forum selection clause, the subscribers appealed. *Held*: Affirmed.

The court held that although the medium used to convey the terms was electronic and not printed, "there is no significant distinction." Caspi v. Microsoft, 732 A.2d 528, 531–32 (N.J. 1999). "The plaintiffs in this case were free to scroll through the various computer screens that presented the terms of their contract before clicking their agreement. [T]here was nothing extraordinary about the size or placement of the forum selection clause text. It was the first item in the last paragraph of the electronic document. We note that a few paragraphs of the contract were presented in upper case typeface, presumably for emphasis, but most provisions, including the forum selection clause, were presented in lower face typeface. We discern nothing about the style or mode of presentation, or the placement of the provision, that can be taken as a basis for concluding that the [clause] was proffered unfairly, or with a design to conceal or de-emphasize its provisions."

Policing Consumer Contracts: Courts, Legislatures, and Agencies

What combination of judicial, legislative, and administrative remedies promise the best result for policing the use of standard form contracts? The following materials review the respective merits and limitations of each. In evaluating the remedies, consider also the competencies of the different state actors to produce and to enforce them.

Judicial Measures. Professor Llewellyn thought that the courts had the solution to problems of standard form contracts ready at hand. As discussed at p. 260 above, it is to recognize a distinction between "dickered" terms and boilerplate clauses. Building on that distinction, he wrote, "the true answer to the whole problem seems, amusingly, to be one which could occur to any court or any lawyer, at any time. . . . " Yet, another thoughtful scholar has countered that "the courts have neither the equipment nor the materials for resolving the basic conflicts of modern society over the limits to be set to the use, or misuse, of economic power." John Dawson, *Economic Duress—An Essay in Perspective*, 45 Mich. L. Rev. 253, 289 (1947). See also Robert Hale, *Bargaining, Duress, and Economic Liberty*, 43 Colum. L. Rev. 603 (1943).

Similarly, the doctrine of unconscionability, at least in some formulations, has also been criticized as a cover for smuggling notions of distributive justice into the judicial process. Alan Schwartz, *Seller Unequal Bargaining Power and the Judicial Process*, 49 Ind. L.J. 367, 396 (1974) ("The unequal bargaining power concept should be abandoned."). Still other scholars have urged the courts to take wide liberties with the terms of standard form contracts and have proposed models more elaborate than anything Llewellyn suggested. See Charles Oldfather Jr., *Toward a Usable Method of Judicial Review of the Adhesion Contractor's Lawmaking*, 16 U. Kan. L. Rev. 303 (1968).

Statutory Measures. Legislation has been the traditional means of constraining the use of economic power in the imposition of contract terms. Congress has addressed imbalances in bargaining power, for example, in laws that permit collective bargaining by workers, through statutes and administrative rules regulating quasi-public industries such as common carriers and utilities, and more generally through antitrust laws aimed at preserving a party's opportunity to choose among firms. Other statutes, such as the Consumer Credit Protection Act of 1968, 15 U.S.C. § 1601 *et seq.*, the Magnuson-Moss Warranty Act, p. 295

above, and various state laws have focused more directly on consumer protection.

Protective legislation can be grouped loosely into three types. The first, prompted by concern about the fairness of particular terms or of the exchange as a whole, seeks to control the terms of exchange. A second type proceeds from the assumption that consumers can best improve their position through well-informed shopping, facilitated by various disclosure requirements. The third type of control, premised on the belief that consumers suffer systemic handicaps in the effective enforcement of their rights, focuses on remedies. These measures, and others, are exemplified by a New York law regulating the dating service industry, and are the subject of the next principle case.

Administrative Measures. The statutory mandate for many administrative agencies often has more to do with setting the price that a given firm (a public utility, say) may charge than with language in the firm's contracts. Yet agencies have on occasion used their powers to exert control over contract language as well as rates. In many business areas—notably insurance—regulating contract terms is a central part of an agency's mandate.

Sometimes an agency acts in a quasi-judicial way, as when the Federal Trade Commission charges a merchant with a deceptive practice. As the FTC has explained:

> Normally we expect the marketplace to be self-correcting, and we rely on consumer choice—the ability of individual consumers to make their own private purchasing decisions without regulatory intervention—to govern the markets. . . . However, it has long been recognized that certain types of sales techniques may prevent consumers from effectively making their own decisions and that corrective action may then be necessary. Most of the Commission's unfairness matters are brought not to second guess the wisdom of particular consumer decisions, but rather to halt some form of seller behavior that unreasonably creates or takes advantage of an obstacle to the free exercise of consumer decisionmaking.

F.T.C. v. IFC Credit Corp., 543 F.Supp.2d 925 (N.D. Ill. 2008).

For example, in F.T.C. v. QT, Inc., 448 F.Supp.2d 908 (N.D. Ill. 2006), the court enjoined the sale of the "Q-Ray Ionized Bracelet" which the defendants had advertised in print and through infomercials as providing "immediate," "significant," and "medically proven" pain relief. During a seven day trial, the court heard testimony from a number of physicians and scientific researchers. The court ordered the defendants to refund the purchase price to buyers and also to disgorge the $22,500,000 in profits it made during the period the infomercials had been broadcast.

What advantages do you see for consumers in agency supervision?

Comparative Approaches. In 1993, the European Commission issued a Directive on unfair terms in consumer contracts (Council Directive 93/13/EEC, since amended in 2011). This sought to protect consumers "against the abuse of power by the seller or supplier, in particular against one-sided standard contracts and the unfair exclusion of essential rights in contracts." Under the Directive, "[a] contractual term which has not been individually negotiated shall be regarded as unfair if, contrary to the requirements of good faith, it causes a significant imbalance in the parties' rights and obligations arising under the contract, to the detriment of the consumer." Art. 3(1).

An Annex to the Directive contains a non-exclusive list of 17 types of terms that are deemed potentially unfair. Among these are terms that would: "inappropriately exclud[e] or limit[ ] the legal rights of the consumer . . . in the event of total or partial non-performance by the seller or supplier;" "irrevocably bind[ ] the consumer to term with which he had no real opportunity of becoming acquainted before the conclusion of the contract;" "enabl[e] the seller or supplier to alter the terms of the contract unilaterally without a valid reason which is specified in the contract;" and "exclud[e] or hinder[ ] the consumer's right to take legal action or exercise any other legal remedy, particularly by requiring the consumer to take disputes exclusively to arbitration not covered by legal provisions . . ."

In addition, the Directive provides that terms in written contracts "must always be drafted in plain, intelligible language," and that "[w]hen there is doubt about the meaning of a term, the interpretation most favourable to the consumer shall prevail." Art. 5. Member states are charged with enacting measures under which unfair terms shall not bind consumers and the continued use of unfair terms shall be prevented. Moreover, the provisions of the Directive are a floor, not a ceiling, for national regulations.

The resulting national legislation varies considerably. At one extreme, some nations have not gone beyond the minimum requirements in the Directive. More commonly, nations have prepared lists of terms that are always considered unfair (the "black" list), terms that are presumptively unfair (the "gray" list), or both. These lists are usually subject to revision by administrative agencies. As a result, the European Union has a hybrid administrative/legislative system for regulating consumer contracts. See generally Paolisa Nebbia, Unfair Contract Terms in European Law: A Study in Comparative and EC Law (2007); Thomas Wilhelmsson, Various Approaches to Unfair Terms and Their Background Philosophies, 14 Juridica Int'l 51 (2008).

Doe v. Great Expectations

Civil Court of the City of New York, New York County, 2005.
809 N.Y.S.2d 819.

■ LEBEDEFF, JUDGE. Two claimants sue to recover, respectively, $1,000 and $3,790 paid under a contract for defendant's services, which offer to expand a client's social horizons primarily through posting a client's video and profile on an Internet site on which other clients can review them and thereafter, as desired, approach a selected client for actual social interaction. Because of the similarities of these two cases, a consolidated decision is issued.[1]

Upon the basis of the contract and testimony, the court determines that the transactions were subject to the Dating Services Law, which regulates defined "social referral services" falling within the scope of General Business Obligations Law § 394–c (Gen. Bus. § 394–c[1][a], "'social referral service' shall include any service for a fee providing matching of members of the opposite sex, by use of computer or any other means, for the purpose of dating and general social contact"). In relation to the application of the Dating Services Law, more than a decade ago, it was judicially determined that the Law did cover services which match members by creating a location and mechanism for members to assess each other by reviewing another member's video, photograph and profile a substantially similar service to the one defined by the written contract terms here (Great Expectations Creative Management, Inc. v. Attorney-General of the State of New York, 616 N.Y.S.2d 917. ("It does not matter whether defendant actually matches its members. It is sufficient if defendant made available the matching of members or supplied the means for matching the members") [citations omitted]. The statute specifically includes services which utilize computers (Gen. Bus. § 394–c[1][a], "'social referral service' shall include any service for a fee providing matching of members by use of computer for the purpose of dating and general social contact").

Because the Dating Service Law is found applicable, the court will review the contract and the service's operation for compliance with the statute. Two types of departures are found. First, there was a massive

---

[1]   The boilerplate printed form contracts has standard terms, reciting that plaintiff would receive a "photo shoot, video, workbook on dating, counseling, background checks, [and] dating etiquette" (para. 2 [a]), and that the defendant "will provide zero number of social referrals" and "is not promising to furnish the Member with any social referrals and the Member does not desire or expect the Company to furnish social referrals."

   Claimant Doe signed a $1,000 contract for a term of six months. Claimant Roe signed a $3,790 contract for a term of 36 months, which was eventually extended to a total duration of 54 months. Although the printed text of both contracts were identical, Ms. Roe's contract bears the additional handwritten notations of "Marriage Program" and "Platinum Shopper" which indicated that the program orally assured her she would be introduced to twelve people through the program and, in Ms. Doe's contract, the personal shopper membership paragraph is stricken. Ms. Roe testified that she was introduced to no prospective suitors and met only one person who approached her after seeing her posted information; Ms. Doe met no one through the service but, at some point, stopped checking with the service to see if any other clients had reached out to her. . . .

overcharge by the dating service. Where, as here, the dating service does not assure it will furnish a client with a specified number of social referrals per month, the service may charge no more than twenty-five dollars (Gen. Bus. § 394–c[3].

Second, in both cases, the defendant's form contract violated every mandate of the Dating Service Law, with the single exception that each contract did contain notice of a three day "cooling off" right to cancel (Gen. Bus. § 394–c[7][a] to [d]). The required provisions omitted from the contracts establish a failure to comply with Gen. Bus. § 394–c subdivision 3 (contracts above twenty-five dollars to state "specified certain number of social referrals per month"), subdivision 4 (contracts above twenty-five dollars to set forth client has "option to cancel the contract and to receive a refund" if minimum referrals not made), subdivision 5 (undertaking service provider will not reveal "any information and material of a personal or private nature" without client's written consent), subdivision 5–a. (granting client "unilateral right to place his or her membership on hold for a period of up to one year"), subdivision 6 (commitment of return to client of "all information and material of a personal or private nature acquired from a purchaser directly or indirectly including but not limited to answers to tests and questionnaires, photographs or background information by certified mail" after conclusion of contract), subdivision 8 (specification of the maximum distance for any face-to-face meeting), and subdivision 8–a (requirement to set forth a policy to be applied if the client "moves to permanently reside at a location outside the service area"). The posture that defendant's services were not governed by the law in any respect also is demonstrated by the failure to provide to the clients written notice of the mandatory "Dating Service Consumer Bill of Rights" (Gen. Bus. § 394–c[7][e].

Turning to the issue of damages, the Dating Service Law states that "[a]ny person who has been injured by reason of a violation of this section may bring an action to recover his or her actual damages or fifty dollars whichever is greater" (Gen. Bus. § 394–c[9][b]). The court is fully satisfied that "actual damages" includes the difference between each contract price and the $25 fee which is the maximum fee permitted under the Dating Service Law for these contracts.

Both claimants seek a return of the full balance paid, which raises the question of whether they establish damages justifying a return of the additional $25 each. This court had its opportunity to "view the witnesses, hear the testimony and observe demeanor." Issues of credibility, as well as the weight to be given to the evidence presented, are primarily questions to be determined by the court in a non-jury trial.

In this case, each claimant, both appearing to be intelligent, well spoken and attractive professional women, carefully negotiated the services to be provided. Defendant had the obligation to assure that each client of the dating service was made aware of statutory rights by providing each with the "Dating Service Consumer Bill of Rights" (Gen.

Bus. § 394–c[7][e]). Based upon the testimony, the court determines that each claimant would not have signed a contract containing terms violating applicable law, had she known of her rights and, accordingly, each claimant is entitled to a refund of the final $25.00 balance at issue, which finding achieves substantial justice in these Small Claims matters (N.Y.C.C.A. § 1805[a]).

Given the foregoing, it is determined that the claimants are entitled to a full refund as restitutionary damages. The statute's reference to "actual damages" was added to the Dating Service law in 1992 (L. 1992, c. 348, § 1, adding subdivision 9(b) to Gen. Bus. § 394–c), and as a part of the same legislation newly authorized the Attorney General to bring enforcement actions and to seek civil penalties of up to $1,000 for each violation (Gen. Bus. § 394–c[9][a]; see, for example, People by Vacco v. Introductions Inc., 252 A.D.2d 631, 632, [3d Dept.1998], suit against dating service sought restitution for 521 customer complaints in the amount of $204,287.10 and penalties of $150,000).

Logic indicates that the 1992 amendment "evened the playing field" by offering a single remedy of restitution to a consumer, which could be achieved by the alternate routes of commencing an individual suit or filing a complaint with the Attorney General. It then follows that the legislature, by adding the "actual damage" language to the statute in 1992 did not erode New York State's commitment to protect consumers from price gouging by dating services. However, such contracts may no longer simply be set aside as contrary to public policy, as was done in the 1991 decision based upon an earlier version of the Dating Service Law (Chassman v. People Resources, supra, 151 Misc.2d at 528–529, 573 N.Y.S.2d 589, given the then existing "statute's silence as to the penalty for non compliance public policy demands non-complying contracts be deemed void and unenforceable. If such contracts were to be enforced social referral services would continue to violate the statute with impunity, secure in the knowledge that the only penalty they face will be a reduction in their fee to the statutory limit").

Based upon the foregoing, the court awards actual damages of the face amount of the contract to each claimant, with interest to commence on the date of the contract payment. Because claimant Doe's contract has expired and claimant Roe's contract is terminated by reason of this determination, defendant may wish to return personal material to each claimant, notwithstanding that such obligation does not appear in this contract (Gen. Bus. § 394–c[6], quoted above). A failure to return personal materials could well lead to adverse consequences outside the scope of this litigation.

Finally, the court considers whether it should exercise its judicial discretion to report the activity found to violate applicable law to appropriate governmental authorities, which in this case would be to the New York State Attorney General's Consumer Fraud Unit, as well as the New York City Department of Consumer Affairs (Gen. Bus. § 394–c[9][c],

"In cities having a population over one million, the provisions of this section may be enforced concurrently with the attorney general by the director of a local or municipal consumer affairs office").

Although "[n]o rule has been adopted as to what is required if a judge receives information indicating that a litigant or witness appears to be guilty of unlawful conduct", it has been recognized that "as a general rule judges are granted the discretion, under the proper circumstances, to report instances of illegal conduct revealed in the course of proceedings before the judge" (New York State Office of Court Administration's Advisory Committee on Judicial Ethics Opinion 03–110, August 13, 2004). As to the exercise of such discretion, in a 1988 opinion, the Advisory Committee wrote (1) that the "desirability or appropriateness depends on all the circumstances, such as the nature of the [offense], the effect of such report on the administration of justice, and, in particular, on the court's truth determining function, and whether it was revealed by the perpetrator's voluntary testimony," (2) that a report could be "undesirable" if it "would dissuade witnesses on trial from telling the whole truth or encourage the threat of possible criminal proceedings as a means of pressure, for settlement purposes or otherwise, by one litigant against another" and (3) a judicial decision to report would be proper if the judge concluded "reporting such a revealed [offense] is in the public interest" (Joint Opinion 88–85 and 88–103, December 8, 1988).

The court considers the following factors: (1) that reporting the wrongful activity found impacts upon the public interest, given that the acts violated rules governing a regulated industry and appear to reflect a continuing pattern and practice on the part of the defendant as indicated by, among other things, the use of a printed boilerplate form found not to be in accordance with applicable laws; (2) the court's past and future truth determining function in each matter has not been, and will not be, impacted by a potential or actual report because no threat of future reporting was posed during the course of these proceedings, and these matters are now disposed; and (3) a question touching upon the administration of justice and the integrity of a court order may be posed in that a similar course of conduct by the same or a related defendant was previously litigated (Great Expectations Creative Management, Inc. v. Attorney-General of the State of New York, supra). As to the manner of the report, it shall be accomplished by forwarding a copy of this decision to the appropriate public officials.

NOTES

(1) *Questions.* What exactly had Great Expectations promised Roe and Doe? What result if Roe and Doe had received the Dating Service Bill of Rights when they signed their contracts? What measure of damages did Roe and Doe receive? How does a civil penalty differ from punitive damages, discussed in White v. Benkowski, p. 43 above?

The court found the claimants were "intelligent" and careful negotiators. What result in a similar case had the claimants been found to be of average ability and nonchalant when signing up for dating services?

(2) *Remedies in Practice Reprised.* The claimants brought their suit in New York Civil Court, which has jurisdiction over civil matters not exceeding $25,000. As stated on the court's website: "Our court is where everyday people come to resolve their everyday legal problems. Whether you are a local merchant, a consumer, a debtor, or a creditor, the Civil Court is dedicated to providing access to fair and efficient justice." http://www.courts.state.ny.us/courts/nyc/smallclaims/index.shtml. Small claims courts, like the New York Civil Court, facilitate the appearance of pro se litigants like Roe and Doe, who represented themselves in the case and appeared without the formal assistance of counsel.

(3) *Scope of Protection.* What factors may have contributed to the decision by the New York legislature to enact, and then to amend, its dating services law?

The Dating Service Law appears to apply only to opposite-sex couples. Does this raise an issue of discrimination on the basis of sex or sexual orientation? See Note 2 on p. 721 below. The topic is left for more focused consideration in courses on constitutional law.

SECTION 3. UNCONSCIONABILITY

In McKinnon v. Benedict, p. 595 above, the court found the inadequacy of consideration "so gross as to be unconscionable and a bar to the plaintiff's invocation of the extraordinary equitable powers of the court." But although the concept of unconscionability itself is by no means new, its embodiment in the Uniform Commercial Code in the early 1960s focused new attention on the doctrine. No longer limited to actions in equity, the doctrine is now a defense in its own right. As with conventional controls, the elements of status, behavior, and substance, in their various combinations, remain a focus of concern.

The statutory starting point is UCC § 2–302, one of the most widely debated sections of the Code. The section authorizes a court to refuse enforcement or to limit the application of a contract or clause that it determines to have been "unconscionable." Comment 1 to that section reads in part:

"This section is intended to make it possible for the courts to police explicitly against the contracts or clauses which they find to be unconscionable. In the past such policing has been accomplished by adverse construction of language, by manipulation of the rules of offer and acceptance or by determinations that the clause is contrary to public policy or to the dominant purpose of the contract. . . . The principle is one of the prevention of oppression and unfair surprise (Cf. Campbell Soup Co. v. Wentz, 172 F.2d 80 (3d Cir.1948) and not of disturbance of allocation of risks because of superior bargaining power."

Campbell Soup Co. v. Wentz, found at p. 886 below, concerned a standard form canner-grower contract. Wentz, a farmer, had committed his entire crop of carrots to Campbell for a price not to exceed $30 a ton. By the time for delivery a scarcity had developed. Carrots were virtually unobtainable, and their price had risen to at least $90 a ton. When Campbell's suppliers, including Wentz, began to sell some of their committed crops to others, it brought an action for specific performance. The court of appeals found several provisions of the contracts to be objectionable and refused to grant equitable relief. For example, the growers were not permitted to sell even those carrots rejected by Campbell to anyone else without Campbell's written permission. As to this provision, the court stated that "[t]his is the kind of provision which the late Francis H. Bohlen would call 'carrying a good joke too far.'" In refusing to enforce the contract on the ground of unconscionability, the court stated that "we are not suggesting that the contract is illegal. Nor are we suggesting any excuse for the grower in this case who has deliberately broken an agreement." Nonetheless, noting that the contract was obviously "drawn by skillful draftsmen with the buyer's interests in mind," the court found it was "too hard a bargain to entitle the plaintiff to relief in a court of conscience."

Campbell Soup, like most of the other cases used by the drafters to illustrate the application of unconscionability, involved commercial sales between businesses. Since the Code's enactment, however, unconscionability has made its mark primarily in the area of consumer contracts. In addition, state codes now regularly include provisions authorizing courts to deny enforcement to all types of contracts, whether in part or in their entirety, on ground of unconscionability. See Cal. Civ. Code § 1670.5; Tex. Bus. & Com. Code Ann. § 17.45(5).

NOTES

(1) *Questions.* Does the *Campbell Soup* decision, cited in Comment 1 to UCC § 2–302, support the Code rule? *Campbell Soup* is the basis for Illustration 1 to Restatement § 208, which states a rule in virtually the same terms as UCC § 2–302(1). The section is without parallel in the First Restatement.

(2) *Overservice by the Profession.* Professor Llewellyn, the Chief Reporter of the Code, defended the section at the hearings of the New York Law Revision Commission in 1954 in these words:

"Business lawyers tend to draft to the edge of the possible. Any engineer makes his construction within a margin of safety, and a wide margin of safety, so that he knows for sure that he is getting what he is gunning for. The practice of business lawyers has been, however—it has grown to be so in the course of time—to draft, as I said before, to the edge of the possible.

"Let me rapidly state that I do not find that this is desired by the business lawyers' clients.... The only doubt that comes up in regard to unconscionability is, if you start drafting to the absolute limit of what the law can conceivably bear. At that point you run into what they run into now, and what you run into now is, the court kicks it over." *Report of the New York State Law Revision Commission for 1954*, N.Y. Leg. Doc. (1954), No. 65, pp. 177–78.

Note that under UCC § 2–302 the issue of unconscionability is not to be submitted to a jury. What do you think explains this reservation by the Code drafters?

Unconscionability: Two Views

The next several cases explore the doctrine of unconscionability in three specific contexts: consumer sales, franchise agreements, and with regard to mandatory arbitration clauses, which are now found in contracts of all types. We begin, however, with excerpts from two wide-ranging essays that indicate the differing degrees of welcome the doctrine of unconscionability has received. Each author is concerned with the relation of unconscionability to classic common law concepts. The first offers a defense and explication of the doctrine; the second raises a fundamental objection.

An Explication. "When the concept of unconscionability was first made explicit by the Uniform Commercial Code, the initial effort was to reconcile it with the bargain principle. A major step in this direction was a distinction, drawn in 1967 by Professor Arthur Leff, between 'procedural' and 'substantive' unconscionability. Leff defined procedural unconscionability as fault or unfairness in the bargaining *process*; substantive unconscionability as fault or unfairness in the bargaining *outcome*—that is, unfairness of terms. The effect (if not the purpose) of this distinction, which influenced much of the later analysis, was to domesticate unconscionability by accepting the concept insofar as it could be made harmonious with the bargain principle (that is, insofar as it was 'procedural'), while rejecting its wider implication that in appropriate cases the courts might review bargains for fairness of terms. Correspondingly, much of the scholarly literature and case law concerning unconscionability has emphasized the element of unfair surprise, in which a major underpinning of the bargain principle— knowing assent—is absent by hypothesis."

"Over the last fifteen years, however, there have been strong indications that the principle of unconscionability authorizes a review of elements well beyond unfair surprise, including, in appropriate cases, fairness of terms. For example, Comment *c* to § 208 of the Restatement (Second) of Contracts states that '[t]heoretically it is possible for a contract to be oppressive taken as a whole, even though there is no weakness in the bargaining process and no single term which is in itself unconscionable.' [A] basic thesis of this Article is that unconscionability is a paradigmatic concept that can never be exhaustively described. It is, however, a major purpose [here] to suggest a methodology by which specific unconscionability norms should be developed. Three general propositions underlie the methodology, and should be stated at the outset: (1) Since the bargain principle rests on arguments of fairness and efficiency, it is appropriate to develop and apply a specific unconscionability norm whenever a class of cases can be identified in which neither fairness nor efficiency support the bargain principle's application. (2) The development and application of specific unconscionability norms is closely related to the manner in which the relevant market deviates from a perfectly competitive market. (3) The distinction between procedural and substantive unconscionability is too rigid to provide significant help in either the development or the application of such norms." Melvin A. Eisenberg, *The Bargain Principle and Its Limits*, 95 Harv. L. Rev. 741, 752–54 (1982).

A Fundamental Objection. "[This paper offers a defense] against modern attacks [on] the principle of freedom of contract which was central to the classical common law. Properly understood, that position does not require a court to enforce every contract brought before it. It does, however, demand that the reasons invoked for not enforcing the contract be of one of two sorts. Either there must be proof of some defect in the process of contract formation (be it duress, fraud or undue influence); or there must be, but only within narrow limits, some incompetence of the party against whom the agreement is to be enforced. The doctrine of unconscionability is important in both these respects because it can, if wisely applied, allow the courts to police these two types of problems, and thereby improve the general administration of the contract law. Yet when the doctrine of unconscionability is used in its substantive dimension, be it in a commercial or consumer context, it serves only to undercut the private right of contract in a manner that is apt to do more social harm than good. The result of the analysis is the same even if we view the question of unconscionability from the lofty perspective of public policy. '[I]f there is one thing which more than another public policy requires, it is that men of full age and competent understanding shall have the utmost liberty of contracting, and that their contracts when entered into freely and voluntarily shall be held sacred and shall be enforced by Courts of justice.'"[f] Richard Epstein, *Unconscionability: A Critical Reappraisal*, 18 J.L. & Econ. 293, 315 (1975).

---

[f]   Printing and Numerical Registering Co. v. Sampson, L.R. 19 Eq. 462, 465 (1875).

Williams v. Walker-Thomas Furniture Co.

United States Court of Appeals, District of Columbia Circuit, 1965.
350 F.2d 445.

■ J. SKELLY WRIGHT, CIRCUIT JUDGE.[g] Appellee, Walker-Thomas Furniture Company, operates a retail furniture store in the District of Columbia. During the period from 1957 to 1962 each appellant in these cases purchased a number of household items from Walker-Thomas, for which payment was to be made in installments. The terms of each purchase were contained in a printed form contract which set forth the value of the purchased item and purported to lease the item to appellant for a stipulated monthly rent payment. The contract then provided, in substance, that title would remain in Walker-Thomas until the total of all the monthly payments made equaled the stated value of the item, at which time appellants could take title. In the event of a default in the payment of any monthly installment, Walker-Thomas could repossess the item.

The contract further provided that "the amount of each periodical installment payment to be made by (purchaser) to the Company under this present lease shall be inclusive of and not in addition to the amount of each installment payment to be made by (purchaser) under such prior leases, bills or accounts; *and all payments now and hereafter made by (purchaser) shall be credited pro rata on all outstanding leases, bills and accounts* due the Company by (purchaser) at the time each such payment is made." (Emphasis added.) The effect of this rather obscure provision was to keep a balance due on every item purchased until the balance due on all items, whenever purchased, was liquidated. As a result, the debt incurred at the time of purchase of each item was secured by the right to repossess all the items previously purchased by the same purchaser, and each new item purchased automatically became subject to a security interest arising out of the previous dealings.

On May 12, 1962, appellant Thorne purchased an item described as a Daveno, three tables, and two lamps, having total stated value of $391.10. Shortly thereafter, he defaulted on his monthly payments and appellee sought to replevy all the items purchased since the first transaction in 1958. Similarly, on April 17, 1962, appellant Williams bought a stereo set of stated value of $514.95.[1] She too defaulted shortly

---

[g] Judge James Skelly Wright (1911–1988). Judge Skelly Wright graduated from Loyola University College of Law in Louisiana. He was appointed by President Truman to the Eastern District of Louisiana in 1949, where he ordered desegregation of the New Orleans transportation system and public schools. In 1962 President Kennedy appointed him to the U.S. Court of Appeals for the District of Columbia where he served for 25 years. He is known for his 1967 decree which led to the end of formal discrimination in D.C. public schools. Other decisions strengthened the rights of tenants, women, and prisoners. He also dissented in a case refusing the publication of the Pentagon Papers by the Washington Post, a decision later reversed by the Supreme Court.

[1] At the time of this purchase her account showed a balance of $164 still owing from her prior purchases. The total of all the purchases made over the years in question came to $1,800. The total payments amounted to $1,400.

thereafter, and appellee sought to replevy all the items purchased since December, 1957.[h] The Court of General Sessions granted judgment for appellee. The District of Columbia Court of Appeals affirmed, and we granted appellants' motion for leave to appeal to this court.

Appellants' principal contention, rejected by both the trial and the appellate courts below, is that these contracts, or at least some of them, are unconscionable and, hence, not enforceable. In its opinion in Williams v. Walker-Thomas Furniture Company, 198 A.2d 914, 916 (1964), the District of Columbia Court of Appeals explained its rejection of this contention as follows:

"Appellant's second argument presents a more serious question. The record reveals that prior to the last purchase appellant had reduced the balance in her account to $164. The last purchase, a stereo set, raised the balance due to $678. Significantly, at the time of this and the preceding purchases, appellee was aware of appellant's financial position. The reverse side of the stereo contract listed the name of appellant's social worker and her $218 monthly stipend from the government. Nevertheless, with full knowledge that appellant had to feed, clothe and support both herself and seven children on this amount, appellee sold her a $514 stereo set.

"We cannot condemn too strongly appellee's conduct. It raises serious questions of sharp practice and irresponsible business dealings. A review of the legislation in the District of Columbia affecting retail sales and the pertinent decisions of the highest court in this jurisdiction disclose, however, no ground upon which this court can declare the contracts in question contrary to public policy. We note that were the Maryland Retail Installment Sales Act, Art. 83 §§ 128–153, or its equivalent, in force in the District of Columbia, we could grant appellant appropriate relief. We think Congress should consider corrective legislation to protect the public from such exploitive contracts as were utilized in the case at bar."

We do not agree that the court lacked the power to refuse enforcement to contracts found to be unconscionable. In other jurisdictions, it has been held as a matter of common law that unconscionable contracts are not enforceable.[2] While no decision of this court so holding has been found, the notion that an unconscionable bargain should not be given full enforcement is by no means novel. In Scott v. United States, 79 U.S. (12 Wall.) 443, 445, 20 L.Ed. 438 (1870), the Supreme Court stated:

---

[h] "The store's records showed that of a combined total claim of $444 as of December 26, 1962, Ora still owed 25¢ on item 1, purchased December 23, 1957 (price $45.65); 3¢ on item 2, purchased December 31, 1957 (price $13.21); . . . and similarly for subsequent purchases . . . ." Robert H. Skilton and Orrin L. Helstad, *Protection of the Installment Buyer of Goods under the UCC*, 65 Mich. L. Rev. 1465, 1477 (1967).

[2] Campbell Soup Co. v. Wentz, 172 F.2d 80 (3d Cir. 1948); Indianapolis Morris Plan Corp. v. Sparks, 132 Ind. App. 145, 172 N.E.2d 899 (1961); Henningsen v. Bloomfield Motors, Inc., 32 N.J. 358, 161 A.2d 69, 84–96 (1960). Cf. 1 Corbin, Contracts Section 128 (1963).

"... If a contract be unreasonable and unconscionable, but not void for fraud, a court of law will give to the party who sues for its breach damages, not according to its letter, but only such as he is equitably entitled to. . . . "

Since we have never adopted or rejected such a rule, the question here presented is actually one of first impression.

Congress has recently enacted the Uniform Commercial Code, which specifically provides that the court may refuse to enforce a contract which it finds to be unconscionable at the time it was made. [Section 2–302] The enactment of this section, which occurred subsequent to the contracts here in suit, does not mean that the common law of the District of Columbia was otherwise at the time of enactment, nor does it preclude the court from adopting a similar rule in the exercise of its powers to develop the common law for the District of Columbia. In fact, in view of the absence of prior authority on the point, we consider the congressional adopting of Section 2–302 persuasive authority for following the rationale of the cases, from which the section is explicitly derived.[3] Accordingly, we hold that where the element of unconscionability is present at the time a contract is made, the contract should not be enforced.

Unconscionability has generally been recognized to include an absence of meaningful choice on the part of one of the parties together with contract terms which are unreasonably favorable to the other party. Whether a meaningful choice is present in a particular case can only be determined by consideration of all the circumstances surrounding the transaction. In many cases the meaningfulness of the choice is negated by a gross inequality of bargaining power.[4] The manner in which the contract was entered is also relevant to this consideration. Did each party to the contract, considering his obvious education or lack of it, have a reasonable opportunity to understand the terms of the contract, or were the important terms hidden in a maze of fine print and minimized by deceptive sales practices? Ordinarily, one who signs an agreement without full knowledge of its terms might be held to assume the risk that

---

[3] See Comment, Sec. 2–302, Uniform Commercial Code (1962). Compare Note, 45 Va.L.Rev. 583, 590 (1959), where it is predicted that the rule of Sec. 2–302 will be followed by analogy in cases which involve contracts not specifically covered by the section. Cf. 1 State of New York Law Revision Commission, Report and Record of Hearings on the Uniform Commercial Code 108–110 (1954) (remarks of Professor Llewellyn).

[4] See Henningsen v. Bloomfield Motors, Inc., supra Note 2, 161 A.2d 69 at 86, and authorities there cited. Inquiry into the relative bargaining power of the two parties is not an inquiry wholly divorced from the general question of unconscionability, since a one-sided bargain is itself evidence of the inequality of the bargaining parties. This fact was vaguely recognized in the common law doctrine of intrinsic fraud, that is, fraud which can be presumed from the grossly unfair nature of the terms of the contract. See the oft-quoted statement of Lord Hardwicke in Earl of Chesterfield v. Janssen, 28 Eng.Rep. 82, 100 (1751):

"... (Fraud) may be apparent from the intrinsic nature and subject of the bargain itself; such as no man in his senses and not under delusion would make ... "

party the chicken litter provisions are and how those provisions are "the personification of the kind of inequality and oppression that courts have found is the hallmark of unconscionability."

In Barnes v. Helfenbein, 1976 OK 33, 548 P.2d 1014, the Court, analyzing the equitable concept of unconscionability in the context of a loan with the Uniform Consumer Credit Code, 14A O.S.1971 § 1–101, *et seq.,* found that "[a]n unconscionable contract is one which no person in his senses, not under delusion would make, on the one hand, and which no fair and honest man would accept on the other." 1976 OK 33, ¶ 23, 548 P.2d at 1020. The Court went on to note:

> The equitable concept of unconscionability is meaningful only within the context of otherwise defined factors of onerous inequality, deception and oppression. Unconscionability is directly related to fraud and deceit. An unconscionable contract is one which no person in his senses, not under delusion would make, on the one hand, and which no fair and honest man would accept on the other. The basic test of unconscionability of a contract is whether under the circumstances existing at the time of making of the contract, and in light of the general commercial background and commercial need of a particular case, clauses are so one-sided as to oppress or unfairly surprise one of the parties. Unconscionability has generally been recognized to include an absence of meaningful choice on the part of one of the parties, together with contractual terms which are unreasonably favorable to the other party.

1976 OK 33, at ¶ 23, 548 P.2d at 1020.

"The question of unconscionability is one of law for the Court to decide." Phillips Machinery Company v. LeBlond, Inc., 494 F.Supp. 318, 322 (N.D.Okla.1980), accord, 12A O.S.2001 § 2–302, Oklahoma Code Comment ("Note that the determination of 'unconscionable' is one of law for the court."). The Oklahoma Legislature, at 12A O.S.2001 § 2–302, has addressed unconscionability in the context of the sale of goods under the Uniform Commercial Code. As is recognized in Restatement (Second) of Contracts, § 208, Comment a, (1981):

> Uniform Commercial Code § 2–302 is literally inapplicable to contracts not involving the sale of goods, but it has proven very influential in non-sales cases. It has many times been used either by analogy or because it was felt to embody a generally accepted social attitude of fairness going beyond its statutory application to sales of goods.

We agree such an analogy is helpful with this analysis. The parties here provided evidence relating to their transaction.

According to Stoll's deposition testimony in the companion case, which testimony is provided to support his motion for summary judgment in this case, it was his idea to include the chicken litter paragraph in the land purchase contract. He testified that one house de-caking of a house like those of Buyers yields about 20 tons of litter. After 2008, rising oil prices drove up the cost of commercial fertilizer, but before then he had not sold litter for more than $12 per ton. Yang testified at deposition that according to Stoll's representations, the litter could be worth $25 per ton. Xiong testified at deposition that they raised five flocks per year in their six houses. Applying these figures, the annual value of the litter from de-caking alone (*i.e.,* which does not include *additional* volumes of litter from a complete clean out) appears to range from roughly $7,200 to $15,000. For thirty years, the estimated value of the de-caked chicken litter using Stoll's $12 value would be $216,000, or roughly an additional $3,325.12 more per acre just from de-caked chicken litter sales than the $2,000 per acre purchase price stated on the first page of the contract. Effectively, Stoll either made himself a partner in their business for no consideration or he would receive almost double to way over double the purchase price for his land over thirty years. Under Stoll's interpretation of paragraph 10, Buyers' separate business would generate an asset for thirty years for which they receive no consideration and would serve as additional payment to him over and above the stated price for the land.

An analogy exists regarding the cancellation of deeds. "Ordinarily the mere inadequacy of consideration is not sufficient ground, in itself, to justify a court in canceling a deed, yet where the inadequacy of the consideration was so gross as to shock the conscience, and the grantor was feeble-minded and unable to understand the nature of his contract, a strong presumption of fraud arises, and unless it is successfully rebutted, a court of equity will set aside the deed so obtained." Fickel v. Webb, 1930 OK 432, 293 P. 206; Morton v. Roberts, 1923 OK 126, 213 P. 297. Under such circumstances, there is no assent to terms. Here, a nearly reverse situation exists in that the consideration actually to be paid under the contract far exceeds that stated. Under Stoll's interpretation of paragraph 10 (which was his "idea"), the land sale contract is onerous to one side of the contracting parties while solely benefitting the other, and the parties to be surcharged with the extra expense were, due to language and education, unable to understand the nature of the contract. Stoll testified he believed his land was worth $2,000 per acre rather than the $1,200 per acre price of nearby land in 2004 due to the work he had done to clear and level it. The actual price Buyers will pay under the paragraph Stoll included in the land sale contract is so gross as to shock the conscience.

Buyers argue no fair and honest person would propose and no rational person would enter into a contract containing a clause imposing a premium for land and which, without any consideration to them, imposes additional costs in the hundreds of thousands over a thirty-year period that both are unrelated to the land itself and exceed the value of the land. We agree. The trial court found the chicken litter clause in the land purchase contract unconscionable as a matter of law and entered judgment in Buyers' favor. That judgment is AFFIRMED.

NOTES

(1) *Why Unconscionability?* Consider the defenses of duress, misrepresentation, incapacity, and undue influence in light of the facts of this case. Would the elements of any of these defenses be met here?

(2) *From Laos to Oklahoma.* In the wake of the Vietnam War, many Hmong (principally from Laos, but from other Southeast Asian nations as well) were political refugees, emigrating to the United States from the mid-1970s into the 1980s. The largest Hmong community in the United States is centered in Minneapolis-St. Paul. Most Hmong were originally subsistence farmers. In the United States, relatively few owned farms, typically for want of capital, though many worked in agriculture-related jobs.

Starting in the 2000s, many Hmong moved from Minnesota to Arkansas, Oklahoma, and Missouri to take advantage of what were billed as outstanding opportunities as contract poultry farmers, to own their own land, and to live in more congenial climates. After only a short time, many faced financial ruin. The reasons are many, but a common theme is inflated appraisals of the chicken farms, together with exaggerated income projections by banks and underestimated living expenses, which resulted in the granting of loans well in excess of the farmers' ability to repay them. Many of the Hmong were marginally literate in English and did not fully understand the loan documents and purchase agreements they were told to sign. Because the loans were federally guaranteed, the banks faced little risk in creating them; indeed, if the Hmong bought farms from failing clients, the banks would have superior security. See Arthur J. Rolnick and David Fettig, Between Two Worlds: How Do Credit Markets Work?: An Investigation into Credit Availability in the Minneapolis-St. Paul Hmong Community, Fed. Reserve Bank of Minneapolis (May 1, 2003) (available at https://www.minneapolisfed.org/publications/the-region/between-two-worlds-how-do-credit-markets-work); Howard Witt, Hmong Poultry Farmers Cry Foul, Sue, Chi. Tribune, May 15, 2006; Laura Yuen, Farm of Failed Dreams, St. Paul Pioneer Press, May 17, 2006.

To what extent did the court take the Xiongs' history into account, and how? Compare their treatment with that of Audrey Vokes, supra p. 483. See Hila Keren, Guilt-Free Markets? Unconscionability, Conscience, and Emotions, 2016 BYU L. Rev. 427.

(3) *Price and Profit.* What remedy did the Xiongs receive? How did the court take Stoll's reasonable profit into account? What if Stoll had used the revenue from chicken litter when setting his price for the land?

PROBLEMS

(1) *Historical Price Unconscionability.* The Indian Claims Commission Act of 1946 authorized tribes to bring claims against the United States resulting from treaties, contracts, or agreements revisable on the basis of

fraud, duress, or unconscionable consideration. The Nez Perce Tribe claimed compensation under the Act for 549,559 acres of farm and timberland it ceded to the U.S. in 1894 for $2.97 per acre. (Under the terms of the sale, the purchase price was put into a trust account for the Tribe at interest for a period of years.) The Tribe claimed the true market value was over $12. The Commission found that the market value at the time of the sale was $4, and that the differential between $4 and $2.97 was not unconscionable. The Tribe appealed. What result? See Nez Perce Tribe of Indians v. United States, 176 Ct. Cl. 815, 828–29 (Ct. Cl. 1966).

(2) *Billable Hours.* Over an 18-month period a law firm billed a client something over $2,000,000 in legal fees for work done on a matter by a lawyer working under contract for the firm. The client later sued the firm for malpractice, claiming also that the firm's fees were unconscionable. To prove the latter, the client sought to discover the firm's profits on his matter. From a judgment denying his motion to produce this information, client appealed. The Rules of Professional Conduct of the State Bar prohibit attorneys from charging unconscionable fees and set out specific guidelines for making that determination. What result on appeal? Is a law firm's profit margin irrelevant to the inquiry? Are profit margins for law firms different from profit margins for freezer sales? See Shaffer v. Superior Court, 39 Cal.Rptr.2d 506 (Ct. App. 1995).

Unconscionability in Franchises

While much of the commentary on unconscionability has focused on its role in consumer cases, the doctrine applies in commercial agreements as well; recall the discussion of *Campbell Soup*, p. 634 above. It is not surprising, however, that courts have been less willing to find unconscionability in agreements where the bargaining position of the parties is more likely to be equal, and where experienced traders are less likely to be confronted with "unfair surprise" in terms. For example, in an action by Continental Airlines against Goodyear Rubber, the Ninth Circuit refused to accept Continental's claim of unconscionability: the doctrine "cannot be invoked by so sophisticated a party as Continental in reference to a contract so laboriously negotiated." Continental Airlines v. Goodyear Tire & Rubber Co., 819 F.2d 1519, 1527 (9th Cir. 1987). Similarly, in U.S. Welding v. Battelle Energy Alliance, 728 F.Supp.2d 1110 (D. Idaho 2010), the court rejected the claim of unconscionability advanced by the plaintiff, "a sophisticated corporate entity, complete with in-house counsel": "This is not a situation in which a powerless consumer is forced into a contract in order to obtain a necessary benefit."

Of course, not all businesses have equal clout. A Michigan court upheld a trial court ruling that a cancellation clause was unconscionable in light of the fact that " 'big sharks' in the garment industry were able to impose these clauses [on] small independent manufacturers." Gianni Sport Ltd. v. Gantos, Inc., 391 N.W.2d 760, 762 (Mich. App. 1986). See generally Larry T. Garvin, *Small Business and the False Dichotomies of Contract Law*, 40 Wake Forest L. Rev. 295 (2005).

One area where the imbalance in positions between commercial parties is sometimes found involves franchise agreements. We have already seen the problems of Hoffman in his efforts to obtain a franchise from Red Owl. And even when the deal is struck, the relationship between franchisor and franchisee remains complex. The franchisor may contend that the franchisee has provided substandard service, damaging the reputation of the product or the services on which royalties and consumer loyalty depend. Diverting from the reputation of the franchise may also injure other franchisees whose interests the franchisor represents. The franchisee may object that the franchisor has skimped on advertising or has siphoned off revenues through a competing franchisee. On the complexities of franchise relationships generally, see Gillian Hadfield, *Problematic Relations: Franchising and the Law of Incomplete Contracts*, 42 Stan. L. Rev. 927 (1990).

Disputes also arise with regard to the basic terms of the underlying contract. Franchise agreements typically take the form of a standardized agreement prepared by the franchisor, containing terms that are not open to negotiation and are strikingly favorable to the franchisor. In particular, a franchisor may reserve the power of termination on short notice [or] "at any time for any reason." See Corenswet, Inc. v. Amana Refrigeration, Inc., 594 F.2d 129 (5th Cir. 1979). The power is defended on the ground that it serves to discipline a slack franchisee tempted by free-rider possibilities to piggy-back on the general quality of the franchise.

Might a termination power, or another provision harsh on a franchisee, be regarded as unconscionable, and so unenforceable? In a case involving a lease between the Shell Oil Company and a service station operator, a New Jersey court held that it was. Shell had terminated the franchise on 10 days' notice, as provided for in the parties' contracts. Among the facts deemed "significant" by the trial court were "the gross disparity in bargaining power between Shell and Marinello, resulting in Shell's ability to dictate the terms of the agreements; the grossly unfair contractual provisions at issue; and the clear tendency to injure the public."

The New Jersey Supreme Court expressed full agreement with the "basic determination . . . that Shell had no legal right to terminate its relationship with Marinello except for good cause. . . . " Shell Oil Co. v. Marinello, 307 A.2d 598 (N.J. 1973).

In contrast, Dairy Mart's termination of one of its franchises on 90 days notice and without cause was found *not* to be unconscionable. In Zapatha v. Dairy Mart, Inc., 408 N.E.2d 1370, 1377 (Mass. 1980), the court stated that:

We find no potential for unfair surprise to the Zapathas. . . . The termination provision was neither obscurely worded, nor buried in fine print in the contract. Contrast Williams v. Walker-Thomas, [p. 637 above], The provision was specifically pointed out to Mr. Zapatha before it was signed; Mr. Zapatha testified that he thought the provision was "straightforward," and that he declined the opportunity to take the agreement to a lawyer for advice.

The court also rejected the argument that the termination clause was oppressive. "As an investment, the Zapathas had only to purchase the inventory of goods to be sold but as Dairy Mart concedes, on termination by it without cause Dairy Mart was obliged to repurchase all the Zapathas' saleable merchandise inventory, including items not purchased from Dairy Mart, at 80% of its retail value. There was no potential for forfeiture or loss of investment."

NOTE

Legislation and Litigation. A number of state and federal fair-practices acts are directed at franchising. For example, the Automobile Dealers' Day in Court Act of 1956 imposed on the automobile manufacturers a duty of good faith "in performing or complying with any of the terms or provisions of [a dealer's] franchise, or in terminating, canceling, or not renewing the franchise." 15 U.S.C. §§ 1221 et seq. The subject of good faith is taken up later in this chapter.

See also The Petroleum Marketing Practices Act of 1978, which substantially preempted state regulation of the termination and renewal of franchise relationships between motor-fuel dispensers and their suppliers, in an attempt to "level the playing field." 15 U.S.C. §§ 2801–2806. See Simmons v. Mobil Oil Corp., 29 F.3d 505 (9th Cir. 1994). In 1979, by rule, the FTC established a minimum federal standard of disclosure applicable to all "franchise and business opportunity offerings." 16 C.F.R. § 436. A number of state disclosure requirements are also operative. On litigation unconscionability in franchise agreements, see Bethany L. Appleby, C. Griffith Towle and Carmen D. Caruso, "Unconscionability and Franchise Litigation," ABA Forum on Franchising (2006).

———

Unconscionability: Arbitration Clauses

Cases concerning the enforceability of mandatory arbitration clauses have generated some of the most contested rulings in contemporary contract law. These clauses are common in employment contracts, often imposed as a condition of employment, and in consumer contracts. As discussed in Chapter 1, pp. 46–47, arbitration as an alternative to litigation has taken on increasing importance over the last few decades. Some of the reasons behind this trend are clear. Many parties choose to arbitrate in order to avoid or lower the costs—in time, in money, in publicity—of seeking a remedy in court. But what if an arbitration clause is not so much chosen as imposed as part of the boilerplate in a standard form or adhesive contract?

This question comes up often in the context of employment contracts. For a baseline answer, one can look to an important 2001 Supreme Court case, which held that mandatory arbitration agreements in employment agreements are generally enforceable under the Federal Arbitration Act (FAA), "save for upon such grounds as exist at law or in equity for the revocation of any contract." Circuit City Stores, Inc. v. Adams, 532 U.S. 105, 112 (2001). The doctrine of unconscionability, of course, is one such ground for revoking a contract. Yet consensus on the standard for invoking the doctrine remains elusive.

The leading California case describing the standard for determining a mandatory arbitration clause in an employment contract is Armendariz v. Foundation Health Psychcare Services, Inc., 24 Cal.4th 83 (2004). The Court in *Armendariz* considered whether an agreement compelling *employees* to arbitrate wrongful termination and employment discrimination claims, *inter alia*, was unconscionable. "We conclude that such claims are in fact arbitrable *if* the arbitration permits an employee to vindicate his or her statutory rights [and], in order for such vindication to occur, the arbitration must meet certain minimum requirements, including neutrality of the arbitrator, the provision of adequate discovery, a written decision that will permit a limited form of judicial review, and limitations on the costs of arbitration." *Id*. at 90–91. The contract had further provided that only employees were compelled to arbitrate any disputes—the employer could bring any claims against employees in court. The Supreme Court of California upheld the trial court's finding "that several of the provisions of the contract are 'so one-sided as to 'shock the conscience.'" *Id*. at 92. Moreover, it held, "[t]he unconscionable one-sidedness of the arbitration agreement is compounded in this case by the fact that it does not permit the full recovery of damages for employees, while placing no such restriction on the employer." *Id*. at 121

In Oblix v. Winiecki, 374 F.3d 488 (2004), the Seventh Circuit Court of Appeals considered a case from the Northern District of Illinois, which had denied an employer's motion to compel arbitration. The arbitration agreement in that case also contained a broad, one-sided mandatory arbitration clause. An employee, Felicia Winiecki, challenged the clause as unconscionable: like the contract in *Armendariz*, here too the contract required the employee to arbitrate all disputes she might have with the employer, while the employer was not so bound. In holding for the employer, Judge Easterbrook stated: "Standard-form agreements are a fact of life, and given [FAA preference for arbitration], arbitration agreements in [employment contracts] must be enforced unless the states would refuse to enforce all off-the-shelf package deals." *Id*. at 491.

Making specific reference to *Armendariz*, Judge Easterbrook asserted, "[i]t is in the end irrelevant whether the Supreme Court of California wants to treat arbitration less favorably than other promises in form contracts; no state can apply to arbitration (when governed by the FAA) any novel rule. Under normal rules of contract, the promises Winiecki made in order to be hired and paid are enforceable. Thus she must arbitrate." *Id.* at 492.

NOTES

(1) *Post-Armendariz.* In California, *Armendariz* has spawned a great deal of litigation as courts attempt to locate the contours of unconscionability as applied to mandatory arbitration in employment agreements. Cases finding unconscionability include Pinedo v. Premium Tobacco, 102 Cal.Rptr.2d 435 (Ct. App. 2000) ("multiple defects") and Villa Milano Homeowner's Association v. Il Davorge, 102 Cal.Rptr.2d 1 (Ct. App. 2000), extending *Armendariz* analysis to arbitration provision in the Covenants, Conditions, and Restrictions (CC&Rs) between a developer and homeowners. Cases finding *no* unconscionability include Pichly v. Nortech Waste LLC, 105 Cal.Rptr.2d 21 (Ct. App. 2001) (arbitration provision in a trucker's employment contract "neither one-sided nor overly harsh") and Baker v. Osborne Development Corp., 71 Cal.Rptr.3d 854 (Ct. App. 2008).

In Shubin v. William Lyon Homes, Inc., 101 Cal.Rptr.2d 390, 402 (Ct. App. 2000), the court addressed the question of whether the circumstances under which the employee signs the arbitration provision may create *procedural* unconscionability. The court found that the office manager "said and did things to hurry or pressure Shubin into signing documents placed before her, without having the time to carefully read their contents . . . [and with] no realistic opportunity to suggest modifications." Procedural unconscionability was established.

Most recently, in Samaniego v. Empire Today LLC, 140 Cal.Rptr.3d 492 (Ct. App. 2012), the plaintiffs were offered form contracts in English and "were told that they were 'required' to sign these documents, including [a mandatory arbitration] agreement, if they wanted to work for Empire. Both Plaintiffs are not able to read English (at all, or sufficiently well) and both Plaintiffs asked for a Spanish translation of the documents (including the agreement) in Spanish [*sic*] but were told none were available." *Id.* at 1145. Additional concerns were raised by the fact that "Empire failed to provide plaintiffs with a copy of the relevant arbitration rules. . . . The Agreement was comprised of 11 pages of densely worded, single-spaced text printed in small typeface. The arbitration clause is the penultimate of 37 sections which[,] were neither flagged by individual headings nor required to be initialed . . . ." *Id.* at 1146. The court held the arbitration clause unconscionable and unenforceable under *Armendariz,* and noted "that the recent decision of the Supreme Court of the United States in AT & T Mobility LLC v. Concepcion (2011) does not change our analysis." *Id.* at 1141–42.

(2) *Severability.* The California Civil Code, modeled after UCC § 2–302, applies the doctrine of unconscionability to *all* contracts, and provides

that in cases of unconscionability a court may refuse to enforce the entire contract, may sever the unconscionable provisions and enforce the remainder, or may "so limit the application of any unconscionable clause as that avoid any unconscionable result." Cal. Civil Code § 1670.5(a). Thus in Graham v. Scissor-Tail, p. 616 above, the California Supreme Court found unconscionable a clause in an entertainment industry contract requiring all arbitrations to be heard by the union of one of the parties. "Although our review of the record has disclosed nothing which would indicate that A.F. of M. procedures operate to deny any party a fair opportunity to present his position prior to decision, we are of the view that the 'minimum levels of integrity' which are requisite to a contractual arrangement for the nonjudicial resolution of disputes are not achieved by an arrangement which designates the union of one of the parties as the arbitrator of disputes arising out of employment—especially when, as here, the arrangement is the product of circumstances indicative of adhesion." 623 P.2d at 177. Recognizing the state's strong public policy of favoring arbitration as a method of dispute resolution, the court severed the objectionable provision appointing the less-than-neutral arbitrator and remanded the case for the selection of a "suitable" arbitrator by the parties, or as a default, by the court.

Compare Bolter v. Superior Court of Orange County, 104 Cal.Rptr.2d 888, 895 (Ct. App. 2001), in which the court found unconscionable a provision requiring "mom-and-pop" carpet cleaning franchisees in California to arbitrate all disputes in Utah, but held that "[i]t is not necessary to throw the baby out with the bath water, i.e., the unconscionable provisions can be severed and the rest of the [arbitration] agreement enforced."

Severability, or divisibility, is discussed further in Chapter 7, below (pp. 822–824).

(3) *Geese and Ganders.* In dismissing the employee's argument in *Oblix*, above, Judge Easterbrook stated: "Businesses regularly agree to arbitrate their disputes with each other; giving employees the same terms and forum (the AAA) that a firm deems satisfactory for commercial dispute resolution is not suspect." 374 F.3d at 491. A roughly contemporaneous study examining the use of arbitration clauses by firms in their contracts with one another suggested that this may not be so: "large corporate actors do not systematically embrace arbitration." Theodore Eisenberg and Geoffrey Miller, *The Flight from Arbitration: An Empirical Study of Ex Ante Arbitration Clauses in the Contracts of Publicly Held Companies*, 56 DePaul L. Rev. 335 (2007). The authors examined 2800 contracts filed by public firms with the Securities and Exchange Commission in 2002 and found that only 11% included arbitration clauses. Eisenberg and Miller conclude that notwithstanding the factors often advanced for including arbitration clauses in consumer contracts—cost savings, simpler procedure—from an economic perspective, it appears that "corporate representatives believe that litigation can add value over arbitration." A recent replication of that study (based on an appreciably expanded sample of the data used by Eisenberg and Miller) identified significantly greater usage of arbitration clauses both over time and across contract type. See Sarath Sanga, *A New Strategy for Regulating Arbitration*, 113 Nw. U. L. Rev. 1121 (2019). For example, 41% of the 140,980

employment agreement analyzed in this study had an arbitration clause, as did 30% of the 4,869 joint venture agreements in the sample. Overall, 19% of the 791,363 contracts in the sample included arbitration agreements. For a thoughtful study of the character of clients and cases brought before arbitrators, see Andrea Cann Chandrasekher and David Horton, *Arbitration Nation: Data from Four Providers*, 107 Calif. L. Rev. (forthcoming 2019). Chandrasekher and Horton examine more than 40,000 cases handled by major arbitration houses (including the American Arbitration Association, AAA), filed in between 2010 and 2016.

Prasad v. Pinnacle Property Management Services, LLC

United States District Court for the Northern District of California, 2018.
2018 WL 4599645.

ORDER GRANTING DEFENDANT'S MOTION TO COMPEL ARBITRATION

■ VIRGINIA K. DEMARCHI, UNITED STATES MAGISTRATE JUDGE.

I. FACTUAL AND PROCEDURAL BACKGROUND

[Stephanie Prasad was hired by Pinnacle in 1996 as a property manager. Her employment ended just under a year later. Ms. Prasad suffers from type I diabetes, which occasionally required such accommodations as a modified work schedule. She claims that, due in part to lengthy work hours, she began experiencing health complications related to her diabetes. Ms. Prasad was placed on medical leave for two weeks. Upon her return, Ms. Prasad's position was filled by another employee, and she was given a new position as a "Roving Manager." Ms. Prasad considered this reassignment a demotion because she says it was temporary in nature and she earned less money than she did as a property manager.]

Claiming that Pinnacle misclassifies its property managers as exempt from overtime pay, Ms. Prasad filed this putative class, collective, and representative action against Pinnacle, asserting eleven claims for relief [under various state and federal statutes and the common law], seven of which are class/collective/representative claims for relief: (1) failure to pay overtime; (2) failure to pay wages; (3) failure to provide meal periods; (4) failure to provide rest periods; (5) failure to provide itemized wage statements; (6) waiting time penalties; and (7) unfair business practices. The remaining four claims are Ms. Prasad's individual claims for relief: (8) disability discrimination; (9) failure to accommodate disability; (10) failure to engage in the interactive process; and (11) intentional infliction of emotional distress.

Pinnacle moved to compel arbitration pursuant to an Issue Resolution Agreement ("IRA" or "Agreement") it claims Ms. Prasad assented to and signed when she applied for employment with the company. The IRA provides, in relevant part:

I agree that I will settle any and all previously unasserted claims, disputes or controversies arising out of or relating to my application or candidacy for employment, employment, and/or cessation of employment with Pinnacle Property Management Services, LLC **exclusively** by final and binding **arbitration** before a neutral Arbitrator.

The Agreement also contains a class action waiver: "Each arbitration proceeding shall cover the claims of only one Employee. Unless the parties mutually agree, the parties agree that the arbitrator has no authority to adjudicate a 'class action.'" As such, Pinnacle contends that Ms. Prasad must arbitrate her individual claims and that the putative class, collective and representative claims must be dismissed without prejudice.

Ms. Prasad opposes Pinnacle's motion, arguing that she never signed the IRA and that the Agreement is unenforceable and unconscionable for a number of reasons.

[The court stayed arbitration pending the Supreme Court's decision in Epic Sys. Corp. v. Lewis, 138 S. Ct. 1612 (2018). There the Court held that the National Labor Relations Act does not reflect a clearly expressed and manifest congressional intention to displace the FAA and to outlaw class and collective action waivers. Ms. Prasad conceded that *Epic* foreclosed her challenge of the class arbitration waiver.]

Ms. Prasad contends that *Epic* does not impact her arguments that the IRA is unconscionable for other reasons. Pinnacle maintains that the IRA is neither procedurally nor substantively unconscionable. To the extent there are any improper provisions, Pinnacle contends that they may be severed from the Agreement and that the remainder properly may be enforced.

[T]he Court grants Pinnacle's motion to compel arbitration as to Ms. Prasad's individual claims and stays these proceedings pending completion of the arbitration.

II. LEGAL STANDARD

[Under the Federal Arbitration Act, a party to an arbitration agreement may seek an order from a federal district court directing that the arbitration proceed.] When ruling on such a petition, the court must determine (1) whether an arbitration agreement exists and (2) whether it encompasses the dispute at issue. *See id.*; *see also* Chiron Corp. v. Ortho Diagnostic Sys., Inc., 207 F.3d 1126, 1130 (9th Cir. 2000). "[A]ny doubts concerning the scope of arbitrable issues should be resolved in favor of arbitration, whether the problem at hand is the construction of the contract language itself or an allegation of waiver, delay, or a like defense to arbitrability." Moses H. Cone Mem'l Hosp. v. Mercury Constr. Corp., 460 U.S. 1, 24–25 (1983).

A court may compel the parties to arbitrate only when they have agreed to arbitrate the dispute at issue. Granite Rock Co. v. Int'l Bhd. of Teamsters, 561 U.S. 287, 302–03 (2010). Additionally, arbitration should be denied if the court finds "grounds as exist at law or in equity for the revocation of any contract," such as fraud, duress, or unconscionability. 9 U.S.C. § 2; Rent-A-Center, West, Inc. v. Jackson, 561 U.S. 63, 68 (2010).

III. DISCUSSION

Ms. Prasad maintains that the IRA should not be enforced because several of its terms are unconscionable. Pinnacle does not dispute that there is some minimal unconscionability presented by at least some of the IRA provisions in question. However, even if this Court finds that the provisions are unconscionable, Pinnacle argues that the Court should sever them from the IRA and enforce the remainder.

A. The Unconscionability Doctrine

In determining whether the IRA is unconscionable, the Court applies "California's general principle of contract unconscionability." Chavarria v. Ralphs Grocery Co., 733 F.3d 916, 921–22 (9th Cir. 2013).

Unconscionability "has both a procedural and a substantive element, the former focusing on oppression or surprise due to unequal bargaining power, the latter on overly harsh or one-sided results." Armendariz v. Foundation Health Psychcare Servs., Inc., 24 Cal.4th 83, 114 (2000) (internal quotations and citation omitted). "The prevailing view is that [procedural and substantive unconscionability] must both be present in order for a court to exercise its discretion to refuse to enforce a contract or clause under the doctrine of unconscionability. But they need not be present in the same degree." . . . "In other words, the more substantively oppressive the contract term, the less evidence of procedural unconscionability is required to come to the conclusion that the term is unenforceable, and vice versa." Id.

1. Procedural Unconscionability

"Procedural unconscionability concerns the manner in which the contract was negotiated and the respective circumstances of the parties at that time, focusing on the level of oppression and surprise involved in the agreement." Chavarria, 733 F.3d at 922. "Oppression addresses the weaker party's absence of choice and unequal bargaining power that results in 'no real negotiation.'" Id. (quoting A & M Produce v. FMC Corp., 135 Cal. App.3d 473, 486 (1982)). "Surprise involves the extent to which the contract clearly discloses its terms as well as the reasonable expectations of the weaker party." Id. (citing Parada v. Super. Ct., 176 Cal.App.4th 1554, 1571 (2009)).

Thus, "[u]nconscionability analysis begins with an inquiry into whether the contract is one of adhesion." Armendariz, 24 Cal.4th at 113. . . . "If the contract is adhesive, the court must then determine whether other factors are present which, under established legal rules—legislative or judicial—operate to render it [unenforceable]." *Id.*

The California Supreme Court has observed that there are degrees of procedural unconscionability:

> At one end of the spectrum are contracts that have been freely negotiated by roughly equal parties, in which there is no procedural unconscionability. . . . Contracts of adhesion that involve surprise or other sharp practices lie on the other end of the spectrum. Ordinary contracts of adhesion, although they are indispensable facts of modern life that are generally enforced, contain a degree of procedural unconscionability even without any notable surprises, and 'bear within them the clear danger of oppression and overreaching'. We have instructed that courts must be particularly attuned to this danger in the employment setting, where economic pressure exerted by employers on all but the most sought-after employees may be particularly acute.

Balthazar v. Forever 21, Inc., 62 Cal.4th 1237, 1244 (2016).

In the present case, Ms. Prasad satisfies the oppression aspect of procedural unconscionability. She contends that the IRA is a non-negotiable contract of adhesion, offered on a take-it-or-leave-it basis. Indeed, Pinnacle documents inform applicants: "You will not be considered as an applicant until you have signed the [IRA]." And, in arguing that Ms. Prasad entered into the Agreement, Pinnacle touts the fact that Ms. Prasad would not have been able to submit her job application unless she first agreed to the IRA. Although the IRA gave Ms. Prasad three days to opt-out, opting out meant that she would have to withdraw her job application.

Moreover, Pinnacle does not dispute that it had superior bargaining power, and the California Supreme Court has observed:

> [I]n the case of preemployment arbitration contracts, the economic pressure exerted by employers on all but the most sought-after employees may be particularly acute, for the arbitration agreement stands between the employee and necessary employment, and few employees are in a position to refuse a job because of an arbitration requirement.

Armendariz, 24 Cal.4th at 115.

As for the element of surprise, Ms. Prasad argues that she has no specific recollection of reviewing the IRA and maintains that the Agreement was signed without her knowledge. As discussed, the Court has rejected that latter assertion.

Ms. Prasad nonetheless contends that she did not make an informed decision with respect to the IRA because the Agreement (1) contains a number of unfavorable terms scattered throughout the IRA and (2) fails to disclose the disadvantages imposed upon her by those terms. Pinnacle argues that the IRA clearly stated that it was an arbitration agreement. . . .

Courts have held that a one-sided explanation of benefits, without a corresponding explanation of disadvantages of arbitration, render an arbitration agreement procedurally unconscionable. . . . Ms. Prasad has established some procedural unconscionability, given that the IRA was a contract of adhesion, with no meaningful opt-out, and that Ms. Prasad's agreement to the IRA was not an informed decision to the extent that the IRA does not explain the potential pitfalls and drawbacks of proceeding with arbitration versus litigation. However, a "finding of procedural unconscionability does not mean that a contract will not be enforced, but rather that courts will scrutinize the substantive terms of the contract to ensure they are not manifestly unfair or one-sided." *Balthazar*, 62 Cal.4th at 1244.

2. Substantive Unconscionability

"Substantive unconscionability addresses the fairness of the term in dispute." Pokorny v. Quixtar, Inc., 601 F.3d 987, 997 (9th Cir. 2010) (internal quotations and citation omitted). "The focus of the inquiry is whether the term is one-sided and will have an overly harsh effect on the disadvantaged party." *Id* "A contract is substantively unconscionable when it is unjustifiably one-sided to such an extent that it 'shocks the conscience.'" *Chavarria*, 733 F.3d at 923 (quoting *Parada*, 176 Cal.App.4th at 1573). "In evaluating the substance of a contract, courts must analyze the contract 'as of the time [it] was made.'" Ingle v. Circuit City Stores, Inc., 328 F.3d 1165, 1172 (9th Cir. 2003) (quoting *A&M Produce*, 135 Cal. App.3d at 487).

Ms. Prasad argues that the IRA is substantively unconscionable for six reasons:

a. Class/Collective Action Waiver

Ms. Prasad agrees that, post-*Epic*, the IRA's concerted action waiver is not a basis for finding unconscionability. Accordingly, the Court concludes that the waiver provision is not unconscionable and that Ms. Prasad cannot maintain the class, collective and representative claims asserted in her original complaint.

b. One-Year Statute of Limitations on Employees' Claims

The IRA requires employees to commence arbitration by filing an "Arbitration Request Form," and imposes a one-sided, one-year limitations period only on employees

Ms. Prasad argues that this provision is unconscionable because the statutes on which her claims are based have limitations periods of more than one year—e.g., two years for FLSA claims and three years for FLSA claims arising out of willful violations . . .; three years for overtime pay under the California Labor Code; and four years for unfair competition claims. Ms. Prasad argues that the IRA is doubly unfair in this respect because it only shortens the limitations period for employees, not Pinnacle.

Pinnacle acknowledges that there is some amount of unfairness inherent in this provision, but says that the level of unconscionability relative to the IRA as a whole is slim. It argues that this is so because the IRA does not affect tolling doctrines under applicable state laws or Ms. Prasad's ability to arbitrate continuing violations. Additionally, Pinnacle argues that the limitations period imposed by this provision is moot as to Ms. Prasad, who timely filed the present suit.

The Court concludes that this provision is unconscionable. The fact that Ms. Prasad filed this action within the one-year contractual limitations period is irrelevant. As discussed above, the Court must assess the IRA as of the time it was made, not as of the time Ms. Prasad filed suit. *Ingle*, 328 F.3d at 1172. Unlike the provision in *Ingle*, the IRA's limitations clause permits employees to benefit from tolling doctrines under applicable state laws and to arbitrate continuing violations. Nevertheless, that does not remedy the fact that the IRA's shortened limitations period applies only to employees. For example, in *Pokorny,* a similar provision was found unconscionable because it shortened a potentially longer statute of limitations period for any claim that the defendant's distributors might wish to bring against the defendant (or another distributor), but did not impose a similar time restriction on the defendant, which remained free to bring an action in court without being subject to the agreement's limitations period. 601 F.3d at 1001–02. Pinnacle having offered no reason why a unilateral reduction in the statute of limitations is required, this provision is substantively unconscionable.

c.   Claim Submission and Filing Fee

To initiate a claim against Pinnacle, the IRA requires employees to pay a $50.00 filing fee to "American Management Services." Ms. Prasad contends that this provision is unconscionable because it essentially requires employees to pay Pinnacle for the privilege of bringing a claim.

In its reply papers, Pinnacle seems to suggest that "American Management Services" is not Pinnacle. Dkt. No. 16 at 9 ("Lastly, the small $50 fee for filing does not go to 'the very entity against which Plaintiff seeks redress'—it goes to American Management Services, which is *not* the entity against which Plaintiff seeks redress.") However, at the initial hearing on the present motion, defense counsel acknowledged that "American Management Services" is Pinnacle. He further stated that the $50 fee goes toward the arbitration costs and is not kept by the company. However, none of that is apparent from the IRA itself. Instead, the IRA indicates that to initiate a claim, an employee must submit an Arbitration Request Form, along with a $50 fee, and then Pinnacle has 30 days to respond to the employee's claim. The claim will proceed to arbitration if the employee is dissatisfied with Pinnacle's response or if Pinnacle fails to respond to the claim within 30 days (or some mutually agreed upon extended period). Dkt. No. 14–1 at ECF p. 11, IRA Rule 4.b.ii.

Pinnacle nevertheless argues that (1) the $50 fee is much smaller than the $400 filing fee Ms. Prasad had to pay to file the present action; and (2) Ms. Prasad never claimed an inability to pay the $400 filing fee by, for example, filing an application to proceed *in forma pauperis*. These arguments are unavailing.

In *Armendariz,* the plaintiff challenged an arbitration agreement that required employees to pay a share of the arbitrator's fees and expenses. The California Supreme Court concluded that the imposition of substantial forum fees is contrary to public policy and, therefore, a ground for invalidating or revoking an arbitration agreement:

> Accordingly, consistent with the majority of jurisdictions to consider this issue, we conclude that when an employer imposes mandatory arbitration as a condition of employment, the arbitration agreement or arbitration process cannot generally require the employee to bear any *type* of expense that the employee would not be required to bear if he or she were free to bring the action in court.

Armendariz, 24 Cal.4th at 110–11. In *Ingle*, the Ninth Circuit found a similar $75 filing fee was unconscionable, because employees were required to pay that fee to the defendant-employer as part of the process for initiating a claim against the company. While *Ingle* acknowledged that a "true filing fee might be appropriate under *Armendariz*," the fee at issue essentially "require[ed] employees to pay the fee to the very entity against which they seek redress," and therefore was not a type of expense that the employee would be required to bear in court. 328 F.3d at 1177.

The IRA's filing fee is substantively unconscionable.

d.   Cost-Splitting

The IRA requires the parties to split the costs of arbitration, no matter what the result, except that the employee's share is limited to $100.

Ms. Prasad objects to this requirement on the ground that requiring employees to pay for a share of the costs is unconscionable. Pinnacle contends that Ms. Prasad's cited cases are inapposite because the IRA limits an employee's share of the costs to no more than $100.

In *Ingle*, the Ninth Circuit rejected a cost-sharing scheme. There, the arbitration agreement provided that "each party shall pay one-half of the costs of arbitration following the issuance of the arbitration award." 328 F.3d at 1177. Additionally, the agreement provided that if the employee was unsuccessful on her claim, then the arbitrator had the discretion to charge the employee for the defendant-employer's share of the arbitration costs. The Ninth Circuit concluded that the fact that the employee potentially could be held responsible for the defendant's arbitration costs if her claim failed was sufficient to find the cost-sharing provision unconscionable. However, the Ninth Circuit found the provision especially unfair because it would require even a successful employee to bear her share of the arbitration costs. *Id.* at 1178. Although other provisions of the agreement apparently limited an employee's liability for fees, the Ninth Circuit was not swayed because the "default rule is that employees will share equally in the cost of arbitration." *Id.* at 1178 n.18.

Pinnacle points out that here, unlike in *Ingle*, the IRA's default rule is that an employee will not pay more than $100 for the arbitration fees and costs (in addition to the filing fee, discussed above). Nevertheless, to the extent that a strict interpretation of *Ingle* counsels against such cost-sharing provisions, the Court finds that the IRA's cost-sharing provision is unconscionable, but that Ms. Prasad has only demonstrated a modicum of unconscionability with respect to that provision.

e.   Pinnacle's Right of Unilateral Modification

Ms. Prasad argues that the IRA is unconscionable because it gives Pinnacle the unilateral right to modify or terminate the agreement's terms [on the last day of the year, after giving 30 days notice, and applicable only to claims filed after the modification took effect] . . .

Pinnacle argues that any measure of unconscionability is minimal because the IRA clearly requires advance notice to employees. For that reason, Pinnacle says that plaintiff's cited cases are inapposite.

In *Ingle*, the Ninth Circuit found a similar provision unconscionable. 328 F.3d at 1179. Even though advance written notice was required, the Ninth Circuit concluded that the provision was unconscionable because "such notice is trivial when there is no meaningful opportunity to negotiate the terms of the agreement. By granting itself the sole authority to amend or terminate the arbitration agreement, [defendant] proscribes an employee's ability to consider and negotiate the terms of her contract." *Id.* . . .

More recently, district courts within the Ninth Circuit have disagreed whether unilateral modification provisions are substantively unconscionable. Mikhak v. Univ. of Phoenix, No. C16-00901 CRB, 2016 WL 3401763, at *10–11 (N.D. Cal., June 21, 2016). As discussed in *Mikhak*, courts upholding unilateral modification provisions have reasoned that such clauses are limited by the duty to exercise the right of modification fairly and in good faith. . . . Borgarding v. JPMorgan Chase Bank, No. CV 16-2485 FMO (RAOx), 2016 WL 8904413, at *8 (C.D. Cal., Oct. 31, 2016) (concluding that a unilateral modification provision was not substantively unconscionable, and noting a consistent trend among California Courts of Appeal upholding unilateral modification provisions because implied in the unilateral right to modify is the obligation to do so upon reasonable and fair notice). . . .

Here, the IRA's unilateral modification provision weighs less heavily in Pinnacle's favor because it requires advance written notice and also prohibits retroactive modifications. As observed in *Mikhak*, however, *Ingle* is controlling authority. Thus, this Court concludes that the unilateral modification provision is unconscionable, because it withholds bargaining power from employees and because the IRA is a contract of adhesion in the first instance.

f.   Confidentiality Provisions

The IRA provides that, "[u]nless otherwise disallowed by statute," all aspects of an arbitration are confidential and not open to the public except (1) to the extent the parties otherwise agree in writing; (2) as may be appropriate in subsequent proceedings between the parties; or (3) as may otherwise be appropriate in response to a government agency or legal process. Dkt. No. 14–1 at ECF p. 15, IRA Rule 9.g.

Ms. Prasad argues that such provisions favor companies over employees because they essentially operate as "gag orders" and make it difficult for a plaintiff to mitigate the effects of bad behavior by a "repeat offender" employer. Pinnacle contends that the confidentiality provision is not unconscionable because it provides that the parties can agree otherwise and also provides that arbitration will not be confidential if confidentiality is disallowed by statute.

Ms. Prasad relies primarily on the Ninth Circuit's decisions in Davis v. O'Melveny & Myers, 485 F.3d 1066 (9th Cir. 2007), abrogated on other grounds as recognized in Ferguson v. Corinthian Colleges, Inc., 733 F.3d 928, 937 (9th Cir. 2013), and *Pokorny*, discussed above. Neither directs a finding of substantive unconscionability here.

Davis concluded that the confidentiality clause in question was so broad that it unconscionably favored the defendant. The clause "preclude[d] even mention to anyone 'not directly involved in the mediation or arbitration' of 'the content of the pleadings, papers, orders, hearings, trials, or awards in the arbitration' or even 'the existence of a controversy and the fact that there is a mediation or an arbitration proceeding.'" 485 F.3d at 1078. Such a clause, the Ninth Circuit reasoned, "would prevent an employee from contacting other employees to assist in litigating (or arbitrating) an employee's case" and would also "handicap if not stifle an employee's ability to investigate and engage in discovery." *Id.* At the same time, the court noted that the clause would put the defendant in a "in a far superior legal posture by preventing plaintiffs from accessing precedent while allowing [defendant] to learn how to negotiate and litigate its contracts in the future." *Id.* (internal quotations omitted and citations omitted). . . .

Several years later, in *Pokorny*, the Ninth Circuit reviewed a confidentiality provision that prevented the defendant's distributors "from disclosing 'to any other person not directly involved in the conciliation or arbitration process (a) the substance of, or basis for, the claim; (b) the content of any testimony or other evidence presented at an arbitration hearing or obtained through discovery; or (c) the terms [or] amount of any arbitration award.'" 601 F.3d at 1001. Further, the confidentiality provision took effect once a distributor became aware that she had a claim. *Id.* Thus, once aware of a potential claim, the distributor was "forever barred from disclosing to anyone not involved in the resolution of that claim the basis for it, the evidence supporting it, or the outcome of the arbitration," whereas the defendant was not similarly barred. *Id. Pokorny* held that the confidentiality provision, like the one in *Davis*, would unfairly hamper the employee's ability to investigate and prepare her case. *Id.* at 1001–02.

The IRA's confidentiality provision is not nearly as broad as those in *Davis* or *Pokorny*. More recently, in Poublon v. C.H. Robinson Co., 846 F.3d 1251 (9th Cir. 2017), the Ninth Circuit reviewed a confidentiality provision that is similar to the one in the IRA. . . . Rejecting the argument that *Pokorny* mandated a finding of substantive unconscionability, the Ninth Circuit reasoned:

> This argument fails. Several years after *Pokorny* was decided, the California Court of Appeal considered a trial court's denial of an employer's motion to compel arbitration. Sanchez v. CarMax Auto Superstores Cal. LLC, 224 Cal.App.4th 398, 168 Cal.Rptr.3d 473 (2014), *review denied* (June 11, 2014). Among the allegedly unconscionable provisions was a confidentiality provision requiring "that the arbitration (including the hearing and record of the proceeding) be confidential and not open to the public unless the parties agree otherwise, or as appropriate in any subsequent proceeding between the parties, or as otherwise may be appropriate in response to governmental or legal process." *Id.* at 408, 168 Cal.Rptr.3d 473. The trial court held that this provision, along with others in the agreement, unreasonably favored the employer because "they inhibit employees from discovering evidence from each other" while "[n]o such restrictions are applied in a court action." *Id.* The California Court of Appeal rejected this reasoning, holding that there is nothing unreasonable or prejudicial about "a secrecy provision with respect to the parties themselves," and the provision requiring confidentiality was not unconscionable. *Id.* (quoting Woodside Homes of Cal., Inc. v. Superior Court, 107 Cal.App.4th 723, 732, 132 Cal.Rptr.2d 35 (2003)).

> This holding is directly on point. The confidentiality provisions in both the Arbitration Procedure at issue here and in *CarMax* are substantially identical . . . Moreover, the California Court of Appeal rejected the same policy argument that Poublon makes

here, namely that such confidentiality provisions "inhibit employees from discovering evidence from each other." *See id.*

Poublon, 846 F.3d at 1266. The IRA's confidentiality provision is much closer to the one at issue in *Poublon* than those in question in *Davis* and *Pokorny*. This Court agrees with *Poublon* and concludes that it directs a finding that the IRA's confidentiality provision is not substantively unconscionable.

3. Severability

As discussed above, Pinnacle argues that any unconscionable terms may be severed from the IRA, and that the remaining terms properly may be enforced. Ms. Prasad contends that any agreement that contains more than one unconscionable term necessarily is permeated with unlawfulness and must be held unenforceable.

California law provides that when a court finds that a contract or any clause in it was unconscionable at the time it was made, the court "may refuse to enforce the contract, or it may enforce the remainder of the contract without the unconscionable clause, or it may so limit the application of any unconscionable clause as to avoid any unconscionable result." Cal. Civ. Code § 1670.5(a). "A court may 'refuse to enforce the entire agreement' only when it is 'permeated' by 'unconscionability.'" *Poublon*, 846 F.3d at 1272 (quoting *Armendariz*, 24 Cal.4th at 122).

"Courts are to look to the various purposes of the contract. If the central purpose of the contract is tainted with illegality, then the contract as a whole cannot be enforced." *Armendariz*, 24 Cal.4th at 124. "If the illegality is collateral to the main purpose of the contract, and the illegal provision can be extirpated from the contract by means of severance or restriction, then such severance and restriction are appropriate." *Id.*; *see also Poublon*, 846 F.3d at 1272 (same).

Courts properly may refuse to enforce an agreement where unconscionable provisions are too numerous and too important to be severed from the whole. *See Armendariz*, 24 Cal.4th at 124 (stating that multiple defects may "indicate a systematic effort to impose arbitration on an employee not simply as an alternative to litigation, but as an inferior forum that works to the employer's advantage.").

Claims of both Pinnacle and its employees are subject to arbitration. Dkt. No. 14–1 at ECF p. 6–7. There is no issue or argument presented as to any unconscionable limitation on the relief available to employees. And, while the Court has found several provisions unconscionable, . . . each of those provisions is collateral to the IRA's central purpose, which is to provide an alternate forum, before the American Arbitration Association or Judicial Arbitration Mediation Services, for the resolution of disputes between Pinnacle and its employees. Thus, the Court does not find that the IRA is so tainted with illegality that there is no lawful object of the contract to enforce. Nor is the Court persuaded by Ms. Prasad's contention that extirpating the unconscionable provisions from the IRA would render the contract a nullity.

The Court will, in its discretion, sever the unconscionable provisions from the IRA and enforce the remainder. Ms. Prasad may not maintain the class, collective and representative claims asserted in her original complaint, and the Court grants Pinnacle's motion to compel arbitration as to Ms. Prasad's individual claims.

IV. CONCLUSION

Based on the foregoing, the portions of the IRA found unconscionable are severed from the Agreement, Pinnacle's motion to compel arbitration is granted as to Ms. Prasad's individual claims, and this matter is stayed pending the completion of the arbitration.

NOTES

(1) *Class Arbitration.* The Prasad opinion makes note of a 2018 Supreme Court decision, Epic Sys. Corp. v. Lewis, 138 S. Ct. 1612 (2018), in support of its uncontested holding that Ms. Prasad's class action demands were preempted by the Federal Arbitration Act. *Epic Systems* is perhaps the climax of a series of Supreme Court decisions starting in 2010 that have broadly validated contractual waivers of class actions and class arbitration. In the most important among them, AT&T Mobility v. Concepcion, 563 U.S. 333 (2011), the Court was faced with a diversity case in which the lower courts, following California law, held that a class arbitration waiver was unconscionable. The plaintiffs argued that California law did not categorically ban class arbitration waivers. Instead, it applied the same unconscionability standard to class arbitration waivers and to class action waivers, thus not discriminating against arbitration. In *Concepcion*, the Court held that California's unconscionability doctrine "interferes with fundamental attributes of arbitration" and thus was preempted by the Federal Arbitration Act. It did not matter whether class *arbitration* and class *litigation* were treated identically; it mattered only whether the treatment of *class* arbitration departed materially from the treatment of *individual* arbitration. Put another way, state law cannot "stand as an obstacle to the accomplishment of the FAA's objectives." Concepcion, 563 U.S. at 344. By that standard, the California approach was problematic; courts almost always invalidated bars of class arbitration when assessed against the doctrine of unconscionability.

Since *Concepcion*, the Court has consistently limited the ability of state courts and state law to invalidate class arbitration. In Am. Express Co. v. Italian Colors Restaurant, 570 U.S. 228 (2013), the Court held that the FAA protected the right to pursue a statutory remedy, not the ability to do so; as a result, it enforced a contract waiving class arbitration even when the costs of individual litigation exceeded by far the potential recovery. Then in DIRECTV, Inc. v. Imburgia, 136 S. Ct. 463 (2015), the Court found a California law invalidating class action waivers to be preempted, even though the contract stated that the entire arbitration provision was unenforceable if state law made class-action waivers unenforceable. And then came *Epic Systems*.

Summing up the case authority yields the following: (1) When a contract is silent about class-action arbitration, the courts will not imply assent, (2) state law that invalidates class-action waivers as substantively unconscionable is inconsistent with the FAA and is preempted; (3) whether the parties can actually maintain individual actions is irrelevant to whether, as the FAA provides, they can "effectively vindicate" their rights.

This does not mean that class-action waivers are now automatically enforceable. *Concepcion* dealt with substantive unconscionability, not procedural unconscionability, so if a state's law allows a contract term, such as a class-action waiver, to be invalidated because of pure procedural unconscionability, that law may be upheld. In addition, it is still possible for class-action waivers to be held unconscionable under generally applicable state law, at least if that state law does not interfere with fundamental attributes of arbitration. But the result in Prasad is the rule, not the exception. See William B. Rubenstein, 2 Newberg on Class Actions § 6:63 (5th ed. 2018).

(2) *Gateway Again*. In Brower v. Gateway, Note 1, p. 296 above, consumers sought to avoid an arbitration clause included among the "Standard Terms and Conditions" that arrived with their mail-order computer, on the grounds that the term was unconscionable "due to the unduly burdensome procedure and cost for the individual consumer." The disputed clause required the New York buyers to arbitrate in Chicago. From an order granting Gateway's motion to dismiss, the consumers appealed. *Held*: Modified in part. Brower v. Gateway 2000, 676 N.Y.S.2d 569, 574 (App. Div. 1998).

Noting that the contract was not one of adhesion ("if any term of the agreement is unacceptable to the consumer, he or she can easily buy a competitor's product instead [and] reject Gateway's agreement by returning the merchandise"), the court found no procedural unconscionability: "any purchaser has 30 days within which to thoroughly examine the contents of their shipment, including the terms of the Agreement. . . . " As to the substantive aspect of the claim, the court found that the inconvenience of arbitrating before the International Chamber of Commerce [ICC] in Chicago was not sufficiently burdensome, but that the *cost* of doing so was. "Barred from resorting to the courts by the arbitration clause in the first instance, the designation of a financially prohibitive forum effectively bars consumers from this forum as well; consumers are thus left with no forum at all in which to resolve a dispute."

The court then noted a new arbitration agreement that Gateway "claims has been extended to all customers, past, present, and future (apparently through publication in a quarterly magazine sent to anyone who has ever purchased a Gateway product)." The new agreement provides for the consumer's choice of arbitration with either the ICC or the American Arbitration Association at any location agreed to by the parties. (The new terms further state that agreement as to location "shall not be unreasonably withheld.") The court remanded the case for the parties to seek appropriate substitution of the arbitrator.

PROBLEM

Add-on Arbitration Agreements. A bank decides that it prefers arbitration, rather than trial, as the mode of resolving potential disputes with its customers. It mails an announcement so stating to holders of accounts in the bank on the subject along with the bank's regular monthly statements. Each depositor has signed a signature card, upon opening an account, which incorporates the bank's rules and charges as set out in a booklet handed at that time to the depositor. According to the booklet, the bank may from time to time alter its rules upon giving notice to customers. The arbitration announcement refers to that provision, specifies an arbitration procedure, and states that either party to a dispute thereafter arising about charges and credits to an account may demand arbitration. In a class action by depositors brought against the bank for a declaratory judgment that the rule change is ineffective, what result? See Bank One v. Coates, 125 F.Supp.2d 819 (S.D. Miss. 2001).

SECTION 4.   PERFORMING IN GOOD FAITH

In Chapter 5, we examined terms, such as gap fillers and warranties, that the law sometimes adds to the parties' actual agreement in determining the full extent of their contractual obligations. The implied duty of good faith in performance and enforcement of a contract—also known as the implied covenant of good faith and fair dealing—is another such term, added to the parties' agreement both by the common law and the UCC. See Restatement § 205 and UCC § 1–304. The duty governs the performance and enforcement of a contract, and not its negotiation and formation. In reading the materials that follow, think about (i) what sorts of contracts include a duty of good faith; (ii) how courts determine the content of the duty; and (iii) the consequences of a party's failure to act in good faith.

Dalton v. Educational Testing Service
Court of Appeals of New York, 1995.
87 N.Y.2d 384, 663 N.E.2d 289.

[In May 1991, Brian Dalton took the Scholastic Aptitude Test (SAT), administered by Educational Testing Service (ETS). In November he took the test a second time and his combined score increased 410 points. Because the increase was more than 350 points, his test results fell within the ETS category of "Large Score Differences" or "discrepant scores," and members of the ETS Test Security Office reviewed his sheets. On finding disparate handwriting, they submitted the answer sheets to a document examiner, who opined that they were completed by different individuals. Dalton's case was then forwarded to the Board of

Review, which preliminarily decided that substantial evidence supported cancelling his November score.

When he registered for the November SAT, Dalton had signed a statement agreeing to the conditions in the New York State edition of the Registration Bulletin, which reserved to ETS "the right to cancel any test score if ETS believes that there is reason to question the score's validity." The Registration Bulletin further provided that, if "the validity of a test score is questioned because it may have been obtained unfairly, ETS [will] notif[y] the test taker of the reasons for questioning the score" and offer the test-taker five options: (1) the opportunity to provide additional information, (2) confirmation of the score by taking a free retest, (3) authorization for ETS to cancel the score and refund all fees, (4) third-party review by any institution receiving the test score, or (5) arbitration.

ETS notified Dalton of its preliminary decision to cancel his November SAT score in a letter informing him that the handwriting disparity and the difference in his scores suggested that someone else may have completed his answer sheet and advising him that he could supply additional information or elect one of the other options. Dalton opted to present additional information, including verification that he was suffering from mononucleosis during the May examination, diagnostic test results from a preparatory course he took prior to the November examination (he had taken no similar course prior to the May SAT) that were consistent with his performance on that test, a statement from an ETS proctor who remembered his presence in November, statements from two students—one previously unacquainted with Dalton—that he had been in the room during the test, and a report from a document examiner obtained by his family who concluded that Dalton was the author of both answer sheets.

After several Board of Review meetings, ETS submitted the handwriting exemplars to a second document examiner who, like its first, opined that the tests were not completed by the same individual. ETS continued to question the validity of Dalton's November score, and Dalton's father commenced an action on his son's behalf to prevent ETS from cancelling the November score and to compel its immediate release.

Following a 12-day nonjury trial, the trial judge found that ETS failed "to make even rudimentary efforts to evaluate or investigate the information" furnished by Dalton. The Board of Review members believed that the sole issue was the disparate handwriting and that evidence regarding Dalton's health or his presence was irrelevant. The judge concluded that ETS had failed to act in good faith as required by its contract and ordered ETS to release the November score. The Appellate Division affirmed.]

■ KAYE, CHIEF JUDGE. [W]e agree that ETS breached its contract with Dalton but differ as to the scope of the relief. By accepting ETS' standardized form agreement when he registered for the November SAT, Dalton entered into a contract with ETS. Implicit in all contracts is a covenant of good faith and fair dealing in the course of contract performance.

Encompassed within the implied obligation of each promisor to exercise good faith [is] a pledge that "neither party shall do anything which will have the effect of destroying or injuring the right of the other party to receive the fruits of the contract" (Kirke La Shelle Co. v. Armstrong Co., 263 N.Y. 79, 87, 188 N.E. 163). Where the contract contemplates the exercise of discretion, this pledge includes a promise not to act arbitrarily or irrationally in exercising that discretion . . . . The duty of good faith and fair dealing, however, is not without limits, and no obligation can be implied that "would be inconsistent with other terms of the contractual relationship" (Murphy v. American Home Prods. Corp., 58 N.Y.2d 293, 304).

The parties here agreed to the provisions in the Registration Bulletin, which expressly permit cancellation of a test score so long as ETS found "reason to question" its validity after offering the test-taker the five specified options. Nothing in the contract compelled ETS to prove that the test-taker cheated. Nor did the invitation to the test-taker to furnish ETS with relevant information reasonably and realistically translate into any requirement that ETS conduct a field investigation or gather evidence to verify or counter the test-taker's documentation. Indeed, such an obligation would be inconsistent with the contractual language placing the burden squarely on the test-taker to overcome the ETS finding of score invalidity. ETS, therefore, was under no duty, express or implied, to initiate an external investigation into a questioned score.

The contract, however, did require that ETS consider any relevant material that Dalton supplied to the Board of Review. Dalton triggered this obligation on the part of ETS by exercising his contractual option to provide ETS with information. Nevertheless, with the exception of the document examiner's report, ETS disputes the relevancy of this information. [However,] ETS expressly framed the dispositive question as one of suspected impersonation. Because the statements from the classroom proctor and November test-takers corroborated Dalton's contention that he was present at and in fact took the November examination, they were relevant to this issue. Likewise, inasmuch as the medical documentation concerning Dalton's health at the time of the May SAT provided an explanation for his poor performance on that examination, and the consistent diagnostic test results demonstrated his ability to achieve such a dramatic score increase, these items were also germane to the question whether it was Dalton or an imposter who completed the November examination.

When ETS fulfills its contractual obligation to consider relevant material provided by the test-taker and otherwise acts in good faith, the testing service—not the courts—must be the final arbiter of both the appropriate weight to accord that material and the validity of the test score. This Court will not interfere with that discretionary determination unless it is performed arbitrarily or irrationally. Where, however, ETS refuses to exercise its discretion in the first instance by declining even to consider relevant material submitted by the test taker, the legal question is whether this refusal breached an express or implied term of the contract, not whether it was arbitrary or irrational. Here, the courts below agreed that ETS did not consider the relevant information furnished by Dalton. By doing so, ETS failed to comply in good faith with its own test security procedures, thereby breaching its contract with Dalton.

We agree with the trial court and Appellate Division that Dalton is entitled to specific performance of the contract. Dalton is not, however, entitled to release of his score as though fully validated. The goal of specific performance is to produce "as nearly as is practicable, the same effect as if the contract had been performed" (Farnsworth, Contracts § 12.5, at 823 [1982]). Had the contract here been performed, ETS would have considered the information provided by Dalton in reaching a final decision. ETS never promised to release a score believed to be invalid, and the validity of Dalton's November SAT score has yet to be determined. Indeed, the trial court specifically noted that it was not resolving the question whether Dalton in fact took the November test.

Dalton is entitled to relief that comports with ETS' contractual promise—good-faith consideration of the material he submitted to ETS. We cannot agree with Dalton's assumption that ETS will merely rubber-stamp its prior determination without good-faith attention to his documentation and that reconsideration by ETS will be an empty exercise. Our conclusion that the contract affords Dalton a meaningful remedy rests also on the provision in the Procedures for Questioned Scores allowing Dalton to utilize one or more of the remaining four options in combination with renewed consideration by the Board of Review. Those options—including third-party review by any institution receiving the test score as well as arbitration—remain available should ETS determine that the information submitted fails to resolve its concerns about the validity of the November score.

Accordingly, the Appellate Division Order should be modified in accordance with this opinion and, as so modified, affirmed, without costs.

NOTES

(1) *Questions.* The court explains that ETS and not the courts must be the final arbiter when ETS "fulfills its contractual obligation to consider relevant material provided by the test-taker and otherwise acts in good faith." It therefore orders "good-faith consideration of the material he submitted to ETS." The court rejects Dalton's contention "that ETS will merely rubber-stamp its prior determination without good-faith attention to his documentation." What criteria would the court use to define "good faith" if it were asked to hold ETS in contempt for failure to comply with the court's

order? Two judges dissented on the ground that "ETS acted within its discretion in continuing the security process rather than releasing the score after considering and rejecting Dalton's evidence" and there was "no evidence that ETS acted arbitrarily in its decision-making process." 663 N.E.2d at 297 (Levine, J. dissenting).

(2) *The Case of the "Dynamic Duo."* Fight promoters Butch Lewis and Don King, doing business as the Dynamic Duo, Inc., made a contract with Hilton Hotels to stage at the Las Vegas Hilton the final four fights in the Unification Series, so called because it was designed to select a single champion from those recognized by three world boxing organizations. Hilton claimed that it was understood that Michael Spinks, the IBF champion, would be available for these events, though the contract was silent as to this. Spinks forfeited his title before the time for the events, and Hilton, claiming that the Dynamic Duo had deliberately induced the forfeiture, sued Dynamic Duo. From judgment for the defendant, plaintiff appealed. *Held*: Reversed and remanded.

"Even though Dynamic Duo did not have a contractual duty to furnish Spinks as a contestant in the Hilton events, it did have a legal duty not to interfere with Spinks' capacity to be a contestant and effectively prevent Spinks from participating in the Hilton events. If Lewis had Spinks stripped of the IBF title in order to undermine the Unification Series and permit Lewis and Dynamic Duo to make more money outside the series, this conduct could be seen as a breach of the covenant of good faith and fair dealing implied in the parties' contract." It was therefore error to exclude the testimony of the Chair of the Nevada Athletic Commission that he had "heard Lewis say that he was going to pull Spinks out of the Unification Series in order to make 'big money' elsewhere." Hilton Hotels Corp. v. Butch Lewis Productions, 808 P.2d 919 (Nev. 1991).

(3) *Statutory Obligation of Good Faith for Sales of Goods.* UCC § 1–304 provides that "Every contract or duty within [the Uniform Commercial Code] imposes an obligation of good faith in its performance and enforcement." Originally, "good faith" was generally defined to mean only "honesty in fact in the conduct or transaction concerned," a purely subjective test. See former UCC § 1–201(19). But Article 2 also contained a special definition of "good faith" for merchants: "honesty in fact and the observance of reasonable commercial standards of fair dealing-in the trade." Former UCC § 2–103(1)(b). When UCC Article 1 was revised in 2001, the heightened "merchant standard" of good faith in Article 2 was incorporated into the general definition of "good faith" in Article 1 and made applicable to all parties, whether or not they are merchants. See UCC § 1–201(b)(20).

(4) *A Comparative Approach.* The notion of an obligation of good faith in the performance of contract duties is a familiar one to civil law systems, most notably the German. Article 242 of the German Civil Code imposes an obligation of "performance according to the requirements of good faith [Treu and Glauben], common habits being duly taken into consideration." At the time of the promulgation of the Uniform Commercial Code, it was not a familiar notion to the common law, and the Code provisions occasioned considerable discussion. E. Allan Farnsworth, *Good Faith Performance and*

Commercial Reasonableness under the Uniform Commercial Code, 30 U. Chi. L. Rev. 666 (1963).

(5) *International Approaches.* Although Article 1.7 of the UNIDROIT Principles requires that a party "act in accordance with good faith and fair dealing in international trade," the CISG contains no comparable provision. Article 7(1) of the Convention provides that in "the interpretation of this Convention, regard is to be had to the observance of good faith in international trade," but this does not speak of a duty of performance by a contracting party.

"At a late stage in the preparation of the Sales Convention this language was adopted as a compromise between two divergent views: (a) Some delegations supported a general rule that the parties must observe principles of 'fair dealing' and must act in 'good faith'; Others resisted this step on the ground that 'fair dealing' and 'good faith' had no fixed meaning and would lead to uncertainty." Ultimately it was "decided that an obligation of 'good faith' should not be imposed loosely and at large, but should be restricted to a principle for interpreting the provisions of the Convention." John Honnold, Uniform Law for International Sales under the 1980 United Nations Convention 99 (3d ed. 1999).

The Content of the Obligation of Good Faith

Courts and commentators have had a much easier time agreeing on the existence of the obligation to perform contracts in good faith than they have had in defining the contours of that duty. The *Dalton* case, quoting an earlier New York decision, stated that the obligation encompassed a pledge that "neither party shall do anything which shall have the effect of destroying or injuring the right of the other party to receive the fruits of the contract." But what does this mean? Certainly, a party's failure to live up to the terms of the agreement can destroy or injure the right of the other party to receive the fruits of the contract, but failure to live up to the terms of the agreement would likely constitute breach even in the absence of an obligation of good faith. What duty is imposed by the obligation of good faith that is not already imposed by the terms of the agreement?

The Uniform Commercial Code addresses the meaning of the obligation through a statutory definition. UCC § 1–201(b)(20) states that good faith "means honesty in fact and the observance of reasonable commercial standards of fair dealing." How would a court applying this standard analyze the situation in *Dalton*?

Both common law courts and those applying the Uniform Commercial Code have struggled with the concept of good faith ever since the obligation began to be seen as an inherent component of contracts in the middle third of the 20th century (a development spurred, in no small part, by the incorporation of the obligation in the Uniform Commercial Code).

As you read the following materials—the first an excerpt from a well-known article by Professor Robert Summers followed by a response to Summers by Professor Steven Burton, who has written extensively on the doctrine of good faith, and concluding with an excerpt from a commentary by the Permanent Editorial Board for the Uniform Commercial Code—consider whether the different approaches to the concept with which each is wrestling are merely different descriptions of the same duty or would yield different results when applied to the facts of particular cases.

(A) ROBERT S. SUMMERS, "GOOD FAITH" IN GENERAL CONTRACT LAW AND THE SALES PROVISIONS OF THE UNIFORM COMMERCIAL CODE

54 Va. L. Rev. 195, 199–206 (1968)

What is the best way to determine a judge's meaning when he uses the phrase "good faith"? In the case law taken as a whole, does the term have a single general meaning of its own, or perhaps several such meanings? (The answers to these questions are closely linked.) Sometimes what a judge means by good faith will be instantly obvious, but frequently it will not be. When not, it may be that he is using the phrase loosely. But even if he is using it with care, there may still be unclarity. He might indicate only that, in a given context, parties are to act in good faith or that a party did or did not act in good faith, without elaborating at all. Or he might elaborate without communicating in any specific way—for example, by laying down some very general definition of good faith, such as acting "honestly" or "being faithful to one's duty or obligation." The analyst of such an opinion is likely to inquire: What is the meaning of good faith itself? He seems to assume that the phrase has some general meaning or meanings, one of which the judge presumably intends.

One of the principal theses of this Article is that in cases of doubt, a lawyer will determine more accurately what the judge means by using the phrase "good faith" if he does not ask what good faith itself means, but rather asks: What, in the actual or hypothetical situation, does the judge intend to rule out by his use of this phrase? Once the relevant form of bad faith is thus identified, the lawyer can, if he wishes, assign a specific meaning to good faith by formulating an "opposite" for the species of bad faith being ruled out. For example, a judge may say: "A public authority must act in good faith in letting bids." And from the facts or the language of the opinion it may appear that the judge is, in effect, saying: "The defendant acted in bad faith because he let bids only as a pretense to conceal his purpose to award the contract to a favored bidder." It can then be said that "acting in good faith" here simply means. letting bids without a preconceived design to award the contract to a favored bidder.

If good faith had a general meaning or meanings of its own—that is, if it were either univocal or ambiguous—there would seldom be occasion to derive a meaning for it from an opposite; its specific uses would almost always be readily and immediately understood. But good faith is not that kind of doctrine. In contract law, taken as a whole, good faith is an "excluder." It is a phrase without general meaning (or meanings) of its own and serves to exclude a wide range of heterogeneous forms of bad faith. In a particular context the phrase takes on specific meaning, but usually this is only by way of contrast with the specific form of bad faith actually or hypothetically ruled out. Aristotle was one of the first to recognize that the function of some words and phrases is not to convey general, "extractable" meanings of their own, but rather is to exclude one or more of a variety of things. He thought "voluntary" was such a word. And the late Professor J. L. Austin of Oxford made much of "excluders." His discussion of the term "real" is instructive:

Good faith, then, takes on specific and variant meanings by way of contrast with the specific and variant forms of bad faith which judges decide to prohibit. From the cases it would be possible to compile a list of forms of bad faith, with an opposite for each listed as the corresponding specific meaning of good faith. The beginnings of such a list might look like this:

Form of Bad Faith Content	*Meaning of Good Faith*
1. seller concealing a defect in what he is selling	fully disclosing material facts
2. builder willfully failing to perform in full, though otherwise substantially performing	substantially performing without knowingly deviating from specifications
3. contractor openly abusing bargaining power to coerce an increase in the contract price	refraining from abuse of bargaining power
4. hiring a broker and then deliberately preventing him from consummating the deal	acting cooperatively
5. conscious lack of diligence in mitigating the other party's damages	acting diligently
6. arbitrarily and capriciously exercising a power to terminate a contract	acting with some reason
7. adopting an overreaching interpretation of contract language	interpreting contract language fairly

8.   harassing the other party for   accepting adequate
       repeated assurances of performance   assurances

This list could run on and on, but it is unnecessary to extend it for present purposes. As it stands, it shows how specific meanings for good faith can be derived and shows that this phrase rules out radically heterogeneous forms of bad faith.

Given the specific meanings of good faith in the foregoing right-hand column, it may seem all the more natural to suppose, contrary to our "excluder" analysis, that there must be some single word or concise phrase which faithfully unifies all such specific meanings into one general meaning of the term. What about "honesty"? Is not acting in good faith equivalent to acting honestly? Numerous judges appear to have thought so, but this is wrong unless, of course, the definition of honesty is stretched beyond recognition. Honesty only rules out dishonesty in its various forms. But good faith, as used by many judges, excludes numerous forms of contractual bad faith besides dishonesty. For one thing, dishonesty is necessarily immoral, but in the eyes of many judges contractual bad faith is not necessarily immoral at all. A party may, for example, abuse his bargaining power, undercut the other party's efforts to perform, or act capriciously without having the "guilty mind" that would make his actions immoral-indeed, a party might even think this conduct is in the other party's own best interest. And despite this purity of mind, many judges could be counted on to say that such conduct conflicts with requirements of contractual good faith. As one judge stated, "Good faith in law . . . is not to be measured always by a man's own standard of right, but by that which it has adopted and prescribed as a standard for the observance of all men in their dealings with each other."

(B) STEVEN J. BURTON, MORE ON GOOD FAITH PERFORMANCE OF A CONTRACT: A REPLY TO PROFESSOR SUMMERS

69 Iowa L. Rev. 497, 498–499 (1984)

Having adopted the excluder approach, Professor Summers classified some bad faith performance cases in one of six general categories, not regarded as exhaustive: evasion of the spirit of the deal; lack of diligence and slacking off; willful rendering of only substantial performance; abuse of a power to specify terms; abuse of a power to determine compliance; and interference with, or failure to cooperate in, the other party's performance. The Restatement (Second) commentary generally follows this approach, adding that "[g]ood faith performance . . . of a contract emphasizes faithfulness to an agreed common purpose and consistency with the justified expectations of the other party; it excludes a variety of types of conduct characterized as involving 'bad faith' because they violate community standards of decency, fairness or reasonableness."

The Restatement-Summers formulation is inspired by the view that the good faith performance doctrine "is of a piece with explicit requirements of 'contractual morality' such as the unconscionability doctrine and various general equitable principles." "Contractual morality" implies a ground for judicial decision that lies outside of and may take precedence over the agreement of the parties. Explaining the good faith performance doctrine in such terms implies that courts typically use the doctrine to render agreed terms unenforceable or to impose obligations that are incompatible with the agreement reached at formation. Moreover, such an explanation implies that the vagueness of doing "justice and justice according to law," or ruling out "abuses" of powers to specify terms or to determine compliance, is a virtue. Such vagueness enables courts to decide each case according to the felt requirements of morality under the particular circumstances.

In my view, courts generally do not use the good faith performance doctrine to override the agreement of the parties. Rather, the good faith performance doctrine is used to effectuate the intentions of the parties, or to protect their reasonable expectations, through interpretation and implication. Courts might override agreed contract terms on grounds of "contractual morality" when the contract is unconscionable or otherwise unenforceable at formation, when estoppel or waiver are properly invoked, or when performance is impossible or commercially impracticable. They might resort to considerations of fairness or justice to interpret or supply terms when the intentions of the parties or their reasonable expectations cannot be reasonably ascertained. But it is hard to see what justifies a court in disregarding the agreement of the parties on grounds of "contractual morality" when the intentions of the parties or their reasonable expectations can be reasonably ascertained, and none of the above-mentioned doctrines properly are invoked.

(C) PERMANENT EDITORIAL BOARD (PEB) COMMENTARY NO. 10 SECTION 1–203 (1994)

UCC § 1–203[m] Does Not Create an Independent Cause of Action

The inherent flaw in the view that [the obligation of good faith codified at UCC § 1–203] supports an independent cause of action is the belief that the obligation of good faith has an existence which is conceptually separate from the underlying agreement. As the above discussion demonstrates, however, this is an incorrect view of the duty. "A party cannot simply 'act in good faith.' One acts in good faith relative to the agreement of the parties. Thus the real question is 'What is the Agreement of the parties?'" Put differently, good faith merely directs

---

[m]   Prior to the 2001 revision of UCC Article 1, the obligation of good faith, now codified in UCC § 1–304, was found in UCC § 1–203.

attention to the parties' reasonable expectations; it is not an independent source from which rights and duties evolve. The language of § 1–203 itself makes this quite clear by providing that the obligation to perform or enforce in good faith extends only to the rights and duties resulting from the parties' contract. The term "contract" is, in turn, defined as "the total legal obligation which results from the parties' agreement . . . ." Consequently, resort to principles of law or equity outside the Code are not appropriate to create rights, duties, and liabilities inconsistent with those stated in the Code. For example, a breach of a contract or duty within the Code arising from a failure to act in good faith does not give rise to a claim for punitive damages unless specifically permitted.

* * *

The correct perspective on the meaning of good faith performance and enforcement is the agreement of the parties. The critical question is, "Has 'X' acted in good faith with respect to the performance or enforcement of some right or duty under the terms of the Agreement?" It is therefore wrong to conclude that as long as the agreement allows a party to do something, it is under all terms and conditions permissible. Such a conclusion overlooks completely the distinction between merely performing or enforcing a right or duty under an agreement on the one hand and, on the other hand, doing so in a way that recognizes that the agreement should be interpreted in a manner consistent with the reasonable expectations of the parties in the light of the commercial conditions existing in the context under scrutiny. The latter is the correct approach. Examples are: (1) Is it reasonable for a buyer in a particular locale or trade to expect that an express quantity term in a contract is "not really" a quantity term, but a mere projection to be adjusted according to market forces?; (2) Does a party to a sales contract that permits discretionary termination have the right to expect that the decision whether to terminate will be made on the basis of sound business criteria?

The Official Comment to § 1–203 is amended by adding the following language at the end of the first paragraph:

> This section does not support an independent cause of action for failure to perform or enforce in good faith. Rather, this section means that a failure to perform or enforce, in good faith, a specific duty or obligation under the contract, constitutes a breach of that contract or makes unavailable, under the particular circumstances, a remedial right or power. This distinction makes it clear that the doctrine of good faith merely directs a court towards interpreting contracts within the commercial context in which they are created, performed, and enforced, and does not create a separate duty of fairness and reasonableness which can be independently breached.

Northwest, Inc. v. Ginsberg

Supreme Court of the United States, 2014.
572 U.S. 273.

■ JUSTICE ALITO[n] delivered the opinion of the Court. Like many airlines, petitioner Northwest, Inc. (Northwest), established a frequent flyer program, its WorldPerks Airline Partners Program, to attract loyal customers. Under this program, members are able to earn "miles" by taking flights operated by Northwest and other "partner" airlines. Members can then redeem these miles for tickets and service upgrades with Northwest or its airline partners.

Respondent became a member of Northwest's WorldPerks program in 1999, and as a result of extensive travel on Northwest flights, he achieved "Platinum Elite" status (the highest level available) in 2005.

In 2008, however, Northwest terminated respondent's membership, apparently in reliance on a provision of the WorldPerks agreement that provided that "[a]buse of the . . . program (including . . . improper conduct as determined by [Northwest] in its sole judgment may result in cancellation of the member's account." According to respondent, a Northwest representative telephoned him in June 2008 and informed him that his "Platinum Elite" status was being revoked because he had "'abused'" the program. In a letter sent about two weeks later, Northwest wrote:

> [Y]ou have contacted our office 24 times since December 3, 2007 regarding travel problems, including 9 incidents of your bag arriving late at the luggage carousel. Since December 3, 2007, you have continually asked for compensation over and above our guidelines. We have awarded you $1,925.00 in travel credit vouchers, 78,500 WorldPerks bonus miles, a voucher extension for your son, and $491.00 in cash reimbursements. Due to our past generosity, we must respectfully advise that we will no longer be awarding you compensation each time you contact us."

Respondent requested clarification of his status, but a Northwest representative sent him an e-mail stating that "[a]fter numerous conversations with not only the Legal Department, but with members of the WorldPerks department, I believe your status with the program should be very clear."

Alleging that Northwest had ended his membership as a cost-cutting measure tied to Northwest's merger with Delta Air Lines, respondent filed a class action in the United States District Court for the Southern

---

[n]   Samuel Anthony Alito Jr. (1950–), an Associate Justice of the Supreme Court of the United States, attended Princeton University and Yale Law School. He served as an Assistant United States Attorney and Deputy Assistant Attorney General before being nominated by President George H. W. Bush, in 1990, to the United States Court of Appeals for the Third Circuit. In 2006 President George W. Bush nominated Alito to serve on the Supreme Court.

District of California on behalf of himself and all other similarly situated WorldPerks members. Respondent's complaint asserted four separate claims. First, his complaint alleged that Northwest had breached its contract by revoking his "Platinum Elite" status without valid cause. Second, the complaint claimed that Northwest violated the duty of good faith and fair dealing because it terminated his membership in a way that contravened his reasonable expectations with respect to the manner in which Northwest would exercise its discretion. Third, the complaint asserted a claim for negligent misrepresentation, and fourth, the complaint alleged intentional misrepresentation. Respondent sought damages in excess of $5 million, as well as injunctive relief requiring Northwest to restore the class members' WorldPerks status and prohibiting Northwest from future revocations of membership.

The District Court held that respondent's claims for breach of the covenant of good faith and fair dealing, negligent misrepresentation, and intentional misrepresentation were pre-empted by the Airline Deregulation Act of 1978 (ADA or Act) as amended, 49 U.S.C. § 41713.

[According to the Court, Ginsberg's claims based on breach of the covenant of good faith and fair dealing would be preempted by the ADA if the Northwest's obligation under the covenant is a state-imposed obligation but not preempted if it the obligation is one that the parties voluntarily undertook.]

[W]e turn to the central issue in this case, i.e., whether respondent's implied covenant claim is based on a state-imposed obligation or simply one that the parties voluntarily undertook.

While most States recognize some form of the good faith and fair dealing doctrine, it does not appear that there is any uniform understanding of the doctrine's precise meaning. "[T]he concept of good faith in the performance of contracts 'is a phrase without general meaning (or meanings) of its own.'" Tymshare, Inc. v. Covell, 727 F.2d 1145, 1152 (C.A.D.C.1984) (Scalia, J.) (quoting Summers, *"Good Faith" in General Contract Law and the Sales Provisions of the Uniform Commercial Code*, 54 Va. L. Rev. 195, 201 (1968)); see also Burton, *Breach of Contract and the Common Law Duty to Perform in Good Faith*, 94 Harv. L. Rev. 369, 371 (1980). Of particular importance here, while some States are said to use the doctrine "to effectuate the intentions of parties or to protect their reasonable expectations," ibid., other States clearly employ the doctrine to ensure that a party does not "'violate community standards of decency, fairness, or reasonableness.'" Universal Drilling Co., LLC v. R & R Rig Service, LLC, 2012 WY 31, 37, 271 P.3d 987, 999[;] Restatement (Second) of Contracts § 205, Comment a (1979). See also Summers, *The General Duty of Good Faith—Its Recognition and Conceptualization*, 67 Cornell L. Rev. 810, 812 (1982).

Whatever may be the case under the law of other jurisdictions, it seems clear that under Minnesota law, which is controlling here, the implied covenant must be regarded as a state-imposed obligation.

Respondent concedes that under Minnesota law parties cannot contract out of the covenant. . . . And as a leading commentator has explained, a State's "unwillingness to allow people to disclaim the obligation of good faith . . . shows that the obligation cannot be implied, but is law imposed." 3A A. Corbin, Corbin on Contracts § 654A, p. 88 (L. Cunningham & A. Jacobsen eds. Supp. 1994). When the law of a State does not authorize parties to free themselves from the covenant, a breach of covenant claim is pre-empted [by the ADA].

Another feature of Minnesota law provides an additional, independent basis for our conclusion. Minnesota law holds that the implied covenant applies to "every contract," with the notable exception of employment contracts. The exception for employment contracts is based, in significant part, on "policy reasons," and therefore the decision not to exempt other types of contracts must be based on a policy determination, namely, that the "policy reasons" that support the rule for employment contracts do not apply (at least with the same force) in other contexts. When the application of the implied covenant depends on state policy, a breach of implied covenant claim cannot be viewed as simply an attempt to vindicate the parties' implicit understanding of the contract.

For these reasons, the breach of implied covenant claim in this case [is pre-empted by the ADA]. A State's implied covenant rules will escape pre-emption only if the law of the relevant State permits an airline to contract around those rules in its frequent flyer program agreement, and if an airline's agreement is governed by the law of such a State, the airline can specify that the agreement does not incorporate the covenant. While the inclusion of such a provision may impose transaction costs and presumably would not enhance the attractiveness of the program, an airline can decide whether the benefits of such a provision are worth the potential costs.

Our holding also does not leave participants in frequent flyer programs without protection. The ADA is based on the view that the best interests of airline passengers are most effectively promoted, in the main, by allowing the free market to operate. If an airline acquires a reputation for mistreating the participants in its frequent flyer program (who are generally the airline's most loyal and valuable customers), customers can avoid that program and may be able to enroll in a more favorable rival program.

NOTE

Common Law Versus the Code. This case involved Minnesota's common-law contractual covenant of good faith and fair dealing. In light of the Permanent Editorial Board Commentary reprinted above on page 681, how would the case have been resolved if it had involved the UCC's duty of good faith in the context of a sale of goods contract?

Market Street Associates v. Frey

United States Court of Appeals, Seventh Circuit, 1991.
941 F.2d 588.

[J.C. Penney, the retail chain, entered into a sale and leaseback arrangement with General Electric Pension Trust in order to finance Penney's growth. Under paragraph 34, the pension trust agreed to give reasonable consideration to requests by Penney for the financing of additional improvements. It went on to provide, in effect, that if the average annual appreciation in the property exceeded 6 percent, a breakdown in the negotiations over the financing of improvements would entitle Penney to buy back the property for less than its market value.

Twenty years later, Market Street Associates, Penney's successor under one of the leases, sought to buy back the property it leased from the pension trust in order to use the property to get financing elsewhere. When Erb of the pension trust, who was responsible for the property, was slow in responding, Orenstein of Market Street Associates then sent two letters to Erb formally requesting $4 million financing but not mentioning paragraph 34. (Orenstein later stated in his deposition that it had occurred to him that Erb might not know about paragraph 34.) Erb responded to the first by saying that the amount requested was below the pension trust's $7 million minimum. Over a month later, Orenstein wrote Erb that Market Street was exercising its option under paragraph 34, which had evidently become advantageous to it.

When the pension trust refused to sell, Market Street Associates sought specific performance. The district judge granted summary judgment for the pension trust, holding that Market Street Associates had violated the duty of good faith. Market Street Associates appealed.]

■ POSNER, JUDGE. [T]he judge emphasized a statement by Orenstein in his deposition that it had occurred to him that Erb mightn't know about paragraph 34, though this was unlikely (Orenstein testified) because Erb or someone else at the pension trust would probably check the file and discover the paragraph and realize that if the trust refused to negotiate over the request for financing, Market Street Associates, as Penney's assignee, would be entitled to walk off with the property for (perhaps) a song. The judge inferred that Market Street Associates didn't want financing from the pension trust—that it just wanted an opportunity to buy the property at a bargain price and hoped that the pension trust wouldn't realize the implications of turning down the request for financing. Market Street Associates should, the judge opined, have advised the pension trust that it was requesting financing pursuant to paragraph 34, so that the trust would understand the penalty for refusing to negotiate.

So we must consider the meaning of the contract duty of "good faith." The Wisconsin cases are cryptic as to its meaning though emphatic about its existence, so we must cast our net wider. The particular confusion to which the vaguely moralistic overtones of "good faith" give rise is the belief that every contract establishes a fiduciary relationship. A fiduciary is required to treat his principal as if the principal were he, and therefore he may not take advantage of the principal's incapacity, ignorance, inexperience, or even naiveté.

But it is unlikely that Wisconsin wishes, in the name of good faith, to make every contract signatory his brother's keeper, especially when the brother is the immense and sophisticated General Electric Pension Trust, whose lofty indifference to small (≤ $7 million) transactions is the signifier of its grandeur. In fact the law contemplates that people frequently will take advantage of the ignorance of those with whom they contract, without thereby incurring liability. The duty of honesty, of good faith even expansively conceived, is not a duty of candor. You can make a binding contract to purchase something you know your seller undervalues. That of course is a question about formation, not performance, and the particular duty of good faith under examination here relates to the latter rather than to the former. But even after you have signed a contract, you are not obliged to become an altruist toward the other party and relax the terms if he gets into trouble in performing his side of the bargain. Otherwise mere difficulty of performance would excuse a contracting party—which it does not.

But it is one thing to say that you can exploit your superior knowledge of the market—for if you cannot, you will not be able to recoup the investment you made in obtaining that knowledge—or that you are not required to spend money bailing out a contract partner who has gotten into trouble. It is another thing to say that you can take deliberate advantage of an oversight by your contract partner concerning his rights under the contract. Such taking advantage is not the exploitation of superior knowledge or the avoidance of unbargained-for expense; it is sharp dealing.

The essential issue bearing on Market Street Associates' good faith was Orenstein's state of mind, a type of inquiry that ordinarily cannot be concluded on summary judgment, and could not be here. If Orenstein believed that Erb knew or would surely find out about paragraph 34, it was not dishonest or opportunistic to fail to flag that paragraph, or even to fail to mention the lease, in his correspondence and (rare) conversations with Erb, especially given the uninterest in dealing with Market Street Associates that Erb fairly radiated. To decide what Orenstein believed, a trial is necessary.

Reversed and remanded.

NOTES

(1) *Opinion on Remand.* After a trial on remand, the district judge held that Market Street Associates was not entitled to specific performance. "While Orenstein initially assumed that the Trust would review the lease

and make its determination as to whether it should provide financing to Market Street in light of paragraph 34, he subsequently recognized that the Trust was not operating under paragraph 34. While Orenstein knew this fact, he did not bring the matter to the Trust's attention, and continued to write ambiguous letters, until he wished to utilize the purchase option, thereby purchasing the property at a discounted cost. By so doing, this court concludes that Orenstein breached his duty to use good faith in his dealings with the Trust, and Market Street is not entitled to specific performance." Market Street Associates v. Frey, 817 F.Supp. 784, 788 (E.D. Wis. 1993).

(2)   *Opportunism.* Note that Judge Posner says that a trial is necessary to determine whether Orenstein was "dishonest or opportunistic." Five years later, Judge Posner's colleague, Judge Easterbrook, discussed opportunism in Industrial Representatives, Inc. v. CP Clare Corp., 74 F.3d 128, 129–30, 132 (7th Cir. 1996). " 'Opportunism' in the law of contracts usually signifies one of two situations. First, there is effort to wring some advantage from the fact that the party who performs first sinks costs, which the other party may hold hostage by demanding greater compensation in exchange for its own performance. The movie star who sulks (in the hope of being offered more money) when production is 90% complete, and reshooting the picture without him would be exceedingly expensive, is behaving opportunistically in this sense. [citing Alaska Packers' Ass'n v. Domenico, p. 438 above.] Second, there is an effort to take advantage of one's contracting partner in a way that could not have been contemplated at the time of drafting, and which therefore was not resolved explicitly by the parties. [citing *Market Street Associates*.] Contract law does not require parties to be fair, or kind, or reasonable, or to share gains or losses equitably. It does require parties to avoid taking advantage of the opportunities that arise from sequential performance, when the contract does not cover a particular subject."

(3)   *Additional Economic Perspectives.* On good faith, Professor Burton, in *Breach of Contract and the Common Law Duty to Perform in Good Faith*, 94 Harv. L. Rev. 369 (1980), concluded his analysis thusly:

> The theory of contract breach by failing to perform in good faith has been derived from a cost perspective on the contractual expectation interest. Cases holding one party's exercise of discretion in performance to constitute a breach of contract and those holding such conduct to be legitimate can be distinguished with reference to facts tending to show that the discretion-exercising party is or is not using discretion to recapture opportunities forgone upon entering the contract. Discretion in performance may be exercised legitimately for the purposes reasonably contemplated by the parties, including ordinary business reasons. It cannot be exercised for the purpose of recapturing forgone opportunities, for such conduct harms the expectation interest of the dependent party.
>
> The good faith performance doctrine, like contract law generally, functions to support the market. It advances the time at which alternative opportunities are deemed to be forgone to the time of formation, when they otherwise would be forgone upon the

expenditure of resources in performance of the contract. A promisee thus may rely not only on the express terms of a contract, but also on the customary implications of the express terms as to opportunities forgone in the commercial setting. The law puts the burden of careful contract planning on the discretion-exercising promisor who wishes to depart from the norm, because such a promisor is in the best position to secure the expectations of both parties. The cost perspective on the contractual expectation interest thus renders the common law good faith performance doctrine reckonable.

See also Richard A. Posner, *Let Us Never Blame a Contract Breaker*, 107 Michigan Law Review 1349 (2009); Todd D. Rakoff, *Good Faith in Contract Performance:* Market Associates Ltd. Partnership v. Frey, 120 Harv. L. Rev. 1187 (2007).

Would the actions of ETS in *Dalton* violate the "recapturing forgone opportunities" standard suggested by Professor Burton?

Bloor v. Falstaff Brewing Corp.

United States Court of Appeals, Second Circuit, 1979.
601 F.2d 609.

■ FRIENDLY, CIRCUIT JUDGE. This action, wherein federal jurisdiction is predicated on diversity of citizenship, 28 U.S.C. § 1332, was brought in the District Court for the Southern District of New York, by James Bloor, Reorganization Trustee of Balco Properties Corporation, formerly named P. Ballantine & Sons (Ballantine), a venerable and once successful brewery based in Newark, N.J. He sought to recover from Falstaff Brewing Corporation (Falstaff) for breach of a contract dated March 31, 1972, wherein Falstaff bought the Ballantine brewing labels, trademarks, accounts receivable, distribution systems and other property except the brewery. The price was $4,000,000 plus a royalty of fifty cents on each barrel of the Ballantine brands sold between April 1, 1972 and March 31, 1978. Although other issues were tried, the appeals concern only two provisions of the contract. These are:

8. Certain Other Covenants of Buyer.

(a) After the Closing Date the [Buyer] will use its best efforts to promote and maintain a high volume of sales under the Proprietary Rights.

2(a)(v) [The Buyer will pay a royalty of $.50 per barrel for a period of 6 years], provided, however, that if during the Royalty Period the Buyer substantially discontinues the distribution of beer under the brand name "Ballantine" (except as the result of a restraining order in effect for 30 days issued by a court of competent jurisdiction at the request of a governmental authority), it will pay to the Seller a cash sum equal to the years and fraction thereof remaining in the Royalty Period times

$1,100,000, payable in equal monthly installments on the first
day of each month commencing with the first month following
the month in which such discontinuation occurs.

Bloor claimed that Falstaff had breached the best efforts clause, 8(a), and
indeed that its default amounted to the substantial discontinuance that
would trigger the liquidated damage clause, 2(a)(v). In an opinion that
interestingly traces the history of beer back to Domesday Book and
beyond, Judge Brieant upheld the first claim and awarded damages but
dismissed the second. Falstaff appeals from the former ruling, Bloor from
the latter. Both sides also dispute the court's measurement of damages
for breach of the best efforts clause.

We shall assume familiarity with Judge Brieant's excellent opinion,
454 F.Supp. 258 (S.D.N.Y. 1978), from which we have drawn heavily, and
will state only the essentials. Ballantine had been a family owned
business, producing low-priced beers primarily for the northeast market,
particularly New York, New Jersey, Connecticut and Pennsylvania. Its
sales began to decline in 1961, and it lost money from 1965 on. On June
1, 1969, Investors Funding Corporation (IFC), a real estate conglomerate
with no experience in brewing, acquired substantially all the stock of
Ballantine for $16,290,000. IFC increased advertising expenditures,
levelling off in 1971 at $1 million a year. This and other promotional
practices, some of dubious legality, led to steady growth in Ballantine's
sales despite the increased activities in the northeast of the "nationals"[1]
which have greatly augmented their market shares at the expense of
smaller brewers. However, this was a profitless prosperity; there was no
month in which Ballantine had earnings and the total loss was
$15,500,000 for the 33 months of IFC ownership.

After its acquisition of Ballantine, Falstaff continued the $1 million
a year advertising program, IFC's pricing policies, and also its policy of
serving smaller accounts not solely through sales to independent
distributors, the usual practice in the industry, but by use of its own
warehouses and trucks—the only change being a shift of the retail
distribution system from Newark to North Bergen, N.J., when brewing
was concentrated at Falstaff's Rhode Island brewery. However, sales
declined and Falstaff claims to have lost $22 million in its Ballantine
brand operations from March 31, 1972 to June 1975. Its other activities
were also performing indifferently, although with no such losses as were
being incurred in the sale of Ballantine products, and it was facing
inability to meet payrolls and other debts. In March and April 1975
control of Falstaff passed to Paul Kalmanovitz, a businessman with 40
years experience in the brewing industry. After having first advanced $3
million to enable Falstaff to meet its payrolls and other pressing debts,
he later supplied an additional $10 million and made loan guarantees, in
return for which he received convertible preferred shares in an amount

---

[1]   Miller's, Schlitz, Anheuser-Busch, Coors, and Pabst.

that endowed him with 35% of the voting power and became the
beneficiary of a voting trust that gave him control of the board of
directors.

Mr. Kalmanovitz determined to concentrate on making beer and
cutting sales costs. He decreased advertising, with the result that the
Ballantine advertising budget shrank from $1 million to $115,000 a
year.[2] In late 1975 he closed four of Falstaff's six retail distribution
centers, including the North Bergen, N.J. depot, which was ultimately
replaced by two distributors servicing substantially fewer accounts. He
also discontinued various illegal practices that had been used in selling
Ballantine products.[3] What happened in terms of sales volume is shown
in plaintiff's exhibit 114 J, a chart which we reproduce in the margin.[4]
With 1974 as a base, Ballantine declined, 29.72% in 1975 and 45.81% in
1976 as compared with a 1975 gain of 2.24% and a 1976 loss of 13.08%
for all brewers excluding the top 15. Other comparisons are similarly
devastating, at least for 1976.[5] Despite the decline in the sale of its own
labels as well as Ballantine's, Falstaff, however, made a substantial
financial recovery. In 1976 it had net income of $8.7 million and its year-

---

[2]   This was for cooperative advertising with purchasers.

[3]   There were two kinds of illegal practices, the testimony on both of which is,
unsurprisingly, rather vague. Certain "national accounts", i.e. large draught beer buyers, were
gotten or retained by "black bagging", the trade term for commercial bribery. On a smaller scale,
sales to taverns were facilitated by the salesman's offering a free round for the house of
Ballantine if it was available ("retention"), or the customer's choice ("solicitation"). Both
practices seem to have been indulged in by many brewers, including Falstaff before Kalmanovitz
took control.

[4]   Percentage Increase or Decline in Sales Volume of Ballantine Beer, Falstaff Beer and
Comparable Brewers for Years Ending December 31, 1972–1976.

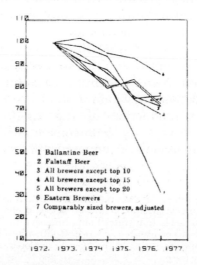

[5]   Falstaff argues that a trend line projecting the declining volume of Ballantine's sales
since 1966, before IFC's purchase, would show an even worse picture. We agree with plaintiff
that the percentage figures since 1974 are more significant; at least the judge was entitled to
think so.

end working capital had increased from $8.6 million to $20.2 million and its cash and certificates of deposit from $2.2 million to $12.1 million.

Seizing upon remarks made by the judge during the trial that Falstaff's financial standing in 1975 and thereafter "is probably not relevant" and a footnote in the opinion, 454 F.Supp. at 267 n. 7,[6] appellate counsel for Falstaff contend that the judge read the best efforts clause as requiring Falstaff to maintain Ballantine's volume by any sales methods having a good prospect of increasing or maintaining sales or, at least, to continue lawful methods in use at the time of purchase, no matter what losses they would cause. Starting from this premise, counsel reason that the judge's conclusion was at odds with New York law, stipulated by the contract to be controlling, as last expressed by the Court of Appeals in Feld v. Henry S. Levy & Sons, Inc., 37 N.Y.2d 466, 373 N.Y.S.2d 102, 335 N.E.2d 320 (1975). The court was there dealing with a contract whereby defendant agreed to sell and plaintiff to purchase all bread crumbs produced by defendant at a certain factory. During the term of the agreement defendant ceased producing bread crumbs because production with existing facilities was "very uneconomical," and the plaintiff sued for breach. This case was governed by § 2–306 of the Uniform Commercial Code [which the opinion quoted].

Affirming the denial of cross-motions for summary judgment, the court said that, absent a cancellation on six months' notice for which the contract provided:

> defendant was expected to continue to perform in good faith and could cease production of the bread crumbs, a single facet of its operation, only in good faith. Obviously, a bankruptcy or genuine imperiling of the very existence of its entire business caused by the production of the crumbs would warrant cessation of production of that item; the yield of less profit from its sale than expected would not. Since bread crumbs were but a part of defendant's enterprise and since there was a contractual right of cancellation, good faith required continued production until cancellation, even if there be no profit. In circumstances such as these and without more, defendant would be justified, in good faith, in ceasing production of the single item prior to cancellation only if its losses from continuance would be more than trivial, which, overall, is a question of fact.

---

[6] "Even if Falstaff's financial position had been worse in mid-1975 than it actually was, and even if Falstaff had continued in that state of impecuniosity during the term of the contract, performance of the contract is not excused where the difficulty of performance arises from financial difficulty or economic hardship. As the New York Court of Appeals stated in 407 E. 61st St. Garage, Inc. v. Savoy Corp., 23 N.Y.2d 275, 281, 296 N.Y.S.2d 338, 344, 244 N.E.2d 37, 41 (1968):

"[W]here impossibility or difficulty of performance is occasioned only by financial difficulty or economic hardship, even to the extent of insolvency or bankruptcy, performance of a contract is not excused. (Citations omitted.)"

37 N.Y.2d 471–72, 373 N.Y.S.2d 106, 335 N.E.2d 323.[7] Falstaff argues from this that it was not bound to do anything to market Ballantine products that would cause "more than trivial" losses.

We do not think the judge imposed on Falstaff a standard as demanding as its appellate counsel argues that he did. Despite his footnote 7, see note 6 supra, he did not in fact proceed on the basis that the best efforts clause required Falstaff to bankrupt itself in promoting Ballantine products or even to sell those products at a substantial loss. He relied rather on the fact that Falstaff's obligation to "use its best efforts to promote and maintain a high volume of sales" of Ballantine products was not fulfilled by a policy summarized by Mr. Kalmanovitz as being:

> We sell beer and you pay for it.

> We sell beer, F.O.B. the brewery. You come and get it.

however sensible such a policy may have been with respect to Falstaff's other products. Once the peril of insolvency had been averted, the drastic percentage reductions in Ballantine sales as related to any possible basis of comparison, see fn. 5, required Falstaff at least to explore whether steps not involving substantial losses could have been taken to stop or at least lessen the rate of decline. The judge found that, instead of doing this, Falstaff had engaged in a number of misfeasances and nonfeasances which could have accounted in substantial measure for the catastrophic drop in Ballantine sales shown in the chart, see 454 F.Supp. at 267–72. These included the closing of the North Bergen depot which had serviced "Mom and Pop" stores and bars in the New York metropolitan area; Falstaff's choices of distributors for Ballantine products in the New Jersey and particularly the New York areas, where the chosen

---

[7]　The text of the Feld opinion did not refer to the case cited by Judge Brieant in the preceding footnote, 407 East 61st Garage, Inc. v. Savoy Fifth Avenue Corporation, 23 N.Y.2d 275, 296 N.Y.S.2d 338, 244 N.E.2d 37 (1968), which might suggest a more onerous obligation here. The Court of Appeals there reversed a summary judgment in favor of the defendant, which had discontinued operating the Savoy Hilton Hotel because of substantial financial losses, in alleged breach of a five-year contract with plaintiff wherein the defendant had agreed to use all reasonable efforts to provide the garage with exclusive opportunity for storage of the motor vehicles of hotel guests. Although the court did use the language quoted by Judge Brieant, the actual holding was simply that "an issue of fact is presented whether the agreement did import an implied promise by Savoy to fulfill its obligations for an entire five-year period." 23 N.Y.2d at 281, 296 N.Y.S.2d at 343.

Other cases suggest that under New York law a "best efforts" clause imposes an obligation to act with good faith in light of one's own capabilities. In Van Valkenburgh v. Hayden Publishing Co., 30 N.Y.2d 34 (1972), the court held a publisher liable to an author when, in clear bad faith after a contract dispute, he hired another to produce a book very similar to plaintiff's and then promoted it to those who had been buying the latter. On the other hand, a defendant having the exclusive right to sell the plaintiff's product may sell a similar product if necessary to meet outside competition, so long as he accounts for any resulting losses the plaintiff can show in the sales of the licensed product. Parev Products Co. v. I. Rokeach & Sons, 124 F.2d 147 (2 Cir. 1941). A summary definition of the best efforts obligation, cited by Judge Brieant, 454 F.Supp. at 266, is given in Arnold Productions, Inc. v. Favorite Films Corp., 176 F.Supp. 862, 866 (S.D.N.Y.1959), aff'd 298 F.2d 540 (2 Cir. 1962), to wit, performing as well as "the average prudent comparable" brewer.

The net of all this is that the New York law is far from clear and it is unfortunate that a federal court must have to apply it.

distributor was the owner of a competing brand; its failure to take advantage of a proffer from Guinness-Harp Corporation to distribute Ballantine products in New York City through its Metrobeer Division; Falstaff's incentive to put more effort into sales of its own brands which sold at higher prices despite identity of the ingredients and were free from the $.50 a barrel royalty burden; its failure to treat Ballantine products evenhandedly with Falstaff's; its discontinuing the practice of setting goals for salesmen; and the general Kalmanovitz policy of stressing profit at the expense of volume. In the court's judgment, these misfeasances and nonfeasances warranted a conclusion that, even taking account of Falstaff's right to give reasonable consideration to its own interests, Falstaff had breached its duty to use best efforts as stated in the Van Valkenburgh decision, supra, 30 N.Y.2d at 46, 330 N.Y.S.2d at 334, 281 N.E.2d at 145.

Falstaff levels a barrage on these findings. The only attack which merits discussion is its criticism of the judge's conclusion that Falstaff did not treat its Ballantine brands evenhandedly with those under the Falstaff name. We agree that the subsidiary findings "that Falstaff but not Ballantine had been advertised extensively in Texas and Missouri" and that "[i]n these same areas Falstaff, although a 'premium' beer, was sold for extended periods below the price of Ballantine," while literally true, did not warrant the inference drawn from them. Texas was Falstaff territory and, with advertising on a cooperative basis, it was natural that advertising expenditures on Falstaff would exceed those on Ballantine. The lower price for Falstaff was a particular promotion of a bicentennial can in Texas, intended to meet a particular competitor.

However, we do not regard this error as undermining the judge's ultimate conclusion of breach of the best efforts clause. While that clause clearly required Falstaff to treat the Ballantine brands as well as its own, it does not follow that it required no more. With respect to its own brands, management was entirely free to exercise its business judgment as to how to maximize profit even if this meant serious loss in volume. Because of the obligation it had assumed under the sales contract, its situation with respect to the Ballantine brands was quite different. The royalty of $.50 a barrel on sales was an essential part of the purchase price. Even without the best efforts clause Falstaff would have been bound to make a good faith effort to see that substantial sales of Ballantine products were made, unless it discontinued under clause 2(a)(v) with consequent liability for liquidated damages. Cf. Wood v. Duff-Gordon, 222 N.Y. 88 (1917) (Cardozo, J.). Clause 8 imposed an added obligation to use "best efforts to promote and maintain a high volume of sales." Although we agree that even this did not require Falstaff to spend itself into bankruptcy to promote the sales of Ballantine products, it did prevent the application to them of Kalmanovitz' philosophy of emphasizing profit über alles without fair consideration of the effect on Ballantine volume. Plaintiff was not obliged to show just what steps Falstaff could reasonably have taken to maintain a high volume for Ballantine products. It was sufficient to show that Falstaff simply didn't care about Ballantine's volume and was content to allow this to plummet so long as that course was best for Falstaff's overall profit picture, an inference which the judge permissibly drew. The burden then shifted to Falstaff to prove there was nothing significant it could have done to promote Ballantine sales that would not have been financially disastrous.

Having correctly concluded that Falstaff had breached its best efforts covenant, the judge was faced with a difficult problem in computing what the royalties on the lost sales would have been. There is no need to rehearse the many decisions that, in a situation like this, certainty is not required; "[t]he plaintiff need only show a 'stable foundation for a reasonable estimate of royalties he would have earned had defendant not breached.'" Contemporary Mission, Inc. v. Famous Music Corp., 557 F.2d 918, 926 (2 Cir.1977), quoting Freund v. Washington Square Press, Inc., 34 N.Y.2d 379, 383 (1974). After carefully considering other possible bases, the court arrived at the seemingly sensible conclusion that the most nearly accurate comparison was with the combined sales of Rheingold and Schaefer beers, both, like Ballantine, being "price" beers sold primarily in the northeast, and computed what Ballantine sales would have been if its brands had suffered only the same decline as a composite of Rheingold and Schaefer.

We also reject plaintiff's complaint on his cross-appeal that the court erred in not taking as its standard for comparison the grouping of all but the top 15 brewers, Ballantine having ranked 16th in 1971. The judge was entirely warranted in believing that the Rheingold-Schaefer combination afforded a better standard of comparison. [Finally, the court rejected plaintiff's contention that Falstaff's actions triggered the liquidated damage clause.]

The judgment is affirmed. Plaintiff may recover two-thirds of his costs.

NOTES

(1) *Best Efforts.* This case involves interpretation and application of a "best efforts" clause in the parties' agreement. Is there a connection between interpretation and application of a best efforts clause and the duty of good faith? Would Falstaff's duties under the contract be any different if the best efforts clause had not appeared in the contract?

(2) *What Efforts Are "Best"?* How can a court determine what a duty of best efforts requires in a particular case? Courts have often looked to the behavior of others engaged in like activities. See the court's reference near the end of footnote 7 to the performance of " 'the average prudent comparable' brewer." UNIDROIT Principles art. 5.1.4(2) requires "such efforts as would be made by a reasonable person of the same kind in the same circumstances."

The question is of interest to lawyers. In Lucas v. Hamm, 364 P.2d 685, 690 (Cal. 1961), the court took a tolerant view of the efforts of a lawyer who, in drafting a will for a client, had failed to apply correctly the rule against perpetuities and restraints on alienation and was sued by the disappointed beneficiaries named in the will. The court, noting that these were subjects that "have long perplexed the courts and the bar," thought "it would not be proper to hold that defendant failed to use such skill, prudence and diligence as lawyers of ordinary skill and capacity ordinarily exercise."

For another test, see Olympia Hotels Corp. v. Johnson Wax Dev. Corp., 908 F.2d 1363, 1373 (7th Cir. 1990), in which Judge Posner said that if a hotel-management firm "worked as hard for [this customer] as it did for its other, but noncomplaining, customers, then it was using best efforts."

(3) *As if a Single Firm*. Professors Goetz and Scott propose a more sophisticated test. They note that "best efforts" contracts are often used instead of vertical integration in a single firm and argue that such contracts "can most sensibly be construed as requiring the level of effort necessary to maximize the joint net product flowing from the contractual relationship. This joint-maximization criterion produces the largest possible net product for ultimate division between the parties." They admit, however, that it is hard to tell from damage computations in cases like *Bloor* what standard of performance has been applied. In *Bloor*, damages were "projected from the behavior of 'comparable' brands that were marketed by integrated non-royalty-paying firms. Thus, the 'comparable brand' volume behavior could be regarded as a good proxy for the joint-maximization outcome for the Ballantine-Falstaff contractual combination. There is, however, no real indication in the decision that the use of integrated firms as comparable entities was understood or intended in this way." Charles Goetz and Robert Scott, *Principles of Relational Contracts*, 67 Va. L. Rev. 1089, 1149–50, 1123 (1981). See also Mark Gergen, *The Use of Open Terms in Contracts*, 92 Colum. L. Rev. 997 (1992).

For support, see Tigg Corp. v. Dow Corning Corp., 962 F.2d 1119, 1125 (3d Cir. 1992), in which the court said that a duty of best efforts requires a buyer under an exclusive dealing agreement "to consider the best interests of the seller and itself as if they were one firm."

(4) *Exclusivity*. Would Otis Wood have broken his contract with Lady Duff Gordon if he had handled the fashions of another designer at the same time? Does a promise to use best efforts imply exclusivity?

In Van Valkenburgh, Nooger & Neville, Inc. v. Hayden Publishing Co., 281 N.E.2d 142 (N.Y. 1972), cited by Judge Friendly, the court concluded that a publisher's undertaking to use efforts to promote an author's works "does not close off the right of a publisher to issue books on the same subject, to negotiate with and pay authors to write such books and to promote them fully according to the publisher's economic interests, even though those later publications adversely affect the contracting author's sales. Although a publisher has a general right to act on its own interests in a way that may incidentally lessen an author's royalties, there may be a point where that activity is so manifestly harmful to the author, and must have been seen by the publisher to be so harmful, as to justify the court in saying there was a breach of the covenant to promote the author's work."

This qualification of a party's "general right to act on its own interests" is illustrated by Joyce Beverages of N.Y., Inc. v. Royal Crown Cola Co., 555 F.Supp. 271 (S.D.N.Y. 1983), in which Joyce had agreed to "devote its best efforts so as to achieve maximum distribution and sale [of Royal Crown] beverages within the territory." The court held that undertaking to distribute Seven-Up beverages was a breach. "A best efforts clause is not per se breached by a mere undertaking of a competitive product line; it depends on the circumstances. [But here the] entire pattern of industry practice since the beginning of the soft drink industry has been for distributors to distribute only one cola. This best efforts clause is properly read in terms of the trade practice and usage." In addition, "Seven-Up's national advertising campaign denigrates the content of Royal Crown cola products. Seven-Up's slogan is 'You don't need caffeine and neither does your cola.' "

SECTION 5.　　PUBLIC POLICY

In the preceding sections the law's concern has been with protecting one party to an agreement against imposition by the other party. In this section the concern shifts to the protection of the public at large against imposition by *both* parties. When will a court refuse to enforce an agreement, fairly and freely entered into, on the ground that to enforce it would contravene "public policy"?

Such agreements fall into two general categories. First are contracts that violate specific criminal laws; these are commonly called "illegal contracts." A court will not generally enforce a private agreement to do what the law explicitly prohibits. The enactment of a criminal code is itself understood as a clear expression of policy, even though statutes proscribing conduct rarely speak to the enforceability of contracts involving the conduct. (Two exceptions are usury and gambling statutes, which characteristically state that contracts in violation of them are "void.")

But what if there is no explicit prohibition against a particular act, product, or type of agreement? When no statute is quite "on point," how do courts determine whether the enforcement of a contract violates public policy? In this second category of cases, courts often detect or derive policy from legislation *related* to the subject of the agreement, again, even when the statutes themselves are silent on contractual enforceability. In other cases, courts have formulated policies from their own sense of social or legal norms. And despite entreaties from one or the other party, courts sometimes find insufficient authority to apply the doctrine of public policy, so that performance will *not* be excused.

Discerning the sources of public policy is an important, and sometimes contentious endeavor. One now classic and much quoted concern was stated by Judge Burrough in 1824:

> If [a contract] be illegal, it must be illegal either on the ground
> that it is against public policy, or against some particular law.
> I, for one, protest . . . against arguing too strongly upon public

> policy;—it is a very unruly horse, and when once you get astride it you never know where it will carry you. It may lead you from the sound law. It is never argued at all but when other points fail.

Richardson v. Mellish, (1824) 130 Eng. Rep. 294, 303.

In Wagenseller v. Scottsdale Memorial Hosp., 710 P.2d 1025, 1033 (Ariz. 1985), the Arizona Supreme Court considered the question of "where 'public policy' may be found and how it may be recognized and articulated." The court stated:

> As the expressions of our founders and those we have elected to our legislature, our state's constitution and statutes embody the public conscience of the people of this state. It is thus in furtherance of their interests to hold that an employer may not with impunity violate the dictates of public policy found in the provisions of our statutory and constitutional law.

> We do not believe, however, that expressions of public policy are contained only in the statutory and constitutional law, nor do we believe that all statements made in either a statute or the constitution are expressions of public policy. Turning first to the identification of other sources, we note our agreement with the following:

> Public policy is usually defined by the political branches of government. Something "against public policy" is something that the Legislature has forbidden. But the Legislature is not the only source of such policy. In common-law jurisdictions the courts too have been sources of law, always subject to legislative correction, and with progressively less freedom as legislation occupies a given field. Lucas v. Brown & Root, 736 F.2d 1202, 1205 (8th Cir. 1984).

Although public policy arguments arise most often when a party argues that it against public policy to enforce a particular contract, positive public policy can also be implemented through contract. For example, non-discrimination has been a policy goal of the Minority Business Enterprise provision of the Public Works Employment Act of 1977; for a case involving this provision, see Note 4 p. 303 above. Other examples include purchasing regulations that favor domestic products, or regional industries, or that require the use of "green" materials in construction, manufacture, or the provision of services. See generally William Leimkuhler, *Enforcing Social and Economic Policy Through Government Contracts*, 1980 Ann. Surv. Am. L. 539; Christopher Yukins, *Making Federal Information Technology Accessible: A Case Study in Social Policy and Procurement*, 33 Pub. Contract L.J. 667 (2004) (discussing Section 508 of the Federal Rehabilitation Act, requiring that all information technology bought into the United States be accessible to persons with disabilities).

Consider also the public policies embodied in the practice of outsourcing. As an increasing number of public functions—schools, prisons, security—are contracted to private parties in the general turn to market competition, might privatization itself be understood as an instance of public policy? See Jody Freeman, *Extending Public Norms Through Privatization*, 116 Harv. L. Rev. 1285 (2003). For thoughtful explorations, see John Donahue, *The Privatization Decision: Public Ends, Private Means* (1989); and Martha Minow and Jody Freeman, eds., *Government by Contract* (2009).

NOTES

(1) *The Unruly Horse?* A recent empirical study of cases in which a public policy defense was raised suggests "that Judge Burrough's metaphorical horse [p. 697 above] is not uniformly 'unruly'—categories of these cases can be discerned, and some categories appear more orderly than others." David Adam Friedman, *Bringing Public Order to Contracts Against Public Policy*, 39 Fla. St. U. L. Rev. 563, 566 (2012). In particular, Professor Friedman's analysis discerned that public policy defenses which appealed to specific statutes or regulations were twice as successful as those that appealed to general notion of public policy.

(2) *Legislative Declarations.* How should courts resolve conflicts between common law understandings of public policy and specific legislative declarations? Consider Hubner v. Spring Valley Equestrian Ctr., 975 A.2d 992 (N.J. Super. Ct. App. Div. 2009), *rev'd*, 1 A.3d 618 (N.J. 2010), in which Gloria Hubner was injured after she was thrown from a horse when it tripped over training logs at the Spring Valley Equestrian Center. Hubner sued for negligence and Spring Valley moved for summary judgment on the ground that Hubner's contract with the Equestrian Center included an exculpatory clause. Hubner argued that the exculpatory clause was void as a matter of New Jersey public policy. The Superior Court granted Spring Valley's summary judgment motion based on the New Jersey Equine Activities Act, N.J.S.A. 5:15. Section 5:15–1 of the Act, legislative findings and declarations, states "The Legislature therefore determines that the allocation of the risks and costs of equine animal activities is an important matter of public policy and it is appropriate to state in law those risks that the participant voluntarily assumes for which there can be no recovery." Specifically addressing the assumption of inherent risk, Section 5:15–3 further declares that "[a] participant and spectator are deemed to assume the inherent risks of equine animal activities created by equine animals, weather conditions, conditions of trails, riding rings, training tracks, equestrians, and all other inherent conditions . . . . " Hubner appealed and the Supreme Court of New Jersey found that, on the specific facts of the case, Hubner's claim fell within explicit statutory exceptions to exculpatory clause enforceability. That decision prompted legislative efforts to clarify its intention regarding the wide scope of exculpatory clauses in the riding industry. See *New Jersey Law Revision Commission Tentative Report Relating to Equine Activities Act* (2012), available at http://www.lawrev.state.nj.us/Equine%20Act/equine TR121012.pdf.

Who has the final say in determining the public policy of the state: the courts or the Legislature? Consider the court's statement in *Hubner* that "use of an exculpatory agreement to permit escape from liability for personal injury authorized by N.J.S.A. 5:15–9 is so likely to upset the Legislature's balance of risks and costs that absent further direction from the Legislature, enforcement as a defense to liability in those circumstances must be denied as contrary to the policy expressed by the Legislature."

PROBLEM

To begin thinking about public policy as a basis for nonenforcement of a contract, consider the following facts ripped from the sports headlines. According to an investigation by the National Football League's security department, from 2009 to 2011, members of the New Orleans professional football team, the Saints, voluntarily funded a special "pay for performance" bounty program under which cash payments were made to players who injured players from opposing teams. Players received $1,500 for a "knockout" (opposing player unable to return to game) and $1,000 for a "cart-off" (opposing player carried off the field), with payments, sometimes for specific players, doubled or tripled during the playoffs. For the National Football League statement on the program, see *Full NFL Statement into 'Bounty' Program Run by New Orleans Saints*, available at http://www.nola.com/saints/index.ssf/2012/03/full_nfl_statement_into_bounty.html.

How would you characterize the contractual structure of the alleged bounty program? As the program is described in the NFL investigation, if a Saints linebacker accomplished a cart-off, could he sue for his bounty? Finally, what, if any, public policies are implicated by the alleged program? What are the sources of such policies? Does it help to know that the NFL has a "Non-Contract Bonuses" provision in its collective bargaining agreement that bans payment for on-field misconduct?

(A) ILLEGAL CONTRACTS

Even in the case of criminal prohibition on conduct, there are subtleties in application. If, for example, the performance of a contract *contributes* to an illegal act, but is not itself prohibited, should the disappointed party be able to sue for damages? Should a contract that is the *product* of an illegal act, such as bribery or an anti-trust conspiracy, be enforced? Should it matter if the statute mandates other specific penalties?

As you read the following materials, consider two contrasting positions on these questions. In 1692, Lord Holt expressed the influential view that "every contract made for or about any matter or thing which is prohibited and made unlawful by any statute, is a void contract, though the statute itself doth not mention that it shall be so, but only inflicts a penalty on the offender, because a penalty implies a prohibition, though there are no prohibitory words in the statute." Bartlett v. Vinor, (1692) 90 Eng. Rep. 750 (K.B.). In 1936, Professor Walter Gellhorn wrote: "The judges are not bound to regard as void every contract which seems in some way to fall within the general aura of the criminal law, but only those whose enforcement, they are persuaded, after respectfully studying the 'public policy' involved, will disserve the general interest as it has been indicated by the legislature." Walter Gellhorn, *Contracts and Public Policy*, 35 Colum. L. Rev. 679, 686 (1936).

Blossom Farm Products Co. v.
Kasson Cheese Co., Inc.

Wisconsin Court of Appeals, 1986.
133 Wis.2d 386, 395 N.W.2d 619.

■ SCOTT, CHIEF JUSTICE. Blossom Farm Products Company (Blossom) appeals from a judgment dismissing its suit on an open-account contract for $138,306 owed by defendant Kasson Cheese Company, Inc. (Kasson) for its last purchase of Isokappacase.[1] Blossom contends that the trial court was in error when it concluded that the contract was illegal and unenforceable. Blossom argues that the contract for the sale of Isokappacase was not illegal because use of a yield-enhancing agent in cheese by Kasson was not illegal, even though Blossom knew Kasson was misbranding the product and selling it as real cheese.[2] In its cross-appeal, Kasson contends that the contract between Blossom and Kasson was illegal because Blossom knew, not only that Kasson's product was labeled illegally, but it participated in and benefited from the illegality.

The trial court held that the contract was illegal and unenforceable because both parties knew and benefited from Kasson's "illegal use" of

---

[1] A brief description of the properties and uses of Isokappacase will help clarify the legal issues regarding Kasson's use of the product. Isokappacase, manufactured by Marvin T. Silverman, president of PTX, was designed for two purposes: (1) as a starter medium; and (2) as a bacteriophage preventive. When used as a starter, Isokappacase would be added to milk, pasteurized with the milk at high temperatures, and inoculated so as to grow a culture that would be put into cheese. When used in this way, the protein in Isokappacase serves a dual purpose: (1) stimulation for nutrient purposes (growth of bacteria); and (2) production of extra yield in the starter medium. For this use, the protein level on a dry basis need be less than 2% or 3% of the total solids of a medium.

If needed as a bacteriophage preventive, Isokappacase protects a specific strain of organism from being killed off by a virus. Because bacteriophage preventive is an insignificant problem with mozzarella and provolone, Kasson's need for Isokappacase as a phage preventive would have been minimal.

A third use for Isokappacase was as a yield enhancer whereby the powder had to be put directly into the *cheese milk*. An important distinction exists between milk and cheese milk. When Isokappacase is used as a starter, it is mixed with milk to begin the starter culture which, in turn, is introduced into the cheese milk. When Isokappacase is introduced directly into cheese milk and is not used in the starter medium to stimulate the growth of bacteria, it is used as a yield enhancer.

Because Isokappacase contains more than 75% protein or caseins, its direct introduction into the cheese milk substantially increases the amount of protein so as to get additional cheese yield to cover the cost of the Isokappacase. When Isokappacase is used as a yield enhancer, however, the resulting product must: (1) be labeled a cheese "analog," an imitation cheese, or a name other than real cheese; and (2) list the ingredients in the end product to reflect the larger percentage of protein or caseins characteristic of imitation cheese.

[2] "Real cheese" must comply with the Federal Standards of Identity as found in 21 CFR, secs. 101.2, 101.3, 133.155 and 133.181 (1986). Wisconsin adopted the federal standards of identity regarding misbranding of food. *See* secs. 97.03 and 97.09, Stats.

Isokappacase. Because we conclude that enforcement of the contract is against public policy, we affirm the trial court's refusal to enforce the contract.

The dispositive issues on appeal are:

(1) whether there is sufficient evidence in the record to support the trial court's findings of fact; and

(2) whether the contract between Blossom and Kasson regarding the sale and purchase of Isokappacase is unenforceable.

Julian Podell, a salesman at Blossom, was sole United States distributor for PTX Food Corporation's (PTX) production of Isokappacase. Blossom sold this product to Kasson from August 1981 until February 13, 1984. The label on Isokappacase indicated that the product was a "starter media, a bacteriophage preventive medium." In fact, however, because Isokappacase contained more than 75% caseins or protein, its composition was characteristic primarily of a yield enhancer. Kasson introduced the Isokappacase directly into the cheese milk to enhance cheese yields from milk but did not label its final product as imitation cheese as required by federal standards.

Blossom was aware of the fact that Kasson's extremely large volume purchases of the product could only be accounted for by Kasson's use of Isokappacase as a yield enhancer. Both Kasson[3] and Blossom[4] benefited economically from this volume purchase and use. When Kasson stopped using Isokappacase as a yield enhancer, PTX stopped making the product.[5] Further facts will be discussed as needed.

Generally, if a promisee has substantially performed its part of the contract, enforcement of a promise is not precluded on grounds of public policy because of some improper use that the promisor intends to make of what he obtains; however, if the promisee acts for the purpose of furthering the promisor's improper use, the promisee is barred from recovering. Restatement (Second) of Contracts § 182 (1981). Whether the promisee has acted for such purpose is a question of fact which may be evidenced by the promisee's "doing of specific acts to facilitate the promisor's improper use" and/or "a course of dealing with persons engaged in improper conduct." *Id.* at comment b. A court engages in a balancing process to determine factually if the improper use or conduct

---

[3] Kasson's yield with the use of Isokappacase was 2.8 pounds of cheese per pound of Isokappacase.

[4] Blossom's list of shipments of Isokappacase to Kasson from August 1981 to February 13, 1984 records a total of 2,699,200 pounds. After the initial order of 20 fifty-pound bags of Isokappacase, the majority of orders were for 840 50-pound bags (42,000 pounds total per order) for a cost of $71,820 per order. Podell testified that two 42,000 pound shipments were missing from the record. As a result of these volume sales, Blossom grossed in excess of $5,000,000.

[5] Kasson stopped its use of Isokappacase approximately three weeks after its receipt of a letter from the Wisconsin Department of Agriculture, Trade and Consumer Protection, stating that protein concentrate or caseins were "illegal ingredients" if added to cheese and would result in an "adulterated" product.

at issue is unenforceable on grounds of public policy. *Id.* at § 178 and § 182 comments a and b.

The trial court held the contract "illegal and unenforceable." We restrict our holding to whether the contract is unenforceable. Our position is in keeping with the Restatement at §§ 178 and 182, which deal with the issue in terms of "unenforceability" rather than "illegality."

We turn to the Restatement because the Wisconsin cases relied on by the parties do not distinguish between illegal contracts which are unenforceable and legal contracts which contravene public policy and are thus unenforceable. See Kryl v. Frank Holton & Co., 217 Wis. 628, 259 N.W. 828 (1935); Lowe v. Crocker, 154 Wis. 497, 143 N.W. 176 (1913). Despite some confusion in these cases regarding this distinction, we read these cases to be consistent with our decision and support our extension of this distinction, in keeping with the Restatement.

SUFFICIENCY OF EVIDENCE

We must first determine whether sufficient facts exist in the record to support the trial court's findings of: (1) Kasson's improper conduct; and (2) Blossom's knowledgeable involvement with Kasson. We conclude sufficient facts exist on both points.

Blossom, as promisee, performed its part of the contract; it delivered the $138,306 shipment of Isokappacase to Kasson. Blossom's contract to sell Isokappacase to Kasson was legal; use of a yield enhancer is legal as long as the end product is properly labeled as an imitation or analog cheese with the concomitant ingredient line listed. Only when a promisor, such as Kasson, intends to use Isokappacase as a yield enhancer and sell its end product as a real cheese that purportedly conforms to federal standards of identity does the use of Isokappacase become improper.[6]

Even with Kasson's intended purpose of improperly labeling its end product, enforcement of Kasson's promise to pay Blossom for sale and delivery of the Isokappacase would not be precluded on grounds of public policy without knowledgeable involvement by Blossom. Testimony from several parties provides sufficient evidence of Blossom's knowledgeable involvement in Kasson's improper conduct.

Podell testified that Blossom knew Kasson was using Isokappacase as a yield enhancer. Podell acknowledged that once he recognized that Kasson was ordering about one hundred times more Isokappacase than would be needed if it were using the product as a starter medium, he

---

[6]   Had Kasson labeled its end product as "mozzarella or provolone cheese analog" or any other comparable label indicating an imitation cheese and listed ingredients so as to remove itself from the requirements of the federal standards of identity, it would have been able to sell its end product for only 70¢ per pound rather than the $1.40 per pound it received for selling it as real cheese.

realized that such large volume orders could only mean that Kasson was using the product as a yield enhancer.[7]

Likewise, Marvin Silverman, president of PTX, testified that while he sold 100% of its production of Isokappacase to Podell who, in turn, sold over 90% to Kasson, he did not know the exact percentage Blossom sold to Kasson because Podell kept "a secret list, confidential." Silverman also testified that he knew Kasson was putting Isokappacase directly into its cheese milk because he was called in to solve a clotting problem at Kasson. In order to facilitate Kasson's use of the product in this way, Silverman suggested the technical assistance of a pump. Based on such use of the product, Silverman testified that: (1) he knew that Kasson had to be using Isokappacase in a way other than as a starter media; and (2) he told Donald Vande Yacht, president of Kasson, that its use of Isokappacase in this manner would necessarily result in an end product not conforming to federal standards for real cheese. He said that he subsequently inferred that Kasson had to be mislabeling its end product as real cheese, for had it not, he believed that Kasson would have suffered huge losses before two and one-half years had passed. He testified that he told Podell of his conclusions about Kasson's improper conduct.

Other testimony confirmed Blossom's knowledgeable dealings in Kasson's improper conduct. Bruce Keller, a consultant for Kasson, testified that all of Podell's figures regarding Kasson's volume use of the product were figures projecting yield and cost analysis only. Vande Yacht said he was told by Podell and Silverman that because Isokappacase was a casein product, the end product would not yield real cheese; nonetheless, Vande Yacht testified that, even though he did not directly tell Podell or Silverman that he was labeling his end product as mozzarella and provolone, he continued to order volume shipments and label his imitation cheese as real cheese, primarily because he considered such practice to be within what he called a "grey area" of the law.

Thus, despite Blossom's direct knowledge of Kasson's use of Isokappacase as a yield enhancer and its tacit knowledge of Kasson's misbranding of its end product as real cheese, it still continued to ship volume orders of Isokappacase to Kasson. Both Podell and Silverman knew or should have known that Kasson's volume use of Isokappacase as a yield enhancer meant that it was also improperly mislabeling its end product because they knew that Kasson could not possibly have survived economically if its end product had been sold as an imitation cheese at its concomitantly lower price.

Based on this evidence, the trial court had sufficient evidence on which to base the factual part of its finding that Blossom, aware of

---

[7]   Had Kasson been using Isokappacase as a starter medium, it would have had to have used nearly a billion pounds of milk per month to achieve the correct proportion; rather, Kasson was using only approximately 60,000,000 pounds of milk per month, a fact which Podell knew. Hence, the small volume of milk and the large volume of Isokappacase used would necessarily lead one familiar with these figures, as was Podell, to conclude that Isokappacase was being used as a yield enhancer.

Kasson's use of Isokappacase and subsequent mislabeling of its end product, nonetheless continued to sell Isokappacase to Kasson in large quantities, thereby facilitating Kasson's improper conduct.

UNENFORCEABILITY OF THE CONTRACT

A decision as to the enforceability of a contract can be reached after a careful balancing, in light of all the circumstances, of the interest in the enforcement of the particular promise against the policy against enforcement of such terms. Restatement (Second) of Contracts § 178 (1981). In weighing a public policy against enforcement of a term, account is taken of: (1) the strength of that policy as manifested by legislation or judicial decisions; (2) the likelihood that a refusal to enforce the term will further that policy; (3) the seriousness of any misconduct involved and the extent to which it was deliberate; and (4) the directness of the connection between that misconduct and the term. *Id.*

A promise may be unenforceable if it involves conduct offensive to public policy, even though the promise does not actually induce the conduct. *Id.* at comments b, c and d. If the conduct to be engaged in by the promisor is deemed improper conduct because it is against public policy, the promisee's doing of specific acts to facilitate the improper use is a bar to recovery. *Id.* at § 182 comment b.

State legislation which adopted federal standards of identity enforces the public policy of accurately distinguishing imitation or analog cheese from real cheese and labeling it accordingly. Sec. 97.09, Stats. Even though Vande Yacht of Kasson testified that neither Podell nor Silverman was directly told about the mislabeling, sufficient evidence reveals that Podell tacitly knew of Kasson's subsequent misbranding of its end product because of the economics of the situation. Furthermore, despite being aware of Kasson's improper conduct, Blossom chose to overlook it and continued to supply volume shipments to Kasson, thereby engaging in a course of dealing which facilitated Kasson in its improper conduct. This course of dealing benefited both Blossom and Kasson. Because mislabeling cheese involves conduct offensive to public policy, the trial court correctly concluded that the transaction which anticipated such improper conduct is unenforceable.

By the Court.—Judgment affirmed.

NOTES

(1) *In Pari Delicto.* Where does the court's holding that the contract is unenforceable leave the parties from a practical point of view? Although the court does not use the phrase, it has in effect found the parties to be *in pari delicto* with regard to their contractual dispute; this mean they should be left as the court found them. The doctrine is this: In circumstances of equal fault, the position of the defendant is the more compelling (*in pari delicto potior est conditio defendantis*). "While it may not always seem an honorable thing to do, a party to an illegal agreement is permitted to set up the illegality as a

defense even though the party may be alleging his or her own turpitude." *Early Detection Center, Inc. v. Wilson*, 811 P.2d 860, 867 (Kan. 1991). Of course, many a claimant has contended that the parties are *not* equally culpable.

In some exceptional cases, a party *in pari delicto* may obtain restitutionary relief, alleviating the harshness that would result if parties to an illegal contract were always "left where they are found, to stew in their own juice." *Id.* According to the Restatement, restitution is available to a party "who would otherwise suffer a forfeiture that is disproportionate in relation to the contravention of public policy involved." See Restatement § 197 cmt. b. (This rule has been somewhat reformulated by Restatement (Third), Restitution and Unjust Enrichment § 32(2).)

(2) *Clean Hands.* Suits for equitable remedies such as specific performance and rescission are sometimes disposed of on the maxim, "He who comes into equity must come with clean hands." Application of the doctrine poses several questions: How clean must hands be? Is cleanliness a relative matter? Must there be a relation between the bad behavior and the suit itself? Consider this case: A lumber wholesaler sought to enforce a non-compete clause against a former employee who had gone on his own in violation of the terms of the covenant. The employee argued that by engaging in unethical practices—eavesdropping on clients in a scheme involving telephone calls and making improper profits on customer claims—the employer had unclean hands and equitable relief should be denied. The wholesaler responded that the employee had engaged in some of the very practices complained about. The trial court dismissed the complaint and awarded the employee his attorney's fees. Both sides appealed. *Held:* Affirmed in part; reversed in part. *North Pacific Lumber Co. v. Oliver*, 596 P.2d 931, 943 (Or. 1979).

Noting that "[e]ven equity does not require saintliness," the Supreme Court of Oregon stated that "the misconduct must bear a certain kind of relationship to the subject matter of the suit before a court will consider it." *Id.* at 939. The court held that the eavesdropping, while perhaps a violation of a state statute, was in this case unconnected with the employee's work and therefore did not implicate the clean hands doctrine. The improper profit scheme was another matter: "A court of equity should not lend its aid to an employer who attempts to enforce a contract of employment the performance of which involves participation by the employee in such wrongdoing." *Id.* at 944. Because the employee had knowingly "participated in the ill-gotten gains," the court reversed the trial court's award of attorney's fees.

X.L.O. Concrete Corp. v. Rivergate Corp.

New York Court of Appeals, 1994.
83 N.Y.2d 513, 611 N.Y.S.2d 786, 634 N.E.2d 158.

■ CIPARICK, JUDGE. The question presented in this action for breach of contract, account stated, and unjust enrichment is whether interposition of an antitrust illegality defense under the Donnelly Act (General

Business Law §§ 340 et seq.) prevents enforcement of the contract between these parties as a matter of law.

The parties, plaintiff X.L.O. Concrete Corp., as subcontractor, and defendant Rivergate Corporation, as general contractor, entered into a written contract on May 12, 1983 for construction of the concrete superstructure and fills of a project located in Manhattan. Plaintiff fully performed its obligations under the contract and sought payment of $844,125.07, the balance due and owing. Defendant refused to pay on the ground that the contract was an integral feature of an extortion and labor bribery operation known as the "Club." [The trial court dismissed the complaint and Rivergate appealed.]

The "Club" was an arrangement between the "Commission" of La Cosa Nostra, a ruling body comprised of four of the five New York City organized crime family bosses, and seven concrete construction companies operating in New York City, and the District Council of Cement and Concrete Workers, Laborers International Union of North America (see United States v. Salerno, 868 F.2d 524, 528–529, [describing the Club and its workings in fuller detail]). The Commission decided which concrete companies would be permitted to undertake construction jobs in New York City worth more than two million dollars; contractors who took jobs over two million were required to pay the Commission two percent of the contract price for guaranteed "labor peace." The Commission not only approved which companies got which jobs, but also rigged the bidding to ensure that the designated company would submit the lowest bid. The Commission enforced compliance through threatened or actual labor unrest or violence. In May 1981, plaintiff became the last concrete contractor doing business in New York City to join the Club.

[The Commission allocated the Rivergate project to X.L.O. who paid the 2% "labor peace" fee. X.L.O. then negotiated a contract with Rivergate for $16,544,125. Since the contract was so large, X.L.O. also gave a representative from the Commission, who was also the president of the District Council of Cement and Concrete Workers, a $50,000 "gift."]

The record indicates that defendant negotiated the contract with full knowledge of the Club and its rules. Plaintiff completed the work agreed upon under the contract and, upon defendant's refusal to pay, commenced this action. [The Supreme Court dismissed the complaint, and certain counterclaims; the Appellate Division modified the judgment to the extent of reinstating the complaint, and in certain other respects.]

The interposition of antitrust defenses in contract actions is not favored (see Kelly v. Kosuga, 358 U.S. 516, 518, 3 L.Ed.2d 475, 79 S.Ct. 429). The concern is that "successful interposition of antitrust defenses is too likely to enrich parties who reap the benefits of a contract and then seek to avoid the corresponding burdens" (Viacom International, Inc. v. Tandem, 526 F.2d 593, 599). Nevertheless, antitrust defenses will be upheld in cases where a court's judgment would result in enforcement of the "precise conduct made unlawful by the Act" (Kelly v. Kosuga, 358 U.S. 516, 520, 3 L.Ed.2d 475, 79 S.Ct. 429). Beyond that point, however, "courts are to be guided by the overriding general policy 'of preventing people from getting other people's property for nothing when they purport to be buying it' " (id. at 520–521 [quoting Continental Wall Paper Co. v. Louis Voight & Sons Co., 212 U.S. 227, 271, 53 L.Ed. 486, 29 S.Ct. 280] [Holmes, J., dissenting]). Thus, a contract which is legal on its face and does not call for unlawful conduct in its performance is not voidable simply because it resulted from an antitrust conspiracy (*see, Kelly, supra but see Continental Wall Paper, supra*).

[T]he critical question is whether the contract is so integrally related to the agreement, arrangement or combination in restraint of competition that its enforcement would result in compelling performance of the precise conduct made unlawful by the antitrust laws (id. at 520). This question we cannot answer on the record before us. Whether the contract was an indivisible, effectuating component of an illegal arrangement that would be consummated by granting the judgment sought in this action is a question that requires further development at trial.

The extent to which the contract price is excessive and discriminatory and fails to reflect fair market value at the contract date because of an unlawful attempt to stifle competition is an important issue requiring development. The unlawful use of market power to inflate the contract price, and the resulting anti-competitive effects, must be assessed in determining whether granting the judgment sought "would be to make the courts a party to the carrying out of one of the very restraints forbidden by the [antitrust laws]" (Kelly, 358 U.S., at 520).

Additionally, the equities of the parties must be examined. Courts should avoid upholding antitrust defenses in contract cases where doing so would work a substantial forfeiture on one party while unjustly enriching the other. A relevant consideration is whether sustaining the illegality defense would render the contract void in its entirety or whether recovery could still be had on a quantum meruit basis. Additionally, the relative culpability, bargaining power, and knowledge of the parties to the contract should also be considered in assessing the possibility of unjust enrichment.

Finally, the public policy in favor of frustrating or discouraging unlawful schemes such as the Club must not be deprecated. However, such a danger is reduced where statutory remedies exist and the State Attorney General can directly attack the alleged antitrust violations.

In light of our analysis, the Court rejects defendant's remaining contention that the contract should be held per se illegal under the Donnelly Act.

Order affirmed, with costs, and certified question answered in the affirmative.

NOTES

(1) *Questions.* Were the parties in this case *in pari delicto?* Did the court decide that further findings in the trial court might warrant a recovery for unjust enrichment, but not of the balance due under the contract? That they might warrant a recovery in excess of the defendant's enrichment? The Attorney General of New York State filed a brief as amicus curiae *opposing* the result in this case. How did the court take account of statutory remedies available to the Attorney General?

(2) *Degrees of Involvement.* Justice Holmes indicated that in selling goods, a merchant may safely exhibit an "understood indifference" to the buyer's intended use of the goods. Graves v. Johnson, 60 N.E. 383 (Mass. 1901). "[A] sale otherwise lawful is not connected with subsequent unlawful conduct by the mere fact that the seller correctly divines the buyer's unlawful intent, closely enough to make the sale unlawful. . . . Of course the [buyer-defendant] was free to change his mind, and there was no communicated desire of the plaintiffs to co-operate with the defendant's present intent. . . . [T]he decisions tend more and more to agree that the connection with the unlawful act in cases like the present is too remote."

The principle was applied in Fineman v. Faulkner, 93 S.E. 384, 385 (N.C. 1917), in which the plaintiff had made a credit sale of a phonograph to a buyer known "by general reputation" to be a prostitute. The defendant, administrator of the buyer's estate, sought to avoid payment on that ground. The court held that "[t]he sale of an Edison talking machine was a legitimate transaction . . . The seller had no control over the use to which it should be put, and did not sell to aid in any illegal purpose, and cannot be held responsible therefor from the simple fact that he knew that the purchaser was carrying on an illegal business." For a case involving the attempted rescission of a real estate sale transacted in North Carolina during the Civil War, see Phillips v. Hooker, 62 N.C. 193 (1867) (buying property with Confederate notes did not "have tendency to aid the rebellion").

(3) *Public Policing of Illegal Contracts.* Although in *X.L.O.* the contracts were between private parties, the problem of illegal contracts is of special interest to city and state governments. Consider the following:

> New York City is one of the biggest contracting entities in the world. Each year City agencies enter into approximately 40,000 contracts worth almost $6.5 billion. These contracts cover everything from pencils to legal services for indigent criminal defendants, from methadone treatment to architectural consultants, from external auditing to massive public works projects. Awarding and monitoring these contracts is one of the city government's great responsibilities.

Frank Anechiarico and James Jacobs, *Purging Corruption from Public Contracting*, 40 N.Y.L. Sch. L. Rev. 143 (1995). The authors describe efforts by the City Comptroller's Office to clean up a system marked by kickbacks and racketeering through competitive bidding and awards to the "lowest responsible bidder."

We now look briefly at three specific types of illegalities: inducing official action, commercial bribery, and violations of licensing laws.

———

Inducing Official Action: Foreign and Domestic

Recall that in Black v. Bush, p. 601 above, the court found that the profits received by Black were not the result of impermissible "dealings with government," and gave as one example inducing governmental action. Influence peddling and influence *buying* are common subjects of judicial denunciation, although not all efforts to procure favorable official action are condemned as such. Consider the role of lobbyists. The proper line has been stated as follows: "The authorities very generally hold that a contract to pay for services to be performed in the endeavor to obtain or defeat legislation by other means than the use of argument addressed to the reason of the legislators, such as, for example, for the exertion of personal or political influence apart from the appeal to reason as applied to the consideration of the merits or demerits of the legislation in question, is an illegal contract." Campbell County v. Howard & Lee, 112 S.E. 876 (Va. 1922).

As with illegality, the bribery of a public official can also be raised as a public policy defense in a contract action see Kevin E. Davis, Contracts Procured Through Bribery of Public Officials: Zero Tolerance Versus Proportional Liability, 50 N.Y.U. J. Int'l L. & Pol. 1261 (2018). In recent years, public policy regarding corruption has also taken on a global dimension, as suggested by the following 2007 arbitration decision. In 1989, Mr. Ali, representing World Duty Free, entered a contract with the Kenyan government to construct and operate certain duty-free shops at the Nairobi and Mombasa airports. Mr. Ali later brought a claim before a private arbitral body, the International Centre for Settlement of Investment Disputes, alleging that the Kenyan government had breached the contract by expropriating Mr. Ali's interests in World Duty Free. During the arbitration Mr. Ali testified that he had paid a $2 million "personal donation" in cash to President Moi of Kenya in order to obtain the contract. Kenya raised a public policy defense, arguing that because bribery is contrary to international public policy, the arbitral tribunal should not enforce the contract. After reviewing national court decisions and international conventions, the tribunal agreed with Kenya, stating:

> [B]ribery is contrary to the international public policy of most, if not all, States or, to use another formula, to transnational public policy. Thus, claims based on contracts of corruption or on contract obtained by corruption cannot be upheld by this Arbitral Tribunal.

World Duty Free Co. v. Republic of Kenya, ICSID Case No. ARB/00/7, Award (Oct. 4, 2006), 46 I.L.M. 339 (2007) (available at http://translex.

uni-koeln.de/output.php?docid=241400). In consequence, the bribe itself was not accounted for, and of course, there was no award of damages for breach. Professor Kevin Davis has characterized this as a "zero tolerance" approach. Kevin E. Davis, Civil Remedies for Corruption in Government Contracting: Zero Tolerance Versus Proportional Liability, IILJ Working Paper No. 2009/4 (2009). Are there other approaches? For a U.S. example of zero tolerance, see Adler v. Federal Republic of Nigeria, 219 F.3d 869 (9th Cir. 2000).

In addition to interposing bribery as a defense in a private contract action, there are also statutory efforts aimed at reducing official corruption. These include the Anti-Kickback Act of 1986, 41 U.S.C. §§ 51–58, and the False Statements Act, 18 U.S.C. § 1001. Recognizing the transnational nature of both commerce and corruption, in 1977 Congress first enacted the Foreign Corrupt Practices Act (FCPA), 15 U.S.C. §§ 78dd–1, et seq. The FCPA prohibits the payment of bribes to foreign governmental officials by individuals and corporations with U. S. ties. FCPA Guidelines issued in 2012 by the Department of Justice and the Securities and Exchange Commission explain the economic, philosophical, and political concerns that motivate the Act: "Corruption has corrosive effects on democratic institutions, undermining public accountability and diverting public resources from important priorities such as health, education, and infrastructure. When business is won or lost based on how much a company is willing to pay in bribes rather than on the quality of its products and services, law-abiding companies are placed at a competitive disadvantage—and consumers lose." See *A Resource Guide to the U.S. Foreign Corrupt Practices Act* (2012), available at www.justice.gov/criminal/fraud/fcpa. The guide is also available at www.sec.gov/spotlight/fcpa.shtml.

The FCPA provides for two kinds of statutory policing, antibribery provisions and accounting requirements:

The antibribery provisions prohibit all U.S. issuers, individuals, and "domestic concerns" from paying, offering, or promising anything of value to a foreign official for the purpose of "obtaining or retaining business." The FCPA's accounting provisions require companies covered by the provisions to keep accurate books and records and to "maintain . . . system[s] of internal accounting controls." Therefore, even if the enforcement agencies cannot find direct evidence of bribe payments, they may charge companies that hide potential bribe payments under the books and records provisions. Moreover, the FCPA is both a criminal and civil statute. Thus, even if the enforcement agencies cannot meet the higher standard of proof required for criminal charges, they can charge companies with civil violations. In short, the statute is tailored to give its enforcers wide scope to deter bribery; it covers a variety of conduct and permits its enforcers to prove that conduct using various standards of proof. (citations omitted)

Rashna Bhojwani, *Deterring Global Bribery: Where Public and Private Enforcement Collide*, 112 Colum. L. Rev. 66 (2012).

For an account of bribery revealed through the accounting provisions, see Charlie Savage, With Wal-Mart Claims, Greater Attention on a Law, *N.Y. Times*, April 25, 2012. See also Matt A. Vega, *The Sarbanes-Oxley Act and the Culture of Bribery: Expanding The Scope of Private Whistleblower Suits to Overseas Employees*, 46 Harv. J. on Legis. 425 (2009). International efforts to combat bribery now include the United Nations Convention against Corruption, available at http://www.unodc.org/documents/treaties/UNCAC/Publications/Convention/08–50026_E.pdf.

NOTES

(1) *Judicial Bribery*. A judge was offered a bribe and consulted the state's attorney, who advised the judge to accept the money. It became evidence in criminal proceedings against the briber, who was convicted and imprisoned. The briber then moved for the return of the money by the state, and that was ordered (by another judge). The state appealed. The court considered the case under the aspect of failure of consideration, or breach by the "bribed" judge. *Held:* Reversed. The appeals court opened its opinion with a definition of "chutzpah" (a term referring to a person with "gall, moxie, nerve and audacity compounded with brazen assertiveness"). It further stated that "[a]ny attempt to bribe a member of the judiciary, or one of the satellites of the judiciary, is a reprehensible, odious act striking at the heart of the judicial system. For the bribe then to be repaid to the briber, on order of a court, erodes the public's confidence in the court's common sense and judgment." The court concluded that the convicted briber could not recover damages for breach of a contract to commit a crime: "Parties of that ilk are left where they are found, to stew in their own juice." State v. Strickland, 400 A.2d 451, 454–55 (Md.App.1979).

Bribery, a form of corruption in office, may also be a ground for judicial impeachment. See, for example, Missouri Constitution, Article VII, Section 1. For a complicated case involving the disbarment of an attorney for judicial bribery, and the attorney's eventual reinstatement, see In re Shelton, 987 So.2d 938 (Miss.2008).

(2) *Undoing Official Corruption*. In 2004, Darlene Druyun, for nine years the Air Force's top civilian acquisition official, pleaded guilty for conspiring to violate a federal statute prohibiting certain government employees from participating in the award of government contracts to firms in which the employee, or the employee's spouse or child, has a financial interest. See 18 U.S.C. § 208(a). Druyun had over a period of years favored the Boeing Corporation in awarding contracts; she admitted that her decisions were influenced by Boeing having hired her future son-in-law and her daughter in 2000, and "her own desire to be employed by Boeing."

Following the exposure of Druyun's malfeasance in 2006, L-3 Communication Integrated Systems, a firm whose bid had been rejected in one of Druyun's deals, filed a "post-award bid protest" alleging that the Air Force had breached its obligation to fairly consider its offer. It sought as damages its bid and proposal preparation costs. The government moved to dismiss that claim on the grounds that claimants must provide "clear and convincing evidence" to overcome the presumption that contracting officers act in "good faith." *Held*: For claimant. L-3 Communications Integrated Systems v. United States, 79 Fed. Cl. 453 (Fed. Cl. 2007).

Acknowledging the "heavy burden" required to overcome the presumption, the court held that L-3 had stated a claim upon which relief could be granted. The court observed that most post-bid protests seek to undo the contract award and secure a recompetition, re-evaluation, or, in rare instances, the "award itself." Here, however, is was "too late for injunctive relief" as the contract had been largely performed, leaving L-3 with the possibility only of its bid and preparation costs.

If L-3 were successful in its claim, might it recover more by receiving its bid preparation costs than by securing a recompetition or re-evaluation of its bid?

Commercial Bribery

Is a contract that is induced by bribery unenforceable on ground of public policy? We have already seen that "[I]t is well settled both in law and in equity that the court will not aid either party to an illegal agreement. . . . While it may not always seem an honorable thing to do, a party to an illegal agreement is permitted to set up the illegality as a defense even though the party may be alleging his or her own turpitude." Early Detection Center, Inc. v. Wilson, 811 P.2d 860, 867 (Kan. 1991).

The following pattern is typical of commercial bribery: a seller bribes a buyer's purchasing agent to buy goods from the seller. After the goods are delivered, the buyer then refuses to pay on grounds of public policy. In a New York case, Sirkin v. Fourteenth St. Store, 108 N.Y.S. 830, 833–834 (App. Div. 1908), the court refused to enforce such a contract, stating that "nothing will be more effective in stopping the growth and spread of this corrupting and now criminal custom . . . ." It denied recovery to the seller, taking guidance from a state statute which made it a misdemeanor for a seller to offer a commission, discount, or bonus to a purchasing agent, and for the agent to receive it. The statute provided for a fine of not more than $500 and imprisonment of not more than a year. (The contract for the bribe itself is unenforceable as a promise inducing violation of an agent's fiduciary duty, see Restatement § 193 and Illustration 12 to Restatement § 178, the latter taken from *Sirkin*.) Two judges dissented, saying that "[i]t is not part of our duty to assume legislative power and prescribe an additional punishment . . . ."

One problem with denying recovery is that the buyer retains the goods without paying for them. This was the result in a later New York case, McConnell v. Commonwealth Pictures Corp., 166 N.E.2d 494 (N.Y. 1960). A movie distributor agreed to pay McConnell $10,000 (plus a percentage of gross receipts) if McConnell negotiated a contract between the distributor and a certain movie producer. McConnell negotiated the contract by paying the producer's agent a $10,000 bribe. When the distributor found out about the bribe, it refused to pay McConnell his percentage of gross receipts on the ground of public policy. McConnell sued, arguing that there was nothing improper about his contract with the distributor, who had known nothing about McConnell's negotiation techniques. Unlike *Sirkin*, he argued, the contract being sued upon had not been obtained by bribery.

The court held that "It is beside the point that the present plaintiff . . . might be able to prove a prima facie case without the bribery being exposed":

> It is argued that [denying enforcement] here means that the doing of any small illegality in the performance of an otherwise lawful contract will deprive the doer of all rights, with the result that the other party will get a windfall. . . . Our ruling does not go as far as that. It is not every minor wrongdoing in the course of contract performance that will insulate the other party from liability for work done or good furnished. There must at least be a direct connection between the illegal transaction and the obligation sued upon.

What, if any, public policies are advanced by permitting recovery on a contract that is itself not illegal?

NOTE

Beneficiary of the Bribe. What becomes of the bribe? It appears, as in *McConnell,* that some "surplus" may be realized by persons not parties to the contract—those who took the bribe. In *Sirkin*, the court said: "The servant would be accountable to his master or employer for any moneys thus received . . . . " Presumably the employer could have gotten that relief *in addition* to retaining the goods without paying for them.

Might not the bribe be disgorged and applied elsewhere? Such dispositions have been proposed, though not as yet adopted in the United States. See Harold Berman, Justice in the U.S.S.R. 141 (1963) (forfeit to the state); Warren Seavey, *Problems in Restitution*, 7 Okla. L. Rev. 257, 259 (1954); see *also* Catherine Sharkey, *Punitive Damages as Social Damages*, 113 Yale L.J. 347, 402 (2003) (suggesting in the context of torts that "[i]t is not difficult to imagine [a court-administered scheme] that would attempt to provide redress or compensation for more diffuse harms to individuals or groups caused by the same, or similar, wrong-doing on the part of the defendant").

Licensing Laws

In Sirkin v. Fourteenth St. Store, discussed in Commercial Bribery, above, the court said that "one who is required by law to procure a license to conduct any trade, calling, or profession may not recover for services rendered or property sold, without first obtaining such license." The statement goes too far. When the purpose of a licensing requirement is ascertained to be raising public revenue, and not the protection of the public's welfare —health, morals or the like—a claimant's want of a license is generally not a bar.

If a person whose vocation is related to the construction industry, such as an architect or a mechanical engineer, performs services without having a mandated license or certification, should the services go uncompensated?

Consider the following. In September, 2005, Trade-Winds Environmental Restoration, Inc. (Trade-Winds) entered into a contract with Stewart Development (Stewart) to perform mold remediation on Stewart's building, which had sustained water damage as a result of Hurricane Katrina. The contract price was to be based on a "rate-sheet" provided by Trade-Winds and estimated at $750,000. At the time the contract was signed, Trade-Winds did not hold a license as a mold remediation contractor. After Trade-Winds completed the work, it submitted an invoice to Stewart for $9,000,000. Stewart paid $7,500,000, but when Trade-Winds failed to provide documentation to support its invoice, Stewart refused further payment, and Trade-Winds sued for the balance. Stewart sued for summary judgment, on the ground that the contract was null and void because Trade-Winds had been unlicensed. *Held*: For Stewart. Trade-Winds Environmental Restoration, Inc. v. Stewart, 2008 WL 236891 (E.D. La. Jan. 28, 2008). Trade-Winds argued that "to void this contract would be against the public policy of facilitating clean-up after [disasters]" and would "cause a chilling effect on the willingness of remediation specialists to perform work in Louisiana." The court noted "the competing policy interest of protecting the public from the unlawful acts of contractors" and pointed to the language of the licensing statute itself: the "purpose of [the mold remediation licensing laws] is to require qualifying criteria in a professional field in which unqualified individuals may injure or mislead the public." The court observed that "the policy decisions made by the legislature are expressly stated in the statutes. . . . [It] is not the place of this court to second guess such decisions." The court rejected Trade-Winds's argument that the Governor had suspended licensing laws with regard to debris removal in the aftermath of other disasters, noting that "while the Executive Branch does have the power to temper legislative intent in times of emergency, no such order was given in this case." Why might Stewart have paid so much of the invoice when it so greatly exceeded the estimate?

NOTES

(1) *Recovery and Restitution?* As a general rule, illegality precludes not only the enforcement of an agreement but also any restitutionary claims. This can produce what appear to be striking injustices in individual cases. Note that Restatement § 178 provides that in weighing the enforcement of a term, account should be taken of "any forfeiture that would result if enforcement were denied."

(2) *Line Drawing.* In Town Planning & Engineering Associates, Inc. v. Amesbury Specialty Co., 342 N.E.2d 706 (Mass. 1976), concerning the plaintiff's want of a certification as an engineer, the court considered the possibility of confining the plaintiff's recovery to "a quantum meruit less than the contract price." It concluded, however, that a "vector of considerations" pointed toward recovery of the contract price. One consideration was whether or not "the characteristics which gave the plaintiff's act its value to the defendant [were] the same as those which made it a violation" of law (quoting from George Gardner, *An Inquiry into the Principles of the Law of Contracts*, 46 Harv. L. Rev. 1, 37 (1932)). *Compare* Kansas City Community Center v. Heritage Industries, Inc., 972 F.2d 185 (8th Cir. 1992) (architect). For a useful distinction between a claim made by an unlicensed contractor in its capacity as a contractor and one made by an unlicensed contractor in its capacity as a joint venturer, see In re Lake Providence Properties, Inc., 168 B.R. 876 (W.D.N.C. 1994).

(B) JUDICIALLY CREATED PUBLIC POLICY

We now turn to the murkier question of how courts should police bargains on policy grounds when there is no clear statutory prohibition against a particular kind of agreement. In such cases, the court must be satisfied nonetheless that a strong public policy can be articulated. The guiding principle is one of protecting "some aspect of the public welfare." See Restatement § 179. That provision identifies two such areas "now rooted in precedents collected over the centuries." They are polices against the restraint of trade and against the impairment of family relations.

Of course, precedents from which policies derive do not always remain rooted over the centuries. As we saw with regard to the disclaimers in standard form contracts, policies may change over time. What sort of facts might lead a court to recognize a change in public policy? An example is found in the instance of cohabitation agreements between unmarried persons. Until the 1970s, such agreements were generally unenforceable on the ground that enforcement would "weaken marriage as the foundation of our family-based society." Hewitt v. Hewitt, Note 3, p. 157. Over time, however, courts have begun to uphold cohabitation contracts, so long as "the business part of a contract between cohabiting or romantically attached partners can be separated from the personal part." Thomas v. LaRosa, 400 S.E.2d 809, 813 (W.Va. 1990).

At moments of possible cultural change, courts may be particularly sensitive about sources of policy guidance. Thus in *Hewitt*, decided in 1979, the court invoked policies *about* policy to deny enforcement to a cohabitation agreement:

"If resolution of this issue rests ultimately on the grounds of public policy, by what body should that policy be determined? [In Marvin v. Marvin, the California court], viewing the issue as governed solely by contract law, found judicial policy-making appropriate. Its decision was facilitated by California precedent and that State's no-fault divorce law. In our view, however, . . . [t]he question whether change is needed in the law governing the rights of parties in this delicate area of marriage-like relationships involves evaluations of sociological data and alternatives we believe best suited to the superior investigative and fact-finding facilities of the legislative branch in the exercise of its traditional authority to declare public policy in the domestic relations field." 394 N.E.2d at 1209.

Are legislatures generally better at fact-finding of this kind than courts? Recall the recourse to sources of fact-finding by judges in both opinions in *O'Callaghan*, p. 610 above.

Restraints of Trade

Hopper v. All Pet Animal Clinic

Supreme Court of Wyoming, 1993.
861 P.2d 531.

■ TAYLOR, JUSTICE. [For three years following her education as a veterinarian, Dr. Glenna Hopper worked—part-time at first—at the All Pet Animal Clinic, Inc., in Laramie, Wyoming. She and her employer executed an agreement, effective in March of 1989, containing this provision:

> This agreement may be terminated by either party upon 30 days' notice to the other party. Upon termination, Dr. Hopper agrees that she will not practice small animal medicine for a period of three years from the date of termination within 5 miles of the corporate limits of the City of Laramie, Wyoming. Dr. Hopper agrees that the duration and geographic scope of that limitation is reasonable.º

Later the president of All Pet, Dr. R.B. Johnson, heard a rumor that Dr. Hopper was investigating the purchase of a competing practice and suggested that she buy her way out of the covenant about competition.

º　This term was part of the first written agreement between Hopper and the Clinic, executed in December 1989 but was antedated to the preceding March, when Hopper had begun work.

In her response she said that she could do anything she wanted. Thereupon she was discharged. In July, 1991, having purchased the other practice, she began operating the Gem City Veterinary Clinic. In November, All Pet sued for an injunction, claiming also damages. (An additional plaintiff was the Alpine Animal Clinic, Inc., in which Dr. Hopper and Dr. Johnson had also been associated.) The case came to trial in the following year, more than two years after Hopper was discharged. The plaintiffs did not seek a temporary injunction.

It appeared that slightly more than half of Hopper's gross income was derived from small-animal practice, and the evidence showed a substantial overlap of clientele in her former and current practices. The trial court granted an injunction, but concluded that the amount of the plaintiff's damages was too speculative to be allowed. Both parties appealed.]

A.   The Enforceability of a Covenant Not to Compete

The common law policy against contracts in restraint of trade is one of the oldest and most firmly established. Restatement (Second) of Contracts §§ 185–188 (1981) (Introductory Note at 35). See Dutch Maid Bakeries v. Schleicher, 58 Wyo. 374, 131 P.2d 630, 634 (1942). The traditional disfavor of such restraints means covenants not to compete are construed against the party seeking to enforce them. . . . The initial burden is on the employer to prove the covenant is reasonable and has a fair relation to, and is necessary for, the business interests for which protection is sought. Tench v. Weaver, 374 P.2d 27, 29 (Wyo.1962).

Two principles, the freedom to contract and the freedom to work, conflict when courts test the enforceability of covenants not to compete. Ridley v. Krout, 180 P.2d 124, 128 (Wyo. 1947). There is general recognition that while an employer may seek protection from improper and unfair competition of a former employee, the employer is not entitled to protection against ordinary competition. See, e.g. Duffner v. Alberty, 718 S.W.2d 111, 112 (Ark. 1986) and American Sec. Services, Inc. v. Vodra, 385 N.W.2d 73, 78 (Neb. 1986). The enforceability of a covenant not to compete depends upon a finding that the proper balance exists between the competing interests of the employer and the employee. See Restatement (Second) of Agency § 393 cmt. e (1958) (noting that without a covenant not to compete, an agent, employee, can compete with a principal despite past employment and can begin preparations for future competition, such as purchasing a competitive business, before leaving present employment).

Wyoming adopted a rule of reason inquiry from the Restatement of Contracts testing the validity of a covenant not to compete. Dutch Maid Bakeries, 131 P.2d 634 (citing Restatement of Contracts §§ 513–515 (1932)); Ridley, 180 P.2d at 127. The present formulation of the rule of reason is contained in Restatement (Second) of Contracts, supra § 188:

. . . See also Restatement (Second) of Contracts, supra, §§ 186–187.[p] An often quoted reformulation of the rule of reason inquiry states that "[a] restraint is reasonable only if it (1) is no greater than is required for the protection of the employer, (2) does not impose undue hardship on the employee, and (3) is not injurious to the public." Harlan M. Blake, *Employee Agreements Not to Compete*, 73 Harv. L. Rev. 625, 648–49 (1960). . . . [W]e turn to the rule of reason inquiry.

The special interests of All Pet and Alpine identified by the district court as findings of fact are not clearly erroneous. Dr. Hopper moved to Laramie upon completion of her degree prior to any significant professional contact with the community. Her introduction to All Pet's and Alpine's clients, client files, pricing policies, and practice development techniques provided information which exceeded the skills she brought to her employment. While she was a licensed and trained veterinarian when she accepted employment, the additional exposure to clients and knowledge of clinic operations her employers shared with her had a monetary value for which the employers are entitled to reasonable protection from irreparable harm. See Reddy [v. Community Health Foundation of Man, 298 S.E.2d 906 (1982)] at 912–14 (discussing the economic analysis applied to restrictive covenants). The proven loss of 187 of All Pet's and Alpine's clients to Dr. Hopper's new practice sufficiently demonstrated actual harm from unfair competition.

The reasonableness, in a given fact situation, of the limitations placed on a former employee by a covenant not to compete are determinations made by the court as a matter of law. See, e.g. Jarrett v. Hamilton, 346 S.E.2d 875, 876 (Ga. 1986). Therefore, the district court's conclusions of law about the reasonableness of the type of activity, geographic, and durational limits contained in the covenant are subject to *de novo* review.

[I]n Cukjati [v. Burkett, 772 S.W.2d 215 (Tex. 1989)] at 216, 218, the Court of Appeals of Texas held a covenant not to compete was unreasonable because it limited a veterinarian from practicing within twelve miles of his former employer's clinic in North Irving, a community within the Dallas-Fort Worth metropolitan area. Because evidence from that proceeding disclosed that Dallas area residents are unlikely to travel more than a few miles for pet care, the court found the restriction unreasonable. Id. at 218. The number of veterinarians and the demands upon their services obviously varies between Laramie, Wyoming and

---

[p]   According to § 187, "A promise to refrain from competition that imposes a restraint that is not ancillary to an otherwise valid transaction or relationship is unreasonably in restraint of trade."

    Comment *b* to the section contains these observations: "The promisee's interest . . . may arise out of a relation between himself as employer or principal and the promisor as employee or agent. . . . In order for a restraint to be ancillary to a transaction or relationship the promise that imposes it must be made as part of that transaction or relationship. A promise made subsequent to the transaction or relationship is not ancillary to it. In the case of an ongoing transaction or relationship, however, it is enough if the promise is made before its termination, as long as it is supported by consideration and meets the other requirements of enforceability."

metropolitan Dallas, Texas, creating a different usage pattern. We believe the reasonableness of individual limitations contained in a specific covenant not to compete must be assessed based upon the facts of that proceeding. Ridley, 180 P.2d at 131.

Enforcement of the practice restrictions Dr. Hopper accepted as part of her covenant not to compete does not create an unreasonable restraint of trade. While the specific terms of the covenant failed to define the practice of small animal medicine the parties' trade usage provided a conforming standard of domesticated dogs and cats along with exotic animals maintained as household pets. As a veterinarian licensed to practice in Wyoming, Dr. Hopper was therefore permitted to earn a living in her chosen profession without relocating by practicing large animal medicine, a significant area of practice in this state. The restriction on the type of activity contained in the covenant was sufficiently limited to avoid undue hardship to Dr. Hopper while protecting the special interests of All Pet and Alpine.

The public will not suffer injury from enforcement of the covenant.

The geographical limit contained in the covenant not to compete restricts Dr. Hopper from practicing within a five mile radius of the corporate limits of Laramie. As a matter of law, this limit is reasonable in this circumstance. The evidence presented at trial indicated that the clients of All Pet and Alpine were located throughout the county. Despite Wyoming's rural character, the five mile restriction effectively limited unfair competition without presenting an undue hardship. Dr. Hopper could, for example, have opened a practice at other locations within the county.

A durational limitation should be reasonably related to the legitimate interest which the employer is seeking to protect. Restatement (Second) of Contracts, supra, § 188 cmt. b.

A one year durational limit sufficiently secures All Pet's and Alpine's interest in pricing policies and practice development information. Pricing policies at All Pet and Alpine were changed yearly, according to Dr. Johnson, to reflect changes in material and service costs provided by the clinics as well as new procedures. Practice development information, especially in a learned profession, loses its value quickly as technological change occurs and new reference material become [sic] available. We hold, as a matter of law, that enforcement of a one year durational limit is reasonable and sufficiently protects the interest of All Pet and Alpine without violating public policy. . . . Because we hold that the covenant's three year durational term imposed a partially unreasonable restraint of trade, we remand for a modification of the judgment to enjoin Dr. Hopper from unfair competition for a duration of one year from the date of termination.

B. *Damages for Violation of a Covenant Not to Compete*

[The court rejected the calculations of damages suggested by the plaintiffs, all of which were "based on figures for gross profits."]

The finding of the district court that the amount of damages suffered was speculative and unproven by a preponderance of the evidence is not clearly erroneous.

■ CARDINE, JUSTICE, dissenting. Glenna Hopper has beaten the system. Just prior to being terminated, Dr. Hopper informed Dr. Johnson that "the [covenant] isn't worth the paper it's written on." And she was right.

The court has now decided as a matter of law that a one-year non-competition restriction is reasonable, and a longer period is unreasonable.

I would require that appellant be enjoined from that part of the practice of veterinary medicine specified in the covenant not to compete from the date the trial court, on remand, enters its modified judgment for at least the one-year period which this court now finds reasonable.

NOTES

(1) *Questions.* The court in *Hopper* discusses the freedom to work and the freedom to contract, two clear public policies. When a covenant not to compete is between doctors, might other, less individualistic public policies in play? Is the provision of health care advanced by enforcing or denying enforcement to a medical covenant not to complete? Compare Mohanty v. St. John Heart Clinic, 866 N.E.2d 85 (Ill. 2006) (noting the adverse effect for patients if enforcement were denied), with Mercho-Roushdi-Shoemaker-Dilley Thoraco-Vascular Corp. v. Blatchford, 900 N.E.2d 786 (Ind. App. 2009) (upholding non-enforcement where there were few suitable alternatives in area).

How might Dr. Johnson's lawyer in the case above have drafted the covenant to provide his client better protection?

(2) *Policy Sources and Limitations.* In 1985, accountant Daniel Miller signed an employment contract with Donald DeMuth. The contract contained a non-competition clause which provided that "if Employer terminates the Agreement for cause, and Employee [engages in accounting work] within a 50-mile radius of any of Employer's current or former clients, [Employee] agrees to pay the Employer 125% of the previous 12 months charges [received from any former client]." Cause was defined to include "moral turpitude, being charged with a felony, . . . intentionally losing clients, engaging in sexual activities in the office, and homosexuality." In 1990, DeMuth fired Miller for cause for appearing on a local television station representing a gay and lesbian coalition. Miller then opened a competing firm and solicited DeMuth's clients, 17 of whom became Miller's clients. DeMuth sought compensation under the non-competition clause. Miller argued that enforcement of the penalty provision would violate his rights to be free from workplace discrimination on the basis of sexual preference. From a judgment for DeMuth, Miller appealed. *Held*: Affirmed.

"[Appellant's] claim [of discrimination] is not actionable under any Pennsylvania statute or its constitution and is certainly not in violation of the doctrines of due process and equal protection in the Fourteenth Amendment to the U.S. Constitution. . . . It surely follows that, because the defendant agreed to the terms of his contract for a period of five years without objection or renegotiation, he must be held to adhere to its (non-competition) terms, absent any evidence of a clear violation of public policy which we have detected here." The court commented in a footnote that "appellant's arguments of discrimination in the workplace, directed at gays and lesbians, would be better directed toward the Legislature (the real body politic) to effectuate a change in the treatment of those whose sexual preferences impact upon their work environment." DeMuth v. Miller, 652 A.2d 891 (Pa. Super. 1995).

(3)   *Practicing Law: A Special Case?* "Should an attorney who leaves a law firm be free to compete with that firm?" That was the question in Howard v. Babcock, 863 P.2d 150, 161 (Cal. 1993) (Justice Kennard, dissenting).

In that case partners in a law firm had agreed that anyone withdrawing from the partnership would receive a share of the firm's net profit for a period following the withdrawal. If, however, that person engaged in a designated type of competitive practice, any profit-sharing would be at the discretion of the remaining partners. Three partners withdrew and the limitation was invoked against them. They sought a declaration that the limitation was unenforceable. From a judgment favoring the defendants, the plaintiffs appealed once, with limited success, and sought further review. *Held:* Reversed (ruling that the non-compete provision was enforceable).

Citing changes in "law firm culture," the court said that "the general rules and habits of commerce have permeated the legal profession." Many other courts have "interpreted the rules of professional conduct of their states . . . as prohibiting all agreements restricting competition among lawyers, including those that merely assess a cost for competition. Upon reflection [however], we have determined that these courts' steadfast concern to assure the theoretical freedom of each lawyer to choose whom to represent and what kind of work to undertake, and the theoretical freedom of any client to select his or her attorney of choice is inconsistent with the reality that both freedoms are actually circumscribed." Howard v. Babcock, 863 P.2d 150 (Cal. 1993).

(4)   *Rejection or Reformation?* If a non-compete clause is found to be unreasonably broad, what becomes of it? Formerly, most courts employed the "all or nothing at all" rule, under which the court either enforced the clause as written or rejected it altogether. See Ehlers v. Iowa Warehouse Co., 188 N.W.2d 368 (Iowa 1971). *Partial* enforcement, as in *Hopper,* was criticized, as by the dissent in that case, as empowering courts to remake the parties' agreement on the court's terms. The trend, however, has been toward *some* form of judicial modification, and courts have taken two approaches.

The first is the "blue pencil" rule under which courts cross out, or "blue pencil," words "to the extent that a grammatically meaningful reasonable restriction remains after the words making the restriction unreasonable are stricken." Central Adjustment Bureau, Inc, v. Ingram, 678 S.W.2d 28 (Tenn. 1984) (explaining that in a restriction on soliciting business clients in "Toledo, Ohio, and the United States," the court could "blue pencil" "Ohio, and the United States" leaving the covenant enforceable in Toledo). While the blue-pencil rule prevents courts from rewriting private agreements in a literal sense, it has been criticized as emphasizing form over substance.

The second approach, employed in *Hopper* above, is the rule of reasonableness, under which the covenant will be enforced only to the extent reasonably necessary to protect the employer's interest. As both Williston and Corbin stated:

"This is not making a new contract for the parties; it is a choice among the possible effects of the one that they made, establishing the one that is the most desirable for the contractors and the public at large." Samuel Williston and Arthur L. Corbin, *On the Doctrine of Beit v. Beit*, 23 Conn. B.J. 40, 49–50 (1949).

The Restatement follows this approach. See Restatement § 184. One objection to the rule is that employers can draft oppressive restrictions knowing that at worst a court will enforce the covenant on reasonable terms. Does the Restatement rule invite abuses by drafters of non-compete clauses?

Public Policy and Termination of At-Will Employees

Since the late 19th century, courts have shown a strong preference for termination at will in employment agreements; see Employment Agreements, p. 83 above. Courts resolutely ignored contrary indications such as description of the employment as "permanent" or "lifetime." Thus the statement that "so long as you do your job you can be here until you're a hundred" was held "insufficient as a matter of law" to vary the at-will rule. Mursch v. Van Dorn Co., 851 F.2d 990, 996 (7th Cir. 1988).

In the mid-1970s, however, a revolution began with decisions that qualified the employer's power to terminate under employment agreements. The seminal case was Monge v. Beebe Rubber Co., 316 A.2d 549 (N.H. 1974), involving a worker fired because she resisted her foreman's sexual advances. There is now general agreement that a plainly opportunistic discharge is actionable. Thus, if an employee is discharged without good cause, "the obligation of good faith and fair dealing imposed on an employer requires that the employer be liable for the loss in compensation that is . . . clearly related to an employee's past service," such as commissions earned by that service. Gram v. Liberty Mut. Ins. Co., 429 N.E.2d 21, 29 (Mass. 1981).

In addition to the demands of good faith, most courts have also fashioned a public policy exception to an employer's right to terminate at-will employees, as discussed in the next case.

Sheets v. Teddy's Frosted Foods

Supreme Court of Connecticut, 1980.
179 Conn. 471, 427 A.2d 385.

■ PETERS, ASSOCIATE JUSTICE.q The issue in this case is whether an employer has a completely unlimited right to terminate the services of an employee whom it has hired for an indefinite term. The plaintiff, Emard H. Sheets, filed a complaint that as amended alleged that he had been wrongfully discharged from his employment as quality control director and operations manager of the defendant, Teddy's Frosted Foods, Inc. The defendant responded with a motion to strike the complaint as legally insufficient. The plaintiff declined to plead further when that motion was granted. From the consequent rendering of judgment for the defendant, the plaintiff has appealed to this court.

The complaint alleges that for a four year period, from November 1973 to November 1977, the plaintiff was employed by the defendant, a producer of frozen food products, as its quality control director and subsequently also as operations manager. In the course of his employment, the plaintiff received periodic raises and bonuses. In his capacity as quality control director and operations manager, the plaintiff began to notice deviations from the specifications contained in the defendant's standards and labels, in that some vegetables were substandard and some meat components underweight. These deviations meant that the defendant's products violated the express representations contained in the defendant's labeling; false or misleading labels in turn violate the provisions of General Statutes § 19–222, the Connecticut Uniform Food, Drug and Cosmetic Act. In May of 1977, the plaintiff communicated in writing to the defendant concerning the use of substandard raw materials and underweight components in the defendant's finished products. His recommendations for more selective purchasing and conforming components were ignored. On November 3, 1977, his employment with the defendant was terminated. Although the stated reason for his discharge was unsatisfactory performance of his duties, he was actually dismissed in retaliation for his efforts to ensure that the defendant's products would comply with the applicable law relating to labeling and licensing.

The plaintiff's complaint alleges that his dismissal by his employer was wrongful in three respects. He claims that there was a violation of an implied contract of employment, a violation of public policy, and a malicious discharge. On this appeal, the claim of malice has not been separately pursued, and we are asked to consider only whether he has stated a cause of action for breach of contract or for intentionally tortious

---

q   Ellen Ash Peters (1930–____) was a member of the faculty of the Yale Law School for over two decades, teaching and writing in the fields of contracts and commercial law and serving as an Adviser for the Restatement (Second) of Contracts. In 1978 she was appointed an associate justice of the Connecticut Supreme Court, serving as Chief Justice from 1984 to 1996. For discussion of her decisions involving the Uniform Commercial Code, see Comment, 21 Conn. L. Rev. 753 (1989).

conduct. On oral argument, it was the tort claim that was most vigorously pressed, and it is upon the basis of tort that we have concluded that the motion to strike was granted in error.

The issue before us is whether to recognize an exception to the traditional rules governing employment at will so as to permit a cause of action for wrongful discharge where the discharge contravenes a clear mandate of public policy. In addressing that claim, we must clarify what is not at stake in this litigation. The plaintiff does not challenge the general proposition that contracts of permanent employment, or for an indefinite term, are terminable at will. Nor does he argue that contracts terminable at will permit termination only upon a showing of just cause for dismissal. Some statutes, such as the Connecticut Franchise Act, General Statutes § 42-133e through 42-133h, do impose limitations of just cause upon the power to terminate some contracts; see § 42-133f; but the legislature has recently refused to interpolate such a requirement into contracts of employment. See H.B. No. 5179, 1974 Sess. There is a significant distinction between a criterion of just cause and what the plaintiff is seeking. "Just cause" substantially limits employer discretion to terminate, by requiring the employer, in all instances, to proffer a proper reason for dismissal, by forbidding the employer to act arbitrarily or capriciously. . . . By contrast, the plaintiff asks only that the employer be responsible in damages if the former employee can prove a demonstrably improper reason for dismissal, a reason whose impropriety is derived from some important violation of public policy.

The argument that contract rights which are inherently legitimate may yet give rise to liability in tort if they are exercised improperly is not a novel one. Although private persons have the right not to enter into contracts, failure to contract under circumstances in which others are seriously misled gives rise to a variety of claims sounding in tort. See Kessler and Fine, *Culpa in Contrahendo*, 77 Harv. L. Rev. 401 (1964). The development of liability in contract for action induced by reliance upon a promise, despite the absence of common law consideration normally required to bind a promisor; see Restatement (Second), Contracts § 90 (1973); rests upon principles derived at least in part from the law of tort. See Gilmore, The Death of Contract 8-90 (1974). By way of analogy, we have long recognized abuse of process as a cause of action in tort whose gravamen is the misuse or misapplication of process, its use "in an improper manner or to accomplish a purpose for which it was not designed." Varga v. Pareles, 137 Conn. 663, 667, 81 A.2d 112, 115 (1951); Schaefer v. O.K. Tool Co., 110 Conn. 528, 532-33, 148 A. 330 (1930); Restatement (Second), Torts § 682 (1977); Wright and Fitzgerald, Connecticut Law of Torts § 163 (1968); Prosser, Torts § 121 (1971).

It would be difficult to maintain that the right to discharge an employee hired at will is so fundamentally different from other contract rights that its exercise is never subject to judicial scrutiny regardless of how outrageous, how violative of public policy, the employer's conduct may be. Cf. General Statutes § 31–126 (unfair employment practices). The defendant does not seriously contest the propriety of cases in other jurisdictions that have found wrongful and actionable a discharge in retaliation for the exercise of an employee's right to: (1) refuse to commit perjury; (2) file a workmen's compensation claim; (3) engage in union activity; (4) perform jury duty. While it may be true that these cases are supported by mandates of public policy derived directly from the applicable state statutes and constitutions, it is equally true that they serve at a minimum to establish the principle that public policy imposes some limits on unbridled discretion to terminate the employment of someone hired at will. No case has been called to our attention in which, despite egregiously outrageous circumstances, the employer's contract rights have been permitted to override competing claims of public policy, although there are numerous cases in which the facts were found not to support the employee's claim.

The issue then becomes the familiar common law problem of deciding where and how to draw the line between claims that genuinely involve the mandates of public policy and are actionable, and ordinary disputes between employee and employer that are not. We are mindful that courts should not lightly intervene to impair the exercise of managerial discretion or to foment unwarranted litigation. We are, however, equally mindful that the myriad of employees without the bargaining power to command employment contracts for a definite term are entitled to a modicum of judicial protection when their conduct as good citizens is punished by their employers.

The central allegation of the plaintiff's complaint is that he was discharged because of his conduct in calling to his employer's attention repeated violations of the Connecticut Uniform Food, Drug and Cosmetic Act. This act prohibits the sale of mislabeled food. General Statutes §§ 19–213, 19–222. The act, in § 19–215, imposes criminal penalties upon anyone who violates § 19–213; subsection (b) of § 19–215 makes it clear that criminal sanctions do not depend upon proof of intent to defraud or mislead, since special sanctions are imposed for intentional misconduct. The plaintiff's position as quality control director and operations manager might have exposed him to the possibility of criminal prosecution under this act. The act was intended to "safeguard the public health and promote the public welfare by protecting the consuming public from injury by product use and the purchasing public from injury by merchandising deceit. "General Statutes § 19–211.

It is useful to compare the factual allegations of this complaint with those of other recent cases in which recovery was sought for retaliatory discharge. In Geary v. United States Steel Corporation, [456 Pa. 171, 319 A.2d 174 (1974)], in which the plaintiff had disputed the safety of tubular steel casings, he was denied recovery because, as a company salesman, he had neither the expertise nor the corporate responsibility to "exercise independent, expert judgment in matters of product safety." Id., 319 A.2d

178. By contrast, this plaintiff, unless his title is meaningless, did have responsibility for product quality control. Three other recent cases in which the plaintiff's claim survived demurrer closely approximate the claim before us.

In the light of these recent cases, which evidence a growing judicial receptivity to the recognition of a tort claim for wrongful discharge, the trial court was in error in granting the defendant's motion to strike. The plaintiff alleged that he had been dismissed in retaliation for his insistence that the defendant comply with the requirements of a state statute, the Food, Drug and Cosmetic Act. We need not decide whether violation of a state statute is invariably a prerequisite to the conclusion that a challenged discharge violates public policy. Certainly when there is a relevant state statute we should not ignore the statement of public policy that it represents. For today, it is enough to decide that an employee should not be put to an election whether to risk criminal sanction or to jeopardize his continued employment.

There is error and the case is remanded for further proceedings.

■ In this opinion BOGDANSKI and HEALEY, JUSTICES, concurred.

■ COTTER, CHIEF JUSTICE (dissenting). The majority by seeking to extend a "modicum" of judicial protection to shield employees from retaliatory discharges instead offers them a sword with which to coerce employers to retain them in their employ. In recognizing an exception to the traditional rules governing employment at will and basing a new cause of action for retaliatory discharge on the facts of this case, the majority is necessarily led to the creation of an overly broad new cause of action whose nuisance value alone may impair employers' ability to hire and retain employees who are best suited to their requirements. Other jurisdictions which have recognized a cause of action for retaliatory discharge have done so on the basis of a much clearer and more direct contravention of a mandate of public policy.

[T]he purposes of the statute the majority would rely on, can only be considered as, at most, marginally affected by an allegedly retaliatory discharge of an employee who observed the supposed sale of shortweight frozen entrees and the use of U.S. Government Certified "Grade B" rather than "Grade A" vegetables. A retaliatory discharge in the present case would not necessarily thwart or inhibit the Connecticut Uniform Food, Drug and Cosmetic Act's purpose of protecting the consumer. The plaintiff, if he desired to protect the consumer, could have communicated, even anonymously, to the commissioner of consumer affairs his concerns that his employer was violating the Food, Drug and Cosmetic Act so as to invoke the statute's enforcement mechanisms. See General Statutes §§ 19–214 through 19–217. To further and comply with the public policy expressed in Connecticut's Uniform Food, Drug and Cosmetic Act and to avoid the exceedingly remote possibility of criminal sanctions, the plaintiff need not have jeopardized his continued employment. There is no indication that the plaintiff has either, before or after his discharge, informed or even attempted to inform the commissioner of consumer protection of violations the plaintiff claims to have first noted in his fourth year as the defendant's quality control director and fourth month as its operations manager. Unlike those cases where an employer allegedly discharged employees for engaging in union activities or filing workmen's compensation claims and the discharge itself contravened a statutory mandate, in the present case the discharge itself at most only indirectly impinged on the statutory mandate.

Consequently, the majority seemingly invites the unrestricted use of an allegation of almost any statutory or even regulatory violation by an employer as the basis for a cause of action by a discharged employee hired for an indefinite term.

■ In this opinion LOISELLE, JUSTICE, concurred.

NOTES

(1) *Discharge for Cause.* Justice Peters explains: "There is a significant distinction between a criterion of just cause and what the plaintiff is seeking. 'Just cause' substantially limits employer discretion to terminate, by requiring the employer, in all instances, to proffer a proper reason for dismissal, by forbidding the employer to act arbitrarily or capriciously." Courts have generally been unwilling to hold that an employer is under a duty of good faith and fair dealing that allows discharge only for good cause. If a duty of good faith and fair dealing is implied in every contract, is an at-will employment agreement a "contract" for this purpose?

Here Justice Peters cautions that "We need not decide whether violation of a state statute is invariably a prerequisite to the conclusion that a challenged discharge violates public policy." Courts differ as to whether the public policy at issue must be reflected in some form of legislation. In Johnson v. McDonnell Douglas Corp., 745 S.W.2d 661, 663 (Mo. 1988), for example, the Supreme Court of Missouri took the extreme view that the public policy exception applied only where the employee has "the benefit of a constitutional provision, a statute, or a regulation based on a statute."

(2) *Absence of a Statute.* In *Sheets*, Chief Justice Cotter, dissenting, protested that "the majority seemingly invites the unrestricted use of an allegation of almost any statutory or even regulatory violation by an employer as the basis for a cause of action by a discharged employee hired for an indefinite term." About two decades later, the Connecticut court revisited the breadth of the exception.

Virginia Daley, who was responsible for design development in Aetna's field offices, gave birth to a son in July 1991. She requested an alternative schedule permitting her to work at home one day a week and was turned down. There were complaints about her inadequate performance, and she was on and off probation. In November 1991, prompted by an award Aetna received for its model family leave programs, Daley drafted an interoffice memo expressing dissatisfaction with her experience and that of unidentified co-workers. After more complaints about her performance, she was fired in

February 1993. She sued for wrongful discharge citing, among other sources of public policy, Connecticut and federal employment and child welfare statutes. From a directed verdict for Aetna, Daley appealed. *Held*: Affirmed.

> [T]he public policy exception to the at will doctrine is a narrow one, and . . . we do not 'lightly intervene to impair the exercise of managerial discretion or to foment unwarranted litigation.' . . . Absent unusual circumstances, we will interfere with a personnel decision only if it implicates an explicit statutory or constitutional provision, or judicially conceived notion of public policy. . . . [W]e are mindful that we should not ignore the statement of public policy that is represented by a relevant statute. . . . [But to] impute a statement of public policy beyond that which is represented . . . would subject the employer who maintains compliance with express statutory obligations to unwarranted litigation for failure to comply with a heretofore unrecognized public policy mandate.

Daley v. Aetna Life & Cas. Co., 734 A.2d 112, 133 (Conn. 1999).

(3) *Presence of a Statute.* Carole Burnham, office manager in a dental office, filed an anonymous complaint with the Connecticut State Dental Association alleging that the dentists engaged in unsanitary practices in violation of the federal Occupational Safety and Health Act. When she was fired two weeks later, she sued for wrongful termination, relying on Connecticut's "whistleblower statute," enacted in 1982 (two years after the decision in *Sheets*). From summary judgment for defendants, she appealed. *Held*: Affirmed.

Connecticut's whistleblower statute "prohibits employers from retaliating against employees who report 'a violation or a suspected violation of any state or federal law . . . to a public body.' " Burnham did not dispute the trial court's conclusion that the Dental Association was not a "public body" within the definition in the whistleblower statute. "Alternatively," the court noted, "plaintiff's claim is precluded by virtue of the existence of a statutory remedy under that statute. . . . The existence of this statutory remedy [of a civil action after exhaustion of administrative remedies] precludes the plaintiff from bringing a common law wrongful discharge action based on an alleged violation" of the statute. The court also concluded that the plaintiff's claim was precluded by the existence of a statutory administrative remedy under federal law. Burnham v. Karl & Gelb, 745 A.2d 178, 182–183 (Conn. 2000).

(4) *Empirical Effects.* What are the economic effects of judicial modification of the at-will doctrine? A study by Professor Thomas Miles found that wrongful-discharge laws had "no statistically significant effects on either employment or unemployment." Thomas Miles, *Common Law Exceptions to Employment at Will and U.S. Labor Markets*, 16 J.L. Econ. & Org. 74 (2000); see also David Autor, John Donohue and Stewart Schwab, *The Employment Consequences of Wrongful-Discharge Laws: Large, Small, or None at All?*, 94 Am. Econ. Rev. 440 (2004).

Consider, in this connection, the arguments of Judge Easterbrook, in dissent, for the importance of giving employers the ability to decide who shall work for them. "It is easy for a jury to mistake a pest, a busybody, for a champion of the law. Firms need to prune their work forces of persons who create more trouble than they are worth; time diverted from business means lower efficiency and higher prices for consumers, undermining still another public policy. Employers fearing litigation—with high legal fees and the risk of punitive damages—will keep troublesome and inefficient employees on the payroll. Everyone loses when that happens." Belline v. K-Mart Corp., 940 F.2d 184, 191 (7th Cir. 1991).

Should judges take account of the effects of common law decisions on workplace practices? If your answer is Yes, what data or other sources of information should judges consider in deciding what those effects are?

PROBLEM

Suppose that an at-will employee is asked by his employer to sign an unreasonable covenant not to compete, and that upon his refusal to do so, he is fired. Would the employee have a claim for wrongful discharge under *Sheets*? D'sa v. Playhut, Inc., 102 Cal. Rptr. 2d 495 (Ct. App. 2000).

Balla v. Gambro, Inc.

Supreme Court of Illinois, 1991.
145 Ill.2d 492, 584 N.E.2d 104.

[Roger Balla, a member of the Illinois bar, was in-house counsel at Gambro, Inc., a distributor of kidney dialysis equipment. In addition to being "responsible for all legal matters," he had non-legal responsibilities including duties as "manager of regulatory affairs." When Balla told the president of Gambro to reject a shipment of dialyzers from its parent corporation in Germany because they did not comply with FDA regulations, the president ignored him and told the parent that they would sell the dialyzers to "a customer who buys only on price." On discovering this, Balla told the president that he would do whatever was necessary to stop their sale. Shortly thereafter the president fired Balla, who then reported the shipment to the FDA, which seized it and determined that it was adulterated. Balla sued Gambro for $22 million in tort for retaliatory discharge. The trial judge granted Gambro's motion for summary judgment, stating that since Balla's decision involved "applying law to fact," the duties that led to his discharge were "clearly within the attorney client relationship" and Gambro had the "absolute right" to discharge its attorney. On appeal by Balla, the Illinois Court of Appeals remanded, holding that Balla's right to sue for retaliatory discharge depended on facts to be determined at a trial. Gambro appealed.]

■ CLARK, JUSTICE. [G]enerally, in house counsel do not have a claim under the tort of retaliatory discharge. Appellee is and was subject to the Illinois Code of Professional Responsibility adopted by this court. The tort of retaliatory discharge is a limited and narrow exception to the general rule of at will employment.

In this case, the public policy to be protected, that of protecting the lives and property of citizens, is adequately safeguarded without extending the tort of retaliatory discharge to in house counsel. Appellee was required under the Rules of Professional Conduct to report Gambro's intention to sell the "misbranded and/or adulterated" dialyzers.

A lawyer *shall* reveal information about a client to the extent it appears necessary to prevent the client from committing an act that would result in death or serious bodily injury (emphasis added.).

Appellee alleges, and the FDA's seizure of the dialyzers indicates, that the use of the dialyzers would cause death or serious bodily injury. Thus, under the above cited rule, appellee was under the mandate of this court to report the sale of these dialyzers.

In his brief to this court, appellee argues that not extending the tort of retaliatory discharge to in house counsel would present attorneys with a "Hobson's choice." According to appellee, in house counsel would face two alternatives: either comply with the client/employer wishes and risk both the loss of a professional license and exposure to criminal sanctions, or decline to comply with client/employer's wishes and risk the loss of a full time job with the attendant benefits. We disagree. . . . [I]n house counsel plainly are not confronted with such a dilemma. In house counsel do not have a choice of whether to follow their ethical obligations as attorneys licensed to practice law, or follow the illegal and unethical demands of their clients. In house counsel must abide by the Rules of Professional Conduct. Appellee had no choice but to report to the FDA Gambro's intention to sell or distribute these dialyzers, and consequently protect the aforementioned public policy.

In addition, we believe that extending the tort of retaliatory discharge to in house counsel would have an undesirable effect on the attorney client relationship that exists between these employers and their in house counsel. Generally, a client may discharge his attorney at any time, with or without cause. This rule applies equally to in house counsel as it does to outside counsel. We believe that if in house counsel are granted the right to sue their employers for retaliatory discharge, employers might be less willing to be forthright and candid with their in house counsel for advice regarding potentially questionable corporate conduct, knowing that their in house counsel could use this information in a retaliatory discharge suit. If extending the tort of retaliatory discharge might have a chilling effect on the communications between the employer/client and the in house counsel, we believe that it is more wise to refrain from doing so.

We also believe that it would be inappropriate for the employer/client to bear the economic costs and burdens of their in house counsel's adhering to their ethical obligations under the Rules of Professional Conduct. The employer/client would be forced to pay damages to its former in house counsel to essentially mitigate the harm the attorney suffered for having to abide by Rules of Professional

Conduct. This, we believe, is impermissible for all attorneys know or should know in their professional career that at certain times they will have to forgo economic gains in order to protect the integrity of the legal profession.

Appellee argues that, if he did learn of Gambro's alleged violation of FDA regulations as manager of regulatory affairs, and acted pursuant to his duties as manager of regulatory affairs, he is merely an "employee" at Gambro and therefore should be entitled to bring a cause of action for retaliatory discharge. [A]lthough appellee may have been the manager of regulatory affairs for Gambro, his discharge resulted from information he learned as general counsel, and from conduct he performed as general counsel.

For the foregoing reasons the decision of the appellate court is reversed and the decision of the trial court is affirmed.

NOTES

(1)   *Questions.* Did Balla's discharge contravene, in the words of *Sheets*, "a clear mandate of public policy"? Do you agree that the policy was, in the words of the court, "adequately safeguarded without extending the tort of retaliatory discharge" to Balla? Do you agree with the court that Balla was not put to a "Hobson's Choice"? Is there any way that in-house counsel can protect themselves from discharge in Balla's circumstances?

(2)   Balla *Extended.* In Jacobson v. Knepper & Moga, 706 N.E.2d 491, 494 (Ill. 1998), the Supreme Court of Illinois extended *Balla* to a claim by a lawyer that he had been discharged by the law firm that had employed him in retaliation for his reporting the firm's illegal practices to a principal partner of the firm. "[P]laintiff, as a licensed attorney employed as such by the defendant law firm, cannot maintain a cause of action for retaliatory discharge because the ethical obligations imposed by the Rules of Professional Conduct provide adequate safeguards to the public policy implicated in this case."

(3)   Balla *Rejected.* The reasoning in *Balla* was rejected by the Supreme Court of California in General Dynamics Corp. v. Superior Court, 876 P.2d 487, 500 (Cal. 1994), a retaliatory discharge suit by an in-house counsel. The court admitted that the Illinois courts had "grappled conscientiously with the conflicting values presented," but added that "one searches in vain for a principled link between the ethical duties of the in-house attorney and the courts' refusal to grant such an employee a tort remedy under conditions that directly implicate those professional obligations. . . . Granted the priest-like license to receive the most intimate and damning disclosures of the client, granted the sanctity of the professional privilege, granted the uniquely influential position attorneys occupy in our society, it is precisely *because of* that role that attorneys should be accorded a retaliatory discharge remedy in those instances in which *mandatory ethical norms* embodied in the Rules of Professional Conduct *collide with illegitimate demands of the employer* and the attorney insists on *adhering to his or her clear professional duty*. It is,

after all, the office of the retaliatory discharge tort to vindicate fundamental public policies by encouraging employees to act in ways that advance them."

In GTE Products Corp. v. Stewart, 653 N.E.2d 161, 166 (Mass. 1995), the Supreme Judicial Court of Massachusetts found the California approach "more persuasive. We would be reluctant to conclude that an employee, solely by reason of his or her status as an attorney, must be denied protection from wrongful discharge arising from the performance of an action compelled by a clearly defined public policy of the Commonwealth."

(4) *Tort or Contract?* Note that in *Sheets,* Justice Peters says that "it is upon the basis of tort that we have concluded that the motion to strike was granted in error" and that *Balla* discusses "the tort of retaliatory discharge." What are the advantages to an employee of a remedy in tort as distinguished from one in contract and what are the disadvantages?

Consider also the issue raised in Corl v. Huron Castings, 544 N.W.2d 278, 286, 291 (Mich. 1996). There the court held, in a 4–3 decision, that where an employee sued for breach of a just-cause employment contract, his "damage award should be reduced by the amount he received in unemployment compensation benefits" because the "collateral source rule, [discussed in Note 3, p. 917 below], does not apply in cases of common law contract." A dissenting judge protested that the "doctrinal foundation of the . . . claim is neither fish nor fowl" and the answer "cannot be found in the rote application of the distinction between contract and tort."

(5) *Emotional Distress.* Claims of emotional distress may also be made in the context of at-will agreements. Some courts have recognized that even where the discharge itself may not have been wrongful, the conduct surrounding the discharge may have been tortious. In Dzinglski v. Weirton Steel Corp., 445 S.E.2d 219, 224, 226, 227 (W.Va. 1994), the court said that it had recognized "the tort of outrage or intentional infliction of emotional distress," even though it had "yet to decide a case where a defendant's conduct was found to be sufficiently outrageous to satisfy the requirements" for that tort. However, though "not unsympathetic to the distress doubtless suffered" by the employee, the court concluded "that the distress stemmed from the discharge itself and not from the investigatory process coincident with the discharge," and it was therefore error to find that the investigation constituted the tort. For a discussion of emotional distress in the context of employment contracts, see Note 5, p. 733 above.

Family Relations

A second category of public policy presented in the Restatement concerns the impairment of family relations. What exactly does the phrase mean? Prohibitions on prenuptial agreements have provided a clear, if increasingly historical, example of a policy thought to be "rooted in precedents collected over the centuries." To enforce a contract that contemplated divorce by agreeing to its financial consequences even before marriage was thought to dangle a lure, enforceable at law, before betrothed couples. Does the attempt to keep spouses together by refusing enforcement of settlement agreements entered into before the marriage make sense in an era of no-fault divorce? On the other hand, does the case below go too far in taking prenuptial agreements out of the protected realm of family contracting by "commodifying" marriage?

Simeone v. Simeone

Supreme Court of Pennsylvania, 1990.
525 Pa. 392, 581 A.2d 162.

■ FLAHERTY, JUSTICE. [In 1975, Catherine Walsh, a twenty-three year old unemployed nurse, was engaged to Frederick Simeone, a thirty-nine year old neurosurgeon. On the eve of their wedding, Frederick's attorney presented Catherine with a prenuptial agreement. Among other provisions, the agreement limited Catherine in the event of a separation or divorce to a maximum total payment from Frederick of $25,000. Without seeking her own counsel and without explanation from Frederick's attorney regarding the legal rights surrendered, Catherine signed the agreement. The parties were married the next day, separated in 1982, and began divorce proceedings in 1984. In 1985, Catherine filed a claim for alimony *pendente lite*. Frederick resisted such payment, arguing that between 1982 and 1984, he had made payments to Catherine satisfying the $25,000 limit. The master upheld the prenuptial agreement; that finding was affirmed on appeal. Catherine appealed to the Supreme Court.

In its decision, the court noted a rule established in Estate of Geyer, 533 A.2d 423 (Pa. 1987), that a prenuptial agreement is valid "if it *either* made a reasonable provision for the spouse *or* was entered after a full and fair disclosure of the general financial positions of the parties and the statutory rights being relinquished." The court stated that "there is need for a reexamination of the foundations upon which *Geyer* and earlier cases rested, and a need for clarification of the standards by which the validity of prenuptial agreements will be judged."]

There is no longer validity in the implicit presumption that supplied the basis for *Geyer* and similar earlier decisions. Such decisions rested upon a belief that spouses are of unequal status and that women are not knowledgeable enough to understand the nature of contracts that they enter. Society has advanced, however, to the point where women are no longer regarded as the "weaker" party in marriage, or in society generally. Indeed, the stereotype that women serve as homemakers while men work as breadwinners is no longer viable. Quite often today both spouses are income earners. Nor is there viability in the presumption that women are uninformed, uneducated, and readily subjected to unfair advantage in marital agreements. Indeed, women nowadays quite often have substantial education, financial awareness, income, and assets.

Accordingly, the law has advanced to recognize the equal status of men and women in our society. See, e.g., Pa. Const. art. 1, § 28 (constitutional prohibition of sex discrimination in laws of the Commonwealth). Paternalistic presumptions and protections that arose to shelter women from the inferiorities and incapacities which they were perceived as having in earlier times have, appropriately, been discarded. It would be inconsistent, therefore, to perpetuate the standards governing prenuptial agreements that were described in *Geyer* and similar decisions, as these reflected a paternalistic approach that is now insupportable.

Further, *Geyer* and its predecessors embodied substantial departures from traditional rules of contract law, to the extent that they allowed consideration of the knowledge of the contracting parties and reasonableness of their bargain as factors governing whether to uphold an agreement. Traditional principles of contract law provide perfectly adequate remedies where contracts are procured through fraud, misrepresentation, or duress. Consideration of other factors, such as the knowledge of the parties and the reasonableness of their bargain, is inappropriate. See Geyer, 533 A.2d at 434–35 (Flaherty, J. dissenting). Prenuptial agreements are contracts, and, as such, should be evaluated under the same criteria as are applicable to other types of contracts.

Contracting parties are normally bound by their agreements, without regard to whether the terms thereof were read and fully understood and irrespective of whether the agreements embodied reasonable or good bargains. See Bollinger v. Central Pennsylvania Quarry Stripping & Construction Co., 229 A.2d 741, 742 (1967). Based upon these principles, the terms of the present prenuptial agreement must be regarded as binding, without regard to whether the terms were fully understood by appellant. *Ignorantia non excusat.*

Accordingly, we find no merit in a contention raised by appellant that the agreement should be declared void on the ground that she did not consult with independent legal counsel. To impose a *per se* requirement that parties entering a prenuptial agreement must obtain independent legal counsel would be contrary to traditional principles of contract law, and would constitute a paternalistic and unwarranted interference with the parties' freedom to enter contracts.

By invoking inquiries into reasonableness, the functioning and reliability of prenuptial agreements is severely undermined. Parties would not have entered such agreements, and, indeed, might not have entered their marriages, if they did not expect their agreements to be strictly enforced. If parties viewed an agreement as reasonable at the time of its inception, as evidenced by their having signed the agreement, they should be foreclosed from later trying to evade its terms by asserting that it was not in fact reasonable. Pertinently, the present agreement contained a clause reciting that "each of the parties considers this agreement fair, just and reasonable."

We are reluctant to interfere with the power of persons contemplating marriage to agree upon, and to act in reliance upon, what *they* regard as an acceptable distribution scheme for their property. A court should not ignore the parties' expressed intent by proceeding to determine whether a prenuptial agreement was, in the court's view, reasonable at the time of its inception or the time of divorce. These are exactly the sorts of judicial determinations that such agreements are designed to avoid.

In discarding the approach of *Geyer,* we do not depart from the longstanding principle that a full and fair disclosure of the financial positions of the parties is required. Absent this disclosure, a material misrepresentation in the inducement for entering a prenuptial agreement may be asserted. Hillegass Estate, 244 A.2d 672, 676–77 (Pa. 1968). Parties to these agreements do not quite deal at arm's length, but rather at the time the contract is entered into stand in a relation of mutual confidence and trust that calls for disclosure of their financial resources. *Id.* at 149. It is well settled that this disclosure need not be exact, so long as it is "full and fair." Kaufmann Estate, 171 A.2d 48, 51 n. 8 (1961). In essence therefore, the duty of disclosure under these circumstances is consistent with traditional principles of contract law.

Appellant's final contention is that the agreement was executed under conditions of duress in that it was presented to her at 5 p.m. on the eve of her wedding, a time when she could not seek counsel without the trauma, expense, and embarrassment of postponing the wedding. The master found this claim not credible. The courts below affirmed that finding, upon an ample evidentiary basis. Appellee testified that, although the final version of the agreement was indeed presented to appellant on the eve of the wedding, he had engaged in several discussions with appellant regarding the contents of the agreement during the six month period preceding that date. . . . Yet another witness confirmed that, during the months preceding the wedding, appellant participated in several discussions of prenuptial agreements. And the legal counsel who prepared the agreement for appellee testified that . . . he was present when the agreement was signed and that appellant expressed absolutely no reluctance about signing. It should be noted, too, that during the months when the agreement was being discussed appellant had more than sufficient time to consult with independent legal counsel if she had so desired. Under these circumstances, there was plainly no error in finding that appellant failed to prove duress.

Order affirmed.

■ PAPADAKOS, JUSTICE, concurring. I cannot join the opinion authored by Mr. Justice Flaherty, because, it must be clear to all readers, it contains a number of unnecessary and unwarranted declarations regarding the "equality" of women. Mr. Justice Flaherty believes that, with the hard-fought victory of the Equal Rights Amendment in Pennsylvania, all vestiges of inequality between the sexes have been erased and women are now treated equally under the law. I fear my colleague does not live in the real world. If I did not know him better I would think that his statements smack of male chauvinism, an attitude that "you women asked for it, now live with it." If you want to know about equality of women, just ask them about comparable wages for comparable work. Just ask them about sexual harassment in the workplace. Just ask them about the sexual discrimination in the Executive Suites of big business. And the list of discrimination based on sex goes on and on.

I view prenuptial agreements as being in the nature of contracts of adhesion with one party generally having greater authority than the other who deals in a subservient role. I believe the law protects the subservient party, regardless of that party's sex, to insure equal protection and treatment under the law.

The present case does not involve the broader issues to which the gratuitous declarations in question are addressed, and it is injudicious to offer declarations in a case which does not involve those issues. Especially when those declarations are inconsistent with reality.

■ MCDERMOTT, JUSTICE, dissenting. Were a contract of marriage, the most intimate relationship between two people, not the surrender of freedom, an offering of self in love, sacrifice, hope for better or for worse, the begetting of children and the offer of effort, labor, precious time and care for the safety and prosperity of their union, then the majority would find me among them.

At the time of dissolution of the marriage, a spouse should be able to avoid the operation of a pre-nuptial agreement upon clear and convincing proof that, despite the existence of full and fair disclosure at the time of the execution of the agreement, the agreement is nevertheless so inequitable and unfair that it should not be enforced in a court of this state. Although the spouse attempting to avoid the operation of the agreement will admittedly have a difficult burden given the standard of proof, and the fact of full and fair disclosure, we must not close our courts to relief where to enforce an agreement will result in unfairness and inequity. The majority holds to the view, without waiver, that parties, having contracted with full and fair disclosure, should be made to suffer the consequences of their bargains. In so holding, the majority has given no weight to the other side of the scales: the state's paramount interest in the preservation of marriage and the family relationship, and the protection of parties to a marriage who may be rendered wards of the state, unable to provide for their own reasonable needs. Our sister states have found such treatment too short a shrift for so fundamental a unit of society.

NOTES

(1) *Questions.* What competing public policies are invoked by Justices Flaherty, Papadakos, and McDermott?

(2) *Reform and Sources of Reform.* In 2012, the Uniform Law Commission (ULC) promulgated the Uniform Premarital and Marital Agreements Act. The Act provides that both premarital and marital (future settlement agreements entered into during marriage) agreements are enforceable unless the challenger proves either that the agreement was not voluntary or that the agreement was unconscionable when executed and that there was inadequate financial disclosure. "In other words, unconscionability by itself is not a basis for voiding an agreement; the challenger must also show a failure of financial disclosure. In that regard, the UPAA makes premarital agreements harder to invalidate than commercial agreements. . . . " See Barbara Ann Atwood and Brian Bix, *A New Uniform Law for Premarital and Marital Agreements*, 46 Fam. L.Q. 313, 322 (2012). Do you see why?

In 2010, the Supreme Court of the United Kingdom held for the first time that a couple's prenuptial agreement "can have decisive or compelling weight," so long as the agreement was "freely entered into by each party with a full appreciation of its implications" and that under prevailing circumstances at the time of enforcement, it would not be unfair to hold the parties to their agreement. Radmacher v. Granatino [2010] UKSC 42. The Supreme Court observed that "it will be natural to infer that parties entering into [such] agreements will intend that effect be given to them".

In the Matter of Baby M

Supreme Court of New Jersey, 1988.
109 N.J. 396, 537 A.2d 1227.

■ WILENTZ, CHIEF JUSTICE. [William Stern and Mary Beth Whitehead entered into a written agreement that, in exchange for $10,000, Whitehead would be inseminated with Stern's sperm, give any resulting baby to Stern, and terminate her own parental rights. In March, 1986, Whitehead delivered a baby girl. When she refused to turn over the baby permanently, Stern sought specific enforcement of the contract. (Stern also obtained an order awarding him custody of the baby until the case was decided.)

Following a lengthy trial, the court upheld the validity of contract, and ordered that Whitehead's parental rights be terminated. Mrs. Whitehead appealed.]

In this matter the Court is asked to determine the validity of a contract that purports to provide a new way of bringing children into a family. For a fee of $10,000, a woman agrees to be artificially inseminated with the semen of another woman's husband; she is to conceive a child, carry it to term, and after its birth surrender it to the natural father and his wife. The intent of the contract is that the child's natural mother will thereafter be forever separated from her child. The wife is to adopt the child, and she and the natural father are to be regarded as its parents for all purposes. The contract providing for this is called a "surrogacy contract," the natural mother inappropriately called the "surrogate mother."

We invalidate the surrogacy contract because it conflicts with the law and public policy of this State. While we recognize the depth of the yearning of infertile couples to have their own children, we find the payment of money to a "surrogate" mother illegal, perhaps criminal, and potentially degrading to women. Although in this case we grant custody to the natural father, the evidence having clearly proved such custody to be in the best interests of the infant, we void both the termination of the surrogate mother's parental rights and the adoption of the child by the wife/stepparent. We thus restore the "surrogate" as the mother of the child. We remand the issue of the natural mother's visitation rights to the trial court, since that issue was not reached below and the record before us is not sufficient to permit us to decide it *de novo*.

We find no offense to our present laws where a woman voluntarily and without payment agrees to act as a "surrogate" mother, provided that she is not subject to a binding agreement to surrender her child. Moreover, our holding today does not preclude the Legislature from altering the current statutory scheme, within constitutional limits, so as to permit surrogacy contracts. Under current law, however, the surrogacy agreement before us is illegal and invalid.

II.

INVALIDITY AND UNENFORCEABILITY OF SURROGACY CONTRACT

We have concluded that this surrogacy contract is invalid. Our conclusion has two bases: direct conflict with existing statutes and conflict with the public policies of this State, as expressed in its statutory and decisional law.

One of the surrogacy contract's basic purposes, to achieve the adoption of a child through private placement, though permitted in New Jersey "is very much disfavored." Sees v. Baber, 377 A.2d 628 (1977). Its use of money for this purpose—and we have no doubt whatsoever that the money is being paid to obtain an adoption and not, as the Sterns argue, for the personal services of Mary Beth Whitehead—is illegal and perhaps criminal. *N.J.S.A.* 9:3–54. In addition to the inducement of money, there is the coercion of contract: the natural mother's irrevocable agreement, prior to birth, even prior to conception, to surrender the child to the adoptive couple. Such an agreement is totally unenforceable in private placement adoption. Sees, 377 A.2d 628. Even where the adoption is through an approved agency, the formal agreement to surrender occurs only *after* birth (as we read N.J.S.A. 9:2–16 and –17, and similar statutes), and then, by regulation, only after the birth mother has been offered counseling. *N.J.A.C.* 10:121A–5.4(c). Integral to these invalid provisions of the surrogacy contract is the related agreement, equally invalid, on the part of the natural mother to cooperate with, and not to contest, proceedings to terminate her parental rights, as well as her contractual concession, in aid of the adoption, that the child's best interests would be served by awarding custody to the natural father and his wife-all of this before she has even conceived, and, in some cases, before she has the slightest idea of what the natural father and adoptive mother are like.

The foregoing provisions not only directly conflict with New Jersey statutes, but also offend long-established State policies. These critical terms, which are at the heart of the contract, are invalid and unenforceable; the conclusion therefore follows, without more, that the entire contract is unenforceable.

A.   Conflict with Statutory Provisions

The surrogacy contract conflicts with: (1) laws prohibiting the use of money in connection with adoptions; (2) laws requiring proof of parental unfitness or abandonment before termination of parental rights is ordered or an adoption is granted; and (3) laws that make surrender of custody and consent to adoption revocable in private placement adoptions.

(1)   Our law prohibits paying or accepting money in connection with any placement of a child for adoption. *N.J.S.A.* 9:3–54a. Violation is a high misdemeanor. Excepted are fees of an approved agency (which must be a non-profit entity), and certain expenses in connection with childbirth. *N.J.S.A.* 9:3–54b.[1]

Considerable care was taken in this case to structure the surrogacy arrangement so as not to violate this prohibition. Nevertheless, it seems clear that the money was paid and accepted in connection with an adoption.

The prohibition of our statute is strong. Violation constitutes a high misdemeanor carrying a penalty of three to five years imprisonment. *N.J.S.A.* 2C:43–6a(3). The evils inherent in baby-bartering are loathsome for a myriad of reasons. The child is sold without regard for whether the purchasers will be suitable parents. N. Baker, *Baby Selling: The Scandal of Black Market Adoption* 7 (1978). The natural mother does not receive the benefit of counseling and guidance to assist her in making a decision that may affect her for a lifetime. In fact, the monetary incentive to sell

---

[1]   N.J.S.A. 9:3–54 reads as follows:

a. No person, firm, partnership, corporation, association or agency shall make, offer to make or assist or participate in any placement for adoption and in connection therewith

(1) Pay, give or agree to give any money or any valuable consideration, or assume or discharge any financial obligation; or

(2) Take, receive, accept or agree to accept any money or any valuable consideration.

b. The prohibition of subsection a. shall not apply to the fees or services of any approved agency in connection with a placement for adoption, nor shall such prohibition apply to the payment or reimbursement of medical, hospital or other similar expenses incurred in connection with the birth or any illness of the child, or to the acceptance of such reimbursement by a parent of the child.

her child may, depending on her financial circumstances, make her decision less voluntary. *Id.* at 44.

The provision in the surrogacy contract, agreed to before conception, requiring the natural mother to surrender custody of the child without any right of revocation is one more indication of the essential nature of this transaction: the creation of a contractual system of termination and adoption designed to circumvent our statutes.

B.   Public Policy Considerations

The surrogacy contract's invalidity, resulting from its direct conflict with the above statutory provisions, is further underlined when its goals and means are measured against New Jersey's public policy. The contract's basic premise, that the natural parents can decide in advance of birth which one is to have custody of the child, bears no relationship to the settled law that the child's best interests shall determine custody.

Under the contract, the natural mother is irrevocably committed before she knows the strength of her bond with her child. She never makes a totally voluntary, informed decision, for quite clearly any decision prior to the baby's birth is, in the most important sense, uninformed, and any decision after that, compelled by a pre-existing contractual commitment, the threat of a lawsuit, and the inducement of a $10,000 payment, is less than totally voluntary. Her interests are of little concern to those who controlled this transaction.

Worst of all, however, is the contract's total disregard of the best interests of the child. There is not the slightest suggestion that any inquiry will be made at any time to determine the fitness of the Sterns as custodial parents, of Mrs. Stern as an adoptive parent, their superiority to Mrs. Whitehead, or the effect on the child of not living with her natural mother.

This is the sale of a child, or, at the very least, the sale of a mother's right to her child, the only mitigating factor being that one of the purchasers is the father. Almost every evil that prompted the prohibition on the payment of money in connection with adoptions exists here.

First, and perhaps most important, all parties concede that it is unlikely that surrogacy will survive without money. Despite the alleged selfless motivation of surrogate mothers, if there is no payment, there will be no surrogates, or very few. That conclusion contrasts with adoption; for obvious reasons, there remains a steady supply, albeit insufficient, despite the prohibitions against payment. The adoption itself, relieving the natural mother of the financial burden of supporting an infant, is in some sense the equivalent of payment.

Second, the use of money in adoptions does not *produce* the problem—conception occurs, and usually the birth itself, before illicit funds are offered. With surrogacy, the "problem," if one views it as such, consisting of the purchase of a woman's procreative capacity, at the risk of her life, is caused by and originates with the offer of money.

Third, with the law prohibiting the use of money in connection with adoptions, the built-in financial pressure of the unwanted pregnancy and the consequent support obligation do not lead the mother to the highest paying, ill-suited, adoptive parents. She is just as well-off surrendering the child to an approved agency. In surrogacy, the highest bidders will presumably become the adoptive parents regardless of suitability, so long as payment of money is permitted.

Fourth, the mother's consent to surrender her child in adoptions is revocable, even after surrender of the child, unless it be to an approved agency, where by regulation there are protections against an ill-advised surrender. In surrogacy, consent occurs so early that no amount of advice would satisfy the potential mother's need, yet the consent is irrevocable.

In the scheme contemplated by the surrogacy contract in this case, a middle man, propelled by profit, promotes the sale. Whatever idealism may have motivated any of the participants, the profit motive predominates, permeates, and ultimately governs the transaction. The demand for children is great and the supply small. The availability of contraception, abortion, and the greater willingness of single mothers to bring up their children has led to a shortage of babies offered for adoption. [citations omitted] The situation is ripe for the entry of the middleman who will bring some equilibrium into the market by increasing the supply through the use of money.

The point is made that Mrs. Whitehead *agreed* to the surrogacy arrangement, supposedly fully understanding the consequences. Putting aside the issue of how compelling her need for money may have been, and how significant her understanding of the consequences, we suggest that her consent is irrelevant. There are, in a civilized society, some things that money cannot buy. In America, we decided long ago that merely because conduct purchased by money was "voluntary" did not mean that it was good or beyond regulation and prohibition. West Coast Hotel Co. v. Parrish, 300 U.S. 379 (1937). Employers can no longer buy labor at the lowest price they can bargain for, even though that labor is "voluntary," 29 U.S.C. § 206 (1982) or purchase the agreement of workers to subject themselves to unsafe or unhealthful working conditions, 29 U.S.C. §§ 651 to 678. (Occupational Safety and Health Act of 1970). There are, in short, values that society deems more important than granting to wealth whatever it can buy, be it labor, love, or life. Whether this principle recommends prohibition of surrogacy, which presumably sometimes results in great satisfaction to all of the parties, is not for us to say. We note here only that, under existing law, the fact that Mrs. Whitehead "agreed" to the arrangement is not dispositive.

The surrogacy contract is based on, principles that are directly contrary to the objectives of our laws. It guarantees the separation of a child from its mother; it looks to adoption regardless of suitability; it totally ignores the child; it takes the child from the mother regardless of her wishes and her maternal fitness; and it does all of this, it accomplishes all of its goals, through the use of money.

Beyond that is the potential degradation of some women that may result from this arrangement. In many cases, of course, surrogacy may bring satisfaction, not only to the infertile couple, but to the surrogate mother herself. The fact, however, that many women may not perceive surrogacy negatively but rather see it as an opportunity does not diminish its potential for devastation to other women.

In sum, the harmful consequences of this surrogacy arrangement appear to us all too palpable. In New Jersey the surrogate mother's agreement to sell her child is void.[2] Its irrevocability infects the entire contract, as does the money that purports to buy it.

CONCLUSION

This case affords some insight into a new reproductive arrangement: the artificial insemination of a surrogate mother. The unfortunate events that have unfolded illustrate that its unregulated use can bring suffering to all involved. Potential victims include the surrogate mother and her family, the natural father and his wife, and most importantly, the child. Although surrogacy has apparently provided positive results for some infertile couples, it can also, as this case demonstrates, cause suffering to participants, here essentially innocent and well-intended.

We have found that our present laws do not permit the surrogacy contract used in this case. Nowhere, however, do we find any legal prohibition against surrogacy when the surrogate mother volunteers, without any payment, to act as a surrogate and is given the right to change her mind and to assert her parental rights. Moreover, the

---

[2] Michigan courts have also found that these arrangements conflict with various aspects of their law. See Doe v. Kelley, 307 N.W.2d 438 (1981), cert. den., 459 U.S. 1183 (1983) (application of sections of Michigan Adoption Law prohibiting the exchange of money to surrogacy is constitutional). . . .

The Supreme Court of Kentucky has taken a somewhat different approach to surrogate arrangements. In Surrogate Parenting Assocs. v. Commonwealth ex. rel. Armstrong, 704 S.W.2d 209 (Ky.1986), the court held that the "fundamental differences" between surrogate arrangements and baby-selling placed the surrogate parenting agreement beyond the reach of Kentucky's baby-selling statute. Id. at 211. . . .

Concomitant with this pro-surrogacy conclusion, however, the court held that a "surrogate" mother has the right to void the contract if she changes her mind during pregnancy or immediately after birth. Id. at 212–13. The court relied on statutes providing that consent to adoption or to the termination of parental rights prior to five days after the birth of the child is invalid, and concluded that consent before conception must also be unenforceable. Id. at 212–13. . . .

In contrast to the law in the United States, the law in the United Kingdom concerning surrogate parenting is fairly well-settled. Parliament passed the Surrogacy Arrangements Act, 1985, ch. 49, which made initiating or taking part in any negotiations with a view to making or arranging a surrogacy contract a criminal offense. The criminal sanction, however, does not apply to the "surrogate" mother or to the natural father, but rather applies to other persons engaged in arranging surrogacy contracts on a commercial basis. . . . It should be noted, however, that certain surrogacy arrangements, i.e., those arranged without brokers and revocable by the natural mother, are not prohibited under current law in the United Kingdom.

Legislature remains free to deal with this most sensitive issue as it sees fit, subject only to constitutional constraints.

If the Legislature decides to address surrogacy, consideration of this case will highlight many of its potential harms. We do not underestimate the difficulties of legislating on this subject. In addition to the inevitable confrontation with the ethical and moral issues involved, there is the question of the wisdom and effectiveness of regulating a matter so private, yet of such public interest. Legislative consideration of surrogacy may also provide the opportunity to begin to focus on the overall implications of the new reproductive biotechnology-*in vitro* fertilization, preservation of sperm and eggs, embryo implantation and the like. The problem is how to enjoy the benefits of the technology-especially for infertile couples-while minimizing the risk of abuse. The problem can be addressed only when society decides what its values and objectives are in this troubling, yet promising, area.

[The court remanded the case for a custody determination based on the best interests of the child].

NOTES

(1) *Questions.* What sources did the court use to inform its decision that the contract is unenforceable? What is the status of an unpaid surrogacy agreement in New Jersey after *Baby M*? A copy of the contract between Stern and Whitehead is found in *Selections*. Do you think all of its terms would be enforceable even if the court had found no public policy violation? On p. 739, the court uses the phrase, and with some disdain, "the coercion of contract." Isn't the coercion of contract one of contract's defining features?

In reading the decision in *Baby M*, when did you first get a sense of how the court might rule? Note 3, pp. 114–115, above describes Judge Cardozo's skill in persuading us to see Lady Duff-Gordon and the transaction in a particular way. What, if any, rhetorical devices does the New Jersey court use to depict paid surrogacy as "against public policy"? Are any public policies *advanced* by enforcing commercial surrogacy contracts? What sources of authority might support that view?

How did the Supreme Court of Kentucky, mentioned by the court in fn. 2, p. 743, above, come to a different conclusion on policy grounds? Would the Pennsylvania Supreme Court, writing in *Simeone*, p. 734, enforce Whitehead's promise to Stern? Should women be permitted to consent to surrogacy agreements? If so, should their consent be subject to any conditions?

(2) *Middlemen and Money.* The importance of middlemen, or intermediaries, in facilitating transactions was discussed in Note 2, p. 604, in connection with defense contracts. In *Baby M,* the court took a less laudatory view, characterizing the middleman as "propelled by profit" to "promot[e] the sale." Is that not the very function of a middleman? Is the problem in *Baby M* that profit was diverted from Whitehead to the middleman? (But see Black v. Bush, p. 601.) Or was the middleman chastised

for performing the search function too well and creating a market for services that themselves offended New Jersey public policy?

Since *Baby M,* women in states where paid surrogacy is legal have opened their own surrogacy agencies, largely dispensing with the middleman. See Carol Sanger, *Developing Markets in Babymaking:* In the Matter of Baby M, 30 Harv. J.L. & Gender 67 (2007). See also Deborah Spar, *The Baby Business: How Money, Science, and Politics Drive the Commerce of Conception* (2006).

(3) *Markets and Legal Regimes.* In *Baby M,* the court noted that the state legislature remained free to deal with surrogacy ("this troubling yet promising area") "as it sees fit." A number of legislatures have done just that. See Va. Code Ann. §§ 20–156 to 20–165 (Michie 2000) (Assisted Conception).

What is the relation between the background legal regime and markets? Certainly law provides a system of property rights against which exchanges take place: Parties want to know with certainty what is theirs to sell and what interests they acquire when they buy something. But as Professor Willard Hurst wrote in his study of the lumber industry in 19th-century Wisconsin, "it was the law of *contract* which supplied the assurances and the procedures and the tools necessary for the immediate operation and steadily expanding energy of the [lumber industry].... For the timber industry as for other business, contract law provided a framework of reasonably assured expectations within which men might plan and venture. The availability of the forms and procedures of contract thus helped the expansion of the market." Willard Hurst, *Law and Economic Growth: The Legal History of the Lumber Industry in Wisconsin 1836–1915,* 285 *et. seq.* (1964) (emphasis added).

"Reasonably assured expectations" may also be at stake in family agreements. As the court noted in *Simeone,* p. 734 above, parties to prenuptial agreements might "not have entered such agreements, and, indeed, might not have entered their marriages, if they did not expect their agreements to be strictly enforced." The certainty of enforcement may be as crucial in markets for reproductive parts and services as it was in the timber industry studied by Professor Hurst. In California, for example, surrogacy providers advertise to potential clients the security provided by the background regime of contract enforceability: "California surrogacy laws are some of the most favorable in the United States for recipient parents." See http://www.thesurrogacysource.com/sanfranciscosurrogate.htm. See also Deborah Spar, *Where Babies Come From: Supply and Demand in an Infant Marketplace,* 84 Harv. Bus. Rev. 133 (2006). Note that brokering surrogacy agreements is a criminal act in the U.K. under the 1985 Surrogacy Arrangements Act. What effect is this likely to have on a market for surrogacy? Might commercial surrogacy disappear? See Lisa C. Ikemoto, *Reproductive Tourism: Equality Concerns in the Global Market for Fertility Services,* 27 J.L. & Inequality 277 (2009).

Of course, acknowledging the relation between background legal rules and market development does not commit us to any view about whether a particular market in a good or service *should* exist.

(4) *Dignity and Public Policy*. In its third paragraph, the court in *Baby M* stated that it found "the payment of money to a 'surrogate' mother illegal, perhaps criminal, and potentially degrading to women." Focusing on the third phrase, does the degradation, or potential degradation, of a party provide a policy ground for judicial nonenforcement of the contract? Certainly there is the problem of what counts as degrading for women, or for anyone else. How might the consensual termination of one's parental rights for payment be considered degrading? Is the court's concern about degradation by contract that the person herself is degraded or that the society is degraded for permitting such a bargain?

In this regard, consider a case from France involving the disturbing practice of dwarf tossing. (The practice involves dwarves or "little people" being thrown by contestants for amusement in bars; the dwarves receive payment for their services.) In 1995, the mayor of Morsang-sur-Orge banned a nightclub from proceeding with the show on public policy grounds. The ban was upheld by Counseil d'Etat, which stated that:

> by its very object, such a show undermines the dignity of the human person; that hence the authority holding the municipal police power may ban it, even in the absence of particular local circumstances, and even where protective measures are in place to ensure the safety of the person concerned and this person lends himself willingly and for reward to this activity.

Manuel Wackenheim v. France, Communication No 854/1999, U.N. Doc. CCPR/C/75/D/854/1999 (2002).

The dwarf, Manuel Wackenheim, then brought a claim against France under the International Covenant on Civil and Political Rights before the U.N. Human Rights Committee. Wackenheim argued that because "there is no work for dwarves in France," the ban itself—and not the activity—constituted the affront to his dignity "since dignity consists in having a job." The Human Rights Committee upheld the French decision on the ground that the ban on dwarf tossing "was necessary in order to protect public order, which brings into play considerations of human dignity that are compatible with the objectives of the Covenant." See Manuel Wackenheim v. France, Communication No 854/1999, U.N. Doc. CCPR/C/75/D/854/1999 (2002).

In thinking about human dignity as a source of public policy that may limit a competent party's right to contract, are there distinctions between the cases of Manuel Wackenheim and Mary Beth Whitehead? Are there other commercial transactions—organ sales? prostitution?—that might be thought to implicate dignity? Should assault to a person's dignity should be a ground for non-enforcement of a contract?

(C) Public Policy Derived from Statutes

In Part (A) of this section, we addressed decisions that considered the enforceability of contracts that were connected to activities made illegal by statute. In this Part, we again examine statutes as possible sources of public policy limitations on contract enforceability. Here, however, the statutes in question are not criminal statutes that *ban* an activity but statutes that may otherwise inform a court's determination regarding public policy.

Shadis v. Beal

United States Court of Appeals for the Third Circuit, 1982.
685 F.2d 824.

■ JAMES HUNTER, III, CIRCUIT JUDGE. [Plaintiffs, medically needy individuals, brought a class action suit against the Commonwealth of Pennsylvania under the 1871 Civil Rights Act, 42 U.S.C. § 1983, alleging the unlawful deprivation of certain medical benefits. The allegations included (1) violations of due process by the individual appellants in terminating Medicaid benefits without prior notice or opportunity for a hearing; and (2) operation of the Medicaid program under illegally low eligibility requirements. The plaintiffs essentially prevailed. Having been successful, plaintiffs moved for an award of attorneys' fees for their counsel, Community Legal Services ("CLS"), pursuant to the Civil Rights Attorney Fees Awards Act, 42 U.S.C. § 1988 ("the Fees Awards Act").]

This appeal raises the question of whether certain provisions of two contracts between the Pennsylvania Department of Public Welfare ("PDPW") and the Pennsylvania Legal Services Center ("PLSC") and between PLSC and CLS, which prohibit CLS from requesting or accepting attorneys' fees in suits against the Commonwealth of Pennsylvania or Commonwealth employees, are void as contrary to public policy. The federal [district] court held that the relevant contractual provisions between CLS and the Commonwealth were void because they conflicted with the public policy underlying by the Fees Awards Act. We agree and will affirm the order of the district court.

FACTS AND PROCEDURAL HISTORY

CLS is a non-profit legal services corporation the sole purpose of which is to provide legal services to the poor. It receives approximately half of its operating budget directly from the federal Legal Services Corporation under the Legal Services Corporation Act. The remaining half is received under Title XX of the Social Security Act. Title XX funding is channeled from the United States Department of Health and Human Services to DPW. DPW then allocates a portion of the federal funds, together with a 25% matching state grant, to various community based legal services programs, including CLS. The actual distribution and administration of Title XX monies for legal services is performed by the conduit organization, PLSC.

Pursuant to this funding arrangement, CLS entered into a series of annual contracts with PLSC for the fiscal years 1978–1981, during which CLS performed much of the work in the preparation of this case. The contracts for the fiscal periods 1979–1980 and 1980–1981 contained the provisions which prevent CLS from requesting attorneys' fees arising out of litigation against the Commonwealth or Commonwealth employees.

Before the no fees clause was inserted into the PLSC-CLS contract, DPW used other arguments in attempts to prevent CLS from obtaining fees when CLS attorneys successfully sued the Commonwealth. Beginning with fiscal year 1978–1979, DPW required, over the objections of PLSC and CLS, that DPW-PLSC funding contracts contain a no fees provision restricting the right of PLSC to receive attorneys' fees in cases against the Commonwealth. Since 1979, DPW has compelled PLSC to include a similar provision in its funding agreements with local legal services programs, including CLS.

In August 1979, PLSC proposed a contract to CLS for the fiscal year 1979–80 which contained a no fees provision. CLS signed and returned the proposed contract on January 11, 1980 with a letter objecting to the provision.

In 1980 DPW again stated that no funding would be forthcoming for any legal services program which did not acquiesce in DPW's demands by signing a contract containing the no fees provision.

Shortly before the end of the fiscal year, DPW and PLSC entered into a contract for fiscal year 1980–1981, which again contained a no fees restraint. On June 30, 1980, CLS received from PLSC the proposed 1980–1981 contract, with a demand that the document be executed and returned no later than the following week. On July 7, 1980, CLS officers, faced with many obligations to poor clients and a severe fiscal crisis, executed and returned the 1980–1981 contract to PLSC. Again, CLS attached a letter asserting that CLS did not, by executing the contract, waive its right to challenge the legality and enforceability of the no fees provision.[r] CLS thus challenged the no fees provision in this case and its position was upheld by the district court. The Commonwealth has appealed.

DISCUSSION

The threshold question in deciding this appeal is whether the district court properly concluded that this case presents a question of federal law, and not one of Pennsylvania of contract law. The district court was clearly correct. The underlying claim in this case is not based on contracts, but is a federal civil rights claim. Part of this claim is a request for attorneys' fees, made under a federal statute, to which a contract provision is raised as a defense. Therefore, the district court was correct

---

[r]   Because we decide this case on the public policy issue, we need not address the appellees' contention that the 1980–81 contract was voidable as the product of economic duress. However, for the sake of factual completeness it is important to stress that DPW had insisted that it would not provide any 1980–81 funding for any social program which had not signed a contract which conformed to DPW demands (including the no fees provision). Appendix at 117a. On June 26, 1980, CLS unexpectedly suffered a $118,000 reduction in its Title XX reimbursements for expenses incurred during April and May of that year. Appendix at 116a. In June 1980, CLS was facing its second successive annual funding cut by the Commonwealth which had already resulted in service reductions and a 20% decrease in attorney staff. Appendix at 115a.

in concluding that it is to federal law that it should turn for its rules of decision.[s] The case before us is clearly at its roots a federal claim. Therefore, we now turn to the question of whether the contract provisions in question conflict with public policy.

Public Policy Underlying the Fees Awards Act

Having decided that federal law is controlling in this case, the district court held that the no fees restraints of the contracts between PLSC and CLS were unenforceable because they counteracted the federal public policy underlying the Fees Awards Act. The court utilized the analysis of the Restatement (Second) of Contracts § 178 (1981). After considering and balancing the factors in favor of enforcement of the contracts against the public policies weighing against enforcement, the court denied effect to the no fees provisions. The district court's conclusion and its approach were correct.

Congress enacted the Fees Awards Act to encourage private citizens to enforce fundamental rights under the civil rights laws. Quite simply, the policy behind the Act is to encourage compliance with and enforcement of those laws. Congress has noted that the primary goal of the Act is "to promote the enforcement of the Federal Civil Rights Acts, as Congress intended, and to achieve uniformity in those statutes and justice for all citizens." Courts have stated that the Act must be liberally construed to achieve these ends.

The district court in this case outlined clearly its view of the public policy involved:

> The public policy embodied in Section 1988 is a vital one. Congress could not have been clearer in its intent or in the seriousness it attached to the attorneys' fees provisions. The use of words such as 'essential' and 'integral' is prevalent in the legislative history and in the cases construing the Act. The policy is, quite clearly, an important one.

520 F.Supp. at 864. The court was referring, among other things, to the Senate Report's unambiguous statement of the policy behind the Act:

> Fee awards are an integral part of the remedies necessary to obtain such compliance (with the civil rights laws) . . . If our civil rights laws are not to become mere hollow pronouncements which the average citizen cannot enforce, we must maintain the traditionally effective remedy of fee shifting in these cases.

S.Rep.No.94–1011 at 5913 (emphasis added).

---

[s] Of course, as the district court noted, the Pennsylvania law of illegal contracts may be instructive. Indeed, in Pennsylvania, as in almost all Anglo-American jurisdictions, contracts that are contrary to public policy, those which tend to be injurious to the public good, are illegal and void. In Book's Estate, 297 Pa. 543, 147 A. 608, 609 (Pa.1929), the Supreme Court of Pennsylvania held that a contract is against public policy if it has "a tendency to injure the public or to be against the public good, or (is) inconsistent with good morals as to the consideration or the thing to be done." See generally 8 Pennsylvania Law Encyclopedia, § 103.

An important aspect of the enforcement scheme designed by Congress is the collection of attorneys' fees from the states when states are losing defendants. It is clear that Congress contemplated that states and state officials would often be the targets of civil rights actions:

> (D)efendants in these (civil rights) cases are often state or local bodies of state or local officials. In such cases, it is intended that attorneys' fees, like other items of costs, will be collected either directly from the official, in his official capacity, from funds of his agency or under his control, or from the state or local government (whether or not the agency or government is a named party).

> S.R.No.94–1011, supra, at 5913 (footnotes omitted).

It is well settled that Congress intended legal service programs, like private attorneys, to receive fees under the Fees Awards Act. Courts have awarded attorney's fees without regard to plaintiffs' ability to pay for counsel or the availability of free legal counsel. In https://1.next. westlaw.com/Link/RelatedInformation/Flag?documentGuid=I34e841c29 18311d9a707f4371c9c34f0&transitionType=InlineKeyCiteFlags&origin ationContext=docHeaderFlag&contextData=(sc.DocLink) Rodriguez v. Taylor, 569 F.2d 1231, 1245 (3d Cir. 1977), we stated:

> The statutory policies underlying the award of fees justify such shifting without regard to whether the individual plaintiff initially assumed the financial burdens of representation. . . . The award of fees to legal aid offices and other groups furnishing pro bono publico representation promotes the enforcement of the underlying statutes as much as an award to privately retained counsel. Legal services organizations often must ration their limited financial and manpower resources. Allowing them to recover fees enhances their capabilities to assist in the enforcement of congressionally favored individual rights. (citations omitted.)

In Dennis v. Chang, the Ninth Circuit agreed that:

> (a)n award (where plaintiff has been represented without charge by a legal service organization) serves the purposes of the (Fees Awards) Act for two reasons: (1) the award encourages the legal services organization to expend its limited resources in litigation aimed at enforcing the civil rights statutes; and (2) the award encourages potential defendants to comply with civil rights statutes.

> 611 F.2d at 1306.

Thus, Legal Aid offices serve a private enforcement role and further the policies contemplated by Congress in the Fees Awards Act. In Rodriguez, we discussed this role in more detail:

. . . legal services organizations may win only modest cash awards or nonmonetized equitable relief for their clients. Despite the often insignificant potential monetary benefits in individual cases, legal services organizations render valuable services to their clients and their communities. Legal aid organizations are often the sole representatives of the economically, socially and culturally deprived in their disputes with landlords, government welfare agencies, employers and creditors.

569 F.2d at 1248 (emphasis added).

Fee incentives to legal aid offices are essential to enable legal services organizations to provide more than individual, routine legal services for poor litigants. To a great extent, legal services organizations must allocate limited resources among various possible clients. Of necessity, the potential for fee recovery will be one of the factors considered in the allocation and use of resources for the maximum benefit of the poor. We are not persuaded by the Commonwealth's contention that the contractual extraction of the financial incentives created by the Fees Awards Act will have no effect on CLS because it is "not free to pick its suits on the basis of pecuniary concerns."

By enacting the Fees Awards Act, Congress reinvested the judiciary with the discretion to grant attorneys' fees in civil rights cases. In this case, we conclude that the Commonwealth has attempted to vitiate, by contract, a significant portion of the power and duty which Congress has granted to the judiciary as an essential tool in the scheme of civil rights enforcement. It is axiomatic to our federal system that neither private parties nor the states can avoid the equitable powers of the federal courts. Here, the existence of a contrary private agreement cannot successfully be asserted as a defense to the district court's statutorily mandated supervisory power over attorneys' fees.

If the Commonwealth could insert and enforce the no fees restraints in its contracts, the policy of economic inducement sought by Congress would be severely impaired. Legal service programs for the poor would have both less incentive and ability to bring civil rights suits against the Commonwealth. Thus, one of the most important types of private attorneys general would be significantly less willing to pursue civil rights litigation against the state. Judge Newcomer stated the issue aptly:

Like any private lawyer, CLS must remain within a budget, and only do the legal work that it can afford to do. What the Commonwealth has attempted to do here is to buy immunity from CLS lawyers. In return for a steady partial subsidy, the Commonwealth has demanded that CLS not seek attorneys' fees in cases brought against the Commonwealth. The obvious effect of this, if the agreement is enforced, is to cause CLS not to bring actions against the Commonwealth. In end result, an important member of the plaintiffs' civil rights bar would be removed from the scene, and the vigorous enforcement of the laws would be materially quelled.

520 F.Supp. at 864 (emphasis added; footnotes and citations omitted). Congress expressed unambiguously the significance it attached to the attorneys' fees provisions, and we conclude that the public policy embodied in § 1988 is a vital one.

Public Policy in Favor of Enforcement

Appellants advance several arguments regarding public policy considerations in favor of enforcement of the contract provision which they contend outweigh the considerations outlined above. Although appellants' arguments have some merit, they do not outweigh the public policy embodied in the Fees Awards Act.

First, the Commonwealth argues that there is a public benefit in funding legal services programs with a fixed and known budget. This is true; but it misses the mark. Attorneys' fees awards to prevailing parties in civil rights litigation are not part of public funding to legal services programs. They are distinct payments of the cost of litigation in accordance with rights and responsibilities determined by Congress. The Commonwealth would have had the burden of paying fees under the Act for violations of civil rights had the litigants' counsel been private. The fact that the taxpayer may be the ultimate payor is not a reason for supporting the no fees restraints. In any event, it is equally plausible to argue that the taxpayer ultimately gains from the payment of attorneys' fees because civil rights litigation is generally recognized as benefiting the public as a whole.

Along similar lines, the Commonwealth argues that its funding of legal service programs is an effective substitute for the provisions of the Fees Awards Act. The Commonwealth contends that the state's funding scheme promotes civil rights litigation "more effectively than does the statute . . . (thereby rendering it) all but superfluous." Obviously funding of a legal services provision by the state furthers the goal of representation of the indigent. However, that basic level of funding provided in the annual grant is not enough to provide incentives to undertake representation in the specific types of civil rights litigation which Congress hoped to encourage. The case at bar is a prime example of the kind of litigation that Congress intended to encourage through the Fees Awards Act. Here, the district court granted injunctive and declaratory relief to two plaintiff classes. The classes comprised, in the first class, recipients of and, in the second class, applicants for, medical assistance to the medically needy. The first class succeeded in proving that the state program conflicted with federal regulations. The second class succeeded in showing that medical assistance benefits had been unconstitutionally terminated. The Commonwealth's argument that its grant to CLS of the minimum amount of money required of it in order to obtain federal funding benefits the poor more than the potential of attorneys' fees awards is disingenuous. The case at bar proves the contrary. Advanced funding does not serve as an inducement to the State to comply with civil rights laws. The prospect of having to pay attorneys' fees does provide such an incentive. Indeed, the state may also have an incentive to settle a case early.

Use of the Restatement of Contracts Standard

In balancing the policy considerations in connection with the contractual fee restraints, the district court used the approach presented in Sections 178 and 179 of the Restatement (Second) of Contracts (1979). Section 178 provides:

> (1) A promise or other term of an agreement is unenforceable on grounds of public policy if legislation provides that it is unenforceable or the interest in its enforcement is clearly outweighted in the circumstances by a public policy against enforcement of such terms.

The Commonwealth argues that the district court's application of the Restatement's formulation was incorrect because it failed to require that the legislation in question either "expressly prohibit(s) the contract or . . . require(s) a performance or a result that directly contradicts what the contract requires." Neither federal nor Pennsylvania law requires such a direct, explicit conflict. Such a requirement would require that a contract be "illegal" in a literal sense before it could be invalid. However, the scope of the public policy doctrine is broader and more encompassing than the concept of illegality.

Section 179 of the Restatement provides that public policy against "the enforcement of promises or other terms may be derived by the court from: (a) legislation relevant to such a policy, or (b) the need to protect some aspect of the public welfare." The Restatement obviously does not require that the legislation in question expressly prohibit or require an act inconsistent with the contract; it is sufficient if the legislature makes an adequate declaration of public policy which is inconsistent with the contract's terms. For example, the Restatement notes:

> The legislation is significant, not as controlling the disposition of the case, but as enlightening the court concerning some specific policy to which it is relevant. A court will examine the particular statute in the light of the whole legislative scheme. . . . It will look to the purpose and history of the statute.

> Comment (b) to Section 179. See generally 6A A. Corbin, Corbin on Contracts § 1375 (1962).

The Commonwealth primarily relied on Westmoreland Hospital, in which we held that certain cost-reimbursement contracts were not illegal or contrary to public policy. However, as noted supra, this court's holding in that case was predicated in part on the absence of a contrary public policy in the relevant legislation and administrative regulations. 605 F.2d at 125. Here, there is such a contrary public policy, the impact of which the state has attempted to avoid.

CONCLUSION

For the foregoing reasons, we rule that the no fees provisions of the contracts between CLS and PLSC are void as contrary to public policy. The judgment of the district court will be affirmed.

NOTES

(1) *Federalism Issues.* Contract law is state law. Which government is the source of the public policy that was used to prevent enforcement of the contract that is the subject of this case? Does it make any difference if the government whose law governs a contract is different than the government that has a strong public policy?

(2) *Judicial Protection or Judicial Intervention?* Congress enacted the Fee Awards Act and did not include a prohibition against lawyers entering contracts to forego seeking fees in certain circumstances. If Congress chose not to enact such a prohibition, should a court do what Congress chose not to do? Does it make a difference if the issue was raised during the legislative process?

CHAPTER 7

PERFORMANCE AND BREACH

An exchange of promises normally leads to an exchange of performances. One who has committed oneself in exchange for a return performance is entitled, as stated in Comment 1 to UCC § 2–609, to "a continuing sense of reliance and security that the promised performance will be forthcoming when due." Much detail in the law of contract is understandable only in light of the principle that a party's fair expectation of return performance deserves protection.

One means of protection is to afford an immediate remedy for breach. But there are other means of at least equal importance for assuring a party's expectations, such as permitting the party to defer or withhold its own performance in the face of a threat that it will not receive what was promised in exchange. Protection in this form is generally described in conditional language. Another means of assuring one's expectation is the right to demand assurance of performance from the other party. That right, recognized in Article 2 of the Uniform Commercial Code and the Restatement, is discussed at the end of this chapter.

Parties have wide liberty both to shape their commitments and to protect their expectations through suitable use of the language of conditions. Section 1 considers what a party may do to establish a condition by language in the agreement. Section 2 introduces the idea of constructive (implied) conditions of exchange. It shows how constructive conditions in a contract are determined according to the order of the performances required by the contract, and how this may afford one party some assurance that the other will perform as agreed. Section 3 examines how Article 2 of the Uniform Commercial Code and the common law deal with the failure of constructive conditions. Section 4 deals with the right to suspend performance and terminate the contract when breach occurs during the course of performance. Section 5 goes through many of the ways that courts mitigate the sometimes harsh results of conditions, whether express or constructive, such as divisibility; restitution; waiver, estoppel, and election; and prevention, hindrance, and cooperation. Finally, Section 6 concerns prospective, as distinguished from actual, nonperformance. Here we consider repudiation and the twentieth-century innovation of the right to demand assurance of a promised performance.

SECTION 1.   CONDITIONS

(A) EFFECTS OF CONDITIONS

Thus far, this book has largely been concerned with the imposition and enforcement of *duties*. What follows deals mainly with how duties are qualified by being subjected to the occurrence of *conditions*. According to Restatement § 224, "A condition is an event, not certain to occur, which must occur, unless its nonoccurrence is excused, before performance under a contract becomes due." The event may or may not be within the control of the parties. If it is not, if it is fortuitous, the promise is sometimes said to be "aleatory." Our present interest is with the interpretation of language relating to such events.

NOTE

Conditions "Precedent" and "Subsequent." "Parties sometimes provide that the occurrence of an event, such as the failure of one of them to commence an action within a prescribed time, will extinguish a duty after performance has become due, along with any claim for breach. Such an event has often been called a 'condition subsequent' while an event of the kind defined in this section has been called a 'condition precedent.' " Restatement § 224 cmt. e. The Restatement abandons the term "condition subsequent" and calls a "condition precedent" simply a "condition." The occurrence of what was called a "condition subsequent" is instead called "termination." Restatement § 230.

The terms "condition precedent" and "condition subsequent" have a significance in the law of procedure that is independent of their significance, or lack of it, in the law of contracts. This significance is best left for the treatment of burdens of pleading and burdens of proof in a course in civil procedure.

Luttinger v. Rosen

Supreme Court of Connecticut, 1972.
164 Conn. 45, 316 A.2d 757.

■ LOISELLE, ASSOCIATE JUSTICE. The plaintiffs contracted to purchase for $85,000 premises in the city of Stamford owned by the defendants and paid a deposit of $8500. The contract was "subject to and conditional upon the buyers obtaining first mortgage financing on said premises from a bank or other lending institution in an amount of $45,000 for a term of not less than twenty (20) years and at an interest rate which does not exceed 8½ per cent per annum." The plaintiffs agreed to use due diligence in attempting to obtain such financing. The parties further agreed that if the plaintiffs were unsuccessful in obtaining financing as provided in the contract, and notified the seller within a specific time, all sums paid on the contract would be refunded and the contract terminated without further obligation of either party.

In applying for a mortgage which would satisfy the contingency clause in the contract, the plaintiffs relied on their attorney who applied at a New Haven lending institution for a $45,000 loan at 8¼ percent per annum interest over a period of twenty-five years. The plaintiffs' attorney knew that this lending institution was the only one which at that time would lend as much as $45,000 on a mortgage for a single-family dwelling. A mortgage commitment was obtained for $45,000 with "interest at the prevailing rate at the time of closing but not less than 8¾%." Since this commitment failed to meet the contract requirement, timely notice was given to the defendants and demand was made for the return of the down payment. The defendants' counsel thereafter offered to make up the difference between the interest rate offered by the bank and the 8½ percent rate provided in the contract for the entire twenty-five years by a funding arrangement, the exact terms of which were not defined. The plaintiffs did not accept this offer and on the defendants' refusal to return the deposit an action was brought. From a judgment rendered in favor of the plaintiffs the defendants have appealed.

The defendants claim that the plaintiffs did not use due diligence in seeking a mortgage within the terms specified in the contract. The unattacked findings by the court establish that the plaintiffs' attorney was fully informed as to the conditions and terms of mortgages being granted by various banks and lending institutions in and out of the area and that the application was made to the only bank which might satisfy the mortgage conditions of the contingency clause at that time. These findings adequately support the court's conclusion that due diligence was used in seeking mortgage financing in accordance with the contract provisions. Brauer v. Freccia, 159 Conn. 289, 293, 268 A.2d 645. The defendants assert that notwithstanding the plaintiffs' reliance on their counsel's knowledge of lending practices, applications should have been made to other lending institutions. This claim is not well taken. The law does not require the performance of a futile act. Vachon v. Tomascak, 155 Conn. 52, 57, 230 A.2d 5; Tracy v. O'Neill, 103 Conn. 693, 699, 131 A. 417; Janulewycz v. Quagliano, 88 Conn. 60, 64, 89 A. 897.

The remaining assignment of error briefed by the defendants is that the court erred in concluding that the mortgage contingency clause of the contract, a condition precedent, was not met and, therefore, the plaintiffs were entitled to recover their deposit. "A condition precedent is a fact or event which the parties intend must exist or take place before there is a right to performance." Lach v. Cahill, 138 Conn. 418, 421, 85 A.2d 481, 482. Lach v. Cahill, supra; Bialeck v. Hartford, 135 Conn. 551, 556, 66 A.2d 610. In this case the language of the contract is unambiguous and clearly indicates that the parties intended that the purchase of the defendants' premises be conditioned on the obtaining by the plaintiffs of a mortgage as specified in the contract. From the subordinate facts found the court could reasonably conclude that since the plaintiffs were unable to obtain a $45,000 mortgage at no more than 8½ percent per annum interest "from a bank or other lending institution" the condition precedent to performance of the contract was not met and the plaintiffs were entitled to the refund of their deposit. Any additional offer by the defendants to fund the difference in interest payments could be rejected by the plaintiffs. See Lach v. Cahill, supra, 138 Conn. 420, 85 A.2d 481.

There was no error in the court's exclusion of testimony relating to the additional offer since the offer was obviously irrelevant.

There is no error.

NOTES

(1) *Whose Performance Is Conditional?* Recall the definition of condition in Restatement § 224. What was the *event* that was the condition in *Luttinger*? Whose *performance* did not become due if the event did not occur? If the Luttingers had won the Connecticut lottery and chosen to proceed without a mortgage, would the Rosens have been justified in refusing on the ground that the Luttingers had not obtained a mortgage with the specified terms?

(2) *Allocation of Risk.* Why was the promise of the Luttingers made conditional? Because an event that is a condition must, according to the Restatement definition, be "not certain to occur," making an event a condition involves an allocation of the risk of the nonoccurrence of the event. Who took that risk and how great was it? Why did the mortgage commitment at 8¾%, together with the Rosens' offer to make up the difference in interest rates, not amount to an occurrence of the stipulated event?

Homebuyers today often secure pre-approval letters from banks even before they have identified a property to purchase. Does any financing risk between the parties remain when pre-approval letters are used? If so, to whom is the risk allocated?

(3) *Why Not?* Assuming that the Rosens' offer to make up the difference in interest rate would have had the same financial consequences as a mortgage with the specified terms from a "bank or other lending institution," what reasons might have induced the Luttingers not to proceed? "Whatever may be the subjective intention of a buyer in any particular case, one can readily think of reasons why a buyer may make an offer contingent upon financing by a specific lending institution or through a particular type of loan. Examples of such reasons are: That the buyer will feel more confident of his own judgment of the price he is to pay if a lending institution is willing to make a loan; That the buyer would rather have the matter, in the event of default, in the hands of an established lending institution than in the hands of an individual who might be less able, if not less willing, to adjust matters reasonably." Fairchild, J., dissenting in Kovarik v. Vesely, 89 N.W.2d 279, 285–86 (Wis. 1958).

(4) *Financing Conditions.* Conditions like that in *Luttinger* are widespread and often give rise to disputes. How long did the Luttingers have to try to get a mortgage with the specified terms? How hard did they have to try to get one? In Informed Physician Services v. Blue Cross, 711 A.2d 1330, 1343 (Md. 1998), the court said that though " 'standing idly by' and falling on one's sword" will not suffice, a party need not "incur extraordinary expense simply to establish reasonableness or good faith." Which standard did the Luttingers have to meet, reasonable efforts or only good faith?

In Barber v. Jacobs, 753 A.2d 430, 434 (Conn. App 2000), a case with facts "analogous to those in Luttinger v. Rosen," the only bank to which the purchasers applied for a loan turned them down because the property failed to comply with wetlands agency standards. The court held that the purchasers had made a sufficient effort to obtain a loan because, "as the attorney in *Luttinger* knew that other loans were not available," here the purchaser's lawyer "drew on his experience to conclude that the wetlands problem could not be easily overcome."

Did the Luttingers in effect have an option to buy the house? Note that the parties had agreed that if the Luttingers could not obtain a mortgage as specified, the contract would be terminated and all sums paid on the contract would be refunded. Do you think that the result would have been different without such a provision? What inference do you draw with respect to the right of the Luttingers to a refund if they had not tried hard enough to get a mortgage with the specified terms? Would the nonoccurrence of the condition then be "excused," to use the Restatement's terminology?

Introduction to Internatio-Rotterdam

Comment *b* to Restatement § 224 explains that because "there is inherent in the concept of condition some degree of uncertainty as to the occurrence of the event. . . . [T]he mere passage of time, as to which there is no uncertainty, is not a condition." But the occurrence of an event *within some period of time* is a common kind of condition. Whether contract language dealing with time is sufficient to impose such a condition is often a disputed question, as in the next case.

Internatio-Rotterdam, Inc. v. River Brand Rice Mills, Inc.

United States Court of Appeals, Second Circuit, 1958.
259 F.2d 137.

■ HINCKS, CIRCUIT JUDGE. Appeal from the United States District Court, Southern District of New York, Walsh, Judge, upon the dismissal of the complaint after plaintiff's case was in.

The defendant-appellee, a processor of rice, in July 1952 entered into an agreement with the plaintiff-appellant, an exporter, for the sale of 95,600 pockets of rice. The terms of the agreement, evidenced by a purchase memorandum, indicated that the price per pocket was to be "$8.25 F.A.S. Lake Charles and/or Houston, Texas"; that shipment was to be "December, 1952, with two weeks call from buyer" and that payment was to be by "irrevocable letter of credit to be opened immediately payable against" dock receipts and other specified documents. In the fall, the appellant, which had already committed itself to supplying this rice to a Japanese buyer, was unexpectedly confronted with United States export restrictions upon its December shipments and was attempting to get an export license from the government. December is a peak month in the rice and cotton seasons in Louisiana and Texas, and the appellee became concerned about shipping instructions under the contract, since congested conditions prevailed at both the mills and the docks. The appellee seasonably elected to deliver 50,000 pockets at Lake Charles and on December 10 it received from the appellant instructions for the Lake Charles shipments. Thereupon it promptly began shipments to Lake Charles which continued until December 23, the last car at Lake Charles being unloaded on December 31. December 17 was the last date in December which would allow appellee the two week period provided in the contract for delivery of the rice to the ports and ships designated. Prior thereto, the appellant had been having difficulty obtaining either a ship or a dock in this busy season in Houston. On December 17, the appellee had still received no shipping instructions for the 45,600 pockets destined for Houston. On the morning of the 18th, the appellee rescinded the contract for the Houston shipments, although continuing to make the Lake Charles deliveries. It is clear that one of the reasons for the prompt cancellation of the contract was the rise in market price of rice from $8.25 per pocket, the contract price, to $9.75. The appellant brought this suit for refusal to deliver the Houston quota.

The trial court, in a reasoned but unreported opinion which dealt with all phases of the case, held that New York would apply Texas law. Auten v. Auten, 308 N.Y. 155, 124 N.E.2d 99, 50 A.L.R.2d 246. We think this ruling right, but will not discuss the point because it is conceded that no different result would follow from the choice of Louisiana law.

The area of contest is also considerably reduced by the appellant's candid concession that the appellee's duty to ship, by virtue of the two-week notice provision, did not arise until two weeks after complete shipping instructions had been given by the appellant. Thus on brief the appellant says: "[w]e concede (as we have done from the beginning) that on a fair interpretation of the contract appellant had a duty to instruct appellee by December 17, 1952 as to the place to which it desired appellee to ship—at both ports, and that, being late with its instructions in this respect, appellant could not have demanded delivery (at either port) until sometime after December 31, 1952." This position was taken, of course, with a view to the contract provision for shipment "December, 1952": a two-week period ending December 31 would begin to run on December 17. But although appellant concedes that the two weeks' notice to which appellee was entitled could not be shortened by the failure to give shipping instructions on or before December 17, it stoutly insists that upon receipt of shipping instructions subsequent to December 17 the appellee thereupon became obligated to deliver within two weeks thereafter. We do not agree.

It is plain that a giving of the notice by the appellant was a condition precedent to the appellee's duty to ship. Corbin on Contracts, Vol. 3, § 640. Id. § 724. Obviously, the appellee could not deliver free alongside ship, as the contract required, until the appellant identified its ship and its location. Jacksboro Stone Co. v. Fairbanks Co., 48 Tex.Civ.App. 639,

107 S.W. 567; Fortson Grocery Co. v. Pritchard Rice Milling Co., Tex.Civ.App., 220 S.W. 1116. Thus the giving of shipping instructions was what Professor Corbin would classify as a "promissory condition": the appellant promised to give the notice and the appellee's duty to ship was conditioned on the receipt of the notice. Op. cit. § 633, p. 523, § 634, footnote 38. The crucial question is whether that condition was performed. And that depends on whether the appellee's duty of shipment was conditioned on notice *on or before December 17,* so that the appellee would have two weeks wholly within December within which to perform, or whether, as we understand the appellant to contend, the appellant could perform the condition by giving the notice later in December, in which case the appellee would be under a duty to ship within two weeks thereafter. The answer depends upon the proper interpretation of the contract: if the contract properly interpreted made shipment *in December* of the essence then the failure to give the notice on or before December 17 was nonperformance by the appellant of a condition upon which the appellee's duty to ship in December depended.

In the setting of this case, we hold that the provision for December delivery went to the essence of the contract. In support of the plainly stated provision of the contract there was evidence that the appellee's mills and the facilities appurtenant thereto were working at full capacity in December when the rice market was at peak activity and that appellee had numerous other contracts in January as well as in December to fill. It is reasonable to infer that in July, when the contract was made, each party wanted the protection of the specified delivery period; the appellee so that it could schedule its production without undue congestion of its storage facilities and the appellant so that it could surely meet commitments which it in turn should make to its customers. There was also evidence that prices on the rice market were fluctuating. In view of this factor it is not reasonable to infer that when the contract was made in July for December delivery, the parties intended that the appellant should have an option exercisable subsequent to December 17 to postpone delivery until January. United Irr. Co. v. Carson Petroleum Co., Tex.Civ.App., 283 S.W. 692; Steiner v. United States, D.C., 36 F.Supp. 496. That in effect would have given the appellant an option to postpone its breach of the contract, if one should then be in prospect, to a time when, so far as could have been foreseen when the contract was made, the price of rice might be falling. A postponement in such circumstances would inure to the disadvantage of the appellee who was given no reciprocal option. Further indication that December delivery was of the essence is found in the letter of credit which was provided for in the contract and established by the appellant. Under this letter, the bank was authorized to pay appellee only for deliveries "during December, 1952." It thus appears that the appellant's interpretation of the contract, under which the appellee would be obligated, upon receipt of shipping instructions subsequent to December 17, to deliver in January, would deprive the appellee of the security for payment of the purchase price for which it had contracted.

Since, as we hold, December delivery was of the essence, notice of shipping instructions *on or before December 17* was not merely a "duty" of the appellant—as it concedes: it was a condition precedent to the performance which might be required of the appellee. The nonoccurrence of that condition entitled the appellee to rescind or to treat its contractual obligations as discharged. Corbin on Contracts, §§ 640, 724 and 1252; Williston on Sales, §§ 452, 457; Restatement, Contracts, § 262. On December 18th the appellant [appellee?] unequivocally exercised its right to rescind. Having done so, its obligations as to the Houston deliveries under the contract were at an end. And of course its obligations would not revive thereafter when the appellant finally succeeded in obtaining an export permit, a ship and a dock and then gave shipping instructions; when it expressed willingness to accept deliveries in January; or when it accomplished a "liberalization" of the outstanding letter of credit whereby payments might be made against simple forwarder's receipts instead of dock receipts.[1]

The appellant urges that by reason of substantial part performance on its part prior to December 17th, it may not be held to have been in default for its failure sooner to give shipping instructions. The contention has no basis on the facts. As to the Houston shipments the appellant's activities prior to December 17th were not in performance of its contract: they were merely preparatory to its expectation to perform at a later time. The mere establishment of the letter of credit was not an act of performance: it was merely an arrangement made by the appellant for future performance which as to the Houston deliveries because of appellant's failure to give shipping instructions were never made. From these preparatory activities the appellee had no benefit whatever.

The appellant also maintains that the contract was single and "indivisible" and that consequently appellee's continuing shipments to Lake Charles after December 17 constituted an election to reaffirm its total obligation under the contract. This position also, we hold untenable. Under the contract, the appellee concededly had an option to split the deliveries betwixt Lake Charles and Houston. The price had been fixed on a per pocket basis, and payment, under the letter of credit, was to be made upon the presentation of dock receipts which normally would be issued both at Lake Charles or Houston at different times. The fact that there was a world market for rice and that in December the market price substantially exceeded the contract price suggests that it would be more to the appellants' advantage to obtain the Lake Charles delivery than to obtain no delivery at all. The same considerations suggest that by continuing with the Lake Charles delivery the appellee did not

---

[1]   The appellee was not informed that the letter of credit had "liberalized" until after it had been rescinded. Moreover, even the liberalized letter did not call for payment of deliveries not made until January.

deliberately intend to waive its right to cancel the Houston deliveries. Conclusions to the contrary would be so greatly against self-interest as to be completely unrealistic. The only reasonable inference from the totality of the facts is that the duties of the parties as to the Lake Charles shipment were not at all dependent on the Houston shipments. We conclude their duties as to shipments at each port were paired and reciprocal and that performance by the parties as to Lake Charles did not preclude the appellee's right of cancellation as to Houston. Cf. Corbin on Contracts §§ 688, 695; Simms-Wylie Co. v. City of Ranger, Tex.Civ.App., 224 S.W.2d 265.

Finally, we hold that the appellant's claims of estoppel and waiver have no basis in fact or in law.

Affirmed.

NOTES

(1) *Questions.* What event was the condition in *Internatio-Rotterdam?* Was the event also the subject of a promise? What did Internatio-Rotterdam argue? What did River Brand argue? What did the court conclude?

(2) *Letters of Credit.* A seller may, as a means of assuring payment for goods, require a buyer to obtain a letter of credit from a bank. The bank, by issuing its letter of credit at the buyer's request, undertakes with the seller that it will pay against the seller's orders in an amount equal to the purchase price, on condition that the orders, known as "drafts" or "bills of exchange," are accompanied by documents affording control over the goods. The documents specified are commonly bills of lading, issued by a carrier. Less commonly they may be documents of other sorts, such as the dock receipts in *Internatio-Rotterdam*, that also carry with them power over the goods. When the seller ships the goods, it forwards to the issuing bank its draft together with the specified document covering the goods. The bank then pays the draft and takes up the document. As soon as the buyer reimburses the bank, the buyer may have the document and use it to obtain the goods from the carrier. Letters of credit reallocate risk of nonpayment away from sellers. Recall the discussion of homebuyer pre-approval letters, Note 2, p. 758 above, which served a similar function. What consideration supports these credit agreements?

(3) *When Time Is of the Essence.* What did the court mean when it said that delivery in December "was of the essence"? Why did the court conclude that this was so? "The importance of prompt delivery by a seller of goods generally derives from the circumstance that goods, as contrasted with land, are particularly likely to be subject to rapid fluctuations in market price." Restatement § 242 cmt. c. Were there other reasons in *Internatio-Rotterdam*? In a case involving the sale of timber on a wooded lot the Supreme Court of New Hampshire said, "Time is generally not of the essence in contract, unless the contract specifically so states, even if a particular time schedule is specified." Fitz v. Coutinho, 622 A.2d 1220, 1223 (N.H. 1993).

Of course it is "open to the parties to make performance or tender by a stated date a condition by their agreement." (Such a date is sometimes called a "drop dead" date.) However, "stock phrases [such] as 'time is of the essence' do not necessarily have this effect." Restatement Second, § 242 cmt. d. And "a specific date for performance does not necessarily mean that performance by that date is of the essence of the contract." Arkla Energy Resources v. Roye Realty & Developing, 9 F.3d 855, 863 (10th Cir. 1993).

For option contracts, however, courts generally presume that time really is of the essence. See Livesey v. Copps Corp., 280 N.W.2d 339 (Wis. 1979) (option expired on November 15, but letter exercising the option was received on November 16; exercise held ineffective). What about option contracts makes their strict enforcement the rule? See Cotter v. James L. Tapp Co., 230 S.E.2d 715 (S.C. 1976).

Separate Contracts

A party's breach of a contract does not allow the other party to terminate a different contract subsisting between the two, or even to suspend performance of the other contract, unless the parties have otherwise agreed. (But see the doctrine of adequate assurance of performance, infra section 6.) "Neither the Uniform Commercial Code nor general contract law gives either party to a contract the right to refuse performance because the other has breached a separate contract between them." Northwest Lumber Sales, Inc. v. Continental Forest Products, Inc., 495 P.2d 744, 749 (Or. 1972). That rule would have made a difference in the foregoing case if the parties there had entered into one contract for "Houston rice" and another for "Lake Charles rice." The authorities do not lay down a rule or standard, it has been said, for "deciding whether a series of transactions constitutes one contract or two." The cases are not numerous and "have not crystallized an identifiable doctrine, though the term 'divisibility' is sometimes used to name the issue." Coplay Cement Company, Inc. v. Willis & Paul Group, 983 F.2d 1435, 1439 (7th Cir. 1993). In that case the judges said

> "The simplest and best rule that we can think of is that if the transactions are embodied in separate documents, each complete in itself, in the sense that ascertaining the terms does not require consulting the document for the other transaction, they are separate contracts."

Id. Does an alternative test come to mind?

One who breaks a contract may anticipate that the other party will, for that reason, lose confidence in the performance of a separate contract between them. If that should happen, the promise breaker might be required to give an assurance of that performance upon demand by the other party, see p. 866 below. If that demand is not satisfied, the breached-against party may terminate the contract, and while awaiting assurance may suspend performance. The right to demand assurance thus tends to tie together separate contracts that would otherwise operate independently of one another.

(B) PROBLEMS OF INTERPRETATION

Condition, Duty, or Both?

A party seeking a particular performance from another party might ask the other party to undertake a duty to render that performance, might make its own performance conditional on the other party rendering that performance, or might do both. As *Internatio-Rotterdam* shows, determining which has been done may pose a difficult question of interpretation from which important consequences follow. Here is an example based on the venerable case Constable v. Cloberie, [1626] 81 Eng. Rep. 1141 (K.B.).

Cargo Owner desires Ship Owner to sail from England to Cadiz and back carrying Cargo Owner's goods. Ship Owner agrees to do so in return for Cargo Owner's promise to pay. In addition, Cargo Owner wants to encourage Ship Owner to sail with the next wind and for this is willing to pay, in addition to the freight, a premium equal to 10% of the freight. Cargo Owner might ask Ship Owner to undertake a duty to sail with the next wind, or might make sailing with the next wind a condition of Cargo Owner's own duty to pay a 10% premium, or might do both. The consequences will be different in each case.

Suppose that Cargo Owner has Ship Owner undertake a duty to sail with the next wind. Sailing with the next wind will discharge Ship Owner's duty. If Ship Owner delays in sailing, however, Cargo Owner will be entitled to any damages caused by Ship Owner's delay. (This ignores the impact of the doctrine of "constructive conditions of exchange," which is taken up in the next section.)

Suppose that Cargo Owner makes sailing with the next wind a condition of the Cargo Owner's duty to pay a 10% premium. Sailing with the next wind will satisfy the condition of Cargo Owner's duty. If Ship Owner delays in sailing, however, Cargo Owner, though not entitled to damages, will not have to pay the premium.

Suppose that Cargo Owner has Ship Owner undertake a duty to sail with the next wind *and* makes sailing with the next wind a condition of Cargo Owner's duty to pay a 10% premium. As was pointed out in *Internatio-Rotterdam*, Corbin used the term "promissory condition" to describe this case. Sailing with the next wind will discharge Ship Owner's duty *and* will satisfy the condition of Cargo Owner's duty. If Ship Owner delays in sailing, however, Cargo Owner will be entitled to any damages caused Ship Owner's delay *and* in addition will not have to pay the premium.

NOTE

Preference in Interpretation. If language is unclear, a court will prefer an interpretation that imposes a duty rather than a condition. As Comment *c* to Restatement § 227(1) explains, "The preferred interpretation avoids the harsh results that might otherwise result from the non-occurrence of a condition and still gives adequate protection to the obligor under the rules . . . relating to promises for an exchange of performances." In the next section, we examine those rules.

PROBLEM

Drafting. Assume that the contract begins: "In consideration of Ship Owner's promise to sail to Cadiz and return with cargo, Cargo Owner promises to pay freight at [a specified rate]." Draft clauses to follow which would make sailing with the next wind: (1) a duty of Ship Owner; (2) a condition of Cargo Owner's duty to pay a 10% premium; (3) both a duty of Ship Owner and a condition of Cargo Owner's duty to pay a 10% premium.

Peacock Construction Co. v. Modern Air Conditioning, Inc.

Supreme Court of Florida, 1977.
353 So.2d 840.

■ BOYD, ACTING CHIEF JUSTICE. We issued an order allowing certiorari in these two causes because the decisions in them of the District Court of Appeal, Second District, conflict with the decision in Edward J. Gerrits, Inc. v. Astor Electric Service, Inc., 328 So.2d 522 (Fla. 3d DCA 1976). The two causes have been consolidated for all appellate purposes in this Court because they involve the same issue. That issue is whether the plaintiffs, Modern Air Conditioning and Overly Manufacturing, were entitled to summary judgments against Peacock Construction Company in actions for breaches of identical contractual provisions.

Peacock Construction was the builder of a condominium project. Modern Air Conditioning subcontracted with Peacock to do the heating and air conditioning work and Overly Manufacturing subcontracted with Peacock to do the "rooftop swimming pool" work. Both written subcontracts provided that Peacock would make final payment to the subcontractors,

> "within 30 days after the completion of the work included in this sub-contract, written acceptance by the Architect and full payment therefor by the Owner."

Modern Air Conditioning and Overly Manufacturing completed the work specified in their contracts and requested final payment. When Peacock refused to make the final payments the two subcontractors separately brought actions in the Lee County Circuit Court for breach of contract. In both actions it was established that no deficiencies had been found in the completed work. But Peacock established that it had not received from the owner[1] full payment for the subcontractors' work. And it defended on the basis that such payment was a condition which, by express term of the final payment provision, had to be fulfilled before it was obligated to perform under the contract. On motions by the plaintiffs, the trial judges granted summary judgments in their favor. The orders of judgment implicitly interpreted the contract not to require payment by the owner as a condition precedent to Peacock's duty to perform.

The Second District Court of Appeal affirmed the lower court's judgment in the appeal brought by Peacock Construction Company. In so doing it adopted the view of the majority of jurisdictions in this country that provisions of the kind disputed here do not set conditions precedent but rather constitute absolute promises to pay, fixing payment by the owner as a reasonable time for when payment to the subcontractor is to be made. When the judgment in the *Overly Manufacturing* case reached the Second District Court, *Modern Air Conditioning* had been decided and the judgment, therefore, was affirmed on the authority of the latter decision. These two decisions plainly conflict with *Gerrits,* supra.

In *Gerrits,* the Court had summarily ordered judgment for the plaintiff/subcontractor against the defendant/general contractor on a contractual provision for payment to the subcontractor which read,

> The money to be paid in current funds and at such times as the General Contractor receives it from the Owner. Id. at 523.

In its review of the judgment, the Third District Court of Appeal referred to the fundamental rule of interpretation of contracts that it be done in accordance with the intention of the parties. Since the defendant had introduced below the issue of intention, a material issue, and since the issue was one that could be resolved through a factual determination by the jury, the Third District reversed the summary judgment and remanded for trial.

Peacock urges us to adopt *Gerrits* as the controlling law in this State. It concedes that the Second District's decisions are backed by the weight of authority. But it argues that they are incorrect because the issue of intention is a factual one which should be resolved after the parties have had an opportunity to present evidence on it. Peacock urges, therefore, that the causes be remanded for trial. If there is produced no evidence that the parties intended there be condition precedents, only then, says Peacock, should the judge, by way of a directed verdict for the subcontractors, be allowed to take the issue of intention from the jury.

The contractual provisions in dispute here are susceptible to two interpretations. They may be interpreted as setting a condition precedent or as fixing a reasonable time for payment. The provision disputed in *Gerrits* is susceptible to the same two interpretations. The questions presented by the conflict between these decisions, then, are whether ambiguous contractual provisions of the kind disputed here may be

---

[1]   The owner, a corporation, had entered proceedings in bankruptcy.

interpreted only by the factfinder, usually the jury, or if they should be interpreted as a matter of law by the court, and if so what interpretation they should be given.

Although it must be admitted that the meaning of language is a factual question, the general rule is that interpretation of a document is a question of law rather than of fact. 4 Williston on Contracts, 3rd Ed., § 616. If an issue of contract interpretation concerns the intention of parties, that intention may be determined from the written contract, as a matter of law, when the nature of the transaction lends itself to judicial interpretation. A number of courts, with whom we agree, have recognized that contracts between small subcontractors and general contractors on large construction projects are such transactions. Cf. Thos. J. Dyer Co. v. Bishop International Engineering Co., 6 Cir., 303 F.2d 655 (1965). The reason is that the relationship between the parties is a common one and usually their intent will not differ from transaction to transaction, although it may be differently expressed.

That intent in most cases is that payment by the owner to the general contractor is not a condition precedent to the general contractor's duty to pay the subcontractors. This is because small subcontractors, who must have payment for their work in order to remain in business, will not ordinarily assume the risk of the owner's failure to pay the general contractor. And this is the reason for the majority view in this country, which we now join.

Our decision to require judicial interpretation of ambiguous provisions for final payment in subcontracts in favor of subcontractors should not be regarded as anti-general contractor. It is simply a recognition that this is the fairest way to deal with the problem. There is nothing in this opinion, however, to prevent parties to these contracts from shifting the risk of payment failure by the owner to the subcontractor. But in order to make such a shift the contract must unambiguously express that intention. And the burden of clear expression is on the general contractor.

The decisions of the Second District Court of Appeal to affirm the summary judgments were correct. We adopt, therefore, these two decisions as the controlling law in Florida and we overrule *Gerrits,* to the extent it is inconsistent with this opinion.

The orders allowing certiorari in these two causes are discharged. It is so ordered.

NOTES

(1) *Fact or Law?* As to the decision of the court in *Peacock* to treat the question of interpretation as "a matter of law," recall the discussion at p. 534 above. Thirteen years later, in DEC Electric, Inc. v. Raphael Construction Corp., 558 So.2d 427 (Fla. 1990), the same court had certified to it a question "of great public importance":

Must all payment provisions in contracts between contractors and subcontractors or suppliers that concern a condition or time of payment provision be construed as a matter of law?

Answering in the affirmative, the court explained that if the provision "is clear and unambiguous, it is interpreted as setting a condition precedent," but if it "is ambiguous it is interpreted as fixing a reasonable time for the general contractor to pay. . . . Once a judge decides that a provision is ambiguous there is nothing for the jury to decide or interpret." How does this differ from a traditional plain meaning rule?

(2) *Public Policy*. In Wm. R. Clarke Corp. v. Safeco Insurance Co., 938 P.2d 372, 376 (Cal. 1997), a "pay if paid" provision was held to be unenforceable as contrary to the public policy evidenced by provisions of the California Constitution and the California Civil Code dealing with mechanic's liens. Under the Civil Code, "a subcontractor may not waive its mechanic's lien rights except under certain specified circumstances . . . and a pay if paid provision is in substance a waiver of mechanic's lien rights because it has the same practical effect as an express waiver of those rights." In addition to California, according to one 2004 study, Nevada and New York are the only states whose courts have invalidated "pay if paid" clauses as against public policy. See Robert F. Carney & Adam Cizek, *Payment Provisions in Construction Contracts and Construction Trust Fund Statutes: A Fifty-State Survey*, Constr. Law, Fall 2004, at 5. And while some state legislatures have enacted statutes making "pay if paid" clauses unenforceable, they are enforced in most jurisdictions. See e.g., BMD Contrs. v. Fid. & Deposit Co., 679 F.3d 643 (7th Cir. 2012).

(3) *Brokers and Conditions*. In Harding Realty, Inc. v. Turnberry Towers Corp., 436 So.2d 983, 984 (Fla. App. 1983), the owner of a condominium development made an agreement with a real estate broker providing that the broker "shall be entitled to a commission of 3%, at time of closing," on the sale of units to purchasers brought by the broker. When two such purchasers defaulted and the owner kept their deposits, the broker sued for its 3% commission. The court affirmed an award of summary judgment to the owner, noting that "the great weight of authority holds that contractual provisions for payment of a brokerage commission at the time of sale, closing, or settlement render such occurrence a condition precedent of payment."

In what ways is the situation of the broker distinguishable from that of the subcontractor?

PROBLEM

Pay If *Paid or Pay* When *Paid?* Redraft the clause in *Peacock* so that it would "unambiguously" shift to the subcontractors the risk of the owner's failure to pay.

Gibson v. Cranage

Supreme Court of Michigan, 1878.
39 Mich. 49.

■ MARSTON, J. Plaintiff in error brought assumpsit to recover the contract price for the making and execution of a portrait of the deceased daughter of defendant. It appeared from the testimony of the plaintiff that he at a certain time called upon the defendant and solicited the privilege of making an enlarged picture of his deceased daughter. He says "I was to make an enlarged picture that he would like, a large one from a small one, and one that he would like and recognize as a good picture of his little girl, and he was to pay me."

The defendant testified that the plaintiff was to take the small photograph and send it away to be finished, "and when returned if it was not perfectly satisfactory to me in every particular, I need not take it or pay for it. I still objected and he urged me to do so. There was no risk about it; if it was not perfectly satisfactory to me I need not take it or pay for it."

There was little if any dispute as to what the agreement was. After the picture was finished it was shown to defendant who was dissatisfied with it and refused to accept it. Plaintiff endeavored to ascertain what the objections were, but says he was unable to ascertain clearly, and he then sent the picture away to the artist to have it changed.

On the next day he received a letter from defendant reciting the original agreement, stating that the picture shown him the previous day was not satisfactory and that he declined to take it or any other similar picture, and countermanded the order. A further correspondence was had, but it was not very material and did not change the aspect of the case. When the picture was afterwards received by the plaintiff from the artist, he went to see defendant and to have him examine it. This defendant declined to do, or to look at it, and did not until during the trial, when he examined and found the same objections still existing.

We do not consider it necessary to examine the charge in detail, as we are satisfied it was as favorable to plaintiff as the agreement would warrant.

The contract (if it can be considered such) was an express one. The plaintiff agreed that the picture when finished should be satisfactory to the defendant, and his own evidence showed that the contract in this important particular had not been performed. It may be that the picture was an excellent one and that the defendant ought to have been satisfied with it and accepted it, but under the agreement the defendant was the only person who had the right to decide this question. Where parties thus deliberately enter into an agreement which violates no rule of public policy, and which is free from all taint of fraud or mistake, there is no hardship whatever in holding them bound by it.

Artists or third parties might consider a portrait an excellent one, and yet it prove very unsatisfactory to the person who had ordered it and who might be unable to point out with clearness or certainty the defects or objections. And if the person giving the order stipulates that the portrait when finished must be satisfactory to him or else he will not accept or pay for it, and this is agreed to, he may insist upon his right as given him by the contract. McCarren v. McNulty, 7 Gray, 141; Brown v. Foster, 113 Mass., 136: 18 Amer., 465.

The judgment must be affirmed with costs.

NOTES

(1) *Questions.* Would the result have been the same if Cranage had refused to look at the portrait at all?

Would the result have been the same if Gibson's promise had been to paint the exterior of Cranage's barn? Does a satisfaction clause impose different risks on a seller of land, a painter of a portrait, and a painter of a barn?

Note that if Gibson had painted Cranage's barn, a question of unjust enrichment might arise. Such questions are taken up in Section 5(b) below.

Observe that the court said that Gibson "agreed that the picture when finished should be satisfactory" to Cranage. Did the court hold that Gibson was under a duty to furnish a picture satisfactory to Cranage? Could Cranage have recovered damages from Gibson for his failure to do so?

(2) *Effect of Forfeiture.* It should be apparent that the law of conditions has a draconian quality. If Gibson's portrait does not satisfy Cranage, Gibson gets nothing for his efforts and is left with a painting that is of no value to him. (Should we assume that Gibson was himself the artist? If not, what should we assume about his agreement with the artist?) Comment b to Restatement § 227 explains that "forfeiture" is used to refer to "the denial of compensation" that results if the non-occurrence of a condition causes the obligee "to lose his right to the agreed exchange after he has relied substantially on the expectation of that exchange, as by preparation or performance." Gibson's risk of forfeiture if Cranage was not satisfied may thus have been greater than Hopper's risk of forfeiture in Mattei v. Hopper, p. 100 above, if Mattei was not satisfied.

(3) *Satisfaction in Real Estate Transactions.* Provisions like that in *Mattei* play an important role in real estate transactions. Suppose that Mattei, the developer, had refused to go through with the purchase of the tract on the ground that the leases were not satisfactory to him and that Hopper had sued Mattei. Would the issue of "satisfaction" be more likely to go to a jury under the standard of "an exercise of judgment in good faith" used by the Supreme Court of California or under "the standard of a reasonable person" rejected by that court? See Note 4 below.

(4) *The Case of the Cheaper Chips.* Potato farmers contracted to sell twelve loads of potatoes that "chipt to buyer satisfaction," at $4.25 per hundredweight. When the market price declined to $2.00 per

hundredweight, the buyer rejected the last nine loads claiming that the potatoes would not chip satisfactorily. The farmers had samples tested by an expert who found them entirely satisfactory. After unsuccessful negotiations—during which the buyer's agent said, "I can buy potatoes all day for $2.00"—the farmers sued. From a judgment for the farmers on a jury verdict, the buyer appealed. *Held:* Affirmed.

> "The law requires such a claim of dissatisfaction to be made in good faith, rather than in an effort to escape a bad bargain." As a "merchant" under UCC § 2–104(1), the buyer was held to the objective standard of UCC § 2–103, which requires "honesty in fact and the observance of reasonable commercial standards of fair dealing in the trade." "Because there was evidence that the potatoes would 'chip' satisfactorily, the jury was not required to accept Buyer's subjective claim to the contrary."

Neumiller Farms, Inc. v. Cornett, 368 So.2d 272 (Ala. 1979). Note that under the current official text of Article 1 of the Code, one no longer has to be a merchant for the heightened definition of good faith to apply. See UCC § 1–203.

Would the farmers necessarily have lost under the standard of good faith used in *Mattei*?

PROBLEM

Drafting. Can you draft language that would make an objective test applicable to the painting of a portrait? That would make a subjective test applicable to the painting of a barn?

In Morin Building Products Co., Inc. v. Baystone Construction, Inc., 717 F.2d 413 (7th Cir. 1983), Judge Richard Posner posed the example of a manager of a steel plant who rejected a shipment of pig iron "because he did not think the pigs had a pretty shape." He concluded that the "reasonable-man standard would be applied even if the contract had an 'acceptability shall rest strictly with the [buyer]' clause, for it would be fantastic to think that the iron supplier would have subjected his contract rights to the whimsy of the buyer's agent." Do you understand Judge Posner to be saying that the "reasonable-man standard" would be applied in the case of painting a barn no matter what you drafted? If so, do you agree?

It might not be necessary to apply a reasonableness standard in the case of the pigs to avoid rejection for their want of "a pretty shape". It has been pointed out that "it is only the decision contracted for that is final" and a decision "not on the question submitted . . . is outside of the contract and is given no effect by it." Devoine Co. v. International Co., 136 A. 37, 38 (Md. 1927).

As to mixed motives, as where a buyer rejects goods both because of dissatisfaction and because of finding a cheaper source of supply, see Columbia Christian Coll. v. Commonwealth Props., 594 P.2d 401, 407–08 (Or. 1979) ("the party's dissatisfaction must relate to the specific subject matter of the condition," but as long as "one of the sources of dissatisfaction gives him a right under the contract to repudiate, the fact that there are other sources of dissatisfaction is immaterial"). Suppose, however, that A had the right to repudiate its contract with B because it was dissatisfied with the goods, but did so almost entirely because a changed market price made the contract undesirable. Would this affect A's right to invoke its condition of satisfaction?

Third-Party Satisfaction

Some of the risk inherent in making the other party's duty conditional on its own satisfaction can be eliminated by making its duty conditional instead on the satisfaction of an independent third party, perhaps an expert of some kind. These terms are common in construction contracts, where the owner's duty to pay the contractor is often conditional on the satisfaction of the architect. It is also possible to make the architect's approval conclusive on the owner, that is, to make approval the sole condition of the owner's duty. As to such provisions see Note 3, p. 803 below.

Despite representing the owner, an architect judging the work of a builder is regarded as a professional of sufficient independence that his or her decisions are generally considered "final" if rendered "in good faith." The usual test is one of honest, not reasonable, satisfaction. Provisions requiring certificates of engineers are usually interpreted in the same way, though the engineer, unlike an architect, is commonly a salaried employee of the owner.

What if the architect exercises honest but egregiously bad judgment? In RaDec Construction v. School District No. 17, 535 N.W.2d 408, 409 (Neb. 1995), the trial court disregarded the architect's determination of the reduction in price under a revised earthworking plan. The architect had, among other things, used the grading subcontractor's figures without verifying them and had ignored the contractor's figures that accurately represented the cost. The Nebraska Supreme Court affirmed on the ground that the architect's determination "constituted a gross mistake" and "was patently erroneous and therefore legally equivalent to bad faith for the purposes of deciding the instant case." Is this consistent with the meaning of "bad faith" in cases you have read? Is it unjustified?

NOTE

The Case of the Refusal Without Reason. A contractor sued an owner, who defended on the ground that the contractor had not procured an architect's certificate. The contractor's complaint alleged "fraud on the part of the architect." A judgment of the trial court for the contractor was reversed on appeal, and the contractor appealed. *Held:* Reversed and judgment of trial court affirmed.

It is inferable from the architect's own testimony that he was ready to issue the certificate, but that the defendants wished to cut down the final payment by several hundred dollars on account of a counterclaim which the architect refused to recognize or support except for a much smaller sum; that he advised the plaintiff to "get after them and get his money"; and that when plaintiff asked for the certificate, it was on the day before suit was begun, after plaintiff had retained counsel, and that he then refused it because he "did not want it to appear that he was issuing a certificate for a case." . . . [H]is refusal under such circumstances was fraudulent. . . . [Otherwise] a corrupt architect would be greatly aided in extorting money from the contractor as a condition of awarding a certificate that was fully earned.

Rizzolo v. Poysher, 99 A. 390 (N.J. 1916).

PROBLEM

Slap Shot. Randy Giunto was selected as a contestant at a Florida Panthers hockey game. He was to shoot a puck at a small slot 118 feet away and if the puck passed "completely through" the slot he would win $1 million. According to the rules the contest judges' decisions were "final in all matters." On Giunto's shot the puck hit the corner, rebounded from side to side, and stopped just slightly within the slot. Giunto insisted that it had passed "completely through," but the contest judge disagreed. Is Giunto entitled to the $1 million? See Giunto v. Florida Coca-Cola Bottling Co., 745 So.2d 1020 (Fla. App. 1999).

_____

Interpretation and the Avoidance of Forfeiture

As we have seen, courts have traditionally preferred interpretations of contract language that avoid forfeiture. Language making a promise conditional may be interpreted in such a way that the condition has occurred, as where a condition of satisfaction is taken to be reasonable satisfaction. Language that does not clearly make a promise conditional may be interpreted as not imposing a condition at all, as when a clause is read as a pay-when-paid rather than a pay-if-paid provision.

Interpretation cannot prevent forfeiture, however, if the drafter of the contract has taken pains to make clear that forfeiture is intended. Even in such a case, the Restatement asserts that a condition may sometimes be excused to avoid "disproportionate forfeiture." Restatement § 229. See Hoosier Energy Rural Elec. Coop. v. Amoco Tax Leasing IV Corp., 34 F.3d 1310, 1320 (7th Cir. 1994) (explaining that though it is unclear whether New York would follow § 229, "New York recognizes equity's abhorrence of a forfeiture"). However, courts have often preferred more traditional methods, some bordering on subterfuge, to avoid forfeiture.

NOTE

The Case of Constructive Fraud. A contract for the construction of low-rent housing required the Housing Authority to extend the time for completing the work "when in its judgment the findings of fact of the [Authority's] Contracting Officer justify such an extension, and his findings of fact thereon shall be final and conclusive upon the parties." The contractor gave notice of a delay resulting from a shortage of plumbers, and the Officer found that a delay of only 15 days was justified. The contractor sued the Authority, complaining that the Officer had arrived at the figure of 15 days by taking 8% of the actual delay of 182 days because the plumbing cost was only that percentage of the cost of the entire contract. The Authority moved for summary judgment. *Held:* Summary judgment denied. The Officer's finding may be set aside, and the issue of allowable delay presented to a jury.

"It is unfortunate that a finding of constructive fraud must be made in so many words when, in fact, we are actually dealing with serious errors in calculations. However, the decisions refer to such miscalculations as constructive fraud and I find it necessary to pin that label upon the contracting officer's erroneous findings here although, actually, there is no hint of bad faith, dishonesty or deliberate wrongful conduct upon the part of the contracting officer or the Authority. I am sure that these errors were the product of inexperience and mistaken judgment." Anthony P. Miller, Inc. v. Wilmington Housing Authority, 179 F.Supp. 199 (D. Del. 1959). Is a contracting officer the same sort of third party as an architect?

Hicks v. Bush

Court of Appeals of New York, 1962.
180 N.E.2d 425.

[Frederick Hicks executed a completely integrated written agreement with shareholders of the Clinton G. Bush Company under which the parties were to merge their corporate interests into a single "holding" company, Bush-Hicks Enterprises. Each party was to subscribe to a specified number of shares of this new company, transferring to it shares representing his existing corporate interest. Hicks transferred his stock, but the others did not, and the merger did not take place. When Hicks sued the others for specific performance, they set up as an affirmative defense that the written agreement was executed "upon a parol condition" that it "was not to operate" as a contract and that the merger was not "to become effective" until "equity expansion funds" of $672,500 were first raised, and they had not been raised. At the trial, the evidence showed that this sum was essential to the successful operation of the merger, and that the parties had agreed that the entire merger deal was subject to the condition that the sum be raised, the writing not to become effective as a binding contract until the specified equity expansion funds were obtained. As one witness said, the understanding was "Get the money or no deal." The Court noted that "Hicks, however, testified that he was 'absolutely positive' that nothing was said about such a condition at the time of the signing and that 'to the best of my knowledge no such language was ever used at any time let alone on the day of the signing.'" Record at pp. 410, 434. From an adverse judgment, Hicks appealed.]

■ FULD, JUDGE. The applicable law is clear, the relevant principles settled. Parol testimony is admissible to prove a condition precedent to the legal effectiveness of a written agreement if the condition does not contradict the express terms of such written agreement. A certain disparity is inevitable, of course, whenever a written promise is, by oral agreement of the parties, made conditional upon an event not expressed in the writing. Quite obviously, though, the parol evidence rule does not bar proof of every orally established condition precedent, but only of those which in a real sense contradict the terms of the written agreement. Upon the present appeal, our problem is to determine whether there is such a contradiction.

There is here no direct or explicit contradiction between the oral condition and the writing; in fact, the parol agreement deals with a matter on which the written agreement, as in some of the cases cited, is silent. The plaintiff, however, contends that, since the written agreement provides in terms that the obligations of the parties were to be terminated if the merged corporation failed to accept any of their stock subscriptions within 25 days, the additional oral condition—that the writing "was [not] to become operative" and that the merger was "not to become effective" until the expansion funds had been raised—is irreconcilable with the written agreement.

As already indicated, and analysis confirms it, the two conditions may stand side by side. The oral requirement that the writing was not to take effect as a contract until the equity expansion funds were obtained is simply a further condition—a condition added to that requiring the acceptance of stock subscriptions within 25 days—and not one which is contradictory. If both provisions had been contained in the written agreement, it is clear that the defendants would not have been under immediate legal duty to transfer the stock in their companies to Bush-Hicks Enterprises until both conditions had been fulfilled and satisfied. And it is equally clear that evidence of an oral condition is not to be excluded as contradictory or "inconsistent" merely because the written agreement contains other conditions precedent.

In short, the parties in the case before us intended that their respective rights and duties with respect to the contemplated transfers of stock in the operating companies to the holding company be subject to two conditions, each independent of the other—the acceptance of the stock subscription within a specified period and the procuring of expansion funds of $672,500. As the courts below found, the parties did not contemplate performance of the written agreement until such funds were first received. In other words, it was their desire and understanding that the merger was to be one of proposal only and that, even though the formal preliminary steps were to be taken, the writing was not to become operative as a contract or the merger effective until $672,500 was raised. It is certainly not improbable that parties contracting in these circumstances would make the asserted oral agreement; the condition precedent at hand is the sort of condition which parties would not be inclined to incorporate into a written agreement intended for public consumption. The challenged evidence was, therefore, admissible and, since there was ample proof attesting to the making of the oral agreement, the trial court was fully warranted in holding that no operative or binding contract ever came into existence.

[Affirmed.]

NOTES

(1) *Questions.* Were the defendants attempting to show that no obligations were to arise under the writing until the funds were procured, or that the obligations that had arisen under the writing were conditional on the procurement of the funds? Is the decision consistent with *W.W.W. Associates*, p. 516 above?

(2) *The Code.* What would have been the result in Hicks v. Bush if UCC § 2–202 had been applicable? See Hunt Foods & Industries v. Doliner, 270 N.Y.S.2d 937 (App. Div. 1966).

(3) *Merger Clauses and Conditions.* In Kryl v. Mechalson, 47 N.W.2d 899 (Wis. 1951), the court held that an oral condition to the contract could be established in spite of the following language: "It is understood that this contract is complete in itself, and that the party of the first part is not bound by any other terms or agreements other than are herein contained." See Edward T. Kelly Co. v. Von Zakobiel, 171 N.W. 75 (Wis. 1919).

(4) *Big MACs.* In Hicks v. Bush the contemplated merger of two corporations was made contingent on the realization of "equity expansion funds" in the amount of $672,500. This was a relatively simple transaction with a clearly stipulated contingency. More complicated mergers and acquisitions typically contain "material adverse change" (MAC) or "material adverse effect" (MAE) clauses that condition the parties' commitments to each other on the non-occurrence of events that would have a material adverse effect on a business, its assets or liabilities, or that would otherwise substantially affect the value of the contemplated deal. What constitutes "material" is often not specified in these clauses, leaving courts to struggle to find the parties' intent. See In re IBP, Inc. v. Tyson Foods, Inc., 789 A.2d 14 (Del. Ch. 2001).

PROBLEMS

(1) *Drafting (Reprise).* Review the clause that you drafted in response to the Problem, p. 774 above. Can you improve it in the light of Hicks v. Bush? Be sure to take account of Note 3 above.

(2) *Conditions Compared.* Suppose that in *Luttinger*, the agreement had contained a merger clause but had not contained a financing condition.

Would the Luttingers have been permitted to testify that the parties had orally agreed on a financing condition as part of their contract? See Luria Bros. & Co. v. Pielet Bros. Scrap Iron & Metal, Inc., 600 F.2d 103 (7th Cir. 1979).

SECTION 2.   CONSTRUCTIVE CONDITIONS OF EXCHANGE

This section introduces problems of performance and non-performance that do not turn on express conditions. Two main instruments of the law's development in this regard are the conceptions of "constructive conditions" and "material breach." A party's failure to *render* a performance—or in some cases its failure to *offer* a performance—is a possible excuse for the non-performance of a duty undertaken by the other party. Moreover, a *prospective* failure to perform may have the same effect. A traditional way of affirming these effects is to say that the commitments exchanged by the parties are "dependent covenants." (And a way of denying these effects is to speak of "independent covenants.") The first case in the section, Kingston v. Preston, is a cornerstone of the law of constructive conditions, reasoned in terms of such dependency.

Kingston v. Preston was regarded in its own time as a notable advance in the doctrine of dependency of covenants, and has been so referred to ever since. To speak in current terms, it is regarded as the chief inspiration for constructive conditions. The views expressed by Lord Mansfield have been commonly seen as modifying an attitude of the common law that was centuries old. Although the dependency of promises was neither invented nor finally resolved in that case, it is the most celebrated of a long series on the subject. On the history of Kingston v. Preston, see Larry T. Garvin, Kingston v. Preston (*and* Goodisson v. Nunn, *sort of*), in *The Best and Worst of Contracts Cases: An Anthology*, 45 Fla. St. U. L. Rev. 889, 914 (2018).

The impact of Kingston v. Preston is suggested by a hypothetical case stated in 1500 concerning a father who covenants to transfer an estate to his daughter and her husband-to-be, as part of a marriage settlement between the two men. According to the old text, even if the prospective husband is faithless—"if I marry another woman"—the father can be compelled to convey. The father's remedy would be a separate action for damages for breach of contract. The result represents in an extreme degree the principle that mutual covenants are independent unless expressed to be otherwise; in current terms we might say that the marriage is not a constructive condition of the father's promise. The result is otherwise, says the note, if the father's covenant refers to the marriage promise as being made "for the same cause."

Y.B.Trin. 15 Hen. 7, f. 10, pl. 17 (1500) [a] In practice, the presumption of independence was less extreme, but the case law establishing when the presumption was overcome was described by one commentator as "quaint technicalities" consisting of "nice and obscure distinctions." Thomas Platt, A Practical Treatise on the Law of Covenants 72, 78 (1829).

The defendant in Kingston v. Preston was in business as a silk mercer, and the plaintiff had entered his business as a "covenant servant," or apprentice. The articles of indenture provided that after a year and a quarter the mercer would retire from the business. Thereafter it was to be carried on by the apprentice and a partner— either a nephew of the mercer or someone else nominated by the defendant. The apprentice was to pay for his share of the business in monthly installments of £250. To assure these payments, the apprentice agreed to give the mercer "good and sufficient security," approved of by him, "at and before the sealing and delivery of the deeds" conveying the business.

The apprentice sued the mercer, alleging that he had refused to surrender the business at the appointed time. The defendant pleaded that the plaintiff had not given sufficient security for the payments. To this the plaintiff demurred, and arguments ensued as reported below.

Kingston v. Preston

King's Bench, 1773.
Lofft 194, 2 Doug. 689, 99 Eng. Rep. 437.

On the part of the plaintiff, the case was argued by Mr. Buller, who contended that the covenants were mutual and independent, and therefore a plea of the breach of one of the covenants to be performed by the plaintiff was no bar to an action for a breach by the defendant of one which he had bound himself to perform, but that the defendant might have his remedy for the breach by the plaintiff in a separate action. On the other side, Mr. Gross insisted that the covenants were dependent in their nature, and therefore performance must be alleged: the security to be given for the money was manifestly the chief object of the transaction, and it would be highly unreasonable to construe the agreement so as to oblige the defendant to give up a beneficial business, and valuable stock-in-trade, and trust to the plaintiff's personal security (who might, and, indeed was admitted to be worth nothing), for the performance of his part.

In delivering the judgment of the Court, Lord Mansfield expressed himself to the following effect: There are three kinds of covenants: 1. Such as are called mutual and independent, where either party may recover damages from the other for the injury he may have received by a breach

---

[a] What may seem to us an illogical assumption in fact followed from the then-current understanding of consideration. If a future act was consideration, then that act must first be performed. If a future promise was consideration, then the existence of the promise would suffice; the promise was present, even if the performance was not.

of the covenants in his favor, and where it is no excuse for the defendant to allege a breach of the covenants on the part of the plaintiff. 2. There are covenants which are conditions and dependent, in which the performance of one depends on the prior performance of another, and, therefore, till this prior condition is performed, the other party is not liable to an action on his covenant. 3. There is also a third sort of covenants, which are mutual conditions to be performed at the same time; and in these, if one party was ready and offered to perform his part, and the other neglected or refused to perform his, he who was ready and offered has fulfilled his engagement, and may maintain an action for the default of the other; though it is not certain that either is obliged to do the first act. His Lordship then proceeded to say, that the dependence or independence of covenants was to be collected from the evident sense and meaning of the parties, and that, however transposed they might be in the deed, their precedency must depend on the order of time in which the intent of the transaction requires their performance. That, in the case before the Court, it would be the greatest injustice if the plaintiff should prevail: the essence of the agreement was, that the defendant should not trust to the personal security of the plaintiff, but, before he delivered up his stock and business, should have good security for the payment of the money. The giving such security, therefore, must necessarily be a condition precedent. Judgment was accordingly given for the defendant, because the part to be performed by the plaintiff was clearly a condition precedent.

PROBLEM

Drafting (Reprise). Refer again to the Drafting Problem, p. 766 above, especially the direction to draft a clause making "sailing with the next wind" the subject of a duty alone. Do you see a difficulty in doing this, not apparent till now? How would you redraft the clause in the light of Kingston v. Preston?

Time for Performance

Because of the doctrine of constructive conditions, fixing the time for performance under a contract has the important effect of allocating the risk that one party will perform but will not receive the other party's return performance. Recall Judge Easterbrook's description, in Note 2, p. 688 above, of an opportunistic situation in which "there is effort to wring some advantage from the fact that the party who performs first sinks costs, which the other party may hold hostage by demanding greater compensation in exchange for its own performance." This situation of opportunism is sometimes referred to as the "holdup problem," and it may lead parties to underinvest in otherwise desirable contracts or not enter into an agreement at all.

The parties themselves can, of course, fix the times for performance in their contract, as the mercer did in Kingston v. Preston by providing that the apprentice was to give security "at and before the sealing and delivery of the deeds." If the contract is silent, default rules may fix the times for performance. One of the most common is that "When the performance of a contract consists in doing (faciendo) on one side, and in giving (dando) on the other side, the doing must take place before the giving." Coletti v. Knox Hat Co., Inc., 169 N.E. 648, 649–650 (N.Y. 1930).

"Centuries ago, the principle became settled that where work is to be done by one party and payment is to be made by the other, the performance of the work must precede payment, in the absence of a showing of a contrary intention. It is sometimes supposed, that this principle grew out of employment contracts, and reflects a conviction that employers as a class are more likely to be responsible than are workmen paid in advance. Whether or not the explanation is correct, most parties today contract with reference to the principle, and unless they have evidenced a contrary intention it is at least as fair as the opposite rule would be." Restatement § 234 cmt. e.

Is there a rationale behind implied conditions? Holmes suggested the following:

> Behind the logical form lies a judgment as to the relative worth and importance of competing legislative grounds, often an inarticulate and unconscious judgment, it is true, and yet the very root and nerve of the whole proceeding. You can give any conclusion a logical form. You can always imply a condition in a contract. But why do you imply it? It is because of some belief as to the practice of a community or of a class, or because of some opinion as to policy, or, in short, because of some attitude of yours upon a matter not capable of exact quantitative measurement, and therefore not capable of founding exact logical conclusions.

O.W. Holmes, *The Path of the Law*, 10 Harv. L. Rev. 457, 465–66 (1897).

Stewart v. Newbury

Court of Appeals of New York, 1917.
220 N.Y. 379, 115 N.E. 984.

■ CRANE, JUDGE. [Stewart, a builder, offered to do the excavation work for Newbury's new foundry building at 65 cents per cubic yard, to furnish labor and forms for the concrete work at $2.05 per cubic yard, and to furnish labor to put in re-enforcing (of the concrete) at $4.00 per ton. Newbury accepted this offer. As a result of a dispute, described in the opinion, over payment, Stewart sued Newbury. From judgment upon a verdict for Stewart, Newbury appealed, the Appellate Division affirmed, and Newbury appealed again.]

Nothing was said in writing about the time or manner of payment. The plaintiff, however, claims that after sending his letter and before receiving that of the defendant he had a telephone communication with Mr. Newbury and said: "I will expect my payments in the usual manner," and Newbury said, "All right, we have got the money to pay for the building." This conversation over the telephone was denied by the defendants.

The custom, the plaintiff testified, was to pay 85 per cent every thirty days or at the end of each month, 15 per cent being retained till the work was completed.

In July the plaintiff commenced work and continued until September 29th, at which time he had progressed with the construction as far as the first floor. He then sent a bill for the work done up to that date for $896.35. The defendants refused to pay the bill and work was discontinued.

The plaintiff claims that the defendants refused to permit him to perform the rest of his contract, they insisting that the work already done was not in accordance with the specifications. The defendants claimed upon the trial that the plaintiff voluntarily abandoned the work after their refusal to pay his bill.

On October 5, 1911, the defendants wrote the plaintiff a letter containing the following: "Notwithstanding you promised to let us know on Monday whether you would complete the job or throw up the contract, you have not up to this time advised us of your intention. . . . Under the circumstances we are compelled to accept your action as being an abandonment of your contract and of every effort upon your part to complete your work on our building. As you know, the bill which you sent us and which we declined to pay is not correct, either in items or amount, nor is there anything due you under our contract as we understand it until you have completed your work on our building."

To this letter the plaintiff replied the following day. In it he makes no reference to the telephone communication agreeing, as he testified, to make "the usual payments," but does say this: "There is nothing in our agreement which says that I shall wait until the job is completed before any payment is due, nor can this be reasonably implied. . . . As to having given you positive date as to when I should let you know what I proposed doing, I did not do so; on the contrary I told you that I would not tell you positively what I would do until I had visited the job, and I promised that I would do this at my earliest convenience. . . . "

The defendant Herbert Newbury testified that the plaintiff "ran away and left the whole thing." And the defendant F.E. Newbury testified that he was told by Mr. Stewart's man that Stewart was going to abandon the job; that he thereupon telephoned Mr. Stewart, who replied that he would let him know about it the next day, but did not.

In this action, which is brought to recover the amount of the bill presented as the agreed price and $95.68 damages for breach of contract, the plaintiff had a verdict for the amount stated in the bill, but not for the other damages claimed, and the judgment entered thereon has been affirmed by the Appellate Division.

The appeal to us is upon exceptions to the judge's charge. The court charged the jury as follows: "Plaintiff says that he was excused from completely performing the contract by the defendant's unreasonable failure to pay him for the work he had done during the months of August and September. . . . Was it understood that the payments were to be made monthly? If it was not so understood the defendant's only obligation was to make payments at reasonable periods, in view of the character of the work, the amount of work being done and the value of it. In other words, if there was no agreement between the parties respecting the payments, the defendants' obligation was to make payments at reasonable times. . . . But whether there was such an agreement or not, you may consider whether it was reasonable or unreasonable for him to exact payment at that time and in that amount."

The court further said, in reply to a request to charge:

"I will say in that connection, if there was no agreement respecting the time of payment, and if there was no custom that was understood by both parties, and with respect to which they made the contract, then the plaintiff was entitled to payments at reasonable times."

The defendants' counsel thereupon made the following request, which was refused: "I ask your Honor to instruct the jury that if the circumstances existed as your Honor stated in your last instruction, then the plaintiff was not entitled to any payment until the contract was completed."

The jury was plainly told that if there were no agreement as to payments, yet the plaintiff would be entitled to part payment at reasonable times as the work progressed, and if such payments were refused he could abandon the work and recover the amount due for the work performed.

This is not the law. Counsel for the plaintiff omits to call our attention to any authority sustaining such a proposition and our search reveals none. In fact the law is very well settled to the contrary. This was an entire contract. (Ming v. Corbin, 142 N.Y. 334, 340, 341, 37 N.E. 105.) Where a contract is made to perform work and no agreement is made as to payment, the work must be substantially performed before payment can be demanded.

This case was also submitted to the jury upon the ground that there may have been a breach of contract by the defendants in their refusal to permit the plaintiff to continue with his work, claiming that he had departed from the specifications, and there was some evidence justifying this view of the case, but it is impossible to say upon which of these two theories the jury arrived at its conclusion. The above errors, therefore, cannot be considered as harmless and immaterial. . . . As the verdict was for the amount of the bill presented and did not include the damages for a breach of contract, which would be the loss of profits, it may well be presumed that the jury adopted the first ground of recovery charged by the court as above quoted and decided that the plaintiff was justified in abandoning work for nonpayment of the installment.

The judgment should be reversed, and a new trial ordered, costs to abide the event.

NOTES

(1) *Questions.* If the jury believed Stewart's evidence about the telephone conversation with Newbury, does it follow that he was justified in abandoning the work? Would it matter whether this conversation occurred before or after the contract was concluded? If it occurred before, how might Stewart's case be affected by the parol evidence rule? If it occurred afterward, what was the consideration for Newbury's promise to pay "in the usual manner"? Might it make a difference if the contract contained a merger clause? A no-oral-modification clause?

(2) *Progress Payments.* For repair work on buildings and chattels, and similar modest jobs, payment is often withheld until completion. But for sizable construction work it is well-nigh universal practice to agree upon periodic progress payments in favor of the contractor. As security for completion, the owner retains a fraction (usually 10–20%) of the amount earned each month by the contractor, and the sums withheld (sometimes called the "retainage") are payable only upon completion. Does this practice indicate that contractors are dissatisfied with the rule in Stewart v. Newbury? Is it a reason for discarding the rule?

————

Concurrent Conditions and Tender

In Kingston v. Preston, Mansfield spoke of promises "which are mutual conditions to be performed at the same time; and in these, if one party was ready and offered to perform his part, and the other neglected or refused to perform his, he who was ready and offered has fulfilled his engagement, and may maintain an action for the default of the other; though it is not certain that either is obliged to do the first act." The case itself, however, turned on a constructive condition *precedent*; Mansfield's observations were dictum.

The Court of King's Bench applied this analysis in Goodisson v. Nunn, [1792] 100 Eng. Rep. 1288 (K.B.), several years after Mansfield's death. A seller of real property alleged that the buyer had failed to pay for the land and therefore was liable for liquidated damages. The buyer replied that the seller had failed to convey the land. The court held that the buyer was not liable because the covenants were mutually dependent:

"They were reciprocal acts, to be performed by each other at the same time." Consequently, "performance, or the offer to perform, must be pleaded on the one part, in order to found the action against the other."

Courts still apply this rule to contracts for the sale of goods where there is no provision for credit or other means of payment. Courts express the mutual dependency of the parties' promises by saying that tender of the goods by the seller and tender of the price by the buyer are "concurrent conditions." "Tender of delivery is a condition to the buyer's duty to accept the goods and . . . to pay for them" (UCC § 2–507(1)), and "tender of payment is a condition to the seller's duty to tender and complete any delivery" (UCC § 2–511(1)).

"A formal tender is seldom made in business transactions," it has been said, "except to lay the foundation for subsequent assertion in a court of justice of rights which spring from refusal of the tender."[b] Courts are not often called on to say what is or is not a formal tender of performance under a contract. Partly for that reason, as the word "tender" is commonly used it suggests a degree of punctilio in conduct that is seldom achieved. Paradoxically, the strict sense of the word is supported by a set of rules dispensing with the necessity of tender in ordinary contract litigation.

The Code states the requisites, under contracts for the sale of goods, for a seller's tender of delivery (UCC § 2–507) and for a buyer's tender of payment (UCC § 2–511). A comment after the former section identifies two senses of the word "tender." In the stricter sense, it "contemplates an offer coupled with a present ability to fulfill all the conditions resting on the tendering party and must be followed by actual performance if the other party shows himself ready to proceed." But the comment indicates that something less than this will suffice to put the other party in default "if he fails to proceed in some manner."

If a buyer has not made an arrangement with the seller for credit, must the buyer proffer payment in money—i.e., "legal tender"? The Code recognizes that it is commercially normal to accept a check from a "seemingly solvent party," and states a rule designed to avoid "commercial surprise." Tendering a check is commonly sufficient under this rule, "unless the seller demands payment in legal tender and gives any extension of time reasonably necessary to procure it." UCC § 2–511(2).

NOTE

Specific Performance. In actions for specific performance, and especially those based on land-sale contracts, constructive conditions of exchange sometimes do not operate with the same effect as in ordinary damage actions. Because the remedy takes the form of an *order,* a court can insert a condition

---

[b]   Lehman, J., dissenting, in Petterson v. Pattberg, 161 N.E. 428, 431 (N.Y. 1928).

that effectively secures the receipt by the defendant of the plaintiff's promised performance.

In McMillan v. Smith, 363 S.W.2d 437, 442 (Tex. 1962), the plaintiffs, purchasers of a ranch, were uncertain what the per-acre price amounted to, in the aggregate. Upon making a deposit into court, they alleged their ability and willingness to pay "such further sum as the Court may order." The court accepted this invitation, saying: "Historically, in a suit for specific performance, the question as to the necessity for a tender of performance by a purchaser has been determined according to equitable rules rather than to those applicable to an action at law. The latter requires the purchaser, as a condition precedent, to tender performance. Courts of equity, on the other hand, have not been bound by strict and inflexible rules."

SECTION 3.   THE CONSEQUENCES OF NON-PERFORMANCE

(A) UCC ARTICLE TWO: THE "PERFECT TENDER RULE"

During the nineteenth century a rule developed that a buyer was entitled to reject goods unless the seller made a "perfect tender." The requirement of perfection covered not only the quantity and quality of the goods but also the details of shipment. In the words of Learned Hand, "There is no room in commercial contracts for the doctrine of substantial performance." Mitsubishi Goshi Kaisha v. J. Aron & Co., 16 F.2d 185, 186 (2d Cir. 1926). This rule of strict performance remained unchallenged during the first half of the twentieth century. In its terms, it applied even though it was not practical for the seller to resell the rejected goods as, for example, if the goods were perishable or specially manufactured. Because the buyer's right to reject did not depend on the buyer's having been harmed by the breach, the rule offered an inviting pretext for buyers that sought to escape their contract obligations on discovering that they no longer needed the goods or that the market price had fallen. The shortcomings of the rule did not escape criticism.

The drafters of the Uniform Commercial Code gave the following reasons for retaining the perfect tender rule in UCC § 2–601: "first, . . . the buyer should not be required to guess at his peril whether a breach is material; second, . . . proof of materiality would sometimes require disclosure of the buyer's private affairs such as secret formulas or processes."

However, the Code softens the rule in several ways. First, UCC § 2–508 gives a seller the power to cure a defective tender "if the time for performance has not yet expired"—and, in some situations, even if that time has expired. Note that under the Code the decision to attempt to cure is within the seller's discretion. Article 46(2)(3) of the CISG, however, gives the buyer a right to *require* the seller to cure. Second, UCC § 2–608 allows a buyer who has already accepted goods to revoke that acceptance (and return the goods to the seller) only if the "non-conformity substantially impairs [their] value to him." Third, UCC § 2–612 similarly allows a buyer under a contract for delivery of goods in installments to reject an installment only if a non-conformity as to the goods "substantially impairs the value of that installment" and to claim a breach of the whole contract only for a breach that "substantially impairs the value of the whole contract."

NOTES

(1) *International Approaches.* The CISG abandons the perfect tender rule in favor of a rule of "fundamental breach." Article 25 defines that term as a breach that "results in such detriment to the other party as substantially to deprive him of what he is entitled to expect under the contract, unless the party in breach did not foresee, and a reasonable person of the same kind in the same circumstances would not have foreseen, such a result."

In *Delchi Carrier,* p. 970 below, the court quoted article 25 and said, "Because the cooling power and energy consumption of an air conditioning compressor are important determinants of the product's value, the district court's conclusion that Rotorex was liable for a fundamental breach of contract under the Convention was proper."

Is the CISG rule of fundamental breach an improvement on the rule in UCC § 2–601? Is the CISG formulation better than that in UCC §§ 2–608 and 2–612?

See UNIDROIT Principles art. 7.3.1, which speaks of "fundamental non-performance" and gives a list of factors to be used in determining whether a non-performance is fundamental.

(2) *Perfect Tender and Good Faith.* The Supermind Publishing Company paid a deposit to a printing firm under a contract for the production of a book. In an action to recover the deposit, a witness for Supermind testified that the books tendered were gray, whereas the defendant's newsprint sample was white; there was also evidence of other defects. On a jury finding that the books failed to conform to the contract, the plaintiff got judgment for the deposit, and the defendant appealed. *Held:* Affirmed.

In dictum the court said that if the printing firm had carried the burden of showing that "the buyer's motivation in rejecting the goods was to escape the bargain," this would have established a breach of the duty of good faith. But there was no evidence that "its primary motivation in rejection of the books was to escape a bad bargain." Such a finding, the court said, might be warranted by evidence of rejection on account of a minor defect, in a falling market. The court cited UCC §§ 1–203 [now UCC § 1–304] and 2–103(1)(b) [now replaced by UCC § 1–201(b)(20)]. Printing Center of Texas, Inc. v. Supermind Publishing Co., Inc., 669 S.W.2d 779 (Tex. Civ. App. 1984). Although the court relied on the Code, it expressed grave doubt that the contract was governed by Article 2.

The issue was addressed more recently in Larson v. Burton Construction, Inc., 421 P.2d 538 (Wyo. 2018). In *Larson,* the court noted "that the obligation of good faith limits a buyer's seemingly unhindered right to reject under the perfect tender rule. The perfect tender rule does not give buyers the power to seize upon the slightest contract deviation, even though it is not important to the buyer, as a pretext for discontinuing the contract . . . . The good faith requirement of the Code effectively prevents such improper strategic behavior, and thus assures that application of the perfect tender rule will occur only in those instances when it is invoked honestly," quoting from William H. Lawrence, *Appropriate Standards for a Buyer's Refusal to Keep Goods Tendered by a Seller*, 35 Wm. & Mary L. Rev. 1635, 1651 (1994).

Bartus v. Riccardi

New York City Court, 1967.
284 N.Y.S.2d 222.

■ HAROLD H. HYMES, JUDGE. The plaintiff is a franchised representative of Acousticon, a manufacturer of hearing aids. On January 15, 1966, the defendant signed a contract to purchase a Model A-660 Acousticon hearing aid from the plaintiff. The defendant specified Model A-660 because he had been tested at a hearing aid clinic and had been informed that the best hearing aid for his condition was this Acousticon model. An ear mold was fitted to the defendant and the plaintiff ordered Model A-660 from Acousticon.

On February 2, 1966, in response to a call from the plaintiff the defendant went to the plaintiff's office for his hearing aid. At that time he was informed that Model A-660 had been modified and improved, and that it was now called Model A-665. This newer model had been delivered by Acousticon for the defendant's use. The defendant denies that he understood this was a different model number. The hearing aid was fitted to the defendant. The defendant complained about the noise, but was assured by the plaintiff that he would get used to it.

The defendant tried out the new hearing aid for the next few days for a total use of 15 hours. He went back to the hearing clinic, where he was informed that the hearing aid was not the model that he had been advised to buy. On February 8, 1966, he returned to the plaintiff's office complaining that the hearing aid gave him a headache, and that it was not the model he had ordered. He returned the hearing aid to the plaintiff, for which he received a receipt. At that time the plaintiff offered to get Model A-660 for the defendant. The defendant neither consented to nor refused the offer. No mention was made by either party about canceling the contract, and the receipt given by the plaintiff contained no notation or indication that the plaintiff considered the contract canceled or rescinded.

The plaintiff immediately informed Acousticon of the defendant's complaint. By letter dated February 14, 1966, Acousticon writing directly to the defendant, informed him that Model A-665 was an improved version of model A-660, and that they would either replace the model that had been delivered to him or would obtain Model A-660 for him. He was asked to advise the plaintiff immediately of his decision so that they could effect a prompt exchange. After receiving this letter the defendant decided that he did not want any hearing aid from the plaintiff, and he refused to accept the tender of a replacement, whether it be Model A 665 or A-660.

The plaintiff is suing for the balance due on the contract. The question before the court is whether or not the plaintiff, having delivered a model which admittedly is not in exact conformity with the contract, can nevertheless recover in view of his subsequent tender of the model that did meet the terms of the contract.

The defendant contends that since there was an improper delivery of goods, the buyer has the right to reject the same under Sections 2–601 and 2–602(2)(c) of the Uniform Commercial Code. He further contends that even if the defendant had accepted delivery he may, under Section 2–608(1)(b) of the U.C.C., revoke his acceptance of the goods because "his acceptance was reasonably induced * * * by the seller's assurances."

The defendant, however, has neglected to take into account Section 2–508 of the Uniform Commercial Code which has added a new dimension to the concept of strict performance. This section permits a seller to cure a non-conforming delivery under certain circumstances. Subparagraph (1) of this section enacts into statutory law what had been New York case law. This permits a seller to cure a non-conforming delivery before the expiration of the contract time by notifying the buyer of his intention to so cure and by making a delivery within the contract period. . . .

The U.C.C. in sub-paragraph (2) of Section 2–508 goes further and extends beyond the contract time the right of the seller to cure a defective performance. Under this provision, even where the contract period has expired and the buyer has rejected a non-conforming tender or has revoked an acceptance, the seller may "substitute a conforming tender" if he had "reasonable grounds to believe" that the nonconforming tender would be accepted, and "if he seasonably notifies the buyer" of his intention "to substitute a conforming tender." (51 NY Jur. Sales, p. 41).

This in effect extends the contract period beyond the date set forth in the contract itself unless the buyer requires strict performance by including such a clause in the contract.

> The section (2–508(2) U.C.C.) rejects the time-honored and perhaps time-worn notion that the proper way to assure effective results in commercial transactions is to require strict performance. Under the Code a buyer who insists upon such strict performance must rely on a special term in his agreement or the fact that the seller knows as a commercial matter that strict performance is required. (48 Cornell Law Quarterly 13; 29 Albany Law Review 260).

This section seeks to avoid injustice to the seller by reason of a surprise rejection by the buyer.

An additional burden, therefore, is placed upon the buyer by this section. "As a result a buyer may learn that even though he rejected or revoked his acceptance within the terms of Sections 2–601 and 2–711, he still may have to allow the seller additional time to meet the terms of the contract by substituting delivery of conforming goods." (Bender's U.C.C. Service—Sales and Bulk Transfers—Vol. 3, Section 14–02(1)(a)(ii)).

Has the plaintiff in this case complied with the conditions of Section 2–508?

The model delivered to the defendant was a newer and improved version of the model than was actually ordered. Of course, the defendant is entitled to receive the model that he ordered even though it may be an older type. But under the circumstances the plaintiff had reasonable grounds to believe that the newer model would be accepted by the defendant.

The plaintiff acted within a reasonable time to notify the defendant of his tender of a conforming model. (Section 1–204 U.C.C.). The defendant had not purchased another hearing aid elsewhere. His position had not been altered by reason of the original non-conforming tender.

The plaintiff made a proper subsequent conforming tender pursuant to Section 2–508(2) of the Uniform Commercial Code.

Judgment is granted to plaintiff.

NOTES

(1) *Questions.* Did Bartus ship the correct goods? What is the consequence of a non-conforming shipment under the UCC? See § 2–601. Why does Bartus get to cure the non-conformity for longer than the contractual time for delivery? What's the statutory basis for this? Why should more time be permitted? What sort of behavior does this encourage? Do we want to discourage good-faith attempts to cure?

(2) *Love Me [Perfect] Tender.* Why should contracts for the sale of goods be subject to a perfect tender rule? How does this affect the balance of power between buyer and seller? Could it be used opportunistically?

(3) *The Timing of Rejection.* Consider the possibility for rejection of the goods. When must rejection take place? What if one accepts the goods? Can one still reject? What can a buyer that has accepted non-conforming goods do? See discussion of revocation, below at p. 792.

(4) *Consolation Prize.* If the buyer accepts the goods in spite of any non-conformity, is it without any UCC remedies?

Wrongful and Ineffective Rejections

Although UCC § 2–602 permits rejection, other sections qualify this right. For a rejection to work perfectly, of course the buyer must be justified in rejecting the goods. Reading UCC §§ 2–601, 2–602, 2–508, and 2–612 together yields the following: First, the buyer must not have accepted the goods, for acceptance precludes rejection. Second, the goods or their tender must not conform to the contract. Third, the seller must either have no cure right or must not have exercised it effectively and rightfully.

Even if these three elements are in place, the buyer still must reject the goods in a procedurally proper way under UCC § 2–602: rejection must be within a reasonable time after delivery or tender and the buyer seasonably notify the seller of the rejection. This makes sense as the seller needs prompt notice so it can cure, if there is a cure right. If the rejection is based on quality, it may need the goods to make its own case against a third party, such as a carrier or a subcontractor. If the goods may perish or decline in value, prompt notice will allow the seller to act and preserve some value. The seller may also need to cart the goods away.

This leaves four possibilities: either the rejection is substantively proper or it is not, and either it is procedurally proper or it is not. A substantively proper rejection is termed *rightful* and a substantively improper rejection is *wrongful*. A procedurally proper rejection is *effective*; a procedurally improper rejection is *ineffective*.

The difference between these categories is critical. If a rejection is rightful but ineffective, it is not a rejection at all. The buyer will, by passage of time, be deemed to have accepted the goods, and its rights will at most be of revocation under UCC § 2–608—a considerably narrower option. The buyer will be liable for the price. If a rejection is wrongful but effective, then it is a real rejection, ending the buyer's obligation to pay. As it is wrongful, though, the buyer will be in breach and will be subject to damages.

This may seem odd. Why does a rightful but ineffective rejection leave the goods on the buyer's hands, but a wrongful but effective rejection give them back to the seller? Shouldn't the breached-against buyer have a more powerful remedy than the buyer whose contract was performed in full? Bear in mind the policies at work here. The seller needs notice for all the reasons given above. With no notice it cannot act. If the buyer loiters, then it will have accepted the goods. Should the seller be in breach, though, the buyer will still have an action for damages under UCC § 2–714. In contrast, if the buyer gives timely notice the seller can take the goods back and preserve their value. This mitigates potential loss. If the buyer erred, then the seller can sue for damages—not under UCC § 2–709, as the seller has the goods, but under UCC § 2–706 or UCC § 2–708.

———

Revocation of Acceptance

As we have seen, if a buyer fails to make an effective rejection, it is deemed to have accepted the goods, whether they conform to the terms of the contract or not. UCC § 2–606(1)(b). This does not entirely deprive the buyer of remedies against the seller. For example, the buyer may still collect damages for breach under UCC § 2–714. Still, the normal buyer would prefer not to have the goods and the consequent obligation to pay.

The circumstances under which the buyer accepted the goods may suggest some limits on the effects of acceptance. Under UCC § 2–513, the buyer has, subject to contrary agreement, a reasonable right to inspect the goods before it accepts them or pays for them. By inspecting the goods, the buyer can find any reasonably obvious defects and resolve any problems with the seller before the transaction proceeds. The buyer has an incentive to make a cost-effective inspection of the goods, because if it does not then it may accept non-conforming goods. But what if the buyer made a reasonable inspection, but a reasonable inspection would not turn up the defect that the products later manifest? The buyer should not be expected to take excessive and inefficient precautions against remote and latent defects. On the other hand, once the buyer has accepted the goods, the seller's bargaining position improves greatly, and it is difficult to see why the ability of the buyer to find a defect at a reasonable cost should have this effect. In addition, the seller generally has a right to cure its non-performance before the buyer rejects the goods. UCC § 2–508. This gives the seller a chance to resolve the buyer's problems informally. But just as the seller needs and gets some finality when the buyer accepts the goods, the buyer needs finality if attempted repairs drag on endlessly and fruitlessly.

Hence the law of revocation of acceptance, codified at UCC § 2–608. As you read the following case, keep in mind (a) the circumstances under which revocation is available and (b) the consequences of making a rightful and effective revocation.

Jorgensen v. Pressnall

Oregon Supreme Court, 1976.
274 Or. 285, 545 P.2d 1382.

■ O'CONNELL, CHIEF JUSTICE. This is a suit for the rescission of a mobile home purchase contract and for the recovery of plaintiffs' down payment and damages. Defendants are Pressnall, the seller of the mobile home, and Commercial Credit Company, the company financing the transaction. Commercial Credit counterclaims for losses incurred in repossession of the mobile home and, in the event rescission is granted, seeks recovery of damages from Pressnall for breach of a warranty. The trial court found for plaintiffs against Pressnall and for Commercial Credit on its cross-complaint against Pressnall. Pressnall appeals.

Plaintiffs purchased a new mobile home from Pressnall, using their old mobile home as a down payment and financing the balance. Pressnall assigned the financing contract to Commercial Credit, warranting the enforceability of the assigned contract.

Pressnall represented the mobile home to plaintiffs as being of 'good, sound construction,' and of 'medium quality.' He also represented to plaintiffs that the mobile home was strong enough to stand up to frequent moves. Plaintiffs were assured that any defects present in the mobile home delivered to them from the factory would be repaired promptly.

The mobile home was delivered to plaintiffs' lot on November 1, 1972. Soon after they moved in plaintiff's discovered water and air leaks, gaps in the 'tip out,'[1] as well as defective doors, cabinets, vents and walls. Plaintiffs promptly gave Pressnall a list of these defects and were assured by Pressnall that the problems would be corrected. Thereafter, a series of repair requests yielded no action except the appearance of workmen who were not prepared to make repairs. Finally, plaintiffs, having decided that it was futile to attempt to have the unit properly repaired through Pressnall's efforts, turned the matter over to their attorney and rejected Pressnall's further efforts to make repairs. Thereafter, negotiations were held with a representative of the mobile home manufacturer and as a result three repairmen worked approximately ten hours each repairing defects. However, plaintiffs were not satisfied with the quality of repairs and when a release was tendered to them they refused to sign it. Although some of the defects were cured, the serious problems such as leakage continued and new problems were created.

Concluding that further requests to repair the unit would be futile, plaintiffs instructed their attorney on December 27th, 1972, to send letters to both defendants notifying them of plaintiffs' decision to rescind the purchase contract. Plaintiffs tendered back the new mobile home, subject to their security interest, and demanded return of the down payment as well as consequential damages. On advice of counsel plaintiffs continued to occupy the mobile home until November 15, 1973, approximately three weeks before the trial. The mobile home was repossessed by Commercial Credit in January of 1974 and resold at a loss.

Pressnall contends that plaintiffs did not prove facts sufficient to justify rescission, asserting (1) that there is no evidence of a material misrepresentation inducing plaintiffs' purchase; (2) that there is no evidence that the uncorrected defects were material or that they rendered the trailer unfit for use as a dwelling; (3) that rescission is not a proper remedy because plaintiffs refused to allow reasonable efforts to repair, and (4) that plaintiffs' continued possession and use of the mobile

---

[1] The 'tip out' is a hinged section that is transported inside the mobile home and then tipped out to widen the living room when the mobile home is set up. This method of construction is necessitated by width limitations for transportation over highways.

home constituted an assertion and exercise of the right of ownership inconsistent with their attempted revocation of acceptance.

The contract in question is governed by the Uniform Commercial Code. Specifically, the buyer's right to revoke acceptance is defined in ORS 72.6080, which provides as follows:

'(1) The buyer may revoke his acceptance of a lot or commercial unit whose nonconformity substantially impairs its value to him if he has accepted it;

'(a) On the reasonable assumption that its nonconformity would be cured and it has not been seasonably cured; or

'(b) Without discovery of such nonconformity if his acceptance was reasonably induced either by the difficulty of discovery before acceptance or by the seller's assurances.

'(2) Revocation of acceptance must occur within a reasonable time after the buyer discovers or should have discovered the ground for it and before any substantial change in condition of the goods which is not caused by their own defects. It is not effective until the buyer notifies the seller of it.

'(3) A buyer who so revokes has the same rights and duties with regard to the goods involved as if he had rejected them.'

Plaintiffs' rescission letter constituted a revocation of acceptance within the meaning of the code. When cast in language of the Uniform Commercial Code, Pressnall's contentions are that there is no proof of nonconformities substantially impairing the value of the goods and that there has been no failure to seasonably cure the nonconformities.

Whether plaintiffs proved nonconformities sufficiently serious to justify revocation of acceptance is a two-step inquiry under the code. Since ORS 72.6080(1) provides that the buyer may revoke acceptance of goods 'whose nonconformity substantially impairs its value to him,' the value of conforming goods to the plaintiff must first be determined. This is a subjective question in the sense that it calls for a consideration of the needs and circumstances of the plaintiff who seeks to revoke; not the needs and circumstances of an average buyer. [UCC § 2–608 cmt. 2] The second inquiry is whether the nonconformity in fact substantially impairs the value of the goods to the buyer, having in mind his particular needs. This is an objective question in the sense that it calls for evidence of something more than plaintiff's assertion that the nonconformity impaired the value to him; it requires evidence from which it can be inferred that plaintiff's needs were not met because of the nonconformity. In short, the nonconformity must substantially impair the value of the goods to the plaintiff buyer. The existence of substantial impairment depends upon the facts and circumstances in each case.

In the present case plaintiffs purchased the mobile home for the purpose of using it as their residence. Because of the defects described above and defendant's failure to cure them, the value of the mobile home to plaintiffs as a residence was substantially impaired. Defendant argues that since plaintiffs did not produce any evidence showing that the cost of repairs were substantial in relation to the purchase price, there was no proof of substantial impairment of value. This argument would have some force if the test for a substantial impairment of value were an objective one. However, since, as we have shown, the test is a subjective one, permitting revocation of acceptance if it is shown that the value to the purchaser is impaired, the relatively small amount of money needed to repair the defect is not necessarily relevant because the impairment of the value to the purchaser may be substantial even though the cost of curing the defect may be relatively small. Thus, in the present case, although the defects in the mobile home probably could have been repaired at a relatively small cost, plaintiffs were deprived of the benefits of a comfortable home for a substantial period of time as a result of defendant's failure to make timely repairs.

Defendant also seems to argue that impairment of value is not shown unless the goods are useless for the purchaser's purposes. This is not true; revocation of acceptance is permissible not only where there is complete impairment, but also where the impairment is substantial but not complete.

Pressnall contends that any failure to cure the nonconformities was excused because plaintiffs unreasonably refused to allow further attempts to repair the unit. The record indicates, however, that Pressnall had ample opportunity to cure the defects before the revocation of acceptance occurred, but that he did not act seasonably. A seller does not have an unlimited amount of time to cure the nonconformity.

Pressnall's final argument is that plaintiffs' use of the mobile home after the notice of rescission constituted a use of the goods inconsistent with the seller's ownership and that therefore a new acceptance of the goods occurred. [UCC § 2–606(1)(c)] The answer to this contention is that plaintiffs retained a security interest in the mobile home after the revocation of acceptance. [UCC § 2–711(3)] This entitled them to continue in possession to preserve their collateral. Continued occupancy was the most feasible method of protecting the mobile home from water damage. The alternative was to find covered storage which would have been expensive. Defendant suffered no loss as a result of plaintiffs' occupancy since the trial court awarded an offset to defendant for the rental value of the mobile home during plaintiffs' occupancy.

Plaintiffs have successfully revoked their acceptance of the mobile home, Pressnall thereby breached the warranty given on assignment of the financing contract to Commercial Credit. Damages were, therefore, properly awarded to Commercial Credit.

The decree of the trial court is affirmed.

NOTES

(1) *Objective or Subjective?* The court employs a two-prong test when determining whether the mobile home's non-conformity substantially impaired its value to the Jorgensens. How, if at all, does proof of the subjective prong differ from proof of the objective prong? How could Pressnall rebut either?

(2) *Wear and Tear.* The trial court awarded Pressnall an offset to compensate for the Jorgensens' continued use of the mobile home. Why? Suppose the Jorgensens had instead rented a reasonably priced apartment while the repairs were in progress. Would they have been able to recover the full cost of the apartment?

(3) *The Road Not Taken.* This case was decided under UCC § 2–608(1)(a), where the buyer accepts the good "on the reasonable assumption that its non-conformity would be cured and it has not been seasonably cured." The other path for revocation comes where the buyer did not discover the non-conformity before accepting the goods, either because the non-conformity was difficult to discover or because of the seller's assurances. For an example of the latter, see N. Am. Lighting, Inc. v. Hopkins Mfg. Corp., 37 F.3d 1253 (7th Cir. 1994) (seller's assurances that machine could be modified to meet the buyer's needs).

(4) *Deeper Pockets.* Suppose Pressnall was judgment-proof. Could the Jorgensens seek to revoke their acceptance from the manufacturer of the mobile home?

(B) THE COMMON LAW: SUBSTANTIAL PERFORMANCE AND MATERIAL BREACH

In *Luttinger* the court required strict compliance with the express financing condition, saying simply that if the condition "is not fulfilled the contract is not enforceable." Where constructive rather than express conditions are concerned, however, the rule is often one of substantial performance. The origin of the rule has been traced to another decision by Mansfield, one about the sale of a plantation in the West Indies. Boone v. Eyre, [1777] 126 Eng. Rep. 160, Note (K.B.) (partial performance as excuse for non-occurrence of a condition); see also Glazebrook v. Woodrow, [1799] 101 Eng. Rep. 1436 (K.B.) (treating the condition as satisfied when a material part of the agreement had been performed).

The rule has found its chief proving ground in suits on construction contracts. Why should this be so? Several considerations suggest the answer. Leases of real property have traditionally been regarded as exempt from the usual contract rules of constructive conditions. As for employment contracts, it is usual for an employer to pay wages at short intervals, and to reserve the power of termination at will. As for contracts for the sale of goods, the seller who is denied a remedy can usually dispose of the goods elsewhere and will not suffer a loss comparable to that of the builder who cannot enforce the contract. As for land sale contracts, enforcement is regularly sought in a court of equity, in which there are specialized rules serving some of the same objects as the doctrine of substantial performance. But neither party to a construction contract ordinarily has access to the remedy of specific performance.

"Through the doctrine of substantial performance," it is said, "the judges installed themselves as administrators of the execution and discharge of contracts. They freed themselves from rigid rules and adopted a broad standard under which they could apply a policy of making contract effective." J. Corry, Law and Policy 41–43 (1959). This must not be understood to mean that the courts will directly administer the performance of a contract, but it means that practical judgments about performance figure in their decisions about money claims. Should courts undertake a more active role as to construction contracts? Having become "administrators of the execution" of such contracts, would judges find it a short and easy next step to order the correction of defective work?

Jacob & Youngs v. Kent

Court of Appeals of New York, 1921.
230 N.Y. 239, 129 N.E. 889, 23 A.L.R. 1429.

■ CARDOZO, JUDGE. The plaintiff built a country residence for the defendant at a cost of upwards of $77,000, and now sues to recover a balance of $3,483.46, remaining unpaid. The work of construction ceased in June, 1914, and the defendant then began to occupy the dwelling. There was no complaint of defective performance until March, 1915. One of the specifications for the plumbing work provides that "all wrought iron pipe must be well galvanized, lap welded pipe of the grade known as 'standard pipe' of Reading manufacture." The defendant learned in March, 1915, that some of the pipe, instead of being made in Reading, was the product of other factories. The plaintiff was accordingly directed by the architect to do the work anew. The plumbing was then encased within the walls except in a few places where it had to be exposed. Obedience to the order meant more than the substitution of other pipe. It meant the demolition at great expense of substantial parts of the completed structure. The plaintiff left the work untouched, and asked for a certificate that the final payment was due. Refusal of the certificate was followed by this suit.

The evidence sustains a finding that the omission of the prescribed brand of pipe was neither fraudulent nor willful. It was the result of the oversight and inattention of the plaintiff's sub-contractor. Reading pipe is distinguished from Cohoes pipe and other brands only by the name of the manufacturer stamped upon it at intervals of between six and seven feet. Even the defendant's architect, though he inspected the pipe upon arrival, failed to notice the discrepancy. The plaintiff tried to show that the brands installed, though made by other manufacturers, were the same in quality, in appearance, in market value and in cost as the brand stated in the contract—that they were, indeed, the same thing, though manufactured in another place. The evidence was excluded, and a verdict directed for the defendant. The Appellate Division reversed, and granted a new trial.

We think the evidence, if admitted, would have supplied some basis for the inference that the defect was insignificant in its relation to the project. The courts never say that one who makes a contract fills the measure of his duty by less than full performance. They do say, however, that an omission, both trivial and innocent, will sometimes be atoned for by allowance of the resulting damage, and will not always be the breach of a condition to be followed by a forfeiture (Spence v. Ham, 163 N.Y. 220, 57 N.E. 412; Woodward v. Fuller, 80 N.Y. 312; Glacius v. Black, 67 N.Y. 563, 566; Bowen v. Kimbell, 203 Mass. 364, 370, 89 N.E. 542.) The distinction is akin to that between dependent and independent promises, or between promises and conditions (Anson on Contracts, Corbin's Ed., sec. 367: 2 Williston on Contracts, sec. 842). Some promises are so plainly independent that they can never by fair construction be conditions of one another. (Rosenthal Paper Co. v. Nat. Folding Box & Paper Co., 226 N.Y. 313, 123 N.E. 766; Bogardus v. N.Y. Life Ins. Co., 101 N.Y. 328, 4 N.E. 522.) Others are so plainly dependent that they must always be conditions. Others, though dependent and thus conditions when there is departure in point of substance, will be viewed as independent and collateral when the departure is insignificant (2 Williston on Contracts, secs. 841, 842; Eastern Forge Co. v. Corbin, 182 Mass. 590, 592, 66 N.E. 419; Robinson v. Mollett, L.R., 7 Eng. & Ir.App. 802, 814; Miller v. Benjamin, 142 N.Y. 613, 37 N.E. 631). Considerations partly of justice and partly of presumable intention are to tell us whether this or that promise shall be placed in one class or another. The simple and the uniform will call for different remedies from the multifarious and the intricate. The margin of departure within the range of normal expectation upon a sale of common chattels will vary from the margin to be expected upon a contract for the construction of a mansion or a "skyscraper." There will be harshness sometimes and oppression in the implication of a condition when the thing upon which labor has been expended is incapable of surrender because united to the land, and equity and reason in the implication of a like condition when the subject-matter, if defective, is in shape to be returned. From the conclusions that promises may not be treated as dependent to the extent of their uttermost minutiae without a sacrifice of justice, the progress is a short one to the conclusion that they may not be so treated without a perversion of intention. Intention not otherwise revealed may be presumed to hold in contemplation the reasonable and probable. If something else is in view, it must not be left to implication. There will be no assumption of a purpose to visit venial faults with oppressive retribution.

Those who think more of symmetry and logic in the development of legal rules than of practical adaptation to the attainment of a just result will be troubled by a classification where the lines of division are so wavering and blurred. Something, doubtless, may be said on the score of consistency and certainty in favor of a stricter standard. The courts have balanced such considerations against those of equity and fairness, and found the latter to be the weightier. The decisions in this state commit us to the liberal view, which is making its way, nowadays, in jurisdictions slow to welcome it (Dakin & Co. v. Lee, 1916, 1 K.B. 566, 579). Where the line is to be drawn between the important and the trivial cannot be settled by a formula. "In the nature of the case precise boundaries are impossible" (2 Williston on Contracts, sec. 841). The same omission may take on one aspect or another according to its setting. Substitution of equivalents may not have the same significance in fields of art on the one side and in those of mere utility on the other. Nowhere will change be tolerated, however, if it is so dominant or pervasive as in any real or substantial measure to frustrate the purpose of the contract (Crouch v. Gutmann, 134 N.Y. 45, 51, 31 N.E. 271). There is no general license to install whatever, in the builder's judgment, may be regarded as "just as good" (Easthampton L. & C., Ltd. v. Worthington, 186 N.Y. 407, 412, 79 N.E. 323). The question is one of degree, to be answered, if there is doubt, by the triers of the facts (Crouch v. Gutmann; Woodward v. Fuller, supra), and, if the inferences are certain, by the judges of the law (Easthampton L. & C. Co., Ltd. v. Worthington, supra). We must weigh the purpose to be served, the desire to be gratified, the excuse for deviation from the letter, the cruelty of enforced adherence. Then only can we tell whether literal fulfillment is to be implied by law as a condition. This is not to say that the parties are not free by apt and certain words to effectuate a purpose that performance of every term shall be a condition of recovery. That question is not here. This is merely to say that the law will be slow to impute the purpose, in the silence of the parties, where the significance of the default is grievously out of proportion to the oppression of the forfeiture. The willful transgressor must accept the penalty of his transgression (Schultze v. Goodstein, 180 N.Y. 248, 251, 73 N.E. 21; Desmond-Dunne Co. v. Friedman-Doscher Co., 162 N.Y. 486, 490, 56 N.E. 995). For him there is no occasion to mitigate the rigor of implied conditions. The transgressor whose default is unintentional and trivial may hope for mercy if he will offer atonement for his wrong (Spence v. Ham, supra). . . .

In the circumstances of this case, we think the measure of the allowance is not the cost of replacement, which would be great, but the difference in value, which would be either nominal or nothing. Some of the exposed sections might perhaps have been replaced at moderate expense. The defendant did not limit his demand to them, but treated the plumbing as a unit to be corrected from cellar to roof. In point of fact, the plaintiff never reached the stage at which evidence of the extent of the allowance became necessary. The trial court had excluded evidence that the defect was unsubstantial, and in view of that ruling there was no occasion for the plaintiff to go farther with an offer of proof. We think, however, that the offer, if it had been made, would not of necessity have been defective because directed to difference in value. It is true that in most cases the cost of replacement is the measure (Spence v. Ham, supra). The owner is entitled to the money which will permit him to complete, unless the cost of completion is grossly and unfairly out of proportion to the good to be attained. When that is true, the measure is the difference in value. Specifications call, let us say, for a foundation built of granite quarried in Vermont. On the completion of the building, the owner learns that through the blunder of a subcontractor part of the foundation has been built of granite of the same quality quarried in New Hampshire. The measure of allowance is not the cost of reconstruction. "There may be omissions of that which could not afterwards be supplied exactly as called for by the contract without taking down the building to its foundations and at the same time the omission may not affect the value of the building for use or otherwise, except so slightly as to be hardly appreciable" (Handy v. Bliss, 204 Mass. 513, 519, 90 N.E. 864. Cf. Foeller v. Heintz, 137 Wis. 169, 178, 118 N.W. 543; Oberlies v. Bullinger, 132 N.Y. 598, 601, 30 N.E. 999; 2 Williston on Contracts, sec. 805, p. 1541). The rule that gives a remedy in cases of substantial performance with compensation for defects of trivial or inappreciable importance, has been developed by the courts as an instrument of justice. The measure of the allowance must be shaped to the same end.

The order should be affirmed, and judgment absolute directed in favor of the plaintiff upon the stipulation, with costs in all courts.

■ McLAUGHLIN, JUDGE. (dissenting). I dissent. The plaintiff did not perform its contract. Its failure to do so was either intentional or due to gross neglect which, under the uncontradicted facts, amounted to the same thing, nor did it make any proof of the cost of compliance, where compliance was possible.[c]

The plaintiff agreed that all the pipe used should be of the Reading Manufacturing Company. It installed between 2,000 and 2,500 feet of pipe, of which only 1,000 feet at most complied with the contract. No explanation was given why pipe called for by the contract was not used, nor was any effort made to show what it would cost to remove the pipe of other manufacturers and install that of the Reading Manufacturing Company. The defendant had a right to contract for what he wanted. He had a right before making payment to get what the contract called for. It is no answer to this suggestion to say that the pipe put in was just as good as that made by the Reading Manufacturing Company, or that the difference in value between such pipe and the pipe made by the Reading Manufacturing Company would be either "nominal or nothing." Defendant contracted for pipe made by the Reading Manufacturing Company. What his reason was for requiring this kind of pipe is of no

---

[c]   An omitted part of the dissent explains that on the first delivery of pipe Jacob & Youngs's superintendent examined the pipe to make certain it was of Reading manufacture, but thereafter the subcontractor's foreman simply left word at its shop that he wanted a certain number of feet without specifying the manufacture, and there was no examination before installation.

importance. He wanted that and was entitled to it. The rule, therefore, of substantial performance, with damages for unsubstantial omissions, has no application.

■ HISCOCK, CHIEF JUDGE, HOGAN and CRANE, JUDGES, concur with CARDOZO, JUDGE; POUND and ANDREWS, JUDGES, concur with MCLAUGHLIN, JUDGE.

NOTES

(1) *Preference in Interpretation (Reprise).* How does the doctrine of substantial performance, which applies only to constructive and not express conditions, relate to the preference in interpretation mentioned in the Note, p. 766 above?

(2) *Variations on the Rule.* Courts have sometimes made arbitrary distinctions in an attempt to give more precision to the vague notion of "substantial performance" in a construction contract.

It is sometimes said that there can be no substantial performance if there are "structural defects." Where the size and placement of girders was faulty, affecting the solidity of the building, these were "deviations from the general plan of so essential a character that they cannot be remedied without partially reconstructing the building, and hence do not come within the rule of substantial performance." Spence v. Ham, 57 N.E. 412, 414 (N.Y. 1900). But see Kizziar v. Dollar, 268 F.2d 914, 917 (10th Cir. 1959), in which the court concluded that "the foundation, although not equal to that specified, was standard and adequate for that type of building."

It is also sometimes said that there is no substantial performance if the defects exceed a certain percent of the contract price. "Under ordinary circumstances . . . a failure to perform 10 percent of the contract price will not admit of the claim of substantial performance." Rochkind v. Jacobson, 110 N.Y.S. 583, 584 (App. Div. 1908). But see Jardine Estates v. Donna Brook Corp., 126 A.2d 372 (N.J. Super. 1956) where the court said, "The matter is not to be determined on a percentage basis, for the cost of remedying defects may sometimes even exceed the outlay for original construction."

(3) *Seriatim Objections.* A builder has put up a dwelling, under contract with the owner of the lot, and considers that all the specifications have been met. If, however, the owner disagrees, the builder means to do corrective work. The builder wishes to do all such work at one time, before moving its crew and equipment away. How can the builder elicit a definitive list of the owner's objections?

In Cawley v. Weiner, 140 N.E. 724 (N.Y. 1923), the owners of a new bungalow moved in before the builder had stopped work, and handed him a list of 17 items that they considered necessary by way of change in or addition to the structure. For about a week after that, apparently, the builder continued work. Not being paid in full, he brought suit against the owners for the price. At the trial, they offered to prove three particulars, not specified in the earlier list, in which the plaintiff had failed of performance. The trial court excluded the evidence on grounds of waiver and estoppel, and gave the plaintiff judgment for virtually the whole amount he claimed. The owners appealed. *Held:* Reversed.

"Unless the plaintiff were in some way harmed by the action of these defendants in furnishing him with a list of the defects, how are they estopped from showing the departures from the plans and specifications?"

(4) *"Willful" Breach.* Cardozo says that Jacob & Youngs' breach was not "willful." It is generally said that a "willful" deviation from the terms of the contract always precludes a finding of substantial performance. (This is often said when the facts seem to show a breach that would prevent substantial performance in any case.)

What kinds of breach by a builder should be regarded as "willful"? Substitution of inferior materials to make a profit? Substitution of equivalent materials to make a profit? What if the builder departs from the plans to meet unforeseen construction problems? What if it is impossible to follow the plans literally?

Is there a better term than "willful" to describe conduct that will bar a builder from claiming substantial performance? Restatement § 241 avoids that word, taking the view that the pertinent inquiry is not simply whether the breach was "willful" but whether the behavior of the party in default "comports with standards of good faith and fair dealing." Even an adverse conclusion on this point is not decisive but is to be weighed with other factors, such as the extent to which the owner will be deprived of a reasonably expected benefit and the extent to which the builder may suffer forfeiture, in deciding whether there has been substantial performance. Whether a breach is willful may also affect the measure of damages, as we shall see in Chapter 8.

(5) *Producing Evidence.* If there is substantial performance, who has the burden of showing how much should be allowed as damages? Some courts require the owner to produce evidence of damages resulting from defects in the builder's work. But see Vance v. My Apartment Steak House, 677 S.W.2d 480 (Tex. 1984), requiring the builder, as plaintiff, to establish the cost of remedying defects. A minority of the justices here thought it "anomalous" to require that the plaintiff provide support for the defendant's position.

Who is in a better position to establish the loss to the defendant? Does the answer depend on the question how that loss is measured?

PROBLEMS

(1) *Credit for Unpaid Price?* Contractor installed a heating system in an office building and did such poor work as to be liable to Owner for $250,000. Owner has withheld $150,000 of the contract price. How much does Contractor owe Owner? $250,000 or only $100,000? See Kirk Reid Company v. Fine, 139 S.E.2d 829 (Va. 1965).

(2) *Drafting.* If you had represented Kent when he made his contract, could you have drafted a provision that would have barred recovery by Jacob & Youngs? Recall Cardozo's dictum in Jacob & Youngs v. Kent: "This is not to say that the parties are not free by apt and certain words to effectuate a

purpose that performance of every term shall be a condition of recovery." In Oppenheimer & Co. v. Oppenheim, Appel, Dixon & Co., 660 N.E.2d 415, 420 (N.Y. 1995), the court quoted this dictum when rejecting the "proposition that the substantial performance doctrine applies universally, including when the language of the agreement leaves no doubt that an express condition precedent was intended."

Under the actual contract between Jacob & Youngs and Kent, payments were to be made monthly as the work progressed, on the certificate of the architect in an amount which "in his judgment" represented the amount due less 15% to be withheld. The specifications attached to the contract provided that where "any particular brand of manufactured article is specified, it is to be considered as a standard," and that a contractor "desiring to use another shall first make application in writing to the Architect . . . and obtain their written approval of the change." The specifications made the architect's decision "as to the character of any material or labor furnished by the Contractor . . . final and conclusive." Furthermore, "Any work furnished by the Contractor, the material or workmanship of which is defective or which is not fully in accordance with the drawings and specifications, in every respect, will be rejected and is to be immediately torn down, removed and remade or replaced in accordance with the drawings and specifications, whenever discovered. . . . The Owner will have the option at all times to allow the defective or improper work to stand and to receive from the Contractor a sum of money equivalent to the difference in value of the work as performed and as herein specified." Record at 98–108. How could these terms have been improved?

(3) *Conclusiveness of Certificate.* A contractor who agrees to procure the certificate of an architect or an engineer as a condition of payment may want to take care lest the provision on the subject be read as leaving the certificate inconclusive when it is issued, so that the contractor remains exposed to a claim that its performance was defective. The other party may wish, naturally, to retain such a claim notwithstanding the issuance of a certificate. What language would you suggest to avert the risk for the contractor? What language to have the opposite effect? How would you interpret the language above?

SECTION 4.   SUSPENDING PERFORMANCE AND TERMINATING THE CONTRACT

Courts developed the doctrine of substantial performance to deal with the relatively simple case in which the party in breach has finished performing and the injured party refuses to pay the price because the performance is defective or incomplete. Often the dispute arises at a much earlier stage of performance, however, and the question is whether a breach justifies the injured party in exercising a right to self-help by suspending performance or by refusing to render performance and terminating the contract. Sometimes the injured party is the defendant, seeking merely to justify its nonperformance in an action that has been brought by the other party. Sometimes the injured party is the plaintiff, seeking to justify its nonperformance in an action that it has brought against the other party for damages for total breach. These cases of breach in the course of performance pose particularly thorny problems of counseling.

It may be useful at this point to have an idea of the analysis used in the Restatement to deal with the problems that arise when an aggrieved party seeks to suspend performance or to refuse to render performance and terminate the contract.

The first step is to determine whether there is an uncured breach by the other party, because the problems we are addressing arise only if there is a breach. If there is, the next question is whether the uncured breach is a breach of a duty of performance that was part of an exchange of promises (as opposed to a duty under a promise on which the injured party's promise does not depend). Under the Restatement analysis it is presumed that this is the case unless "a contrary intention is clearly manifested." Restatement § 232 cmt. a. A third question is whether the breach went to a performance that was to take place before that of the aggrieved party. See Restatement § 237. If not, then we would have to determine which breach happened first; under the constructive conditions of exchange, the first material breach may excuse any later breaches by the other party.

The final issue is the subject of much litigation. Suppose that the other party has breached, its breach has not been cured, and the breach went to a performance that was due before the other party was to perform. Is the breach serious enough to justify self-help in the form of suspension or termination? Is it what is called a *material* breach? See Restatement § 241 for a list of factors relevant when deciding whether a breach is material. If the breach is *not* a material breach—in other words, if there has been substantial performance—the aggrieved party has no choice but to continue performance and treat the breach as a *partial* breach. This gives rise to a right to any damages incurred to that point, but it does not give rise to a right to suspend or terminate. If the breach *is* material, however, the aggrieved party has a choice: either continue performance and treat the breach as a partial breach or stop performing and treat the breach as a *total* breach. (It may help to realize that in the Restatement vernacular, whether a breach is to be characterized as *material* or *not material* is not within the control of the aggrieved party, but whether to treat a material breach as *partial* or *total* is a matter for decision by the aggrieved party.) Treating the breach as a total breach has drastic consequences. First, because of the constructive conditions of exchange, the breached-against party has the right to terminate its own performance. Restatement § 237. Second, the breached-against party may collect damages for breach of the entire contract, not just the part as to which the performance was defective. Restatement § 236(1).

As an illustration, suppose Arnold made a contract with an athletic trainer for six months of twice-weekly hour-long individual sessions, payment for the sessions due at the end of each month. Everything went well until the sixth session, which the trainer cut short by five minutes. That certainly would be a breach. If the trainer didn't provide some acceptable alternative, the breach would be uncured. The breach would also be part of a performance that was to take place before Arnold's (that is, Arnold's obligation to pay). But was the trainer's breach material? Almost certainly not, given its brevity in the context of the whole contract. The breach thus would give rise only to an action for partial breach. Arnold would have the right to sue for the value of the lost five minutes, but he would not have the right to terminate the contract.

Suppose instead that the trainer failed to show up for four straight sessions and didn't respond to any messages. Now the breach looks material. Arnold would have the right to sue for partial breach—that is, for the value of the missed sessions—while continuing to seek the trainer's performance. He would alternatively have the right to sue for total breach. This would allow him to stop his own performance and to sue for damages for the breach of the entire agreement, including, for example, any increased costs for hiring another trainer. Cf. UCC § 2–612.

If the circumstances make it appropriate for the aggrieved party to suspend performance and give the other party a chance to cure, the aggrieved party is expected to do so before treating the breach as total. Circumstances that are significant in determining how long an aggrieved party, having suspended, must wait before terminating are listed in Restatement § 242. Cf. UCC § 2–508(2).

For an analysis in Restatement terms, see Farnsworth on Contracts §§ 8.16–8.18.

Walker & Co. v. Harrison

Supreme Court of Michigan, 1957.
347 Mich. 630, 81 N.W.2d 352.

■ SMITH, JUSTICE. This is a suit on a written contract. The defendants are in the dry-cleaning business. Walker & Company, plaintiff, sells, rents, and services advertising signs and billboards. These parties entered into an agreement pertaining to a sign. The agreement is in writing and is termed a "rental agreement." It specifies in part that:

"The lessor agrees to construct and install, at its own cost, one 18′9″ high × 8′8″ wide pylon type d.f. neon sign with electric clock and flashing lamps. . . . The lessor agrees to and does hereby lease or rent unto the said lessee the said SIGN for the term, use and rental and under the conditions, hereinafter set out, and the lessee agrees to pay said rental. . . .

"(a) The term of this lease shall be 36 months.

"(b) The rental to be paid by lessee shall be $148.50 per month for each and every calendar month during the term of this lease;

"(d) Maintenance. Lessor at its expense agrees to maintain and service the sign together with such equipment as supplied and installed by the lessor to operate in conjunction with said sign under the terms of this lease; this service is to include cleaning and repainting of sign in original color scheme as often as deemed necessary by lessor to keep sign in first class advertising condition and make all necessary repairs to sign and equipment installed by lessor."

At the "expiration of this agreement," it was also provided, "title to this sign reverts to lessee." This clause is in addition to the printed form of agreement and was apparently added as a result of defendants' concern over title, they having expressed a desire "to buy for cash" and the salesman, at one time, having "quoted a cash price."

The sign was completed and installed in the latter part of July, 1953. The first billing of the monthly payment of $148.50 was made August 1, 1953, with payment thereof by defendants on September 3, 1953. The first payment was also the last. Shortly after the sign was installed, someone hit it with a tomato. Rust, also, was visible on the chrome, complained defendants, and in its corners were "little spider cobwebs." In addition, there were "some children's sayings written down in here." Defendant Herbert Harrison called Walker for the maintenance he believed himself entitled to under subparagraph (d) above. It was not forthcoming. He called again and again. "I was getting, you might say, sorer and sorer. Occasionally, when I started calling up, I would walk around where the tomato was and get mad again. Then I would call up on the phone again." Finally, on October 8, 1953, plaintiff not having responded to his repeated calls, he telegraphed Walker that:

"You Have Continually Voided Our Rental Contract By Not Maintaining Signs As Agreed As We No Longer Have A Contract With You Do Not Expect Any Further Remuneration."

[Walker answered by letter, pointing out that the telegram did not "make any specific allegations as to what the failure of maintenance comprises," and concluding:]

"We would like to call your attention to paragraph G in our rental contract, which covers procedures in the event of a Breach of Agreement. In the event that you carry out your threat to make no future monthly payments in accordance with the agreement, it is our intention to enforce the conditions outlined under paragraph G[1]. . . . Unless we receive both

---

[1] "(g) Breach of Agreement. Lessee shall be deemed to have breached this agreement by default in payment of any installment of the rental herein provided for; abandonment of the sign or vacating premises where the sign is located; termination or transfer of lessee's interest in the premises by insolvency, appointment of a receiver for lessee's business; filing of a voluntary or involuntary petition in bankruptcy with respect to lessee or the violation of any of the other terms or conditions hereof. In the event of such default, the lessor may, upon notice to the lessee, which notice shall conclusively be deemed sufficient if mailed or delivered to the premises where the sign was or is located, take possession of the sign and declare the balance of the rental herein provided for to be forthwith due and payable, and lessee hereby agrees to pay such balance upon any such contingencies. Lessor may terminate this lease and without notice, remove and repossess said sign and recover from the lessee such amounts as may be

the September and October payments by October 25th, this entire matter will be placed in the hands of our attorney for collection in accordance with paragraph G which stipulates that the entire amount is forthwith due and payable."

No additional payments were made and Walker sued in assumpsit for the entire balance due under the contract, $5,197.50, invoking paragraph (g) of the agreement. Defendants filed answer and claim of recoupment, asserting that plaintiff's failure to perform certain maintenance services constituted a prior material breach of the agreement, thus justifying their repudiation of the contract and grounding their claim for damages. The case was tried to the court without a jury and resulted in a judgment for the plaintiff. The case is before us on a general appeal.

Defendants urge upon us again and again, in various forms, the proposition that Walker's failure to service the sign, in response to repeated requests, constituted a material breach of the contract and justified repudiation by them. The legal proposition is undoubtedly correct. Repudiation is one of the weapons available to an injured party in event the other contractor has committed a material breach. But the injured party's determination that there has been a material breach, justifying his own repudiation, is fraught with peril, for should such determination, as viewed by a later court in the calm of its contemplation, be unwarranted, the repudiator himself will have been guilty of material breach and himself have become the aggressor, not an innocent victim.

What is our criterion for determining whether or not a breach of contract is so fatal to the undertaking of the parties that it is to be classed as "material"? There is no single touchstone. Many factors are involved. They are well stated in section 275 of Restatement [first] of Contracts in the following terms:

"In determining the materiality of a failure fully to perform a promise the following circumstances are influential:

"(a) The extent to which the injured party will obtain the substantial benefit which he could have reasonably anticipated;

"(b) The extent to which the injured party may be adequately compensated in damages for lack of complete performance;

---

unpaid for the remaining unexpired term of this agreement. Time is of the essence of this lease with respect to the payment of rentals herein provided for. Should lessee after lessor has declared the balance of rentals due and payable, pay the full amount of rental herein provided, he shall then be entitled to the use of the sign, under all the terms and provisions hereof, for the balance of the term of this lease. No waiver by either party hereto of the nonperformance of any term, condition or obligation hereof shall be a waiver of any subsequent breach of, or failure to perform the same, or any other term, condition or obligation hereof. It is understood and agreed that the sign is especially constructed for the lessee and for use at the premises now occupied by the lessee for the term herein provided; that it is of no value unless so used and that it is a material consideration to the lessor in entering into this agreement that the lessee shall continue to use the sign for the period of time provided herein and for the payment of the full rental for such term."

"(c) The extent to which the party failing to perform has already partly performed or made preparations for performance;

"(d) The greater or less hardship on the party failing to perform in terminating the contract;

"(e) The wilful, negligent or innocent behavior of the party failing to perform;

"(f) The greater or less uncertainty that the party failing to perform will perform the remainder of the contract."

We will not set forth in detail the testimony offered concerning the need for servicing. Granting that Walker's delay (about a week after defendant Herbert Harrison sent his telegram of repudiation Walker sent out a crew and took care of things) in rendering the service requested was irritating, we are constrained to agree with the trial court that it was not of such materiality as to justify repudiation of the contract, and we are particularly mindful of the lack of preponderant evidence contrary to his determination. Jones v. Eastern Michigan Motorbuses, 287 Mich. 619, 283 N.W. 710. The trial court, on this phase of the case, held as follows:

"Now Mr. Harrison phoned in, so he testified, a number of times. He isn't sure of the dates but he sets the first call at about the 7th of August and he complained then of the tomato and of some rust and some cobwebs. The tomato, according to the testimony, was up on the clock; that would be outside of his reach, without a stepladder or something. The cobwebs are within easy reach of Mr. Harrison and so would the rust be. I think that Mr. Bueche's argument that these were not materially a breach would clearly be true as to the cobwebs and I really can't believe in the face of all the testimony that there was a great deal of rust seven days after the installation of this sign. And that really brings it down to the tomato. And, of course, when a tomato has been splashed all other (sic) your clock, you don't like it. But he says he kept calling their attention to it, although the rain probably washed some of the tomato off. But the stain remained, and they didn't come. I really can't find that that was such a material breach of the contract as to justify rescission. I really don't think so."

Nor, we conclude, do we. There was no valid ground for defendants' repudiation and their failure thereafter to comply with the terms of the contract was itself a material breach, entitling Walker, upon this record, to judgment.

The question of damages remains. [The court concluded that it need not address the question "whether this contract is one of sale or of lease" because the parties have agreed that the remedy sought is "acceleration of 'rentals' due."] The trial court cut down such sum by the amount that service would have cost Walker during the unexpired portion of the agreement (Restatement, Contracts, § 335) and as to such diminution Walker does not complain or cross-appeal. Judgment was, therefore, rendered for the cash price of the sign, for such services and maintenance as were extended and accepted, and interest upon the amount in default. There was no error.

Affirmed. Costs to appellee.

NOTES

(1) *Counseling.* If Harrison had consulted you before he sent the telegram, what would you have advised him to do?

It would have been safe for Harrison to have hired someone to clean off the sign and then sue Walker for partial breach, claiming what he paid. Would it have been safe for Harrison to have deducted that amount from the amount due under paragraph (b)? (The right of a party to withhold payment due on this ground is taken up later in connection with the next case.)

(2) *Condition Versus Promise.* Maintenance of the sign by Walker with some diligence, and in some degree of respectability, was of course a constructive condition of Harrison's duty to keep up the rental payments. Walker's duty of maintenance, as stated in paragraph (d), would not be met by anything less than punctilious performance. But the condition of performance by Harrison need not be so stringent. Obviously there is some softening effect, or "play," in the process of deriving a condition from a promise. Compare the effect the paragraph might have had if it had been written in terms of an express condition.

In *Delta Dynamics,* p. 512 above, Pixey was required to sell a minimum of 50,000 units in its first year but sold only 10,000. When you read that case you were asked what remedies would have been available to Delta if the agreement had not contained a provision allowing Delta to terminate if Pixey did not meet the minimum. What would be your answer now? What remedies would have been available if Pixey had taken only 49,999 locks? At what point would Pixey's breach have been *material*?

(3) *Question of Law or Fact?* Did the court make its own judgment whether or not Walker's conduct amounted to a material breach? Or did it accept the trial judge's determination as a permissible finding on the evidence? Should the issue of materiality of a breach ever be submitted to a jury? And if so, should they be directed to balance the factors mentioned in Restatement § 241, or in some similar list? What merit or demerit do you find in treating the issue as a "question of law"?

(4) *Irrelevance of Good Faith.* Good faith will not prevent a statement from being a repudiation. In United California Bank v. Prudential Ins. Co., 681 P.2d 390, 431 (Ariz. App. 1983), the court declined to "engraft a vague fault principle onto one branch of settled contract doctrine. If a 'good faith' contract interpretation is made as a defense to a claim of breach by anticipatory repudiation, then it should be a defense where the repudiating party believes wrongly but in 'good faith' that there is no contract at all or that the contract has been terminated, modified, or rescinded." Cf. Lorang v. Fortis Ins. Co., 192 P.3d 186 (Mont. 2008) ("Although the parties dispute

whether the denial was a mistake or an intentional act, that issue is not relevant in determining whether Fortis repudiated its contractual duty.").

(5) *Delay Under the CISG.* Recall that the CISG abandons the "perfect tender" rule in favor of a rule of "fundamental breach" (Note 1, p. 787 above). If a seller delays delivery of the goods under a contract that does not make time "of the essence," how can the buyer know how much delay will make the seller's breach "fundamental"?

Article 47(1) empowers the buyer to "fix an additional period of time of reasonable length for performance by the seller of his obligations." If the seller fails to deliver the goods within this additional period, article 49(1)(b) provides that the buyer may declare the contract avoided, regardless of whether the failure amounts to a "fundamental breach." Articles 63(1) and 64(1)(b) set out comparable rules for the seller in the event of a breach by the buyer.

These provisions of the CISG were inspired by the *Nachfrist* provisions of German law. Under German law, however, failure to give a *Nachfrist* notice may preclude termination, whereas under the Convention it gives an alternative ground for avoidance. See John O. Honnold, Uniform Law for International Sales under the 1980 United Nations Convention ¶¶ 27, 289, 305 (Harry M. Flechtner ed., 4th ed. 2009).

PROBLEMS

(1) *Drafting.* How might Harrison's telegram have been drafted to put pressure on Walker without risk to Harrison? Would it have been safe for Harrison to have demanded Walker's assurance of proper maintenance in the future? (The right of a party that has become insecure about the other party's performance to demand assurance of due performance is dealt with in Section 6(B) below.)

If Harrison had consulted you before signing the agreement, what proposals would you have made for changes in its terms? Do the provisions of the CISG described above give you any ideas for changes?

(2) *Liquidated Damages or Penalty?* Is the provision providing for recovery of unpaid amounts in the third sentence of paragraph (g), see footnote 1 above, enforceable?

K & G Construction Co. v. Harris

Court of Appeals of Maryland, 1960.
223 Md. 305, 164 A.2d 451.

[A case was stated for appeal in an action by a Contractor against a Subcontractor, and the following facts were given. K & G Construction Company was the owner and general contractor for a housing subdivision project. Harris and Brooks contracted with it to do excavating and earth-moving work on the project. Certain provisions of the agreement were as follows:

"Section 4. (b) Progress payments will be made each month during the performance of the work. Subcontractor will submit to Contractor, by the 25th of each month, a requisition for work performed during the preceding month. Contractor will pay these requisitions, less a retainer equal to ten per cent (10%), by the 10th of the months in which such requisitions are received.[1]

"(c) No payments will be made under this contract until the insurance requirements of Sec. 9 hereof have been complied with.

"Section 8. . . . All work shall be performed in a workmanlike manner, and in accordance with the best practices.

"Section 9. Subcontractor agrees to carry, during the progress of the work, . . . liability insurance against . . . property damage, in such amounts and with such companies as may be satisfactory to Contractor and shall provide Contractor with certificates showing the same to be in force."

While in the course of his employment by the Subcontractor on the project, a bulldozer operator drove his machine too close to Contractor's house while grading the yard, causing the immediate collapse of a wall and other damage to the house. Contractor was generally satisfied with Subcontractor's work and progress as required by the contract until September 12, 1958, with the exception of the bulldozer accident which occurred on August 9. The Subcontractor and its insurance carrier refused to repair damage or compensate Contractor for damage to the house, claiming that there was no liability on the part of the Subcontractor.

For work done prior to July 25, the Subcontractor submitted a requisition payable under the terms of the contract on or before August 10. Contractor refused to pay it because the bulldozer damage had not been repaired or paid for. Subcontractor continued to work on the project until September 12, when it discontinued work because of Contractor's refusal to pay the said requisition, but notified Contractor by registered letter of its willingness to return to the job upon payment. Contractor later requested it to return and complete work, which Subcontractor refused to do because of nonpayment of work requisitions of July 25 and thereafter. Contractor had another excavating concern complete the work, for which it paid $450 above the contract price.

Contractor's suit against Subcontractor contained two counts: (1) for the bulldozer damage, alleging negligence, and (2) for $450 as damages for breach of contract. Subcontractor filed a counterclaim for work done and not paid for and for profit it lost by not being permitted to finish the job, totalling $2,824.50. The bulldozer damage claim was submitted to a jury, who found in favor of Contractor in the amount of $3,400, and that judgment has been paid. The other claims were submitted to the trial

---

[1]   This section is not a model for clarity.

(A) DIVISIBILITY

Gill v. Johnstown Lumber Co.

Supreme Court of Pennsylvania, 1892.
151 Pa. 534, 25 A. 120.

[Assumpsit for driving logs under a written contract, the terms of which are set forth in the opinion. John L. Gill agreed to drive some four million feet of logs, and to begin driving at once, "if sufficient natural water, or by the use of splash dams." The trial court directed a verdict for the Johnstown Lumber Co. on the ground that the contract was "entire" and that Gill defaulted when a flood carried a considerable proportion of the logs past the Johnstown Lumber Co.'s boom.[e] Gill appealed.]

■ HEYDRICK, JUSTICE. The single question in this cause is whether the contract upon which the plaintiff sued is entire or severable. If it is entire it is conceded that the learned court below properly directed a verdict for the defendant; if severable, it is not denied that the cause ought to have been submitted to the jury. The criterion by which it is to be determined to which class any particular contract shall be assigned is thus stated in 1 Parsons on Contracts, 29–31: "If the part to be performed by one party consists of several and distinct items, and the price to be paid by the other is (1) apportioned to each item to be performed, or (2) is left to be implied by law, such a contract will generally be held to be severable. But if the consideration to be paid is single and entire the contract must be held to be entire, although the subject of the contract may consist of several distinct and wholly independent items." The rule thus laid down was applied in Ritchie v. Atkinson, 10 East, 295, a case not unlike the present. There the master and freighter of a vessel of four hundred tons mutually agreed that the ship should proceed to St. Petersburg, and there load from the freighter's factors a complete cargo of hemp and iron and deliver the same to the freighter at London on being paid freight for hemp £5 per ton, for iron 5s. per ton, and certain other charges, one half to be paid on delivery and the other at three months. The vessel proceeded to St. Petersburg, and when about half loaded was compelled by the imminence of a Russian embargo upon British vessels to leave, and returning to London deliver to the freighter so much of the stipulated cargo as had been taken on board. The freighter, conceiving that the contract was entire and the delivery of a complete cargo a condition precedent to a recovery of any compensation, refused to pay at the stipulated rate for so much as was delivered. Lord Ellenborough said: "The delivery of the cargo is in its nature, divisible, and therefore I think it is not a condition precedent; but the plaintiff is entitled to recover freight in proportion to

---

e   On May 31, 1889, ten days after the date of the contract, what has been called the largest earthen dam in the world, above Johnstown, broke. More than 2,000 lives were lost. That and other flooding in the area, caused by a great rain, carried log booms estimated at many millions of feet of timber into the Potomac River and the Chesapeake Bay. R. O'Connor, *Johnstown— The Day the Dam Broke* 29 (1957).

the extent of such delivery; leaving the defendant to his remedy in damages for the short delivery."

Applying the test of an apportionable or apportioned consideration to the contract in question, it will be seen at once that it is severable. The work undertaken to be done by the plaintiff consisted of several items, viz., driving logs, first, of oak, and second of various other kinds of timber, from points upon Stony creek and its tributaries above Johnstown to the defendant's boom at Johnstown, and also driving cross-ties from some undesignated point or points, presumably understood by the parties, to Bethel in Somerset county, and to some other point or points below Bethel. For this work the consideration to be paid was not an entire sum, but was apportioned among the several items at the rate of one dollar per thousand feet for the oak logs; seventy-five cents per thousand feet for all other logs; three cents each for cross-ties driven to Bethel, and five cents each for cross-ties driven to points below Bethel. But while the contract is severable, and the plaintiff entitled to compensation at the stipulated rate for all logs and ties delivered at the specified points, there is neither reason nor authority for the claim for compensation in respect to logs that were swept by the flood to and through the defendant's boom, whether they had been driven part of the way by the plaintiff or remained untouched by him at the coming of the flood. In respect to each particular log the contract in this case is like a contract of common carriage, which is dependent upon the delivery of the goods at the designated place, and if by *casus* the delivery is prevented the carrier cannot recover pro tanto for freight for part of the route over which the goods were taken: Wharton, Law of Contracts, sec. 714. Indeed this is but an application of the rule already stated. The consideration to be paid for driving each log is an entire sum per thousand feet for the whole distance and is not apportioned or apportionable to parts of the drive.

The judgment is reversed and a venire facias de novo is awarded.

NOTES

(1) *Questions.* If some of the oak logs had been driven halfway, might the plaintiff have recovered at the rate of 50 cents per thousand feet for them? Why was the contract not divisible by distances?

(2) *The Case of the Magic Tees.* The Army Signal Corps made an "Industrial Preparedness Contract" with Lerner under which Lerner was to equip itself for the production, in volume, of an item called a microwave magic tee. The work was to be done in four steps, the first three of which involved a pilot run and the acquisition of equipment. Step IV was to be taken on Government order only in case of a national emergency and required volume production of the magic tees. Lerner was obligated to maintain a status of readiness for this over a six-year period. When the first three steps had been substantially completed and the Government had paid Lerner about $128,000, Lerner transferred all its assets to assignees for the benefit of creditors, as an alternative to bankruptcy. The assignees sued the

Government for about $45,000, the sum owed for completing the first three steps. The Government counterclaimed for damages and moved for summary judgment. *Held:* Summary judgment granted.

The court considered the purpose of the contract and concluded that the first three steps were "merely incidental to Step IV, which was the ultimate objective. . . . The duty to stand by and be ready to perform Step IV was the essential element of the bargain. The contract was not divisible." The assignment for the benefit of creditors operated as a total breach, for it is an implied condition in every contract that the promisor will not permit itself to be disabled from performing. Pennsylvania Exchange Bank v. United States, 170 F.Supp. 629 (Ct. Cl. 1959).

(3)   *Uses of Divisibility.* Reconsider *Internatio-Rotterdam*, p. 759 above. What argument did the buyer try to combat by maintaining that the contract was not divisible? Compare the plaintiff's claim in that case and the defendant's contention in Gill v. Johnstown Lumber Co. Does it seem that the doctrine of divisibility has various uses?

In the rice case, would the seller have been *justified* in withholding further shipments to Lake Charles after December 17th? If it had done so, how would you compare the merits of the buyer's claim with that in Gill v. Johnstown Lumber Co.? With the claim in Pennsylvania Exchange Bank v. United States?

(4)   *Divisibility and Conditions.* Divisibility is most commonly seen as a means of reducing the consequences of material breach. It also can be used as a means of reducing the consequences of the non-occurrence of a condition. Consider Grease Monkey Int'l, Inc. v. Godat, 916 S.W.2d 257 (Mo. Ct. App. 1995). There a contract for the sale of real property was made subject to a condition that the buyer secure financing. The contract also contained a clause stating that if the parties litigated a dispute, the prevailing party would be entitled to recover its fees and costs from the other. The buyer did not obtain financing, and the seller sued, seeking specific performance. The court held that the condition in the sales contract did not occur, so no duties under the contract arose. However, it held as well that the fee-shifting provision should be severed from the rest of the contract and enforced, with the result that the seller had to pay the fees and costs of the buyer.

(B) RESTITUTION

We have seen a variety of situations in which restitution may be available as a basis for liability. In many of these situations there is no agreement that can be enforced. The parties may not have dealt with one another (Chapter 1), or they may have engaged in negotiations that fell short of a contract (Chapter 2), or they may have made an agreement that proved to be unenforceable for some reason, such as the statute of frauds (Chapter 3), or a contravention of public policy (Chapter 4). Restitution will also be discussed under the heading of remedies (Chapter 8) and as a remedy when an agreement is rendered unenforceable via mistake, impracticability, or frustration (Chapter 9).

As we will see, even when there is a breach of an enforceable agreement, the *aggrieved* party may prefer restitution to other forms of relief, and it is commonly available (see Note 4, p. 19 above and *Algernon Blair,* p. 939 below). But what of restitution for a party *in breach* of an enforceable agreement? If that party has performed in part, and is unable to enforce the contract because it has failed to complete performance, may it nevertheless get restitution? Such claims have met serious resistance, especially when the plaintiff's breach may be characterized as "willful." The remarks of the court in the venerable case of Lawrence v. Miller, 86 N.Y. 131, 140 (1881), represent the traditional response. "To allow a recovery of this money would be to sustain an action by a party on his own breach of his own contract, which the law does not allow. . . . That would be ill doctrine."

Some other responses are shown in this section. The following case is a watershed.

Britton v. Turner

Supreme Court of Judicature of New Hampshire, 1834.
6 N.H. 481.

Assumpsit, for work and labor, performed by the plaintiff, in the service of the defendant, from March 9, 1831, to December 27, 1831.

The declaration contained the common counts, and among them a count in quantum meruit, for the labor, averring it to be worth $100.

At the trial in the C.C. Pleas, the plaintiff proved the performance of the labor as set forth in the declaration.

The defense was that it was performed under a special contract; that the plaintiff agreed to work one year, from some time in March, 1831, to March, 1832, and that the defendant was to pay him for said year's labor the sum of $120; and the defendant offered evidence tending to show that such was the contract under which the work was done. Evidence was also offered to show that the plaintiff left the defendant's service without his consent, and it was contended by the defendant that the plaintiff had no good cause for not continuing in his employment. There was no evidence offered of any damage arising from the plaintiff's departure, farther than was to be inferred from his nonfulfillment of the entire contract.

The court instructed the jury that, if they were satisfied from the evidence that the labor was performed under a contract to labor a year, for the sum of $120, and if they were satisfied that the plaintiff labored only the time specified in the declaration, and then left the defendant's service, against his consent, and without any good cause, yet the plaintiff was entitled to recover, under his quantum meruit count, as much as the labor he performed was reasonably worth, and under this direction the jury gave a verdict for the plaintiff for the sum of $95.

The defendant excepted to the instructions thus given to the jury.

■ PARKER, JUSTICE, delivered the opinion of the court. It may be assumed that the labor performed by the plaintiff, and for which he seeks to recover a compensation in this action, was commenced under a special contract to labor for the defendant the term of one year, for the sum of $120, and that the plaintiff has labored but a portion of that time, and has voluntarily failed to complete the entire contract.

It is clear, then, that he is not entitled to recover upon the contract itself, because the service, which was to entitle him to the sum agreed upon, has never been performed.

But the question arises: Can the plaintiff, under these circumstances, recover a reasonable sum for the service he has actually performed, under the count in quantum meruit? Upon this, and questions of a similar nature, the decisions to be found in the books are not easily reconciled.

It has been held, upon contracts of this kind for labor to be performed at a specified price, that the party who voluntarily fails to fulfill the contract by performing the whole labor contracted for, is not entitled to recover anything for the labor actually performed, however much he may have done towards the performance, and this has been considered the settled rule of law upon this subject. [Citations of Massachusetts, New York and English cases omitted.]

That such rule in its operation may be very unequal, not to say unjust, is apparent. A party who contracts to perform certain specified labor, and who breaks his contract in the first instance, without any attempt to perform it, can only be made liable to pay the damages which the other party has sustained by reason of such non-performance, which in many instances may be trifling; whereas a party who in good faith has entered upon the performance of his contract, and nearly completed it, and then abandoned the further performance, although the other party has had the full benefit of all that has been done, and has perhaps sustained no actual damage, is in fact subjected to a loss of all which has been performed, in the nature of damages for the non-fulfillment of the remainder, upon the technical rule, that the contract must be fully performed in order to [sustain] a recovery of any part of the compensation.

By the operation of this rule, then, the party who attempts performance may be placed in a much worse situation than he who wholly disregards his contract, and the other party may receive much more, by the breach of the contract, than the injury which he has sustained by such breach, and more than he could be entitled to were he seeking to recover damages by an action.

The case before us presents an illustration. Had the plaintiff in this case never entered upon the performance of his contract, the damage could not probably have been greater than some small expense and trouble incurred in procuring another to do the labor which he had contracted to perform. But having entered upon the performance, and labored nine and a half months, the value of which labor to the defendant as found by the jury is $95, if the defendant can succeed in this defense, he in fact receives nearly five-sixths of the value of a whole year's labor, by reason of the breach of contract by the plaintiff, a sum not only utterly disproportionate to any probable, not to say possible damage which could have resulted from the neglect of the plaintiff to continue the remaining two and a half months, but altogether beyond any damage which could have been recovered by the defendant, had the plaintiff done nothing towards the fulfillment of his contract.

Another illustration is furnished in Lantry v. Parks, 8 Cow., N.Y., 63. There the defendant hired the plaintiff for a year, at ten dollars per month. The plaintiff worked ten and a half months, and then left saying he would work no more for him. This was on Saturday—on Monday the plaintiff returned, and offered to resume his work, but the defendant said he would employ him no longer. The court held that the refusal of the defendant [plaintiff?] on Saturday was a violation of his contract, and that he could recover nothing for the labor performed.

There are other cases, however, in which principles have been adopted leading to a different result.

It is said, that where a party contracts to perform certain work, and to furnish materials, as, for instance, to build a house, and the work is done, but with some variations from the mode prescribed by the contract, yet if the other party has the benefit of the labor and materials he should be bound to pay so much as they are reasonably worth. 2 Stark.Ev. 97, 98; Hayward v. Leonard, 7 Pick., Mass., 181. . . .

A different doctrine seems to have been holden in Ellis v. Hamlen, 3 Taunt. 52, and it is apparent, in such cases, that if the house has not been built in the manner specified in the contract, the work has not been done. The party has no more performed what he contracted to perform, than he who has contracted to labor for a certain period, and failed to complete the time.

It is in truth virtually conceded in such cases that the work has not been done, for, if it had been, the party performing it would be entitled to recover upon the contract itself, which it is held he cannot do.

Those cases are not to be distinguished, in principle, from the present, unless it be in the circumstance, that where the party has contracted to furnish materials, and do certain labor, as to build a house in a specified manner, if it is not done according to the contract, the party for whom it is built may refuse to receive it—elect to take no benefit from what has been performed—and therefore, if he does receive, he shall be bound to pay the value; whereas in a contract for labor, merely, from day to day, the party is continually receiving the benefit of the contract under an expectation that it will be fulfilled, and cannot, upon the breach of it, have an election to refuse to receive what has been done, and thus discharge himself from payment.

But we think this difference in the nature of the contracts does not justify the application of a different rule in relation to them. The party who contracts for labor merely, for a certain period, does so with full knowledge that he must, from the nature of the case, be accepting part performance from day to day, if the other party commences the performance, and with knowledge also that the other may eventually fail of completing the entire term. If under such circumstances he actually receives a benefit from the labor performed, over and above the damage occasioned by the failure to complete, there is as much reason why he should pay the reasonable worth of what has thus been done for his benefit, as there is when he enters and occupies the house which has been built for him, but not according to the stipulations of the contract, and which he perhaps enters, not because he is satisfied with what has been done, but because circumstances compel him to accept it such as it is, that he should pay for the value of the house.

Where goods are sold upon a special contract as to their nature, quality, and price, and have been used before their inferiority has been discovered, or other circumstances have concurred which have rendered it impracticable or inconvenient for the vendee to rescind the contract in toto, it seems to have been the practice formerly to allow the vendor to recover the stipulated price, and the vendee recovered by a cross-action damages for the breach of the contract. "But according to the later and more convenient practice, the vendee in such case is allowed, in an action for the price, to give evidence of the inferiority of the goods in reduction of damages, and the plaintiff who has broken his contract is not entitled to recover more than the value of the benefits which the defendant has actually derived from the goods; and where the latter has derived no benefit, the plaintiff cannot recover at all." 2 Stark.Ev. 640, 642; Okell v. Smith, 1 Starkie's Rep. 107.

There is a close analogy between all these classes of cases, in which such diverse decisions have been made.

If the party who has contracted to receive merchandise takes a part and uses it, in expectation that the whole will be delivered, which is never done, there seems to be no greater reason that he should pay for what he has received than there is that the party who has received labor in part, under similar circumstances, should pay the value of what has been done for his benefit.

It is said that in those cases where the plaintiff has been permitted to recover there was an acceptance of what had been done. The answer is that where the contract is to labor from day to day, for a certain period, the party for whom the labor is done in truth stipulates to receive it from day to day, as it is performed, and although the other may not eventually do all he has contracted to do, there has been, necessarily, an acceptance of what has been done in pursuance of the contract, and the party must have understood when he made the contract that there was to be such acceptance.

If, then, the party stipulates in the outset to receive part performance from time to time, with a knowledge that the whole may not be completed, we see no reason why he should not equally be holden to pay for the amount of value received, as where he afterwards takes the benefit of what has been done, with a knowledge that the whole which was contracted for has not been performed. In neither case has the contract been performed. In neither can an action be sustained on the original contract. In both the party has assented to receive what is done. The only difference is that in the one case the assent is prior, with a knowledge that all may not be performed; in the other it is subsequent, with a knowledge that the whole has not been accomplished.

We have no hesitation in holding that the same rule should be applied to both classes of cases, especially as the operation of the rule will be to make the party who has failed to fulfill his contract liable to such amount of damages as the other party has sustained, instead of subjecting him to an entire loss for a partial failure, and thus making the amount received in many cases wholly disproportionate to the injury. 1 Saund. 320, c; 2 Stark.Ev. 643. It is as "hard upon the plaintiff to preclude him from recovering at all, because he has failed as to part of his entire undertaking," where his contract is to labor for a certain period, as it can be in any other description of contract, provided the defendant has received a benefit and value from the labor actually performed.

We hold, then, that where a party undertakes to pay upon a special contract for the performance of labor, or the furnishing of materials, he is not to be charged upon such special agreement until the money is earned according to the terms of it, and where the parties have made an express contract the law will not imply and raise a contract different from that which the parties have entered into, except upon some farther transaction between the parties.

In case of a failure to perform such special contract, by the default of the party contracting to do the service, if the money is not due by the terms of the special agreement he is not entitled to recover for his labor, or for the materials furnished, unless the other party receives what has been done, or furnished, and upon the whole case derives a benefit from it. Taft v. Montague, 14 Mass. 282; 2 Stark.Ev. 644.

But if, where a contract is made of such a character, a party actually receives labor, or materials, and thereby derives a benefit and advantage, over and above the damage which has resulted from the breach of the contract by the other party, the labor actually done, and the value received, furnish a new consideration, and the law thereupon raises a promise to pay to the extent of the reasonable worth of such excess. This may be considered as making a new case, one not within the original agreement, and the party is entitled to "recover on his new case, for the work done, not as agreed, but yet accepted by the defendant." 1 Dane's Abr. 224.

If on such failure to perform the whole, the nature of the contract be such that the employer can reject what has been done, and refuse to receive any benefit from the part performance, he is entitled so to do, and in such case is not liable to be charged, unless he has before assented to and accepted of what has been done, however much the other party may have done towards the performance. He has in such case received nothing, and having contracted to receive nothing but the entire matter contracted for, he is not bound to pay, because his express promise was only to pay on receiving the whole, and having actually received nothing the law cannot and ought not to raise an implied promise to pay. But where the party receives value—takes and uses the materials, or has advantage from the labor, he is liable to pay the reasonable worth of what he has received. Farnsworth v. Garrard, 1 Camp. 38. And the rule is the same whether it was received and accepted by the assent of the party prior to the breach, under a contract by which, from its nature, he was to receive labor, from time to time until the completion of the whole contract, or whether it was received and accepted by an assent subsequent to the performance of all which was in fact done. If he received it under such circumstances as precluded him from rejecting it afterwards, that does not alter the case—it has still been received by his assent.

In fact, we think the technical reasoning—that the performance of the whole labor is a condition precedent, and the right to recover anything dependent upon it; that, the contract being entire, there can be no apportionment; and that, there being an express contract, no other can be implied, even upon the subsequent performance of service—is not properly applicable to this species of contract, where a beneficial service has been actually performed; for we have abundant reason to believe, that the general understanding of the community is that the hired laborer shall be entitled to compensation for the service actually performed, though he do not continue the entire term contracted for, and such contracts must be presumed to be made with reference to that understanding, unless an express stipulation shows the contrary. . . .

It is easy, if parties so choose, to provide by an express agreement that nothing shall be earned, if the laborer leaves his employer without having performed the whole service contemplated, and then there can be no pretense for a recovery if he voluntarily deserts the service before the expiration of the time.

The amount, however, for which the employer ought to be charged, where the laborer abandons his contract, is only the reasonable worth, or the amount of advantage he receives upon the whole transaction (Wadleigh v. Sutton, 6 N.H. 15), and, in estimating the value of the labor, the contract price for the service cannot be exceeded.

If a person makes a contract fairly, he is entitled to have it fully performed; and, if this is not done, he is entitled to damages. He may maintain a suit to recover the amount of damage sustained by the non-performance. The benefit and advantage which the party takes by the labor, therefore, is the amount of value which he receives, if any, after deducting the amount of damage; and if he elects to put this in defense he is entitled so to do, and the implied promise which the law will raise, in such case, is to pay such amount of the stipulated price for the whole labor, as remains after deducting what it would cost to procure a completion of the residue of the service and also any damage which has been sustained by reason of the nonfulfillment of the contract. If in such case it be found that the damages are equal to or greater than the amount of the labor performed, so that the employer, having a right to the full performance of the contract, has not upon the whole case received a beneficial service, the plaintiff cannot recover.

Applying the principles thus laid down, to this case, the plaintiff is entitled to judgment on the verdict. The defendant sets up a mere breach of the contract in defense of the action, but this cannot avail him. He does not appear to have offered evidence to show that he was damnified by such breach, or to have asked that a deduction should be made upon that account. The direction to the jury was therefore correct, that the plaintiff was entitled to recover as much as the labor performed was reasonably worth, and the jury appear to have allowed a pro rata compensation, for the time which the plaintiff labored in the defendant's service.

As the defendant has not claimed or had any adjustment of damages, for the breach of the contract, in this action, if he has actually sustained damage he is still entitled to a suit to recover the amount.

Judgment on the verdict.

NOTES

(1) *Pay Periods.* Was the contract divisible by months? How much would Britton have recovered if it were?

Employee claims, based either on divisibility or restitution, are of little importance today because statutes generally require that employees be paid no less frequently than monthly. See Cal. Labor Code § 204; N.Y. Labor L. § 191.

(2) *Trend.* In 1978, Professor George Palmer reported that the doctrine of Britton v. Turner was still a minority position. 1 G. Palmer, Law of Restitution § 5.13 (1978). Thirty years later, Professor Robert Gordon observed that "legislation mandating regular wage payments ha[s] rendered the doctrine of the case mostly irrelevant." Robert W. Gordon, Britton v. Turner: *A Signpost on the Crooked Road to "Freedom" in the Employment Contract,* in Contracts Stories (Douglas G. Baird, ed., 2007) 186, 187. The trend, however, is plainly in its favor. UCC § 2–718(2), Restatement § 374, and Restatement (Third) of Restitution and Unjust Enrichment § 36 state rules in accord with the doctrine from the case.

(3) *Licensed Workers.* Current estimates suggest that anywhere from a quarter to more than a third of the U.S. labor force is subject to professional licensing or government certification. Morris M. Kleiner & Alan B. Krueger, *Analyzing the Extent and Influence of Occupational Licensing on the Labor Market*, 31 J. Labor Econ. 173 (2013). What result if failure of licensing renewal or professional certification prevents completion of employment?

In David M. Somers & Assocs. v. Busch, 927 A.2d 832 (Conn. 2007) an attorney, unable to perform under a contract for legal services after he was disbarred, sought his accrued fees from a client. "The trial court ultimately concluded that the plaintiff could not recover contract damages because he had failed to perform the 'single, indivisible task' that he had agreed to perform under the agreement, namely, the representation of the defendant [through the] final dissolution of her marriage. The trial court also concluded that the plaintiff could recover only under the doctrine of unjust enrichment, because the work for which the plaintiff sought recovery had been performed pursuant to a valid express contract that he had breached due to his disbarment." *Held:* Affirmed. See also Restatement (Third) of the Law Governing Lawyers § 37, on Partial or Complete Forfeiture of a Lawyer's Compensation, and Restatement (Third) of Restitution and Unjust Enrichment § 36 cmt. *e.*

(4) *Faithless Servants.* Breach of some service contracts involving special confidence or trust, such as, for instance, the lawyer-client relationship and agency generally, may give rise to forfeiture of compensation otherwise owed. Charles A. Sullivan, *Mastering the Faithless Servant?: Reconciling Employment Law, Contract Law, and Fiduciary Duty*, 2011 Wis. L. Rev. 777; see also Restatement, Third, of Agency § 801; Restatement (Third) of Restitution and Unjust Enrichment § 36 cmt. *e* & ills. 15–17. In many cases, however, promisors may still receive compensation through restitution even when the breach violates a most sacred trust. For example, in Menorah Chapels v. Needle, 899 A.2d 316 (N.J. Super. App. Div. 2008) a funeral home agreed to arrange a funeral for an Orthodox Jew. This entailed hiring *shomrim,* men who would watch over the casket until the funeral and periodically recite sacred texts. Some time after the funeral, the relatives of the decedent learned that the funeral home had not hired the requisite number of shomrim. The estate refused to pay and filed suits for breach. The court held that (a) the funeral home did breach the contract, (b) the plaintiffs were entitled to damages for emotional distress, and (c) the unpaid funeral home was entitled to a cause of action in restitution for the reasonable value of its services. Restatement (Third) of Restitution and Unjust Enrichment § 36.

On remand, how should the two offsetting claims be measured? First, how might the finder of fact measure the estate's damages for the funeral home's breach? On the other side, how would one measure the reasonable value of the funeral home's services? By the value to someone indifferent to the presence of the shomrim? By the market price for a similar funeral, prorated to account for the breach? How, if at all, would this value take into account the special harm caused to the estate?

PROBLEM

Lawyer-Client Relations. Begovich, who was charged with murder, retained Murphy to defend him and paid him a total of $6,500. Murphy consulted with his client and made two appearances on his behalf, these services not being worth more than $2,500. At that point Begovich committed suicide. The administrator of the estate sued Murphy for $4,000, and Murphy demurred. What decision? See Begovich v. Murphy, 101 N.W.2d 278 (Mich. 1960).

Kirkland v. Archbold

Court of Appeals of Ohio, Cuyahoga County, 1953.
113 N.E.2d 496.

[The plaintiff contracted to make alterations and repairs on a dwelling house owned by the defendant. Paragraph 20 of the contract provided: "The Owner agrees to pay the Contractor, as follows: $1,000 when satisfactory work has been done for ten days; an additional $1,000 when twenty days work has been completed; an additional $1,000 when thirty days work has been completed, and $1,000 on completion of the contract. $2,000 shall be paid within thirty days after the completion of the contract." After the plaintiff had worked for two months on the job he was prevented from proceeding further. He claims that he and his sub-contractors had reasonably expended $2,985 at that point. He has been paid only $800, and he sues for damages in the amount of the difference.

The trial court found that the plaintiff was in default in attempting to plaster the house over wood lath instead of rock lath, and without the use of rock wool. Paragraph 4 of the contract provided: "All outside walls are to be lined with rock wool and rock lathe, superimposed thereon." Thus the defendant was within her rights in preventing the plaintiff from proceeding. However, the court held that her payment of $800 was an admission that the first installment of the price was earned, and gave the plaintiff judgment for $200. The plaintiff appealed.]

■ SKEEL, PRESIDING JUDGE. The court committed error prejudicial to the rights of plaintiff in holding that the provisions of the contract were severable. The plaintiff agreed to make certain repairs and improvements on the defendant's property for which he was to be paid $6,000. The total consideration was to be paid for the total work specified in the contract. The fact that a schedule of payments was set up based on the progress of the work does not change the character of the agreement. Newman Lumber Co. v. Purdum, 41 Ohio St. 373.

The court found that the plaintiff and not the defendant breached the agreement, leaving the job without just cause, when the work agreed upon was far from completed. In fact, the plaintiff by his pleadings and evidence does not attempt to claim substantial performance on his part. The question is, therefore, clearly presented on the facts as the court found them to be, as to whether or not the plaintiff being found in default can maintain a cause of action for only part performance of his contract.

The earlier case law of Ohio has refused to permit a plaintiff to found an action on the provisions of a contract where he himself is in default. The only exception to the rule recognized is where the plaintiff has substantially performed his part of the agreement. . . .

The result of decisions which deny a defaulting contractor all right of recovery even though his work has enriched the estate of the other party to the contract is to penalize the defaulting contractor to the extent of the value of all benefit conferred by his work and materials upon the property of the other party. This result comes from unduly emphasizing the technical unity and entirety of contracts. Some decisions permit such result only when the defaulting contractor's conduct was willful or malicious.

An ever-increasing number of decisions of courts of last resort now modify the severity of this rule and permit defaulting contractors, where their work has contributed substantial value to the other contracting party's property, to recover the value of the work and materials expended on a quantum meruit basis, the recovery being diminished, however, to the extent of such damage as the contractor's breach causes the other party. These decisions are based on the theory of unjust enrichment. The action is not founded on the broken contract but on a quasi-contract to pay for the benefits received, which cannot be returned, diminished by the damages sustained because of the contractor's breach of his contract.

The leading case supporting this theory of the law is Britton v. Turner, 6 N.H. 481, 26 Am.Dec. 713.

Williston on Contracts, Vol. 5, p. 4123, par. 1475, says: "The element of forfeiture in wholly denying recovery to a plaintiff who is materially in default is most strikingly exemplified in building contracts. It has already been seen how, under the name of substantial performance, many courts have gone beyond the usual principles governing contracts in allowing relief in an action on the contract. But many cases of hardship cannot be brought within the doctrine of substantial performance, even if it is liberally interpreted; and the weight of authority strongly supports the statement that a builder, whose breach of contract is merely negligent, can recover the value of his work less the damages caused by his default; but that one who has wilfully abandoned or broken his contract cannot recover. The classical English doctrine, it is true, has denied recovery altogether where there has been a material breach even though it was due to negligence rather than wilfulness; and a few decisions in the United States follow this rule, where the builder has not substantially performed. But the English court has itself abandoned it and now holds that where a builder has supplied work and labor for the erection or repair of a house under a lump sum contract, but has departed from the terms of the contract, he is entitled to recover for his services and materials, unless (1) the work that he has done has been of no benefit to the owner; (2) the work he has done is entirely different from the work which he has contracted to do; or (3) he has abandoned the work and left it unfinished. The courts often do not discuss the question whether one who has intentionally abandoned the contract did so merely to get out of a bad bargain or whether he acted in a mistaken belief that a just cause existed for the abandonment. Where the latter situation exists, however, it would seem that the defaulter might properly be given recovery for his part performance. It seems probable that the tendency of decisions will favor a builder who has not been guilty of conscious moral fault in abandoning the contract or in its performance."

The drastic rule of forfeiture against a defaulting contractor who has by his labor and materials materially enriched the estate of the other party should in natural justice, be afforded relief to the reasonable value of the work done, less whatever damage the other party has suffered.

We conclude, therefore, that the judgment is contrary to law as to the method by which the right to judgment was determined. . . .

For the foregoing reasons the judgment is reversed and the cause is remanded for further proceedings.

NOTES

(1) *Divisibility.* Can the court's holding that the contract was not divisible because the "total consideration was to be paid for the total work" be reconciled with the decision in *Internatio-Rotterdam,* p. 759 above? Would the trial court's treatment of the contract in *Kirkland* as divisible have been justified if the *defendant* had broken the contract rather than the plaintiff?

(2) *Sales of Goods.* UCC § 2–718(2), which gives a defaulting buyer a right to restitution, follows the trend set by Britton v. Turner. The Code provision was examined in *Diasonics,* p. 932 below, where the court explained that absent proof of Diasonics' damages as a lost volume seller, Davis would have been entitled to the return of all but $500 of its $300,000 down payment.

If a seller delivers part of the goods contracted for, and defaults as to the rest, having received no payment, is the seller entitled to the price fixed by the contract for the goods delivered, or to the amount by which the buyer is enriched? See UCC § 2–607(1).

(3) *Sales of Land.* The traditional rule that denies restitution to a party in breach has been particularly tenacious in connection with down payments by purchasers of land.

In 1986, the New York Court of Appeals declined to overrule its century-old decision in Lawrence v. Miller, quoted at p. 825 above. "The rule permitting a party in default to seek restitution for part performance has much to commend it in its general applications. But as applied to real estate down payments approximating 10% it does not appear to offer a better or more workable rule than the long-established 'usage' in this State with respect to the seller's right to retain a down payment upon default." In a footnote, however, the court emphasized that it expressed no view as to payments in excess of 10%. Maxton Builders, Inc. v. Lo Galbo, 502 N.E.2d 184, 188–89 (N.Y. 1986).

In 1980, the Supreme Court of Connecticut arrived at a similar result from the opposite direction. In Vines v. Orchard Hills, Inc., 435 A.2d 1022, 1027, 1029 (Conn. 1980), the court (Peters, J.) began by explaining "that a purchaser whose breach is not willful has a restitutionary claim to recover moneys that unjustly enrich his seller." But it concluded that the seller was entitled to retain the buyer's down payment of 10%, which had been designated in the contract as liquidated damages, because a "liquidated damages clause allowing the seller to retain 10 percent of the contract price as earnest money is presumptively a reasonable allocation of the risks associated with default." The presumption is a rebuttable one.

In 1991, the Supreme Court of New Jersey overruled cases adhering to the common law rule and adopted "the modern approach" of Restatement § 374(1). In Kutzin v. Pirnie, 591 A.2d 932, 941 (N.J. 1991), the court held that the defaulting purchasers were entitled "to restitution for any benefit that they conferred by way of part performance or reliance in excess of the loss that they caused by their own breach," but noted that they had the burden of proving unjust enrichment. The holding was "not affected by the fact that the $36,000 deposit was less than ten percent of the $365,000 purchase price." However, the contract said nothing about liquidated damages. See also Restatement (Third) of Restitution and Unjust Enrichment § 36 & ill. 6.

(4) *Restitution and Conditions.* The connection between restitution and the constructive conditions of exchange is discussed above in *Kirkland.* Restitution and express conditions are on the surface an uneasy pairing. The failure of a condition does not mean that there is no contract; it means that the contract is not enforceable. In the presence of a contract, there ordinarily is no action in unjust enrichment.

All that is true, but restitution can nevertheless be used as a means of mitigating the effect of the non-occurrence of a condition. Suppose, for example, that A has made a contract with B for the sale of B's estate, Blackacre, for $500,000, on the condition that A secure financing that meets certain standards—somewhat like *Luttinger,* at p. 756 above. But suppose as well that A has already paid $50,000 toward the purchase price. If the condition fails, may B keep the $50,000? Unless their contract provides otherwise, no; the failure of the condition means that the transaction will not occur, so retaining the partial payment would unjustly enrich B.

(C) WAIVER, ESTOPPEL, AND ELECTION

A requirement that a condition occur or that a duty be performed may of course be eliminated by agreement between the parties. Furthermore, after a contract is made, an obligor whose duty is conditional may promise to perform despite the nonoccurrence of a condition or despite a delay in its occurrence. See Restatement § 84. Such a promise is commonly termed a *waiver.* In other contexts, it is often said that a waiver is "the intentional relinquishment of a known right," but this is not a useful formulation in a contractual setting. What is involved is not the relinquishment of a right and the termination of the reciprocal duty, but rather the excuse of the nonoccurrence of a condition of a duty. The creditor who discharges a debt by release or renunciation does not "waive" the debt in the strict sense of that word. However, as Corbin said, the word is one "of indefinite connotation" that, "like a cloak, . . . covers a multitude of sins." Arthur L. Corbin, *Conditions in the Law of Contracts*, 28 Yale L.J. 739, 754 (1919).

A party that, without consideration, has waived a condition that is within the other party's control *before* the time for occurrence of the condition can retract the waiver and reinstate the requirement that the condition occur unless the other party has relied to such an extent that retraction would be unjust. See Restatement § 84(2); UCC § 2–209(5). If there has been such reliance, *estoppel* will preclude retraction. However, a party that has waived a condition *after* the time for occurrence of the condition is subject to a dramatically different rule under which the waiver cannot be retracted, even in the absence of reliance. See Restatement § 84(1). Such waivers smack of election.

The word *election* signifies a choice, one that is binding on the party that makes it, even without reliance by the other party. When the time for occurrence of a condition has expired, the party whose duty is conditional has a choice between, on the one hand, taking advantage of the nonoccurrence of the condition and treating the duty as discharged or, on the other hand, disregarding the nonoccurrence of the condition and treating the duty as unconditional. Under the rule just stated, a party that chooses to disregard the nonoccurrence of a condition is bound by an election to treat the duty as unconditional. The parties that have most often been bound by such elections are insurers.

The same applies when an injured party treats a breach as partial, but then reconsiders and wishes to treat it as total. This decision often can be inferred from conduct. If, for example, a buyer of goods accepts them in spite of their known defects, the buyer has signaled that she is treating the seller's breach as partial, and her obligations under the original contract—here, to pay for the goods—are not discharged.

NOTES

(1) *Anti-Waiver Clauses Redux.* A party may have a better chance to fend off a claim of waiver if the contract contains an anti-waiver clause. Such a clause typically states that no action or inaction by that party shall amount to a waiver of any condition of any duty of that party. However, such clauses are not always honored by courts. See Hovnanian Land Inv. Group v. Annapolis Towne Centre, 25 A.3d 967 (Md. 2011) ("[O]ur caselaw shows a persistent unwillingness to give dispositive and preclusive effect to contractual limitations on future changes to that contract. This approach applies to the entire catalogue of possible alterations in contractual rights

and obligations, whether it is mutual modification, novation, waiver of remedies, or, as here, a waiver of condition precedent."). As Judge Posner has pointed out, though, "the waiver of a no-waiver clause must be proved by clear and convincing evidence." Wis. Elec. Power v. Union Pac. R.R., 557 F.3d 504 (7th Cir. 2009).

(2) *Waiver or Course of Performance.* It is often argued that conduct results in a waiver. How do these two effects of conduct differ? As one court has pointed out, in contrast to course of dealings, "the conduct of the parties in *performing* an agreement may be relevant to show a modification or waiver of a provision inconsistent with their conduct in the performance of that agreement." J.R. Hale Contracting Co. v. United New Mexico Bank, 799 P.2d 581, 587 (N.M. 1990). According to Comment 3 to UCC § 2–208, "Where it is difficult to determine whether a particular act merely sheds light on the meaning of the agreement or represents a waiver of a term of the agreement, the preference is in favor of 'waiver' whenever such construction, plus the application of the provisions on the reinstatement of rights waived (see Section 2–209), is needed to preserve the flexible character of commercial contracts and to prevent surprise or other hardship."

(3) *Prevention and Waiver.* Prevention is sometimes coupled with waiver. In McCarthy v. Tobin, 706 N.E.2d 629 (Mass. 1999), the court concluded that the vendor had waived the deadline for the execution of a more formal purchase and sale agreement for real estate. The vendor's lawyer, "acting as her agent, voluntarily undertook the task of drafting the purchase and sale agreement. He did not produce the final draft until it was impossible for [the purchaser] to sign it before the deadline. He also did not object to the passage of the deadline in the telephone calls and facsimile transmissions that followed. Instead he continued to deal with [the purchaser's] lawyer in an effort to craft a mutually satisfactory agreement."

McKenna v. Vernon

Supreme Court of Pennsylvania, 1917.
258 Pa. 18, 101 A. 919.

[McKenna undertook to build a moving picture theatre in Philadelphia for Vernon. The contract price, $8,750, was to be paid in installments for the first 80% of the work, and the final installment within 30 days after completion of the work. The work was to be done under the direction of an architect, whose certificate of work done was to be the condition of each payment by Vernon. McKenna received several payments, amounting in all to $6,000, and brought this action for the remainder of the contract price. Vernon asserted that the work was defective, but the architect testified that there were no unauthorized departures from the specifications, and McKenna had judgment for $2,500. Vernon appealed on the theory that no right of action existed in the absence of a certificate from the architect of final completion of the building. *Held:* Affirmed.]

■ STEWART, JUSTICE. All payments were to be made only on certificate of the architect, and yet with a single exception each of the seven payments made as the work progressed was made without a certificate being asked for. With such constant and repeated disregard on the part of the owner to exact compliance with this provision in the contract, it is too late now for him to insist that failure on the part of the plaintiff to secure such certificate before suit defeats his right of action. . . . If he waived it repeatedly, as he did here, during the progress of the work, he cannot complain if he be held to have waived it when he seeks to defend against a final payment for work shown to have been honestly and substantially performed, especially when almost daily he has had the work under his own observation, without remonstrance or complaint at any time with respect to either the work done or materials employed.

NOTE

The Benefits of Lenience. In Sethness-Greenleaf v. Green River Corp., 65 F.3d 64, 67 (7th Cir. 1995), involving a soft drink manufacturer's claim for delayed payments from buyers of concentrate for Green River Soda, Judge Easterbrook wrote that "a vendor who cuts the buyer some slack—even 14 months worth of slack—does not thereby 'agree' to forbear indefinitely. The buyer may enjoy the extra breathing room, but when the vendor's patience runs out the buyer must pay up or face the consequences. . . . Were it otherwise, vendors would be inclined to cut off supplies at the first sign of trouble, and buyers as a whole would lose the benefits of lenience."

After giving McKenna "the benefits of lenience" by making several payments without certificates, could Vernon have insisted on certificates for subsequent payments? How? If McKenna had asked for and received, early in the course of performance, Vernon's promise that he would not insist on compliance with the condition, enforcement of the promise would present an obvious problem of consideration. Was there no problem of consideration in McKenna v. Vernon?

PROBLEMS

(1) *A Change of Mind.* Suppose that in *Luttinger*, after the Luttingers had failed to get a mortgage, a relative offered to provide the financing and they assured the Rosens that they would proceed with the transaction. What would be the legal position of the Luttingers if the relative then reneged and they told the Rosens that they had changed their mind and did not want to buy the house? Would it make a difference if the Rosens could prove that they had relied on the assurance? Loda v. H.K. Sargeant & Associates, 448 A.2d 812 (Conn. 1982); Williams v. Ubaldo, 670 A.2d 913 (Me. 1996).

(2) *Another Change of Mind.* Suppose that in *Mattei*, p. 100 above, Mattei had told Hopper that he was not satisfied with the leases obtained but the next day, still within the 120-day period, had changed his mind and said he was satisfied. Would Hopper have been bound? See Beverly Way Associates v. Barham, 276 Cal. Rptr. 240 (Ct. App. 1990).

(3)   *Variations on a Theme.* Suppose that in *Luttinger*, p. 756 above, the Luttingers had not made any attempt to get a mortgage. Could the Rosens have retained the $8,500 or any part of it? Would the answer be different if the amount had been $12,750 instead of $8,500? Would the answers be different if the house had been in New York? In New Jersey? Would it make a difference if the contract had provided that in case of default by the Luttingers the Rosens could retain the $8,500 "as liquidated damages"? If it had provided that they could retain the $8,500 "as liquidated damages at their option"?

(D) HINDRANCE, PREVENTION, AND COOPERATION

The duty of good faith performance applies to all parts of a contract, whether they are express conditions, constructive conditions, or covenants. The boundaries of this duty are, as we have seen, sometimes obscure. Not particularly obscure is the idea that if a party to a contract interferes unduly with the other party's performance, the result may be a breach of the duty of good faith.

But may one party to a contract sit on its hands while the other struggles to perform? If the parties are linked, not just by contract, but with a fiduciary duty, then the party owing the duty does have some obligations to act on behalf of the other. In the more common arm's length transaction, however, does either party have a right to more than sullen acquiescence by the other?

————

Hindrance and Prevention

We have seen that breach of the duty of good faith may not yield an independent cause of action, though it may affect how a party to a contract can legally exercise its discretion. The question, common to the law of express conditions and the law of constructive conditions, is how far good faith limits the ability of a party to hinder or prevent the other party from acquiring or exercising her contractual rights.

Consider United States v. Peck, 102 U.S. 64 (1880), described this way in the next case: "Peck contracted to sell the government a certain quantity of hay for the Tongue River station, and the trial court found it was mutually understood the hay was to be cut on government lands called 'the Big Meadows,' in the Yellowstone valley, which was the only available source of supply, also that thereafter the government caused all of that hay to be cut for it by other parties, in view of which Peck was relieved from his contract." The Supreme Court of the United States held that "the conduct of one party to a contract which prevents the other from performing his part is an excuse for nonperformance."

Questions of prevention often arise in cases involving real-estate brokers. Refer to Note 3, p. 769 above, which dealt with the right of a broker whose commission was payable "at time of closing." If a broker's right is so conditioned, can the broker nevertheless recover the commission if the sale is not consummated because the *seller,* rather than the *buyer,* backs out? For an affirmative answer, see Drake v. Hosley, 713 P.2d 1203 (Alaska 1986), in which the court held that the condition was excused by the seller's "frustrating conduct" in selling the property to a third party.

Hindrance arises frequently in disputes about insurance coverage, in which the insured argues that the insurer's wrongful denial of liability has prevented her from performing her own duties. Where the insurer's failure to pay is a breach of the insurance contract, the courts generally do not limit the doctrine of prevention to conduct in bad faith. See D & S Realty, Inc. v. Markel Ins. Co., 816 N.W.2d 1 (Neb. 2012). But this sort of prevention may merely suspend the insured's obligations until the insurer pays the claim or the insured can no longer feasibly perform.

NOTES

(1) *A Coup at the NRA.* At an annual meeting of the National Rifle Association (NRA), the organization was "taken over" by dissident members. Earlier, the decision had been made to sell its headquarters in the District of Columbia and move to Colorado, and the president had signed a contract of sale to a purchaser procured by Shear, as broker, and selected by the Management Committee, "subject to the approval of the Board." His $150,000 commission was confirmed before the takeover, under an agreement making it "contingent on settlement." After the takeover, the Management Committee declined to recommend the sale to the Board, and the NRA by-laws were amended to prohibit changing the headquarters and to strip the Board of power to approve the sale. Shear sued the NRA and, from dismissal of his complaint, he appealed. *Held:* Reversed.

The court discussed an "assumption of risk" exception to the prevention doctrine, to the effect that the doctrine does not apply if the contract authorizes prevention. But it ruled that the doctrine of prevention and not the exception applied. The court thought it "somewhat inaccurate to call the assumption of risk rule an 'exception' to the prevention doctrine." Since prevention is a breach of contract, it is a corollary "that there is no prevention when the contract authorizes a party to prevent a condition from occurring. Shear did not assume the risk that the Management Committee would refuse to recommend the contract, or that the Board would be deprived of authority to approve the contract." Shear v. National Rifle Association, 606 F.2d 1251 (D.C. Cir. 1979).

The court also rejected the Association's contention that "nothing but abject speculation could show that 'the condition [settlement] would have occurred.'" Shear also alleged that when he signed his contingent-on-settlement agreement the NRA official who signed for it knew of the impending coup, and that he (Shear) would not have signed if he had known of it. What sort of claim does this allegation support?

(2) *The Case of the School Board's Lesson.* The New York City Board of Education let a contract for work on a school building, containing a

condition that the agreement should be binding only if "the comptroller shall indorse hereon his certificate" that appropriated and unexpended funds were on hand to meet the estimated expense. After the contractor had done some preliminary work, the Board "rescinded" the contract. Although it did not question that the required funds were available, it justified its action by the comptroller's failure to certify the contract. He had withheld certification at the Board's request. The contractor sued the Board. From a judgment for the defendant, the plaintiff appealed. *Held:* Reversed.

The Board's action could not be justified by the comptroller's failure to certify the contract. "The general rule is, as it has been frequently stated, that a party to a contract cannot rely on the failure of another to perform a condition precedent where he has frustrated or prevented the occurrence of the condition." Kooleraire Service & Installation Corp. v. Board of Education, 268 N.E.2d 782 (N.Y. 1971).

———

Cooperation

In many situations a contracting party is responsible for taking affirmative steps to cooperate with the other party, even though the parties have not troubled to express such a duty in their agreement. This is likely to be so if it can be shown that such cooperative effort is essential to the other party's performance. This principle is frequently applied in construction cases. Under building contracts it is understood that a contractor, or subcontractor, cannot proceed effectively until a site is provided and prepared in a way appropriate for the work. See R.G. Pope Constr. Co., Inc. v. Guard Rail of Roanoke, Inc., 244 S.E.2d 774 (Va. 1978) (subcontractor's "performance of the duty to install guardrail was subject to certain conditions, the most important of which was the implied condition that a site would be available for such installation").

Similar reasoning was applied in Kehm Corp. v. United States, 93 F.Supp. 620 (Ct. Cl. 1950), in which the Government was held accountable for a supplier's delays in producing concrete bombs for practice in the Navy. When the Navy lost interest in the concrete bomb program, the Government delayed in providing tail assemblies, and Kehm's casting work became extended, sporadic, and costly. Speaking of Kehm's obligation, the court said: "The promisor's undertaking normally gives rise to an implied complementary obligation on the part of the promisee: He must not only not hinder his promisor's performance, he must do whatever is necessary to enable him to perform. The implied obligation is as binding as if it were spelled out. Wood v. Lucy, Lady Duff-Gordon [p. 111 above]."

Of course, cooperation has its limits. Consider a settlement agreement between a state agency and an individual which contained a clause conditioning the agreement on the approval of the governor and the state's department of transportation. When approval did not come forth, the individual sued for breach. The state supreme court held that there was indeed a duty of good faith in the settlement agreement, and that this duty encompassed the requirement of approval. But the court went on to hold that the duty of good faith consisted only of an obligation "to consider that approval in good faith," not actually to secure the approval. Indiana State Highway Comm'n v. Curtis, 704 N.E.2d 1015 (Ind. 1998). There are also contracting parties who, in a spirit of self-pity or worse, demand more than their fair share of cooperation. There is a countervailing principle that "enthusiasm is not required in performing contractual obligations." Esmieu v. Hsieh, 580 P.2d 1105, 1109 (Wash. App. 1978).

Who carries the burden of proof in prevention cases has occasioned some dispute. The breached-against party must prove that the promisor did not perform its contractual duties. If these duties are subject to a condition, then the breached-against party must also prove that the condition is not an obstacle to enforcement. But what if the condition did not occur, but the breached-against party argues that it did not occur because the promisor prevented it from coming about? The best answer appears to be that the breached-against party has the initial burden of showing that the promisor's action or inaction was at least a partial cause of the failure of the condition. Once that is met, the promisor has the burden of establishing that any misfeasance or nonfeasance on its part did not contribute materially to the non-occurrence of the condition. See Shear v. Nat'l Rifle Ass'n, 606 F.2d 1251 (D.C. Cir. 1979).

NOTE

Influences in Cooperation Cases. "While not every act or omission by the obligor which may expedite performance by the obligee (of his promise or of a condition) is required, the acts or omissions which are clearly within the obligor's control and which are the normal or obvious means of the obligee's performance, are presumably required of the obligor, or he assumes the risk of their non-occurrence. The justifiable reliance by the obligee, the usages of the trade or activity, the mores of the community, are obviously influential in determining what co-operation is required in a particular transaction. Judicial opinions reveal these influences. The moral notions of carelessness or diligence, malice or inadvertence, have sporadic influence. The avoidance of unjust enrichment seems also influential." Edwin W. Patterson, *Constructive Conditions in Contracts*, 42 Colum. L. Rev. 903, 937–38 (1942).

Iron Trade Products Co. v. Wilkoff Co.

Supreme Court of Pennsylvania, 1922.
272 Pa. 172, 116 A. 150.

■ WALLING, JUSTICE. In July, 1919, plaintiff entered into a written contract with defendant for the purchase of 2,600 tons of section relaying rails, to be delivered in New York harbor at times therein specified for $41 a ton. Defendant failed to deliver any of the rails, and plaintiff brought this suit, averring, by reason of such default, it had been compelled to purchase the rails elsewhere (2,000 tons thereof at $49.20 per ton and 600 tons at $49 per ton), also that the market or current price of the rails at the time and place of delivery was approximately $50 per ton, and claiming as damages the difference between what it had been compelled to pay and the contract price. Defendant filed an affidavit of defense and a supplement thereto, both of which the court below held insufficient and entered judgment for plaintiff, from which defendant brought this appeal.

In effect, the affidavit of defense avers the supply of such rails was very limited, there being only two places in the United States (one in Georgia and one in West Virginia) where they could be obtained in quantities to fill the contract, and that pending the time for delivery defendant was negotiating for the required rails when plaintiff announced to the trade its urgent desire to purchase a similar quantity of like rails, and in fact bought 887 tons and agreed to purchase a much larger quantity from the parties with whom defendant had been negotiating, further averring this conduct on behalf of plaintiff reduced the available supply of relaying rails and enhanced the price to an exorbitant sum, rendering performance by defendant impossible. The affidavit, however, fails to aver knowledge on part of plaintiff that the supply of rails was limited or any intent on its part to prevent, interfere with, or embarrass defendant in the performance of the contract; and there is no suggestion of any understanding, express or implied, that defendant was to secure the rails from any particular source, or that plaintiff was to refrain from purchasing other rails; hence it was not required to do so. The true rule is stated in Williston on Contracts, p. 1308, as quoted by the trial court, viz.:

"If a party seeking to secure all the merchandise of a certain character which he could entered into a contract for a quantity of the required goods, and subsequently made performance of the contract by the seller more difficult by making other purchases which increased the scarcity of the available supply, his conduct would furnish no excuse for refusal to perform the prior contract."

Mere difficulty of performance will not excuse a breach of contract. Corona C. & C. Co. v. Dickinson, 261 Pa. 589, 104 A. 741; Janes v. Scott, 59 Pa. 178, 98 Am.Dec. 328; 35 Cyc. 245. Defendant relies upon the rule stated in United States v. Peck, 102 U.S. 64, 26 L.Ed. 46, that—

"The conduct of one party to a contract which prevents the other from performing his part is an excuse for nonperformance."

The cases are not parallel. Here plaintiff's conduct did not prevent performance by defendant, although it may have added to the difficulty and expense thereof. There is no averment that plaintiff's purchases exhausted the supply of rails, and the advance in price caused thereby is no excuse. The *Peck* Case stands on different ground.

The affidavit "denies that there was any market or market price or current price for such relaying rails" at any time from the date of the contract to the beginning of this suit, but other statements therein amount to an admission of a market price. For example, it speaks of "the trade in Pittsburgh, New York, and other centers of such trade"; also of "the very small quantity of such rails in the market." The affidavit further states that—

"After making the said contract with the plaintiff the defendant began negotiations with the persons from whom the said rails in Georgia and West Virginia might be purchased; and in each of the two cases referred to such negotiations had proceeded so far that defendant could have purchased 2,600 tons of such rails either in Georgia or West Virginia at some such price as that contracted to the plaintiff, or less, or not greatly in excess thereof.

"In fact, the plaintiff bought a quantity of such rails, to wit, 887 tons, and at one time had contracted for the purchase of a much larger quantity thereof, from the same persons with whom the defendant had been negotiating for the same, and at higher prices than had been offered to the defendant by the same persons within the terms of the said contract.

"And affiant, while denying, as aforesaid, that the plaintiff was compelled to purchase the said rails or any of them, avers that, if the plaintiff was so compelled, it was only as the result of plaintiff's own interference with the defendant's performance of the said contract, and avers that but for the said interference the defendant would have made full performance of its said contract."

The above and the admitted facts that plaintiff actually bought the 2,600 tons and had previously resold the same indicate a market value, and the specific averment thereof, in the statement of claim is not sufficiently denied in the affidavit. An affidavit of defense must be considered as a whole, and therein a general denial is of no avail against an admission of the same fact. An affidavit that is contradictory or equivocal is insufficient. See Noll v. Royal Exchange Assurance Corp., 76 Pa.Super.Ct. 510.

The supplemental affidavit avers that when the contract in suit was made plaintiff, to the knowledge of defendant, had resold the 2,600 tons of rails at $42.25 per ton, and, furthermore, that the purchaser at such resale released plaintiff from all claim for damages under the contract. . . . The fact that a vendee has resold the goods contracted for is of no moment unless made a part of the contract; for, if not, he is entitled to the benefit of his bargain, regardless of the disposition he may intend to make of the property involved. To hold otherwise would inject collateral issues in trials for breaches of such contracts.

The assignments of error are overruled, and the judgment is affirmed.

NOTE

The Case of the Overbidding Buyer. Anna Meyerhofer was interested in some houses in Brooklyn that were to be offered at a foreclosure sale. Since Benjamin Patterson was in a favorable position to buy them, they entered into a contract of sale under which Meyerhofer agreed to pay Patterson $23,000 for the houses, no mention being made of the fact that he did not own them. When Patterson attended the foreclosure sale, Meyerhofer was also there, and whenever he made a bid she bid higher. The houses were struck down to her for $22,380. Patterson sued for $620 damages and, from a judgment for Meyerhofer, he appealed. *Held:* Reversed and remanded.

"In the case of every contract there is an implied undertaking on the part of each party that he will not intentionally and purposely do anything to prevent the other party from carrying out the agreement on his part." Patterson v. Meyerhofer, 97 N.E. 472 (N.Y. 1912).

What distinguishes this case from *Iron Trade Products*?

SECTION 6.   PROSPECTIVE NONPERFORMANCE

(A) ANTICIPATORY REPUDIATION

In Walker & Co. v. Harrison, the court referred to Harrison's telegram as one "of repudiation." What is a repudiation? "In order to constitute a repudiation, a party's language must be sufficiently positive to be reasonably interpreted to mean that the party will not or cannot perform. [L]anguage that under a fair reading 'amounts to a statement of intention not to perform except on conditions which go beyond the contract' constitutes a repudiation. Comment 2 to Uniform Commercial Code § 2–610." Restatement § 250 cmt. *b*.

The "announcement of an intention not to perform" need not be in words. When, in Stewart v. Newbury, Stewart "voluntarily abandoned the work," his conduct without more amounted to a repudiation. See Wholesale Sand & Gravel v. Decker, 630 A.2d 710, 711 (Me. 1993) (after second weekend of work, contractor "removed its equipment and did not return"). Whatever the form may be, the courts do not lightly declare that the promisor's behavior amounts to a repudiation. "[I]t should be shown that the announcement of an intention not to perform was positive and unequivocal." Tenavision, Inc. v. Neuman, 379 N.E.2d 1166, 1168 (N.Y. 1978).

What are the consequences of a repudiation? If the repudiation is accompanied by a breach by nonperformance, it "gives rise to a claim for damages for total breach" (with an exception to be considered shortly). Restatement § 253(1). Thus Harrison's repudiation in Walker & Co. v. Harrison, coupled with his breach by nonpayment of rent, would have given Walker a claim for damages for total breach quite without regard to whether Harrison's breach was material.

Our concern is with the consequences of a repudiation when it is not accompanied by a breach by nonperformance. Such a repudiation is often called an "anticipatory repudiation" because it occurs before the time for performance has arrived.[f]

We will consider five questions relating to the consequences of an anticipatory repudiation. First, is the recipient of a repudiation free to make other arrangements? Second, can the recipient of a repudiation go to court immediately, even before the time for performance has arrived? Third, can the recipient of a repudiation ignore the repudiation and await performance? Fourth, what are the consequences if the recipient of a repudiation urges retraction of the repudiation? Fifth, can a party that has repudiated withdraw the repudiation?

NOTE

Repudiation by Conduct. Claims of repudiation by conduct are sometimes troublesome in real estate transactions. In Neves v. Wright, 638 P.2d 1195, 1198 (Utah 1981), the court explained: "The rule that a seller of real estate need not have title at all times during the executory period of a contract, is not designed to favor sellers over buyers; rather, the purpose is to enhance the alienability of real estate by providing necessary flexibility in real estate transactions. Nevertheless, it is essential that in every case there be a close scrutiny of the facts, and the rule must be carefully applied to avoid unfairness, sharp practice, and outright dishonesty. If it plainly appears that a seller has lost or encumbered his ownership so that he will not be able to fulfill his contract, he cannot insist that a buyer continue to make payments." Suppose that in *Mattei*, p. 100 above, Hopper had given an option to another prospective buyer during the 120-day period. Would this have been a repudiation?

PROBLEM

You Know Quite as Well as We Do. When a buyer of iron rails complained that the first two shipments were short, and expressed the wish to be relieved from the contract, the seller, in England, asked "to know definitely what is your intention." The buyer, in New York, replied: "You ask us to determine whether we will or will not object to receive further shipments because of past defaults. We tell you we will if we are entitled to do so, and will not if we are not entitled to do so. We do not think you have the right to compel us to decide a disputed question of law to relieve you from the risk of deciding it yourself. You know quite as well as we do what is the rule and its uncertainty of application." Has the buyer repudiated? See Norrington v. Wright, 115 U.S. 188 (1885).

---

[f] The term "anticipatory breach" is sometimes used in place of "anticipatory repudiation." Comment *a* to Restatement § 253 calls the term "anticipatory breach" an elliptical expression for a "breach by anticipatory repudiation, because it occurs before there is any breach by non-performance."

Hochster v. De La Tour
Queen's Bench, 1853.
2 E. & B. 678, 118 Eng.Rep. 922.

[Action of assumpsit.] Declaration: "for that, heretofore, to wit, on 12th April 1852, in consideration that plaintiff, at the request of defendant would agree with the defendant to enter into the service and employ of the defendant in capacity of a courier, on a certain day then to come, to wit, the 1st day of June, 1852, and to serve the defendant in that capacity, and travel with him on the continent of Europe as a courier for three months certain from the day and year last aforesaid, and to be ready to start with the defendant on such travels on the day and year last aforesaid, at and for certain wages or salary, to wit," £10 per month of such service, "the defendant then agreed with the plaintiff, and then promised him, that he, the defendant, would engage and employ the plaintiff in the capacity of a courier on and from the said 1st day of June, 1852, for three months" on these terms; "and to start on such travels with the plaintiff on the day and year last aforesaid, and to pay the plaintiff" on these terms. [Further averments of the plaintiff were that he did make the agreement, "confiding in" the defendant's promise, and that—as the defendant always knew—from that time until the defendant broke his promise the plaintiff was "always ready and willing" to start travels with the defendant on the day aforesaid, and would have entered the defendant's service on that day but for the defendant's breach. "(Y)et the defendant, not regarding the said agreement . . . before the said 1st June, 1852, wrongfully wholly refused" to employ the plaintiff for the three months agreed upon, or for any other time, and then "absolved" the plaintiff from performance of the agreement and from "being ready and willing to perform," and put an end to the engagement, to the plaintiff's damage.] The writ was dated on the 22d of May, 1852.

Pleas: 1. That defendant did not agree or promise in manner, and form, & c.: conclusion to the country. Issue thereon.

2.   That plaintiff did not agree with defendant in manner and form, & c.: conclusion to the country. Issue thereon.

3.   That plaintiff was not ready and willing, nor did defendant absolve, exonerate, or discharge plaintiff from being ready and willing, in manner and form, & c.: conclusion to the country. Issue thereon.

4.   That defendant did not refuse or decline, nor wrongfully absolve, exonerate, or discharge, nor wrongfully break, put an end to or determine, in manner and form, & c.: conclusion to the country. Issue thereon.

On the trial before Erle, J., at the London sittings in last Easter term, it appeared that plaintiff was a courier, who in April, 1852, was engaged by defendant to accompany him on a tour, to commence on 1st June, 1852, on the terms mentioned in the declaration. On the 11th May, 1852, defendant wrote to plaintiff that he had changed his mind, and declined his services. He refused to make him any compensation. The action was commenced on 22d May. The plaintiff, between the commencement of the action and the 1st of June, obtained an engagement with Lord Ashburton, on equally good terms, but not commencing till 4th July. The defendant's counsel objected that there could be no breach of the contract before the 1st of June. The learned judge was of contrary opinion, but reserved leave to enter a nonsuit on this objection. The other questions were left to the jury, who found for plaintiff.

■ LORD CAMPBELL, CHIEF JUSTICE,[g] now delivered the judgment of the court:

On this motion in arrest of judgment, the question arises whether if there be an engagement between A. and B. whereby B. engages to employ A. on and from a future day for a given period of time, to travel with him into a foreign country as a courier, and to start with him in that capacity on that day, A. being to receive a monthly salary during the continuance of such service, B. may, before the day, refuse to perform the agreement and break and renounce it, so as to entitle A. before the day to commence an action against B. to recover damages for breach of the agreement, A. having been ready and willing to perform it, till it was broken and renounced by B.

The defendant's counsel very powerfully contended that, if the plaintiff was not contented to dissolve the contract, and to abandon all remedy upon it, he was bound to remain ready and willing to perform it till the day when the actual employment as courier in the service of the defendant was to begin; and that there could be no breach of the agreement, before that day, to give a right of action. But it cannot be laid down as a universal rule that, where by agreement an act is to be done on a future day, no action can be brought for a breach of the agreement till the day for doing the act has arrived. If a man promises to marry a woman on a future day, and before that day marries another woman, he is instantly liable to an action for breach of promise of marriage. Short v. Stone, 8 Q.B. 358. If a man contracts to execute a lease on and from a future day for a certain term, and, before that day, executes a lease to another for the same term, he may be immediately sued for breaking the contract. Ford v. Tiley, 6 B. & C. 325. So if a man contracts to sell and deliver specific goods on a future day, and before the day he sells and delivers them to another he is immediately liable to an action at the suit

g   John Campbell (1779–1861), a Scot of ancient lineage, matriculated at St. Andrews University at the age of eleven. Upon entering the English bar he predicted that he would become Lord Chancellor. His name is associated with a number of law reform statutes which he pressed as a member of Parliament, as Attorney General, and in the House of Lords. As a reward for his services to the government, he was made the first Baron Campbell. He won literary fame with his "Lives of the Lord Chancellors," followed by the "Lives of the Chief Justices," works full of good stories, inaccuracies, and harsh judgments; it was said that they had added a new sting to death. He held judicial office briefly as Lord Chancellor of Ireland, where he was not popular, and as Chief Justice of England from 1850 to 1859. He became Lord Chancellor of England at the age of eighty.

of the person with whom he first contracted to sell and deliver them. Bowdell v. Parsons, 10 East, 359.

One reason alleged in support of such an action is, that the defendant has, before the day, rendered it impossible for him to perform the contract at the day; but this does not necessarily follow; for, prior to the day fixed for doing the act, the first wife may have died, a surrender of the lease executed might be obtained, and the defendant might have repurchased the goods so as to be in a situation to sell and deliver them to the plaintiff. Another reason may be that, where there is a contract to do an act on a future day, there is a relation constituted between the parties in the meantime by the contract, and that they impliedly promise that in the meantime neither will do anything to the prejudice of the other inconsistent with that relation. As an example, a man and woman engaged to marry are affianced to one another during the period between the time of the engagement and the celebration of the marriage. In this very case of traveller and courier, from the day of the hiring till the day when the employment was to begin, they were engaged to each other; and it seems to be a breach of an implied contract if either of them renounced the engagement. This reasoning seems in accordance with the unanimous decisions of the Exchequer Chamber in Elderton v. Emmens, 6 C.B. 160, which we have followed in subsequent cases in this court.

The declaration in the present case, in alleging a breach, states a great deal more than a passing intention on the part of the defendant which he may repent of, and could only be proved by evidence that he had utterly renounced the contract, or done some act which rendered it impossible for him to perform it. If the plaintiff has no remedy for breach of the contract unless he treats the contract as in force, and acts upon it down to the 1st June, 1852, it follows that, till then, he must enter into no employment which will interfere with his promise "to start with the defendant on such travels on the day and year," and that he must then be properly equipped in all respects as a courier for a three months' tour on the continent of Europe. But it is surely much more rational, and more for the benefit of both parties, that, after the renunciation of the agreement by the defendant, the plaintiff should be at liberty to consider himself absolved from any future performance of it, retaining his right to sue for any damage he has suffered from the breach of it. Thus, instead of remaining idle and laying out money in preparations which must be useless, he is at liberty to seek service under another employer, which would go in mitigation of the damages to which he would otherwise be entitled for a breach of the contract.

It seems strange that the defendant, after renouncing the contract, and absolutely declaring that he will never act under it, should be permitted to object that faith is given to his assertion, and that an opportunity is not left to him of changing his mind. If the plaintiff is barred of any remedy by entering into an engagement inconsistent with starting as a courier with the defendant on the 1st June, he is prejudiced by putting faith in the defendant's assertion; and it would be more consistent with principle if the defendant were precluded from saying that he had not broken the contract when he declared that he entirely renounced it. Suppose that the defendant, at the time of his renunciation, had embarked on a voyage for Australia, so as to render it physically impossible for him to employ the plaintiff as a courier on the continent of Europe in the months of June, July and August, 1852; according to decided cases, the action might have been brought before the 1st June; but the renunciation may have been founded on other facts, to be given in evidence, which would equally have rendered the defendant's performance of the contract impossible. The man who wrongfully renounces a contract into which he has deliberately entered cannot justly complain if he is immediately sued for a compensation in damages by the man whom he has injured; and it seems reasonable to allow an option to the injured party, either to sue immediately, or to wait till the time when the act was to be done, still holding it as prospectively binding for the exercise of this option, which may be advantageous to the innocent party, and cannot be prejudicial to the wrongdoer.

An argument against the action before the 1st of June is urged from the difficulty of calculating the damages; but this argument is equally strong against an action before the 1st of September, when the three months would expire. In either case, the jury in assessing the damages would be justified in looking to all that happened, or was likely to happen, to increase or mitigate the loss of the plaintiff down to the day of trial. We do not find any decision contrary to the view we are taking of this case. Leigh v. Paterson, 8 Taunt, 540, only shows that upon a sale of goods to be delivered at a certain time, if the vendor before the time gives information to the vendee that he cannot deliver them, having sold them, the vendee may calculate the damages according to the state of the market when they ought to have been delivered.

If it should be held that, upon a contract to do an act on a future day, a renunciation of the contract by one party dispenses with a condition to be performed in the meantime by the other, there seems no reason for requiring that other to wait till the day arrives before seeking his remedy by action; and the only ground on which the condition can be dispensed with seems to be, that the renunciation may be treated as a breach of contract.

Upon the whole, we think that the declaration in this case is sufficient. It gives us great satisfaction to reflect that, the question being on the record, our opinion may be reviewed in a Court of Error. In the meantime, we must give judgment for the plaintiff.

Judgment for plaintiff.

NOTES

(1) *A Non Sequitur.* According to Lord Campbell, if Hochster "has no remedy for breach of the contract unless he treats the contract as in force, and acts upon it down to the 1st June, 1852, it follows that, till then, he must enter into no employment which will interfere with his promise." Does this statement conflate the first and second of the five questions listed above relating to the consequences of an anticipatory repudiation? Why does it follow that if Hochster could not have gone to court until June 1 he would not have been free to make another arrangement with Lord Ashburton before then?

Whatever the logic of Lord Campbell's opinion, Hochster v. De La Tour has generally been followed in the United States. See Restatement § 253; UCC § 2–610. Massachusetts is a notable exception. See Pedersen v. Klare, 910 N.E.2d 382 (Mass. App. 2009) ("As a general matter, Massachusetts has not recognized the doctrine of anticipatory repudiation").

(2) *Exception for One-Sided Contracts.* It was mentioned earlier, p. 846 above, that there was an exception to the rule that a repudiation accompanied by a breach by nonperformance gives rise to a claim for damages for total breach. It is generally accepted that if, at the time of the breach, the aggrieved party has fully performed and the only remaining duty of performance of the party in breach is to pay money in independent installments, the failure to pay one or more installments, whether or not coupled with a repudiation, will not give rise to a claim for damages for total breach. Nor will a repudiation alone give rise to such a claim. The breach will not, in other words, accelerate the time for payment of the balance of the debt, and therefore suit must be brought for the installments as they come due.

The exception can be found in Restatement §§ 243(3) & 253. Note that while the former section is limited to obligations "for the payment of money in installments," the latter section is not so limited. What might be the reason for this difference?

(3) *Acceleration Clauses.* The exception just described is almost invariably avoided by the inclusion of an acceleration clause. A typical clause might read, "On any default in payment of principal or interest, the creditor may declare all amounts remaining payable immediately due and payable." UCC § 1–309 imposes limits on a party's right to accelerate payment "at will" or "when he deems himself insecure," but not in the event of a default.

(4) *The Rose Bowl Affair.* The University of Southern California advertised "economy" season tickets to its football games, promising that if its team went to the Rose Bowl each holder of such a season ticket would be given an option to buy a Rose Bowl ticket. Roger Diamond, a lawyer and Trojan football fan, bought an "economy" season ticket, but when the Trojans were selected for the Rose Bowl the University wrote Diamond that, for reasons beyond its control, first-time economy season ticket holders could not be given the promised options. Diamond brought a class action on behalf of economy season ticket holders. From summary judgment for the University, Diamond appealed. *Held:* Affirmed.

"[P]laintiff forgets that, logically or not, it is the general rule, recognized in this state, that the doctrine of breach by anticipatory repudiation does not apply to contracts which are unilateral in their inception or have become so by complete performance by one party." Diamond v. University of Southern California, 89 Cal. Rptr. 302, 305 (Ct. App. 1970).

Kanavos v. Hancock Bank & Trust Co.

Supreme Judicial Court of Massachusetts, 1985.
395 Mass. 199, 479 N.E.2d 168.

■ WILKINS, JUSTICE. This appeal presents two basic questions. First, if, for valid consideration, the owner of stock in a corporation has agreed to give A the opportunity to purchase that stock at the price at which the owner intends to sell it to another in the future (a right of first refusal) but the owner instead sells the stock to a third party without giving A the opportunity to match the third party's offer and thus acquire the stock, does A's right to recover in an action for breach of contract in any way depend on whether A had the financial ability to purchase the stock during the relevant time? Second, if A's right does so depend, as we conclude it does, does A have the burden of proving his financial ability to perform or is the burden on the repudiating former stockholder to prove A's inability to perform?

The plaintiff Harold J. Kanavos (Kanavos) is A in the example given, an individual to whom the defendant Hancock Bank & Trust Company (bank) gave the right to acquire all the stock of 1025 Hancock, Inc., before the bank sold the stock to anyone else on the same terms. This corporation owned a fourteen-story apartment building, known as Executive House, on Hancock Street in Quincy. The corporation was a G.L. c. 121A limited dividend corporation, and the first mortgage was guaranteed by the Federal Housing Administration of the Department of Housing and Urban Development. On July 16, 1976, James M. Brown, then executive vice president of the bank, gave Kanavos a letter in which the bank agreed to pay him $40,000 for surrendering an option to purchase the stock and further gave Kanavos "the option to match the price of sale of said property to extend for a 60 day period from the time our offer is received." In November, 1976, the bank entered into a purchase and sale agreement to sell the stock for $760,000 to a third person and, early in December, the bank sold the stock accordingly without giving Kanavos notice and the opportunity to purchase the stock.

For the purpose of determining Kanavos's contract damages, apart from the $40,000 to be paid for the surrender of his option, the parties and the trial judge treated the value of the stock as equal to the value of the equity in the apartment building. The balance on the first mortgage was $2,500,000 at the relevant times. When the jury, in response to a special verdict question, concluded that the apartment complex was worth $4,000,000, contract damages were determined by subtracting from $4,000,000 the balance due on the mortgage ($2,500,000) and the sale price of the stock ($760,000). That damage figure ($740,000) equaled the amount by which the fair market value of the stock exceeded the price at which it was sold. The $40,000 option surrender payment was then added to arrive at a final judgment of $780,000.

The judge presented the case to the jury seeking a special verdict. . . . The bank's only challenge to the special verdict and resulting judgment is that the judge failed to instruct the jury (and give them an associated special verdict question) that the plaintiff had to be ready, willing, and able, pursuant to the letter creating the right of first refusal, to pay the bank $760,000 (i.e., within the sixty days, to match the offer the bank received and accepted).

The judge ruled, over objection, that Kanavos's ability to pay $760,000 was not material to this case. This is the first issue we stated above in the abstract. We conclude that Kanavos's financial ability was material because he should not recover contract damages, even from a repudiating promisor, under an agreement to sell stock unless he could have complied with his concurrent obligation to pay for the stock (or, as is not the case here, unless the bank's conduct substantially prevented Kanavos from being able to meet his obligation).

When the bank received an offer for the stock that it was prepared to accept, the bank was obliged to give Kanavos the right to match that offer. At that point, Kanavos had an option to purchase the stock on the same terms, although, of course, in this case he was unaware that such an offer (and hence the option) existed. He could have exercised his option by tendering the purchase price, and the bank would have been obliged to deliver the shares of stock. In the circumstances of this case, Kanavos was not obliged to make a meaningless tender of the purchase price. The stock had already been sold. However, one party's repudiation of a bilateral contract containing simultaneous obligations does not normally make immaterial the question whether the other party could perform his obligation. "It is the general rule 'that when performance under a contract is concurrent, one party cannot put the other in default unless he is ready, able, and willing to perform and has manifested this by some offer of performance' although a tender of performance is not necessary 'if the other party has shown that he cannot or will not perform.' " Mayer v. Boston Metropolitan Airport, Inc., 355 Mass. 344, 354, 244 N.E.2d 568 (1969), quoting Leigh v. Rule, 331 Mass. 664, 668, 121 N.E.2d 854 (1954).

The weight of authority in this country is that the financial ability of a prospective buyer of property is a material issue in his action for damages against a repudiating defendant for breach of an agreement to sell that property for an established price. See 5 S. Williston, Contracts § 699, at 352–353 (Jaeger ed. 1961), and 6 S. Williston, Contracts § 882, at 394 (Jaeger ed. 1962); 4 A. Corbin, Contracts § 978, at 924–925 (1951); Restatement (Second) of Contracts § 254 cmt. a (1981) (the duty of a repudiating party "to pay damages is discharged if it subsequently appears that there would have been a total failure of performance by the injured party"); Farnsworth, *The Problems of Nonperformance in Contract*, 17 New Eng. L. Rev. 249, 306 (1982) (If a seller repudiates an option to sell land, "[a]lthough the holder of the option is under no duty to pay the price of the land, his payment of the price is a condition of the seller's repudiated duty"); Taylor, *The Impact of Article 2 of the U.C.C. on the Doctrine of Anticipatory Repudiation*, 9 B.C. Indus. & Com. L. Rev. 917, 927 (1967)[h]. . . . We have taken the view that, even where promises were not concurrent, a plaintiff could only recover nominal or small damages against a defendant who repudiated a contract, where it would have been impossible for the plaintiff to perform a contractual obligation arising shortly after the defendant's breach. See Randall v. Peerless Motor Car Co., 212 Mass. 352, 382, 99 N.E. 221 (1912).

Here, the bank's obligation to sell the shares and Kanavos's obligation to pay for them were concurrent obligations. If neither could perform, even if the bank repudiated the contract, neither could recover. 6 S. Williston, supra § 882, at 389–391. Kanavos did not have to show that he was ready, willing, and able to purchase the stock on the day the bank repudiated its agreement with him by selling the stock. Thomas v. Christensen, 12 Mass.App.Ct. 169, 177, 422 N.E.2d 472 (1981). That principle does not mean, however, that his ability to purchase the stock during the option period is irrelevant.

Kanavos relies, as the trial judge apparently did, on a statement in Lowe v. Harwood, 139 Mass. 133, 135, 29 N.E. 538 (1885), that, when a seller repudiates a purchase and sale agreement by selling land to a third person, the inability of the plaintiff to pay the purchase price according to the contract terms is unimportant in an action for breach of contract.[1] The *Lowe* opinion cites no relevant authority for the proposition that a repudiating seller is liable in damages to a buyer who could not have carried out his end of the bargain. That principle . . . appears now to be extinct. . . . There is no compelling reason to adopt such a rule at this time.[2]

---

[h] "Under general contract law there was, however, a twist: If the nonrepudiating party was not in a position to perform either at the time of repudiation or at sometime thereafter prior to the date for performance, he had no remedy. The fact that the repudiation may have been unjustified did not change this result, and the burden of proving the necessary ability to perform was on the nonrepudiating plaintiff." Id.

[1] The relevant language of the opinion is as follows: "It is suggested that it does not appear that the plaintiff was able to pay the money which he was to pay. But he was personally bound for it, and the degree of his ability at any moment before he was called on to pay was no concern of the defendant's. The way for the defendant to test that was to tender performance on his side conditionally upon the plaintiff's performing his part of the agreement. See Brown v. Davis, 138 Mass. 458."

[2] We perceive no reason why Kanavos's ability to purchase the stock should be any less significant than the ability of a person who had the right to buy property under a purchase and sale agreement or of a person who held an option to purchase property. Once the bank determined that it would sell the property to a third person, Kanavos's rights were substantially equivalent to an option to buy. Once the bank repudiated its obligation to Kanavos by selling the stock to a third person, Kanavos's rights and his burden of proof were the same as they would have been if he had been a buyer under a repudiated purchase and sale or option

If, as we have concluded, Kanavos's ability to match the offer which the bank accepted is material to his right to recover, the question then is whether the burden of proof should be placed on Kanavos to show his ability or on the bank to show his lack of ability. The general rule is that the plaintiff must prove his ability to perform his obligations under a contract of the type involved here. See Wolbarsht v. Donnelly, 302 Mass. 568, 570–571, 20 N.E.2d 415 (1939); 5 S. Williston, supra § 699, at 352–353; 4 A. Corbin, supra § 978, at 925; Taylor, 9 B.C.Indus. & Com.L.Rev. supra at 927 ("the burden of proving the necessary ability to perform was on the nonrepudiating plaintiff"). Cf. Restatement (Second) of Contracts § 245 cmt. b (1981) (where an express condition of the defendant's liability has not occurred but the defendant has already repudiated the contract, the repudiating defendant has the burden of proving that the condition would not have occurred). There is not, however, a unanimity of view in this country on the placing of the burden of proof in such a case.

The burden was on Kanavos to prove his ability to finance the purchase of the stock. The fact of his ability to do so was an essential part of establishing the defendant's liability. Circumstances concerning his ability to raise $760,000 for the stock were far better known to him than to the bank. It is, of course, true that the bank created the problem by selling the stock to another in violation of its contractual obligation, and one could argue that, therefore, it should take the risk of failing to establish Kanavos's inability to purchase the stock. Such an argument, however, has not been generally accepted, for to do so would in effect place on the defendant the burden of disproving a fact essential to the plaintiff's case.

There was evidence from which the jury would have been warranted in finding that Kanavos had the ability to finance the purchase of the stock. Although he admitted that he was in financial difficulty during the relevant times, he had connections with people who might have assisted him. He testified that he could have purchased the stock if the bank had given him timely notice of his rights. Moreover, the jury found that the apartment complex was worth $1,500,000 more than the principal balance of the first mortgage, and thus $780,000 more than Kanavos would have had to have paid the bank for the stock (the sale price of $760,000 less the $40,000 the bank owed him). This differential suggests that financing was not an impossibility for Kanavos. Considering Kanavos's admitted financial difficulties at that time, the question of his ability to purchase the stock (or to sell his rights to another) may depend on whether the earnings of the apartment complex were sufficient to support some arrangement to finance the acquisition within the various limitations applicable under the federally guaranteed first mortgage (assuming it were not to be discharged in the process).

---

agreement. The bank's repudiation of the agreement giving Kanavos a right of first refusal did not estop the bank from arguing that Kanavos lacked the ability to pay for the stock.

The question of Kanavos's ability to purchase the stock should have been submitted to the jury. We see no reason, however, for a retrial of those issues already decided by the jury. We remand the case for a retrial on the question whether, if he had had proper notice of his right to purchase the stock, Kanavos would have been ready, willing, and able to do so during the option period.

So ordered.

NOTES

(1) *Analogy to Express Conditions.* The first question addressed by the court is analogous to one that arises in the case of an express condition. In Shear v. National Rifle Association, discussed in Note 1, p. 841 above, the NRA argued that, even if the Management Committee had recommended the sale and even if the by-laws had not been amended, "nothing but abject speculation could show that 'the condition [settlement] would have occurred.'" The court rejected this argument, noting that "almost all cases in which prevention is alleged will involve speculation as to what would have happened had the defendant's conduct not taken place." 606 F.2d at 1257.

In American List Corp. v. U.S. News & World Report, 549 N.E.2d 1161, 1165 (N.Y. 1989), the court rejected the argument "that in discounting the total amount due under the contract to its present value, the court may factor in the risk that the nonrepudiating party will be unable to perform the contract in the future" since such a rule "would require the nonrepudiating party to prove its ability to perform in the future, despite the fact that the doctrine [of anticipatory breach] is intended to operate to relieve the nonrepudiating party of that very performance." Is this consistent with the decision in *Kanavos*?

(2) *An Offer You Can Refuse.* A demand that a contract be modified is not itself a repudiation. See O'Connor v. Sleasman, 830 N.Y.S.2d 377 (App. Div. 2007) (where "not a single word or inference threatened non-performance under the contract if the suggested modifications were not accepted," there was no unequivocal refusal to perform, making plaintiff's immediate termination of the contract wrongful). But if a party wrongfully states that it will not perform unless the other party consents to a modification of the contract, that statement amounts to a repudiation. Austin Instrument, Inc. v. Loral Corp., p. 455, is a variation on this theme.

Permissible Responses to Repudiation

Recall Lord Campbell's statement in Hochster v. De La Tour, p. 848, "that the renunciation may be treated as a breach of contract." His use of "may" suggests that the recipient of a repudiation can choose to treat the repudiation as a breach or not, much as the recipient of an offer can choose to accept the offer or not. However, the temptation to analogize a repudiation to an offer leads to unsatisfactory results when the recipient of the repudiation disregards it.

If the recipient disregards the repudiation, will the rights of the parties be determined as if the repudiation had never occurred, as would be the case if the recipient of an offer disregarded it? Lord Cockburn seemed to think so when he said, in Frost v. Knight, (1872) L.R. 7 Ex. 111, 112, that the aggrieved party, "if he pleases, may treat the notice of intention as inoperative . . . but in that case he keeps the contact alive for the benefit of the other party as well as his own." But the court in Rockingham County v. Luten Bridge Co., p. 943 below, dismissed Lord Cockburn's view as "not in harmony with the decisions in this country." Would not Lord Cockburn's view have allowed the Luten Bridge Co. "to pile up damages by proceeding with the erection of a useless bridge"? Where, however, the recipient's disregard of a repudiation involves nothing more than waiting for the other party to perform despite the repudiation, Lord Cockburn's view has had more appeal.

That was the situation in Phillpotts v. Evans, [1839] 151 Eng. Rep. 200, 201, a suit by a seller on a contract for the sale of wheat. The market having fallen, the buyer repudiated before the time for delivery. The market price continued to fall between the day of the repudiation and the last day when the seller could have delivered. The question was whether the damages should be calculated with reference to the market price at the time of the buyer's repudiation, or to the price at the later time. Naturally, the buyer preferred the earlier date. The seller, however, prevailed for, according to Lord Abinger, the seller was not bound at the time of the repudiation "to sell in order to reduce damages." The Supreme Court of the United States took the same approach in Roehm v. Horst, 178 U.S. 1 (1900), a leading American case on anticipatory breach of contract.

――――――

Retracting a Repudiation

When a promisor breaches a contract, the promisee may generally sue for damages from breach. If the breach is material, then the promisee may also cease its own performance or preparation. But what if the promisor repudiates the contract anticipatorily? Anticipatory repudiation is by definition material, but it is not quite a breach. The promisor may still be able to perform its contractual obligations, notwithstanding her vigorous insistence that she will not. So what if she has had second thoughts, perhaps after consulting with lawyers who have painted lurid pictures of ruinous damages?

Before Hochster v. De La Tour this would not have been a problem. The promisee would have had to await performance until the time set for it had passed; there would thus be no harm in permitting the promisor to retract its repudiation. But much of the point of anticipatory repudiation is to permit the aggrieved party to declare a total breach and therefore to end its own obligations. It might become impracticable or even impossible for the promisee to accept performance from the original promisor—say, if the promisee has arranged for an alternative, or if by stopping its own preparations it could no longer keep its part of the bargain.

The law of anticipatory repudiation allows for all this. It is indeed possible for a promisor to retract its anticipatory repudiation, at least if it does so within a reasonable time. That reasonable time ends, however, when the aggrieved party materially changes its position in reliance on the repudiation. Restatement § 256; UCC § 2–610. As the Restatement points out, this is rather "a vague criterion," so an aggrieved party may not know just when the promisor's right to retract ends. Restatement § 256 cmt. c. The aggrieved party may thus make the repudiation final simply by saying so, even in the absence of reliance. This provides the certainty otherwise lacking. On retraction, see E. Allan Farnsworth, Changing Your Mind: The Law of Regretted Decisions 62–63 (1998).

United States v. Seacoast Gas Co., 204 F.2d 709 (5th Cir. 1953), is a good example of repudiation, retraction, and reliance at work. Seacoast Gas contracted to supply natural gas to a federal housing project from April of 1947 to June of 1948. On October 7, 1947, Seacoast wrote to the housing authority that, because the authority had breached the contract, Seacoast intended to cancel the contract on November 15, 1947. The housing authority immediately told Seacoast that it had no right to cancel the contract and that the authority would seek bids for alternative suppliers if Seacoast persisted. The housing authority went forward with bidding and, on November 6, 1947, wrote to Seacoast that unless it retracted its repudiation within three days, the authority would accept the low bid and Seacoast would be liable for breach. Seacoast did not retract its repudiation, so on November 10 the authority accepted the low bid (as it happens, from a company owned by the same person who owned Seacoast). It signed a contract with the low bidder on November 17. But on November 13, two days before its stated termination date, Seacoast retracted its repudiation. The housing authority sued Seacoast; Seacoast pointed to its retraction as a defense. The appellate court thought otherwise. Seacoast could have retracted its repudiation until the housing authority relied upon it or otherwise treated the repudiation as final—in the piquant words of the court, until the agency "close[d] the door to repentance." When the housing authority stated in its letter of November 6 that it would do so three days later, Seacoast's right to retract its repudiation ended, even if, as Seacoast's owner claimed, he did not receive the letter. Nor did it matter that the agency had not yet signed the contract when Seacoast attempted to retract its repudiation, because the agency had already declared its intent to treat the repudiation as final.

NOTE

The Rose Bowl Affair (Reprise). After the class action was brought in the case discussed in Note 4, p. 852 above, the University had what the trial court called a "sudden affluence in the matter of tickets" and offered tickets to members of the plaintiff's class. The Court of Appeals decided the case on the assumption, "at least for the sake of argument, that the filing of an action is a sufficient change in position to destroy the power to retract an anticipatory repudiation." What does *Seacoast* say about the correctness of this assumption?

PROBLEMS

(1) *Speculation by Repudiation.* Seller contracts to sell Buyer goods for $100,000. A week later, when the market price of the goods has risen to $110,000, Seller repudiates and Buyer does nothing in response. A week later when the market price of the goods has fallen to $90,000, Seller retracts its repudiation. Is the retraction effective?

(2) *Repudiation Plus More.* On June 1, seller and buyer contracted for the sale of a house, closing to be on June 30, "time is of the essence." On June 20, the buyer repudiated and the seller urged performance. Nothing further happened until September 1 when the buyer sent a letter of retraction and sought to perform. The seller refused. Need the seller prove reliance? Glass v. Anderson, 596 S.W.2d 507 (Tex. 1980).

(3) *Jarbeau's Case.* The Jarbeau Comedy Company arranged to appear at the Buffalo Academy of Music for three days in December under a contract calling for equal division of gross receipts. In August the Company's impresario sent the Academy a draft contract increasing his share, explaining that he could not think of playing for less than 60%. The Academy returned the contract unsigned "for the reason that we have a contract signed by you and do not need any other for the appearance of Verona Jarbeau and company at our Academy." On November 17 the impresario wrote again, sending advertising material and saying, "Please keep Miss Jarbeau before the public as much as possible. I want to see her turn them away in your town." Owing to the itinerant habits of both parties, the plaintiff did not receive the defendants' response for about a month. It expressed surprise that Miss Jarbeau intended to play the Academy and explained that the Academy was booked to other performers. The Company sued the Academy for damages based on its expenses. What result? Bernstein v. Meech, 29 N.E. 255 (N.Y. 1891).

McCloskey & Co. v. Minweld Steel Co.

United States Court of Appeals, Third Circuit, 1955.
220 F.2d 101.

Suit by contractor against subcontractor alleging anticipatory breach of three contracts entered into by parties. The United States District Court for the Western District of Pennsylvania, Joseph P. Willson, J., granted defendant's motion for judgment on ground that plaintiff had not made out prima facie case, and entered order denying plaintiff's motion for findings of fact, to vacate judgments and for new trial, and plaintiff appealed.

Order affirmed.

■ McLAUGHLIN, CIRCUIT JUDGE. Plaintiff-appellant, a general contractor, sued on three contracts alleging an anticipatory breach as to each. At the close of the plaintiff's case the district judge granted the defense motions for judgment on the ground that plaintiff had not made out a cause of action.

By the contracts involved the defendant, a fabricator and erector of steel, agreed to furnish and erect all of the structural steel required on two buildings to be built on the grounds of the Hollidaysburg State Hospital, Hollidaysburg, Pa. and to furnish all of the long span steel joists required in the construction of one of the two buildings. Two of the contracts were dated May 1, 1950 and the third May 26, 1950. By Article V of each of the contracts "Should the Sub-Contractor [the defendant herein] at any time refuse or neglect to supply a sufficiency of materials of the proper quality, in and about the performance of the work required to be done pursuant to the provisions of this agreement, or fail, in the performance of any of the agreements herein contained, the Contractor shall be at liberty, without prejudice, to any other right or remedy, on two days' written notice to the Sub-Contractor, either to provide any such materials and to deduct the cost thereof from any payments then or thereafter due the Sub-Contractor, or to terminate the employment of the Sub-Contractor for the said work and to enter upon the premises."

There was no stated date in the contracts for performance by the defendant subcontractor. Article VI provided for completion by the subcontractor of its contract work "by and at the time or times hereafter stated to-wit:

"Samples, Shop Drawings and Schedules are to be submitted in the quantities and manner required by the Specifications, for the approval of the Architects, immediately upon receipt by the Sub-Contractor of the contract drawings, or as may be directed by the Contractor. All expense involved in the submission and approval of these Samples, Shop Drawings and Schedules shall be borne by the Sub-Contractor.

"All labor, materials and equipment required under this contract are to be furnished at such times as may be directed by the Contractor, and in such a manner so as to at no time delay the final completion of the building.

"It being mutually understood and agreed that prompt delivery and installation of all materials required to be furnished under this contract is to be the essence of this Agreement."

Appellee Minweld Steel Co., Inc., the subcontractor, received contract drawings and specifications for both buildings in May, 1950. On June 8, 1950, plaintiff McCloskey & Co. wrote appellee asking when it might "expect delivery of the structural steel" for the buildings and "also the time estimated to complete erection." Minweld replied on June 13, 1950, submitting a schedule estimate of expecting to begin delivery of the steel by September 1, and to complete erection approximately November 15. On July 20, 1950 plaintiff wrote Minweld threatening to terminate the contracts unless the latter gave unqualified assurances that it had effected definite arrangements for the procurement, fabrication and delivery within thirty days of the required materials. On July 24, 1950 Minweld wrote McCloskey & Co. explaining its difficulty in obtaining the necessary steel. It asked McCloskey's assistance in procuring it and stated that "We are as anxious as you are that there be no delay in the final completion of the buildings or in the performance of our contract."[1]

---

[1]   This letter in full is as follows:

Minweld Steel Company
Incorporated
Shaler and Wabash Streets
Pittsburgh 20, Pa.

July 24, 1950.

McClosky & Company
1620 Thompson Street
Philadelphia 21, Penna.

In re: New Hospital Buildings
            Hollidaysburg State Hospital
            Hollidaysburg, Pennsylvania

Attention of J.C. McCloskey,
Vice President

Dear Sir:

This will acknowledge receipt of your letter of July 20th, 1950, which was received by us today.

Upon receipt of the architect's specifications, we completed the engineering and erection plans on the said specifications. Immediately after those details were available, we attempted to place orders for the steel with the Bethlehem Steel Company. Our order was held in the offices of the Bethlehem Steel Company for two weeks before we were notified that it could not be supplied. Since that time, we have tried the U.S. Steel Corporation and Carnegie Illinois, both companies informing us that they were under contract for approximately one year and could not fulfill the order.

The recent directive by the President of the United States, with which we assume you are familiar, has further tightened up the steel market so that at the present writing we cannot give you any positive promise as to our ability to obtain the steel or delivery dates.

In view of the directive from Washington and the tightening up of the entire steel industry, we solicit your help and that of the General State Authority in aiding us to obtain the steel for these contracts.

We are as anxious as you are that there be no delay in the final completion of the buildings or in the performance of our contract, but we have nowhere else to turn at the present time for the supply of steel necessary under said contracts, unless through your aid and assistance, and that of the General State Authority, a supplier can be induced to give us the materials needed.

The U.S. Steel Corporation informs us that you have discussed this matter with them and are presently aware of our present difficulties.

If steel is to be supplied to these hospital buildings by governmental directive, we feel that the steel should be supplied to us for completion under our contract.

Plaintiff-appellant claims that by this last letter, read against the relevant facts, defendant gave notice of its positive intention not to perform its contracts and thereby violated same.[2] Some reference has already been made to the background of the July 24th letter. It concerned Minweld's trouble in securing the steel essential for performance of its contract. Minweld had tried unsuccessfully to purchase this from Bethlehem Steel, U.S. Steel and Carnegie-Illinois. It is true as appellant urges that Minweld knew and was concerned about the tightening up of the steel market.[3] And as is evident from the letter it, being a fabricator and not a producer, realized that without the help of the general contractor on this hospital project particularly by it enlisting the assistance of the General State Authority,[4] Minweld was in a bad way for the needed steel. However, the letter conveys no idea of contract repudiation by Minweld. That company admittedly was in a desperate situation. Perhaps if it had moved earlier to seek the steel its effort might have been successful. But that is mere speculation for there is no showing that the mentioned producers had they been solicited sooner would have been willing to provide the material.

Minweld from its written statement did, we think, realistically face the problem confronting it. As a result it asked its general contractor for the aid which the latter, by the nature of the construction, should have been willing to give. Despite the circumstances there is no indication in the letter that Minweld had definitely abandoned all hope of otherwise receiving the steel and so finishing its undertaking. One of the mentioned producers might have relented. Some other supplier might have turned up. It was McCloskey & Co. who eliminated whatever chance there was. That concern instead of aiding Minweld by urging its plea for the hospital construction materials to the State Authority which represented the Commonwealth of Pennsylvania took the position that the subcontractor had repudiated its agreement and then moved quickly to have the work completed. Shortly thereafter, and without the slightest trouble as far as appears, McCloskey & Co. procured the steel from Bethlehem[5] and

---

Very truly yours,

Minweld Steel Company, Inc.

J.A. Roberts

Sales Manager

JAR/fs

c/c   Travelers Indemnity Co.,
        Hartford, Conn.
        General State Authority,
        Harrisburg, Penna.

[2]   Plaintiff cancelled the contracts on July 26, 1950 on the ground that the July 24th letter constituted an admission of defendant's inability to perform the required work.

[3]   The Korean War broke out on June 24, 1950.

[4]   The Pennsylvania state agency which represented and owned the Hollidaysburg State Hospital.

[5]   Bethlehem had originally submitted a bid in competition with Minweld. Its new proposals were dated July 28, 1950 and were finally accepted by McCloskey & Co. on August 7,

brought in new subcontractors to do the work contemplated by the agreement with Minweld.

Under the applicable law Minweld's letter was not a breach of the agreement. The suit is in the federal court by reason of diversity of citizenship of the parties. Though there is no express statement to that effect the contracts between the parties would seem to have been executed in Pennsylvania with the law of that state applicable. In McClelland v. New Amsterdam Cas. Co., 1936, 322 Pa. 429, 433, 185 A. 198, 200, the Pennsylvania Supreme Court held in a case where the subcontractor had asked for assistance in obtaining credit, "In order to give rise to a renunciation amounting to a breach of contract there must be an absolute and unequivocal refusal to perform or a distinct and positive statement of an inability to do so." Minweld's conduct is plainly not that of a contract breaker under that test. See also Dingley v. Oler, 1886, 117 U.S. 490. Restatement of Contracts, Comment (i) to Sec. 318 (1932) speaks clearly on the point saying:

"Though where affirmative action is promised mere failure to act, at the time when action has been promised, is a breach, failure to take preparatory action before the time when any performance is promised is not an anticipatory breach, even though such failure makes it impossible that performance shall take place, and though the promisor at the time of the failure intends not to perform his promise." See Williston on Contracts, Vol. 5, Sec. 1324 (1937), Corbin on Contracts, Vol. 4, Sec. 973 (1951).

Appellant contends that its letter of July 20, requiring assurances of arrangements which would enable appellee to complete delivery in thirty days, constituted a fixing of a date under Article VI of the contracts. The short answer to this is that the thirty-day date, if fixed, was never repudiated. Appellee merely stated that it was unable to give assurances as to the preparatory arrangements. There is nothing in the contracts which authorized appellant to demand or receive such assurances.

The district court acted properly in dismissing the actions as a matter of law on the ground that plaintiff had not made out a prima facie case.

The order of the district court of July 14, 1954 denying the plaintiff's motion for findings of facts, to vacate the judgments and for new trials will be affirmed.

NOTES

(1) *What Is a Repudiation (Reprise)?* If the test for determining what is a repudiation is an objective one, it is surely no better to say "I cannot perform the contract" than to say "I will not perform it." Is it any better to

---

1950. The long span steel joists required by the third contract were procured from the Frederick Grundy Iron Works.

say, "I will try to perform, though I see no prospect of succeeding"? How does that differ from what Minweld wrote to McCloskey in the main case?

A party who is delinquent in performance, or threatened with inability, can surely plead with the other for leniency without being guilty of a repudiation. If pressed, one may hope to skirt a repudiation with cautiously written letters, perhaps drafted with the aid of counsel. How may the other party force the issue? Would it be easier to do so in a face-to-face encounter than by correspondence? Which party is likely to call for a conference? See Plunkett v. Comstock-Cheney Co., 208 N.Y.S. 93 (App. Div. 1925).

In formulating tests for repudiation, what bearing might it have if a party having grounds to expect a breach by the other had a right to demand assurance of due performance?

(2) *Counseling (Reprise)*. If McCloskey had asked for your help in drafting its letter of July 20, what would you have advised? What were the risks of a badly drafted letter? Might a face-to-face encounter have been preferable for McCloskey? If McCloskey had asked you how it should respond to Minweld's letter of July 24, what would you have advised? Could McCloskey have made use of Article V, which allowed McCloskey to either provide the materials itself and deduct the cost or terminate the contract if Minweld should "at any time refuse or neglect to supply a sufficiency . . . of materials"?

If Minweld had asked for your help in drafting its letter of July 24, what would you have advised? What were the risks of a badly drafted letter? Might a face-to-face encounter have been preferable for Minweld?

PROBLEM

Spam or Beef? In a series of contracts made from November of 2007 to March of 2008, Validsa, a food commodities trader, and PSI, an agent of the Republic of Venezuela, agreed that Validsa would sell beef, sugar, and other foodstuffs to PSI. Under these contracts, Validsa was to begin its performance when it received partial payments from PSI and would receive the balance shortly after it delivered the food. By April of 2008, PSI had fallen behind on both its initial payments and its payments due after delivery.

On April 15, 2008, a Validsa employee received an email inadvertently sent by a PSI employee. The email contained a string of highly disquieting messages. For example, an email of April 8 directed certain PSI employees to cancel one of its orders from Validsa, and another email stated that PSI was to suspend payments to Validsa. In a letter of April 17, Validsa demanded an explanation from PSI for the messages it had received. PSI instead proposed that PSI would make no further payments until all outstanding deliveries were complete, and that it would make future payments on less favorable terms. Validsa rejected this proposal and once again requested an explanation for the emails. Validsa also requested that the statements about suspending payments and cancelling a contract be retracted, and that PSI give Validsa tangible assurances that PSI would honor its commitments. PSI responded with a proposal to modify the contract, in part to Validsa's disadvantage. Validsa rejected the proposal and continued performing for a time. After PSI continued not to pay, Validsa finally suspended its own performance. PSI owed Validsa about $6,000,000 for the goods delivered; Validsa held about $44,500,000 in partial payments from PSI.

Validsa sued PSI for breach. PSI countersued, claiming that Validsa had breached its contracts by ceasing its own performance and demanding restitution of its partial payments. PSI argued that it had not repudiated the pending contracts, but rather had proposed different terms; as for the emails, it argued that they were sent unintentionally and were meant as points for discussion rather than items for action. Did PSI repudiate its pending contracts with Validsa? Did Validsa breach those contracts by suspending its own performance? See Validsa, Inc. v. PDVSA Servs., 424 Fed. Appx. 862 (11th Cir. 2011).

(B) ASSURANCE OF DUE PERFORMANCE

We have seen several examples of parties who might have wished, as things developed, to have some assurance that the other party would perform as agreed. The common law, however, gave no right to such assurance. "A party does not contract for oral assurances of performance, but for performance of the contract." BAII Banking Corp. v. UPG, Inc., 985 F.2d 685, 703 (2d Cir. 1993).

The drafters of the Code saw the need for an exception, and this exception was carried over into the Restatement. "Ordinarily an obligee has no right to demand reassurance by the obligor that the latter will perform when his performance is due. However, a contract 'imposes an obligation on each party that the other's expectation of receiving due performance will not be impaired.' Uniform Commercial Code § 2–609(1). When, therefore, an obligee reasonably believes that the obligor will commit a breach by nonperformance that would of itself give him a claim for damages for total breach (§ 243), he may, under the rule stated in this Section, be entitled to demand assurance of performance." Restatement § 251 cmt. a. Section 251 had no counterpart in the first Restatement. It is a generalization from UCC § 2–609, which was itself a legislative innovation.

McCloskey v. Minweld typifies the sort of case that gave rise to UCC § 2–609—one in which a seller committed itself to supply goods for payment thereafter, and received signals before making delivery that the buyer was in financial distress. What should the anxious seller do? Simply *being* insolvent is not an anticipatory repudiation. Naturally, if the buyer told the seller that it was not going to perform, then the buyer would have repudiated the contract anticipatorily. As we have seen, that would give the seller the right to treat the repudiation as a breach, and its own duties would not come into being because of the doctrine of constructive conditions. But what if the buyer responds by saying "Yes, I can't pay my bills now, but by the time for performance I have every reason to believe that I will be able to pay you in full"? The seller might be forgiven for taking that statement at a heavy discount.

A few options were available to insecure parties before the advent of adequate assurance. One was the seller's right to stop the goods in transit if it learned of the buyer's insolvency after putting the goods in the hands of a carrier. Another was the implied condition of solvency. Until relatively recently, it was not common for a contract to state expressly that the debtor would be in breach if it became insolvent. Nineteenth-century courts therefore found an implied condition in credit contracts that the debtor would remain solvent. If the debtor became insolvent, the condition failed and the duty to give credit never arose. The balance of the contract was, however, unaffected, so in essence what had been a credit contract became one for payment on delivery. Still another was for the parties to define breach and default in a way that swept in the main causes for insecurity, or even conditioned performance on the seller's satisfaction that the buyer's credit was not impaired.

None of these options was entirely satisfactory, however. The first two still required that the seller either place the goods in the hands of a carrier or actually tender them, which reduces the savings that repudiation can effect. Careful drafters could solve the problem contractually, but this was rare; perhaps commercial parties resisted putting a vague clause about insecurity and reasonableness into an otherwise clear agreement. Karl Llewellyn solved the problem with adequate assurance of performance, which he described as a way to prevent the promisor from wasteful preparation for a promisee that would not reciprocate and to encourage adjusting contracts rather than litigating over their breach.

Look at the formulation in UCC § 2–609 (or in Restatement § 251, which was largely drawn from the Code). Do these increase or decrease commercial certainty? Are these likely to affect contracting behavior? Behavior in the shadow of breach? Litigating positions?

NOTE

(1) *Opportunism.* It was pointed out in the discussion of "Time for Performance," p. 780 above, that one answer to opportunism is to insist that the other party perform first, so as to have the protection afforded by the doctrine of constructive conditions. Another is to require the other party to furnish a guarantee of performance by a reliable third party. The right to demand assurances is yet another answer.

(2) *Breach of a Separate Contract (Reprise).* Recall that the doctrine of constructive conditions cannot be invoked where there has been a breach of a separate contract. This is so even if the separate contract has been repudiated. UCC § 2–610 applies only when a party "repudiates *the* contract." But might UCC § 2–609 help an apprehensive party in such a situation? According to comment 3 to UCC § 2–609, "under commercial

standards and in accord with commercial practice, a ground for insecurity need not arise from or be directly related to the contract in question."

PROBLEM

You Know Quite as Well as We Do (Reprise). Review the letter in the Problem at p. 847 above. Would the seller be justified in demanding assurance of due performance under UCC § 2–609?

By-Lo Oil Co. v. ParTech, Inc.

United States Court of Appeals, Sixth Circuit, 2001.
11 Fed. Appx. 538.

■ KENNEDY, CIRCUIT JUDGE. Plaintiff, By-Lo Oil Company, appeals the district court's grant of summary judgment to defendant, ParTech, Incorporated, in this diversity contract dispute. On appeal, By-Lo makes two claims. . . . Second, it argues in analyzing the issue of whether the continuing support provision of the contract required ParTech to update the software, the district court improperly decided a factual question in determining that under Michigan's Uniform Commercial Code section 2–609. ParTech had provided By-Lo with adequate assurance that ParTech would perform under the contract.

We find no merit in either argument. As to the continuing support provision, while questions of whether a party provided "adequate assurance" and whether the other party had "reasonable grounds for insecurity" to ask for that assurance are generally fact questions left to the jury, we hold that as a matter of law, no reasonable jury could find that ParTech's assurance was inadequate nor could it find that By-Lo had reasonable grounds for insecurity to ask for that assurance. Accordingly, we affirm the district court's judgment.

We begin with a brief factual background before moving to our analysis.

I.

[ParTech agreed to supply By-Lo with software used in managing its accounting, its convenience stores, and its oil and gas supplies. Their contract stated that ParTech would provide continuing support to By-Lo for a fixed monthly fee, which the parties read to require that ParTech make the software Y2K-compliant. In September of 1997, By-Lo's Controller, Thomas Masters, wrote "Terry" at ParTech to inquire about "software and hardware options with [ParTech's] software and the concern of reaching the year 2000." The letter requested that Mary Beth Eng, director of ParTech's Host Accounting Systems, contact Mr. Masters to discuss the matter. Ms. Eng did not respond. Masters wrote again, this time to Ms. Eng, on January 7, 1998. He demanded "a written response from [Ms. Eng] by January 31, 1998 of Par[Tech]'s commitment that the software [By-Lo] own[s] will function after *December 31, 1999* with no problems." (emphasis added). Masters also threatened a lawsuit if he did not receive such response, warning that By-Lo would replace the software with that of another company and would seek the replacement cost from ParTech.

Ms. Eng responded by letter on January 30, 1998. She stated she could give Masters no answer to the question of "whether . . . the software would be changed by Par[Tech] to handle year 2000" because the "decision will be made by upper level management within Par[Tech] once they have the appropriate data to make an informed decision." She assured him that "[o]nce the decision [was] made, [he would] be notified."

According to Masters, he made another attempt to secure more definitive assurances by traveling to ParTech's Arlington, Texas headquarters where he was again told he would be informed when a decision was made. Unsatisfied with these responses, By-Lo, on May 1, 1998, filed a lawsuit against a Partech company located in New York. It obtained a default judgment in the suit. It later realized that the New York ParTech was not the Partech with which it had an agreement. In June of 1998, concerned about the looming Y2K problem, By-Lo purchased a new computer system—both software and hardware—for over $175,000.00. At oral argument, By-Lo explained that the software needed a different hardware system to run.

Unaware of these events, ParTech, on November 20, 1998, gave By-Lo the definitive answer for which it had been looking. ParTech's letter stated ParTech would supply the needed software at no cost and that the software needed to be installed prior to January 1, 1999, because the programs run on a "date check plus one" system by which a year is added to certain dates the user enters. *See* Appellant's Br. at 7. (By-Lo, however, was unaware of the "date check plus one" system when it initiated its lawsuit and changed computer equipment.) On December 18, 1998, ParTech, as promised, sent By-Lo the necessary software with detailed instructions for loading it. Of course, because By-Lo was now operating on a different system, it did not install the software.

Meanwhile, By-Lo, having realized its mistake in filing its May 1998 lawsuit against the wrong ParTech, refiled in May of 1999 in Michigan state court against the correct ParTech; ParTech removed the action to federal district court. By-Lo argued it had a right to obtain new computer equipment because of ParTech's actions, which it characterized as an anticipatory breach under Michigan's UCC sections 2–609 and 2–610. In response, ParTech moved for summary judgment on the grounds that (1) it had not made an overt communication of intent to repudiate the contract and therefore there was not a breach under 2–610; and (2) By-Lo did not have the reasonable grounds for insecurity necessary to seek assurance and the assurance ParTech gave was adequate and therefore there was no basis to find a breach under 2–609. The district court agreed and granted ParTech's motion.]

This appeal followed.

II.

B.

We also find without merit By-Lo's argument that the district court improperly decided questions of fact in analyzing the anticipatory repudiation claim. In reaching its conclusion, the district court assumed for the sake of argument that there were reasonable grounds for By-Lo's insecurity and held that ParTech's assurance-given almost two years before what By-Lo had indicated was the date it was concerned about-that it was looking into the matter was adequate assurance under the UCC. Accordingly, it concluded, By-Lo did not have the right to purchase equipment from another company in June of 1998 nor did it have the right to instigate a lawsuit in May of 1998. In passing, By-Lo argues it had reasonable grounds for insecurity because of the impending deadline coupled with the failure of ParTech to respond to its September 7, 1997 letter and several phone calls. *See* Appellant's Br. at 22.

Under Michigan's UCC,

> (1)   A contract for sale imposes an obligation on each party that the other's expectation of receiving due performance will not be impaired. When *reasonable grounds for insecurity* arise with respect to the performance of either party the other may in writing demand adequate assurance of due performance and until he receives such assurance may if commercially reasonable suspend any performance for which he has not already received the agreed return.
>
> (2)   Between merchants the reasonableness of grounds for insecurity and the adequacy of any assurance offered shall be determined by commercial standards.
>
> . . . .
>
> (4)   After receipt of a justified demand failure to provide within a reasonable time not exceeding 30 days such *assurance of due performance as is adequate* under the circumstances of the particular case is a repudiation of the contract.

Mich. Comp. Laws Ann. § 440.2609 (emphasis added). As a general matter what constitutes reasonable grounds for insecurity under subsection (1) and adequate assurance under subsections (1) and (4) are factual questions left to the trier of fact. *See id.* cmt. 4; *see also* 1 JAMES J. WHITE & ROBERT S. SUMMERS, UNIFORM COMMERCIAL CODE § 6–2 (4th ed. 2000) ("[T]he trier of fact must normally answer whether grounds for insecurity exist."); Larry T. Garvin, *Adequate Assurance of Performance: Of Risk, Duress, and Cognition*, 69 U. COLO. L.REV. 71, 102 (1998). As indicated, this is the general rule; there are exceptions. *See* BAII Banking Corp. v. UPG, Inc., 985 F.2d 685, 702 (2nd Cir. 1993). And indeed, By-Lo does not argue that district courts possess no power to make such determinations as a matter of law; it argues this is just not one of those cases. We disagree. We believe that, as a matter of law, By-

Lo did not have reasonable grounds for insecurity and that the court was correct to rule as a matter of law that ParTech's assurance was adequate.

1.   Reasonable Grounds

As general guidance, the comments to the section indicate that the grounds need not be the actions or inactions of a contracting party-outside circumstances may be sufficient. The question to be answered is whether a reasonable merchant in By-Lo's position would "feel that his expectation of receiving full performance was threatened." 2 HAWKLAND UNIFORM COMMERCIAL CODE SERIES § 2–609:2 (2000). The grounds that give rise to this feeling have to be something that occurred after the contract was in place. *See id.*

In essence By-Lo's argument that it had reasonable grounds for insecurity is based on the contention that ParTech was due to perform (in two years) and if ParTech failed to perform, it would be costly to By-Lo. Of course, this is generally the case in any contract. Hence, it is clear that the mere fact that performance was to come due is not sufficient under 2–609. *See* Cole v. Melvin, 441 F.Supp. 193, 202 (D.S.D. 1977) ("Clearly, the drafters of the code did not intend that one party to a contract can go about demanding security for the performance of the other whenever he gets nervous about a contract. Some reason for the demand for assurance must precede the demand."); SPS Industries, Inc. v. Atlantic Steel Co., 186 Ga.App. 94, 366 S.E.2d 410 (1988). Although the Y2K problem was not widely recognized prior to the contract, it is not entirely clear that that fact allows it to function as the incident that would create reasonable insecurity. The provision for continuing support contemplates that without such support the software may not function as well or at all. If this is considered in conjunction with the alleged failure of ParTech to return calls, it might have given rise to reasonable grounds for insecurity at some point before Y2K. *See* 295 N.W.2d 172 (S.D. 1980) (finding that growing amount of credit extended by the seller to the buyer coupled with the buyer's failure to return the seller's calls to discuss the situation constituted reasonable grounds for insecurity).

The question still remains whether January 7, 1998 was that time. By-Lo offers little reason to conclude that a date nearly two years prior to the date performance was necessary would be a time at which one would reasonably feel insecure. Michigan courts have not addressed the question so we must look to cases from other jurisdictions. In analyzing the question, we look to (1) whether time was running short for By-Lo to make alternative arrangements, *see* In re Coast Trading Co., 26 B.R. 737, 740 (Bankr. D. Or. 1982); (2) whether it would take By-Lo nearly that amount of time to install any modifications or updates sent by ParTech; (3) whether ParTech had proved unreliable in the past, *see* T & S Brass & Bronze Works, Inc. v. Pic-Air, Inc., 790 F.2d 1098, 1105 (4th Cir. 1986); and (4) whether By-Lo had reason to believe that ParTech would be unable to perform, *see* 731 F.Supp. 1484 (D. Kan. 1990). Looking at these factors, it is clear that as of January 7, 1998, By-Lo had no reasonable grounds to feel insecure. By-Lo does not complain about ParTech's previous service nor is there any indication that it was in time pinch to obtain a new system if ParTech did not respond quickly. There is no indication that By-Lo had reason to believe it would take a lengthy period of time to make any corrections ParTech required. By-Lo attempts to characterize the affidavit of Ronda Ryan, a computer programmer and software developer, as evidence that as of May 1998, it had little time to obtain new software and implement it or to install any software sent by ParTech:

> By May 1998, timing became an issue for By-Lo, which perceived that it had a Hobson's choice: purchase a new computer system to ensure installation and readiness when the year 2000 dates would be utilized . . . , or roll the dice and wait to see [whether] Partech would decide to honor its contractual obligations. . . . Because By-Lo had no in-house information systems department, it would have to contract with a third party to do the installation . . . but, by this time, due to the substantial demand for computer upgrades to handle the year 2000 dates, the supply of qualified computer systems personnel was becoming scarce.

Appellant's Br. at 7–8 (citing Ms. Ryan's affidavit). Of course, May of 1998 is of no consequence in evaluating whether By-Lo had reasonable grounds for insecurity in January of 1998 when it asked ParTech for assurance. Moreover, Ms. Ryan's affidavit does not say what By-Lo claims it says. The "this time" referred to in the above passage appears to be May of 1998. The language from By-Lo's brief almost mirrors a passage from Ms. Ryan's affidavit. However, that passage does not refer to May or June of 1998, but rather to December of 1998. In her affidavit, she states,

> It is my professional opinion that *13 days over the December holiday* is not adequate time to install and test a software upgrade to mission critical computer applications given the tremendous demand for computer consultants caused by the Year 2000 bug. By-Lo, which does not have an in-house information systems department, would have found it very difficult to retain a computer consultant to install and test the software upgrade and to ensure that it was compatible with other aspects of the computer system *during that 13-day period in December 1998*.

J.A. 171 (emphasis added). Finally, the only thing that could be seen as an indication that ParTech would be unable to perform was ParTech's initial delay in responding. In sum, there was little reason for By-Lo to be concerned at such an early date-so little that no reasonable jury could have found for By-Lo.

2. Adequate Assurance

The same is true as to the adequate assurance issue. The question to be answered is "what are the minimum kinds of promises or acts on the part of the promisor that would satisfy a reasonable merchant in the position of the promisee that his expectation of receiving due performance will be fulfilled?" 2 HAWKLAND UNIFORM COMMERCIAL CODE SERIES § 2–609:03. Generally, when a promisor's assurance is something less than what was sought, courts find the assurance inadequate. *See* Garvin, *supra* at 105. Again, that is generally the case. In evaluating the assurance, the court should keep in mind the reputation of the promisor, the grounds for insecurity, and the kinds of assurance available. *See id.; see also* Mich. Comp. Laws Ann. § 440.2609 cmt. 4.

With those factors in mind, we conclude the district court was correct to hold that as a matter of law, ParTech's assurance that it was evaluating the matter was adequate despite the fact that it was less than requested. As noted, By-Lo did not have reasonable grounds for insecurity in January of 1998. The Y2K problem was almost two years away. There is absolutely no indication that ParTech had failed to fulfill its obligations in the past nor is there any evidence that ParTech's reputation should have given By-Lo cause for concern. And, moreover, it is not clear what else ParTech could have done.

III.

For the foregoing reasons, we affirm the district court's judgment.

NOTES

(1) *Questions.* How many ill-advised things did By-Lo do? To whom should a demand for assurances be directed? Who should be asked to furnish the assurances? How specific should the demand be? Is the recipient justified in demanding to know what specific form of assurance would be satisfactory? If the promisee demands a specific form of assurance (*e.g.*, a bank guarantee) that is inconvenient or impossible for the recipient to give, but another form would serve the purpose equally well, is the demand effective? And why should the insecure party be able to demand more than the original contract provided for? Couldn't it have bargained for reasonable assurances in advance? If so, then doesn't adequate assurance doctrine effectively let one party rewrite the contract to reduce its own risk?

For more on UCC § 2–609, see Richard Craswell, *Insecurity, Repudiation, and Cure*, 19 J. Legal Stud. 399 (1990); Gregory Crespi, *The Adequate Assurances Doctrine after U.C.C. § 2–609: A Test of the Efficiency of the Common Law*, 38 Vill. L. Rev. 179 (1993); Larry T. Garvin, *Adequate Assurance of Performance: Of Risk, Duress, and Cognition*, 69 U. Colo. L. Rev. 71 (1998).

(2) *Oral Demand.* Notwithstanding that UCC § 2–609(1) requires a demand for adequate assurance to be in writing, it has been held that an oral demand may suffice under UCC § 2–609 "as long as the demand provides a

'clear understanding' of the insecure party's intent to suspend performance until receipt of adequate assurances from the other party." See Atwood-Kellogg, Inc. v. Nickeson Farms, 602 N.W.2d 749, 753 (S.D. 1999). Is there any reason for requiring a writing? There is no such requirement in Restatement § 251. On the other hand, what justifies reading UCC § 2–609 *not* to require a writing?

(3) *International Approaches.* Article 71 of the CISG allows a party "to suspend the performance of his obligations if, after the conclusion of the contract, it becomes apparent that the other party will not perform a substantial part of his obligations," but the party "must continue with performance if the other party provides adequate assurance of his performance." How does this provision differ from UCC § 2–609?

UNIDROIT Principles art. 7.3.4 follows the language of UCC § 2–609 more closely. How does this provision differ from UCC § 2–609?

PROBLEMS

(1) *Drafting for the Textile Trade.* Suppose that you have been asked by the Associations that have promulgated the Standard Textile Salesnote ("Worth Street Rules"), widely used in the textile trade, to review these Rules under the Uniform Commercial Code. The Rules provide that on Buyer's breach of any term "of this and any other contracts with Seller, all sums owing under this or any other contract between Buyer and Seller, shall at the option of Seller . . . at once become due." This paragraph also requires payments by Buyer in the event that net balances under all their contracts exceed Buyer's established credit limit, and provides that on Buyer's failure "to make any such payment within five (5) days after demand in writing, Seller shall have the option to cancel this and other contracts between Buyer and Seller."

Under UCC § 1–302(b), is this a "manifestly unreasonable" standard of performance of a seller's non-disclaimable duty of reasonableness prescribed in the Code? Is it a permissible variation of the effect of UCC § 2–609? How would you advise the Associations?

(2) *Drafting for the Lumber Business.* Suppose that you have been asked by a trade association of lumber dealers for your opinion on the following provision.

> The seller shall have the right to cancel on account of any arbitrary deductions made by the buyer with respect to, or failure to comply with, contract terms in respect to any prior shipment, or on account of any transfer of or change in the buyer's business, its insolvency, suit by other creditors, failure of buyer to meet financial obligations to seller, impairment of buyer's credit information, or for unfavorable credit reports made to seller through usual channels of credit information unless the buyer shall promptly furnish to the seller's satisfaction guaranty of full payment for any shipment made or to be made. Notice of such cancellation shall be given in writing.

Recall the discussion of acceleration clauses in Note 3, p. 852 above. Is UCC § 1–309 applicable to the term quoted above? Is there any other reason to expect that that term would not be effective? See UCC § 1–302(b). How would you advise the trade association?

(3) *Spam or Beef? (Reprise).* Review the Validsa-PSI problem at p. 865. Does Validsa have grounds to demand adequate assurance of due performance? What might Validsa reasonably demand? Would it be commercially reasonable for Validsa to suspend its own performance?

Rocheux Int'l of N.J. v. U.S. Merchants Fin. Group

United States District Court, District of New Jersey, 2010.
741 F.Supp.2d 651.

■ BROWN, CHIEF JUDGE. [U.S. Merchants Financial Group, a provider of plastic product-packaging services, ordered large amounts of raw plastics (PVC and APET) from Rocheux, a plastics distributor, in 2005 and 2006. Rocheux delivered some of the plastics that U.S. Merchants ordered, but U.S. Merchants did not pay for most, if not all, of the 2006 deliveries. At the time of the litigation, U.S. Merchants owed Rocheux over two million dollars for the plastics delivered in 2006. Additionally, in 2005 and 2006 Rocheux delivered over a million and a half dollars worth of plastics to a warehouse designated by U.S. Merchants; these too were not paid for. On September 24, 2006, Rocheux President Wendy Steed sent an email to Defendants' President and CEO Jeffrie Green requesting the delinquent payments for the 2006 deliveries and the warehouse goods by September 29, 2009, and notifying Defendants that their failure to pay would result in Rocheux selling the warehouse goods and seeking any deficiency from Defendants pursuant to UCC § 2–706. Rocheux eventually sold the warehouse goods to third parties for $1,194,582.68, resulting in a deficiency of $387,699.70 compared to the original purchase price for the warehouse goods.

U.S. Merchants argued that the 2006 deliveries substantially failed to conform with the contract descriptions, and that it frequently had told Rocheux that it could not use the defective material. Because the plastics were supplied in large rolls, most defects appeared only when the plastics were used in the assembly lines, often well after U.S. Materials had received the plastics. After it heard nothing from Rocheux, U.S. Materials sold the defective goods as scrap.

For its part, Rocheux claimed that it was not notified of problems with the 2006 deliveries until its president received an email from Defendants' president on September 6, 2006. Before that email, Rocheux claimed that Defendants had generally acknowledged that they owed payments for the 2006 deliveries, and that U.S. Materials had not complained of more than occasional and minor problems with the quality of the plastics. If it had, Rocheux stated that it would have requested an opportunity to inspect the goods, and that Rocheux would have returned any defective goods to the original manufacturer for credits. To support this claim, Rocheux notes that its representatives met with Defendants' president in California on three occasions: April 1, 2006, May 31, 2006, and July 17, 2006. According to these representatives, Defendants never expressed any concerns with the 2006 deliveries at these meetings, and Defendants' president acknowledged that Defendants owed the amounts listed in Rocheux's invoices, but that the delay in payments for the 2006 deliveries was attributable to problems with Defendants' new accounting software.

After Rocheux received the September 6 email, its president replied the following day with an email asking U.S. Materials to "please provide [Rocheux] full details" regarding his assertion of defects with delivered goods. Her response further asserted "We stand behind our product and will send a team to investigate any problems you may be having with our material. Any defective materials should be returned for a full credit." Rocheux asserted that Defendants never responded to her request for inspection or return of defective goods. Defendants concede that "the vast majority" of the 2006 deliveries had been discarded as scrap when they received Rocheux's September 7, 2006 email requesting the return or inspection of defective goods. Rocheux sued U.S. Materials for breach of contract, and U.S. Materials countersued. Rocheux now moves for summary judgment on its claims for the 2006 deliveries and warehouse goods, seeking $4,635,761.18 in damages, interest, attorneys' fees, and costs.[1]]

* * *

Rocheux next argues that Defendants are liable for the deficiency between the original purchase price and the subsequent resale value of the warehouse goods, as well as the costs Rocheux incurred by storing and reselling the same. Defendants respond that Rocheux cannot recover these sums as a matter of law because Rocheux improperly repudiated its contracts with Defendants under N.J. Stat. Ann. § 12A:2–609 without demanding adequate assurance and despite receiving such assurance from Defendants. Defendants do not seek any offset or damages related to the warehouse goods; accordingly, the Court considers whether Rocheux demanded adequate assurance and whether Defendants provided such assurance. . . .

With regard to Defendants' first contention that Rocheux did not demand adequate assurances, Defendants appear to challenge not only the language used by Rocheux in its correspondence, but also Rocheux's grounds for insecurity. Defendants argue that Rocheux did not demand adequate assurance, as was required by § 12A:2–609 prior to repudiating the parties' contracts, because Rocheux "conditioned its own future

---

[1]   Rocheux's damages calculation consists of $2,116,571.76 in damages for the 2006 deliveries, $387,699.70 for the deficiency related to the resale of the warehouse goods, and $18,562.36 and $56,622.67 in freight and storage charges related to the resale of the warehouse goods. (Pl.'s Br. at 5–6.) According to the Declaration of Mr. Stephanoff and its accompanying Exhibit A, Rocheux seeks $2,056,304.68 in interest on the 2006 deliveries and warehouse goods as of May 31, 2010.

performance on Defendants' payment of prior contracts." Specifically, Defendants point to the September 21, 2006 letter sent by Rocheux's President Wendy Steed to Defendants' President Jeffrie Green, which states in pertinent part:

> Unless payment of [past-due invoices] is received by September 29th, 2006, Rocheux will have no alternative but to commence an action and seek all appropriate remedies to recover said amount together with all applicable 1.5% interest per month late fees, attorney's fees and other damages available to Rocheux under its terms of sale. This letter shall also constitute notice of Rocheux's intent, in the event payment is not forthcoming, to sell or otherwise dispose of the material remaining in our warehouse pursuant to UCC § 2–706 and recover any deficiency from you.

Defendants cite a number of cases for the proposition that a party's breach of a collateral contract does not authorize the aggrieved party to refuse performance under a separate and distinct contract. However, comment 3 to § 12A:2–609 provides that, "[u]nder commercial standards and in accord with commercial practice, a ground for insecurity need not arise from or be directly related to the contract in question. . . . Thus a buyer who falls behind in 'his account' with the seller, even though the items involved have to do with separate and legally distinct contracts, impairs the seller's expectation of due performance." Furthermore, the correspondence relied upon by Defendants indicates that Rocheux's insecurity arose from Defendants' failure to pay for both the 2006 deliveries and the warehouse goods. Defendants overlook the fact that Rocheux's September 21 letter, as well as Ms. Steed's prior email of August 2, 2006, sought to remedy Defendants' non-payment on the purchase orders that comprised *both* the 2006 deliveries and the warehouse goods. Rocheux's correspondence indicates that it sought nothing more than the *performance due* under the parties' contracts, which was Defendants' payment for and receipt of the warehouse goods, in addition to Defendants' payment for the 2006 deliveries. Considering the parties' course of dealings, which included Defendants' undisputed failure to pay more than $2 million of the purchase price for the 2006 deliveries and the warehouse goods, this Court cannot say that Rocheux's insecurity was unreasonable as a matter of law.

Turning to the actual language of Rocheux's correspondence of August 2 and September 21, 2006, which must be read in the context of the parties' prior dealings, the Court notes that Rocheux both (1) clearly conveyed its reasons for insecurity—Defendants' failure to pay substantial sums related to invoices for the 2006 deliveries and the warehouse goods, and (2) clearly indicated that it intended to suspend its own performance. Specifically, the August 2 email recognized that Defendants had recently sent a check on an invoice, and presented the following proposal to resolve Defendants' problem with past-due invoices:

Based on your consistent weekly payments and with a full understanding of your short term computer problems I will throw out a proposal for your consideration.

We will ship you on a two to one payment ratio; i.e. for every two truckload invoices you pay we will release one truckload. In other words if you pay past due invoices of $100,000 we will release $50,000. This will move us in the right direction so we can be on track when your computer problems are finally resolved.

Please let me know if you have any interest in this option.

As noted above, the September 21 letter indicated that Rocheux would dispose of the warehouse goods if Defendants did not pay on their past-due invoices. Although neither message included the exact term "adequate assurance," courts have generally eschewed applying formalistic requirements for the demand of adequate assurances, instead opting for a case-specific approach that considers a party's demands in the context of its course of dealings with the adverse party. See, e.g., AMF, Inc. v. McDonald's Corp., 536 F.2d 1167, 1170–71 (7th Cir. 1976) (rejecting a "formalistic" approach to § 2–609, and looking instead to the parties' "clear understanding that [one party] had suspended performance until it should receive adequate assurance of due performance from [the other party]"); Atwood-Kellogg, Inc. v. Nickeson Farms, 602 N.W.2d 749, 753 (S.D. 1999) (agreeing with the *AMF* court that "a demand for adequate assurances may be either written or oral, as long as the demand provides a 'clear understanding' of the insecure party's intent to suspend performance until receipt of adequate assurances from the other party"); see also Cumberland County Improvement Auth. v. GSP Recycling Co., 358 N.J. Super. 484, 499, 818 A.2d 431 (App. Div. 2003) (finding that plaintiff failed to demand adequate assurance because "plaintiff is unable to point to any written or verbal demand that conveyed plaintiff's intent to terminate deliveries if defendant either refused to pay the past-due invoices, or refused to pay for future deliveries"); Koch Materials Co. v. Shore Slurry Seal, Inc., 205 F.Supp.2d 324, 332 (D.N.J. 2002) (noting that "courts have routinely accepted as sufficient under § 609 requests for assurances of a far less formal nature" than statements specifically citing § 609); but see Scotts Co. v. Central Garden & Pet Co., No. 2:00-CV-755, 2002 WL 1578781, at *4 (S.D.Ohio Apr. 22, 2004) (applying UCC's requirement that a demand for adequate assurance be made in writing in accordance with the decisions of Ohio courts). Considering the parties' course of dealings, which included multiple in-person meetings between Rocheux and Defendants concerning Defendants' failure to pay accounts on time, the Court cannot say as a matter of law that Rocheux's correspondence of August 2 and September 21, 2006 did not constitute a demand for adequate assurance.

Finally, with regard to assurances provided, Defendants argue that Mr. Green's October 4 letter provided adequate assurance that Defendants would continue to perform under the contract. This letter generally disputed Defendants' liability for Rocheux's invoices, asserting that "Rocheux alone is responsible for its failure to ship and bill product which we ordered," but nevertheless indicated that Defendants "[we]re willing to purchase the undelivered PVC . . . ordered under [purchase orders] 20491 and 21920." The letter also indicated a willingness to purchase "APET which Rocheux did not deliver . . . at the price and terms set forth on our orders. . . . " Both of these proposals were conditioned on the assumption that Rocheux would provide "first quality virgin" and "RF sealable" material. The letter appears to adopt quantities and prices from the parties' 2005–2006 purchase orders. Defendants further proposed in the letter that:

> [t]he additional PVC and APET may be delivered to us FOB our Ontario facility as we request it. We hereby advise you that the first delivery may be made the week of October 23, 2006. We anticipate that the balance of the additional PVC and APET will be requested for delivery prior to April 30, 2007. Please confirm in writing by no later than Friday, October 5, 2006, that Rocheux will make these deliveries when and as requested. Upon receipt of your written confirmation, we will advise you in writing of each delivery which we request. We will also advise you whether the payment will be made on a C.O.D. basis by Company check or whether we will arrange for a letter of credit payable Net 120 days from our receipt of each delivery.

Rocheux's president responded by letter of October 6, 2006, which stated that Defendants' "continuing failure to pay Rocheux's outstanding invoices relieved [Rocheux] of any obligation to ship any material to [Defendants]," but proposed that withheld materials would be released to Defendants "only on the condition that, prior to shipment, [Defendants] open [ ] an irrevocable letter of credit in favor of Rocheux for an amount not less than the total amount of the open invoices." The letter concluded "[t]he aforesaid letter of credit need be your only reply." The October 6, 2006 letter appears to have been the last correspondence between the parties on this matter.

Defendants argue that, by offering to pay on a C.O.D. basis or extend a letter of credit in the October 4 letter, they provided adequate assurance as a matter of law. While Defendants correctly note that courts have generally recognized that letters of credit provide adequate assurance of performance due, see, e.g., Lustrelon, Inc. v. Prutscher, 178 N.J. Super. 128, 139, 428 A.2d 518 (App. Div. 1981), it is undisputed that Defendants did not provide a letter of credit for the warehouse goods, even after Rocheux's October 6 response indicated that the "letter of credit need be [Defendants'] only reply." Furthermore, while some courts have recognized that an insecure party may request C.O.D. payments, see, e.g., Coke Lumber & Mfg. Co. v. First Nat'l Bank in Dallas, 529 S.W.2d 612 (Tex. Civ. App. 1975), the Court is aware of no authority for the proposition that an insecure party must accept an assurance of C.O.D. where the delinquent party had fallen in arrears more than $2 million on goods delivered at the time that the insecure party sought assurances of performance. "Between merchants the reasonableness of grounds for insecurity and the adequacy of any assurance offered shall be determined according to commercial standards," N.J. Stat. Ann. § 12A:2–609(2), and comment 4 to this section notes that "repeated delinquencies must be viewed as cumulative." Comment 4 further provides:

> What constitutes "adequate" assurance of due performance is subject to the same test of factual conditions. For example, where the buyer can make use of a defective delivery, a mere promise by a seller of good repute that he is giving the matter his attention and that the defect will not be repeated, is normally sufficient. Under the same circumstances, however, a similar statement by a known corner-cutter might well be considered insufficient without the posting of a guaranty or, if so demanded by the buyer, a speedy replacement of the delivery involved.

Given Defendants' continued failure to pay outstanding invoices regarding the 2006 deliveries and warehouse goods, this Court cannot say as a matter of law that Rocheux's demand for a letter of credit covering these goods was unreasonable. Cf. Creusot-Loire Int'l, Inc. v. Coppus Eng'g Corp., 585 F.Supp. 45, 50 (S.D.N.Y. 1983) (finding that an insecure party's requests for "an extension of contractual guarantee and the posting of a letter of credit were not unreasonable").

Furthermore, it appears Defendants' October 4 letter sought to change the terms of delivery of the warehouse goods. The October 4 letter expressly contemplates extending the delivery period for the retained goods through April 2007, and that Defendants would reserve 60–120 days to pay upon the deliveries if it provided a letter of credit. Alternatively, it requested that Rocheux propose a "discount for immediate C.O.D. payment rather than payment on extended terms." Generally speaking, a buyer's refusal to perform except upon conditions not required by the contract constitutes repudiation. E.g., Aero Consulting Corp. v. Cessna Aircraft Co., 867 F.Supp. 1480, 1491 (D. Kan. 1994) (finding that a buyer's refusal to pay except upon conditions not required by the contract constituted a repudiation); see also Kaiser-Francis Oil Co. v. Producer's Gas Co., 870 F.2d 563, 569 (10th Cir. 1989) (finding assurance inadequate where the party "indicated it would perform only if the contract was amended"). Considering Defendants' history of late payments, this Court cannot say as a matter of law that Rocheux's decision to respond to the October 4 letter by requesting a letter of credit in the October 6 letter was unreasonable as a matter of law.

However, nor can this Court determine as a matter of law that Defendants' letter of October 4 constituted repudiation or provided inadequate assurance. These issues usually present questions of fact to be determined according to commercial standards. See, e.g., Timmerman v. Grain Exchange, LLC, 394 Ill.App.3d 189, 333 Ill.Dec. 592, 915 N.E.2d 113, 124 (2009) ("Whether an anticipatory repudiation has occurred is a question of fact. . . ."); Upton v. Ginn, 231 S.W.3d 788, 791 (Ky.Ct.App.2007) (same); S & S, Inc., 478 N.W.2d at 863 (noting that adequacy of assurance presents a question of fact). This Court finds that a reasonable jury could conclude that Defendants' October 4 letter provided adequate assurance and did not repudiate the parties' contracts. Accordingly, the Court will deny both parties' cross-motions for summary judgment with regard to the warehouse goods.

NOTES

(1) *Questions.* Based on the facts presented, did Rocheux make a sufficient demand for assurances? What facts would you seek to introduce at trial to bolster this argument? Given that credit risks are present in all credit contracts, why should Rocheux have been entitled to *any* assurances of due performance? What if U.S. Materials had responded with a letter from its bank certifying that it had the funds necessary to pay Rocheux's bills?

(2) *Extension by Analogy.* In Conference Center Ltd. v. TRC—The Research Corp., 455 A.2d 857, 864–65 (Conn. 1983), a landlord sued a tenant for wrongful abandonment of the premises. The tenant, claiming constructive eviction, had summary judgment, but the Supreme Court of Connecticut reversed and remanded. Justice Ellen Peters noted "that courts in other jurisdictions have required a tenant who contemplates abandonment of the premises because of constructive eviction first to give his landlord notice and a reasonable opportunity to provide adequate assurance. . . . That case law provides a further link to Uniform Commercial Code § 2–609, for the cases and the statute both recognize the desirability of providing an opportunity for dialogue to establish whether the parties intend to repudiate or to fulfill their contractual obligations. . . . [W]e find support for recourse to § 2–609 as a source of general law in the provisions of § 251 of the Restatement (Second) of Contracts. . . . Only a full trial can establish whether the defendant was in fact constructively evicted or was entitled, for lack of adequate assurance, to infer that its lease had been terminated."

Adequate Demands for Adequate Assurances

As the court in *Rocheux International* notes, it is not necessary that a demand for adequate assurances in a sales transaction state specifically that the demand has been made under UCC § 2–609. Very often the demand looks as though it was drafted by a lawyer—for example, the demand in Koch Materials Co. v. Shore Slurry Seal, 205 F.Supp.2d 324 (D.N.J. 2002), cited to in *Rocheux*, stated that "once Shore has provided Koch with adequate assurance of performance of its obligations to Koch the process which we began with this letter can be terminated." It is hard to imagine that someone unencumbered with a legal education would throw around phrases like "adequate assurance of performance." But at least as often the language presented as a demand falls well short of paraphrasing the statute. It is then the litigator's job to fight about whether words probably uttered without adequate assurance in mind can be said after the fact to have been a demand for adequate assurance. The argument in *Rocheux International* is typical.

Did that language make sufficiently clear that Rocheux sought adequate assurances, the implication being that it could declare a repudiation if U.S. Materials didn't come forth? Was it as clear as the language required to repudiate a contract? If not, then why was it acceptable in the context of adequate assurance of due performance? On this issue, consider Judge Posner's opinion in C.L. Maddox, Inc. v. Coalfield Services, Inc., 51 F.3d 76 (7th Cir. 1995). There Maddox, who had a contract with Old Ben Coal Company to demolish and replace a loading facility in one of the company's mines, decided to subcontract everything except the fabrication of the new facility. In February, Maddox met with the president of Coalfield, who offered to do the job for $230,000 in the three weeks that Maddox wished because of his commitments to Old Ben.

Coalfield's crew traveled to the mine on March 19. On the same day Coalfield faxed a proposed contract to Maddox, specifying a price of $230,000, completion within three weeks, and biweekly progress payments. Maddox called Coalfield the same day and said that he would sign the proposal, but he never did. Coalfield's crew began work the next day, March 20. Progress was slower than expected. On April 8, after Maddox had failed to reply to repeated requests to sign the proposal, Coalfield ordered its crew to stop work and come to the surface with its tools and equipment. It faxed Maddox that it would not proceed unless Maddox accepted the proposed contract and paid an invoice for $103,500, which was 45 percent of the contract price, the percentage of the job that Coalfield claimed it had completed.

Maddox replied by fax the same day, apologizing for not having responded sooner, and saying, from information received from the project superintendent, that "your 45 percent completion is a little high, . . . we shall in good faith accept the 45 percent completion figure and pay accordingly less 10 percent retention." But Maddox appeared to condition this promise on Coalfield's signing an enclosed "acceptance letter" extending the deadline for completion of the work from three weeks to four and adding a liquidated-damages clause requiring Coalfield to pay $1,000 for each day's delay beyond the four-week deadline. Coalfield balked. It had been working for three weeks and estimated that completion might take another five weeks beyond this new deadline, with a potential liability of $35,000 if it agreed to liquidated damages.

Coalfield faxed Maddox the same day, rejecting the acceptance letter and refusing to complete the project unless Maddox paid the $103,500 invoice and accepted Coalfield's May 19 offer, with an exception for the date of completion. It added, "if you decide to accept the above conditions, we will proceed with work starting April 16," eight days from the date of the fax. Maddox replied that if Coalfield did not resume work by April 9, it would be in breach. Coalfield never resumed work.

Maddox sued for damages based on the cost of paying another contractor to finish the job in time to avoid a breach of its contract with Old Ben. Coalfield counterclaimed for $103,500 based on the percentage of the job that it claimed it had completed. The parties consented to a trial before a magistrate judge, who found for Coalfield. Maddox appealed.

Judge Posner observed that Coalfield would have had a right to demand assurance of Maddox's performance if the case had been governed by the Uniform Commercial Code, and that the principle behind UCC § 2–609 was a "sound one." "Coalfield's repeated requests to Maddox to sign a proposal that, so far as the record shows, contained no unusual, coercive, or one-sided terms . . . were in effect reasonable requests for assurances, or close enough to be treated the same by the law. Maddox's failure to provide any assurances entitled Coalfield in the circumstances . . . to anticipate that Maddox would commit a breach, to suspend its own performance for the sake of self-protection, and to demand payment for the work done to date. . . . Against this it can be argued that since the parties already had a contract, Coalfield need not have required Mr. Maddox to sign anything and therefore did not have to worry about his failure to respond to the repeated demands to sign Coalfield's written offer, and could treat Maddox's counteroffer as a request for modification and ignore it. . . .

"We are mindful of the standard formula . . . that an anticipatory breach occurs only when a party makes a clear and unequivocal statement of his intention to break the contract when his performance comes due. . . . We have no quarrel with the formula. But obviously it is meant for cases in which the claim of anticipatory repudiation is based on a statement. Here, as in cases based on section 2–609 of the Uniform Commercial Code, the claim is based on silence in the face of a request for the equivalent of assurances. . . . By the time Coalfield brought its crew to the surface, Maddox had repeatedly failed to respond to Coalfield's demand for confirmation of their agreement. Had Coalfield not acted and instead had completed the job and sued, it might have been faced with a defense of failure to mitigate its damages."

How, if at all, can we distinguish the demand in *C.L. Maddox* from a routine notice of breach? Is any such difference material? Is there anything to be said for requiring some degree of form in a demand for adequate assurance?

NOTE

Self-Help Remedies Under the Code. Under the doctrine of constructive conditions of exchange, an injured party may suspend performance and ultimately terminate. As long as the injured party does not claim damages, that party does not need to go to court. Suspension and termination are "self-help" remedies. In UCC §§ 2–609 and 2–717, the Code expands the array of such remedies available under contracts for the sale of goods. What might be the reason for this expansion? Do you see any drawback? See Celia Taylor, *Self-Help in Contract Law: An Exploration and Proposal*, 33 Wake Forest L. Rev. 839 (1998).

PROBLEM

Spam or Beef? (Second Encore). Look back at the Validsa-PSI problem at p. 865 and the reprise on p. 875. Consider the assurances you thought Validsa might reasonably demand. If PSI had responded with a revised contract that provided marginally greater security with less favorable payment terms, would Validsa's demands have been met sufficiently, though not ideally? Are there any ways to avoid this mess through foresighted contract drafting?

CHAPTER 8

REMEDIES FOR BREACH

The remedy for breach of contract is presumptively monetary, or *substitutional* relief, in the form of a judgment awarding money damages to be paid to the aggrieved promisee, rather than injunctive, or *specific* relief, in the form of a court order directing the promisor to perform its promise. In both its specific and substitutional forms, contract remedies may be seen as serving various functions. Recent academic writings have suggested that the primary purpose of contract remedies is to provide optimal performance incentives, particularly among commercial and sophisticated parties, or to deter socially undesirable behavior under the contract. Close inspection of the remedial doctrines, however, clearly reveals that compensation is the principal aim of relief, specific and substitutional.

Remedies for breach assume a chiefly compensatory purpose, which isn't to say that is their only function. A remedy designed to compensate harm may also deter breach and encourage reliance. It is easy to see the primary compensatory design from a payment of money following a breach of contract. Less apparent, but no less germane to the American remedial approach, is the point that specific relief also seeks primarily to compensate promisees for breach rather than to compel promisors to perform. Traditionally, it was only when conventional legal remedies for breach of contract failed, or when monetary relief was otherwise deemed inadequate, that equity's specific relief kicked in—itself then merely a substitute for the inadequacy of money damages.

Courts of equity also issued remedial orders over matters for which they had original or exclusive jurisdiction, such as claims arising in trust law. However, for claims concerning breach of contract, equity by and large played a supplemental role, serving as a fail-safe when the primary system of law was unable to offer an adequate remedy. It was a compromise reached over time. "When, during the long jurisdictional struggle between the two systems of courts, some means of accommodation was needed, an adequacy test was developed to prevent the chancellor from encroaching on the powers of the common law judges. Equity would stay its hand if the remedy of an award of damages at law was 'adequate.' To this test was added the gloss that damages were ordinarily adequate—a gloss encouraged by the philosophy of free enterprise with its confidence that a market economy ought to enable the injured party to arrange a substitute transaction." See Farnsworth on Contracts § 12.4, at 162–66.

Courts today continue to observe the historical compromise between legal and equitable remedies for breach of contract, even though the separate courts of law and equity have been largely, but not entirely, merged. Contracts for the sale of real property, for instance, remain subject to specific enforcement, an exception to the presumption of compensatory payment long ago granted because English tradition viewed land as so distinctive and singular that money damages were treated as categorically inadequate. Family heirlooms constituted another traditional exception. At the same time, new categories, such as output and requirement contracts, are said to reflect a modern trend favoring an "extension of specific relief at the expense of the traditional primacy of damages." Id. This trend is identifiable in the next case, Campbell Soup Co. v. Wentz, which we first encountered on p. 633, in the materials on unconscionability.

In the excerpt of the case below, Judge Goodrich's expression of the modern trend toward liberalizing specific performance is quite apparent. Nonetheless, the Court refused to grant an order of equitable relief. "The reason" he offered for denying "specific performance is found in the contract itself. We think it is too hard a bargain and too one-sided an agreement to entitle the plaintiff to relief in a court of conscience." 172 F.2d 80, 83. Here we see another traditional restriction on the availability of equitable relief, conveyed in the ancient equitable maxims: "one who seeks equity must do equity" and "one who comes into equity must come with clean hands." Note, however, that this restriction is imposed by the practice of equity itself, and not as a result of a compromise with law or public policy. As you read the cases in the next section, attend to the articulated and underlying policies leading the courts to award or deny specific relief.

SECTION 1. SPECIFIC RELIEF

Campbell Soup Co. v. Wentz

United States Court of Appeals, Third Circuit, 1948.
172 F.2d 80.

■ GOODRICH, CIRCUIT JUDGE. These are appeals from judgments of the District Court denying equitable relief to the buyer under a contract for the sale of carrots. The defendants in No. 9648 are the contract sellers. The defendant in No. 9649 is the second purchaser of part of the carrots which are the subject matter of the contract.

The transactions which raise the issues may be briefly summarized. On June 21, 1947, Campbell Soup Company (Campbell), a New Jersey corporation, entered into a written contract with George B. Wentz and Harry T. Wentz, who are Pennsylvania farmers, for delivery by the Wentzes to Campbell of all the Chantenay red cored carrots to be grown on fifteen acres of the Wentz farm during the 1947 season.

Where the contract was entered into does not appear. The contract provides, however, for delivery of the carrots at the Campbell plant in Camden, New Jersey. The prices specified in the contract ranged from

$23 to $30 per ton according to the time of delivery. The contract price for January, 1948 was $30 a ton.

The Wentzes harvested approximately 100 tons of carrots from the fifteen acres covered by the contract. Early in January, 1948, they told a Campbell representative that they would not deliver their carrots at the contract price. The market price at that time was at least $90 per ton, and Chantenay red cored carrots were virtually unobtainable. The Wentzes then sold approximately 62 tons of their carrots to the defendant Lojeski, a neighboring farmer. Lojeski resold about 58 tons on the open market, approximately half to Campbell and the balance to other purchasers.

On January 9, 1948, Campbell, suspecting that Lojeski was selling it "contract carrots," refused to purchase any more, and instituted these suits against the Wentz brothers and Lojeski to enjoin further sale of the contract carrots to others, and to compel specific performance of the contract. The trial court denied equitable relief. We agree with the result reached, but on a different ground from that relied upon by the District Court.

[The court said that the form of relief was for it to decide, as a federal court. Yet it noted that the federal rule on the point did not appear to differ from that of either state whose law might be applied—New Jersey or Pennsylvania.] A party may have specific performance of a contract for the sale of chattels if the legal remedy is inadequate. Inadequacy of the legal remedy is necessarily a matter to be determined by an examination of the facts in each particular instance.

We think that on the question of adequacy of the legal remedy the case is one appropriate for specific performance. It was expressly found that at the time of the trial it was "virtually impossible to obtain Chantenay carrots in the open market." This Chantenay carrot is one which the plaintiff uses in large quantities, furnishing the seed to the growers with whom it makes contracts. It was not claimed that in nutritive value it is any better than other types of carrots. Its blunt shape makes it easier to handle in processing. And its color and texture differ from other varieties. The color is brighter than other carrots. The trial court found that the plaintiff failed to establish what proportion of its carrots is used for the production of soup stock and what proportion is used as identifiable physical ingredients in its soups. We do not think lack of proof on that point is material. It did appear that the plaintiff uses carrots in fifteen of its twenty-one soups. It also appeared that it uses these Chantenay carrots diced in some of them and that the appearance is uniform. The preservation of uniformity in appearance in a food article marketed throughout the country and sold under the manufacturer's name is a matter of considerable commercial significance and one which is properly considered in determining whether a substitute ingredient is just as good as the original.

With this in mind we have carefully reviewed the very complete record on appeal and conclude that the trial court should grant the injunctive relief prayed. We are satisfied that this case falls within that category in which specific performance should be ordered as a matter of right.

Amoco contends that four of the requirements for specific performance have not been met. Its claims are: (1) there is no mutuality of remedy in the contract; (2) the remedy of specific performance would be difficult for the court to administer without constant and long-continued supervision; (3) the contract is indefinite and uncertain; and (4) the remedy at law available to Laclede is adequate. The first three contentions have little or no merit and do not detain us for long.

There is simply no requirement in the law that both parties be mutually entitled to the remedy of specific performance in order that one of them be given that remedy by the court.

While a court may refuse to grant specific performance where such a decree would require constant and long-continued court supervision, this is merely a discretionary rule of decision which is frequently ignored when the public interest is involved.

Here the public interest in providing propane to the retail customers is manifest, while any supervision required will be far from onerous.

Section 370 of the Second Restatement of Contracts (1932) provides:

> Specific enforcement will not be decreed unless the terms of the contract are so expressed that the court can determine with reasonable certainty what is the duty of each party and the conditions under which performance is due.

We believe these criteria have been satisfied here. As discussed in part I of this opinion, as to all developments for which a supplemental agreement has been signed, Amoco is to supply all the propane which is reasonably foreseeably required, while Laclede is to purchase the required propane from Amoco and pay the contract price therefor. The parties have disagreed over what is meant by "Wood River Area Posted Price" in the agreement, but the district court can and should determine with reasonable certainty what the parties intended by this term and should mold its decree, if necessary accordingly. Likewise, the fact that the agreement does not have a definite time of duration is not fatal since the evidence established that the last subdivision should be converted to natural gas in 10 to 15 years. This sets a reasonable time limit on performance and the district court can and should mold the final decree to reflect this testimony.

It is axiomatic that specific performance will not be ordered when the party claiming breach of contract has an adequate remedy at law. Jamison Coal & Coke Co. v. Goltra, 143 F.2d 889, 894 (8th Cir.), cert. denied, 323 U.S. 769 (1944). This is especially true when the contract involves personal property as distinguished from real estate.

However, in Missouri, as elsewhere, specific performance may be ordered even though personalty is involved in the "proper circumstances." Mo. Rev. Stat. § 400.2–716(1); Restatement of Contracts, supra, § 361. And a remedy at law adequate to defeat the grant of specific performance "must be as certain, prompt, complete, and efficient to attain the ends of justice as a decree of specific performance." National Marking Mach. Co. v. Triumph Mfg. Co., 13 F.2d 6, 9 (8th Cir. 1926). Accord, Snip v. City of Lamar, 239 Mo. App. 824, 201 S.W.2d 790, 798 (1947).

One of the leading Missouri cases allowing specific performance of a contract relating to personalty because the remedy at law was inadequate is Boeving v. Vandover, 240 Mo. App. 117, 218 S.W.2d 175, 178 (1949). In that case the plaintiff sought specific performance of a contract in which the defendant had promised to sell him an automobile. At that time (near the end of and shortly after World War II) new cars were hard to come by, and the court held that specific performance was a proper remedy since a new car "could not be obtained elsewhere except at considerable expense, trouble or loss, which cannot be estimated in advance."

We are satisfied that Laclede has brought itself within this practical approach taken by the Missouri courts. As Amoco points out, Laclede has propane immediately available to it under other contracts with other suppliers. And the evidence indicates that at the present time propane is readily available on the open market. However, this analysis ignores the fact that the contract involved in this lawsuit is for a long-term supply of propane to these subdivisions. The other two contracts under which Laclede obtains the gas will remain in force only until March 31, 1977, and April 1, 1981, respectively; and there is no assurance that Laclede will be able to receive any propane under them after that time. Also it is unclear as to whether or not Laclede can use the propane obtained under these contracts to supply the Jefferson County subdivisions, since they were originally entered into to provide Laclede with propane with which to "shave" its natural gas supply during peak demand periods. Additionally, there was uncontradicted expert testimony that Laclede probably could not find another supplier of propane willing to enter into a long-term contract such as the Amoco agreement, given the uncertain future of worldwide energy supplies. And, even if Laclede could obtain supplies of propane for the affected developments through its present contracts or newly negotiated ones, it would still face considerable expense and trouble which cannot be estimated in advance in making arrangements for its distribution to the subdivisions.

Specific performance is the proper remedy in this situation, and it should be granted by the district court.

[Reversed and remanded.]

NOTES

(1) *The Code and Specific Performance.* Comments 1 and 2 to UCC § 2–716 say: "[W]ithout intending to impair in any way the exercise of the court's sound discretion in the matter, this Article seeks to further a more liberal attitude than some courts have shown in connection with the specific performance of contracts of sale. In view of this Article's emphasis on the commercial feasibility of replacement, a new concept of what are 'unique' goods is introduced under this section. Specific performance is no longer limited to goods which are already specific or ascertained at the time of contracting. The test of uniqueness under this section must be made in terms of the total situation which characterizes the contract. Output and requirements contracts involving a particular or peculiarly available source or market present today the typical commercial specific performance situation, as contrasted with contracts for the sale of heirlooms or priceless works of art which were usually involved in the older cases. However, uniqueness is not the sole basis of the remedy under this section for the relief may also be granted 'in other proper circumstances'."

In the case of a long-term output or requirements contract, might the difficulty of proving damages amount to "other proper circumstances" even if there is no "particular or peculiarly available source or market"? If Laclede were limited to damages, how would its damages be calculated under the Code? In Eastern Rolling Mill Co. v. Michlovitz, 145 A. 378 (Md. 1929), a five-year output contract for scrap steel was broken by the seller in the first year. Part of the court's justification for ordering specific performance was that any estimate of damages "would be speculative and conjectured, and not, therefore, compensatory. To substitute damages by guess for due performance of contract could only be because 'there's no equity stirring.'"

(2) *Another Form of Specific Relief.* In addition to the possibility of specific relief in the form of a decree of specific performance under UCC § 2–716(1), a buyer of goods may in some circumstances also obtain specific relief through an action to replevy the goods under UCC § 2–716(3).

A seller may in some circumstances obtain what amounts to specific relief through an action for the price under UCC § 2–709(1)(b). Can the seller do so if it can resell? What would you advise an aggrieved seller to do following breach in order to lay the foundation for a possible action for the price under this section?

Northern Delaware Industrial Development Corp. v. E.W. Bliss Co.

Court of Chancery of Delaware, 1968.
245 A.2d 431.

Bliss, a general contractor, contracted to modernize the plant of the Phoenix Steel Corporation, for $27,500,000. [Phoenix was, along with Northern Delaware, a party to the contract and a plaintiff in the case.] The plant was spread over a 60-acre site. Work did not progress as rapidly as contemplated in the contract, and Phoenix sought an order to have Bliss put 300 more workers on the job, as required by the contract, to make up a full second shift during the period that one of Phoenix's mills had to be shut down because of the work. The court denied specific performance.

■ MARVEL, VICE CHANCELLOR. It is not that a court of equity is without jurisdiction in a proper case to order the completion of an expressly designed and largely completed construction contract, particularly where the undertaking is tied in with a contract for the sale of land and the construction in question is largely finished. The point is that a court of equity should not order specific performance of any building contract in a situation in which it would be impractical to carry out such an order, unless there are special circumstances or the public interest is directly involved. I conclude that to grant specific performance would be inappropriate in view of the imprecision of the contract provision relied upon and the impracticability if not impossibility of effective enforcement by the Court of a mandatory order designed to keep a specific number of men on the job at the site of a steel mill which is undergoing extensive modernization and expansion. If plaintiffs have sustained loss as a result of actionable building delays, they may, at an appropriate time, resort to law for a fixing of their claimed damages. [On a motion for reargument, Phoenix argued that it sought only an order "directing the performance of a ministerial act, namely the hiring by defendant of more workers." The court denied the motion, relying on "the well established principle that performance of a contract for personal services, even of a unique nature, will not be affirmatively and directly enforced."]

NOTES

(1) *Distinctions.* Consider the remark of Chancellor Walworth in denying a decree of specific performance against an opera singer: "I am not aware that any officer of this court has that perfect knowledge of the Italian language, or possesses that exquisite sensibility in the auricular nerve, which is necessary to understand and to enjoy with a proper zest the peculiar beauties of the Italian opera, so fascinating to the fashionable world." De Rivafinoli v. Corsetti, 4 Paige Ch. 264, 270 (N.Y. 1833). Is this point distinguishable from that in *Northern Delaware*?

Courts have shown increased willingness to order specific performance of construction contracts. In most of these cases, however, the construction was to take place on the defendant's land with a conveyance or lease to follow. See, *e.g.*, Floyd v. Watson, 254 S.E.2d 687, 690 (W.Va. 1979), where the court noted that the agreement "includes a provision for conveyance of land, and therefore specific performance is proper." *Cf.* City Stores Co. v. Ammerman, 266 F.Supp. 766 (D.D.C. 1967), *aff'd*, 394 F.2d 950 (D.C.Cir. 1968).

(2) *Specific Performance in Arbitration.* Recall the inquiry at p. 331, concerning whether an arbitral award—which would not survive judicial scrutiny if the court sought to issue the award directly—may nonetheless be

enforceable in courts. Now suppose that Bliss and Phoenix had included in their construction contract the American Arbitration Association's arbitration clause. Would the court have enforced an arbitral award granting the relief that the court would have refused if it had heard the actual case rather than the arbitrators? See Sarath Sanga, *A New Strategy for Regulating Arbitration*, 113 Nw. U. L. Rev. 1121, 1144–1149 (2019). The New York Court of Appeals held that such an award was enforceable in Grayson-Robinson Stores, Inc. v. Iris Construction Corp., 168 N.E.2d 377 (N.Y. 1960).

Walgreen Co. v. Sara Creek Property Co.

United States Court of Appeals, Seventh Circuit, 1992.
966 F.2d 273.

[For decades, Walgreen, a "discount" chain, had operated a pharmacy in the Southgate Mall in Milwaukee. Under its lease, the landlord, Sara Creek, promised not to lease space in the mall to another store operating a pharmacy. In 1990, fearful that its "anchor [largest] tenant" was about to close its store, Sara Creek informed Walgreen that it intended to buy out that tenant and install in its place a store operated by Phar-Mor, a "deep discount" chain that would contain a pharmacy. Its entrance was to be within a couple of hundred feet of Walgreen's. Walgreen sought an injunction against Sara Creek. After a hearing, the trial judge entered a permanent injunction against Sara Creek's letting the premises to Phar-Mor until Walgreen's lease expired. At the hearing Sara Creek's expert witnesses had testified that Walgreen's damages could be readily estimated, whereas Walgreen's employees had testified to the contrary, asserting among other reasons that those damages included intangibles such as good will. Sara Creek appealed.]

■ POSNER, CIRCUIT JUDGE. Sara Creek reminds us that damages are the norm in breach of contract as in other cases. Many breaches, it points out, are "efficient" in the sense that they allow resources to be moved into a more valuable use. Perhaps this is one—the value of Phar-Mor's occupancy of the anchor premises may exceed the cost to Walgreen of facing increased competition. If so, society will be better off if Walgreen is paid its damages, equal to that cost, and Phar-Mor is allowed to move in rather than being kept out by an injunction. That is why injunctions are not granted as a matter of course, but only when the plaintiff's damages remedy is inadequate. Northern Indiana Public Service Co. v. Carbon County Coal Co., 799 F.2d 265, 279 (7th Cir. 1986). Walgreen's is not, Sara Creek argues; the projection of business losses due to increased competition is a routine exercise in calculation. Damages representing either the present value of lost future profits or (what should be the equivalent, the diminution in the value of the leasehold) have either been awarded or deemed the proper remedy in a number of reported cases for breach of an exclusivity clause in a shopping-center lease. Why, Sara Creek asks, should they not be adequate here?

The benefits of substituting an injunction for damages are twofold. First, it shifts the burden of determining the cost of the defendant's conduct from the court to the parties. If it is true that Walgreen's damages are smaller than the gain to Sara Creek from allowing a second pharmacy into the shopping mall, then there must be a price for dissolving the injunction that will make both parties better off. Thus, the effect of upholding the injunction would be to substitute for the costly processes of forensic fact determination the less costly processes of private negotiation. Second, a premise of our free-market system, and the lesson of experience here and abroad as well, is that prices and costs are more accurately determined by the market than by government. A battle of experts is a less reliable method of determining the actual cost to Walgreen of facing new competition than negotiations between Walgreen and Sara Creek over the price at which Walgreen would feel adequately compensated for having to face that competition.

That is the benefit side of injunctive relief but there is a cost side as well. Many injunctions require continuing supervision by the court, and that is costly. Some injunctions are problematic because they impose costs on third parties. A more subtle cost of injunctive relief arises from the situation that economists call "bilateral monopoly," in which two parties can deal only with each other: the situation that an injunction creates. The sole seller of widgets selling to the sole buyer of that product would be an example. But so will be the situation confronting Walgreen and Sara Creek if the injunction is upheld. Walgreen can "sell" its injunctive right only to Sara Creek, and Sara Creek can "buy" Walgreen's surrender of its right to enjoin the leasing of the anchor tenant's space to Phar-Mor only from Walgreen. The lack of alternatives in bilateral monopoly creates a bargaining range, and the costs of negotiating to a point within that range may be high. Suppose the cost to Walgreen of facing the competition of Phar-Mor at the Southgate Mall would be $1 million, and the benefit to Sara Creek of leasing to Phar-Mor would be $2 million. Then at any price between those figures for a waiver of Walgreen's injunctive right both parties would be better off, and we expect parties to bargain around a judicial assignment of legal rights if the assignment is inefficient. R.H. Coase, "The Problem of Social Cost," 3 J. Law & Econ. 1 (1960). But each of the parties would like to engross as much of the bargaining range as possible—Walgreen to press the price toward $2 million, Sara Creek to depress it toward $1 million. With so much at stake, both parties will have an incentive to devote substantial resources of time and money to the negotiation process. The process may even break down, if one or both parties want to create for future use a reputation as a hard bargainer; and if it does break down, the injunction will have brought about an inefficient result. All these are in one form or another costs of the injunctive process that can be avoided by substituting damages.

The costs and benefits of the damages remedy are the mirror of those of the injunctive remedy. The damages remedy avoids the cost of continuing supervision and third-party effects, and the cost of bilateral monopoly as well. It imposes costs of its own, however, in the form of diminished accuracy in the determination of value, on the one hand, and of the parties' expenditures on preparing and presenting evidence of damages, and the time of the court in evaluating the evidence, on the other.

The weighing up of all these costs and benefits is the analytical procedure that is or at least should be employed by a judge asked to enter a permanent injunction, with the understanding that if the balance is even the injunction should be withheld. The judge is not required to explicate every detail of the analysis and he did not do so here, but as long as we are satisfied that his approach is broadly consistent with a proper analysis we shall affirm; and we are satisfied here. The determination of Walgreen's damages would have been costly in forensic resources and inescapably inaccurate. The lease had ten years to run. So Walgreen would have had to project its sales revenues and costs over the next ten years, and then project the impact on those figures of Phar-Mor's competition, and then discount that impact to present value. All but the last step would have been fraught with uncertainty.

Affirmed.

NOTES

(1) *Preliminary Injunctive Relief.* In *Van Wagner*, the Special Term denied Van Wagner's motion for a preliminary injunction, because it concluded he was not likely to succeed on the merits. In determining whether to grant a preliminary injunction courts consider, *inter alia*, the plaintiff's likelihood of ultimate success on the merits and the degree to which failure to grant injunctive relief will cause the plaintiff irreparable harm, and weigh that against the defendant's likelihood of success and the irreparable harm for the defendant from granting the injunction. For a formalization of this this balancing by Judge Posner, see American Hospital Supply Corp. v. Hospital Products Ltd., 780 F.2d 589 (7th Cir. 1986). What other factors might a court consider in awarding or denying a preliminary injunction? See John Leubsdorf, *The Standard for Preliminary Injunctions*, 91 Harv. L. Rev. 525 (1978); Richard R.W. Brooks & Warren Schwartz, *Legal Uncertainty, Economic Efficiency, and the Preliminary Injunction Doctrine*, 58 Stan. L. Rev. 381 (2005).

(2) *Weighing of Harms from Permanent Injunctions.* In *Walgreen*, Judge Posner described the weighing of costs and benefits in granting a permanent injunction. Does he consider the competing irreparable harms, if any, to Walgreen and Sara Creek? Should he? On the distinct standards used for evaluating permanent and preliminary injunctions, see Douglas Laycock, *The Death of the Irreparable Injury Rule,* 103 Harv. L. Rev. 687 (1990).

SECTION 2.   MEASURING EXPECTATION

The usual remedy for breach of contract is an award of damages, typically based on the *expectation interest*. Recall from Chapter 1 that an award of expectation damages is a sum of money that will, to the extent that money can, put the promisee in the position he would have been in had the promise been performed. The promisee is then said to have received "the benefit of the bargain" or to have been "made whole."

Although this is an intuitive and simple principle, its practical implementation can be challenging. Unlike restitution damages (based on the *actual* benefit the promisee has conferred on the promisor) or reliance damages (based on the *actual* amount the promisee has expended in reliance on the promise), expectation damages pose a counterfactual difficulty: What value would the promisee have received had the breach not occurred? Finding a monetary equivalent to this value is straightforward in some instances, "as, for example, where the injured party has simply had to pay an additional amount to arrange a substitute transaction and can be adequately compensated by damages based on the amount." Restatement § 347, cmt. *a*. Similarly, where the promisee's expected advantage consists largely or exclusively of the realization of profit, as is the case for most commercially significant exchanges, the expectation interest can be expressed in money with some assurance. This is particularly true in well-defined or "thick" markets, where there are many buyers and sellers trading over particular goods.

Cases of defective, as distinguished from merely incomplete, performance often present challenging remedial questions. If the breach consists merely of incomplete performance, the injured party can usually arrange to have someone else complete the contract at less than the loss in value to the injured party. Again, this is especially common in thick markets. "Cover" or "resale" are the names given by UCC Article 2 to such arrangements, where a buyer, for instance, finds another party to provide the sought-after performance, or where a seller finds another buyer after the first breaches. Special difficulties regarding cover and resale are taken up later in this section, but observe now that much of the difficulty in determining the monetary award after cover or resale is removed by the affirmative act of the injured party. Proof of damages tends to be more easily established because cover and resale remedies are determined retrospectively, which is to say after expenditures of money, time, and effort have been made.

When a promisee does not or cannot act affirmatively to address a defective or incomplete performance, the court must find a monetary award to supplement the received nonconforming performance in order to make the injured party whole. We are returned to the counterfactual challenge of determining what value a promisee would have appreciated had the breach not occurred. Courts often look to the difference in market value between that which was contracted for and that which was received as a useful approximation of the expectation ideal, particularly where a transaction occurs in thick markets. In principle, of course, the expectation interest is based on that of the particular promisee at hand, quite without regard to that of the hypothetical reasonable promisee, and depends on the particular promisee's unique circumstances or those of its enterprise. Markets merely facilitate the identification of a promisee's expectation interest, either because the market approximates the promisee's interests well or because it allows the promisee to realize that interest through a substitute transaction.

Market value, however, is neither the sole nor often the best measure of the expectation interest. Competing with the difference in market value measure of expectancy is the cost of completion measure, which is based on the costs of completing or curing the partial or defective performance. Several cases are presented below that highlight the distinctions between the "difference in value" and "cost of completion" proxies of the expectation award. It is important to emphasize, however, as Lord Mustill did, that these "are not two alternative measures of damage, at opposite poles, but only one: namely the loss truly suffered by the promisee. In some cases the loss cannot be fairly measured except by reference to the full cost of repairing the deficiency in performance. In others, and in particular those where the contract is designed to fulfill a purely commercial purpose, the loss will very often consist only of the monetary detriment brought about by the breach of contract." Ruxley Electronics & Construction, Ltd. v. Forsyth, [1995] 3 W.L.R. 118 (H.L.). The aim is always, and essentially, how best to measure a promisee's expectation interest.

In pursuit of this aim, Restatement § 347 suggests three broad factors for measuring a party's expectation interest:

"(a) the loss in the value to him of the other party's performance caused by its failure or deficiency, plus

(b) any other loss, including incidental or consequential loss, caused by the breach, *less*

(c) any cost or other loss that he has avoided by not having to perform."

Consider these factors in turn. First, the breach may cause the injured party a loss by limiting or eliminating the expected return, or value, of performance itself. The difference between the value to the injured party of the performance that should have been received and the value to that party of what, if anything, was actually received is the injured party's *loss in value* (a).

Second, the breach may cause the injured party loss other than *loss in value,* such as physical harm to that party's person or property or expenses incurred in an attempt to salvage the transaction after breach. This residual category is the injured party's *other loss* (b).

Any breach, regardless of its seriousness, may result in *loss in value* (a) and in *other loss* (b). A serious breach may give the injured party a choice between continuing performance and stopping performance and treating the contract as terminated.

If the injured party chooses to stop performance and treat the contract as terminated, the breach may affect it in a third way. The breach may have a beneficial effect on the injured party by saving that party further expense that would have been incurred had performance continued. Moreover, the breach may have an additional effect on the injured party by allowing that party to avoid some loss by salvaging and reallocating some or all of the resources that it otherwise would have had to devote to performance of the contract. These savings are the injured party's *costs and other loss avoided* (c) and should be subtracted from any expectation damage award that a breaching promisor would have to pay.[b] Hence the general measure of damages is the sum of these factors, which can be expressed as a simple formula:

Damages = (a) loss in value + (b) other loss − (c) cost and loss avoided.

Hold aside *other loss* (b) for a moment and focus on the two remaining factors in the equation above—*loss in value* (a) and *cost and loss avoided* (c). Estimation of *loss in value* and *cost and loss avoided* pose different challenges depending on which party is in breach. In most agreements, one of the parties (say, a buyer) is simply required to pay money while the other party (say, a seller) is required to furnish goods, land, or services in return for a money payment. When the seller is the injured party, and the breach consists of the buyer's failure to pay, the difficulty largely lies in the determination of the seller's *cost and loss avoided,* since its *loss in value* is simply the amount of money that the buyer has failed to pay. When the seller is in breach, the difficulty lies in the determination of the buyer's *loss in value,* since its *cost and loss avoided* is simply the amount of money that it has not yet paid.

Now consider the *other loss* category, which consists mainly of incidental and consequential losses. "Incidental losses include costs incurred in a reasonable effort, whether successful or not, to avoid loss, as where a party [*e.g.*, a buyer] pays brokerage fees in arranging or attempting to arrange a substitute transaction." Restatement § 347, comment *c*. Typically, for a seller of goods, they include costs incurred in halting delivery and in transporting, housing and caring for goods after breach by the recipient. See, *e.g.*, UCC § 2–710 (Seller's Incidental Damages). Consequential losses encompass, but are not limited to, harm to persons or property as a result of breach. As between the buyer and

---

[b]   It may help in understanding the distinction between *cost avoided* and *loss avoided* to imagine a contract for the sale of two products to be manufactured by the seller. Suppose that the buyer repudiates after the seller has manufactured one of the products. The saving that results when the seller stops production of the second product is the seller's *cost avoided*. The saving that results when the seller sells the first product to another buyer is the seller's *loss avoided.*

the seller, one might expect consequential losses to be suffered more likely by the former.

The cases that follow illustrate these basic factors and how they operate in the context of conventional measures and components of expectation damages, including lost profits, difference in value, cost of completion, cover and resale damages among other considerations. Our first case focuses on lost profits with an additional and important complication of how to treat overhead costs in this measure of the expectation interest.

———

Lost Profits

The venerated British economist John Maynard Keynes once famously quipped that "[i]n the long run we are all dead." *A Tract on Monetary Reform* (1923). The more prosaic distinction economists typically draw between the long run and the short run involves the variability of inputs used by firms in producing goods and services. Inputs, also called factors of production, include such things as raw materials, machinery, and labor. The short run is defined by economists as the period during which at least one input is fixed—that is, not variable. A factory is a common example of a short-run fixed input. With enough time, or in the long run, new factories may be built and existing ones modified, but in the short run a factory is not variable.

The costs associated with fixed inputs are called, uninspiringly, fixed costs. Those costs must be borne before any goods can be produced. For example, a factory must be established before any goods can be manufactured. How then do these fixed costs relate to the profits expected from subsequent agreements to produce goods? This question is thoughtfully taken up in the next case. The opinion introduces the lost-profits measure of expectation damages. Lost profits are simply the profits that a firm would have earned had the breach not occurred. In commercial transactions, where parties are largely motivated by expected profits, lost profits are excellent approximations of the *expectation interest*; the connection between profits and expectancy is simple and direct. But there's often a devil in the details. Recall the observation above that when a seller is the injured party, the difficulty in determining damages lies largely in the estimation of its *cost and loss avoided* (c). How do fixed costs figure in this calculation?

Vitex Manufacturing Corp. v. Caribtex Corp.

United States Court of Appeals, Third Circuit, 1967.
377 F.2d 795.

■ STALEY, CHIEF JUDGE. This is an appeal by Caribtex Corporation from a judgment of the District Court of the Virgin Islands finding Caribtex in breach of a contract entered into with Vitex Manufacturing Company, Ltd., and awarding $21,114 plus interest to Vitex for loss of profits. The only substantial question raised by Caribtex is whether it was error for the district court, sitting without a jury, not to consider overhead as part of Vitex's costs in determining the amount of profits lost. We conclude that under the facts presented, the district court was not compelled to consider Vitex's overhead costs, and we will affirm the judgment.

Before discussing the details of the controversy between the parties, it will be helpful to briefly describe the peculiar legal setting in which this suit arose. At the time of the events in question, there were high tariff barriers to the importation of foreign wool products. However, under § 301 of the Tariff Act of 1930, 19 U.S.C.A. § 1301a, repealed but the provision continued under Revised Tariff Schedules, 19 U.S.C.A. § 1202, note 3(a)(i)(ii) (1965), if such goods were imported into the Virgin Islands and were processed in some manner so that their finished value exceeded their importation value by at least 50%, then the high tariffs to importation into the continental United States would be avoided. Even after the processing, the foreign wool enjoyed a price advantage over domestic products so that the business flourished. However, to keep the volume of this business at such levels that Congress would not be stirred to change the law, the Virgin Islands Legislature imposed "quotas" on persons engaging in processing, limiting their output. 33 V.I.C. § 504 (Supp. 1966).

Vitex was engaged in the business of chemically shower-proofing imported cloth so that it could be imported duty-free into the United States. For this purpose, Vitex maintained a plant in the Virgin Islands and was entitled to process a specific quantity of material under the Virgin Islands quota system. Caribtex was in the business of importing cloth into the islands, securing its processing, and exporting it to the United States.

In the fall of 1963, Vitex found itself with an unused portion of its quota but no customers, and Vitex closed its plant. Caribtex acquired some Italian wool and subsequently negotiations for a processing contract were conducted between the principals of the respective companies in New York City. Though the record below is clouded with differing versions of the negotiations and the alleged final terms, the trial court found upon substantial evidence in the record that the parties did enter into a contract in which Vitex agreed to process 125,000 yards of Caribtex's woolen material at a price of 26 [25?] cents per yard.

Vitex proceeded to re-open its Virgin Islands plant, ordered the necessary chemicals, recalled its work force and made all the necessary preparations to perform its end of the bargain. However, no goods were forthcoming from Caribtex, despite repeated demands by Vitex, apparently because Caribtex was unsure that the processed wool would be entitled to duty-free treatment by the customs officials. Vitex subsequently brought this suit to recover the profits lost through Caribtex's breach.

Vitex alleged, and the trial court found, that its gross profits for processing said material under the contract would have been $31,250 and that its costs would have been $10,136, leaving Vitex's damages for loss of profits at $21,114. On appeal, Caribtex asserted numerous objections to the detailed computation of lost profits. While the record below is sometimes confusing, we conclude that the trial court had substantial evidence to support its findings on damages. It must be remembered that the difficulty in exactly ascertaining Vitex's costs is due to Caribtex's wrongful conduct in repudiating the contract before performance by Vitex. Caribtex will not be permitted to benefit by the uncertainty it has caused. Thus, since there was a sufficient basis in the record to support the trial court's determination of substantial damages, we will not set aside its judgment. Stentor Elec. Mfg. Co. v. Klaxon Co., 115 F.2d 268 (C.A.3, 1940), rev'd other grounds 313 U.S. 487 (1941); 5 Williston, Contracts § 1345 (rev. ed. 1937).

Caribtex first raised the issue at the oral argument of this appeal that the trial court erred by disregarding Vitex's overhead expenses in determining lost profits. In general, overhead ". . . may be said to include broadly the continuous expenses of the business, irrespective of the outlay on a particular contract." Grand Trunk W.R.R. Co. v. H.W. Nelson Co., 116 F.2d 823, 839 (C.A.6, 1941). Such expenses would include executive and clerical salaries, property taxes, general administration expenses, etc. Although Vitex did not expressly seek recovery for overhead, if a portion of these fixed expenses should be allocated as costs to the Caribtex contract, then under the judgment of the district court Vitex tacitly recovered these expenses as part of its damages for lost profits, and the damages should be reduced accordingly. Presumably, the portion to be allocated to costs would be a pro rata share of Vitex's annual overhead according to the volume of business Vitex would have done over the year if Caribtex had not breached the contract.

Although there is authority to the contrary, we feel that the better view is that normally, in a claim for lost profits, overhead should be treated as a part of gross profits and recoverable as damages, and should not be considered as part of the seller's costs. A number of cases hold that since overhead expenses are not affected by the performance of the particular contract, there should be no need to deduct them in computing lost profits. E.g., Oakland California Towel Co. v. Sivils, 52 Cal.App.2d 517, 520, 126 P.2d 651, 652 (1942); Jessup & Moore Paper Co. v. Bryant Paper Co., 297 Pa. 483, 147 A. 519, 524 (1929); Annot., 3 A.L.R.3d 689 (1965) (collecting cases on both sides of the controversy). The theory of these cases is that the seller is entitled to recover losses incurred and gains prevented in excess of savings made possible, Restatement, Contracts § 329 (made part of the law of the Virgin Islands, 1 V.I.C. § 4);

since overhead is fixed and nonporformance of the contract produced no overhead cost savings, no deduction from profits should result.

The soundness of the rule is exemplified by this case. Before negotiations began between Vitex and Caribtex, Vitex had reached a lull in business activity and had closed its plant. If Vitex had entered into no other contracts for the rest of the year, the profitability of its operations would have been determined by deducting its production costs and overhead from gross receipts yielded in previous transactions. When this opportunity arose to process Caribtex's wool, the only additional expenses Vitex would incur would be those of re-opening its plant and the direct costs of processing, such as labor, chemicals and fuel oil. Overhead would have remained the same whether or not Vitex and Caribtex entered their contract and whether or not Vitex actually processed Caribtex's goods. Since this overhead remained constant, in no way attributable-to or affected-by the Caribtex contract, it would be improper to consider it as a cost of Vitex's performance to be deducted from the gross proceeds of the Caribtex contract.

However, Caribtex may argue that this view ignores modern accounting principles, and that overhead is as much a cost of production as other expenses. It is true that successful businessmen must set their prices at sufficient levels to recoup all their expenses, including overhead, and to gain profits. Thus, the price the businessman should charge on each transaction could be thought of as that price necessary to yield a pro rata portion of the company's fixed overhead, the direct costs associated with production, and a "clear" profit. Doubtless this type of calculation is used by businessmen and their accountants. Pacific Portland Cement Co. v. Food Mach. & Chem. Corp., 178 F.2d 541 (C.A.9, 1949). However, because it is useful for planning purposes to allocate a portion of overhead to each transaction, it does not follow that this allocate share of fixed overhead should be considered a cost factor in the computation of lost profits on individual transactions.

First, it must be recognized that the pro rata allocation of overhead costs is only an analytical construct. In a similar manner one could allocate a pro rata share of the company's advertising cost, taxes and/or charitable gifts. The point is that while these items all are paid from the proceeds of the business, they do not normally bear such a direct relationship to any individual transaction to be considered a cost in ascertaining lost profits.

Secondly, even were we to recognize the allocation of overhead as proper in this case, we should uphold the tacit award of overhead expense to Vitex as a "loss incurred." Conditioned Air Corp. v. Rock Island Motor Transit Co., 253 Iowa 961, cert. denied, 371 U.S. 825 (1962). By the very nature of this allocation process, as the number of transactions over which overhead can be spread becomes smaller, each transaction must bear a greater portion or allocate share of the fixed overhead cost. Suppose a company has fixed overhead of $10,000 and engages in five similar transactions; then the receipts of each transaction would bear $2000 of overhead expense. If the company is now forced to spread this $10,000 over only four transactions, then the overhead expense per transaction will rise to $2500, significantly reducing the profitability of the four remaining transactions. Thus, where the contract is between businessmen familiar with commercial practices, as here, the breaching party should reasonably foresee that his breach will not only cause a loss of "clear" profit, but also a loss in that the profitability of other transactions will be reduced. Resolute Ins. Co. v. Percy Jones, Inc., 198 F.2d 309 (C.A.10, 1952); Cf. In re Kellett Aircraft Corp., 191 F.2d 231 (C.A.3, 1951). Therefore, this loss is within the contemplation of "losses caused and gains prevented," and overhead should be considered to a compensable item of damage.

Significantly, the Uniform Commercial Code, adopted in the Virgin Islands, 11A V.I.C. § 1–101 et seq., and in virtually every state today, provides for the recovery of overhead in circumstances similar to those presented here. Under 11A V.I.C. § 2–708, the seller's measure of damage for non-acceptance or repudiation is the difference between the contract price and the market price, but if this relief is inadequate to put the seller in as good position as if the contract had been fully performed, ". . . then the measure of damages is the *profit (including reasonable overhead)* which the seller would have made from full performance by the buyer. . . . " 11A V.I.C. § 2–708(2). (Emphasis added.) While this contract is not controlled by the Code, the Code is persuasive here because it embodies the foremost modern legal thought concerning commercial transactions. Indeed, it may overrule some of the cases denying recovery for overhead. E.g., Wilhelm Lubrication Co. v. Brattrud, 197 Minn. 626, 632, 268 N.W. 634, 636, 106 A.L.R. 1279 (1936).

Caribtex also argued that the contract should not be enforced because it was unconscionable. While Vitex was to make a large profit on the processing and Caribtex did bear the risk of failure to meet customs standards, the contract was freely entered-into, after much negotiation, between parties of apparently equal bargaining strength. This was not a contract of adhesion—Vitex was not the only processor in the Virgin Islands and Caribtex's bargaining strength was evidenced by the successive and substantial price reductions it wrested from Vitex during the negotiations. Compare, Campbell Soup Co. v. Wentz, 172 F.2d 80 (C.A.3, 1948); Henningsen v. Bloomfield Motors, Inc., 32 N.J. 358, 161 A.2d 69, 75 A.L.R.2d 1 (1960).

The judgment of the district court will be affirmed.

NOTES

(1) *Cost and Loss Avoided*. In *Vitex*, the court observed that "since overhead is fixed and nonperformance of the contract produced no overhead cost savings, no deduction from profits should result." In terms of the damages formula above (*Damages* = (a) *loss in value* + (b) *other loss* − (c) *cost*

and loss avoided), this means that the overhead to which the court referred was not a part of the third component. Are all overhead expenses fixed and unavoidable? See Kansas Gas & Elec. Co v. United States, 95 Fed. Cl. 257 (2010), aff'd in part, rev'd in part, 685 F.3d 1361 (Fed. Cir. 2012), for a useful overview of the types of overhead.

(2) *Profit at the Margin.* Profit is the difference between revenue earned and all expenditures required to generate that revenue. These expenditures include fixed and non-fixed costs. But to determine the lost profit from a particular contract, as the court sought to do in *Vitex*, one would look to *marginal* revenue and *marginal* cost—not to total revenue and total cost, or average revenue and average cost. The marginal revenue a party receives from a contract is the additional revenue resulting from that contract. (Often, but not always, that amount is the contract price.) The marginal cost of a contract is the cost of completing performance of that contract. Therefore, so far as the fixed costs of performing have been expended already, they are not part of the marginal cost of performing. Only the further expenditures required to perform the contract enter into marginal cost.

(3) *Overhead Costs.* The *Vitex* court relied on the marginal-cost logic above in reaching its conclusions regarding Vitex's overhead costs in the lost-profit calculation. But the court also said that "even were we to recognize the allocation of overhead as proper in this case, we should uphold the tacit award of overhead expense to Vitex as a 'loss incurred.'" Under which loss category—*i.e.*, *loss in value* (a), or *other loss* (b)—would this loss fall? Note that UCC § 2–708 gives little guidance as to how overhead is to be taken into account.

(4) *Sunk Costs.* Suppose that a firm leases a fleet of trucks for $500,000 in order to deliver goods as required by a large sale contract. If, following a breach by the buyer, the firm sublets the fleet for $400,000, then only $100,000 of this expenditure is "sunk." Sunk costs are those that cannot be avoided or recouped once they have been made. How much effort should a court require of an injured party to limit its losses to sunk costs alone?

Laredo Hides Co., Inc. v. H & H Meat Products Co., Inc.

Court of Civil Appeals of Texas, 1974.
513 S.W.2d 210.

■ Bissett, Justice. This is a breach of contract case. Laredo Hides Company, Inc., the buyer, sued H & H Meat Products Company, Inc., the seller, to recover damages for breach of a written contract for the sale of cattle hides. Trial was to the court without a jury. A take nothing judgment in favor of defendant was rendered. Plaintiff has appealed.

The controlling facts of the case are undisputed. H & H Meat Products Company, Inc. (H & H) is a meat processing and packing corporation, located in Mercedes, Texas. It sells cattle hides as a by-product of its business. Laredo Hides Company, Inc. (Laredo Hides) is a corporation, located in Laredo, Texas. It purchases cattle hides from various meat packers in the United States and ships them to tanneries in Mexico.

A written contract dated February 29, 1972, was executed whereby Laredo Hides agreed to buy H & H's entire cattle hide production during the period March through December, 1972. [After two deliveries of hides, a $9,000 check sent by Laredo Hides to H & H in payment for the second shipment was delayed in the mail. Before it arrived, H & H gave Laredo Hides an ultimatum demanding payment within a few hours. When the demand was not met, H & H notified Laredo Hides on March 30, 1972, that H & H regarded. this as a breach justifying cancellation of the contract and that it would deliver no more hides. In an omitted part of the opinion, the court held that H & H's precipitous action was unjustified, that its refusal to deliver more hides was itself a breach by repudiation of the contract that relieved Laredo Hides of tendering performance during the remaining months of the contract, and that the trial court's disposition of the case was error.]

Laredo Hides, on March 3, 1972, had contracted with a Mexican tannery for the sale of all the hides which it expected to purchase from H & H under the February 29, 1972, contract. Following the cancellation by H & H of the contract, Laredo Hides, in order to meet the requirements of its contract with the tannery, was forced to purchase hides on the open market in substitution for the hides which were to have been delivered to it under the contract with H & H.

H & H's total production during the months April through December, 1972, was 17,218 hides. Under the contract with H & H, the price was $9.75 per hide for bull, steer and heifer hides, and $9.75 per hide for cow hides if the shipment was under 5% cow hides. In the event the shipment was more than 5% cow hides, the price on the excess of cow hides over 5% was reduced to $7.50 per cow hide. The market price for hides steadily increased following the execution of the contract in question. By December 31, 1972, the average cost of bull hides was about $33.00 each and the average cost of cow, heifer and steer hides was about $22.00 each. The total additional cost to Laredo Hides of purchasing substitute hides from other suppliers was $142,254.48. The additional costs (transportation and handling charges) to Laredo Hides which resulted because of the purchases from third parties amounted to $3,448.95.

Since this case must be reversed, we now confront the issue of damages. The guidelines for determining a buyer's remedies in a case where there is a breach of a contract for the sale of goods by a seller are found in Chapter 2 of the Texas Business and Commerce Code [the Uniform Commercial Code, as enacted in Texas]. Among other remedies afforded by the Code, when there is a repudiation of the contract by the seller or a failure to make delivery of the goods under contract, the buyer may cover under § 2.711. He may have damages under § 2.712 "by making in good faith and without unreasonable delay any reasonable purchase of or contract to purchase goods in substitution for those due from the seller", and "may recover from the seller as damages the difference between the cost of cover and the contract price together with any incidental or consequential damages" provided by the chapter; or, he may, under § 2.713, have damages measured by "the difference between the market price at the time when the buyer learned of the breach and the contract price together with any incidental and consequential damages" provided by the chapter.

Laredo Hides instituted suit in May, 1972, and filed its amended petition (its trial pleading) on October 24, 1972, when performance was still due by H & H under the contract. It prayed for specific performance, or in the alternative ". . . damages at least in the amount of one hundred thousand dollars ($100,000), the same being the damages proximately caused by defendant's breach of the contract . . . " There was never a trial amendment of this petition. There were no exceptions by H & H to Laredo Hides' pleadings. Trial commenced on February 28, 1973, was recessed on March 2, 1973, resumed on May 15, 1973, and ended May 16, 1973. Judgment was signed and rendered on August 6, 1973.

Laredo Hides offered uncontroverted evidence of the hide production of H & H from April to December, 1972. It also established the price for the same number of hides which it was forced to buy elsewhere. There was testimony that purchases had to be made periodically throughout 1972 since Laredo Hides had no storage facilities, and the hides would decompose if allowed to age. Furthermore, White, a C.P.A., testified as to statistical summaries which he made showing the cost of buying substitute hides. These summaries were made from invoices which are also in evidence. All of this evidence was admitted without objection. Clearly, Laredo Hides elected to pursue the remedy provided by § 2.712 of the Code, and by its pleadings and evidence brought itself within the purview of the "cover" provisions contained therein.

It is not necessary under § 2.712 that the buyer establish market price. Duesenberg and King, Sales and Bulk Transfers under the U.C.C. § 14.04 Matthew Bender (1974). Where the buyer complies with the requirements of § 2.712, his purchase is presumed proper and the burden of proof is on the seller to show that "cover" was not properly obtained. Spies, *Sales, Performance and Remedies*, 44 Tex. L. Rev. 629, 638 (1966). There was no evidence offered by H & H to negate this presumption or to "establish expenses saved in consequence of the seller's breach", as permitted by § 2.712.

The difference between the cover price and the contract price is shown to be $134,252.82 for steer hides and $8,001.66 for bull hides, or a total of $142,254.48. In addition, Laredo Hides offered evidence of increased transportation costs of $1,435.77, and increased handling charges of $2,013.18. These are clearly recoverable as incidental damages where the buyer elects to "cover". §§ 2.715(a); 2.712(b).

There is no evidence that Laredo Hides, in any manner, endeavored to increase its damages sustained when H & H refused to deliver any more hides to it. Laredo Hides, in purchasing the hides in substitution of the hides which should have been delivered under the contract, acted promptly and in a reasonable manner. The facts of this case regarding the issue of liability of H & H and the issues pertaining to damages suffered by Laredo Hides, have been fully and completely developed in the court below. The facts upon which judgment should have been rendered for Laredo Hides by the trial court are conclusively established. It, therefore, becomes the duty of this Court to render judgment which the trial court should have rendered.

Applying the rules announced by the above cited cases and authorities to the instant case, we hold that the record does not support the findings of fact made by the trial judge and there is no legal justification for the conclusion of law reached by the court. Accordingly, the judgment of the trial court is reversed, and judgment is here rendered for Laredo Hides in the amount of $152,960.04, together with interest thereon at the rate of 6% per annum from August 6, 1973, the date judgment was rendered by the trial court, until paid.

Reversed and rendered.

NOTES

(1) *What Is Cover?* Note that although Laredo Hides' contract with H & H was for a term of 10 months, its substitute purchases were on the "spot" market. What statutory language justified the court in treating these purchases as cover? Compare McGinnis v. Wentworth Chevrolet Co., 668 P.2d 365 (Or. 1983) (rental of car in lieu of purchase), and Cives Corp. v. Callier Steel Pipe & Tube, Inc., 482 A.2d 852 (Me. 1984) (manufacture of goods in lieu of purchase). What result if the hides purchased on the spot market had been of a better quality than those that H & H had contracted to supply? See Martella v. Woods, 715 F.2d 410 (8th Cir. 1983) (heifer buyer's purchase of better heifers); Handicapped Children's Education Board v. Lukaszewski, 332 N.W.2d 774 (Wis. 1983) (Board's hire of better-qualified teacher).

Would it make a difference if other hides of the quality contracted for were available on the spot market?

If Laredo Hides had been denied recovery under UCC § 2–712 (because the goods in the second transaction were held not to be "in substitution for those due from the seller"), then to what relief would it have been entitled?

(2) *Substitute Transactions: Goods.* Often, following breach, the injured party arranges a substitute transaction and claims damages based on that transaction rather than on one of the damage formulas set out earlier. Laredo Hides did that by arranging substitute purchases of hides and basing its damages on the cover price in those transactions under UCC § 2–712. The rule of that section is a Code innovation. It has no antecedent in prior law. (For comparable provisions, see CISG art. 75 and UNIDROIT

Principles art. 7.4.5.) Had this case arisen before the enactment of the Code, Laredo Hides would have had to prove damages based on the difference between market price and contract price under the common law rule of Texas that was the antecedent of UCC § 2–713. What disadvantages would that have had for Laredo Hides?

In connection with the foregoing question, consider what the Supreme Court of Maine said in Williams v. Ubaldo, 670 A.2d 913 (Me. 1996), a case involving the sale of a home. "The reports of professional appraisers have been accepted as evidence of the fair market value of real estate. Evidence of the price resulting from a subsequent sale is also probative of a property's fair market value." *Id.* at 917.

(3) *Substitute Transactions: Services.* If an employee is fired in breach of a contract and does other work as a result of being freed from that contract, the employee's damages are based on the salary that would have been earned under the broken contract less that earned by doing the other work. In State ex rel. Schilling v. Baird, 222 N.W.2d 666, 670 (Wis. 1974), Schilling, a deputy sheriff who was wrongfully suspended, argued that he was not required to deduct his earnings from other work because they were not made between midnight and 8 in the morning, the shift to which he was assigned as a deputy. "With this conclusion the Court cannot agree. It lends itself to an almost absurd result. Under this interpretation all Schilling had to do was to refrain from getting a third shift job and could then earn as much as he wanted or was fortunate enough to earn and would not be required to deduct any of it."

Under the "collateral source" rule that prevails in some states, an employee's recovery in tort is reduced by sums received from a collateral source, such as unemployment compensation and similar benefits, in order to avoid double recovery. Courts in states with the rule have divided over whether an employee who sues in contract must deduct such sums. See Farnsworth on Contracts § 12.9 n. 14.

Sometimes it is no simple matter to decide whether another comparable opportunity accepted by the injured party after breach should be treated as a "substitute" in calculating damages. Often a seller or other supplier claims that a subsequent transaction *was not* a substitute in order to have not only the benefit of that transaction but also damages based on profits lost on the original transaction.

A person fired from a full-time job cannot expect to make gainful use of the released time and to have the gain disregarded in an action based on wrongful firing. That is so whether or not the old and new jobs are in the same line. Recall the wrongfully suspended deputy sheriff in Schilling, above.

Unlike sheriffs, schoolteachers, and stars of the stage, persons in the building trades commonly apply their personal services to the simultaneous performance of multiple contracts; and firms in those trades may not apply the personal service of any specified individual to a contract. Hence it is generally assumed that a person or firm can undertake a new repair or construction job while continuing work on jobs already booked, adding as necessary to the work force and the stock of tools and materials. On that assumption, earnings on a new job are not credited against a builder's claim for having been dismissed, wrongfully, from an "old" one. The breach has resulted in "lost volume" for the builder.

(4) *An "Alternative Product" Rule.* On occasion a seller of goods, in breach, has contested the buyer's claim of loss by contending that, aside from the contract in question, nothing would have averted the loss. The argument amounts to saying that a recovery of a claimant's lost expectation cannot be justified if, when the contract was made, that party could not have accomplished its purpose by dealing with someone else, and so lost no opportunity. One court has subscribed to that rule. Overstreet v. Norden Laboratories, 669 F.2d 1286 (6th Cir. 1982). Norden Labs had supplied Dr. Overstreet with a vaccine for horses, said by him to have been ineffective. In an appeal by Norden, one issue was the trial court's instruction to a jury about damages. Norden persuaded two of the judges that it could limit its liability by showing that no effective vaccine had been available to Overstreet. One judge opposed that limitation, ascribing it to what he called an "alternative product" rule. A contrasting decision is that in Chatlos Systems v. National Cash Register [NCR] Corp., 670 F.2d 1304 (3d Cir. 1982). NCR, having warranted the performance of its computer system, contended, in effect, that no other computer system in the same price range could have achieved the performance expected by the buyer of its system. The buyer presented testimony of the high value of a system that would serve the buyer as NCR had warranted that its system would. NCR sought to counter that valuation. It had gotten the witness to concede that the price of the high-value system would exceed by far the price paid to NCR for its system. Given that fact, NCR said, the testimony was like substituting a Rolls-Royce for a Ford. The analogy did not move a majority of the court.

In Overstreet's case the court drew a different analogy. It said:

> "Let us assume, as appears to be the case, that nothing will reverse or prevent baldness. . . . Suppose a warrantor, in good faith, represents to a man who is beginning to go bald that use of the warrantor's product will prevent the loss of his hair. The product fails to work and the man goes bald. . . . If in reliance on the warranty he gave away his assortment of wigs he could recover from the warrantor the cost of replacing them. However, he could not recover for the loss of his hair. The breach simply had no effect on the presence or absence of the hair."

Id. at 1296–97. Should the bald man recover for his lost expectation? The court thought not. It called its ruling a straightforward application of the requirement of causation.

PROBLEM

A Lucky Star. Star Paving subcontracted with Drennan to do for $15,000 the paving required under Drennan's contract to build a school for the Lancaster School District. Drennan wrongfully ordered Star to stop work at a time when it would have cost Star $5,000 to complete it. Luckily for Star, it was able at once to make a contract with the School District to finish the job at a price of $7,000. Star demands $10,000 ($15,000 minus $5,000) from Drennan. Drennan offers to pay $8,000 ($15,000 minus $7,000). Who is right? See Olds v. Mapes-Reeves Constr. Co., 58 N.E. 478 (Mass. 1900). Would it make a difference if one or more terms of the second contract (*e.g.*, one about liability in the event of breach) were significantly different from those of the first?

Cost of Completion and Diminished Value

Parties seeking a remedy following partial or defective performance must overcome a preliminary hurdle of showing that the nonconforming performance justifies the remedy sought. The issue is often resolved under the substantial performance doctrine —explored more fully in the prior chapter—but which is usefully borne in mind when reading the cases involving nonconforming construction and land grading claims that follow. How much performance is enough to satisfy a party's contractual duty is a question with which courts commonly wrestle. As Justice Hallows observed in Plante v. Jacobs, "[s]ubstantial performance as applied to construction of a house does not mean that every detail must be in strict compliance with the specifications and the plans. Something less than perfection is the test. No mathematical rule relating to the percentage of the price, of cost of completion, or of completeness can be laid down to determine substantial performance of a building contract."

After working through questions of substantial performance and breach, the court must then turn to the matter of relief, which particularly in construction or building contracts often entails a choice between the difference in market value of the expected and received performances on the one hand, and the cost of completing or remedying the nonconforming performance on the other hand. Often these two measures track each other somewhat closely. The cost of procuring some performance typically bears a close relationship to its value as measured by the market. In some cases, however, these measures may diverge substantially, along with the interests of the parties, with the promisor advocating vehemently for the lesser sum and the promisee the greater. The cases that follow explore the competing interests in these two measures in the context of such divergence.

Plante v. Jacobs
Supreme Court of Wisconsin, 1960.
10 Wis.2d 567, 103 N.W.2d 296.

[Eugene Plante contracted with Frank and Carol Jacobs to furnish the materials and construct a house upon their lot in Brookfield, in accordance with plans and specifications, for the sum of $26,765. During the course of construction, Plante was paid $20,000. Disputes arose between the parties, the Jacobses refused to continue payment, and Plante did not complete the house. He sued to establish a lien on the property as a way of recovering the unpaid balance of the contract price, plus extras. The owners—who are the appellants—answered with allegations of faulty workmanship and incomplete construction.]

■ HALLOWS, JUSTICE. The defendants argue the plaintiff cannot recover any amount because he has failed to substantially perform the contract. The plaintiff conceded he failed to furnish the kitchen cabinets, gutters and downspouts, sidewalk, closet clothes poles, and entrance seat amounting to $1,601.95. This amount was allowed to the defendants. The defendants claim some 20 other items of incomplete or faulty performance by the plaintiff and no substantial performance because the cost of completing the house in strict compliance with the plans and specifications would amount to 25 or 30 per cent of the contract price. The defendants especially stress the misplacing of the wall between the living room and the kitchen, which narrowed the living room in excess of one foot. The cost of tearing down this wall and rebuilding it would be approximately $4,000. The record is not clear why and when this wall was misplaced, but the wall is completely built and the house decorated and the defendants are living therein. Real estate experts testified that the smaller width of the living room would not affect the market price of the house. Although the defendants received a house with which they are dissatisfied in many respects, the trial court was not in error in finding the contract was substantially performed.

The next question is what is the amount of recovery when the plaintiff has substantially, but incompletely, performed. For substantial performance the plaintiff should recover the contract price less the damages caused the defendant by the incomplete performance. Both parties agree. Venzke v. Magdanz, 1943, 243 Wis. 155, 9 N.W.2d 604, states the correct rule for damages due to faulty construction amounting to such incomplete performance, which is the difference between the value of the house as it stands with faulty and incomplete construction and the value of the house if it had been constructed in strict accordance with the plans and specifications. This is the diminished-value rule. The cost of replacement or repair is not the measure of such damage, but is an element to take into consideration in arriving at value under some circumstances. The cost of replacement or the cost to make whole the omissions may equal or be less than the difference in value in some cases and, likewise, the cost to rectify a defect may greatly exceed the added value to the structure as corrected. The defendants argue that under the Venzke rule their damages are $10,000. The plaintiff on review argues the defendants' damages are only $650. Both parties agree the trial court applied the wrong rule to the facts.

The trial court applied the cost-of-repair or replacement rule as to several items, relying on Stern v. Schlafer, 1943, 244 Wis. 183, 11 N.W.2d 640, 12 N.W.2d 678, wherein it was stated that when there are a number of small items of defect or omission which can be remedied without the reconstruction of a substantial part of the building or a great sacrifice of work or material already wrought in the building, the reasonable cost of correcting the defect should be allowed. However, in Mohs v. Quarton, 1950, 257 Wis. 544, 44 N.W 2d 580, the court held when the separation of defects would lead to confusion, the rule of diminished value could apply to all defects.

In this case no such confusion arises in separating the defects. The trial court disallowed certain claimed defects because they were not proven. This finding was not against the great weight and clear preponderance of the evidence and will not be disturbed on appeal. Of the remaining defects claimed by the defendants, the court allowed the cost of replacement or repair except as to the misplacement of the living-room wall. Whether a defect should fall under the cost-of-replacement rule or be considered under the diminished-value rule depends upon the nature and magnitude of the defect. This court has not allowed items of such magnitude under the cost-of-repair rule as the trial court did. Viewing the construction of the house as a whole and its cost we cannot say, however, that the trial court was in error in allowing the cost of repairing the plaster cracks in the ceilings, the cost of mud jacking and repairing the patio floor, and the cost of reconstructing the non-weight-bearing and nonstructural patio wall. Such reconstruction did not involve an unreasonable economic waste.

The item of misplacing the living-room wall under the facts of this case was clearly under the diminished-value rule. There is no evidence that defendants requested or demanded the replacement of the wall in the place called for by the specifications during the course of construction. To tear down the wall now and rebuild it in its proper place would involve a substantial destruction of the work, if not all of it, which was put into the wall and would cause additional damage to other parts of the house and require replastering and redecorating the walls and ceilings of at least two rooms. Such economic waste is unreasonable and unjustified. The rule of diminished value contemplates the wall is not going to be moved. Expert witnesses for both parties, testifying as to the value of the house, agreed that the misplacement of the wall had no effect on the market price. The trial court properly found that the defendants suffered no legal damage, although the defendants' particular desire for specified room size was not satisfied. For a discussion of these rules of damages for defective or unfinished construction and their application see Restatement, 1 Contracts, pp. 572–573, sec. 346(1)(a) and illustrations.

Judgment affirmed.

NOTES

(1) *Proving Diminution in Value.* The problem of determining loss in value is most acute when, as in the principal case, there is great disparity between the minimum of diminution in market price and the maximum of

cost to remedy the defect. Which better approximates loss in value? Who should have the burden with respect to diminution in value?

One court has said that if the builder "thought that the cost of repairs was an unreasonable measure of damages given what it believed to be the relatively small decrease in value resulting from the breach, it clearly had the burden to present evidence from which the jury could find the diminution in value." Advanced, Inc. v. Wilks, 711 P.2d 524, 527 (Alaska 1985) (quoted in Note 2 above). But the builder could do this simply by presenting evidence of market price. Another court has said that, as plaintiff, the owner "had the burden of producing evidence that afforded the jury a reasonable basis to measure" the owner's loss. But that court went on to say, "It is undisputed that homeowners are qualified to testify as to their personal opinion regarding the value, or diminution in value, of their properties." This is so even though the homeowner may rely in part on the cost of repairs in forming that opinion. The appropriate vehicle for challenging such an opinion is cross-examination. Tessmann v. Tiger Lee Constr. Co., 634 A.2d 870, 873 (Conn. 1993).

(2) *Value to Whom?* Recall Jacob & Youngs v. Kent, p. 797, a substantial performance case, where the breach involved the substitution of comparable plumbing (Cohoes pipes) for the "Reading" pipes stipulated in the contract. Judge Cardozo wrote that the "difference in value" to Kent "would be either nominal or nothing." Do you agree? It may be that the difference between the *market price* of a house with Reading pipes and one with Cohoes pipe is zero, because buyers of houses consider the two kinds of pipe to be of equal value *to them.* But why should Kent's recovery be limited by this? "If a proud householder, who plans to live out his days in the home of his dreams, orders a new roof of red barrel tile and the roofer instead installs a purple one, money damages for the reduced value of his house may not be enough to offset the strident offense to aesthetic sensibilities, continuing over the life of the roof." Gory Associated Industries v. Jupiter Roofing & Sheet Metal, 358 So.2d 93, 95 (Fla. Ct. App. 1978).

(3) *Relevance of Diminution in Value.* Diminution in market price is useful in fixing a lower limit for recovery, since the value of property to its owner is usually no less than the net price at which the owner could sell it. Similarly, cost to remedy the defect is useful in fixing an upper limit for recovery since, even if that cost is less than the loss in value to the owner, the lesser sum will enable the owner to complete and avoid any loss in value.

"An owner's recovery is not necessarily limited to diminution in value whenever that figure is less than the cost of repair. It is true that in a case where the cost of repair exceeds the damages under the value formula, an award under the cost of repair measure may place the owner in a better economic position than if the contract had been fully performed, since he could pocket the award and then sell the defective structure. On the other hand, it is possible that the owner will use the damage award for its intended purpose and turn the structure into the one originally envisioned. He may do this for a number of reasons, including personal esthetics or a hope for increased value in the future. If he does this his economic position will equal the one he would have been in had the contractor fully performed. The fact finder is the one in the best position to determine whether the owner will actually complete performance, or whether he is only interested in obtaining the best immediate economic position he can. In some cases, such as where the property is held solely for investment, the court may conclude as a matter of law that the damage award can not exceed the diminution in value. Where, however, the property has special significance to the owner and repair seems likely, the cost of repair may be appropriate even if it exceeds the diminution in value." Wilks, 711 P.2d at 526 (quoted in Note 1 above).

PROBLEMS

(1) *The Deep End.* Stephen Forsyth made a contract with Ruxley for a swimming pool on his estate. The price was $100,000, and the contract specified that the depth of the pool was to be 7 feet 9 inches at the deep end. However, Ruxley encountered unexpected rock and, after Forsyth had paid the price in full, he discovered that the pool was only 6 feet 6 inches deep at the deep end. (A depth of 5 feet 6 inches is considered safe for diving and, in any case, Forsyth had no plans to install a diving board.) To increase the depth to that required by the contract would involve demolishing and replacing the pool, with additional excavation, at a cost of $180,000, and Forsyth testified that he had no intention of having this done. Forsyth sued for damages based on the $180,000 cost. The jury awarded him $10,000 on an instruction that they could award damages for "loss of pleasure and amenity." Both parties appealed. What result? Ruxley Electronics & Construction, Ltd. v. Forsyth, [1995] 3 W.L.R. 118 (H.L.).

Would your answer be affected if Forsyth had testified that he planned to demolish and rebuild the pool if he recovered the $180,000? Would it be affected if it had been proved that Ruxley saved $50,000 by building the shallower pool?

(2) *The Thinned Blue Line.* Security Services contracted with Engulf & Devour, Inc., a multinational corporation, to provide 20 plainclothed guards for a price of $18,000, paid in advance, in order to prevent disruption by protestors at its annual meeting of shareholders. Because no protestors appeared at the meeting, the guards were not needed. However, Engulf & Devour later learned that Security Services provided only 14 guards. Does Engulf & Devour have a claim for damages against Security Services?

Groves v. John Wunder Co.

Supreme Court of Minnesota, 1939.
205 Minn. 163, 286 N.W. 235.

■ STONE, JUSTICE. Action for breach of contract. Plaintiff got judgment for a little over $15,000. Sorely disappointed by that sum, he appeals.

In August, 1927 S.J. Groves & Sons Company, a corporation (hereinafter mentioned simply as Groves), owned a tract of 24 acres of Minneapolis suburban real estate. It was served or easily could be reached by railroad trackage. It is zoned as heavy industrial property. But for lack of development of the neighborhood its principal value thus far may have been in the deposit of sand and gravel which it carried. The

Groves company had a plant on the premises for excavating and screening the gravel. Nearby defendant owned and was operating a similar plant.

In August, 1927, Groves and defendant made the involved contract. For the most part it was a lease from Groves, as lessor, to defendant, as lessee; its term seven years. Defendant agreed to remove the sand and gravel and to leave the property "at a uniform grade, substantially the same as the grade now existing at the roadway . . . on said premises, and that in stripping the overburden . . . it will use said overburden for the purpose of maintaining and establishing said grade."

Under the contract defendant got the Groves screening plant. The transfer thereof and the right to remove the sand and gravel made the consideration moving from Groves to defendant, except that defendant incidentally got rid of Groves as a competitor. On defendant's part it paid Groves $105,000. So that from the outset, on Groves' part the contract was executed except for defendant's right to continue using the property for the stated term. (Defendant had a right to renewal which it did not exercise.)

Defendant breached the contract deliberately. It removed from the premises only "the richest and best of the gravel" and wholly failed, according to the findings, "to perform and comply with the terms, conditions, and provisions of said lease . . . with respect to the condition in which the surface of the demised premises was required to be left." Defendant surrendered the premises, not substantially at the grade required by the contract "nor at any uniform grade." Instead, the ground was "broken, rugged and uneven." Plaintiff sues as assignee and successor in right of Groves.

As the contract was construed below, the finding is that to complete its performance 288,495 cubic yards of overburden would need to be excavated, taken from the premises, and deposited elsewhere. The reasonable cost of doing that was found to be upwards of $60,000. But, if defendant had left the premises at the uniform grade required by the lease, the reasonable value of the property on the determinative date would have been only $12,160. The judgment was for that sum, including interest, thereby nullifying plaintiff's claim that cost of completing the contract rather than difference in value of the land was the measure of damages. The gauge of damage adopted by the decision was the difference between the market value of plaintiff's land in the condition it was [in] when the contract was made and what it would have been if defendant had performed. The one question for us arises upon plaintiff's assertion that he was entitled, not to that difference in value, but to the reasonable cost to him of doing the work called for by the contract which defendant left undone.

1.   Defendant's breach of contract was wilful. There was nothing of good faith about it. Hence, that the decision below handsomely rewards bad faith and deliberate breach of contract is obvious. That is not

allowable. Here the rule is well settled, and has been since Elliott v. Caldwell, 43 Minn. 357, 45 N.W. 845, 9 L.R.A. 52, that, where the contractor wilfully and fraudulently varies from the terms of a construction contract, he cannot sue thereon and have the benefit of the equitable doctrine of substantial performance. That is the rule generally. See Annotation, "Wilful or intentional variation by contractor from terms of contract in regard to material or work as affecting measure of damages," 6 A.L.R. 137.

Jacob & Youngs, Inc. v. Kent, 230 N.Y. 239, 243, 244, 129 N.E. 889, 891, 23 A.L.R. 1429, is typical. It was a case of substantial performance of a building contract. (This case is distinctly the opposite.) Mr. Justice Cardozo, in the course of his opinion, stressed the distinguishing features. "Nowhere," he said, "will change be tolerated, however, if it is so dominant or pervasive as in any real or substantial measure to frustrate the purpose of the contract." Again, "the willful transgressor must accept the penalty of his transgression."

2.   In reckoning damages for breach of a building or construction contract, the law aims to give the disappointed promisee, so far as money will do it, what he was promised. 9 Am.Jur. Building and Construction Contracts, sec. 152. It is so ruled by a long line of decisions in this state beginning with Carli v. Seymour, Sabin & Co., 26 Minn. 276, 3 N.W. 348, where the contract was for building a road. There was a breach. Plaintiff was held entitled to recover what it would cost to complete the grading as contemplated by the contract. For our other similar cases, see 2 Dunnell, Minn.Dig., 2 Ed. & Supp., secs. 2561, 2565.

Never before, so far as our decisions show, has it even been suggested that lack of value in the land furnished to the contractor who had bound himself to improve it [gave] any escape from the ordinary consequences of a breach of the contract.

Even in case of substantial performance in good faith, the resulting defects being remediable, it is error to instruct that the measure of damage is "the difference in value between the house as it was and as it would have been if constructed according to contract." The "correct doctrine" is that the cost of remedying the defect is the "proper" measure of damages. Snider v. Peters Home Building Co., 139 Minn. 413, 414, 416, 167 N.W. 108.

Value of the land (as distinguished from the value of the intended product of the contract, which ordinarily will be equivalent to its reasonable cost) is no proper part of any measure of damages for wilful breach of a building contract. The reason is plain.

The summit from which to reckon damages from trespass to real estate is its actual value at the moment. The owner's only right is to be compensated for the deterioration in value caused by the tort. That is all he has lost. But not so if a contract to improve the same land has been breached by the contractor who refuses to do the work, especially where, as here, he has been paid in advance. The summit from which to reckon damages for that wrong is the hypothetical peak of accomplishment (not value) which would have been reached had the work been done as demanded by the contract.

The owner's right to improve his property is not trammeled by its small value. It is his right to erect thereon structures which will reduce its value. If that be the result, it can be of no aid to any contractor who declines performance. As said long ago in Chamberlain v. Parker, 45 N.Y. 569, 572: "A man may do what he will with his own, and if he chooses to erect a monument to his caprice or folly on his premises, and employs and pays another to do it, it does not lie with a defendant who has been so employed and paid for building it, to say that his own performance would not be beneficial to the plaintiff." To the same effect is Restatement, Contracts, sec. 346, p. 576, Illustrations of Subsection (1), par. 4.

Suppose a contractor were suing the owner for breach of a grading contract such as this. Would any element of value, or lack of it, in the land have any relevance in reckoning damages? Of course not. The contractor would be compensated for what he had lost, i.e., his profit. Conversely, in such a case as this, the owner is entitled to compensation for what he has lost, that is, the work or structure which he has been promised, for which he has paid, and of which he has been deprived by the contractor's breach.

To diminish damages recoverable against him in proportion as there is presently small value in the land would favor the faithless contractor. It would also ignore and so defeat plaintiff's right to contract and build for the future. To justify such a course would require more of the prophetic vision than judges possess. This factor is important when the subject matter is trackage property in the margin of such an area of population and industry as that of the Twin Cities.

The genealogy of the error pervading the argument contra is easy to trace. It begins with Seely v. Alden, 61 Pa. 302, 100 Am.Dec. 642, a tort case for pollution of a stream. Resulting depreciation in value of plaintiff's premises, of course, was the measure of damages. About 40 years later, in Bigham v. Wabash-Pittsburg T. Ry., 223 Pa. 106, 72 A. 318, the measure of damages of the earlier tort case was used in one for breach of contract, without comment or explanation to show why.

It is at least interesting to note Morgan v. Gamble, 230 Pa. 165, 79 A. 410, decided two years after the *Bigham* case. The doctrine of substantial performance is there correctly stated, but plaintiff was denied its benefit because he had deliberately breached his building contract. It was held that: "Where a building contractor agrees to lay an extra strong lead water pipe, and he substitutes therefor an iron pipe, he will be required to allow to the owners in a suit upon the contract, not the difference [in value] between the iron and lead pipes, but the cost of laying a lead pipe as provided in the agreement."

To show how remote any factors of value were considered, it was also held that: "Where a contractor of a building agrees to construct two gas lines, one for natural gas, and one for artificial gas, he will not be relieved from constructing both lines, because artificial gas was not in use in the town in which the building was being constructed."

The objective of this contract of present importance was the improvement of real estate. That makes irrelevant the rules peculiar to damages to chattels, arising from tort or breach of contract. In tort, the thing lost is money value, nothing more. But under a construction contract, the thing lost by a breach such as we have here is a physical structure or accomplishment, a promised and paid for alteration in land. That is the "injury" for which the law gives him compensation. Its only appropriate measure is the cost of performance.

It is suggested that because of little or no value in his land the owner may be unconscionably enriched by such a reckoning. The answer is that there can be no unconscionable enrichment, no advantage upon which the law will frown, when the result is but to give one party to a contract only what the other has promised; particularly where, as here, the delinquent has had full payment for the promised performance.

3. It is said by the Restatement, Contracts, sec. 346, Comment *b*: "Sometimes defects in a completed structure cannot be physically remedied without tearing down and rebuilding, at a cost that would be imprudent and unreasonable. The law does not require damages to be measured by a method requiring such economic waste. If no such waste is involved, the cost of remedying the defect is the amount awarded as compensation for failure to render the promised performance."

The "economic waste" declaimed against by the decisions applying that rule has nothing to do with the value in money of the real estate, or even with the product of the contract. The waste avoided is only that which would come from wrecking a physical structure, completed, or nearly so, under the contract. The cases applying that rule go no further. Illustrative are Buchholz v. Rosenberg, 163 Wis. 312, 156 N.W. 946; Burmeister v. Wolfgram, 175 Wis. 506, 185 N.W. 517. Absent such waste, as it is in this case, the rule of the Restatement, Contracts, sec. 346, is that "the cost of remedying the defect is the amount awarded as compensation for failure to render the promised performance." That means that defendants here are liable to plaintiff for the reasonable cost of doing what defendants promised to do and have wilfully declined to do.

It follows that there must be a new trial. The initial question will be as to the proper construction of the contract. Thus far the case has been considered from the standpoint of the construction adopted by plaintiff and acquiesced in, very likely for strategic reasons, by defendants. The question has not been argued here, so we intimate no opinion concerning it, but we put the question whether the contract required removal from the premises of any overburden. The requirement in that respect was that the overburden should be used for the purpose of "establishing and maintaining" the grade. A uniform slope and grade were doubtless required. But whether, if it could not be accomplished without removal and deposit elsewhere of large amounts of overburden, the contract required as a condition that the grade everywhere should be as low as the one recited as "now existing at the roadway" is a question for initial consideration below.

The judgment must be reversed with a new trial to follow.

So ordered.

■ [JUSTICE OLSON, dissenting in an opinion in which Justice Holt joined, urged that the diminished value rule be applied in the absence of evidence to show that the completed product was to satisfy the personal taste of the promisee, and denied that the wilfulness of the breach should affect the measure of damages.]

NOTES

(1) *Explanation.* In 1927, when the parties were bargaining over the terms of their contract, they would surely not knowingly have agreed to have Wunder assume such a burdensome task if it would have been of so slight a benefit to Groves. What is the explanation for the circumstances that, after seven years, Wunder's task was so burdensome and Groves's benefit was apparently so slight? That Wunder had underestimated the burden? That Groves had overestimated the benefit? That the cost of Wunder's performance had risen? That the amount of the benefit to Groves had fallen? That Wunder's performance would not have been so burdensome if it had done the restoration as the work progressed? That the actual benefit to Groves would have been greater than that reflected in the market price of the land? Some combination of these? Which of these possible explanations would justify the court's decision?

According to one critic, "not enforcing the contract would have given the defendant a windfall. But enforcing the contract gave the plaintiff an equal and opposite windfall, in the form of a cushion, which almost certainly the parties had not intended, against the impact of the Depression on land values." Richard A. Posner, Economic Analysis of Law 121 (7th ed. 2007).

After the decision in *Groves*, Wunder paid Groves $55,000 to settle the claim. The land was left until 1951, when some grading was done on a portion at a cost of $6,000, and in 1953 this portion was sold for $45,000 to a buyer who planned to use it for a factory. Does this suggest anything about the proper measure of recovery?

(2) *"Wilfulness."* The court says that Wunder's "breach of contract was wilful." In H.P. Droher & Sons v. Toushin, 85 N.W.2d 273 (Minn. 1957), the court distinguished *Groves* on the ground that, "The majority opinion is based, at least in part, on the fact that the breach of the contract was wilful and in bad faith". What does "wilful" mean in this context? Holmes said that for breach of contract "the measure of damages generally is the same, whatever the cause of the breach." Globe Refining Co. v. Landa Cotton Oil Co., 190 U.S. 540, 544 (1903). Is the *Groves* case an exception? If Wunder

must pay over $47,000 more in damages if its breach is "wilful," is this not a penalty for "wilfulness"? Is that consistent with the goals of contract remedies?

PROBLEM

Advising Wunder. If you had been counsel for Wunder and had been asked by your client whether it should perform its promise to do the grading at a cost of $60,000 if the benefit to Groves would be under $13,000, what advice would you have given? If Wunder then refused to perform, would its breach be "wilful"?

Peevyhouse v. Garland Coal & Mining Co.

Supreme Court of Oklahoma, 1963.
1962 OK 267, 382 P.2d 109.

[In 1954 Willie and Lucille Peevyhouse leased their farm for five years to Garland Coal & Mining Co. to strip mine coal. In addition to the usual covenants, Garland agreed to perform specified restorative and remedial work at the end of the lease. It failed to do this work, which would have involved the moving of many thousands of cubic yards of dirt at a cost of about $29,000. Had the work been done, the market price of the farm would have been increased by only $300. The Peevyhouses sued for $25,000 in damages. The trial court gave judgment on a verdict for $5,000. Both parties appealed.]

■ JACKSON, JUSTICE. On appeal, the issue is sharply drawn. Plaintiffs contend that the true measure of damages in this case is what it will cost plaintiffs to obtain performance of the work that was not done because of defendant's default. Defendant argues that the measure of damages is the cost of performance "limited, however, to the total difference in the market value before and after the work was performed". It appears that this precise question has not heretofore been presented to this court.

Plaintiffs rely on Groves v. John Wunder Co., 205 Minn. 163, 286 N.W. 235, 123 A.L.R. 502. In that case, the Minnesota court, in a substantially similar situation, adopted the "cost of performance" rule as opposed to the "value" rule. The result was to authorize a jury to give plaintiff damages in the amount of $60,000, where the real estate concerned would have been worth only $12,160, even if the work contracted for had been done.

It may be observed that Groves v. John Wunder Co., supra, is the only case which has come to our attention in which the cost of performance rule has been followed under circumstances where the cost of performance greatly exceeded the diminution in value resulting from the breach of contract. Incidentally, it appears that this case was decided by a plurality rather than a majority of the members of the court.

We do not think [that] either [the] analogy [of a "building and construction" or a "grading and excavation" contract] is strictly applicable to the case now before us. The primary purpose of the lease contract between plaintiffs and defendant was neither "building and construction" nor "grading and excavation". It was merely to accomplish the economical recovery and marketing of coal from the premises, to the profit of all parties. The special provisions of the lease contract pertaining to remedial work were incidental to the main object involved.

Even in the case of contracts that are unquestionably building and construction contracts, the authorities are not in agreement as to the factors to be considered in determining whether the cost of performance rule or the value rule should be applied. The American Law Institute's Restatement of the Law, Contracts, Volume 1, Sections 346(1)(a)(i) and (ii) submits the proposition that the cost of performance is the proper measure of damages "if this is possible and does not involve *unreasonable economic waste*"; and that the diminution in value caused by the breach is the proper measure "if construction and completion in accordance with the contract would involve *unreasonable economic waste*". (Emphasis supplied.) In an explanatory comment immediately following the text, the Restatement makes it clear that the "economic waste" referred to consists of the destruction of a substantially completed building or other structure. Of course no such destruction is involved in the case now before us.

On the other hand, in McCormick, Damages, Section 168, it is said with regard to building and construction contracts that ". . . in cases where the defect is one that can be repaired or cured without *undue expense*" the cost of performance is the proper measure of damages, but where ". . . the defect in material or construction is one that cannot be remedied without *an expenditure for reconstruction disproportionate to the end to be attained*" (emphasis supplied) the value rule should be followed. The same idea was expressed in Jacob & Youngs, Inc. v. Kent, 230 N.Y. 239, 129 N.E. 889, 23 A.L.R. 1429, as follows: "The owner is entitled to the money which will permit him to complete, unless the cost of completion is grossly and unfairly out of proportion to the good to be attained. When that is true, the measure is the difference in value."

It thus appears that the prime consideration in the Restatement was "economic waste"; and that the prime consideration in McCormick, Damages, and in Jacob & Youngs, Inc. v. Kent, supra, was the relationship between the expense involved and the "end to be attained"—in other words, the "relative economic benefit".

We hold that where, in a coal mining lease, lessee agrees to perform certain remedial work on the premises concerned at the end of the lease period, and thereafter the contract is fully performed by both parties except that the remedial work is not done, the measure of damages in an action by lessor against lessee for damages for breach of contract is ordinarily the reasonable cost of performance of the work; however, where the contract provision breached was merely incidental to the main purpose in view, and where the economic benefit which would result to lessor by full performance of the work is grossly disproportionate to the cost of performance, the damages which lessor may recover are limited to the diminution in value resulting to the premises because of the non-performance.

[Judgment reduced to $300 and affirmed (4–3).]

■ IRWIN, JUSTICE (dissenting). Although the contract speaks for itself, there were several negotiations between the plaintiffs and defendant before the contract was executed. Defendant admitted in the trial of the action, that plaintiffs insisted that the above provisions be included in the contract and that they would not agree to the coal mining lease unless the above provisions were included.

[I]n my opinion, the plaintiffs were entitled to specific performance of the contract and since defendant has failed to perform, the proper measure of damages should be the cost of performance. Any other measure of damage would be holding for naught the express provisions of the contract; would be taking from the plaintiffs the benefits of the contract and placing those benefits in defendant which has failed to perform its obligations; would be granting benefits to defendant without a resulting obligation; and would be completely rescinding the solemn obligation of the contract for the benefit of the defendant to the detriment of the plaintiffs by making an entirely new contract for the parties.

NOTES

(1) Groves *and* Peevyhouse. Are *Groves* and *Peevyhouse* distinguishable? Is it clear that the loss in value to the Peevyhouses was not $5,000? Did Garland get a "windfall"? See E. Allan Farnsworth, *Your Loss or My Gain? The Dilemma of the Disgorgement Principle in Breach of Contract*, 94 Yale L.J. 1339 (1985). What result in these cases under Restatement § 348(2)? For the background of *Peevyhouse*, see Judith Maute, Peevyhouse v. Garland Coal Co. *Revisited: The Ballad of Willie and Lucille*, 89 Nw. U. L. Rev. 1341 (1995).

Peevyhouse was reconsidered in Schneberger v. Apache Corp., 890 P.2d 847, 850, 854, 855 (Okla. 1994), an action for breach of a contract to reduce water pollution that had been caused during the defendant's drilling operations. The plaintiffs argued "that recent statutory enactments and federal case law reflect a change in Oklahoma policy regarding protecting the environment from pollution caused by oil and gas drilling operations," and that this policy change "clearly indicates that the diminution in value rule established in *Peevyhouse* is outdated and that the cost of remediation is the proper measure of damages for pollution caused by oil and gas operations." The Supreme Court of Oklahoma, however, adhered to *Peevyhouse*, noting that the parties to the contract "were free to specify in the contract what the measure of damages would be in the event of a breach," and that even if the court were to use the more generous measure, nothing would require "a plaintiff to apply the award to reclaiming the land."

(2) *"Economic Waste."* The first Restatement, we are told by the court in *Peevyhouse*, speaks of "economic waste" in the sense of destruction of a substantially completed structure.

Similarly Justice Hallows in Plante v. Jacobs emphasizes that "[t]o tear down the wall now and rebuild it in its proper place would involve a substantial destruction of the work, if not all of it, which was put into the wall and would cause additional damage to other parts of the house and require replastering and redecorating the walls and ceilings of at least two rooms. Such economic waste is unreasonable and unjustified." Perhaps a more extreme example is found in the facts of Jacob & Youngs v. Kent. If Kent had been awarded damages measured by the cost to replace the pipe with Reading pipe, would he then have been required to replace it? Does it seem likely that he would have done so? In what sense is there "economic waste" if he is awarded damages measured by the cost to complete? See Restatement § 348 cmt. c.

PROBLEM

Threatening Inefficient Performance. Suppose that the value to the Peevyhouses of having the land graded is $8,000, that the cost to Garland of grading it is $30,000, and that the parties are confident that a court will award $30,000 as damages for breach of contract by Garland. If Garland has not decided whether or not to grade the land and offers to split the $22,000 difference and pay the Peevyhouses $19,000 ($8,000 + $11,000), should the Peevyhouses accept? Suppose that Garland threatens to grade the land if they do not accept? Does this call into question the wisdom of a rule that would result in an award of $30,000 as damages? See Ian Ayres & Kristin Madison, *Threatening Inefficient Performance of Injunctions and Contracts*, 148 U. Pa. L. Rev. 45, 52–53 (1999) (noting that, as compared to litigation, "actual performance potentially saves attorney fees").

Lost Volume

R.E. Davis Chemical Corp. v. Diasonics, Inc.

United States Court of Appeals, Seventh Circuit, 1987.
826 F.2d 678.

■ CUDAHY, CIRCUIT JUDGE. Diasonics, Inc. appeals from the orders of the district court denying its motion for summary judgment and granting R.E. Davis Chemical Corp.'s summary judgment motion. Diasonics also appeals from the order dismissing its third-party complaint against Dr. Glen D. Dobbin and Dr. Galdino Valvassori. We affirm the dismissal of the third-party complaint, reverse the grant of summary judgment in favor of Davis and remand for further proceedings.

1.

Diasonics is a California corporation engaged in the business of manufacturing and selling medical diagnostic equipment. Davis is an Illinois corporation that contracted to purchase a piece of medical diagnostic equipment from Diasonics. On or about February 23, 1984, Davis and Diasonics entered into a written contract under which Davis agreed to purchase the equipment. Pursuant to this agreement, Davis paid Diasonics a $300,000 deposit on February 29, 1984. Prior to entering into its agreement with Diasonics, Davis had contracted with Dobbin and Valvassori to establish a medical facility where the equipment was to be used. Dobbin and Valvassori subsequently breached their contract with Davis. Davis then breached its contract with Diasonics; it refused to take delivery of the equipment or to pay the balance due under the agreement. Diasonics later resold the equipment to a third party for the same price at which it was to be sold to Davis.

Davis sued Diasonics, asking for restitution of its $300,000 down payment under section 2–718(2) of the Uniform Commercial Code (the "UCC" or the "Code"). Diasonics counterclaimed. Diasonics did not deny that Davis was entitled to recover its $300,000 deposit less $500 as provided in section 2–718(2)(b). However, Diasonics claimed that it was entitled to an offset under section 2–718(3). Diasonics alleged that it was a "lost volume seller," and, as such, it lost the profit from one sale when Davis breached its contract. Diasonics' position was that, in order to be put in as good a position as it would have been in had Davis performed, it was entitled to recover its lost profit on its contract with Davis under section 2–708(2) of the UCC.

Diasonics subsequently filed a third-party complaint against Dobbin and Valvassori, alleging that they tortiously interfered with its contract with Davis. Diasonics claimed that the doctors knew of the contract between Davis and Diasonics and also knew that, if they breached their contract with Davis, Davis would have no use for the equipment it had agreed to buy from Diasonics.

The district court dismissed Diasonics' third-party complaint for failure to state a claim upon which relief could be granted, finding that the complaint did not allege that the doctors intended to induce Davis to breach its contract with Diasonics. The court also entered summary judgment for Davis. The court held that lost volume sellers were not entitled to recover damages under 2–708(2) but rather were limited to recovering the difference between the resale price and the contract price along with incidental damages under section 2–706(1). Davis was awarded $322,656, which represented Davis' down payment plus prejudgment interest less Diasonics' incidental damages. Diasonics appeals the district court's decision respecting its measure of damages as well as the dismissal of its third-party complaint.

II.

We consider first Diasonics' claim that the district court erred in holding that Diasonics was limited to the measure of damages provided in 2–706 and could not recover lost profits as a lost volume seller under 2–708(2). Surprisingly, given its importance, this issue has never been addressed by an Illinois court, nor, apparently, by any other court construing Illinois law. Thus, we must attempt to predict how the Illinois Supreme Court would resolve this issue if it were presented to it. Courts applying the laws of other states have unanimously adopted the position that a lost volume seller can recover its lost profits under 2–708(2). Contrary to the result reached by the district court, we conclude that the Illinois Supreme Court would follow these other cases and would allow a lost volume seller to recover its lost profit under 2–708(2).

We begin our analysis with 2–718(2) and (3). Under 2–718(2)(b), Davis is entitled to the return of its down payment less $500. Davis' right to restitution, however, is qualified under 2–718(3)(a) to the extent that Diasonics can establish a right to recover damages under any other provision of Article 2 of the UCC. Article 2 contains four provisions that concern the recovery of a seller's general damages (as opposed to its incidental or consequential damages): 2–706 (contract price less resale price); 2–708(1) (contract price less market price); 2–708(2) (profit); and 2–709 (price). The problem we face here is determining whether Diasonics' damages should be measured under 2–706 or 2–708(2). To answer this question, we need to engage in a detailed look at the language and structure of these various damage provisions.

The Code does not provide a great deal of guidance as to when a particular damage remedy is appropriate. The damage remedies provided under the Code are catalogued in section 2–703, but this section does not indicate that there is any hierarchy among the remedies. One method of approaching the damage sections is to conclude that 2–708 is relegated to a role inferior to that of 2–706 and 2–709 and that one can turn to 2–708 only after one has concluded that neither 2–706 nor 2–709 is applicable. Under this interpretation of the relationship between 2–706 and 2–708, if the goods have been resold, the seller can sue to recover damages measured by the difference between the contract price and the resale price under 2–706. The seller can turn to 2–708 only if it resells in a commercially unreasonable manner or if it cannot resell but an action for the price is inappropriate under 2–709. The district court adopted this reading of the Code's damage remedies and, accordingly, limited Diasonics to the measure of damages provided in 2–706 because it resold the equipment in a commercially reasonable manner.

The district court's interpretation of 2–706 and 2–708, however, creates its own problems of statutory construction. There is some suggestion in the Code that the "fact that plaintiff resold the goods [in a commercially reasonable manner] does *not* compel him to use the resale remedy of § 2–706 rather than the damage remedy of § 2–708." Harris, *A*

Radical Restatement of the Law of Seller's Damages: Sales Act and Commercial Code Results Compared, 18 Stan. L. Rev. 66, 101 n. 174 (1965) (emphasis in original). Official Comment 1 to 2–703, which catalogues the remedies available to a seller, states that these "remedies are essentially cumulative in nature" and that "[w]hether the pursuit of one remedy bars another depends entirely on the facts of the individual case." See also State of New York, Report of the Law Revision Comm'n for 1956, 396–97 (1956).

Those courts that found that a lost volume seller can recover its lost profits under 2–708(2) implicitly rejected the position adopted by the district court; those courts started with the assumption that 2–708 applied to a lost volume seller without considering whether the seller was limited to the remedy provided under 2–706. None of those courts even suggested that a seller who resold goods in a commercially reasonable manner was limited to the damage formula provided under 2–706. We conclude that the Illinois Supreme Court, if presented with this question, would adopt the position of these other jurisdictions and would conclude that a reselling seller, such as Diasonics, is free to reject the damage formula prescribed in 2–706 and choose to proceed under 2–708.

Concluding that Diasonics is entitled to seek damages under 2–708, however, does not automatically result in Diasonics being awarded its lost profit. Two different measures of damages are provided in 2–708. Subsection 2–708(1) provides for a measure of damages calculated by subtracting the market price at the time and place for tender from the contract price. The profit measure of damages, for which Diasonics is asking, is contained in 2–708(2). However, one applies 2–708(2) only if "the measure of damages provided in subsection (1) is inadequate to put the seller in as good a position as performance would have done. . . . " Diasonics claims that 2–708(1) does not provide an adequate measure of damages when the seller is a lost volume seller. To understand Diasonics' argument, we need to define the concept of the lost volume seller. Those cases that have addressed this issue have defined a lost volume seller as one that has a predictable and finite number of customers and that has the capacity either to sell to all new buyers or to make the one additional sale represented by the resale after the breach. According to a number of courts and commentators, if the seller would have made the sale represented by the resale whether or not the breach occurred, damages measured by the difference between the contract price and market price cannot put the lost volume seller in as good a position as it would have been in had the buyer performed. The breach effectively cost the seller a "profit," and the seller can only be made whole by awarding it damages in the amount of its "lost profit" under 2–708(2).

We agree with Diasonics' position that, under some circumstances, the measure of damages provided under 2–708(1) will not put a reselling seller in as good a position as it would have been in had the buyer performed because the breach resulted in the seller losing sales volume.

However, we disagree with the definition of "lost volume seller" adopted by other courts. Courts awarding lost profits to a lost volume seller have focused on whether the seller had the capacity to supply the breached units in addition to what it actually sold. In reality, however, the relevant questions include, not only whether the seller could have produced the breached units in addition to its actual volume, but also whether it would have been profitable for the seller to produce both units. Goetz & Scott, *Measuring Sellers' Damages: The Lost-Profits Puzzle*, 31 Stan. L. Rev. 323, 332–33, 346–47 (1979). As one commentator has noted, under

> the economic law of diminishing returns or increasing marginal costs[,] . . . as a seller's volume increases, then a point will inevitably be reached where the cost of selling each additional item diminishes the incremental return to the seller and eventually makes it entirely unprofitable to conclude the next sale.

Shanker, supra n. 1, at 705. Thus, under some conditions, awarding a lost volume seller its presumed lost profit will result in overcompensating the seller, and 2–708(2) would not take effect because the damage formula provided in 2–708(1) does place the seller in as good a position as if the buyer had performed. Therefore, on remand, Diasonics must establish, not only that it had the capacity to produce the breached unit in addition to the unit resold, but also that it would have been profitable for it to have produced and sold both. Diasonics carries the burden of establishing these facts because the burden of proof is generally on the party claiming injury to establish the amount of its damages; especially in a case such as this, the plaintiff has easiest access to the relevant data.

One final problem with awarding a lost volume seller its lost profits was raised by the district court. This problem stems from the formulation of the measure of damages provided under 2–708(2) which is "the profit (including reasonable overhead) which the seller would have made from full performance by the buyer, together with any incidental damages provided in this Article (Section 2–710), due allowance for costs reasonably incurred and due credit for payments or *proceeds of resale*." (emphasis added). The literal language of 2–708(2) requires that the proceeds from resale be credited against the amount of damages awarded which, in most cases, would result in the seller recovering nominal damages. In those cases in which the lost volume seller was awarded its lost profit as damages, the courts have circumvented this problem by concluding that this language only applies to proceeds realized from the resale of uncompleted goods for scrap. See, e.g., Neri [v. Retail Marine Corp., 30 N.Y.2d 393, 399 & n. 2, 334 N.Y.S.2d 165, 169 & n. 2, 285 N.E.2d 311, 314 & n. 2 (1972)]; see also J. White & R. Summers, Handbook of the Law under the Uniform Commercial Code § 7–13, at 285 ("courts should simply ignore the 'due credit' language in lost volume cases") (footnote omitted). Although neither the text of 2–708(2) nor the official comments limit its application to resale of goods for scrap, there is evidence that the drafters of 2–708 seemed to have had this more limited application in mind when they proposed amending 2–708 to include the phrase "due credit for payments or proceeds of resale." We conclude that the Illinois Supreme Court would adopt this more restrictive interpretation of this phrase rendering it inapplicable to this case.

We therefore reverse the grant of summary judgment in favor of Davis and remand with instructions that the district court calculate Diasonics' damages under 2–708(2) if Diasonics can establish, not only that it had the capacity to make the sale to Davis as well as the sale to the resale buyer, but also that it would have been profitable for it to make both sales. Of course, Diasonics, in addition, must show that it probably would have made the second sale absent the breach.

[In an omitted part of the opinion, the court went on to uphold dismissal of the third-party complaint.]

NOTES

(1)   *Appeal After Remand.* On remand, after a three-day bench trial, the district judge concluded that Diasonics had adequately established damages for lost profits amounting to $453,050 and entered judgment for that sum less the $300,000 deposit retained by Diasonics. On appeal by Davis, the Court of Appeals upheld this conclusion as not clearly erroneous. "The evidence is undisputed that Diasonics possessed the capacity to manufacture one more MRI. Diasonics also demonstrated that it was . . . 'beating the bushes for all possible sales.' Diasonics was still a young company struggling to acquire business in an extremely competitive market. The mere fact that Diasonics was unable to specify the particular unit Davis contracted to buy and trace the exact resale buyer for that unit should not foreclose it from recovering lost profits." R.E. Davis Chemical Corp. v. Diasonics, Inc., 924 F.2d 709, 711–12 (7th Cir. 1991).

(2)   *Lost Opportunities.* Many hundreds of pages of economic analysis have been devoted to the subject of sellers' claims of lost volume resulting from buyers' breaches. Two helpful sources are Robert Cooter & Melvin A. Eisenberg, *Damages for Breach of Contract*, 73 Cal. L. Rev. 1432, 1444–77 (1985); Victor Goldberg, Framing Contract Law (2006). See also PurCo Fleet Servs. v. Koenig, 240 P.3d 435 (Colo. Ct. App. 2010), for a useful case analysis of lost opportunity.

In practice, the outcome may turn on who has the burden of proof on the issue of lost volume. Courts have generally placed the burden of proof on the seller. See Famous Knitwear Corp. v. Drug Fair, Inc., 493 F.2d 251 (4th Cir. 1974). But in Islamic Republic of Iran v. Boeing Co., 771 F.2d 1279 (9th Cir. 1985), the court rejected the argument that to take advantage of UCC § 2–708(2) a seller must prove that the market is one "in which supply exceeds demand." "We will not . . . impose rigid and complex burdens of proof on this section. . . . Most other jurisdictions have held that to qualify as a 'lost volume' seller under section 2–708(2), the seller needs to show only that it *could have* supplied both the breaching purchaser and the resale purchaser."

PROBLEM

A Paradox. How do you explain the following paradox? In order to justify allowing recovery for breach of a contract on which neither party appears to have relied, a court reasons that the injured party might have passed up the opportunity of making a similar alternative contract but should not be required to prove this. Then, in calculating the injured party's damages, the court reasons that the injured party lost volume because it would not have passed up the opportunity of making a similar alternative contract but would have made both contracts. Judicial inconsistency?

———

Losing Contracts

If a lottery operator failed to deliver a purchased ticket, the purchaser could "get his money back whether or not he eventually would have won the lottery." Does this mean that an aggrieved party is generally entitled to restitution under a "losing contract"—even though that party would have sustained a loss had that contract been performed?

Consider the following as a possible solution.

In cases where the venture would have proved profitable to the promisee, there is no reason why he should not recover his expenses. On the other hand, on those occasions in which the performance would not have covered the promisee's outlay, such a result imposes the risk of the promisee's contract upon the promisor. We cannot agree that the promisor's default in performance should under this guise make him an insurer of the promisee's venture; yet it does not follow that the breach should not throw upon him the duty of showing that the value of the performance would in fact have been less than the promisee's outlay. It is often very hard to learn what the value of the performance would have been; and it is a common expedient, and a just one, in such situations to put the peril of the answer upon that party who by his wrong has made the issue relevant to the rights of the other. On principle therefore the proper solution would seem to be that the promisee may recover his outlay in preparation for the performance, subject to the privilege of the promisor to reduce it by as much as he can show that the promisee would have lost, if the contract had been performed.

L. Albert & Son v. Armstrong Rubber Co., 178 F.2d 182, 189 (2d Cir. 1949) (Learned Hand, J.).

The case just quoted from involved material delay by a seller of machines to be used by the buyer to reclaim old rubber during World War II. The buyer did not ask for loss of profits when the delay caused this speculative venture to fall through, but did claim expenses in reliance on tho seller's promise to deliver on time, including the cost of laying foundations for the machines. It was this claim to which Judge Hand spoke. For a defense of expectation-based recovery in such cases, see Andrew Kull, *Restitution as a Remedy for Breach of Contract*, 67 S. Calif. L. Rev. 1465 (1994); Henry Mather, *Restitution as a Remedy for Breach of Contract: The Case of the Partially Performing Seller*, 92 Yale L.J. 14 (1982).

UCC § 2–718(2) provides for some restitution when a party has pre-paid. Notice that this section applies to pre-paying buyers. What about a pre-delivering seller? See UCC § 2–709.

PROBLEM

Flour Markets. Buyer made a $500,000 payment on a contract for the sale of flour for a total price of $1,400,000. Seller broke the contract by failing to deliver the flour, although the market price of the flour had dropped to $1,100,000 by the time of delivery. Is Buyer entitled to restitution of $500,000 from Seller? See Bush v. Canfield, 2 Conn. 485 (1818).

United States v. Algernon Blair, Inc.

United States Court of Appeals, Fourth Circuit, 1973.
479 F.2d 638.

■ CRAVEN, CIRCUIT JUDGE. May a subcontractor, who justifiably ceases work under a contract because of the prime contractor's breach, recover in quantum meruit the value of labor and equipment already furnished pursuant to the contract irrespective of whether he would have been entitled to recover in a suit on the contract? We think so, and, for reasons to be stated, the decision of the district court will be reversed.

The subcontractor, Coastal Steel Erectors, Inc., brought this action under the provisions of the Miller Act, 40 U.S.C.A. § 270a et seq., in the name of the United States against Algernon Blair, Inc., and its surety, United States Fidelity and Guaranty Company. Blair had entered a contract with the United States for the construction of a naval hospital in Charleston County, South Carolina. Blair had then contracted with Coastal to perform certain steel erection and supply certain equipment in conjunction with Blair's contract with the United States. Coastal commenced performance of its obligations, supplying its own cranes for handling and placing steel. Blair refused to pay for crane rental, maintaining that it was not obligated to do so under the subcontract. Because of Blair's failure to make payments for crane rental, and after completion of approximately 28 percent of the subcontract, Coastal terminated its performance. Blair then proceeded to complete the job with a new subcontractor. Coastal brought this action to recover for labor and equipment furnished.

The district court found that the subcontract required Blair to pay for crane use and that Blair's refusal to do so was such a material breach as to justify Coastal's terminating performance. This finding is not questioned on appeal. The court then found that under the contract the amount due Coastal, less what had already been paid, totaled approximately $37,000. Additionally, the court found Coastal would have lost more than $37,000 if it had completed performance. Holding that any amount due Coastal must be reduced by any loss it would have incurred by complete performance of the contract, the court denied recovery to Coastal. While the district court correctly stated the " 'normal' rule of contract damages," we think Coastal is entitled to recover in quantum meruit.

In United States for Use of Susi Contracting Co. v. Zara Contracting Co., 146 F.2d 606 (2d Cir.1944), a Miller Act action, the court was faced with a situation similar to that involved here—the prime contractor had unjustifiably breached a subcontract after partial performance by the subcontractor. The court stated:

> For it is an accepted principle of contract law, often applied in the case of construction contracts, that the promisee upon breach has the option to forego any suit on the contract and claim only the reasonable value of his performance.

146 F.2d at 610. Quantum meruit recovery is not limited to an action against the prime contractor but may also be brought against the Miller Act surety, as in this case. Further, that the complaint is not clear in regard to the theory of a plaintiff's recovery does not preclude recovery under quantum meruit. Narragansett Improvement Co. v. United States, 290 F.2d 577 (1st Cir.1961). A plaintiff may join a claim for quantum meruit with a claim for damages from breach of contract.

In the present case, Coastal has, at its own expense, provided Blair with labor and the use of equipment. Blair, who breached the subcontract, has retained these benefits without having fully paid for them. On these facts, Coastal is entitled to restitution in quantum meruit.

> The "restitution interest," involving a combination of unjust impoverishment with unjust gain, presents the strongest case for relief. If, following Aristotle, we regard the purpose of justice as the maintenance of an equilibrium of goods among members of society, the restitution interest presents twice as strong a claim to judicial intervention as the reliance interest, since if A not only causes B to lose one unit but appropriates that unit to himself, the resulting discrepancy between A and B is not one unit but two.

Fuller & Perdue, *The Reliance Interest in Contract Damages*, 46 Yale L.J. 52, 56 (1936).

The impact of quantum meruit is to allow a promisee to recover the value of services he gave to the defendant irrespective of whether he would have lost money on the contract and been unable to recover in a suit on the contract. Scaduto v. Orlando, 381 F.2d 587, 595 (2d Cir. 1967). The measure of recovery for quantum meruit is the reasonable value of the performance, Restatement of Contracts § 347 (1932); and recovery is undiminished by any loss which would have been incurred by complete performance. 12 Williston on Contracts § 1485, at 312 (3d ed. 1970). While the contract price may be evidence of reasonable value of the services, it does not measure the value of the performance or limit recovery. Rather, the standard for measuring the reasonable value of the services rendered is the amount for which such services could have been purchased from one in the plaintiff's position at the time and place the services were rendered.

Since the district court has not yet accurately determined the reasonable value of the labor and equipment use furnished by Coastal to Blair, the case must be remanded for those findings. When the amount has been determined, judgment will be entered in favor of Coastal, less payments already made under the contract. Accordingly, for the reasons stated above, the decision of the district court is

Reversed and remanded with instructions.

NOTES

(1) *Measure of Restitution Interest.* What recovery for a builder under the losing contract according to *Algernon Blair?* What is the court's justification for measuring Coastal's restitution interest by "the reasonable value of the performance"? Is this a proper measure of the "benefits" that Blair "retained without having fully paid for"? How does it differ from Coastal's reliance interest? See Restatement § 371. The conclusion that "the property owner is enriched by each stroke of the hammer or the paint brush" is characterized as "Pickwickian" in Edwin Patterson, *The Scope of Restitution and Unjust Enrichment*, 1 Mo. L. Rev. 223, 230 (1936). What if the Peevyhouses had sought damages based on their restitution interest?

A claimant that, like Coastal, asks for restitution must account for any benefits that it has received. In Coastal's case, its benefits were "what had already been paid," its progress payments. Accounting for a claimant's benefits is not always so simple. In EarthInfo v. Hydrosphere Resource Consultants, 900 P.2d 113, 120–21 (Colo. 1995), Hydrosphere sought restitution, having "rescinded" its software development contracts with EarthInfo because of the latter's "substantial" breach in suspending royalty payments. The court allowed restitution based on EarthInfo's profits during the time the contract was in effect and then turned to EarthInfo's claim to the benefit it had conferred on Hydrosphere during that time. The Supreme Court of Colorado said that on remand the trial court "must determine which part of the profit results from [EarthInfo's] own independent efforts and which part results from the benefits provided by [Hydrosphere]. The allocation may be affected by such factors as the seriousness of [EarthInfo's] wrongdoing and the extent to which [Hydrosphere's] contribution was at risk in the profit making enterprise." The burden of establishing the parties' relative contributions was on EarthInfo.

(2) *Contract Price as a Ceiling.* An injured party who has fully performed and then been refused payment cannot recover more than the contract price. Should an injured party who has not fully performed be allowed to recover "the reasonable value of the performance" even if it exceeds the contract price? Using the contract price as a ceiling on recovery in such a case will not entirely avoid problems of measurement of the benefit conferred on the party in breach, since that benefit must, at least in principle, be measured before it can be known whether the ceiling has been reached. On the other hand, not using the contract price as a ceiling on recovery may result in a more generous recovery for partial performance than would have been allowed for full performance.

For authority that the contract price is a ceiling, see Johnson v. Bovee, 574 P.2d 513 (Colo. App. 1978). *Cf.* John T. Brady & Co. v. City of Stamford, 599 A.2d 370, 377 (Conn. 1991), in which the court, through Peters, C.J., held that where "work on the project was 99 percent complete," restitution was precluded by the rule that after "full performance . . . the appropriate measure of the value of the benefit conferred is the value that the parties themselves, in their contract, have assigned to that performance." For authority that it is not, see Southern Painting Co. v. United States, 222 F.2d 431 (10th Cir. 1955). Restatement § 373 states that the contract price is not a ceiling; Restatement (Third) of Restitution and Unjust Enrichment § 38(2)(b) states that it is.

PROBLEM

Kansas City to Atlantic City and Back. Security Stove in Kansas City had developed a furnace which it was anxious to exhibit at a trade association convention in Atlantic City, although it was not yet on the market. Since it was too late to ship it by freight, Security Stove made a contract for its shipment with Express Company, explaining its need, asking that it be shipped to arrive by October 8, and reminding Express Company of the urgency shortly before the date for shipment. Express Company picked up the shipment of 21 numbered packages, but the package containing the gas manifold, the most important part of the exhibit, was mislaid and did not arrive until the convention closed. Security Stove sues to recover from Express Company for express charges to Atlantic City, freight charges back to Kansas City, travel and hotel expenses and salaries for its employees who went to the convention to exhibit the furnace, and rental for the booth. What decision? See Security Stove & Mfg. Co. v. American Railway Express Co., 51 S.W.2d 572 (Mo. App. 1932).

SECTION 3.   LIMITATIONS ON DAMAGES

The cases and materials in Section 2 focused on various measures of the expectation award. We now turn to three general limits placed on that award of a party's expectancy. The first, mitigation, recognizes a requirement on the victim of breach to take reasonable steps to limit the accrual of damages. The second, foreseeability, limits the award to those damages that are reasonably foreseeable by the promisor, which will often, but not always, imply limits on the recovery of sentimental value and damages for emotional distress. The third limitation, certainty, is grounded in ordinary rules of evidence as much as substantive contract law. Simply stated it restricts a party's recovery to only those damages that can be proven with sufficient certainty. These three limitations on the expectation measure are considered in turn.

(A) AVOIDABILITY

In Virtue v. Bird, (1678) 84 Eng. Rep. 1000, 86 Eng. Rep. 200 (K.B.), a quaint case from three centuries ago, the plaintiff contracted to carry goods to Ipswich and to deliver them to a place to be appointed by the defendant. When the plaintiff arrived in Ipswich, however, "the defendant delayed by the space of six hours the appointment of the place; insomuch that his horses being so hot and standing in aperto aere, they died soon after." The court denied him recovery of this loss on the ground that "it was the plaintiff's folly to let the horses stand," for he "might have taken his horses out of the cart, or have laid down the [goods] any where in Ipswich."

Under an important limitation on expectation, an aggrieved promisee is not allowed to recover loss that it could reasonably have avoided. See Restatement § 350. Although the term is often used, there is in fact no "duty to mitigate"; the injured party is simply precluded from recovering for loss that it could reasonably have avoided. Yet while it is true that the injured party incurs no liability to the party in breach for a failure to mitigate, the converse is not true. The promisor must compensate the injured party for costs associated with reasonable mitigation efforts and attempts, whether or not mitigation occurs. Hence recovery is not necessarily the same regardless of whether the injured party takes steps in mitigation or not. Some duties *are* entailed.

Where there is a market for goods, a buyer's damages are based on the assumption that the buyer could reasonably have avoided greater loss by obtaining substitute goods on the market. See UCC § 2–713, under which "the measure of damages . . . is the difference between the market price . . . and the contract price." See also CISG arts. 76(1), 77; UNIDROIT Principles arts. 7.4.6, 7.4.8.

Rockingham County v. Luten Bridge Co.

United States Circuit Court of Appeals, Fourth Circuit, 1929.
35 F.2d 301, 66 A.L.R. 735.

[Action at law, instituted in the district court, to recover an amount alleged to be due under a contract for the construction of a bridge in North Carolina. The contract was entered into by the Board of County Commissioners on January 7, 1924; but there was considerable public opposition to the building of the bridge, and on February 21, 1924, the board notified the plaintiff not to proceed any further under the contract, which it refused (unjustifiably, as the court found) to recognize as valid. At that time plaintiff had expended about $1900 for labor done and material on the ground. Despite this notice from the county commissioners, plaintiff continued to build the bridge in accordance with the terms of the contract. The present action is brought to recover $18,301.07, the amount alleged to be due plaintiff for work done before November 3, 1924. The trial court directed a verdict for plaintiff for this sum. Defendant appealed.]

■ PARKER, CIRCUIT JUDGE. Coming, then, to the third question—i.e., as to the measure of plaintiff's recovery—we do not think that, after the county had given notice, while the contract was still executory, that it did not desire the bridge built and would not pay for it, plaintiff could proceed to build it and recover the contract price. It is true that the county had no right to rescind the contract, and the notice given plaintiff amounted to a breach on its part; but, after plaintiff had received notice of the breach, it was its duty to do nothing to increase the damages flowing therefrom. If A enters into a binding contract to build a house for B, B, of course, has no right to rescind the contract without A's consent. But if, before the house is built, he decides that he does not want it, and notifies A to that effect, A has no right to proceed with the building and thus pile up damages. His remedy is to treat the contract as broken when he receives the notice, and sue for the recovery of such damages as he may have sustained from the breach, including any profit which he would have realized upon performance, as well as any other losses which may have resulted to him. In the case at bar, the county decided not to build the road of which the bridge was to be a part, and did not build it. The bridge, built in the midst of the forest, is of no value to the county because of this change of circumstances. When, therefore, the county gave notice to the plaintiff that it would not proceed with the project, plaintiff should have desisted from further work. It had no right thus to pile up damages by proceeding with the erection of a useless bridge.

The contrary view was expressed by Lord Cockburn in Frost v. Knight, L.R. 7 Ex. 111, but, as pointed out by Prof. Williston (Williston on Contracts, vol. 3, p. 2347), it is not in harmony with the decisions in this country. The American rule and the reasons supporting it are well stated by Prof. Williston as follows:

"There is a line of cases running back to 1845 which holds that, after an absolute repudiation or refusal to perform by one party to a contract, the other party cannot continue to perform and recover damages based on full performance. This rule is only a particular application of the general rule of damages that a plaintiff cannot hold a defendant liable for damages which need not have been incurred; or, as it is often stated, the plaintiff must, so far as he can without loss to himself, mitigate the damages caused by the defendant's wrongful act. The application of this rule to the matter in question is obvious. If a man engages to have work done, and afterwards repudiates his contract before the work has been begun or when it has been only partially done, it is inflicting damage on the defendant without benefit to the plaintiff to allow the latter to insist on proceeding with the contract. The work may be useless to the defendant, and yet he would be forced to pay the full contract price. On the other hand, the plaintiff is interested only in the profit he will make out of the contract. If he receives this it is equally advantageous for him to use his time otherwise."

Judgment reversed.

NOTE

The Code. Under UCC § 2–704(2), a seller that is to manufacture goods may proceed to complete their manufacture upon the buyer's repudiation, instead of halting manufacture and salvaging them while in process, "in the exercise of reasonable commercial judgment for the purposes of avoiding loss and of effective realization." The seller that does so may then base recovery on the goods as completed, even if the "reasonable commercial judgment" turned out to be wrong. Is the manufacturer's situation in any way distinguishable from that of the Luten Bridge Co.? See Barak Richman, Jordi Weinstock and Jason Mehta, *A Bridge, a Tax Revolt, and the Struggle to Industrialize: The Story and Legacy of* Rockingham County v. Luten Bridge Co., 84 N.C. L. Rev. 1841 (2006) for background on the case.

PROBLEM

Walking Across the Brooklyn Bridge. In the Brooklyn Bridge hypothetical (p. 238 above), assume that on finishing the walk across the bridge, B will have to spend $10 to take a taxi back to where A is waiting. If A attempts to revoke the $100 offer after B has taken only a few steps, can B recover $100 after continuing to walk across the bridge and spending the $10 on a taxi? See Restatement § 45(2). What do you think B should do when A attempts to revoke? What answer if A's offer had been to pay B $100 in return for B's *promise* to walk across the bridge? Is § 45(2) consistent with the principle of avoidability?

Mitigation and Contracts for the Sale of Goods

It is one thing to say, as the court did in the *Luten Bridge* case, that the injured party cannot recover for cost that could have been avoided by simply *stopping performance*. It is another to take a second step and say that the injured party cannot recover for loss that could have been avoided by taking *affirmative steps* to arrange a substitute transaction. This second step is the basis for some of the most important rules governing damages for breach of contract for the sale of goods.

In a market economy, it is assumed that the injured party can generally arrange a substitute transaction and, under the principle of mitigation, it is expected to do so. If the seller fails to deliver goods, the buyer can go into the market and "cover" by obtaining substitute goods, so that the buyer's damages should be based on the difference between the presumably greater price that the buyer will have to pay on the market and the lesser contract price. See UCC § 2–712. If the buyer fails to take and pay for goods, the seller can go into the market and resell to a substitute buyer, so that the seller's damages should be based on the difference between the presumably greater contract price and a lesser price it will receive on the market. See UCC § 2–706.

For the injured party that fails to take advantage of the availability of a substitute transaction on the market, the principle of mitigation results in a formula based on the difference between the contract price and the market price at which it could have arranged a hypothetical substitute transaction. If, when the seller fails to deliver goods, the buyer fails to go into the market and "cover," its damages are based on "the difference between the market price . . . and the contract price." UCC § 2–713. If, when the buyer fails to take and pay for goods, the seller fails to go into the market and resell, its damages are based on "the difference between the market price and the unpaid contract price." UCC § 2–708. On proof of market price, see UCC §§ 2–723, 2–724.

NOTE

Windfalls? The Code rules in this area have occasioned criticism on the ground that they sometimes seem to give the injured party a "windfall" by allowing that party to recover more than its actual loss, in disregard of the goal stated in UCC § 1–305(a) of putting that party "in as good a position as if the other party had fully performed."

Suppose, for example, that the injured party has arranged an actual substitute transaction for a price *more* favorable than the market price. Can the injured party recover damages based on market price even though those damages exceed that party's actual loss? Comment 5 to UCC § 2–713 suggests that a buyer cannot do so by explaining that the section "provides a remedy which is completely alternative to cover and applies only when and to the extent that the buyer has not covered." See also UCC §§ 2–703, 2–711. But the Code nowhere suggests that a seller is subject to a similar restriction after a resale for more than market price. Should the Code be read as giving a "windfall" to a seller but not to a buyer? To neither? To both?

PROBLEM

Waiting for a Windfall? Seller contracts to sell Buyer goods for $100,000. Buyer then makes a contract to resell the goods to another purchaser at $125,000. Seller fails to deliver. The market price of similar goods at and immediately after the delivery date is $110,000. Since Buyer's resale contract does not require delivery for six months, Buyer waits and does not go into the market for six months, by which time the market price has dropped to $90,000. How much should Buyer recover? Would $10,000 give Buyer a "windfall"? (Suppose that the market price had *risen* to $120,000 during Buyer's delay. How much should Buyer recover?) Is the applicable section UCC § 2–712 or § 2 713?

The following case wrestles with the problem under the Uniform Commercial Code.

Cosden Oil & Chemical Co. v. Karl O. Helm Aktiengesellschaft

United States Court of Appeals, Fifth Circuit, 1984.
736 F.2d 1064.

■ REAVLEY, CIRCUIT JUDGE. We must address one of the most difficult interpretive problems of the Uniform Commercial Code—the appropriate time to measure buyer's damages where the seller anticipatorily repudiates a contract and the buyer does not cover. The district court applied the Texas version of Article 2 and measured buyer's damages at a commercially reasonable time after seller's repudiation. We affirm, but remand for modification of damages on another point.

Case History

This contractual dispute arose out of events and transactions occurring in the first three months of 1979, when the market in polystyrene, a petroleum derivative used to make molded products, was steadily rising. During this time Iran, a major petroleum producer, was undergoing political turmoil. Karl O. Helm Aktiengesellschaft (Helm or Helm Hamburg), an international trading company based in Hamburg, West Germany, anticipated a tightening in the world petrochemical supply and decided to purchase a large amount of polystyrene. Acting on orders from Helm Hamburg, Helm Houston, a wholly-owned subsidiary, initiated negotiations with Cosden Oil & Chemical Company (Cosden), a Texas-based producer of chemical products, including polystyrene.

Negotiating over the telephone and by telex, the parties agreed to the purchase and sale of 1250 metric tons[1] of high impact polystyrene at $.2825 per pound and 250 metric tons of general purpose polystyrene at $.265 per pound. [The confirmations of these contracts gave Helm options for additional amounts of each type of polystyrene. Upon the proper exercise of these options, Helms held four confirmations, numbered 04 through 07. Numbers 04 and 06 represented the "high impact" product.

[On or about January 26 Cosden shipped 90,000 pounds of this product. After encountering difficulties described in the note,[c] Cosden

---

[1]   One metric ton equals approximately 2,204.5 pounds.

[c]   "As Helm had expected, polystyrene prices began to rise in late January, and continued upward during February and March. Cosden also experienced problems at two of its plants in late January. Normally, Cosden supplied its Calumet City, Illinois, production plant with styrene monomer, the 'feed stock' or main ingredient of polystyrene, by barges that traveled from Louisiana up the Mississippi and Illinois Rivers to a canal that extended to Cosden's plant. Due to the extremely cold winter of 1978–79, however, the Illinois River and the canal froze, suspending barge traffic for a few weeks. A different problem beset Cosden's Windsor, New Jersey, production plant. A new reactor, used in the polystyrene manufacturing process, had recently been installed at the Windsor plant. A manufacturing defect soon became apparent,

notified Helm in late January that delivery under the 04 contract might be delayed. On February 6, Cosden informed Helm that it "was cancelling orders 05, 06, and 07 because two plants were 'down' and it did not have sufficient product to fill the orders." In mid-February Cosden shipped some 1,260,000 pounds under order 04. It refused, as "not possible," a request to make the final delivery under 04 by March 16; and near the end of March it cancelled the remainder of 04. Meanwhile, Cosden remained unpaid for product it had delivered.[d]]

Cosden sued Helm, seeking damages for Helm's failure to pay for delivered polystyrene. Helm counterclaimed for Cosden's failure to deliver polystyrene as agreed. The jury found on special verdict that Cosden had agreed to sell polystyrene to Helm under all four orders.[e] The jury also found that Cosden anticipatorily repudiated orders 05, 06, and 07 and that Cosden cancelled order 04 before Helm's failure to pay for the second 04 delivery constituted a repudiation. The jury fixed the per pound market prices for polystyrene under each of the four orders at three different times: when Helm learned of the cancellation, at a commercially reasonable time thereafter, and at the time for delivery.

The district court determined that Helm was entitled to recover $628,676 in damages representing the difference between the contract price and the market price at a commercially reasonable time after Cosden repudiated its polystyrene delivery obligations and that Cosden was entitled to an offset of $355,950 against those damages for polystyrene delivered, but not paid for, under order 04.

Time for Measuring Buyer's Damages

Both parties find fault with the time at which the district court measured Helm's damages for Cosden's anticipatory repudiation of orders 05, 06, and 07.[2] Cosden argues that damages should be measured when Helm learned of the repudiation. Helm contends that market price as of the last day for delivery—or the time of performance—should be used to compute its damages under the contract-market differential. We reject both views, and hold that the district court correctly measured

---

however, and Cosden returned the reactor to the manufacturer for repair, which took several weeks. At the time of the reactor breakdown, Cosden was manufacturing only general purpose at the Windsor plant. Cosden had planned on supplying Helm's high impact orders from the Calumet City plant." 736 F.2d at 1068.

[d] After Helm Hamburg learned of Cosden's cancellation, apparently in February, "Wolfgang Gordian, a member of Helm's executive board, sent an internal memorandum to Helm Houston outlining a strategy. Helm would urge that Cosden continue to perform under 04 and, after receiving the high impact polystyrene, would offset amounts owing under 04 against Helm's damages for nondelivery of the balance of polystyrene."

[e] It found also that the four orders comprised one contract, and, according to a stipulation, Cosden was not in breach prior to March 19.

[2] The damages measurement problem does not apply to Cosden's breach of order 04, which was not anticipatorily repudiated. The time Helm learned of Cosden's intent to deliver no more polystyrene under 04 was the same time as the last date of performance, which had been extended to the end of March.

damages at a commercially reasonable point after Cosden informed Helm that it was cancelling the three orders.

Article 2 of the Code has generally been hailed as a success for its comprehensiveness, its deference to mercantile reality, and its clarity. Nevertheless, certain aspects of the Code's overall scheme have proved troublesome in application. The interplay among sections 2.610, 2.711, 2.712, 2.713, and 2.723, Tex. Bus. & Com. Code Ann. (Vernon 1968), represents one of those areas, and has been described as "an impossible legal thicket." J. White & R. Summers, Uniform Commercial Code § 6–7 at 242 (2d ed. 1980). The aggrieved buyer seeking damages for seller's anticipatory repudiation presents the most difficult interpretive problem.[3] Section 2.713 describes the buyer's damages remedy:

Buyer's Damages for Non-Delivery or Repudiation

(a)   Subject to the provisions of this chapter with respect to proof of market price (Section 2.723), the measure of damages for non-delivery or repudiation by the seller is the difference between the market price *at the time when the buyer learned of the breach* and the contract price together with any incidental and consequential damages provided in this chapter (Section 2.715), but less expenses saved in consequence of the seller's breach.

(emphasis added).

Courts and commentators have identified three possible interpretations of the phrase "learned of the breach." If seller anticipatorily repudiates, buyer learns of the breach:

(1)   When he learns of the repudiation;

(2)   When he learns of the repudiation plus a commercially reasonable time; or

(3)   When performance is due under the contract.

We would not be free to decide the question if there were a Texas case on point. [But] no Texas case has addressed the Code question of buyer's damages in an anticipatory repudiation context.[f]

We do not doubt, and Texas law is clear, that market price at the time buyer learns of the breach is the appropriate measure of section 2.713 damages in cases where buyer learns of the breach at or after the time for performance. This will be the common case, for which section

---

[3]   The only area of unanimous agreement among those that have studied the Code provisions relevant to this problem is that they are not consistent, present problems in interpretation, and invite amendment.

[f]   Before Texas adopted the Code, its courts applied the traditional time-of-performance measure of damages in repudiation cases. See, e.g., Henderson v. Otto Goedecke, Inc., 430 S.W.2d 120, 123–24 (Tex.Civ.App.—Tyler 1968, writ ref'd n.r.e.); Roy R. Anderson, *Learning of Breaches Under Section 2–713 of the Code,* 40 Tex. B.J. 317, 318 & n. 7 (1977). By interpreting the time buyer learns of the breach to mean a commercially reasonable time after buyer learns of the repudiation, we depart from pre-Code law.

2.713 was designed. See Peters, *Remedies for Breach of Contracts Relating to the Sale of Goods Under the Uniform Commercial Code: A Roadmap for Article Two*, 73 Yale L.J. 199, 264 (1963). In the relatively rare case where seller anticipatorily repudiates and buyer does not cover, see Anderson, supra, at 318, the specific provision for anticipatory repudiation cases, section 2.610, authorizes the aggrieved party to await performance for a commercially reasonable time before resorting to his remedies of cover or damages.

In the anticipatory repudiation context, the buyer's specific right to wait for a commercially reasonable time before choosing his remedy must be read together with the general damages provision of section 2.713 to extend the time for measurement beyond when buyer learns of the breach. Comment 1 to section 2.610 states that if an aggrieved party "awaits performance beyond a commercially reasonable time he cannot recover resulting damages which he should have avoided." This suggests that an aggrieved buyer can recover damages where the market rises during the commercially reasonable time he awaits performance. To interpret 2.713's "learned of the breach" language to mean the time at which seller first communicates his anticipatory repudiation would undercut the time that 2.610 gives the aggrieved buyer to await performance.

The buyer's option to wait a commercially reasonable time also interacts with section 2.611, which allows the seller an opportunity to retract his repudiation. Thus, an aggrieved buyer "learns of the breach" a commercially reasonable time after he learns of the seller's anticipatory repudiation. The weight of scholarly commentary supports this interpretation. See J. Calamari & J. Perillo, Contracts § 14–20 (2d ed. 1977); Sebert, *Remedies Under Article Two of the Uniform Commercial Code: An Agenda for Review*, 130 U. Pa. L. Rev. 360, 372–80 (1981); Wallach, *Anticipatory Repudiation and the UCC*, 13 U.C.C. L.J. 48 (1980); Peters, supra, at 263–68.

Typically, our question will arise where parties to an executory contract are in the midst of a rising market. To the extent that market decisions are influenced by a damages rule, measuring market price at the time of seller's repudiation gives seller the ability to fix buyer's damages and may induce seller to repudiate, rather than abide by the contract. By contrast, measuring buyer's damages at the time of performance will tend to dissuade the buyer from covering, in hopes that market price will continue upward until performance time.

Allowing the aggrieved buyer a commercially reasonable time, however, provides him with an opportunity to investigate his cover possibilities in a rising market without fear that, if he is unsuccessful in obtaining cover, he will be relegated to a market-contract damage remedy measured at the time of repudiation. The Code supports this view. While cover is the preferred remedy, the Code clearly provides the option to seek damages. See § 2.712(c) & cmt. 3. If "[t]he buyer is always free to choose between cover and damages for non-delivery," and if 2.712 "is not intended to limit the time necessary for [buyer] to look around and decide as to how he may best effect cover," it would be anomalous, if the buyer chooses to seek damages, to fix his damages at a time before he investigated cover possibilities and before he elected his remedy. See id. cmt. 2 & 3; Dura-Wood Treating Co. v. Century Forest Industries, Inc., 675 F.2d 745, 754 (5th Cir. 1982) ("buyer has some time in which to evaluate the situation"). Moreover, comment 1 to section 2.713 states, "The general baseline adopted in this section uses as a yardstick the market in which the buyer would have obtained cover had he sought that relief." See § 2.610 cmt. 1. When a buyer chooses not to cover, but to seek damages, the market is measured at the time he could have covered—a reasonable time after repudiation. See §§ 2.711 & 2.713.

Persuasive arguments exist for interpreting "learned of the breach" to mean "time of performance," consistent with the pre-Code rule. See J. White & R. Summers, supra, § 6–7; Anderson, supra. If this was the intention of the Code's drafters, however, phrases in section 2.610 and 2.712 lose their meaning. If buyer is entitled to market-contract damages measured at the time of performance, it is difficult to explain why the anticipatory repudiation section limits him to a commercially reasonable time to await performance. See § 2.610 cmt. 1. Similarly, in a rising market, no reason would exist for requiring the buyer to act "without unreasonable delay" when he seeks to cover following an anticipatory repudiation. See § 2.712(a).

The interplay among the relevant Code sections does not permit, in this context, an interpretation that harmonizes all and leaves no loose ends. We therefore acknowledge that our interpretation fails to explain the language of section 2.723(a) insofar as it relates to aggrieved buyers. We note, however, that the section has limited applicability—cases that come to trial before the time of performance will be rare. Moreover, the comment to section 2.723 states that the "section is not intended to exclude the use of any other reasonable method of determining market price or of measuring damages. . . ." In light of the Code's persistent theme of commercial reasonableness, the prominence of cover as a remedy, and the time given an aggrieved buyer to await performance and to investigate cover before selecting his remedy, we agree with the district court that "learned of the breach" incorporates section 2.610's commercially reasonable time.[4]

---

[4]   We note that two circuits arrived at a similar conclusion by different routes. In Cargill, Inc. v. Stafford, 553 F.2d 1222 (10th Cir. 1977), the court began its discussion of damages by embracing the "time of performance" interpretation urged by Professors White and Summers. Id. at 1226. Indeed, the court stated that "damages normally should be measured from the time when performance is due and not from the time when the buyer learns of repudiation." Id. Nevertheless, the court conclude[d] that under § 4–2–713 a buyer may urge continued performance for a reasonable time. At the end of a reasonable period he should cover if substitute goods are readily available. If substitution is readily available and buyer does not cover within a reasonable time, damages should be based on the price at the end of that

"Cover" as a Ceiling

At trial Cosden argued that Helm's purchases of polystyrene from other sources in early February constituted cover. Helm argued that those purchases were not intended to substitute for polystyrene sales cancelled by Cosden. Helm, however, contended that it did cover by purchasing large amounts of high impact polystyrene from other sources late in February and around the first of March. Cosden claimed that these purchases were not made reasonably and that they should not qualify as cover. The jury found that none of Helm's purchases of polystyrene from other sources were cover purchases.

Now Cosden argues that the prices of polystyrene for the purchases that Helm claimed were cover should act as a ceiling for fixing market price under section 2.713. We refuse to accept this novel argument. Although a buyer who has truly covered may not be allowed to seek higher damages under section 2.713 than he is granted by section 2.712, see § 2.713 cmt. 5; J. White & R. Summers, supra, § 6–4 at 233–34, in this case the jury found that Helm did not cover. We cannot isolate a reason to explain the jury's finding: it might have concluded that Helm would have made the purchases regardless of Cosden's nonperformance or that the transactions did not qualify as cover for other reasons. Because of the jury's finding, we cannot use those other transactions to determine Helm's damages.

[The jury found that Cosden was excused by commercial impracticability—UCC § 2–615—from performing under orders 05 and 07, but that Cosden had failed to allocate its production as that section requires. At the trial court's direction, the jury therefore assessed damages based on the amount of general purpose polystyrene that Cosden should have allocated to Helm. On appeal, this was held to be

---

reasonable time rather than on the price when performance is due. Id. at 1227. The Cargill court would employ the time of performance measure only if buyer had a valid reason for not covering.

In First Nat'l Bank of Chicago v. Jefferson Mortgage Co., 576 F.2d 479 (3d Cir. 1978), the court initially quoted with approval legislative history that supports a literal or "plain meaning" interpretation of New Jersey's section 2–713. Nevertheless, the court hedged by interpreting that section "to measure damages within a commercially reasonable time after learning of the repudiation." Id. at 492. In light of the unequivocal repudiation and because cover was "easily and immediately . . . available . . . in the well-organized and easily accessible market," id. at 493 (quoting Oloffson v. Coomer, 11 Ill.App.3d 918, 296 N.E.2d 871 (1973)), a commercially reasonable time did not extend beyond the date of repudiation.

We agree with the First National court that "the circumstances of the particular market involved should determine the duration of a 'commercially reasonable time.'" 576 F.2d at 492; see Tex.Bus. & Com.Code § 1.204(b). In this case, however, there was no showing that cover was easily and immediately available in an organized and accessible market and that a commercially reasonable time expired on the day of Cosden's cancellation. We recognize that § 2.610's "commercially reasonable time" and § 2.712's "without unreasonable delay" are distinct concepts. Often, however, the two time periods will overlap, since the buyer can investigate cover possibilities while he awaits performance. See Sebert, supra, at 376–77 & n. 80.

Although the jury in the present case did not fix the exact duration of a commercially reasonable time, we assume that the jury determined market price at a time commercially reasonable under all the circumstances, in light of the absence of objection to the form of the special issue.

error: owing to the misallocation, Cosden should have been allowed no credit for commercial impracticability.]

Affirmed, but, in part, reversed and remanded.

NOTES

(1) *The Reverse Case.* Suppose that the market price of polystyrene had dropped rather than risen after Cosden made its sale agreements with Helm, and that Helm, the buyer, rather than Cosden, the seller, had repudiated in February, 1979. For that case UCC § 2–708(1) provides for damages based on the difference between the unpaid contract price and the market price *"at the time and place for tender."* UCC § 2–708(1). If that rule were different, the decision in the main case would be easier to accept, would it not? What might account for the difference?

If Helm had repudiated the contract, might Cosden have recovered under UCC § 2–706?

(2) *Retraction.* The court observes that the "buyer's option to wait a commercially reasonable time" interacts with UCC § 2–611, "which allows the seller an opportunity to retract his repudiation." An offer and an anticipatory repudiation have virtually nothing in common except that each may be withdrawn, an offer by revocation and a repudiation by retraction. An anticipatory repudiation thus differs from a breach by nonperformance, since in the case of the latter there is nothing that the defaulting party can do to deprive the other of a claim for damages, at least nominal. See Restatement § 256.

(3) *Urging Retraction.* The modern view is that the recipient of a repudiation may urge its retraction without becoming committed to further performance if it is not retracted. See UCC § 2–610(b), Restatement § 257.

PROBLEMS

(1) *Repudiation and Arbitration.* If Cosden had succeeded in getting Helm to agree to the inclusion of an arbitration clause calling for arbitration in Texas, where Cosden's headquarters were located, would Cosden's repudiation disable it from insisting on that clause? See Kulukundis Shipping Co. v. Amtorg Trading Corp., 126 F.2d 978 (2d Cir. 1942). What answer if the clause, instead of providing for arbitration, provided that "all disputes and matters . . . shall be litigated . . . before a Court located in the State of Texas, to the exclusion of the Courts of any other state or country"? See the clause in Carnival Cruise Lines v. Shute, p. 293 above; see Marra v. Papandreou, 216 F.3d 1119 (D.C. Cir. 2000).

If you represented Cosden, what arguments could you muster for your client?

(2) *A Matter of an Option.* Charles Hermanowski, former president of Acton Corporation, was given a five-year non-cancelable stock option to purchase 50,000 shares of Acton's common stock at $2 per share. One year later, when the market price of the stock was $3 per share, Acton, in the mistaken belief that the option was cancelable, notified Hermanowski that

it had cancelled it. At the end of three years, the price had risen to $5 per share. At the end of four years, the price stood at $4 per share, and Hermanowski notified Acton that he exercised the option. When Acton reiterated that it had cancelled the option, Hermanowski sued. How much should Hermanowski recover? $50,000? $100,000? $150,000? See Hermanowski v. Acton Corp., 580 F.Supp. 140 (E.D.N.Y. 1983), *aff'd per curiam*, 729 F.2d 921 (2d Cir. 1984).

Does Hermanowski's right to enforce the option depend on whether he objected to Acton's initial notification of cancellation? On whether he tendered $100,000 when he notified Acton that he exercised the option?

Tongish v. Thomas

Supreme Court of Kansas, 1992.
251 Kan. 728, 840 P.2d 471.

[Dennis Tongish, a farmer, made a contract with the Decatur Coop Association under which he was to grow 116.8 acres of sunflower seeds, to be purchased by Coop at $13 per hundredweight for large seeds and $8 per hundredweight for small seeds, delivery to be in thirds by December 31, 1988, March 31, 1989, and May 31, 1989. Coop had a contract to deliver the seeds to Bambino Bean & Seed for the same price it paid Tongish plus a 55 cent per hundredweight handling fee, Coop's only anticipated profit. Owing to a short crop, bad weather, and other factors, the market price of sunflower seeds in January 1989 had risen to double that in the Tongish contract. Tongish notified Coop that he would make no more deliveries and sold the balance of his crop to Danny Thomas for about $20 per hundredweight or $14,714, which was $5,153 more than the Coop contract price. Coop sued Tongish and recovered $455 in damages, based on its loss of handling charges. Coop appealed and the Court of Appeals reversed for determination of damages based on market price under UCC § 2–713. Tongish appealed, arguing that under UCC § 1–106 the trial court was correct.]

■ MCFARLAND, JUSTICE. This case presents the narrow issue of whether damages arising from the nondelivery of contracted-for sunflower seeds should be computed on the basis of K.S.A. 84–1–106 or K.S.A. 84–2–713. The analyses and rationale of the Court of Appeals utilized in resolving the issue are sound and we adopt the following portion thereof:

"There is authority for appellee's position that K.S.A. 84–2–713 should not be applied in certain circumstances. In Allied Canners & Packers, Inc. v. Victor Packing Co., 162 Cal.App.3d 905, 209 Cal.Rptr. 60 (1984), Allied contracted to purchase 375,000 pounds of raisins from Victor for 29.75 cents per pound with a 4% discount. Allied then contracted to sell the raisins for 29.75 cents per pound expecting a profit of $4,462.50 from the 4% discount it received from Victor. 162 Cal.App.3d at 907–08 [209 Cal.Rptr. 60].

"Heavy rains damaged the raisin crop and Victor breached its contract, being unable to fulfill the requirement. The market price of raisins had risen to about 80 cents per pound. Allied's buyers agreed to rescind their contracts so Allied was not bound to supply them with raisins at a severe loss. Therefore, the actual loss to Allied was the $4,462.50 profit it expected, while the difference between the market price and the contract price was about $150,000. 162 Cal.App.3d at 908–09 [209 Cal.Rptr. 60].

"The California appellate court, in writing an exception, stated: 'It has been recognized that the use of the market-price contract-price formula under section 2–713 does not, absent pure accident, result in a damage award reflecting the buyer's actual loss. [Citations omitted.]' 162 Cal.App.3d at 912 [209 Cal.Rptr. 60]. The court indicated that section 2–713 may be more of a statutory liquidated damages clause and, therefore, conflicts with the goal of section 1–106. The court discussed that in situations where the buyer has made a resale contract for the goods, which the seller knows about, it may be appropriate to limit 2–713 damages to actual loss. However, the court cited a concern that a seller not be rewarded for a bad faith breach of contract. 162 Cal.App.3d at 912–14 [209 Cal.Rptr. 60].

"In *Allied,* the court determined that if the seller knew the buyer had a resale contract for the goods, and the seller did not breach the contract in bad faith, the buyer was limited to actual loss of damages under section 1–106. 162 Cal.App.3d at 915 [209 Cal.Rptr. 60].

"The similarities between the present case and *Allied* are that the buyer made a resale contract which the seller knew about. (Tongish knew the seeds eventually went to Bambino, although he may not have known the details of the deal.) However, in examining the breach itself, Victor could not deliver the raisins because its crop had been destroyed. Victor had no raisins to sell to any buyer, while Tongish took advantage of the doubling price of sunflower seeds and sold to Danny Thomas. Although the trial court had no need to find whether Tongish breached the contract in bad faith, it did find there was no valid reason for the breach. Therefore, the nature of Tongish's breach was much different than Victor's in *Allied.*

"Section 2–713 and the theories behind it have a lengthy and somewhat controversial history. In 1963, it was suggested that 2–713 was a statutory liquidated damages clause and not really an effort to try and accurately predict what actual damages would be. Peters, *Remedies for Breach of Contracts Relating to the Sale of Goods Under the Uniform Commercial Code: A Roadmap for Article Two*, 73 Yale L.J. 199, 259 (1963).

"In 1978, Robert Childres called for the repeal of section 2–713. Childres, *Buyer's Remedies: The Danger of Section 2–713*, 72 Nw. U. L. Rev. 837 (1978). Childres reflected that because the market price/contract price remedy 'has been the cornerstone of Anglo-American damages' that it has been so hard to see that this remedy 'makes no sense whatever when applied to real life situations.' 72 Nw. U. L. Rev. at 841–42.

"In 1979, David Simon and Gerald A. Novack wrote a fairly objective analysis of the two arguments about section 2–713 and stated:

'For over sixty years our courts have divided on the question of which measure of damages is appropriate for the supplier's breach of his delivery obligations. The majority view, reinforced by applicable codes, would award market damages even though in excess of plaintiff's loss. A persistent minority would reduce market damages to the plaintiff's loss, without regard to whether this creates a windfall for the defendant. Strangely enough, each view has generally tended to disregard the arguments, and even the existence, of the opposing view.' Simon and Novack, *Limiting the Buyer's Market Damages to Lost Profits: A Challenge to the Enforceability of Market Contracts*, 92 Harv. L. Rev. 1395, 1397 (1979).

"Although the article discussed both sides of the issue, the authors came down on the side of market price/contract price as the preferred damages theory. The authors admit that market damages fly in the face 'of the familiar maxim that the purpose of contract damages is to make the injured party whole, not penalize the breaching party.' 92 Harv. L. Rev. at 1437. However, they argue that the market damages rule discourages the breach of contracts and encourages a more efficient market. 92 Harv. L. Rev. at 1437.

"The *Allied* decision in 1984, which relied on the articles cited above for its analysis to reject market price/contract price damages, has been sharply criticized. In Schneider, *UCC § Section 2–713: A Defense of Buyers' Expectancy Damages*, 22 Cal. W. L. Rev. 233, 266 (1986), the author stated that *Allied* 'adopted the most restrictive [position] on buyer's damages. This Article is intended to reverse that trend.' Schneider argued that by following section 1–106, 'the court ignored the clear language of section 2–713's compensation scheme to award expectation damages in accordance with the parties' allocation of risk as measured by the difference between contract price and market price on the date set for performance.' 22 Cal. W. L. Rev. at 264.

"Recently in Scott, *The Case for Market Damages: Revisiting the Lost Profits Puzzle*, 57 U. Chi. L. Rev. 1155, 1200 (1990), the *Allied* result was called 'unfortunate.' Scott argues that section 1–106 is 'entirely consistent' with the market damages remedy of 2–713. 57 U. Chi. L. Rev. at 1201. According to Scott, it is possible to harmonize sections 1–106 and 2–713. Scott states, 'Market damages measure the expectancy ex ante, and thus reflect the value of the option; lost profits, on the other hand, measure losses ex post, and thus only reflect the value of the completed exchange.' 57 U. Chi. L. Rev. at 1174. The author argues that if the nonbreaching party has laid off part of the market risk (like Coop did) the lost profits rule creates instability because the other party is now encouraged to breach the contract if the market fluctuates to its advantage. 57 U. Chi. L. Rev. at 1178.

"We are not persuaded that the lost profits view under *Allied* should be embraced. It is a minority rule that has received only nominal support. We believe the majority rule or the market damages remedy as contained in K.S.A. 84–2–713 is more reasoned and should be followed as the preferred measure of damages. While application of the rule may not reflect the actual loss to a buyer, it encourages a more efficient market and discourages the breach of contracts." Tongish v. Thomas, 16 Kan. App. 2d at 811–17 [829 P.2d 916].

At first blush, the result reached herein appears unfair. However, closer scrutiny dissipates this impression. By the terms of the contract Coop was obligated to buy Tongish's large sunflower seeds at $13 per hundredweight whether or not it had a market for them. Had the price of sunflower seeds plummeted by delivery time, Coop's obligation to purchase at the agreed price was fixed. If loss of actual profit pursuant to K.S.A. 84–1–106(1) would be the measure of damages to be applied herein, it would enable Tongish to consider the Coop contract price of $13 per hundredweight plus 55 cents per hundredweight handling fee as the "floor" price for his seeds, take advantage of rapidly escalating prices, ignore his contractual obligation, and profitably sell to the highest bidder. Damages computed under K.S.A. 84–2–713 encourage the honoring of contracts and market stability.

[Judgment of the Court of Appeals affirmed.]

NOTES

(1) *Questions.* If Coop had gone into the market after Tongish's repudiation and bought seeds to deliver to Bambino for $14,714, could it have recovered $5,153 from Tongish under UCC § 2–712? If Coop bought no seeds to deliver to Bambino and therefore had to pay damages to Bambino, could Coop recover those damages from Tongish? Note that Allied's buyers had agreed to rescind their contracts. Should the result in *Tongish* be different if Bambino had agreed to rescind its contract with Coop? Compare Iron Trade Products v. Wilkoff, p. 843 below, with H-W-H Cattle Co. v. Schroeder, 767 F.2d 437 (8th Cir. 1985). Should the result in *Tongish* be different if Coop had protected itself by reserving the power to cancel the contract with Bambino on breach by Tongish? See E. Allan Farnsworth, *Legal Remedies for Breach of Contract*, 70 Colum. L. Rev. 1145, 1190 n.189 (1970).

(2) *A Cautionary Note on Efficient Breach.* Recall the discussion of *The Economics of Remedies* at p. 34 above. It would be a mistake to assume that a seller like Tongish, who deals with a commodity that has a market, can often commit such a breach when there is a rise in the market.

If Tongish had not made his contract with Coop, he would, of course, have been free to take advantage of the risen market for sunflower seeds and sell his crop on the market, as he did to Thomas. But he had a contract with Coop. If we suppose that the contract price was $13 per hundredweight and that the risen market price was $20 per hundredweight, he would have gained an additional $7 per hundredweight by breaking his contract with Coop and selling on the risen market.

How much of that gain would be left after paying damages to Coop under the decision in *Tongish* to apply UCC § 2–713? How much of the gain would be left after paying damages to Coop under the decision in *Allied*? Can the difference in your answers be justified on the ground, noted by the court in *Tongish,* that "the nature of Tongish's breach" was much different than Victor's in *Allied*?

How can one explain the difference between a case such as *Naval Institute*, which seems to invite thoughts of efficient breach, and *Tongish*, which seems to discourage such thoughts?

(3)   *More Middlemen.* Coop acted like a middleman between Tongish and Bambino Bean & Seed. Coop's expected profit for this service was 55 cent per hundredweight handling fee, or about $455. But recall that there were two separate contracts: one between Coop and Tongish; the other between Coop and Bambino Bean & Seed. If Bambino Bean & Seed breached or renegotiated its contract with Coop, then Coop's damages from Tongish's breach would not have been $455. Should the damages available to Coop depend on what might have happened to Bambino? See Victor Goldberg, Framing Contract Law 225 (2006) on the middleman's damages.

PROBLEM

Tongish *Topsy-Turvy?* Seller contracts to sell Buyer goods for $100,000. Seller then makes a contract to purchase the goods from a supplier for $90,000. The market price for similar goods then falls to $75,000, and Buyer repudiates the contract. (The market price then remains constant through the delivery date.) Seller has neither received the goods from its supplier nor resold them to another buyer. How much should Seller recover? Would $25,000 give Seller a "windfall"? Does UCC § 2–708(2) apply if a seller will be overcompensated by UCC § 2–708(1)? Compare Nobs Chemical, U.S.A., Inc. v. Koppers Co., Inc., 616 F.2d 212 (5th Cir. 1980), with Trans World Metals, Inc. v. Southwire Co., 769 F.2d 902 (2d Cir. 1985), and Robert Scott, *The Case for Market Damages: Revisiting the Lost Profits Puzzle*, 57 U. Chi. L. Rev. 1155, 1175–79 (1990).

―――――――

Mitigation and Contracts for Services

The application of the principle of mitigation to contracts of employment has proved particularly troublesome. In Gandell v. Pontigny, (1816) 171 Eng.Rep. 119, the court simply refused to apply the principle. A merchant was sued by his clerk, whom he had wrongfully discharged in the middle of a quarter. The clerk was allowed to recover the agreed compensation for the entire quarter, including the part when he had not worked, on Lord Ellenborough's reasoning that:

Having served a part of the quarter and being willing to serve the residue, in contemplation of law he may be considered to have served the whole.

In Howard v. Daly, 61 N.Y. 362 (1875), a leading American case, Commissioner Theodore W. Dwight[g] rejected this doctrine of "constructive service" as

> so wholly irreconcilable to that great and beneficent rule of law, that a person discharged from service must not remain idle, but must accept employment elsewhere if offered, that we cannot accept it. The doctrine of "constructive service" is not only at war with principle but with the rules of political economy, as it encourages idleness and gives compensation to men who fold their arms and decline service, equal to those who perform with willing hands their stipulated amount of labor.

The case that follows is premised on rejection of the doctrine of constructive service and on applicability of the principle of mitigation.

Parker v. Twentieth Century-Fox Film Corp.

Supreme Court of California, 1970.
3 Cal.3d 176, 474 P.2d 689.

■ BURKE, JUSTICE. Defendant Twentieth Century-Fox Film Corporation appeals from a summary judgment granting to plaintiff the recovery of agreed compensation under a written contract for her services as an actress in a motion picture. As will appear, we have concluded that the trial court correctly ruled in plaintiff's favor and that the judgment should be affirmed.

Plaintiff is well known as an actress, and in the contract between plaintiff and defendant is sometimes referred to as the "Artist.[h]" Under the contract, dated August 6, 1965, plaintiff was to play the female lead in defendant's contemplated production of a motion picture entitled "Bloomer Girl." The contract provided that defendant would pay plaintiff a minimum "guaranteed compensation" of $53,571.42 per week for 14 weeks commencing May 23, 1966, for a total of $750,000. Prior to May 1966 defendant decided not to produce the picture and by a letter dated

---

[g] Theodore W. Dwight (1822–1892) served as professor of law at Hamilton College, and then as professor of law and later as warden of the law school at Columbia from 1858 to 1891. His principal field was contracts. His method of teaching involved interrogation of his students on an assigned text, and it is reported that, "He could so cross-examine a dunce that the dunce would come off amazed at his own unconscious cerebration." From 1873 to 1875 he was a member of the New York Commission of Appeals, which had been created to help the Court of Appeals dispose of its backlog of undecided cases. It was said that his 68 opinions were "monographs, exhausting the particular subject," and it was doubted "whether in any reports a greater amount of learning is anywhere condensed into an equal number of pages."

[h] Shirley MacLaine, born in 1934, is an American singer, dancer, and actress of film and theater. She was born Shirley MacLean, later married to Steve Parker, businessman, from 1954 to 1982.

April 4, 1966, it notified plaintiff of that decision and that it would not "comply with our obligations to you under" the written contract.

By the same letter and with the professed purpose "to avoid any damage to you," defendant instead offered to employ plaintiff as the leading actress in another film tentatively entitled "Big Country, Big Man" (hereinafter, "Big Country"). The compensation offered was identical, as were 31 of the 34 numbered provisions or articles of the original contract. Unlike "Bloomer Girl," however, which was to have been a musical production, "Big Country" was a dramatic "western type" movie. "Bloomer Girl" was to have been filmed in California; "Big Country" was to be produced in Australia. Also, certain terms in the proffered contract varied from those of the original. Plaintiff was given one week within which to accept; she did not and the offer lapsed. Plaintiff then commenced this action seeking recovery of the agreed guaranteed compensation.

The complaint sets forth two causes of action. The first is for money due under the contract; the second, based upon the same allegations as the first, is for damages resulting from defendant's breach of contract. Defendant in its answer admits the existence and validity of the contract, that plaintiff complied with all the conditions, covenants and promises and stood ready to complete the performance, and that defendant breached and "anticipatorily repudiated" the contract. It denies, however, that any money is due to plaintiff either under the contract or as a result of its breach, and pleads as an affirmative defense to both causes of action plaintiff's allegedly deliberate failure to mitigate damages, asserting that she unreasonably refused to accept its offer of the leading role in "Big Country."

Plaintiff moved for summary judgment under Code of Civil Procedure section 437c, the motion was granted, and summary judgment for $750,000 plus interest was entered in plaintiff's favor. This appeal by defendant followed.

The general rule is that the measure of recovery by a wrongfully discharged employee is the amount of salary agreed upon for the period of service, less the amount which the employer affirmatively proves the employee has earned or with reasonable effort might have earned from other employment. However, before projected earnings from other employment opportunities not sought or accepted by the discharged employee can be applied in mitigation, the employer must show that the other employment was comparable, or substantially similar, to that of which the employee has been deprived; the employee's rejection of or failure to seek other available employment of a different or inferior kind may not be resorted to in order to mitigate damages.

In the present case defendant has raised no issue of *reasonableness of efforts* by plaintiff to obtain other employment; the sole issue is whether plaintiff's refusal of defendant's substitute offer of "Big Country" may be used in mitigation. Nor, if the "Big Country" offer was of employment different or inferior when compared with the original "Bloomer Girl" employment, is there an issue as to whether or not plaintiff acted reasonably in refusing the substitute offer. Despite defendant's arguments to the contrary, no case cited or which our research has discovered holds or suggests that reasonableness is an element of a wrongfully discharged employee's option to reject, or fail to seek different or inferior employment lest the possible earnings therefrom be charged against him in mitigation of damages.

Applying the foregoing rules to the record in the present case, with all intendments in favor of the party opposing the summary judgment motion—here, defendant—it is clear that the trial court correctly ruled that plaintiff's failure to accept defendant's tendered substitute employment could not be applied in mitigation of damages because the offer of the "Big Country" lead was of employment both different and inferior, and that no factual dispute was presented on that issue. The mere circumstance that "Bloomer Girl" was to be a musical review calling upon plaintiff's talents as a dancer as well as an actress, and was to be produced in the City of Los Angeles, whereas "Big Country" was a straight dramatic role in a "Western Type" story taking place in an opal mine in Australia, demonstrates the difference in kind between the two employments; the female lead as a dramatic actress in a western style motion picture can by no stretch of imagination be considered the equivalent of or substantially similar to the lead in a song-and-dance production. Additionally, the substitute "Big Country" offer proposed to eliminate or impair the director and screenplay approvals accorded to plaintiff under the original "Bloomer Girl" contract (see fn. 2, ante), and thus constituted an offer of inferior employment. No expertise or judicial notice is required in order to hold that the deprivation or infringement of an employee's rights held under an original employment contract converts the available "other employment" relied upon by the employer to mitigate damages, into inferior employment which the employee need not seek or accept. (See Gonzales v. Internat. Assn. of Machinists, supra, 213 Cal.App.2d 817, 823–824, 29 Cal.Rptr. 190; and fn. 3, ante.).

In view of the determination that defendant failed to present any facts showing the existence of a factual issue with respect to its sole defense—plaintiff's rejection of its substitute employment offer in mitigation of damages—we need not consider plaintiff's further contention that for various reasons, including the provisions of the original contract set forth in footnote 1, ante, plaintiff was excused from attempting to mitigate damages.

The judgment is affirmed.

■ SULLIVAN, ACTING CHIEF JUSTICE (dissenting). Over the years the courts have employed various phrases to define the type of employment which the employee, upon his wrongful discharge, is under an obligation to accept. Thus in California alone it has been held that he must accept employment which is "substantially similar"; "comparable employment";

employment "in the same general line of the first employment"; "equivalent to his prior position"; "employment in a similar capacity"; employment which is "not . . . of a different or inferior kind".

For reasons which are unexplained, the majority select from among the various judicial formulations which contain one particular phrase, "Not of a different or inferior kind," with which to analyze this case. I have discovered no historical or theoretical reason to adopt this phrase, which is simply a negative restatement of the affirmative standards set out in the above cases, as the exclusive standard. Indeed, its emergence is an example of the dubious phenomenon of the law responding not to rational judicial choice or changing social conditions, but to unrecognized changes in the language of opinions or legal treatises. However, the phrase is a serviceable one and my concern is not with its use as the standard but rather with what I consider its distortion.

The relevant language excuses acceptance only of employment which is of a *different kind*. It has never been the law that the mere existence of *differences between two jobs in the same field* is sufficient, as a matter of law, to excuse an employee wrongfully discharged from one from accepting the other in order to mitigate damages. Such an approach would effectively eliminate any obligation of an employee to attempt to minimize damage arising from a wrongful discharge. The only alternative job offer an employee would be required to accept would be an offer of his former job by his former employer.

Although the majority appear to hold that there was a difference "in kind" between the employment offered plaintiff in "Bloomer Girl" and that offered in "Big Country", an examination of the opinion makes crystal clear that the majority merely point out differences between the two *films* (an obvious circumstance) and then apodictically assert that these constitute a difference in the *kind of employment*. The entire rationale of the majority boils down to this: that the "*mere circumstances*" that "Bloomer Girl" was to be a musical review while "Big Country" was a straight drama "demonstrates the difference in kind" since a female lead in a western is not "the equivalent of or substantially similar to" a lead in a musical. This is merely attempting to prove the proposition by repeating it. It shows that the vehicles for the display of the star's talents are different but it does not prove that her employment as a star in such vehicles is of necessity different *in kind* and either inferior or superior.

I believe that the approach taken by the majority (a superficial listing of differences with no attempt to assess their significance) may subvert a valuable legal doctrine. The inquiry in cases such as this should not be whether differences between the two jobs exist (there will always be differences) but whether the differences which are present are substantial enough to constitute differences in the *kind* of employment or, alternatively, whether they render the substitute work employment of an *inferior kind*.

I remain convinced that the relevant question in such cases is whether or not a particular contract provision is so significant that its omission creates employment of an inferior kind. This question is, of course, intimately bound up in what I consider the ultimate issue: whether or not the employee acted reasonably. This will generally involve a factual inquiry to ascertain the importance of the particular contract term and a process of weighing the absence of that term against the countervailing advantages of the alternate employment. In the typical case, this will mean that summary judgment must be withheld.

NOTES

(1) *Questions.* Would it have made a difference if the studio's offer of substitute employment had been conditioned on Parker's surrender of her rights under the old contract?

Who should bear the burden of proof on the issue of mitigation? In Delliponti v. DeAngelis, 681 A.2d 1261, 1265 (Pa. 1996), the court placed the burden on the defendant employer and held that it had failed to meet that burden. Although the plaintiff, a municipal employee, testified only "that she made telephone inquiries regarding three job openings she read about in the newspaper but did not pursue any other jobs," the court concluded that the municipality's "assertion that there were unquestionably comparable jobs available does not establish that there were actual vacant positions available" to the employee.

(2) *"Honor and Respect."* Personal service contracts often involve considerations not common in the case of other kinds of contracts. "If the general counsel of a large corporation is wrongfully discharged, he is not required, in order to mitigate his damages, to take a job as a dishwasher. . . . Our case involves a contract to build a sewer. There is no suggestion that the contractor, a corporation rather than an individual, would have lost 'honor and respect' by taking steps to mitigate its damages. And we cannot imagine how any such steps could be thought to degrade or humiliate the corporation." S.A. Healy Co. v. Milwaukee Metropolitan Sewerage District, 50 F.3d 476, 481 (7th Cir. 1995) (Posner, C.J.).

The court in *Parker* laid no stress on the fact that the offer of substitute employment came from the employer that had broken the contract in suit. Might this circumstance call "honor and respect" into question? Might the answer depend on the circumstances of the breach? In Voorhees v. Guyan Machinery Co., 446 S.E.2d 672, 679 (W.Va. 1994), the court explained that "an offer of reemployment by an employer will not diminish the employee's recovery if the offer is not accepted if circumstances are such as to render further association between the parties offensive or degrading to the employee." The court went on to observe that the former employer's offer of reemployment came after it had caused the employee to lose his job with his new employer and after he had sued his former employer, and concluded that expecting him to return to work for his former employer "in such circumstances would be tantamount to expecting that Sulla and Gaius

Marius might form a productive working relationship after Sulla's march on Rome."

(3) *An Equal-Opportunity Exception?* Does the mitigation principle apply even if the party in breach has an equal opportunity to reduce the damages by the same act? In Shea-S & M Ball v. Massman-Kiewit-Early, 606 F.2d 1245, 1249–50 (D.C. Cir. 1979), one contractor sued another for damage caused by the other's failure to control groundwater and prevent a sewer from overflowing.[i] The Court of Appeals held that it was error for the trial court to conclude that the plaintiff "had not properly mitigated its damages by failing to build a dike. 'The duty to mitigate damages is not applicable where the party whose duty it is primarily to perform a contract has equal opportunity for performance and equal knowledge of the consequences of nonperformance.' " Here the defendant "had the primary responsibility for controlling its water runoff and had the same opportunity as [the plaintiff] to build a dike that would have prevented the damages." A few courts have taken a similar position, severely criticized in Cates v. Morgan Portable Building Corp., 780 F.2d 683, 689 (7th Cir. 1985) (Posner, C.J.: this position is "discordant with common law principles" by not preserving injured party's "incentive to consider a wide range of possible methods of mitigation of damages").

PROBLEMS

(1) *A Classic Problem.* First Bank repossessed a collection of classic automobiles together with thousands of rare parts no longer manufactured. It contracted to sell them to Frederick Simeone, a private collector of vintage automobiles, for $400,000. Because of legal problems arising from the repossession, First Bank refused Simeone's tender of the price and later, mistakenly thinking it was relieved of its obligation to Simeone because of a provision in their contract, sold the cars and parts to SMB, Inc., which resold them for $1,000,000. Simeone sued First Bank and recovered $2,600,000, based on expert testimony that the cars and parts were worth $3,000,000. First Bank appealed on the ground that Simeone "could have mitigated his damages by purchasing the vehicles and parts from SMB, Inc. at the increased price." What result on appeal? See Simeone v. First Bank National Assn., 73 F.3d 184 (8th Cir. 1996).

(2) *Diasonics (Reprise).* Suppose that in *Diasonics*, p. 932 above, a company affiliated with Davis had offered to buy the equipment if Davis did not, so that Davis would not lose its deposit. What result if Diasonics had ignored the offer? See Schiavi Mobile Homes, Inc. v. Gironda, 463 A.2d 722 (Me. 1983).

(B) FORESEEABILITY

Until the 19th century, judges left the assessment of damages for breach of contract largely to the discretion of the jury. It was no accident that the development of rules to curb this discretion, and the "outrageous

---

[i]   The first contractor was an intended beneficiary of the second contractor's contract with the owner, the Washington Metropolitan Area Transit Authority.

and excessive" verdicts that resulted, coincided with the end of the Industrial Revolution and with a consequent solicitude for burgeoning enterprise. Hadley v. Baxendale is the leading case in this development.

Hadley v. Baxendale
Court of Exchequer, 1854.
9 Ex. 341, 156 Eng.Rep. 145.

[Plaintiffs, who operated a mill at Gloucester, sued defendants, who were common carriers, for damages for breach of a contract of carriage. The declaration contained two counts, but prior to the trial, plaintiffs entered a *nolle prosequi* as to the first. In the second count plaintiffs alleged that they were forced to shut their mill down because the crank shaft of the steam engine, by which their mill was operated, became broken; that they arranged with W. Joyce & Co., of Greenwich, the manufacturers of the engine, to make a new shaft from the pattern of the old one; that they delivered the broken shaft to defendants who, in consideration of the payment of their charges, promised to use due care to deliver it to W. Joyce & Co. within a reasonable time but that defendants failed to do so; that by reason of defendants' negligence the completion of the new shaft and the reopening of plaintiffs' mill were delayed five days longer than would otherwise have been the case; and that during that period plaintiffs were compelled to pay wages and lost profits aggregating 300£ for which amount plaintiffs sought judgment. Defendants pleaded that they had paid 25£ into court in satisfaction of plaintiffs' claim; plaintiffs replied that this sum was insufficient for that purpose; and issue was joined upon this replication.]

At the trial before Crompton, J., at the last Gloucester Assizes, it appeared that the plaintiffs carried on an extensive business as millers at Gloucester; and that, on the 11th of May, their mill was stopped by a breakage of the crank shaft by which the mill was worked. The steam-engine was manufactured by Messrs. Joyce & Co., the engineers at Greenwich, and it became necessary to send the shaft as a pattern for a new one to Greenwich. The fracture was discovered on the 12th, and on the 13th the plaintiffs sent one of their servants to the office of the defendants, who are the well known carriers trading under the name of Pickford & Co., for the purpose of having the shaft carried to Greenwich. The plaintiffs' servant told the clerk that the mill was stopped, and that the shaft must be sent immediately; and in answer to the inquiry when the shaft would be taken, the answer was, that if it was sent up by twelve o'clock any day, it would be delivered at Greenwich on the following day. On the following day the shaft was taken by the defendants, before noon, for the purpose of being conveyed to Greenwich, and the sum of 2£ 4s. was paid for its carriage for the whole distance; at the same time the defendants' clerk was told that a special entry, if required, should be made to hasten its delivery. The delivery of the shaft at Greenwich was delayed by some neglect; and the consequence was, that the plaintiffs did not receive the new shaft for several days after they would otherwise have done, and the working of their mill was thereby delayed, and they thereby lost the profits they would otherwise have received.

On the part of the defendants, it was objected that these damages were too remote, and that the defendants were not liable with respect to them. The learned Judge left the case generally to the jury, who found a verdict with 25£ damages beyond the amount paid into Court.

Whateley, [for defendants], in last Michaelmas Term, obtained a rule nisi for a new trial, on the ground of misdirection. * * *

■ ALDERSON, BARON. We think that there ought to be a new trial in this case; but, in so doing, we deem it to be expedient and necessary to state explicitly the rule which the Judge, at the next trial, ought, in our opinion, to direct the jury to be governed by when they estimate the damages.

It is, indeed, of the last importance that we should do this; for, if the jury are left without any definite rule to guide them, it will, in such cases as these, manifestly lead to the greatest injustice. The Courts have done this on several occasions; and, in Blake v. Midland Railway Company, 21 L.J., Q.B. 237, the Court granted a new trial on this very ground, that the rule had not been definitely laid down to the jury by the learned judge at Nisi Prius.

"There are certain established rules," this Court says, in Alder v. Keighley, 15 M. & W. 117, "according to which the jury ought to find." And the Court, in that case, adds: "and here there is a clear rule, that the amount which would have been received if the contract had been kept is the measure of damages if the contract is broken."

Now we think the proper rule in such a case as the present is this: Where two parties have made a contract which one of them has broken, the damages which the other party ought to receive in respect of such breach of contract should be such as may fairly and reasonably be considered either arising naturally, i.e., according to the usual course of things, from such breach of contract itself, or such as may reasonably be supposed to have been in the contemplation of both parties, at the time they made the contract, as the probable result of the breach of it. Now, if the special circumstances under which the contract was actually made were communicated by the plaintiffs to the defendants, and thus known to both parties, the damages resulting from the breach of such a contract, which they would reasonably contemplate, would be the amount of injury which would ordinarily follow from a breach of contract under these special circumstances so known and communicated. But, on the other hand, if these special circumstances were wholly unknown to the party breaking the contract, he, at the most, could only be supposed to have had in his contemplation the amount of injury which would arise generally, and in the great multitude of cases not affected by any special circumstances, from such a breach of contract. For, had the special circumstances been known, the parties might have specially provided for the breach of contract by special terms as to the damages in that case; and of this advantage it would be very unjust to deprive them.

Now the above principles are those by which we think the jury ought to be guided in estimating the damages arising out of any breach of contract. It is said, that other cases, such as breaches of contract in the nonpayment of money, or in the not making a good title to land, are to be treated as exceptions from this, and as governed by a conventional rule. But as, in such cases, both parties must be supposed to be cognizant of that well-known rule, these cases may, we think, be more properly classed under the rule above enunciated as to cases under known special circumstances, because there both parties may reasonably be presumed to contemplate the estimation of the amount of damages according to the conventional rule.

Now, in the present case if we are to apply the principles above laid down, we find that the only circumstances here communicated by the plaintiffs to the defendants at the time the contract was made, were, that the article to be carried was the broken shaft of a mill, and that the plaintiffs were the millers of that mill. But how do these circumstances show reasonably that the profits of the mill must be stopped by an unreasonable delay in the delivery of the broken shaft by the carrier to the third person? Suppose the plaintiffs had another shaft in their possession put up or putting up at the time, and that they only wished to send back the broken shaft to the engineer who made it; it is clear that this would be quite consistent with the above circumstances, and yet the unreasonable delay in the delivery would have no effect upon the intermediate profits of the mill. Or, again, suppose that, at the time of the delivery to the carrier, the machinery of the mill had been in other respects defective, then, also, the same results would follow. Here it is true that the shaft was actually sent back to serve as a model for a new one, and that the want of a new one was the only cause of the stoppage of the mill, and that the loss of profits really arose from not sending down the new shaft in proper time, and that this arose from the delay in delivering the broken one to serve as a model. But it is obvious that, in the great multitude of cases of millers sending off broken shafts to third persons by a carrier under ordinary circumstances, such consequences would not, in all probability, have occurred; and these special circumstances were here never communicated by the plaintiffs to the defendants.

It follows, therefore, that the loss of profits here cannot reasonably be considered such a consequence of the breach of contract as could have been fairly and reasonably contemplated by both the parties when they made this contract. For such loss would neither have flowed naturally from the breach of this contract in the great multitude of such cases occurring under ordinary circumstances, nor were the special circumstances, which, perhaps, would have made it a reasonable and natural consequence of such breach of contract, communicated to or known by the defendants. The Judge ought, therefore, to have told the jury that, upon the facts then before him, they ought not to take the loss of profits into consideration at all in estimating the damages. There must therefore be a new trial in this case.

Rule absolute.

NOTES

(1) *Rule of* Hadley v. Baxendale. Do you think that in Hadley v. Baxendale the court applied the rule that it formulated correctly or incorrectly? *Cf.* Victoria Laundry (Windsor) Ltd. v. Newman Industries Ltd., (1949) 2 K.B. 528, 537: "In considering the meaning and application of these rules, it is essential to bear clearly in mind the facts on which Hadley v. Baxendale proceeded. The head-note is definitely misleading in so far as it says that the defendant's clerk, who attended at the office, was told that the mill was stopped and that the shaft must be delivered immediately. The same allegation figures in the statement of facts which are said . . . to have 'appeared' at the trial before Crompton J. If the Court of Exchequer had accepted these facts as established, the court must, one would suppose, have decided the case the other way round. . . . But it is reasonably plain from Baron Alderson's judgment that the court rejected this evidence, for . . . he says: 'We find that the only circumstances here communicated by the plaintiffs to the defendants at the time when the contract was made were that the article to be carried was the broken shaft of a mill and that the plaintiffs were the millers of that mill.' "

Hadley v. Baxendale has prompted much discussion. For criticism of the rule, see Barry Adler, *The Questionable Ascent of* Hadley v. Baxendale, 51 Stan. L. Rev. 1547 (1999); Melvin A. Eisenberg, *The Principle of* Hadley v. Baxendale, 80 Calif. L. Rev. 563 (1992). For a thorough discussion of the background of the case, see Richard Danzig, Hadley v. Baxendale*: A Study in the Industrialization of the Law*, 4 J. Legal Stud. 249 (1975).

The House of Lords has recently overturned Hadley v. Baxendale, replacing the doctrine, it seems, with an objective version of the tacit agreement test. See Transfield Shipping v. Mercator Shipping (The Achilleas), [2008] UKHL 48, [2009] 1 A.C. 61. On the tacit agreement test, see Note 1 below at p. 977.

The common law rule laid down in Hadley v. Baxendale may be usefully contrasted with other the formulations of foreseeability in contracts, see Restatement § 351 and UCC § 2–715(2), as well as torts, see Restatement (Second) of Torts § 435.

(2) *Limitation of Risk.* "The rule of Hadley v. Baxendale is an attempt to restrict the promisor's liability for breach of promise to those consequences, the risk of which he knew about, or must be taken to have known about, when he made the contract. The scope of damage for breach of contract is much narrower than the 'proximate consequence' rule which prevails in actions to recover for a tort. If we may assume that the defaulting promisor is usually an *entrepreneur*, a business man who has undertaken a

risky enterprise, the law here manifests a policy to encourage the *entrepreneur* by reducing the extent of his risk below that amount of damage which, it might be plausibly argued, the promisee has actually been caused to suffer." Edwin Patterson, *The Apportionment of Business Risks Through Legal Devices*, 24 Colum. L. Rev. 335, 342 (1924).

In British Columbia Saw Mill Co. v. Nettleship, (1868) L.R. 3 C.P. 499, Willes, J., criticized the result reached in an old case "said to have been decided two centuries ago where a man going to be married to an heiress, his horse having cast a shoe on the journey, employed a blacksmith to replace it, who did the work so unskilfully that the horse was lamed, and the rider not arriving in time, the lady married another; and the blacksmith was held liable for the loss of the marriage." *But cf.* Coppola v. Kraushaar, 92 N.Y.S. 436 (App. Div. 1905), in which a disappointed suitor whose betrothed broke their engagement after their wedding was delayed sued to recover five hundred dollars, expended uselessly on the wedding, from the defendant, whose failure to deliver two gowns, ordered for the bride, had caused the postponement of the wedding. "Before the defendant can be held to these alleged damages I think that the parties must have had in contemplation that the wedding would never occur if the defendant failed to furnish the 'two dresses' on the day before the appointed time. While such a disappointment would naturally be keen to any prospective bride, it was hardly to be contemplated, in the absence of specific warning, that she would forever refuse to wed if those 'two dresses' were not forthcoming before the day set for the ceremony. The damages are too remote."

(3) *Allocation of Risk*. Restatement § 351(3) confronts the problem of risk by stating that a court may limit damages even for foreseeable loss "if it concludes that in the circumstances justice so requires in order to avoid disproportionate compensation." In Sundance Cruises Corp. v. American Bureau of Shipping, 7 F.3d 1077, 1084 (2d Cir. 1993), the court held that a shipowner was "not entitled to rely on a classification certificate as a guarantee to the owner that the vessel is soundly constructed." The court reasoned that "the great disparity between the fee charged ($85,000) by ABS for its services and the damages sought by Sundance ($264,000,000) is strong evidence that such a result was not intended by the parties. Citing Restatement § 351, the court concluded "that the small fees charged could not have been intended to cover the risk of such liability; the ship classification industry could not continue to exist under such terms." See Larry T. Garvin, *Disproportionality and the Law of Consequential Damages: Default Theory and Cognitive Reality*, 59 Ohio St. L.J. 339 (1998).

(4) *Consequential Damages*. Damages that, in Baron Alderson's words, would not be considered as "arising naturally," but only as a result of "the special circumstances under which the contract was actually made," are often called "consequential" damages. The Code has given special significance to this term by providing in UCC § 2–712(2) for buyer's recovery of "any incidental or consequential damages" while providing in UCC § 2–708(1) for seller's recovery of only "any incidental damages." In addition, UCC § 2–715 refers to both "incidental" and "consequential" damages "resulting from seller's breach," while UCC § 2–710 speaks only of

"incidental damages to an aggrieved seller." Can you justify such a distinction between buyers and sellers?

Courts have read the Code as precluding recovery by sellers of consequential damages, a reading that has resulted in attempts by sellers to characterize claims such as those for additional interest costs resulting from breach as "incidental" rather than "consequential" and therefore allowable under UCC § 2–710. In St. Paul Structural Steel Co. v. ABI Contracting, Inc., 364 N.W.2d 83 (N.D. 1985), the court accepted a seller's argument that "interest payments incurred as a result of a buyer's breach of a sales agreement do constitute incidental damages."

Disputes over the meaning of "consequential" also arise when the contract contains a provision precluding recovery of "consequential damages." For a case involving such a clause, see Reynolds Metals Co. v. Westinghouse Electric Corp., 758 F.2d 1073 (5th Cir. 1985) (where the seller of a transformer failed to provide a competent engineer to install it, buyer was limited to "difference-in-value losses" based on the fee that the competent engineer would have charged and could not recover consequential damages for the cost of repairing the damage to the transformer caused by the breach).

(5) *Availability of Cover.* Courts have often assumed that in our market economy there is ordinarily a market on which an injured buyer can cover. They have therefore concluded that losses resulting from the buyer's inability to cover do not follow from the breach in the ordinary course and are foreseeable by the seller only if the seller was aware of facts making the buyer's inability to cover foreseeable. See Marcus & Co. v. K.L.G. Baking Co., 3 A.2d 627 (N.J. 1939). Does UCC § 2–715(2)(a) dispense with the requirement that the buyer's inability to cover be foreseeable?

Delchi Carrier Spa v. Rotorex Corp.

United States Court of Appeals, Second Circuit, 1995.
71 F.3d 1024.

[Rotorex, a New York corporation, agreed to supply compressors to Delchi, an Italian manufacturer of air conditioners, in three shipments. While the second shipment was en route, Delchi discovered that the first shipment had both higher power consumption and lower cooling capacity than the contract required. Delchi asked Rotorex to supply conforming compressors and, when Rotorex refused, Delchi cancelled the contract and sought another source. Delchi sued Rotorex seeking incidental and consequential damages. From a $1,248,332 judgment for Delchi, both parties appealed.]

■ WINTER, CIRCUIT JUDGE. [T]he instant matter is governed by the CISG, a self-executing agreement between the United States and other signatories, including Italy. Because there is virtually no caselaw under the Convention, we look to its language and to "the general principles" upon which it is based. See CISG art. 7(2). The Convention directs that its interpretation be informed by its "international character and the need to promote uniformity in its application and the observance of good faith in international trade." See CISG art. 7(1). Caselaw interpreting analogous provisions of Article 2 of the Uniform Commercial Code ("UCC") may also inform a court where the language of the relevant CISG provisions tracks that of the UCC.

The CISG [art. 74] provides

> Damages for breach of contract may not exceed the loss which the party in breach foresaw or ought to have foreseen at the time of the conclusion of the contract, in the light of the facts and matters of which he then knew or ought to have known, as a possible consequence of the breach of contract.

Rotorex contends that the district court improperly awarded lost profits for unfilled orders from Delchi affiliates in Europe and from sales agents within Italy. We disagree. The CISG requires that damages by limited by the familiar principle of foreseeability established in Hadley v. Baxendale. However, it was objectively foreseeable that Delchi would take orders for sales based on the number of compressors it had ordered and expected to have ready for the season.

On its cross-appeal, Delchi challenges the district court's denial of various consequential and incidental damages on the ground that an award would constitute a double recovery for Delchi. We disagree. The expenses incurred by Delchi for shipping, customs, and related matters for the two returned shipments of Rotorex compressors, including storage expenses for the second shipment at Genoa, [along with the] unreimbursed tooling expenses and the cost of useless insulation and tubing materials are legitimate [incidental and] consequential damages that in no way duplicate lost profits damages.

The labor expense incurred as a result of the production line shutdown is also a reasonably foreseeable result of delivering nonconforming compressors for installation in air conditioners. Whether Delchi's labor costs during this four-day period are variable or fixed costs is in large measure a fact question that we cannot answer because we lack factual findings by the district court. We therefore remand to the district court on this issue.

[Affirmed in part and reversed and remanded in part.]

NOTES

(1) *"Possible" or "Probable"?* Judge Winter explains that cases under the Code may "inform a court where the language of the relevant CISG provisions tracks that of the UCC." The relevant CISG provision speaks of "a *possible* consequence of the breach." Do you find this language in the Code? Recall that in Hadley v. Baxendale Baron Alderson spoke of "the *probable* result of the breach," language that has been carried over into Restatement § 351(1), which speaks of "a *probable* result of the breach." Is the difference

between "possible" and "probable" significant? See also UNIDROIT Principles 7.4.4 ("likely").

(2) *Buyer for Resale.* The court's decision on Delchi's "lost profits for unfilled orders" is not surprising. If a seller knows it is selling to a buyer for resale, loss of such profits is generally regarded as foreseeable. Loss of profits on future contracts is another matter.

Nevertheless, Hendricks, an import agent, overcame this obstacle under a contract to buy garments from Daewoo, a Korean manufacturer. As Daewoo knew, Hendricks needed the garments for resale to Champion, a wholesaler of sporting apparel, with whom Hendricks had developed a continuing relationship. The garments had serious defects ("too risky to market"), and Champion terminated its relationship with Hendricks. Hendricks sued Daewoo for damages including its loss of future Champion contracts and had judgment based on a $375,000 jury verdict. Daewoo appealed. As to foreseeability, the court said: "We think that a rational jury could conclude in these circumstances that Daewoo could have foreseen that a nonconforming tender, as severe and pervasive as the present evidence demonstrates, probably would cause Hendricks, in the ordinary course of events, to lose future Champion contracts." Hendricks & Associates v. Daewoo Corp., 923 F.2d 209, 215 (1st Cir. 1991). For the court's disposition of the case, see Note 1, p. 982 below.

PROBLEM

Sweetening a Damage Claim. Federal contracted to sell 75,000 tons of sugar to Czarnikow, to be delivered directly to Czarnikow's customers. In the contracts that Czarnikow then made in turn with its customers, it provided that the sugar was to be "Federal" brand, but this provision was not known to Federal. (Recall that in *Tongish*, p. 954 above, the court noted that "Tongish knew the seeds eventually went to Bambino, although he may not have known the details of the deal.") When the sugar delivered by Federal turned out to be defective, Czarnikow spent $340,000 in the settlement of claims and the defense of law suits brought by its customers, an amount that was inflated because Czarnikow's obligations to them could not be met by delivery of sugar from other suppliers, which it might have obtained on the market. Is Federal liable for $340,000? Czarnikow-Rionda Co. v. Federal Sugar Refining Co., 173 N.E. 913 (N.Y. 1930).

Assuming that Federal is liable for $340,000, could Czarnikow recover an additional $100,000 by showing that it had lost this much in profits when its volume dropped because it was deprived of $340,000 in capital? See Lewis v. Mobil Oil Corp., 438 F.2d 500 (8th Cir. 1971).

Might these questions be answered differently under Article 2 of the UCC and the CISG?

Kenford Co. v. County of Erie

Court of Appeals of New York, 1989.
73 N.Y.2d 312, 537 N.E.2d 176.

■ MOLLEN, JUDGE. This appeal arises out of breach of contract litigation spanning 18 years and involving the proposed construction and operation of a domed stadium facility in the County of Erie. The issue is whether the plaintiff Kenford Company, Inc. (Kenford) is entitled to recover damages against the defendant County of Erie (County) for the loss of anticipated appreciation in the value of the land which Kenford owned in the periphery of the proposed stadium site. Under the circumstances of this case, we conclude that Kenford is not entitled to recovery on this claim since there is no evidence to support a determination that the parties contemplated, prior to or at the time of the contract, assumption by the County of liability for these damages.

By way of background, the County of Erie adopted enabling legislation in May 1968 authorizing it to finance and construct a domed sports stadium in the vicinity of the City of Buffalo. The County, simultaneously, adopted a resolution authorizing a $50 million bond resolution for the purpose of financing the construction of the proposed stadium. Kenford, through its president and sole shareholder, Edward H. Cottrell, submitted an offer to donate to the County the land upon which the stadium was to be built, in exchange for which the County was to permit the management company of Dome Stadium, Inc. (DSI), to lease or manage the proposed stadium facility.

In June 1969, the County adopted a resolution accepting Kenford's offer, after which the parties engaged in contract negotiations. During this period of time, Cottrell, as agent for Kenford, exercised his options on several parcels of land located in the Town of Lancaster. On August 8, 1969, the County, Kenford and DSI executed a contract which provided, in pertinent part, that Kenford would donate 178 acres of land located in the Town of Lancaster to the County for use in construction of the stadium and necessary access roadways. In consideration therefor, the County agreed to commence construction of the stadium within 12 months. The County also agreed to negotiate a 40-year lease with DSI for the operation of the facility which was to provide, inter alia, that the County would receive, as its consideration, lease revenues of not less than $63.75 million over the 40-year term to be comprised of (1) all tax revenues received by the County generated by the operation of the stadium site area; (2) rental payments from DSI; and (3) increased real property taxes resulting from increased assessments and other tax revenues received from or generated by "the peripheral lands and development thereof". The term "peripheral lands" was defined as "those lands presently owned, contracted for or hereinafter acquired by Edward H. Cottrell or Kenford, and located within the area of the Town of Lancaster". If a mutually satisfactory lease could not be agreed upon within three months of the contract signing, the County and DSI were to execute a 20-year management agreement which was annexed to the contract.

[When the County learned] that the proposed project would cost approximately $72 million which was $22 million in excess of the County's prior bond resolution [it terminated the contract and] Kenford and DSI instituted the instant breach of contract action and sought specific performance thereof, or, in the alternative, damages in the amount of $90 million. [A damage trial] resulted in a jury award to Kenford in the sum of $18 million for its lost appreciation in the value on its property located on the periphery of the proposed stadium site and an award of over $6 million in out-of-pocket expenses. DSI was awarded $25.6 million in lost profits under the parties' 20-year management contract.

On appeal, the Appellate Division, while affirming the major portion of the $6 million jury award for Kenford's mitigation and reliance damages, reversed the award to DSI for loss of profits as well as a portion of the award to Kenford for out-of-pocket expenses and directed a new trial on the damage award for loss of anticipated appreciation in the value of Kenford's peripheral lands. On this latter point, the majority of the Appellate Division determined that Kenford's loss of land appreciation was both a foreseeable and certain damage for which it was entitled to recover. The majority, however, found that the award was based upon improper appraisal evidence [and remanded]. Two Justices dissented and took the position that these damages were not foreseeable and, in any event, were inherently speculative and, therefore, not recoverable.

DSI subsequently sought review of the Appellate Division's dismissal of its breach of contract claim against the County. This court, addressing itself solely to the denial of DSI's right to recover its loss of profits under the 20-year management contract, affirmed that portion of the Appellate Division's decision. Therein, we determined that those damages were not recoverable on the twofold basis that the County's liability for DSI's loss of profits was not in the contemplation of the parties at the time of the execution of the contract and, secondly, the damages were too speculative and, thus, did not satisfy the legal requirements of proof with reasonable certainty.

[On retrial on the issue of damages for Kenford's loss of anticipated land appreciation, the jury awarded Kenford the sum of $6.5 million. The Appellate Division affirmed, and the County appealed, raising the issue whether Kenford was entitled to recover damages for lost anticipated appreciation in the value of its peripheral lands.]

It is well established that in actions for breach of contract, the nonbreaching party may recover general damages which are the natural and probable consequence of the breach. "[In] order to impose on the defaulting party a further liability than for damages [which] naturally and directly [flow from the breach], i.e., in the ordinary course of things, arising from a breach of contract, such unusual or extraordinary damages must have been brought within the contemplation of the parties as the probable result of a breach at the time of or prior to contracting" (Chapman v. Fargo, 223 N.Y. 32, 36, 119 N.E.76); see also Czarnikow Rionda Co. v. Federal Sugar Ref. Co., 255 N.Y 33, 173 N.E. 913; Hadley v. Baxendale, 9 Exch. 341, 156 Eng. Rep. 145. In determining the reasonable contemplation of the parties, the nature, purpose and particular circumstances of the contract known by the parties should be considered as well as "what liability the defendant fairly may be supposed to have assumed consciously, or to have warranted the plaintiff reasonably to suppose that it assumed, when the contract was made" (Globe Ref. Co. v. Landa Cotton Oil Co., 190 U.S. 540, 544 [Holmes, J.]).

In the case before us, it is beyond dispute that at the time the contract was executed, all parties thereto harbored an expectation and anticipation that the proposed domed stadium facility would bring about an economic boom in the County and would result in increased land values and increased property taxes. This expectation is evidenced by the terms of the provision of the parties' contract requiring the County and DSI to undertake negotiations of a lease which would provide for specified revenues to be derived from, inter alia, the increased taxes on the peripheral lands. We cannot conclude, however, that this hope or expectation of increased property values and taxes necessarily or logically leads to the conclusion that the parties contemplated that the County would assume liability for Kenford's loss of anticipated appreciation in the value of its peripheral lands if the stadium were not built. On this point, our decision in the prior appeal regarding DSI's right to recover damages for lost profits under the 20-year management contract is particularly instructive: "Initially, the proof does not satisfy the requirement that liability for loss of profits over a 20-year period was in the contemplation of the parties at the time of the execution of the basic contract or at the time of its breach. . . . Indeed, the provisions in the contract providing remedy for a default do not suggest or provide for such a heavy responsibility on the part of the County. In the absence of any provision for such an eventuality, *the commonsense rule to apply is to consider what the parties would have concluded had they considered the subject.* The evidence here fails to demonstrate that liability for loss of profits over the length of the contract would have been in the contemplation of the parties at the relevant time" ([Kenford Co. v. County of Erie,] 67 N.Y.2d 257, 262, 493 N.E.2d 234 [emphasis added]).

Similarly, there is no provision in the contract between Kenford and the County, nor is there any evidence in the record to demonstrate that the parties, at any relevant time, reasonably contemplated or would have contemplated that the County was undertaking a contractual responsibility for the lack of appreciation in the value of Kenford's peripheral lands in the event the stadium was not built. This conclusion is buttressed by the fact that Kenford was under no contractual obligation to the County to acquire or maintain ownership of any land surrounding the 178 acres it was required to donate to the County. Although the County was aware that Kenford had acquired and intended to further acquire peripheral lands, this knowledge, in and of itself, is insufficient, as a matter of law, to impose liability on the County for the loss of anticipated appreciation in the value of those lands since the County never contemplated at the time of the contract's execution that it assumed legal responsibility for these damages upon a breach of the contract. [In] Hadley v. Baxendale, 9 Exch. 341, 156 Eng. Rep. 145, supra [the common carrier was not liable for the loss of profits at the plaintiffs' flour mill since the carrier, who knew that the mill was closed, was not aware that the mill's continued operation was dependent solely on prompt delivery of the mill's broken shaft].

Undoubtedly, Kenford purchased the peripheral lands in question with the hope of benefiting from the expected appreciation in the value of those lands once the stadium was completed and became operational. In doing so, Kenford voluntarily and knowingly assumed the risk that, if the stadium were not built, its expectations of financial gain would be unrealized. There is no indication that either Kenford or the County reasonably contemplated at the time of the contract that this risk was assumed, either wholly or partially, by the County. To hold otherwise would lead to the irrational conclusion that the County, in addition to promising to build the domed stadium, provided a guarantee that if for any reason the stadium were not built, Kenford would still receive all the hoped for financial benefits from the peripheral lands it anticipated to receive upon the completion of the stadium. According to Kenford's version of the facts, Kenford was to realize all of its anticipated gains with or without the stadium. Clearly, such a result is illogical and without any basis whatsoever in the record.

Thus, the constant refrain which flows throughout the legion of breach of contract cases dating back to the leading case of Hadley v. Baxendale (9 Exch. 341, 156 Eng. Rep. 145, supra) provides that damages which may be recovered by a party for breach of contract are restricted to those damages which were reasonably foreseen or contemplated by the parties during their negotiations or at the time the contract was executed. The evident purpose of this well-accepted principle of contract law is to limit the liability for unassumed risks of one entering into a contract and, thus, diminish the risk of business enterprise. In the case before us, although Kenford obviously anticipated and expected that it would reap financial benefits from an anticipated dramatic increase in the value of its peripheral lands upon the completion of the proposed domed stadium facility, these expectations did not ripen or translate into cognizable breach of contract damages since there is no indication whatsoever that the County reasonably contemplated at any relevant time that it was to assume liability for Kenford's unfulfilled land appreciation expectations in the event that the stadium was not built.

Thus, under the principles set forth in Hadley v. Baxendale (supra) and its progeny of cases in this State Kenford is not entitled to recovery, as a matter of law, for its lost appreciation in the value of its peripheral lands caused by the County's breach of the parties' contract.

[Reversed and] award for loss of anticipated profits from appreciation in the value of peripheral lands stricken.

NOTES

(1) *Limitation of Risk (Reprise).* Note the court's quotation from Globe Refining Co. v. Landa Cotton Oil Co. In that case Holmes laid down a "tacit agreement" test, declaring that "the extent of liability . . . should be worked out on terms which it fairly may be presumed he would have assented to if they had been presented to his mind. . . . [It] depends on what liability the defendant fairly may be supposed to have assumed consciously, or to have warranted the plaintiff reasonably to suppose that it assumed, when the contract was made. . . . [M]ere notice to a seller of some interest or probable action of the buyer is not enough." For the history and analysis of the test, see Larry T. Garvin, Globe Refining Co. v. Landa Cotton Oil Co. *and the Dark Side of Reputation*, 12 Nev. L.J. 659 (2012).

This test has not generally found favor. According to Comment 2 to UCC § 2–715, "The 'tacit agreement' test for the recovery of consequential damages is rejected." What does *Kenford's* use of the test show about the attitude of the New York Court of Appeals toward limitation of risk?

(2) *Jury Instructions.* Because the issue of foreseeability is often one for the jury, it is of interest to see how judges instruct juries on the issue. In Redgrave v. Boston Symphony Orchestra, Inc., 602 F.Supp. 1189 (D.Mass. 1985), the actress Vanessa Redgrave sued the Boston Symphony Orchestra for breach of a contract under which she was to appear as narrator in the orchestra's centenary performances of Stravinsky's opera-oratorio Oedipus Rex, claiming, among other things, damages for harm to her professional career. She alleged that the orchestra had cancelled the performances in retaliation for her public expressions on political issues, and the orchestra argued that it had done so because Redgrave's statements in support for the Palestine Liberation Organization caused it to fear a disruption of the performances. Here is the judge's instruction on the issue of foreseeability.[j]

> Damages are allowed for consequential harm to her professional career only if the harm was a foreseeable consequence within the contemplation of the parties to the contract when it was made.
>
> By the phrase "harm that is a foreseeable consequence within the contemplation of the parties" we mean harm of a kind within one or more of the following groups:
>
> (1) harm of a kind that was referred to in communications between the parties while they were negotiating at or before the time the contract was made; (2) any other harm of a kind foreseeable as

---

[j]   The judge was Robert E. Keeton, an author of a leading textbook on insurance, R. Keeton & A. Widiss, *Insurance Law* (1988).

sufficiently likely to result from cancellation that it would have been taken into account in the exercise of reasonable care in assessing the possible costs and benefits of the proposed contract and in deciding whether or not to enter into the contract. The test of foreseeable harm is an objective one based on what a party to the contract, at the time of making the contract, knew or had reason to foresee or had reason to know or ought to have known would be harm which could result from the breach of the contract. To be within the contemplation of the parties, the harm must be of a kind that either was foreseen or else was foreseeable by a reasonable person in the position of the party now being sued, taking into account the facts and circumstances that party or its agents knew, as well other facts and circumstances, if any, which a reasonable person in that position would have known through the exercise of reasonable care. Thus, in order to find that consequential harm was within the contemplation of both parties in this case, you must find that BSO's agents knew or should have known, when the contract was made, that there was a substantial likelihood that a cancellation would be likely to cause Vanessa Redgrave to lose other professional work.

The plaintiffs have the burden of proving by a preponderance of the evidence that the harm was a foreseeable consequence within the contemplation of the parties. You are not allowed to speculate on this question.

The jury found that harm to Redgrave's professional career was foreseeable and awarded $100,000 in consequential damages. The trial judge concluded that this award was supported by the evidence, but that, on principles analogous to the law of defamation, Redgrave could not recover for such harm on the facts of the case. Therefore, he limited Redgrave's recovery to $27,500, the amount she was to be paid for the performances less expenses that she would have incurred to perform the contract. The Court of Appeals held that it was error so to limit damages but concluded that, though the quoted instruction was "appropriate," Redgrave's evidence was sufficient to support only some $12,000 in consequential damages. Redgrave v. Boston Symphony Orchestra, Inc., 855 F.2d 888 (1st Cir. 1988).

PROBLEM

Cold Steel. In September, Torrington, the successful bidder with the New York State Department of Transportation on a highway reconstruction job in northern New York, made a subcontract with Fort Pitt for the structural steel to be used for a bridge, "Delivery to be mutually agreed upon." In November, Torrington advised that it would need the steel the following June, and Fort Pitt replied that it was tentatively scheduling delivery accordingly. In January, however, Fort Pitt advised that it could not meet the June date. When most of the steel did not arrive until mid-September, this delayed the pouring of the concrete until the end of October when there was danger of freezing. To mitigate damages, Torrington had the concrete poured on a crash basis in a single day, which entailed additional costs including overtime pay and extra equipment. Torrington sued Fort Pitt for damages based on these additional costs.

Fort Pitt argued that when it made the contract in September it was advised that the total work was to be completed in two years and could not reasonably have anticipated that Torrington would so expedite the work that steel delivery would be called for within a year. It claimed that, under Hadley v. Baxendale, whatever knowledge it received after the contract was made cannot expand its liability. Torrington, on the other hand, argued that Fort Pitt should be charged with whatever knowledge it had in November when the June delivery date was agreed upon, and Fort Pitt, as an experienced bridge fabricator, must have then realized that any delay beyond August would jeopardize the pouring of the concrete and force postponement of the work until spring.

Is Fort Pitt or Torrington right? See Spang Industries, Inc. v. Aetna Casualty & Surety Co., 512 F.2d 365 (2d Cir. 1975).

Sentimental Value

In Mieske v. Bartell Drug Co., 593 P.2d 1308 (Wash. 1979), the court said this in connection with a claim for damages caused by the loss of a home-movie record of a couple's wedding and later family life. "The fact that damages are difficult to ascertain and measure does not diminish the loss to the person whose property has been destroyed. . . The problem is to establish the value to the owner. . . . Recognizing that value to the owner encompasses a subjective element, the rule has been established that compensation for sentimental or fanciful values will not be allowed. . . .

"What is sentimental value? The broad dictionary definition is that sentimental refers to being 'governed by feeling, sensibility or emotional idealism. . . .' *Webster's Third New International Dictionary* (1963). Obviously that is not the exclusion contemplated by the statement that sentimental value is not to be compensated. If it were, no one would recover for the wrongful death of a spouse or a child. Rather, the type of sentiment which is not compensable is that which relates to 'indulging in feeling to an unwarranted extent' or being 'affectedly or mawkishly emotional . . .' *Webster's Third New International Dictionary* (1963).

"Under these rules, the court's damages instruction was correct. In essence it allowed recovery for the actual or intrinsic value to the plaintiffs but denied recovery for any unusual sentimental value of the film to the plaintiffs or a fanciful price which plaintiffs, for their own special reasons, might place thereon."

Was the value of Keno to Archie Sparrow in Morris v. Sparrow, p. 27 above, sentimental or something else?

Emotional Distress

Courts have been reluctant to allow damages for emotional distress resulting from breach of contract. See Restatement § 353. Sometimes emotional distress is not foreseeable, and, even if it is foreseeable, the resulting damages are often particularly difficult to establish and to measure. See Charlotte K. Goldberg, *Emotional Distress Damages and Breach of Contract: A New Approach*, 20 U.C. Davis L. Rev. 57 (1986).

Consider the following case: Blummer Lamm employed the Shingletons, undertakers, to inter her husband in a vault guaranteed to be watertight. About three months later, during a heavy rain, the vault rose above the ground, and the Shingletons undertook to reinter the body. They raised the vault in Lamm's presence and found that the casket was wet. The sight "caused her considerable shock and made her extremely nervous as a result of which she became a nervous wreck." One of the Shingletons said he would not get the mud out of the vault and "to hell with the whole damned business, it's no concern of mine." This made Lamm "so nervous she could hardly stand up." She sued for breach of contract and, from judgment that she take nothing, she appealed. *Held:* Reversed.

Although "as a general rule," damages for mental anguish are not recoverable in a contract action, the law is "in a state of flux. . . . Where the contract is personal in nature and the contractual duty or obligation is so coupled with matters of mental concern or solicitude, or with the sensibilities of the party to whom the duty is owed, that a breach of that duty will necessarily or reasonably result in mental anguish or suffering, and it should be known to the parties from the nature of the contract that such suffering will result from its breach, compensatory damages therefor may be recovered. . . . The contract was predominantly personal in nature and no substantial pecuniary loss would follow its breach." Lamm v. Shingleton, 55 S.E.2d 810, 813 (N.C. 1949).

For an unusual case granting recovery for "mental anguish" resulting from the defective construction of a new home, see B & M Homes v. Hogan, 376 So.2d 667 (Ala. 1979). The court noted that the "largest single investment the average American family will make is the purchase of a home" and concluded that "any reasonable builder could easily foresee that an individual would undergo extreme mental anguish if their newly constructed house contained defects as severe as those shown to exist in this case." For a contrary and more traditional view, see Ostrowe v. Darensbourg, 377 So.2d 1201 (La. 1979).

NOTES

(1) *Employment Contracts.* Claims of damages for emotional distress are common in actions for breach of employment contracts. In Francis v. Lee

Enterprises, 971 P.2d 707, 713 (Haw. 1999), the court held that though "damages for emotional distress . . . are generally not recoverable in contract," they may be awarded where "the contract is of such a kind that serious emotional disturbance is a particularly foreseeable result if a breach occurs. . . . [I]n deciding whether such damages are recoverable, we shift the focus of the inquiry away from the *manner* of the breach and to the *nature* of the contract."

Several recent decisions have allowed emotional distress damages when employees have been discharged following harassment by fellow employees or supervisors. Morris Newspaper Corp. v. Allen, 932 So.2d 810 (Miss. App. 2005); Cabaness v. Thomas, 232 P.3d 486 (Utah 2010). While these also entail some, more or less, tortious behavior by the employer, the torts did not appear to be a necessary condition for recovery of damages for emotional distress.

Most courts, however, exclude emotional distress damages for breach of an employment contract. Carraway Methodist Health Sys. v. Wise, 986 So.2d 387 (Ala. 2007). For example, in Saporoso v. Aetna Life & Cas. Co., 603 A.2d 1160, 1166–67 (Conn. 1992), the Supreme Court of Connecticut concluded that there "is no reasonable basis in the evidence for a jury to have found that . . . when the plaintiff resumed her employment with Aetna, it was reasonably foreseeable that if the plaintiff's employment should be terminated, with or without cause, she would suffer a continuing disability from a psychiatric disorder related to her employment or the circumstances of her discharge." See also Gaglidari v. Denny's Restaurants, 815 P.2d 1362, 1370, 1373 (Wash. 1991), where the court said that its research had found only one state, Colorado, that rejects the "traditional common law doctrine . . . that tort damages for emotional distress caused by breach of an employment contract are not recoverable" and added that "the overwhelming majority of courts deny recovery for mental distress damages even though they might be foreseeable within the rule stated in Hadley v. Baxendale."

(2) *The Sacred and Profane.* Cases involving religious observance sometimes lead to damages for emotional distress. See e.g., Gupta v. Asha Enters., 27 A.3d 953 (N.J. Super. App. Div. 2011), in which damages for emotional or spiritual injury were awarded under UCC 2–313 and 2–715 after a restaurant filled an order for vegetarian samosas from Hindu vegetarians with meat-filled samosas.

(3) *The Case of the Designer Dress.* The purchaser of a custom-made wedding dress sued "the high fashion designer . . . known to the cognoscenti simply as Halston" for "mental anguish" caused because the dress was allegedly improperly made and could not be worn by the purchaser's daughter at her wedding. *Held:* Cause of action dismissed. Levin v. Halston Ltd., 398 N.Y.S.2d 339 (N.Y. City Ct. 1977).

(C) CERTAINTY

In an omitted part of the opinion you just read in *Kenford*, the court discussed its earlier decision in Kenford Co. v. County of Erie, 493 N.E.2d 234 (N.Y. 1986). It recalled that in that decision it had reviewed DSI's award of $25.6 million in lost profits under its 20-year management contract and had "determined that those damages were not recoverable on the twofold basis that the County's liability for DSI's profits was not in the contemplation of the parties at the time of the execution of the contract and, secondly, the damages were too speculative and, thus, did not satisfy the legal requirement of proof with reasonable certainty."

You may remember that the term "speculative" also appeared in the opinion in *Naval Institute*, p. 21 above. There Berkley challenged as "speculative" the premise "that, but for the breach by Berkley, Naval would have sold in September the same number of hardcover copies it sold in August." In that case the court rejected the challenge, saying that "it is not error to lay the normal uncertainty in such hypotheses at the door of the wrongdoer who altered the proper course of events."

These two cases point out an important limitation on the disappointed promisee's right to contract damages. As put in a seminal New York case decided in 1858, damages for breach of contract must "be shown, by clear and satisfactory evidence, to have been actually sustained" and "be shown with certainty, and not left to speculation or conjecture." Griffin v. Colver, 16 N.Y. 489, 491 (1858).

Contemporary formulations, however, insist only on "reasonable certainty" rather than on "certainty" itself. Restatement § 352, for example, precludes recovery "for loss beyond an amount that the evidence permits to be established with reasonable certainty." Comment 1 to UCC § 1–106 explains that damages need not "be calculable with mathematical accuracy," are "at best approximate," and "have to be proved with whatever definiteness and accuracy the facts permit, but no more." And UNIDROIT Principles art. 7.4.3 requires only "a reasonable degree of certainty." Nevertheless, it is clear that in this regard the injured party has a more onerous burden than that imposed by the ordinary requirement to make its case by the "preponderance of evidence."

NOTES

(1) *Buyer for Resale (Reprise)*. Recall that in Note 2, p. 972 above, the Court of Appeals upheld Hendricks's damage award against Daewoo in the face of a challenge based on Hadley v. Baxendale. As to certainty of proof of lost profits, however, Hendricks did not fare as well. *Held:* Affirmed conditioned on a remittitur of damages in excess of $45,000, otherwise Daewoo's motion for new trial to be granted.

"We can only conclude that no loss of prospective profits in an amount even approaching the $375,000 consequential damages award was proven in the manner required by Massachusetts law. With no evidence of *past* profits, future profit margins, future business revenues or expenses, beyond [the year of the breach], and no formula or method for divining any other element in a rational projection or calculation of prospective profits, the jury was left entirely to guesswork . . . The jury could have found, without impermissible resort to surmise and speculation, that Hendricks was entitled to recover no more than $45,000 for loss of prospective profits. . . . " Hendricks & Associates v. Daewoo Corp., 923 F.2d 209, 217, 220, 221 (1st Cir. 1991).

(2) *The Value of a Chance.* In Collatz v. Fox Wisconsin Amusement Corp., 239 Wis. 156, 300 N.W. 162 (1941), the plaintiff, one of two finalists in a quiz contest held at the defendant's theater, claimed a half interest in the automobile offered as a prize, on the ground that it had been arbitrarily awarded to the other finalist before completion of the contest. The court held for the defendant. The plaintiff "suffered no damage because of the defendant's breach of the contract, for it cannot be assumed nor is it susceptible of proof that had the contest proceeded to a proper finish he would have become the winner." The classic case to the contrary is Chaplin v. Hicks, [1911] 2 K.B. 786 (Eng.), in which the winner of a preliminary round in a beauty contest prevailed. *Accord* Wachtel v. National Alfalfa Journal Co., 176 N.W. 801 (Iowa 1920). See Restatement § 348(3); UNIDROIT Principles art. 7.4.3(2). How would a court set a value on a lost chance for a lottery, if the ticket would have lost? Might unjust enrichment provide an alternative basis for recovery? See Melvin A. Eisenberg, *Probability and Chance in Contract Law,* 45 UCLA L. Rev. 1005 (1998).

(3) *The Right to Work.* In *Parker,* could Shirley MacLaine have recovered more than $750,000? Would not starring in "Bloomer Girl" have enhanced her reputation as an actress? A few courts have favored recovery for lost reputation. See Herbert Clayton & Jack Waller, Ltd. v. Oliver, [1930] A.C. 209 (Eng.), in which the court said: "Here both parties knew that as flowing from the contract the plaintiff would be billed and advertised as appearing at the Hippodrome, and in the theatrical profession this is a valuable right."

See also Malik v. Bank of Credit & Commerce Intl., [1997] 3 All E.R. 1, 11 (H.L.) (Lord Steyn: "there is no good reason why in the field of employment law recovery of financial loss in respect of damage to reputation caused by breach of contract is necessarily excluded"). Compare the discussion of sentimental value, p. 979 above.

American courts, however, have generally denied recovery for lost reputation on grounds of either uncertainty or unforeseeability. Cases are discussed in Redgrave v. Boston Symphony Orchestra, Note 2, p. 977 above. The court there noted that she did not claim that "her general reputation as a professional actress has been tarnished" but rather "that a number of specific movie and theater performances that would have been offered to her in the usual course of events were not offered to her." How did Redgrave's situation differ from MacLaine's?

Fera v. Village Plaza, Inc.

Supreme Court of Michigan, 1976.
396 Mich. 639, 242 N.W.2d 372.

■ T.G. KAVANAGH, CHIEF JUSTICE. Plaintiffs received a jury award of $200,000 for loss of anticipated profits in their proposed new business as a result of defendants' breach of a lease. The Court of Appeals reversed. We reverse and reinstate the jury's award.

On August 20, 1965 plaintiffs and agents of Fairborn-Village Plaza executed a ten-year lease for a "book and bottle" shop in defendants' proposed shopping center. This lease provided for occupancy of a specific location at a rental of $1,000 minimum monthly rent plus 5% of annual receipts in excess of $240,000. A $1,000 deposit was paid by plaintiffs.

After this lease was executed, plaintiffs gave up approximately 600 square feet of their leased space so that it could be leased to another tenant. In exchange, it was agreed that liquor sales would be excluded from the percentage rent override provision of the lease.

Complications arose, including numerous work stoppages. Bank of the Commonwealth received a deed in lieu of foreclosure after default by Fairborn and Village Plaza. Schostak Brothers managed the property for the bank.

When the space was finally ready for occupancy, plaintiffs were refused the space for which they had contracted because the lease had been misplaced, and the space rented to other tenants. Alternative space was offered but refused by plaintiffs as unsuitable for their planned business venture.

Plaintiffs initiated suit in Wayne Circuit Court, alleging *inter alia* a claim for anticipated lost profits. The jury returned a verdict for plaintiffs against all defendants for $200,000.

The Court of Appeals reversed and remanded for new trial on the issue of damages only, holding that the trial court "erroneously permitted lost profits as the measure of damages for breach of the lease." 52 Mich.App. 532, 542, 218 N.W.2d 155, 160.

In Jarrait v. Peters, 145 Mich. 29, 31–32, 108 N.W. 432 (1906), plaintiff was prevented from taking possession of the leased premises. The jury gave plaintiff a judgment which included damages for lost profits. This Court reversed:

> "It is well settled upon authority that the measure of damages when a lessor fails to give possession of the leased premises is the difference between the actual rental value and the rent reserved. 1 Sedgwick on Damages (8th Ed.) par. 185. Mr. Sedgwick says:
>
> " 'If the business were a new one, since there could be no basis on which to estimate profits, the plaintiff must be content to recover according to the general rule.'
>
> "The rule is different where the business of the lessee has been interrupted. . . .
>
> "The evidence admitted tending to show the prospective profits plaintiff might have made for the ensuing two years should therefore have been excluded under the objections made by

defendant, and the jury should have been instructed that the plaintiff's damages, if any, would be the difference between the actual rental value of the premises and the rent reserved in the lease."

Six years later, in Isbell v. Anderson Carriage Co., 170 Mich. 304, 318, 136 N.W. 457, 462 (1912), the Court wrote:

"It has sometimes been stated as a rule of law that prospective profits are so speculative and uncertain that they cannot be recognized in the measure of damages. This is not because they are profits, but because they are so often not susceptible of proof to a reasonable degree of certainty. Where the proof is available, prospective profits may be recovered, when proven, as other damages. But the jury cannot be asked to guess. They are to try the case upon evidence, not upon conjecture."

These cases and others since should not be read as stating a rule of law which prevents every new business from recovering anticipated lost profits for breach of contract. The rule is merely an application of the doctrine that "[i]n order to be entitled to a verdict, or a judgment, for damages for breach of contract, the plaintiff must lay a basis for a reasonable estimate of the extent of his harm, measured in money". 5 Corbin on Contracts, § 1020, p. 124. The issue becomes one of sufficiency of proof. "The jury should not [be] allowed to speculate or guess upon this question of the amount of loss of profits." Kezeli v. River Rouge Lodge IOOF, 195 Mich. 181, 188, 161 N.W. 838, 840 (1917). . . .

The rule was succinctly stated in Shropshire v. Adams, 40 Tex.Civ.App. 339, 344, 89 S.W. 448, 450 (1905):

"Future profits as an element of damage are in no case excluded merely because they are profits but because they are uncertain. In any case when by reason of the nature of the situation they may be established with reasonable certainty they are allowed."

It is from these principles that the "new business"/"interrupted business" distinction has arisen.

"If a business is one that has already been established a reasonable prediction can often be made as to its future on the basis of its past history. * * * If the business * * * has not had such a history as to make it possible to prove with reasonable accuracy what its profits have been in fact, the profits prevented are often but not necessarily too uncertain for recovery." 5 Corbin on Contracts, § 1023, pp. 147, 150–151. Cf. Jarrait v. Peters, supra.

The Court of Appeals based its opinion reversing the jury's award on two grounds: First, that a new business cannot recover damages for lost profits for breach of a lease. We have expressed our disapproval of that rule. Secondly, the Court of Appeals held plaintiffs barred from recovery because the proof of lost profits was entirely speculative. We disagree.

The trial judge in a thorough opinion made the following observations upon completion of the trial.

"On the issue of lost profits, there were days and days of testimony. The defendants called experts from the Michigan Liquor Control Commission and from Cunningham Drug Stores, who have a store in the area, and a man who ran many other stores. The plaintiffs called experts and they, themselves, had experience in the liquor sales business, in the book sales business and had been representatives of liquor distribution firms in the area.

"The issue of the speculative, conjectural nature of future profits was probably the most completely tried issue in the whole case. Both sides covered this point for days on direct and cross-examination. The proofs ranged from no lost profits to two hundred and seventy thousand dollars over a ten-year period as the highest in the testimony. A witness for the defendants, an expert from Cunningham Drug Company, testified the plaintiffs probably would lose money. Mr. Fera, an expert in his own right, testified the profits would probably be two hundred and seventy thousand dollars. The jury found two hundred thousand dollars. This is well within the limits of the high and the low testimony presented by both sides, and a judgment was granted by the jury.

"The Court cannot invade the finding of fact by the jury, unless there is no testimony to support the jury's finding. There is testimony to support the jury's finding. We must realize that witness Stein is an interested party in this case, personally. He is an officer or owner in Schostak Brothers. He may personally lose money as a result of this case. The jury had to weigh this in determining his credibility. How much credibility they gave his testimony was up to them. How much weight they gave to counter-evidence was up to them.

"The Court must decide whether or not the jury had enough testimony to take this fact from the speculative-conjecture category and find enough facts to be able to make a legal finding of fact. This issue [damages for lost profits] was the most completely tried issue in the whole case. Both sides put in testimony that took up days and encompassed experts on both sides. This fact was adequately taken from the category of speculation and conjecture by the testimony and placed in the position of those cases that hold that even though loss of profits is hard to prove, if proven they should be awarded by the jury. In this case, the jury had ample testimony to make this decision from both sides. . . . "

As Judge Wickens observed, the jury was instructed on the law concerning speculative damages. The case was thoroughly tried by all the parties. Apparently, the jury believed the plaintiffs. That is its prerogative.

The testimony presented during the trial was conflicting. The weaknesses of plaintiffs' specially prepared budget were thoroughly explored on cross-examination. Defendants' witnesses testified concerning the likelihood that plaintiffs would not have made profits if the contract had been performed. There was conflicting testimony concerning the availability of a liquor license. All this was spread before the jury. The jury weighed the conflicting testimony and determined that plaintiffs were entitled to damages of $200,000.

As we stated in Anderson v. Conterio, 303 Mich. 75, 79, 5 N.W.2d 572, 574 (1942):

> "The testimony . . . is in direct conflict, and that of plaintiff . . . was impeached to some extent. However, it cannot be said as a matter of law that the testimony thus impeached was deprived of all probative value or that the jury could not believe it. The credibility of witnesses is for the jury, and it is not for us to determine who is to be believed."

The trial judge, who also listened to all of the conflicting testimony, denied defendants' motion for a new trial, finding that the verdict was justified by the evidence. We find no abuse of discretion in that decision. . . .

While we might have found plaintiffs' proofs lacking had we been members of the jury, that is not the standard of review we employ. "As a reviewing court we will not invade the fact finding of the jury or remand for entry of judgment unless the factual record is so clear that reasonable minds may not disagree." Hall v. Detroit, 383 Mich. 571, 574, 177 N.W.2d 161, 163 (1970). This is not the situation here.

The Court of Appeals is reversed and the trial court's judgment on the verdict is reinstated.

■ COLEMAN, JUSTICE (concurring in part, dissenting in part). Although anticipated profits from a new business may be determined with a reasonable degree of certainty such was not the situation regarding loss of profits from liquor sales as proposed by plaintiffs.

First, plaintiffs had no license and a Liquor Control Commission regional supervisor and a former commissioner testified that the described book and bottle store could not obtain a license. Further, the proofs of possible profits from possible liquor sales—if a license could have been obtained—were too speculative. The speculation of possible licensing plus the speculation of profits in this case combine to cause my opinion that profits from liquor sales should not have been submitted to the jury.

I . . . would have allowed proof of loss from the bookstore operation to go to the jury, but not proof of loss from liquor sales. . . . I would affirm the trial court judgment conditioned upon plaintiffs' consenting within 30 days following the release of this opinion, to "remitting that portion of the judgment in excess of $60,000. Otherwise, the judgment should be reversed and a new trial had." Plaintiffs are also entitled to the $1,000 deposit.

NOTES

(1) *Royalties from Artistic Creations.* The requirement of reasonable certainty has plagued plaintiffs whose claims are based on lost royalties from artistic creations. In Contemporary Mission, Inc. v. Famous Music Corp., 557 F.2d 918, 926, 927 (2d Cir. 1977), a generous result was reached under New York law. The plaintiffs, a group of Roman Catholic priests who wrote musical compositions and recordings, sued Famous Music for breach of its contract to make and sell records on a royalty basis from the master tape recording of the priests' rock opera "Virgin."

The Court of Appeals held that the trial court erred in excluding a statistical analysis, together with expert testimony, in order to prove how successful the most successful of the opera's single recordings, "Fear No Evil," would have been. The court acknowledged that the requirement of certainty "operates with particular severity in cases involving artistic creations such as books, . . . movies, . . . and, by analogy, records." Nevertheless, at the time of the breach, "the record was real, the price was fixed, the market was buying and the record's success, while modest, was increasing. Even after the promotional efforts ended, the record was withdrawn from the marketplace, it was carried, as a result of its own momentum, to an additional 10,000 sales and to a rise from approximately number 80 on the 'Hot Soul Singles' chart of Billboard magazine to number 61." The court, however, rejected the plaintiff's "domino theory" of projected damages under which, if "Fear No Evil" had become a "hit," it would have generated opportunities for concert and theatrical tours and similar benefits, on the ground that "these additional benefits are too dependent upon taste or fancy to be considered anything other than speculative and uncertain."

(2) *Good Will.* The requirement of certainty is likely to be particularly troublesome to a claimant that seeks to recover for loss of business reputation, or what is commonly termed "good will." For many years, Pennsylvania refused to allow recovery for loss of good will on the ground that "damages of this nature would be entirely too speculative." Harry Rubin & Sons v. Consolidated Pipe Co., 153 A.2d 472, 476 (Pa. 1959) (wholesaler's loss of good will due to manufacturer's failure to deliver hula hoops). In 1990, however, Pennsylvania joined the overwhelming majority of states by overruling such cases "to the extent they prohibit a plaintiff from alleging a claim for damage to good will as a matter of law." AM/PM Franchise Ass'n v. Atlantic Richfield Co., 584 A.2d 915, 926 (Pa. 1990) (gasoline franchisee's loss of good will due to franchisor's breach of warranty).

Causation

It is often relatively straightforward to establish when a breach has caused damages, although the amount of damages may be difficult to prove. Even unforeseeable damages may have clear causation. Sometimes, however, the causal links are more attenuated and there the law of causation steps in. See generally H.L.A. Hart & Tony Honoré, Causation in the Law 308–324 (2d ed. 1985). Causation-in-fact is a bare minimum. As in tort law, there may be liability despite the presence of other causes. See, e.g., Ind. Mich. Power Co. v. U.S., 422 F.3d 1369 (Fed. Cir. 2005) (requiring that "the breach is a substantial causal factor in the damages"). As the links multiply, though, the judicial decisions become less and less predictable. In Nirdlinger v. Am. Dist. Tel. Co., 91 A. 883 (Pa. 1914), for instance, the court had to determine whether the failure of a burglar alarm system was the cause of an ensuing burglary. In that case the court held it was not. The following chestnut illustrates the factor of remoteness in establishing causation.

Newsome v. Western Union Telegraph Co.

Supreme Court of North Carolina, 1910.
153 N.C. 153, 69 S.E. 10.

■ BROWN, JUDGE. The facts of this case are stated fully in 137 N.C. 513, 50 S.E. 279, and 144 N.C. 178, 56 S.E. 863. The alleged negligence consists in transmitting a telegram to one Royal, Benson, N.C., ordering four gallons corn whisky to be sent by express to Mints Siding, in Sampson county, N.C. The signature was transcribed on the delivered telegram as T.J. Sessons, instead of T.J. Newsom. The plaintiff alleges that he ordered the whisky by agreement with his raft hands, who were preparing to construct rafts and take his timber and rosin to Wilmington during a freshet in February 1902, and that they refused to go into the water without it, in consequence of which he lost the benefit of the freshet, and was greatly endamaged.

The defendant requested an instruction that in no view of the evidence can plaintiff recover more than nominal damage, which was refused. The courts will be careful not to apply to a contract of this character a rule of damage which will impose upon the defendant an unreasonable and speculative liability, which an individual may avoid by declining to enter into the contract. The fact that the plaintiff informed the defendant's operator that he needed the whisky in order to get his rafting done will not allow us to hold the defendant to damages which from the very nature of the case must be purely speculative and remote. It should be borne in mind that the defendant, being a public agency, was compelled to accept the telegram, and to agree with the plaintiff, at the price fixed by the North Carolina Corporation Commission to transmit it. Under such circumstances it cannot be said that the defendant contracted with reference to the damages claimed by the plaintiff simply because its agent was informed of the purpose for which the plaintiff wanted the whisky. While we apply the rule of Hadley v. Baxendale to this kind of a contract, yet that rule will not justify the imposition of remote and speculative damages upon a public service corporation.

In Tanning Co. v. Telegraph Co., 143 N.C. 376, 55 S.E. 777, cited and approved in Manufacturing Co. v. Telegraph Co., 152 N.C. 157, 67 S.E. 329, this court said: "Damages are measured in matters of contract, not only by the well-known rule laid down in Hadley v. Baxendale, 9 Exch. 341, but they must not be the remote, but the proximate, consequence of a breach of contract, and must not be speculative or contingent." See, also, Byrd v. Express Co., 139 N.C. 273, 51 S.E. 851. It is an elementary principle that all damages must flow directly and naturally, and that they must be certain both in their nature and in respect to the cause from which they proceed. Damages which are uncertain and speculative, or which are not the natural and probable result of the breach, are too remote to be recoverable. It is universally held that damages are not to be based upon mere conjectural probability of future loss or gain. 8 Am. & Eng. 610, and cases cited. Something more than a possible result must appear.

The fact that the whisky was not sent may have caused the hands not to go into the water, but it is a far cry between constructing the raft at Thomas and marketing the product at Wilmington. The whisky may have arrived and still the raft remain unconstructed. The raft may have been constructed and loaded, and still never have reached Wilmington. It requires a stretch of the imagination to conceive that, had the four gallons of corn whisky arrived at Thomas, the raft would have been properly constructed, loaded, and safely conducted over a heavy freshet to Wilmington, and the merchandize duly and profitably marketed. Whisky is very potent at times, but it cannot be relied upon to produce such beneficent results as is claimed for it in this case. It is a singular fact in the county where the four gallons of corn whisky were expected to produce such unusual results its use was decried and its sale prohibited by law. It was contraband, outlawed, and dealing in it made a crime.

We are of opinion that the plaintiff is entitled to recover nominal damages only.

Error.

NOTES

(1) *Nothing Amusing About It.* In Evergreen Amusement Corp. v. Milstead, 112 A.2d 901 (Md. 1955), an action was brought against a contractor for damages for delay in the opening of a drive-in theater from June 1 to mid-August. The operator of the theater proffered a witness who had built a majority of the drive-in theaters in the area and who would have testified as to reasonably anticipated profits for the months in question by comparison with the theater's profits for the same months of the following year. The court held that it was not error to refuse to hear the witness. "[T]he

general rule clearly is that loss of profit is a definite element of damages in an action for breach of contract or in an action for harming an established business which has been operating for a sufficient length of time to afford a basis of estimation with some degree of certainty as to the probable loss of profits, but that, on the other hand, loss of profits from a business which has not gone into operation may not be recovered because they are merely speculative and incapable of being ascertained with the requisite degree of certainty. . . . While this Court has not laid down a flat rule (and does not hereby do so), nevertheless, no case has permitted recovery of lost profits under comparable circumstances."

(2)   *The New Business Rule*. As *Evergreen Amusement* illustrates, there was a time when proof of profits for a new business were held as a matter of law too speculative to permit recovery. Today most jurisdictions allow an aggrieved new business owner to attempt to prove lost profits, though naturally the proof is trickier and more open to challenge than it would be for an established business. See Victor P. Goldberg, *The New-Business Rule and Compensation for Lost Profits*, 1 Criterion J. Innov. 341 (2016).

SECTION 4.   STIPULATED, LIQUIDATED, AND PUNITIVE DAMAGES

It was observed in the introductory comments on remedying breach in Chapter 1 that parties may stipulate their own remedy for breach. They may agree to limit their remedies to specific actions, such as receiving a refund or a right to repair or replace defective goods. Parties may also stipulate an amount or means of calculating money damages, so-called "liquidated damages." One thing they may not stipulate is a "punishment" for breach. Hence when a stipulated damage remedy seems too one-sided or does not appear reasonably related to the actual harm suffered from breach, courts often interpret such liquidated damage clauses as "penalty clauses," which are unenforceable. Punitive damages are rarely awarded for breach of contract, and never by a stipulated agreement of the parties. When courts award punitive damages the breach is generally accompanied by some other wrong, such as a tort, or egregious conduct where public policy or statutes sanction punishment. The materials that follow provide an overview of stipulated, liquidated, and punitive damages for breach of contract.

————

Stipulating Remedies and Limiting Damages

We first encountered the next case, *Figgie International v. Destileria Serralles*, in Chapter 5, at p. 553. Recall that Figgie, a manufacturer of bottle-labeling equipment, agreed to supply Serralles with "equipment capable of placing a clear label on a clear bottle of 'Cristal' rum within a raised glass oval." From the start there were significant problems with the bottle-labeling equipment, which Figgie attempted unsuccessfully to repair; Figgie ultimately refunded Serralles' purchase price. Serralles, in turn, returned the equipment, but then sought damages for breach of the contract. Figgie counterclaimed, seeking a declaratory judgment that Serralles is limited by its agreement to the exclusive remedy of repair or replacement of the equipment, or refund of the purchase price upon the return of the equipment.

Figgie International, Inc. v. Destileria Serralles, Inc.

United States Court of Appeals, Fourth Circuit, 1999.
190 F.3d 252.

■ TRAXLER, CIRCUIT JUDGE. With regard to the alleged limitation of remedy in the sales agreement, Figgie asserts that standard terms and conditions accompanying the sales agreement contained the following language:

> Buyer's exclusive remedies for all claims arising out of this agreement and the transaction to which it pertains shall be the right to return the product at buyer's expense, and, at seller's option, receive repayment of the purchase price plus reasonable depreciation for the repair and/or replacement of the product. Seller shall not be subject to any other obligations or liabilities whatsoever with respect to this transaction, and shall under no circumstances be liable for delays, or for any consequential, contingent or incidental damages.

Because the crux of this appeal centers on whether the agreement between the parties limited Serralles' remedy for breach to repair, replacement, or refund of the purchase price, we begin with the language of [UCC § 2–719], which governs modifications or limitations to the remedies otherwise provided by the UCC for the breach of a sales agreement. Section 2–719 provides that:

> (1) Subject to the provisions of subsections (2) and (3) of this section and of the preceding section (§ 2–318) on liquidation of damages,

> (a)   the agreement may provide for remedies in addition to or in substitution for those provided in this chapter and may limit or alter the measure of damages recoverable under this chapter, as by limiting the buyer's remedies to return of the goods and repayment of the price or to repair and replacement of nonconforming goods or parts; and

> (b)   resort to a remedy as provided is optional unless the remedy is expressly agreed to be exclusive, in which case it is the sole remedy.

> (2)   Where circumstances cause an exclusive or limited remedy to fail of its essential purpose, remedy may be had as provided in this act.

(3) Consequential damages may be limited or excluded unless the limitation or exclusion is unconscionable. Limitation of consequential damages for injury to the person in the case of consumer goods is prima facie unconscionable but limitation of damages where the loss is commercial is not.

Having determined that usage of trade supplemented the agreement between the parties with the exclusive remedy of repair, replacement, or return [eds., *see* pp. 553–555], we turn to Serralles' contention that the limited remedy "fail[ed] of its essential purpose," entitling it to nevertheless pursue the full array of UCC remedies. We conclude that it did not.

Section 2–719(1)(a) specifically contemplates that parties to an agreement may, as they did in this case, limit available remedies in the event of a breach to "return of the goods and repayment of the price or to repair and replacement of nonconforming goods or parts." Section 2–719(2), however, provides that the general remedies of the UCC will apply, notwithstanding an agreed-upon exclusive remedy, if the "circumstances cause [the remedy] to fail of its essential purpose." Under this provision, "where an apparently fair and reasonable clause because of circumstances fails in its purpose or operates to deprive either party of the substantial value of the bargain, it must give way to the general remedy provisions of [the Code].'" Bishop Logging Co. v. John Deere Indus. Equip. Co., 317 S.C. 520. In the instant case, however, there is no evidence that the limited remedy of repair, replacement, or return has failed of its essential purpose or that the contracting parties have been deprived of the substantial value of the bargain.

Serralles argues that Figgie, by first attempting to repair the equipment, elected to pursue repair as the exclusive remedy and, thereby, forgo enforcement of the remedy of return and reimbursement. From this premise, Serralles contends that Figgie's failure to repair the machines resulted in the remedy failing of its essential purpose. We find no support in the language of the UCC or in the cases interpreting it for this novel argument, and no evidence that this contemplated remedy of return and refund, once invoked, failed of its essential purpose.

While Serralles is correct that a limited remedy of repair or replacement can fail of its essential purpose where the seller's repair or replacement is unsuccessful, Serralles' remedies were limited to repair, replacement, or return. Figgie installed the bottle-labeling equipment in April and, over the course of the next several months, attempted to find solutions to resolve the problems encountered. In November, when attempts to fix the equipment had so far failed, the equipment was returned and the purchase price refunded. Hence, the remedies invoked were exactly those envisioned by § 2–719(1)(a) and contemplated by the agreement.

Serralles' contention that a seller eliminates the remedy of "refund" simply by electing to attempt repair or replacement is unpersuasive. On the contrary, one would expect a manufacturer or seller to first attempt to repair or replace equipment in order to meet its contractual obligations to the purchaser, and only resort to a return and refund if unsuccessful in doing so-particularly in the context of an agreement between two commercial entities for the purchase of sophisticated equipment. Accordingly, the district court correctly concluded that the limited remedy of repair, replacement, or return did not fail of its essential purpose.

NOTES

(1) *Broad Disclaimers?* Figgie's standard terms and conditions disclaimed both consequential and incidental damages. By what standard is the enforceability of these disclaimers judged? See UCC § 2–719(3). Is the standard of enforceability the same for consequential damages and incidental damages? Why might it differ?

(2) *Fair Dealing.* Is Figgie's broad disclaimer of consequential and incidental damages unfair? Recall from the discussion of the case in Chapter 5, at p. 553 that the disclaimer was incorporated from local trade usages.

(3) *Risk Allocations.* Without disclaimers in commercial transactions sellers would face significant and hard-to-predict risks of liability from consequential damages. Consider the following observations by Roy Anderson:

> As a general matter, consequential damages exclusions are hands down the most significant limitation of liability in a contract for the sale of goods. Potential liability for consequential damages in commercial contexts, usually in the form of the buyer's lost profits from the use or resale of the goods in its business, is enormous in comparison to the contract price of the goods. On the other hand, the general or direct damages that a buyer may suffer upon a seller's breach are finite and can be gauged at a maximum amount either in terms of the contract price or market price of the goods to be sold. Potential consequential losses are a much different proposition. They can exceed, and most likely will exceed, the value of the goods by an unknown quantum, depending not so much on the actions and machinations of the seller as on the individual operating structure of the buyer and on the buyer's contracts and relationships with third parties.

Roy R. Anderson, *Failure of Essential Purpose and Essential Failure on Purpose: A Look at Section 2–719 of the Uniform Commercial Code*, 32 Sw. L.J. 759, 774 (1977). Such observations have informed the conclusion that "[i]n a commercial setting, the seller's right to exclusion of consequential damages is recognized as a beneficial risk-allocation device that reduces the seller's exposure in the event of breach." Kearney & Trecker v. Master Engraving, 107 N.J. 584 (1987). Do the observations and conclusion above apply with equal force if applied to a commercial exchange between merchants to a consumer context?

Penalties and Liquidated-Damage Clauses

It is well-settled law that contracting parties may not stipulate punishments for breach of contract. A party to a contract, however, may be concerned with compelling the promisor to perform, rather than punishing the promisor *per se*. Consider the following explanation, given by a bridge engineer for the California Division of Highways, of the completion assessment—the per day assessment for each day the contractor overruns the specified contract time. "The sole purpose of a completion assessment is to assure that the contract work will be done within the time specified, . . . to threaten the Contractor with sufficient monetary loss so that he will find it advantageous to apply sufficient men and equipment to the work to get it done on time. Whereas moderate liquidated damages such as $100 per day may well be used to insure the completion of a normal project having no special urgency, higher amounts are used to force faster work on jobs which must be finished in less than a normal construction time. High assessments may be used to emphasize the need for haste and should be of sufficient size to make it economically desirable that the contractor expedite his work by the use of multiple shifts or additional equipment." A. Elliott, Cal. Div. Hwys., *A Study of Liquidated Damages on Highway Contracts* 5 (1956). Should courts lend their aid to the enforcement of such penalties where the parties have bargained for and agreed to them? When reading the brief excerpted opinion below, consider what other purposes, beyond punishment, may be served by an apparent penalty in a liquidated damages clause.

Dave Gustafson & Co. v. State
Supreme Court of South Dakota, 1968.
156 N.W.2d 185.

[Gustafson surfaced a new state highway that paralleled an older road that remained open during and after the construction. From the $530,724.14 due for the work, the state withheld $14,070 that it claimed as liquidated damages for a delay of 67 days. The contract provided a graduated scale of "liquidated damages per day" under which damages of $210 per day were fixed for a contract in an amount of over $500,000 but not more than $1,000,000. This daily damage multiplied by 67 gave $14,070. When Gustafson sued, the trial court upheld the state's claim and Gustafson appealed.]

■ HANSON, PRESIDING JUDGE. . . . [As this court said in an earlier case,] "A provision for payment of a stipulated sum as a liquidation of damages will ordinarily be sustained if it appears that at the time the contract was made the damages in the event of a breach will be incapable or very difficult of accurate estimation, that there was a reasonable endeavor by the parties as stated to fix fair compensation, and that the amount stipulated bears a reasonable relation to probable damages and not disproportionate to any damages reasonably to be anticipated."

This case reflects the modern tendency not to "look with disfavor upon 'liquidated damages' provisions in contracts. When they are fair and reasonable attempts to fix just compensation for anticipated loss caused by breach of contract, they are enforced . . . They serve a particularly useful function when damages are uncertain in nature or amount or are unmeasurable, as is the case in many government contracts." Priebe & Sons v. United States, 332 U.S. 407.

Judged in this light and by the standards established in Anderson v. Cactus Heights Country Club, 80 S.D. 417, 125 N.W.2d 491, the provision in question must be considered to be one for liquidated damages rather than a penalty for the following reasons: I. Damages for delay in constructing a new highway are impossible of measurement. II. The amount stated in the contract as liquidated damages indicates an endeavor to fix fair compensation for the loss, inconvenience, added costs, and deprivation of use caused by delay. Daily damage is graduated according to total amount of work to be performed. It may be assumed that a large project involves more loss than a small one and each day of delay adds to the loss, inconvenience, cost and deprivation of use. For the same reasons we must conclude the amount stipulated in the contract bears a reasonable relation to probable damages and is not, as a matter of law, disproportionate to any and all damage reasonably to be anticipated from the unexcused delay in performance.

Affirmed.

NOTES

(1) *Questionable Categories.* As this chapter has suggested, an injured party may have difficulty in recovering for losses that fall in a variety of specific categories. These include sentimental value, value of a chance, emotional distress, lost volume, loss of reputation, and loss of good will. To what extent will losses in these categories, if not recoverable in the absence of agreement, serve to support the enforceability of a clause stipulating damages? See Wassenaar v. Panos, 331 N.W.2d 357 (Wis. 1983), discussed in Wasserman's Inc. v. Township of Middletown below. Recall that in Schneberger v. Apache Co., Note 1, p. 931 above, the Supreme Court of Oklahoma, in adhering to *Peevyhouse*, noted that the parties to the contract "were free to specify in the contract what the measure of damages would be in the event of a breach."

(2) *Equitable Relief.* Should a valid liquidated damages clause bar equitable relief that would otherwise be available? See Bowen v. Carlsbad Ins. & Real Estate, Inc., 724 P.2d 223 (N.M. 1986).

Can parties by explicit provision bar equitable relief that would otherwise be available? Can parties by explicit provision make equitable relief available where it would not be otherwise? For a case holding that specific performance was available against farmers who had contracted to sell the cotton that they produced where at trial "the parties stipulated that the cotton involved was unique," see R.L. Kimsey Cotton Co., Inc. v. Ferguson, 214 S.E.2d 360 (Ga. 1975). See Note 2, p. 901 above.

PROBLEMS

(1) Suppose that in the Dave Gustafson case the state highway had connected with a bridge that was also under construction, but by a different contractor. Would the result have been the same if, because of a delay by that contract, the bridge had also been closed for 67 days, so that the highway could not have been used even if it had been completed on time?

Would it affect your answer if the contractor responsible for the bridge had had a similar clause stipulating damages and had argued that it was invalid because the delay in the highway would have prevented the use of the bridge even if it had been completed on time?

Compare Massman Constr. Co. v. City Council of Greenville, 147 F.2d 925 (5th Cir. 1945), with California & Hawaiian Sugar Co. v. Sun Ship, Inc., 794 F.2d 1433 (9th Cir. 1986), and Southwest Engineering Co. v. United States, 341 F.2d 998 (8th Cir. 1965).

(2) Seller contracts to deliver to Buyer a machine that is readily available on the market for $1,000 more than the contract price. If Seller fails to deliver, what are the rights of the parties under each of the following provisions?

a. In the event of Seller's failure to deliver, Seller shall pay Buyer a penalty of $10,000.

b. In the event of Seller's failure to deliver, Seller shall be liable to Buyer for $10,000 in liquidated damages.

c. Seller hereby agrees, at Seller's option, to either deliver the machine to Buyer or to pay Buyer $10,000.

Lake River Corp. v. Carborundum Co.

United States Court of Appeals, Seventh Circuit, 1985.
769 F.2d 1284.

■ POSNER, CHIEF JUDGE. This diversity suit between Lake River Corporation and Carborundum Company requires us to consider questions of Illinois commercial law, and in particular to explore the fuzzy line between penalty clauses and liquidated-damages clauses.

Carborundum manufactures "Ferro Carbo," an abrasive powder used in making steel. To serve its midwestern customers better, Carborundum made a contract with Lake River by which the latter agreed to provide distribution services in its warehouse in Illinois. Lake River would receive Ferro Carbo in bulk from Carborundum, "bag" it, and ship the bagged product to Carborundum's customers. The Ferro Carbo would remain Carborundum's property until delivered to the customers.

Carborundum insisted that Lake River install a new bagging system to handle the contract. In order to be sure of being able to recover the cost of the new system ($89,000) and make a profit of 20 percent of the contract price, Lake River insisted on the following minimum-quantity guarantee:

> In consideration of the special equipment [i.e., the new bagging system] to be acquired and furnished by LAKE-RIVER for handling the product, CARBORUNDUM shall, during the initial three-year term of this Agreement, ship to LAKE-RIVER for bagging a minimum quantity of [22,500 tons]. If, at the end of the three-year term, this minimum quantity shall not have been shipped, LAKE-RIVER shall invoice CARBORUNDUM at the then prevailing rates for the difference between the quantity bagged and the minimum guaranteed.

If Carborundum had shipped the full minimum quantity that it guaranteed, it would have owed Lake River roughly $533,000 under the contract.

After the contract was signed in 1979, the demand for domestic steel, and with it the demand for Ferro Carbo, plummeted, and Carborundum failed to ship the guaranteed amount. When the contract expired late in 1982, Carborundum had shipped only 12,000 of the 22,500 tons it had guaranteed. Lake River had bagged the 12,000 tons and had billed Carborundum for this bagging, and Carborundum had paid, but by virtue of the formula in the minimum-guarantee clause Carborundum still owed Lake River $241,000—the contract price of $533,000 if the full amount of Ferro Carbo had been shipped, minus what Carborundum had paid for the bagging of the quantity it had shipped.

When Lake River demanded payment of this amount, Carborundum refused, on the ground that the formula imposed a penalty. At the time, Lake River had in its warehouse 500 tons of bagged Ferro Carbo, having a market value of $269,000, which it refused to release unless Carborundum paid the $241,000 due under the formula. Lake River did offer to sell the bagged product and place the proceeds in escrow until its dispute with Carborundum over the enforceability of the formula was resolved, but Carborundum rejected the offer and trucked in bagged Ferro Carbo from the East to serve its customers in Illinois, at an additional cost of $31,000.

Lake River brought this suit for $241,000, which it claims as liquidated damages. Carborundum counterclaimed for the value of the bagged Ferro Carbo when Lake River impounded it and the additional cost of serving the customers affected by the impounding. The theory of the counterclaim is that the impounding was a conversion, and not as Lake River contends the assertion of a lien. The district judge, after a bench trial, gave judgment for both parties. Carborundum ended up roughly $42,000 to the good: $269,000 + $31,000 – $241,000 – $17,000, the last figure representing prejudgment interest on Lake River's damages. (We have rounded off all dollar figures to the nearest thousand.) Both parties have appealed.

The only issue that is not one of damages is whether Lake River had a valid lien on the bagged Ferro Carbo that it refused to ship to Carborundum's customers-that, indeed, it holds in its warehouse to this day. [The Court held the lien invalid since its purpose was not to assure payment for services performed, but rather "to put pressure on Carborundum to pay a for services not performed".]

The hardest issue in the case is whether the formula in the minimum-guarantee clause imposes a penalty for breach of contract or is merely an effort to liquidate damages. Deep as the hostility to penalty clauses runs in the common law, see Loyd, *Penalties and Forfeitures*, 29 Harv. L. Rev. 117 (1915), we still might be inclined to question, if we thought ourselves free to do so, whether a modern court should refuse to enforce a penalty clause where the signator is a substantial corporation, well able to avoid improvident commitments. Penalty clauses provide an earnest of performance. The clause here enhanced Carborundum's credibility in promising to ship the minimum amount guaranteed by showing that it was willing to pay the full contract price even if it failed to ship anything. On the other side it can be pointed out that by raising the cost of a breach of contract to the contract breaker, a penalty clause increases the risk to his other creditors; increases (what is the same thing and more, because bankruptcy imposes "deadweight" social costs) the risk of bankruptcy; and could amplify the business cycle by increasing the number of bankruptcies in bad times, which is when contracts are most likely to be broken. But since little effort is made to prevent businessmen from assuming risks, these reasons are no better than makeweights.

A better argument is that a penalty clause may discourage efficient as well as inefficient breaches of contract. Suppose a breach would cost the promisee $12,000 in actual damages but would yield the promisor $20,000 in additional profits. Then there would be a net social gain from breach. After being fully compensated for his loss the promisee would be no worse off than if the contract had been performed, while the promisor would be better off by $8,000. But now suppose the contract contains a penalty clause under which the promisor if he breaks his promise must pay the promisee $25,000. The promisor will be discouraged from breaking the contract, since $25,000, the penalty, is greater than $20,000, the profits of the breach; and a transaction that would have increased value will be forgone.

On this view, since compensatory damages should be sufficient to deter inefficient breaches (that is, breaches that cost the victim more than the gain to the contract breaker), penal damages could have no effect other than to deter some efficient breaches. But this overlooks the earlier point that the willingness to agree to a penalty clause is a way of making the promisor and his promise credible and may therefore be essential to inducing some value-maximizing contracts to be made. It also overlooks the more important point that the parties (always assuming they are fully competent) will, in deciding whether to include a penalty clause in their contract, weigh the gains against the costs-costs that include the possibility of discouraging an efficient breach somewhere down the road-and will include the clause only if the benefits exceed those costs as well as all other costs.

On this view the refusal to enforce penalty clauses is (at best) paternalistic-and it seems odd that courts should display parental solicitude for large corporations. But however this may be, we must be on guard to avoid importing our own ideas of sound public policy into an area where our proper judicial role is more than usually deferential. The responsibility for making innovations in the common law of Illinois rests with the courts of Illinois, and not with the federal courts in Illinois. And like every other state, Illinois, untroubled by academic skepticism of the wisdom of refusing to enforce penalty clauses against sophisticated promisors, see, e.g., Goetz & Scott, *Liquidated Damages, Penalties and the Just Compensation Principle*, 77 Colum. L. Rev. 554 (1977), continues steadfastly to insist on the distinction between penalties and liquidated damages. . . . To be valid under Illinois law a liquidation of damages must be a reasonable estimate at the time of contracting of the likely damages from breach, and the need for estimation at that time must be shown by reference to the likely difficulty of measuring the actual damages from a breach of contract after the breach occurs. If damages would be easy to determine then, or if the estimate greatly exceeds a reasonable upper estimate of what the damages are likely to be, it is a penalty . . .

Mindful that Illinois courts resolve doubtful cases in favor of classification as a penalty[,] we conclude that the damage formula in this case is a penalty and not a liquidation of damages, because it is designed always to assure Lake River more than its actual damages. The formula-full contract price minus the amount already invoiced to Carborundum-is invariant to the gravity of the breach. When a contract specifies a single sum in damages for any and all breaches even though it is apparent that all are not of the same gravity, the specification is not a reasonable effort to estimate damages; and when in addition the fixed sum greatly exceeds the actual damages likely to be inflicted by a minor breach, its character as a penalty becomes unmistakable. . . . This case is within the gravitational field of these principles even though the minimum-guarantee clause does not fix a single sum as damages.

Suppose to begin with that the breach occurs the day after Lake River buys its new bagging system for $89,000 and before Carborundum ships any Ferro Carbo. Carborundum would owe Lake River $533,000. Since Lake River would have incurred at that point a total cost of only $89,000, its net gain from the breach would be $444,000. This is more than four times the profit of $107,000 (20 percent of the contract price of

$533,000) that Lake River expected to make from the contract if it had been performed: a huge windfall.

Next suppose (as actually happened here) that breach occurs when 55 percent of the Ferro Carbo has been shipped. Lake River would already have received $293,000 from Carborundum. To see what its costs then would have been (as estimated at the time of contracting), first subtract Lake River's anticipated profit on the contract of $107,000 from the total contract price of $533,000. The difference—Lake River's total cost of performance—is $426,000. Of this, $89,000 is the cost of the new bagging system, a fixed cost. The rest ($426,000 – $89,000 = $337,000) presumably consists of variable costs that are roughly proportional to the amount of Ferro Carbo bagged; there is no indication of any other fixed costs. Assume, therefore, that if Lake River bagged 55 percent of the contractually agreed quantity, it incurred in doing so 55 percent of its variable costs, or $185,000. When this is added to the cost of the new bagging system, assumed for the moment to be worthless except in connection with the contract, the total cost of performance to Lake River is $274,000. Hence a breach that occurred after 55 percent of contractual performance was complete would be expected to yield Lake River a modest profit of $19,000 ($293,000 – $274,000). But now add the "liquidated damages" of $241,000 that Lake River claims, and the result is a total gain from the breach of $260,000, which is almost two and a half times the profit that Lake River expected to gain if there was no breach. And this ignores any use value or salvage value of the new bagging system, which is the property of Lake River—though admittedly it also ignores the time value of money; Lake River paid $89,000 for that system before receiving any revenue from the contract.

To complete the picture, assume that the breach had not occurred till performance was 90 percent complete. Then the "liquidated damages" clause would not be so one-sided, but it would be one-sided. Carborundum would have paid $480,000 for bagging. Against this, Lake River would have incurred its fixed cost of $89,000 plus 90 percent of its variable costs of $337,000, or $303,000. Its total costs would thus be $392,000, and its net profit $88,000. But on top of this it would be entitled to "liquidated damages" of $53,000, for a total profit of $141,000—more than 30 percent more than its expected profit of $107,000 if there was no breach.

The reason for these results is that most of the costs to Lake River of performing the contract are saved if the contract is broken, and this saving is not reflected in the damage formula. As a result, at whatever point in the life of the contract a breach occurs, the damage formula gives Lake River more than its lost profits from the breach—dramatically more if the breach occurs at the beginning of the contract; tapering off at the end, it is true. Still, over the interval between the beginning of Lake River's performance and nearly the end, the clause could be expected to generate profits ranging from 400 percent of the expected contract profits to 130 percent of those profits. And this is on the assumption that the bagging system has no value apart from the contract. If it were worth only $20,000 to Lake River, the range would be 434 percent to 150 percent.

Lake River argues that it would never get as much as the formula suggests, because it would be required to mitigate its damages. This is a dubious argument on several grounds. First, mitigation of damages is a doctrine of the law of court-assessed damages, while the point of a liquidated-damages clause is to substitute party assessment; and that point is blunted, and the certainty that liquidated-damages clauses are designed to give the process of assessing damages impaired, if a defendant can force the plaintiff to take less than the damages specified in the clause, on the ground that the plaintiff could have avoided some of them. It would seem therefore that the clause in this case should be read to eliminate any duty of mitigation, [b]ut in any event mitigation would not mitigate the penal character of this clause.

The fact that the damage formula is invalid does not deprive Lake River of a remedy. The parties did not contract explicitly with reference to the measure of damages if the agreed-on damage formula was invalidated, but all this means is that the victim of the breach is entitled to his common law damages. See, e.g., Restatement, Second, Contracts § 356, comment a (1981). In this case that would be the unpaid contract price of $241,000 minus the costs that Lake River saved by not having to complete the contract (the variable costs on the other 45 percent of the Ferro Carbo that it never had to bag). The case must be remanded to the district judge to fix these damages.

NOTES

(1) *Paying for Nothing?* As suggested in the note above, promisors should be expected to demand compensation for facing a risk of paying high liquidated damages in the event of breach. If, following a breach by the promisor, the court refuses to enforce the liquidated damages clause, has the promisor been unjustly enriched?

Consider again the study of liquidated damages in California highway contracts mentioned above: "High liquidated damages have a tendency to make the contractors jittery. A fear of the high cost of delay will cause an involuntary rise in bid prices. All of the bidders' thinking on prices must inevitably be colored by the specter of the high damages lurking in the background. This only emphasizes the need to use this specialized treatment and high liquidated damages only on those projects where the urgency really exists. Otherwise the State will be paying extra for expediting jobs which do not need the hurry and will not justify the higher cost. High liquidated damages make a contractor susceptible to considerable labor pressure. When a contractor is working under high liquidated damages, it gives the unions a powerful lever to force compliance with demands which may or may not be justified. The contractor is forced to give in because he cannot afford a delaying argument or strike. This pressure also may have a widespread effect. When labor unions make an advance by this sort of a squeeze play against the contractor working under high liquidated damages, other contractors in the area find that they too must give the same benefits or face considerable trouble." A. Elliott, Cal. Div. Hwys., *A Study of Liquidated Damages on Highway Contracts* 21–22 (1956).

(2) *Take-or-Pay.* Contracts in the petroleum industry sometimes contain what are known as "take-or-pay" clauses, which have been attacked as penalty provisions. In an excerpted part of the *Lake River* opinion above, Judge Posner observed, "[w]e do not mean by this discussion to cast a cloud of doubt over the 'take or pay' clauses that are a common feature of contracts between natural gas pipeline companies and their customers."

Here is analysis from another court: "Under a take-and-pay clause, the pipeline is required annually to take and pay for a minimum contract quantity of gas. A take-and-pay clause benefits the producer by maximizing revenue through the steady depletion of gas reserves. . . . Under a take-or-pay clause, the pipeline is required annually to take and pay for a minimum contract quantity of gas *or* pay for a specified quantity. A take-or-pay clause differs from a take-and-pay clause in that it assures the producer a constant cash flow rather than the actual purchase of the contract quantity of gas over the term of the contract. . . . In addition, a take-or-pay clause adds some measure of flexibility in a long-term gas purchase contract by allowing the pipeline to pay for a specified quantity in lieu of taking the contract quantity without endangering its long-term source of supply. . . . Because one of the alternative performances in a take-or-pay contract is the payment of money, courts have distinguished the 'pay' provision from a liquidated damage provision." Prenalta Corp. v. Colorado Interstate Gas Co., 944 F.2d 677, 680, 689 (10th Cir.1991).

(3) *Preventing Penalties or Paternalism of Both?* In 1977 California enacted a statute under which "a provision in a contract liquidating the damages for the breach of the contract is valid unless the party seeking to invalidate the provision establishes that the provision was unreasonable under the circumstances existing at the time the contract was made." Cal. Civil Code § 1671. The statute does not apply against a consumer and in certain other situations. What concerns might justify a limitation on freedom of contract with respect to penalties? Are terms providing for penalties more onerous than other terms?

(4) *Policing of Penalties by Courts, Legislatures and Agencies.* In In re Cellphone Termination Fee Cases, 122 Cal. Rptr. 3d 726 (Ct. App. 2011), a California Court ruled that early termination fees of $150 or $200 were illegal penalties in part because the same liquidated fee would be charged to a customer who terminated service on the first day of the contract as one who terminated on the penultimate day. Since the harm to the service provider under these two breach scenarios would no doubt differ, the single fixed fee would appear unrelated to actual harm. Many cellphone providers now offer graduated termination fees to avoid the penalty interpretation. See Oren Bar-Gill & Omri Ben-Shahar, *Exit From Contract*, 6 J. Leg. Anal. 151 (2014)

Wasserman's v. Middletown

In addition to courts, state and federal legislatures are increasingly policing early termination and prepayment penalties. Section 1414(a) of the Dodd-Frank Wall Street Reform and Consumer Protection Act, Pub. L. No. 111–203, prohibits certain prepayment penalties as well as providing that "[a] creditor may not offer a consumer a residential mortgage loan product that has a prepayment penalty for paying all or part of the principal after the loan is consummated as a term of the loan without offering the consumer a residential mortgage loan product that does not have a prepayment penalty as a term of the loan." 15 U.S.C. § 1639c(c)(4).

While termination clauses are not the same as liquidated damages clauses, both are policed for penalties. How else are these clauses similar?

Wasserman's Inc. v. Township of Middletown

Supreme Court of New Jersey, 1994.
137 N.J. 238, 645 A.2d 100.

■ POLLOCK, J. Pursuant to a public advertisement for bids, plaintiff Wasserman's Inc. (Wasserman's) and defendant, Township of Middletown (the Township or Middletown), entered into a commercial lease for a tract of municipally-owned property. The agreement contained a clause providing that if the Township cancelled the lease, it would pay the lessee, Wasserman's, a pro-rata reimbursement for any improvement costs and damages of twenty-five percent of the lessee's average gross receipts for one year. In 1989, the Township cancelled the lease and sold the property, but refused to pay the agreed damages.

[Wasserman's and a man doing business as "Jo-Ro" sued for damages according to the terms of the lease. (Jo-Ro was a plaintiff because Wasserman's had ceased doing business, apparently, and had sublet the store to Jo-Ro. The sublease provided that the parties to it would share any payments made by the Township under the cancellation provision.) The Township answered, and sought a declaration that part of the cancellation provision was invalid—the part about paying Wasserman's 25% of its average yearly gross receipts.]

On cross-motions for summary judgment, the Law Division held that the lease and the cancellation clause were enforceable. It subsequently required the Township to pay damages in the amount of $346,058.44 plus interest. [On a first appeal, that was affirmed. This court granted certification.] We conclude that the lease is enforceable. We affirm the award of renovation costs and remand to the Law Division the issue of the enforceability of the stipulated damages clause.

I

[Wasserman's had won the lease by bidding for it. It provided for a monthly rental of $458.33 throughout a thirty-year term. Wasserman's object was to run a general store. The Township set the value of the property at $47,500. Initially the store comprised 3,200 square feet. During its occupancy, Wasserman's enlarged it. It sublet the premises to

Jo-Ro not much more than two years after beginning its occupancy, charging Jo-Ro a monthly rent of $1,850.]

[The Township's cancellation of the lease was effective on the last day of 1988. Some six months later the Township sold the property at public auction for $610,000.]

At the center of the dispute is the cancellation clause in the lease. [The clause provided that, if the Township should cancel the lease, it would pay some of the cost of any improvements made by Wasserman's. (For any improvement, the amount was to be calculated by reference to the period of the tenancy remaining when the improvement was made, in relation to the entire term of the lease.] More controversial is the second half of the clause. . . . That provision requires the Township to pay "twenty-five percent of the lessee[']s average gross receipts for one year (to be computed by + (adding) the lessee[']s total gross receipts for the lessee[']s three full fiscal years immediately preceding the time of cancellation of the lease and ÷ (dividing by) 12 (twelve). . . . "

II

The Law Division initially granted plaintiffs a partial summary judgment according "full force and effect" to the lease and the cancellation clause. On a subsequent motion, the court awarded plaintiffs damages of $346,058.44 plus ten-percent prejudgment interest. The trial court calculated damages as follows:

$142,336.01 (construction costs) multiplied by 11.75 (remaining years) divided by 30 years (term of lease) for a total of $55,748.27.

$3,483,722.25 (Jo-Ro's gross receipts for the years 1985, 1986, 1987) divided by 12 equalling $290,310.18.

Construction compensation	$55,748.27
Gross receipts compensation	+ 290,310.18
Total amount due	$346,058.45

III

[In a part of the opinion omitted here, the court rejected the Township's argument that the lease did not meet the requirements for a valid public contract.]

IV

The provision in the termination clause providing for damages based on the lessee's gross receipts presents a more difficult issue. The issue is whether that provision is an enforceable liquidated damages provision or is an unenforceable penalty clause.

Disapproval of penalty clauses originated at early common law when debtors bound themselves through sealed penalty bonds for twice the amount of their actual debts. Charles J. Goetz & Robert E. Scott, *Liquidated Damages, Penalties and the Just Compensation Principle: Some Notes on an Enforcement Model and a Theory of Efficient Breach*, 77 Colum. L. Rev. 554, 554 (1977) (hereinafter Goetz & Scott). Because clauses in penalty bonds "carried an unusual danger of oppression and extortion," equity courts refused to enforce them. Id. at 555. "This equitable rule, designed to prevent overreaching and to give relief from unconscionable bargains, was later adopted by courts of law." John D. Calamari & Joseph M. Perillo, The Law of Contracts, § 14–31 at 639 (3d ed. 1987) (hereinafter Calamari & Perillo). In a sense, judicial reluctance to enforce penalty clauses is a product of history.

For more than five centuries, courts have scrutinized contractual provisions that specify damages payable in the event of breach. Wassenaar v. Panos, 331 N.W.2d 357 (Wis.1983) . . . [Hereafter, references to this case give page numbers only.] The validity of these "stipulated damage clauses" has depended on a judicial assessment of the clauses as an unenforceable penalty or as an enforceable provision for "liquidated damage." Thus, " '[l]iquidated damages' and 'penalties' are terms used to reflect legal conclusions as to the enforceability or nonenforceability, respectively, of stipulated damage clauses." Kenneth W. Clarkson et al., *Liquidated Damages v. Penalties: Sense or Nonsense?*, 1978 Wis. L. Rev. 351, 351 n. 1 (hereinafter Clarkson).

Thirty years ago, the Appellate Division distinguished liquidated damages and penalty clauses:

> *Liquidated damages* is the sum a party to a contract agrees to pay if he breaks some promise, and which, having been arrived at by a good faith effort to estimate in advance the actual damages that will probably ensue from the breach, is legally recoverable as agreed damages if the breach occurs. A *penalty* is the sum a party agrees to pay in the event of a breach, but which is fixed, not as a pre-estimate of probable actual damages, but as a punishment, the threat of which is designed to prevent the breach. Parties to a contract may not fix a penalty for its breach. The settled rule in this State is that such a contract is unlawful.

[Westmount Country Club v. Kameny, 82 N.J.Super. 200, 205, 197 A.2d 379 (1964) (citations omitted).]

Stating the distinction, however, has been easier than describing its underlying rationale. " '[T]he ablest judges have declared that they felt themselves embarrassed in ascertaining the principle on which the decisions [distinguishing penalties from liquidated damages] were founded.' " E. Allan Farnsworth, Contracts § 12.18 at 937 (2d ed. 1990) (alterations in original) (quoting Cotheal v. Talmage, 9 N.Y. 551, 553 (1854)). . . .

As the law has evolved, a stipulated damage clause "must constitute a reasonable forecast of the provable injury resulting from breach;

otherwise, the clause will be unenforceable as a penalty and the non-breaching party will be limited to conventional damage measures." Goetz & Scott, supra, 77 Colum.L.Rev. at 554. So viewed, "reasonableness" emerges as the standard for deciding the validity of stipulated damages clauses. See *Wassenaar* at 361 (noting that "[t]he overall single test of validity is whether the clause is reasonable under the totality of circumstances").

The reasonableness test has developed as a compromise between two competing viewpoints concerning stipulated damages clauses. The Wisconsin Supreme Court has described the policy considerations underlying these viewpoints:

> Enforcement of stipulated damages clauses is urged because the clauses serve several purposes. The clauses allow the parties to control their exposure to risk by setting the payment for breach in advance. They avoid the uncertainty, delay, and expense of using the judicial process to determine actual damages. They allow the parties to fashion a remedy consistent with economic efficiency in a competitive market, and they enable the parties to correct what the parties perceive to be inadequate judicial remedies by agreeing upon a formula which may include damage elements too uncertain or remote to be recovered under rules of damages applied by the courts. In addition to these policies specifically relating to stipulated damages clauses, considerations of judicial economy and freedom of contract favor enforcement of stipulated damages clauses.
>
> A competing set of policies disfavors stipulated damages clauses, and thus courts have not been willing to enforce stipulated damages clauses blindly without carefully scrutinizing them. Public law, not private law, ordinarily defines the remedies of the parties. Stipulated damages are an exception to this rule. Stipulated damages allow private parties to perform the judicial function of providing the remedy in breach of contract cases, namely, compensation of the nonbreaching party, and courts must ensure that the private remedy does not stray too far from the legal principle of allowing compensatory damages. Stipulated damages substantially in excess of injury may justify an inference of unfairness in bargaining or an objectionable *in terrorem* agreement to deter a party from breaching the contract, to secure performance, and to punish the breaching party if the deterrent is ineffective.

[*Wassenaar* at 362.]

Consistent with the principle of reasonableness, New Jersey courts have viewed enforceability of stipulated damages clauses as depending on whether the set amount "is a reasonable forecast of just compensation for the harm that is caused by the breach" and whether that harm "is incapable or very difficult of accurate estimate." Westmount Country Club, supra, 82 N.J.Super. at 206, 197 A.2d 379.

Uncertainty or difficulty in assessing damages is best viewed not as an independent test, Calamari and Perillo, *supra*, § 14–31 at 641; Goetz & Scott, supra, 77 Colum.L.Rev. at 559 (stating, "liquidated damages provisions have seldom been voided solely because the damages were easy to estimate"), but rather as an element of assessing the reasonableness of a liquidated damages clause, *Wassenaar* at 363. Thus, "[t]he greater the difficulty of estimating or proving damages, the more likely the stipulated damages will appear reasonable." *Ibid.*

Some courts in other jurisdictions have also considered whether the parties intended the clause to be one for liquidated damages. Clarkson, supra, 1978 Wis.L.Rev. at 353. Even those courts recognize that "subjective intent has little bearing on whether the clause is objectively reasonable." *Wassenaar* at 363.

Although the Appellate Division has indicated that courts should determine the enforceability of a stipulated damages clause as of the time of the making of the contract. Westmount Country Club, supra, 82 N.J.Super. at 206, 197 A.2d 379, the modern trend is towards assessing reasonableness either at the time of contract formation or at the time of the breach. Calamari & Perillo, *supra*, § 14–31 at 642 (stating, "there are two moments at which the liquidated damages clause may be judged rather than just one").

Actual damages, moreover, reflect on the reasonableness of the parties' prediction of damages. "If the damages provided for in the contract are grossly disproportionate to the actual harm sustained, the courts usually conclude that the parties' original expectations were unreasonable." *Wassenaar* at 364; see 5A Corbin on Contracts § 1063 (1951) (Corbin) ("It is to be observed that hindsight is frequently better than foresight, and that, in passing judgment upon the honesty and genuineness of the pre-estimate made by the parties, the court cannot help but be influenced by its knowledge of subsequent events."). Determining enforceability at the time either when the contract is made or when it is breached encourages more frequent enforcement of stipulated damages clauses. Calamari & Perillo, supra, § 14–31 at 642.

Two of the most authoritative statements concerning liquidated damages are contained in the Uniform Commercial Code and the Restatement (Second) of Contracts, both of which emphasize reasonableness as the touchstone. Farnsworth, *supra*, § 12.18 at 938. [Here the court set out UCC § 2–718(1) and Restatement § 356(1).]

Consistent with the trend toward enforcing stipulated damages clauses, the Appellate Division has recognized that such clauses should be deemed presumptively reasonable and that the party challenging such a clause should bear the burden of proving its unreasonableness.

Similarly, most courts today place the burden on the party challenging a stipulated damages clause.

In commercial transactions between parties with comparable bargaining power, stipulated damage provisions can provide a useful and efficient remedy. See Priebe & Sons v. United States, 332 U.S. 407, 411–13 (1947). . . . Sophisticated parties acting under the advice of counsel often negotiate stipulated damages clauses to avoid the cost and uncertainty of litigation. Such parties can be better situated than courts to provide a fair and efficient remedy. Absent concerns about unconscionability, courts frequently need ask no more than whether the clause is reasonable. We do not reach the issue of the enforceability of liquidated damage clauses in consumer contracts. Notwithstanding the presumptive reasonableness of stipulated damage clauses, we are sensitive to the possibility that, as their history discloses, such clauses may be unconscionable and unjust.

V

The purpose of a stipulated damages clause is not to compel the promisor to perform, but to compensate the promisee for non-performance. Farnsworth, supra, § 12.18 at 936. Thus, the subject cancellation clause is unreasonable if it does more than compensate plaintiffs for their approximate actual damages caused by the breach.

Whether measured from the time of execution of the contract or from the termination of the lease damages based on gross receipts run the risk of being found unreasonable. Generally speaking, gross receipts do not reflect actual losses incurred because of the cancellation. Gross receipts, unlike net profits, do not account for ordinary expenses; nor do they account for the expenses specifically attributable to the breach. Here, we cannot determine whether the stipulated amount was based on damages that would likely flow from a breach or whether it is an arbitrary figure unrelated to any such damages.

Courts also have disapproved the use of gross receipts as a measure of damages apart from stipulated damages clauses. Evaluating damages based on gross income is problematic partly because such damages would be too speculative or uncertain. Furthermore, basing damages on gross profits could award the plaintiff a windfall.

We cannot determine from plaintiffs' gross receipts the losses they sustained because of the Township's cancellation of the lease. The subject clause requires the Township to pay damages of twenty-five percent of the lessee's average gross receipts for one year. Under the lease, average gross receipts are calculated by taking an average of the lessee's total gross receipts for three fiscal years immediately preceding the cancellation. So calculated, Jo-Ro's average yearly gross was $1,161,240.75. Twenty-five percent of this figure amounts to $290,310.18.

This amount, however, does not necessarily reflect plaintiffs' actual losses on considering operating expenses or relocation costs and other expenses attributable to defendant's breach. As reflected in Jo-Ro's income-tax returns, Jo-Ro earned a net profit of $3,649 in 1985, $414 in 1986, and sustained a loss of $323 in 1987. We recognize the difference between tax losses and actual losses. Yet, to the extent that tax returns reflect actual profit or loss, they demonstrate the unreasonableness of damages exceeding $290,000, which were calculated on the basis of gross receipts.

The decision whether a stipulated damages clause is enforceable is a question of law for the court. Although the question is one of law, it may require resolution of underlying factual issues.

On balance, we believe we should remand this matter to the trial court to consider the reasonableness of the clause in light of this opinion. In resolving that issue, the court should consider, among other relevant considerations, the reasonableness of the use of gross receipts as the measure of damages no matter when the cancellation occurs; the significance of the award of damages based on twenty-five percent of one year's average gross receipts, rather than on some other basis such as total gross receipts computed for each year remaining under the lease; the reasoning of the parties that supported the calculation of the stipulated damages; the lessee's duty to mitigate damages; and the fair market rent and availability of replacement space. We leave to the sound discretion of the trial court the extent to which additional proof is necessary on the reasonableness of the clause. Because stipulated damages clauses are presumptively reasonable the burden of production and of persuasion rests on the Township.

To summarize, we affirm the judgment of the Appellate Division that the Township is liable to plaintiffs for terminating the lease. We also affirm the judgment of the Appellate Division awarding plaintiffs damages of $55,748.27 for renovation costs. We remand to the Law Division the issue whether the clause requiring payment of stipulated damages based on the lessee's gross receipts is a valid liquidated damages clause.

NOTES

(1) *Arguments on Remand.* If you were the lawyer for the defendant Township on remand, what arguments and evidence would you use to meet the "burden" of challenging the clause? If you were the lawyer for the plaintiffs, Wasserman's and Jo-Ro, how would you counteract Justice Pollock's critical remarks on gross receipts as a standard? Is it relevant that on termination the plaintiffs lost the use for twelve more years, at an annual rental of only $5,500, of property then worth some $600,000? Does their unproductive use of the property affect your answer?

(2) *A "Second Look"?* Note that Justice Pollock reports that "the modern trend is towards assessing reasonableness either at the time of

contract formation or at the time of the breach." This echoes the language of UCC § 2–718, which speaks of the "anticipated or actual harm." But Article 2A of the Code, dealing with leases of goods, departs from the language of Article 2 and speaks of only the "anticipated harm." UCC § 2A–504(1).

In Kelly v. Marx, 705 N.E.2d 1114, 1117 (Mass. 1999), the court, in allowing the seller of a house to keep the purchaser's 5% deposit as liquidated damages, rejected the "second look" approach described by Justice Pollock in favor of a "single look" approach. "In addition to meeting the parties' expectations, the 'single look' approach helps resolve disputes efficiently by making it unnecessary to wait until actual damages from a breach are proved. The 'second look,' by contrast, undermines the 'peace of mind and certainty of result' the parties sought when they contracted for liquidated damages. It increases the potential for litigation by inviting the aggrieved party to attempt to show evidence of damage flowing from the breach . . . ." The court rejected the argument that the " 'second look' approach would allow the court to guard against undue windfalls, such as the one the defendants would receive here, . . . because the defendants suffered no loss from the breach."

(3) *Subterfuge?* Can a party by the use of subterfuge accomplish the same purpose that a penalty would accomplish? Instead of providing a penalty of $10,000 a day for each day's delay in construction beyond June 1, up to a maximum of $100,000, an owner might adjust the price and provide a *bonus* of $10,000 a day for each day's early completion before June 10, up to a maximum of $100,000.

The proscription of penalties might not extend to alternative performances. Instead of having an employee promise not to compete or pay a penalty of $100,000, an employer might have the employee promise either not to compete or, in the alternative, pay $100,000. Is this a "subterfuge" or a different sort of agreement? Is it arguable that the provision in *Wasserman's* was such an agreement?

(4) *Arbitration and Liquidated Damages.* Suppose that Wasserman's lease had included the arbitration clause recommended by the American Arbitration Association. See Note 2, p. 901 above. Would the court have enforced an arbitration award granting damages under the clause even if the court had considered it a penalty clause? In Matter of Associated General Contractors, 335 N.E.2d 859, 859 (N.Y. 1975), New York's highest court concluded that a party, having "chosen the arbitration forum for the resolution of disputes," was bound by the arbitrators' determination "that the damages clause was not a penalty and was therefore enforceable."

PROBLEMS

(1) *A Corvette Stalled.* Jim Steinke contracted with Circle B to restore its vintage Corvette car. Circle B paid $2,000 down, leaving a balance of $10,000. For delay, the contract provided for "a penalty of $100 per day assessed and deducted from the amount of $10,000." When Steinke finished the work 160 days late, Circle B refused to pay the $10,000 balance and claimed an additional $6,000. What result? How would you have drafted the

clause on behalf of Circle B? Circle B Enterprises v. Steinke, 584 N.W.2d 97 (N.D. 1998).

(2) *Paradise Lost.* A travel bureau offers a kosher Passover vacation at a resort hotel in Puerto Rico, including two complete Seders. Its contract includes a provision for "liquidated damages" based on a sliding scale and culminating in forfeiture of 100% of the price for cancellations made within 14 days of departure. Is the provision enforceable against a client who cancels 13 days before departure? See Turner-Schraeter v. Brighton Travel Bureau, 685 N.Y.S.2d 692 (App. Div. 1999).

———

Punitive Damages in Breach of Contract

At the beginning of this chapter it was emphasized that contract law's main remedial aim is directed at compensatory relief of promisees rather than at punishing promisors or compelling performance, and that for this reason punitive damages are not ordinarily awarded for breach of contract. We close the chapter with an exception to this traditional rule, which we first encountered in White v. Benkowski, p. 31.

Bains LLC v. Arco Prod. Co.

United States Court of Appeals, Ninth Circuit, 2005.
405 F.3d 764.

■ KLEINFELD, CIRCUIT JUDGE. In 1999 an Olympic Pipeline Company petroleum pipeline ruptured, interfering with the transportation of fuel from refineries in Northwest Washington to a distribution center in Seattle. It took two years to fix the pipeline. During that period ARCO hired a number of companies to truck fuel from its Blaine, Washington refinery to the distribution center.

Paul, Gary, and Deep Bains are American citizens who were born in the Punjab region of India. The Bains brothers bought a gas station and convenience store in Okanogan, Washington. They were the first Sikh family in the area. They did business under the name "Flying B," signifying that the Bains brothers were flying high in the American business world. Flying B soon owned five gas stations and employed thirty people. The brothers bought a tanker truck for about $100,000 and got the necessary permits to haul gasoline to their stations. That investment put the Bains brothers in an excellent position to make some money when the Olympic pipeline ruptured and ARCO needed help. In March 2000 they signed a contract with ARCO to haul fuel. By then Flying B was doing business as a corporation, the stock of which was owned solely by the three Bains brothers.

In June 2000, Flying B started hauling fuel for ARCO, and in August, after getting the necessary permits and safety clearances from ARCO, the company bought three more trucks and hired more drivers, although the Bains brothers themselves continued to drive trucks as well. But after four and a half months, about 600 loads (or 6.5 million gallons of gasoline), and 130,000 miles, Flying B's work ended on October 30, 2000, when ARCO terminated it.

During the period that Flying B transported fuel for ARCO, the Bains brothers and their drivers had to endure a considerable measure of abuse from Bill Davis, the lead man at ARCO's Seattle terminal where the drivers dropped off their fuel. Davis did not like the Flying B drivers and purposely made their unloading work at the Seattle terminal difficult. He made a point of delaying the Flying B drivers by ignoring their presence when they needed their papers signed after a delivery. Because ARCO paid by the load (about $460 for each load), the delays meant that Flying B's drivers could haul fewer loads and make less money. Davis made them stand out in the rain while other drivers were allowed to stay in their trucks or seek shelter. Davis also falsely accused Flying B drivers of various safety violations and made them clean up spills left by other drivers instead of making those responsible clean up their own spills.

Davis's rudeness included—and by inference arose from—his ethnic animus against Sikhs. Paul and Deep Bains, and many of the other Flying B drivers, were religiously observant Sikhs who wore turbans and long beards. Davis started his relationship with Paul Bains by refusing to shake his hand. He called Paul a "diaperhead" to his face despite Paul's protest that his turban was an important religious symbol. "Mr. Bains" or "Paul" were apparently too hard for Davis to say—he preferred "raghead." One of Flying B's hired drivers said Davis commonly called him "stupid Indian," "motherfucking Indian," and similar sobriquets, and when he asked for a rag after Davis had told him to clean up a spill, Davis refused and told him to take the "fucking rag from your head and clean it."

After months of Davis's abuse, the morale of Flying B drivers suffered and drivers threatened to quit. Even the non-Sikh Flying B drivers felt degraded by Davis's attitude toward their association with their company. Davis asked both Patrick Dauer and A.C. Morgan, the only two Caucasian Flying B drivers, "How did you get hooked up with these fuckers?"

Eventually the Bains brothers decided to report Davis's abuse to Al Lawrence, the manager of the Seattle terminal and Davis's boss. The brothers decided that Deep would talk to Lawrence. . . . Lawrence responded that perhaps Davis was upset about something and asked Deep to let him know if anything happened in the future.

But the problems continued and Davis kept up his abuse. . . . Deep complained to Lawrence again, but it did not do any good. . . . Gary Bains went to Lawrence and advised him yet again of the continuing abuse. But instead of stopping Davis's abuse, Lawrence and ARCO stopped Flying B. ARCO terminated Flying B without giving a reason and without notice, not even the thirty-day minimum notice required by their contract. Flying B was forced to lay off a number of employees and to sell their now superfluous trucks. Deep Bains contacted Tim Reichert, the Los Angeles central dispatch manager, who was above Lawrence in the ARCO hierarchy, to contest the termination, but to no effect. Reichert claimed that there were too many trucks for the job.

An important part of the case was whether the ethnic nastiness and coarse language was only Davis's independent foray into obnoxiousness, or whether ARCO, through Davis's supervisor, Al Lawrence, ought to have known about Davis's behavior and done something about it. The parties also disputed whether ARCO's termination of Flying B had anything to do with the racism. In addition to the Bains' testimony that they had complained to Lawrence, a driver for another company, Torrance Holmes, testified that once he started chatting with the Bains brothers, Lawrence quit talking to him. Holmes also testified that he heard Davis brag that "we kicked those ragheads out of here and they're never coming back."

In his own testimony, Bill Davis admitted that he had used the term "raghead" "once in a while" when referring to the Bains brothers in conversations with coworkers, typically when other people complained about Flying B drivers. . . . [T]he gist of Davis's testimony was that he called the Flying B drivers "ragheads" only behind their backs, not to their faces. Lawrence never disciplined or reprimanded Davis, but Davis claimed that he quit using the term after his chat with Lawrence.

An economist testified that Flying B suffered a $576,000 loss on account of the termination. He calculated this based solely on the profits the company would have made from November 1, 2000, when Flying B was terminated, to June 30, 2001, when the pipeline was fixed and ARCO no longer needed drivers to move the fuel.

The jury delivered a special verdict. It found that ARCO had breached Flying B's contract, a state law claim, and awarded $50,000 in compensatory damages for the breach. The verdict also established that ARCO had discriminated against Flying B on account of race, in violation of 42 U.S.C. § 1981, but that the actual damages to the corporation on account of this discrimination were nominal. The jury therefore awarded only one dollar in compensatory damages on the § 1981 claim. In addition, however, the jury awarded five million dollars in punitive damages for the racial discrimination. ARCO moved for judgment as a matter of law or a new trial, or alternatively, to set aside or remit the punitive damages. The district court denied the motions. The district court awarded $392,065 in attorneys' fees and $10,017.40 in costs, plus $50,000 in additional fees and $916.36 in additional costs, based on the post-trial proceedings. ARCO appeals.

Analysis

ARCO argues that it was entitled to judgment as a matter of law, or alternatively, a new trial, because a corporation cannot suffer racial discrimination actionable under 42 U.S.C. § 1981,[1] and because even if that is incorrect, the award of only nominal damages establishes that firing Flying B was not motivated by race discrimination.

[The Court summarized the relevant caselaw—holding that a corporation has standing to bring a § 1981 claim—before turning to Arco's twin claim that (i) there is no injury to a corporation without economic harm and (ii) the jury award of nominal damages implies no economic injury to the corporation.]

ARCO argues that the jury verdict-awarding one dollar in nominal damages for the § 1981 violation—establishes that the ethnic discrimination caused no economic harm (as opposed to the breach of contract, for which $50,000 was awarded), and that there can be no injury to a corporation without economic damages. ARCO moved for a new trial, which the district court denied. We review the district court's denial of a motion for a new trial for abuse of discretion. Because we are reviewing a case that resulted in a jury verdict, we interpret the evidence, and state our account, most favorably to the parties successful at trial.

First, the district court instructed the jury that, because the plaintiff was a corporation, the jury could award damages, even nominal damages, only for harm to the corporation, not for the emotional distress to its owners or employees. We must presume that the jury followed that instruction.

Second, the one dollar in nominal damages for the § 1981 violation was not the whole of the jury's verdict. The jury also found that ARCO had in fact discriminated against Flying B because of race, that it caused a $50,000 loss by breaking its contract with Flying B, and that ARCO deserved to be punished for its racial discrimination to the extent of $5 million. These verdicts could be viewed as inconsistent, but, as we held in White v. Ford Motor Co., a court has a duty under the Seventh Amendment to harmonize a jury's seemingly inconsistent answers if a fair reading allows for it. The district court was therefore obligated to ask "not whether the verdict necessarily makes sense under any reading, but whether it can be read in light of the evidence to make sense."

We agree with the district court that the verdict is not inconsistent and does not establish the absence of economic harm. The district court

---

[1]   42 U.S.C. § 1981(a)–(b) states: (a) Statement of equal rights—All persons within the jurisdiction of the United States shall have the same right in every State and Territory to make and enforce contracts, to sue, be parties, give evidence, and to the full and equal benefit of all laws and proceedings for the security of persons and property as is enjoyed by white citizens, and shall be subject to like punishment, pains, penalties, taxes, licenses, and exactions of every kind, and to no other. (b) "Make and enforce contracts"—Defined for purposes of this section, the term "make and enforce contracts" includes the making, performance, modification, and termination of contracts, and the enjoyment of all benefits, privileges, terms, and conditions of the contractual relationship.

correctly held that the jury may have found that Flying B's claimed damages for lost profits were not "shown with reasonable certainty" as required by jury instruction number 18. On the evidence in this record, the jury could well have concluded that (1) racial discrimination had caused lost profits by delaying Flying B's drivers and thereby reducing the number of loads Flying B hauled; but (2) the jury did not have testimony that would enable it to put a number on how many loads were lost; so (3) even though lost profits were proved, the "amount" of lost profits could not be established "with reasonable certainty," as the jury instruction required.

The damages to Flying B, as a predicate for punitive damages, do not have to be from the termination. Section 1981 extends its prohibition against racial discrimination in the making and enforcement of contracts to cover all phases and incidents of the contractual relationship, not just the termination of a contract. The testimony established that ARCO employees made Flying B's drivers wait longer to fill their trucks and to use slower pumps than other drivers, and that Flying B drivers suffered damaged morale. The jury could have concluded that Flying B suffered economic harm during the contractual relationship from the intentional delays and its drivers' damaged morale, which resulted in a reduced number of loads-and therefore less money under a contract that paid by the load-and that all of this was caused by Davis's racial harassment. Flying B's economics expert testified that Flying B would have made $576,000 if it had continued to haul the same number of loads it did until the broken pipeline was fixed, but he did not offer testimony on how much money Flying B lost because of the slowdowns caused by Davis's racial harassment. The jury could reasonably have concluded that Flying B had made less money while it was hauling because of Davis's racial harassment, yet reasonably have found no number that it could attach to the harm, and therefore awarded nominal damages.

The district court, having heard all the evidence, was able to reconcile the verdicts, and on our review of the evidence and arguments, we find no irreconcilable conflict.

An award of nominal damages does not mean that there were not actual economic damages, just that the exact amount of damages attributable to the improper conduct was not proven.

III. Amount of Punitive Damages

ARCO argues that the $5 million in punitive damages awarded by the jury was excessive in light of BMW of North America, Inc. v. Gore and In re Exxon Valdez. We review the excessiveness of punitive damages de novo. The guideposts we follow are: (1) the degree of reprehensibility, (2) the disparity between the harm suffered and the punitive damages award, and (3) the difference between this remedy and the civil penalties authorized or imposed in comparable cases. The gist of ARCO's argument is that the harm to Flying B was purely economic, and that the amount of punitive damages is too great relative to the amount of economic damages awarded. As to the amount of punitive damages, ARCO's argument is partially correct.

State Farm Mutual Automobile Insurance Co. v. Campbell enumerates the factors to be used when evaluating the reprehensibility of a defendant's conduct. We look to whether "the harm caused was physical as opposed to economic; the tortious conduct evinced an indifference to or a reckless disregard of the health or safety of others; the target of the conduct had financial vulnerability; the conduct involved repeated actions or was an isolated incident; and the harm was the result of intentional malice, trickery, or deceit, or mere accident." Here the harm to Flying B was economic and did not evince reckless disregard of health or safety. More than in Exxon Valdez, where we noted that the wrongdoing did not kill anyone, here there was no threat of physical harm. That reduces reprehensibility. On the other hand, the conduct was not an isolated incident but repeated, the target was highly vulnerable financially, and the harm resulted from intentional malicious conduct. An Exxon oil tanker that performs a socially valuable task can accidentally run aground causing damage. By contrast there can be no excuse for intentional, repeated ethnic harassment, so the reprehensibility here is worse than conduct that might have some legitimate purpose. In Exxon Valdez, we held that "[r]eprehensibility should be discounted if defendants act promptly and comprehensively to ameliorate any harm they cause in order to encourage such socially beneficial behavior." Here, given ARCO's clear failure to remedy or even address the discriminatory effects of its employee's conduct, the jury could properly have concluded that punitive damages were necessary to prevent such discrimination from occurring in the future.

As to the other two BMW factors, the disparity between the harm suffered and the punitive damages award, and the difference between this remedy and civil penalties authorized or imposed in comparable cases, ARCO is on stronger ground.

On the facts of this case, in determining the correct amount of punitive damages, the jury could properly consider not only the one dollar in nominal damages awarded for discrimination under § 1981, but also the $50,000 in compensatory damages awarded for breach of contract. The conduct was intertwined and the jury could conclude that, even if Tim Reichert would have terminated Flying B based on the safety reports that Al Lawrence gave him, those safety reports would never have come to Reichert had Lawrence not decided to back up his racist leadman or to exercise his authority to lock Flying B out of the terminal. Thus we take $50,000 as the harm suffered.

Flying B argues that because "potential harm" may properly be considered under TXO Production Corp. v. Alliance Resources Corp., a much higher punitive damages award is appropriate. But TXO was speaking of the potential harm "if the wrongful plan had succeeded, as well as the possible harm to other victims." Here the wrongful conduct did succeed. It is not as though Davis had fired a shot at Flying B and missed. Davis bragged that he had "gotten rid of those ragheads." As for the harm to the individual drivers, the award to Flying B did not impair their own rights to sue for whatever common law or state statutory torts that might lie, such as intentional infliction of mental distress. Potential harm to others is best considered when victims are not in a position to vindicate the wrongs against themselves, not where, as here, they are in such a position.

In State Farm, the Supreme Court held that "in practice, few awards exceeding a single-digit ratio between punitive and compensatory damages, to a significant degree, will satisfy due process." The rare exception might be a case where "a particularly egregious act has resulted in only a small amount of economic damages." This is not a "small amount" case because the economic damages were substantial-$50,000. The controlling Supreme Court authority therefore implies a punitive damages ceiling in this case of, at most, $450,000 (nine times the compensatory damages)-not anywhere near the $5,000,000 (100 times the compensatory damages) that was awarded by the jury.

In Zhang v. American Gem Seafoods, Inc., a post-State Farm § 1981 race discrimination case, we took note that "few awards exceeding a single digit ratio" will satisfy due process, although this is not a "brightline rule," and upheld the award because it was only seven times the amount of compensatory damages. We need not rely solely on the ratio, because the third BMW guidepost—which looks to the difference between the amount of punitive damages awarded and the civil penalties authorized or imposed in comparable cases—provides us with another measure that restrains the permissible amount. [I]n Zhang, we noted that the $300,000 statutory limitation on punitive damages in Title VII cases was an appropriate benchmark for reviewing § 1981 damage awards, even though the statute did not apply to § 1981 cases.

Flying B argues that the huge corporate assets of ARCO justify a higher award than might be justified for a defendant less able to pay it. A punitive damages award is supposed to sting so as to deter a defendant's reprehensible conduct, and juries have traditionally been permitted to consider a defendant's assets in determining an award that will carry the right degree of sting. But there are limits. "The wealth of a defendant cannot justify an otherwise unconstitutional punitive damages award," and "cannot make up for the failure of other factors, such as 'reprehensibility,' to constrain significantly an award that purports to punish a defendant's conduct."

Thus what we are left with is a case of highly reprehensible conduct, though not threatening to life or limb, that caused economic harm to a corporation. The jury found $50,000 of actual harm, and, as this is not the "rare case" for which State Farm leaves room, the ratio approach suggests that punitive damages could not, consistent with due process, exceed $450,000. Comparing the award to the civil penalty authorized in

Title VII for comparable harm suggests that Congress regards $300,000 as the highest appropriate amount in somewhat comparable cases.

Conclusion

We affirm the jury verdict and the rulings of the district court on all issues, except for the amount of punitive damages, which we vacate. The award exceeds constitutional limits, so on de novo review, we are required to reduce it or to remand so that the district court may order a new trial, unless the plaintiff accepts a remittitur. The level of punitive damages is not a finding of "fact" that must be determined by the jury; it may be determined de novo by the court. Because the district court tried the case and has greater understanding of the facts than we do, we remand the case and leave the amount, within the $300,000 to $450,000 range, to the district court.

Each party shall bear its own costs on appeal.

NOTES

(1) *Breach Plus.* As illustrated in a number of cases through the book, the general and strong disposition in the American law of contracts is to award no punitive damages for breach of contract. Exceptions tend to follow only where the breach is combined with some other wrong, such as a tort or fraud (including perhaps especially promissory fraud) or a statutory violation providing for a punitive award.

(2) *Nominal, Not Nothing.* What was the importance in the outcome of the case of the award of $1 in damages?

(3) *Standing and Standing-in for the Corporation.* Many of the cases we have read involve breach of a contract where the counterparties are corporations. A significant aspect of this case (largely edited out of the excerpt here) concerned whether the employees and owners of Flying B could assert a claim themselves or on behalf of the corporation, and whether the Arco corporation is liable for wrongs committed by its employees apparently acting within the scope of their employment. These considerations are the subject of a course on the law of business organization; however, they cannot be entirely separated from the matters of remedies for breach of contract. Where breach causes some person harm, that harm must not only be legally cognizable, but the person harmed must have standing to bring a claim against the breaching party for a remedy to the injury. See Domino's Pizza, Inc. v. McDonald, 546 U.S. 470 (2006).

CHAPTER 9

BASIC ASSUMPTIONS: MISTAKE, IMPRACTICABILITY, AND FRUSTRATION

Contracting parties often encounter obstacles to performance that they failed to account for when making the contract. For this reason, a court will occasionally—but only very occasionally—excuse or suspend a contract obligation, sometimes replacing the original obligation with a new duty. This chapter addresses occasions of these types.

When a party's performance is impeded, or when a party's expectations are seriously thwarted by circumstances existing but unknown to the parties at the time they enter into the contract, a common ground for claiming an excuse is mistake. That is the focus of Section 1, mutual mistake, and Section 2, unilateral mistake. In contrast, Sections 3 and 4 largely feature obligations that are subverted by events occurring *after* the parties have contracted.

When a promisor seeks relief on the ground that a supervening turn of events has impeded its performance, the conventional legal basis is "impossibility" now more commonly called "impracticability." We have already seen a number of cases in which a performance was impeded by a "turn of events," such as floods (Gill v. Johnstown Lumber Co., p. 822), outbreak of war (McCloskey & Co. v. Minweld Steel Co., p. 860) and temperature (Cosden Oil & Chemical Co. v. Karl O. Helm, p. 947). Events over the recent decade have provided ample sources for consideration. In Dryland Steamboat Road, LLC v. GRC Realty Corp., 2010 WL 4276761 (Sup. Ct. Conn. July 20, 2010), for instance, the plaintiff, having failed to close on a high-end commercial office building, sought return of its $22.5 million deposit based on the "sudden, unforeseeable collapse of Lehman Brothers [that] sent shock waves through the financial markets, effectively freezing those markets and rendering it impossible for [the plaintiff] to obtain third party, first mortgage financing from any source, in a reasonable amount and under any reasonable terms. Effectively, the commercial financing markets were frozen in place." The doctrine of impracticability, the topic of Section 3, describes the additional circumstances that must attend such events—whether freezing temperatures or frozen markets—in order to excuse the performance of a party: although important, it is not sufficient that the party's performance is simply more difficult or costly than anticipated.

While our discussion of impracticability is significantly informed by considerations of the cost of performance, the topic of Section 4, "frustration of purpose," focuses on the value or purpose of performance. The typical situation presented in this section is somewhat singular in that the party claiming an excuse cannot say that performance itself was impeded by a supervening event; rather, some turn of events has thwarted that party's purpose in making the contract, and for that reason—not the impracticability of performance—the party seeks to be excused from performing.

Being relieved of an obligation through an excuse doctrine is often not the end of the story. There may well be a sequel to the story when one party's expectations are defeated because another party has succeeded, for one of the reasons mentioned above, in disclaiming an obligation. Some compensating adjustment may be possible, especially in the name of *restitution*. Section 5 provides some instances.

SECTION 1.   MUTUAL MISTAKE

The cases considered in this section involve *mutual* mistake, where both parties to the contract are mistaken as to the same basic assumption. Mistaken beliefs and misunderstandings concerning material aspects of an agreement may undermine assent and the very basis of the contract. Restatement § 20 cmt. h; Raffles v. Wichelhaus, p. 559 above. But even when a belief, contrary to fact, does not defeat formation of a contract, courts will sometimes allow a party to avoid performance of the contract through the doctrine of mistake.

The background principle against which the mistake doctrine operates is that agreements are to be observed—*pacta sunt servanda*—notwithstanding the regret that a party may experience when fresh information comes to light. This principle underlies a dictum in Watkins & Son v. Carrig, p. 445. The contract there called for the excavation of a cellar, and the parties seemed to be surprised when the excavator encountered rock. "In this situation," the court said, "a defense of mutual mistake is not available." Similarly, in the case that follows, a builder, Leonard, encountered an unfavorable soil condition. In writing about Leonard's responsibility, the court did not indicate that he made an explicit appeal to the law of mistake. But it is clear from the opinion that the court would have been deaf to that appeal.

Stees v. Leonard

Supreme Court of Minnesota, 1874.
20 Minn. 494, 20 Gil. 448.

[The statement of facts is taken in part from the 1882 edition by Gilfillan of 20 Minnesota Reports.] The action was brought to recover damages for a failure of defendants to erect and complete a building on a lot of plaintiffs, on Minnesota Street, between Third and Fourth streets, in the city of St. Paul, which, by an agreement under seal between them and plaintiffs, the defendants had agreed to build, erect, and complete, according to plans and specifications annexed to and made part of the agreement. The defendants commenced the construction of the building, and had carried it to the height of three stories when it fell to the ground. The next year, 1869, they began again and carried it to the height as before, when it again fell to the ground, whereupon defendants refused to perform the contract. They claimed that in their attempts to erect the building they did the work in all respects according to the plans and specifications and that the failure to complete the building and its fall on the two occasions was due to the fact that the soil upon which it was to be constructed was composed of quicksand, and when water flowed into it, was incapable of sustaining the building. The specifications annexed to the contract are very full, and provide, (among other things,) that "All the walls shall be of the following thickness: foundation walls, two feet thick, and shall have footings six inches thick, which shall run clear across walls and project six inches on each side of wall above it." The specifications contain no other provisions relating to the character of the foundation for the building. [The plaintiffs alleged that the specifications, signed by both parties to the contract, had been prepared by a firm of architects named Sheire & Bro. Two persons named Sheire were named as defendants along with Leonard.]

The plaintiffs allege that the fall of the building was owing to the negligence and unskilful work of the defendants, and the poor quality of the material furnished by them. Judgment is demanded for the sum of $5,214.80, with interest, as the damages sustained by the plaintiffs; being $3,745.80 paid, pursuant to the contract, during the progress of the work, $1,000 as damages for loss of the use of the lot on which the building was to be erected, and $469, as damages, occasioned by the fall of the building, to an adjacent house of plaintiffs, and property stored therein.

The jury found for the plaintiffs. The defendants moved, upon a bill of exceptions, for a new trial, and appeal from the order denying their motion.

■ YOUNG, JUSTICE. The general principle of law which underlies this case is well established. If a man bind himself, by a positive, express contract, to do an act in itself possible, he must perform his engagement, unless prevented by the act of God, the law, or the other party to the contract. No hardship, no unforeseen hindrance, no difficulty short of absolute impossibility, will excuse him from doing what he has expressly agreed to do. This doctrine may sometimes seem to bear heavily upon contractors; but, in such cases, the hardship is attributable, not to the law, but to the contractor himself, who has improvidently assumed an absolute, when he might have undertaken only a qualified, liability. The law does no more than enforce the contract as the parties themselves have made it.

School Trustees v. Bennett, 3 Dutcher, N.J., 513, is almost identical, in its material facts, with the present case. The contractors agreed to build and complete a schoolhouse, and find all materials therefor, according to specifications annexed to the contract; the building to be located on a lot owned by plaintiff, and designated in the contract. When the building was nearly completed it was blown down by a sudden and violent gale of wind. The contractors again began to erect the building, when it fell, solely on account of the soil on which it stood having become soft and miry, and unable to sustain the weight of the building; although, when the foundations were laid, the soil was so hard as to be penetrated with difficulty by a pickax, and its defects were latent. The plaintiff had a verdict for the amount of the installments paid under the contract as the work progressed. The verdict was sustained by the supreme court, which held that the loss, although arising solely from a latent defect in the soil, and not from a faulty construction of the building, must fall on the contractor.

[The court referred to Dermott v. Jones, 69 U.S. (2 Wall.) 1 (1864), a case in which "the foundation of the building sank, owing to a latent defect in the soil." From the opinion there the court quoted a statement that the applicable principle "regards the sanctity of contracts. It requires a party to do what he has agreed to do. If unexpected impediments lie in the way, and a loss ensue, it leaves the loss where the contract places it."]

Nothing can be added to the clear and cogent arguments we have quoted in vindication of the wisdom and justice of the rule which must govern this case, unless it is in some way distinguishable from the cases cited.

It is no defense to the action that the specifications directed that "footings" should be used as the foundation of the building, and that the defendants, in the construction of those footings, as well as in all other particulars, conformed to the specifications. The defendants contracted to "erect and complete the building." Whatever was necessary to be done in order to complete the building, they were bound by the contract to do. If the building could not be completed without other or stronger foundations than the footings specified, they were bound to furnish such other foundations. If the building could not be erected without draining the land, then they must drain the land, "because they have agreed to do everything necessary to erect and complete the building." (3 Dutcher, N.J., 520; and see Dermott v. Jones, supra, where the same point was made by the contractor, but ruled against him by the court.)

As the draining of the land was, in fact, necessary to the erection and completion of the building, it was a thing to be done, under the contract, by the defendants. The prior parol agreement that plaintiffs should drain the land, related therefore, to a matter embraced within the terms of the written contract, and was not, as claimed by defendants' counsel, collateral thereto. It was, accordingly under the familiar rule, inadmissible in evidence to vary the terms of the written contract, and was properly excluded.

[In the remainder of the opinion the court considered evidence offered by the defendants that *after* the work was begun the plaintiffs made promises to drain the site of the building, and that the failure to do so caused the collapse. The court held that the evidence was properly excluded because the defendants had failed to allege consideration for the promises, or justifiable reliance upon them.]

There was, therefore, no error in the exclusion of the evidence offered, and the order appealed from is affirmed.

NOTES

(1) *Questions.* Note that Stees did not get, nor did he ask for, his expectation interest—the value to him of the building less any savings. Do you see any significance in that? As a test of your answer, suppose that Leonard detected the problem before beginning work and refused to begin, whereupon Stees paid a higher price to another builder for doing the work. What of a claim for the additional cost?

Charles Fried, in his influential book *Contract as Promise* (1981), has called the result in *Stees* a harsh and silly one. Id. at 64. Do you agree? If so, do you object also to what was said in Watkins & Son, as quoted before the *Stees* opinion, about an excavator's liability?

(2) *Owner's Responsibility?* In Dermott v. Jones, relied on in *Stees*, counsel for the owner cautioned the Court against the theory that a building contract makes the owner "an insurer to the builder of the stability and solidity of the soil on which such builder contracts to build work." In *Stees*, the defendants urged a modified version of that theory on the court. The court rejected the argument, concluding that it was foreclosed by the pleadings. The argument has impressive support, however, at least when the contract requires building according to plans prepared by the owner. That being the case, it has been said that "the contractor will not be responsible for the consequences of defects in the plans and specifications." United States v. Spearin, 248 U.S. 132, 136 (1918). There, the Court ruled that specifications in the contract about a projected sewer, including its location in the Brooklyn Navy Yard, "imported a warranty that, if the specifications were complied with, the sewer would be adequate." See also the "soft soil" case, Ridley Investment Co. v. Croll, 192 A.2d 925 (Del. 1963) (plans and specifications "defective for the location in question").

Courts have distinguished between a "performance specification," which requires a contractor to produce a specific result without specifying the means for achieving that result, and a "design specification," which specifies the design, materials, and methods, and impliedly warrants their adequacy. Which kind of specification was involved in *Stees*? In *Spearin*?

(3) *Act of God.* Changing the facts in *Stees*, suppose that Leonard had no foundation trouble in putting up the building, but that when he had nearly finished the job the building was struck by lightning and destroyed by an ensuing fire. He would have been accountable for breach, it seems, if he did not begin to build again. "It is well established law that where one contracts to furnish labor and materials, and construct a chattel, or build a

house, on land of another, he will not ordinarily be excused from performance of his contract by the destruction of the chattel or building without his fault before the time fixed for the delivery of it." Butterfield v. Byron, 27 N.E. 667 (Mass. 1891)—a case of lightning. (Nonetheless, the court found in the facts a reason to avoid applying the rule quoted.)

(4) *Parol Evidence.* Consider Leonard's offer to prove a "prior parol agreement" by Stees to drain the site, in relation to this statement: "The parol evidence rule does not preclude the use of prior or contemporaneous agreements or negotiations to establish that the parties were mistaken." Restatement § 152 cmt. a. Evidence of the supposed agreement could not have helped Leonard to establish a mutual mistake, it seems. What, then, of using that evidence to establish that the parties were *not* mistaken? One can imagine that Stees—not Leonard—offered evidence of his own promise. Expecting that the parol evidence rule would prevent enforcement of the promise, Stees might want to use the evidence to show that no mistake was made. (Anyone believing the evidence would infer that the parties knew the site was waterlogged.)

Renner v. Kehl

Supreme Court of Arizona, 1986.
150 Ariz. 94, 722 P.2d 262.

[Two couples, the Kehls and the Moyles, doing business together, decided to sell their interest in unimproved land near Yuma, Arizona. They held leases on more than two thousand acres. Roy Renner and some associates contracted to pay about $100 an acre for the leases. Before that, the purchasers made it clear to the sellers that they were interested in the property only for the cultivation of jojoba and required adequate water supplies. The property appeared to be ideal for that purpose; the soil and climate were good and both parties were of the opinion that sufficient water was available beneath the land to sustain jojoba production. (Jojoba ["ha-ho'ba"] is a shrub, the seeds of which yield a valuable oil.)

The purchasers abandoned the project after making a down payment, taking a conveyance, and drilling five test wells. None of the wells produced water of sufficient quantity or quality for commercial jojoba cultivation. Then the purchasers brought an action against the sellers for rescission. The trial court directed the sellers to reimburse the purchasers, upon receiving a reassignment of the leases. The Court of Appeals affirmed, on a first appeal, and the sellers appealed again.]

■ Gordon, Vice Chief Justice. Mutual mistake of fact is an accepted basis for rescission. Amos Flight Operations, Inc. v. Thunderbird Bank, 112 Ariz. 263, 540 P.2d 1244 (1975); Mortensen v. Berzell Investment Company, 102 Ariz. 348, 429 P.2d 945 (1967). See Restatement (Second) of Contracts § 152. In Arizona a contract may be rescinded when there is a mutual mistake of material fact which constitutes "an essential part and condition of the contract." [*Mortensen* at 350, 947.] The trial court found that the sole purpose of the contract was to enable respondents to grow jojoba, which depends upon an adequate water supply. The trial court specifically found that "There would have been no sale if both sellers and buyers had not believed it was possible to grow jojoba commercially on the leased acres. . . . " and that "[b]ased upon the factual data available, all parties were of the opinion that there would be sufficient good quality water for commercial jojoba production, and that it would be close enough to the surface that it would be economically feasible to pump it for irrigation of large acreages." Consequently, the trial court concluded that "[p]laintiffs are entitled to rescind the purchase agreement because of the mutual mistake of fact and because there was a total failure of consideration."[1]

The belief of the parties that adequate water supplies existed beneath the property was "a basic assumption on which both parties made the contract," Restatement (Second) of Contracts § 152 Comment *b*, and their mutual mistake "ha[d] such a material effect on the agreed exchange of performances as to upset the very bases of the contract." Id. Comment *a*. The contract was therefore voidable and the respondents were entitled to rescission.[2]

[The trial court had ordered the sellers to reimburse the purchasers in the amount of $309,849.84. This amount included $80,200, which the sellers had received as a down payment for the leases. (The purchasers had agreed to pay $142,000 more in annual installments.) The remainder of the reimbursement consisted of expenses that the purchasers had incurred in developing the property, including the cost of drilling test wells.]

The court of appeals upheld the full award. The petitioners challenge the $229,649.84 awarded as an improper grant of "consequential damages".[a] [The parties and the court seem to have used this expression as an alias for a recovery of reliance expenses.]

We are dealing with a rescission based upon mutual mistake, which implies freedom from fault on the part of both parties. [W]e hold that absent proof of breach for fraud or misrepresentation a party who rescinds a contract may not recover consequential damages.

---

[1]   The petitioner challenges the sufficiency of the evidence in support of the trial court's conclusions of fact and law, but failed to provide a record of the trial. . . . Without a record we must presume that the trial court properly exercised its discretion and that there was substantial evidence in the complete record to support the findings of the trial court. . . .

[2]   The failure of the parties to make a thorough investigation of the water supply prior to signing the contract does not preclude rescission where the risk of mistake was not allocated among the parties and the mistake is material and relates to a basic assumption on which the contract was made. Restatement (Second) of Contracts § 152 Comment *a*. See id., illustration 1:

"A contracts to sell and B to buy a tract of land, the value of which has depended mainly on the timber on it. Both A and B believe that the timber is still there, but in fact it has been destroyed by fire. The contract is voidable by B."

[a]   Consequential or "incidental" damages represent a plaintiff's expenses incurred in reliance upon the contract. *See* Fousel v. Ted Walker Mobile Homes, Inc., 124 Ariz. 126, 602 P.2d 507 (App. 1979). In *Fousel* these expenses included the cost of custom-made awnings, skirting and steps purchased for their mobile home, *see* discussion, *infra*; in this case they would represent the cost of developing the land for jojoba production.

This does not mean, however, that the respondents are entitled only to recover their down payment. When a party rescinds a contract on the ground of mutual mistake he is entitled to restitution for any benefit that he has conferred on the other party by way of part performance or reliance. Restatement (Second) of Contracts § 376. Restitutionary recoveries are not designed to be compensatory; their justification lies in the avoidance of unjust enrichment on the part of the defendant. D. Dobbs, Remedies § 4.1 p. 224 (1973). Thus the defendant is generally liable for restitution of a benefit that would be unjust for him to keep, even though he gained it honestly. Id; Restatement (Second) of Contracts § 376 Comment *a*. The issue we must now address is the proper measure of the restitutionary interest.

The first step determining the proper measure of restitution requires that the rescinding party return or offer to return, conditional on restitution, any interest in property that he has received in the bargain. Restatement (Second) of Contracts § 384(1)(a). In Arizona this includes reimbursement for the fair market value of the use of the property. Thus the respondents were obliged to return the land to the petitioners in exchange for their down payment, and in addition to pay the petitioners the fair rental value of the land for the duration of their occupancy.

However, to avoid unjust enrichment the petitioners must pay the respondents a sum equal to the amount by which their property has been enhanced in value by the respondents' efforts. The Restatement (Second) of Contracts § 376 provides that "[i]f [a party] has received and must return land he may have made improvements on the land in reliance on the contract and he is entitled to recover the reasonable value of those improvements. The rule stated in this section applies to avoidance on any ground, including . . . mistake. . . . " Comment *a*. The reasonable value of any improvements is measured by "the extent to which the other party's property has been increased in value or his other interests advanced." Restatement (Second) of Contracts § 371(b). Thus the petitioners must pay to the respondents that amount of money which represents the enhanced value of the land due to the respondents' development efforts. In short, the respondents are entitled to their down payment, plus the amount by which their efforts increased the value of the petitioners' property, minus an amount which represents the fair rental value of the land during their occupancy. They are not entitled to the $229,649.84 expended upon development, because that would shift the entire risk of mistake onto the petitioners, which is incompatible with equitable rescission.

CONCLUSION

The respondents were entitled to rescind the contract, but may not recover the costs of developing the land in the form of consequential damages. The respondents are entitled to restitution of their down payment and any amount by which the value of the land was enhanced, but in turn the respondents must pay petitioners the fair rental value of the tenancy. Accordingly, the trial court is affirmed in part and reversed in part and the court of appeals' decision is approved in part and vacated in part. The case is remanded to the trial court for further proceedings not inconsistent with this opinion.

NOTES

(1) *Enforcement Possibilities.* It is well to defer consideration of the court's rulings about restitution for the purchasers and the rental-value charge, and for the present to consider only the ruling that the purchasers were entitled to rescission. (As to monetary adjustments, see below.)

Suppose that the buyers had learned of the water problem earlier, and had refused to take a conveyance. Suppose also that the court had ruled otherwise on the issue of mistake. It would follow that the sellers could have recovered damages based on the contract price. Does it also follow that the sellers could have won an order for specific performance, as is usual for contracts for real-property transfers? Recall the element of judicial discretion in actions for specific performance, and see McKinnon v. Benedict, p. 595 above.

(2) *The Converse Case.* Changing the facts in *Renner*, suppose that the buyers' test drilling had disclosed not only an ample and accessible supply of water but also valuable minerals. In that case one might anticipate an action for rescission brought by the *sellers*, not the buyers. Except that, by all indications, that action would fail. "[I]t is commonly understood that the seller of farm land generally cannot avoid the contract of sale upon later discovery by both parties that the land contains valuable mineral deposits, even though the price was negotiated on the basic assumption that the land was suitable only for farming and the effect on the agreed exchange of performances is material." Restatement § 154 cmt. a. Can this be explained on any ground other than *caveat vendor*?

SECTION 2. UNILATERAL MISTAKE

Reprieve under the doctrine of unilateral mistake is most commonly sought in situations involving erroneous bids, as in Elsinore School District v. Kastorff, p. 200, where a bidder for building work got relief for his mistaken offer. Yet construction bids are not the only site of application for the doctrine of unilateral mistake, as our next case illustrates. When reading the opinion below, take note of how the court applies the doctrine variably to the questions of formation and avoidance.

Sumerel v. Goodyear Tire & Rubber Co.

Colorado Court of Appeals, 2009.
232 P.3d 128.

■ JUDGE GABRIEL. Defendant, Goodyear Tire & Rubber Company (Goodyear), appeals from the district court's order holding that Goodyear had entered into a valid and enforceable settlement agreement with Bob and Sallie Sumerel, Steven and Ann Berzin, Dane and Kerry Dicke, and Bart Kaufman (collectively plaintiffs). Because we conclude that the November 2, 2006 email and erroneous charts that Goodyear's counsel sent to plaintiffs' counsel did not constitute an offer capable of acceptance, and because even if there were such an offer, any agreement based on it would be unenforceable, we reverse and remand to allow the parties to file a satisfaction of judgment for the amounts already paid by Goodyear.

I.   Background

In 2002, plaintiffs and two entities successfully tried a products liability action against Chiles Power Supply Company, which is not a party to this appeal, and Goodyear, which designed and manufactured a defective hose that was installed in plaintiffs' and the two entities' heating systems. After trial, the jury awarded plaintiffs and the two entities approximately $1.3 million against Goodyear, including, as applicable to plaintiffs and the two entities, repair and replacement costs, diminution in value damages, and "other costs and losses" incident to having to repair and replace their heating systems. In addition, the jury found that Goodyear was responsible for 36% of such "other costs and losses" suffered by the Berzins and Dickes and 48% of those incurred by the Sumerels and Mr. Kaufman.

The district court entered judgment on the jury's verdict and awarded prejudgment interest on the repair costs but not on the "other costs and losses" awarded to plaintiffs. Both sides then appealed. Specifically, plaintiffs appealed, among other things, the court's decision not to award prejudgment interest with respect to the "other costs and losses" awarded them. Goodyear appealed, among other things, the award of the "other costs and losses" damages. As pertinent here, a division of this court upheld the award of "other costs and losses" to plaintiffs and further held that plaintiffs were entitled to prejudgment interest on those damages. Sumerel v. Goodyear Tire & Rubber Co., 2005 WL 1476425 (Colo. App. No. 02 CA 1997, June 23, 2005) (not published pursuant to C.A.R. 35(f)). The division, however, remanded the case to the district court "to determine from the existing record the proper accrual dates for prejudgment interest on other costs and losses" and to calculate and award such interest. Id.

After the case was remanded, Goodyear's lead attorney, Roger Thomasch of Ballard Spahr Andrews & Ingersoll, LLP, discussed with plaintiffs' lead attorney, William Maywhort of Holland & Hart LLP, a potential compromise on the applicable accrual dates. Thomasch proposed certain accrual dates and advised Maywhort of the amount of prejudgment interest that would result from using these proposed dates. Thomasch's calculation of these amounts took into account the jury's 36% and 48% allocations of fault, and Thomasch expressly conveyed that fact to Maywhort.

Following up on the discussion between Thomasch and Maywhort, co-counsel for plaintiffs, Lee Gray, an associate at Holland & Hart, called Michael Brooks of Wells Anderson & Race, co-counsel for Goodyear. Although the parties appear to have agreed on the applicable accrual dates with little difficulty, they had trouble getting their calculations of prejudgment interest based on these dates to match. Thus, in mid-October 2006, Brooks advised Gray that his calculations showed a total amount owed by Goodyear of approximately $2.7 million. At some point within the following few days, Gray responded that this amount appeared to be larger than his own estimates by "about six figures." Gray did not elaborate or share any more information regarding his calculations.

After attempting to determine the source of the discrepancy, on October 23, 2006, Brooks called Gray and speculated that the "six-figure" discrepancy may have resulted from a failure by plaintiffs to include in their calculations the full amount of post-judgment interest applicable to Mr. Kaufman, who had been awarded additional sums as a result of the prior appeal. Gray responded, "[T]hat could be it," "[T]hat might be it," or words to that effect. Brooks took from Gray's response that Gray either agreed or had no basis to disagree that Brooks had found the source of the discrepancy, although the parties had not yet exchanged their respective calculations. Without Gray's calculations, Brooks could not be sure whether he had, in fact, resolved the discrepancy.

Believing that he may have discovered the source of the discrepancy, however, on November 2, 2006, Brooks sent Gray an email, stating, "Here are our charts providing the numers [sic] that Goodyear believes are appropriate. Please review these, then let's discuss." Attached to this email were charts that reflected Goodyear's then existing calculations as to the total amounts due to each plaintiff.

After reviewing these charts, Maywhort noticed that Goodyear's calculations did not agree with plaintiffs' numbers. Moreover, as plaintiffs concede, plaintiffs' counsel recognized that Goodyear's calculations had failed to reduce the damages for "other costs and losses" according to the jury's finding that Goodyear was only liable for 36% of the Berzins' and Dickes' and 48% of the Sumerels' and Mr. Kaufman's "other costs and losses." Instead, Goodyear's calculations were erroneously based on an allocation of 100% of those costs and losses to Goodyear. This was in contrast to other categories of damages set forth in Goodyear's charts, in which Goodyear had correctly applied the jury's fault allocations. Goodyear's error resulted in an overstatement of the damages due by more than $550,000.

Plaintiffs' counsel did not call this obvious error to Brooks's attention or to the attention of any other representative of Goodyear. Instead, Maywhort later claimed that he and his firm had surmised that since Goodyear alone had invited the jury to award "other costs and losses," Goodyear may have concluded that it was solely responsible for any such damages awarded. Maywhort took this position even though (1) the parties had tried the allocation of fault issue and the jury had allocated only 36% and 48% of such losses to Goodyear, and (2) Maywhort had previously discussed prejudgment interest calculations with Thomasch, Thomasch provided calculations that were based on the correct allocated fault percentages, and Thomasch called these allocations to Maywhort's attention.

Gray, in contrast, attributed the more than $550,000 overstatement of damages to a possible desire on Goodyear's part to "sweeten the pot." As noted above, however, the jury had already determined liability, and the record shows that the parties were not negotiating the amounts due but rather were attempting to determine why there was a discrepancy in their mathematical calculations. Accordingly, the record belies the existence of any pot to be sweetened.

Ultimately, neither Gray nor any of plaintiffs' co-counsel called Brooks to discuss his charts, as Brooks had requested. Rather, Maywhort, who had not been directly involved in the more recent discussions regarding the calculations, left a voicemail message for Thomasch, who also had not been directly involved, stating that plaintiffs accepted Goodyear's November 2, 2006 "offer." Maywhort then followed his voicemail with a fax confirming plaintiffs' acceptance of that purported "offer." Notably, neither Maywhort nor Gray informed Brooks of plaintiffs' "acceptance," nor was Brooks copied on Maywhort's fax to Thomasch.

Thereafter, Brooks and Gray discussed, among other things, whether the parties needed a settlement agreement or release, or whether a satisfaction of judgment would suffice to conclude the case. They agreed on the latter, and Brooks prepared a form of satisfaction of judgment that he sent to Gray on November 16, 2006, with a notation that the document was a draft for discussion purposes only. That same day, before anyone had signed the satisfaction of judgment, Brooks realized the error in his earlier calculations. He immediately called the error to Gray's attention and sent Gray corrected versions of the charts and a revised satisfaction of judgment with corrected numbers.

Rather than acknowledging the error, signing the revised satisfaction, and concluding the action for the amounts actually awarded by the jury, Gray indicated that he needed to consult with his colleagues and would get back to Brooks. Then, on November 21, 2006, Maywhort wrote Brooks and demanded that Goodyear adhere to the parties' alleged agreement, which would have resulted in plaintiffs' receiving over $550,000 more than what was due them. When Goodyear refused to do so, plaintiffs filed a motion to enforce the purported "settlement agreement." The district court granted plaintiffs' motion, and Goodyear now appeals, having paid, and plaintiffs having accepted, the amounts that the parties agreed were due and owing, without prejudice to plaintiffs' claims for the additional amounts.

II. Existence of an Offer

Goodyear first argues that the district court erred by concluding that Goodyear and plaintiffs formed a valid and enforceable agreement because the November 2, 2006 email and erroneous charts that Brooks sent to Gray did not constitute an offer. We agree.

[W]e conclude that Goodyear's November 2, 2006 email and attached erroneous charts did not constitute an offer that was properly capable of acceptance. Accordingly, we hold for several reasons that there was no agreement that could be enforced.

First, the email and charts were sent in a context in which the parties were attempting to complete a mathematical computation but had a discrepancy in their respective calculations, which Brooks was attempting to resolve. Specifically, by the time the email and charts were sent, the parties had already reached agreement on the relevant accrual dates. Accordingly, the record demonstrates that the parties were not negotiating dollar amounts or anything else at this point in time. Rather, they were beginning to exchange mathematical calculations based on the agreed accrual dates, while simultaneously attempting to identify the six-figure discrepancy in those calculations. Thus, Brooks's email, using qualifying and indefinite language, noted that the calculations were what "Goodyear believes are appropriate" See Citywide Bank, 978 F.Supp. at 977–79 (use of qualifying language showed no definitive offer).

Second, Brooks's email did not solicit an acceptance but rather solicited a return call: "Please review these, then let's discuss." Accordingly, on their face, Brooks's email and charts represented a continuation of the parties' preliminary discussions, particularly as to their effort to determine the source of the discrepancy in their respective calculations. See Nations Enters., 40 Colo. App. at 394, 579 P.2d at 658 (letter recognizing need for further negotiations was not an offer); Restatement (Second) of Contracts § 24 (offer must justify another in understanding that his assent is invited and will conclude a bargain).

For these reasons alone, Brooks's email and charts did not constitute an offer capable of acceptance.

Our conclusion finds additional support in the "well-settled rule" that "an offeree may not snap up an offer that is on its face manifestly too good to be true." See Lange v. United States, 120 F.2d 886, 889 (4th Cir. 1941).

In our view, the present case is a prototype for a purported offer that was "on its face manifestly too good to be true." The jury had already spoken, and the parties had agreed on the relevant accrual dates. All that should have been left was a simple mathematical calculation. Moreover, when plaintiffs' counsel received Goodyear's calculations, they immediately recognized that Brooks's calculations assumed that Goodyear was 100% liable for the "other costs and losses," rather than the 36% and 48% allocation of fault that the jury had found, resulting in an error in their favor of over \$550,000. On these undisputed facts, we conclude that Brooks's email and erroneous charts raised a presumption of error because they were inconsistent with (1) the jury's award; (2) Thomasch's prior discussion with Maywhort, in which Thomasch specifically pointed out that the calculations that he had provided were based on the percentages of fault that the jury had allocated to Goodyear; and (3) other calculations in the same charts, in which Goodyear consistently used the jury's allocations of fault. At a minimum, these obvious inconsistencies gave rise to a duty on the part of plaintiffs' counsel to inquire before attempting to accept the purported "offer." See Speckel, 364 N.W.2d at 893–94. Without such an inquiry, there was no offer capable of acceptance here. See Limestone Realty, 256 A.2d at 679.

For the foregoing reasons, we conclude that the November 2, 2006 email and charts did not constitute an offer by Goodyear.

III. Unilateral Mistake

Goodyear also contends that, even if its counsel's November 2, 2006 email and attached erroneous charts constituted an offer, any agreement based on such an offer would be unenforceable. We again agree and thus hold, in the alternative, that any agreement reached by the parties here is unenforceable.

Regarding unilateral mistake, Professor Corbin states, "[T]here is practically universal agreement that, if the material mistake of one party was . . . known by the other or was of such character and accompanied by such circumstances that the other had reason to know of it, the mistaken party has the power to avoid the contract." 7 Joseph M. Perillo, Corbin on Contracts § 28.41, at 255 (rev. ed.2002). Corbin further states that relief due to unilateral mistake is available even if the offeree neither knew of nor had reason to know of the mistake, if enforcement of the contract would be "oppressive" to the mistaken party, and relief from the contract "would impose no substantial hardship" on the other party. Id. § 28.39, at 224.

Pronouncements by our supreme court and the Restatement (Second) of Contracts are consistent with these principles. Thus, in Powder Horn Constructors, Inc. v. City of Florence, 754 P.2d 356, 363 (Colo.1988), the supreme court held that a contractor was entitled to equitable relief from the consequences of a bid containing mathematical or clerical errors where the errors were made in good faith and related to a material part of the bid, and where the city that received the bid had not relied to its detriment on the mistaken bid. In such circumstances, the court held that equitable relief was appropriate because the bid that was apparently accepted was not the bid that was intended and, therefore, was not a valid bid. Id. The supreme court further stated that the contractor was entitled to equitable relief, because, where the contractor acted in good faith and where the city knew of the mistake before accepting the bid, it would "contravene fundamental principles of fairness" to allow the city to "take advantage of [the contractor's] mistake and gain a windfall profit." Id. at 364.

Similarly, Restatement (Second) of Contracts §§ 153–54 (1981), which have not yet been expressly adopted in Colorado (although § 153 was cited with approval in Powder Horn), are fully consistent with these principles.

Restatement (Second) of Contracts § 153 provides:

Where a mistake of one party at the time a contract was made as to a basic assumption on which he made the contract has a material effect on the agreed exchange of performances that is adverse to him, the contract is voidable by him if he does not bear the risk of the mistake under the rule stated in § 154, and

(a) the effect of the mistake is such that enforcement of the contract would be unconscionable, or

(b) the other party had reason to know of the mistake or his fault caused the mistake.

Restatement (Second) of Contracts § 154 in turn provides:

A party bears the risk of a mistake when

(a) the risk is allocated to him by agreement of the parties, or

(b) he is aware, at the time the contract is made, that he has only limited knowledge with respect to the facts to which the mistake relates but treats his limited knowledge as sufficient, or

(c) the risk is allocated to him by the court on the ground that it is reasonable in the circumstances to do so.

Notably, comment f to § 153 states, "It is, of course, unusual for a party to bear the risk of a mistake that the other party had reason to know of . . . ." Restatement (Second) of Contracts § 153 cmt. f.

Applying these principles here, we conclude for the following reasons that even if an agreement had been formed, it was voidable under the circumstances.

First, it cannot reasonably be disputed that Goodyear's calculations were in error, and plaintiffs admit that they knew or had reason to know of the error.

Second, the purported agreement would clearly be oppressive and unconscionable, and relief from such an agreement would pose no substantial hardship on plaintiffs. Simply stated, plaintiffs are attempting to exploit Goodyear's mistake to gain a windfall of over $550,000 more than the jury in this case awarded to them. Such a windfall is most certainly oppressive to Goodyear and, in our view, would be unconscionable. Conversely, avoiding the purported agreement and awarding plaintiffs only what the jury awarded works no hardship on plaintiffs. They would receive the amount to which they are entitled.

Third, we reject plaintiffs' assertion that the risk of mistake here rested with Goodyear. As in Powder Horn, we perceive no basis for a determination that Goodyear did not act in good faith. Moreover, as noted above, it is unusual for a party to bear the risk of a mistake that the other party had reason to know of. Restatement (Second) of Contracts § 153 cmt. f. Nor do we perceive any basis for concluding, as plaintiffs contend, that Brooks chose to charge ahead in conscious ignorance, believing that his limited knowledge was sufficient. The record reflects that someone had to share the first set of calculations here. Brooks did so, knowing that there was still a possible six-figure discrepancy. Hence, he asked Gray to review the calculations and to call him to discuss the numbers. Further, as was obvious from the November 2, 2006 email, Brooks was continuing to try to identify the discrepancy and, thus, was seeking further discussion. In short, the record demonstrates that Brooks did not seek an agreement through conscious ignorance. Rather, the record shows that he sought further dialogue because he knew of the discrepancy in the parties' calculations.

For these reasons, we hold that even if Brooks's November 2, 2006 email and charts could be characterized as an offer and that offer was accepted, Goodyear may properly avoid the resulting agreement on the facts presented here.

IV. Conclusion

The current phase of this litigation could, and should, have been avoided. When plaintiffs' counsel reviewed Brooks's charts, they immediately recognized the cause of the parties' six-figure discrepancy. At this point, the proper course was obvious to us: plaintiffs' counsel should have called Brooks, identified the discrepancy, and concluded the matter without further delay. Had plaintiffs' counsel done so, plaintiffs would have immediately received the considerable sums to which they were entitled, and all parties would have been spared the undoubtedly substantial expense of the current litigation over what can only be viewed as a quest by plaintiffs to obtain a substantial windfall. For the reasons set forth above, on the facts presented here, the law will not countenance the patently inequitable result that plaintiffs seek. See, e.g., Lange, 120 F.2d at 889.

In light of our foregoing disposition, we need not address Goodyear's remaining contention on appeal.

The order is reversed, and the case is remanded for the sole purpose of allowing the parties to file a satisfaction of judgment for the amounts already paid by Goodyear.

■ JUDGE RUSSEL and JUDGE J. JONES concur.

NOTES

(1) *Questions.* Compare Restatement § 152 on mutual mistake with Restatement § 153 on unilateral mistake. How do they differ? Why is unilateral mistake less readily available than mutual mistake? More generally, what purposes are served by these limits on unilateral mistake?

(2) *Mental Blunders.* Mistakes based on computational, mathematical, clerical and transcription errors—what Professor Melvin Eisenberg called "mechanical errors" or "mental blunders"—are common to unilateral mistake claims because the error is usually made by one party. See Melvin Eisenberg, *Mistake in Contract Law*, 91 Calif. L. Rev. 1573 (2003). Mental blunders are best considered apart from errors in judgment, misunderstandings, and mispredictions, which courts look upon with disfavor when considering whether to grant relief for mistakes. One reason that courts offer for favoring release from mental blunders that would otherwise be enforced is that these errors are impossible or "difficult to prevent, and that no useful social purpose is served by enforcing the mistaken term." S.T.S. Transport Service, Inc. v. Volvo White Truck Corp., 766 F.2d 1089, 1093 (7th Cir. 1985). Might one find some social purpose from enforcement in that it provides an incentive to create systems to screen for these errors?

(3) *Bounded Rationality, Human Fallibility, and Technology.* The source of mistakes may also be distinguished by bounded rationality and human fallibility. Bounded rationality is a capacious term, roughly capturing the notion that while people intend to be rational they have limited capacity to realize their rational ideals. The bounds of our rationality, however, may be expanded through learning, intentional structures, and technological improvements. "One rough analogy here is to a network of computers, each with limited capacity, such that many of them together can fully accomplish the computational task at hand." Human fallibility, on the other hand, cannot be unlearned and is said to be less subject to systems corrections. Communication among humans, in particular, reveals the intractability of the problem. "Communicating facts with full precision and comprehensiveness, is difficult and prohibitively expensive in any language[,] which makes communicative errors persistent no matter how many individuals work together or how they are organized." Raaj K. Sah, *Fallibility in Human Organizations and Political Systems*, 5 J. Econ. Persp. 67, 67–68 (1991). What role, if any, did the technology available to Brooks in the case above affect the making and communication of the erroneous settlement offer?

(4) *Bounded Morality.* Is it permissible for a lawyer to take advantage of mistaken beliefs held by opposing counsel in negotiating a settlement? Rule 4.1 of the ABA Model Rules of Professional Conduct states, "In the course of representing a client a lawyer shall not knowingly: (a) make a false statement of material fact or law to a third person; or (b) fail to disclose a material fact to a third person when disclosure is necessary to avoid assisting a criminal or fraudulent act by a client, unless disclosure is prohibited by Rule 1.6." Lawyers are required to be truthful in their professional conduct,

but as a general matter, they have no affirmative duty to inform or educate opposing counsel as to relevant facts, yet as Chief Justice Marshall observed of contracting parties generally, "each party must take care not to say or do any thing tending to impose upon the other." Laidlaw v. Organ, 15 U.S. 178 (1817). Did plaintiff's counsel in *Sumerel* impose on the counterparty, and if so, do you believe the imposition breached the bounds of professional conduct? The comment to Rule 4.1 provides that "[a] misrepresentation can occur if the lawyer incorporates or affirms a statement of another person that the lawyer knows is false. Misrepresentations can also occur by partially true but misleading statements or omissions that are the equivalent of affirmative false statements."

(5) *Unilateral Mistake and Misrepresentation.* Mistake and doctrines related to misrepresentation, p. 468, often coincide as the decision in *Sumerel* indicates. In English law the doctrines are even more closely linked, with misrepresentation viewed as a subcategory of mistake—namely, induced mistake. See J. Cartwright, *Misrepresentation*, para. 1.02 (2002). Situations of so-called "innocent misrepresentation," where a party asserts mistaken facts that he or she had reason to believe were otherwise, offer a clear example of this coincidence. Take the following case. The Detroit Downtown Development Authority (the Authority), Wayne County, the Detroit Lions and Detroit Tigers, professional football and baseball clubs, respectively, entered into a memorandum of understanding to build a new downtown sports stadium. The Authority began negotiations with Freda Alibri in 1996 to acquire her property as needed parking for the stadium project and threatened to acquire her property through eminent domain, if it came to that. In January of 1997, Alibri conveyed her property for $264,551.94 to the Authority, which later downsized the Stadium project, including the requisite parking. In an action brought by Alibri to rescind the contact, the Supreme Court of Michigan held: "The defendant represented that all of the west side properties, including plaintiff's, were needed by the stadium project for parking. It was later determined that this was not correct. While there is no indication that the defendant knew of the inaccuracy of its representation, this justifies rescission on the ground of innocent misrepresentation." Alibri v. Detroit Wayne County Stadium Authority, 470 Mich. 895 (2004).

PROBLEMS

(1) Bryan, a twelve-year-old baseball card collector who owned around 40,000 cards, saw a 1968 Nolan Ryan rookie card in a display case in a sports card store. The price of the card read "1200/"; the standard price guide for baseball cards listed the card at between $800 and $1200. Bryan looked at the card and asked the sales clerk, who was unfamiliar with the value of baseball cards, "Is the price for this card $12?" The clerk said Yes, and Bryan bought the card. Joe, the owner of the store, learned of the sale a few days later, located Bryan, and demanded the card back. Upon Bryan's refusal, Joe sued Bryan (more accurately, Bryan's parents), seeking rescission and restitution on the grounds of unilateral mistake. Result? See Andrew Kull, *Unilateral Mistake: The Baseball Card Case*, 70 Wash. U.L.Q. 57 (1992)

(2) Larry, another twelve year old baseball card collector, was looking through a rack of common 1969 baseball cards displayed by a dealer at a baseball card convention when he saw two Reggie Jackson rookie cards. At the time the cards had a catalog price of around $100. Larry asked the clerk, "Are all the cards in this rack twenty cents?", which was the price posted on the rack. When he was told Yes, he bought the two Jackson cards, along with several other cards he had previously selected. Suppose the dealer discovered the sale, found Larry, and, as with Bryan, unsuccessfully sought the return of the cards. Should this dealer be able to avoid the sale because of unilateral mistake? Do any differences in facts between problem 1 and problem 2 lead you to different conclusions?

Sale of Goods: Two Famous Cases

We have so far considered land and building contracts. We now turn to two well-known cases involving the sale of goods.

The first case is Wood v. Boynton, 25 N.W. 42 (Wis. 1885), the so-called "Diamond in the Rough Case." S.B. Boynton, of the firm Boynton & Boynton, jewelers, was accepting a pin for repair when the customer (Clarissa Wood) showed him a stone she had found. "I thought I would ask him what the stone was," Wood said later. After Boynton looked over the stone, "[Wood] told him [she] had been told it was a topaz, and he said it might be." The conversation progressed something like this: B—"I would buy this; would you sell it?" W—"What would it be worth?" Boynton said he did not know; he would give me a dollar and keep it as a specimen. Wood said she would not sell, and that the stone was "certainly pretty to look at." Two or three months later Wood visited Boynton again. "I needed money pretty badly," she later said, "and thought every dollar would help, and I [told] Mr. Boynton . . . I had brought back the topaz, and he says, 'Well, yes; what did I offer you for it?' and I says, 'One dollar;' and he stepped to the change drawer and gave me the dollar, and I went out." The stone was straw-colored, and about the size and shape of a canary egg. It was later found to be a rough diamond, worth about $700. Wood demanded that it be returned, tendering $1.10 (ten cents as interest) to the Boyntons. Wood brought an action for the return of the diamond. The foregoing report of the parties' dealings is drawn from her testimony at the trial. Boynton's testimony did not differ materially. He added that he had never seen an uncut diamond, and that "it never entered his brain at the time" that the stone was a diamond. The trial court dismissed the action and Wood appealed. *Held*: Affirmed. Aside from fraud, the court said, it knew of only one possible ground for recovery: "that there was a mistake made by the vendor in delivering an article which was not the article sold,—a mistake in fact as to the identity of the thing sold with the thing delivered."

The second case is Sherwood v. Walker, 33 N.W. 919 (Mich. 1887): the "Pregnant-Cow Case." Hiram Walker, a cattle breeder, agreed with

Theodore Sherwood, a banker, to sell him a cow of distinguished ancestry known as Rose 2d of Aberlone. The price was $80, both parties believing Rose to be sterile. When Walker discovered that she was pregnant and therefore worth between $750 and $1,000, he refused to deliver her. Sherwood sued in replevin and prevailed in the trial court, but lost on appeal. "A barren cow is substantially a different creature than a breeding one," the court explained. Rose "was not in fact the animal, or the kind of animal, the defendants had intended to sell or the plaintiff to buy."

NOTES

(1) *Distinctions*. Which of the following suggestions serves better as the operative distinction between the rough-diamond case and the pregnant-cow case? Are there other distinctions?

   a. In the former case the party adversely affected by the mistake (the seller, Wood) had delivered the diamond before the mistake was discovered, and sought to retrieve it, whereas in the latter that party (Walker) had not performed, and sought only to retain the cow. Though this distinction has been advocated, it is generally discounted. It would not explain Renner v. Kehl, above.

   b. Possibly the price/value ratios differentiate the two cases. That is, $80 for a titled cow would indicate a basic assumption that she was not fertile, whereas one dollar is a fair compromise between the prospect of great value in a small rock—a dim prospect—and the going price of the vast majority of rocks, even those "pretty to look at" (zero).

(2) *Background Principles*. These cases preceded the UCC, but were they to arise today they would fall within the scope of Article 2. Yet Article 2 does not directly address mistake (but see UCC § 1–103).

(3) *Essence and Quality*. Courts use varying terminology when discussing the avoidance of a contract for mistake. One is represented in the expression, "basic assumption on which the contract was made," as used in the Restatement and in Renner v. Kehl, above. In an earlier period, discourse about "essences" and "attributes," or "substances" and "qualities," was common. For an English example, see Leaf v. International Galleries, [1950] 2 K.B. 86 (C.A.), about the sale of a painting that was supposed to be, but was not, the work of a master. One justice observed that the mistake was one about "quality and value rather than [about] the substance of the thing itself." Such a mistake, Lord Denning said, "does not avoid the contract: there was no mistake at all about the subject-matter of the sale. It was a specific picture: 'Salisbury Cathedral' "—whether or not painted by Constable. Because the seller had told the buyer that the painting was a "Constable," might the buyer have recovered damages for breach of warranty?

Does it matter how the critical distinction is expressed? Reasoning about essences has been denounced as metaphysical and "conclusory." The

Restatement speaks with disapproval of "such artificial and specious distinctions as are sometimes drawn between 'intrinsic' and 'extrinsic' mistakes or between mistakes that go to the 'identity' or 'existence' of the subject matter and those that go merely to its 'attributes,' 'quality' or 'value.'" Restatement § 154 cmt. a. Is the Restatement criterion any less conclusory? Not all scholars think so. See Andrew Kull, *Mistake, Frustration, and the Windfall Principle of Contract Remedies*, 43 Hastings L.J. 1, 13 (1991) (concluding "less quaint, but no less conclusory"). That criterion may be more conducive to relief. But reasoning about essences can be somewhat flexible. Witness the pregnant-cow case, in which the court said: "A barren cow is substantially a different creature than a breeding one."

Long after the Supreme Court of Michigan court decided the pregnant-cow case, it abandoned the test used there. Lenawee County Bd. of Health v. Messerly, 331 N.W.2d 203, 211 (1982). In the more recent case, the buyer and the seller of an apartment building mistakenly believed that the building was suitable for human habitation and would generate rental income. The court concluded that "the distinctions which may be drawn from [the opinion in the cow case] do not provide a satisfactory analysis of the nature of a mistake sufficient to invalidate a contract." The "better reasoned approach," it said, is that of the Restatement. The court held, however, that the buyer bore the risk of the parties' mistake because the contract contained an "as is" clause, stating that the buyer "has examined this property and agrees to accept the same in its present condition."

(4) *Defining Mistake.* The conception of "mistake" is open to differing views. The Restatement defines mistake as "a belief that is not in accord with the facts." Section 151. It speaks also of a situation in which it is "sometimes said . . . that, in a sense, there was not mistake but 'conscious ignorance.'" § 154, cmt *c*. That situation has also been characterized as one of "recognized uncertainty." For that situation, however, the overarching solution is that one of the parties "bears the risk of a mistake." The divide between mistake and ignorance is more pronounced in some sources. And sometimes when a court denies relief, it may offer a curious combination of reasons: the risk of mistake was assumed, and there was "no mistake." See Note 1 below.

The Risks of Limited Knowledge

What obligations do parties have to investigate facts concerning their dealings? The administrators of the Estate of Martha Nelson advertised a public sale of some estate assets. At the sale, they asked $60 for two oil paintings bearing the signature "Martin Johnson Heade" (an American painter of scenery, 1819–1904). Carl Rice paid that price. He assumed the paintings were not originals, but he liked the frame on one and the subject matter of the other. Later, after consulting a notable dealer in art (Christie's), Rice sold the paintings at auction for more than $1 million. Rice's wife enjoyed some of the after-tax proceeds. "[T]he Rices paid income taxes of $337,000 on the profit from the sale of the paintings, purchased a home, created a family trust, and spent some of the funds on living expenses." Having learned of the Rices' good fortune, the administrators proceeded against the Rices, asking that the sale contract be either rescinded or reformed on ground of mutual mistake.[b] The trial court granted summary judgment for the Rices. It found that the Estate bore the risk of mistake. It relied on Restatement § 154(b), which states that a party bears the risk of mistake when "he is aware, at the time the contract is made, that he has only limited knowledge with respect to the facts to which the mistake relates but treats his limited knowledge as sufficient." On appeal, *held*: Affirmed. Estate of Nelson v. Rice, 12 P.3d 238 (Ariz. App. 2000).

The court quoted, as "clearly" applicable, Comment *c* to § 154 ("Conscious ignorance"). The administrators cited Renner v. Kehl, above, saying that the facts of the two cases were similar. To that the court answered: "The Estate's reliance on *Renner* is unavailing because, as stated above, the Estate bore the risk of mistake based on its own conscious ignorance."[c]

In support of its ruling, the court recited findings that the administrators had consulted an appraiser before the sale—one who told them that she was not qualified to appraise fine art. That reservation did not concern one of the administrators, he testified, because he had supposed that the Estate contained little of significant value. Is it possible that there was no mistake at all on the part of the administrators?

The court found yet another reason for denying relief based on § 154(c) of the Restatement. The court said—including quotations from Comment *d*—that it could "allocate the risk of mistake to one party 'on the ground that it is reasonable in the circumstances to do so.' In making this determination, 'the court will consider the purposes of the parties and will have recourse to its own general knowledge of human behavior in bargain transactions.' Here, the Estate had had ample opportunity to discover what it was selling and failed to do so; instead, it ignored the possibility that the paintings were valuable and attempted to take action only after learning of their worth as a result of the efforts of the Rices. Under these circumstances, the Estate was a victim of its own folly and it was reasonable for the court to allocate to it the burden of its mistake."

---

[b]   Unconscionability was another ground asserted by the administrators. As to that the appellate court said: "In refusing to rescind the sale on [that basis], the trial court stated that, 'while the results of the transaction may seem unconscionable to the [Estate] in hindsight, the terms of the contract certainly were not.' We agree . . . . "

[c]   In its reply brief, the Estate argues that a party's negligence does not bar avoidance or reformation of a contract for mutual mistake, claiming that § 157 of the Restatement requires bad faith or gross negligence. This argument is waived by the Estate's failure to raise it in its opening brief. General Motors Corp. v. Arizona Dep't of Revenue, 189 Ariz. 86, 938 P.2d 481 (App. 1996); Wasserman v. Low, 143 Ariz. 4, 691 P.2d 716 (App. 1984).

NOTES

(1) *Risk Controls.* A distinction like that in the pregnant-cow case appears in Watkins & Son v. Carrig, p. 445 above. There the court said that a contract for excavating a cellar was not voidable by reason of the parties' supposition that rock would not be encountered. Suppose it had been shown that excavators habitually make test borings before committing themselves. Would that have reinforced the court's view of the mistake issue? Changing the facts in the case, let it be supposed that, before making the contract, the *owner* had made a boring at the site to test for rock and, by mischance, had detected none. Would that have reinforced the court's view, or have changed it? Recall that, in Renner v. Kehl, the purchasers drilled test wells *after* committing themselves. Should the court have given weight to that fact? (See the court's footnote 2.)

(2) *Expert Knowledge.* Consider again the Diamond in the Rough (*Wood*) and the Pregnant-Cow (*Sherwood*) cases. One difference between *Wood* and *Sherwood* concerns the vocations of the parties. By vocation, the buyer of the diamond and the seller of the cow were presumably more discriminating with respect to pretty stones and breedable cattle, respectively, than the parties they dealt with. The buyer prevailed in the one case, and the seller in the other. Is this a difference without a distinction? Should expertness have counted against the winner in either case? Where a retail dealer in coins deals for a rare coin under a mutual mistake with a *part-time* dealer, would you expect the former to bear the risk of mistake? See Beachcomber Coins, Inc. v. Boskett, 400 A.2d 78 (N.J. Super. Ct. 1979).

PROBLEMS

(1) *A Case of Rare Gas.* The buyer of a tract of land is led to pay a premium for it by seismic studies indicating to both parties that a supply of natural gas may underlie the property. Upon drilling, the buyer finds instead a deposit of helium, making the property worth three times what the buyer paid. Is the seller entitled to rescission?

(2) *The Putative Poussin.* By family tradition, the owners of a painting believed it to be the work of the great 17th century painter Nicholas Poussin. They consulted an auctioneer about selling it. In turn, the auctioneer consulted an art expert, and the owners were persuaded that the painting was the work of an unknown minor painter. The painting was exhibited for sale under the modest designation "school of the Carraci." The buyer was the "Reunion des musées nationaux," which, exercising a right of preemption under French law, paid about $500. The painting was later authenticated as a Poussin by an expert connected with the Louvre and exhibited there as a Poussin. Other experts continued to doubt this attribution, however, and the question remained in doubt. On these facts, can the owners recover the painting?

See (Réunion des Musées Nationaux c/Saint-Arromans), Versailles, Jan. 7, 1987, Gaz. Pal. 1987 Jur. 34—the last of six opinions which, nearly twenty years after the sale, concluded a dispute that, as one commentator wrote, "had caused more ink than paint to flow." Cf. Firestone & Parson, Inc. v. Union League of Philadelphia, 672 F.Supp. 819 (E.D. Pa. 1987).

———

Mistake and Restitution

Review the opinion in Renner v. Kehl, p. 1026 above, attending to the concluding paragraphs, in which the court instructed the trial court how to determine what amount of reimbursement the sellers should pay to the purchasers (no "consequential damages" as such). The court did not mention the payment of interest. In the case of the pretty stone (diamond), p. 1039 above, Wood, the seller, met one condition on rescission by making a tender of money to Boynton, the buyer. She tendered $1.10—the price she had received plus interest of ten cents. Should one dollar be enough? In *Renner*, should the sellers have been charged with interest on the deposit they had received?

As a general question, to what extent should a court readjust the parties' legal relations to account for performances, expenditures, and lost opportunities prior to their discovery of the mistake? Should it matter whether the discovery was a pleasant or unpleasant one? (In a case of pleasant surprise, as in Wood v. Boynton, the result is a gain in the joint wealth of the parties as they perceive it. In a case of unpleasant surprise, as in *Renner*, there is a loss.) Professor Kull found in contemporary cases a strong inclination to make adjustments—stronger in "loss" cases than in "gain" cases, "though why this should be so is not entirely clear." Andrew Kull, *Mistake, Frustration, and the Windfall Principle of Contract Remedies*, 43 Hastings L.J. 1, 41 (1991).

Professor Kull argued for leaving matters as they stand.[d] The effect of his solution in *Renner* would have been, apparently, to confer the leases on the buyers, leaving the sellers with the down payment and no further rights. If the courts were to go that way, might there be a reaction against avoiding contracts for mistakes?

Support for monetary "reparations" in cases of rescission is found in the Restatement § 158 and in other scholarly work.[e] But attitudes differ about the appropriate computation. Opposing judgments depend in part on diverse views about why parties contract for "down payments," advance payments, and deferred payments. Why, in *Renner*, might the parties have agreed on a down payment of 36%?

Settlements of disputed claims, though intended to be conclusive, are sometimes not, owing to mistake. The overpayment of a claim often generates a right of restitution if it was based on a mistake, but usually

---

[d]   He was anticipated in this by Professor Victor Goldberg, who wrote: "Anglo-American law appears to be moving in the wrong direction." *Impossibility and Related Excuses*, 144 J. of Inst'l & Theoretical Econ. 100, 112–14 (1988).

[e]   See Eric Kades, *Windfalls*, 108 Yale L.J. 1489, 1526 (1999); for a defense of loss sharing, see Charles Fried, Contract as Promise 69–73 (1981).

not if the payment was one implementing the settlement of a disputed claim. Likewise, a claimant who settles for an underpayment usually has no further entitlement. As to consideration and compromise in a claim-release case, see Fiege v. Boehm, p. 66 above.

An exceptional case is one in which the settlement contract itself can be avoided for mutual mistake. Suppose, for example, a claim by a woman against an insurance company, based on a contract insuring the life of her husband (known as the *cestui que vie* (CQV), the person whose life determines the duration of a trust, an estate or, in this case, an insurance agreement), and on a report that he was a wartime casualty. Suppose also that the claim was compromised at 50%, owing to a dispute about premium payments. Upon the surprise reappearance of the husband, the CQV, it is likely that the insurer could recapture its payment—but would be embroiled again in a dispute about the premiums. The release of a personal-injury claim may become questionable when an injury comes to light that the parties were not aware of at the time of settlement.

Comment *f* to Restatement § 152 speaks to the problem. It indicates some circumstances bearing on the basic assumptions of the parties, including "the amount received by the claimant in settlement of his claim."

A settlement may be vitiated for a misperception of law as well as for one of fact, by the better view. Or, as the Restatement puts it, "Facts include law." § 151 cmt. b. If, however, the parties have made an inference about the state of the law, relying on inconclusive precedents, and are taught by a later decision that their inference was wrong, the case is not one of relievable mistake. Krantz v. University of Kansas, 21 P.3d 561 (Kan. 2001). In order to support a finding of *mistake*, as the word is defined in the Restatement, "the erroneous belief must relate to the facts as they exist at the time of the making of the contract." § 151 cmt. a.

If the courts were to find a vitiating mistake in a large proportion of settlement agreements, what consequence would you expect in the practices of litigants?

NOTE

Arithmetic in the Rubble. Refer again to the amounts recovered in Stees v. Leonard, above. If in that case Leonard had sought to avoid the contract on the ground of mistake, and had succeeded, what reparations would have been appropriate?

PROBLEMS

(1) *The Sham Stradivarius.* A violin supposed to be the work of a master craftsman of the Renaissance was sold for $9,000 by an amateur collector of rare instruments (not a dealer). The buyer, a renowned concert violinist, paid $3,000 down. Before he paid more, the violin was found to be

Rst
152

a recent knockoff, worth $500 at most. Each party has made a claim against the other: the seller for the unpaid part of the price, and the buyer (who has tendered the return of the item) for the down payment. How should the claims be decided? See Smith v. Zimbalist, 38 P.2d 170 (Cal. App. 1934).

(2) *Make or Change?* To settle a dispute under a contract, Creditor and Debtor make a settlement agreement under which Debtor is to pay Creditor $1,000,000 in return for a release from all of Creditor's claims based on the underlying contract. The parties assume that that contract does not offend public policy and is clearly enforceable. Their assumption rests on the advice of their lawyers and on a ten-year-old decision of the state's highest court. Soon after the settlement agreement is made, that court overrules its earlier decision, holding that contracts like the one that generated the dispute are unenforceable, being contrary to public policy. You represent Debtor. Mistake or erroneous prediction? (Do judges make the law or only declare it?) What difference does it make whether or not the settlement rests on a mistake? See Kleinwort Benson v. Lincoln City Council, [1998] 4 All E.R. 513 (H. L.).

(3) *Trading Aces.* Consider problem 1 on p. 1038 [the first baseball card problem]. Suppose that before the store owner demanded the return of the card, Bryan traded it for two other cards worth approximately $1200 to $1500. Suppose instead that, before the store owner demanded return of the card, Bryan lost it. What should the store owner receive by way of restitution? See Restatement (Third) of Restitution and Unjust Enrichment § 58.

SECTION 3. IMPRACTICABILITY OF PERFORMANCE

Recall *Stees v. Leonard*: "If a man bind himself, by a positive, express contract, to do an act in itself possible, he must perform his engagement, unless prevented by the act of God, the law, or the other party to the contract. No hardship, no unforeseen hindrance, no difficulty short of absolute impossibility, will excuse him from doing what he has expressly agreed to do."

Of course, many contractual undertakings are not "absolute" in this sense. Take, for example, the obligations of Otis Wood (p. 111 above) and Falstaff Brewing (p. 689 above) to use reasonable efforts. In the rest of this chapter, however, we explore the limits of more specific undertakings. To what extent is even an "absolute" contractual undertaking affected by a change of circumstances after the contract is made? This principle underlies a dictum in *Watkins & Son*. "In this situation," the court said, "a defense of mutual mistake is not available." In the following case that follows, a contractor encounters unfavorable soil conditions, raising the costs of its performance—similar to the situation in *Watkins & Son*, where a contractor unexpectedly encountered a boulder in the excavation of a cellar, and to the situation in *Stees v. Leonard*, where a builder unknowingly erected a building on quicksand, twice.

Mineral Park Land Co. v. Howard

Supreme Court of California, 1916.
172 Cal. 289, 156 P. 458.

■ SLOSS, JUSTICE. The defendants appeal from a judgment in favor of plaintiff for $3,650. The appeal is on the judgment roll alone.

The plaintiff was the owner of certain land in the ravine or wash known as the Arroyo Seco, in South Pasadena, Los Angeles county. The defendants had made a contract with the public authorities for the construction of a concrete bridge across the Arroyo Seco. In August, 1911, the parties to this action entered into a written agreement whereby the plaintiff granted to the defendants the right to haul gravel and earth from plaintiff's land, the defendants agreeing to take therefrom all of the gravel and earth necessary in the construction of the fill and cement work on the proposed bridge, the required amount being estimated at approximately 114,000 cubic yards. Defendants agreed to pay 5 cents per cubic yard for the first 80,000 yards, the next 10,000 yards were to be given free of charge, and the balance was to be paid for at the rate of 5 cents per cubic yard.

The complaint was in two counts. The first alleged that the defendants had taken 50,131 cubic yards of earth and gravel, thereby becoming indebted to plaintiff in the sum of $2,506.55, of which only $900 had been paid, leaving a balance of $1,606.55 due. The findings support plaintiff's claim in this regard, and there is no question of the propriety of so much of the judgment as responds to the first count. The second count sought to recover damages for the defendants' failure to take from plaintiff's land any more than the 50,131 yards.

It alleged that the total amount of earth and gravel used by defendants was 101,000 cubic yards, of which they procured 50,869 cubic yards from some place other than plaintiff's premises. The amount due the plaintiff for this amount of earth and gravel would, under the terms of the contract, have been $2,043.45. The count charged that plaintiff's land contained enough earth and gravel to enable the defendants to take therefrom the entire amount required, and that the 50,869 yards not taken had no value to the plaintiff. Accordingly the plaintiff sought, under this head, to recover damages in the sum of $2,043.45.

The answer denied that the plaintiff's land contained any amount of earth and gravel in excess of the 50,131 cubic yards actually taken, and alleged that the defendants took from the said land all of the earth and gravel available for the work mentioned in the contract.

The court found that the plaintiff's land contained earth and gravel far in excess of 101,000 cubic yards of earth and gravel, but that only 50,131 cubic yards, the amount actually taken by the defendants, was above the water level. No greater quantity could have been taken "by ordinary means," or except by the use, at great expense, of a stream dredger, and the earth and gravel so taken could not have been used without first having been dried at great expense and delay. On the issue raised by the plea of defendants that they took all the earth and gravel that was available the court qualified its findings in this way: It found that the defendants did take all of the available earth and gravel from plaintiff's premises, in this, that they took and removed 'all that could have been taken advantageously to defendants, or all that was practical to take and remove from a financial standpoint'; that any greater amount could have been taken only at a prohibitive cost, that is, at an expense of 10 or 12 times as much as the usual cost per yard. It is also declared that the word "available" is used in the findings to mean capable of being taken and used advantageously. It was not "advantageous or practical" to have taken more material from plaintiff's land, but it was not impossible. There is a finding that the parties were not under any mutual misunderstanding regarding the amount of available gravel, but that the contract was entered into without any calculation on the part of either of the parties with reference to the amount of available earth and gravel on the premises.

The single question is whether the facts thus found justified the defendants in their failure to take from the plaintiff's land all of the earth and gravel required. This question was answered in the negative by the court below. The case was apparently thought to be governed by the principle—established by a multitude of authorities—that where a party has agreed, without qualification, to perform an act which is not in its nature impossible of performance, he is not excused by difficulty of performance, or by the fact that he becomes unable to perform.

It is, however, equally well settled that, where performance depends upon the existence of a given thing, and such existence was assumed as the basis of the agreement, performance is excused to the extent that the thing ceases to exist or turns out to be nonexistent.

We think the findings of fact make a case falling within the rule of these decisions. The parties were contracting for the right to take earth and gravel to be used in the construction of the bridge. When they stipulated that all of the earth and gravel needed for this purpose should be taken from plaintiff's land, they contemplated and assumed that the land contained the requisite quantity, available for use. The defendants were not binding themselves to take what was not there. And, in determining whether the earth and gravel were "available," we must view the conditions in a practical and reasonable way. Although there was gravel on the land, it was so situated that the defendants could not take it by ordinary means, nor except at a prohibitive cost. To all fair intents then, it was impossible for defendants to take it.

"A thing is impossible in legal contemplation when it is not practicable; and a thing is impracticable when it can only be done at an excessive and unreasonable cost." 1 Beach on Contr. § 216. We do not mean to intimate that the defendants could excuse themselves by showing the existence of conditions which would make the performance of their obligation more expensive than they had anticipated, or which would entail a loss upon them. But, where the difference in cost is so great as here, and has the effect, as found, of making performance impracticable, the situation is not different from that of a total absence of earth and gravel.

On the facts found, there should have been no recovery on the second count.

The judgment is modified by deducting therefrom the sum of $2,043.45, and, as so modified, it stands affirmed.

■ We concur: SHAW, JUSTICE.; LAWLOR, JUSTICE.

NOTES

(1) *Mistake or Impracticability?* A distinction is sometimes drawn between a performance that becomes impracticable because of some event occurring after the contract is formed and a performance that is impracticable for reasons that existed at the time of contract formation but were unknown to the parties. The former is called supervening impracticability, while the latter is often referred to as existing impracticability. A party who claims existing impracticability may also have a claim of mistake under the common law. What difficulties would Mineral Park have encountered if it had based its defense on mistake? What difficulties would the excavating contractor in *Watkins & Son* have encountered if he had claimed that he was relieved on the ground of impracticability?

(2) *Not Earth Moving.* Cases involving impracticability typically entail realized performance costs that are substantially greater than anticipated costs. In these cases, the value of performance, while exceeding anticipated cost, may be less than the actual cost of performance. Compelling performance in such circumstances, where the value of performance is less than the cost of performance, would be an inefficient allocation of resources. Should the doctrine of impracticability be motivated by efficiency, or basic fairness—or something else?

Does the opinion in *Mineral Park* suggest that Howard placed any value on the removal of the gravel beyond the price offered by Mineral Park? Do you think Howard would have objected if Mineral Park simply offered to pay 5 cents per cubic yard for the remaining 50,869 cubic yards (less the "10,000 yards [that] were to be given free of charge" after the first 80,000 cubic yard) without removing any more earth and gravel? Was there any risk that earth and gravel would have been inefficiently moved from the ground if Mineral Park's obligation was not excused?

(3) *Risky Business.* Though the excavating contractor, in *Watkins & Son*, struck solid rock, "a defense of mutual mistake [was] not available." The court said, "[i]f the plaintiff was unwise in taking chances, it is not relieved, on the ground of mistake, from the burden incurred in being faced with them." Courts often look to see if the risks of impracticability are assigned to one party or the other by the agreement or context of the parties. And what

if the risks are not allocated by the agreement or the background rules against which the parties contract? Does the court make its own independent risk allocation decision by granting or refusing the sought-after excuse?

————

Supervening Events

Centuries ago, in Paradine v. Jane, Aleyn 26, [1647] 82 Eng. Rep. 897 (K.B.), the court gave reasons for the proposition that a contract duty—in this instance, a duty to pay rent—is "absolute," in the sense that no excuse based on changed conditions has been recognized. First, the court said that even if a change makes a party's performance impossible, "he might have provided against it in his contract." (If that was ever the rule, it has long since been subjected to some important qualifications.) Second, the court said that because a party "is to have the advantage of casual profits, so he must run the hazard of casual losses." In other words, a contract should impose matching burdens on the parties, so that a party that could take advantage of a favorable change in circumstances ought to bear the risk of an unfavorable one. Both of these reasons are echoed in later cases and continue to be effective arguments, on occasion. The next case depicts an early departure from the absolute rule.

Taylor v. Caldwell
King's Bench, 1863.
3 B. & S. 826, 122 Eng. Rep. 309.

[Action for breach of a written agreement by which defendants contracted to "let" the Surrey Gardens and Music Hall, at Newington, Surrey, to plaintiffs, for four days, for the purpose of giving four grand concerts and day and night fêtes in the hall; plaintiffs agreeing to pay £100 at the close of each day. The defendants agreed to furnish a band and certain other amusements in connection with plaintiffs' entertainments, but the plaintiffs were to have all moneys paid for entrance to the music hall and gardens. The plaintiffs alleged the defendants' breach, "Whereby the plaintiffs lost divers moneys paid by them for printing advertisements of and in advertising the concerts, and also lost divers sums expended and expenses incurred by them in preparing for the concerts and otherwise in relation thereto, and on the faith of the performance by the defendants of the agreement on their part". The defendants pleaded that the Gardens and Music Hall were accidentally destroyed by fire on June 11, 1861, without the default of the defendants. A verdict was returned for the plaintiffs, with leave reserved to enter a verdict for defendants.]

■ BLACKBURN, JUDGE. In this case the plaintiffs and defendants had, on the 27th May, 1861, entered into a contract by which the defendants agreed to let the plaintiffs have the use of The Surrey Gardens and Music Hall on four days then to come, viz., the 17th June, 15th July, 5th August and 19th August, for the purpose of giving a series of four grand concerts, and day and night fêtes at the Gardens and Hall on those days respectively; and the plaintiffs agreed to take the Gardens and Hall on those days, and pay £100 for each day.

[The court interpreted the agreement not to be a lease, and concluded that the entertainments provided for in the agreement could not be given without the existence of the Music Hall.]

After the making of the agreement, and before the first day on which a concert was to be given, the Hall was destroyed by fire. This destruction, we must take it on the evidence, was without the fault of either party, and was so complete that in consequence the concerts could not be given as intended. And the question we have to decide is whether, under these circumstances, the loss which the plaintiffs have sustained is to fall upon the defendants. The parties when framing their agreement evidently had not present to their minds the possibility of such a disaster, and have made no express stipulation with reference to it, so that the answer to the question must depend upon the general rules of law applicable to such a contract.

There seems no doubt that where there is a positive contract to do a thing, not in itself unlawful, the contractor must perform it or pay damages for not doing it, although in consequence of unforeseen accidents, the performance of his contract has become unexpectedly burdensome or even impossible. The law is so laid down in 1 Roll.Abr. 450, Condition (G), and in the note (2) to Walton v. Waterhouse, 2 Wms.Saund. 421a. 6th Ed., and is recognised as the general rule by all the Judges in the much discussed case of Hall v. Wright (E.B. & E. 746). But this rule is only applicable when the contract is positive and absolute, and not subject to any condition either express or implied: and there are authorities which, as we think, establish the principle that where, from the nature of the contract, it appears that the parties must from the beginning have known that it could not be fulfilled unless when the time for the fulfillment of the contract arrived some particular specified thing continued to exist, so that, when entering into the contract, they must have contemplated such continuing existence as the foundation of what was to be done; there, in the absence of any express or implied warranty that the thing shall exist, the contract is not to be construed as a positive contract, but as subject to an implied condition that the parties shall be excused in case, before breach, performance becomes impossible from the perishing of the thing without default of the contractor.

There seems little doubt that this implication tends to further the great object of making the legal construction such as to fulfil the intention of those who entered into the contract. For in the course of affairs men in making such contracts in general would if it were brought to their minds, say that there should be such a condition.

Accordingly, in the Civil law, such an exception is implied in every obligation of the class which they call obligatio de certo corpore. The rule is laid down in the Digest, lib. XLV, tit. 1, de verborum obligationibus,

1.33. "Si Stichus certo die dari promissus, ante diem moriatur: non tenetur promissor." The principle is more fully developed in 1.23. "Si ex legati causa, aut ex stipulatu hominem certum mihi debeas: non aliter post mortem ejus tenearis mihi, quam si per te steterit, quominus vivo eo eum mihi dares: quod ita fit, si aut interpellatus non dedisti, aut occidisti eum." The examples are of contracts respecting a slave, which was the common illustration of a certain subject used by the Roman lawyers, just as we are apt to take a horse; and no doubt the propriety, one might almost say necessity, of the implied condition is more obvious when the contract relates to a living animal, whether man or brute, than when it relates to some inanimate thing (such as in the present case a theatre) the existence of which is not so obviously precarious as that of the live animal, but the principle is adopted in the Civil law as applicable to every obligation of which the subject is a certain thing. The general subject is treated of by Pothier, who in his Traite des Obligations, partie 3, chap. 6, art. 3, sec. 668, states the result to be that the debtor corporis certi is freed from his obligation when the thing has perished, neither by his act, nor his neglect, and before he is in default, unless by some stipulation he has taken on himself the risk of the particular misfortune which has occurred.[f]

Although the Civil law is not of itself authority in an English Court, it affords great assistance in investigating the principles on which the law is grounded. And it seems to us that the common law authorities establish that in such a contract the same condition of the continued existence of the thing is implied by English law.

[The court referred to instances of a performance unfulfilled at the death of the promisor, saying, "[I]t was very early determined that, if the performance is personal, the executors are not liable." (See Note 2 above.)]

These are instances where the implied condition is of the life of a human being, but there are others in which the same implication is made as to the continued existence of a thing.

[In *Williams v. Lloyd W. Jones*, 179] the count, which was in assumpsit, alleged that the plaintiff had delivered a horse to the defendant, who promised to redeliver it on request. Breach, that though requested to redeliver the horse he refused. Plea, that the horse was sick and died, and the plaintiff made the request after its death; and on demurrer it was held a good plea, as the bailee was discharged from his promise by the death of the horse without default or negligence on the part of the defendant. "Let it be admitted," say the Court "that he promised to deliver it on request, if the horse die before, that is become impossible by the act of God, so the party shall be discharged as much as

---

f   For a criticism of the Roman law authorities relied upon by Blackburn, J., see William Warwick Buckland, *Casus and Frustration in Roman and Common Law*, 46 Harv. L. Rev. 1281, 1287–89 (1933).

if an obligation were made conditioned to deliver the horse on request, and he died before it."[g]

It may, we think, be safely asserted to be now English law, that in all contracts of loan of chattels or bailments if the performance of the promise of the borrower or bailee to return the things lent or bailed, becomes impossible because it [sic] has perished, this impossibility (if not arising from the fault of the borrower or bailee from some risk which he has taken upon himself) excuses the borrower or bailee from the performance of his promise to redeliver the chattel.

The great case of Coggs v. Bernard (1 Smith's L.C. 171, 5th ed.; 2 L. Raym. 909) is now the leading case on the law of bailments, and Lord Holt, in that case, referred so much to the Civil law that it might perhaps be thought that this principle was there delivered direct from the civilians, and was not generally applicable in English law except in the case of bailments; but the case of Williams v. Lloyd (W. Jones, 179), above cited, shows that the same law had been already adopted by the English law as early as The Book of Assizes. The principle seems to us to be that, in contracts in which the performance depends on the continued existence of a given person or thing, a condition is implied that the impossibility of performance arising from the perishing of the person or thing shall excuse the performance.

In none of these cases is the promise in words other than positive, nor is there any express stipulation that the destruction of the person or thing shall excuse the performance; but that excuse is by law implied, because from the nature of the contract it is apparent that the parties contracted on the basis of the continued existence of the particular person or chattel. In the present case, looking at the whole contract, we find that the parties contracted on the basis of the continued existence of the Music Hall at the time when the concerts were to be given; that being essential to their performance.

We think, therefore, that the Music Hall having ceased to exist, without fault of either party, both parties are excused, the plaintiffs from taking the gardens and paying the money, the defendants from performing their promise to give the use of the Hall and Gardens and other things. Consequently the rule must be absolute to enter the verdict for the defendants.

NOTES

(1) *"Tiger Days Excepted."* By 1922 it was possible, in a British court, to ridicule the notion that when a post-contract event impedes the performance of a party, and so excuses that performance, the result depends on a condition, explicit or implicit, in the parties' agreement. In that year, a

---

[g] But at an earlier period the bailee was not excused. O.W. Holmes, *The Common Law* 176, *et seq.* (1881).

Scottish judge felt bound to that notion, owing to its acceptance in the House of Lords. But he expressed doubt, saying:

> It does seem to me somewhat far-fetched to hold that the non-occurrence of some event, which was not within the contemplation or even the imagination of the parties, was an implied term of the contract. . . . A tiger has escaped from a travelling menagerie. The milkgirl fails to deliver the milk. Possibly the milkman may be exonerated from any breach of contract; but, even so, it would seem hardly reasonable to base that exoneration on the ground that "tiger days excepted" must be held as if written into the milk contract.

Scott & Sons v. Del Sel, (1922) S.C. 592, 596–97, aff'd, 1923 S.C. 37 (H.K.).

Compare this passage in the Introductory Note to Restatement Chapter 11 (Impracticability of Performance and Frustration of Purpose): "An extraordinary circumstance may make performance so vitally different from what was reasonably to be expected as to alter the essential nature of that performance. In such a case the court must determine whether justice requires a departure from the general rule that the obligor bear the risk that the contract may become more burdensome or less desirable. This Chapter is concerned with the principles that guide that determination. . . . In recent years courts have shown increasing liberality in discharging obligors on the basis of such extraordinary circumstances."

(2) *Death and Illness.* A duty to perform a "personal" service (one that cannot be delegated to another to perform) is usually excused when the person required to perform suffers death or illness. Cardozo stated the point in connection with the death of a person while engaged in decorative work on a structure: "The contract being personal, the effect of his death was to terminate the duty of going forward with performance. . . . " Buccini v. Paterno Construction Co., 170 N.E. 910, 911 (N.Y. 1930).

Not only a death, but also a malady, may discharge a contract obligation. In Oneal v. Colton Consolidated School District No. 306, 557 P.2d 11 (Wash. App. 1976), a school teacher's duty was discharged by deterioration of his vision. Moreover, not only illness but the "apprehension" of illness may excuse. See Wasserman Theatrical Enterprise v. Harris, 77 A.2d 329 (Conn. 1950), in which Walter Huston, the actor, was excused from appearing on stage because of a minor throat ailment.

(3) *Specific Result or Reasonable Efforts?* Whether a commitment is one to achieve a specific result, or only to use reasonable effort to do so, is sometimes unclear. The difference may be critical if changed circumstances have made the result harder to achieve. In City of Mounds View v. Walijarvi, 263 N.W.2d 420 (Minn. 1978), the court that decided Stees v. Leonard rejected the argument that an architect's undertaking was to achieve a specific result—an implied warranty that the structure was fit for its intended purpose—and had this to say:

"Architects, doctors, engineers, attorneys, and others deal in somewhat inexact sciences and are continually called upon to exercise their skilled judgment in order to anticipate and provide for random factors which are incapable of precise measurement. The indeterminate nature of these factors makes it impossible for professional service people to gauge them with complete accuracy in every instance. Thus, doctors cannot promise that every operation will be successful; a lawyer can never be certain that a contract he drafts is without latent ambiguity; and an architect cannot be certain that a structural design will interact with natural forces as anticipated. Because of the inescapable possibility of error which inheres in these services, the law has traditionally required, not perfect results, but rather the exercise of that skill and judgment which can be reasonably expected from similarly situated professionals."

For a different view, see Tamarac Development Co., Inc. v. Delamater, Freund & Associates, P.A., 675 P.2d 361 (Kan. 1984), reasoning that the "work performed by architects and engineers is an exact science; that performed by doctors and lawyers is not." Do professionals *never* undertake to achieve a specific result? See Sullivan v. O'Connor, p. 13 above.

Do nonprofessionals *ever* undertake to achieve a specific result? See *Bloor v. Falstaff Brewing Corp.*, p. 689 above. Absent explicit provision, what factors other than professionalism might affect the classification? See Milau Associates, Inc. v. North Avenue Development Corp., 368 N.E.2d 1247 (N.Y. 1977). For a distinction between a duty of best efforts and a duty to achieve a specific result, see articles 5.1.4 and 5.1.5 of the UNIDROIT Principles.

Impossibility and Impracticability of Performance Under Article 2

Article 2 of the Uniform Commercial Code contains a series of provisions that may afford relief in the event of changed circumstances. The narrowest of these is UCC § 2–613, which provides that a contract is "avoided" if goods that are required for performance of the contract suffer a "casualty" without the fault of either party before the risk of loss passes to the buyer. ("Risk of loss" is an Article 2 term of art that indicates which party will bear the loss if something happens to the goods at any particular time.) UCC § 2–613 is limited to situations in which the goods that suffer the casualty are the only goods that would satisfy the contract. It does not apply when the seller could satisfy its obligation by tendering goods other than those destroyed. Section 2–613 is analogous to the common law doctrine of impossibility. Section 2–615 provides relief when the seller's performance "has been made impracticable by the occurrence of a contingency the non-occurrence of which was a basic assumption on which the contract was made." As noted in the comments to that section, the standard for impracticability is high—a mere increase in cost is not sufficient. Finally, UCC § 2–614 provides relief when the agreed method of delivery becomes commercially impracticable. Both UCC § 2–614 and UCC § 2–615 are considered in the *Transatlantic* case, which follows, even though the case is not governed by Article 2.

Transatlantic Financing Corporation
v. United States

United States Court of Appeals, D.C. Circuit, 1966.
363 F.2d 312.

■ J. SKELLY WRIGHT, CIRCUIT JUDGE. This appeal involves a voyage charter between Transatlantic Financing Corporation, operator of the SS CHRISTOS, and the United States covering carriage of a full cargo of wheat from a United States Gulf port to a safe port in Iran. The District Court dismissed a libel filed by Transatlantic against the United States for costs attributable to the ship's diversion from the normal sea route caused by the closing of the Suez Canal. We affirm.

On July 26, 1956, the Government of Egypt nationalized the Suez Canal Company and took over operation of the Canal. On October 2, 1956, during the international crisis which resulted from the seizure, the voyage charter in suit was executed between representatives of Transatlantic and the United States. The charter indicated the termini of the voyage but not the route. On October 27, 1956, the SS CHRISTOS sailed from Galveston for Bandar Shapur, Iran, on a course which would have taken her through Gibraltar and the Suez Canal. On October 29, 1956, Israel invaded Egypt. On October 31, 1956, Great Britain and France invaded the Suez Canal Zone. On November 2, 1956, the Egyptian Government obstructed the Suez Canal with sunken vessels and closed it to traffic.[h]

On or about November 7, 1956, Beckmann, representing Transatlantic, contacted Potosky, an employee of the United States Department of Agriculture, who appellant concedes was unauthorized to bind the Government, requesting instructions concerning disposition of the cargo and seeking an agreement for payment of additional compensation for a voyage around the Cape of Good Hope. Potosky advised Beckmann that Transatlantic was expected to perform the charter according to its terms, that he did not believe Transatlantic was entitled to additional compensation for a voyage around the Cape, but that Transatlantic was free to file such a claim. Following this discussion, the CHRISTOS changed course for the Cape of Good Hope and eventually arrived in Bandar Shapur on December 30, 1956.

Transatlantic's claim is based on the following train of argument. The charter was a contract for a voyage from a Gulf port to Iran. Admiralty principles and practices, especially stemming from the

---

[h] For another chronology of events see Fry, The Suez Crisis, 1956, 15, 19, and 24 (Georgetown Institute for the Study of Diplomacy 1992). Among the events listed are these:

Britain and France began military planning for an invasion of Egypt on August 2. On September 12, they informed the U.N. Security Council that Egypt's rejection of certain proposals constituted a threat to international peace and security. The European canal pilots left Egypt on September 15. Israeli forces attacked Egypt in Sinai on October 29. Egypt sank ships in the canal, thereby blocking it, on November 4. On the following day British and French paratroops were dropped at the north end of the canal. On November 7 (Middle East time) a cease-fire went into effect.

doctrine of deviation, require us to imply into the contract the term that the voyage was to be performed by the "usual and customary" route. The usual and customary route from Texas to Iran was, at the time of contract, via Suez, so the contract was for a voyage from Texas to Iran via Suez. When Suez was closed this contract became impossible to perform. Consequently, appellant's argument continues, when Transatlantic delivered the cargo by going around the Cape of Good Hope, in compliance with the Government's demand under claim of right, it conferred a benefit upon the United States for which it should be paid in *quantum meruit.*

The doctrine of impossibility of performance has gradually been freed from the earlier fictional and unrealistic strictures of such tests as the "implied term" and the parties' "contemplation." Page, *The Development of the Doctrine of Impossibility of Performance*, 18 Mich. L. Rev. 589, 596 (1920). See generally 6 Corbin, Contracts §§ 1320–1372 (rev. ed. 1962); 6 Williston, Contracts §§ 1931–1979 (rev. ed. 1938). It is now recognized that " 'A thing is impossible in legal contemplation when it is not practicable; and a thing is impracticable when it can only be done at an excessive and unreasonable cost.' " Mineral Park Land Co. v. Howard, 172 Cal. 289, 293, 156 P. 458, 460, L.R.A.1916F, 1 (1916). Accord, Whelan v. Griffith Consumers Company, D.C.Mun.App., 170 A.2d 229 (1961); Restatement, Contracts § 454 (1932); Uniform Commercial Code (U.L.A.) § 2–615, comment 3. The doctrine ultimately represents the ever-shifting line, drawn by courts hopefully responsive to commercial practices and mores, at which the community's interest in having contracts enforced according to their terms is outweighed by the commercial senselessness of requiring performance.[1] When the issue is raised, the court is asked to construct a condition of performance[2] based on the changed circumstances, a process which involves at least three reasonably definable steps. First, a contingency—something unexpected—must have occurred. Second, the risk of the unexpected occurrence must not have been allocated either by agreement or by custom. Finally, occurrence of the contingency must have rendered performance commercially impracticable.[3] Unless the court finds these three requirements satisfied, the plea of impossibility must fail.

---

[1] While the impossibility issue rarely arises, as it has here, in a suit to recover the cost of an alternative method of performance, compare Annot., 84 A.L.R.2d 12, 19 (1962), there is nothing necessarily inconsistent in claiming commercial impracticability for the method of performance actually adopted; the concept of impracticability assumes performance was physically possible. Moreover, a rule making nonperformance a condition precedent to recovery would unjustifiably encourage disappointment of expectations.

[2] Patterson, *Constructive Conditions in Contracts*, 42 Colum. L. Rev. 903, 943–954 (1942).

[3] Compare Uniform Commercial Code § 2–615(a), which provides that, in the absence of an assumption of greater liability, delay or non-delivery by a seller is not a breach if performance as agreed is made "impracticable" by the occurrence of a "contingency" the non-occurrence of which was a "basic assumption on which the contract was made." To the extent this limits relief to "unforeseen" circumstances, comment 1, see the discussion below, and compare Uniform Commercial Code § 2–614(1). There may be a point beyond which agreement cannot go, Uniform Commercial Code § 2–615, Comment 8, presumably the point at which the obligation would be

The first requirement was met here. It seems reasonable, where no route is mentioned in a contract, to assume the parties expected performance by the usual and customary route at the time of contract.[4] Since the usual and customary route from Texas to Iran at the time of contract[5] was through Suez, closure of the Canal made impossible the expected method of performance. But this unexpected development raises rather than resolves the impossibility issue, which turns additionally on whether the risk of the contingency's occurrence had been allocated and, if not, whether performance by alternative routes was rendered impracticable.[6]

Proof that the risk of a contingency's occurrence has been allocated may be expressed in or implied from the agreement. Such proof may also be found in the surrounding circumstances, including custom and usages of the trade. See 6 Corbin, supra, § 1339, at 394–397; 6 Williston, supra, § 1948, at 5457–5458. The contract in this case does not expressly condition performance upon availability of the Suez route. Nor does it

---

"manifestly unreasonable," § 1–102(3), in bad faith, § 1–203, or unconscionable, § 2–302. For an application of these provisions see Judge Friendly's opinion in United States v. Wegematic Corporation, 2 Cir., 360 F.2d 674 (1966).

[4]   Uniform Commercial Code § 2–614, Comment 1, states: "Under this Article, in the absence of specific agreement, the normal or usual facilities enter into the agreement either through the circumstances, usage of trade or prior course of dealing." So long as this sort of assumption does not necessarily result in construction of a condition of performance, it is idle to argue over whether the usual and customary route is an "implied term." The issue of impracticability must eventually be met. One court refused to imply the Suez route as a contract term, but went on to rule the contract had been "frustrated." Carapanayoti & Co. Ltd. v. E.T. Green Ltd., [1959] 1 Q.B. 131. The holding was later rejected by the House of Lords. Tsakiroglou & Co. Ltd. v. Noblee Thorl G.m.b.H., [1960] 2 Q.B. 348.

[5]   The parties have spent considerable energy in disputing whether the "usual and customary" route by which performance was anticipated is defined as of the time of contract or of performance. If we were automatically to treat the expected route as a condition of performance, this matter would be crucial, and we would be compelled to choose between unacceptable alternatives. If we assume as a constructive condition the usual and customary course always to mean the one in use at the time of contract, any substantial diversion (we assume the diversion would have to be substantial) would nullify the contract even though its effect upon the rights and obligations of the parties is insignificant. Nor would it be desirable, on the other hand, to assume performance is conditioned on the availability of *any* usual and customary route at the time of performance. It may be that very often the availability of a customary route at the time of performance other than the route expected to be used at the time of contract should result in denial of relief under the impossibility theory; certainly if *no* customary route is available at the time of performance the contract is rendered impossible. But the same customarily used alternative route may be practicable in one set of circumstances and impracticable in another, as where the goods are unable to survive the extra journey. Moreover, the "time of performance" is no special point in time; it is every moment in a performance. Thus the alternative route, in our case around the Cape, may be practicable at some time during performance, for example while the vessel is still in the Atlantic Ocean, and impracticable at another time during performance, for example after the vessel has traversed most of the Mediterranean Sea. Both alternatives, therefore, have their shortcomings, and we avoid choosing between them by refusing automatically to treat the usual and customary route as of any time as a condition of performance.

[6]   In criticizing the "contemplation" test for impossibility Professor Patterson pointed out: " 'Contemplation' is appropriate to describe the mental state of philosophers but is scarcely descriptive of the mental state of business men making a bargain. It seems preferable to say that the promisee *expects* performance by [the] means . . . the promisor expects to (or which on the facts known to the promisee it is probable that he will) use. It does not follow as an inference of fact that the promisee expects performance by *only* that means. . . . " Patterson, supra Note 2, at 947.

specify "via Suez" or, on the other hand, "via Suez or Cape of Good Hope."[7] Nor are there provisions in the contract from which we may properly imply that the continued availability of Suez was a condition of performance.[8] Nor is there anything in custom or trade usage, or in the surrounding circumstances generally, which would support our constructing a condition of performance. The numerous cases requiring performance around the Cape when Suez was closed, see e.g., *Ocean Tramp Tankers Corp. v. V/O Sovfracht (The Eugenia)*, [1964] 2 Q.B. 226, and cases cited therein, indicate that the Cape route is generally regarded as an alternative means of performance. So the implied expectation that the route would be via Suez is hardly adequate proof of an allocation to the promisee of the risk of closure. In some cases, even an express expectation may not amount to a condition of performance.[9] The doctrine of deviation supports our assumption that parties normally

---

[7] In Glidden Company v. Hellenic Lines, Limited, 2 Cir., 275 F.2d 253 (1960), the charter was for transportation of materials from India to America "via Suez Canal or Cape of Good Hope, or Panama Canal," and the court held performance was not "frustrated." In his discussion of this case, Professor Corbin states: "Except for the provision for an alternative route, the defendant would have been discharged, for the reason that the parties contemplated an open Suez Canal as a specific condition or means of performance." 6 Corbin, supra, § 1339, at 399 n. 57. Appellant claims this supports its argument, since the Suez route was contemplated as usual and customary. But there is obviously a difference, in deciding whether a contract allocates the risk of a contingency's occurrence, between a contract specifying no route and a contract specifying Suez. We think that when Professor Corbin said, "Except for the provision for an alternative route," he was referring, not to the entire *provision*—"via Suez Canal or Cape of Good Hope" etc.—but to the fact that *an alternative route* had been provided for. Moreover, in determining what Corbin meant when he said "the parties contemplated an open Suez Canal as a specific condition or means of performance," consideration must be given to the fact, recited by Corbin, that in *Glidden* the parties were specifically aware when the contract was made the Canal might be closed, and the promisee had refused to include a clause excusing performance in the event of closure. Corbin's statement, therefore, is most accurately read as referring to cases in which a route is specified after negotiations reflecting the parties' awareness that the usual and customary route might become unavailable. Compare Held v. Goldsmith, 153 La. 598, 96 So. 272 (1919).

[8] The charter provides that the vessel is "in every way fitted for *the voyage*" (emphasis added), and the "P. & I. Bunker Deviation Clause" refers to "the contract voyage" and the "direct and/or customary route." Appellant argues that these provisions require implication of a voyage by the direct and customary route. Actually they prove only what we are willing to accept—that the parties expected the usual and customary route would be used. The provisions in no way condition performance upon nonoccurrence of this contingency.

There are two clauses which allegedly demonstrate that time is of importance in this contract. One clause computes the remuneration "in steaming time" for diversions to other countries ordered by the charterer in emergencies. This proves only that the United States wished to reserve power to send the goods to another country. It does not imply in any way that either was in a rush about the matter. The other clause concerns demurrage and despatch. The charterer agreed to pay Transatlantic demurrage of $1,200 per day for all time in excess of the period agreed upon for loading and unloading, and Transatlantic was to pay despatch of $600 per day for any saving in time. Of course this provision shows the parties were concerned about time, see Gilmore & Black, The Law of Admiralty § 4–8 (1957), but the fact that they arranged so minutely the consequences of any delay or speedup of loading and unloading operates against the argument that they were similarly allocating the risk of delay or speed-up of the voyage.

[9] Uniform Commercial Code § 2–614(1) provides: "Where without fault of either party . . . the *agreed* manner of delivery . . . becomes commercially impracticable but a commercially reasonable substitute is available, such substitute performance must be tendered and accepted." (Emphasis added.) Compare Mr. Justice Holmes' observation: "You can give any conclusion a logical form. You always can imply a condition in a contract. But why do you imply it? It is because of some belief as to the practice of the community or of a class, or because of some opinion as to policy. . . . " Holmes, *The Path of the Law*, 10 Harv. L. Rev. 457, 466 (1897).

expect performance by the usual and customary route, but it adds nothing beyond this that is probative of an allocation of the risk.[10]

If anything, the circumstances surrounding this contract indicate that the risk of the Canal's closure may be deemed to have been allocated to Transatlantic. We know or may safely assume that the parties were aware, as were most commercial men with interests affected by the Suez situation, see The Eugenia, supra, that the Canal might become a dangerous area. No doubt the tension affected freight rates, and it is arguable that the risk of closure became part of the dickered terms. Uniform Commercial Code § 2–615, Comment 8. We do not deem the risk of closure so allocated, however. Foreseeability or even recognition of a risk does not necessarily prove its allocation.[11] Compare Uniform Commercial Code § 2–615, Comment 1; Restatement, Contracts § 457 (1932). Parties to a contract are not always able to provide for all the possibilities of which they are aware, sometimes because they cannot agree, often simply because they are too busy. Moreover, that some abnormal risk was contemplated is probative but does not necessarily establish an allocation of the risk of the contingency which actually occurs. In this case, for example, nationalization by Egypt of the Canal Corporation and formation of the Suez Users Group did not necessarily indicate that the Canal would be blocked even if a confrontation resulted.[12] The surrounding circumstances do indicate, however, a willingness by Transatlantic to assume abnormal risks, and this fact should legitimately cause us to judge the impracticability of performance by an alternative route in stricter terms than we would were the contingency unforeseen.

---

[10] The deviation doctrine, drawn principally from admiralty insurance practice, implies into all relevant commercial instruments naming the termini of voyages the usual and customary route between those points. 1 Arnould, Marine Insurance and Average § 376, at 522 (10th ed. 1921). Insurance is cancelled when a ship unreasonably "deviates" from this course, for example by extending a voyage or by putting in at an irregular port, and the shipowner forfeits the protection of clauses of exception which might otherwise have protected him from his common law insurer's liability to cargo. See Gilmore & Black, supra Note 8, § 2–6, at 59–60. This practice, properly qualified, see id. § 3–41, makes good sense, since insurance rates are computed on the basis of the implied course, and deviations in the course increasing the anticipated risk make the insurer's calculations meaningless. Arnould, supra, § 14, at 26. Thus the route, so far as insurance contracts are concerned, is crucial, whether express or implied. But even here, the implied term is not inflexible. Reasonable deviations do not result in loss of insurance, at least so long as established practice is followed. . . . The doctrine's only relevance, therefore, is that it provides additional support for the assumption we willingly make that merchants agreeing to a voyage between two points expect that the usual and customary route between those points will be used. The doctrine provides no evidence of an allocation of the risk of the route's unavailability.

[11] See Note, *The Fetish of Impossibility in the Law of Contracts*, 53 Colum. L. Rev. 94, 98 n. 23 (1953), suggesting that foreseeability is properly used "as a *factor* probative of assumption of the risk of impossibility." (Emphasis added.)

[12] Sources cited in the briefs indicate formation of the Suez Canal Users Association on October 1, 1956, was viewed in some quarters as an implied threat of force. See N.Y. Times, Oct. 2, 1956, p. 1, col. 1, noting, on the day the charter in this case was executed, that "Britain has declared her freedom to use force as a last resort if peaceful methods fail to achieve a satisfactory settlement." Secretary of State Dulles was able, however, to view the statement as evidence of the canal users' "dedication to a just and peaceful solution." The Suez Problem 369–370 (Department of State Pub. 1956).

We turn then to the question whether occurrence of the contingency rendered performance commercially impracticable under the circumstances of this case. The goods shipped were not subject to harm from the longer, less temperate Southern route. The vessel and crew were fit to proceed around the Cape.[13] Transatlantic was no less able than the United States to purchase insurance to cover the contingency's occurrence. If anything, it is more reasonable to expect owner-operators of vessels to insure against the hazards of war. They are in the best position to calculate the cost of performance by alternative routes (and therefore to estimate the amount of insurance required), and are undoubtedly sensitive to international troubles which uniquely affect the demand for and cost of their services. The only factor operating here in appellant's favor is the added expense, allegedly $43,972.00 above and beyond the contract price of $305,842.92, of extending a 10,000 mile voyage by approximately 3,000 miles. While it may be an overstatement to say that increased cost and difficulty of performance never constitute impracticability, to justify relief there must be more of a variation between expected cost and the cost of performing by an available alternative than is present in this case, where the promisor can legitimately be presumed to have accepted some degree of abnormal risk, and where impracticability is urged on the basis of added expense alone.[14]

We conclude, therefore, as have most other courts considering related issues arising out of the Suez closure, that performance of this contract was not rendered legally impossible. Even if we agreed with appellant, its theory of relief seems untenable. When performance of a contract is deemed impossible it is a nullity. In the case of a charter party involving carriage of goods, the carrier may return to an appropriate port and unload its cargo, The Malcolm Baxter, Jr., 277 U.S. 323 (1928), subject of course to required steps to minimize damages. If the performance rendered has value, recovery in *quantum meruit* for the entire performance is proper. But here, Transatlantic has collected its contract price, and now seeks *quantum meruit* relief for the additional expense of the trip around the Cape. If the contract is a nullity, Transatlantic's theory of relief should have been *quantum meruit* for the entire trip, rather than only for the extra expense. Transatlantic attempts to take its profit on the contract, and then force the Government

---

[13] The issue of impracticability should no doubt be "an objective determination of whether the promise can reasonably be performed rather than a subjective inquiry into the promisor's capability of performing as agreed." Symposium, *The Uniform Commercial Code and Contract Law: Some Selected Problems*, 105 U. Pa. L. Rev. 836, 880, 887 (1957). Dealers should not be excused because of less than normal capabilities. But if both parties are aware of a dealer's limited capabilities, no objective determination would be complete without taking into account this fact.

[14] See Uniform Commercial Code § 2–615, Comment 4: "Increased cost alone does not excuse performance unless the rise in cost is due to some unforeseen contingency which alters the essential nature of the performance." See also 6 Corbin, supra, § 1333; 6 Williston, supra, § 1952, at 5468.

to absorb the cost of the additional voyage.[15] When impracticability without fault occurs, the law seeks an equitable solution, see 6 Corbin, supra, § 1321, and *quantum meruit* is one of its potent devices to achieve this end. There is no interest in casting the entire burden of commercial disaster on one party in order to preserve the other's profit. Apparently the contract price in this case was advantageous enough to deter appellant from taking a stance on damages consistent with its theory of liability. In any event, there is no basis for relief.

NOTES

(1) *Unexpected Events.* "First, a contingency . . . must have occurred." So said the court in stating three requirements for an excuse by reason of impossibility. A seller that wants to be excused from delivering goods is unlikely to meet even this first requirement simply by showing that its cost of producing the goods has spiked upward. On inquiry, however, it may be possible to identify an unexpected event underlying the increase of cost that is more likely to count as a contingency—"something unexpected"—than higher cost. If, for example, the seller is a miller and supplier of lumber, and has encountered unusual cost in buying timber, it may be possible to attribute the added cost to new environmental regulations, to a sharp upswing in construction, or to the coincidence of vast forest fires. With respect to a lumber-sale contract, which of these events is the most likely to count as a contingency? As to which is the risk most likely have been allocated—"either by agreement or by custom"—to the seller?

(2) *Impracticability and Risk.* In response to an invitation from the Federal Reserve Board, the Wegematic Corporation submitted the winning proposal for a new computing system, which Wegematic described as "a truly revolutionary system utilizing all of the latest technical advances." Delivery was to be a year later. After delays of nearly four months, Wegematic finally announced that it was "impracticable to deliver the . . . Computing System at this time." After another year, the Board succeeded in procuring comparable equipment elsewhere. When sued by the United States, Wegematic argued that it was excused because it was unable to achieve the revolutionary breakthrough that it had anticipated because of "basic engineering difficulties" that would have taken up to two years and a million and a half dollars to correct, with success likely but not certain. The United States prevailed. (In *Transatlantic Financing* the court cited the decision in its footnote 3.)

Was there a "contingency" in the *Wegematic* case? The court referred to UCC § 2–615, and said that the "basic assumption" part of the Code's test "seems a somewhat complicated way of putting Professor Corbin's question of how much risk the promisor assumed." It went on: "We see no basis for

---

[15] The argument that the Uniform Commercial Code requires the buyer to pay the additional cost of performance by a commercially reasonable substitute was advanced and rejected in Symposium, supra Note 13, 105 U. Pa. L. Rev. at 884 n. 205. In Dillon v. United States, 156 F.Supp. 719, 140 Ct. Cl. 508 (1957), relief was afforded for some of the cost of delivering hay from a commercially unreasonable distance, but the suit was one in which the plaintiff had suffered losses far in excess of the relief given.

thinking that when an electronics system is promoted by its manufacturer as a revolutionary breakthrough, the risk of the revolution's occurrence falls on the purchaser; the reasonable supposition is that it has already occurred or, at least, that the manufacturer is assuring the purchaser that it will be found to have when the machine is assembled. If a manufacturer wishes to be relieved of the risk that what looks good on paper may not prove so good in hardware, the appropriate exculpatory language is well known and often used."

Note that UCC § 2–615 begins with an exception where a seller has "assumed a greater obligation," recognizing that a party may assume the risk of being unable to do the impracticable—even the impossible. As compared with impracticability, would mistake have been a better ground for Wegematic's defense?

(3) *Other Suez Cases.* The court relied for support on the *Glidden* case, partially described in footnote 7. A further fact in that case was a provision of the charter that gave the shipper power to designate a destination (on the Atlantic seaboard) "not later than on Vessel's passing Gibraltar." In which case—*Glidden* or the main case—did the carrier come closer to establishing a defense under the doctrine of impracticability?

In footnotes not reproduced here, the court also referred to two English "Suez cases" for support. One was *The Eugenia.* There the court said that performance is not excused by a cost increase that is merely onerous: "It must be positively unjust to hold the parties bound." Ocean Tramp Tankers Corp. v. V/O Sovfracht (The Eugenia), [1964] 2 Q.B. 226, 239. The other case concerned a sale-of-goods contract requiring the seller to pay, among other charges, the freight for transporting the goods from Sudan to Hamburg. (The case was *Tsakiroglou & Co.*, cited in the court's footnote 4.) Assume that, before the Canal closure, the seller had contracted for a carrier to move the goods. If the carrier were to be excused by the closure, does it follow that the seller should be? In *Transatlantic Financing*, Judge Wright seemed to be disconcerted by the thought that the seller might be committed to the buyer although the carrier was not committed to the seller. Are you?

Foreseeability

"Foreseeability or even recognition of a risk does not necessarily prove its allocation." So said Judge Wright in *Transatlantic Financing.* A passage in the Restatement squares with this: Though anticipating a possible turn of events, "the parties may not have thought it sufficiently important a risk to have made it a subject of their bargaining." Introductory Note to Restatement Chapter 11. In some quarters—not all—the test of foreseeability has been treated with scorn, or, at best, with lukewarm regard.[i] Yet it is difficult, on hearing a party's plea of

---

[i]   See Hans Smit, *Frustration of Contract: A Comparative Attempt at Consolidation*, 58 Colum. L. Rev. 287 (1958); Paul Joskow, *Commercial Impossibility, the Uranium Market and the Westinghouse Case*, 6 J. Legal Stud. 119, 173 (1977) (test tolerated as imposing a penalty on

changed circumstances, to refrain from asking "Weren't you worried that
. . .?" Notice that Judge Wright adverted to worrisome events before
Transatlantic made the contract before him, and inferred its "willingness
. . . to assume abnormal risks." A Comment to UCC § 2–615 contains a
lengthy, Delphic sentence about an event "foreshadowed" at the time of
contracting: that being so, possibly "the exemptions of this section do not
apply." Do you find that thought in the text of the section?

If the foreseeability of an impeding event counts for little, what of a
showing that the event was *not* foreseeable? This is significant, according
to the Restatement Introductory Note quoted above, as suggesting that
the nonoccurrence of the impeding event was a basic assumption on
which the contract was made. Is it easy to believe that foreseeability is
less significant than unforeseeability?

NOTE

The Case of the Foreseeable Finale. By an agreement with the Wolf Trap
Foundation for the Performing Arts, the Opera Company of Boston was to
stage four summertime performances at the Foundation's concert center.
The final performance was cancelled when a thunderstorm caused an
electrical outage and left the stage dark. Wolf Trap declined to pay the price
of that performance. In an action against it by the Opera Company, evidence
was given of some remarks following the mishap that were unfortunate for
Wolf Trap. "We have experienced power outages on several occasions,"
according to its agent who had negotiated the contract. He had also
expressed his feeling that a theater without an adequate generator is
incomplete. The trial court said, in granting judgment against Wolf Trap,
that, if it could have foreseen the mishap, it was "absolutely barred" from
relying on the doctrine of impossibility. Wolf Trap appealed. *Held*: Reversed
and remanded.

The reviewing court was divided. According to the majority,
"Foreseeability . . . is at best but one fact to be considered. . . . " Opera
Company v. Wolf Trap Foundation, 817 F.2d 1094, 1102 (4th Cir. 1987).

———————

Risk-Bearing Analyses

Look again at the three sentences in the opinion in *Transatlantic
Financing* following the court's footnote 13. These sentences compare the
capacities of the parties to anticipate "troubles" and to calculate
additional costs of performance. As between Transatlantic and the
United States, the court thought it reasonable to expect that
Transatlantic be the one to insure itself against war risks. In a well-

———————

the "suboptimal use of available information"). But it has been said that foreseeability "has been
central to impossibility cases for as long as they have been around." Richard Duesenberg,
Contract Impracticability: Courts Begin to Shape § 2–615, 32 Bus. Law. 1089, 1095 (1977).

known economic analysis, this passage is quoted with approval and is amplified as follows:

> The shipowner is the superior risk bearer because he is better able to estimate the magnitude of the loss ... and the probability of the unexpected event. Furthermore, shipowners who own several ships and are engaged in shipping along several routes can spread the risks of delay on any particular route without purchasing market insurance.

Richard Posner and Andrew Rosenfield, *Impossibility and Related Doctrines in Contract Law*, 6 J. Legal Stud. 83, 104 (1977). Having ready access to an appropriate insurance market is one mark of a well-qualified risk bearer, according to this analysis. A mode of risk distribution, alternative to buying insurance and more cost-effective, is open to some firms: diversification, as suggested in *Transatlantic Financing*. Other marks of a well-qualified risk bearer are some ability to avert the event that impeded performance, and to mitigate its loss when the event occurs.

The thesis of the authors is that once a court has identified the "superior risk bearer" in a case like *Transatlantic Financing*, it should rule in favor of the other party as to the dispensing effect of a mischance. Some underlying assumptions are these: (i) If the parties had had the mischance in mind during their negotiations, as a possibility, they would have assigned the risk to the superior risk bearer—possibly adjusting the price or another term to balance that assignment; (ii) For the court to make the same assignment would spare the parties the cost, time, and effort ("transaction costs") of negotiating to the position they would prefer.

Posner and Rosenfield acknowledged that uncertainties creating the risk of error in identifying superior risk bearers tend to undercut the potential savings in transaction costs. As to *Transatlantic Financing*, they acknowledged also that the United States was a candidate for the position of superior risk bearer, as the holder of a well-diversified portfolio of contracts. But, they concluded, "decision should (and here did) turn on the characteristics of shippers *as a class*, if an unduly particularistic analysis is to be avoided." (emphasis supplied).

For a detailed rebuttal of the authors' analysis see John Elofson, *The Dilemma of Changed Circumstances in Contract Law: An Economic Analysis of the Foreseeability and Superior Risk Bearer Tests*, 30 Colum. J.L. & Soc. Probs. 1 (1996), seizing on the acknowledgments just mentioned and on other supposed defects. Although the analysis has drawn widespread attention in academic circles, it has not been cited often in judicial opinions. The Supreme Court has referred to it, however, for these propositions: "parties generally rely on contract law 'to reduce the costs of contract negotiation by supplying contract terms that the parties would probably have adopted explicitly had they negotiated over them' "; and "subject to certain constraints, 'the contracting parties' chosen allocation of risk' should always be honored as the most efficient one possible." United States v. Winstar Corporation, 518 U.S. 839, 884 n.27, 909 n.56 (1996).

At a time when price inflation was unusually brisk in the United States, Professor Alan Schwartz developed an argument for imposing at least the inflation risk on sellers. To do so, he reasoned, would help to popularize price-indexing terms in sale contracts. And that, in turn, would complement government efforts to control inflation. See Alan Schwartz, *Sales Law and Inflation*, 50 So. Cal. L. Rev. 1, 21–22 (1976).

Selland Pontiac-GMC, Inc. v. King

Minnesota Court of Appeals, 1986.
384 N.W.2d 490.

■ RANDALL, JUDGE. Buyer, Selland Pontiac-GMC, Inc., sued seller, George King, for breach of contract. After a one-day bench trial the court granted judgment for King. The trial court denied Selland's motion for a new trial and/or amended findings of fact and conclusions of law and entered judgment. Selland appeals. We affirm.

FACTS

Selland contracted with King (doing business as King's Superior Bus Sales) to buy four school bus bodies. The oral agreement made in April, 1983, was reduced to a writing dated May 12, 1983. King was to supply the bodies, which would be built on top of chassis provided by Selland. The written agreement indicates that the bodies would be manufactured by Superior Manufacturing, which was located in Morris, Manitoba. The written agreement contains no completion date. King was aware that Selland's customer needed the buses by late August for the start of the school year. The contract price was $47,660. The writing contained no escape clause excusing King's performance should his source of supply fail.

In reliance on the contract, Selland ordered four bus chassis from General Motors. They arrived at Superior's entry point in Pembina, North Dakota, in June and early July, 1983.

Superior went into receivership on July 7, 1983, and King learned of this on July 8. King informed Selland of the receivership on August 12. The parties do not agree on what happened afterwards. Selland claims that King assured Selland that the buses would be completed on time. King claims that Selland, fully advised of Superior's status, decided to wait and see if Superior would come out of receivership able to supply and install the bus bodies. The trial court found that "after receiving notice of the receivership, Selland acquiesced to the delay in production."

The bodies were never manufactured. The Superior plant was operated by a new company from approximately late July to September or October. For some time after that, different individuals expressed interest in buying and operating the plant. Finally it was purchased, moved to Oklahoma, and it began production in 1985. Superior went out of business. In December, 1983, Selland's customer (Chief Auto Sales) cancelled their order. Selland sold the chassis at a loss.

ANALYSIS

On appeal this court will not set aside the trial court's findings unless they are clearly erroneous. Peterson v. Johnston, 254 N.W.2d 360, 362 (Minn. 1977). Selland questions the trial court's finding that the contract identified Superior as King's supplier, and that the contract contemplated that the bodies would be manufactured by Superior. This finding is supported by the contract which states that Superior bus bodies were being sold.

[Selland contested the finding by the trial court that it had acquiesced in King's delay in making delivery. The court sustained that finding.]

[The court quoted from clauses (a) and (c) of UCC § 2–615, enacted as Minn. Stat. § 336.2–615.] Supply of Superior bus bodies was a basic assumption on which the contract was made. These became impracticable to supply when Superior ceased manufacturing.

Appellant argues that the trial court improperly applied § 336.2–615. In Barbarossa & Sons v. Iten Chevrolet, Inc., 265 N.W.2d 655 (Minn. 1978) the supreme court applied § 336.2–615 and affirmed judgment for the buyer where the manufacturer's supply of seller's order was not a basic assumption of the contract and the contract contained no escape clause. The manufacturer, General Motors, was not mentioned in the contract as the source of supply. General Motors had cancelled several orders at this time due to a shortage. The court stated:

> A partial failure of a seller's source of supply generally has been treated as a foreseeable contingency, the risk of which is allocated to the seller absent a specific provision to the contrary in the contract.

Id. at 659–60 (citations omitted).

The trial court's finding of no breach of contract here is consistent with Barbarossa's holding that the contract was breached under § 336.2–615. Here the seller's supplier was specified in the contract. Superior was also specified in King's price quotation to Selland. In *Barbarossa* the supplier did not cease to manufacture, but simply cancelled the orders of some of its dealers. Here both parties testified that they had no knowledge of Superior's questionable financial circumstances when they contracted and King did not expressly assume the risk of Superior's ceasing production.

[Finally, the court dealt with Selland's contention that King had failed to give it seasonable notice of nondelivery. Although the court agreed with Selland that "notice of delay does not necessarily constitute notice of nondelivery," it sustained the trial court's conclusion on the point. Selland had cancelled the contract, the court said, before such notice could be given.]

DECISION

The trial court did not clearly err in finding that the contract contemplated that the bus bodies would be manufactured by Superior and that Selland acquiesced to the delay in delivery. The trial court did not err in its application of Minn. Stat. § 336.2–615.

Affirmed.

NOTES

(1) *Authorities*. The court suggested two ways of distinguishing the decision in *Barbarossa & Sons v. Iten Chevrolet*: (a) In that case, unlike this one, "[t]he manufacturer . . . was not mentioned in the contract as the source of supply"; and (b) In that case the manufacturer (General Motors), unlike Superior Manufacturing, had not ceased producing, but had "simply cancelled the orders of some of its dealers." Which of these distinctions is the more satisfying one?

Restatement § 261, Comment *e* includes this statement: "Even if a party contracts to render a performance that depends on some act by a third party, he is not ordinarily discharged because of a failure by that party because this is also a risk that is commonly understood to be on the obligor." What made *Selland* an exceptional case, outside this observation?

(2) *Parol Evidence*. Because the King-Selland contract indicated that the bus bodies were to be manufactured by Superior Manufacturing, King had no need to rely on parol evidence that the parties had agreed on Superior as a particular source of supply. Would the decision have been different if the contract—an integrated one—had omitted any reference to Superior, but Selland could otherwise be shown to have known where King expected to get the bodies? Suppose that knowledge to be proved by convincing evidence of a conversation King had with Selland when the contract was executed. Would the decision be the same on those facts? For a negative answer, see Luria Bros. & Co. v. Pielet Bros. Scrap Iron & Metal, Inc., 600 F.2d 103, 112 n.7 (7th Cir. 1979). Do you agree that the effect of the supposed evidence is to contradict the writing, or instead to introduce an additional term?

PROBLEM

The School-Bus Resale. "In December, 1983," we are told, "Selland's customer (Chief Auto Sales) cancelled their order." Assume that the "order" was in truth a contract of sale, Selland to Chief. Possibly Chief's cancellation was warranted by Selland's delay in delivery: Chief needed the buses for the start of the school year. Was Selland's duty of timely delivery excused by commercial impracticability? A further question arises if it is assumed that Chief effected cover in September and claimed damages against Selland: Was Selland discharged of its duty to deliver by impracticability?

How would you answer these questions? What undisclosed facts would be especially helpful in answering them?

Force Majeure Clauses

When, during the negotiation of a contract, a party anticipates one or more events that it cannot readily prevent and that might impede its performance, it may well introduce a term intended to excuse it from performing if the impediment arises. "*Force majeure* clause" is the generic name for such a provision. Would you expect such a clause to be broader in scope in a seller's or a buyer's contract? In a short-term or long-term contract? In *Selland Pontiac* the court remarked that the written agreement between the parties "contained no escape clause excusing King's performance should his source of supply fail." If King had been quizzed about that at the trial, what answer might he have made?

The drafting of a *force majeure* clause calls for a certain level of craft. A threat to a careless drafter is the maxim *ejusdem generis*. (See the discussion of maxims, p. 527 above.)

An example of a *force majeure* clause is found in OWBR LLC v. Clear Channel Communications, Inc., 266 F.Supp.2d 1214 (D. Haw. 2003). The Outrigger Waliea Resort (OWBR) in Hawaii agreed to hold 2,270 "sleeping room nights" for the attendees of a convention, "Power Jam 2002, a music industry event/conference produced by Defendants (Clear Channel Communications) and scheduled for February 13–17, 2002." Id. at 1215. Rates went from $235 to $900 a night. The agreement also contained a liquidated damages clause, providing for a payment of 100% of the "Total Guest Room Revenue," plus taxes, in case the agreement were cancelled. There was also a *force majuere* clause that included terrorism as an acceptable reason for either party to cancel the contract. However, on January 16, 2002, less than 30 days before the event, Clear Channel Communications indicated it wished to cancel because "[t]he events of September 11th coupled with the fragile condition of the U.S. and international consumer economies have resulted in the withdrawal of commitments to this event from many of our sponsors and participants." Id. at 1216. According to the defendants (Clear Channel Communications), out of the 102 companies who participated last year, only 38 planned to attend after 9/11. The basic disagreement between the parties was whether the "terrorism" portion of the Force Majeure clause covered the economic effects of terrorism (although Clear Channel was arguing that it was basically *caused* by 9/11, while Outrigger argued that it was in fact the economic downturn resulting from 9/11 that caused the cancellation—and therefore it wasn't covered by the *force majuere* clause). The court used Section 261 of the Restatement (Second) of Contracts to interpret the *force majuere* provision, and found that an unexpected drop in market prices was not covered by the provision. The court also noted that had Power Jam 2002 been scheduled immediately after 9/11, when travel was still difficult and cancelled in many places, they would have had a stronger argument. The court granted the plaintiffs' (Outrigger's) motion for summary judgment on this issue.

Another example of a *force majeure* clause appears in Kama Rippa Music, Inc. v. Schekeryk, 510 F.2d 837 (2d Cir. 1975). The clause pertained to an undertaking by the company, a music publisher, to make prompt payment of royalties to a songwriter and performer known professionally as Melanie. In stated eventualities, it was provided, "Publisher may, upon notice to writers, suspend its obligations including its obligations to make payments hereunder for the duration of such delay, impossibility, impracticability, as the case may be." The clause contained a "specific enumeration" of some dozen excusing events, typified by these: Act of God, earthquake, strike, civil commotion, acts of government, and delays in the delivery of material and supplies. The list concluded with this phrase: "for any similar or dissimilar reason." The trial court disregarded this general term. On appeal, that was said to be "a tack supported by New York contract law." The appellate court said also:

> Alternatively, the [trial] court might have assimilated the clause to the remainder of the provision by invoking *ejusdem generis* and, hence, construing this final and most generic term in a series in light of the more specific terms preceding it.

Id. at 841 n.5.

A similar fate has befallen other generic terms adjoining specific ones. See, for example, Rothenberg v. Lincoln Farm Camp, Inc., 755 F.2d 1017 (2d Cir. 1985), accepting "any other *similar* reason" as a reading of "any other reason." But see Eastern Air Lines, Inc. v. McDonnell Douglas Corp., 532 F.2d 957 (5th Cir. 1976). In that case, growing out of the Vietnam War, McDonnell Douglas had been persuaded by government officials to defer the production of civilian aircraft. As a seller, resisting Eastern's claim, it relied on a provision in the contract between them that referred to delays

> due to causes beyond Seller's control and not occasioned by its fault or negligence, *including but not being limited to* governmental priorities [and other specific eventualities].

"Unambiguous," the court said, referring to the words italicized in this quotation. Are they any less ambiguous than those in *Kama Rippa Music* ("any similar or dissimilar reason")? How did the drafting on behalf of the music producer go wrong?

NOTES

(1)   Force Majeure *Clauses and the UCC.* Agreed-upon restrictions on a party's undertakings, presumably including *force majeure* clauses, are broadly recognized in the Code. In a Comment to the section about discordant offers and acceptances (UCC § 2–207, Comment 5), mention is made of a clause "setting forth and perhaps enlarging slightly upon the seller's

exemption due to supervening causes, similar to those covered by [UCC § 2–615]"; that is given as an example of a term in an acceptance that does not materially alter the offer. On the other hand, Comment 8 to UCC § 2–615 contains this obscure sentence:

> Generally, express agreements as to exemptions designed to enlarge upon or supplant the provisions of this section are to be read in the light of mercantile sense and reason, for this section itself sets up the commercial standard for normal and reasonable interpretation *and provides a minimum beyond which agreement may not go.*

Does the phrase emphasized here mean a minimum of obligation or a minimum of exemption from obligation?

In *Eastern Air Lines v. McDonnell Douglas Corp.*, cited in the foregoing text, the court referred to the sentence quoted above, and drew this conclusion: "where there is doubt concerning the parties' intention, exemption clauses should not be construed as broadening the excuses available under the Code's impracticability rule." Plainly the sentence is a bad omen for a drafter intent on writing an extensive *force majeure* provision. Why should that purpose require especially explicit drafting?

(2) *Opting In and Opting Out.* It has been suggested that express terms "offer two distinct options for using particularized instructions to enhance a framework of implied terms. The first of these enables one to augment or *supplement* the implied terms ('opting in'). . . . By contrast, parties sometimes desire to countermand or trump one or more of the pre-formulated provisions ('opting out')." Charles Goetz & Robert Scott, *The Limits of Expanded Choice: An Analysis of the Interactions Between Express and Implied Contract Terms*, 73 Calif. L. Rev. 261, 281 (1985). Did the *force majeure* clause used by McDonnell Douglas involve supplementing or trumping?

PROBLEMS

(1) *Practice.* As a test of your drafting skill, consider the word "strike" in the music publisher's contract quoted above. What would you add to the list of specifics in order to protect the publisher in the event of labor difficulties not amounting to a strike? An answer is suggested by the full provision, as set out in the opinion cited.

(2) *A Hospital Case.* The Brighten Company made a contract with T-Square Inc. to restore and replace a neon sign marquee on a theater that T-Square was renovating. Brighten's contract contained the following clause:

> The Company shall not be liable for any failure in the performance of its obligations under this agreement which may result from strikes or acts of labor unions, fires, floods, earthquakes, or acts of God, war or other conditions or contingencies beyond its control.

Shortly after making the contract, Brighten learned that its expert on sheetmetal work required hospitalization for an indeterminate period. Because this was the only employee who could do the sheet metal work on the marquee, Brighten explained to T-Square that it would be unable to do that part of the work, and it returned an uncashed deposit check. T-Square had work done by another firm, for a higher price, and brought an action against Brighten for the difference between the two prices. What result? Seitz v. Mark-O-Lite Sign Contractors, Inc., 510 A.2d 319 (N.J. Super. 1986).

Canadian Industrial Alcohol Co. v. Dunbar Molasses Co.

Court of Appeals of New York, 1932.
258 N.Y. 194, 179 N.E. 383.

[At the end of 1927, the plaintiff Alcohol Company contracted with Dunbar to purchase a quantity of molasses, shipments to begin after the following April 1, and to be spread out during the warm weather. The goods were described as "approximately 1,500,000 wine gallons Refined Blackstrap (Molasses) of the usual run from the National Sugar Refinery, Yonkers, N.Y., to test around 60 per cent sugars." While the contract was in force, that refinery produced much less molasses than its capacity—less than half a million gallons. Dunbar shipped to the Alcohol Company its entire allotment of the refinery's output (344,083 gallons), but failed to deliver any more molasses. Upon being sued for damages, Dunbar contended that its duty was conditioned, by an implied term, on the refinery's producing enough molasses to fill the plaintiff's order. From a judgment for the buyer, Dunbar appealed.]

■ CARDOZO, CHIEF JUDGE. The contract, read in the light of the circumstances existing at its making, or more accurately in the light of any such circumstances apparent from this record, does not keep the defendant's duty within boundaries so narrow. The defendant does not even show that it tried to get a contract from the refinery during the months that intervened between the acceptance of the plaintiff's order and the time when shipments were begun. It has wholly failed to relieve itself of the imputation of contributory fault (3 Williston on Contracts, sec. 1959). So far as the record shows, it put its faith in the mere chance that the output of the refinery would be the same from year to year, and finding its faith vain, it tells us that its customer must have expected to take a chance as great. We see no reason for importing into the bargain this aleatory element. The defendant is in no better position than a factor who undertakes in his own name to sell for future delivery a special grade of merchandise to be manufactured by a special mill. The duty will be discharged if the mill is destroyed before delivery is due. The duty will subsist if the output is reduced because times turn out to be hard and labor charges high.

[Affirmed.]

NOTES

(1) *Back-to-Back Contracts.* If Dunbar had made a contract with the refinery, as Cardozo suggested, would the result in the case have been different? Could Dunbar, in its contract with Alcohol Company, have relieved itself of the risk that its source of supply would fail as it did? If so, would Dunbar be expected to turn over to Alcohol Company any rights of Dunbar against the refinery? Compare Comment 5 to UCC § 2–615, with InterPetrol Bermuda Ltd. v. Kaiser Aluminum Int'l Corp., 719 F.2d 992 (9th Cir. 1983).

(2) *Stranded Sellers.* Each seller in the two previous cases—George King in *Selland Pontiac*, and Dunbar Molasses in *Canadian Industrial Alcohol*—had a designated supplier, and the supply for each seller failed. "Stranded seller" is an apt name for a seller in that position. As to the seller's liability it matters why the supply fails, according to the latter case: "The [seller's] duty will be discharged if the mill is destroyed . . . . " Why is that? The result would be different, we are told, if the supply fails because "times turn out to be hard." Does this mean that what has been called "economic *force majeure*" does not count? If it does not, how can we explain the decision in *Selland Pontiac*?

(3) *Labor Difficulties.* In the foregoing opinion the court spoke dismissively of high labor costs. But what of strikes, sick-outs, and other job actions against a supplier of goods or services? In *force majeure* clauses, strikes are commonly associated with acts of God; see *Kama Rippa Music*, p. 1070 above. Apart from a *force majeure* clause, might a work stoppage at the Yonkers refinery justify it in withholding molasses from Dunbar if there had been a sale contract between them? Might a work stoppage excuse a subcontractor from completing its work on time, under a contract with a general contractor?

It has been suggested that experience in the line of business concerned, as known to the parties, might be dispositive. Mishara Construction Co v. Transit-Mixed Concrete Corp., 310 N.E.2d 363 (Mass. 1974). Although the court had some difficulty envisaging an industry in which labor relations were consistently amicable, it indicated that the picketing of a firm in such an industry would be more likely to limit its contract obligations than the picketing of a firm engaged in a business "with a long record of labor difficulties."

(4) *International Approaches.* Article 79 of the CISG, in paragraph (1), relieves a party from liability "for a failure to perform any of his obligations if he proves that the failure was due to an impediment beyond his control and that he could not reasonably be expected to have taken the impediment into account at the time of the conclusion of the contract or to have avoided or overcome it or its consequences." Does this test seem more or less strict than that of UCC § 2–615? The article has been criticized as having a "chameleon-like character that permits it to take on that meaning that best conforms to the reader's own legal background." Farnsworth, *Perspective of Common Law Countries, in La Vendita Internazionale* 3, 19 (Congress at S. Margherita Ligure 1981). The comparable provision of the UNIDROIT

b. Suppose that the carload is destroyed by lightning while it is still on Seller's premises on August 1, Buyer not yet having taken possession. Can Seller recover the price from Buyer? Can Buyer recover damages from Seller?

See UCC §§ 2–709(1)(a) and 2–613.

Eastern Air Lines, Inc. v. Gulf Oil Corporation

United States District Court, Southern District of Florida, 1975.
415 F.Supp. 429.

■ JAMES LAWRENCE KING, DISTRICT JUDGE. Eastern Air Lines, Inc., hereafter Eastern, and Gulf Oil Corporation, hereafter Gulf, have enjoyed a mutually advantageous business relationship involving the sale and purchase of aviation fuel for several decades.

This controversy involves the threatened disruption of that historic relationship and the attempt, by Eastern, to enforce the most recent contract between the parties. On March 8, 1974 the correspondence and telex communications between the corporate entities culminated in a demand by Gulf that Eastern must meet its demand for a price increase or Gulf would shut off Eastern's supply of jet fuel within fifteen days.

Eastern responded by filing its complaint with this court, alleging that Gulf had breached its contract and requesting preliminary and permanent mandatory injunctions requiring Gulf to perform the contract in accordance with its terms. By agreement of the parties, a preliminary injunction preserving the status quo was entered on March 20, 1974, requiring Gulf to perform its contract and directing Eastern to pay in accordance with the contract terms, pending final disposition of the case.

Gulf answered Eastern's complaint, alleging that the contract was not a binding requirements contract, was void for want of mutuality, and, furthermore, was "commercially impracticable" within the meaning of UCC § 2–615; Fla. Stat. §§ 672.614, 672.615.

The extraordinarily able advocacy by the experienced lawyers for both parties produced testimony at the trial from internationally respected experts who described in depth economic events that have, in recent months, profoundly affected the lives of every American.

The Contract

On June 27, 1972, an agreement was signed by the parties which, as amended, was to provide the basis upon which Gulf was to furnish jet fuel to Eastern at certain specific cities in the Eastern system. Said agreement supplemented an existing contract between Gulf and Eastern which, on June 27, 1972, had approximately one year remaining prior to its expiration.

The contract is Gulf's standard form aviation fuel contract and is identical in all material particulars with the first contract for jet fuel, dated 1959, between Eastern and Gulf and, indeed, with aviation fuel contracts antedating the jet age. It is similar to contracts in general use in the aviation fuel trade. The contract was drafted by Gulf after substantial arm's length negotiation between the parties. Gulf approached Eastern more than a year before the expiration of the then-existing contracts between Gulf and Eastern, seeking to preserve its historic relationship with Eastern. Following several months of negotiation, the contract, consolidating and extending the terms of several existing contracts, was executed by the parties in June, 1972, to expire January 31, 1977.

The parties agreed that this contract, as its predecessor, should provide a reference to reflect changes in the price of the raw material from which jet fuel is processed, i.e., crude oil, in direct proportion to the cost per gallon of jet fuel.

Both parties regarded the instant agreement as favorable, Eastern, in part, because it offered immediate savings in projected escalations under the existing agreement through reduced base prices at the contract cities; while Gulf found a long term outlet for a capacity of jet fuel coming on stream from a newly completed refinery, as well as a means to relate anticipated increased cost of raw material (crude oil) directly to the price of the refined product sold. The previous Eastern/Gulf contracts contained a price index clause which operated to pass on to Eastern only one-half of any increase in the price of crude oil. Both parties knew at the time of contract negotiations that increases in crude oil prices would be expected, were "a way of life", and intended that those increases be borne by Eastern in a direct proportional relationship of crude oil cost per barrel to jet fuel cost per gallon.

Accordingly, the parties selected an indicator (West Texas Sour); a crude which is bought and sold in large volume and was thus a reliable indicator of the market value of crude oil. From June 27, 1972 to the fall of 1973, there were in effect various forms of U.S. government imposed price controls which at once controlled the price of crude oil generally, West Texas Sour specifically, and hence the price of jet fuel. As the government authorized increased prices of crude those increases were in turn reflected in the cost of jet fuel. Eastern has paid a per gallon increase under the contract from 11 cents to 15 cents (or some 40%).

The indicator selected by the parties was "the average of the posted prices for West Texas sour crude, 30.0–30.9 gravity of Gulf Oil Corporation, Shell Oil Company, and Pan American Petroleum Corporation". The posting of crude prices under the contract "shall be as listed for these companies in Platts Oilgram Service—Crude Oil Supplement."

"Posting" has long been a practice in the oil industry. It involves the physical placement at a public location of a price bulletin reflecting the current price at which an oil company will pay for a given barrel of a specific type of crude oil. Those posted price bulletins historically have, in addition to being displayed publicly, been mailed to those persons evincing interest therein, including sellers of crude oil, customers whose price of product may be based thereon, and, among others, Platts Oilgram, publishers of a periodical of interest to those related to the oil industry.

In recent years, the United States has become increasingly dependent upon foreign crude oil, particularly from the "OPEC" nations most of which are in the Middle East. OPEC was formed in 1970 for the avowed purpose of raising oil prices, and has become an increasingly cohesive and potent organization as its member nations have steadily enhanced their equity positions and their control over their oil production facilities. Nationalization of crude oil resources and shutdowns of production and distribution have become a way of life for oil companies operating in OPEC nations, particularly in the volatile Middle East. The closing of the Suez Canal and the concomitant interruption of the flow of Mid-East oil during the 1967 "Six-Day War", and Libya's nationalization of its oil industry during the same period, are only some of the more dramatic examples of a trend that began years ago. By 1969 "the handwriting was on the wall" in the words of Gulf's foreign oil expert witness, Mr. Blackledge.

During 1970 domestic United States oil production "peaked"; since then it has declined while the percentage of imported crude oil has been steadily increasing. Unlike domestic crude oil, which has been subject to price control since August 15, 1971, foreign crude oil has never been subject to price control by the United States Government. Foreign crude oil prices, uncontrolled by the Federal Government, were generally lower than domestic crude oil prices in 1971 and 1972; during 1973 foreign prices "crossed" domestic prices; by late 1973 foreign prices were generally several dollars per barrel higher than controlled domestic prices. It was during late 1973 that the Mid-East exploded in another war, accompanied by an embargo (at least officially) by the Arab oil-producing nations against the United States and certain of its allies. World prices for oil and oil products increased.

Mindful of that situation and for various other reasons concerning the nation's economy, the United States government began a series of controls affecting the oil industry culminating, in the fall of 1973, with the implementation of price controls known as "two-tier." In practice "two-tier" can be described as follows: taking as the bench mark the number of barrels produced from a given well in May of 1972, that number of barrels is deemed "old" oil. The price of "old" oil then is frozen by the government at a fixed level. To the extent that the productivity of a given well can be increased over the May, 1972, production, that increased production is deemed "new" oil. For each barrel of "new" oil produced, the government authorized the release from price controls of an equivalent number of barrels from those theretofore designated "old" oil. For example, from a well which in May of 1972, produced 100 barrels of oil; all of the production of that well would, since the imposition of "two-tier" in August of 1973, be "old" oil. Increased productivity to 150 barrels would result in 50 barrels of "new" oil and 50 barrels of "released" oil; with the result that 100 barrels of the 150 barrels produced from the well would be uncontrolled by the "two-tier" pricing system, while the 50 remaining barrels of "old" would remain government price controlled.

The implementation of "two-tier" was completely without precedent in the history of government price control action. Its impact, however, was nominal, until the imposition of an embargo upon the exportation of crude oil by certain Arab countries in October, 1973. Those countries deemed sympathetic to Israel were embargoed from receiving oil from the Arab oil producing countries. The United States was among the principal countries affected by that embargo, with the result that it experienced an immediate "energy crises".

Following closely after the embargo, OPEC (Oil Producing Export Countries) unilaterally increased the price of their crude to the world market some 400% between September, 1973, and January 15, 1974. Since the United States domestic production was at capacity, it was dependent upon foreign crude to meet its requirements. New and released oil (uncontrolled) soon reached parity with the price of foreign crude, moving from approximately $5 to $11 a barrel from September, 1974 to January 15, 1974.

Since imposition of "two-tier", the price of "old oil" has remained fixed by government action, with the oil companies resorting to postings reflecting prices they will pay for the new and released oil, not subject to government controls. Those prices, known as "premiums", are the subject of supplemental bulletins which are likewise posted by the oil companies and furnished to interested parties, including Platts Oilgram.

Platts, since the institution of "two-tier" has not published the posted prices of any of the premiums offered by the oil companies in the United States, including those of Gulf Oil Corporation, Shell Oil Company and Pan American Petroleum, the companies designated in the agreement. The information which has appeared in Platts since the implementation of "two-tier" with respect to the price of West Texas Sour crude oil has been the price of "old" oil subject to government control.

Under the court's restraining order, entered in this cause by agreement of the parties, Eastern has been paying for jet fuel from Gulf on the basis of the price of "old" West Texas Sour crude oil as fixed by government price control action, i.e., $5 a barrel. Approximately 40 gallons of finished jet fuel product can be refined from a barrel of crude.

Against this factual background we turn to a consideration of the legal issues.

I

The "Requirements" Contract

[The court rejected Gulf's claims that the contract between it and Eastern is not a valid contract because it lacks mutuality of obligation and is too vague and indefinite.]

II

Breach of Contract

[The court determined that Eastern's performance under the contract "did not constitute a breach of its agreement with Gulf" and was "consistent with good faith and commercial practices as required by UCC § 2–306."]

III

Commercial Impracticability

Gulf's commercial impracticability defenses are premised on two sections of the Uniform Commercial Code specifically §§ 2–614 (F.S. 672.614) and 2–615 (F.S. 672.615). The modern U.C.C. § 2–615 doctrine of commercial impracticability has its roots in the common law doctrine of frustration or impossibility and finds its most recognized illustrations in the so-called "Suez Cases", arising out of the various closings of the Suez Canal and the consequent increases in shipping costs around the Cape of Good Hope. Those cases offered little encouragement to those who would wield the sword of commercial impracticability. As a leading British case arising out of the 1957 Suez closure declared, the unforeseen cost increase that would excuse performance "must be more than merely onerous or expensive. It must be positively unjust to hold the parties bound." Ocean Tramp Tankers v. V/O Sovfracht (The Eugenia), 2 Q.B. 226, 239 (1964). These British precedents were followed by the District of Columbia Circuit, which gave specific consideration to U.C.C. 2–615, Comment 4, in Transatlantic Financing Corp. v. United States, 124 U.S. App. D.C. 183, 363 F.2d 312, 319 (1966).

Other recent American cases similarly strictly construe the doctrine of commercial impracticability. For example, one case found no U.C.C. defense, even though costs had doubled over the contract price, the court stating, "It may have been unprofitable for defendant to have supplied the pickers, but the evidence does not establish that it was impossible. A mere showing of unprofitability, without more, will not excuse the performance of a contract." Schafer v. Sunset Packing Co., 256 Or. 539, 474 P.2d 529, 530 (1970).

Gulf's argument on commercial impracticability has two strings to its bow. First, Gulf contends that the escalator indicator does not work as intended by the parties by reason of the advent of so-called "two-tier" pricing under Phase IV government price controls.[1] Second, Gulf alleges

---

[1]   One tier being "old" price-controlled oil, and the second tier being the unregulated oil.

that crude oil prices have risen substantially without a concomitant rise in the escalation indicator, and, as a result, that performance of the contract has become commercially impracticable.[2]

The short and dispositive answer to Gulf's first argument under U.C.C. § 2–615, that the price escalation indicator (posting in Platt's Oilgram Crude Oil Supplement) no longer reflects the intent of the parties by reason of the so-called "two-tier" pricing structure, is that the language of the contract is clear and unambiguous. The contract does not require interpretation and requires no excursion into the subjective intention of the parties. The intent of the parties is clear from the four corners of the contract; they intended to be bound by the specified entries in *Platt's,* which has been published at all times material here, which is published today, and which prints the contract reference prices. Prices under the contract can be and still are calculated[3] by reference to Platt's publication.[4]

It should be noted that Platt's Oilgram Crude Oil Supplement states on its face that its postings since the advent of "two-tier" are basically comparable to the postings historically quoted in Platt's, and that postings listed in Platt's were price controlled at the time of negotiation and execution of the contract, just as they are today and have been at all times in between. In addition, Gulf's expert witness Mr. Coates testified that oil companies, including Gulf, continue to use "old oil" prices (the prices reported in Platt's) for contracts between themselves. Finally, as to the indicator crude (West Texas Sour) there is no showing that the Platt's postings do not reflect the market price for that oil today. The testimony is in substantial dispute but the court finds, with respect to domestic oil, some 60 percent of Gulf's 1974 domestic production was old oil. With respect to foreign crude oil, domestic prices were considerably lower than imported price at the beginning of the period in question so that the West Texas Sour Crude postings unquestionably did not reflect foreign crude oil postings. In the absence of any evidence to the contrary it may be reasonably inferred that virtually all transactions in West Texas Sour Crude Oil take place at the postings reflected in *Platt's,* since most of the production in that field is "old" oil.

With regard to Gulf's contention that the contract has become "commercially impracticable" within the meaning of U.C.C. § 2–615,

---

[2] The average price paid by Eastern to Gulf has risen more than 40% over the life of the contract.

[3] The parties have stipulated that Eastern has been paying prices mandated by the contract terms.

[4] Gulf's contention that the publication of the postings has been "suspended" and therefore that a proviso of Article II of the contract, declaring the consequences of "suspension", has been triggered, is without merit. The Proviso deals, in the clearest of terms, with *Platt's* ceasing to publish either *in toto* or in regard to the specified postings, neither of which is the case here. Furthermore, the proviso contains its own prescription for remedial action in the case of suspension, including notice and substitution of other indicators. Gulf has never attempted to follow the prescribed remedy; thus its argument fails for procedural as well as substantive reasons.

because of the increase in market price of foreign crude oil and certain domestic crude oils, the court finds that the tendered defense has not been proved. On this record the court cannot determine how much it costs Gulf to produce a gallon of jet fuel for sale to Eastern, whether Gulf loses money or makes a profit on its sale of jet fuel to Eastern, either now or at the inception of the contract, or at any time in between. Gulf's witnesses testified that they could not make such a computation. The party undertaking the burden of establishing "commercial impracticability" by reason of allegedly increased raw material costs undertakes the obligation of showing the extent to which he has suffered, or will suffer, losses in performing his contract. The record here does not substantiate Gulf's contention on this fundamental issue.

Gulf presented evidence tending to show that its "costs" of crude oil have increased dramatically over the past two years.

However, the "costs" to which Gulf adverts are unlike any "costs" that might arguably afford ground for any of the relief sought here. Gulf's claimed "costs" of an average barrel of crude oil at Gulf's refineries (estimated by Gulf's witness Davis at about $10.00 currently, and about $9.50 during 1974) include intra-company profits, as the oil moved from Gulf's overseas and domestic production departments to its refining department. The magnitude of that profit was not revealed.

With respect to Gulf's foreign crude oil "costs", the record shows that at the very time Gulf was in the process of repudiating its contract with Eastern (January 1974), Gulf's profit margin on foreign crude oil brought into the United States (Cabindan and Nigerian) was approximately $4.43 to $3.88 per barrel compared with profits of $0.92 and $0.88 respectively, one year earlier.[5] That margin may now have declined, but the record discloses that Gulf's overseas subsidiaries have enjoyed substantial profits from crude oil transactions and that those profits are included in the "average" crude oil "costs" of which Gulf now complains. The "transfer" prices at which Gulf "sells" its foreign oil to its domestic subsidiaries are set by a pricing committee in Gulf's Pittsburgh home office.[j]

Intra-company profit can be and is allocated among those 400-plus corporate subsidiaries of Gulf, largely through the transfer price device, to optimize overall benefit to the corporation, as documents from the committee reveal. Internal memoranda from the pricing committee introduced into evidence showed for instance that the committee had before it the view of one of its tax experts that every $1 increase in Nigerian oil prices resulted in a 50 to 90 cent benefit to the company; other memoranda describe how profits might be assigned, through

---

[5]   Gulf's international oils expert, Mr. Blackledge testified that foreign oil costs were up four-fold during 1973–74 but Gulf's profits also went up four-fold in that period.

[j]   Transfer pricing is the practice, not unusual within segmented firms, of assigning a cost to goods as they are acquired by one segment from another (*e.g.*, by the assembly division from the parts division).

intercompany sales, to various other offshore subsidiaries to obtain favorable tax treatment for the purpose of maximizing the advantages to the corporation for the benefit of the parent corporation. Similarly, there are memoranda reflecting a policy of charging the highest prices possible to the United States.

In like manner, the "per barrel" cost calculations which Gulf introduced at trial reflect "in house" profits from Gulf's domestic production. During the discovery process, Gulf developed for Eastern certain "cost" figures. Those data show that a Gulf-produced barrel of domestic crude oil is reflected on Gulf's books at a cost of approximately $2.44 for the nine-month period ending September 30, 1974. Yet, for purposes of computing an overall average "cost" to Gulf of a barrel of crude oil for trial purposes (estimated by Gulf's economist witness Davis on the stand at about $9.50 for that period), Gulf used, not the $2.44 actual booked cost, but a "transfer" price, equal to "postings" and including intra-company profit. To the extent "old oil" postings are reflected in the domestic oil "transfer price", the intra-company profit would be on the order of $2.76 per barrel, measured against the $5.20 posting listed in *Platt's* for West Texas Sour Crude; "new" oil "transfer prices" would include an even larger profit margin. Gulf estimated that some 70 percent of domestic oil going into Gulf's refineries was its own proprietary production.

Again, these are not the kinds of "costs" against which to measure hardship, real or imagined, under the Uniform Commercial Code. Under no theory of law can it be held that Gulf is guaranteed preservation of its intra-company profits, moving from the left-hand to the right-hand, as one Gulf witness so aptly put it. The burden is upon Gulf to show what its real costs are, not its "costs" inflated by its internal profits at various levels of the manufacturing process and located in various foreign countries.

No criticism is implied of Gulf's rational desire to maximize its profits and take every advantage available to it under the laws. However, these factors cannot be ignored in approaching Gulf's contention that it has been unduly burdened by crude oil price increases.

No such hardship has been established. On the contrary, the record clearly establishes that 1973, the year in which the energy crises began, was Gulf's best year ever, in which it recorded some $800 million in net profits after taxes. Gulf's 1974 year was more than 25% better than 1973's record-$1,065,000,000 profits were booked by Gulf in 1974 after paying all taxes.[6]

For the foregoing reasons, Gulf's claim of hardship giving rise to "commercial impracticability" fails.

---

[6] Gulf stipulated in the parties' pretrial stipulation that it had the capability to perform the contract.

But even if Gulf had established great hardship under U.C.C. § 2–615, which it has not, Gulf would not prevail because the events associated with the so-called energy crises were reasonably foreseeable at the time the contract was executed. If a contingency is foreseeable, it and its consequences are taken outside the scope of U.C.C. § 2–615, because the party disadvantaged by fruition of the contingency might have protected himself in his contract, Ellwood v. Nutex Oil Co., 148 S.W.2d 862 (Tex. Civ. App. 1941).

The record is replete with evidence as to the volatility of the Middle East situation, the arbitrary power of host governments to control the foreign oil market, and repeated interruptions and interference with the normal commercial trade in crude oil. Even without the extensive evidence present in the record, the court would be justified in taking judicial notice of the fact that oil has been used as a political weapon with increasing success by the oil-producing nations for many years, and Gulf was well aware of and assumed the risk that the OPEC nations would do exactly what they have done.

With respect to Gulf's argument that "two-tier" was not "foreseeable", the record shows that domestic crude oil prices were controlled at all material times, that Gulf foresaw that they might be de-controlled, and that Gulf was constantly urging to the Federal Government that they should be de-controlled. Government price regulations were confused, constantly changing, and uncertain during the period of the negotiation and execution of the contract. During that time frame, high ranking Gulf executives, including some of its trial witnesses, were in constant repeated contact with officials and agencies of the Federal Government regarding petroleum policies and were well able to protect themselves from any contingencies.

Even those outside the oil industry were aware of the possibilities. Eastern's principal contract negotiator advised his superior in recommending this contract to him:

> "While Gulf is apparently counting on crude price increases, such increases are a fact of life for the future, except as the government may inhibit by price controls, therefore all suppliers have such anticipation."

> "1975 is the year during which the full effect of energy shortages will be felt in the United States according to most estimates."

Knowing all the factors, Gulf drafted the contract and tied the escalation to certain specified domestic postings in *Platt's*. The court is of the view that it is bound thereby.

The court is further of the opinion that U.C.C. § 2–614(2) is not applicable to this case. It is clear that this section dealing with "means or manner of payment" speaks, by way of illustration, to the blocking by governmental interference with the contemplated mode of monetary exchange (e.g., when a contract provides for payment in gold specie and the government subsequently forbids payment in gold). No such issue appears in the case at bar and U.C.C. § 2–614 is inapposite here.

NOTES

(1) *Questions.* If Eastern's supplier had been a firm other than Gulf, one whose dealings in hydrocarbons was restricted to refining crude oil and marketing the products, might that firm have found it easier to establish the "great hardship" that Gulf failed to establish? Might it be possible to establish the requisite injury without showing that operations under the contract in question have begun to show a loss? How, exactly, was it germane that, overall, Gulf had record and rising profits in 1973 and 1974?

Consider the court's discussion of the cost to Gulf of crude oil, as affected by its transfer pricing. Is the court's reasoning linked to the concept of self-imposed impracticability?

(2) *Promisor's Good Faith?* An obstacle to a promisor's performance is not an excuse for the promisor if it might have been overcome easily. Neither are obstacles that the promisor has put in its own way. "A man may habitually leave his house by the front door to keep his appointments; but, if the front door is stuck, he would hardly be excused for not leaving by the back." So said Lord Radcliffe in Tsakiroglou & Co. v. Noblee Thorl G.m.b.H., [1960] 2 Q.B. 318. "To recognize impossibility where . . . the party pleading the defense has intentionally incapacitated itself from performing would defy . . . all good sense." Kama Rippa Music, Inc. v. Schekeryk, 510 F.2d 837, 843–43 (2d Cir. 1975).

These observations may be self-evident, but they do not solve all the problems about a promisor's responsibility. What of an obstacle that the promisor might have overcome by strenuous effort? And what of one resulting from the promisor's carelessness? Consider the following observations: (i) In *Kama Rippa Music*: "The party pleading impossibility as a defense must demonstrate that it took virtually every action within its power to perform its duties under the contract." (ii) According to Comment 5 to UCC § 2–615, concerning the defense of commercial impracticability for a "stranded seller," the section provides no excuse for a seller unless he has "employed all due measures to assure himself that his source will not fail." (iii) "Some day it may have to be finally determined whether a *prima donna* is excused by complete loss of voice from an executory contract to sing if it is proved that her condition was caused by her carelessness in not changing her wet clothes after being out in the rain." Viscount Simon, in Joseph Constantine Steamship Line v. Imperial Smelting Corp., [1942] A.C. 154, [1941] 2 All E.R. 165 (C.A.). The limitations on a promisor's excuse indicated above might be ascribed, loosely, to its duty to perform in good faith.

(3) *Promisee's Good Faith?* A want of good faith on the part of the promisee may serve as an excuse for the promisor. More precisely, an obstacle to the promisor's performance that is chargeable to the promisee may well be an excuse for the promisor under the rubric "prevention." See the discussion of Hindrance and Prevention, p. 840 above.

(4) *Governmental Acts.* In United States v. Winstar Corporation, 518 U.S. 839 (1996), discussed at, pp. 1065–1066, above, the Supreme Court considered an impracticability defense presented by the United States. It considered also the "sovereign act" doctrine, restricting contractual liability of the United States for engaging in "public and general acts." The claimants in the case were three banks. The Government pinned a defense on a change in federal banking law: the enactment of a statute known as FIRREA.[k] Earlier, the claimants had been promised favorable accounting treatment by federal authorities supervising them. This promise led them to absorb weaker institutions the failure of which would have been a drain on the Federal Savings & Loan Insurance Corporation. FIRREA sought to foreclose the accounting practice desired by and promised to the claimants. If considered as an ordinary litigant, the Government was in a poor position to rely on its inability to perform the promise, for the disabling statute was its own doing. But the United States is not an ordinary litigant. As a contractor, the Court said, it is relieved from "the traditional blanket rule that a contracting party may not obtain discharge if its own act rendered performance impossible." Hence, while rejecting the Government's defense, the Court proceeded to take it seriously.

Governmental interference with a seller's means of performance may and may not excuse the seller, according to Comment 10 to UCC § 2–615. "[T]his section," we are told, "disregards any technical distinction between 'law,' 'regulation,' 'order' and the like." But there are more-than-technical distinctions to be made. Judicial opinions commonly purport to refine existing law, rather than to promulgate fresh rules. It would not be surprising, therefore, to be told that a seller had assumed the risk of a new, pro-buyer precedent about, say, a reasonable time for tendering goods. When a court announces a novel ruling, should its effect on outstanding contracts depend on whether or not the court portrays the ruling as a novelty?

On occasion, a buyer has complained that its supplier acquiesced too readily in governmental opposition to performance of the supplier's undertaking. Officials, fearful that performance may give comfort to an enemy, have been known to forestall performance by "jawboning" a supplier rather than by promulgating a regulation. In Harriscom Svenska, AB v. Harris Corp., 3 F.3d 576 (2d Cir. 1993), a seller found shelter under a *force majeure* clause ("governmental interference") without having resisted governmental influence to a degree that would have been, in the court's view, "unusually foolhardy." Cf. MG Refining & Mktg. v. Knight Enters., 25 F.Supp.2d 175 (S.D.N.Y. 1998).

(5) *Temporary Impracticability.* An obstacle to performance that makes it impracticable may prove to be temporary; it may abate before the period required for full performance has elapsed. Promisors have sometimes sought excuses from any further performance based on obstacles that endured only for a time. Gene Autry, for example, a star of cowboy movies, refused to resume the performance of an acting contract with his studio, following his Army service during World War II. That was not a breach, it

---

[k]   The Financial Institutions Reform, Recovery, and Enforcement Act of 1989.

was held. Autry v. Republic Productions, Inc., 180 P.2d 888 (Cal. 1947). A different but related question is this· When may a party justifiably terminate a contract because the other party suffers from a short-term disability? A party who announces termination too hastily is chargeable with having repudiated the contract.

(6) *The Westinghouse Litigation.* The most widely observed litigation over UCC § 2–615 arose out of long term contracts made by Westinghouse Electric to supply uranium oxide ("yellowcake") to electric utility companies in connection with sales of nuclear power plants. The price of uranium oxide rose from about $6 a pound in 1972 to about $40 a pound in 1976. Late in 1975 Westinghouse wrote seventeen utilities, saying that it was excused because of commercial impracticability from delivering the total of some 80 million pounds that it had agreed to supply, and that it would prorate among the utilities some 15 million pounds that it could command. From that event a fountain of litigation flowed, resulting in many settlements. Most interesting is the interim decision in the Richmond case, in which the suits of several utilities were consolidated for trial.

Westinghouse arranged, with court approval, to deliver the uranium oxide at its disposal, subject to a later determination. After nine months of hearings, the judge ruled that Westinghouse was not wholly excused, but he expressed willingness to hear argument that a judicial limitation of the remedy was appropriate. Submissions on issues of damages and an "equitable adjustment" were then made. Eventually all claims were settled on terms relatively favorable to Westinghouse. For background, see Paul Joskow, *Commercial Impossibility, the Uranium Market and the Westinghouse Case*, 6 J. Legal Stud. 119 (1977).[1]

SECTION 4.   FRUSTRATION OF PURPOSE

Krell v. Henry
Court of Appeal, 1903.
2 K.B. 740.

[By a contract in writing of June 20, 1902, the defendant agreed to hire from the plaintiff a flat in Pall Mall, London for June 26 and 27, on which days it had been officially announced that the coronation processions (i.e., to be held in connection with the coronation of Edward VII) would take place and pass along Pall Mall. The contract contained no express reference to the coronation processions, or to any other purpose for which the flat was taken. A deposit was paid when the contract was entered into. As, owing to the serious illness of the King, the processions did not take place on the days originally fixed, the defendant declined to pay the balance of the rent.]

---

[1]   For a later episode in Westinghouse's travails arising out of nuclear power contracts, see Florida Power & Light Co. v. Westinghouse Electric Corp., 826 F.2d 239 (4th Cir. 1987). The court there noted a trial court's finding that "while Westinghouse was supposedly more expert in the field of nuclear energy, Florida was more expert in the drafting of agreements and that it had demonstrated this superior expertise by 'out-negotiating' Westinghouse."

■ VAUGHN WILLIAMS, LORD JUDGE. The real question in this case is the extent of the application in English law of the principle of the Roman law which has been adopted and acted on in many English decisions, and notably in the case of Taylor v. Caldwell, (3 B. & S. 826). I do not think that the principle of the civil law as introduced into the English law is limited to cases in which the event causing the impossibility of performance is the destruction or non-existence of some thing which is the subject matter of the contract or of some condition or state of things expressly specified as a condition of it. I think that you first have to ascertain, not necessarily from the terms of the contract, but, if required, from necessary inferences, drawn from surrounding circumstances recognized by both contracting parties, what is the substance of the contract, and then to ask the question whether that substantial contract needs for its foundation the assumption of the existence of a particular state of things. If it does, this will limit the operation of the general words, and in such case, if the contract becomes impossible of performance by reason of the non-existence of the state of things assumed by both contracting parties as the foundation of the contract, there will be no breach of the contract thus limited. Now what are the facts of the present case? The contract is contained in two letters of June 20 which passed between the defendant and the plaintiff's agent, Mr. Cecil Bisgood. These letters do not mention the coronation, but speak merely of the taking of Mr. Krell's chambers, or, rather, of the use of them, in the daytime of June 26 and 27, for the sum of 75*l.*, 25*l.* then paid, balance 50*l.* to be paid on the 24th. But the affidavits, which by agreement between the parties are to be taken as stating the facts of the case, show that the plaintiff exhibited on his premises, third floor, 56A, Pall Mall, an announcement to the effect that windows to view the Royal coronation procession were to be let, and that the defendant was induced by that announcement to apply to the housekeeper on the premises, who said that the owner was willing to let the suite of rooms for the purpose of seeing the Royal procession for both days, but not nights, of June 26 and 27.[m] In my judgment the use of the rooms was let and taken for the purpose of seeing the Royal procession. It was not a demise of the rooms,

---

[m] Two processions were planned in connection with the coronation: that on Coronation Day, and a "Pageant" on the following day. *Experience of the Diamond Jubilee* (1897) provided some guidance for the pricing of space to see the processions. At that time a club-house had been "let to a speculator for £200, who realized £500 by his bargain." C. Pascoe, *The Pageant & Ceremony of The Coronation* 213 (1902). But there were complications in the early summer of 1902, in that the routes of the processions had not been determined. Pall Mall—"club-land of the empire"—was thought to be a certainty for the Pageant procession; but for Coronation Day two shorter routes, not including Pall Mall, were thought to be under consideration. One writer of the time estimated that prices for the Pageant ought not to exceed those paid for Victoria's Jubilee—"that is to say, if the Route be not [curtailed]. Of course, the lesser the opportunity of seeing the Pageant, the higher will be the prices asked for accommodation." Id. at 212.

On June 22 Commons was informed that the King had just undergone an operation for appendicitis, and that the Coronation was indefinitely postponed. V. Cowles, *Edward VII and His Circle* 240 (1956). It was performed on August 9. Though some of the captains and the princes (kings were not invited) had departed London, the splendor of the ceremony was "scarcely dimmed." Pall Mall was on the coronation route. London Illustrated News, Aug. 14, 1902.

or even an agreement to let and take the rooms. It is a license to use rooms for a particular purpose and none other. And in my judgment the taking place of those processions on the days proclaimed along the proclaimed route, which passed 56A, Pall Mall, was regarded by both contracting parties as the foundation of the contract; and I think that it cannot reasonably be supposed to have been in the contemplation of the contracting parties, when the contract was made, that the coronation would not be held on the proclaimed days, or the processions not take place on those days along the proclaimed route; and I think that the words imposing on the defendant the obligation to accept and pay for the use of the rooms for the named days, although general and unconditional, were not used with reference to the possibility of the particular contingency which afterwards occurred. It was suggested in the course of the argument that if the occurrence, on the proclaimed days, of the coronation and the procession in this case were the foundation of the contract, and if the general words are thereby limited or qualified, so that in the event of the non-occurrence of the coronation and procession along the proclaimed route they would discharge both parties from further performance of the contract, it would follow that if a cabman was engaged to take someone to Epsom on Derby Day at a suitable enhanced price for such a journey, say 10*l.*, both parties to the contract would be discharged in the contingency of the race at Epsom for some reason becoming impossible; but I do not think this follows, for I do not think that in the cab case the happening of the race would be the foundation of the contract. No doubt the purpose of the engager would be to go to see the Derby, and the price would be proportionately high; but the cab had no special qualification for this particular occasion. Any other cab would have done as well.

Appeal dismissed.

NOTES

(1) *Twin Doctrines.* The foregoing decision is the best-known example of the doctrine known as "frustration of purpose." In this country, frustration affords an excuse distinct from that of impracticability of performance. In *Krell v. Henry*, the court pitched its decision on the "impossibility" principle of the music-hall case, *Taylor v. Caldwell*, above. But the postponement of the coronation did not impede performance of the contract either by Krell or by Henry. After the King's illness, as before, it was perfectly possible for Henry to occupy the rooms and to pay the agreed price; it was only that the occupancy would have been relatively valueless to him.

A comparable California case is Lloyd v. Murphy, 153 P.2d 47 (1944). Murphy's business as a car dealer, in leased quarters, was severely curtailed when wartime orders of the federal government placed sharp restrictions on sales of new cars. When he withheld rent payments, his landlords brought an action to enforce the lease terms. The court identified Murphy's defense as one of frustration. "Although [that] doctrine is akin to the doctrine of impossibility of performance . . . frustration is not a form of impossibility. . . .

Performance remains possible but the expected value of performance to the party seeking to be excused has been destroyed by a fortuitous event. . . . " For a tenant in a different kind of difficulty, see Kel Kim Corp. v. Central Markets, Inc., 519 N.E.2d 295 (N.Y. 1987). Kel Kim sought to maintain its lease without complying with its undertaking to maintain a sizable amount of liability insurance; a crisis in the insurance market had prevented it from complying, Kel Kim said. The landlord prevailed in each case.

(2) *Efficient Non-Performance?* When parties enter into a contract, the value of performance to each party often exceeds the cost of performance. In the introductory note on the Economics of Remedies, p. 34, we presented a hypothetical where a buyer purchased a piece of machinery from a seller. The machinery, which would cost the seller $300 to produce, was worth $1,000 to the buyer. The parties entered into a contract for the sale of the machinery for a price of $600.

However, the relationship between value and costs may change before performance is rendered. For example, a more valuable opportunity may present itself to the seller, as it did in the introductory note. Another occurrence that may change the relationship between value and costs is when a party's cost of performance increases significantly, as we saw in the cases on impracticability, such as *Transatlantic*.

Like impracticability, frustration of purpose may also lead to a change in the relative magnitude of value and cost of performance. With frustration of purpose, however, it is the value of performance to the party receiving it (rather than the cost) that turns out to be significantly different than expected.

Suppose, in our hypothetical, that before the seller produces and delivers the machinery to the buyer, the buyer's factory burns to the ground—frustrating the buyer's purpose of entering into the contract with the seller. The machinery now has little value to the buyer. In such a circumstance, does excusing the buyer promote efficiency? Does it promote fairness? What would inform your response? Different conceptions of efficiency? Different conceptions of fairness? Something else?

(3) *Occurrence and Assumption.* Was it so inconceivable that illness or bad weather or some other unfortunate event would lead to cancellation or postponement of the coronation of Edward VII, thereby frustrating Krell's purpose in letting the room on the announced day of the event? Perhaps it was difficult for a lay person to foresee this eventuality. But, "[i]n fact, Krell did not let his rooms directly; rather, he left that to his solicitor." Victor Goldberg, *Framing Contract Law* 340 (2006). Is this a significant fact? Should excuse doctrines apply equally to those represented by counsel and those that are not?

PROBLEMS

(1) *The Lost Weekend.* A major university, Gridiron U., is situated in the town of Touchdown, which is otherwise a small community that is somewhat isolated. There is one hotel in the town, and a few motels, but rooms for transient visitors are not abundant. You represent several alumni

of Gridiron who have suffered a disappointment. They had planned to attend the school's homecoming, a major annual event in Touchdown. This year the event was canceled, owing to a tragic tornado strike. Your clients, however, already arranged for weekend lodgings in Touchdown, paying substantial advance deposits to the hotelkeeper. As your clients well knew, the usual room charges in Touchdown are more than doubled for homecoming weekends. If you can establish that your clients' lodging contracts were terminated by Gridiron's cancellation of its homecoming, you can expect to succeed in a class action on behalf of your clients and other alumni who have made similar arrangements, seeking recovery of the deposits.

Do you find support for that action in *Krell*? Can you distinguish the case of the cab on Derby Day, suggested by counsel for Krell? Are you prepared to dispute the court's dictum on that case?

(2) *A Bride Bereaved*. For a promise of $500 P promises to provide a wedding dress for D by June 1. D's marriage to X is scheduled for a week after that. When the dress is all but ready, X suffers a fatal accident. Is D bound to pay anything?

Swift Canadian Co. v. Banet

United States Court of Appeals, Third Circuit, 1955.
224 F.2d 36.

Action to recover from buyer of goods, for breach of contract. In the United States District Court for the Eastern District of Pennsylvania, George A. Welsh, District Judge, each party moved for summary judgment upon stipulated facts, and the buyer's motion was granted. The seller appealed to the Court of Appeals.

Judgment reversed with instructions to enter judgment for plaintiff.

■ GOODRICH, CIRCUIT JUDGE. This is an action on the part of a seller of goods to recover against the buyer for breach of contract. In the trial court each party, following the filing of a stipulation of facts, moved for summary judgment. The court granted the motion of the defendant. Plaintiff here says that it should have had the summary judgment or, at the worst, that the case should be remanded for trial on the facts.

The one point presented is both interesting and elusive. The seller is a Canadian corporation. It entered into an agreement with defendant buyers who do business as Keystone Wool Pullers in Philadelphia. By this contract Keystone agreed to purchase a quantity of lamb pelts at a stipulated price. Part of the quantity was delivered on board railroad cars at Toronto and shipped to Keystone in Philadelphia. On or about March 12, 1952, Swift advised Keystone of its readiness to deliver the remaining pelts to the buyer on board railroad cars in Toronto for shipment to Philadelphia. The parties have stipulated that on or about that day the government of the United States by its agency, the Bureau of Animal Industry, had issued stricter regulations for the importation of lamb pelts into the United States. The parties have stipulated that "pursuant to these regulations, the importation into the United States of these lamb pelts by Keystone was prevented." They have also stipulated that for the reasons just stated Keystone then and thereafter refused to accept delivery of the pelts and the loading and shipment of the car did not occur.

From an inspection of the contract made between the parties it appears that the seller agreed to sell the pelts:

"all at $3.80 each U.S. Funds"

"F.O.B. Toronto."[n]

Below this an approximate time was stipulated for shipment and then there were shipping directions in the following form:

>   Note   Frankford
>
>   Via: Buffalo—Penna. R.R. to
>
>   ~~Broad & Washington Ave.~~
>
>   Freight Sta. Penna. R.R. Delivery.

Following this appears the terms and method of payment.

Two additional conditions of sale should be stated. There was a provision that neither party is to be liable for "orders or acts of any government or governmental agency...." And there was a provision that "when pelts are sold F.O.B. seller's plant title and risk of loss shall pass to buyer when product is loaded on cars at seller's plant."

The one question in this case is the legal effect of this agreement between the parties. If the seller's obligation was performed when it delivered, or offered to deliver, the pelts to the railroad company in Toronto, we think it is entitled to recovery. If the seller did fulfill its obligation, when it did so deliver, of course it is clear that when it failed to load the pelts because the buyer had signified his refusal to accept them, the seller may assert the same rights as though he had loaded them. A party is not obligated to do the vain thing of performing, assuming that he is ready to perform, when the other party has given notice of refusal to accept performance. 3 Williston on Sales, § 586 (Rev. ed., 1948); Restatement, Contracts, §§ 280, 306; Leonard Seed Co. v. Lustig Burgerhoff Co., 1923, 81 Pa. Super. 499. See also Uniform Commercial Code, § 2–610(c); Pa. Stat. Ann. tit. 12A, § 2–610(c) (1954).

The argument for the buyer must rest on the fact that the shipping directions in the contract showed that what the parties had in mind was such kind of performance by the seller as would start the goods to the

---

[n]   F.O.B. is a common trade term that means, in this context, that for the stated price the seller will place the pelts "free on board" a train at the named place, here Toronto. See the similar term "F.A.S." described in footnote g, p. 536 above.

buyer in Philadelphia. This coupled with the stipulation that, in consequence of the stiffening of federal regulations, "the importation into the United States of these lamb pelts by Keystone was prevented," forms the basis for the argument that the carrying out of the agreement was prevented by governmental agency and the buyer is therefore excused.

The validity of this argument depends upon what effect we give to a provision for shipment of the goods to the buyer via Pennsylvania R.R., destination Philadelphia. We do not think that this is any more than a shipping direction which the buyer could have changed to any other destination in the world had it so desired. Suppose the buyer had found that it wanted the goods in New York, could it not have directed such a change in destination without any violation of the contract? Could the seller have insisted that it would ship to Philadelphia and nowhere else? We think that authority in general regards these shipping directions as simply inserted for the convenience of the buyer and subject to change by him. Dwight v. Eckert, 1888, 117 Pa. 490, 12 A. 32; Hocking v. Hamilton, 1893, 158 Pa. 107, 27 A. 836; Richter v. Zoccoli, 1930, 150 A. 1, 8 N.J. Misc. 289; 1 & 2 Williston on Sales, §§ 190, 457 (Rev. ed., 1948). See also Uniform Commercial Code, § 2–319(3); Pa. Stat. Ann. tit. 12A, § 2–319(3) (1954).

If the contract in this case had called for performance "F.O.B. seller's plant" a provision of the contract itself would clearly have indicated when the seller's responsibility was finished and the buyer's had begun.[1] Here the provision in the earlier part of the contract was simply "F.O.B. Toronto" and it was not specifically provided that the sale was delivery at the seller's plant. We think the provision shows what the parties meant by "F.O.B." and can see no difference, so far as this expressed meaning goes, between F.O.B. at seller's plant and F.O.B. Toronto.

The general rule on this subject is pretty clear. Williston points out that when goods are delivered "free on board" pursuant to contract the presumption is that the property passes thereupon. Williston on Sales, § 280(b) (Rev. ed., 1948). It is agreed that this is a presumption and that the phrase F.O.B. is not one of iron-clad meaning. Seabrook Farms Co. v. Commodity Credit Corp., 206 F.2d 93 (3d Cir. 1953). There is nothing in this case, however, to counteract the effect of such a presumption. When the shipper had made his delivery he was to send bill of lading and draft through a Philadelphia bank. His part of the agreement would have been fully performed when the goods were delivered F.O.B. at Toronto. We think both the risk of loss and the possibility of profit if the market advanced, were in the buyer from then on. Even if the goods could not be imported into the United States under the then existing regulations, the rest of the world was free to the buyer, so far as we know, as destination for the shipment. If he did not care to accept them under the circumstances and his expectation of a profitable transaction was

---

[1]   See the second additional condition of sale quoted in the text above.

disappointed, nevertheless, the seller having performed or being ready, able and willing to perform, was entitled to the value of his bargain.

[The court found that the law of Pennsylvania and that of Ontario were identical on the issue involved here, and that the seller's damages were sufficiently proved.]

The judgment of the district court will be reversed with instructions to enter judgment for the plaintiff for the difference between the contract price and the price at which the goods were sold.

NOTE

Variations. Would the decision have been different if the sale contract had provided for delivery F.O.B. Philadelphia rather than Toronto? UCC § 2–319(1) distinguishes between "F.O.B. the place of shipment" and "F.O.B. the place of destination." Given the latter expression, "the seller must at his own expense and risk transport the goods to that place and there tender delivery. . . . " But the entire subsection is qualified by the opening phrase, "Unless otherwise agreed. . . . "

If the seller had undertaken to deliver the pelts in Philadelphia, and had failed to do so because of United States import regulations, would that necessarily be a breach of its duty?

If Canada had regulated the *export* of lamb pelts, so as to require a license, would the Canadian seller have borne the risk that one could not be obtained? Look in the opinion for a remark that might be used to distinguish import from export restrictions. See also Amtorg Trading Corp. v. Miehle Printing Press & Mfg. Co., 206 F.2d 103 (2d Cir.1953).

Chase Precast Corp. v. John J. Paonessa Co.

Supreme Judicial Court of Massachusetts, 1991.
409 Mass. 371, 566 N.E.2d 603.

■ LYNCH, JUSTICE. This appeal raises the question whether the doctrine of frustration of purpose may be a defense in a breach of contract action in Massachusetts, and, if so, whether it excuses the defendant John J. Paonessa Company, Inc. (Paonessa), from performance.

The claim of the plaintiff, Chase Precast Corporation (Chase), arises from the cancellation of its contracts with Paonessa to supply median barriers in a highway reconstruction project of the Commonwealth. Chase brought an action to recover its anticipated profit on the amount of median barriers called for by its supply contracts with Paonessa but not produced. Paonessa brought a cross action against the Commonwealth for indemnification in the event it should be held liable to Chase. After a jury-waived trial, a Superior Court judge ruled for Paonessa on the basis of impossibility of performance.[1] Chase and

---

[1] The judge also ruled that the Department of Public Works had the right to cancel the order for median barriers under its general contracts with Paonessa, particularly under subsection 4.06 of those contracts. See note [5], *infra.*

Paonessa cross appealed. The Appeals Court affirmed, noting that the doctrine of frustration of purpose more accurately described the basis of the trial judge's decision than the doctrine of impossibility. Chase Precast Corp. v. John J. Paonessa Co., 28 Mass. App. Ct. 639, 554 N.E.2d 868 (1990). We agree. We allowed Chase's application for further appellate review, and we now affirm.

The pertinent facts are as follows. In 1982, the Commonwealth, through the Department of Public Works (department), entered into two contracts with Paonessa for resurfacing and improvements to two stretches of Route 128. Part of each contract called for replacing a grass median strip between the north and southbound lanes with concrete surfacing and precast concrete median barriers. Paonessa entered into two contracts with Chase under which Chase was to supply, in the aggregate, 25,800 linear feet of concrete median barriers according to the specifications of the department for highway construction. The quantity and type of barriers to be supplied were specified in two purchase orders prepared by Chase.

The highway reconstruction began in the spring of 1983. By late May, the department was receiving protests from angry residents who objected to use of the concrete median barriers and removal of the grass median strip. Paonessa and Chase became aware of the protest around June 1. On June 6, a group of about 100 citizens filed an action in the Superior Court to stop installation of the concrete median barriers and other aspects of the work. On June 7, anticipating modification by the department, Paonessa notified Chase by letter to stop producing concrete barriers for the projects. Chase did so upon receipt of the letter the following day. On June 17, the department and the citizens' group entered into a settlement which provided, in part, that no additional concrete median barriers would be installed. On June 23, the department deleted the permanent concrete median barriers item from its contracts with Paonessa.

Before stopping production on June 8, Chase had produced approximately one-half of the concrete median barriers called for by its contracts with Paonessa, and had delivered most of them to the construction sites. Paonessa paid Chase for all that it had produced, at the contract price. Chase suffered no out-of-pocket expense as a result of cancellation of the remaining portion of barriers.

This court has long recognized and applied the doctrine of impossibility as a defense to an action for breach of contract. See, e.g., Boston Plate & Window Glass Co. v. John Bowen Co., 335 Mass. 697, 141 N.E.2d 715 (1957); Butterfield v. Byron, 153 Mass. 517, 27 N.E. 667 (1891). Under that doctrine, "where from the nature of the contract it appears that the parties must from the beginning have contemplated the continued existence of some particular specified thing as the foundation of what was to be done, then, in the absence of any warranty that the thing shall exist . . . the parties shall be excused . . . [when] performance becomes impossible from the accidental perishing of the thing without the fault of either party." Boston Plate & Window Glass Co., supra, 335 Mass. at 700, 141 N.E.2d 715, quoting Hawkes v. Kehoe, 193 Mass. 419, 423, 79 N.E. 766 (1907).

On the other hand, although we have referred to the doctrine of frustration of purpose in a few decisions, we have never clearly defined it. See Mishara Constr. Co. v. Transit-Mixed Concrete Corp., 365 Mass. 122, 128–129, 310 N.E.2d 363 (1974). Other jurisdictions have explained the doctrine as follows: when an event neither anticipated nor caused by either party, the risk of which was not allocated by the contract, destroys the object or purpose of the contract, thus destroying the value of performance, the parties are excused from further performance. See Lloyd v. Murphy, 25 Cal.2d 48, 153 P.2d 47 (1944).

In Mishara Constr. Co., supra, 365 Mass. at 129, 310 N.E.2d 363, we called frustration of purpose a "companion rule" to the doctrine of impossibility. Both doctrines concern the effect of supervening circumstances upon the rights and duties of the parties. The difference lies in the effect of the supervening event. Under frustration, "[p]erformance remains possible but the expected value of performance to the party seeking to be excused has been destroyed by [the] fortuitous event. . . . "[2] Lloyd v. Murphy, supra, 25 Cal.2d at 53, 153 P.2d 47. The principal question in both kinds of cases remains "whether an unanticipated circumstance, the risk of which should not fairly be thrown on the promisor, has made performance vitally different from what was reasonably to be expected." See Lloyd, supra at 54, 153 P.2d 47 (frustration); Mishara Constr. Co., supra, 365 Mass. at 129, 310 N.E.2d 363 (impossibility).

Since the two doctrines differ only in the effect of the fortuitous supervening event, it is appropriate to look to our cases dealing with impossibility for guidance in treating the issues that are the same in a frustration of purpose case.[3] The trial judge's findings with regard to those issues are no less pertinent to application of the frustration defense because they were considered relevant to the defense of impossibility.

Another definition of frustration of purpose is found in the Restatement (Second) of Contracts § 265 (1981):

> "Where, after a contract is made, a party's principal purpose is
> substantially frustrated without his fault by the occurrence of
> an event the non-occurrence of which was a basic assumption on
> which the contract was made, his remaining duties to render

---

[2]   Clearly frustration of purpose is a more accurate label for the defense argued in this case than impossibility of performance, since, as the Appeals Court pointed out, "[p]erformance was not literally impossible. Nothing prevented Paonessa from honoring its contract to purchase the remaining sections of median barrier, whether or not the [department] would approve their use in the road construction." 28 Mass. App. Ct. 639, 644 n. 5, 554 N.E.2d 868 (1990).

[3]   Those issues include the foreseeability of the supervening event, allocation of the risk of occurrence of the event, and the degree of hardship to the promisor. . . .

performance are discharged, unless the language or the circumstances indicate the contrary."

This definition is nearly identical to the defense of "commercial impracticability," found in the Uniform Commercial Code, G.L. c. 106, § 2–615 (1988 ed.),[4] which this court, in Mishara Constr. Co., supra at 127–128, 310 N.E.2d 363, held to be consistent with the common law of contracts regarding impossibility of performance. It follows, therefore, that the Restatement's formulation of the doctrine is consistent with this court's previous treatment of impossibility of performance and frustration of purpose.

Paonessa bore no responsibility for the department's elimination of the median barriers from the projects. Therefore, whether it can rely on the defense of frustration turns on whether elimination of the barriers was a risk allocated by the contracts to Paonessa. Mishara Constr. Co., supra, 365 Mass. at 129, articulates the relevant test:

> "The question is, given the commercial circumstances in which the parties dealt: Was the contingency which developed one which the parties could reasonably be thought to have foreseen as a real possibility which could affect performance? Was it one of that variety of risks which the parties were tacitly assigning to the promisor by their failure to provide for it explicitly? If it was, performance will be required. If it could not be so considered, performance is excused."

This is a question for the trier of fact. Id. at 127, 130, 310 N.E.2d 363.

Paonessa's contracts with the department contained a standard provision allowing the department to eliminate items or portions of work found unnecessary.[5] The purchase order agreements between Chase and Paonessa do not contain a similar provision. This difference in the contracts does not mandate the conclusion that Paonessa assumed the risk of reduction in the quantity of the barriers. It is implicit in the judge's findings that Chase knew the barriers were for department projects. The record supports the conclusion that Chase was aware of the department's power to decrease quantities of contract items. The judge found that Chase had been a supplier of median barriers to the

---

[4] That section states that performance is excused when it has been made "impracticable by the occurrence of a contingency the non-occurrence of which was a basic assumption on which the contract was made." G.L. c. 106, § 2–615.

[5] The contracts contained the following provision:

"4.06 Increased or Decreased Contract Quantities."

"When the accepted quantities of work vary from the quantities in the bid schedule, the Contractor shall accept as payment in full, so far as contract items are concerned, payment at the original contract unit prices for the accepted quantities of work done."

"The Engineer may order omitted from the work any items or portions of work found unnecessary to the improvement and such omission shall not operate as a waiver of any condition of the Contract nor invalidate any of the provisions thereof, nor shall the Contractor have any claim for anticipated profit."

"No allowance will be made for any increased expenses, loss of expected reimbursement therefor or from any other cause."

department in the past. The provision giving the department the power to eliminate items or portions thereof was standard in its contracts. See Standard Specifications for Highways and Bridges, Commonwealth of Massachusetts Department of Public Works § 4.06 (1973). The judge found that Chase had furnished materials under and was familiar with the so-called "Unit Price Philosophy" in the construction industry, whereby contract items are paid for at the contract unit price for the quantity of work actually accepted. Finally, the judge's finding that "[a]ll parties were well aware that lost profits were not an element of damage in either of the public works projects in issue" further supports the conclusion that Chase was aware of the department's power to decrease quantities, since the term prohibiting claims for anticipated profit is part of the same sentence in the standard provision as that allowing the engineer to eliminate items or portions of work.

In Mishara Constr. Co., supra at 130, 310 N.E.2d 363, we held that, although labor disputes in general cannot be considered extraordinary, whether the parties in a particular case intended performance to be carried out, even in the face of a labor difficulty, depends on the facts known to the parties at the time of contracting with respect to the history of and prospects for labor difficulties. In this case, even if the parties were aware generally of the department's power to eliminate contract items, the judge could reasonably have concluded that they did not contemplate the cancellation for a major portion of the project of such a widely used item as concrete median barriers, and did not allocate the risk of such cancellation.[6]

Our opinion in Chicopee Concrete Serv., Inc. v. Hart Eng'g Co., 398 Mass. 476, 498 N.E.2d 121 (1986), does not lead to a different conclusion. Although we held there that a provision of a prime contract requiring city approval of subcontractors was not incorporated by reference into the subcontract, id. at 478, 498 N.E.2d 121, we nevertheless stated that, if the record had supported the conclusion that the subcontractor knew, or at least had notice of, the approval clause, the result might have been different. Id. at 478–479, 498 N.E.2d 121.[7]

---

[6]   The judge did not explicitly find that cancellation of the barriers was not contemplated and that the risk of their elimination was not allocated by the contracts. However, the judge's decision imports every finding essential to sustain it if there is evidence to support it. Mailer v. Mailer, 390 Mass. 371, 373, 455 N.E.2d 1211 (1983).

[7]   This court held in John Soley & Sons v. Jones, 208 Mass. 561, 566–567, 95 N.E. 94 (1911), that, where by its terms the prime contract could be cancelled if the defendant was not making sufficient progress on the work, and the plaintiff knew of the article of cancellation, nevertheless, even if it was mutually understood that the defendant did not intend to perform unless the prime contract remained in force, the defendant was not relieved from performance on the ground of impossibility where it failed to provide for the risk of cancellation in its contract with the plaintiff. To the extent that holding is contrary to our decision in this case, we decline to follow it, and refer to our adoption in Mishara Constr. Co., supra, 365 Mass. at 130, 310 N.E.2d 363, of the following statement: "Rather than mechanically apply any fixed rule of law, where the parties themselves have not allocated responsibility, justice is better served by appraising all of the circumstances, the part the various parties played, and thereon determining liability," quoting Badhwar v. Colorado Fuel & Iron Corp., 138 F.Supp. 595, 607 (S.D.N.Y.1955), aff'd, 245 F.2d 903 (2d Cir.1957). See West Los Angeles Inst. for Cancer

Judgment affirmed.

NOTE

Stranded Buyers. In Note 2, p. 1073 above, the term "stranded seller" is used for sellers who plead impracticability because their supplies were choked off. The situation of Paonessa was the converse: its contract with Chase Precast designated a customer, and it lost the patronage of that customer. Paonessa was a "stranded buyer," one might say.

It is a striking fact about UCC § 2–615 that, on its face, the section has no bearing on the problem in *Chase Precast*: it makes no provision for a stranded buyer. In the case next presented, a buyer ("NIPSCO") sought to be excused under the doctrine of frustration. The court alluded to the question whether or not a buyer can ever claim excuse under UCC § 2–615. That part of the opinion is omitted; it provides no answer. If applicable, the court concluded, UCC § 2–615 would be of no more avail to the buyer than the common law of frustration. The enactment of the Code did not displace that law, the court said, citing UCC § 1–103.

As to the question of whether or not UCC § 2–615 can be applied in favor of a buyer, in an appropriate case, the court considered Indiana law. It quoted from Comment 9 to the section: "the reason of the present section may well apply and entitle the buyer to the exemption." The court cited several precedents, although in none of the cases was a buyer exempted. The court noted, on the other hand, that the Indiana legislature had not enacted the Code comments. No legislature has. Most states, like Indiana, have their own state comments—none of them having been enacted either.

Laying aside the case of severe currency deflation, and the case of a buyer's cash shortage (usually an allocated risk), it is not easy to suppose situations in which it is impracticable for a buyer to pay. Considering the "reason" of UCC § 2–615, does it support the decision in the main case?

PROBLEMS

(1)   Heavyside Company was a franchised dealer in farm equipment for the International Harvester Company (IH). After a dramatic downturn in the market for farm equipment, which caused IH to lose $4 billion in four years, it concluded that it had no alternative but to go into bankruptcy or to sell off its farm implement division. It decided to do the latter, receiving for its assets hundreds of millions, in cash and stock, from J.I. Case Company and an affiliate. Although Case did not acquire the IH franchise network, it offered franchises to many IH dealers. Heavyside was not one of these, for Case already had a dealer in the area. Heavyside sued IH for breach of contract. Does IH have the defense of impracticability? Of frustration? See Karl Wendt Farm Equip. Co. v. International Harvester Co., 931 F.2d 1112 (6th Cir. 1991).

Research v. Mayer, 366 F.2d 220, 225 (9th Cir.1966), cert. denied, 385 U.S. 1010 (1967) ("foreseeability of the frustrating event is not alone enough to bar rescission if it appears that the parties did not intend the promisor to assume the risk of its occurrence").

(2) The Precision Parts Company contracted with Micro Manufacturing, Inc. to produce and deliver a specialized machine part, a custom gear box. Micro cancelled the contract when Precision's work was almost complete. It did so as a consequence of the first Gulf War in the early 1990s. Micro's reason for buying the gear box was to incorporate it into a piece of equipment called a human centrifuge. Iraqi Airways had ordered that equipment from Micro. But Micro lost interest in the gear box when, in connection with the war, the United Nations placed an embargo on shipments to Iraq like the one Micro had counted on. In an action by Precision against Micro for breach of the gear-box contract, Micro defended on the ground of frustration of purpose. It appeared that (a) Precision had not been told, before the cancellation, what the gear box was wanted for. Also that (b) after the cancellation, Precision had completed work on the item and sold it to the Macro Corporation for very nearly the price Micro had agreed to pay. Do both of these circumstances—(a) and (b)—run counter to Micro's frustration defense? If so, which is the more compelling? See Power Engineering & Mfg. v. Krug International, 501 N.W.2d 490 (Iowa 1993).

Northern Indiana Public Service Co. v. Carbon County Coal Co.

United States Court of Appeals, Seventh Circuit, 1986.
799 F.2d 265.

■ POSNER, CIRCUIT JUDGE. These appeals bring before us various facets of a dispute between Northern Indiana Public Service Company (NIPSCO), an electric utility in Indiana, and Carbon County Coal Company, a partnership that until recently owned and operated a coal mine in Wyoming. In 1978 NIPSCO and Carbon County signed a contract whereby Carbon County agreed to sell and NIPSCO to buy approximately 1.5 million tons of coal every year for 20 years, at a price of $24 a ton subject to various provisions for escalation which by 1985 had driven the price up to $44 a ton.

NIPSCO's rates are regulated by the Indiana Public Service Commission. In 1983 NIPSCO requested permission to raise its rates to reflect increased fuel charges. Some customers of NIPSCO opposed the increase on the ground that NIPSCO could reduce its overall costs by buying more electrical power from neighboring utilities for resale to its customers and producing less of its own power. Although the Commission granted the requested increase, it directed NIPSCO, in orders issued in December 1983 and February 1984 (the "economy purchase orders"), to make a good faith effort to find, and wherever possible buy from, utilities that would sell electricity to it at prices lower than its costs of internal generation. The Commission added ominously that "the adverse effects of entering into long-term coal supply contracts which do not allow for renegotiation and are not requirement contracts, is a burden which must rest squarely on the shoulders of NIPSCO management." Actually the contract with Carbon County did provide for renegotiation of the contract price—but one-way renegotiation in favor of Carbon County; the price fixed in the contract (as adjusted from time to time in accordance with the escalator provisions) was a floor. And the contract was indeed not a requirements contract: it specified the exact amount of coal that NIPSCO must take over the 20 years during which the contract was to remain in effect. NIPSCO was eager to have an assured supply of low-sulphur coal and was therefore willing to guarantee both price and quantity.

Unfortunately for NIPSCO, as things turned out it was indeed able to buy electricity at prices below the costs of generating electricity from coal bought under the contract with Carbon County; and because of the "economy purchase orders," of which it had not sought judicial review, NIPSCO could not expect to be allowed by the Public Service Commission to recover in its electrical rates the costs of buying coal from Carbon County. NIPSCO therefore decided to stop accepting coal deliveries from Carbon County, at least for the time being; and on April 24, 1985, it brought this diversity suit against Carbon County in a federal district court in Indiana, seeking a declaration that it was excused from its obligations under the contract either permanently or at least until the economy purchase orders ceased preventing it from passing on the costs of the contract to its ratepayers. In support of this position it argued that the contract violated section 2(c) of the Mineral Lands Leasing Act of 1920, 30 U.S.C. § 202, because of Carbon County's affiliation with a railroad (Union Pacific), and that in any event NIPSCO's performance was excused or suspended—either under the contract's *force majeure* clause or under the doctrines of frustration or impossibility—by reason of the economy purchase orders.

On May 17, 1985, Carbon County counterclaimed for breach of contract and moved for a preliminary injunction requiring NIPSCO to continue taking delivery under the contract. On June 19, 1985, the district judge granted the preliminary injunction, from which NIPSCO has appealed. Also on June 19, rejecting NIPSCO's argument that it needed more time for pretrial discovery and other trial preparations, the judge scheduled the trial to begin on August 26, 1985. Trial did begin then, lasted for six weeks, and resulted in a jury verdict for Carbon County of $181 million. The judge entered judgment in accordance with the verdict, rejecting Carbon County's argument that in lieu of damages it should get an order of specific performance requiring NIPSCO to comply with the contract. Upon entering the final judgment the district judge dissolved the preliminary injunction, and shortly afterward the mine—whose only customer was NIPSCO—shut down. NIPSCO has appealed from the damage judgment, and Carbon County from the denial of specific performance.

[Here the court considered a provision of the contract, saying, "This is what is known as a *force majeure* clause." The provision permitted NIPSCO to stop taking delivery of coal.]

[for any cause beyond (its) reasonable control . . . including but not limited to . . . orders or acts of civil . . . authority . . . which wholly or partly prevent . . . the utilizing . . . of the coal.]

[According to NIPSCO, the "economy purchase orders" of the Indiana Public Service Commission had prevented it, at least in part, from using the coal that it had agreed to buy. To that the court answered: "It is evident that the clause was not triggered by the orders."]

All that those orders do is tell NIPSCO it will not be allowed to pass on fuel costs to its ratepayers in the form of higher rates if it can buy electricity cheaper than it can generate electricity internally using Carbon County's coal. Such an order does not "prevent," whether wholly or in part, NIPSCO from using the coal; it just prevents NIPSCO from shifting the burden of its improvidence or bad luck in having incorrectly forecasted its fuel needs to the backs of the hapless ratepayers. By signing the kind of contract it did, NIPSCO gambled that fuel costs would rise rather than fall over the life of the contract; for if they rose, the contract price would give it an advantage over its (hypothetical) competitors who would have to buy fuel at the current market price. If such a gamble fails, the result is not *force majeure*.

This is all the clearer when we consider that the contract price was actually fixed just on the downside; it put a floor under the price NIPSCO had to pay, but the escalator provisions allowed the actual contract prices to rise above the floor, and they did. This underscores the gamble NIPSCO took in signing the contract. It committed itself to paying a price at or above a fixed minimum and to taking a fixed quantity at that price. It was willing to make this commitment to secure an assured supply of low-sulphur coal, but the risk it took was that the market price of coal or substitute fuels would fall. A *force majeure* clause is not intended to buffer a party against the normal risks of a contract. The normal risk of a fixed-price contract is that the market price will change. If it rises, the buyer gains at the expense of the seller (except insofar as escalator provisions give the seller some protection); if it falls, as here, the seller gains at the expense of the buyer. The whole purpose of a fixed-price contract is to allocate risk in this way. A *force majeure* clause interpreted to excuse the buyer from the consequences of the risk he expressly assumed would nullify a central term of the contract.

[Here, the court compared the market in which NIPSCO operated—a regulated one—with unregulated ones. Assuming an unregulated and fully competitive market, Judge Posner observed, if fuel costs were to drop after NIPSCO made a long-term, fixed price contract for coal, it could expect to suffer a loss. Conversely, if fuel costs were to increase, it could expect a gain at the expense of competitors. "The chance of this 'windfall' gain offsets, on an ex ante (before the fact) basis, the chance of a windfall loss if fuel costs drop."]

The Indiana Public Service Commission is a surrogate for the forces of competition, and the economy fuel orders are a device for simulating the effects in a competitive market of a drop in input prices. The orders say to NIPSCO, in effect: "With fuel costs dropping, and thus reducing the costs of electricity to utilities not burdened by long-term fixed-price contracts, you had better substitute those utilities' electricity for your own when their prices are lower than your cost of internal generation. In a freely competitive market consumers would make that substitution; if you do not do so, don't expect to be allowed to pass on your inflated fuel costs to those consumers." If as is likely the Public Service Commission would require NIPSCO to pass on any capital gain from an advantageous contract to the ratepayers, then it ought to allow NIPSCO to pass on to them some of the capital loss from a disadvantageous contract—provided that the contract, when made, was prudent. Maybe it was not; maybe the risk that NIPSCO took was excessive. But all this was a matter between NIPSCO and the Public Service Commission, and NIPSCO did not seek judicial review of the economy purchase orders.

If the Commission had ordered NIPSCO to close a plant because of a safety or pollution hazard, we would have a true case of *force majeure*. As a regulated firm NIPSCO is subject to more extensive controls than unregulated firms and it therefore wanted and got a broadly worded *force majeure* clause that would protect it fully (hence the reference to partial effects) against government actions that impeded its using the coal. But as the only thing the Commission did was prevent NIPSCO from using its monopoly position to make consumers bear the risk that NIPSCO assumed when it signed a long-term fixed-price fuel contract, NIPSCO cannot complain of *force majeure;* the risk that has come to pass was one that NIPSCO voluntarily assumed when it signed the contract.

The district judge refused to submit NIPSCO's defenses of impracticability and frustration to the jury, ruling that Indiana law does not allow a buyer to claim impracticability and does not recognize the defense of frustration.

Section 2–615 of the Uniform Commercial Code takes this approach. It provides that "delay in delivery . . . by a seller . . . is not a breach of his duty under a contract for sale if performance as agreed has been made impracticable by the occurrence of a contingency the non-occurrence of which was a basic assumption on which the contract was made. . . . " Performance on schedule need not be impossible, only infeasible— provided that the event which made it infeasible was not a risk that the promisor had assumed. Notice, however, that the only type of promisor referred to is a seller; there is no suggestion that a buyer's performance might be excused by reason of impracticability. The reason is largely semantic. Ordinarily all the buyer has to do in order to perform his side of the bargain is pay, and while one can think of all sorts of reasons why, when the time came to pay, the buyer might not have the money, rarely would the seller have intended to assume the risk that the buyer might, whether through improvidence or bad luck, be unable to pay for the seller's goods or services. To deal with the rare case where the buyer or (more broadly) the paying party might have a good excuse based on some unforeseen change in circumstances, a new rubric was thought necessary, different from "impossibility" (the common law term) or "impracticability" (the Code term, picked up in Restatement (Second) of Contracts § 261 (1979)), and it received the name "frustration." Rarely is it impracticable or impossible for the payor to pay; but if something has happened to make the performance for which he would be paying worthless to him, an excuse for not paying, analogous to impracticability or impossibility, may be proper. See Restatement, supra, § 265, Comment *a*.

NIPSCO is the buyer in the present case, and its defense is more properly frustration than impracticability; but the judge held that frustration is not a contract defense under the law of Indiana. At all events, the facts of the present case do not bring it within the scope of the frustration doctrine, so we need not decide whether the Indiana Supreme Court would embrace the doctrine in a suitable case.

For the same reason, we need not decide whether a *force majeure* clause should be deemed a relinquishment of a party's right to argue impracticability or frustration, on the theory that such a clause represents the integrated expression of the parties' desires with respect to excuses based on supervening events; or whether such a clause either in general or as specifically worded in this case covers any different ground from these defenses; or whether a buyer can urge impracticability under section 2–615 of the Uniform Commercial Code, which applies to this suit. [Much of what the court had to say about the latter question is indicated in the Note, p. 1099 above.]

Whether or not Indiana recognizes the doctrine of frustration, and whether or not a buyer can ever assert the defense of impracticability under section 2–615 of the Uniform Commercial Code, these doctrines, so closely related to each other and to *force majeure* as well, cannot help NIPSCO. All are doctrines for shifting risk to the party better able to bear it, either because he is in a better position to prevent the risk from materializing or because he can better reduce the disutility of the risk (as by insuring) if the risk does occur.

Since impossibility and related doctrines are devices for shifting risk in accordance with the parties' presumed intentions, which are to minimize the costs of contract performance, one of which is the disutility created by risk, they have no place when the contract explicitly assigns a particular risk to one party or the other. As we have already noted, a fixed-price contract is an explicit assignment of the risk of market price increases to the seller and the risk of market price decreases to the buyer, and the assignment of the latter risk to the buyer is even clearer where, as in this case, the contract places a floor under price but allows for escalation. If, as is also the case here, the buyer forecasts the market incorrectly and therefore finds himself locked into a disadvantageous contract, he has only himself to blame and so cannot shift the risk back to the seller by invoking impossibility or related doctrines. It does not matter that it is an act of government that may have made the contract less advantageous to one party. Government these days is a pervasive factor in the economy and among the risks that a fixed-price contract allocates between the parties is that of a price change induced by one of government's manifold interventions in the economy. Since "the very purpose of a fixed price agreement is to place the risk of increased costs on the promisor (and the risk of decreased costs on the promisee)," the fact that costs decrease steeply (which is in effect what happened here—the cost of generating electricity turned out to be lower than NIPSCO thought when it signed the fixed price contract with Carbon County) cannot allow the buyer to walk away from the contract.

[Affirmed.]

NOTES

(1) *We're All Frustrated.* In the case above, the court went on to hold that Carbon County was not entitled to specific performance which "would force the continuation of production that has become uneconomical." The workers and merchants where Carbon County's mine was located suffered hardship when the mine shutdown, although they were not parties to the contract or third party beneficiaries. But, assume that some of these workers and merchants entered into contracts with other parties, contracts of little value following the mine closing. Might some have plausible claims of frustration of purpose? How foreseeable is the closing of a coal mine in a highly fluctuating market for coal and electricity? More or less foreseeable than a King's coronation being cancelled?

(2) *Market Discipline and Government Discipline.* Judge Posner, in the opinion above, made these further observations about the market for electricity, assuming it to be unregulated and fully competitive:

> If NIPSCO signed a long-term fixed-price fixed-quantity contract to buy coal, and during the life of the contract competing electrical companies were able to produce and sell electricity at prices below the cost to NIPSCO of producing electricity from that coal, NIPSCO would have to swallow the excess cost of the coal. It could not raise its electricity prices in order to pass on the excess cost to its consumers, because if it did they would buy electricity at lower prices from NIPSCO's competitors. Admittedly, the comparison between competition and regulation is not exact. [But the] purpose of public utility regulation is to provide a substitute for competition in markets (such as the market for electricity) that are naturally monopolistic.

Id. at 275.

In discussing NIPSCO's prospect of a "windfall gain," the court did not suppose that this was NIPSCO's object in making the contract. Rather: "NIPSCO it appears was seeking a secure source of low-sulphur coal. . . . " As one reason for thinking that, the court surmised that the Public Service

Commission would not have permitted NIPSCO to translate such a gain into profit. Do you see a suggestion in the opinion that the Commission should— within limits—permit that?

(3) *Take-or-Pay: Reprise.* The character of a take-or-pay clause is described, and contrasted with that of a take-and-pay clause, p. 1003 above. Consider a change of circumstances that would excuse a buyer from taking and paying, owing to frustration of purpose. Does it follow that the same buyer would be excused, in the same circumstances, if its contract required it to take *or* pay? For an indication that *force majeure* clauses, identical in terms, might—other things being equal—excuse an "and pay" obligation, but not an "or pay" obligation, see International Minerals & Chemical Corp. v. Llano, Inc., 770 F.2d 879 (10th Cir. 1985). (There, however, the buyer got relief under a provision about adjusting its minimum purchase requirements.)

SECTION 5.   HALF MEASURES

What further consequences follow when a party is excused from performance on the ground of impracticability or frustration? One consequence is that, because of the operation of the concept of constructive conditions of exchange, the other party is excused from having to render any further performance. But this will not serve to compensate either party for losses incurred in reliance on the contract before the parties were excused. To what extent have courts in such situations been receptive to "half measures"°—to relief that stands somewhere between strict enforcement and complete excuse?

If the contract can be treated as divisible, a court may hold that the parties are excused only as to part of their performances. See Gill v. Johnstown Lumber Co., p. 822 above. If the losses incurred in reliance have resulted in a benefit to the other party, usually restitution will be allowed. Beyond that, however, courts have not ventured far. The Restatement states, in one of its more audacious pronouncements, that if the traditional rules "will not avoid injustice, the court may grant relief on such terms as justice requires including protection of the parties' reliance interests." Restatement § 272. Materials below examine some of the support for that assertion.

NOTE

A Test Case. The problems addressed in this section are illustrated by the facts of a well-known British case. The outbreak of World War II made it impossible for a British firm to perform an export contract it had made to manufacture and deliver industrial (flax-hackling) machines. It had received an advance payment of £1,000 from the buyer, a Polish firm. The buyer brought the action to recover that payment. The seller objected that it had

---

° See William Young, *Half Measures*, 81 Colum. L. Rev. 19, 20 (1981), noting "that half measure relief is equivalent to a court-imposed compromise."

incurred expenses in preparing the machines that it could not recapture. For this discussion let it be assumed that these expenses amounted to £800.

Several ways of assigning rights to these parties can be imagined. One is to award £200 to the buyer, recognizing the buyer's restitution interest, but offsetting it by the seller's reliance interest. The House of Lords chose to award full recovery—£1000—to the buyer. Fibrosa Spolka Akcyjna v. Fairbairn Lawson Combe Barbour, Ltd., [1943] A.C. 32, 144 A.L.R. 1298. Being dissatisfied with that, Parliament redirected the law by a statute described below (p. 1112).

Another possibility is to deny any recovery to the buyer, leaving matters as they stand. A "do nothing" rule has scholarly support in the United States, see p. 1044 above. That was once the so-called English rule: "that the loss must remain where it first falls, and that neither of the parties can recover of the other for anything done under the contract." Butterfield v. Byron, 27 N.E. 667, 668 (Mass. 1891). In Krell v. Henry, above, it is reported that Henry made an advance payment of £25 for the use of Krell's rooms to view the coronation. The *Fibrosa* decision indicates that Krell would owe Henry restitution of that amount. Earlier, however, restitution had been denied in other cases concerning the coronation of Edward VII.

On reading the materials that follow, consider how a United States court might deal with the facts of *Fibrosa*.

Impracticability and Reliance

To the extent that before a party's performance became impracticable, it has conferred a benefit on the other party through part performance, the courts are receptive to a claim for restitution. Similarly, restitutionary relief is often available when a contract has been terminated by the doctrine of frustration. (*Fibrosa* is an example.) Restatement § 272 recognizes restitution as one form of relief available in these situations. A restitution award may be made also when a contract is rescinded for mistake. (Renner v. Kehl, p. 1026 above, is an illustration.)

The amount of compensable benefit is sometimes debatable. A judicial pronouncement by Cardozo has been influential. The case was Buccini v. Paterno Construction Company, 170 N.E. 910 (N.Y. 1930). The company had engaged Alberto Buccini to give personal attention to some decorative design work, and he had died before completing it. As indicated in Note 2, p. 1054 above, further performance by Buccini was excused. Recognizing that, Cardozo proceeded, in dictum,[p] as follows:

> The parties may say by their contract what compensation shall be made in the event of that excuse. The award will then

---

[p] The action was one brought by Flora Buccini, as executrix of her husband's estate, to compel arbitration of the estate's claim. The court approved an award of relief, relying on an arbitration term in the contract.

conform to the expression of their will. They may leave the subject open, to be governed by the law itself. The award will then conform to the principles of liability in quasi-contract and to the considerations of equity and justice by which that liability is governed. . . . The interrupted work may have been better than any called for by the plans. . . . The value proportionately distributed may be greater than the contract price. Even so, the price, and not the value, will be the maximum beyond which the judgment may not go (Clark v. Gilbert, 26 N.Y. 279, 283). "The recovery in such a case cannot exceed the contract price, or the rate of it for the part of the service performed" (Clark v. Gilbert, *supra*). The question to be determined is not the value of the work considered by itself and unrelated to the contract. The question to be determined is the benefit to the owner in advancement of the ends to be promoted by the contract.

The final sentence suggests a generous measure of restitution claims.

NOTES

(1) *The Case of Cutter's Contingency.* Cutter, a seaman of the 18th century, signed on in Jamaica as second mate aboard the ship *Governor Parry*. His pay was to be thirty guineas [one guinea being worth £1.05], "provided the proceeds, continues and does his duty as second mate in the said ship from hence to the port of Liverpool." The ship sailed from Jamaica on August 2 with Cutter on board and arrived at Liverpool on October 9, but Cutter had died on September 20. The usual wage for a second mate on such a voyage, if fixed by the month for a round-trip voyage, was £4 per month, roughly a quarter of what Cutter had been promised. Cutter's administratrix sued for the thirty guineas. *Held:* Judgment for defendant.

> "[I]f there been no contract between these parties, all that the intestate could have recovered . . . for the voyage would have been eight pounds; whereas here the defendant contracted to pay thirty guineas provided the mate continued to do his duty as mate during the whole voyage, in which case the latter would have received nearly four times as much as if he were paid for the number of months he served. He stipulated to receive the larger sum if the whole duty were performed, and nothing unless the whole of that duty were performed; it was a kind of insurance."

Cutter v. Powell, [1795] 101 Eng. Rep. 573 (K.B.).

Do you agree? In what sense was there "a kind of insurance"? Does Cutter v. Powell illustrate what Cardozo said with reference to death as an excuse: "The parties may say by their contract what compensation shall be made in the event of that excuse"?

(2) *The Case of the House Halfway.* Owner contracted with Mover to have a building on Third Street relocated to First Street, at a fixed price. When Mover had gotten it about halfway, and quit work for the night, it was consumed by fire, through no fault of Mover. Owner disclaimed any liability,

and Mover sued for the fair value of the services rendered in the work down to the time of the fire. Mover obtained a judgment on a jury verdict (amount unspecified), and Owner appealed. *Held:* Affirmed. Angus v. Scully, 57 N.E. 674 (Mass. 1900). Do you find support for this decision in Cardozo's statement, "The question to be determined is the benefit to the owner in advancement of the ends to be promoted by the contract"?

Young v. City of Chicopee

Supreme Judicial Court of Massachusetts, 1904.
186 Mass. 518, 72 N.E. 63.

■ HAMMOND, JUSTICE. This is an action to recover for work and materials furnished under a written contract providing for the repair of a wooden bridge forming a part of the highway across the Connecticut river. While the work was in progress the bridge was totally destroyed by fire without the fault of either party, so that the contract could not be performed. The specifications required that the timber and other woodwork of the carriageway, wherever decayed, should be replaced by sound material, securely fastened, so that the way should be in "a complete and substantial condition." As full compensation both for work and materials, the plaintiff was to receive a certain sum per thousand feet for the lumber used "on measurements made after laying and certified by the engineers"; or, in other words, the amount of the plaintiff's compensation was measured by the number of feet of new material wrought into the bridge. That the public travel might not be interfered with more than was reasonably necessary, the contract provided that no work should be begun until material for at least one-half of the repairs contemplated should be "upon the job." With this condition the plaintiff complied, the lumber, which, at the time of the fire had not been used, being distributed "all along the bridge" and upon the river banks. Some of this lumber was destroyed by the fire. At the trial the defendant did not dispute its liability to pay for the work done upon and materials wrought into the structure at the time of the fire (Angus v. Scully, 176 Mass. 357, 57 N.E. 674, 49 L.R.A. 562, 79 Am.St.Rep. 318, and cases there cited), and the only question before us is whether it was liable for the damage to the lumber which was distributed as above stated and had not been used. It is to be noted that there had been no delivery of this lumber to the defendant. It was brought "upon the job," and kept there as the lumber of the plaintiff. The title to it was in him, and not in the defendant. Nor did the defendant have any care or control over it. No part of it belonged to the defendant until wrought into the bridge. The plaintiff could have exchanged it for other lumber. If at any time during the progress of the work before the fire the plaintiff had refused to proceed, the defendant, against his consent, could not lawfully have used it. Indeed, had it not been destroyed, it would have remained the property of the plaintiff after the fire. Nor is the situation changed, so far as respects the question before us, by the fact that the lumber was brought there in compliance with the condition relating to the commencement of the work. This condition manifestly was inserted to insure the rapid progress of the work, and it has no material bearing upon the rights of the parties in relation to the lumber. It is also to be borne in mind in this connection that the compensation for the whole job was to be determined by the amount of lumber wrought into the bridge. The contract was entire. By the destruction of the bridge each party was excused from further performance, and the plaintiff could recover for partial performance. The principle upon which the plaintiff can do this is sometimes said to rest upon the doctrine that there is an implied contract upon the owner of the structure upon which the work is to be done that it shall continue to exist, and therefore, if it is destroyed, even without his fault, still he must be regarded as in default, and so liable to pay for what has been done. Niblo v. Binsse, 40 N.Y. 476; Whelen v. Ansonia Clock Co., 97 N.Y. 293. In Butterfield v. Byron, 153 Mass. 523, 12 L.R.A. 571, 25 Am. St. Rep. 654, it was said by Knowlton, J., that there was "an implied assumpsit for what has properly been done by either [of the parties], the law dealing with it as done at the request of the other, and creating a liability to pay for it its value." In whatever way the principle may be stated, it would seem that the liability of the owner in a case like this should be measured by the amount of the contract work done which at the time of the destruction of the structure had become so far identified with it as that, but for the destruction, it would have inured to him as contemplated by the contract. In the present case the defendant, in accordance with this doctrine, should be held liable for the labor and materials actually wrought into the bridge. To that extent it insured the plaintiff. But it did not insure the plaintiff against the loss of lumber owned by him at the time of the fire, which had not then come into such relations with the bridge as, but for the fire, to inure to the benefit of the defendant, as contemplated by the contract. The cases of Haynes v. Second Baptist Church, 88 Mo. 285, 57 Am. Rep. 413, and Rawson v. Clark, 70 Ill. 656, cited by the plaintiff, seem to us to be distinguishable from this case.

The exceptions therefore must be sustained, and the verdict set aside. In accordance with the terms of the statement contained in the bill of exceptions, judgment should be entered for the plaintiff in the sum of $584 damages, and it is so ordered.

NOTES

(1) *You're Both Excused.* In *Chicopee*, the court observes that "[b]y the destruction of the bridge each party was excused from further performance." On what basis do you imagine an excuse was granted for each party?

(2) *Multiple and Divisible Contracts.* As a variation on the facts of Young's case, suppose that he had made separate contracts with the City— one for the sale of materials, requiring payment by the City when they arrived at the work site, and another for doing the repair work. Would the fire have had different consequences? If so, how different?

Given a single contract, for work and materials, assume that the fire was confined to the bridge, not consuming lumber stacked aside the river. How would you assess a claim by the City that it could appropriate that lumber for other projects, on the ground that the contract was divisible?

(3) *Repair Versus Building.* Young's case would have been quite different if he had contracted to erect a bridge from scratch, rather than to repair one. In that case, the risk of chance destruction of the bridge would have rested entirely on him, it seems, absent an agreement to the contrary. See Note 3, p. 1054 above. Aside from the analogy of Taylor v. Caldwell, above, what might account for the difference between construction contracts and repair contracts?

Reliance Interests

Restatement Chapter 11, which states rules about impracticability of performance and frustration of purpose, concludes with the statement that, in some circumstances, a court may grant relief "on such terms as justice requires including protection of the parties' reliance interests." Section 272(2). Reliance expenditures were the basis of a recovery by a subcontractor against a general contractor in Albre Marble and Tile Co. v. John Bowen Co., 155 N.E.2d 437 (Mass. 1959). The court took pains to distinguish Young v. Chicopee, above. One distinction was that the court was able to ascribe the dislocating event in *Albre Marble* to some degree of fault on the part of the general contractor, whereas the event that prevented performance in Young v. Chicopee was "a fire not shown to have been caused by the fault of either party." The court found some support in its decision in Angus v. Scully, represented as "The Case of the House Halfway" in Note 2, p. 1108 above.

NOTES

(1) *Coordination of Interests.* What does justice require, when competing interests are deserving of protection: a restitution interest on one side and a reliance interest on the other? Let it be supposed that a buyer has prepaid $1,000 and the seller has incurred preparatory expenses of $800, which cannot otherwise be recouped. (Compare Note, p. 1106 above.) Two eminent British jurists have advocated differing solutions: $200 to the buyer, according to one, and $600 according to the other. Professor Glanville Williams would have each party shoulder half of the unavoidable loss ($800). Lord Chancellor Simon argued for giving more protection to the seller's reliance interest, saying, "I think that will commend itself to everybody as good sense." Glanville Williams, *Law Reform (Frustrated Contracts) Act* 35–36 (1944). For other proposals about apportioning losses, see Leon Trakman, *Winner Take Some: Loss Sharing and Commercial Impracticability*, 69 Minn. L. Rev. 471 (1985); Philip D. Weiss, Note, *Apportioning Loss After Discharge of a Burdensome Contract: A Statutory Solution*, 69 Yale L.J. 1054 (1960).

(2) *Why the Hurry?* In setting an appropriate amount of recovery for a prepaying buyer, such as the Polish firm Fibrosa Spolka Akcyjna (see the note at p. 1106 above), it may help to know what the seller's object was in requiring an advance payment. Possibly it was to maintain the seller's cash flow. Possibly it was to avert or limit loss to the seller if the buyer should lack the resources to pay. Possibly it was to avert or limit loss to the seller if it should happen that a supervening event (*e.g.*, a war) terminated the contract after the seller had made an investment in the contract. One of these objects might, of course, operate in conjunction with another. Buyers and sellers are not usually actuated to provide for prepayments by the latter object, it is said. If they contemplate a disabling event, "their usual reaction is to take out a policy of insurance, not to provide for payment in advance." Williams, *Law Reform* at 36. But see the discussion of "reparations," pp. 1044–1045 above.

On facing a claim for restitution of an advance payment, might a seller undercut the claim by establishing that, as the buyer understood, the seller had negotiated for the payment for one of the reasons suggested above?

(3) *Statutes.* The note at p. 1111 above mentions a English statute concerning reliance interests: the Law Reform (Frustrated Contracts) Act of 1943. The statute addresses the case of a seller of goods who has received a prepayment and has incurred expenses in preparing the goods. According to the Act, "the court may, if it considers it just to do so having regard to all the circumstances of the case, allow him to retain [part of the prepayment], not being an amount in excess of the expenses so incurred." Section 1(2). This text was the subject of the views reported in Note 1 above.

Section 1514 of the California Civil Code, part of the Field Code, provides for apportionment, upon excuse from performance of an obligation, "of the consideration to which [the obligor] would have been entitled upon full performance, according to the benefits" received by the other party.

Compare Restatement § 272(2). How does it differ from these enactments?

PROBLEM

Ex Post. Reconsider Chase Precast Corp. v. Paonessa Co., p. 1094 above. What would have been the result if Chase had, in accordance with its contract, produced all of the median barriers before receiving Paonessa's letter notifying it to stop?

———

The *Alcoa* Case

One of the most controversial decisions dealing with changed circumstances is Aluminum Company of America v. Essex Group, Inc., 499 F.Supp. 53 (W.D. Pa. 1980). Late in 1967, after more than six months of negotiations, ALCOA contracted with Essex to convert Essex's alumina into molten aluminum by a smelting process. Performance was to take place over 16 years, with an option in Essex to extend for another five years, for a flexible price. (Alan Greenspan, the economist, assisted ALCOA in devising the pricing formula.) One of the variables in the formula represented changing production costs other than labor; for this the Wholesale Price Index—Industrial Commodities (WPI) was used as a proxy. At all events the charge to Essex was limited to 65% of an aluminum market price periodically published (the "65% cap"). In each of the first six years of operations ALCOA's profit exceeded 4 cents per pound, but by the tenth year ALCOA was incurring losses that threatened to mount to more than 75 million dollars. Other than the labor cost, that of electricity is the chief outlay in converting alumina. Since energy costs are a relatively small component of the WPI, electricity rates had begun swiftly to outpace that index, owing to OPEC's influence on oil prices and to anti-pollution regulations.

In litigation between ALCOA and Essex, the trial court found, in an opinion of some forty pages, that though ALCOA had sought a profit of four cents per pound, the parties had foreseen that the profit might vary either way, between one cent and seven cents per pound, and reformed the price term so as to yield ALCOA not less than a one cent per pound profit (unless the 65% cap should be less). The case was settled while on appeal.

NOTES

(1) *The Ground in ALCOA.* It is not certain that the *ALCOA* decision was one dependent on a change of circumstances. The court first concluded that the parties had contracted under the influence of a mutual mistake, warranting some kind of relief for ALCOA. Then it gave reasons for continuing with a discussion of changed circumstances.

The parties' mistake, according to the court, concerned the capacity of the WPI "to work as [they] expected it to work." The court found that they chose the WPI after a careful investigation, showing that it had, for a number of years, tracked fairly well ALCOA's non-labor costs. According to Comment *a* to Restatement § 151, a party's "prediction or judgment as to events to occur in the future, even if erroneous, is not a 'mistake' as that word is defined here." See also the discussion of claim settlements, p. 1045 above. Is *ALCOA* consistent with the Comment? The court said that the parties had made an error "of fact rather than one of simple prediction of future events"— had made a mistaken assumption that "was essentially a present actuarial error." Are you convinced?

(2) *The Remedy in ALCOA.* The ALCOA case occasioned extensive scholarly comment. The court's remedy—reformation of the price—played to mixed reviews. Professor Richard Speidel expressed reservations, but was generally sympathetic. He referred to the case as "a trail blazer" and has written of its "new 'spirit' of contract law." See Richard E. Speidel, *Court-Imposed Price Adjustments Under Long-Term Supply Contracts*, 76 Nw. U. L. Rev. 369 (1981). Professor John Dawson took issue with Speidel. He described the case as "grotesque." It was, he said "the only instance in which

an American judge has tried to dictate entirely different substantive terms . . . in a contract that was still being actively performed." Also: "Does anyone seriously contend that a judge . . . becomes better equipped than the parties concerned to reconcile their divergent, often conflicting interests, to devise the terms that can govern a complex enterprise and ensure its future survival?" John Dawson, *Judicial Revision of Frustrated Contracts: The United States*, 64 B.U. L. Rev. 1, 26, 35–36 (1984). For the results of a survey of general counsel, indicating approval of judicial price adjustment, see Russell J. Weintraub, *A Survey of Contract Practice and Policy*, 1992 Wis. L. Rev. 1, 41–45. In Unihealth v. U.S. Healthcare, Inc., 14 F.Supp.2d 623 (D.N.J. 1998), the court, relying on *ALCOA*, asserted its "right to fashion an equitable remedy by modifying the price term of a contract the principal purpose of which had been frustrated."

(3) *Significance of Concessions.* Scholars have occasionally suggested that changed circumstances may place a party under an obligation to negotiate in good faith with respect to a modification. See Speidel, as cited above. But courts have not been receptive to this suggestion. See, for example, L.C. Williams Oil Co., Inc. v. Exxon Corp., 625 F.Supp. 477 (M.D.N.C. 1985), rejecting the argument "that Exxon was under a good faith obligation to modify the existing contract terms when Williams's circumstances changed."

This is not to say, however, that a court will ignore a party's reasonable proposal for a concession in the face of changed circumstances. See Lloyd v. Murphy, 153 P.2d 47 (Cal. 1944), in which a dealer in new cars suffered from wartime restrictions and ultimately vacated his leased quarters. Before that, the landlords had offered to reduce the rent and to waive prohibitions in the lease against uses they had not consented to, and against subletting. In a major statement on the law of frustration of purpose, Justice Traynor denied relief to the tenant, emphasizing the value of the landlord's concession. The inference might be that the tenant's obligation turned on how the landlords chose to refashion the terms of the lease.

(4) *Renegotiation Clauses.* On entering into a long-term contract, the parties may perceive a high risk of changing conditions and so may choose to provide for renegotiation in specified circumstances. The drafter faces several challenging questions. How, first, to specify those circumstances? Second, what standards should govern the process of renegotiation? And third, what consequence should follow from a failure to agree? For a case involving a provision under which the parties to a long-term coal supply contract agreed to address revising the price on the occurrence "of material unforeseen events or changed conditions" which caused the price to be inequitable to one of the parties, see Kentucky Utilities Co. v. South East Coal Co., 836 S.W.2d 392 (Ky. 1992).

The International Chamber of Commerce (ICC) has addressed these questions in "drafting suggestions" for so-called hardship provisions. The suggested occasion for renegotiation is an occurrence "not contemplated by the parties [that] fundamentally alter[s] the equilibrium" of the contract and places "an excessive burden on one of the parties" in its performance, followed by a party's request for revision. Thereupon, according to the suggested term, the parties are to consult one another "with a view to revising the contract on an equitable basis, in order to ensure that neither party suffers excessive prejudice." For cases in which no agreed revision results, drafters are offered several choices. One is a provision that "the contract remains in force in accordance with its original terms." Another is to draw on third parties, either as advisers or as arbiters, leading possibly to a judicial revision. ICC, *Force Majeure and Hardship* 18 ff. (1985). Compare the orders entered in Oglebay Norton Co. v. Armco, p. 332 above.

PROBLEM

Seller contracted to sell a pile of lumber located on its premises to Buyer, who was to assume the risk of loss immediately and was to remove the lumber as soon as practicable. Unknown to either party, when the contract was made an underground fire was burning nearby and was likely to consume the lumber before it could be removed. In fact, it did. You represent the Buyer. Mistake or erroneous prediction? What difference does it make? See Richardson Lumber Co. v. Hoey, 189 N.W. 923 (Mich. 1922).

CHAPTER 10

THIRD PARTIES: RIGHTS AND RESPONSIBILITIES

When relief is sought for the breach of a contract, an objection often made is that the claimant is not in *privity* with the promisor—that is, that the claim is not based on a contract between the claimant and the promisor. A claim for relief may fail on that ground, but the requirement of privity has limitations. This chapter deals with two of its major limitations. First, a claimant may be eligible to enforce a contract, although not a party to it, because the claimant is a *third-party beneficiary*. And second, a claimant may be eligible to enforce a contract right by virtue of a transfer (an *assignment*) to the claimant of that right, made by one who was a party to the contract. As it is sometimes put, "the assignee stands in the shoes of the assignor."

The chapter deals also with agreements in which a contracting party delegates a duty to a third party, and that party assumes the duty that the contract imposes on the one making the *delegation*. It will be seen that when an effective delegation is made, the other contracting party—the one entitled to the performance in question—is usually a third-party beneficiary of the delegation.

SECTION 1. THIRD-PARTY-BENEFICIARY CONTRACTS

The modern development of third-party-beneficiary law, at least in this country, is usually dated from the 1859 case Lawrence v. Fox, the first in this chapter. Long before then, however, claims on contracts had been made by persons who were not parties to them. The results were mixed. In 17th-century England it was successfully argued that a promise to pay a woman £1,000 was enforceable by her, although it was made to her father, and although she gave nothing in exchange for the promise. Dutton v. Poole, 83 Eng.Rep. 523 (K.B. 1677). Later this case was disapproved. According to a 19th-century English judge, "It would be a monstrous proposition to say that a person was a party to the contract for the purpose of suing upon it for his own advantage, and not for the purpose of being sued." Tweddle v. Atkinson, 121 Eng.Rep. 762 (Q.B. 1861).

As the case law developed in this country, it became generally accepted that an action may sometimes be maintained on a contract by one who had no part in creating it. Probably the class of third-party-beneficiary contracts most familiar to the public at large is contracts of life insurance. The beneficiary of a life insurance policy may enforce a right to the death benefits even though the beneficiary did not apply for it, pay for it, or have any other connection with it.

Of course, most contracts are not third party beneficiary contracts, even when they affect greatly the rights of non-parties. Together, the initial Restatement and the Restatement Second have popularized the term "incidental beneficiary" for a third party who may enjoy an advantage through the performance of a contract, but has no enforceable interest in its performance. To take an unusual example, a basketball referee called a foul in a game between Iowa and Purdue. Iowa lost. In Iowa City there was a novelty store stocked with Iowa University sports memorabilia. The store owners made a claim against the referee for losses due to his alleged incompetence; the game had cost Iowa its chance of a championship. One basis for the claim was an alleged contract between the referee and the Big Ten Conference, requiring him to exhibit competence in his calls. The trial court granted summary judgment for the referee. On appeal, *held:* Affirmed. Bain v. Gillispie, 357 N.W.2d 47 (Iowa App.1984).

As the example of life insurance shows, contracts that create rights in third parties can be very useful. We will see other settings—construction contracts, contracts to draft wills, government contracts—in which one who is not a party to a contract may derive benefit from it, and may wish to vindicate its rights directly rather than through a contracting party. The contracting party that conferred the benefit on the third party may be unable or unwilling to pursue the third party's rights. Without the ability to sue directly on the contract, the third party may simply be out of luck, whatever the intent of the contracting parties might have been.

Nevertheless, there are complications and inconveniences in the law of third-party beneficiaries. The parties to a contract may wish to prevent third parties from enforcing its terms. They may wish to limit the scope of third-party rights. This can pose a challenge to the drafter seeking to remove doubts and promote the goals of the agreement. And even if the contract does not limit these rights expressly, perhaps the default rule should be that there are no third-party rights. As we go through the law of third-party beneficiaries, you may find it useful to think about the advantages and disadvantages of allowing third parties to sue on the kinds of contracts we study.

———

Restatement Formulations

In the initial Restatement of Contracts, and in the Restatement Second, each of the chapters on contract beneficiaries opens with a section classifying beneficiaries. The two sections have much in common, but differ in significant ways. Each section identifies a class of "beneficiaries" called *incidental*; these are ineligible to enforce a contract between other parties, even though they would benefit from its performance. Beneficiaries eligible to enforce a contract between other parties are designated in Restatement Second § 302 as *intended* beneficiaries. A claimant is in this class only if "recognition of a right to performance in [the claimant] is appropriate to effectuate the intention of the [contracting] parties." (Although the parties' intention is a focus of the section, Comment *d* expands on that: "In some cases an overriding policy, which may be embodied in a statute, requires recognition of [a third party's right] without regard to the intention of the parties.")

According to Section 302, a claimant must also meet one of two qualifications. One of these is that "the performance of the promise will satisfy an obligation of the promisee to pay money to [the claimant]." The other is that "the circumstances indicate that the promisee intends to give [the claimant] the benefit of the promised performance." As to the first qualification, see the case that follows. As to the second, see Seaver v. Ransom, p. 1125 below.

NOTE

Circumventing Privity. A person or firm may qualify to enforce a contract because it was made on behalf of that entity by a person acting as an agent for the claimant—the claimant being known, in that case, as the "principal." Governments, as well as corporations, use the law of agency when taking part in commerce. When they do, the requirement of privity is affected by that body of law. We leave the large body of agency law for other courses.

In some situations various doctrinal ideas work together to moderate the requirement of privity. The following example is given in the Restatement: "[T]he rights of employees under a collective bargaining agreement are sometimes treated as rights of contract beneficiaries, sometimes as rights based on agency principles, sometimes as rights analogous to the rights of trust beneficiaries. Or the collective bargaining agreement may be treated as establishing a usage incorporated in individual employment contracts, or as analogous to legislation." Introductory Note to Restatement Chapter 14.

Introduction to Lawrence v. Fox

Lawrence won a judgment in this case as what would now be called an *intended* beneficiary of a contract between the promisor (Fox) and the promisee (Holly). The judgment was affirmed by a vote of 6–2 in the Court of Appeals. But two of the six judges would have said that Holly made the contract as a self-professed agent of Lawrence. That left only four judges committed to the general proposition that when "a promise [is] made to one for the benefit of another, he for whose benefit it is made may bring an action for its breach."

The arguments about that proposition centered on the law of trusts, which provides a way around the requirement of privity. "If A delivers money or property to B, which the latter accepts upon a trust for the benefit of C, the latter can enforce the trust by an appropriate action for that purpose." All the judges agreed that far. But what if no property has been placed in trust with B? Might C nevertheless enforce a *promise* made by B to A? On that question the judges were divided.

A person might become a trustee by having goods delivered to him and accepting responsibility for them. Say that the owner of a batch of plastic, A, delivers it to B with instructions to mold the plastic into Supreme Court bobblehead dolls and to deliver the dolls to C. If B accepts that charge, the plastic is the subject of an express trust, B is the trustee, and C is the beneficiary ("*cestui que trust*"). That would not be so, however, if B had instead contracted with A to buy plastic, mold it, and deliver the dolls to C. Having bargained for those promises, A could enforce them. As indicated above, some judges thought that C could not, distinguishing the case in which C is the beneficiary of a trust. What differentiates the two situations supposed is the existence in one of an asset—a batch of plastic or a crate of dolls—as the subject of an agreement between A and B. The existence of a trust asset, or *res*, is a requisite of a trust. For a comparison of agency and trust relationships with those growing out of third-party-beneficiary contracts, see Restatement § 302, cmt. *f*.

Lawrence v. Fox

Court of Appeals of New York, 1859.
20 N.Y. 268.

Appeal from the Superior Court of the City of Buffalo. On the trial before Mr. Justice Masten, it appeared by the evidence of a bystander that one Holly, in November, 1857, at the request of the defendant [Fox], loaned and advanced to him $300, stating at the time that he owed that sum to the plaintiff [Lawrence] for money borrowed of him, and had agreed to pay it to him the then next day; that the defendant, in consideration thereof, at the time of receiving the money, promised to pay it to the plaintiff the then next day. Upon this state of facts the defendant moved for a nonsuit, upon three several grounds, viz.: That there was no proof tending to show that Holly was indebted to the plaintiff, that the agreement by the defendant with Holly to pay the plaintiff was void for want of consideration, and that there was no privity between the plaintiff and defendant. The court overruled the motion, and the counsel for the defendant excepted. The cause was then submitted to the jury, and they found a verdict for the plaintiff for the amount of the loan and interest, $344.66, upon which judgment was entered, from which the defendant appealed to the Superior Court, at General Term, where the judgment was affirmed, and the defendant appealed to this court. The cause was submitted on printed argument.

■ H. GRAY, JUDGE. The first objection raised on the trial amounts to this: That the evidence of the person present, who heard the declarations of

Holly giving directions as to the payment of the money he was then advancing to the defendant, was mere hearsay and, therefore, not competent. Had the plaintiff sued Holly for this sum of money no objection to the competency of this evidence would have been thought of; and if the defendant had performed his promise by paying the sum loaned to him to the plaintiff, and Holly had afterwards sued him for its recovery, and the evidence had been offered by the defendant, it would doubtless have been received without an objection from any source. All the defendant had the right to demand in this case was evidence which, as between Holly and the plaintiff, was competent to establish the relation between them of debtor and creditor. For that purpose the evidence was clearly competent; it covered the whole ground and warranted the verdict of the jury.

But it is claimed that notwithstanding this promise was established by competent evidence, it was void for the want of consideration. It is now more than a quarter of a century since it was settled by the supreme court of this state—in an able and painstaking opinion by the late Chief Justice Savage, in which the authorities were fully examined and carefully analyzed—that a promise in all material respects like the one under consideration was valid; and the judgment of that court was unanimously affirmed by the court for the correction of errors. Farley v. Cleveland, 4 Cow. 432, 15 Am.Dec. 387; s. c. in error, 9 Cow. 639. In that case one Moon owed Farley and sold to Cleveland a quantity of hay, in consideration of which Cleveland promised to pay Moon's debt to Farley; and the decision in favor of Farley's right to recover was placed upon the ground that the hay received by Cleveland from Moon was a valid consideration for Cleveland's promise to pay Farley, and that the subsisting liability of Moon to pay Farley was no objection to the recovery. The fact that the money advanced by Holly to the defendant was a loan to him for a day, and that it thereby became the property of the defendant, seemed to impress the defendant's counsel with the idea that because the defendant's promise was not a trust fund placed by the plaintiff in the defendant's hands, out of which he was to realize money as from the sale of a chattel or the collection of a debt, the promise although made for the benefit of the plaintiff could not inure to his benefit. The hay which Cleveland bought of Moon was not to be paid to Farley, but the debt incurred by Cleveland for the purchase of the hay, like the debt incurred by the defendant for money borrowed, was what was to be paid.

That case has been often referred to by the courts of this state, and has never been doubted as sound authority for the principle upheld by it. Barker v. Bucklin, 2 Denio 45, 43 Am.Dec. 726; Canal Co. v. Westchester County Bank, 4 Denio 97. It puts to rest the objection that the defendant's promise was void for want of consideration. The report of that case shows that the promise was not only made to Moon but to the plaintiff Farley. In this case the promise was made to Holly and not expressly to the plaintiff; and this difference between the two cases presents the question, raised by the defendant's objection, as to the want of privity between the plaintiff and defendant.

But it is urged that because the defendant was not in any sense a trustee of the property of Holly for the benefit of the plaintiff, the law will not imply a promise. I agree that many of the cases where a promise was implied were cases of trusts, created for the benefit of the promisor. The case of Felton v. Dickinson, 10 Mass. 287, and others that might be cited are of that class; but concede them all to have been cases of trusts, and it proves nothing against the application of the rule to this case. The duty of the trustee to pay the cestui que trust, according to the terms of the trust, implies his promise to the latter to do so. In this case the defendant, upon ample consideration received from Holly, promised Holly to pay his debt to the plaintiff; the consideration received and the promise to Holly made it as plainly his duty to pay the plaintiff as if the money had been remitted to him for that purpose, and as well implied a promise to do so as if he had been made a trustee of property to be converted into cash with which to pay. The fact that a breach of the duty imposed in the one case may be visited, and justly, with more serious consequences than in the other, by no means disproves the payment to be a duty in both. The principle illustrated by the example so frequently quoted (which concisely states the case in hand) "that a promise made to one for the benefit of another, he for whose benefit it is made may bring an action for its breach," has been applied to trust cases, not because it was exclusively applicable to those cases, but because it was a principle of law, and as such applicable to those cases.

It was also insisted that Holly could have discharged the defendant from his promise, though it was intended by both parties for the benefit of the plaintiff, and, therefore, the plaintiff was not entitled to maintain this suit for the recovery of a demand over which he had no control. It is enough that the plaintiff did not release the defendant from his promise, and whether he could or not is a question not now necessarily involved.

The cases cited and especially that of Farley v. Cleveland, established the validity of a parol promise; it stands then upon the footing of a written one. Suppose the defendant had given his note in which for value received of Holly, he had promised to pay the plaintiff and the plaintiff had accepted the promise, retaining Holly's liability. Very clearly Holly could not have discharged that promise, be the right to release the defendant as it may. No one can doubt that he owes the sum of money demanded of him or that in accordance with his promise it was his duty to have paid it to the plaintiff; nor can it be doubted that whatever may be the diversity of opinion elsewhere, the adjudications in this state, from a very early period, approved by experience, have established the defendant's liability; if, therefore, it could be shown that a more strict and technically accurate application of the rules applied, would lead to a different result (which I by no means concede), the effort should not be made in the face of manifest justice.

The judgment should be affirmed.

■ JOHNSON, CH. JUDGE, DENIO, SELDEN, ALLEN and STRONG, JUDGES, concurred. JOHNSON, CHIEF JUDGE, and DENIO, JUDGE, were of opinion that the promise was to be regarded as made to the plaintiff through the medium of his agent, whose action he could ratify when it came to his knowledge, though taken without his being privy thereto.

■ COMSTOCK, JUDGE (dissenting). The plaintiff had nothing to do with the promise on which he brought this action. It was not made to him, nor did the consideration proceed from him. If he can maintain the suit, it is because an anomaly has found its way into the law on this subject. In general, there must be privity of contract. The party who sues upon a promise must be the promisee, or he must have some legal interest in the undertaking. In this case, it is plain that Holly who loaned the money to the defendant, and to whom the promise in question was made, could at any time have claimed that it should be performed to himself personally. He had lent the money to the defendant, and at the same time directed the latter to pay the sum to the plaintiff. This direction he could countermand, and if he had done so, manifestly the defendant's promise to pay according to the direction would have ceased to exist. The plaintiff would receive a benefit by a complete execution of the arrangement, but the arrangement itself was between other parties, and was under their exclusive control. If the defendant had paid the money to Holly, his debt would have been discharged thereby. So Holly might have released the demand or assigned it to another person, or the parties might have annulled the promise now in question, and designated some other creditor of Holly as the party to whom the money should be paid. It has never been claimed that in a case thus situated the right of a third person to sue upon the promise rested on any sound principle of law. We are to inquire whether the rule has been so established by positive authority.

If A. delivers money or property to B., which the latter accepts upon a trust for the benefit of C., the latter can enforce the trust by an appropriate action for that purpose. There is some authority even for saying that an express promise founded on the possession of a trust fund may be enforced by an action at law in the name of the beneficiary, although it was made to the creator of the trust. Thus, in Comyn, Dig. "Action on the Case upon Assumpsit," B. 15, it is laid down that if a man promise a pig of lead to A. and his executor give lead to make a pig to B., who assumes to deliver it to A., an assumpsit lies by A. against him. [P]erhaps there is no gross violation of principle in permitting the equitable owner of [a fund held in trust] it to sue upon an express promise to pay it over. Having a specific interest in the thing, the undertaking to account for it may be regarded as in some sense made with him through the author of the trust. But further than this we cannot go without violating plain rules of law. In the case before us there was nothing in the nature of a trust or agency. The defendant borrowed the money of Holly and received it as his own. The plaintiff had no right in the fund, legal or equitable. The promise to repay the money created an obligation in favor of the lender to whom it was made and not in favor of any one else.

The judgment of the court below should, therefore, be reversed, and a new trial granted.

■ GROVER, JUDGE, also dissented.

Judgment affirmed.

NOTES

(1) *Restitution.* Could the decision in Lawrence v. Fox have been based on quasi-contract? Does it seem that the court would have affirmed if there had been no evidence of a promise made by Fox to Holly? Compare Callano v. Oakwood Park Homes Corp., p. 148 above.

"The underlying premise on which the third-party beneficiary doctrine is based," it has been said, "is the same as that of unjust enrichment. It must appear that one party is holding sums of money which *rightfully belong* to another party." Litton Systems, Inc. v. Frigitemp Corp., 613 F.Supp. 1377 (S.D.Miss. 1985). Does this statement ignore the discussion in Lawrence v. Fox of "cases of trusts"? See Restatement (Third) of Restitution and Unjust Enrichment § 48 ("If a third person makes a payment to the defendant to which (as between claimant and defendant) the claimant has a better legal or equitable right, the claimant is entitled to restitution from the defendant as necessary to prevent unjust enrichment.").

(2) *Durability of Rights.* In Lawrence v. Fox the dissenting judges saw no merit in recognizing an entitlement that was readily defeasible. They assumed that the contracting parties could have divested Lawrence of his right at will. "[T]he arrangement . . . was under their exclusive control. . . . So Holly might have released the demand or assigned it to another person, or the parties might have annulled the promise now in question, and designated some other creditor of Holly as the party to whom the money should be paid." The other judges brushed this objection aside: "It is enough that the plaintiff [Lawrence] did not release the defendant from his promise, and whether he could or not is a question not now necessarily involved." (Both of these passages are omitted above.)

That question has generated controversy. It is addressed in the discussion at p. 1154 below, Vesting of Third-Party Rights.

(3) *Commentary.* For a history of the litigation in Lawrence v. Fox see Anthony Waters, *The Property in the Promise: A Study of the Third Party Beneficiary Rule*, 98 Harv. L. Rev. 1109 (1985). Professor Waters's investigations led him to believe that the promisee (not "Holly" but actually one Samuel Hawley) made the loan to Fox for the purpose of gambling, as Hawley knew. For an appraisal of the case see Melvin A. Eisenberg, *Third Party Beneficiary Contracts*, 92 Colum. L. Rev. 1358, 1392–93 (1992) [cited hereafter as "Eisenberg"].

Seaver v. Ransom

Court of Appeals of New York, 1918.
224 N.Y. 233, 120 N.E. 639.

Action by Marion E. Seaver against Matt. C. Ransom and another, as executors, etc., of Samuel A. Beman, deceased. From a judgment of the Appellate Division (180 App.Div. 734, 168 N.Y.S. 454), affirming judgment for plaintiff, defendants appeal. Affirmed.

■ POUND, JUDGE. Judge Beman and his wife were advanced in years. Mrs. Beman was about to die. She had a small estate consisting of a house and lot in Malone and little else. Judge Beman drew his wife's will according to her instruction. It gave $1,000 to plaintiff, $500 to one sister, plaintiff's mother, and $100 each to another sister and her son, the use of the house to her husband for life, and remainder to the American Society for the Prevention of Cruelty to Animals. She named her husband as residuary legatee and executor. Plaintiff was her niece, 34 years old, in ill health, sometimes a member of the Beman household. When the will was read to Mrs. Beman, she said that it was not as she wanted it. She wanted to leave the house to the plaintiff. She had no other objection to the will, but her strength was waning, and, although the judge offered to write another will for her, she said she was afraid she would not hold out long enough to enable her to sign it. So the judge said, if she would sign the will, he would leave plaintiff enough in his will to make up the difference. He avouched the promise by his uplifted hand with all solemnity and his wife then executed the will. When he came to die, it was found that his will made no provision for the plaintiff.

This action was brought, and plaintiff recovered judgment in the trial court, on the theory that Beman had obtained property from his wife and induced her to execute the will in the form prepared by him by his promise to give plaintiff $6,000, the value of the house, and that thereby equity impressed his property with a trust in favor of the plaintiff. Where a legatee promises the testator that he will use property given him by the will for a particular purpose, a trust arises. O'Hara v. Dudley, 95 N.Y. 103, 47 Am.Rep. 53; Trustees of Amherst College v. Ritch, 151 N.Y. 282, 45 N.E. 876, 37 L.R.A. 305; Aherns v. Jones, 169 N.Y. 555, 62 N.E. 666, 88 Am.St.Rep. 620. Beman received nothing under his wife's will but the use of the house in Malone for life. Equity compels the application of property thus obtained to the purpose of the testator, but equity cannot so impress a trust, except on property obtained by the promise. Beman was bound by his promise, but no property was bound by it; no trust in plaintiff's favor can be spelled out.

An action on the contract for damages, or to make the executors trustees for performance, stands on different ground. Farmers' Loan & Trust Co. v. Mortimer, 219 N.Y. 290, 294, 295. The Appellate Division properly passed to the consideration of the question whether the judgment could stand upon the promise made to the wife, upon a valid consideration, for the sole benefit of plaintiff. The judgment of the trial court was affirmed by a return to the general doctrine laid down in the great case of Lawrence v. Fox, 20 N.Y. 268, which has since been limited as herein indicated.

Contracts for the benefit of third persons have been the prolific source of judicial and academic discussion. Williston, *Contracts for the Benefit of a Third Person*, 15 Harvard Law Review, 767; Corbin, *Contracts for the Benefit of Third Persons*, 27 Yale Law Review, 1008. The general rule, both in law and equity (Phalen v. United States Trust Co., 186 N.Y. 178, 186, 78 N.E. 943, 7 L.R.A., N.S., 734, 9 Ann.Cas. 595), was that privity between a plaintiff and a defendant is necessary to the maintenance of an action on the contract. The consideration must be furnished by the party to whom the promise was made. The contract cannot be enforced against the third party, and therefore it cannot be enforced by him. On the other hand, the right of the beneficiary to sue on a contract made expressly for his benefit has been fully recognized in many American jurisdictions, either by judicial decision or by legislation, and is said to be "the prevailing rule in this country." Hendrick v. Lindsay, 93 U.S. 143; Lehow v. Simonton, 3 Colo. 346. It has been said that "the establishment of this doctrine has been gradual, and is a victory of practical utility over theory, of equity over technical subtlety." Brantly on Contracts, 2d Ed., p. 253. The reasons for this view are that it is just and practical to permit the person for whose benefit the contract is made to enforce it against one whose duty it is to pay. Other jurisdictions still adhere to the present English Rule (7 Halsbury's Laws of England, 342, 343; Jenks' Digest of English Civil Law, sec. 229) that a contract cannot be enforced by or against a person who is not a party. Exchange Bank v. Rice, 107 Mass. 37. But see, also, Forbes v. Thorpe, 209 Mass. 570; Gardner v. Denison, 217 Mass. 492.

In New York the right of the beneficiary to sue on contracts made for his benefit is not clearly or simply defined. It is at present confined: First. To cases where there is a pecuniary obligation running from the promisee to the beneficiary, "a legal right founded upon some obligation of the promisee in the third party to adopt and claim the promise as made for his benefit." [Cases cited.] Secondly. To cases where the contract is made for the benefit of the wife (Buchanan v. Tilden, 52 N.E. 724; Bouton v. Welch, 63 N.E. 539), affianced wife (De Cicco v. Schweizer, 117 N.E. 807), or child (Todd v. Weber, 95 N.Y. 181, 193; Matter of Kidd, 80 N.E. 924) of a party to the contract. The close relationship cases go back to the early King's Bench case (1677), long since repudiated in England, of Dutton v. Poole, 2 Lev. 211 (s.c., 1 Ventris, 318, 332). See Schemerhorn v. Vanderheyden, 1 Johns, 139, 3 Am.Dec. 304. The natural and moral duty of the husband or parent to provide for the future of wife or child sustains the action on the contract made for their benefit. "This is the furthest the cases in this state have gone," says Cullen, J., in the marriage settlement case of Borland v. Welch, 162 N.Y. 104, 110, 56 N.E. 556.

The right of the third party is also upheld in, thirdly, the public contract cases [cases cited] where the municipality seeks to protect its inhabitants by covenants for their benefit; and, fourthly, the cases where, at the request of a party to the contract, the promise runs directly to the beneficiary although he does not furnish the consideration [cases cited]. It may be safely said that a general rule sustaining recovery at the suit of the third party would include but few classes of cases not included in these groups, either categorically or in principle.

The desire of the childless aunt to make provisions for a beloved and favorite niece differs imperceptibly in law or in equity from the moral duty of the parent to make testamentary provision for a child. The contract was made for the plaintiff's benefit. She alone is substantially damaged by its breach. The representatives of the wife's estate have no interest in enforcing it specifically. It is said in Buchanan v. Tilden that the common law imposes moral and legal obligations upon the husband and the parent not measured by the necessaries of life. It was, however, the love and affection or the moral sense of the husband and the parent that imposed such obligations in the cases cited, rather than any common-law duty of husband and parent to wife and child. If plaintiff had been a child of Mrs. Beman, legal obligation would have required no testamentary provision for her, yet the child could have enforced a covenant in her favor identical with the covenant of Judge Beman in this case. De Cicco v. Schweizer, supra. The constraining power of conscience is not regulated by the degree of relationship alone. The dependent or faithful niece may have a stronger claim than the affluent or unworthy son. No sensible theory of moral obligation denies arbitrarily to the former what would be conceded to the latter. We might consistently either refuse or allow the claim of both, but I cannot reconcile a decision in favor of the wife in Buchanan v. Tilden, based on the moral obligations arising out of near relationship, with a decision against the niece here on the ground that the relationship is too remote for equity's ken. No controlling authority depends upon so absolute a rule. In Sullivan v. Sullivan, 161 N.Y. 554, 56 N.E. 116, the grandniece lost in a litigation with the aunt's estate, founded on a certificate of deposit payable to the aunt "or in case of her death to her niece;" but what was said in that case of the relations of plaintiff's intestate and defendant does not control here, any more than what was said in Durnherr v. Rau [135 N.Y. 219, 32 N.E. 49], on the relation of husband and wife, and the inadequacy of mere moral duty, as distinguished from legal or equitable obligation, controlled the decision in Buchanan v. Tilden. Borland v. Welch, supra, deals only with the rights of volunteers under a marriage settlement not made for the benefit of collaterals. Kellogg, P.J., writing for the court below, well said:

> "The doctrine of Lawrence v. Fox is progressive, not retrograde. The course of the late decisions is to enlarge, not limit, the effect of that case."

The court in that leading case attempted to adopt the general doctrine that any third person, for whose direct benefit a contract was intended, could sue on it. [Next the court referred to a number of later New York precedents, some stating the doctrine in general terms, and others narrowing its application.]

But, on principle, a sound conclusion may be reached. If Mrs. Beman had left her husband the house on condition that he pay the plaintiff $6,000, and he had accepted the devise, he would have become personally liable to pay the legacy, and plaintiff could have recovered in an action at law against him, whatever the value of the house. That would be because the testatrix had in substance bequeathed the promise to plaintiff, and not because close relationship or moral obligation sustained the contract. The distinction between an implied promise to a testator for the benefit of a third party to pay a legacy and an unqualified promise on a valuable consideration to make provision for the third party by will is discernible, but not obvious. The tendency of American authority is to sustain the gift in all such cases and to permit the donee beneficiary to recover on the contract. Matter of Edmundson's Estate (1918) 259 Pa. 429, 103 A. 277. The equities are with the plaintiff, and they may be enforced in this action, whether it be regarded as an action for damages or an action for specific performance to convert the defendants into trustees for plaintiff's benefit under the agreement.

Judgment affirmed.

NOTE

Qualified Enforcers. The New York Court of Appeals has intimated that Marion Seaver prevailed because no one else was qualified to enforce Judge Beman's promise to his wife. See Fourth Ocean Putnam Corp. v. Interstate Wrecking Co., 485 N.E.2d 208 (N.Y. 1985). There, on re-reading the *Seaver* opinion, the court was struck by the statement that only Seaver was substantially damaged by Judge Beman's breach. The court wrote: "we have emphasized when upholding the third party's right to enforce the contract that no one other than the third party can recover if the promisor breaches the contract." Following this, the court cited *Seaver*. Was that citation apt?

According to § 307 of the Restatement, a duty owed to an intended beneficiary may be enforced by the promisee in an action for specific performance if that remedy is otherwise appropriate. A supporting authority is Croker v. New York Trust Co., 156 N.E. 81 (N.Y.1927). That was a case like *Seaver*, except that the promisee was the suitor. The court said: "That plaintiff's remedy in law would be inadequate is obvious." Id. at 82.

PROBLEMS

(1) Tobi, the long-time owner of "Tobi's Tulips," recently sold her business to Lee. When Tobi began the business she had help from her mother Ruth, in the form of a startup loan. As part of the sale transaction, Lee agreed to pay business debts as listed by Tobi. One entry on Tobi's list was Ruth's

name and the amount of Ruth's loan. Actually, by that time Ruth was barred from collecting from Tobi by a statute of limitations. May she now collect from Lee? See Spiklevitz v. Markmil Corp., 357 N.W.2d 721 (Mich.App.1984).

Tobi may have put Ruth in the list of her creditors because she thought it would be unbecoming to use what some people regard as a "technical" defense so as to withhold payment from anyone who had given her credit. Is there another possible reason that would make Ruth's claim stronger? One that would make it weaker?

(2) The United Kingdom Ministry of Defence (the Ministry) expected that its cruise missile program would benefit from goods supplied by Trimble Navigation Ltd.; those goods would permit the Ministry to latch onto the global positioning system of the U.S. Air Force. The Air Force, having received payment from the Ministry for the goods in advance, contracted with Trimble for it to supply the goods to the Ministry. (Congress has authorized sales of military goods to foreign authorities in this manner.) The Ministry has complained that defects in the goods have imposed a cost on it. The Air Force has decided not to take action against Trimble. May the Ministry do so, as a third-party beneficiary? See United Kingdom Ministry of Defence v. Trimble Navigation Ltd., 422 F.3d 165 (4th Cir. 2005).

Detroit Institute of Arts Founders Society v. Rose

United States District Court, D. Connecticut, 2001.
127 F.Supp.2d 117 (D.Conn.2001).

[This case concerned the disposition of a puppet that was revered as the central figure in a popular 1950's children's TV show. The original "Howdy Doody" was owned by the National Broadcasting Company (NBC). After the show closed, the puppet was held in storage and for servicing by Rufus C. Rose. After some sparring, Rose and NBC entered into an agreement represented by letters between him and a member of the NBC legal department. According to one letter from NBC, Rose and another would "arrange for the disposition of the various Howdy Doody puppets (except for *the* HOWDY DOODY, of course)," and Rose would inform NBC which puppets would be "going into the PUPPET MUSEUM," along with Howdy Doody. (Several similar puppets had been created, including a "Double Doody" which appeared as a stand-in while repairs were made on "Howdy.") Read with others, the court said, this letter indicated that the puppet in question was to go to the Detroit Institute of Arts, which, according to Rose, housed "the recognized museum of Puppetry in America."

After the death of Rose and his widow, not having received the puppet, the Institute brought an action against several Rose defendants (one being the executor of the widow's estate).]

■ CHRISTOPHER F. DRONEY, DISTRICT JUDGE. Two parties may enter into a contract to benefit a third party beneficiary who is then entitled to enforce contractual obligations without being a party to the contract and thus may sue the obligor for breach. To be valid, there need not be express language in the contract creating a direct obligation to the third party beneficiary. See Grigerik v. Sharpe [p. 1150 below]. However, a contract can only result in an obligation to a third party if both parties to the contract intended to create a direct obligation from the promisor to the third party. In other words, the fact a third party may gain an incidental benefit is not enough to support third-party beneficiary status. The intent of the parties is to be "determined from the terms of the contract read in light of the circumstances attending the making of the contract, including the motives and the purposes of the parties." Delacroix [v. Lublin Graphics, Inc., 993 F.Supp. 74 (D.Conn. 1997)] at 83.

[The court entered a partial summary judgment in favor of the Institute.]

NOTE

Tangled Strings? This case was the converse of Seaver v. Ransom. Although it featured a donative intent, the would-be donor was not the promisee (NBC), but was the promisor (R.C. Rose). Possibly NBC was indifferent about the disposition of the puppet.

Consult Restatement § 302(1). Can the Institute be fitted into either clause (a) or clause (b)? If not, wasn't it only an incidental beneficiary? Possible conclusions are that the court was in error, and that the Restatement section is unduly restrictive.

———

Distribution Networks

Now and then, a distributor of goods holding an exclusive marketing license has portrayed itself as a third-party beneficiary of an agreement between its supplier and another licensee. A representative distribution network was described this way:

> Exercycle Corporation of New York sells its machines through a national system of territorial distributorships. During the period in question here, each contract between Exercycle Corporation and the various distributors, including those of plaintiff and defendants, granted the distributor an exclusive right to sell exercycles within a specified area and each contract contained a provision similar to that of clause 11 of defendants' contract. In that clause the distributor agreed "Not to sell Exercycles in any territory other than that assigned to him by the Company under clause 1."

Exercycle of Michigan, Inc. v. Wayson, 341 F.2d 335, 336 (7th Cir.1965). Exercycle of Michigan complained that its territory had been invaded by other licensees, in violation of clause 11. That clause was intended, the court said, "for the protection of other distributors, including plaintiff." Id. at 337. For a contrasting case see Piccoli A/S v. Calvin Klein

Jeanswear Co., 19 F.Supp.2d 157 (S.D.N.Y. 1998), a case about sales of jeans in Scandinavia. Each of the contestants held a license to distribute gear trademarked by Calvin Klein Inc. (CKI). The agreement between CKI and the defendant Jeanswear prohibited Jeanswear from selling Calvin Klein products outside North America and also from selling to third parties whom it knew or should have known would sell the products outside North America. Piccoli charged that Calvin Klein jeans had showed up in Scandinavian discount stores owing to a breach of that part of the Jeanswear license agreement.

Piccoli purported to be a third-party beneficiary of that agreement. The court rejected that characterization. First, Calvin Klein had the contractual right to go after a licensee that violated the terms of the license and collect damages for breach. It thus was not necessary that Piccoli be a intended beneficiary of the contract in order to make certain that *someone* would have the right to go after the promisor. Second, the contract between Calvin Klein and Jeanswear did not expressly grant to third parties the right to enforce the contract. Indeed, it stated that the rights created under the contract could not be assigned without Calvin Klein's approval, and that the benefits deriving from the contract inured to the parties and their successors. The court reasoned from this that the parties did not want to make assignments freely available, in large part because the inurement clause specified a class of beneficiaries but did not include the plaintiff.

NOTES

(1) *Eligible Enforcers—Reprise.* An effort to enforce a promise by someone other than the recipient may gain some traction from the assumption that the promisee could not enforce it: "*Someone* ought to be in a position to enforce." That effect was suggested in Fourth Ocean Putnam Corp. v. Interstate Wrecking Co., 485 N.E.2d 208 (N.Y. 1985), which was cited to in *Piccoli*.

Conversely, a third party's effort to enforce may lose traction because the court assumes that the recipient of the promise might have enforced it. This happened when a bottler of Pepsi-Cola, Bottling Company of Pittsburg, sought to enforce a promise made by another bottler to PepsiCo, Inc. The other bottler's promise was to refrain from marketing PepsiCo products outside a specified territory. A reason given for repelling the bottler's claim was that PepsiCo might have enforced the promise. The court was influenced by *Piccoli*. Pepsi-Cola Bottling Company of Pittsburg v. PepsiCo, Inc., 431 F.3d 1241 (10th Cir. 2006).

The enforcement power of a promisee is the subject of the Note at p. 1128 above. That Note points out some apparent slippage in the reasoning in *Fourth Ocean Putnam*. Possibly some slippage occurred also in *Pepsi-Cola Bottling*, for the promisee had some solid business reasons to indulge the defendant in trespassing on the claimant's territory. One was a call by nationwide customers of PepsiCo (*e.g.*, Sam's Club) for the opportunity to purchase at a single point. Another was the creation by Coca-Cola of a single "anchor" distributor. Should considerations like these weigh in a decision whether or not to entertain a third-party-beneficiary claim?

(2)   *Anti-Assignment Clauses*. An illustrative clause of this sort is this:

> Neither this Agreement nor any right, remedy, obligation or liability arising hereunder or by reason thereof shall be assignable by any party to this Agreement without the prior written consent of the other parties.

Anti-assignment clauses have been invoked against distributors asserting third-party-beneficiary status. Courts sometimes conclude that they show "an intent to limit the obligation of the contract to the original parties." Subaru Distributors Corp. v. Subaru of America, Inc., 425 F.3d 119, 125 (2d Cir.2005). By limiting the promisee's right to assign the contract, the parties implicitly intend to bar all others from suing for the equivalent of performance. More often, though, these clauses are read as evidence that the parties intended to eliminate third-party claims, but not as conclusive evidence.

Something might be said for any of three positions about an anti-assignment clause in relation to a third-party-beneficiary claim: (a) It defeats the claim, (b) It indicates that the claim has no merit, and (c) It has no bearing on the issue. Which do you consider the best position?

(3)   *Get out and Stay out!* Another way to avoid third-party-beneficiary claims is more direct—by excluding them expressly. Consider, for example, an important case of data theft. In 2007, TJX Companies, which operates several chains of discount stores (including TJMaxx), announced that its computer systems had been hacked and that credit card data for millions of its customers had been stolen. As a result, the customers whose data had been stolen were hurt, as were the banks issuing the credit cards when they had to reimburse their customers for the fraudulent use of their cards. The banks then sued TJX and Fifth Third Bancorp, the bank that processed the credit-card receivables, alleging that they had failed to safeguard the data as required by contracts between Fifth Third and TJX and between Fifth Third and credit card organizations, such as Visa and MasterCard. The court held that these contracts did not give the issuing banks the right to sue Fifth Third and TJX. As Restatement § 302(1) states, the parties to a contract may agree to exclude otherwise intended beneficiaries. The Fifth Third-TJX contract stated that "This Agreement is for the benefit of, and may be enforced only by, Bank and Merchant . . . and is not for the benefit of, and may not be enforced by any third party." That was sufficient to bar the issuing banks from suing for breach of contract. In re TJX Cos. Retail Sec. Breach Litig., 564 F.3d 489 (1st Cir. 2009).

But excluding putative beneficiaries is not as easy as it may seem. For one thing, the contract has to be consistent. If a contract contains both a general statement barring third parties from suing and a more specific provision granting rights to third parties, basic principles of contract interpretation suggest that the more specific clause will control. *See, e.g.,* Prouty v. Gores Tech. Group, 18 Cal. Rptr. 3d 178 (Ct. App. 2004) (specific clause granting severance benefits to employees prevails over general provision precluding third-party beneficiary status). For another, the contract had better exclude the third parties expressly, not by implication. A contract may state that one particular entity has the right to sue for breach. That does not necessarily mean that all other entities are excluded. *Compare* Limbach Co. v. City of Philadelphia, 905 A.2d 567 (Pa. Commw. 2006) (no exclusion) *with* Ahmad v. Wells Fargo Bank, 861 F.Supp.2d 818 (E.D. Mich. 2012) (exclusion). The drafters could instead have written, not that entity X has the right to sue, but that *only* entity X has the right to sue.

Contracts for Public Services

The opinion in Seaver v. Ransom cites "public contract" cases in which municipalities bargained for benefits to be conferred on their inhabitants. The first of these concerned a contract made on behalf of the State of New York with A. Bleecker Banks, a publisher. Banks had agreed to supply copies of the New York Reports "to all alike," and to allot a specified quantity to any other law-book dealer. In the event of his breach, Banks was to pay liquidated damages of $100 to any aggrieved person. Banks had declined to sell to another dealer, named Little. In Little v. Banks, 85 N.Y. 258 (N.Y. 1881), the court affirmed a judgment against Banks, citing Lawrence v. Fox. Apparently the court perceived a way to distinguish that case, for it said that it need not rely on the rule laid down there. It cited other New York cases in support of "a broad principle of public policy essential to the public welfare," and applicable where officers of the State had entered into a contract "for the advantage and welfare of the public." (Judges of the Court of Appeals naturally saw an inestimable advantage to the public in having their opinions distributed widely.)

Subsequent decisions by the New York Court of Appeals have placed some bounds on the broad principle of Little v. Banks. One concerned a contract by a water company to supply the City of Rensselaer with water for homes and commercial users, and for various city purposes. In an action against the company, the claimant alleged that a fire had spread to its warehouse owing to the company's failure to supply enough water at the pressure needed for firefighting, and that the warehouse and its contents had been destroyed. The trial court dismissed the claim. The Court of Appeals approved. Distinguishing Lawrence v. Fox, the court said: "No legal duty rests upon a city to supply its inhabitants with protection against fire." City uses of water were the subject of separate "branches" of the contract. No intention was discernible to "assume an obligation of indefinite extension to every member of the public. . . . [Such an intention] is seen to be the more improbable when we recall the crushing burden that the obligation would impose." As to liability in the event that a fire should lay low an entire city, "A promisor will not be deemed to have had in mind the assumption of a risk so overwhelming for any trivial reward." The court applied the method of analogy: "A promisor undertakes to supply fuel for heating a public building. He is not liable for breach of contract to a visitor who finds the building without fuel, and thus contracts a cold." H.R. Moch Co. v. Rensselaer Water Co., 159 N.E. 896, 897 (N.Y. 1928) (Cardozo, C.J.). See also Ultramares Corp. v. Touche, 174 N.E. 441 (N.Y. 1931) (Cardozo, C.J.), in which the court spoke of liability "in an indeterminate amount for an indeterminate time to an indeterminate class."

The New York high court has gone on to moderate liabilities that might have been "crushing" by means other than rejecting third-party claims. For example, it reversed a judgment for roughly half a million dollars, stemming from the death of the claimant's husband. The claimant alleged that his death was caused by an undue delay in responding to a call for help after a mishap on the State Thruway. The defendant was an oil company which had contracted with the Thruway Authority to sell gas and make service calls. The court found in the contract an intention by the Authority to serve the interests of motorists in some ways, as well as its own interest. But the court said that a personal-injury claim was "another matter." It relied on the doctrine of Hadley v. Baxendale, p. 965 above. Kornblut v. Chevron Oil Co., 389 N.Y.S.2d 232 (Sup. Ct. 1976), *rev'd,* 407 N.Y.S.2d 498 (App. Div. 1978), *aff'd on opinion below,* 400 N.E.2d 368 (N.Y. 1979).

On the other hand, in Koch v. Consolidated Edison Co., 468 N.E.2d 1 (N.Y. 1984), the court was faced with claims by New York City and fourteen public benefit corporations for losses due to looting and vandalism that followed a massive power failure in New York City. Some of the claimants relied on agreements made by the power supplier ("Con Ed") with the State's Power Authority to provide customers with service of a stated quality. The court said that power users were "precisely the consumers for whose benefit . . . the agreements [were] made." It distinguished *Moch* and *Kornblut* because "[i]n neither of those cases did the operative contract provide that the service was to be rendered other than for the contracting party, city or authority. Moreover, in *Moch* we noted the distinction between the agreement of the water company, there in issue, to furnish water at the hydrants and the agreement of the water company to provide direct service to members of the public at their homes and factories. In the present instance, the purpose of the enabling legislation was expressly stated to be "To preserve reliability of electric service in the metropolitan area of the city of New York" (Public Authorities Law, § 1001–a, subd. 1), and the service agreement contained the express obligation to "operate and maintain all the facilities necessary to deliver power to Astoria-Indian Point Customers [which included plaintiffs] in accordance with good utility operating practice". Indeed, the essence of the responsibility of a public utility is to provide services to the consuming public." 468 N.E.2d at 7. However, the court limited the utility's liability to damages resulting from looting and vandalism. It specifically barred recovery of the extra costs for safety and sanitation personnel resulting from the blackout and for taxes and other revenues not collected for that reason. The former was prevented because of a general public policy against recovering public expenditures made in the performance of governmental functions. The latter was prevented by the overly speculative nature of those damages and by "strong considerations of public policy which militate against recognition of losses sustained by municipal and public benefit corporations in consequence of adverse effects on the general economy." 468 N.E.2d at 8.

The facts of the next principal cases bring them within the realm of contracts for public services, although the claimant was not a member of the public at large. (The claimant in each, Sisney, was a prisoner.)

NOTES

(1) *Reasoning About* H.R. Moch. Most owners of improved real property maintain insurance against serious fire losses. If the Moch Company was insured against the damage to its warehouse, and the insurer had paid it for the loss, the insurer might well have made a claim against the Water Company. As between those parties, how should the loss be allocated? Thinking about that question might lead to a choice between raising the cost of fire insurance and raising the cost of water in fire hydrants. Is that an easy choice? All the City's taxpayers had to contribute to the cost of water, whereas some of them could have done without insurance. Does that matter? (For what it is worth, the City had agreed to pay the Water Company $42.50 a year for supplying each of its hydrants.)

(2) *Salmon Versus Farmers.* Farmers have sought to qualify as third-party beneficiaries of contracts about waters subject to management by the U.S. Bureau of Reclamation. Decisions on the point are mixed. The Court of Appeals for the Ninth Circuit has resisted, saying:

> Parties that benefit from a government contract are generally assumed to be incidental beneficiaries, and may not enforce the contract absent a clear intent to the contrary. Government contracts often benefit the public, but individual members of the public are treated as incidental beneficiaries unless a different intention is manifested.

Orff v. United States, 358 F.3d 1137 (9th Cir. 2004) (quoting from Klamath Water Users Protective Ass'n v. Patterson, 204 F.3d 1206, 1211 (9th Cir. 1999)).

Orff was one of a long line of cases involving the nation's largest federal water-management project, the Central Valley [California] Project. The farmers sought relief under a contract between their water district and the United States. The Bureau had reduced the diversion of water from the Sacramento River for the protection of Chinook salmon.

According to Professor Eisenberg, "a third party should be allowed to enforce a contract where enforcement is supported by an independent reason of policy or morality and would not conflict with the contracting parties' performance objectives"; and this proposition tends to favor the enforcement of government contracts by third-party beneficiaries. Eisenberg at 1409. Can the Ninth Circuit decision in *Orff* be made to comport with that? The cases that follow test that proposition.

Sisney v. State

South Dakota Supreme Court, 2008.
754 N.W.2d 639.

■ ZINTER, JUSTICE. Charles E. Sisney, an inmate in the South Dakota State Penitentiary (SDSP), filed a *pro se* complaint against the State of South Dakota, Douglas Weber, and CBM Inc. (Defendants). Sisney alleged that CBM breached a state contract under which CBM agreed to provide food services to the State at Department of Correction (DOC) facilities. Sisney sought damages for breach of contract as a third-party beneficiary. The circuit court dismissed for failure to state claim, concluding that Sisney was not a third-party beneficiary who could enforce a public contract. We affirm, finding no third-party beneficiary status.

I

Sisney pleaded that he is Jewish and follows a kosher diet as a part of his religion. Douglas Weber is the Director of Prison Operations for the State of South Dakota, and CBM is a corporation that provides food services to the State of South Dakota.

In July or August of 2002, the State entered into a contract with CBM to provide food services at DOC facilities, including prisons. Under the contract, the services were to be provided "to the State" in a manner that would meet the needs and concerns of the facilities' residents, inmates and staff. The contract provided that "[t]he proposed menu . . . [was to] have an average caloric base of 2700 to 2500 calories per day." The contract further provided that "[f]ood substitutions [were to] be available to accommodate food avoidances due to religious beliefs/practices/observances[.]"

In April of 2007, CBM began serving different food at DOC facilities in which prisoners had requested a kosher diet. Sisney filed an administrative grievance through the DOC, claiming that the new kosher diet averaged 400 to 500 fewer calories than the minimum required under the State's contract with CBM. He also alleged that the food did not meet the dictates of his religious beliefs. Sisney based his grievance on his study of the kosher diet. Weber responded that Sisney's study was incomplete and underestimated the actual caloric content of the meals served. Weber informed Sisney that no action would be taken. Sisney grieved Weber's response. Weber again rejected Sisney's claims, indicating that no further action would be taken on his grievance.

Sisney then brought this suit premising his state and federal claims on allegations that Defendants had "conspired together to cause, permit, and allow a breach of contract to the detriment of [Sisney] because of his religious beliefs; and that this breach of contract resulted in financial gain to the Defendants." Sisney claimed standing to sue for breach of contract "because the contract directly affect[ed] him and his well-being."

Defendants moved to dismiss for failure to state a claim upon which relief could be granted under SDCL 15–6–12(b)(5). Defendants argued that Sisney's claims were barred by statutory immunity and a lack of standing to assert breach of a public contract between the State and CBM.

The circuit court granted Defendants' motion. The court concluded that "[e]ven assuming as true all of [Sisney's] factual allegations contained in the [c]omplaint, it cannot be said that he has standing to assert a breach of contract claim for a contract which he was not a party, and was not a third-party beneficiary." Sisney now appeals the dismissal and the denial of an opportunity to amend his pleadings.

* * *

III

Sisney asserts that he has standing to sue for breach of the State's contract with CBM, arguing that he is a third-party beneficiary of that contract.

SDCL 53–2–6 governs the right to enforce a contract as a third-party beneficiary. The statute provides, "[a] contract made *expressly* for the benefit of a third person may be enforced by him at any time before the parties thereto rescind it." SDCL 53–2–6 (emphasis added). This does not, however, entitle every person who received some benefit from the contract to enforce it. As this Court stated in Thompson Yards v. Van Nice, 59 S.D. 306, 308, 239 N.W. 753, 755 (1931):

> The [third-party beneficiary] statute is not applicable to every contract made by one person with another for the performance of which a third person will derive a benefit; the intent to make the contract inure to the benefit of a third party must be clearly manifested. In the language of the statute, the contract must be one "made expressly for the benefit of a third person."

(Citations omitted.) *See also* Trouten v. Heritage Mut. Ins. Co., 2001 SD 106, ¶ 13, 632 N.W.2d 856, 858; Kary v. Kary, 318 N.W.2d 334, 336 (S.D.1982); Fry v. Ausman, 29 S.D. 30, 135 N.W. 708, 710 (1912). Thus, the rule requires that *at the time the contract was executed,* it was the contracting parties' intent to *expressly* benefit the third party. And, even then, not all beneficiaries qualify: incidental beneficiaries are not entitled to third-party beneficiary status. North Dakota, in construing language similar to SDCL 53–2–6, explained that even "the mention of one's name in an agreement does not give rise to a right to sue for enforcement of the agreement where that person is only incidentally benefited." First Fed. Sav. & Loan Ass'n of Bismarck v. Compass Inv. Inc., 342 N.W.2d 214, 218 (N.D.1983). The party claiming third-party beneficiary status must show "that the contract was entered into by the parties directly and primarily for his benefit." Mercado v. Mitchel, 83 Wis.2d 17, 28, 264 N.W.2d 532, 538 (1978). "The benefit must be more than merely incidental to the agreement." *Id.*

"Government contracts . . . pose unique difficulties in the area of third-party beneficiary rights because, to some extent, every member of the public is directly or indirectly intended to benefit from such a contract." Clifton v. Suburban Cable TV Co. Inc., 434 Pa.Super. 139, 144, 642 A.2d 512, 515 (1994). Therefore, as a general rule, a private party who contracts with the public government entity does not open itself to liability at the hands of the public. Restatement (Second) of Contracts § 302 (1981). A private third-party right of enforcement is not properly inferred because of the potential burden that expanded liability would impose. *See id.* The right of enforcement in public contracts can only arise from the plain and clear language of the contract. *See id.* Consequently, when a public contract is involved, private citizens are presumed not to be third-party beneficiaries. Drummond v. Univ. of Pa., 651 A.2d 572, 578–79 (Pa.Cmwlth.1994). The Pennsylvania court observed that "[t]here must be language evincing an intent that the party contracting with the government will be liable to third parties in the event of nonperformance." *Id.* at 579.

Under these rules, it is generally held that inmates lack standing to enforce public contracts. *Clifton,* 642 A.2d at 514. *See also* Gay v. Ga. Dep't of Corrections, 270 Ga.App. 17, 606 S.E.2d 53, 57–59 (2004)[1] (stating, "the mere fact that the [third party] would benefit from performance of the agreement is not alone sufficient" to render that party a third-party beneficiary). The rationale underlying these decisions is that public contracts are intended to benefit everyone, and therefore, the inmate's benefit is only incidental to the contract.

In this case, the contract was a public contract between the State of South Dakota and CBM, and the contract did not expressly indicate that it was intended for Sisney's direct benefit or enforcement. On the contrary, the contract reflects that it was made for the express benefit of the State, and the collective benefit that inmates may have received was only incidental to that of the State. Sisney concedes as much, indicating that his relationship with the contract involved a mere "benevolent nexus between the promisee [State] and the beneficiary [Sisney]." Brief of Appellant at 12.

Nevertheless, Sisney argues that because the contract provided that "[t]he contractor shall describe the complaint resolution process in place for addressing complaints," Sisney possessed a right of enforcement. Sisney, however, conceded that the complaint resolution mechanism is a

---

[1]   Sisney argues that *Clifton* and *Gay* are inapplicable because the contracts in those cases contained clauses that specifically provided only the State could enforce the contract. This distinction is irrelevant, however, because both cases were decided on the basis that, similar to Sisney's case, there was no indication or language in the contracts that clearly expressed the signatory parties' intent to benefit the specific inmates at issue: they were only incidentally benefited, and therefore they lacked standing. *Clifton,* 642 A.2d at 512; *Gay,* 606 S.E.2d at 53.

general administrative remedy: *See* SDDOC Policy 1.3.E.2. Because this remedy is a general institutional remedy provided to all inmates to address numerous confinement complaints, and because that remedy is provided independent of the State's food service contract with CBM, the contract's reference to that policy does not confer contractual third-party beneficiary status on Sisney to *enforce* the contract.

* * *

We affirm the circuit court's dismissal of Sisney's complaint.

Sisney v. Reisch

South Dakota Supreme Court, 2008.
754 N.W.2d 813.

■ ZINTER, JUSTICE. Charles E. Sisney, an inmate in the South Dakota State Penitentiary (SDSP), filed a *pro se* complaint alleging that he was a third-party beneficiary of a settlement agreement between the Department of Corrections (DOC) and a former inmate. Sisney claimed that DOC and penitentiary officials breached the settlement agreement when they did not provide him with pre-packaged, certified kosher meals. The circuit court dismissed for failure to state a claim. We reverse, concluding that Sisney pleaded sufficient facts to support the inference that defendants were responsible for enforcing the settlement agreement; that Sisney was a third-party beneficiary of the agreement; and that suit on the agreement was not barred by sovereign immunity.

I

Sisney pleaded that he is Jewish and follows a kosher diet as part of his religion. Defendant Tim Reisch is the Secretary of the DOC, and Defendant Douglas Weber is the Director of Prison Operations.

In 1998, inmate Philip Heftel filed a suit under 42 U.S.C. § 1983 alleging that the DOC had deprived Heftel of his constitutional right to free exercise of the Jewish religion. The parties ultimately entered into a settlement agreement (hereinafter "Heftel Agreement" or "Agreement"), which Heftel and Jeffrey Bloomberg (then Secretary of the DOC) signed in February 2000. The Heftel Agreement provided that the DOC "agree[d] to provide a kosher diet to all Jewish inmates who request it," and that the kosher diet would include "[p]repackaged meals which are certified kosher for noon and evening meals[.]"

In February of 2007, the SDSP's food service provider, CBM Inc., quit serving prepackaged kosher meals and began serving a new kosher diet, including a rice and bean mixture prepared and cooked in the SDSP kitchen. Sisney alleged that this change violated the Heftel Agreement and his religious beliefs. Sisney subsequently submitted a grievance through DOC administrative procedures. Weber responded that Sisney was not a party to the Heftel Agreement. Sisney then brought this suit against Reisch and Weber in their individual and official capacities.

Sisney alleged that Reisch and Weber breached the Heftel Agreement "in violation of South Dakota Law and Statute(s)."

The circuit court dismissed the suit, concluding that Sisney's claim was barred by statutory immunity, and in addition, the complaint did not contain sufficient factual assertions supporting an inference that either Reisch or Weber was responsible for enforcing the Agreement. The circuit court did not reach the issue of whether Sisney had third-party standing to enforce the Heftel Agreement. Sisney now appeals the dismissal and the denial of an opportunity to amend his pleadings.

* * *

III

A

The circuit court first concluded that the complaint failed to state a claim because it contained "no factual assertions supporting an inference that it was the Defendants' responsibility to carry out the [Heftel Agreement]." We disagree with this conclusion.

The complaint alleged that Reisch is the current Secretary of Corrections. The Agreement reflects that it was executed on behalf of the DOC by Jeffrey Bloomberg, the former Secretary of Corrections. These facts create a legal inference that Reisch, as the current Secretary of Corrections, is the superseding party responsible for carrying out the Agreement. *See* SDCL 24–1–4 (providing, [t]he state penitentiary and its ancillary facilities shall be under the direction and government of the Department of Corrections); SDCL 1–15–1.3 (providing, "the secretary of corrections shall be qualified by training and experience to administer the programs of the Department of Corrections"). Similarly, as the alleged Director of Prison Operations for the DOC, Weber's position creates the inference that he may be responsible for enforcing the Agreement at the penitentiary. At this stage in the proceedings, Sisney is entitled to the inference that it was Reisch's and Weber's responsibility to enforce the Heftel Agreement at the SDSP.

B

On appeal, Defendants reassert their circuit court argument that Sisney was not entitled to enforce the Agreement as a third-party beneficiary. SDCL 53–2–6–provides, "[a] contract made expressly for the benefit of a third person may be enforced by him at any time before the parties thereto rescind it." In Trouten v. Heritage Mut. Ins. Co., 2001 SD 106, ¶ 13, 632 N.W.2d 856, 858–59, we highlighted the express benefit requirement, noting that the purported third-party beneficiary must clearly show that the contract was entered into with intent to benefit that party:

[W]henever two parties enter into an agreement that appears to have been made expressly for the benefit of a third party, and such agreement has a good and sufficient consideration, the agreement itself creates all the privity there need be between the person for whose benefit the agreement was entered into and the party assuming the obligation, and an action at law should lie regardless of whether there was any obligation existing between the other party to the agreement and the third party. *But, before the third party can adopt the agreement entered into and recover thereon, he must show clearly that it was entered into with the intent on the part of the parties thereto that such third party should be benefited thereby.*

(Emphasis added). Standing to enforce an agreement as a third-party beneficiary may also be conferred upon a class of individuals. "[T]he terms of the contract must clearly express intent to benefit that party or an identifiable class of which the party is a member." Verni v. Cleveland Chiropractic College, 212 S.W.3d 150, 153 (Mo.2007) [p. 1147 below]. "This intent might, in a given case, sufficiently appear from the contract itself [.]" *Trouten*, 2001 SD 106, ¶ 13, 632 N.W.2d at 859.

In this case, the Heftel Agreement clearly expressed that the DOC agreed to provide a kosher diet to an identifiable class of which Sisney was a member; i.e., "to all Jewish inmates who request it." Agreement, ¶ 3. Further, the Agreement expressly reflected an intent to benefit all members of that class: "[i]nmates who request a kosher diet will receive kosher meals regardless of their custody status;" and the DOC "will provide inmates who request a kosher diet a kosher meal prior to the beginning of the fast day and at the conclusion of the fast." Agreement, ¶¶ 3, 4. At the pleading stage of the suit, this explicit contractual language reflected the signatories' intent to provide more than an incidental benefit: the foregoing contractual language raised the inference that the Heftel Agreement was intended to expressly benefit all Jewish inmates who requested a kosher diet. Because Sisney alleged that he was a member of that class, we conclude that Sisney's complaint was sufficient to state a claim that he is a third-party beneficiary with standing to enforce the Heftel Agreement.

* * *

Considering Sisney's factual assertions in a light most favorable to the pleader, the complaint stated a third-party beneficiary cause of action for enforcement of the Heftel Agreement and for declaratory relief. In light of this conclusion, we do not consider Sisney's argument regarding amendment of the complaint.

Reversed and remanded.

NOTE

A Tale of Two Sisneys. Why the different results in *Sisney v. State* and *Sisney v. Reisch*? In particular, how can a prisoner who requires kosher food not be an intended beneficiary of a contract to supply prisons with kosher food? Why else does the contract exist? And what is the practical difference between giving Sisney the right to sue in one case and not giving him the right to sue in the other? Bear in mind that the relief available from different defendants may vary, depending on the extent to which each defendant may invoke sovereign immunity to avoid liability.

First Restatement

§ 133.   Definition   of   Donee   Beneficiary,   Creditor   Beneficiary, Incidental Beneficiary

(1)   Where performance of a promise in a contract will benefit a person other than the promisee, that person is [exception omitted]:

(a)   a donee beneficiary if it appears from the terms of the promise in view of the accompanying circumstances that the purpose of the promisee in obtaining the promise of all or part of the performance thereof is to make a gift to the beneficiary or to confer upon him a right against the promisor to some performance neither due nor supposed or asserted to be due from the promisee to the beneficiary;

(b)   a creditor beneficiary if no purpose to make a gift appears from the terms of the promise in view of the accompanying circumstances and performance of the promise will satisfy an actual or supposed or asserted duty of the promisee to the beneficiary, or a right of the beneficiary against the promisee which has been barred by the Statute of Limitations or by a discharge in bankruptcy, or which is unenforceable because of the Statute of Frauds;

(c)   an incidental beneficiary if neither the facts stated in Clause (a) nor those stated in Clause (b) exist.

NOTE

New Diction; New(ish) Law. The comparable section in the Restatement Second is different, at least in phrasing. It retains the expression "incidental beneficiary," but it uses the expression "intended beneficiary" where the original Restatement would have said "donee beneficiary" or "creditor beneficiary." There may be less here than meets the eye. In *Seaver v. Ransom,* Marion Seaver fit the definition of "donee beneficiary," and she fits comfortably within the category of what may now be called "intended subsection (1)(b) beneficiary." In *Lawrence v. Fox,* Lawrence fit the definition of "creditor beneficiary," and he fits comfortably within the category "intended subsection (1)(a) beneficiary." For these cases, at least, the revision was only a rewording. Some courts have continued to use the discarded expressions well into this century.

For other situations the revision made a substantive difference. To name just one, the Restatement Second requires that the duty owed by the promisee to the beneficiary be the duty to pay money or its near equivalent. Restatement Second § 302 cmt. *b.* In contrast, the original Restatement had no such limitation. Restatement First § 133(1)(b). On the other hand, recall the phrasing of Restatement Second § 90(1) on promissory estoppel—that the promisor must reasonably expect the promise to induce "action or forbearance on the part of the promisee *or a third person*" (emphasis added). Thus, even an incidental beneficiary of a promise may have a right against the promisor because of her reliance on the promise. (What would be the biggest hurdle a third party would have under Restatement Second § 90(1)?)

PROBLEM

The Tenant Mix. In Gianni v. R. Russell & Co., 126 A. 791 (Pa. 1924), a provision of Gianni's lease of a room used as a store in an office building was that he would not sell tobacco in any form. Suppose the owner of the office building had leased other space to a lessee who would use that space for tobacco sales. If so, should the lessee of the other space be treated as a third-party beneficiary of Gianni's promise not to sell tobacco? Is this case provided for in Restatement Second § 302(1)(a)? Is it provided for in First Restatement § 133(2)(b)? Does the law of restitution warrant a claim against Gianni by the other tenant, on the facts supposed?

In a similar case, the claimant was defeated, but the ruling was based on a statute curtailing the rights of third-party beneficiaries. Tusa v. Roffe, 791 So.2d 512 (Fla.App.2001).

Statutes

Many state statutes deal with some aspect of third-party claims, either to support or to suppress them. Three of those statutes are presented here.

Oklahoma: 15 Okla.Stat. § 29—Beneficiary may enforce

> A contract, made expressly for the benefit of a third person, may be enforced by him at any time before the parties thereto rescind it.

West Virginia: Code § 55–8–12

> If a covenant or promise be made for the sole benefit of a person with whom it is not made, or with whom it is made jointly with others, such person may maintain, in his own name, any action thereon which he might maintain in case it had been made with him only, and the consideration had moved from him to the party making such covenant or promise.

Michigan: Compiled Laws § 600.1405

Any person for whose benefit a promise is made by way of contract, as hereinafter defined, has the same right to enforce said promise that he would have had if the said promise had been made directly to him as the promisee.

> (1) A promise shall be construed to have been made for the benefit of a person whenever the promisor of said promise had

undertaken to give or to do or refrain from doing something directly to or for said person.

NOTES

(1) *Direct Performance.* "A's son C is indebted to D. With the purpose of assisting C, A secures from B a promise to pay the debt to D." On these facts, according to the Restatement, D is an intended beneficiary of the promise. And so is C. Restatement § 302, ill. 6. According to the Michigan statute, should the promise be construed to have been made for the benefit of D? For the benefit of C?

The test of direct performance is criticized in Eisenberg at 1380–81. See also Stowe v. Smith, 441 A.2d 81 (Conn.1981): "Contracts for the benefit of a third party are enforceable without any requirement that the promisor's performance be rendered directly to the intended beneficiary." Id. at 83.

(2) *Third-Party Beneficiaries and Private Rights of Action.* Many statutes provide specifically for private rights of action. For example, under CERCLA—The Comprehensive Environmental Reponse, Compensation and Liability Act—also known as the "Superfund" statute, a potentially responsible party ("PRP") may sue another PRP to recover its environmental response costs. CERCLA § 107(a), 42 U.S.C. § 9607(a); U.S. v. Atlantic Research Corp., 551 U.S. 128 (2007). When a statute is silent, often those affected by it will argue for an implied right of action. But the Supreme Court has made clear the reluctance with which it finds those rights. See Stoneridge Inv. Partners v. Scientific-Atlanta, Inc., 552 U.S. 148, 164–65 (2008) ("[T]here is an implied cause of action only if the underlying statute can be interpreted to disclose the intent to create one. Concerns with the judicial creation of a private cause of action caution against its expansion. The decision to extend the cause of action is for Congress, not for us."). In response, private parties often have tried to sue as third-party beneficiaries of contracts regulated by statute, seeking to assert statutory rights violated by one party and not enforced by the other. This has been especially common when one of the parties is governmental.

Until fairly recently, these private parties met with occasional success. See Amaral v. Cintas Corp., 78 Cal. Rptr. 3d 572 (Ct. App. 2008) (employees were intended beneficiaries of employer's agreement with city pursuant to ordinance that employer would pay living wage). At least for federal statutes, the Supreme Court recently slammed this door shut in Astra USA v. Santa Clara County, 563 U.S. 110 (2011). There a county and its medical facilities sued pharmaceutical manufacturers for breach of the manufacturers' pricing agreements with the federal government. The statute providing for this program did not create a private right of action. The county therefore sued as a third-party beneficiary of the pricing agreements. The Court held unanimously that this wouldn't wash. The pricing agreements "simply incorporate statutory obligations and record the manufacturers' agreement to abide by them. A third-party suit to enforce an HHS-drug manufacturer agreement, therefore, is in essence an suit to enforce the statute itself." 563 U.S. at 118. *Astra USA* doesn't put the kibosh on all third-party-beneficiary suits intended to avoid the absence of a private cause of action. Should the private party seek to enforce an aspect of the contract other than one arising from statutory obligations, the Court's decision in *Astra USA* would not apply. But the great majority of these suits center upon violations of statutory requirements, and these are clearly foreclosed.

PROBLEMS

(1) A college enters into a contract for the renovation of its football stadium. The general contractor subcontracts the job of reinforcing the bleachers. Given a breach by the subcontractor, would it be plausible for the college to make a claim as a third-party beneficiary of the subcontract?

(2) Suppose that a breach by the subcontractor causes a delay in reopening the stadium, and cancellation of the first game of the season. Would it be plausible for a disappointed fan, holding a ticket for that game, to make a claim as a third-party beneficiary of the subcontract? Instead suppose that a breach by the general contractor caused the cancellation. Would it be plausible for the fan to make a claim as a third-party beneficiary of the general contract?

Third-Party Claims for Bad-Faith Breach

The victim of a breach of contract can sometimes enhance recovery by showing that the breach was a *bad-faith* breach, see discussion on p. 34 above. May a third-party beneficiary do so as well? If so, one can imagine that courts would be inclined to withhold relief altogether from third-party claimants as a way to curtail the doctrine of bad-faith breach. But that would go overboard; a better means is to discriminate among classes of beneficiaries, or types of contracts, so that only some of them sustain recoveries for bad-faith breach.

Third-party claims on insurance contracts are especially important here, because the doctrine of bad-faith breach focuses largely on insurers. As one court put it, an insurer's duty to deal fairly and act in good faith "does not extend to every party entitled to payment of insurance benefits." Anderson v. American Int'l Specialty Lines Ins. Co., 38 P.3d 240, 241 (Okla.App. 2001), echoing Roach v. Atlas Life Ins. Co., 769 P.2d 158, 161 (Okla. 1989). In deciding about third parties to whom that duty *does* extend, a court might nominate any or all of the following persons and firms:

> One that qualifies as a person insured by the policy in question;

> One on whom the insurer is bound by the policy to confer a direct payment or other benefit;

> One of whom, as the insurer should understand, a buyer of the coverage was solicitous.

Rather than endowing entities—persons and firms—with bad-faith claims according to the favor intended by a particular buyer, a court might select one or more *coverages* commonly bought as benevolences, and assign duties of good faith to those.

The opinion in *Roach* proceeds along that line. The court said: "There must be either a contractual or statutory relationship between the insurer and the party asserting the bad faith claim before the duty arises. The beneficiary of a life insurance contract meets both criteria for assertion of the right. [T]he failure to afford a cause of action for bad faith to the beneficiary of a life insurance policy would negate a substantial reason for the insured's purchase of the policy—the peace of mind and security which it provides in the event of loss." Id. at 161–62.

Doubtless medical-expense coverages often are bought for the same purpose. But Oklahoma courts have held otherwise in cases about that coverage bought in conjunction with premises-liability coverage. *Anderson*, above, and Rednour v. JC & P Partnership, 996 P.2d 487 (Okla.Civ.App. 1999). In *Rednour* the court said: "the primary purpose behind a business owner's purchase of liability insurance is the protection of assets. Medical expense provisions in such policies principally serve that goal by reducing the likelihood of further litigation through the prompt payment of medical expenses of parties injured on the premises without the necessity of them suing the business owner and proving negligence." Id. at 490. Hence punitive damages were unavailable to a third-party claimant who charged that the insurer was slow to pay expenses resulting from a fall he had suffered.

PROBLEM

Howard bought auto liability insurance on his car. He allowed his daughter Margo to drive it. That made Margo an insured driver, according to an omnibus clause included in the policy. Margo gave a lift to a friend named Arielle. Arielle was injured in a collision. She made a claim against Margo, charging her with negligent driving, and a claim against Howard under an owners' liability statute. Margo and Howard demanded that the insurer provide defenses against Arielle's claims, as required by its policy. The insurer treated the demands with unwarranted contempt. Arielle won judgments against Howard and Margo. She then demanded payment from the insurer, who treated that demand with the same contempt.

Now Howard, Margo, and Arielle make claims against the insurer for punitive damages by reason of bad-faith breach. Going by Oklahoma law, which of those claims is viable, if any?

Does it matter that an Oklahoma statute required Howard's policy to contain the omnibus clause? See Gianfillippo v. Northland Casualty Co., 861 P.2d 308 (Okla. 1993); 47 Okl.St. § 7–324.

Verni v. Cleveland Chiropractic College

Missouri Supreme Court, 2007.
212 S.W.3d 150.

[Leonard Verni was enrolled in a dermatology class conducted by Dr. Aleksandr Makarov at the College. The faculty handbook required that members of the faculty observe some standards of decency in dealing with students. Verni brought an action against Makarov, charging that Makarov had dealt with him in violation of the handbook, and so had violated Makarov's employment contract with the College. (Verni had been dismissed by the school for having sold advance copies of Makarov's exam. He made claims against the College also, but not on the same theory.) Verni won a verdict and judgment against Makarov for $10,000. Makarov appealed.]

■ MICHAEL A. WOLFF, CHIEF JUSTICE.

Verni is not a third-party beneficiary of the contract.

Verni's breach of contract claim asserts that he is a third-party beneficiary of the employment contract between Dr. Makarov and Cleveland. Dr. Makarov argues that Verni was not a party to the contract or a third-party beneficiary of the contract and, thus, did not have standing to raise the claim.

Whether Verni had standing to raise the breach of contract claim is a matter of law that this Court reviews de novo. Where a question of standing has been raised, this Court has a duty to resolve that question before reaching substantive issues.

Only parties to a contract and any third-party beneficiaries of a contract have standing to enforce that contract. Andes v. Albano, 853 S.W.2d 936, 942 (Mo. banc 1993). "To be bound as a third-party beneficiary, the terms of the contract must clearly express intent to benefit that party or an identifiable class of which the party is a member." Nitro Distributing, Inc. v. Dunn, 194 S.W.3d 339, 345 (Mo. banc 2006). "In cases where the contract lacks an express declaration of that intent, there is a strong presumption that the third party is not a beneficiary and that the parties contracted to benefit only themselves." *Id.* "Furthermore, a mere incidental benefit to the third party is insufficient to bind that party." *Id.*

This matter is resolved by examining the contract's language. OFW Corp. v. City of Columbia, 893 S.W.2d 876, 879 (Mo.App. 1995). The contract is a one-page document providing that Dr. Makarov would be a full-time faculty member of Cleveland for one year. The contract required him to be on campus a certain amount of time each week and outlined his teaching duties. In return, the contract provided Dr. Makarov's salary and employment benefits. Although the contract might incidentally provide a benefit to Cleveland students, it does not clearly express any intent that Dr. Makarov was undertaking a duty to benefit Verni or a class of students.

The contract also required Dr. Makarov to comply with the policies and procedures stated in Cleveland's faculty handbook and with any institutional modification thereof. Verni alleges that Dr. Makarov violated the handbook's requirement that faculty members treat students with courtesy, respect, fairness, and professionalism. The handbook also provides that students are entitled to expect such treatment. Assuming, for the sake of argument, that the faculty handbook is a binding part of the employment contract, this language does not overcome the strong presumption that the contract was executed solely for the parties' own benefit.

Undoubtedly, Verni and all of Cleveland's students are incidental beneficiaries of employment contracts between the college and faculty members, but not every person who is benefited by a contract may bring suit to enforce that contract. Rather, only those third-parties who are clearly intended beneficiaries may do so. Verni is not entitled to third-party beneficiary status under the contract between Cleveland and Dr. Makarov because the terms of the contract do not directly and clearly express the intent to benefit Verni or any class of which Verni claims to be a member.

The judgment of the circuit court against Dr. Makarov on Verni's breach of contract claim is reversed.

———

Attorney-Client Contracts and Third Parties

The courts have looked with some favor on charges against attorneys of substandard performance of contracts with their clients, brought by persons and firms other than clients. The Restatement (Third) of the Law Governing Lawyers states some circumstances in which a lawyer owes a duty of care to a non-client, and says that the enforcement of that duty "may promote the lawyer's loyal and effective pursuit of the client's objectives." Section 51. Illustration 2 to that section states a case in which an attorney botched the execution of a will, so that a person named in it—"Nonclient"—was deprived of an intended benefit. According to the illustration, the attorney would be accountable to Nonclient for negligence. A well-known supporting authority is Lucas v. Hamm, 364 P.2d 685 (Cal.1961). An attorney pursuing a claim may also have an obligation to someone other than the client—someone whose hopes ride on the claim. See Oxendine v. Overturf, 973 P.2d 417 (Utah 1999).

On the other hand, courts and scholars have often taken note of countervailing considerations. In the words of the South Carolina Supreme Court, "The imposition of a duty on an attorney to a prospective beneficiary of a nonexistent will would wreak havoc on the attorney's ethical duty of undivided loyalty to the client and force an impermissible wedge in the attorney-client relationship." Rydde v. Morris, 675 S.E.2d 431, 435 (S.C. 2009) (How?) Indeed, in *Lucas* itself the court declined to castigate the defendant attorney, saying that he had stumbled over a rule of property law that had "long perplexed the courts and the bar"—namely, the rule against perpetuities, the bane of suffering property students nationwide. Also, the case is distinguishable when a non-client tries to show that a will is less favorable to him than the testator wished it to be. See Stowe v. Smith, 441 A.2d 81 (Conn.1981), where the court observed that a claim of that kind may be especially difficult to win. Difficult, perhaps, but winnable on extreme facts; see Young v. Williams, 645 S.E.2d 624 (Ga.App. 2007).

A non-client suing on a promise made by an attorney to a client cannot expect an easy victory when it appears that the interests of the claimant and the client were at odds. For illustrations, see California Public Employees' Retirement System [CalPERS] v. Shearman & Sterling, 741 N.E.2d 101 (N.Y.2000), and Baker v. Coombs, 219 S.W.3d 204 (Ky.App.2007). In *CalPERS*, the law firm was charged with fault in documenting an investment. The court observed that CalPERS and the client were on opposite sides of an agreement between the two, and "did not share at all times the same interests." Janice Baker's claim against Coombs grew out of his representation of James Collins when she brought a divorce proceeding against Collins. Disapproving her claim, the court said that Coombs "had a contractual obligation to represent Collins *against* Baker" (emphasis by the court).

NOTES

(1) *Putting the Client First*. The Restatement (Third) of the Law Governing Lawyers alludes to situations in which enforcement would "significantly impair the lawyer's performance of obligations to the client." One such situation arises when an attorney hesitates to prepare a will for a client. If the attorney has a doubt about the client's mental capacity, and imagines a successful will contest, she might worry about being held liable to the winner of that contest—a rightful heir—for the legal expense of winning. A worry like that might deter an attorney from providing a service meritorious in itself. See § 51 and Comment *f* and Illustration 4 thereto. See also Caba v. Barker, 145 P.3d 174 (Or.2006), indicating that a client cannot fairly expect a lawyer, drafting a will, to make it invulnerable to a will contest—cannot, that is, absent an express undertaking to that effect.

(2) *Wanted: Enforcers*. A court resisting a third-party claim against a lawyer may take comfort in the fact that the client may press a claim for negligence by the lawyer. See Ferguson v. Cramer, above. But that is cold comfort if the client has died. When a will is defective, the normal case is that the testator's estate "is not injured . . . except to the extent of fees paid. . . . Unless the beneficiaries can recover against the attorney, no one could do so and the social policy of preventing future harm would be frustrated." Bucquet v. Livingston, 129 Cal.Rptr. 514, 521 (Cal.App.1976). See also the Note at p. 1128 above.

Grigerik v. Sharpe

Supreme Court of Connecticut, 1998.
247 Conn. 293.

[Joseph Grigerik contracted to buy a tract of undeveloped land from Edward Lang for $16,000. He had offered $9,000 for the property "as is," but agreed to the higher price because of Lang's undertaking to get the town's approval of the tract as a building lot. Because the tract was adjacent to a reservoir, the town sanitarian had told the parties that they needed an engineer to prepare a site plan for drainage. Lang contracted for that work—including the design of a septic sewage-disposal system—with Gary Sharpe and a firm with which Sharpe was associated. According to evidence in the case (although Sharpe denied it), Lang told Sharpe that he needed the site plan in order to obtain approval of the land as a building lot and that he had a buyer for the land if the town granted approval. The site plan having been prepared, and approved by the sanitarian, the sale went through. Later, however, when Grigerik applied for a building permit, it was denied. The town sanitarian (a new one) and state authorities concluded that the tract was not suited to a septic system.

Grigerik brought this action against Sharpe and his firm, alleging (i) professional negligence, and (ii) an entitlement as third-party beneficiary of the services contracts. A judgment was entered for Grigerik, on the jury's verdict. (The facts as stated above were those that might reasonably have been found by the jury.) On an appeal by Sharpe, the judgment was reversed by the Appellate Court. That court ruled that (i) the negligence claim was barred by a statute of limitations, and (ii) there was error in charging the jury about third party beneficiary law. For the latter point the Appellate Court relied on the decision in Stowe v. Smith, 441 A.2d 81 (Conn.1981), saying, "we have concluded that the implications of that decision have changed the law and that such a mutual intent of the promisor and promisee is no longer necessary for a beneficiary to have a right to enforce the contract." Grigerik v. Sharpe, 699 A.2d 189, 196 (Conn.App.1997).

Against those rulings Grigerik brought the present appeal. The court disagreed with the first ruling, and wrote as follows about the second.]

■ BORDEN, JUSTICE. The dispositive issues in this certified appeal are: (2) whether it is the intent of the promisee of a contractual obligation, rather than the intent of both of the parties to the contract, which determines whether a third party is a beneficiary of the contract in question. We conclude that: (1) [a] seven year limitations period applies to this action; and (2) it is the intent of both parties to a contract that determines whether a third party is a beneficiary of a contract. Accordingly, we reverse the judgment of the Appellate Court.

With respect to the breach of contract count, the trial court instructed the jury that, in order for the plaintiff to recover as a third party beneficiary to the contract, he was required to establish that he was either an intended, a contemplated, or a foreseeable beneficiary of the contract between Lang and the defendants.[1]

With respect to the breach of contract count, the Appellate Court concluded that the trial court's instructions were flawed in two respects: first, in favor of the plaintiff, by permitting him to recover as a foreseeable, rather than an intended beneficiary of the contract; second, in favor of the defendants, by requiring that both parties, rather than just the promisee of the contractual obligation in question, intended to benefit the plaintiff. Accordingly, the Appellate Court reversed the judgment of the trial court, ordered that judgment be rendered for the defendants on the negligence count, and ordered a new trial on the breach of contract count.

As noted earlier, the jury found that the plaintiff was a foreseeable third party beneficiary of the contract between the defendants and Lang, and returned a verdict in favor of the plaintiff on the plaintiff's breach of contract count.

[Here the court considered its decision in Stowe v. Smith, 441 A.2d 81 (1981), as support for the Grigeriks' claim. The court concluded that its traditional rule about third-party-beneficiary claims had not been changed, "by *Stowe* or any other decision of this court," and that "the intent of both parties to a contract determines whether a third party has contract rights as a third party beneficiary." The court conceded that, in *Stowe*, it had made reference to some remarks by Professor Arthur Corbin in opposition to taking guidance from the intent of the parties.[a]

---

[1]   The trial court instructed the jury as follows: "In light of all the evidence, you must determine whether [the plaintiff] was an intended, contemplated or foreseeable third party which was to derive a benefit from the contract for professional services entered into between the defendants and [Lang]. You must determine that it was intended, contemplated and foreseeable that any buyer of the property would derive a benefit from the contract or you may determine that it was intended, contemplated or foreseeable that [the plaintiff] specifically would derive a benefit from the contract. If you find that it was intended that [the plaintiff] was an intended, contemplated or foreseeable beneficiary to the contract, then you must find that [the plaintiff] was a third party beneficiary to the contract. In summary, if you determine that [the plaintiff] was a third party beneficiary to the contract and that the defendants breached the contract, then [the plaintiff] is entitled to the damages caused him as a result of the breach."

[a]   The passage in *Stowe* is this, as adapted from 441 A.2d 83 n. 1: "Commentators generally look upon the intent of the promisee, if the promisee had any relevant intent, as governing whether a third party may enforce a contract as a donee beneficiary. Restatement (Second), Contracts, c. 6, Introductory Note and § 133 (Tent. Draft 1973); 2 Williston, Contracts (3d Ed.) § 356A, pp. 836, 839 n.19; 4 Corbin, Contracts § 776, p. 16.

"Williston has criticized Colonial Discount Co. v. Avon Motors, Inc., 75 A.2d 507 (1950), and Byram Lumber & Supply Co. v. Page, 146 A. 293 (1929), for proposing as a universal test of third party rights the intent of the contracting parties to impose on the promisor a direct obligation to the third party. 2 Williston, op.cit. § 356A, pp. 838–39.

"Corbin views the ideas that lie behind such terms as 'purpose,' 'motive,' and 'intention' as obscure and elusive. 4 Corbin, op.cit. § 776, pp. 14–15. The problem before the courts, he says, 'is to draw the line between those third persons whose benefit is so indirect and incidental that it is not sound policy to let them enforce the contract, and those other persons whose benefit is so direct and substantial and so closely connected with that of the promisee that it is economically desirable to let them enforce it. The law would profit greatly if the courts would concentrate upon this aspect of the problem and cease to state the questions merely in terms of the supposed 'intent' of the parties. 4 Corbin, op.cit. § 786, p. 95."

But the passage, taken as a whole, did not support Grigerik's argument, the court said.]

Moreover, we disagree with Professor Corbin's view that the concept of "intent" is too "obscure and elusive" to be helpful in determining the contract rights of third parties. 4 A. Corbin, Contracts (1951) § 776, pp. 14–15. We traditionally have relied on the intent of the parties to determine whether a contract has been formed, as well as to determine the meaning of the terms of the contract. See [three cases cited]. We are unpersuaded, therefore, that the concept of intent is any more elusive in the context of determining whether third parties have enforceable rights under the contract.

In support of the view that the presence of a third party beneficiary issue is determined solely by the intention of the promisee, the Appellate Court also relied on 2 Restatement (Second), Contracts § 302 (1981), and concluded that "the notion that the promisor and promisee must share the same intent is at variance with most authorities." Grigerik v. Sharpe, *supra*, 45 Conn.App. 784. Our reading of § 302 of the Restatement (Second) does not support that reliance. That provision provides in relevant part: "Unless otherwise agreed between promisor and promisee, a beneficiary of a promise is an intended beneficiary if recognition of a right to performance in the beneficiary is *appropriate to effectuate the intention of the parties and* . . . the circumstances indicate that the promisee intends to give the beneficiary the benefit of the promised performance." 2 Restatement (Second), *supra*, § 302(1)(b). Thus, the language of the Restatement (Second) suggests that the right to performance in a third party beneficiary is determined both by the intention of the contracting parties and by the intention of one of the parties to benefit the third party.

We decline, therefore, to alter our traditional test for determining whether a third party has enforceable contract rights. We reaffirm that the intent of both parties, rather than just one of the parties to a contract, determines whether a third party is to be afforded third party beneficiary status under a contract.

Applying this standard to the facts of the present case, we conclude that the plaintiff cannot prevail on his breach of contract claim. The jurors specifically found that the plaintiff had not proven that he was an intended beneficiary of the contract between Lang and the defendants. See [editors' footnote a, above]. The plaintiff, therefore, did not establish that it was the intent of the parties that he be a third party beneficiary of the contract.

Although the jury found that the plaintiff was a foreseeable beneficiary of the contract, we agree with the Appellate Court that foreseeability is a tort concept, and the fact that a person is a foreseeable beneficiary of a contract is not sufficient for him to claim rights as a third party beneficiary. To import the concept of foreseeability into the law governing contracts, which is premised "on the concept that mutual obligations entered into voluntarily should be enforced," would significantly reduce contracting parties' ability to control, through the negotiated exchange of promises and consideration, the scope of their contractual duties and obligations.

With respect to the negligence count, the judgment of the Appellate Court is reversed and the case is remanded to that court [with directions]. With respect to the breach of contract count, the judgment of the Appellate Court is reversed and the case is remanded to that court with direction to remand it to the trial court with direction to render judgment for the defendants on that count.

NOTES

(1) *Mutual Intent.* The court stood by an inquiry into the intent of the promisor, as well as an inquiry into the intent of the promisee. It found support in Section 302 of the Restatement. The section speaks both of "the intention of the parties" and the intention of the promisee. A reader might well wonder why.

Conceivably the "intention of the parties" is not an intention "to give the beneficiary the benefit of the promised performance," but is an intention about something else. What that something else might be is not clear. The *Grigerik* opinion simplifies matters, no doubt, with its test of mutual intent. But some readers of the Restatement may consider that test an over-simplification.

(2) *Beneficiaries of Construction Contracts.* Many third-party claims concern construction work. The contract in question is sometimes a subcontract, on which the owner makes a claim; sometimes the general contract, on which a subcontractor makes a claim; and sometimes a sub-subcontract, on which either the owner or the general contractor makes a claim.

These claims are usually rebuffed. Can that be explained without reference to the intent of *both parties* to the contract in question?

(3) *A Professorial Principle.* Professor Melvin A. Eisenberg has harsh words for the test "intent to benefit the claimant," as generalized in the Restatement and elsewhere: *inadequate, largely meaningless.* "[T]he entire enterprise of finding [that] intent . . . is misguided. . . . [T]he intent of the contracting parties is typically to further their own interests. . . . " Eisenberg at 1381. He qualified this, however, in two ways. One concerns a promisee who acts in favor of a third party as a means to serve the promisee's own interests. The other concerns what he called "true donee beneficiaries" (*e.g.*, Marion Seaver, in *Seaver v. Ransom*). He was critical also of the reference in the Restatement to what the claimant might have relied upon with reason, believing that the reasonableness of reliance depends on the decision whether or not that party has an entitlement under the contract—the very issue in question. Id. at 1384.

What Professor Eisenberg instead proposed was a principle allowing for third-party entitlements "supported by reasons of policy or morality independent of contract law," and otherwise only as important means of effectuating the "objectives of the enterprise embodied in the contract"— objectives not necessarily manifested in the parties' language, but only those that the promisor knew or should have known. Id. at 1385.

Vesting of Third-Party Rights

The parties to a contract are generally free to modify it or cancel it, so long as both parties assent to the modification or cancellation. Indeed, they cannot contractually preclude themselves from modifying or cancelling their agreement. This situation becomes more complex when the parties to a contract create a third-party beneficiary. Certainly the parties to a contract may state in that contract that the beneficiary's rights cannot be altered without the beneficiary's assent. Restatement § 311(1), (3). But if the contract does not address vesting expressly, under what circumstances may the parties to it alter or eliminate the rights it gives to a third party?

The Restatement and the courts begin with the assumption that the parties who form a contract have the right to change it or cancel it. Restatement § 311(2). *Any* change to a contract will have effects on non-parties, so the mere existence of affected non-parties isn't sufficient to limit this right. If, however, the parties to a contract intend it to create rights in a non-party and tell the non-party about those rights, the non-party might reasonably consider those rights fixed and definite. The law recognizes this possibility by making contract rights irrevocable when the beneficiary "materially changes its position in justifiable reliance on the promise." Restatement § 311(3). As a result, third-party rights under a contract are treated much the same as offers to enter into unilateral contracts, or promises lacking consideration, or anticipatory repudiations, for example. All of these are legal acts which may normally be revocable but which may create reasonable expectations in those to whom they are directed. Along the same lines, if the beneficiary assents to the promise, then the promise becomes irrevocable by the promisor and promisee. Restatement § 311(3) & cmt. *h.*

The earlier rule of vesting was invoked on behalf of Mrs. Roxanne Scott in Detroit Bank and Trust Co. v. Chicago Flame Hardening Co., 541 F.Supp. 1278 (N.D.Ind.1982). As her guardian, the Detroit Bank referred to a rule stated in the Restatement of 1932. By that rule, applicable to the rights of donee beneficiaries only, those rights vest when they arise. The court described the competing rules as follows:

> The old Restatement rule provided that the promisor and promisee could make no change in the promise made to a donee beneficiary unless such a power is reserved. Restatement of Contracts § 142. Nor could a change be made by the promisor and promisee in their promise to a creditor beneficiary if he has

changed his position in reliance on that promise. *Id.*; see Page, *The Power of Contracting Parties to Alter a Contract for Rendering Performance to a Third Person*, 12 Wis. L. Rev. 141, 149–50 (1937). Evolutionary changes in the law, however, have transformed the aforementioned position of the original Restatement. The Second Restatement of Contracts eliminates this distinction between a donee and creditor beneficiary and recognizes that modification on the part of the promisor and promisee is ineffective only if the agreement so provides, unless the third party beneficiary has changed his position in reliance on the promise or has accepted, adopted or acted upon it.

Id. at 1282–83. The court rejected the "old Restatement rule," and said that it was "not followed by the vast majority of states even at the time of its adoption." The result was that the rescission of a contract for the benefit of Mrs. Scott deprived her of that benefit.

NOTES

(1) *A Statutory Position.* The Michigan statute partly quoted on p. 1143 above contains, in subsection (2), rules about the vesting of the rights of a third party as stated in subsection (1). A two-step sketch of those rules, omitting some significant features, is as follows:

(a) *Cases of the type of Lawrence v. Fox.* The parties to a third-party-beneficiary contract may, subject to two qualifications, divest a right to payment that it confers on a creditor of the promisee, if performance of the promise in question was intended to discharge the promisee's debt. They may not do so with intent to hinder, delay or defraud the creditor, and may do so only *"before he has taken any legal steps to enforce said promise."*

(b) *General rule.* Otherwise, a third party's entitlement under the section becomes vested "without any act or knowledge on his part, the moment the promise becomes legally binding on the promisor." That rule can be overridden by a provision in the contract to the contrary. Also, it is subject to "conditions, limitations, or infirmities of the contract" to which the promise is subject.

What merits and demerits can be found in the Michigan statute, as described here?

(2) *Full and Partial Vesting.* The directors of a corporation adopt a resolution conferring a pension on Mrs. Anna Sachs Feinberg, a long-time employee, payment to begin when she chooses to retire. On being told of the resolution, Mrs. Feinberg transfers her holding of stock in the firm to her daughter as a gift. "I won't need that for my retirement," she says. The stock is worth $10,000 at all material times.

Suppose that the cost to the corporation of the pension is anticipated, reasonably, to be at least $25,000. Compare two possibilities: (a) The corporation can withdraw the pension promise only upon paying Mrs.

Feinberg $10,000, and (b) It cannot withdraw the promise at all. Which is the better rule? The Restatement appears to adopt the latter. But cf. Restatement § 90(1): "The remedy . . . may be limited as justice requires." And see Eisenberg at 1418–19.

————

Claims and Defenses That Apply to the Third-Party Beneficiary

An intended beneficiary derives its rights from the contract between the promisor and the promisee. As a corollary, the beneficiary's rights are subject to the same limits as were the rights of the promisee in the original contract. For example, the third-party beneficiary is vulnerable to such defenses as lack of consideration, failure to satisfy the statute of frauds, mistake, and incapacity. *See, e.g.,* Herd v. Am. Sec. Ins. Co., 556 F.Supp.2d 992 (W.D. Mo. 2008) (mutual mistake defense regarding the presence of other insurance coverage); Holt v. First Nat'l Bank, 418 So.2d 77 (Ala. 1982) (statute of frauds bars claim by daughter under father's and stepmother's pre-nuptial agreement). He is also subject to any claims the promisor might have for breach of promise by the promisee, up to the point at which the promisor's claim against the promisee would extinguish the beneficiary's claim against the promisor. *See* Souza v. Westlands Water Dist., 38 Cal. Rptr. 3d 78 (Ct. App. 2006). But he is not subject to unrelated claims that the promisor may have against the promisee, because those claims arise from contracts not involving the third-party beneficiary. *See* J.G.B. Enters. v. U.S., 497 F.3d 1259 (Fed. Cir. 2007) (right of setoff).

Arbitration clauses have been the subject of much litigation in this area. Commonly a third-party to a contract wants to pursue its claims in court, but the underlying contract contains an arbitration clause. The courts generally hold that the beneficiary must take the bitter with the sweet; if she wants to pursue a claim created under a contract, she can do so only in the venue chosen by the contracting parties. *See* In re Labatt Food Serv., 279 S.W.3d 640 (Tex. 2009) (arbitration clause in employment agreement binds wrongful death beneficiaries of employee). In the pithy words of one court, "A nonparty cannot both have his contract and defeat it too." In re Weekley Homes, 180 S.W.3d 127, 135 (Tex. 2005). But this is true only when the third party is an intended beneficiary of the contract at issue. Thus, for example, the beneficiaries of a life insurance policy were not bound by an arbitration clause in a contract between the insured and the insurance broker; their suit was based on bad investment advice given by the broker that lowered the value of the insurance policy, not on the contract creating the policy. Thompson v. Witherspoon, 12 A.3d 685 (Md. App. 2011). These cases rest more on estoppel than on the law of third-party beneficiaries; indeed, the doctrine under which the third party is bound even by obnoxious clauses is called *direct benefit estoppel*.

SECTION 2.   DELEGATION OF DUTIES

Some contractual duties are delegable, others not.

To say that a duty is delegable signifies that the holder of the reciprocal right cannot object to having the duty performed by someone other than the initial obligor. Many cases presented above illustrate delegable duties. One appears as far back as p. 364: Langman v. Alumni Association. Dr. Langman was an initial obligor, having incurred a debt upon acquiring a property that she later donated to the UVA Alumni Association. In connection with the "gift", the Alumni Association undertook to satisfy Langman's debt. That is, she *delegated* her duty to the Association. A money debt is a paradigm of delegable duty. If the Association had tendered payment to Langman's creditor, the creditor would not have been heard to object that the money should have come from her. It is not that the creditor would have been likely to make that objection; almost all creditors are content to take payment from any source. That fact goes a long way toward explaining why an obligation to pay a fixed sum of money is within the category "delegable duty." A similar delegation was made in *Lawrence v. Fox,* p. 1120 above, Holly having delegated to Fox the duty to pay Lawrence.

At the extreme, nondelegable duties are easy to distinguish. A standard example is that of a singer, engaged to perform in public. In this connection, one court has mentioned the exceptional talent of the late Luciano Pavarotti ("the great tenor"). The court supposed this case: Pavarotti contracts with the agency operating a city airport to sing in its terminal "in order to soothe the souls of weary travelers." Pavarotti enters bankruptcy and a trustee is appointed to manage his bankruptcy estate. Relying on a provision of the Bankruptcy Code about executory contracts, the trustee attempts to delegate the responsibility for singing to the pop-star Michael Jackson. After stating that case, the court said that the agency could not be compelled to accept performance by Jackson. The performance is of a type, the court suggested, "that depends upon the identity of the party that is to perform" (*e.g.,* Pavarotti). Metropolitan Airports Comm'n v. Northwest Airlines, Inc., 6 F.3d 492 (7th Cir. 1993). Presumably the converse would hold: If Jackson had made the contract and had entered bankruptcy, the agency could not be compelled to accept a vocal recital by Pavarotti instead. If a more extreme example of non-delegable duties is wanted, consider those undertaken by the parties entering into a contract of marriage. The Restatement criterion is whether or not the obligee has "a substantial interest in having [a particular] person perform or control the acts promised." Section 318(2).

Metropolitan Airports Comm'n was actually a case about a lease of airport space. The tenant being in bankruptcy, the question was whether or not the Airports Commission could be compelled to deal with a substitute tenant. As to that, the court said that the payment of rent pursuant to a lease is "hardly the type of performance that depends upon the identity of . . . the lessee." Of course a lease may require action by the lessee of some other type, as to which the lessor can decline to accept performance by a surrogate.

NOTE

Delegation as a Threat. It may be that the "substantial interest" test does not capture fully the interest of a promisee in shunning strangers as potential delegates of the promised undertaking. A commentator has suggested that a stranger "may have a greater willingness [than the initial promisor] to breach in the hope of getting some collateral gain." Richard Epstein, *Why Restrain Alienation?*, 85 Colum. L. Rev. 970, 983 (1985). (Oddly, this observation appears in connection with assignments, although many assignments are not accompanied by a delegation.)

Professor Epstein's observation can be countered, at least in part, by two others. First, a promisor is likely to be averse to making a delegation to anyone prone to breach; see the text that follows. And second, if a person or firm bargaining for a promise is fearful that the other party will delegate performance to someone prone to breach, the concern can be allayed by an appropriate "no delegation" term. See the text below at p. 1160: UCC Article 2 and the Restatement.

<hr>

Delegation ≠ Absolution

The delegation of a contract obligation does not of itself absolve the obligor of its duty. For absolution, the assent of the obligee is required. Given that assent, the result is a novation; see p. 364 above. The rule of ongoing obligation is so firmly established that any deviation from it can be regarded as an aberration. (The case described in the Note that follows appears to be an aberration.) The rule is exemplified by the liability fixed on an insurer, CIGNA, as to which the court said:

> CIGNA is still liable.
>
> Many a debtor wishes that by such an expression of an intention to delegate he could get rid of his debts. [Nonetheless, t]he debtor's duty remains absolutely unchanged. The performance required by a duty can often be delegated; but by such a delegation the duty itself is not escaped.

In re Integrated Res. Life Ins. Co., 562 N.W.2d 179, 182–83 (Iowa 1997) (quoting 4 Arthur L. Corbin, Corbin on Contracts § 866 (1951) (citations and alterations omitted)).

NOTES

(1) *Running with the Land.* Aldon Companies, Inc., a housing developer, sold a lot in a "subdivision" unit (Lot 9, Unit 1) to John and Kathy Paniaguas ["the couple"], and improved it according to their specifications. According to Aldon's contract with the couple, it was required that a uniform quality of improvements be maintained on other lots within the subdivision. That covenant was not observed, the couple charged, saying that its breach diminished the value of their home. The trial court dismissed their claim against Aldon, and they appealed.

Another transaction critical to the decision had occurred some years after the Aldon-Paniaguas sale: Aldon had sold to another developer, Endor, Inc. the lots in Unit 1 that it had not disposed of. That sale transferred to Endor the rights and obligations of Aldon arising from its dealings with the couple, including the one stated above, about quality. It was Endor's work on the lots it acquired that offended the couple.

The ruling below was affirmed in Paniaguas v. Endor, Inc., 847 N.E.2d 967 (Ind.App.2006). The court's reasoning followed this line:

> (a) Aldon's obligation to the claimants was delegable. "[T]his court cannot conclude that Aldon's personal development of the [ ] subdivision is so essential to the purchase agreements between [the claimants] and Aldon as to preclude the assignment of the obligation to Endor."

> (b) Aldon "assigned" its obligation to Endor. Alson's obligation to "maintain a specified level of quality development was effectively transferred to Endor."

> (c) Thereafter the obligation was Endor's, not Aldon's.

The court concluded that the claimants' remedy, if any, "lies . . . against Endor."

It is possible that the court was misled by its own observation, in an earlier case, about covenants affecting real property:

> Covenants are either personal, enforceable only by the original parties to an agreement, *or* they "run with the land." When covenants run with the land, they may be enforced against remote grantees. The ruling in *Paniaguas* appears to rest on reading the foregoing sentence as if it ended ". . . remote grantees *only*."

(2) *Duty Bonded to Status.* The expression "non-delegable duty" has a different meaning when used at one remove or more from contract law. It refers, often, to a duty attendant on a *status*.

According to the Restatement, Second, of Torts, the expression is used to describe, for example, a duty of one (an "employer") who engages an independent contractor—a duty that the employer "is not free to delegate to the contractor. [The duty] requires the person upon whom it is imposed to answer for it that care is exercised by anyone, even though he be an independent contractor, to whom the performance of the duty is entrusted." Liability may rest on an employer who has not himself been at fault. "The liability imposed is closely analogous to that of a master for the negligence of his servant." But it is not that. The quotations above are taken from the Introductory Note to Restatement Chapter 15, Topic 2 titled "Harm Caused by Negligence of a Carefully Selected Independent Contractor"—Chapter 15, Topic 2.

Another non-delegable duty is that of an attorney appointed as the guardian of an incompetent person. A sanction can be imposed on the attorney for having delegated responsibility for managing that person's assets to an assistant and having failed to supervise the assistant. Disciplinary Counsel v. Young, 862 N.E.2d 504 (Ohio 2007).

UCC Article 2 and the Restatement

The primary Article 2 provisions about delegation of duties appear in UCC § 2–210. They resemble those of the Restatement in important ways, but are more detailed. As to the Restatement, see § 318, quoted in part on p. 1157 above. The Code section is similar in that it deprives a party—seller or buyer—of the power to perform its duties through a delegate if "the other party has a substantial interest in having the original promisor perform or control the acts required by the contract." UCC § 210(1). As between a manufacturer of goods and its customer, which is the more likely to have that interest?

Both the Restatement and the Code use the phrase "unless otherwise agreed", but they do so in opposite directions. In the former the phrase serves to liberate a promisor to make a delegation that would otherwise be foreclosed by the "substantial interest" standard, whereas in the Code the phrase appears to foreclose delegation even when that standard would not. Compare Restatement § 318(2) with UCC § 2–210(1), and compare § 318(1): ". . . contrary to . . . the terms of his promise."

Both sections concur with the statement above that the delegation of a contract obligation does not of itself absolve the obligor of its duty. Section 318(3) and UCC § 2–210(1).

The opinions in the case presented next (*Sally Beauty*, p. 1162) concern the first sentence of UCC § 2–210(1): "A party may perform its duties through a delegate unless. . . ."

Terms of Delegation

A hospital terminated a contract it had made with a firm it had engaged to do construction work; the firm ("Walsh") was in default. Walsh had engaged a subcontractor to do structural steel and other work on the project. The subcontractor alleged in its complaint against the hospital that some of its work had been done before the termination and not been paid for. Following the termination of the main contract, the hospital had received from Walsh a document reading, in part, "Walsh hereby assigns to Presbyterian Hospital . . . the contract between Walsh and Metropolitan Steel [the subcontractor]." The subcontractor contended that, by accepting that assignment, the hospital became chargeable with making good on Walsh's duty to pay. *Held*: Complaint dismissed. A.C. Associates v. Metropolitan Steel Industries, Inc., 1989 U.S.Dist.Lexis 15053 (S.D.N.Y.1989), (Apparently the claimant was actually a sub-sub-contractor, but the court dealt with the matter as if the facts were as stated here.)

UCC § 2–210 did not govern the case. But it speaks to analogous cases in which a seller or buyer of goods makes an assignment in terms that are similarly indeterminate: "of 'the contract' or of 'all my rights under the contract' or an assignment in similar general terms". For those cases Subsection (5) states that, unless the language or the circumstances indicate the contrary, the assignment "is also a delegation of performance of the duties of the assignor."

The Restatement tracks that statement in Subsection (1) of § 328. And in Subsection (2) it adds, as the Code does, a provision about the claim of Metropolitan Steel against Presbyterian Hospital ("intended beneficiary" versus recipient of the assignment, given an acceptance). But that subsection is not wholehearted; see Note (1) below.

NOTES

(1) *Land-Sale Contracts*. With respect to land-sale contracts and the responsibilities of assignees, the authorities are in disarray. New York courts have never accepted it that a person taking an assignment of the purchaser's "contract" thereby becomes accountable to the vendor. The leading case is Langel v. Betz, 164 N.E. 890 (1928). (The opinion there cites *Seaver v. Ransom,* p. 1125 above.) When, in 1967, the matter came before the American Law Institute, in connection with the Restatement Second, there was a face-off between advocates of the *Langel* rule and advocates of a *Caveat*:

> The Institute expresses no opinion as to whether the rule stated in Subsection (2) applies to an assignment by a purchaser of his rights under a contract for the sale of land.

The *Caveat* won, 47–44.

(2) *Common Sense?* S, a manufacturer of goods, contracts to sell a quantity of them to a customer, B. The contract prohibits B from delegating its duty to pay for the goods. B makes an assignment to D of "all my rights under the contract", describing the contract, and D accepts. S now finds it desirable to deliver the goods to D and to collect the price from D. (The price is over-market, and B is insolvent.) An applicable statute provides that the prohibition on delegation is enforceable, and that an attempt at delegation in violation of the prohibition is "not effective." Does the statute bar S from enforcing the contract against D?

What does common sense say about appending a delegation of duty to B's assignment of "all my rights"? What does common sense say about nullifying the delegation, when enforcing it would be to the benefit of S?

Introduction to Sally Beauty Co. v. Nexxus Products Co.

There is an idea in the law that "in dealing with a corporation a party cannot rely on what may be termed the human equation in the company." New York Bank Note Co. v. Hamilton Bank Note Engraving & Printing Co., 73 N.E. 48, 52 (N.Y.1905). A reading of cases from New York courts has raised a doubt that they "would impose the same implied duty of personal service upon a contracting corporation as [they] would on an individual under the same circumstances." Arnold Productions, Inc. v. Favorite Films Corp., 298 F.2d 540 (2d Cir.1962). In contrast, when there is a change in the membership of a professional partnership, having ongoing services contracts with clients, there is often good reason to doubt that the "new firm" may maintain the entitlements of the former partnership as of right.

Yet the decisions relating to delegation of contract obligations do not insist on a sharp dichotomy. Something of a "personal character" has been ascribed to a corporation, owing to its distinctive charter powers and the applicable laws governing the liabilities of its officers and stockholders. See the first case cited above. For partnership cases an illustration is City of North Kansas City v. Sharp, 414 F.2d 359 (8th Cir.1969). "The essence of the professional service cases," the court said, "is that the critical partner, for one reason or another, is no longer available to render those services. Here the critical partners were available and the record indicates . . . that they were able to, and did, function collectively."

In the opinions that follow, serious questions are raised about the degree of "personal trust and confidence" that existed in an inter-corporate relation, as compared with that between, say, a lawyer and a client.

Sally Beauty Co. v. Nexxus Products Co.
United States Court of Appeals, Seventh Circuit, 1986.
801 F.2d 1001.

[In July of 1981 the Best Barber Beauty & Supply Company was acquired by, and merged into, the Sally Beauty Company, a Dallas-based firm. Both firms were distributors of hair care and beauty products to retail stores and hair styling salons. Sally Beauty succeeded to Best's rights and interests in all of Best's contracts. One of those was a letter agreement of August 2, 1979, with Nexxus Products, a California firm founded in that year, which formulated and marketed hair care products through independent distributors. The agreement provided for introducing and promoting Nexxus products in the Texas market; it made Best the exclusive distributor of these in Texas (except for El Paso). Prices to Best were specified; and Nexxus agreed to provide support, such as maintaining a technician in the territory and helping to pay for an annual seminar, with "guest artist." Nexxus agreed not to terminate the agreement except on an anniversary date, and then upon 120 days' notice and upon buying back Best's inventory of Nexxus products at cost. "[We] look forward to a long and successful business relationship," Best wrote.

Nexxus renounced its obligations when Best was merged into Sally Beauty. Sally Beauty was a wholly-owned subsidiary of a company (Alberto-Culver) which was a major manufacturer of hair-care products and, thus, a direct competitor of Nexxus in the hair-care market: "we have great reservations about allowing our NEXXUS products to be distributed by a company which is, in essence, a direct competitor."

Sally Beauty sued Nexxus, charging it with breach of contract and violation of the antitrust laws. Nexxus made a motion for summary judgment on the former claim.]

■ CUDAHY, CIRCUIT JUDGE. Nexxus argued that the distribution agreement it entered into with Best was a contract for personal services, based upon a relationship of personal trust and confidence between Reichek and the Redding family. As such, the contract could not be assigned to Sally without Nexxus's consent.

In opposing this motion Sally Beauty argued that the contract was freely assignable because (1) it was between two corporations, not two individuals and (2) the character of the performance would not be altered by the substitution of Sally Beauty for Best.

In ruling on this motion, the district court [said]:

[I]n this case the circumstances surrounding the contract's formation support the conclusion that the agreement was not simply an ordinary commercial contract but was one which was based upon a relationship of personal trust and confidence between the parties. Specifically, Stephen Redding, Nexxus's vice-president, travelled to Texas and met with Best's president personally for several days before making the decision to award the Texas distributorship to Best. Best itself had been in the hair care business for 40 years and its president Mark Reichek had extensive experience in the industry. It is reasonable to conclude that Stephen Redding and Nexxus would want its distributor to be experienced and knowledgeable in the hair care field and that the selection of Best was based upon personal factors such as these.

We cannot affirm this summary judgment on the grounds relied on by the district court. Although it might be "reasonable to conclude" that Best and Nexxus had based their agreement on "a relationship of personal trust and confidence," and that Reicheck's participation was considered essential to Best's performance, this is a finding of fact.

We may affirm this summary judgment, however, on a different ground if it finds support in the record. Sally Beauty contends that the distribution agreement is freely assignable because it is governed by the provisions of the Uniform Commercial Code (the "UCC" or the "Code"), as adopted in Texas.[1]

III.

Texas applies the "dominant factor" test to determine whether the UCC applies to a given contract or transaction: was the essence of or dominant factor in the formation of the contract the provision of goods or services? We are confident that a Texas court would find the sales aspect of this contract dominant and apply the majority rule that such a distributorship is a contract for "goods" under the UCC.

IV.

We are concerned here with the delegation of Best's duty of performance under the distribution agreement, as Nexxus terminated the agreement because it did not wish to accept Sally Beauty's substituted performance.[2]

In the exclusive distribution agreement before us, Nexxus had contracted for Best's "best efforts" in promoting the sale of Nexxus products in Texas. UCC § 2–306(2). It was this contractual undertaking which Nexxus refused to see performed by Sally.

[We] hold that Sally Beauty's position as a wholly-owned subsidiary of Alberto-Culver is sufficient to bar the delegation of Best's duties under the agreement.

We do not believe that our holding will work the mischief with our national economy that the appellants predict. We hold merely that the duty of performance under an exclusive distributorship may not be delegated to a competitor in the market place—or the wholly-owned subsidiary of a competitor—without the obligee's consent. We believe that such a rule is consonant with the policies behind section 2–210, which is concerned with preserving the bargain the obligee has struck. Nexxus should not be required to accept the "best efforts" of Sally Beauty when those efforts are subject to the control of Alberto-Culver. It is entirely reasonable that Nexxus should conclude that this performance would be a different thing than what it had bargained for. At oral argument, Sally Beauty argued that the case should go to trial to allow it to demonstrate that it could and would perform the contract as

---

[1]   The parties agree that the contract is governed by the law of Texas.

[2]   If this contract is assignable, Sally Beauty would also, of course, succeed to Best's rights under the distribution agreement. But the fact situation before us must be distinguished from the assignment of contract rights that are no longer executory (*e.g.*, the right to damages for breach or the right to payment of an account), which is considered in UCC § 2–210(2), Tex.Bus. & Com.Code Ann. § 2–210(b) (Vernon 1968), and in several of the authorities relied on by appellants. The policies underlying these two situations are different and, generally, the UCC favors assignment more strongly in the latter. See UCC § 2–210(2) (non-executory rights assignable even if agreement states otherwise).

impartially as Best. It stressed that Sally Beauty is a "multi line" distributor, which means that it distributes many brands and is not just a conduit for Alberto-Culver products. But we do not think that this creates a material question of fact in this case.[3] When performance of personal services is delegated, the trier merely determines that it is a personal services contract. If so, the duty is *per se* nondelegable. There is no inquiry into whether the delegate is as skilled or worthy of trust and confidence as the original obligor: the delegate was not bargained for and the obligee need not consent to the substitution.[4] And so here: it is undisputed that Sally Beauty is wholly owned by Alberto-Culver, which means that Sally Beauty's "impartial" sales policy is at least acquiesced in by Alberto-Culver—but could change whenever Alberto-Culver's needs changed. Sally Beauty may be totally sincere in its belief that it can operate "impartially" as a distributor, but who can guarantee the outcome when there is a clear choice between the demands of the parent-manufacturer, Alberto-Culver, and the competing needs of Nexxus? The risk of an unfavorable outcome is not one which the law can force Nexxus to take. Nexxus has a substantial interest in not seeing this contract performed by Sally Beauty, which is sufficient to bar the delegation under section 2–210. Because Nexxus should not be forced to accept performance of the distributorship agreement by Sally, we hold that the contract was not assignable without Nexxus' consent.[5]

The judgment of the district court is Affirmed.

■ POSNER, CIRCUIT JUDGE, dissenting.[b] My brethren find this a simple case—as simple (it seems) as if a lawyer had undertaken to represent the party opposing his client. But notions of conflict of interest are not the same in law and in business, and judges can go astray by assuming that the legal-services industry is the pattern for the entire economy. The lawyerization of America has not reached that point. Sally Beauty, though a wholly owned subsidiary of Alberto-Culver, distributes "hair care" supplies made by many different companies, which so far as appears compete with Alberto-Culver as vigorously as Nexxus does. Steel

---

[3]   We do not address here the situation in which the assignee is not completely under the control of a competitor. If the assignee were only a partially-owned subsidiary, there presumably would have to be fact-finding about the degree of control the competitor-parent had over the subsidiary's business decisions.

[4]   Of course, the obligee makes such an assessment of the prospective delegate. If it thinks the delegated performance will be as satisfactory, it is of course free to consent to the delegation. Thus, the dissent is mistaken in its suggestion that we find it improper—a "conflict of interest"— for one competitor to distribute another competitor's products. Rather, we believe only that it is commercially reasonable that the supplier in those circumstances have consented to such a state of affairs. To borrow the dissent's example, Isuzu allows General Motors to distribute its cars because it considers this arrangement attractive.

Nor is distrust of one's competitors a trait unique to lawyers (as opposed to ordinary businessmen), as the dissent may be understood to suggest.

[5]   This disposition makes it unnecessary to address Nexxus' argument that Sally Beauty breached the distribution agreement by not giving Nexxus 120 days' notice of the Best-Sally Beauty merger.

[b]   Judge Posner observed that Alberto-Culver's products "mostly are cheaper than Nexxus's, and are sold to the public primarily through grocery stores and drugstores."

companies both make fabricated steel and sell raw steel to competing fabricators. General Motors sells cars manufactured by a competitor, Isuzu. What in law would be considered a fatal conflict of interest is in business a commonplace and legitimate practice. The lawyer is a fiduciary of his client; Best was not a fiduciary of Nexxus.

How likely is it that the acquisition of Best could hurt Nexxus? Not very. Suppose Alberto-Culver had ordered Sally Beauty to go slow in pushing Nexxus products, in the hope that sales of Alberto-Culver "hair care" products would rise. Even if they did, since the market is competitive Alberto-Culver would not reap monopoly profits. Moreover, what guarantee has Alberto-Culver that consumers would be diverted from Nexxus to it, rather than to products closer in price and quality to Nexxus products? In any event, any trivial gain in profits to Alberto-Culver would be offset by the loss of goodwill to Sally Beauty; and a cost to Sally Beauty is a cost to Alberto-Culver, its parent. Remember that Sally Beauty carries beauty supplies made by other competitors of Alberto-Culver; Best alone carries "hair care" products manufactured by Revlon, Clairol, Bristol-Myers, and L'Oreal, as well as Alberto-Culver. Will these powerful competitors continue to distribute their products through Sally Beauty if Sally Beauty displays favoritism for Alberto-Culver products? Would not such a display be a commercial disaster for Sally Beauty, and hence for its parent, Alberto-Culver? Is it really credible that Alberto-Culver would sacrifice Sally Beauty in a vain effort to monopolize the "hair care" market, in violation of section 2 of the Sherman Act? Is not the ratio of the profits that Alberto-Culver obtains from Sally Beauty to the profits it obtains from the manufacture of "hair care" products at least a relevant consideration?

Another relevant consideration is that the contract between Nexxus and Best was for a short term. Could Alberto-Culver destroy Nexxus by failing to push its products with maximum vigor in Texas for a year? In the unlikely event that it could and did, it would be liable in damages to Nexxus for breach of the implied best-efforts term of the distribution contract. Finally, it is obvious that Sally Beauty does not have a bottleneck position in the distribution of "hair care" products, such that by refusing to promote Nexxus products vigorously it could stifle the distribution of those products in Texas; for Nexxus has found alternative distribution that it prefers—otherwise it wouldn't have repudiated the contract with Best when Best was acquired by Sally Beauty.

Not all businessmen are consistent and successful profit maximizers, so the probability that Alberto-Culver would instruct Sally Beauty to cease to push Nexxus products vigorously in Texas cannot be reckoned at zero. On this record, however, it is slight. And there is no principle of law that if something happens that trivially reduces the probability that a dealer will use his best efforts, the supplier can cancel the contract. At most, so far as the record shows, Nexxus may have had grounds for "insecurity" regarding the performance by Sally Beauty of its obligation to use its best efforts to promote Nexxus products, but if so its remedy was not to cancel the contract but to demand assurances of due performance. See UCC § 2–609; Official Comment 5 to § 2–306. No such demand was made. An anticipatory repudiation by conduct requires conduct that makes the repudiating party unable to perform. The merger did not do this. At least there is no evidence it did. The judgment should be reversed and the case remanded for a trial on whether the merger so altered the conditions of performance that Nexxus is entitled to declare the contract broken.

NOTES

(1) *A Case for Contrast.* O.R. Concepts, Inc. (ORC) was a producer of health-care products, one of which was "Thermadrape", used to prevent hypothermia. Shareholders of the firm sold 95% of the stock in the firm to Vital Signs, Inc. (VSI). Thereafter the sales staff of VSI began distributing Thermadrape. These developments led to an action against ORC, brought by the Baxter Healthcare Corporation (Baxter). Earlier, Baxter had contracted with ORC to buy quantities of Thermadrape at a price of at least $3 million, for distribution to Baxter's customers. Baxter charged ORC with having violated UCC § 2–210, and with breach of the implied covenant of good faith and fair dealing. Baxter relied on *Sally Beauty.* The court that decided that case approved the trial court's dismissal of Baxter's action. Baxter Healthcare Corp. v. O.R. Concepts, Inc., 69 F.3d 785 (7th Cir. 1995).

What distinctions can be drawn between *Sally Beauty* and *Baxter Healthcare*? See In re Nedwick Steel Company, 289 B.R. 95 (Bankr.Ct.N.D.Ill. 2003). (The court offered distinctions between *Sally Beauty* and the trial court's decision in *Baxter Healthcare*, not noticing, apparently, the affirmance of the latter, as cited above.)

(2) *A Case for Comparison.* The decision in *Sally Beauty* was cited by the Bronco Wine Company when Bronco was sued by Scher Enterprises, Inc. Scher, formerly a wholesaler of wine, had sold its business to the J. Lewis Cooper Company. It had sold at a "greatly reduced price", Scher alleged, because Bronco had refused assent to the sale. That refusal, Scher contended, was a violation of the Michigan Liquor Control Code, in particular § 436.1305, the purpose of which is "to provide a structure for the business relations" between suppliers and wholesalers of wine. One provision of the section is this:

> A supplier shall not withhold consent to any transfer of a wholesaler's business if the proposed transferee meets the material and reasonable qualifications and standards required by the supplier.

At one point in discussion between Scher and Bronco, Bronco wrote: "You have sold your business to a distributorship which already represents our single largest competitor [Gallo]. It is simply not in the best interests of our brands to play 'second fiddle' to any product line where other alternatives are available."

Upon Bronco's motion for summary judgment, the court invited submissions by the parties which yielded much evidence. One telling bit of evidence was that Bronco supplied wine to 31 distributors who also distributed Gallo wine. A witness for Bronco sought to discount that fact in various ways. Among other things, he noted that Bronco used hundreds of distributors, and that the number 31 reflected "a 92.5% consistency in adhering to Bronco's requirements" about competing wines.

The court denied Bronco's motion. Of *Sally Beauty* it said simply that the case was "not factually analogous or legally relevant." Scher Enterprises, Inc. v. Bronco Wine Co., 178 F.Supp.2d 780, 788 (E.D.Mich. 2001). Is that right?

SECTION 3.   ASSIGNMENTS OF RIGHTS

An illustration in the Restatement supposes that "B contracts with A to furnish A's family with all the oil it shall need for the ensuing year at a fixed price." Illustration 3 to § 334. The supposed contract suggests the question whether or not either party might transfer—*assign*—to someone else its rights: A to X, A's right to a supply of oil, or B to Y, B's right to payment.

With respect to an attempt by A to assign to X her right to a supply of oil, one must make a fundamental distinction. It is one thing to call it "success" if, should B fall short of supplying A's family with oil, it must pay damages to X. It is quite another to say that success in assigning means that B must thereafter supply the needs of *X's family*, rather than those of A's family. The Restatement illustration mentioned above goes on to say that an assignment by A cannot confer on some other person a right that that person's family be supplied with oil. The Restatement rule on the subject appears in § 317(2), cited in the opinion that follows. The section begins: "A contractual right can be assigned unless. . . ." One of the restrictions stated there applies when "the substitution of a right of the assignee [X] for the right of the assignor [A] would materially change the duty of the obligor [B]." That restriction appears to apply, unless the requirements of X's family are known to be nearly identical to those of A's family.

A comparable case, now dated, is Crane Ice Cream Co. v. Terminal Freezing & Heating Co., 128 A. 280 (Md. 1925), concerning a sale of ice. Terminal Freezing had agreed to supply, within a limit, the requirements of one Frederick, the operator of a "simple" ice-cream plant in Baltimore. Frederick attempted to assign his rights and to delegate his duties under the contract to a much larger, multi-state operator, Crane Ice Cream. According to the court, that attempt constituted a repudiation by Frederick of his contract with Terminal.

Now that the Code is in place, it would govern on the facts of *Crane Ice Cream* and on the others supposed above, all of which concern sales of goods. UCC § 2–210(2) was the pattern for the Restatement rule quoted above. Subject to some stated exceptions, it provides that "all rights of either seller or buyer can be assigned." It is not so, however, "when the assignment would materially change the duty of the other party."

With respect to an attempt by B to assign her right to payment to Y, several questions must be addressed. First, what must occur for the assignment from B to Y to be effective between those two parties? Second, what additional steps, if any, must occur in order for this assignment to be effective against third parties who may trace their claim to the payment right to a subsequent voluntary or involuntary transfer by B? Third, what is the effect of the assignment on the rights and duties of A, the party that owes payment, especially if the contract between A and B purports to limit the ability of B to assign the payment right? The analysis of these questions is complicated by the existence of an Article of the Uniform Commercial Code that does not otherwise play a significant role in contract law—Article 9. Article 9 is implicated in this matter because it governs the sale of most payment rights. This means that Article 9 governs most assignments of payment rights inasmuch as most such assignments are not gifts but, rather, are assignments in exchange for consideration—in other words, sales. UCC Article 9 is largely beyond the scope of this course, but aspects of it are addressed in the materials below.

NOTES

(1) *Delegation and Repudiation*. Article 2 does not track the statement about repudiation in *Crane Ice Cream*. What it says is that *any* assignment which delegates performance entitles the other party—B, in the illustrative case above—to demand adequate assurance of due performance from the assignee—X, in that case. It says also that the "other party" may treat the assignment as "creating reasonable grounds for insecurity." Presumably that would entitle B to demand assurance from the assigning party, A. See UCC § 2–609. One's failure to make an adequate response to a justified demand amounts, by that section, to a repudiation. (Both entitlements are stated in Subsection 6 of UCC § 2–210.)

It would seem sensible to say that B cannot require adequate assurances from *both* A and X, but must be content with an assurance from one or the other. But that is not what Subsection 6 says.

(2) *Lost Leverage*. Professor Richard Epstein has described a burden that an assignment may place on a promisor even though the assignment does not alter the prior legal position of the promisor. "The promisee is a known quantity chosen and selected by the promisor. Even if the legal system gives the promisor the same rights against the promisee's assignee, the value of those rights still may be reduced by the assignment. The promisor may not have any informal leverage against the assignee. . . . Preventing the assignment reduces the cost to the promisor by fixing the content of the obligation that would otherwise run to an unidentified party." Epstein, *Why Restrain Alienation?*, 85 Colum. L. Rev. 970, 983 (1985).

Is any "informal leverage" against a chosen promisee lost if the promisee assigns only its rights and delegates none of its duties?

PROBLEM

Ice Lifting. Disregard the problem of delegation in *Crane Ice Cream*, and consider only the problem of assignment there, in relation to UCC § 2–210(2). Does the Code validate Frederick's assignment of his right to ice? Does it matter that Crane, having access to Terminal's ice, might adjust its production of ice cream as between its newly acquired Baltimore plant and one it already owned in Philadelphia, to take account of differences between its ice costs at the two points? How likely would that adjustment be?

Herzog v. Irace

Supreme Judicial Court of Maine, 1991.
594 A.2d 1106.

■ BRODY, JUSTICE. Anthony Irace and Donald Lowry appeal from an order entered by the Superior Court (Cumberland County, *Cole, J.*) affirming a District Court (Portland, Goranites, J.) judgment in favor of Dr. John P. Herzog in an action for breach of an assignment to Dr. Herzog of personal injury settlement proceeds[c] collected by Irace and Lowry, both attorneys, on behalf of their client, Gary G. Jones. On appeal, Irace and Lowry contend that the District Court erred in finding that the assignment was valid and enforceable against them. They also argue that enforcement of the assignment interferes with their ethical obligations toward their client. Finding no error, we affirm.

The facts of this case are not disputed. Gary Jones was injured in a motorcycle accident and retained Irace and Lowry to represent him in a personal injury action. Soon thereafter, Jones dislocated his shoulder, twice, in incidents unrelated to the motorcycle accident. Dr. Herzog examined Jones's shoulder and concluded that he needed surgery. At the time, however, Jones was unable to pay for the surgery and in consideration for the performance of the surgery by the doctor, he signed a letter dated June 14, 1988, written on Dr. Herzog's letterhead stating:

> I, Gary Jones, request that payment be made directly from settlement of a claim currently pending for an unrelated incident, to John Herzog, D.O., for treatment of a shoulder injury which occurred at a different time.

Dr. Herzog notified Irace and Lowry that Jones had signed an "assignment of benefits" from the motorcycle personal injury action to cover the cost of surgery on his shoulder and was informed by an employee of Irace and Lowry that the assignment was sufficient to allow the firm to pay Dr. Herzog's bills at the conclusion of the case. Dr. Herzog

---

[c]   This case involves the assignment of proceeds from a personal injury action, not an assignment of the cause of action itself.

performed the surgery and continued to treat Jones for approximately one year.

In May, 1989, Jones received a $20,000 settlement in the motorcycle personal injury action. He instructed Irace and Lowry not to disburse any funds to Dr. Herzog indicating that he would make the payments himself. Irace and Lowry informed Dr. Herzog that Jones had revoked his permission to have the bill paid by them directly and indicated that they would follow Jones's directions. Irace and Lowry issued a check to Jones for $10,027 and disbursed the remaining funds to Jones's other creditors. Jones did send a check to Dr. Herzog but the check was returned by the bank for insufficient funds and Dr. Herzog was never paid.

Dr. Herzog filed a complaint in District Court against Irace and Lowry seeking to enforce the June 14, 1988 "assignment of benefits." The matter was tried before the court on the basis of a joint stipulation of facts. The court entered a judgment in favor of Dr. Herzog finding that the June 14, 1988 letter constituted a valid assignment of the settlement proceeds enforceable against Irace and Lowry. Following an unsuccessful appeal to the Superior Court, Irace and Lowry appealed to this court. Because the Superior Court acted as an intermediate appellate court, we review the District Court's decision directly. See Brown v. Corriveau, 576 A.2d 200, 201 (Me.1990).

[W]e will set aside trial court findings based solely upon documentary evidence and stipulated facts only if clearly erroneous.

Validity of Assignment

An assignment is an act or manifestation by the owner of a right (the assignor) indicating his intent to transfer that right to another person (the assignee). See Shiro v. Drew, 174 F.Supp. 495, 497 (D.Me.1959). For an assignment to be valid and enforceable against the assignor's creditor [debtor?] (the obligor), the assignor must make clear his intent to relinquish the right to the assignee and must not retain any control over the right assigned or any power of revocation. *Id.* The assignment takes effect through the actions of the assignor and assignee and the obligor need not accept the assignment to render it valid. Palmer v. Palmer, 112 Me. 149, 153, 91 A. 281, 282 (1914). Once the obligor has notice of the assignment, the fund is "from that time forward impressed with a trust; it is . . . impounded in the [obligor's] hands, and must be held by him not for the original creditor, the assignor, but for the substituted creditor, the assignee." *Id.* at 152, 91 A. 281. After receiving notice of the assignment, the obligor cannot lawfully pay the amount assigned either to the assignor or to his other creditors and if the obligor does make such a payment, he does so at his peril because the assignee may enforce his rights against the obligor directly. *Id.* at 153, 91 A. 281.

Ordinary rights, including future rights, are freely assignable unless the assignment would materially change the duty of the obligor, materially increase the burden or risk imposed upon the obligor by his contract, impair the obligor's chance of obtaining return performance, or materially reduce the value of the return performance to the obligor, and unless the law restricts the assignability of the specific right involved. See Restatement (Second) Contracts § 317(2)(a) (1982). In Maine, the transfer of a future right to *proceeds* from pending litigation has been recognized as a valid and enforceable equitable assignment. McLellan v. Walker, 26 Me. 114, 117–18 (1896). An equitable assignment need not transfer the entire future right but rather may be a partial assignment of that right. Palmer, 112 Me. at 152, 91 A. 281. We reaffirm these well established principles.

Irace and Lowry contend that Jones's June 14, 1988 letter is invalid and unenforceable as an assignment because it fails to manifest Jones's intent to permanently relinquish all control over the assigned funds and does nothing more than request payment from a specific fund. We disagree. The June 14, 1988 letter gives no indication that Jones attempted to retain any control over the funds he assigned to Dr. Herzog. Taken in context, the use of the word "request" did not give the court reason to question Jones's intent to complete the assignment and, although no specific amount was stated, the parties do not dispute that the services provided by Dr. Herzog and the amounts that he charged for those services were reasonable and necessary to the treatment of the shoulder injury referred to in the June 14 letter. Given that Irace and Lowry do not dispute that they had ample notice of the assignment, the court's finding on the validity of the assignment is fully supported by the evidence and will not be disturbed on appeal.

Ethical Obligations

Next, Irace and Lowry contend that the assignment, if enforceable against them, would interfere with their ethical obligation to honor their client's instruction in disbursing funds. Again, we disagree.

The Bar Rules [of Maine] require that an attorney "promptly pay or deliver to the client, as requested by the client, the funds, securities, or other properties in the possession of the lawyer which the client is entitled to receive." M.Bar R. 3.6(f)(2)(iv). The rules say nothing, however, about a client's power to assign his right to proceeds from a pending lawsuit to third parties. Because the client has the power to assign his right to funds held by his attorney, McLellan v. Walker, 26 Me. at 117–18, it follows that a valid assignment must be honored by the attorney in disbursing the funds on the client's behalf. Irace and Lowry were under no ethical obligation, and the record gives no indication that they were under a contractual obligation, to honor their client's instruction to disregard a valid assignment. The District Court correctly concluded that the assignment is valid and enforceable against Irace and Lowry.

———

Means of Assignment

Both the Uniform Commercial Code and the Restatement recognize that an intention to assign payment rights of some kinds can be implemented by making a delivery. These are rights represented by what the Restatement calls "a writing of a type customarily accepted as a symbol or as evidence of the right assigned." Restatement § 332(1)(b) (applying concept to gratuitous assignments). An instance is a savings bond; in the not-too-distant past, another was a passbook symbolizing a bank savings account. The Code provides for comparable transfers of certain interests that are not payment rights. It provides also for implementing transfers of some payment rights, and some other interests, by establishing "control" in the transferee. These include transfers of deposit accounts generally. See UCC § 9–203(b) as to both delivery and control. These modes of assignment are not addressed further in this book. What follows next is about language as a means of assignment.

According to § 324 of the Restatement, an intention to transfer a contract right may be manifested, except as provided by statute or by contract, either orally or by a writing. But what language to use requires some discrimination. The language used by Gary Jones, in *Herzog*, is less dispositive than that customarily used by competent attorneys wishing to effect an assignment. Several other forms of expression are now to be illustrated. Some of them constitute assignments; others do not. Each of them should be compared with the language used by Jones.

(a) Words of assignment were used by the firm JVS Powersports USA (JVS) with respect to payment rights it held against its customers, buyers of motorbikes and other vehicles. JVS used these payment rights—"accounts", or "accounts receivable"—to obtain several millions of dollars from a financier named Rexford Funding. The financing agreement contained this term:

> [JVS] hereby assigns and sells to [Rexford], as absolute owner, and [Rexford] hereby purchases from [JVS], certain Accounts which arise from [JVS's] sale of merchandise or rendition of services.

That was an assignment.

(b) One can imagine that Rexford transferred funds to JVS by way of a document much like this:

```
┌─────────────────────────────────────────────────────────────────┐
│                                          April 1, 2005            │
│  Rexford Funding, Inc.                                            │
│                                                                   │
│  PAY TO THE ORDER OF JVS Powersports USA        $ _____     │
│  _____ DOLLARS            │
│                                                                   │
│  YOUR BANK                              /s/ Rexford Funding, Inc. │
│                                                                   │
└─────────────────────────────────────────────────────────────────┘
```

That would not be an assignment. A check is not an assignment. "A person with an account at a bank enjoys a claim against the bank for funds in an amount equal to the account balance. Under the UCC, a check is simply an order to the drawee bank to pay the sum stated, signed by the maker and payable on demand. Receipt of a check does not, however, give the recipient a right against the bank. The recipient may present the check, but, if the drawee bank refuses to honor it, the recipient has no recourse against the drawee." Barnhill v. Johnson, 503 U.S. 393, 398 (1992). Also: "A check or other draft does not of itself operate as an assignment of any funds in the hands of the drawee available for its payment, and the drawee is not liable on the instrument until he accepts it." (The court quoted this from the 1989 Official Text of UCC Article 3. The current Official Text contains a virtually identical provision, § 3–408.)

(c) A writes to B, "Please pay to C the balance you owe me." That looks even less like an assignment than a check does.

(d) A firm named Fiberlast needs financing to fulfill a contract to build a "radome"; the work is to be done for the Counter Company. Fiberlast gets a substantial loan from a friendly investor named Gordon Drew, and gives him a memo, signed, saying:

> Any money advanced by Mr. Drew for the purpose of manufacturing the Radome will be paid immediately to him upon receipt of Counter's remittance, irrespective of any other demands from other creditors.

See Shiro v. Drew, 174 F.Supp. 495, 498 (D.Me. 1959): "Language of present transfer is wholly lacking."

A passage in the *Shiro* opinion is virtually quoted in *Herzog*; see the paragraph above that follows "Validity of Assignment." According to the *Shiro* opinion, at 497–98, "the courts have uniformly recognized that an agreement to pay out of a particular fund, without more, is not an assignment. . . . " For that the court cited Christmas v. Russell, 1871, 14 Wall. 69, 84, 81 U.S. 69, 84.

NOTES

(1) *Ebb and Flow.* This sentence in Christmas v. Russell has been quoted often: "An agreement to pay out of a particular fund, however clear

in its terms, is not an equitable assignment." In some quarters words of present transfer are regarded as essential to an effective assignment. But the courts have not been altogether faithful to the proposition quoted. Early in the 20th century the Supreme Court detoured around it. In Barnes v. Alexander, 232 U.S. 117 (1914), the Court ruled that a fee earned by William Barnes, an attorney, had become subject to an equitable lien because, in soliciting the assistance of another attorney, he had earlier said "I will give you one third of the [contingent] fee which I have coming to me. . . . "

After *Barnes*, it was still possible to think that the decision represented a limited exception to the general rule. See B. Kuppenheimer & Co. v. Mornin, 78 F.2d 261 (8th Cir.1935). There it was said that the Supreme Court had "mellowed" the strict requirements set down in the *Christmas* case, but only for certain situations—*e.g.*, "in cases involving contingent fees of attorneys." *Id.* at 264. Also:

> Many cases are to be found sustaining the rule that a promise to pay out of a particular fund, when it shall come into existence, does not create an equitable assignment of that fund. As counsel for defendants on argument aptly said, in effect, that business and commerce will be greatly harmed, hamstrung, and impeded if every agreement of an Iowa farmer to pay a debt out of a crop of corn, when he shall have sold the corn, is to be held to be an equitable assignment of the proceeds of such corn.

Id. at 265. The opinion in Spiro v. Drew cited *B. Kuppenheimer*, and distinguished *Barnes*.

In this century, however, *Barnes* was revivified. See Sereboff v. Mid Atlantic Medical Services, Inc., 547 U.S. 356 (2006), where a unanimous Court rebuffed an argument for applying the "typical rules regarding equitable liens by assignment," and denied that *Barnes* "announced a special rule for attorneys claiming an equitable lien over funds promised under a contingency fee arrangement." In *Barnes* the Court rested its ruling on an ancient principle of general law. Now that the Court defers largely to state courts in elaborating general law, it may well be that the ruling is authoritative only for questions strongly influenced by a federal interest. *Sereboff* was, in the main, a construction of the Employee Retirement Income Security Act, "ERISA."

(2) *Legal Effect Without Assignment.* To say that a check and the documents in (c) and (d) above do not amount to assignments is not to say that they are without legal significance. It is clear, for instance, that a bank may charge the checking account of a customer upon payment of a check properly drawn and issued, and indorsed and presented by the payee. Indeed, assuming that the account balance is ample, the bank usually owes it to its customer—the drawer of the check—to honor it. Are the elements of a contract apparent in the transactions described in (c) or (d) above?

(3) *Gift Assignments.* A striking distinction exists between "for value" assignments and gift assignments. As to many payment rights an oral assignment is ineffective as part of a commercial transaction. So it is provided in UCC § 9–203(b)(3), setting out some conditions on the

enforceability of a "security agreement" with respect to the "collateral." As indicated above, if the collateral is embodied in a document, handing over possession of the document may make the agreement enforceable. Otherwise the agreement may well be unenforceable unless the assignor has "authenticated" the agreement. In contrast, an oral assignment by way of gift is effective, given appropriate wording.

On the other hand, the recipient of an oral gift assignment is likely to have only a tenuous hold on the right transferred. According to Section 332 of the Restatement, "Except as stated in this Section, a gratuitous assignment is revocable," and is terminated by any one of a number of incidents, including the making of a conflicting assignment and the assignor's death.

The section states various ways in which a gift assignment may be made, or may become, more durable than that. One of these is the delivery of a written and signed assignment. (In this connection, a New York statute dispenses with delivery: Gen.Oblig.L. § 5–1107.) Another is the delivery of a symbolic or evidentiary writing. Another, sometimes operative, is expectable action or inaction on the part of the assignee, induced by the assignment. A California statute is largely parallel to the Restatement section (taking *verbal* to mean *oral*): "A verbal gift is not valid, unless. . . . " Civil Code § 1147. It omits any thought of reliance, however.

————

Sale Versus Loan

Two firms mentioned above, JVS Powersports and Rexford Funding, entered into a *factoring* agreement by which Rexford received an advance of some $3 million. Rexford does a like business across the United States. In litigation between the two firms, the court quoted as follows from Black's Law Dictionary (8th ed. 2004), saying: "Factoring is '[t]he buying of accounts receivable at a discount. The price is discounted because the factor (who buys them) assumes the risk of delay in collection and loss on the accounts receivable.'" The accounts concerned were, of course, payment rights arising from sales by JVS to its customers, the *account debtors*.

Some tension is apparent in the foregoing paragraph. A merchant making an outright *sale* of its accounts thereby sheds the risk of nonpayment by its customers, or by a disproportionate number of them. In contrast, in using its accounts as collateral for a loan (an *advance*), a merchant retains that risk. The parties disagreed about the extent to which the factoring agreement shifted the nonpayment risk to Rexford.

A term of the agreement, quoted above at p. 1173, used the word *sale*. On the other hand, the agreement assigned to JVS some responsibilities with respect to its nonpaying customers. To that end it defined the word *disputes*, making it mean "any cause for nonpayment of an Account . . . except for financial inability of [JVS's] Customers to pay an Account at maturity." JVS undertook to give Rexford prompt notice of any disputes, and to "settle all Disputes at no cost or expense to [Rexford]. . . . " Upon a failure by JVS to settle a customer dispute, it was to become liable for all of the unpaid factored accounts.

The court considered evidence about a representative nonpaying customer, and was unsure whether or not that customer's account was in dispute. Hence it denied a motion by Rexford for a partial summary judgment. Rexford Funding, LLC v. JVS Powersports USA, Inc., 2007 WL 2822771 (W.D.Mich. Sept. 26, 2007).

Whether or not Rexford's "advance" to JVS represented a loan is open to doubt; it might fairly be called a prepayment. JVS assigned to Rexford invoices having face values of nearly $6 million in the aggregate. The case illustrates the hybrid character of many assignments.

For many purposes the sale/loan distinction was reduced in importance by the Uniform Commercial Code. Section 9–109(a) provides that, subject to a number of qualifications, Article 9—"Secured Transactions"—applies not only to a transaction that creates a personal-property security interest but also to a sale of accounts. The Comment to a predecessor section (9–102) gave this explanation: "Commercial financing on the basis of accounts . . . is often so conducted that the distinction between a security transfer and a sale is blurred, and a sale of such property is therefore covered. . . . " Article 9 applies to transfers of payment rights by way of sales, as well as to those that support loans, a broadly applicable rule that an assignee's interest is enforceable only if the assignor has "authenticated a security agreement." UCC § 9–203(b)(3)(A). (Subparagraph (A) speaks of authentication by a *debtor*; but by definition that word comprises a selling assignor.) The rule is in effect a statute of frauds. Other parts of paragraph (3) describe some transactions not subject to it.

Although the Code has reduced the sale/loan distinction, it has not obliterated it: witness *Rexford Funding*, on page 1177 above.

———

Anti-Assignment Provisions

A contract between a general contractor, Caristo Construction, and a subcontractor, Kroo Painting, contained this provision:

> The assignment by [Kroo] of this contract or any interest therein, or of any money due or to become due by reason of the terms hereof without the written consent of [Caristo] shall be void.

Without having obtained the written consent of Caristo, Kroo purported to assign to a bank its right to "moneys due and to become due" under the subcontract. In turn, the bank assigned the right to Herman Allhusen, who sought to enforce it. That action was dismissed by reason of the anti-assignment provision. Allhusen appealed twice, without success. The power to contract trumped the power to transfer. The ultimate ruling, made in 1952, is cited in the opinion that follows.

The enactment of the Uniform Commercial Code superseded the ruling in *Allhusen* and others like it. UCC § 9–406(d) provides, with some qualifications, that a term in an agreement between an *account debtor* [*e.g.,* Caristo] and an assignor is ineffective to the extent that it:

> (1) prohibits, restricts, or requires the consent of the *account debtor* to the assignment or transfer of the *account*.

[The terms italicized here are given definitions in UCC § 9–102(a)].

In the opinion that follows the court considered the possibility that an assignment of contract rights was barred by a provision in the contract that generated those rights. The court did not refer to the Code. That omission would be surprising but for the fact that the rights in question were not "accounts," as defined in Section 9–102(a). As defined there, the word is limited, among other ways, to a right to payment of a monetary obligation for goods, for services, or for various other benefits. Hence the Code would not have suppressed an anti-assignment provision, properly drafted. Neither would it have suppressed a provision directed at the right of a buyer of goods to receive delivery. That sort of provision appears in Trubowitch v. Riverbank Canning Co., 182 P.2d 182 (Cal.1947), a case concerning a large quantity of canned tomato paste. The provision was: "This contract is not assignable and goods sold hereunder are not to be shipped or diverted to any destination other than that herein specified, without consent of seller."

An anti-assignment provision, as follows, appears in a standard form widely used for deals in California real estate: "Buyer may not assign any rights hereunder without the prior written consent of Seller." The Code definition of *account* does not comprise the principal entitlement conferred on a buyer by the form—the right to a conveyance of property. Nor does it comprise the seller's principal entitlement—the right to be paid.

The three anti-assignment provisions quoted above are perceptibly different in tenor, each from the others. Whether or not they differ in effect should be considered in light of the opinion that follows.

Bel-Ray Company v. Chemrite (Pty) Ltd.

United States Court of Appeals, Third Circuit, 1999.
181 F.3d 435.

[The Bel-Ray Company, a New Jersey corporation, makes specialty lubricants, using formulas and technology that it maintains in the highest confidentiality. Over a period of years, Bel-Ray entered into a series of agreements—the Trade Agreements, or "Agreements"—with a South African corporation, Chemrite Ltd., for the blending and distribution of Bel-Ray products in South Africa. In 1996, a newly formed firm named Lubritene Ltd. acquired Chemrite's lubricant business, including rights under the Agreements. Bel-Ray was informed of the transfer. Business went on as before, under the Agreements. Four persons who had been shareholders and officeholders in Chemrite took similar positions in Lubritene.

Bel-Ray brought an action in New Jersey against Lubritene, charging it with fraud and other torts, and with violations of the Agreements. In the trial court, Bel-Ray got an order compelling Lubritene to arbitrate the Bel-Ray claims. The basis for this order was a provision in the most recent Agreement requiring arbitration, in New Jersey, of "any and all disputes relating to the agreement or its breach."

Appealing, Lubritene relied on provisions in the Chemrite/Bel-Ray Agreements that required Bel-Ray's written consent to any assignment of Chemrite's interests under the Agreements.]

■ STAPLETON, CIRCUIT JUDGE. Under the Federal Arbitration Act ("FAA"), a court may only compel a party to arbitrate where that party has entered into a written agreement to arbitrate that covers the dispute. See 9 U.S.C. §§ 2 & 206. The arbitration clauses in the Trade Agreements are the only written agreements to arbitrate offered in this case. It is undisputed that these agreements were entered into by Chemrite and Bel-Ray, and that Chemrite subsequently assigned the agreements to Lubritene. If these assignments are effective, then the District Court's order should be affirmed. Lubritene, however, contends that the assignments are ineffective because Bel-Ray did not consent to the assignments in writing as the Trade Agreements require. They therefore argue that there is no written agreement to arbitrate and we must reverse the District Court's order.

Thus, according to Lubritene, this case turns on the effect to be given to the Trade Agreements' requirement that Bel-Ray consent in writing to any assignment of Chemrite's interest.

[After observing that the law of South Africa might be controlling, the court concluded that it should apply New Jersey law—"forum law"— owing to Lubritene's failure both to raise the issue and to provide information about foreign law.]

The New Jersey Supreme Court has not yet addressed the effect of contractual provisions limiting or prohibiting assignments. Nevertheless, we are not without guidance because the Superior Court's Appellate Division recently addressed this issue in Garden State Buildings L.P. v. First Fidelity Bank, N.A., 305 N.J. Super. 510, 702 A.2d 1315 (N.J.Super.Ct.App.Div.1997). There, a partnership had entered a loan agreement with Midatlantic Bank for the construction of a new hotel. The parties subsequently entered into a modification agreement to extend the loan's maturity date, which provided that: "No party hereto shall assign this Letter Agreement (or assign any right or delegate any obligation contained herein) without the prior written consent of the other party hereto and any such assignment shall be void." 702 A.2d at 1318. Midatlantic subsequently assigned the loan to Starwood without obtaining the partnership's prior written consent. The partnership acknowledged Starwood's rights under the loan agreement by making payments to, and eventually entering a settlement agreement with, Starwood. Nonetheless, the partnership filed suit against Midatlantic for damages arising from its breach of the modification agreement's assignment clause. It argued that it was not required to void the assignment, but could recognize its validity while still preserving its right to sue Midatlantic for breach of its covenant not to assign without the partnership's written consent.

To resolve this claim the Appellate Division looked to § 322 of the Restatement (Second) of Contracts, which provides in relevant part:

> (2)   A contract term prohibiting assignment of rights under the contract, unless a different intention is manifested.
>
> (b)   gives the obligor a right to damages for breach of the terms forbidding assignment *but does not render the assignment ineffective.*

Restatement (Second) of Contracts § 322 (1981) (emphasis added). The Court, distinguished between an assignment provision's effect upon a party's "power" to assign, as opposed to its "right" to assign. A party's "power" to assign is only limited where the parties clearly manifest a different intention. According to the Court:

> "to reveal the intent necessary to preclude the power to assign, or cause an assignment violative of contractual provisions to be wholly void, such clause must contain express provisions that any assignment shall be void or invalid if not made in a certain specified way." Otherwise, the assignment is effective, and the obligor has the right to damages.

Garden State, 702 A.2d at 1321 (quoting University Mews Assoc's v. Jeanmarie, 471 N.Y.S.2d 457, 461 (N.Y.Sup.Ct.1984)). The Court concluded that the parties had sufficiently manifested their intent to limit Midatlantic's power to assign the loan because the anti-assignment clause clearly provided that assignments without the other party's written consent "shall be void." 702 A.2d at 1322.

In adopting § 322, New Jersey joins numerous other jurisdictions that follow the general rule that contractual provisions limiting or prohibiting assignments operate only to limit a parties' right to assign the contract, but not their power to do so, unless the parties' manifest an intent to the contrary with specificity. See Allhusen v. Caristo Const. Corp., 303 N.Y. 446, 103 N.E.2d 891, 893 (N.Y. 1952) [and six other cases cited]. To meet this standard the assignment provision must generally state that non-conforming assignments (i) shall be "void" or "invalid," or (ii) that the assignee shall acquire no rights or the non-assigning party shall not recognize any such assignment. See *Garden State*, 702 A.2d at 1321 ("clause must contain express provisions that any assignment shall be void or invalid if not made in a certain specified way"). In the absence of such language, the provision limiting or prohibiting assignments will be interpreted merely as a covenant not to assign, or to follow specific procedures—typically obtaining the non-assigning party's prior written consent—before assigning. Breach of such a covenant may render the assigning party liable in damages to the non-assigning party. The assignment, however, remains valid and enforceable against both the assignor and the assignee.

[After quoting from the Agreements,[d] the court continued:] None contain terms specifically stating that an assignment without Bel-Ray's written consent would be void or invalid. Several courts have considered virtually identical clauses and concluded that they did not contain the necessary express language to limit the assigning party's power to assign.

The Trade Agreements' assignment clauses do not contain the requisite clear language to limit Chemrite's "power" to assign the Trade Agreements. Chemrite's assignment to Lubritene is therefore enforceable, and Lubritene is bound to arbitrate claims "relating to" the Trade Agreements pursuant to their arbitration clauses. We therefore agree with the District Court that Bel-Ray was entitled to an order compelling Lubritene to arbitrate.

NOTES

(1) *Question*. Consider the three anti-assignment clauses quoted in the text preceding the main case. What differences among them in legal effect, if any, are indicated in *Bel-Ray*?

(2) *Meddling with a Mortgage*. Roy Haggett was much disturbed by a letter he received from a person, K.E. Norton, with whom he had had some arguments. The letter said that Norton had bought, from a savings bank, a note that Haggett had given the bank, and the accompanying mortgage on Haggett's home. These facts emerged in litigation between the two men. Norton v. Haggett, 85 A.2d 571 (Vt.1952). The opinion does not say why Haggett was disturbed. One can speculate that he counted on the bank for mercy in the event of his delay in paying the note, and did not expect mercy from Norton. If so, Haggett may have wished he had gotten the bank's agreement not to make an assignment of the note and mortgage without his consent. In another case about a contested assignment, the court said that

---

[d] "(i) the Distributor Sales Agreement § 7.06 provides that the 'Agreement and the obligations and rights under this Agreement will not be assignable by [Chemrite] without express prior written consent of Bel-Ray, which may be withheld at the sole discretion of Bel-Ray'; (ii) the Blending and Manufacturing License Agreement 7.05 provides that the 'Agreement and the obligations and rights hereunder will not be assignable by [Chemrite] without the express prior written consent of BEL-RAY'; and (iii) the License Agreement to Trade Name § 6.06 provides that the 'Agreement, and the obligations and rights under this agreement will not be assignable without the express written consent of all Parties to this Agreement.'"

to withhold approval of it would have served no interest of the contestant. The court emphasized the somewhat singular facts. Trubowitch v. Riverbank Canning Co., 182 P.2d 182 (Cal.1947). These cases suggest the question why a debtor should care whether the creditor is this or that entity.

The suggestion has been made that a promisee's assignment may impose a burden on a promisor by depriving it of informal leverage that it had over the promisee; see Note 2, p. 1169 above. Could that have been a concern for Haggett upon receiving Norton's letter? Eventually, federal and state officials began to put serious pressure on banks to defer home foreclosures. But that followed the decision in *Norton* by more than fifty years.

Note that Norton v. Haggett was an action bought by Norton. It emerged that he had made a mistake in dealing with the bank: instead of buying Haggett's note he had *paid* it. On learning of his mistake, he brought the action to reinstate the note and mortgage in his favor. Otherwise, Norton thought, Haggett would be unjustly enriched. The court thought otherwise, concluding that Norton had acted as a meddler in Haggett's affairs, and was simply out his money.

SECTION 4.   CONTESTS BETWEEN ASSIGNEES AND OBLIGORS

OBLIGOR'S DUTY TO ASSIGNEE: SOME VARIATIONS

If an assignment of an account has been made effective by Article 9 of the UCC, and the account debtor has received an appropriate notification of the assignment, a payment made on the account to the original creditor will not be credited to the account debtor. (As to the terms *account* and *account debtor* in this statement, see p. 1176 above.) The Restatement makes a comparable statement, generalized to *obligors* rather than account debtors. The Restatement section reads, in part,

> The right of an assignee is not [subject to] defenses or claims [of the obligor] which accrue [after the obligor receives notification of the assignment] except as stated in this Section or as provided by statute.

Section 336(2). Observe that an obligor's defense "I have paid that," when faced with a claim by an assignee, constitutes a defense which accrued after notification unless the payment was made before the notification. The same section speaks also to the case of prior payment:

> The right of an assignee is subject to any defense or claim of the obligor which accrues before the obligor receives notification.

The Code rule about post-notification payments appears, with particulars added, in UCC § 9–406.

The rule about pre-notification payments appears in paragraph (2) of UCC § 9–404(a), which, like the Restatement, speaks in terms of the time when a defense accrues. The defense "I have paid that" is not one "arising from the transaction that gave rise to the contract." A defense so arising is, for example, "Your claim is based on a contract that I may avoid, owing to fraud by your assignor." The distinction is important because both the Code and the Restatement give more leeway to that kind of defense. As for the Code, a comparison between paragraphs (1) and (2) of Section 9–404(a) demonstrates that. As for the Restatement, see Section 336(1).

In the opinion that follows the court set out both paragraphs and applied paragraph (1). The defense concerned was based on a *failure* to pay—a failure on the part of the assignor to satisfy a debt that it owed to the account debtor.

Introduction to Delacy Investments v. Thurman

The contestants in this appeal were Delacy Investments, as assignee, and Re/Max, as account debtor. Re/Max had won a default judgment below against Steven Thurman, assignor, owing to his failure to plead; Thurman was not a party to the appeal. A Note after the opinion speaks to his legal position.

By reason of the assignment from Thurman to Delacy, Delacy held a *security interest* in the account in question. That interest was the nub of a *security agreement* between those parties. Hence Delacy was a *secured party*. The three terms in italics are the subject of interrelated definitions in the Uniform Commercial Code. See UCC § 1–201(b)(35), and paragraphs (72) and(73) of UCC § 9–102(a). The opinion reports that Delacy had "perfected its security interest by filing a UCC financing statement with the Minnesota Secretary of State." Something of the mechanics and effect of that precaution is described in text below at p. 1189. It had little effect, if any, on the contest between Delacy and Re/Max.

The court quoted and referred to Minnesota statutes that track the Uniform Commercial Code; *e.g.*, "Minn. Stat. § 336.9–404," which tracks UCC § 9–404. As presented here, the opinion invariably substitutes "UCC" for the prefix "Minn. Stat. § 336."

The court stated the issue before it this way: "Did the district court err by granting summary judgment to respondent based on its interpretation of article 9 of the Uniform Commercial Code as to assignment of an account receivable?"

Delacy Investments, Inc. v. Thurman & Re/Max Real Estate Guide, Inc.

Minnesota Court of Appeals, 2005.
693 N.W.2d 479.

■ HALBROOKS, JUDGE.

FACTS

Appellant Delacy Investments, Inc., d/b/a Commission Express (CE), is in the business of factoring receivables from real-estate agents. In this business, a real-estate agent can assign or sell his future receivable or commission to CE in exchange for immediate funds. Respondent Re/Max Real Estate Guide, Inc. (Re/Max) is a real-estate brokerage company.

On November 11, 2001, defendant Steven Thurman, a licensed real-estate agent, entered into a master repurchase and security agreement (MRSA) with CE. The substance of the MRSA "granted to CE a security interest under the [UCC] in all of [Thurman's] right, title and interest in and to [Thurman's] current and future accounts receivable. . . . " CE perfected its security interest by filing a UCC financing statement with the Minnesota Secretary of State.

On February 25, 2003, Thurman entered into a standard independent-contractor agreement with Re/Max. The agreement details the employment relationship between the two, whereby Thurman agreed to pay Re/Max certain overhead expenses. The agreement explains how Thurman will receive his "commission" from Re/Max and certain "nonpayment remedies." In pertinent part, the agreement states:

> [Thurman] shall be deemed entitled only to 100 percent of the amount by which commissions generated by [Thurman's] efforts *exceed* past-due financial obligations imposed by the terms of Paragraphs 4 and 5 of the Agreement. That portion of commissions which *does not exceed* past-due financial obligations shall be deemed to belong to RE/MAX and shall be used by RE/MAX first to offset arrearages owed by [Thurman].

(Emphasis added.) Thus, in terms of the legal relationships that exist here, CE is an "assignee," having accepted Thurman's assignment of his commission by the MRSA. Thurman, in turn, is an "assignor," having assigned his right of commission to CE. Re/Max is an "account debtor" by virtue of its independent-contractor agreement with Thurman, whereby Re/Max possesses the potential right to receipt of that which Thurman assigned to CE.

In April 2003, Re/Max executed an acknowledgement of CE's security interest in Thurman's account receivable from the sale of a home on Javelin Avenue and directed that Thurman's commission from that sale be paid directly to CE. On April 22, 2003, CE and Thurman entered into an Account Receivable Sale and Assignment Agreement (assignment agreement), whereby CE agreed to purchase a $10,000 receivable related to Thurman's sale of a property on Keller Lake Drive in Burnsville (Keller Lake property).[1]

On June 7, Re/Max terminated Thurman as a real-estate agent for poor performance, failure to deposit earnest-money payments in a timely manner, and customer complaints. Re/Max asserts that at the time of his termination, Thurman had accumulated $11,126.38 in overhead debts owed to Re/Max. As a result, Re/Max refused to pay the assigned receivable and "applied the commission to Thurman's balance in accordance with [the independent-contractor agreement]," claiming a right of setoff based on the overhead expenses that Thurman owed. In Re/Max's words, "because the commissions earned by Re/Max as a result of Thurman's services did not exceed his past-due financial obligation to Re/Max, Thurman was entitled to no compensation at the Keller Lake closing, and so nothing was paid to CE pursuant to the assignment."

In June 2003, CE sent Re/Max a demand for immediate payment of the Keller Lake account receivable and sent a notice of default to Thurman. Re/Max did not pay. CE then filed a complaint in district court. Re/Max answered and counterclaimed against Thurman.[2] Both parties moved for summary judgment. The district court denied CE's motion and granted Re/Max's, finding that "[CE's] ability to receive a commission from Re/Max is based upon Thurman's assignment of a contractual right to receive a commission from Re/Max." Therefore, the district court determined that "Thurman was not entitled to a commission at the time of the Keller Lake property closing." As a result, it was "impossible for [CE] to obtain a greater right in the commission than Thurman had in the commission." This appeal follows.

ANALYSIS

On an appeal from summary judgment, we ask two questions: (1) whether there are any genuine issues of material fact, and (2) whether the district court erred in its application of the law.

A.   The District Court's Application of UCC 9–404

In granting Re/Max's motion for summary judgment, the district court determined that Thurman was not entitled to a commission at the time of the Keller Lake property closing. The court stated:

> Under UCC 9–404, an assignee's rights are subject to "(1) all terms of the agreement between the account debtor and the assignor[.]" "A valid assignment generally operates to vest in the assignee the same right, title, or interest that the assignor had in the thing assigned." Ill. Farmers Ins. Co. v. Glass Service

---

[1]   Pursuant to the assignment agreement, CE immediately paid $8,000 to Thurman and promised to pay him an additional $1,000 upon the receipt of the assigned receivable, in exchange for Thurman's assignment of a $10,000 receivable to be paid at the closing on the Keller Lake property.

[2]   Thurman is not a party to this appeal. A default judgment was entered against him following his failure to plead.

Co. [ ], 669 N.W.2d 420, 424 (Minn.App. 2003) (citation omitted), [*rev'd on other grounds,* 683 N.W.2d 792 (Minn. 2004)].

In the present action, Thurman was not entitled to collect a commission while his fees were in arrears. There is no question that at the time of the closing on the Keller Lake property, Thurman was in arrears in his fees to Re/Max in the amount of approximately $11,126.38. The court, therefore, finds that Thurman was not entitled to a commission at the time of the Keller Lake property closing and that it is impossible for [CE] to obtain a greater right in the commission than Thurman had in the commission.

[The Court of Appeals quoted from UCC § 9–404 as follows, adding emphasis.]

(a) Assignee's rights subject to terms, claims, and defenses; exceptions. Unless an account debtor has made an enforceable agreement not to assert defenses or claims, and subject to subsections (b) through (e), *the rights of an assignee are subject to*:

(1) *all terms of the agreement between the account debtor and assignor* and any defense or claim in recoupment arising from the transaction that gave rise to the contract; and

(2) any other defense or claim of the account debtor against the assignor which accrues before the account debtor receives a notification of the assignment authenticated by the assignor or assignee.

The official comment to the provision further explains its meaning:

Subsection (a) provides that an assignee generally takes an assignment subject to defenses and claims of an account debtor. Under subsection (a)(1), if the account debtor's defenses on an assigned claim arise from the transaction that gave rise to the contract with the assignor, *it makes no difference* whether the defense or claim accrues before or after the account debtor is notified of the assignment.

UCC 9–404 cmt. 2 (emphasis added); *see also* Restatement (Second) of Contracts § 336, cmt. b (1981) (explaining that an assignor can assign "only what he has" and "is subject to limitations imposed by the terms of that contract [creating the right] and to defenses which would have been available against the [account debtor] had there been no assignment"). The particular issue presented here is one of first impression in Minnesota.[3]

---

[3] Both parties cite to Nat'l Trade Trust, Inc. v. Merrimac Constr., 524 N.W.2d 14 (Minn.App.1994). In that case, we held that "an account debtor that erroneously pays the assignor after receiving notice of assignment waives any claim to a setoff against the assignor raised for the first time *after* the assigned debt was paid." *Id.* at 17 (emphasis in original). Because that case was decided on narrow grounds factually distinguishable from the issue presented here, its application is of little value.

Under UCC 9–404(a)(1), because the rights of CE are subject to *all* terms of the agreement between Re/Max and Thurman—namely, the independent-contractor agreement giving CE a right to all of Thurman's commissions which *exceed* past-due financial obligations to Re/Max—we conclude that CE cannot collect from Re/Max because the commissions earned by Re/Max as a result of Thurman's sales do not exceed his past-due financial obligations to Re/Max. As we recently explained, "it is black-letter law that an assignee of a claim take no other or greater rights than the original assignor and cannot be in a better position than the assignor." *Ill. Farmers Ins. Co.*, 669 N.W.2d at 424. This most basic principle of commercial law is reflected in the Latin phrase *nemo dat qui non habet*—or, "no one may transfer more than he owns." Commerce Bank, N.A. v. Chrysler Realty Corp., 244 F.3d 777, 780 (10th Cir. 2001).

Our decision is further supported by a number of courts across the country interpreting former § 9–318(1) and revised § 9–404 of the UCC. The Sixth Circuit has interpreted the same UCC provision to "clearly limit[ ] the rights of the assignee, to those of the assignor and make[ ] its right to accounts receivable *subject to the provisions of* [the account debtor's] contract with [the assignor]." Nat'l. City Bank, Northwest v. Columbian Mut. Life Ins. Co., 282 F.3d 407, 410 (6th Cir. 2002) (emphasis added). In that case, the court concluded that "there is no authority for the proposition that a perfected assignment to a third person takes precedence over a right of recoupment created between the original contracting parties in their contract."[4] *Id.*

[The court found support in a decision that an assignee was bound by an arbitration term in the agreement between the account debtor and the assignor: Systran Fin. Servs. Corp. v. Giant Cement Holding, Inc., 252 F.Supp.2d 500 (N.D.Ohio 2003). From the opinion there the court quoted as follows:

> [If the assignee] did not want to arbitrate disputes over collections from account debtors, it could have contracted with [the assignor] to prevent it from entering into any agreement that contained arbitration clauses. Because it did not do so, it is bound by the arbitration clause.]

Similarly, here, if CE did not want to be bound by the independent-contractor agreement between Re/Max and Thurman, it could have contracted otherwise. But it did not, and CE is thereby bound by the independent-contractor agreement between Re/Max and Thurman. As the assignee, CE cannot assume greater rights than Thurman, the assignor.

---

[4] The case distinguishes between a right of "recoupment" and "setoff." "[A] right of 'recoupment' arises from the same transaction or contract that creates an asset whereas 'setoff' is a broader term referring to any claim or demand, however created, that the holder of the asset has against the debtor." [*Id.*] at 409 (citing *Black's Law Dictionary* 1439–40 (4th ed. 1968)).

B.   Subsection (a)(2)

But CE also argues that UCC 9–404(a)(2) does not permit an account debtor to contract away the rights of an assignee *after* having received notice of a previously-executed assignment. According to CE, subsection (a)(2) limits which setoffs an account debtor may assert against a payment to an assignee after notice of the assignment. CE contends that Re/Max had notice of the assignment on three separate occasions: (1) statutory notice by CE's filing of the financing statement with the Secretary of State on November 14, 2001, after Thurman's execution of the MRSA; (2) actual notice that CE was entitled to all of the Thurman receivables when a notice of default regarding the Javelin Avenue property was delivered by certified mail on March 12, 2003; and (3) actual notice from the assignment of the Keller Lake receivable on April 22, 2003. CE argues that Thurman signed the MRSA with CE, giving CE a right to his commission, before Thurman signed the independent-contractor agreement with Re/Max.

[The court quoted from UCC § 1–201(25) and (26), as enacted in Minnesota.] It therefore appears that Re/Max had notice of the assignment between Thurman and CE before its independent-contractor agreement with Thurman.

A perfected security interest is generally effective against creditors "*except as otherwise provided* in the Uniform Commercial Code." UCC 9–201(a) (emphasis added). UCC 9–404(a)(1) provides otherwise. UCC 9–404(a)(2) does not govern the dispute here.

The plain language of UCC 9–404(a)(1) makes clear that the rights of CE (as an assignee) "are subject to . . . all terms of the agreement between the account debtor and assignor." *Id.* Here, the independent-contractor agreement between Re/Max and Thurman limited payment to Thurman to those commissions that exceeded his past-due financial obligations to Re/Max. Because CE can take no greater rights nor be in a better position than Thurman by recovering a commission when Thurman, himself, was not entitled to the commission, the district court did not err by granting summary judgment to Re/Max.

DECISION

[W]e affirm the district court's grant of summary judgment in favor of respondent.

NOTES

(1) *The Thurman Factor.* The court indicated, inferentially, that Delacy made a claim against Thurman, without indicating the character of that claim. Perhaps it was a claim of fraud, or other tort. Or perhaps Delacy contended that the account in question was collateral for an unpaid loan. Or that Thurman had warranted that the account was collectible. Whatever the terms of the assignment were, they did not impair Re/Max's defense. Recall that a sale of the account, by which Delacy took all the risk of collectibility,

would have generated an Article 9 security interest just as much as a transfer securing a loan. See the text, *Sale versus Loan*, at p. 1176 above.

(2) *Financing Statements and "Perfection."* "UCC-1" is the informal name given to an official form used to put the public on notice of a security interest like that of CE, and of a host of other security interests governed by Article 9. It is designed for filing in one or more public offices, as designated by the adopting state. It is a simple, one-page document. It requires few entries, chiefly these three: names and addresses for the debtor and the secured party, and something in a space after "This FINANCING STATEMENT covers the following collateral:". A suitable entry for that space would be "accounts that have arisen and may arise against Re/Max." CE could have achieved the same effect by filing its agreement with Thurman, or another document they might have devised.

The object of a filing is to achieve *perfection* of a security interest. The object of that is to prevent competing claimants from appropriating the collateral at the expense of the secured party. The court alluded to an important class of competitors, saying that a perfected security interest "is generally effective against creditors." As applied to the facts of *Delacy Investments*, that would be a reference to creditors of Thurman. If he had entered bankruptcy, it would include that gargantuan hypothetical creditor, the bankruptcy trustee. Some further particulars about perfection, and about competitors of assignees, are presented in Section 3 of this chapter.

The *attachment* of a security interest is another matter, having to do with its efficacy against not only against competitors but even against the debtor.

(3) *Timing.* The Thurman-CE security agreement was made in 2001. The Thurman-Re/Max agreement was made in 2003. Because the account in question was generated by the latter, CE could not have had a security interest in it before 2003. UCC § 9–203(a) and (b)(2).

The court was not required to say when CE received a notification of the assignment. It did say that Re/Max had notice of the assignment before it agreed to pay commissions to Thurman. That may have been a rash statement. It can be argued that notification could not occur until the Re/Max-Thurman agreement was in place. That would have been important if Re/Max's only defense was that it had paid the account to Thurman. CE offered three possible "notification dates," one in 2001 and two in 2003. Assignees have a natural disposition to favor early notification dates.

Modification

Following an assignment of rights under a contract, it is sometimes possible for the parties to the contract to impair the assignee's interest by agreeing on a modification of the contract. The Code addresses the matter in Section 9–405, "Modification of Assigned Contract." Subsection (a) states rules about the effect on the assignee. Rule #1 is this:

A modification of or substitution for an assigned contract is effective against an assignee if made in good faith.

But the rules of subsection (a) are qualified in further subsections. For example, they apply only to the extent that the right to payment has not been fully earned by performance or, if it has been fully earned by performance, the account debtor has not received notification of the assignment under Section 9–406(1). That qualification leaves much room for modifications effective against assignees, many of whom must rely for protection on the requirement of good faith. "Good faith" means, in this context, "honesty in fact and the observance of reasonable commercial standards of fair dealing." UCC § 1–201(b)(20).

Further rules in subsection (a) are that, upon a modification or substitution, the assignee acquires "corresponding rights" under the modified or substituted contract, and that the assignment may provide that the modification or substitution is a breach of contract by the assignor.

NOTE

Rescission. When a bank made a claim as assignee of rent due under a computer-equipment lease, it was faced with the defense that the parties to the lease had rescinded it. On a review of Article 9, it was found that no such defense works against an assignee. Modification, yes, in the right circumstances, but not rescission. The defendant contended that the distinction creates an anomaly. The court conceded that "the functional difference between a modification of the lease amount to a dollar and the rescission of the contract is nugatory in financial terms." As to the former, the legislature may have supposed that a trier of fact would withhold a finding of good faith. "But regardless of the reason the Legislature chose to differentiate between modification and rescission, it did." Wells Fargo Bank Minnesota, N.A. v. B.C.B.U., 49 Cal.Rptr.3d 324, 332 (Cal.App.2006). (Also, an agreement to rescind does not amount to *paying* the assignor, as described in UCC § 9–406.)

PROBLEMS

(1)   Mayflower Motel, Inc. received this letter from the Plymouth Bank:

The Plank Company tells us that it expects you to call on it to supply you with lumber, on credit, as needed to repair your property damaged in the recent fire. We notify you hereby that Plank is a customer of ours, that we have extended a line of credit to it, and that we hold an assignment from Plank of all its accounts now on its books and of those hereafter to arise. That assignment secures all advances we have made and will make to Plank. You are to make payment for any lumber you buy from Plank directly to us.

After that, Mayflower did indeed contract to purchase lumber from Plank, on credit. Plank has yet to deliver most of the goods. Now the parties to the lumber-sale contract wish to reduce the price by 10%, owing to a general drop in lumber prices. They want to know whether or not, if they do, the change will affect the bank's entitlement against Mayflower.

In part, the answer is determined by UCC § 2–209(1), and in part by UCC § 9–405. How would you advise Mayflower and Plank?

(2) The facts are the same as in Problem 1, except that Plank delivered all the lumber ordered by Mayflower before the drop in prices. Might it be argued that a good-faith reduction in the lumber price would be effective against the bank, in that there has not yet been notification to the account debtor of the assignment?

A dictum in *Delacy Investments*, above, indicates the answer No. The court said that Re/Max had notice of Thurman's assignment before it entered into the contract that generated the account in question. Does that make sense? As to UCC § 9–406(a), the juncture specified there is when "the account debtor receives a notification that the amount due or to become due has been assigned and that payment is to be made to the assignee." When Mayflower received the bank's letter, was it an account debtor? Should that matter?

(3) Suppose that UCC § 9–405 would make effective, against the bank, a 10% change in the contract price, as suggested in the foregoing problems. Suppose also, however, these further facts: On learning of the lumber-sale contract, the bank increased Plank's line of credit by the amount of the contract price, and Plank drew down the full amount of the credit. Mayflower has been informed of these transactions. How might it be argued that Mayflower cannot now, as against the bank, enjoy the benefit of a price reduction? Would it matter that Mayflower does not know of the two transactions described?

Agreement Not to Assert Defenses Against Assignee

The heading of this part, "Agreement . . .", is the caption of UCC § 9–403, a section mentioned below at p. 1192. The section empowers the parties to some agreements—account debtor and assignor—to contract, to some extent, around this other provision, also mentioned above: "[T]he rights of an assignee are subject to any defense or claim in recoupment arising from the transaction that gave rise to the contract." UCC § 9–404(a)(1). Clauses having that object are known commonly as *waiver-of-defenses* clauses. The Restatement touches only lightly on the subject, referring to statutes affecting certain defenses.

For several reasons waiver-of-defenses clauses are the subject of widespread obloquy. Almost always they appear in standard-form contracts, at the instance of firms that take assignments as a vocation. They may lead to serious misfortune for subscribing obligors, who may not appreciate this threat when they sign. Hence both federal and state authorities have moved to counteract them. Moves of that kind are exemplified in Title 16, § 433.2, of the Code of Federal Regulations ("Preservation of consumers' claims and defenses . . . "), and in § 2986.10 of the California Civil Code, both quoted in the Notes below.

An example of misfortune occasioned by a waiver-of-defenses clause is that of a firm desiring the use of computer equipment. During negotiations for a lease, the prospective lessor induced an agent of the firm to sign lease documents, saying that it was common industry practice to execute undated documents "in advance," and promised to hold the documents in escrow until a deal was reached. No deal was reached, and the would-be lessee never received the equipment. Nevertheless, it had to pay according to the "lease" because of an assignment and because of a waiver-of-defenses clause in the documents. (The waiver-of-defenses clause was, "Lessee shall not assert against the assignee any defense, counterclaim or set-off that Lessee may have against Lessor.") Wells Fargo Bank Minnesota, N.A. v. B.C.B.U., 49 Cal.Rptr.3d 324 (Cal.App.2006). For another example of misfortune for a lessee, this one a law firm, see Chemical Bank v. Rinden Professional Ass'n, p. 1196 below. The leased property was an office telephone system.

One might think that a waiver-of-defenses clause cannot override defenses more appealing than the ones in those cases—fraud, for example. But a waiver-of-defenses clause can override a defense based on fraud of the worst type.

The Code places significant limits on the class of assignees who can enjoy the benefit of waiver-of-defenses clauses under UCC § 9–403. An assignee qualifies only if it has taken the assignment for value, and in good faith. The definition of "good faith" is that appearing on p. 1190 above. A further requirement is that the assignee take without notice of some truly fundamental defenses, including an especially egregious kind of fraud and most defenses of duress and incapacity. This qualification manifests some mistrust of the good-faith requirement. (The qualification speaks of defenses "of a type that may be asserted against a holder in due course of a negotiable instrument under Section 3–305(b)." The particulars of negotiable instrument law are not pursued here.)

UCC Section 9–403 makes two references to "other" laws protective of obligors. One of the laws referred to is the federal regulation cited above, 16 C.F.R. § 433.2. It requires that certain contracts include a prominent "anti-waiver-of-defenses" clause; see Note 1 below. In the absence of the required clause, subsection (d) of UCC § 9–403 undercuts a waiver-of-defenses clause to the extent that the required clause would have done if included.

Subsection (e) of UCC § 9–403 provides that the section is "subject to law other than this article which establishes a different rule for an account debtor who is an individual and who incurred the obligation primarily for personal, family, or household purposes." A "different rule" would be one preserving an account debtor's defenses against an assignee. The subsection has no bearing on the cases last cited, *Wells Fargo Bank* and *Chemical Bank*, for the goods concerned in those cases were wanted for business purposes. But the subsection applied in LaChapelle v. Toyota Motor Credit Corp., 126 Cal.Rptr.2d 32 (Cal.App.2002), assuming that the Toyota 4-Runner concerned was leased to Ms. LaChapelle for her personal use. See Note 2 below.

NOTES

(1) *A Federal Riposte.* "ANY HOLDER OF THIS ... CONTRACT IS SUBJECT TO ALL CLAIMS AND DEFENSES WHICH THE DEBTOR COULD ASSERT AGAINST THE SELLER OF GOODS OR SERVICES OBTAINED PURSUANT HERETO OR WITH THE PROCEEDS HEREOF. ... "

A failure to include this text, in ten-point bold-face type, in a consumer credit contract, may be a federal offense, in connection with a sale or lease of goods or services to a consumer. The offense is that of the "seller." It can be committed only in a transaction "in or affecting commerce as 'commerce' is defined in the Federal Trade Commission Act." 16 C.F.R. § 433.2.

(2) *A California Riposte.* "An assignee of the lessor's rights is subject to all equities and defenses of the lessee against the lessor, notwithstanding an agreement to the contrary. ... "

This provision applies to leases by which a natural person acquires the use of a registered motor vehicle, primarily for personal, family or household purposes, for a term exceeding four months. Cal.Civil Code §§ 2985.7(d) and 2986.10. In UCC § 9–403, according to subsection (e), the section is subject to these provisions of the California Vehicle Leasing Act.

Note the word "all" the California statute—"all equities and defenses"—and in the notice quoted in Note 1—"ALL CLAIMS AND DEFENSES." Presumably the word comprises some defenses that would preclude recovery by a holder in due course.

Financiers Versus Consumers

The Uniform Commercial Code is relatively dispassionate about consumers who express assent to waiver-of-defenses clauses. See Robert Skilton & Orrin Helstad, Protection of the Installment Buyer of Goods under the UCC, 65 Mich.L.Rev.1465 (1967). That may be so partly because the topic has engendered much passion.

To some extent rules that protect consumers against waiver-of-defense clauses reflect only concern about the more general problems of standard form contracts. But attempts have been made to show that the waiver-of-defenses problem is a singular one, deserving of specialized treatment. The following considerations figure in the argument. (1) Financing institutions are in a superior position, by comparison with ordinary consumers, to evaluate the reliability of a retail merchant or firm. A bank or finance company supplying a merchant with funds is equipped to form judgments about the matter more accurately than the merchant's ordinary customers. (2) Customers of a retail firm are poorly situated to exercise discipline against it for substandard business practices, whereas corrective measures may readily be forced on it by a financier if its retail operations give rise to an undue number of complaints. (3) Pooling of information is an effective means of reducing substandard performance by merchants. Financing institutions are capable of organizing exchanges of information, such that a merchant who proves unworthy of trust will be promptly foreclosed from the credit market. By contrast, information exchanges among consumers are feebly organized, so that a retail firm may maintain a certain reputation with the public even though many of its customers suffer from its delinquencies.

None of these arguments need be taken at face value, of course. What countervailing considerations are there? It has been argued forcefully that, if merchants cannot give the assurances to financing institutions through waiver-of-defenses clauses, they will find credit more expensive, or inaccessible, and that the cost to merchants must be reflected in retail prices. Persuasive? If so, would the effect show in cash transactions, or only in credit transactions?

It is instructive to compare the remedies of a disappointed buyer who uses credit with those of one who does not. Withholding payment, while not a remedy available to a cash buyer, may be a remedy available to a buyer on credit. Possibly, then, a disappointed cash buyer never has a better prospect of relief than one who uses credit, and often has a worse one. Does that state of affairs make sense?

————

Linkage, Assignor and Assignee

A firm that takes assignments repeatedly or continuously from a merchant whose dealings with customers are substandard may become entangled with defenses of customers, notwithstanding waiver-of-defenses clauses. At some point a question may arise about that firm's good faith.

Aside from that, customers' defenses have succeeded simply because of the ongoing link between assignor and assignee. Notable authorities on the subject are Unico v. Owen, 232 A.2d 405 (N.J.1967), and Leasing Service Corp. v. River City Const., Inc., 743 F.2d 871 (11th Cir.1984). In each case the claimant sought to override a buyer's defense by presenting itself as a holder in due course of a negotiable instrument.

In *Unico* the court wrote an elaborate opinion, referring to Williams v. Walker-Thomas Furniture Co., p. 637 above, among other cases. "Many courts have solved the problem", the court said, "by denying to the holder of the paper the status of holder in due course where the financer maintains a close relationship with the dealer whose paper he buys. . . . " The court described signs of close cooperation between dealers and assignees. "The transaction is looked upon, as a species of tripartite proceeding, and the tenor of the cases is that the financer should not be permitted 'to isolate itself behind the fictional fence' of the Negotiable Instruments Law, and thereby achieve an unfair advantage over the buyer." *Unico* at 412.

In *Leasing Service Corp.* the court said: "There are, of course, commercial cases in which a court has held that the seller and the alleged holder in due course were so closely linked that the entities were indistinguishable for purposes of the holder in due course doctrine. . . . In those cases the manufacturer's representative either assisted or participated in the sale by the dealer, and the manufacturer's course of dealing was, to furnish blank sales contracts to its dealer and to have the dealer assign the contract routinely as soon as the sale was made."

Is a decision like that justifiable on the ground that a closely-connected financier is in a position to monitor the merchant's selling practices and the quality of its products? The opinion that follows speaks to the point.

Introduction to *Chemical Bank v. Rinden Professional Association*

The ruling here depended on the following sentence in a Massachusetts statute now superseded:

> Subject to any statute or decision which establishes a different rule for buyers of consumer goods, an agreement by a buyer that he will not assert against an assignee any claim or defense which he may have against the seller is enforceable by an assignee who takes his assignment for value, in good faith and without notice of a claim or defense, except as to defenses of a type which may be asserted against a holder in due course of a negotiable instrument under the Article on Negotiable Instruments (Article 3).

The sentence was very like the first of three in a section of the Uniform Commercial Code—Section 9–206—that was the predecessor of current UCC § 9–403. The current section was later enacted in Massachusetts as Gen.Laws ch. 106, § 9–402.

The sentence quoted above differs notably from the corresponding one in UCC § 9–403. The closing "except" phrase entrenched certain defenses which can be foreclosed under the section as revised. But that difference is not germane to the case.

As presented here, the opinion does not include chapter or section references to the General Laws, and refers to former Code Section 9–206 as "the Code section".

Chemical Bank v. Rinden Professional Association

Supreme Court of New Hampshire, 1985.
126 N.H. 688, 498 A.2d 706.

[A firm named Intertel installed an office telephone system for a law firm (Rinden) under a lease-purchase agreement made in April, 1974. The contract required monthly payments into 1982, at which time Rinden might purchase the equipment for a dollar. Thereafter Rinden received written notice that the Chemical Bank expected to purchase from Intertel the payment rights. This document required Rinden's assent to its terms; on June 11 Rinden's office manager, John Satterfield, read and signed it. One of its terms included this provision:

> As Lessee, you . . . agree as follows: (a) that your obligation to pay directly to the Assignee [bank] the amounts which come due as rentals as set forth in said Lease shall be absolutely unconditional and shall be payable whether or not the Lease is terminated [in any way] and you promise to pay the same notwithstanding any defense, set-off or counterclaim whatsoever, [by] breach or otherwise, which you may or might now or hereafter have as against the Lessor [Intertel].

After the bank received the signed document, it received also an assignment by Intertel of Intertel's payment rights, for which it paid. About a week after Satterfield signed, Rinden received a letter from the bank saying that the assignment had been completed and that Rinden was obligated to make its monthly payments to the bank.

After nearly three years of payments to the bank, the phone system began to malfunction seriously. Rinden replaced it and refused to make further payments to the bank. A three-party lawsuit ensued, which resulted in a master's report in 1984. In the meanwhile, Intertel had gone into bankruptcy.

The report favored the bank. Rinden appealed, contesting a finding that the waiver clause was enforceable.]

■ DOUGLAS, JUSTICE. This case is governed by the Uniform Commercial Code (UCC) as enacted in Massachusetts. The version of the provision of article 9 of the UCC applicable to this case is entitled "Agreement Not to Assert Defenses Against Assignee; Modification of Sales Warranties Where Security Agreement Exists". [Here the court set out the statute. With one qualification, it was identical to UCC § 9–206(1), as it stood prior to the revision of Article 9 effective 2001. The difference was that the statute omitted references, found in the Code section, to lessors and lessees of goods, as well as to sellers and buyers. The court concluded, however, that the statute applied because the Intertel-Rinden "lease" fit the UCC definition of a security agreement.]

The requirements of a valid waiver are that there was an agreement by a buyer, who is not a consumer, to waive defenses against an assignee and that the assignment was made for value, in good faith, and without notice of a claim or defense. We find that these requirements were met so that the defendant validly waived his defenses against Chemical Bank.

The master found that Rinden agreed to the waiver of defenses clause, and the evidence supports this view.

The defendant does not claim that it is a consumer so as to make [the statute] inapplicable on that account. The defendant is a professional association, a law firm, not in need of special protections often provided for unwary consumers.

Next we must determine whether there is sufficient evidence to support the master's findings that Chemical Bank took the assignment for value, in good faith, and without notice of a claim or defense. As to the first issue, Chemical Bank paid Intertel over $8,800 for the assignment of Intertel's rights in the defendant's contract.

As to the next requirement, the defendant asserts that Chemical Bank is not a good faith purchaser, mainly because the plaintiff and Intertel were too closely connected. Nothing in the record indicates, however, that the relationship between Intertel and Chemical Bank was anything other than an arms-length commercial relationship.

William Tupka, the Chemical Bank employee in charge of the Intertel account, testified that Chemical Bank's course of dealing in purchasing the rights to the Rinden contract from Intertel was typical of its transactions with hundreds of other clients with which it had entered into similar agreements. Chemical Bank and Intertel were not related corporations, having common directors or owning shares of stock in each other. Nor was Chemical the only bank to lend to Intertel.

Finally, the facts that Chemical Bank checked Rinden's credit rating and insisted upon an insertion of a waiver of defenses clause, before it would purchase the assignment, certainly do not prove lack of good faith as Rinden claims. Both Mr. Tupka and Kenneth Barron, former president of Intertel, testified that these actions were standard procedure for a bank extending credit. Moreover, even if there was any evidence of interrelatedness, Massachusetts law appears to look with disfavor on the admission of past dealings between parties to show bad faith, absent some other indications of bad faith by the holder. See Bowling Green, Inc. v. State Street Bank and Trust Co., 425 F.2d 81, 85 (1st Cir. 1970) (citing Universal C.I.T. Credit Corp. v. Ingel, 196 N.E.2d 847, 852 (Mass. 1964)).

There is also no basis to conclude that the master erred in finding that Chemical Bank took the assignment without notice of a claim or defense. Mr. Tupka testified that he came across nothing in his investigation of the Intertel account which would indicate that Rinden might have some kind of claim or defense relating to the lease agreement between it and Intertel. No evidence was introduced to contradict this testimony.

The defendant next argues that even if the terms of [the statute] were complied with, the waiver of defenses is ineffective because it was given without consideration. The short answer to this is that none was required. Mass.Gen.Laws Ann. ch. 106 § 2–209(1) states that "[a]n agreement modifying a contract within this Article needs no consideration to be binding."

[The opinion next turned to the defendant's contention that a provision of Article 2, such as that last cited, is inapplicable to a transaction within Article 9 of the Code. The court concluded that "Article 2 does apply to transactions in goods which involve both a sales contract and a security agreement." The court rejected an argument grounded in public policy.]

We note that our decision today is in accord with the policy of the UCC in general, and of [the Code section] in particular, "to encourage the supplying of credit for the buying of goods by insulating the [institutional] lender from lawsuits over the quality of the goods." Massey-Ferguson Credit Corp. v. Brown, 547 P.2d 846, 850 (Mont. 1976) (quoting Massey-Ferguson, Inc. v. Utley, 439 S.W.2d 57, 60 (Ky.1969)). "A contrary holding would not only have a chilling effect on loans made by financial institutions but would mean that the law allows the plain meaning of covenants to be declared nugatory whenever a bad bargain results." B.V.D. Co. v. Marine Midland Bank-New York, 360 N.Y.S.2d 901, 904 (App.Div. 1974).

Affirmed.

NOTES

(1) *Unconscionability*. Rinden argued that the waiver of defense clause it had assented to was unenforceable because it was unconscionable. The court rejected that argument in a part of the opinion omitted here. What were the weaknesses in the argument?

(2) *Alternate Rationale*. The facts of *Chemical Bank* might have supported a finding that Rinden made a promise directly to the bank that the bank would be paid notwithstanding any defense that Rinden might have against Intertel. If that promise was made, would it have served as a basis for the decision without reference to Article 9 of the Code?

There might be a question of consideration for the promise: What was given in exchange for Rinden's undertaking? The question would be especially acute if the supposed promise was made after the bank had invested in the contract. (Rinden could of course bargain with the bank for it to make an advance, or a payment, to Intertel, if the bank had not already acted.) Possibly a promise by Rinden to the bank, if one was made, could be enforced on the basis of promissory estoppel. A showing of something in the way of reliance by the bank would be required. What kind of reliance might be shown?

(3) *Variant State Rules*. The stance of Article 9 toward waivers by consumers of their defenses was sharply debated in the councils of the Code

sponsors. As to the Code's neutrality on consumer-credit issues see Robert Skilton & Orrin Helstad, *Protection of the Installment Buyer of Goods under the UCC*, 65 Mich.L.Rev. 1465 (1967). The decision was, of course, not to strive for uniformity on the issue of consumer protection. Does that fact suggest any attitude that should be taken toward the business buyer?

The issue of consumer protection has also been hard-fought in the legislatures and the courts. A number of states virtually deprive waiver-of-defense clauses—and holder-in-due-course status, with respect to notes—of their efficacy in ordinary consumer transactions. See Uniform Consumer Credit Code § 3.307 and other sections cited in the Comment. Other statutes provide the consumer with a limited period for raising objections against paying the assignee. In states of this persuasion, the inception and the duration of this period are variables. A description and compilation of retail installment sales statutes as they affect assignment law appear in the Introductory Note to Chapter 15 of the Restatement.

––––––

Assignees' Liabilities

Efforts, now to be described, have been made to impose no-fault liabilities on assignees, sometimes by consumers, sometimes by others. The end point of these efforts, which is not in sight, might be put this way: When a dispenser of goods or services has obtained financing by assigning a customer's account, and the dispenser is found to have imposed on the customer, the customer may require the assignee to account for its gain or may charge the assignee with the customer's loss.

Statutory and regulatory texts have given some impetus to claims against assignees, but also have put them in check. An example is the FTC "holder rule," which requires that consumer credit contracts contain this notice: ANY HOLDER OF THIS . . . CONTRACT IS SUBJECT TO ALL CLAIMS . . . WHICH THE DEBTOR COULD ASSERT AGAINST THE SELLER OF GOODS OR SERVICES OBTAINED PURSUANT HERETO.

Restitution Claims

Long before that rule was thought of, restitution was thought of as a basis for a claim against an assignee. In Merchants' Insurance Company v. Abbott, 131 Mass. 397 (1881), the facts were such that, if the company had paid anything to Abbott, "it could be recovered back as money paid under the influence of a mistake." The mistake was that the company was indebted to Abbott under a policy of insurance on a mill which had been destroyed by fire. In fact, the company owed him nothing because he had instigated the fire. And it had paid him nothing. Instead, the company had paid the amount of the loss to a firm—Denny, Rice & Company—to which Abbott had assigned his "claim" on the policy. On learning of the arson, the company sought to recover from Denny, Rice the payment it had made. Denny, Rice was exonerated. Abbott had made the assignment to satisfy a debt that he owed to Denny, Rice. Hence it took the assignment "for value." Denny, Rice was not unjustly enriched by having received money that Abbott owed to it. A comparable claim was made in Michelin Tires (Canada) Ltd. v. First Nat. Bank of Boston, 666 F.2d 673 (1st Cir. 1981). This one had some support in UCC Article 9: "the rights of an assignee are subject to . . . all the terms of the contract between the account debtor and assignor and *any . . . claim arising therefrom. . . .* " (emphasis supplied). Nevertheless, the assignee was exonerated. The section quoted was the predecessor of what is now subsection (a) of UCC § 9–404. The current provision contains language disfavoring the claim. For one thing, the former reference to "any . . . claim" has been changed to "any . . . claim in recoupment". Also, the revision inserted subsection (b), the rule of which, applicable to the facts of *Michelin Tire*, is: "[T]he claim of an account debtor against an assignor may be asserted against an assignee under subsection (a) only to reduce the amount the account debtor owes."

NOTE

Monitoring Costs. In *Michelin Tires* the court made a policy argument against affirmative actions, based on transaction costs. Michelin complained of its contractor, one Corrigan, in an action against his assignee, the bank. The court compared the Corrigan-Michelin connection with the Corrigan-bank connection. To charge financiers with liability would compel them, the court thought, to supervise performance by their customers of the job being financed. A party in Michelin's position would not, however, relax its supervision. "The party most interested in adequate performance would be the other contracting party. Given this natural interest, it seems likely to us that while [on charging them with affirmative actions] the banks will be given additional burdens of supervision, there would be no corresponding reduction in vigilance by the contracting parties, thus creating two inspections where there was formerly one. Costs for everyone thus increase, without any discernible benefit." Also: "We simply do not believe that the banks are best suited to monitor contract compliance."

Does this reasoning cut too deep? That is, does it tend to show that Corrigan's default should be no defense for Michelin when the bank is the claimant?

Holder Rules

By an Act of the Michigan legislature concerning the financing of motor-vehicle sales, an installment sale contract governed by the Act is to contain this notice:

> Any holder of this consumer credit contract is subject to all claims and defenses which the debtor could assert against the seller of goods or services obtained pursuant hereto or with the proceeds hereof. Recovery hereunder by the debtor shall not exceed amounts paid by the debtor hereunder.

Mich. Comp. Laws § 492.114a(c). Before the second sentence was added, this provision was held (as that sentence intimates) to impose vicarious liability on a holder.

It may be noticed that the first sentence parallels the language required by the Federal Trade Commission in its "holder rule." One might suppose, then, that federal law also opens financiers to vicarious liability. But the Congress has acted to limit that liability. It added the following provision to the Truth-in-Lending Act (15 U.S.C. § 1601 *et seq.*), which governs applications of the FTC holder rule:

> [Subject to a qualification] any civil action for a violation of this subchapter . . . which may be brought against a creditor may be maintained against any assignee of such creditor only if the violation for which such action or proceeding is brought is apparent on the face of the disclosure statement, except where the assignment was involuntary.

The statute goes on to restrict the kinds of "apparent" violation.

Among the debtors who have been balked by this provision was Susanne Ramadan, when she made a claim against the Hyundai Motor Finance Corporation. See Ramadan v. Chase Manhattan Corp., 229 F.3d 194 (3d Cir. 2000) (Chase Manhattan was another of her targets). That case is of special interest, in part because it evoked an interesting response from Judge Louis H. Pollak, eminent as a law-school dean before becoming a judge. Dissenting, he wrote:

> [I]t seems to me that a finance company, feeling that the Holder Notice is in place via force majeure and intending to defend against its applicability in any litigation that may arise, should, before accepting assignment of a finance agreement, insist that the Holder Notice be garlanded with caveat emptors that warn the purchaser-borrower of the finance company's view that the 1980 TILA amendment robs the Holder Notice of substantive effect. A finance company has no ground for supposing that more than one in tens of thousands of purchaser-borrowers (the Ramadans of the world) will be conversant with the interplay between the FTC regulation and TILA. Given the disparity in the possession of crucial information, I would conclude that an assignee finance company that failed to insist on inclusion of an appropriate warning adjacent to the Holder Notice should be estopped from invoking the Holder Notice in litigation.

Id. at 203, 204.

INDEX

References are to Pages

Force majeure clauses, 1102
Half measures substituted for
    performance, 1106
Hardships, 1105
Impossibility distinguished, 1090, 1096–
    97
Impracticability distinguished, 1089–90
Lease, 1087–88
Occurrence and assumptions, 1090
Output and requirements contracts, 1099
Overview, 1021
Reliance interests, recovery of, 1111
Remedies, 1106
Renegotiation clauses, 1114–15
Rental of property, 1087–88
Risk assumptions, 1090
Sales of goods, 1091–92, 1099
Stranded buyers, 1099
Supervening events, 1096

GAP FILLERS
Generally, 568–69
Sales of goods, 570–72
Statutory, 569–70
Supplementary nature of, 567–68
    See also: Good Faith Duties.

GENTLEMEN'S AGREEMENTS, 187

GIFTS
Charitable Subscriptions, 122–24, 126–27
Conditional, 81, 83
    See also: Consideration, Promises.

GOOD FAITH DUTIES
Generally, 554
Agreement to negotiate in good faith,
    181–82
Ambiguity, 684, 686
Bad faith and punitive damages, 34
Bargaining *vs.* performance good faith
    standards, 181–82
Best efforts undertakings, 113–14, 689–95
Candor, 687
Capacity of parties and, 565
Common Law *vs.* the Code, 685
Comparative Approach, 628, 676–77
Condition, prevention of, 742
Content of the obligation, 677–82
Cooperation, hindrance and prevention,
    840–46
Definition, 677
Evaluating evidence, 675–76
Express terms, duty in relation to, 672–75
Honesty in fact formulation, 677
Interference with performance, 840–46
International Approaches, 677
Mandated good-faith term, 592
Modification, 441–42, 666
Negotiations, 304–10, 315–16, 320–23
Opportunism, 688
Performance, in, 593–94, 672–77
Repudiation, 809–10
Requirements contracts, 108–10
Sales of goods, 676
Satisfaction provisions, 102, 104
Settlement of claims, in, 62–66

Third party claims for bad faith breach,
    1145–46
Uniform Commercial Code
    Generally, 592, 676
    Article 2 and Article 1 formulations,
        676
    Independent duty proposal, 681–82
        See also: At-Will Employment,
            Best Efforts,
            Concealment,
            Constructive Conditions,
            Definiteness, Fraud;
            Misrepresentation
            Insurance Contracts,
            Negotiation,
            Repudiation.

GOVERNMENT CONTRACTS
Bribery and Corruption, 710–13
Contracts for public services, 1133–36
Excessive profits and public policy, 602,
    605–06
Liquidated damages provisions, 996
Military supplier, 455–60
Third party beneficiaries, 1118, 1135
Unfairness, 605
    See also: Unfairness, Construction
        Contracts, Public Policy
        Considerations, Third Party
        Beneficiaries.

GRATUITOUS PROMISES
See Consideration

GUARANTEE
Indemnity Agreements, 276–77, 287, 508–
    11
    See also: Suretyship Contracts.

ILLEGAL CONTRACTS
Generally, 700–16
Bribe money, disposition of, 714
Burden to show, 578
Clean hands doctrine, 706
Construction contract, 706–08
Criminal law, guidance from, 697
Enforcement
    Supporting public interest, 705
    Withheld, 705, 710
Government contracts, 710–13
Illegal *vs.* unenforceable, 703
Inducing official action
    Generally, 710–13
    Commercial bribery, 713
    Judicial bribery, 712
    Lobbying, 710
In pari delicto, 705–06
Licensing laws
    Generally, 715–16
    Concerning construction, 715
    Revenue measures, 587
Regulatory and public policy, 705, 710
Restitution of benefits conferred, 716
Sale of goods, 582
Severability, 699
Statutory remedies, 709